Programming and Problem Solving with C++

Second Edition

Programming and Problem Solving with C++

Second Edition

Nell Dale
University of Texas, Austin

Chip Weems
University of Massachusetts, Amherst

Mark Headington
University of Wisconsin—La Crosse

JONES AND BARTLETT PUBLISHERS
Sudbury, Massachusetts
BOSTON   TORONTO   LONDON   SINGAPORE

World Headquarters
Jones and Bartlett Publishers
40 Tall Pine Drive
Sudbury, MA 01776
978-443-5000
info@jbpub.com
www.jbpub.com

Jones and Bartlett Publishers Canada
2406 Nikanna Rd.
Suite 6-272
Mississauga, Ontario
Canada L5C 2W6

Jones and Bartlett Publishers International
Barb House, Barb Mews
London W6 7PA
UK

CHIEF EXECUTIVE OFFICER: Clayton Jones
CHIEF OPERATING OFFICER: Don Jones, Jr.
PUBLISHER: Tom Walker
V.P., SALES AND MARKETING: Tom Manning
V.P., COLLEGE EDITORIAL DIRECTOR: Brian L. McKean
V.P., DIRECTOR OF INTERACTIVE TECHNOLOGY: Mike Campbell
V.P., MANAGING EDITOR: Judith H. Hauck
MARKETING DIRECTOR: Rich Pirozzi
MARKETING MANAGER: Jennifer M. Jacobson
DIRECTOR OF DESIGN AND PRODUCTION: Anne Spencer
SENIOR ACQUISITIONS EDITOR: J. Michael Stranz
PRODUCTION EDITOR: Rebecca S. Marks
DIRECTOR OF MANUFACTURING AND INVENTORY CONTROL: Therese Bräuer
COVER DESIGN: Anne Spencer
TEXT DESIGN: George McLean
COMPOSITION: PageMasters & Company
PRINTING AND BINDING: Courier Companies
COVER PRINTING: Courier Companies

Library of Congress Cataloging-in-Publication Data
Dale, Nell B.
   Programming and problem solving in C++ / Nell Dale, Chip Weems,
and Mark Headington.--2nd ed.
      p.   cm.
   ISBN 0–7637–1063–6
   1. C++ (Computer program language)   I. Weems, Chip.
II. Headington, Mark R.   III. Title.
QA76.73C153D34   1999
005.13'3—dc21   99-25436
                                                        CIP

ISBN: 0-7637-1063-6

Printed in the United States of America
03 02 01 00   10 9 8 7 6 5 4 3

Cover image © James Archambeault.

To you, and to all of our other students for whom it was begun and without whom it would never have been completed.

N.D.   C.W.   M.H.

To the memory of my parents, Rog and Anne, who fostered in me a lifelong love of reading and learning.

M.H.

Programming and Problem Solving with C++, Second Edition Program Disk

Jones and Bartlett Publishers offers free to students and instructors a program disk with all the complete programs found in *Programming and Problem Solving with C++*, Second Edition. The program disk is available through the Jones and Bartlett World Wide Web site on the Internet.*

Download Instructions

1. Connect to the Jones and Bartlett student diskette home page (www.jbpub.com/disks).
2. Choose *Programming and Problem Solving with C++*, Second Edition.
3. Follow the instructions for downloading and saving the *Programming and Problem Solving with C++*, Second Edition data disk.
4. If you need assistance downloading a Jones and Bartlett student diskette, please send email to: help@jbpub.com.

---

* Downloading the *Programming and Problem Solving with C++*, Second Edition program disk via the Jones and Bartlett home page requires access to the Internet and a World Wide Web browser, such as Netscape Navigator or Microsoft Internet Explorer. Instructors at schools without Internet access may call 1-800-832-0034 and request a copy of the program disk. Jones and Bartlett grants adopters of *Programming and Problem Solving with C++*, Second Edition the right to duplicate copies of the program disk or to store the files on any stand-alone computer or network.

Contents

1   Overview of Programming and Problem Solving   1

Overview of Programming   2
What Is Programming?   2
How Do We Write a Program?   3
Theoretical Foundations: 8
     Binary Representation of Data

What Is a Programming Language?   10
Background Information: 13
     Compilers and Interpreters

What Is a Computer?   16
Background Information: 19
     PCs, Workstations, and Mainframes
Background Information: 24
     The Origins of C++

Ethics and Responsibilities in the Computing Profession   25
Software Piracy   26
Privacy of Data   27
Use of Computer Resources   28
Software Engineering   29

Problem-Solving Techniques   30
Ask Questions   30
Look for Things That Are Familiar   31
Solve by Analogy   31
Means-Ends Analysis   32
Divide and Conquer   33
The Building-Block Approach   34
Merging Solutions   34
Mental Blocks: The Fear of Starting   35
Algorithmic Problem Solving   36

Problem-Solving Case Study:
An Algorithm for a Company Payroll   36

Summary 41
   Quick Check 42
   Exam Preparation Exercises 43
   Programming Warm-up Exercises 44
   Case Study Follow-Up 45

2 **C++ Syntax and Semantics, and the Program Development Process** 47

The Elements of C++ Programs 48
   C++ Program Structure 48
   Syntax and Semantics 51
   Theoretical Foundations:
      Metalanguages 52
   Syntax Templates 53
   Naming Program Elements: Identifiers 56
   Matters of Style:
      Using Meaningful, Readable Identifiers 57
   Data and Data Types 58
   Background Information:
      Data Storage 58
   Naming Elements: Declarations 61
   Matters of Style:
      Capitalization of Identifiers 65
   Taking Action: Executable Statements 66
   Beyond Minimalism: Adding Comments to a Program 72

Program Construction 73
   Blocks (Compound Statements) 75
   The C++ Preprocessor 78
   An Introduction to Namespaces 79

More About Output 81
   Creating Blank Lines 81
   Inserting Blanks Within a Line 82

Program Entry, Correction, and Execution 83
   Entering a Program 83
   Compiling and Running a Program 84

Finishing Up | 86

Problem-Solving Case Study:
   Contest Letter | **86**

Testing and Debugging | **91**

Summary | **92**
Quick Check | 93
Exam Preparation Exercises | 95
Programming Warm-up Exercises | 98
Programming Problems | 99
Case Study Follow-Up | 100

3 Numeric Types, Expressions, and Output | 101

Overview of C++ Data Types | **102**

Numeric Data Types | **103**
Integral Types | 103
Floating-Point Types | 104

Declarations for Numeric Types | **105**
Named Constant Declarations | 105
Software Engineering Tip:
   Using Named Constants Instead of Literals | 106
Variable Declarations | 106

Simple Arithmetic Expressions | **107**
Arithmetic Operators | 107
Increment and Decrement Operators | 110

Compound Arithmetic Expressions | **112**
Precedence Rules | 112
Type Coercion and Type Casting | 113
May We Introduce:
   Blaise Pascal | 117

Function Calls and Library Functions | **118**
Value-Returning Functions | 118
Library Functions | 120
Void Functions | 122

Formatting the Output   123
Integers and Strings   123
Floating-Point Numbers   126
Matters of Style:
   Program Formatting   129

Additional `string` Operations   131
The `length` and `size` Functions   131
The `find` Function   132
The `substr` Function   134
Software Engineering Tip:
   Understanding Before Changing   136

Problem-Solving Case Study:
Map Measurements   137

Testing and Debugging   141

Summary   142
Quick Check   142
Exam Preparation Exercises   145
Programming Warm-up Exercises   148
Programming Problems   151
Case Study Follow-Up   152

4   Program Input and the Software Design Process   153

Getting Data into Programs   154
Input Streams and the Extraction Operator (>>)   155
The Reading Marker and the Newline Character   158
Reading Character Data with the `get` Function   160
Theoretical Foundations:
   More About Functions and Arguments   162
Skipping Characters with the `ignore` Function   162
Reading String Data   163

Interactive Input/Output   165

Noninteractive Input/Output   167

File Input and Output   167

Files 168
Using Files 168
An Example Program Using Files 172
Run-Time Input of File Names 174

Input Failure 175

Software Design Methodologies 177

What Are Objects? 178

Object-Oriented Design 179

Functional Decomposition 181
Modules 182
Implementing the Design 185
A Perspective on Design 191
Software Engineering Tip:
Documentation 191

Problem-Solving Case Study:

Stretching a Canvas 192
Background Information:
Programming on Many Scales 198

Testing and Debugging 200
Testing and Debugging Hints 201

Summary 202
Quick Check 203
Exam Preparation Exercises 204
Programming Warm-up Exercises 206
Programming Problems 208
Case Study Follow-Up 209

5 Conditions, Logical Expressions, and Selection Control Structures 211

Flow of Control 212
Selection 213

Conditions and Logical Expressions 214
The `bool` Data Type 214

Background Information:
Before the `bool` Type   215

Logical Expressions   216

May We Introduce:
George Boole   224

Precedence of Operators   225

Software Engineering Tip:
Changing English Statements into Logical Expressions   227

Relational Operators with Floating-Point Types   228

The If Statement   **229**
The If-Then-Else Form   229

Blocks (Compound Statements)   232

Matters of Style:
Braces and Blocks   233

The If-Then Form   234

A Common Mistake   236

Nested If Statements   **236**
The Dangling `else`   240

Testing the State of an I/O Stream   **241**

Problem-Solving Case Study:

Warning Notices   **243**

Testing and Debugging   **249**
Testing in the Problem-Solving Phase:
The Algorithm Walk-Through   249

Testing in the Implementation Phase   253

The Test Plan   259

Tests Performed Automatically During Compilation
and Execution   260

Testing and Debugging Hints   262

Summary   **264**
Quick Check   264

Exam Preparation Exercises   265

Programming Warm-up Exercises   268

Programming Problems   271

Case Study Follow-Up   274

6 Looping 275

The While Statement *276*

Phases of Loop Execution *278*

Loops Using the While Statement *280*

Count-Controlled Loops 280

Event-Controlled Loops 282

Looping Subtasks 288

How to Design Loops *292*

Designing the Flow of Control 292

Designing the Process Within the Loop 294

The Loop Exit 295

Nested Logic *296*

Designing Nested Loops 300

Theoretical Foundations:

Analysis of Algorithms 302

Problem-Solving Case Study:

Average Income by Gender *307*

Testing and Debugging *313*

Loop-Testing Strategy 313

Test Plans Involving Loops 314

Testing and Debugging Hints 315

Summary *317*

Quick Check 318

Exam Preparation Exercises 318

Programming Warm-up Exercises 321

Programming Problems 322

Case Study Follow-Up 324

7 Functions 325

Functional Decomposition with Void Functions *326*

When to Use Functions 327

Writing Modules as Void Functions 327

May We Introduce:

Charles Babbage 331

An Overview of User-Defined Functions — 332
Flow of Control in Function Calls 332
Function Parameters 333

Syntax and Semantics of Void Functions — 336
Function Call (Invocation) 336
Function Declarations and Definitions 337
Local Variables 340
The Return Statement 341
Matters of Style:

Naming Void Functions 343
Header Files 343

Parameters — 344
Value Parameters 345
Reference Parameters 346
An Analogy 350
Matching Arguments with Parameters 350
Theoretical Foundations:

Argument-Passing Mechanisms 353

Designing Functions — 354
Writing Assertions as Program Comments 356
Matters of Style:

Function Preconditions and Postconditions 358
Documenting the Direction of Data Flow 358
Matters of Style :

Formatting Function Headings 360
Software Engineering Tip :

Conceptual Versus Physical Hiding
of a Function Implementation 361

Problem-Solving Case Study:

Comparison of Furniture-Store Sales — 363

Testing and Debugging — 372
The assert Library Function 374
Testing and Debugging Hints 376

Summary **376**

    Quick Check 377

    Exam Preparation Exercises 378

    Programming Warm-up Exercises 383

    Programming Problems 385

    Case Study Follow-Up 390

8   Scope, Lifetime, and More on Functions   391

Scope of Identifiers **392**

    Scope Rules 395

    Variable Declarations and Definitions 399

    Namespaces 400

Lifetime of a Variable **403**

    Initializations in Declarations 404

Interface Design **405**

    Side Effects 406

    Global Constants 409

    May We Introduce:

        Ada Lovelace 409

Value-Returning Functions **411**

    Boolean Functions 416

    Matters of Style:

        Naming Value-Returning Functions 419

    Interface Design and Side Effects 420

    When to Use Value-Returning Functions 421

    Background Information:

        Ignoring a Function Value 421

Problem-Solving Case Study:

Reformat Dates **423**

    Software Engineering Tip:

        Control Abstraction, Functional Cohesion,
        and Communication Complexity 434

Problem-Solving Case Study:

Starship Weight and Balance **435**

Testing and Debugging **446**
Stubs and Drivers 447
Testing and Debugging Hints 449

Summary **450**
Quick Check 451
Exam Preparation Exercises 452
Programming Warm-up Exercises 455
Programming Problems 457
Case Study Follow-Up 459

9 Additional Control Structures **461**

The Switch Statement **462**
May We Introduce:
Admiral Grace Murray Hopper 466

The Do-While Statement **468**

The For Statement **471**

The Break and Continue Statements **474**

Guidelines for Choosing a Looping Statement **477**

Problem-Solving Case Study:
Monthly Rainfall Averages **478**

Testing and Debugging **484**
Testing and Debugging Hints 484

Summary **485**
Quick Check 485
Exam Preparation Exercises 486
Programming Warm-up Exercises 488
Programming Problems 489
Case Study Follow-Up 491

10 Simple Data Types: Built-In and User-Defined **493**

Built-In Simple Types **494**
Integral Types 496
Floating-Point Types 500

Additional C++ Operators — *502*
Assignment Operators and Assignment Expressions — 503
Increment and Decrement Operators — 505
Bitwise Operators — 505
The Cast Operation — 506
The `sizeof` Operator — 507
The `?:` Operator — 507
Operator Precedence — 508

Working with Character Data — *511*
Character Sets — 511
C++ `char` Constants — 513
Programming Techniques — 515

More on Floating-Point Numbers — *520*
Representation of Floating-Point Numbers — 520
Arithmetic with Floating-Point Numbers — 523
Implementation of Floating-Point Numbers in the Computer — 524
Background Information
Practical Implications of Limited Precision — 530
Software Engineering Tip
Choosing a Numeric Data Type — 531

User-Defined Simple Types — *532*
The Typedef Statement — 532
Enumeration Types — 533
Named and Anonymous Data Types — 541
User-Written Header Files — 542

More on Type Coercion — *543*
Type Coercion in Arithmetic and Relational Expressions — 544
Type Coercion in Assignments, Argument Passing,
and Return of a Function Value — 545

Problem-Solving Case Study:
Finding the Area Under a Curve — *547*

Problem-Solving Case Study:
Rock, Paper, Scissors — *555*

Testing and Debugging — *565*
Floating-Point Data — 565

Coping with Input Errors 566

Testing and Debugging Hints 567

Summary **568**

Quick Check 569

Exam Preparation Exercises 570

Programming Warm-up Exercises 572

Programming Problems 573

Case Study Follow-Up 574

11 Structured Types, Data Abstraction, and Classes 577

Simple Versus Structured Data Types **578**

Records (C++ Structs) **579**

Accessing Individual Components 582

Aggregate Operations on Structs 583

More About Struct Declarations 585

Hierarchical Records 587

Unions **589**

Data Abstraction **590**

Abstract Data Types **592**

Theoretical Foundations:

Categories of Abstract Data Type Operations 595

C++ Classes **596**

Matters of Style:

Declaring Public and Private Class Members 599

Classes, Class Objects, and Class Members 600

Built-in Operations on Class Objects 601

Class Scope 603

Information Hiding 604

Specification and Implementation Files **606**

The Specification File 606

The Implementation File 608

Compiling and Linking a Multifile Program 613

Guaranteed Initialization with Class Constructors   **616**

Invoking a Constructor   617

Revised Specification and Implementation
Files for `TimeType`   618

Guidelines for Using Class Constructors   620

Problem-Solving Case Study:

Manipulating Dates   **621**

Problem-Solving Case Study:

Birthday Calls   **634**

Testing and Debugging   **644**

Testing and Debugging Hints   648

Summary   **649**

Quick Check   650

Exam Preparation Exercises   652

Programming Warm-up Exercises   656

Programming Problems   658

Case Study Follow-Up   661

12 Arrays   **663**

One-Dimensional Arrays   **664**

Declaring Arrays   666

Accessing Individual Components   667

Out-of-Bounds Array Indexes   670

Initializing Arrays in Declarations   671

(Lack of) Aggregate Array Operations   671

Examples of Declaring and Accessing Arrays   673

Passing Arrays as Arguments   676

Background Information:

C, C++, and Arrays as Arguments   679

Assertions About Arrays   679

Using Typedef with Arrays   680

Arrays of Records and Class Objects   **681**

Arrays of Records   681

Arrays of Class Objects   683

Special Kinds of Array Processing — 684
Subarray Processing — 684

Indexes with Semantic Content — 684

Two-Dimensional Arrays — 685

Processing Two-Dimensional Arrays — 689
Sum the Rows — 690

Sum the Columns — 691

Initialize the Array — 692

Print the Array — 694

Passing Two-Dimensional Arrays as Arguments — 695

Another Way of Defining Two-Dimensional Arrays — 698

Multidimensional Arrays — 700

Problem-Solving Case Study:
Comparison of Two Lists — 703

Problem-Solving Case Study:
City Council Election — 710

Testing and Debugging — 721
One-Dimensional Arrays — 721

Complex Structures — 722

Multidimensional Arrays — 723

Testing and Debugging Hints — 725

Summary — 726
Quick Check — 726

Exam Preparation Exercises — 729

Programming Warm-up Exercises — 734

Programming Problems — 737

Case Study Follow-Up — 741

13 Array-Based Lists — 743

The List as an Abstract Data Type — 744

Unsorted Lists — 748
Basic Operations — 748

Insertion and Deletion — 751

Sequential Search   752

Sorting   755

Sorted Lists   **758**

Basic Operations   761

Insertion   761

Sequential Search   764

Binary Search   765

Deletion   770

Theoretical Foundations:

   Complexity of Searching and Sorting 772

Understanding Character Strings   **773**

Initializing C Strings   776

C String Input and Output   777

C String Library Routines   781

String Class or C Strings?   783

Problem-Solving Case Study:

 Exam Attendance   **783**

Testing and Debugging   **792**

Testing and Debugging Hints   792

Summary   **793**

Quick Check   793

Exam Preparation Exercises   795

Programming Warm-up Exercises   797

Programming Problems   798

Case Study Follow-Up   799

14 **Object-Oriented Software Development**   **801**

Object-Oriented Programming   **802**

Objects   **804**

Inheritance   **805**

Deriving One Class from Another   807

Software Engineering Tip:

 Inheritance and Accessibility   810

Specification of the ExtTime Class   811

Implementation of the `ExtTime` Class   812

Avoiding Multiple Inclusion of Header Files   816

Composition   *817*

Design of a `TimeCard` Class   818

Implementation of the `TimeCard` Class   820

Dynamic Binding and Virtual Functions   *822*

The Slicing Problem   823

Virtual Functions   825

Object-Oriented Design   *827*

Step 1: Identify the Objects and Operations   828

Step 2: Determine the Relationships Among Objects   829

Step 3: Design the Driver   830

Software Engineering Tip:

The Iterative Nature of Object-Oriented Design   830

Implementing the Design   *831*

Problem-Solving Case Study:

Time Card Lookup   *832*

Testing and Debugging   *854*

Testing and Debugging Hints   854

Summary   *855*

Quick Check   856

Exam Preparation Exercises   858

Programming Warm-up Exercises   862

Programming Problems   863

Case Study Follow-Up   864

15 Pointers, Dynamic Data, and Reference Types   867

Pointers   *868*

Pointer Variables   869

Pointer Expressions   875

Dynamic Data   *879*

Reference Types   *884*

Classes and Dynamic Data *890*
Class Destructors 894
Shallow Versus Deep Copying 895
Class Copy-Constructors 897

Problem-Solving Case Study:

Personnel Records *901*
Problem-Solving Case Study:

Dynamic Arrays *917*
Testing and Debugging *928*
Testing and Debugging Hints 930

Summary *931*
Quick Check 932
Exam Preparation Exercises 934
Programming Warm-up Exercises 937
Programming Problems 939
Case Study Follow-Up 940

16 Linked Structures 943

Sequential Versus Linked Structures *944*
Array Representation of a Linked List *946*
Dynamic Data Representation of a Linked List *948*
Algorithms on Dynamic Linked Lists 956
Pointer Expressions 975
Classes and Dynamic Linked Lists 976

Choice of Data Representation *977*
Problem-Solving Case Study:

Simulated Playing Cards *979*
Problem-Solving Case Study:

Solitaire Simulation *986*
Testing and Debugging *1006*
Testing and Debugging Hints 1006

Summary *1006*

Quick Check   1007
Exam Preparation Exercises   1008
Programming Warm-up Exercises   1010
Programming Problems   1011
Case Study Follow-Up   1012

17 Recursion   1013

What Is Recursion?   1014

Recursive Algorithms with Simple Variables   1018

Towers of Hanoi   1021

Recursive Algorithms with Structured Variables   1026

Recursion Using Pointer Variables   1029
Printing a Dynamic Linked List in Reverse Order   1029
Copying a Dynamic Linked List   1032

Recursion or Iteration?   1036

Problem-Solving Case Study:
Converting Decimal Integers to Binary Integers   1037

Problem-Solving Case Study
Minimum Value in an Integer Array   1040

Testing and Debugging   1043
Testing and Debugging Hints   1043

Summary   1043
Quick Check   1044
Exam Preparation Exercises   1044
Programming Warm-up Exercises   1046
Programming Problems   1048
Case Study Follow-Up   1049

Appendix A   Reserved Words   A1

Appendix B   Operator Precedence   A1

Appendix C   A Selection of Standard Library Routines   A3

Appendix D   Using This Book with a Prestandard Version of C++   A12

Appendix E   Character Sets   *A16*

Appendix F   Program Style, Formatting, and Documentation   *A18*

Glossary   *A27*

Answers to Selected Exercises   *A37*

Index   *A67*

Preface

Shortly after its introduction in 1996, the first edition of *Programming and Problem Solving with C++* became one of the best-selling computer science textbooks in the United States. Although this second edition incorporates numerous changes, including reorganization of chapter material, one thing has not changed: our commitment to the student. As always, our efforts are directed toward making the sometimes difficult concepts of computer science more accessible to all students.

The first edition and the Pascal and Ada versions of this book have been widely accepted as model textbooks for the ACM-recommended curriculum for CS1 and the Advanced Placement AP exam in computer science. The content and organization have been guided by the ACM-recommended curriculum for CS1 (October 1984) and the following knowledge units from the ACM/IEEE Computing Curricula 1991 recommendations for a C101 course: AL1–AL4, AL6, NU1, PL3–PL5, and SE1–SE5.

This edition of *Programming and Problem Solving with C++* continues to reflect our experience that topics once considered too advanced can be taught in the first course. For example, we address metalanguages explicitly as the formal means of specifying programming language syntax. We introduce Big-*O* notation early and use it to compare algorithms in later chapters. We discuss modular design in terms of abstract steps, concrete steps, functional equivalence, and functional cohesion. Preconditions and postconditions are used in the context of the algorithm walk-through, in the development of testing strategies, and as interface documentation for user-written functions. The discussion of function interface design includes encapsulation, control abstraction, and communication complexity. Data abstraction and abstract data types (ADTs) are explained in conjunction with the C++ class mechanism, forming a natural lead-in to object-oriented programming.

Changes in the Second Edition

The second edition incorporates the following changes:

- *Conformance to ISO/ANSI standard C++.* ISO/ANSI standard C++ (officially approved in July 1998) is used throughout the book, including relevant portions of the new C++ standard library. However, readers with pre–standard C++ compilers are also supported. A new appendix discusses how to modify the textbook's programs to compile and run successfully with an earlier compiler.

- *An earlier introduction to classes, data abstraction, and object-oriented concepts.* Chapters 11–19 of the first edition have been reorganized into the following Chapters 11–17:
  11 Structured Types, Data Abstraction, and Classes
  12 Arrays
  13 Array-Based Lists
  14 Object-Oriented Software Development
  15 Pointers, Dynamic Data, and Reference Types
  16 Linked Structures
  17 Recursion

  The visible changes are the deletion of two chapters ("Records" and "Multidimensional Arrays"), whose contents have been merged into Chapters 11 and 12, respectively, and the movement of the chapter "Structured Types, Data Abstraction, and Classes" (Chapter 15 in the first edition) to become Chapter 11. With this reorganization, the concept of the C++ class as both a structuring mechanism and a tool for abstraction now comes earlier in the book.

  Introducing classes before arrays has several benefits. In their first exposure to composite types, many students find it easier to comprehend accessing a component by name rather than by position. Chapter 12 on arrays can now rather easily introduce the idea of an array of class objects or an array of structs. Also, Chapter 13, which deals with the list as an ADT, can now be handled in a better way, namely, encapsulating both the data representation (an array) and the length variable within a class, rather than the first edition's approach of using two loosely coupled variables (an array and a separate length variable) to represent the list. Finally, with three chapters' worth of exposure to classes and objects, students reading Chapter 14 can focus on the more difficult aspects of the chapter: inheritance, composition, and dynamic binding.

  A natural result of this reorganization is that the chapter "Object-Oriented Software Development" comes earlier in the sequence: Chapter 14 rather than the first edition's Chapter 16.

- *Attention to length.* In response to feedback from our users and reviewers about the length of the first edition, we have made the following changes:
  - Presentations of certain topics have been streamlined or moved elsewhere. (For example, the material on loop invariants has been moved to the *Instructor's Guide*.)
  - The number of case studies has been reduced substantially. Whereas the first edition presented two or three case studies per chapter, most chapters now have one case study.
  - The first edition's two chapters on one-dimensional arrays and multidimensional arrays have been combined into a single chapter.

- The first edition's appendix containing all syntax templates in one location has been moved to the publisher's Web site.

C++ and Object-Oriented Programming

Some educators reject the C++ language as too permissive and too conducive to writing cryptic, unreadable programs. Our experience does not support this view, *provided that the use of language features is modeled appropriately*. That C++ permits a terse, compact programming style cannot be labeled simply as "good" or "bad." Almost any programming language can be used to write in a style that is too terse and clever to be easily understood. C++ may indeed be used in this manner more often than are other languages, but we have found that with careful instruction in software engineering and a programming style that is straightforward, disciplined, and free of intricate language features, students can learn to use C++ to produce clear, readable code.

It must be emphasized that although we use C++ as a vehicle for teaching computer science concepts, the book is not a language manual and does not attempt to cover all of C++. Certain language features—templates, exceptions, operator overloading, default arguments, and mechanisms for advanced forms of inheritance, to name a few—are omitted in an effort not to overwhelm the beginning student with too much too fast.

Currently, there are diverse opinions about when to introduce the topic of object-oriented programming (OOP). Some educators advocate an immersion in OOP from the very beginning, whereas others (for whom this book is intended) favor a more heterogeneous approach in which both functional decomposition and object-oriented design are presented as design tools. The chapter organization of *Programming and Problem Solving with C++* reflects a transitional approach to OOP. Although we provide an early preview of object-oriented design in Chapter 4, we delay a focused discussion until Chapter 14. The sequence of topics in Chapters 1 through 13 mirrors our belief that OOP is best understood after a firm grounding in algorithm design, control abstraction, and data abstraction with classes. As one reviewer of the first edition, who was originally critical of the delayed introduction to OOP, stated in a subsequent review, "The logical flow of the chapters is excellent. In the earlier review, I commented on the late introduction to OOP. I now (having nearly completed teaching a CS1 with C++) believe that is a good strategy."

Synopsis

Chapter 1 is designed to create a comfortable rapport between students and the subject. The basics of hardware and software are presented, and problem-solving techniques are discussed and reinforced in a Problem-Solving Case Study. We have added a section on ethics to round out this introduction.

Chapters 2 and 3 have been revised as follows. Chapter 2, instead of overwhelming the student right away with the various numeric types available in C++, concentrates on two types only: char and string. (The string type is the ISO/ANSI string class provided by the standard library.) With fewer data types to keep track of, students can focus on overall program structure and get an earlier start on creating and running a simple program. Chapter 3 then begins with a discussion of the C++ numeric types and proceeds as in the first edition, with material on arithmetic expressions, function calls, and output. Unlike many books that detail *all* of the C++ data types and *all* of the C++ operators at once, these two chapters focus only on the int, float, char, and string types and the basic arithmetic operators. Details of the other data types and the more elaborate C++ operators are postponed until Chapter 10.

The functional decomposition and object-oriented design methodologies are a major focus of Chapter 4, and the discussion is written with a healthy degree of formalism. This early in the book, the treatment of object-oriented design is necessarily more superficial than that of functional decomposition. However, students gain the perspective that there are two—not one—design methodologies in widespread use and that each serves a specific purpose. Chapter 4 also covers input and file I/O. The early introduction of files permits the assignment of programming problems that require the use of sample data files.

Students learn to recognize functions in Chapters 1 and 2, and they learn to use standard library functions in Chapter 3. Chapter 4 reinforces the basic concepts of function calls, argument passing, and function libraries. Chapter 4 also relates functions to the implementation of modular designs and begins the discussion of interface design that is essential to writing proper functions.

Chapter 5 begins with Boolean data, but its main purpose is to introduce the concept of flow of control. Selection, using If-Then and If-Then-Else structures, is used to demonstrate the distinction between physical ordering of statements and logical ordering. We also develop the concept of nested control structures. Chapter 5 concludes with a lengthy Testing and Debugging section that expands on the modular design discussion by introducing preconditions and postconditions. The algorithm walk-through and code walk-through are introduced as means of preventing errors, and the execution trace is used to find errors that made it into the code. We also cover data validation and testing strategies extensively in this section.

Chapter 6 is devoted to loop control strategies and looping operations using the syntax of the While statement. Rather than introducing multiple syntactical structures, our approach is to teach the concepts of looping using only the While statement. However, because many instructors have told us that they prefer to show students the syntax for all of C++'s looping statements at once, the discussion of For and Do-While statements in Chapter 9 can be covered optionally after Chapter 6.

By Chapter 7, the students are already comfortable with breaking problems into modules and using library functions, and they are receptive to the idea of writing their own functions. Chapter 7 focuses on passing arguments by value and covers flow of control in function calls, arguments and parameters, local variables, and interface design. The last topic includes preconditions and postconditions in the interface documentation, control abstraction, encapsulation, and physical versus conceptual hiding of an implementation. Chapter 8 expands the discussion to include reference parameters, scope and lifetime, stubs and drivers, and more on interface design, including side effects.

Chapter 9 covers the remaining "ice cream and cake" control structures in C++ (Switch, Do-While, and For), along with the Break and Continue statements. Chapter 9 forms a natural ending point for the first quarter of a two-quarter introductory course sequence.

Chapter 10 begins a transition between the control structures orientation of the first half of the book and the abstract data type orientation of the second half. We examine the built-in simple data types in terms of the set of values represented by each type and the allowable operations on those values. We introduce more C++ operators and discuss the problems of floating-point representation and precision at length. User-defined simple types, user-written header files, and type coercion are among the other topics covered in this chapter.

We begin Chapter 11 with a discussion of simple versus structured data types. We introduce the record (`struct` in C++) as a heterogeneous data structure, describe the syntax for accessing its components, and demonstrate how to combine record types into a hierarchical record structure. From this base, we make a transition to the concept of data abstraction and give a precise definition to the notion of an ADT, emphasizing the separation of specification from implementation. The C++ class mechanism is introduced as a programming language representation of an ADT. The concepts of encapsulation, information hiding, and public and private class members are stressed. We describe the separate compilation of program files, and students learn the technique of placing a class's declaration and implementation into two separate files: the specification (`.h`) file and the implementation file.

In Chapter 12, the array is introduced as a homogeneous data structure whose components are accessed by position rather than by name. One-dimensional arrays are examined in depth, including arrays of structs and arrays of class objects. Material on multidimensional arrays, formerly a separate chapter in the first edition, has been moved to this chapter to complete the discussion.

Chapter 13 integrates the material from Chapters 11 and 12 by defining the list as an ADT. Because we have already introduced classes and arrays, we can clearly differentiate the concepts of array and list from the beginning. The array is a built-in, fixed-size data structure. The list is a user-defined, variable-size structure represented as a length and an array of items, bound together in a class object. The elements in the list are those elements in the array from position 0 through position *length* − 1. In this chapter, we design C++ classes for unsorted and sorted list ADTs, and we code the list algorithms as class member functions. We use Big-*O* notation to compare the various searching and sorting algorithms developed for these ADTs. Finally, we examine C strings in order to give students some insight into how a higher-level abstraction (a string as a list of characters) might be implemented in terms of a lower-level abstraction (a null-terminated `char` array).

Chapter 14 extends the concepts of data abstraction and C++ classes to an exploration of object-oriented software development. Object-oriented design, introduced briefly in Chapter 4, is revisited in greater depth. Students learn to distinguish between inheritance and composition relationships during the design phase, and C++'s derived classes are used to implement inheritance. This chapter also introduces C++ virtual functions, which support polymorphism in the form of run-time binding of operations to objects.

Chapter 15 examines pointer and reference types. We present pointers as a way of making programs more efficient and of allowing the run-time allocation of program data. The coverage of dynamic data structures continues in Chapter 16, in which we present linked lists, linked-list algorithms, and alternative representations of linked lists.

Chapter 17 covers recursion. There is no consensus as to the best place to introduce this subject. We believe that it is better to wait until at least the second semester to cover this topic. However, we have included recursion for those instructors who have requested it. Although Chapter 17 is the last chapter, we divide the examples into two parts: those that require only simple data types and those that require structured data types. Instructors can cover the first part after Chapter 8. The second part contains examples from simple arrays to dynamic linked lists. These examples could be used individually after the appropriate chapter (for example, simple arrays after Chapter 12) or as a unit after Chapter 16.

Additional Features

Web Links Special Web icons found in the Special Sections (see below) prompt students to visit the text's companion Web site located at `www.jbpub.com/dale` for additional information about selected topics. These Web Links give students instant access to real-world applications of material presented in the text. The Web Links are updated on a regular basis to ensure that students receive the most recent information available on the Internet.

Special Sections Five kinds of features are set off from the main text. Theoretical Foundations sections present material related to the fundamental theory behind various branches of computer science. Software Engineering Tips discuss methods of making programs more reliable, robust, or efficient. Matters of Style address stylistic issues in the coding of programs. Background Information sections explore side issues that enhance the student's general knowledge of computer science. May We Introduce sections contain biographies of computing pioneers such as Blaise Pascal, Ada Lovelace, and Grace Murray Hopper. Web Links appear in most of these Special Sections prompting students to visit the companion Web site at www.jbpub.com/dale for expanded material.

Goals Each chapter begins with a list of learning objectives for the student. These goals are reinforced and tested in the end-of-chapter exercises.

Problem-Solving Case Studies Problem solving is best demonstrated through case studies. In each case study, we present a problem and use problem-solving techniques to develop a manual solution. Next, we expand the solution to an algorithm, using functional decomposition, object-oriented design, or both; then we code the algorithm in C++. We show sample test data and output and follow up with a discussion of what is involved in thoroughly testing the program.

Testing and Debugging Following the case studies in each chapter, this section considers in depth the implications of the chapter material with regard to thorough testing of programs. The section concludes with a list of testing and debugging hints.

Quick Checks At the end of each chapter are questions that test the student's recall of major points associated with the chapter goals. Upon reading each question, the student immediately should know the answer, which he or she can then verify by glancing at the answers at the end of the section. The page number on which the concept is discussed appears at the end of each question so that the student can review the material in the event of an incorrect response.

Exam Preparation Exercises These questions help the student prepare for tests. The questions usually have objective answers and are designed to be answerable with a few minutes of work. Answers to selected questions are given in the back of the book, and the remaining questions are answered in the *Instructor's Guide.*

Programming Warm-up Exercises This section provides the student with experience in writing C++ code fragments. The student can practice the syntactic constructs in each chapter without the burden of writing a complete program. Solutions to selected questions from each chapter appear in the back of the book; the remaining solutions may be found in the *Instructor's Guide*.

Programming Problems These exercises, drawn from a wide range of disciplines, require the student to design solutions and write complete programs.

Case Study Follow-Up These questions require the student to analyze or modify the case studies in the chapter. The exercises afford experience in reading and understanding the documentation and code for existing programs.

Supplements

Instructor's Guide and Test Bank The *Instructor's Guide* features chapter-by-chapter teaching notes, answers to the balance of the exercises, and a compilation of exam questions with answers. The *Instructor's Guide* is available to adopters on request from Jones and Bartlett.

Instructor's ToolKit CD-ROM Also available to adopters upon request from the publisher is a powerful teaching tool entitled "Instructor's ToolKit." This CD-ROM contains an electronic version of the *Instructor's Guide,* a computerized test bank, PowerPoint lecture presentations containing over 900 slides, and the complete programs from the text (see below).

Programs The programs contain the source code for all of the complete programs that are found within the textbook. They are available on the Instructor's ToolKit CD-ROM and also as a free download for instructors and students from the publisher's Web site: www.jbpub.com/disks. The programs from all the case studies, plus several programs that appear in the chapter bodies, are included. Fragments or snippets of program code are not included nor are the solutions to the chapter-ending "Programming Problems." These program files can be viewed or edited using any standard text editor, but in order to compile and run the programs, a C++ compiler must be used.

Companion Web Site This Web site features integrated Web Links from the textbook, the complete programs from the text, and Appendix D entitled "Using this Book with a Prestandard Version of C++," which describes the changes needed to allow the programs in the textbook to run successfully with a prestandard compiler. The Web site also includes the syntax templates in one location. These appeared as an appendix in the last edition.

A Laboratory Course in C++, Second Edition   Written by Nell Dale, this lab manual follows the organization of the second edition of the text. The lab manual is designed to allow the instructor maximum flexibility and may be used in both open and closed laboratory settings. Each chapter contains three types of activities: Prelab, Inlab and Postlab. Each lesson is broken into exercises that thoroughly demonstrate the concept covered in the chapter. A disk that contains the programs, program shells (partial programs), and data files accompanies the lab manual.

Student Lecture Notebook   Designed from the PowerPoint presentations developed for this text, the Student Lecture Notebook is an invaluable tool for learning. The notebook is designed to encourage students to focus their energies on listening to the lecture as they fill in additional details. The skeletal outline concept helps students organize their notes and readily recognize the important concepts in each chapter.

About the Cover

The broken and scrambled cover image was created from a unique aspect of the 40-room Centre Family Dwelling, a building in The Shaker Village of Pleasant Hill, Kentucky. Built to accommodate 100 celibate inhabitants, Centre Family Dwelling boasts two entranceways, dual stairways, and a wide common passageway on each floor that separates brothers' and sisters' apartments.

Completed in 1834, the massive building's exterior is hand-hewn Kentucky River Limestone which was quarried from the nearby Kentucky Palisades. In the hallways, the floors are covered in quarter-sawed white oak.

Centre Family Dwelling's high ceilings and vast windows are exceptional features for architecture of the time. These unusual characteristics reflect a concern for proper ventilation and lighting, embracing small, high interior windows and transoms to permit light into intimate spaces.

Acknowledgments

We would like to thank the many individuals who have helped us in the preparation of this second edition. We are indebted to the members of the faculties of the Computer Science Departments at the University of Texas at Austin, the University of Massachusetts at Amherst, and the University of Wisconsin–La Crosse.

We extend special thanks to Jeff Brumfield for developing the syntax template metalanguage and allowing us to use it in the text.

For their many helpful suggestions, we thank the lecturers, teaching assistants, consultants, and student proctors who run the courses for which this book was written, and the students themselves.

We are grateful to the following people who took the time to review our manuscript: J. Ken Collier, Northern Arizona State; Lee Cornell, Mankato State University; Charles Dierbach, Towsen State University; Judy Etchison, Collin County Community College; David Galles, University of San Francisco; Susan Gauch, University of Kansas; Wagar Haque, University of Northern British Columbia; Ilga Higbee, Black Hawk College; Jeanine Ingber, University of New Mexico; Paula Jech, Pennsylvania State University; Hikyoo Koh, Lamar University; I. Stephen Leach, Florida State University; Joseph Marti, College of the Canyons; Kenrick Mock, Oregon State University; Viera Proulx, Northeastern University; Howard Pyron, University of Missouri-Rolla; Dennis Ray, Old Dominion University; Sujan Sarkar, Santa Rosa Junior College; Lynn Stauffer, Sonoma State University; Greg Steuben, Rensselaer Polytechnic Institute.

We also thank Karen Jolie and PageMasters & Company along with the many people at Jones and Bartlett who contributed so much, especially Tom Walker, Rebecca Marks, Jennifer Jacobson, Anne Spencer, J. Michael Stranz, W. Scott Smith, and Mike DeFronzo.

Anyone who has ever written a book—or is related to someone who has—can appreciate the amount of time involved in such a project. To our families—all the Dale clan and the extended Dale family (too numerous to name); to Lisa, Charlie, and Abby; to Anne, Brady, and Kari—thanks for your tremendous support and indulgence.

N. D.
C. W.
M. H.

1

Overview of Programming and Problem Solving

GOALS

- To understand what a computer program is.
- To be able to list the basic stages involved in writing a computer program.
- To understand what an algorithm is.
- To learn what a high-level programming language is.
- To be able to describe what a compiler is and what it does.
- To understand the compilation and execution processes.
- To learn the history of the C++ programming language.
- To learn what the major components of a computer are and how they work together.
- To be able to distinguish between hardware and software.
- To learn about some of the basic ethical issues confronting computing professionals.
- To be able to choose an appropriate problem-solving method for developing an algorithmic solution to a problem.

Overview of Programming

---

com•put•er \kəm-'pyüt-ər\ *n, often attrib* (1646): one that computes; *specif.* a programmable electronic device that can store, retrieve, and process data*

What a brief definition for something that has, in just a few decades, changed the way of life in industrialized societies! Computers touch all areas of our lives: paying bills, driving cars, using the telephone, shopping. In fact, it would be easier to list those areas of our lives that are not affected by computers.

It is sad that a device that does so much good is so often maligned and feared. How many times have you heard someone say, "I'm sorry, our computer fouled things up" or "I just don't understand computers; they're too complicated for me"? The very fact that you are reading this book, however, means that you are ready to set aside prejudice and learn about computers. But be forewarned: This book is not just about computers in the abstract. This is a text to teach you how to program computers.

What Is Programming?

Much of human behavior and thought is characterized by logical sequences. Since infancy, you have been learning how to act, how to do things. And you have learned to expect certain behavior from other people.

A lot of what you do every day you do automatically. Fortunately, it is not necessary for you to consciously think of every step involved in a process as simple as turning a page by hand:

1. Lift hand.
2. Move hand to right side of book.
3. Grasp top right corner of page.
4. Move hand from right to left until page is positioned so that you can read what is on the other side.
5. Let go of page.

Think how many neurons must fire and how many muscles must respond, all in a certain order or sequence, to move your arm and hand. Yet you do it unconsciously.

Much of what you do unconsciously you once had to learn. Watch how a baby concentrates on putting one foot before the other while learning to walk. Then watch a group of three-year-olds playing tag.

---

* By permission. From *Merriam-Webster's Collegiate Dictionary*, Tenth Edition. © 1994 by Merriam-Webster Inc.

On a broader scale, mathematics never could have been developed without logical sequences of steps for solving problems and proving theorems. Mass production never would have worked without operations taking place in a certain order. Our whole civilization is based on the order of things and actions.

We create order, both consciously and unconsciously, through a process we call **programming.** This book is concerned with the programming of one of our tools, the **computer.**

Programming   Planning or scheduling the performance of a task or an event.

Computer   A programmable device that can store, retrieve, and process data.

Computer programming   The process of planning a sequence of steps for a computer to follow.

Just as a concert program lists the order in which the players perform pieces, a **computer program** lists the sequence of steps the computer performs. From now on, when we use the words *programming* and *program*, we mean *computer programming* and *computer program*.

Computer program   A sequence of instructions to be performed by a computer.

The computer allows us to do tasks more efficiently, quickly, and accurately than we could by hand—if we could do them by hand at all. In order to use this powerful tool, we must specify what we want done and the order in which we want it done. We do this through programming.

How Do We Write a Program?

A computer is not intelligent. It cannot analyze a problem and come up with a solution. A human (the *programmer*) must analyze the problem, develop a sequence of instructions for solving the problem, and then communicate it to the computer. What's the advantage of using a computer if it can't solve problems? Once we have written the solution as a sequence of instructions for the computer, the computer can repeat the solution very quickly and consistently, again and again. The computer frees people from repetitive and boring tasks.

To write a sequence of instructions for a computer to follow, we must go through a two-phase process: *problem solving* and *implementation* (see Figure 1-1).

Problem-Solving Phase

1. *Analysis and specification.* Understand (define) the problem and what the solution must do.
2. *General solution (algorithm).* Develop a logical sequence of steps that solves the problem.
3. *Verify.* Follow the steps exactly to see if the solution really does solve the problem.

Implementation Phase

1. *Concrete solution (program).* Translate the algorithm into a programming language.
2. *Test.* Have the computer follow the instructions. Then manually check the results. If you find errors, analyze the program and the algorithm to determine the source of the errors, and then make corrections.

Once a program has been written, it enters a third phase: *maintenance*.

Maintenance Phase

1. *Use.* Use the program.
2. *Maintain.* Modify the program to meet changing requirements or to correct any errors that show up in using it.

The programmer begins the programming process by analyzing the problem and developing a general solution called an **algorithm**. Understanding and analyzing a problem take up much more time than Figure 1-1 implies. They are the heart of the programming process.

FIGURE 1-1
Programming
Process

PROBLEM-SOLVING PHASE   IMPLEMENTATION PHASE

Algorithm   A step-by-step procedure for solving a problem in a finite amount of time.

If our definitions of a computer program and an algorithm look similar, it is because all programs are algorithms. A program is simply an algorithm that has been written for a computer.

An algorithm is a verbal or written description of a logical sequence of actions. We use algorithms every day. Recipes, instructions, and directions are all examples of algorithms that are not programs.

When you start your car, you follow a step-by-step procedure. The algorithm might look something like this:

1. Insert the key.
2. Make sure the transmission is in Park (or Neutral).
3. Depress the gas pedal.
4. Turn the key to the start position.
5. If the engine starts within six seconds, release the key to the ignition position.
6. If the engine doesn't start in six seconds, release the key and gas pedal, wait ten seconds, and repeat steps 3 through 6, but not more than five times.
7. If the car doesn't start, call the garage.

Without the phrase "but not more than five times" in step 6, you could be trying to start the car forever. Why? Because if something is wrong with the car, repeating steps 3 through 6 over and over again will not start it. This kind of never-ending situation is called an *infinite loop*. If we leave the phrase "but not more than five times" out of step 6, the procedure does not fit our definition of an algorithm. An algorithm must terminate in a finite amount of time for all possible conditions.

Suppose a programmer needs an algorithm to determine an employee's weekly wages. The algorithm reflects what would be done by hand:

1. Look up the employee's pay rate.
2. Determine the number of hours worked during the week.
3. If the number of hours worked is less than or equal to 40, multiply the number of hours by the pay rate to calculate regular wages.
4. If the number of hours worked is greater than 40, multiply 40 by the pay rate to calculate regular wages, and then multiply the difference between the number of hours worked and 40 by $1\frac{1}{2}$ times the pay rate to calculate overtime wages.
5. Add the regular wages to the overtime wages (if any) to determine total wages for the week.

The steps the computer follows are often the same steps you would use to do the calculations by hand.

After developing a general solution, the programmer tests the algorithm, walking through each step mentally or manually. If the algorithm doesn't work, the programmer repeats the problem-solving process, analyzing the problem again and coming up with another algorithm. Often the second algorithm is just a variation of the first. When the programmer is satisfied with the algorithm, he or she translates it into a **programming language.** We use the C++ programming language in this book.

Programming language   A set of rules, symbols, and special words used to construct a computer program.

A programming language is a simplified form of English (with math symbols) that adheres to a strict set of grammatical rules. English is far too complicated a language for today's computers to follow. Programming languages, because they limit vocabulary and grammar, are much simpler.

Although a programming language is simple in form, it is not always easy to use. Try giving someone directions to the nearest airport using a vocabulary of no more than 45 words, and you'll begin to see the problem. Programming forces you to write very simple, exact instructions.

FIGURE 1-2

Differences in
Implementation

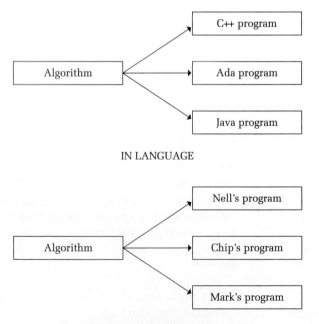

IN LANGUAGE

IN PERSONAL PROGRAMMING STYLE

Translating an algorithm into a programming language is called *coding* the algorithm. The product of that translation—the program—is tested by running (*executing*) it on the computer. If the program fails to produce the desired results, the programmer must *debug* it—that is, determine what is wrong and then modify the program, or even the algorithm, to fix it. The combination of coding and testing an algorithm is called *implementation*.

There is no single way to implement an algorithm. For example, an algorithm can be translated into more than one programming language. Each translation produces a different implementation. Even when two people translate an algorithm into the same programming language, they are likely to come up with different implementations (see Figure 1-2). Why? Because every programming language allows the programmer some flexibility in how an algorithm is translated. Given this flexibility, people adopt their own styles in writing programs, just as they do in writing short stories or essays. Once you have some programming experience, you develop a style of your own. Throughout this book, we offer tips on good programming style.

Some people try to speed up the programming process by going directly from the problem definition to coding the program (see Figure 1-3). A shortcut here is very tempting and at first seems to save a lot of time. However, for many reasons that will become obvious to you as you read this book, this kind of shortcut actually takes *more* time and effort. Developing a general solution before you write a program helps you manage the problem, keep your thoughts straight, and avoid mistakes. If you don't take the time at the beginning to think out and polish your algorithm, you'll spend a lot of extra time debugging and revising your program. So think first and code later! The sooner you start coding, the longer it takes to write a program that works.

Once a program has been put into use, it is often necessary to modify it. Modification may involve fixing an error that is discovered during the use of the program or changing the program in response to changes in the user's requirements. Each time the program is modified, it is necessary to repeat the problem-solving and implementation phases for those aspects of

FIGURE 1-3

Programming
Shortcut?

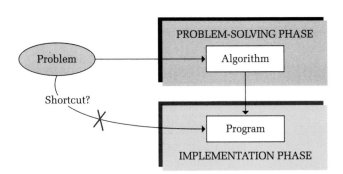

the program that change. This phase of the programming process is known as maintenance and actually accounts for the majority of the effort expended on most programs. For example, a program that is implemented in a few months may need to be maintained over a period of many years. Thus, it is a cost-effective investment of time to develop the initial problem solution and program implementation carefully. Together, the problem-solving, implementation, and maintenance phases constitute the program's *life cycle.*

In addition to solving the problem, implementing the algorithm, and maintaining the program, **documentation** is an important part of the programming process. Documentation includes written explanations of the problem being solved and the organization of the solution, comments embedded within the program itself, and user manuals that describe how to use the program. Most programs are worked on by many different people over a long period of time. Each of those people must be able to read and understand your code.

Documentation The written text and comments that make a program easier for others to understand, use, and modify.

After you write a program, you must give the computer the information or data necessary to solve the problem. **Information** is any knowledge that can be communicated, including abstract ideas and concepts such as "the earth is round." **Data** is information in a form the computer can use—for example, the numbers and letters making up the formulas that relate the earth's radius to its volume and surface area. But data is not restricted to numbers and letters. These days, computers also process data that represents sound (to be played through speakers), graphic images (to be displayed on a computer screen or printer), video (to be played on a VCR), and so forth.

Information Any knowledge that can be communicated.

Data Information in a form a computer can use.

---

*T*HEORETICAL FOUNDATIONS

Binary Representation of Data

In a computer, data is represented electronically by pulses of electricity. Electric circuits, in their simplest form, are either on or off. Usually a circuit that is on is represented by the number 1; a circuit that is off is represented by the number 0. Any kind of data can be represented by combinations of enough 1s and 0s. We simply have to choose which combination represents each piece of data we are using. For example, we could arbitrarily choose the pattern 1101000110 to represent the name *C++*.

Data represented by 1s and 0s is in *binary form*. The binary (base-2) number system uses only 1s and 0s to represent numbers. (The decimal [base-10] number system uses the digits 0 through 9.) The word *bit* (short for **b**inary dig**it**) often is used to refer to a single 1 or 0. The pattern 1101000110 thus has 10 bits. A binary number with 10 bits can represent 2^{10} (1024) different patterns. A *byte* is a group of 8 bits; it can represent 2^8 (256) patterns. Inside the computer, each character (such as the letter *A*, the letter *g*, or a question mark) is usually represented by a byte. Four bits, or half of a byte, is called a *nibble* or *nybble*—a name that originally was proposed with tongue in cheek but now is standard terminology. Groups of 16, 32, and 64 bits are generally referred to as *words* (although the terms *short word* and *long word* are sometimes used to refer to 16-bit and 64-bit groups, respectively).

The process of assigning bit patterns to pieces of data is called *coding*—the same name we give to the process of translating an algorithm into a programming language. The names are the same because the only language that the first computers recognized was binary in form. Thus, in the early days of computers, programming meant translating both data and algorithms into patterns of 1s and 0s.

Binary coding schemes are still used inside the computer to represent both the instructions that it follows and the data that it uses. For example, 16 bits can represent the decimal integers from 0 to $2^{16} - 1$ (65,535). Characters also can be represented by bit combinations. In one coding scheme, 01001101 represents *M* and 01101101 represents *m*. More complicated coding schemes are necessary to represent negative numbers, real numbers, numbers in scientific notation, sound, graphics, and video. In Chapter 10, we examine in detail the representation of numbers and characters in the computer.

The patterns of bits that represent data vary from one computer to another. Even on the same computer, different programming languages can use different binary representations for the same data. A single programming language may even use the same pattern of bits to represent different things in different contexts. (People do this too. The word formed by the four letters *tack* has different meanings depending on whether you are talking about upholstery, sailing, sewing, paint, or horseback riding.) The point is that patterns of bits by themselves are meaningless. It is the way in which the patterns are used that gives them their meaning.

Fortunately, we no longer have to work with binary coding schemes. Today the process of coding is usually just a matter of writing down the data in letters, numbers, and symbols. The computer automatically converts these letters, numbers, and symbols into binary form. Still, as you work with computers, you will continually run into numbers that are related to powers of 2—numbers such as 256, 32,768, and 65,536—reminders that the binary number system is lurking somewhere nearby.

What Is a Programming Language?

In the computer, all data, whatever its form, is stored and used in binary codes, strings of 1s and 0s. Instructions and data are stored together in the computer's memory using these binary codes. If you were to look at the binary codes representing instructions and data in memory, you could not tell the difference between them; they are distinguished only by the manner in which the computer uses them. It is thus possible for the computer to process its own instructions as a form of data.

When computers were first developed, the only programming language available was the primitive instruction set built into each machine, the **machine language,** or *machine code.*

Machine language   The language, made up of binary-coded instructions, that is used directly by the computer.

Even though most computers perform the same kinds of operations, their designers choose different sets of binary codes for each instruction. So the machine code for one computer is not the same as for another.

When programmers used machine language for programming, they had to enter the binary codes for the various instructions, a tedious process that was prone to error. Moreover, their programs were difficult to read and modify. In time, **assembly languages** were developed to make the programmer's job easier.

Assembly language   A low-level programming language in which a mnemonic is used to represent each of the machine language instructions for a particular computer.

Instructions in an assembly language are in an easy-to-remember form called a *mnemonic* (pronounced ni-MON-ik). Typical instructions for addition and subtraction might look like this:

Assembly Language	Machine Language
ADD	100101
SUB	010011

Although assembly language is easier for humans to work with, the computer cannot directly execute the instructions. One of the fundamental discoveries in computer science is that, because a computer can process its own instructions as a form of data, it is possible to write a program to translate the assembly language instructions into machine code. Such a program is called an **assembler**.

Assembler   A program that translates an assembly language program into machine code.

Assembly language is a step in the right direction, but it still forces programmers to think in terms of individual machine instructions. Eventually, computer scientists developed high-level programming languages. These languages are easier to use than assembly languages or machine code because they are closer to English and other natural languages (see Figure 1-4).

FIGURE 1-4

Levels of Abstraction

Human thought

Natural language (English, French, German, etc.)

High-level language (C++, FORTRAN, COBOL, etc.)

Low-level language (assembly language)

Machine code (computer)

A program called a **compiler** translates programs written in certain high-level languages (C++, Pascal, FORTRAN, COBOL, Modula-2, and Ada, for example) into machine language. If you write a program in a high-level language, you can run it on any computer that has the appropriate compiler. This is possible because most high-level languages are *standardized*, which means that an official description of the language exists.

Compiler   A program that translates a high-level language into machine code.

A program in a high-level language is called a **source program.** To the compiler, a source program is just input data. It translates the source program into a machine language program called an **object program** (see Figure 1-5). Some compilers also output a *listing*—a copy of the program with error messages and other information inserted.

Source program   A program written in a high-level programming language.

Object program   The machine language version of a source program.

A benefit of standardized high-level languages is that they allow you to write *portable* (or *machine-independent*) code. As Figure 1-5 emphasizes,

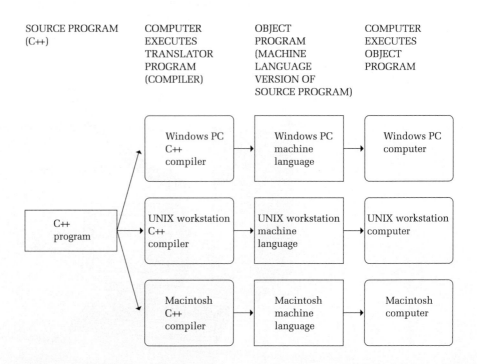

FIGURE 1-5

High-Level Programming Languages Allow Programs to Be Compiled on Different Systems

SOURCE PROGRAM (C++)

COMPUTER EXECUTES TRANSLATOR PROGRAM (COMPILER)

OBJECT PROGRAM (MACHINE LANGUAGE VERSION OF SOURCE PROGRAM)

COMPUTER EXECUTES OBJECT PROGRAM

C++ program

Windows PC C++ compiler → Windows PC machine language → Windows PC computer

UNIX workstation C++ compiler → UNIX workstation machine language → UNIX workstation computer

Macintosh C++ compiler → Macintosh machine language → Macintosh computer

FIGURE 1-6

Compilation and
Execution

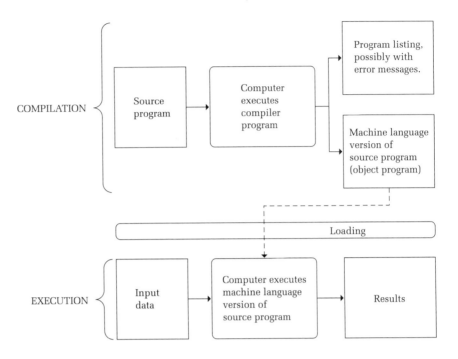

a single C++ program can be used on different machines, whereas a program written in assembly language or machine language is not portable from one computer to another. Because each computer has its own machine language, a machine language program written for computer A will not run on computer B.

It is important to understand that *compilation* and *execution* are two distinct processes. During compilation, the computer runs the compiler program. During execution, the object program is loaded into the computer's memory unit, replacing the compiler program. The computer then runs the object program, doing whatever the program instructs it to do (see Figure 1-6).

*B*ACKGROUND INFORMATION

Compilers and Interpreters

Some programming languages—LISP, Prolog, and many versions of BASIC, for example—are translated by an *interpreter* rather than a compiler. An interpreter translates *and executes* each instruction in the source program, one at a time. In contrast, a compiler translates the entire source program into machine language, after which execution of the object program takes place.

The Java language uses both a compiler and an interpreter. First, a Java program is compiled, not into a particular computer's machine language, but into an intermediate code called bytecode. Next, a program called the Java Virtual Machine (JVM) takes the bytecode program and interprets it (translates a bytecode instruction into machine language and executes it, translates the next one and executes it, and so on). Thus, a Java program compiled into bytecode is portable to many different computers, as long as each computer has its own specific JVM that can translate bytecode into the computer's machine language

---

The instructions in a programming language reflect the operations a computer can perform:

- A computer can transfer data from one place to another.
- A computer can input data from an input device (a keyboard or mouse, for example) and output data to an output device (a screen, for example).
- A computer can store data into and retrieve data from its memory and secondary storage (parts of a computer that we discuss in the next section).
- A computer can compare two data values for equality or inequality.
- A computer can perform arithmetic operations (addition and subtraction, for example) very quickly.

Programming languages require that we use certain *control structures* to express algorithms as programs. There are four basic ways of structuring statements (instructions) in most programming languages: sequentially, conditionally, repetitively, and with subprograms (see Figure 1-7). A *sequence* is a series of statements that are executed one after another. *Selection*, the conditional control structure, executes different statements depending on certain conditions. The repetitive control structure, the *loop*, repeats statements while certain conditions are met. The *subprogram* allows us to structure a program by breaking it into smaller units. Each of these ways of structuring statements controls the order in which the computer executes the statements, which is why they are called control structures.

Imagine you're driving a car. Going down a straight stretch of road is like following a sequence of instructions. When you come to a fork in the road, you must decide which way to go and then take one or the other branch of the fork. This is what the computer does when it encounters a selection control structure (sometimes called a *branch* or *decision*) in a program. Sometimes you have to go around the block several times to find a place to park. The computer does the same sort of thing when it encounters a loop in a program.

A subprogram is a process that consists of multiple steps. Every day, for example, you follow a procedure to get from home to work. It makes sense, then, for someone to give you directions to a meeting by saying, "Go

FIGURE 1-7

Basic Structures of Programming Languages

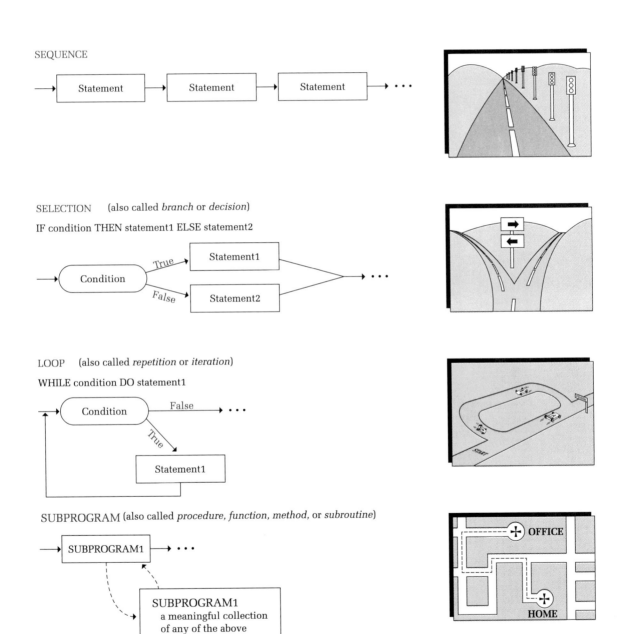

SEQUENCE

Statement → Statement → Statement → ...

SELECTION   (also called *branch* or *decision*)

IF condition THEN statement1 ELSE statement2

Condition —True→ Statement1
          —False→ Statement2   → ...

LOOP   (also called *repetition* or *iteration*)

WHILE condition DO statement1

Condition —False→ ...
          —True→ Statement1

SUBPROGRAM (also called *procedure, function, method,* or *subroutine*)

SUBPROGRAM1 → ...

SUBPROGRAM1
a meaningful collection
of any of the above

FIGURE 1-8

Basic Components
of a Computer

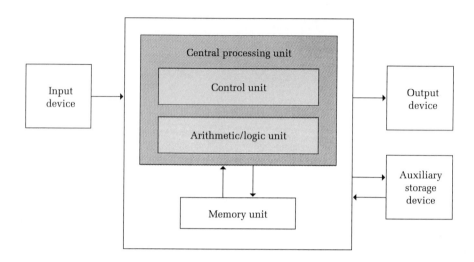

to the office, then go four blocks west" without specifying all the steps you have to take to get to the office. Subprograms allow us to write parts of our programs separately and then assemble them into final form. They can greatly simplify the task of writing large programs.

What Is a Computer?

You can learn a programming language, how to write programs, and how to run (execute) these programs without knowing much about computers. But if you know something about the parts of a computer, you can better understand the effect of each instruction in a programming language.

Most computers have six basic components: the memory unit, the arithmetic/logic unit, the control unit, input devices, output devices, and auxiliary storage devices. Figure 1-8 is a stylized diagram of the basic components of a computer.

The **memory unit** is an ordered sequence of storage cells, each capable of holding a piece of data. Each memory cell has a distinct address to which we refer in order to store data into it or retrieve data from it. These storage cells are called *memory cells*, or *memory locations.** The memory unit holds data (input data or the product of computation) and instructions (programs), as shown in Figure 1-9.

Memory unit   Internal data storage in a computer.

---

* The memory unit is also referred to as RAM, an acronym for **r**andom **a**ccess **m**emory (so called because we can access any location at random).

FIGURE 1-9

Memory

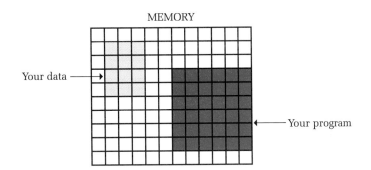

The part of the computer that follows instructions is called the **central processing unit (CPU).** The CPU usually has two components. The **arithmetic/logic unit (ALU)** performs arithmetic operations (addition, subtraction, multiplication, and division) and logical operations (comparing two values). The **control unit** controls the actions of the other components so that program instructions are executed in the correct order.

Central processing unit (CPU)   The part of the computer that executes the instructions (program) stored in memory; made up of the arithmetic/logic unit and the control unit.

Arithmetic/logic unit (ALU)   The component of the central processing unit that performs arithmetic and logical operations.

Control unit   The component of the central processing unit that controls the actions of the other components so that instructions (the program) are executed in the correct sequence.

For us to use computers, there must be some way of getting data into and out of them. **Input/output (I/O) devices** accept data to be processed (input) and present data values that have been processed (output). A keyboard is a common input device. Another is a *mouse*, a pointing device. A video display is a common output device, as are printers and liquid crystal display (LCD) screens. Some devices, such as a connection to a computer network, are used for both input and output.

Input/output (I/O) devices   The parts of the computer that accept data to be processed (input) and present the results of that processing (output).

For the most part, computers simply move and combine data in memory. The many types of computers differ primarily in the size of their memories, the speed with which data can be recalled, the efficiency with which data can be moved or combined, and limitations on I/O devices.

When a program is executing, the computer proceeds through a series of steps, the *fetch-execute cycle:*

1. The control unit retrieves (*fetches*) the next coded instruction from memory.
2. The instruction is translated into control signals.
3. The control signals tell the appropriate unit (arithmetic/logic unit, memory, I/O device) to perform (execute) the instruction.
4. The sequence repeats from step 1.

Computers can have a wide variety of **peripheral devices** attached to them. An **auxiliary storage device,** or *secondary storage device*, holds coded data for the computer until we actually want to use the data. Instead of inputting data every time, we can input it once and have the computer store it onto an auxiliary storage device. Whenever we need to use the data, we tell the computer to transfer the data from the auxiliary storage device to its memory. An auxiliary storage device therefore serves as both an input and an output device. Typical auxiliary storage devices are disk drives and magnetic tape drives. A *disk drive* is a cross between a compact disc player and a tape recorder. It uses a thin disk made out of magnetic material. A read/write head (similar to the record/playback head in a tape recorder) travels across the spinning disk, retrieving or recording data. A *magnetic tape drive* is like a tape recorder and is most often used to *back up* (make a copy of) the data on a disk in case the disk is ever damaged.

Other examples of peripheral devices include the following:

- Scanners, which "read" visual images on paper and convert them into binary data
- CD-ROM (compact disc–read-only memory) drives, which read (but cannot write) data stored on removable compact discs
- CD-R (compact disc–recordable) drives, which can write to a particular CD once only but can read from it many times
- CD-RW (compact disc–rewritable) drives, which can both write to and read from a particular CD many times
- DVD-ROM (digital video disc [or digital versatile disc]–read-only memory) drives, which use CDs with far greater storage capacity than conventional CDs
- Modems (modulator/demodulators), which convert back and forth between binary data and signals that can be sent over conventional telephone lines
- Audio sound cards and speakers
- Voice synthesizers
- Digital cameras

Together, all of these physical components are known as **hardware.** The programs that allow the hardware to operate are called **software.** Hardware usually is fixed in design; software is easily changed. In fact, the ease with which software can be manipulated is what makes the computer such a versatile, powerful tool.

Peripheral device   An input, output, or auxiliary storage device attached to a computer.

Auxiliary storage device   A device that stores data in encoded form outside the computer's main memory.

Hardware   The physical components of a computer.

Software   Computer programs; the set of all programs available on a computer.

---

*B*ACKGROUND INFORMATION

PCs, Workstations, and Mainframes

There are many different sizes and kinds of computers. *Mainframes* are very large (they can fill a room!) and very fast. A typical mainframe computer consists of several cabinets full of electronic components. Inside those cabinets are the memory, the central processing unit, and input/output units. It's easy to spot the various peripheral devices: Separate cabinets contain the disk drives and tape drives. Other units are obviously printers and terminals (monitors with keyboards). It is common to be able to connect hundreds of terminals to a single mainframe. For example, all of the cash registers in a chain of department stores might be linked to a single mainframe.

At the other end of the spectrum are *personal computers (PCs)*. These are small enough to fit comfortably on top of a desk. Because of their size, it can be difficult to spot the individual parts inside personal computers. Many PCs are just a single box with a screen, a keyboard, and a mouse. You have to open up the case to see the central processing unit, which is usually just an electronic component called an *integrated circuit* or *chip.*

Some personal computers have tape drives, but most operate only with disk drives, CD-ROM drives, and printers. The CD-ROM and disk drives for personal computers typically hold much less data than disks used with mainframes. Similarly, the printers that are attached to personal computers typically are much slower than those used with mainframes.

Laptop or *notebook* computers are PCs that have been reduced to the size of a large notebook and operate on batteries so that they are portable. They typically consist of two parts that are connected by a hinge at the back of the case. The upper part holds a flat, liquid crystal display (LCD) screen, and the lower part has the keyboard, pointing device, processor, memory, and disk drives.

Mainframe Computer

Inside a PC, system unit broken down

Personal Computer, Macintosh

Personal Computer, IBM

Inside a PC, close-up of a system board

Notebook Computer

Workstation

Supercomputer

Between mainframes and personal computers are *workstations.* These intermediate-sized computer systems are usually less expensive than mainframes and more powerful than personal computers. Workstations are often set up for use primarily by one person at a time. A workstation may also be configured to act like a small mainframe, in which case it is called a *server.* A typical workstation looks very much like a PC. In fact, as PCs have grown more powerful and workstations have become more compact, the distinction between them has begun to fade.

One last type of computer that we should mention is the *supercomputer,* the most powerful class of computer in existence. Supercomputers typically are designed to perform scientific and engineering calculations on immense sets of data with great speed. They are very expensive and thus are not in widespread use.

In addition to the programs that we write or purchase, there are programs in the computer that are designed to simplify the user/computer **interface,** making it easier for us to use the machine. The interface between user and computer is a set of I/O devices—for example, a keyboard, mouse, and screen—that allow the user to communicate with the computer. We work with the keyboard, mouse, and screen on our side of the interface boundary; wires attached to these devices carry the electronic pulses that the computer works with on its side of the interface boundary. At the boundary itself is a mechanism that translates information for the two sides.

Interface   A connecting link at a shared boundary that allows independent systems to meet and act on or communicate with each other.

When we communicate directly with the computer, we are using an **interactive system.** Interactive systems allow direct entry of programs and data and provide immediate feedback to the user. In contrast, *batch systems* require that all data be entered before a program is run and provide feedback only after a program has been executed. In this text we focus on interactive systems, although in Chapter 4 we discuss file-oriented programs, which share certain similarities with batch systems.

The set of programs that simplify the user/computer interface and improve the efficiency of processing is called *system software*. It includes the compiler as well as the operating system and the editor (see Figure 1-10). The **operating system** manages all of the computer's resources. It can input programs, call the compiler, execute object programs, and carry out any other system commands. The **editor** is an interactive program used to create and modify source programs or data.

Interactive system   A system that allows direct communication between user and computer.

Operating system   A set of programs that manages all of the computer's resources.

Editor   An interactive program used to create and modify source programs or data.

Although solitary (*stand-alone*) computers are often used in private homes and small businesses, it is very common for many computers to be connected together, forming a *network*. A *local area network* (*LAN*) is one in which the computers are connected by wires and must be reasonably close together, as in a single office building. In a *wide area network* (*WAN*) or *long-haul network*, the computers can be far apart geographically and communicate through phone lines, fiber optic cable, and other media. The most well-known long-haul network is the Internet, which was originally devised as a means for universities, businesses, and government agencies to exchange research information. The Internet exploded in popularity with the establishment of the World Wide Web, a system of linked Internet computers that support specially formatted documents (*Web pages*) that contain text, graphics, audio, and video.

FIGURE 1-10

User/Computer
Interface

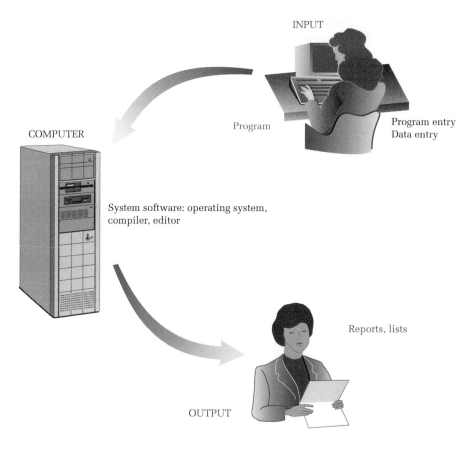

INPUT

Program

Program entry
Data entry

COMPUTER

System software: operating system,
compiler, editor

Reports, lists

OUTPUT

---

*B*ACKGROUND INFORMATION

The Origins of C++

In the late 1960s and early 1970s, Dennis Ritchie created the C programming language at AT&T Bell Labs. At the time, a group of people within Bell Labs were designing the UNIX operating system. Initially, UNIX was written in assembly language, as was the custom for almost all system software in those days. To escape the difficulties of programming in assembly language, Ritchie invented C as a system programming language. C combines the low-level features of an assembly language with the ease of use and portability of a high-level language. UNIX was reprogrammed so that approximately 90 percent was written in C, and the remainder in assembly language.

People often wonder where the cryptic name C came from. In the 1960s a programming language named BCPL (Basic Combined Programming Language) had a small but loyal following, primarily in Europe. From BCPL, another language arose with its name abbreviated to B. For his language, Dennis Ritchie adopted features from the B language and decided that the successor to B naturally should be named C. So the progression was from BCPL to B to C.

In 1985 Bjarne Stroustrup, also of Bell Labs, invented the C++ programming language. To the C language he added features for data abstraction and object-oriented programming (topics we discuss later in this book). Instead of naming the language D, the Bell Labs group in a humorous vein named it C++. As we see later, ++ signifies the increment operation in the C and C++ languages. Given a variable x, the expression $x++$ means to increment (add one to) the current value of x. Therefore, the name C++ suggests an enhanced ("incremented") version of the C language.

In the years since Dr. Stroustrup invented C++, the language began to evolve in slightly different ways in different C++ compilers. Although the fundamental features of C++ were nearly the same in all companies' compilers, one company might add a new language feature, whereas another would not. As a result, C++ programs were not always portable from one compiler to the next. The programming community agreed that the language needed to be standardized, and a joint committee of the International Standards Organization (ISO) and the American National Standards Institute (ANSI) began the long process of creating a C++ language standard. After several years of discussion and debate, the ISO/ANSI language standard for C++ was officially approved in mid-1998. Most of the current C++ compilers support the ISO/ANSI standard (hereafter called *standard C++*). To assist you if you are using a pre–standard compiler, throughout the book we point out discrepancies between older language features and new ones that may affect how you write your programs.

Although C originally was intended as a system programming language, both C and C++ are widely used today in business, industry, and personal computing. C++ is powerful and versatile, embodying a wide range of programming concepts. In this book you will learn a substantial portion of the language, but C++ incorporates sophisticated features that go well beyond the scope of an introductory programming course.

Ethics and Responsibilities in the Computing Profession

Every profession operates with a set of ethics that help to define the responsibilities of people who practice the profession. For example, medical professionals have an ethical responsibility to keep information about their patients confidential. Engineers have an ethical responsibility to their employers to protect proprietary information, but they also have a responsibility to protect the public and the environment from harm that may result from their work. Writers are ethically bound not to plagiarize the work of others, and so on.

The computer presents us with a vast new range of capabilities that can affect people and the environment in dramatic ways. It thus challenges society with many new ethical issues. Some of our existing ethical practices apply to the computer, whereas other situations require new ethical rules. In some cases, there may not be established guidelines, but it is up to you to decide what is ethical. In this section we examine some common situations encountered in the computing profession that raise particular ethical issues.

A professional in the computing industry, like any other professional, has knowledge that enables him or her to do certain things that others cannot do. Knowing how to access computers, how to program them, and how to manipulate data gives the computer professional the ability to create new products, solve important problems, and help people to manage their interactions with the ever more complex world in which we all live. Knowledge of computers can be a powerful means to effect positive change.

Knowledge also can be used in unethical ways. A computer can be programmed to trigger a terrorist's bomb, to sabotage a competitor's production line, or to steal money. Although these blatant examples make an extreme point and are unethical in any context, there are more subtle examples that are unique to computers.

Software Piracy

Computer software is easy to copy. But just like books, software is usually copyrighted. It is illegal to copy software without the permission of its creator. Such copying is called **software piracy.**

Software piracy   The unauthorized copying of software for either personal use or use by others.

Copyright laws exist to protect the creators of software (and books and art) so that they can make a profit from the effort and money spent developing the software. A major software package can cost millions of dollars to develop, and this cost (along with the cost of producing the package, shipping it, supporting customers, and allowing for retailer markup) is reflected in the purchase price. If people make unauthorized copies of the software, then the company loses those sales and either has to raise its prices to compensate or spend less money to develop improved versions of the software—in either case, a desirable piece of software becomes harder to obtain.

Software pirates sometimes rationalize their software theft with the excuse that they're just making one copy for their own use. It's not that they're selling a bunch of bootleg copies, after all. But if thousands of people do the same, then it adds up to millions of dollars in lost revenue for the company, which leads to higher prices for everyone.

Computing professionals have an ethical obligation to not engage in software piracy and to try to stop it from occurring. You should never copy software without permission. If someone asks you for a copy of a piece of software, you should refuse to supply it. If someone says that he or she just wants to "borrow" the software to "try it out," tell that person that he or she is welcome to try it out on your machine (or at a retailer's shop) but not to make a copy.

This rule isn't restricted to duplicating copyrighted software; it includes plagiarism of all or part of code that belongs to anyone else. If someone gives you permission to copy some of his or her code, then, just like any responsible writer, you should acknowledge that person with a citation in the code.

Privacy of Data

The computer enables the compilation of databases containing useful information about people, companies, geographic regions, and so on. These databases allow employers to issue payroll checks, banks to cash a customer's check at any branch, the government to collect taxes, and mass merchandisers to send out junk mail. Even though we may not care for every use of databases, they generally have positive benefits. However, they also can be used in negative ways.

For example, a car thief who gains access to the state motor vehicle registry could print out a shopping list of valuable car models together with their owners' addresses. An industrial spy might steal customer data from a company database and sell it to a competitor. Although these are obviously illegal acts, computer professionals face other situations that are not so obvious.

Suppose your job includes managing the company payroll database. In that database are the names and salaries of the employees in the company. You might be tempted to poke around in the database to see how your salary compares with your associates; however, this act is unethical and an invasion of your associates' right to privacy, because this information is confidential. Any information about a person that is not clearly public should be considered confidential. An example of public information is a phone number listed in a telephone directory. Private information includes any data that has been provided with an understanding that it will be used only for a specific purpose (such as the data on a credit card application).

A computing professional has a responsibility to avoid taking advantage of special access that he or she may have to confidential data. The professional also has a responsibility to guard that data from unauthorized access. Guarding data can involve such simple things as shredding old printouts, keeping backup copies in a locked cabinet, and not using passwords that are easy to guess (such as a name or word) as well as more complex measures such as *encryption* (keeping data stored in a secret coded form).

Use of Computer Resources

If you've ever bought a computer, you know that it costs money. A personal computer can be relatively inexpensive, but it is still a major purchase. Larger computers can cost millions of dollars. Operating a PC may cost a few dollars a month for electricity and an occasional outlay for paper, disks, and repairs. Larger computers can cost tens of thousands of dollars per month to operate. Regardless of the type of computer, whoever owns it has to pay these costs. They do so because the computer is a resource that justifies its expense.

The computer is an unusual resource because it is valuable only when a program is running. Thus, the computer's time is really the valuable resource. There is no significant physical difference between a computer that is working and one that is sitting idle. By contrast, a car is in motion when it is working. Thus, unauthorized use of a computer is different from unauthorized use of a car. If one person uses another's car without permission, that individual must take possession of it physically—that is, steal it. If someone uses a computer without permission, the computer isn't physically stolen, but just as in the case of car theft, the owner is being deprived of a resource that he or she is paying for.

For some people, theft of computer resources is a game—like joyriding in a car. The thief really doesn't want the resources, just the challenge of breaking through a computer's security system and seeing how far he or she can get without being caught. Success gives a thrilling boost to this sort of person's ego. Many computer thieves think that their actions are acceptable if they do no harm, but whenever real work is displaced from the computer by such activities, then harm is clearly being done. If nothing else, the thief is trespassing in the computer owner's property. By analogy, consider that even though no physical harm may be done by someone who breaks into your bedroom and takes a nap while you are away, such an action is certainly disturbing to you because it poses a threat of potential physical harm. In this case, and in the case of breaking into a computer, mental harm can be done.

Other thieves can be malicious. Like a joyrider who purposely crashes a stolen car, these people destroy or corrupt data to cause harm. They may feel a sense of power from being able to hurt others with impunity. Sometimes these people leave behind programs that act as time bombs, to cause harm long after they have gone. Another kind of program that may be left is a virus—a program that replicates itself, often with the goal of spreading to other computers. Viruses can be benign, causing no other harm than to use up some resources. Others can be destructive and cause widespread damage to data. Incidents have occurred in which viruses have cost millions of dollars in lost computer time and data.

Virus   A computer program that replicates itself, often with the goal of spreading to other computers without authorization, and possibly with the intent of doing harm.

Computing professionals have an ethical responsibility never to use computer resources without permission, which includes activities such as doing personal work on an employer's computer. We also have a responsibility to help guard resources to which we have access—by using unguessable passwords and keeping them secret, by watching for signs of unusual computer use, by writing programs that do not provide loopholes in a computer's security system, and so on.

Software Engineering

Humans have come to depend greatly on computers in many aspects of their lives. That reliance is fostered by the perception that computers function reliably; that is, they work correctly most of the time. However, the reliability of a computer depends on the care that is taken in writing its software.

Errors in a program can have serious consequences, as the following examples of real incidents involving software errors illustrate. An error in the control software of the F-18 jet fighter caused it to flip upside down the first time it flew across the equator. A rocket launch went out of control and had to be blown up because there was a comma typed in place of a period in its control software. A radiation therapy machine killed several patients because a software error caused the machine to operate at full power when the operator typed certain commands too quickly.

Even when the software is used in less critical situations, errors can have significant effects. Examples of such errors include the following:

- An error in your word processor that causes your term paper to be lost just hours before it is due
- An error in a statistical program that causes a scientist to draw a wrong conclusion and publish a paper that must later be retracted
- An error in a tax preparation program that produces an incorrect return, leading to a fine

Programmers thus have a responsibility to develop software that is free from errors. The process that is used to develop correct software is known as **software engineering.**

Software engineering   The application of traditional engineering methodologies and techniques to the development of software.

Software engineering has many aspects. The software life cycle described at the beginning of this chapter outlines the stages in the development of software. Different techniques are used at each of these stages. We address many of the techniques in this text. In Chapter 4 we introduce methodologies for developing correct algorithms. We discuss strategies for testing and validating programs in every chapter. We use a modern programming language that enables us to write readable, well-organized programs, and so on. Some aspects of software engineering, such as the development of a formal, mathematical specification for a program, are beyond the scope of this text.

Problem-Solving Techniques

You solve problems every day, often unaware of the process you are going through. In a learning environment, you usually are given most of the information you need: a clear statement of the problem, the necessary input, and the required output. In real life, the process is not always so simple. You often have to define the problem yourself and then decide what information you have to work with and what the results should be.

After you understand and analyze a problem, you must come up with a solution—an algorithm. Earlier we defined an algorithm as a step-by-step procedure for solving a problem in a finite amount of time. Although you work with algorithms all the time, most of your experience with them is in the context of *following* them. You follow a recipe, play a game, assemble a toy, take medicine. In the problem-solving phase of computer programming, you will be *designing* algorithms, not following them. This means you must be conscious of the strategies you use to solve problems in order to apply them to programming problems.

Ask Questions

If you are given a task orally, you ask questions—When? Why? Where?—until you understand exactly what you have to do. If your instructions are written, you might put question marks in the margin, underline a word or a sentence, or in some other way indicate that the task is not clear. Your questions may be answered by a later paragraph, or you might have to discuss them with the person who gave you the task.

These are some of the questions you might ask in the context of programming:

- What do I have to work with—that is, what is my data?
- What do the data items look like?
- How much data is there?

- How will I know when I have processed all the data?
- What should my output look like?
- How many times is the process going to be repeated?
- What special error conditions might come up?

Look for Things That Are Familiar

Never reinvent the wheel. If a solution exists, use it. If you've solved the same or a similar problem before, just repeat your solution. People are good at recognizing similar situations. We don't have to learn how to go to the store to buy milk, then to buy eggs, and then to buy candy. We know that going to the store is always the same; only what we buy is different.

In programming, certain problems occur again and again in different guises. A good programmer immediately recognizes a subtask he or she has solved before and plugs in the solution. For example, finding the daily high and low temperatures is really the same problem as finding the highest and lowest grades on a test. You want the largest and smallest values in a set of numbers (see Figure 1-11).

Solve by Analogy

Often a problem reminds you of a similar problem you have seen before. You may find solving the problem at hand easier if you remember how you

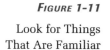

FIGURE 1-11

Look for Things
That Are Familiar

FIGURE 1-12

Analogy

A library catalog system can give insight into how to organize a parts inventory.

solved the other problem. In other words, draw an analogy between the two problems. For example, a solution to a perspective projection problem from an art class might help you figure out how to compute the distance to a landmark when you are on a cross-country hike. As you work your way through the new problem, you come across things that are different than they were in the old problem, but usually these are just details that you can deal with one at a time.

Analogy is really just a broader application of the strategy of looking for things that are familiar. When you are trying to find an algorithm for solving a problem, don't limit yourself to computer-oriented solutions. Step back and try to get a larger view of the problem. Don't worry if your analogy doesn't match perfectly—the only reason for using an analogy is that it gives you a place to start (see Figure 1-12). The best programmers are people who have broad experience solving all kinds of problems.

Means-Ends Analysis

Often the beginning state and the ending state are given; the problem is to define a set of actions that can be used to get from one to the other. Suppose you want to go from Boston, Massachusetts, to Austin, Texas. You know the beginning state (you are in Boston) and the ending state (you

FIGURE 1-13

Means-Ends Analysis

Start: Boston **Goal:** Austin	**Means:** *Fly*, walk, hitchhike, bike, drive, sail, bus
Start: Boston **Goal:** Austin	**Revised Means:** Fly to Chicago and then Austin; *fly to Newark and then Austin:* fly to Atlanta and then Austin
Start: Boston **Intermediate Goal:** Newark **Goal:** Austin	**Means to Intermediate Goal:** *Commuter flight*, walk, hitchhike, bike, drive, sail, bus
Solution: Take commuter flight to Newark and then catch cheap flight to Austin	

want to be in Austin). The problem is how to get from one to the other. In this example, you have lots of choices. You can fly, walk, hitchhike, ride a bike, or whatever. The method you choose depends on your circumstances. If you're in a hurry, you'll probably decide to fly.

Once you've narrowed down the set of actions, you have to work out the details. It may help to establish intermediate goals that are easier to meet than the overall goal. Let's say there is a really cheap, direct flight to Austin out of Newark, New Jersey. You might decide to divide the trip into legs: Boston to Newark and then Newark to Austin. Your intermediate goal is to get from Boston to Newark. Now you only have to examine the means of meeting that intermediate goal (see Figure 1-13).

The overall strategy of means-ends analysis is to define the ends and then to analyze your means of getting between them. The process translates easily to computer programming. You begin by writing down what the input is and what the output should be. Then you consider the actions a computer can perform and choose a sequence of actions that can transform the data into the results.

Divide and Conquer

We often break up large problems into smaller units that are easier to handle. Cleaning the whole house may seem overwhelming; cleaning the rooms one at a time seems much more manageable. The same principle applies to programming. We break up a large problem into smaller pieces that we can solve individually (see Figure 1-14). In fact, the functional

FIGURE 1-14

Divide and Conquer

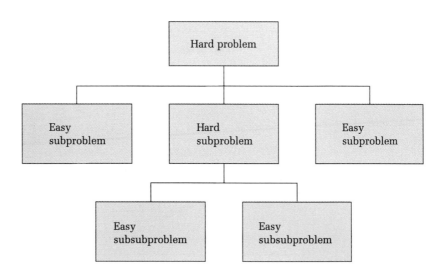

decomposition and object-oriented methodologies, which we describe in Chapter 4, are based on the principle of divide and conquer.

The Building-Block Approach

Another way of attacking a large problem is to see if any solutions for smaller pieces of the problem exist. It may be possible to put some of these solutions together end to end to solve most of the big problem. This strategy is just a combination of the look-for-familiar-things and divide-and-conquer approaches. You look at the big problem and see that it can be divided into smaller problems for which solutions already exist. Solving the big problem is just a matter of putting the existing solutions together, like mortaring together blocks to form a wall (see Figure 1-15).

Merging Solutions

Another way to combine existing solutions is to merge them on a step-by-step basis. For example, to compute the average of a list of values, we must both sum and count the values. If we already have separate solutions for summing values and for counting values, we can combine them. But if we first do the summing and then do the counting, we have to read the list twice. We can save steps if we merge these two solutions: Read a value and then add it to the running total and add 1 to our count before going on to the next value. Whenever the solutions to subproblems duplicate steps, think about merging them instead of joining them end to end.

Figure 1-15

Building-Block Approach

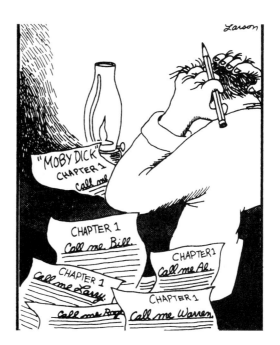

Mental Blocks: The Fear of Starting

Writers are all too familiar with the experience of staring at a blank page, not knowing where to begin. Programmers have the same difficulty when they first tackle a big problem. They look at the problem and it seems overwhelming (see Figure 1-16).

Remember that you always have a way to begin solving any problem: Write it down on paper in your own words so that you understand it. Once you paraphrase the problem, you can focus on each of the subparts individually instead of trying to tackle the entire problem at once. This process gives you a clearer picture of the overall problem. It helps you see pieces of the problem that look familiar or that are analogous to other problems you have solved, and it pinpoints areas where something is unclear, where you need more information.

As you write down a problem, you tend to group things together into small, understandable chunks, which may be natural places to split the problem up—to divide and conquer. Your description of the problem may collect all of the information about data and results into one place for easy reference. Then you can see the beginning and ending states necessary for means-ends analysis.

Most mental blocks are caused by not really understanding the problem. Rewriting the problem in your own words is a good way to focus on the subparts of the problem, one at a time, and to understand what is required for a solution.

Algorithmic Problem Solving

Coming up with a step-by-step procedure for solving a particular problem is not always a cut-and-dried process. In fact, it is usually a trial-and-error process requiring several attempts and refinements. We test each attempt to see if it really solves the problem. If it does, fine. If it doesn't, we try again. Solving any nontrivial problem typically requires a combination of the techniques we've described.

Remember that the computer can only do certain things (see p. 14). Your primary concern, then, is how to make the computer transform, manipulate, calculate, or process the input data to produce the desired output. If you keep in mind the allowable instructions in your programming language, you won't design an algorithm that is difficult or impossible to code.

In the case study that follows, we develop a program for calculating employees' weekly wages. It typifies the thought processes involved in writing an algorithm and coding it as a program, and it shows you what a complete C++ program looks like.

*P*ROBLEM-SOLVING CASE STUDY

An Algorithm for a Company Payroll

Problem: A small company needs an interactive program (the payroll clerk will input the data) to figure its weekly payroll. The input data and each employee's wages should be saved in a secondary storage file, and the total wages for the week should be displayed on the screen so that the payroll clerk can transfer the appropriate amount into the payroll account.

Discussion: At first glance, this seems like a simple problem. But if you think about how you would do it by hand, you see that you need to ask questions about the specifics of the process. What employee data is input? How are wages computed? In what file should the results be stored? How does the clerk indicate that all of the data has been entered?

- The data for each employee includes an employee identification number, the employee's hourly pay rate, and the hours worked that week.
- Wages equal the employee's pay rate times the number of hours worked, up to 40 hours. If an employee worked more than 40 hours, wages equal the employee's pay rate times 40 hours, plus $1\frac{1}{2}$ times the employee's regular pay rate times the number of hours worked above 40.
- The results should be stored in a file called payFile.

PROBLEM-SOLVING CASE STUDY cont'd.

▪ There is no employee number 0, so the clerk can indicate the end of the data by entering a 0 when asked for an employee number.

Let's apply the *divide-and-conquer* approach to this problem. There are three obvious steps in almost any problem of this type:

1. Get the data.
2. Compute the results.
3. Output the results.

First we need to get the data. (By *get*, we mean *read* or *input* the data.) We need three pieces of data for each employee: employee identification number, hourly pay rate, and number of hours worked. So that the clerk will know when to enter each value, we must have the computer output a message that indicates when it is ready to accept each of the values (this is called a *prompting message*, or a *prompt*). Therefore, to input the data, we take these steps:

Prompt the user for the employee number (put a message on the screen)
Read the employee number
Prompt the user for the employee's hourly pay rate
Read the pay rate
Prompt the user for the number of hours worked
Read the number of hours worked

The next step is to compute the wages. Let's apply *means-ends analysis*. Our starting point is the set of data values that was input; our desired ending, the payroll for the week. The means at our disposal are the basic operations that the computer can perform, which include calculation and control structures. Let's begin by working backward from the end.

We know that there are two formulas for computing wages: one for regular hours and one for overtime. If there is no overtime, wages are simply the pay rate times the number of hours worked. If the number of hours worked is greater than 40, however, wages are 40 times the pay rate, plus the number of overtime hours times $1\frac{1}{2}$ times the pay rate. The number of overtime hours is computed by subtracting 40 from the total number of hours worked. Here are the two formulas:

wages = *hours worked* × *pay rate*
wages = (40.0 × *pay rate*) + (*hours worked* − 40.0) × 1.5 × *pay rate*

We now have the means to compute wages for each case. Our intermediate goal is to execute the correct formula given the input data. We must decide which formula to use and employ a branching control structure to make the computer execute the appropriate formula. The decision that controls the branching structure is simply whether more than 40 hours have been worked. We now have the means to get from our starting point to the desired end. To figure the wages, then, we take the following steps:

If hours worked is greater than 40.0, then
    wages = (40.0 × pay rate) + (hours worked − 40.0) × 1.5 × pay rate
otherwise
    wages = hours worked × pay rate

The last step, outputting the results, is simply a matter of directing the computer to write the employee number, the pay rate, the number of hours worked, and the wages into `payFile`:

Write the employee number, pay rate, hours worked, and wages into payFile

There are two things we've overlooked. First, we must repeat this process for each employee, and second, we must compute the total wages for the week. Let's use the *building-block approach* to combine our three main steps (getting the data, computing the wages, and outputting the results) with a structure that repeats the steps for each employee as long as the employee number is not 0. When the employee number is 0, this structure should skip to the end of the algorithm. Next we should insert a step just after the wages are computed that adds them to a running total.

Finally, we must take care of a couple of housekeeping chores. Before we start processing, we must prepare the output file to receive the results and set the running total to zero. At the end of the algorithm, we must tell the computer to stop processing.

What follows is the complete algorithm. Calculating the wages is written as a separate subalgorithm that is defined below the main algorithm. Notice that the algorithm is simply a very precise description of the same steps you would follow to do this process by hand.

Main Algorithm

Prepare to write a list of the employees' wages (open file payFile)
Set the total payroll to zero
Prompt the user for the employee number (put a message on the screen)
Read the employee number
As long as the employee number is not 0, repeat the following steps:
    Prompt the user for the employee's hourly pay rate
    Read the pay rate
    Prompt the user for the number of hours worked
    Read the number of hours worked

Perform the subalgorithm for calculating pay (below)
Add the employee's wages to the total payroll
Write the employee number, pay rate, hours worked, and wages onto the list (file payFile)
Prompt the user for the employee number
Read the employee number
When an employee number equal to 0 is read, continue with the following steps:
Write the total company payroll on the screen
Stop

Subalgorithm for Calculating Pay

If hours worked is greater than 40.0, then
    wages = (40.0 × pay rate) + (hours worked − 40.0) × 1.5 × pay rate
otherwise
    wages = hours worked × pay rate

Before we implement this algorithm, we should test it. Case Study Follow-Up Exercise 2 asks you to carry out this test.

What follows is the C++ program for this algorithm. It's here to give you an idea of what you'll be learning. If you've had no previous exposure to programming, you probably won't understand most of the program. Don't worry; you will soon. In fact, throughout this book as we introduce new constructs, we refer you back to the Payroll program. One more thing: The remarks following the symbols // are called comments. They are here to help you understand the program; the compiler ignores them. Words enclosed by the symbols /* and */ also are comments and are ignored by the compiler.

```cpp
//*****************************************************************
// Payroll program
// This program computes each employee's wages and
// the total company payroll
//*****************************************************************
#include <iostream>
#include <fstream>      // For file I/O

using namespace std;

void CalcPay( float, float, float& );

const float MAX_HOURS = 40.0;   // Maximum normal work hours
const float OVERTIME = 1.5;     // Overtime pay rate factor

int main()
{
```

PROBLEM-SOLVING CASE STUDY cont'd.

```cpp
    float    payRate;             // Employee's pay rate
    float    hours;               // Hours worked
    float    wages;               // Wages earned
    float    total;               // Total company payroll
    int      empNum;              // Employee ID number
    ofstream payFile;             // Company payroll file

    payFile.open("payfile.dat");          // Open the output file
    total = 0.0;                          // Initialize total
    cout << "Enter employee number: ";    // Prompt
    cin >> empNum;                        // Read employee ID no.
    while (empNum != 0)                   // While employee number
    {                                     //    isn't zero
        cout << "Enter pay rate: ";       // Prompt
        cin >> payRate;                   // Read hourly pay rate
        cout << "Enter hours worked: ";   // Prompt
        cin >> hours;                     // Read hours worked
        CalcPay(payRate, hours, wages);   // Compute wages
        total = total + wages;            // Add wages to total
        payFile << empNum << payRate      // Put results into file
                << hours << wages;
        cout << "Enter employee number: ";   // Prompt
        cin >> empNum;                    // Read ID number
    }
    cout << "Total payroll is "           // Print total payroll
         << total << endl;                //    on screen
    return 0;                             // Indicate successful
}                                         //    completion


//*******************************************************************

void CalcPay( /* in */  float  payRate,      // Employee's pay rate
              /* in */  float  hours,        // Hours worked
              /* out */ float& wages )       // Wages earned

// CalcPay computes wages from the employee's pay rate
// and the hours worked, taking overtime into account

{
    if (hours > MAX_HOURS)                    // Is there overtime?
        wages = (MAX_HOURS * payRate) +       // Yes
                (hours - MAX_HOURS) * payRate * OVERTIME;
    else
        wages = hours * payRate;              // No
}
```

Summary

We think nothing of turning on the television and sitting down to watch it. It's a communication tool we use to enhance our lives. Computers are becoming as common as televisions, just a normal part of our lives. And like televisions, computers are based on complex principles but are designed for easy use.

Computers are dumb; they must be told what to do. A true computer error is extremely rare (usually due to a component malfunction or an electrical fault). Because we tell the computer what to do, most errors in computer-generated output are really human errors.

Computer programming is the process of planning a sequence of steps for a computer to follow. It involves a problem-solving phase and an implementation phase. After analyzing a problem, we develop and test a general solution (algorithm). This general solution becomes a concrete solution—our program—when we write it in a high-level programming language. The sequence of instructions that makes up our program is then compiled into machine code, the language the computer uses. After correcting any errors ("bugs") that show up during testing, our program is ready to use.

Once we begin to use the program, it enters the maintenance phase. Maintenance involves correcting any errors discovered while the program is being used and changing the program to reflect changes in the user's requirements.

Data and instructions are represented as binary numbers (numbers consisting of just 1s and 0s) in electronic computers. The process of converting data and instructions into a form usable by the computer is called coding.

A programming language reflects the range of operations a computer can perform. The basic control structures in a programming language—sequence, selection, loop, and subprogram—are based on these fundamental operations. In this text, you will learn to write programs in the high-level programming language called C++.

Computers are composed of six basic parts: the memory unit, the arithmetic/logic unit, the control unit, input and output devices, and auxiliary storage devices. The arithmetic/logic unit and control unit together are called the central processing unit. The physical parts of the computer are called hardware. The programs that are executed by the computer are called software.

System software is a set of programs designed to simplify the user/computer interface. It includes the compiler, the operating system, and the editor.

Computing professionals are guided by a set of ethics, as are members of other professions. Among the responsibilities that we have are copying software only with permission and including attribution to other programmers when we make use of their code, guarding the privacy of confidential data, using computer resources only with permission, and carefully engineering our programs so that they work correctly.

We've said that problem solving is an integral part of the programming process. Although you may have little experience programming computers, you have lots of experience solving problems. The key is to stop and think about the strategies you use to solve problems, and then to use those strategies to devise workable algorithms. Among those strategies are asking questions, looking for things that are familiar, solving by analogy, applying means-ends analysis, dividing the problem into subproblems, using existing solutions to small problems to solve a larger problem, merging solutions, and paraphrasing the problem in order to overcome a mental block.

The computer is widely used today in science, engineering, business, government, medicine, consumer goods, and the arts. Learning to program in C++ can help you use this powerful tool effectively.

Quick Check

The Quick Check is intended to help you decide if you've met the goals set forth at the beginning of each chapter. If you understand the material in the chapter, the answer to each question should be fairly obvious. After reading a question, check your response against the answers listed at the end of the Quick Check. If you don't know an answer or don't understand the answer that's provided, turn to the page(s) listed at the end of the question to review the material.

1. What is a computer program? (p. 3)
2. What are the three phases in a program's life cycle? (p. 4)
3. Is an algorithm the same as a program? (p. 5)
4. What is a programming language? (p. 6)
5. What are the advantages of using a high-level programming language? (p. 11)
6. What does a compiler do? (p. 12)
7. What part does the object program play in the compilation and execution processes? (p. 12)
8. Name the four basic ways of structuring statements in C++ and other languages. (p. 15)
9. What are the six basic components of a computer? (p. 16)
10. What is the difference between hardware and software? (p. 19)
11. In what regard is theft of computer time like stealing a car? How are the two crimes different? (p. 28)
12. What is the divide-and-conquer approach? (p. 33)

Answers   **1.** A computer program is a sequence of instructions performed by a computer.   **2.** The three phases of a program's life cycle are problem solving, implementation, and maintenance.   **3.** No. All programs are algorithms, but not all algorithms are programs.   **4.** A set of rules, symbols, and special words used to construct a program.   **5.** A high-level programming language is easier to use than an assembly language or a machine language. Also, programs written in a high-level language can be run on many different computers.   **6.** The compiler translates a program written in a high-level language into machine language.   **7.** The object program is the machine language version of a program. It is created by a compiler. The object program is what is loaded into the computer's memory and executed.   **8.** Sequence, selection, loop, and subprogram. **9.** The basic components of a computer are the memory unit, arithmetic/logic unit, control unit, input and output devices, and auxiliary storage devices. **10.** Hardware is the physical components of the computer; software is the collection of programs that run on the computer. **11.** Both crimes deprive the owner of access to a resource. A physical object is taken in a car theft, whereas time is the thing being stolen from the computer owner. **12.** The divide-and-conquer approach is a problem-solving technique that breaks a large problem into smaller, simpler subproblems.

Exam Preparation Exercises

1. Explain why the following series of steps is not an algorithm, then rewrite the series so it is.

   Shampooing
   (1) Rinse.
   (2) Lather.
   (3) Repeat.

2. Describe the input and output files used by a compiler.
3. In the following recipe for chocolate pound cake, identify the steps that are branches (selection) and loops, and the steps that are references to subalgorithms outside the algorithm.

   Preheat the oven to 350 degrees
   Line the bottom of a 9-inch tube pan with wax paper
   Sift $2^3/_4$ c flour, $^3/_4$ t cream of tartar, $^1/_2$ t baking soda, $1^1/_2$ t salt, and $1^3/_4$ c sugar
       into a large bowl
   Add 1 c shortening to the bowl
   If using butter, margarine, or lard, then
       add $^2/_3$ c milk to the bowl,
   else
       (for other shortenings) add 1 c minus 2 T of milk to the bowl
   Add 1 t vanilla to the mixture in the bowl
   If mixing with a spoon, then
       see the instructions in the introduction to the chapter on cakes,
   else
       (for electric mixers) beat the contents of the bowl for 2 minutes at medium
       speed, scraping the bowl and beaters as needed
   Add 3 eggs plus 1 extra egg yolk to the bowl
   Melt 3 squares of unsweetened chocolate and add to the mixture in the bowl
   Beat the mixture for 1 minute at medium speed
   Pour the batter into the tube pan
   Put the pan into the oven and bake for 1 hour and 10 minutes
   Perform the test for doneness described in the introduction to the chapter on
       cakes
   Repeat the test once each minute until the cake is done
   Remove the pan from the oven and allow the cake to cool for 2 hours
   Follow the instructions for removing the cake from the pan, given in the
       introduction to the chapter on cakes
   Sprinkle powdered sugar over the cracks on top of the cake just before serving

4.   Put a check next to each item below that is a peripheral device.

_____   a.   Disk drive
_____   b.   Arithmetic/logic unit
_____   c.   Magnetic tape drive
_____   d.   Printer
_____   e.   CD-ROM drive
_____   f.   Memory
_____   g.   Auxiliary storage device
_____   h.   Control unit
_____   i.   LCD screen
_____   j.   Mouse

5.   Next to each item below, indicate whether it is hardware (H) or software (S).

_____   a.   Disk drive
_____   b.   Memory
_____   c.   Compiler
_____   d.   Arithmetic/logic unit
_____   e.   Editor
_____   f.   Operating system
_____   g.   Object program
_____   h.   Mouse
_____   i.   Central processing unit

6.   Means-ends analysis is a problem-solving strategy.
     a.   What are three things you must know in order to apply means-ends analysis to a problem?
     b.   What is one way of combining this technique with the divide-and-conquer strategy?

7.   Show how you would use the divide-and-conquer approach to solve the problem of finding a job.

Programming Warm-up Exercises

1.   Write an algorithm for driving from where you live to the nearest airport that has regularly scheduled flights. Restrict yourself to a vocabulary of 74 words plus numbers and place names. You must select the appropriate set of words for this task. An example of a vocabulary is given in Appendix A, the list of reserved words (words with special meaning) in the C++ programming language. Notice that there are just 74 words in that list. The purpose of this exercise is to give you practice writing simple, exact instructions with an equally small vocabulary.

2.   Write an algorithm for making a peanut butter and jelly sandwich, using a vocabulary of just 74 words (you choose the words). Assume that all ingredients are in the refrigerator and that the necessary tools are in a drawer under the kitchen counter. The instructions must be very simple and exact because the person making the sandwich has no knowledge of food preparation and takes every word literally.

3.   In Exercise 1 above, identify the sequential, conditional, repetitive, and subprogram steps.

Case Study Follow-Up

1. Using Figure 1-14 as a guide, construct a divide-and-conquer diagram of the Problem-Solving Case Study, "An Algorithm for a Company Payroll."
2. Use the following data set to test the payroll algorithm presented on pages 38–39. Follow each step of the algorithm just as it is written, as if you were a computer. Then check your results by hand to be sure that the algorithm is correct.

ID Number	Pay Rate	Hours Worked
327	8.30	48
201	6.60	40
29	12.50	40
166	9.25	51
254	7.00	32
0		

3. In the Company Payroll case study, we used means-ends analysis to develop the subalgorithm for calculating pay. What are the *ends* in the analysis? That is, what information did we start with and what information did we want to end up with?
4. In the Payroll program, certain remarks are preceded by the symbols //. What are these remarks called, and what does the compiler do with them? What is their purpose?

2

C++ Syntax and Semantics, and the Program Development Process

- To understand how a C++ program is composed of one or more subprograms (functions).
- To be able to read syntax templates in order to understand the formal rules governing C++ programs.
- To be able to create and recognize legal C++ identifiers.
- To be able to declare named constants and variables of type `char` and `string`.
- To be able to distinguish reserved words in C++ from user-defined identifiers.
- To be able to assign values to variables.
- To be able to construct simple string expressions made up of constants, variables, and the concatenation operator.
- To be able to construct a statement that writes to an output stream.
- To be able to determine what is printed by a given output statement.
- To be able to use comments to clarify your programs.
- To be able to construct simple C++ programs.
- To learn the steps involved in entering and running a program.

The Elements of C++ Programs

Programmers develop solutions to problems using a programming language. In this chapter, we start looking at the rules and symbols that make up the C++ programming language. We also review the steps required to create a program and make it work on a computer.

C++ Program Structure

In Chapter 1, we talked about the four basic structures for expressing actions in a programming language: sequence, selection, loop, and subprogram. We said that subprograms allow us to write parts of our program separately and then assemble them into final form. In C++, all subprograms are referred to as **functions,** and a C++ program is a collection of one or more functions.

Each function performs some particular task, and collectively they all cooperate to solve the entire problem.

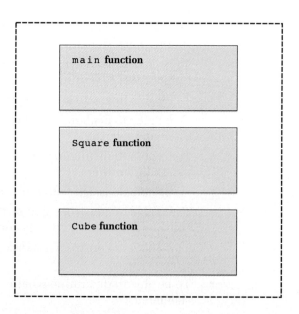

Function   A subprogram in C++.

Every C++ program must have a function named `main`. Execution of the program always begins with the `main` function. You can think of `main` as the master and the other functions as the servants. When `main` wants the function `Square` to perform a task, `main` *calls* (or *invokes*) `Square`. When the `Square` function completes execution of its statements, it obediently returns control to the master, `main`, so the master can continue executing.

Let's look at an example of a C++ program with three functions: `main`, `Square`, and `Cube`. Don't be too concerned with the details in the program—just observe its overall look and structure.

```cpp
#include <iostream>

using namespace std;

int Square( int );
int Cube( int );

int main()
{
    cout << "The square of 27 is " << Square(27) << endl;
    cout << "and the cube of 27 is " << Cube(27) << endl;
    return 0;
}

int Square( int n )
{
    return n * n;
}

int Cube( int n )
{
    return n * n * n;
}
```

In each of the three functions, the left brace ({) and right brace (}) mark the beginning and end of the statements to be executed. Statements appearing between the braces are known as the *body* of the function.

Execution of a program always begins with the first statement of the `main` function. In our program, the first statement is

```cpp
cout << "The square of 27 is " << Square(27) << endl;
```

This is an output statement that causes information to be printed on the computer's display screen. You will learn how to construct output statements like this later in the chapter. Briefly, this statement prints two items. The first is the message

```
The square of 27 is
```

The second to be printed is the value obtained by calling (invoking) the `Square` function, with the value 27 as the number to be squared. As the servant, the `Square` function performs its task of squaring the number and sending the computed result (729) back to its *caller*, the `main` function. Now `main` can continue executing by printing the value 729 and proceeding to its next statement.

In a similar fashion, the second statement in `main` prints the message

```
and the cube of 27 is
```

and then invokes the `Cube` function and prints the result, 19683. The complete output produced by executing this program is, therefore,

```
The square of 27 is 729
and the cube of 27 is 19683
```

Both `Square` and `Cube` are examples of *value-returning functions*. A value-returning function returns a single value to its caller. The word `int` at the beginning of the first line of the `Square` function

```
int Square( int n )
```

states that the function returns an integer value.

Now look at the `main` function again. You'll see that the first line of the function is

```
int main()
```

The word `int` indicates that `main` is a value-returning function that should return an integer value. And it does. After printing the square and cube of 27, `main` executes the statement

```
return 0;
```

to return the value 0 to its caller. But who calls the `main` function? The answer is: the computer's operating system.

When you work with C++ programs, the operating system is considered to be the caller of the `main` function. The operating system expects `main` to return a value when `main` finishes executing. By convention, a return value of 0 means everything went OK. A return value of anything else (typically 1, 2, ...) means something went wrong. Later in this book we look at situations in which you might want to return a value other than 0 from `main`. For the time being, we always conclude the execution of `main` by returning the value 0.

We have looked only briefly at the overall picture of what a C++ program looks like—a collection of one or more functions, including `main`. We have also mentioned what is special about the `main` function—it is a required function, execution begins there, and it returns a value to the operating system. Now it's time to begin looking at the details of the C++ language.

Syntax and Semantics

A programming language is a set of rules, symbols, and special words used to construct a program. There are rules for both **syntax** (grammar) and **semantics** (meaning).

Syntax The formal rules governing how valid instructions are written in a programming language.

Semantics The set of rules that determines the meaning of instructions written in a programming language.

Syntax is a formal set of rules that defines exactly what combinations of letters, numbers, and symbols can be used in a programming language. There is no room for ambiguity in the syntax of a programming language because the computer can't think; it doesn't "know what we mean." To avoid ambiguity, syntax rules themselves must be written in a very simple, precise, formal language called a **metalanguage.**

Metalanguage A language that is used to write the syntax rules for another language.

Learning to read a metalanguage is like learning to read the notations used in the rules of a sport. Once you understand the notations, you can read the rule book. It's true that many people learn a sport simply by watching others play, but what they learn is usually just enough to allow them to take part in casual games. You could learn C++ by following the examples in this book, but a serious programmer, like a serious athlete, must take the time to read and understand the rules.

Syntax rules are the blueprints we use to build instructions in a program. They allow us to take the elements of a programming language—the basic building blocks of the language—and assemble them into *constructs*, syntactically correct structures. If our program violates any of the rules of the language—by misspelling a crucial word or leaving out an important comma, for instance—the program is said to have *syntax errors* and cannot compile correctly until we fix them.

*T*HEORETICAL FOUNDATIONS

Metalanguages

Metalanguage is the word *language* with the prefix *meta-*, which means "beyond" or "more comprehensive." A metalanguage is a language that goes beyond a normal language by allowing us to speak precisely about that language. It is a language for talking about languagesOne of the oldest computer-oriented metalanguages is *Backus-Naur Form* (*BNF*), which is named for John Backus and Peter Naur, who developed it in 1960. BNF syntax definitions are written out using letters, numbers, and special symbols. For example, an *identifier* (a name for something in a program) in C++ must be at least one letter or underscore (_), which may or may not be followed by additional letters, underscores, or digits. The BNF definition of an identifier in C++ is

\<Identifier\> ::= \<Nondigit\> | \<Nondigit\> \<NondigitOrDigitSequence\>

\<NondigitOrDigitSequence\> ::= \<NondigitOrDigit\> | \<NondigitOrDigit\> \<NondigitOrDigitSequence\>

\<NondigitOrDigit\> ::= \<Nondigit\> | \<Digit\>

\<Nondigit\> ::= _ | A | B | C | D | E | F | G | H | I | J | K | L | M | N | O | P | Q | R | S | T | U | V | W | X | Y | Z |
        a | b | c | d | e | f | g | h | i | j | k | l | m | n | o | p | q | r | s | t | u | v | w | x | y | z

\<Digit\> ::= 0 | 1 | 2 | 3 | 4 | 5 | 6 | 7 | 8 | 9

where the symbol ::= is read "is defined as," the symbol | means "or," the symbols \< and \> are used to enclose words called *nonterminal symbols* (symbols that still need to be defined), and everything else is called a *terminal symbol.*

The first line of the definition reads as follows: "An identifier is defined as either a nondigit or a nondigit followed by a nondigit-or-digit sequence." This line contains nonterminal symbols that must be defined. In the second line, the nonterminal symbol NondigitOrDigitSequence is defined as either a NondigitOrDigit or a NondigitOrDigit followed by another NondigitOrDigitSequence. The self-reference in the definition is a roundabout way of saying that a NondigitOrDigitSequence can be a series of one or more nondigits or digits. The third line defines NondigitOrDigit to be either a Nondigit or a Digit. In the fourth and last lines, we finally encounter terminal symbols, which define Nondigit to be an underscore or any upper- or lowercase letter and Digit as any one of the numeric symbols 0 through 9.

BNF is an extremely simple language, but that simplicity leads to syntax definitions that can be long and difficult to read. An alternative metalanguage, the *syntax diagram*, is easier to follow. It uses arrows to indicate how symbols can be combined. The syntax diagrams that define an identifier in C++ appear on the next page.

To read the diagrams, start at the left and follow the arrows. When you come to a branch, take any one of the branch paths. Symbols in boldface are terminal symbols, and words not in boldface are nonterminal symbols.

The first diagram shows that an identifier consists of a nondigit followed, optionally, by any number of nondigits or digits. The second diagram defines the nonterminal symbol Nondigit to be an underscore or any one of the alphabetic characters. The third diagram defines Digit to be one of the numeric characters. Here, we have eliminated the BNF nonterminal symbols NondigitOrDigitSequence and NondigitOrDigit by using arrows in the first syntax diagram to allow a sequence of consecutive nondigits or digits.

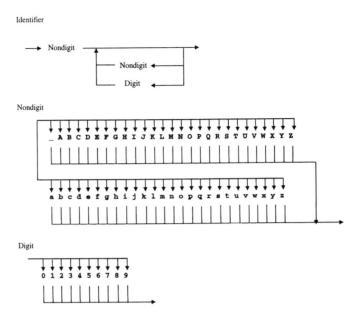

Syntax diagrams are easier to interpret than BNF definitions, but they still can be difficult to read. In this text, we introduce another metalanguage, called a *syntax template*. Syntax templates show at a glance the form a C++ construct takes.

One final note: Metalanguages only show how to write instructions that the compiler can translate. They do not define what those instructions do (their semantics). Formal languages for defining the semantics of a programming language exist, but they are beyond the scope of this text. Throughout this book, we describe the semantics of C++ in English.

Syntax Templates

In this book, we write the syntax rules for C++ using a metalanguage called a *syntax template*. A syntax template is a generic example of the C++ construct being defined. Graphic conventions show which portions are optional and which can be repeated. A boldface word or symbol is a literal word or symbol in the C++ language. A nonboldface word can be replaced by another template. A curly brace is used to indicate a list of items, from which one item can be chosen.

Let's look at an example. This template defines an identifier in C++:

Identifier

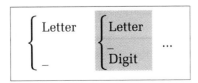

The shading indicates a part of the definition that is optional. The three dots (. . .) mean that the preceding symbol or shaded block can be repeated. Thus, an identifier in C++ must begin with a letter or underscore and is optionally followed by one or more letters, underscores, or digits.

Remember that a word not in boldface type can be replaced with another template. These are the templates for Letter and Digit:

Letter   **Digit**

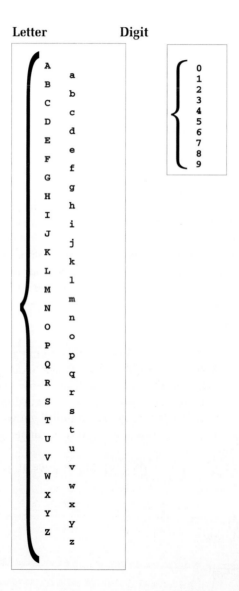

In these templates, the braces again indicate lists of items from which any one item can be chosen. So a letter can be any one of the upper- or lower-case letters, and a digit can be any of the numeric characters 0 through 9.

Now let's look at the syntax template for the C++ `main` function:

MainFunction

```
int main()
{
      Statement
        ⋮

}
```

The `main` function begins with the word `int`, followed by the word `main` and then left and right parentheses. This first line of the function is the *heading*. After the heading, the left brace signals the start of the statements in the function (its body). The shading and the three dots indicate that the function body consists of zero or more statements. (In this diagram we have placed the three dots vertically to suggest that statements usually are arranged vertically, one above the next.) Finally, the right brace indicates the end of the function.

In principle, the syntax template allows the function body to have no statements at all. In practice, however, the body should include a Return statement because the word `int` in the function heading states that `main` returns an integer value. Thus, the shortest C++ program is

```
int main()
{
    return 0;
}
```

As you might guess, this program does absolutely nothing useful when executed!

As we introduce C++ language constructs throughout the book, we use syntax templates to display the proper syntax. At the publisher's Web site, you will find these syntax templates gathered into one central location.*

When you finish this chapter, you should know enough about the syntax and semantics of statements in C++ to write simple programs. But before we can talk about writing statements, we must look at how names are written in C++ and at some of the elements of a program.

---

* The publisher's Web site is www.jbpub.com/dale

Naming Program Elements: Identifiers

As we noted in our discussion of metalanguages, **identifiers** are used in C++ to name things—things such as subprograms and places in the computer's memory. Identifiers are made up of letters (A–Z, a–z), digits (0–9), and the underscore character (_), but must begin with a letter or underscore.

Identifier   A name associated with a function or data object and used to refer to that function or data object.

Remember that an identifier *must* start with a letter or underscore:

Identifier

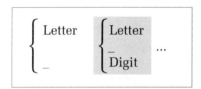

(Identifiers beginning with an underscore have special meanings in some C++ systems, so it is best to begin an identifier with a letter.)

Here are some examples of valid identifiers:

sum_of_squares   J9   box_22A   GetData   Bin3D4   count

And here are some examples of invalid identifiers and the reasons why they are invalid:

Invalid Identifier	Explanation
40Hours	Identifiers cannot begin with a digit.
Get Data	Blanks are not allowed in identifiers.
box-22	The hyphen (–) is a math symbol (minus) in C++.
cost_in_$	Special symbols such as $ are not allowed.
int	The word int is predefined in the C++ language.

The last identifier in the table, int, is an example of a **reserved word.** Reserved words are words that have specific uses in C++; you cannot use them as programmer-defined identifiers. Appendix A lists all of the reserved words in C++.

Reserved word   A word that has special meaning in C++; it cannot be used as a programmer-defined identifier.

The Payroll program in Chapter 1 uses the programmer-defined identifiers listed below. (Most of the other identifiers in the program are C++ reserved words.) Notice that we chose the names to convey how the identifiers are used.

Identifier	*How It Is Used*
MAX_HOURS	Maximum normal work hours
OVERTIME	Overtime pay rate factor
payRate	An employee's hourly pay rate
hours	The number of hours an employee worked
wages	An employee's weekly wages
total	The sum of weekly wages for all employees (total company payroll)
empNum	An employee's identification number
payFile	The output file (where the employee's number, pay rate, hours, and wages are written)
CalcPay	A function for computing an employee's wages

 ATTERS OF STYLE

Using Meaningful, Readable Identifiers

The names we use to refer to things in our programs are totally meaningless to the computer. The computer behaves in the same way whether we call the value 3.14159265 pi or cake, as long as we always call it the same thing. However, it is much easier for somebody to figure out how a program works if the names we choose for elements actually tell something about them. Whenever you have to make up a name for something in a program, try to pick one that is meaningful to a person reading the program.

C++ is a *case-sensitive* language. Uppercase letters are different from lowercase letters. The identifiers

PRINTTOPPORTION   printtopportion   pRiNtToPpOrTiOn   PrintTopPortion

are four distinct names and are not interchangeable in any way. As you can see, the last of these forms is the easiest to read. In this book, we use combinations of uppercase letters, lowercase letters, and underscores in identifiers. We explain our conventions for choosing between uppercase and lowercase as we proceed through this chapter.

Now that we've seen how to write identifiers, we look at some of the things that C++ allows us to name.

Data and Data Types

A computer program operates on data (stored internally in memory, stored externally on disk or tape, or input from a device such as a keyboard, scanner, or electrical sensor) and produces output. In C++, each piece of data must be of a specific **data type.** The data type determines how the data is represented in the computer and the kinds of processing the computer can perform on it.

Data type   A specific set of data values, along with a set of operations on those values.

Some types of data are used so frequently that C++ defines them for us. Examples of these *standard* (or *built-in*) *types* are int (for working with integer numbers), float (for working with real numbers having decimal points), and char (for working with character data).

Additionally, C++ allows programmers to define their own data types—*programmer-defined* (or *user-defined*) *types*. Beginning in Chapter 10, we show you how to define your own data types.

In this chapter, we focus on two data types—one for representing data consisting of a single character, the other for representing strings of characters. In the next chapter, we examine the numeric types (such as int and float) in detail.

*B*ACKGROUND INFORMATION

Data Storage

Where does a program get the data it needs to operate? Data is stored in the computer's memory. Remember that memory is divided into a large number of separate locations or cells, each of which can hold a piece of data. Each memory location has a unique address we refer to when we store or retrieve data. We can visualize memory as a set of post office boxes, with the box numbers as the addresses used to designate particular locations.

Of course, the actual address of each location in memory is a binary number in a machine language code. In C++ we use identifiers to name memory locations; the compiler then translates them into binary for us. This is one of the advantages of a high-level programming language: It frees us from having to keep track of the numeric addresses of the memory locations in which our data and instructions are stored.

The* char *Data Type The built-in type char describes data consisting of one alphanumeric character—a letter, a digit, or a special symbol:

```
'A'    'a'    '8'    '2'    '+'    '-'    '$'    '?'    '*'    ' '
```

Each machine uses a particular *character set*, the set of alphanumeric characters it can represent. (See Appendix E for some sample character sets.) Notice that each character is enclosed in single quotes (apostrophes). The C++ compiler needs the quotes to differentiate, say, between the character data '8' and the integer value 8 because the two are stored differently inside the machine. Notice also that the blank, ' ', is a valid character.*

---

* Most programming languages use ASCII (the American Standard Code for Information Interchange) to represent the English alphabet and other symbols. Each ASCII character is stored in a single byte of memory.

A newly developed character set called Unicode includes the larger alphabets of many international human languages. A single Unicode character occupies two bytes of memory. C++ provides the data type wchar_t (for "wide character") to accommodate larger character sets such as Unicode. In C++, the notation L'*something*' denotes a value of type wchar_t, where the *something* depends on the particular wide character set being used. We do not examine wide characters any further in this book.

You wouldn't want to add the character 'A' to the character 'B' or subtract the character '3' from the character '8', but you might want to compare character values. Each character set has a *collating sequence*, a predefined ordering of all the characters. Although this sequence varies from one character set to another, 'A' always compares less than 'B', 'B' less than 'C', and so forth. And '1' compares less than '2', '2' less than '3', and so on. None of the identifiers in the Payroll program is of type char.

The string *Data Type*   Whereas a value of type char is limited to a single character, a *string* is a sequence of characters, such as a word, name, or sentence, enclosed in double quotes. For example, the following are strings in C++:

```
"Problem Solving"     "C++"     "Programming and "     " . "
```

A string must be typed entirely on one line. For example, the string

```
"This string is invalid because it
is typed on more than one line."
```

is not valid because it is split across two lines. In this situation, the C++ compiler issues an error message at the first line. The message may say something like "UNTERMINATED STRING," depending on the particular compiler.

The quotes are not considered to be part of the string but are simply there to distinguish the string from other parts of a C++ program. For example, "amount" (in double quotes) is the character string made up of the letters *a, m, o, u, n,* and *t* in that order. On the other hand, amount (without the quotes) is an identifier, perhaps the name of a place in memory. The symbols "12345" represent a string made up of the characters *1, 2, 3, 4,* and *5* in that order. If we write 12345 without the quotes, it is an integer quantity that can be used in calculations.

A string containing no characters is called the *null string* (or *empty string*). We write the null string using two double quotes with nothing (not even spaces) between them:

```
""
```

The null string is not equivalent to a string of spaces; it is a special string that contains no characters.

To work with string data, this book uses a data type named string. This data type is not part of the C++ language (that is, it is not a built-in type). Rather, string is a programmer-defined type that is supplied by the C++ *standard library*, a large collection of prewritten functions and data types that any C++ programmer can use. Operations on string data include comparing the values of strings, searching a string for a particular character, and joining one string to another. We look at some of these operations later in this chapter and cover additional operations in subsequent chapters. None of the identifiers in the Payroll program is of type `string`, although string values are used directly in several places in the program.

Naming Elements: Declarations

Identifiers can be used to name both constants and variables. In other words, an identifier can be the name of a memory location whose contents are not allowed to change or it can be the name of a memory location whose contents can change.

How do we tell the computer what an identifier represents? By using a **declaration,** a statement that associates a name (an identifier) with a description of an element in a C++ program (just as a dictionary definition associates a name with a description of the thing being named). In a declaration, we name an identifier and what it represents. For example, the Payroll program uses the declaration

```
int empNum;
```

to announce that `empNum` is the name of a variable whose contents are of type `int`. When we declare a variable, the compiler picks a location in memory to be associated with the identifier. We don't have to know the actual address of the memory location because the computer automatically keeps track of it for us.

Declaration   A statement that associates an identifier with a data object, a function, or a data type so that the programmer can refer to that item by name.

Suppose that when we mailed a letter, we only had to put a person's name on it and the post office would look up the address. Of course, everybody in the world would need a different name; otherwise, the post office wouldn't be able to figure out whose address was whose. The same is true in C++. Each identifier can represent just one thing (except under special circumstances, which we talk about in Chapters 7 and 8). Every identifier you use in a program must be different from all others.

Constants and variables are collectively called *data objects*. Both data objects and the actual instructions in a program are stored in various memory locations. You have seen that a group of instructions—a function—can be given a name. A name also can be associated with a programmer-defined data type.

In C++, you must declare every identifier before it is used. This allows the compiler to verify that the use of the identifier is consistent with what it was declared to be. If you declare an identifier to be a constant and later try to change its value, the compiler detects this inconsistency and issues an error message.

There is a different form of declaration statement for each kind of data object, function, or data type in C++. The forms of declarations for variables and constants are introduced here; others are covered in later chapters.

Variables   A program operates on data. Data is stored in memory. While a program is executing, different values may be stored in the same memory location at different times. This kind of memory location is called a **variable,** and its content is the *variable value.* The symbolic name that we associate with a memory location is the *variable name* or *variable identifier* (see Figure 2-1). In practice, we often refer to the variable name more briefly as the *variable.*

Variable   A location in memory, referenced by an identifier, that contains a data value that can be changed.

Declaring a variable means specifying both its name and its data type. This tells the compiler to associate a name with a memory location whose contents are of a specific type (for example, char or string). The following statement declares myChar to be a variable of type char:

```
char myChar;
```

In C++, a variable can contain a data value only of the type specified in its declaration. Because of the above declaration, the variable myChar can contain *only* a char value. If the C++ compiler comes across an instruction that tries to store a float value into myChar, it generates extra instructions to convert the float value to the proper type. In Chapter 3, we examine how such type conversions take place.

Here's the syntax template for a variable declaration:

VariableDeclaration

DataType Identifier , Identifier . . . ;

where DataType is the name of a data type such as char or string. Notice that a variable declaration always ends with a semicolon.

FIGURE 2-1
Variable

From the syntax template, you can see that it is possible to declare several variables in one statement:

```
char letter, middleInitial, ch;
```

Here, all three variables are declared to be `char` variables. Our preference, though, is to declare each variable with a separate statement:

```
char letter;
char middleInitial;
char ch;
```

With this form it is easier, when modifying a program, to add new variables to the list or delete ones you no longer want.

Declaring each variable with a separate statement also allows you to attach comments to the right of each declaration, as we do in the Payroll program:

```
float payRate;        // Employee's pay rate
float hours;          // Hours worked
float wages;          // Wages earned
float total;          // Total company payroll
int   empNum;         // Employee ID number
```

These declarations tell the compiler to reserve memory space for four `float` variables—payRate, hours, wages, and total—and one `int` variable, empNum. The comments explain to someone reading the program what each variable represents.

Now that we've seen how to declare variables in C++, let's look at how to declare constants.

Constants All single characters (enclosed in single quotes) and strings (enclosed in double quotes) are constants.

```
'A'   '@'    "Howdy boys"    "Please enter an employee number:"
```

In C++ as in mathematics, a constant is something whose value never changes. When we use the actual value of a constant in a program, we are using a **literal value** (or *literal*).

Literal value   Any constant value written in a program.

An alternative to the literal constant is the **named constant** (or **symbolic constant**), which is introduced in a declaration statement. A named constant is just another way of representing a literal value. Instead of using the literal value in an instruction, we give it a name in a declaration statement, then use that name in the instruction. For example, we can write an instruction that prints the title of this book using the literal string `"Programming and Problem Solving with C++"`. Or we can declare a named constant called `BOOK_TITLE` that equals the same string and then use the constant name in the instruction. That is, we can use either

```
"Programming and Problem Solving with C++"
```

or

```
BOOK_TITLE
```

in the instruction.

Named constant (symbolic constant)   A location in memory, referenced by an identifier, that contains a data value that cannot be changed.

Using the literal value of a constant may seem easier than giving it a name and then referring to it by that name. But, in fact, named constants make a program easier to read because they make the meaning of literal constants clearer. Named constants also make it easier to change a program later on.

This is the syntax template for a constant declaration:

ConstantDeclaration

```
const DataType  Identifier = LiteralValue ;
```

Notice that the reserved word `const` begins the declaration, and an equal sign (=) appears between the identifier and the literal value.

The following are examples of constant declarations:

```
const string STARS = "********";
const char   BLANK = ' ';
const string BOOK_TITLE = "Programming and Problem Solving with C++";
const string MESSAGE = "Error condition";
```

As we have done above, many C++ programmers capitalize the entire identifier of a named constant and separate the English words with an underscore. The idea is to let the reader quickly distinguish between variable names and constant names when they appear in the middle of a program.

It's a good idea to add comments to constant declarations as well as variable declarations. In the Payroll program, we describe in comments what each constant represents:

```
const float MAX_HOURS = 40.0;    // Maximum normal work hours
const float OVERTIME = 1.5;      // Overtime pay rate factor
```

*M*ATTERS OF STYLE

Capitalization of Identifiers

Programmers often use capitalization as a quick visual clue to what an identifier represents. Different programmers adopt different conventions for using uppercase letters and lowercase letters. Some people use only lowercase letters, separating the English words in an identifier with the underscore character:

```
pay_rate   emp_num  pay_file
```

The conventions we use in this book are as follows:

- For identifiers representing variables, we begin with a lowercase letter and capitalize each successive English word.

  ```
  lengthInYards   middleInitial   hours
  ```

- Names of programmer-written functions and programmer-defined data types (which we examine later in the book) are capitalized in the same manner as variable names except that they begin with capital letters.

  ```
  CalcPay(payRate, hours, wages)   Cube(27)   MyDataType
  ```

Capitalizing the first letter allows a person reading the program to tell at a glance that an identifier represents a function name or data type rather than a variable. However, we cannot use this capitalization convention everywhere. C++ expects every program to have a function named `main`—all in lowercase letters—so we cannot name it `Main`. Nor can we use `Char` for the built-in data type `char`. C++ reserved words use all lowercase letters, as do most of the identifiers declared in the standard library (such as `string`).

- For identifiers representing named constants, we capitalize every letter and use underscores to separate the English words.

```
BOOK_TITLE    OVERTIME    MAX_LENGTH
```

This convention, widely used by C++ programmers, is an immediate signal that `BOOK_TITLE` is a named constant and not a variable, a function, or a data type.

These conventions are only that—conventions. C++ does not require this particular style of capitalizing identifiers. You may wish to capitalize in a different fashion. But whatever system you use, it is essential that you use a consistent style throughout your program. A person reading your program will be confused or misled if you use a random style of capitalization.

Taking Action: Executable Statements

Up to this point, we've looked at ways of declaring data objects in a program. Now we turn our attention to ways of acting, or performing operations, on data.

Assignment The value of a variable can be set or changed through an **assignment statement.** For example,

```
lastName = "Lincoln";
```

assigns the string value `"Lincoln"` to the variable `lastName` (that is, it stores the sequence of characters "Lincoln" into the memory associated with the variable named `lastName`).

Assignment statement A statement that stores the value of an expression into a variable.

Here's the syntax template for an assignment statement:

AssignmentStatement

> Variable = Expression ;

The semantics (meaning) of the assignment operator (=) is "store"; the value of the **expression** is *stored* into the variable. Any previous value in the variable is destroyed and replaced by the value of the expression.

Expression   An arrangement of identifiers, literals, and operators that can be evaluated to compute a value of a given type.

Only one variable can be on the left-hand side of an assignment statement. An assignment statement is *not* like a math equation ($x + y = z + 4$); the expression (what is on the right-hand side of the assignment operator) is **evaluated,** and the resulting value is stored into the single variable on the left of the assignment operator. A variable keeps its assigned value until another statement stores a new value into it.

Evaluate   To compute a new value by performing a specified set of operations on given values.

Given the declarations

```
string firstName;
string middleName;
string lastName;
string title;
char   middleInitial;
char   letter;
```

the following assignment statements are valid:

```
firstName = "Abraham";
middleName = firstName;
middleName = "";
lastName = "Lincoln";
title = "President";
middleInitial = ' ';
letter = middleInitial;
```

However, these assignments are not valid:

Invalid Assignment Statement	Reason
`middleInitial = "A.";`	`middleInitial` is of type char; `"A."` is a string.
`letter = firstName;`	`letter` is of type char; `firstName` is of type string.
`firstName = Thomas;`	Thomas is an undeclared identifier.
`"Edison" = lastName;`	Only a variable can appear to the left of =.
`lastName = ;`	The expression to the right of = is missing.

String Expressions Although we can't perform arithmetic on strings, the `string` data type provides a special string operation, called *concatenation*, that uses the + operator. The result of concatenating (joining) two strings is a new string containing the characters from both strings. For example, given the statements

```
string bookTitle;
string phrase1;
string phrase2;

phrase1 = "Programming and ";
phrase2 = "Problem Solving";
```

we could write

```
bookTitle = phrase1 + phrase2;
```

This statement retrieves the value of `phrase1` from memory and concatenates the value of `phrase2` to form a new, temporary string containing the characters

```
"Programming and Problem Solving"
```

This temporary string (which is of type `string`) is then assigned to (stored into) `bookTitle`.

The order of the strings in the expression determines how they appear in the resulting string. If we instead write

```
bookTitle = phrase2 + phrase1;
```

then `bookTitle` contains

```
"Problem SolvingProgramming and "
```

Concatenation works with named `string` constants, literal strings, and `char` data as well as with `string` variables. The only restriction is that at least one of the operands of the + operator *must* be a `string` variable or named constant (so you cannot use expressions like `"Hi"` + `"there"` or `'A'` + `'B'`). For example, if we have declared the following constants:

```
const string WORD1 = "rogramming";
const string WORD3 = "Solving";
const string WORD5 = "C++";
```

then we could write the following assignment statement to store the title of this book into the variable `bookTitle`:

```
bookTitle = 'P' + WORD1 + " and Problem " + WORD3 + " with " + WORD5;
```

As a result, `bookTitle` contains the string

```
"Programming and Problem Solving with C++"
```

The preceding example demonstrates how we can combine identifiers, `char` data, and literal strings in a concatenation expression. Of course, if we simply want to assign the complete string to `bookTitle`, we can do so directly:

```
bookTitle = "Programming and Problem Solving with C++";
```

But occasionally we encounter a situation in which we want to add some characters to an existing string value. Suppose that `bookTitle` already contains `"Programming and Problem Solving"` and that we wish to complete the title. We could use a statement of the form

```
bookTitle = bookTitle + " with C++";
```

Such a statement retrieves the value of `bookTitle` from memory, concatenates the string `" with C++"` to form a new string, and then stores the new string back into `bookTitle`. The new string replaces the old value of `bookTitle` (which is destroyed).

Keep in mind that concatenation works only with values of type `string`. Even though an arithmetic plus sign is used for the operation, we cannot concatenate values of numeric data types, such as `int` and `float`, with strings.

If you are using pre–standard C++ (any version of C++ prior to the ISO/ANSI standard) and your standard library does not provide the `string` type, see Section D.1 of Appendix D for a discussion of how to proceed.

Output Have you ever asked someone, "Do you know what time it is?" only to have the person smile smugly, say, "Yes, I do," and walk away? This situation is like the one that currently exists between you and the computer. You now know enough C++ syntax to tell the computer to assign values to variables and to concatenate strings, but the computer won't give you the results until you tell it to write them out.

In C++ we write out the values of variables and expressions by using a special variable named `cout` (pronounced "see-out") along with the *insertion operator* (`<<`):

```
cout << "Hello";
```

This statement displays the characters `Hello` on the *standard output device*, usually the video display screen.

The variable `cout` is predefined in C++ systems to denote an *output stream*. You can think of an output stream as an endless sequence of characters going to an output device. In the case of `cout`, the output stream goes to the standard output device.

The insertion operator `<<` (often pronounced as "put to") takes two operands. Its left-hand operand is a stream expression (in the simplest case, just a stream variable such as `cout`). Its right-hand operand is an expression, which could be as simple as a literal string:

```
cout << "The title is ";
cout << bookTitle + ", 2nd Edition";
```

The insertion operator converts its right-hand operand to a sequence of characters and inserts them into (or, more precisely, appends them to) the output stream. Notice how the `<<` points in the direction the data is going—*from* the expression written on the right *to* the output stream on the left.

You can use the `<<` operator several times in a single output statement. Each occurrence appends the next data item to the output stream. For example, we can write the preceding two output statements as

```
cout << "The title is " << bookTitle + ", 2nd Edition";
```

If `bookTitle` contains `"American History"`, both versions produce the same output:

```
The title is American History, 2nd Edition
```

The output statement has the following form:

OutputStatement

> `cout << ` Expression `<< ` **Expression** `...;`

The following output statements yield the output shown. These examples assume that the `char` variable ch contains the value `'2'`, the `string` variable firstName contains `"Marie"`, and the `string` variable lastName contains `"Curie"`.

Statement	What Is Printed (□ means blank)
`cout << ch;`	2
`cout << "ch = " << ch;`	ch□=□2
`cout << firstName + " " + lastName;`	Marie□Curie
`cout << firstName << lastName;`	MarieCurie
`cout << firstName << ' ' << lastName;`	Marie□Curie
`cout << "ERROR MESSAGE";`	ERROR□MESSAGE
`cout << "Error=" << ch;`	Error=2

An output statement prints literal strings exactly as they appear. To let the computer know that you want to print a literal string—not a named constant or variable—you must remember to use double quotes to enclose the string. If you don't put quotes around a string, you'll probably get an error message (such as "UNDECLARED IDENTIFIER") from the C++ compiler. If you want to print a string that includes a double quote, you must type a backslash (\) character and a double quote, with no space between them, in the string. For example, to print the characters

```
Al "Butch" Jones
```

the output statement looks like this:

```
cout << "Al \"Butch\" Jones";
```

To conclude this introductory look at C++ output, we should mention how to terminate an output line. Normally, successive output statements cause the output to continue along the same line of the display screen. The sequence

```
cout << "Hi";
cout << "there";
```

writes the following to the screen, all on the same line:

```
Hithere
```

To print the two words on separate lines, we can do this:

```
cout << "Hi" << endl;
cout << "there" << endl;
```

The output from these statements is

```
Hi
there
```

The identifier `endl` (meaning "end line") is a special C++ feature called a *manipulator*. We discuss manipulators in the next chapter. For now, the important thing to note is that `endl` lets you finish an output line and go on to the next line whenever you wish.

Beyond Minimalism: Adding Comments to a Program

All you need to create a working program is the correct combination of declarations and executable statements. The compiler ignores comments, but they are of enormous help to anyone who must read the program. Comments can appear anywhere in a program except in the middle of an identifier, a reserved word, or a literal constant.

C++ comments come in two forms. The first is any sequence of characters enclosed by the `/*  */` pair. The compiler ignores anything within the pair. Here's an example:

```
string idNumber;    /* Identification number of the aircraft */
```

The second, and more common, form begins with two slashes (`//`) and extends to the end of that line of the program:

```
string idNumber;    // Identification number of the aircraft
```

The compiler ignores anything after the two slashes.

Writing fully commented programs is good programming style. A comment should appear at the beginning of a program to explain what the program does:

```
// This program computes the weight and balance of a Beechcraft
// Starship-1 airplane, given the amount of fuel, number of
// passengers, and weight of luggage in fore and aft storage.
// It assumes that there are two pilots and a standard complement
// of equipment, and that passengers weigh 170 pounds each
```

Another good place for comments is in constant and variable declarations, where the comments explain how each identifier is used. In addition, comments should introduce each major step in a long program and should explain anything that is unusual or difficult to read (for example, a lengthy formula).

It is important to make your comments concise and to arrange them in the program so that they are easy to see and it is clear what they refer to. If comments are too long or crowd the statements in the program, they make the program more difficult to read—just the opposite of what you intended!

Program Construction

We have looked at basic elements of C++ programs: identifiers, declarations, variables, constants, expressions, statements, and comments. Now let's see how to collect these elements into a program. As you saw earlier, C++ programs are made up of functions, one of which must be named main. A program also can have declarations that lie outside of any function. The syntax template for a program looks like this:

Program

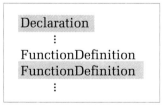

A function definition consists of the function heading and its body, which is delimited by left and right braces:

FunctionDefinition

```
Heading
{
      Statement
         ⋮
}
```

Here's an example of a program with just one function, the `main` function:

```cpp
//*******************************************************************
// PrintName program
// This program prints a name in two different formats
//*******************************************************************
#include <iostream>
#include <string>

using namespace std;

const string FIRST = "Herman";      // Person's first name
const string LAST = "Smith";        // Person's last name
const char   MIDDLE = 'G';          // Person's middle initial

int main()
{
    string firstLast;      // Name in first-last format
    string lastFirst;      // Name in last-first format

    firstLast = FIRST + " " + LAST;
    cout << "Name in first-last format is " << firstLast << endl;

    lastFirst = LAST + ", " + FIRST + ", ";
    cout << "Name in last-first-initial format is ";
    cout << lastFirst << MIDDLE << '.' << endl;

    return 0;
}
```

The program begins with a comment that explains what the program does. Immediately after the comment, the following lines appear:

```cpp
#include <iostream>
#include <string>

using namespace std;
```

The #include lines instruct the C++ system to insert into our program the contents of the files named iostream and string. The first file contains information that C++ needs in order to output values to a stream such as cout. The second file contains information about the programmer-defined data type string. We discuss the purpose of these #include lines and the using statement a little later in the chapter.

Next comes a declaration section in which we define the constants FIRST, LAST, and MIDDLE. Comments explain how each identifier is used. The rest of the program is the function definition for our main function. The first line is the function heading: the reserved word int, the name of the function, and then opening and closing parentheses. (The parentheses inform the compiler that main is the name of a function, not a variable or named constant.) The body of the function includes the declarations of two variables, firstLast and lastFirst, followed by a list of executable statements. The compiler translates these executable statements into machine language instructions. During the execution phase of the program, these are the instructions that are executed.

Our main function finishes by returning 0 as the function value:

```
return 0;
```

Remember that main returns an integer value to the operating system when it completes execution. This integer value is called the *exit status*. On most computer systems, you return an exit status of 0 to indicate successful completion of the program; otherwise, you return a nonzero value.

Notice how we use spacing in the PrintName program to make it easy for someone to read. We use blank lines to separate statements into related groups, and we indent the entire body of the main function. The compiler doesn't require us to format the program this way; we do so only to make it more readable. We have more to say in the next chapter about formatting a program.

Blocks (Compound Statements)

The body of a function is an example of a *block* (or *compound statement*). This is the syntax template for a block:

Block

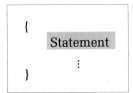

A block is just a sequence of zero or more statements enclosed (delimited) by a { } pair. Now we can redefine a function definition as a heading followed by a block:

FunctionDefinition

Heading
Block

In later chapters when we learn how to write functions other than `main`, we define the syntax of Heading in detail. In the case of the `main` function, Heading is simply

```
int main()
```

Here is the syntax template for a statement, limited to the C++ statements discussed in this chapter:

Statement

NullStatement
Declaration
AssignmentStatement
OutputStatement
Block

A statement can be empty (the *null statement*). The null statement is just a semicolon (;) and looks like this:

```
;
```

It does absolutely nothing at execution time; execution just proceeds to the next statement. It is not used often.

As the syntax template shows, a statement also can be a declaration, an executable statement, or even a block. The latter means that you can use an entire block wherever a single statement is allowed. In later chapters in which we introduce the syntax for branching and looping structures, this fact is very important.

We use blocks often, especially as parts of other statements. Leaving out a { } pair can dramatically change the meaning as well as the execution of a program. This is why we always indent the statements inside a block—the indentation makes a block easy to spot in a long, complicated program.

Notice in the syntax templates for the block and the statement that there is no mention of semicolons. Yet the PrintName program contains many semicolons. If you look back at the templates for constant declaration, variable declaration, assignment statement, and output statement, you can see that a semicolon is required at the end of each kind of statement. However, the syntax template for the block shows no semicolon after the right brace. The rule for using semicolons in C++, then, is quite simple: Terminate each statement *except* a compound statement (block) with a semicolon.

One more thing about blocks and statements: According to the syntax template for a statement, a declaration is officially considered to be a statement. A declaration, therefore, can appear wherever an executable statement can. In a block, we can mix declarations and executable statements if we wish:

```
{
    char ch;
    ch = 'A';
    cout << ch;
    string str;
    str = "Hello";
    cout << str;
}
```

It's far more common, though, for programmers to group the declarations together before the start of the executable statements:

```
{
    char    ch;
    string str;

    ch = 'A';
    cout << ch;
    str = "Hello";
    cout << str;
}
```

The C++ Preprocessor

Imagine that you are the C++ compiler. You are presented with the following program. You are to check it for syntax errors and, if there are no syntax errors, you are to translate it into machine language code.

```
//***********************************
// This program prints Happy Birthday
//***********************************

int main()
{
    cout << "Happy Birthday" << endl;
    return 0;
}
```

You, the compiler, recognize the identifier int as a C++ reserved word and the identifier main as the name of a required function. But what about the identifiers cout and endl? The programmer has not declared them as variables or named constants, and they are not reserved words. You have no choice but to issue an error message and give up.

To fix this program, the first thing we must do is insert a line near the top that says

```
#include <iostream>
```

just as we did in the PrintName program (as well as in the sample program at the beginning of this chapter and the Payroll program of Chapter 1).

The line says to insert the contents of a file named iostream into the program. This file contains declarations of cout, endl, and other items needed to perform stream input and output. The #include line is not handled by the C++ compiler but by a program known as the *preprocessor*.

The preprocessor concept is fundamental to C++. The preprocessor is a program that acts as a filter during the compilation phase. Your source program passes through the preprocessor on its way to the compiler (see Figure 2-2).

A line beginning with a pound sign (#) is not considered to be a C++ language statement (and thus is not terminated by a semicolon). It is called a *preprocessor directive*. The preprocessor expands an #include directive by physically inserting the contents of the named file into your source program. A file whose name appears in an #include directive is called a *header file*. Header files contain constant, variable, data type, and function declarations needed by a program.

FIGURE 2-2
C++ Preprocessor

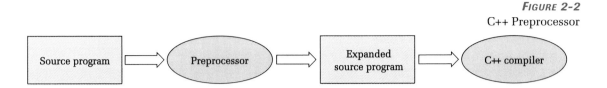

In the directives

```
#include <iostream>
#include <string>
```

the angle brackets < > are required. They tell the preprocessor to look for the files in the standard *include directory*—a location in the computer system that contains all the header files that are related to the C++ standard library. The file `iostream` contains declarations of input/output facilities, and the file `string` contains declarations about the `string` data type. In Chapter 3, we make use of standard header files other than `iostream` and `string`.

In the C language and in pre–standard C++, the standard header files end in the suffix `.h` (for example, `iostream.h`), where the *h* suggests "header file." In ISO/ANSI C++, the standard header files no longer use the `.h` suffix.

An Introduction to Namespaces

In our Happy Birthday program, even if we add the preprocessor directive `#include <iostream>`, the program will not compile. The compiler *still* doesn't recognize the identifiers `cout` and `endl`. The problem is that the header file `iostream` (and, in fact, every standard header file) declares all of its identifiers to be in a *namespace* called `std`:

```
namespace std
{
    :       Declarations of variables, data types, and so forth
}
```

An identifier declared within a namespace block can be accessed directly only by statements within that block. To access an identifier that is "hidden" inside a namespace, the programmer has several options. We describe two options here. Chapter 8 describes namespaces in more detail.

The first option is to use a *qualified name* for the identifier. A qualified name consists of the name of the namespace, then the `::` operator (the *scope resolution operator*), and then the desired identifier:

```
std::cout
```

With this approach, our program looks like the following:

```
#include <iostream>

int main()
{
    std::cout << "Happy Birthday" << std::endl;
    return 0;
}
```

Notice that both `cout` and `endl` must be qualified.

The second option is to use a statement called a **using** *directive:*

```
using namespace std;
```

When we place this statement near the top of the program before the `main` function, we make *all* the identifiers in the `std` namespace accessible to our program without having to qualify them:

```
#include <iostream>

using namespace std;

int main()
{
    cout << "Happy Birthday" << endl;
    return 0;
}
```

This second option is the one we used in the PrintName program and the sample program at the beginning of the chapter. In many of the following chapters, we continue to use this method. However, in Chapter 8 we discuss why it is not advisable to use the method in large programs.

If you are using a pre–standard C++ compiler that does not recognize namespaces and the newer header files (`iostream`, `string`, and so forth), you should turn to Section D.2 of Appendix D for a discussion of incompatibilities.

More About Output

We can control both the horizontal and vertical spacing of our output to make it more appealing (and understandable). Let's look first at vertical spacing.

Creating Blank Lines

We control vertical spacing by using the `endl` manipulator in an output statement. You have seen that a sequence of output statements continues to write characters across the current line until an `endl` terminates the line. Here are some examples:

Statements	*Output Produced**
`cout << "Hi there, ";` `cout << "Lois Lane. " << endl;`	Hi there, Lois Lane.
`cout << "Have you seen ";` `cout << "Clark Kent?" << endl;`	Have you seen Clark Kent?
`cout << "Hi there, " << endl;`	Hi there,
`cout << "Lois Lane. " << endl;`	Lois Lane.
`cout << "Have you seen " << endl;`	Have you seen
`cout << "Clark Kent?" << endl;`	Clark Kent?
`cout << "Hi there, " << endl;`	Hi there,
`cout << "Lois Lane. ";`	
`cout << "Have you seen " << endl;`	Lois Lane. Have you seen
`cout << "Clark Kent?" << endl;`	Clark Kent?

*The output lines are shown next to the output statement that ends each of them. There are no blank lines in the actual output from these statements.

What do you think the following statements print out?

```
cout << "Hi there, " << endl;
cout << endl;
cout << "Lois Lane." << endl;
```

The first output statement causes the words *Hi there,* to be printed; the `endl` causes the screen cursor to go to the next line. The next statement prints nothing but goes on to the next line. The third statement prints the words *Lois Lane.* and terminates the line. The resulting output is the three lines

```
Hi there,

Lois Lane.
```

Whenever you use an `endl` immediately after another `endl`, a blank line is produced. As you might guess, three consecutive uses of `endl` produce two blank lines, four consecutive uses produce three blank lines, and so forth.

Note that we have a great deal of flexibility in how we write an output statement in a C++ program. We could combine the three preceding statements into two statements:

```
cout << "Hi there, " << endl << endl;
cout << "Lois Lane." << endl;
```

In fact, we could do it all in one statement. One possibility is

```
cout << "Hi there, " << endl << endl << "Lois Lane." << endl;
```

Here's another:

```
cout << "Hi there, " << endl << endl
     << "Lois Lane." << endl;
```

The last example shows that you can spread a single C++ statement onto more than one line of the program. The compiler treats the semicolon, not the physical end of a line, as the end of a statement.

Inserting Blanks Within a Line

To control the horizontal spacing of the output, one technique is to send extra blank characters to the output stream. (Remember that the blank character, generated by pressing the spacebar on a keyboard, is a perfectly valid character in C++.)

For example, to produce this output:

```
*   *   *   *   *   *   *   *   *

*   *   *   *   *   *   *   *   *   *

  *   *   *   *   *   *   *   *   *
```

you would use these statements:

```
cout << "  *   *   *   *   *   *   *   *   *" << endl << endl;
cout << "*   *   *   *   *   *   *   *   *" << endl << endl;
cout << "  *   *   *   *   *   *   *   *   *" << endl;
```

All of the blanks and asterisks are enclosed in double quotes, so they print literally as they are written in the program. The extra `endl` manipulators give you the blank lines between the rows of asterisks.

If you want blanks to be printed, you *must* enclose them in quotes. The statement

```
cout << '*' <<                                  '*';
```

produces the output

```
**
```

Despite all of the blanks we included in the output statement, the asterisks print side by side because the blanks are not enclosed by quotes.

Program Entry, Correction, and Execution

Once you have a program on paper, you must enter it on the keyboard. In this section, we examine the program entry process in general. You should consult the manual for your specific computer to learn the details.

Entering a Program

The first step in entering a program is to get the computer's attention. With a personal computer, this usually means turning it on if it is not already running. Workstations connected to a network are usually left running all the time. You must *log on* to such a machine to get its attention. This means entering a user name and a password. The password system protects information that you've stored in the computer from being tampered with or destroyed by someone else.

Once the computer is ready to accept your commands, you tell it that you want to enter a program by having it run the editor. The editor is a program that allows you to create and modify programs by entering information into an area of the computer's secondary storage called a **file.**

File   A named area in secondary storage that is used to hold a collection of data; the collection of data itself.

A file in a computer system is like a file folder in a filing cabinet. It is a collection of data that has a name associated with it. You usually choose the name for the file when you create it with the editor. From that point on, you refer to the file by the name you've given it.

There are so many different types of editors, each with different features, that we can't begin to describe them all here. But we can describe some of their general characteristics.

The basic unit of information in an editor is a display screen full of characters. The editor lets you change anything that you see on the screen. When you create a new file, the editor clears the screen to show you that the file is empty. Then you enter your program, using the mouse and keyboard to go back and make corrections as necessary. Figure 2-3 shows an example of an editor's display screen.

Compiling and Running a Program

Once your program is stored in a file, you compile it by issuing a command to run the C++ compiler. The compiler translates the program, then stores the machine language version into a file. The compiler may display a window with messages indicating errors in the program. Some systems

FIGURE 2-3
Display Screen for
an Editor

```
Payroll.cpp                                                        _ □ ×
Payroll.cpp                                                       ← ▾ → ▾

//***********************************************************************
// Payroll program
// This program computes each employee's wages and
// the total company payroll
//***********************************************************************
#include <iostream>
#include <fstream>      // For file I/O

using namespace std;

void CalcPay( float, float, float& );

const float MAX_HOURS = 40.0;    // Maximum normal work hours
const float OVERTIME = 1.5;      // Overtime pay rate factor

int main()
{
    float    payRate;        // Employee's pay rate
    float    hours;          // Hours worked
    float    wages;          // Wages earned
    float    total;          // Total company payroll
    int      empNum;         // Employee ID number
    ofstream payFile;        // Company payroll file

1: 1   Modified     Insert
```

let you click on an error message to automatically position the cursor in the editor window at the point where the error was detected.

If the compiler finds errors in your program (syntax errors), you have to determine their cause, go back to the editor and fix them, and then run the compiler again. Once your program compiles without errors, you can run (execute) it.

Some systems automatically run a program when it compiles successfully. On other systems, you have to issue a separate command to run the program. Still other systems require that you specify an extra step called *linking* between compiling and running a program. Whatever series of commands your system uses, the result is the same: Your program is loaded into memory and executed by the computer.

Even though a program runs, it still may have errors in its design. The computer does exactly what you tell it to do, even if that's not what you wanted it to do. If your program doesn't do what it should (a *logic error*), you have to go back to the algorithm and fix it, and then go to the editor and fix the program. Finally, you compile and run the program again. This *debugging* process is repeated until the program does what it is supposed to do (see Figure 2-4).

FIGURE 2-4
Debugging Process

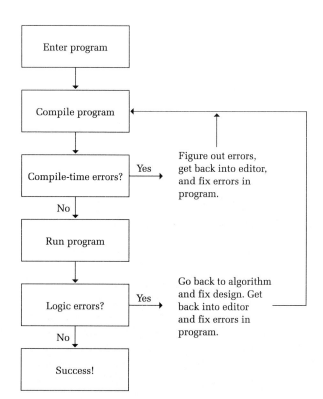

Finishing Up

On a workstation, once you finish working on your program you have to *log off* by issuing a command with the mouse or keyboard. This frees up the workstation so that someone else can use it. It also prevents someone from walking up after you leave and tampering with your files.

On a personal computer, when you're done working you save your files and quit the editor. Turning off the power wipes out what's in the computer's memory, but your files are stored safely on disk. It is a wise precaution to periodically back up (make a copy of) your program files onto a removable diskette. When a disk in a computer suffers a hardware failure, it is often impossible to retrieve your files. With a backup copy on a diskette, you can restore your files to the disk once it is repaired.

Be sure to read the manual for your particular system and editor before you enter your first program. Don't panic if you have trouble at first—almost everyone does. It becomes much easier with practice. That's why it's a good idea to first go through the process with a program such as PrintName, where mistakes don't matter—unlike a class programming assignment!

*P*ROBLEM-SOLVING CASE STUDY

Contest Letter

Problem: You've taken a job with a company that is running a promotional contest. They want you to write a program to print a personalized form letter for each of the contestants. As a first effort, they want to get the printing of the letter straight for just one name. Later on, they plan to have you extend the program to read a mailing list file, so the output should use variables in which the name appears in the letter.

Output: A form letter with a name inserted at the appropriate points so that it appears to be a personal letter.

Discussion: The marketing department for the company has written the letter already. Your job is to write a program that prints it out. The majority of the letter must be entered verbatim into a series of output statements, with a person's name inserted at the appropriate places.

In some places the letter calls for printing the full name, in others it uses a title (such as Mr. or Mrs.), and in others it uses just the first name. Because you plan to eventually use a data file that provides each name in four parts (title, first name, middle initial, last name), you decide that this preliminary program should start with a set of named string constants containing the four parts of a name. The program can then use concatenation expressions to form `string` variables in the different formats required by the letter. In that way, all the name strings can be created before the output statements are executed.

The form letter requires the name in four formats: the full name with the title, the last name preceded by the title, the first name alone, and the first and last names without the title or middle initial. Here is the algorithmic solution:

Define Constants

```
TITLE = "Dr."
FIRST_NAME = "Margaret"
MIDDLE_INITIAL = "H"
LAST_NAME = "Sklaznick"
```

Create First Name with Blank

```
Set first = FIRST_NAME + " "
```

Create Full Name

```
Set fullName = TITLE + " " + first + MIDDLE_INITIAL
Set fullName = fullName + ". " + LAST_NAME
```

Create First and Last Name

```
Set firstLast = first + LAST_NAME
```

Create Title and Last Name

```
Set titleLast = TITLE + " " + LAST_NAME
```

Print the Form Letter

Series of output statements containing the text of the letter with the names inserted in the appropriate places

From the algorithm we can create tables of constants and variables that help us write the declarations in the program.

Constants

Name	Value	Description
TITLE	"Dr."	Salutary title for the name
FIRST_NAME	"Margaret"	First name of addressee
MIDDLE_INITIAL	"H"	Middle initial of addressee
LAST_NAME	"Sklaznick"	Last name of addressee

Variables

Name	Data Type	Description
first	string	Holds the first name plus a blank
fullName	string	Complete name, including title
firstLast	string	First name and last name
titleLast	string	Title followed by the last name

Now we're ready to write the program. Let's call it FormLetter. We can take the declarations from the tables and create the executable statements from the algorithm and the draft of the letter. We also include comments as necessary.

(The following program is written in ISO/ANSI standard C++. If you are working with pre–standard C++, see the alternate version of the program in the PRE_STD directory of the program disk, available at the publisher's Web site, www.jbpub.com/disks.)

```
//****************************************************************
// FormLetter program
// This program prints a form letter for a promotional contest.
// It uses the four parts of a name to build name strings in four
// different formats to be used in personalizing the letter
//****************************************************************
#include <iostream>
#include <string>

using namespace std;
```

PROBLEM-SOLVING CASE STUDY cont'd.

```cpp
const string TITLE = "Dr.";              // Salutary title
const string FIRST_NAME = "Margaret";    // First name of addressee
const string MIDDLE_INITIAL = "H";       // Middle initial
const string LAST_NAME = "Sklaznick";    // Last name of addressee

int main()
{
    string first;         // Holds the first name plus a blank
    string fullName;      // Complete name, including title
    string firstLast;     // First name and last name
    string titleLast;     // Title followed by the last name

    // Create first name with blank

    first = FIRST_NAME + " ";

    // Create full name

    fullName = TITLE + " " + first + MIDDLE_INITIAL;
    fullName = fullName + ". " + LAST_NAME;

    // Create first and last name

    firstLast = first + LAST_NAME;

    // Create title and last name

    titleLast = TITLE + " " + LAST_NAME;

    // Print the form letter

    cout << fullName << " is a GRAND PRIZE WINNER!!!!!!" << endl
        << endl;
    cout << "Dear " << titleLast << "," << endl << endl;
    cout << "Yes it's true! " << firstLast << " has won our"
        << endl;
    cout << "GRAND PRIZE -- your choice of a 42-INCH* COLOR"
        << endl;
    cout << "TELEVISION or a FREE WEEKEND IN NEW YORK CITY.**"
        << endl;
    cout << "All that you have to do to collect your prize is"
        << endl;
    cout << "attend one of our fun-filled all-day presentations"
        << endl;
    cout << "on the benefits of owning a timeshare condominium"
        << endl;
```

```
        cout << "trailer at the Happy Acres Mobile Campground in"
             << endl;
        cout << "beautiful Panhard, Texas! Now " << first << "I realize"
             << endl;
        cout << "that the three-hour drive from the nearest airport"
             << endl;
        cout << "to Panhard may seem daunting at first, but isn't"
             << endl;
        cout << "it worth a little extra effort to receive such a"
             << endl;
        cout << "FABULOUS PRIZE? So why wait? Give us a call right"
             << endl;
        cout << "now to schedule your visit and collect your" << endl;
        cout << "GRAND PRIZE!" << endl << endl;
        cout << "Most Sincerely," << endl << endl;
        cout << "Argyle M. Sneeze" << endl << endl << endl << endl;
        cout << "* Measured around the circumference of the packing"
             << endl;
        cout << "crate. ** Includes air fare and hotel accommodations."
             << endl;
        cout << "Departure from Nome, Alaska; surcharge applies to"
             << endl;
        cout << "other departure airports. Accommodations within"
             << endl;
        cout << "driving distance of New York City at the Cheap-O-Tel"
             << endl;
        cout << "in Plattsburgh, NY." << endl;
        return 0;
}
```

The output from the program is

Dr. Margaret H. Sklaznick is a GRAND PRIZE WINNER!!!!!!

Dear Dr. Sklaznick,

Yes it's true! Margaret Sklaznick has won our
GRAND PRIZE -- your choice of a 42-INCH* COLOR
TELEVISION or a FREE WEEKEND IN NEW YORK CITY.**
All that you have to do to collect your prize is
attend one of our fun-filled all-day presentations
on the benefits of owning a timeshare condominium
trailer at the Happy Acres Mobile Campground in
beautiful Panhard, Texas! Now Margaret I realize
that the three-hour drive from the nearest airport
to Panhard may seem daunting at first, but isn't
it worth a little extra effort to receive such a
FABULOUS PRIZE? So why wait? Give us a call right
now to schedule your visit and collect your

PROBLEM-SOLVING CASE STUDY cont'd.

GRAND PRIZE!

Most Sincerely,

Argyle M. Sneeze

* Measured around the circumference of the packing
crate. ** Includes air fare and hotel accommodations.
Departure from Nome, Alaska; surcharge applies to
other departure airports. Accommodations within
driving distance of New York City at the Cheap-O-Tel
in Plattsburgh, NY.

Testing and Debugging

1. Every identifier that isn't a C++ reserved word must be declared. If you use a name that hasn't been declared—either by your own declaration statements or by including a header file—you get an error message.
2. If you try to declare an identifier that is the same as a reserved word in C++, you get an error message from the compiler. See Appendix A for a list of reserved words.
3. C++ is a case-sensitive language. Two identifiers that are capitalized differently are treated as two different identifiers. The word `main` and all C++ reserved words use only lowercase letters.
4. To use identifiers from the standard library, such as `cout` and `string`, you must either (a) give a qualified name such as `std::cout` or (b) put a `using` directive near the top of your program:

    ```
    using namespace std;
    ```

5. Check for mismatched quotes in `char` and string literals. Each `char` literal begins and ends with an apostrophe (single quote). Each string literal begins and ends with a double quote.
6. Be sure to use only the apostrophe (`'`) to enclose `char` literals. Most keyboards also have a reverse apostrophe (`` ` ``), which is easily confused with the apostrophe. If you use the reverse apostrophe, the compiler issues an error message.
7. To use a double quote within a literal string, use the two symbols `\"` in a row. If you use just a double quote, it ends the string, and the compiler then sees the remainder of the string as an error.

8. In an assignment statement, be sure that the identifier to the left of = is a variable and not a named constant.
9. In assigning a value to a string variable, the expression to the right of = must be a string expression, a literal string, or a char.
10. In a concatenation expression, at least one of the two operands of + must be of type string. For example, the operands cannot both be literal strings or char values.*
11. Make sure your statements end in semicolons (except compound statements, which do not have a semicolon after the right brace).

Summary

The syntax (grammar) of the C++ language is defined by a metalanguage. In this text, we use a form of metalanguage called syntax templates. We describe the semantics (meaning) of C++ statements in English.

Identifiers are used in C++ to name things. Some identifiers, called reserved words, have predefined meanings in the language; others are created by the programmer. The identifiers you invent are restricted to those *not* reserved by the C++ language. Reserved words are listed in Appendix A.

Identifiers are associated with memory locations by declarations. A declaration may give a name to a location whose value does not change (a constant) or to one whose value can change (a variable). Every constant and variable has an associated data type. C++ provides many built-in data types, the most common of which are int, float, and char. Additionally, C++ permits programmer-defined types such as the string type from the standard library.

The assignment operator is used to change the value of a variable by assigning it the value of an expression. At execution time, the expression is evaluated and the result is stored into the variable. With the string type, the plus sign (+) is an operator that concatenates two strings. A string expression can concatenate any number of strings to form a new string value.

Program output is accomplished by means of the output stream variable cout, along with the insertion operator (<<). Each insertion operation sends output data to the standard output device. When an endl manipulator appears instead of a data item, the computer terminates the current output line and goes on to the next line.

Output should be clear, understandable, and neatly arranged. Messages in the output should describe the significance of values. Blank lines (produced by successive uses of the endl manipulator) and blank spaces within lines help to organize the output and improve its appearance.

---

* The invalid concatenation expression "Hi" + "there" results in a syntax error message such as "INVALID POINTER ADDITION." This can be confusing, especially because the topic of pointers is not covered until much later in this book.

A C++ program is a collection of one or more function definitions (and optionally some declarations outside of any function). One of the functions *must* be named `main`. Execution of a program always begins with the `main` function. Collectively, the functions all cooperate to produce the desired results.

Quick Check

1. Every C++ program consists of at least how many functions? (p. 51)
2. Use the following syntax template to decide whether your last name is a valid C++ identifier. (pp. 53–55)

Identifier

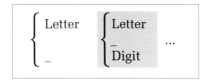

3. Write a C++ constant declaration that gives the name ZED to the value 'z'. (pp. 64–65)
4. Which of the following words are reserved words in C++? (*Hint:* Look in Appendix A.)

    const   pi   float   integer   sqrt

   (pp. 56–57)
5. Declare a char variable named `letter` and a string variable named `street`. (pp. 62–63)
6. Assign the value "Elm" to the string variable `street`. (pp. 67–68)
7. Write an output statement to print out the title of this book (*Programming and Problem Solving with C++*). (pp. 70–72)
8. What does the following code segment print out?

```
string str;

str = "Abraham";
cout << "The answer is " << str + "Lincoln" << endl;
```

   (pp. 68–72)
9. The following program code is incorrect. Rewrite it, using correct syntax for the comment.

```
string address;    / Employee's street address,
                   / including apartment
```

   (pp. 72–73)

10. Fill in the blanks in this program.

```
#include _____

#include _____

using _____

const string TITLE = "Mr";     // First part of salutary title

int _____()

____

    string guest1;     // First guest

    string guest2;     // Second guest

    guest1 _____ TITLE + ". Jones";

    guest2 _____ TITLE + "s. Smith";

    _____ << "The guests in attendance were" _____ endl;

    _____ << guest1 << " and ";

    _____ << guest2 _____ endl;

    return _____;

_____
```

(pp. 73–80)

11. Show precisely the output produced by running the program in Question 10 above.

12. If you want to print the word *Hello* on one line and then print a blank line, how many consecutive `endl` manipulators should you insert after the output of `"Hello"`? (pp. 81–82)

Answers   1. A program must have at least one function—the `main` function.   2. Unless your last name is hyphenated, it probably is a valid C++ identifier.

3. `const char ZED = 'Z';`   4. `const, float`

5. `char letter;`
   `string street;`

6. `street = "Elm";`

7. `cout << "Programming and Problem Solving with C++" << endl;`

8. The answer is AbrahamLincoln

9. `string address;     // Employee's street address,`
   `                    // including apartment`

   or

   `string address;     /* Employee's street address, */`
   `                    /* including apartment        */`

```
10.#include <iostream>
   #include <string>

   using namespace std;

   const string TITLE = "Mr";      // First part of salutary title

   int main()
   {
       string guest1;      // First guest
       string guest2;      // Second guest

       guest1 = TITLE + ". Jones";
       guest2 = TITLE + "s. Smith";
       cout << "The guests in attendance were" << endl;
       cout << guest1 << " and ";
       cout << guest2 << endl;
       return 0;
   }
```
11.The guests in attendance were
   Mr. Jones and Mrs. Smith
12. Two consecutive endl manipulators are necessary.

Exam Preparation Exercises

1. Mark the following identifiers either valid or invalid.

	Valid	Invalid
a. item#1	_____	_____
b. data	_____	_____
c. y	_____	_____
d. 3Set	_____	_____
e. PAY_DAY	_____	_____
f. bin-2	_____	_____
g. num5	_____	_____
h. Sq Ft	_____	_____

2. Given these four syntax templates:

Dwit

Twitnit . . .

Twitnit

Twit . . . Nit . . .

Twit

{ X
  Y
  Z

Nit

{ 1
  2
  3

mark the following "Dwits" either valid or invalid.

	Valid	*Invalid*
a. XYZ	_____	_____
b. 123	_____	_____
c. X1	_____	_____
d. 23Y	_____	_____
e. XY12	_____	_____
f. Y2Y	_____	_____
g. ZY2	_____	_____
h. XY23X1	_____	_____

3. Match each of the following terms with the correct definition (1 through 15) given below. There is only one correct definition for each term.

_____ a. program	_____ g. variable
_____ b. algorithm	_____ h. constant
_____ c. compiler	_____ i. memory
_____ d. identifier	_____ j. syntax
_____ e. compilation phase	_____ k. semantics
_____ f. execution phase	_____ l. block

(1) A symbolic name made up of letters, digits, and underscores but not beginning with a digit

(2) A place in memory where a data value that cannot be changed is stored

(3) A program that takes a program written in a high-level language and translates it into machine code

(4) An input device

(5) The time spent planning a program

(6) Grammar rules

(7) A sequence of statements enclosed by braces

(8) Meaning

(9) A program that translates assembly language instructions into machine code

(10) When the machine code version of a program is being run

(11) A place in memory where a data value that can be changed is stored

(12) When a program in a high-level language is converted into machine code

(13) A part of the computer that can hold both program and data

(14) A step-by-step procedure for solving a problem in a finite amount of time

(15) A sequence of instructions that enables a computer to perform a particular task

4. Which of the following are reserved words and which are programmer-defined identifiers?

	Reserved	*Programmer-Defined*
a. char	_____	_____
b. sort	_____	_____
c. INT	_____	_____
d. long	_____	_____
e. Float	_____	_____

5. Reserved words can be used as variable names. (True or False?)

6. In a C++ program consisting of just one function, that function can be named either main or Main. (True or False?)

7. If s1 and s2 are `string` variables containing "blue" and "bird", respectively, what output does each of the following statements produce?

   a. cout << "s1 = " << s1 << "s2 = " << s2 << endl;
   b. cout << "Result:" << s1 + s2 << endl;
   c. cout << "Result: " << s1 + s2 << endl;
   d. cout << "Result: " << s1 << ' ' << s2 << endl;

8. Show precisely what is output by the following statement.

   ```
   cout << "A rolling" << endl
        << "stone" << endl << endl
        << "gathers" << endl
        << endl << endl << endl << "no"
        << "moss" << endl;
   ```

9. How many characters can be stored into a variable of type `char`?
10. How many characters are in the null string?
11. A variable of type `string` can be assigned to a variable of type `char`. (True or False?)
12. A literal string can be assigned to a variable of type `string`. (True or False?)
13. What is the difference between the literal string `"computer"` and the identifier `computer`?
14. What is output by the following code segment? (All variables are of type `string`.)

    ```
    street = "Elm St.";
    address = "1425B";
    city = "Amaryllis";
    state = "Iowa";
    firstLine = address + ' ' + street;
    cout << firstLine << endl;
    cout << city;
    cout << ", " << state << endl;
    ```

15. Identify the syntax errors in the following program.

    ```
    // This program is full of errors
    #include <iostream

    constant string FIRST : Martin";
    constant string MID : "Luther;
    constant string LAST : King

    int main
    {
        string name;
        character initial;

        name = Martin + Luther + King;
        initial = MID;
        LAST = "King Jr.";
        count << 'Name = ' << name << endl;
    ```

```
cout << mid
cout << endl;
```

Programming Warm-up Exercises

1. Write an output statement that prints your name.
2. Write three consecutive output statements that print the following three lines:

   ```
   The moon
   is
   blue.
   ```

3. Write declaration statements to declare three variables of type string and two variables of type char. The string variables should be named make, model, and color. The char variables should be named plateType and classification.
4. Write a series of output statements that print out the values in the variables declared in Exercise 3. The values should each appear on a separate line, with a blank line between the string and char values. Each value should be preceded by an identifying message on the same line.
5. Change the PrintName program (page 74) so that it also prints the name in the format

   First-name Middle-initial. Last-name

   Make MIDDLE a string constant rather than a char constant. Define a new string variable to hold the name in the new format and assign it the string using the existing named constants, any literal strings that are needed for punctuation and spacing, and concatenation operations. Print the string, labeled appropriately.
6. Write C++ output statements that produce exactly the following output.

   a. ```
      Four score
      and seven years ago
      ```
   b. ```
      Four score
      and seven
      years ago
      ```
   c. ```
      Four score
      and

      seven
      years ago
      ```
   d. ```
      Four
          score
              and
      seven
          years
              ago
      ```

7. Enter and run the following program. Be sure to type it exactly as it appears here.

```
//*************************************************************
// HelloWorld program
// This program prints two simple messages
//*************************************************************
#include <iostream>
#include <string>

using namespace std;

const string MSG1 = "Hello world.";

int main()
{
    string msg2;

    cout << MSG1 << endl;
    msg2 = MSG1 + " " + MSG1 + " " + MSG1;
    cout << msg2 << endl;
    return 0;
}
```

Programming Problems

1. Write a C++ program that prints your initials in large block letters, each letter made up of the same character it represents. The letters should be a minimum of seven printed lines high and should appear all in a row. For example, if your initials were DOW, your program should print out

```
DDDDDDD           OOOOO        W           W
D     D          O     O       W           W
D      D        O       O      W           W
D      D        O       O      W     W     W
D      D        O       O      W   W   W   W
D     D          O     O       W  W     W  W
DDDDDDD           OOOOO         WW         WW
```

   Be sure to include appropriate comments in your program, choose meaningful identifiers, and use indentation as we do in the programs in this chapter.

2. Write a program that simulates the child's game "My Grandmother's Trunk." In this game, the players sit in a circle, and the first player names something that goes in the trunk: "In my grandmother's trunk, I packed a pencil." The next player restates the sentence and adds something new to the trunk: "In my grandmother's trunk, I packed a pencil and a red ball." Each player in turn adds something to the trunk, attempting to keep track of all the items that are already there.

   Your program should simulate just five turns in the game. Starting with the null string, simulate each player's turn by concatenating a new word or phrase to the existing string, and print the result on a new line. The output should be formatted as follows:

```
In my grandmother's trunk, I packed
a flower.
In my grandmother's trunk, I packed
a flower and a shirt.
In my grandmother's trunk, I packed
a flower and a shirt and a cup.
In my grandmother's trunk, I packed
a flower and a shirt and a cup and a blue marble.
In my grandmother's trunk, I packed
a flower and a shirt and a cup and a blue marble and a ball.
```

3. Write a program that prints its own grading form. The program should output the name and number of the class, the name and number of the programming assignment, your name and student number, and labeled spaces for scores reflecting correctness, quality of style, late deduction, and overall score. An example of such a form is the following:

```
CS-101 Introduction to Programming and Problem Solving

Programming Assignment 1

Sally A. Student
ID Number 431023877

Grade Summary:

    Program Correctness:
    Quality of Style:
    Late Deduction:
    Overall Score:
    Comments:
```

Case Study Follow-Up

1. Change the FormLetter program so that the name of the town is Wormwood, Massachusetts, instead of Panhard, Texas.
2. In the FormLetter program, explain what takes place in each of the two statements that assign values to the string variable fullName.
3. For obvious reasons, the president of the company wants more space inserted between the signature and the footnotes describing the prizes. How would you accomplish this?
4. Change the FormLetter program so that your name is printed in the appropriate places in the letter. (*Hint:* You need to change only four lines in the program.)

3

Numeric Types, Expressions, and Output

GOALS

- To be able to declare named constants and variables of type `int` and `float`.
- To be able to construct simple arithmetic expressions.
- To be able to evaluate simple arithmetic expressions.
- To be able to construct and evaluate expressions that include multiple arithmetic operations.
- To understand implicit type coercion and explicit type conversion.
- To be able to call (invoke) a value-returning function.
- To be able to recognize and understand the purpose of function arguments.
- To be able to use C++ library functions in expressions.
- To be able to call (invoke) a void function (one that does not return a function value).
- To be able to use C++ manipulators to format the output.
- To learn and be able to use additional operations associated with the `string` type.
- To be able to format the statements in a program in a clear and readable fashion.

In Chapter 2, we examined enough C++ syntax to be able to construct simple programs using assignment and output. We focused on the `char` and `string` types and saw how to construct expressions using the concatenation operator. In this chapter we continue to write programs that use assignment and output, but we concentrate on additional built-in data types: `int` and `float`. These numeric types are supported by numerous operators that allow us to construct complex arithmetic expressions. We show how to make expressions even more powerful by using *library functions*—prewritten functions that are part of every C++ system and are available for use by any program.

We also return to the subject of formatting the output. In particular, we consider the special features that C++ provides for formatting numbers in the output. We finish by looking at some additional operations on `string` data.

Overview of C++ Data Types

The C++ built-in data types are organized into simple types, structured types, and address types (see Figure 3-1). Do not feel overwhelmed by the quantity of data types shown in this figure. Our purpose is simply to give you an overall picture of what is available in C++. This chapter concentrates on the integral and floating types. Details of the other types come later in the book. First we look at the integral types (those used primarily to represent integers), and then we consider the floating types (used to represent real numbers containing decimal points).

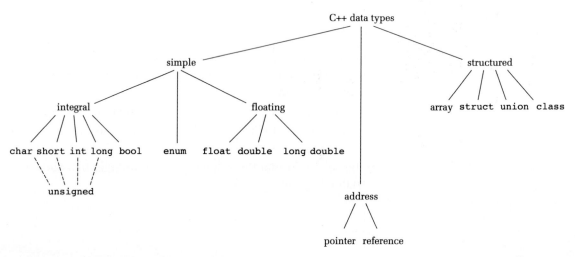

FIGURE 3-1
C++ Data Types

Numeric Data Types

You already are familiar with the basic concepts of integer and real numbers in math. However, as used on a computer, the corresponding data types have certain limitations, which we now consider.

Integral Types

The data types `char`, `short`, `int`, and `long` are known as integral types (or integer types) because they refer to integer values—whole numbers with no fractional part. (We postpone talking about the remaining integral type, `bool`, until Chapter 5.)

In C++, the simplest form of integer value is a sequence of one or more digits:

```
22   16   1   498   0   4600
```

Commas are not allowed.

In most cases, a minus sign preceding an integer value makes the integer negative:

```
-378   -912
```

The exception is when you explicitly add the reserved word `unsigned` to the data type name:

```
unsigned int
```

An `unsigned` integer value is assumed to be only positive or zero. The `unsigned` types are used primarily in specialized situations. With a few exceptions later in this chapter, we rarely use `unsigned` in this book.

The data types `char`, `short`, `int`, and `long` are intended to represent different sizes of integers, from smaller (fewer bits) to larger (more bits). The sizes are machine dependent (that is, they may vary from machine to machine). For one particular machine, we might picture the sizes this way:

`char` memory cell

`short` memory cell

`int` memory cell

`long` memory cell

On another machine, the size of an int might be the same as the size of a long. In general, the more bits there are in the memory cell, the larger the integer value that can be stored.

Although we used the char type in Chapter 2 to store character data such as 'A', there are reasons why C++ classifies char as an integral type. Chapter 10 discusses the reasons.

int is by far the most common data type for manipulating integer data. In the Payroll program, the identifier for the employee number, empNum, is of data type int. You nearly always use int for manipulating integer values, but sometimes you have to use long if your program requires values larger than the maximum int value. (On some personal computers, the range of int values is from −32768 through +32767. More commonly, ints range from −2147483648 through +2147483647.) If your program tries to compute a value larger than your machine's maximum value, the result is *integer overflow*. Some machines give you an error message when overflow occurs, but others don't. We talk more about overflow in later chapters.

One caution about integer values in C++: A literal constant beginning with a zero is taken to be an octal (base-8) number instead of a decimal (base-10) number. If you write

015

the C++ compiler takes this to mean the decimal number 13. If you aren't familiar with the octal number system, don't worry about why an octal 15 is the same as a decimal 13. The important thing to remember is not to start a decimal integer constant with a zero (unless you simply want the number 0, which is the same in both octal and decimal). In Chapter 10, we discuss the various integral types in more detail.

Floating-Point Types

Floating-point types (or floating types), the second major category of simple types in C++, are used to represent real numbers. Floating-point numbers have an integer part and a fractional part, with a decimal point in between. Either the integer part or the fractional part, but not both, may be missing. Here are some examples:

18.0   127.54   0.57   4.   193145.8523   .8

Starting 0.57 with a zero does not make it an octal number. It is only with integer values that a leading zero indicates an octal number.

Just as the integral types in C++ come in different sizes (char, short, int, and long), so do the floating-point types. In increasing order of size, the floating-point types are float, double (meaning double precision), and `long double`. Again, the exact sizes are machine dependent. Each larger size potentially gives us a wider range of values and more precision (the number of significant digits in the number), but at the expense of more memory space to hold the number.

Floating-point values also can have an exponent, as in scientific notation. (In scientific notation, a number is written as a value multiplied by 10 to some power.) Instead of writing 3.504×10^{12}, in C++ we write `3.504E12`. The E means exponent of base 10. The number preceding the letter E doesn't need to include a decimal point. Here are some examples of floating-point numbers in scientific notation:

```
1.74536E-12    3.652442E4    7E20
```

Most programs don't need the `double` and `long double` types. The `float` type usually provides sufficient precision and range of values for floating-point numbers. Even personal computers provide `float` values with a precision of six or seven significant digits and a maximum value of about `3.4E+38`. In the Payroll program, the identifiers MAX_HOURS, OVER-TIME, payRate, hours, wages, and `total` are all of type `float` because they are identifiers for data items that may have fractional parts.

We talk more about floating-point numbers in Chapter 10. But there is one more thing you should know about them now. Computers cannot always represent floating-point numbers exactly. You learned in Chapter 1 that the computer stores all data in binary (base-2) form. Many floating-point values can only be approximated in the binary number system. Don't be surprised if your program prints out the number 4.8 as 4.7999998. In most cases, slight inaccuracies in the rightmost fractional digits are to be expected and are not the result of programmer error.

Declarations for Numeric Types

Just as with the types `char` and `string`, we can declare named constants and variables of type `int` and `float`. Such declarations use the same syntax as before, except that the literals and the names of the data types are different.

Named Constant Declarations

In the case of named constant declarations, the literal values in the declarations are numeric instead of being characters in single or double quotes. For example, here are some constant declarations that define values of type `int` and `float`. For comparison, declarations of `char` and `string` values are included.

```
const float   PI = 3.14159;
const float   E = 2.71828;
const int     MAX_SCORE = 100;
const int     MIN_SCORE = -100;
const char    LETTER = 'W';
const string  NAME = "Elizabeth";
```

Although character and string literals are put in quotes, literal integers and floating-point numbers are not, because there is no chance of confusing them with identifiers. Why? Because identifiers must start with a letter or underscore, and numbers must start with a digit or sign.

SOFTWARE ENGINEERING TIP

Using Named Constants Instead of Literals

It's a good idea to use named constants instead of literals. In addition to making your program more readable, named constants can make your program easier to modify. Suppose you wrote a program last year to compute taxes. In several places you used the literal 0.05, which was the sales tax rate at the time. Now the rate has gone up to 0.06. To change your program, you must locate every literal 0.05 and change it to 0.06. And if 0.05 is used for some other reason—to compute deductions, for example—you need to look at each place where it is used, figure out what it is used for, and then decide whether to change it.

The process is much simpler if you use a named constant. Instead of using a literal constant, suppose you had declared a named constant, TAX_RATE, with a value of 0.05. To change your program, you would simply change the declaration, setting TAX_RATE equal to 0.06. This one modification changes all of the tax rate computations without affecting the other places where 0.05 is used.

C++ allows us to declare constants with different names but the same value. If a value has different meanings in different parts of a program, it makes sense to declare and use a constant with an appropriate name for each meaning.

Named constants also are reliable; they protect us from mistakes. If you mistype the name PI as PO, the C++ compiler tells you that the name PO has not been declared. On the other hand, even though we recognize that the number 3.14149 is a mistyped version of pi (3.14159), the number is perfectly acceptable to the compiler. It won't warn us that anything is wrong.

Variable Declarations

We declare numeric variables the same way in which we declare char and string variables, except that we use the names of numeric types. The following are valid variable declarations:

```
int     studentCount;    // Number of students
int     sumOfScores;     // Sum of their scores
float   average;         // Average of the scores
char    grade;           // Student's letter grade
string  stuName;         // Student's name
```

Given the declarations

```
int   num;
int   alpha;
float rate;
char  ch;
```

the following are appropriate assignment statements:

Variable	Expression
alpha =	2856;
rate =	0.36;
ch =	'B';
num =	alpha;

In each of these assignment statements, the data type of the expression matches the data type of the variable to which it is assigned. Later in the chapter we see what happens if the data types do not match.

Simple Arithmetic Expressions

Now that we have looked at declaration and assignment, we consider how to calculate with values of numeric types. Calculations are performed with expressions. We first look at simple expressions that involve at most one operator so that we may examine each operator in detail. Then, we move on to compound expressions that combine multiple operations.

Arithmetic Operators

Expressions are made up of constants, variables, and operators. The following are all valid expressions:

```
alpha + 2   rate - 6.0   4 - alpha   rate   alpha * num
```

The operators allowed in an expression depend on the data types of the constants and variables in the expression. The *arithmetic operators* are

+ Unary plus
− Unary minus
+ Addition
− Subtraction
∗ Multiplication
/ { Floating-point division (floating-point result)
      Integer division (no fractional part)
% Modulus (remainder from integer division)

The first two operators are **unary operators**—they take just one operand. The remaining five are **binary operators**, taking two operands. Unary plus and minus are used as follows:

```
-54    +259.65    -rate
```

Programmers rarely use the unary plus. Without any sign, a numeric constant is assumed to be positive anyway.

Unary operator   An operator that has just one operand.

Binary operator   An operator that has two operands.

You may not be familiar with integer division and modulus (%). Let's look at them more closely. Note that % is used only with integers. When you divide one integer by another, you get an integer quotient and a remainder. Integer division gives only the integer quotient, and % gives only the remainder. (If either operand is negative, the sign of the remainder may vary from one C++ compiler to another.)

$$
\begin{array}{ll}
3 & \leftarrow 6\ /\ 2 \\
2)\overline{6} & \\
\underline{6} & \\
0 & \leftarrow 6\ \%\ 2
\end{array}
\qquad
\begin{array}{ll}
3 & \leftarrow 7\ /\ 2 \\
2)\overline{7} & \\
\underline{6} & \\
1 & \leftarrow 7\ \%\ 2
\end{array}
$$

In contrast, floating-point division yields a floating-point result. The expression

```
7.0 / 2.0
```

yields the value 3.5.

Here are some expressions using arithmetic operators and their values:

Expression	Value
3 + 6	9
3.4 - 6.1	−2.7
2 * 3	6
8 / 2	4
8.0 / 2.0	4.0
8 / 8	1
8 / 9	0
8 / 7	1
8 % 8	0
8 % 9	8
8 % 7	1
0 % 7	0
5 % 2.3	error (both operands must be integers)

Be careful with division and modulus. The expressions 7.0 / 0.0, 7 / 0, and 7 % 0 all produce errors. The computer cannot divide by zero.

Because variables are allowed in expressions, the following are valid assignments:

```
alpha = num + 6;
alpha = num / 2;
num = alpha * 2;
num = 6 % alpha;
alpha = alpha + 1;
num = num + alpha;
```

As we saw with assignment statements involving string expressions, the same variable can appear on both sides of the assignment operator. In the case of

```
num = num + alpha;
```

the value in num and the value in alpha are added together, and then the sum of the two values is stored back into num, replacing the previous value stored there. This example shows the difference between mathematical equality and assignment. The mathematical equality

$$num = num + alpha$$

is true only when *alpha* equals 0. The assignment statement

```
num = num + alpha;
```

is valid for *any* value of `alpha`.

Here's a simple program that uses arithmetic expressions:

```
//*************************************************************
// FreezeBoil program
// This program computes the midpoint between
// the freezing and boiling points of water
//*************************************************************
#include <iostream>

using namespace std;

const float FREEZE_PT = 32.0;    // Freezing point of water
const float BOIL_PT = 212.0;     // Boiling point of water

int main()
{
    float avgTemp;                    // Holds the result of averaging
                                      //   FREEZE_PT and BOIL_PT

    cout << "Water freezes at " << FREEZE_PT << endl;
    cout << " and boils at " << BOIL_PT << " degrees." << endl;

    avgTemp = FREEZE_PT + BOIL_PT;
    avgTemp = avgTemp / 2.0;

    cout << "Halfway between is ";
    cout << avgTemp << " degrees." << endl;

    return 0;
}
```

The program begins with a comment that explains what the program does. Next comes a declaration section where we define the constants `FREEZE_PT` and `BOIL_PT`. The body of the `main` function includes a declaration of the variable `avgTemp` and then a sequence of executable statements. These statements print a message, add `FREEZE_PT` and `BOIL_PT`, divide the sum by 2, and finally print the result.

Increment and Decrement Operators

In addition to the arithmetic operators, C++ provides *increment* and *decrement operators*:

```
++        Increment
--        Decrement
```

These are unary operators that take a single variable name as an operand. For integer and floating-point operands, the effect is to add 1 to (or subtract 1 from) the operand. If num currently contains the value 8, the statement

```
num++;
```

causes num to contain 9. You can achieve the same effect by writing the assignment statement

```
num = num + 1;
```

but C++ programmers typically prefer the increment operator. (Recall from Chapter 1 how the C++ language got its name: C++ is an enhanced ["incremented"] version of the C language.)

The ++ and -- operators can be either *prefix operators*

```
++num;
```

or *postfix operators*

```
num++;
```

Both of these statements behave in exactly the same way; they add 1 to whatever is in num. The choice between the two is a matter of personal preference.

C++ allows the use of ++ and -- in the middle of a larger expression:

```
alpha = num++ * 3;
```

In this case, the postfix form of ++ does *not* give the same result as the prefix form. In Chapter 10, we explain the ++ and -- operators in detail. In the meantime, you should use them only to increment or decrement a variable as a separate, stand-alone statement:

IncrementStatement

$$\left\{ \begin{array}{l} \text{Variable ++ ;} \\ \text{++ Variable ;} \end{array} \right.$$

DecrementStatement

$$\left\{ \begin{array}{l} \text{Variable -- ;} \\ \text{-- Variable ;} \end{array} \right.$$

Compound Arithmetic Expressions

The expressions we've used so far have contained at most a single arithmetic operator. We also have been careful not to mix integer and floating-point values in the same expression. Now we look at more complicated expressions—ones that are composed of several operators and ones that contain mixed data types.

Precedence Rules

Arithmetic expressions can be made up of many constants, variables, operators, and parentheses. In what order are the operations performed? For example, in the assignment statement

```
avgTemp = FREEZE_PT + BOIL_PT / 2.0;
```

is FREEZE_PT + BOIL_PT calculated first or is BOIL_PT / 2.0 calculated first?

The basic arithmetic operators (unary +, unary –, + for addition, – for subtraction, * for multiplication, / for division, and % for modulus) are ordered the same way mathematical operators are, according to *precedence rules:*

Highest precedence level:	Unary + Unary –
Middle level:	* / %
Lowest level:	+ –

Because division has higher precedence than addition, the expression in the example above is implicitly parenthesized as

```
FREEZE_PT + (BOIL_PT / 2.0)
```

That is, we first divide BOIL_PT by 2.0 and then add FREEZE_PT to the result.

You can change the order of evaluation by using parentheses. In the statement

```
avgTemp = (FREEZE_PT + BOIL_PT) / 2.0;
```

FREEZE_PT and BOIL_PT are added first, and then their sum is divided by 2.0. We evaluate subexpressions in parentheses first and then follow the precedence of the operators.

When an arithmetic expression has several binary operators with the same precedence, their *grouping order* (or *associativity*) is from left to right. The expression

```
int1 - int2 + int3
```

means (int1 − int2) + int3, not int1 − (int2 + int3). As another example, we would use the expression

```
(float1 + float2) / float1 * 3.0
```

to evaluate the expression in parentheses first, then divide the sum by float1, and multiply the result by 3.0. Below are some more examples.

Expression	Value
10 / 2 * 3	15
10 % 3 - 4 / 2	−1
5.0 * 2.0 / 4.0 * 2.0	5.0
5.0 * 2.0 / (4.0 * 2.0)	1.25
5.0 + 2.0 / (4.0 * 2.0)	5.25

In C++, all unary operators (such as unary + and unary −) have right-to-left associativity. Though this fact may seem strange at first, it turns out to be the natural grouping order. For example, − + x means − (+ x) rather than the meaningless (− +) x.

Type Coercion and Type Casting

Integer values and floating-point values are stored differently inside a computer's memory. The pattern of bits that represents the constant 2 does not look at all like the pattern of bits representing the constant 2.0. (In Chapter 10, we examine why floating-point numbers need a special representation inside the computer.) What happens if we mix integer and floating-point values together in an assignment statement or an arithmetic expression? Let's look first at assignment statements.

Assignment Statements   If you make the declarations

```
int    someInt;
float someFloat;
```

then someInt can hold *only* integer values, and someFloat can hold *only* floating-point values. The assignment statement

```
someFloat = 12;
```

may seem to store the integer value 12 into someFloat, but this is not true. The computer refuses to store anything other than a float value into someFloat. The compiler inserts extra machine language instructions that first convert 12 into 12.0 and then store 12.0 into someFloat. This implicit (automatic) conversion of a value from one data type to another is known as **type coercion.**

The statement

```
someInt = 4.8;
```

also causes type coercion. When a floating-point value is assigned to an int variable, the fractional part is truncated (cut off). As a result, someInt is assigned the value 4.

With both of the assignment statements above, the program would be less confusing for someone to read if we avoided mixing data types:

```
someFloat = 12.0;
someInt = 4;
```

More often, it is not just constants but entire expressions that are involved in type coercion. Both of the assignments

```
someFloat = 3 * someInt + 2;
someInt = 5.2 / someFloat - anotherFloat;
```

lead to type coercion. Storing the result of an int expression into a float variable generally doesn't cause loss of information; a whole number such as 24 can be represented in floating-point form as 24.0. However, storing the result of a floating-point expression into an int variable can cause loss of information because the fractional part is truncated. It is easy to overlook the assignment of a floating-point expression to an int variable when we try to discover why our program is producing the wrong answers.

To make our programs as clear (and error free) as possible, we can use explicit **type casting** (or **type conversion**). A C++ *cast operation* consists of a data type name and then, within parentheses, the expression to be converted:

```
someFloat = float(3 * someInt + 2);
someInt = int(5.2 / someFloat - anotherFloat);
```

Type coercion   The implicit (automatic) conversion of a value from one data type to another.

Type casting   The explicit conversion of a value from one data type to another; also called type conversion.

Both of the statements

```
someInt = someFloat + 8.2;
someInt = int(someFloat + 8.2);
```

produce identical results. The only difference is in clarity. With the cast operation, it is perfectly clear to the programmer and to others reading the program that the mixing of types is intentional, not an oversight. Countless errors have resulted from unintentional mixing of types.

Note that there is a nice way to round off rather than truncate a floating-point value before storing it into an `int` variable. Here is the way to do it:

```
someInt = int(someFloat + 0.5);
```

With pencil and paper, see for yourself what gets stored into `someInt` when `someFloat` contains 4.7. Now try it again, assuming `someFloat` contains 4.2. (This technique of rounding by adding 0.5 assumes that `someFloat` is a positive number.)

Arithmetic Expressions   So far we have been talking about mixing data types across the assignment operator (=). It's also possible to mix data types within an expression:

```
someInt * someFloat
4.8 + someInt - 3
```

Such expressions are called **mixed type** (or **mixed mode**) **expressions.**

Mixed type expression   An expression that contains operands of different data types; also called mixed mode expression.

Whenever an integer value and a floating-point value are joined by an operator, implicit type coercion occurs as follows.

1. The integer value is temporarily coerced to a floating-point value.
2. The operation is performed.
3. The result is a floating-point value.

Let's examine how the machine evaluates the expression 4.8 + someInt - 3, where someInt contains the value 2. First, the operands of the + operator have mixed types, so the value of someInt is coerced to 2.0. (This conversion is only temporary; it does not affect the value that is stored in someInt.) The addition takes place, yielding a value of 6.8. Next, the subtraction (-) operator joins a floating-point value (6.8) and an integer value (3). The value 3 is coerced to 3.0, the subtraction takes place, and the result is the floating-point value 3.8.

Just as with assignment statements, you can use explicit type casts within expressions to lessen the risk of errors. Writing expressions such as

```
float(someInt) * someFloat
4.8 + float(someInt - 3)
```

makes it clear what your intentions are.

Explicit type casts are not only valuable for program clarity, but also are mandatory in some cases for correct programming. Given the declarations

```
int    sum;
int    count;
float  average;
```

suppose that sum and count currently contain 60 and 80, respectively. If sum represents the sum of a group of integer values and count represents the number of values, let's find the average value:

```
average = sum / count;      // Wrong
```

Unfortunately, this statement stores the value 0.0 into average. Here's why. The expression to the right of the assignment operator is not a mixed type expression. Both operands of the / operator are of type int, so integer division is performed. 60 divided by 80 yields the integer value 0. Next, the machine implicitly coerces 0 to the value 0.0 before storing it into average. The way to find the average correctly, as well as clearly, is this:

```
average = float(sum) / float(count);
```

This statement gives us floating-point division instead of integer division. As a result, the value 0.75 is stored into average.

As a final remark about type coercion and type conversion, you may have noticed that we have concentrated only on the int and float types. It is also possible to stir char values, short values, and double values into the pot. The results can be confusing and unexpected. In Chapter 10, we return to the topic with a more detailed discussion. In the meantime, you should avoid mixing values of these types within an expression.

Mᴀʏ ᴡᴇ ɪɴᴛʀᴏᴅᴜᴄᴇ

Blaise Pascal

One of the great historical figures in the world of computing was the French mathematician and religious philosopher Blaise Pascal (1623–1662), the inventor of one of the earliest known mechanical calculators.

Pascal's father, Etienne, was a noble in the French court, a tax collector, and a mathematician. Pascal's mother died when Pascal was 3 years old. Five years later, the family moved to Paris and Etienne took over the education of the children. Pascal quickly showed a talent for mathematics. When he was only 17, he published a mathematical essay that earned the jealous envy of René Descartes, one of the founders of modern geometry. (Pascal's work actually had been completed before he was 16.) It was based on a theorem, which he called the *hexagrammum mysticum*, or mystic hexagram, that described the inscription of hexagons in conic sections (parabolas, hyperbolas, and ellipses). In addition to the theorem (now called Pascal's theorem), his essay included over 400 corollaries.

When Pascal was about 20, he constructed a mechanical calculator that performed addition and subtraction of eight-digit numbers. That calculator required the user to dial in the numbers to be added or subtracted; the sum or difference then appeared in a set of windows. It is believed that his motivation for building this machine was to aid his father in collecting taxes. The earliest version of the machine does indeed split the numbers into six decimal digits and two fractional digits, as would be used for calculating sums of money. The machine was hailed by his contemporaries as a great advance in mathematics, and Pascal built several more in different forms. It achieved such popularity that many fake, nonfunctional copies were built by others and displayed as novelties. Several of Pascal's calculators still exist in various museums.

Pascal's box, as it is called, was long believed to be the first mechanical calculator. However, in 1950 a letter from Wilhelm Shickard to Johannes Kepler written in 1624 was discovered. This letter described an even more sophisticated calculator built by Shickard 20 years prior to Pascal's box. Unfortunately, the machine was destroyed in a fire and never rebuilt.

During his twenties, Pascal solved several difficult problems related to the cycloid curve, indirectly contributing to the development of differential calculus. Working with Pierre de Fermat, he laid the foundation of the calculus of probabilities and combinatorial analysis. One of the results of this work came to be known as Pascal's triangle, which simplifies the calculation of the coefficients of the expansion of $(X + Y)^N$, where N is a positive integer.

Pascal also published a treatise on air pressure and conducted experiments that showed that barometric pressure decreases with altitude, helping to confirm theories that had been proposed by Galileo and Torricelli. His work on fluid dynamics forms a significant part of the foundation of that field. Among the most famous of his contributions is Pascal's law, which states that pressure applied to a fluid in a closed vessel is transmitted uniformly throughout the fluid.

When Pascal was 23, his father became ill, and the family was visited by two disciples of Jansenism, a reform movement in the Catholic Church that had begun six years earlier. The family converted, and five years later one of his sisters entered a convent. Initially, Pascal was not so taken with the new movement, but by the time he was 31, his sister had persuaded him to abandon the world and devote himself to religion.

His religious works are considered no less brilliant than his mathematical and scientific writings. Some consider *Provincial Letters*, his series of 18 essays on various aspects of religion, as the beginning of modern French prose.

Pascal returned briefly to mathematics when he was 35, but a year later his health, which had always been poor, took a turn for the worse. Unable to perform his usual work, he devoted himself to helping the less fortunate. Three years later, he died while staying with his sister, having given his own house to a poor family.

Function Calls and Library Functions

Value-Returning Functions

At the beginning of Chapter 2, we showed a program consisting of three functions: `main`, `Square`, and `Cube`. Here is a portion of the program:

```
int main()
{
    cout << "The square of 27 is " << Square(27) << endl;
    cout << "and the cube of 27 is " << Cube(27) << endl;
    return 0;
}

int Square( int n )
{
    return n * n;
}

int Cube( int n )
{
    return n * n * n;
}
```

We said that all three functions are value-returning functions. `Square` returns to its caller a value—the square of the number sent to it. `Cube` returns a value—the cube of the number sent to it. And `main` returns to the operating system a value—the program's exit status.

Let's focus for a moment on the Cube function. The main function contains a statement

```
cout << " and the cube of 27 is " << Cube(27) << endl;
```

In this statement, the master (main) causes the servant (Cube) to compute the cube of 27 and give the result back to main. The sequence of symbols

```
Cube(27)
```

is a **function call** or **function invocation.** The computer temporarily puts the main function on hold and starts the Cube function running. When Cube has finished doing its work, the computer goes back to main and picks up where it left off.

Function call (function invocation)   The mechanism that transfers control to a function.

In the above function call, the number 27 is known as an *argument* (or *actual parameter*). Arguments make it possible for the same function to work on many different values. For example, we can write statements like these:

```
cout << Cube(4);
cout << Cube(16);
```

Here's the syntax template for a function call:

FunctionCall

FunctionName (ArgumentList)

The **argument list** is a way for functions to communicate with each other. Some functions, like Square and Cube, have a single argument in the argument list. Other functions, like main, have no arguments in the list. And some functions have two, three, or more arguments in the argument list, separated by commas.

Argument list   A mechanism by which functions communicate with each other.

Value-returning functions are used in expressions in much the same way that variables and constants are. The value computed by a function simply takes its place in the expression. For example, the statement

```
someInt = Cube(2) * 10;
```

stores the value 80 into `someInt`. First the `Cube` function is executed to compute the cube of 2, which is 8. The value 8—now available for use in the rest of the expression—is multiplied by 10. Note that a function call has higher precedence than multiplication, which makes sense if you consider that the function result must be available before the multiplication takes place.

Here are several facts about value-returning functions:

- The function call is used within an expression; it does not appear as a separate statement.
- The function computes a value (*result*) that is then available for use in the expression.
- The function returns exactly one result—no more, no less.

The `Cube` function expects to be given (or *passed*) an argument of type `int`. What happens if the caller passes a `float` argument? The answer is that the compiler applies implicit type coercion. The function call `Cube(6.9)` computes the cube of 6, not 6.9.

Although we have been using literal constants as arguments to `Cube`, the argument could just as easily be a variable or named constant. In fact, the argument to a value-returning function can be any expression of the appropriate type. In the statement

```
alpha = Cube(int1 * int1 + int2 * int2);
```

the expression in the argument list is evaluated first, and only its result is passed to the function. For example, if `int1` contains 3 and `int2` contains 5, the above function call passes 34 as the argument to `Cube`.

An expression in a function's argument list can even include calls to functions. For example, we could use the `Square` function to rewrite the above assignment statement as follows:

```
alpha = Cube(Square(int1) + Square(int2));
```

Library Functions

Certain computations, such as taking square roots or finding the absolute value of a number, are very common in programs. It would be an enormous waste of time if every programmer had to start from scratch and create functions to perform these tasks. To help make the programmer's life easier, every C++ system includes a standard library—a large collection of prewritten functions, data types, and other items that any C++ programmer may use. Here is a very small sample of some standard library functions:

Header File*	Function	Argument Type(s)	Result Type	Result (Value Returned)
<cstdlib>	abs(i)	int	int	Absolute value of i
<cmath>	cos(x)	float	float	Cosine of x (x is in radians)
<cmath>	fabs(x)	float	float	Absolute value of x
<cstdlib>	labs(j)	long	long	Absolute value of j
<cmath>	pow(x, y)	float	float	x raised to the power y (if x = 0.0, y must be positive; if x ≤ 0.0, y must be a whole number)
<cmath>	sin(x)	float	float	Sine of x (x is in radians)
<cmath>	sqrt(x)	float	float	Square root of x (x ≥ 0.0)

* The names of these header files are not the same as in pre–standard C++. If you are working with pre–standard C++, see Section D.2 of Appendix D.

Technically, the entries in the table marked `float` should all say `double`. These library functions perform their work using double-precision floating-point values. But because of type coercion, the functions work just as you would like them to when you pass `float` values to them.

Using a library function is easy. First, you place an `#include` directive near the top of your program, specifying the appropriate header file. This directive ensures that the C++ preprocessor inserts declarations into your program that give the compiler some information about the function. Then, whenever you want to use the function, you just make a function call.* Here's an example:

```
#include <iostream>
#include <cmath>        // For sqrt() and fabs()

using namespace std;
  ⋮
float alpha;
float beta;
  ⋮
alpha = sqrt(7.3 + fabs(beta));
```

* Some systems require you to specify a particular compiler option if you use the math functions. For example, with some versions of UNIX, you must add the option –lm when compiling your program.

Remember from Chapter 2 that all identifiers in the standard library are in the namespace `std`. If we omit the `using` directive from the above code, we must use qualified names for the library functions (`std::sqrt`, `std::fabs`, and so forth).

The C++ standard library provides dozens of functions for you to use. Appendix C lists a much larger selection than we have presented here. You should glance briefly at this appendix now, keeping in mind that much of the terminology and C++ language notation will make sense only after you have read further into the book.

Void Functions

In this chapter, the only kind of function that we have looked at is the value-returning function. C++ provides another kind of function as well. If you look at the Payroll program in Chapter 1, you see that the function definition for `CalcPay` begins with the word `void` instead of a data type like `int` or `float`:

```
void CalcPay( ... )
{
    ⋮
}
```

`CalcPay` is an example of a function that doesn't return a function value to its caller. Instead, it just performs some action and then quits. We refer to a function like this as a *non-value-returning function,* a *void-returning function,* or, most briefly, a **void function.** In many programming languages, a void function is known as a **procedure.**

Void functions are invoked differently from value-returning functions. With a value-returning function, the function call appears in an expression. With a void function, the function call is a separate, stand-alone statement. In the Payroll program, `main` calls the `CalcPay` function like this:

```
CalcPay(payRate, hours, wages);
```

From the caller's perspective, a call to a void function has the flavor of a command or built-in instruction:

```
DoThis(x, y, z);
DoThat();
```

In contrast, a call to a value-returning function doesn't look like a command; it looks like a value in an expression:

```
y = 4.7 + Cube(x);
```

Value-returning function A function that returns a single value to its caller and is invoked from within an expression.

Void function (procedure) A function that does not return a function value to its caller and is invoked as a separate statement.

For the next few chapters, we won't be writing our own functions (except `main`). Instead, we'll be concentrating on how to use existing functions, including functions for performing stream input and output. Some of these functions are value-returning functions; others are void functions. Again, we emphasize the difference in how you invoke these two kinds of functions: A call to a value-returning function occurs in an expression, whereas a call to a void function occurs as a separate statement.

Formatting the Output

To format a program's output means to control how it appears visually on the screen or on a printer. In Chapter 2, we considered two kinds of output formatting: creating extra blank lines by using the `endl` manipulator and inserting blanks within a line by putting extra blanks into literal strings. In this section, we examine how to format the output values themselves.

Integers and Strings

By default, consecutive integer and string values are output with no spaces between them. If the variables i, j, and k contain the values 15, 2, and 6, respectively, the statement

```
cout << "Results: " << i << j << k;
```

outputs the stream of characters

```
Results: 1526
```

Without spacing between the numbers, this output is difficult to interpret.
To separate the output values, you could print a single blank (as a `char` constant) between the numbers:

```
cout << "Results: " << i << ' ' << j << ' ' << k;
```

This statement produces the output

```
Results: 15 2 6
```

If you want even more spacing between items, you can use literal strings containing blanks, as we discussed in Chapter 2:

```
cout << "Results: " << i << "    " << j << "    " << k;
```

Here, the resulting output is

```
Results: 15    2    6
```

Another way to control the horizontal spacing of the output is to use *manipulators*. For some time now, we have been using the endl manipulator to terminate an output line. In C++, a manipulator is a rather curious thing that behaves like a function but travels in the disguise of a data object. Like a function, a manipulator causes some action to occur. But like a data object, a manipulator can appear in the midst of a series of insertion operations:

```
cout << someInt << endl << someFloat;
```

Manipulators are used *only* in input and output statements.

Here's a revised syntax template for the output statement, showing that not only arithmetic and string expressions but also manipulators are allowed:

OutputStatement

```
cout << ExpressionOrManipulator  << ExpressionOrManipulator ... ;
```

The C++ standard library supplies many manipulators, but for now we look at only five of them: endl, setw, fixed, showpoint, and setprecision. The endl, fixed, and showpoint manipulators come "for free" when we #include the header file iostream to perform I/O. The other two manipulators, setw and setprecision, require that we also #include the header file iomanip:

```
#include <iostream>
#include <iomanip>

using namespace std;
   ⋮
cout << setw(5) << someInt;
```

The manipulator `setw`—meaning "set width"—lets us control how many character positions the next data item should occupy when it is output. (`setw` is only for formatting numbers and strings, not `char` data.) The argument to `setw` is an integer expression called the *fieldwidth specification;* the group of character positions is called the *field.* The next data item to be output is printed *right-justified* (filled with blanks on the left to fill up the field).

Let's look at an example. Assuming two `int` variables have been assigned values as follows:

```
ans = 33;
num = 7132;
```

then the following output statements produce the output shown to their right.

Statement	Output (□ *means blank*)

1. `cout << setw(4) << ans`
`      << setw(5) << num`
`      << setw(4) << "Hi";`
	□□33□7132□□Hi
	  4 5 4

2. `cout << setw(2) << ans`
`      << setw(4) << num`
`      << setw(2) << "Hi";`
	337132Hi
	 2 4 2

3. `cout << setw(6) << ans`
`      << setw(3) << "Hi"`
`      << setw(5) << num;`
	□□□□33□Hi□7132
	   6 3 5

4. `cout << setw(7) << "Hi"` `      << setw(4) << num;`	□□□□□Hi7132 7 4
5. `cout << setw(1) << ans` `      << setw(5) << num;`	33□7132 ↑ 5 Field automatically expands to fit the two-digit value

In (1), each value is specified to occupy enough positions so that there is at least one space separating them. In (2), the values all run together because the fieldwidth specified for each value is just large enough to hold the value. This output obviously is not very readable. It's better to make the fieldwidth larger than the minimum size required so that some space is left between values. In (3), there are extra blanks for readability; in (4), there are not. In (5), the fieldwidth is not large enough for the value in ans, so it automatically expands to make room for all of the digits.

Setting the fieldwidth is a one-time action. It holds only for the very next item to be output. After this output, the fieldwidth resets to 0, meaning "extend the field to exactly as many positions as are needed." In the statement

```
cout << "Hi" << setw(5) << ans << num;
```

the fieldwidth resets to 0 after ans is output. As a result, we get the output

```
Hi    337132
```

Floating-Point Numbers

You can specify a fieldwidth for floating-point values just as for integer values. But you must remember to allow for the decimal point when you specify the number of character positions. The value 4.85 requires four output positions, not three. If x contains the value 4.85, the statement

```
cout << setw(4) << x << endl
     << setw(6) << x << endl
     << setw(3) << x << endl;
```

produces the output

```
4.85
  4.85
4.85
```

In the third line, a fieldwidth of 3 isn't sufficient, so the field automatically expands to accommodate the number.

There are several other issues related to output of floating-point numbers. First, large floating-point values are printed in scientific (E) notation. The value 123456789.5 may print on some systems as

```
1.23457E+08
```

You can use the manipulator named `fixed` to force all subsequent floating-point output to appear in decimal form rather than scientific notation:

```
cout << fixed << 3.8 * x;
```

Second, if the number is a whole number, C++ doesn't print a decimal point. The value 95.0 prints as

```
95
```

To force decimal points to be displayed in subsequent floating-point output, even for whole numbers, you can use the manipulator `showpoint`:

```
cout << showpoint << floatVar;
```

(If you are using a pre–standard version of C++, the `fixed` and `showpoint` manipulators may not be available. See Section D.3 of Appendix D for an alternative way of achieving the same results.)

Third, you often would like to control the number of *decimal places* (digits to the right of the decimal point) that are displayed. If your program is supposed to print the 5% sales tax on a certain amount, the statement

```
cout << "Tax is $" << price * 0.05;
```

may output

```
Tax is $17.7435
```

Here, you clearly would prefer to display the result to two decimal places. To do so, use the `setprecision` manipulator as follows:

```
cout << fixed << setprecision(2) << "Tax is $" << price * 0.05;
```

Provided that `fixed` has already been specified, the argument to `setprecision` specifies the desired number of decimal places. Unlike `setw`, which applies only to the very next item printed, the value sent to `setprecision` remains in effect for all subsequent output (until you change it with another call to `setprecision`). Here are some examples of using `setprecision` in conjunction with `setw`:

Value of x	Statement	Output (□ means blank)

310.0	`cout << fixed;`
	`cout << setw(10)`
	`    << setprecision(2) << x;`
		□□□□310.00

310.0	`cout << setw(10)` `    << setprecision(5) << x;`	□310.00000
310.0	`cout << setw(7)` `    << setprecision(5) << x;`	310.00000 (expands to nine positions)
4.827	`cout << setw(6)` `    << setprecision(2) << x;`	□□4.83 (last displayed digit is rounded off)
4.827	`cout << setw(6)` `    << setprecision(1) << x;`	□□□4.8 (last displayed digit is rounded off)

Again, the total number of print positions is expanded if the fieldwidth specified by setw is too narrow. However, the number of positions for fractional digits is controlled entirely by the argument to setprecision.

The following table summarizes the manipulators we have discussed in this section. Manipulators without arguments are available through the header file iostream. Those with arguments require the header file iomanip.

Header File	Manipulator	Argument Type	Effect
`<iostream>`	endl	None	Terminates the current output line
`<iostream>`	showpoint	None	Forces display of decimal point in floating-point output
`<iostream>`	fixed	None	Suppresses scientific notation in floating-point output
`<iomanip>`	setw(n)	int	Sets fieldwidth to n*
`<iomanip>`	setprecision(n)	int	Sets floating-point precision to n digits

*setw is only for numbers and strings, not char data. Also, setw applies only to the very next output item, after which the fieldwidth is reset to 0 (meaning "use only as many positions as are needed").

*M*ATTERS OF STYLE

Program Formatting

As far as the compiler is concerned, C++ statements are *free format:* They can appear anywhere on a line, more than one can appear on a single line, and one statement can span several lines. The compiler only needs blanks (or comments or new lines) to separate important symbols, and it needs semicolons to terminate statements. However, it is extremely important that your programs be readable, both for your sake and for the sake of anyone else who has to examine them.

When you write an outline for an English paper, you follow certain rules of indentation to make it readable. These same kinds of rules can make your programs easier to read. It is much easier to spot a mistake in a neatly formatted program than in a messy one. Thus, you should keep your program neatly formatted while you are working on it. If you've gotten lazy and let your program become messy while making a series of changes, take the time to straighten it up. Often the source of an error becomes obvious during the process of formatting the code.

Take a look at the following program for computing the cost per square foot of a house. Although it compiles and runs correctly, it does not conform to any formatting standards.

```cpp
// HouseCost program
// This program computes the cost per square foot of
    // living space for a house, given the dimensions of
// the house, the number of stories, the size of the
// nonliving space, and the total cost less land
#include <iostream>
#include <iomanip>// For setw() and setprecision()
using namespace
std;
const float WIDTH = 30.0; // Width of the house
    const float LENGTH = 40.0; // Length of the house
const float STORIES = 2.5; // Number of full stories
const float NON_LIVING_SPACE = 825.0;// Garage, closets, etc.

const float PRICE = 150000.0; // Selling price less land
int main() { float grossFootage;// Total square footage
    float livingFootage;        // Living area
float costPerFoot;      // Cost/foot of living area
   cout << fixed << showpoint;    // Set up floating-pt.
//   output format

grossFootage = LENGTH * WIDTH * STORIES; livingFootage =
grossFootage - NON_LIVING_SPACE; costPerFoot = PRICE /
livingFootage; cout << "Cost per square foot is "
<< setw(6) << setprecision(2) << costPerFoot << endl;
return 0; }
```

Now look at the same program with proper formatting:

```
//******************************************************************
// HouseCost program
// This program computes the cost per square foot of
// living space for a house, given the dimensions of
// the house, the number of stories, the size of the
// nonliving space, and the total cost less land
//******************************************************************
#include <iostream>
#include <iomanip>       // For setw() and setprecision()

using namespace std;

const float WIDTH = 30.0;                   // Width of the house
const float LENGTH = 40.0;                  // Length of the house
const float STORIES = 2.5;                  // Number of full stories
const float NON_LIVING_SPACE = 825.0;       // Garage, closets, etc.
const float PRICE = 150000.0;               // Selling price less land

int main()
{
    float grossFootage;       // Total square footage
    float livingFootage;      // Living area
    float costPerFoot;        // Cost/foot of living area

    cout << fixed << showpoint;              // Set up floating-pt.
                                             //   output format

    grossFootage = LENGTH * WIDTH * STORIES;
    livingFootage = grossFootage - NON_LIVING_SPACE;
    costPerFoot = PRICE / livingFootage;

    cout << "Cost per square foot is "
         << setw(6) << setprecision(2) << costPerFoot << endl;
    return 0;
}
```

Need we say more?

Appendix F talks about programming style. Use it as a guide when you are writing programs.

▊ *Additional* string *Operations*

Now that we have introduced numeric types and function calls, we can take advantage of additional features of the string data type. In this section, we introduce four functions that operate on strings: length, size, find, and substr.

The length and size Functions

The length function, when applied to a string variable, returns an unsigned integer value that equals the number of characters currently in the string. If myName is a string variable, a call to the length function looks like this:

```
myName.length()
```

You specify the name of a string variable (here, myName), then a dot (period), and then the function name and argument list. The length function requires no arguments to be passed to it, but you still must use parentheses to signify an empty argument list. Also, length is a value-returning function, so the function call must appear within an expression:

```
string firstName;
string fullName;

firstName = "Alexandra";
cout << firstName.length() << endl;       // Prints 9
fullName = firstName + " Jones";
cout << fullName.length() << endl;         // Prints 15
```

Perhaps you are wondering about the syntax in a function call like

```
firstName.length()
```

This expression uses a C++ notation called *dot notation*. There is a dot (period) between the variable name firstName and the function name length. Certain programmer-defined data types, such as string, have functions that are tightly associated with them, and dot notation is required in the function calls. If you forget to use dot notation, writing the function call as

```
length()
```

you get a compile-time error message, something like "UNDECLARED IDENTIFIER." The compiler thinks you are trying to call an ordinary function named `length`, not the `length` function associated with the `string` type. In Chapter 4, we discuss the meaning behind dot notation.

Some people refer to the length of a string as its *size*. To accommodate both terms, the `string` type provides a function named `size`. Both `firstName.size()` and `firstName.length()` return the same value.

We said that the `length` function returns an unsigned integer value. If we want to save the result into a variable `len`, as in

```
len = firstName.length();
```

then what should we declare the data type of `len` to be? To keep us from having to guess whether `unsigned int` or `unsigned long` is correct for the particular compiler we're working with, the `string` type defines a data type `size_type` for us to use:

```
string firstName;
string::size_type len;

firstName = "Alexandra";
len = firstName.length();
```

Notice that we must use the qualified name `string::size_type` (just as we do with identifiers in namespaces) because the definition of `size_type` is otherwise hidden inside the definition of the `string` type.

Before leaving the `length` and `size` functions, we should make a remark about capitalization of identifiers. In the guidelines given in Chapter 2, we said that in this book we begin the names of programmer-defined functions and data types with uppercase letters. We follow this convention when we write our own functions and data types in later chapters. However, we have no control over the capitalization of items supplied by the C++ standard library. Identifiers in the standard library generally use all-lowercase letters.

The `find` Function

The `find` function searches a string to find the first occurrence of a particular substring and returns an unsigned integer value (of type `string::size_type`) giving the result of the search. The substring, passed as an argument to the function, can be a literal string or a `string` expression. If `str1` and `str2` are of type `string`, the following are valid function calls:

```
str1.find("the")        str1.find(str2)        str1.find(str2 + "abc")
```

In each case above, str1 is searched to see if the specified substring can be found within it. If so, the function returns the position in str1 where the match begins. (Positions are numbered starting at 0, so the first character in a string is in position 0, the second is in position 1, and so on.) For a successful search, the match must be exact, including identical capitalization. If the substring could not be found, the function returns the special value string::npos, a named constant meaning "not a position within the string." (string::npos is the largest possible value of type string::size_type, a number like 4294967295 on many machines. This value is suitable for "not a valid position" because the string operations do not let any string become this long.)

Given the code segment

```
string phrase;
string::size_type position;

phrase = "The dog and the cat";
```

the statement

```
position = phrase.find("the");
```

assigns to position the value 12, whereas the statement

```
position = phrase.find("rat");
```

assigns to position the value string::npos, because there was no match.

The argument to the find function can also be a char value. In this case, find searches for the first occurrence of that character within the string and returns its position (or string::npos, if the character was not found). For example, the code segment

```
string theString;

theString = "Abracadabra";
cout << theString.find('a');
```

outputs the value 3, which is the position of the first occurrence of a lower-case *a* in theString.

Below are some more examples of calls to the find function, assuming the following code segment has been executed:

```
string str1;
string str2;

str1 = "Programming and Problem Solving";
str2 = "gram";
```

Function Call	Value Returned by Function
str1.find("and")	12
str1.find("Programming")	0
str2.find("and")	string::npos
str1.find("Pro")	0
str1.find("ro" + str2)	1
str1.find("Pr" + str2)	string::npos
str1.find(' ')	11

Notice in the fourth example that there are two copies of the substring "Pro" in str1, but find returns only the position of the first copy. Also notice that the copies can be either separate words or parts of words—find merely tries to match the sequence of characters given in the argument list. The final example demonstrates that the argument can be as simple as a single character, even a single blank.

The substr Function

The substr function returns a particular substring of a string. Assuming myString is of type string, here is a sample function call:

```
myString.substr(5, 20)
```

The first argument is an unsigned integer that specifies a position within the string, and the second is an unsigned integer that specifies the length of the desired substring. The function returns the piece of the string that starts with the specified position and continues for the number of characters given by the second argument. Note that substr doesn't change myString; it returns a new, temporary string value that is a copy of a portion of the string. Below are some examples, assuming the statement

```
myString = "Programming and Problem Solving";
```

has been executed.

Function Call	String Contained in Value Returned by Function
myString.substr(0, 7)	"Program"
myString.substr(7, 8)	"ming and"
myString.substr(10, 0)	""
myString.substr(24, 40)	"Solving"
myString.substr(40, 24)	None. Program terminates with an execution error message.

In the third example, specifying a length of 0 produces the null string as the result. The fourth example shows what happens if the second argument specifies more characters than are present after the starting position: substr returns the characters from the starting position to the end of the string. The last example illustrates that the first argument, the position, must not be beyond the end of the string.

Because substr returns a value of type string, you can use it with the concatenation operator (+) to copy pieces of strings and join them together to form new strings. The find and length functions can be useful in determining the location and end of a piece of a string to be passed to substr as arguments.

Here is a code segment that uses several of the string operations:

```
string fullName;
string name;
string::size_type startPos;

fullName = "Jonathan Alexander Peterson";
startPos = fullName.find("Peterson");
name = "Mr. " + fullName.substr(startPos, 8);
cout << name << endl;
```

This code outputs Mr. Peterson when it is executed. First it stores a string into the variable fullName, and then it uses find to locate the start of the name Peterson within the string. Next, it builds a new string by concatenating the literal "Mr. " with the characters Peterson, which are copied from the original string. Last, it prints out the new string. As we see in later chapters, string operations are an important aspect of many computer programs.

The following table summarizes the string operations we have looked at in this chapter.

Function Call (s is of type string)	Argument Type(s)	Result Type	Result (Value Returned)
s.length() s.size()	None	string::size_type	Number of characters in the string
s.find(arg)	string, literal string, or char	string::size_type	Starting position in s where arg was found. If not found, result is string::npos
s.substr(pos,len)	string::size_type	string	Substring of at most len characters, starting at position pos of s. If len is too large, it means "to the end" of string s. If pos is too large, execution of the program is terminated.*

*Technically, if pos is too large, the program generates what is called an out-of-range *exception*—a topic we do not discuss at this time. Unless we write additional program code to deal explicitly with this out-of-range exception, the program simply terminates with a message such as "ABNORMAL PROGRAM TERMINATION."

SOFTWARE ENGINEERING TIP

Understanding Before Changing

When you are in the middle of getting a program to run and you come across an error, it's tempting to start changing parts of the program to try to make it work. *Don't!* You'll nearly always make things worse. It's essential that you understand what is causing the error and that you carefully think through the solution. The only thing you should try is running the program with different data to determine the pattern of the unexpected behavior.

There is no magic trick—inserting an extra semicolon or right brace, for example—that can automatically fix a program. If the compiler tells you that a semicolon or a right brace is missing, you need to examine the program in light of the syntax rules and determine precisely what the problem is. Perhaps you accidentally typed a colon instead of a semicolon. Or maybe there's an extra left brace.

If the source of a problem isn't immediately obvious, a good rule of thumb is to leave the computer and go somewhere where you can quietly look over a printed copy of the program. Studies show that people who do all of their debugging away from the computer actually get their programs to work in less time *and in the end produce better programs* than those who continue to work on the machine—more proof that there is still no mechanical substitute for human thought.*

---

*Basili, V. R., and Selby, R. W., "Comparing the Effectiveness of Software Testing Strategies," *IEEE Trans. on Software Engineering* SE-13, no. 12 (1987): 1278–1296.

PROBLEM-SOLVING CASE STUDY

Map Measurements

Problem: You're spending a day in the city. You plan to visit the natural history museum, a record store, a gallery, and a bookshop, and then go to a concert. You have a tourist map that shows where these places are located. You want to determine how far apart they are and how far you'll walk during the entire day. Then you can decide when it would be better to take a taxi. According to the map's legend, one inch on the map equals one quarter of a mile on the ground.

Output: The distance between each of the places and the total distance, rounded to the nearest tenth of a mile. The values on which the calculations are based should also be printed for verification purposes.

Discussion: You can measure the distances between two points on the map with a ruler. The program must output miles, so you need to multiply the number of inches by 0.25. You then write down the figure, rounded to the nearest tenth of a mile. When you've done this for each pair of places, you add the distances to get the total mileage. This is essentially the algorithm we use in the program.

The only tricky part is how to round a value to the nearest tenth of a mile. In this chapter, we showed how to round a floating-point value to the nearest integer by adding 0.5 and using a type cast to truncate the result:

```
int(floatValue + 0.5)
```

To round to the nearest tenth, we first multiply the value by 10, round the result to the nearest integer, and then divide by 10 again. For example, if floatValue contains 5.162, then

```
float(int(floatValue * 10.0 + 0.5)) / 10.0
```

gives 5.2 as its result.

Let's treat all of the quantities as named constants so that it is easier to change the program later. From measuring the map, you know that the distance from the museum to the record store is 1.5 inches, from the record store to the gallery is 2.3 inches, from the gallery to the bookshop is 5.9 inches, and from the bookshop to the concert is 4.0 inches. Here is the algorithmic solution:

Define Constants

```
DISTANCE1 = 1.5
DISTANCE2 = 2.3
DISTANCE3 = 5.9
DISTANCE4 = 4.0
SCALE = 0.25
```

Initialize the Total Miles

```
Set totMiles = 0.0
```

Compute Miles for Each Distance on the Map

```
Set miles = float(int(DISTANCE1 * SCALE * 10.0 + 0.5)) / 10.0
Print DISTANCE1, miles
Add miles to totMiles
Set miles = float(int(DISTANCE2 * SCALE * 10.0 + 0.5)) / 10.0
Print DISTANCE2, miles
Add miles to totMiles
Set miles = float(int(DISTANCE3 * SCALE * 10.0 + 0.5)) / 10.0
Print DISTANCE3, miles
Add miles to totMiles
Set miles = float(int(DISTANCE4 * SCALE * 10.0 + 0.5)) / 10.0
Print DISTANCE4, miles
Add miles to totMiles
```

Print the Total Miles

```
Print a blank line
Print totMiles
```

From the algorithm we can create tables of constants and variables that help us write the declarations in the program.

PROBLEM-SOLVING CASE STUDY cont'd.

Constants

Name	Value	Description
DISTANCE1	1.5	Measurement for first distance
DISTANCE2	2.3	Measurement for second distance
DISTANCE3	5.9	Measurement for third distance
DISTANCE4	4.0	Measurement for fourth distance
SCALE	0.25	Scale factor of map

Variables

Name	Data Type	Description
totMiles	float	Total of rounded mileages
miles	float	An individual rounded mileage

Now we're ready to write the program. Let's call it Walk. We take the declarations from the tables and create the executable statements from the algorithm. We have labeled the output with explanatory messages and formatted the values to one decimal place. We've also added comments where needed.

(The following program is written in ISO/ANSI standard C++. If you are working with pre–standard C++, see the alternate version of the program in the PRE_STD directory of the program disk, available at the publisher's Web site, www.jbpub.com/disks.)

```
//*****************************************************************
// Walk program
// This program computes the mileage (rounded to tenths of a mile)
// for each of four distances between points in a city, given
// the measurements on a map with a scale of one inch equal to
// one quarter of a mile
//*****************************************************************
#include <iostream>
#include <iomanip>      // For setprecision()

using namespace std;

const float DISTANCE1 = 1.5;      // Measurement for first distance
const float DISTANCE2 = 2.3;      // Measurement for second distance
const float DISTANCE3 = 5.9;      // Measurement for third distance
const float DISTANCE4 = 4.0;      // Measurement for fourth distance
const float SCALE = 0.25;         // Map scale (miles per inch)
```

```cpp
int main()
{
    float totMiles;       // Total of rounded mileages
    float miles;          // An individual rounded mileage

    cout << fixed << showpoint            // Set up floating-pt.
         << setprecision(1);              //    output format

    // Initialize the total miles

    totMiles = 0.0;

    // Compute miles for each distance on the map

    miles = float(int(DISTANCE1 * SCALE * 10.0 + 0.5)) / 10.0;
    cout << "For a measurement of " << DISTANCE1
         << " the first distance is " << miles << " mile(s) long."
         << endl;
    totMiles = totMiles + miles;

    miles = float(int(DISTANCE2 * SCALE * 10.0 + 0.5)) / 10.0;
    cout << "For a measurement of " << DISTANCE2
         << " the second distance is " << miles << " mile(s) long."
         << endl;
    totMiles = totMiles + miles;

    miles = float(int(DISTANCE3 * SCALE * 10.0 + 0.5)) / 10.0;
    cout << "For a measurement of " << DISTANCE3
         << " the third distance is " << miles << " mile(s) long."
         << endl;
    totMiles = totMiles + miles;

    miles = float(int(DISTANCE4 * SCALE * 10.0 + 0.5)) / 10.0;
    cout << "For a measurement of " << DISTANCE4
         << " the fourth distance is " << miles << " mile(s) long."
         << endl;
    totMiles = totMiles + miles;

    // Print the total miles

    cout << endl;
    cout << "Total mileage for the day is " << totMiles << " miles."
         << endl;
    return 0;
}
```

PROBLEM-SOLVING CASE STUDY cont'd.

The output from the program is

```
For a measurement of 1.5 the first distance is 0.4 mile(s) long.
For a measurement of 2.3 the second distance is 0.6 mile(s) long.
For a measurement of 5.9 the third distance is 1.5 mile(s) long.
For a measurement of 4.0 the fourth distance is 1.0 mile(s) long.

Total mileage for the day is 3.5 miles.
```

Testing and Debugging

1. An `int` constant other than 0 should not start with a zero. If it starts with a zero, it is an octal (base-8) number.
2. Watch out for integer division. The expression `47 / 100` yields 0, the integer quotient. This is one of the major sources of wrong output in C++ programs.
3. When using the `/` and `%` operators, remember that division by zero is not allowed.
4. Double-check every expression according to the precedence rules to be sure that the operations are performed in the desired order.
5. Avoid mixing integer and floating-point values in expressions. If you must mix them, consider using explicit type casts to reduce the chance of mistakes.
6. For each assignment statement, check that the expression result has the same data type as the variable to the left of the assignment operator (=). If not, consider using an explicit type cast for clarity and safety. And remember that storing a floating-point value into an `int` variable truncates the fractional part.
7. For every library function you use in your program, be sure to `#include` the appropriate header file.
8. Examine each call to a library function to see that you have the right number of arguments and that the data types of the arguments are correct.
9. With the `string` type, positions of characters within a string are numbered starting at 0, not 1.
10. If the cause of an error in a program is not obvious, leave the computer and study a printed listing. Change your program only after you understand the source of the error.

Summary

C++ provides several built-in numeric data types, of which the most commonly used are int and float. The integral types are based on the mathematical integers, but the computer limits the range of integer values that can be represented. The floating-point types are based on the mathematical notion of real numbers. As with integers, the computer limits the range of floating-point numbers that can be represented. Also, it limits the number of digits of precision in floating-point values. We can write literals of type float in several forms, including scientific (E) notation.

Much of the computation of a program is performed in arithmetic expressions. Expressions can contain more than one operator. The order in which the operations are performed is determined by precedence rules. In arithmetic expressions, multiplication, division, and modulus are performed first, then addition and subtraction. Multiple binary (two-operand) operations of the same precedence are grouped from left to right. You can use parentheses to override the precedence rules.

Expressions may include function calls. C++ supports two kinds of functions: value-returning functions and void functions. A value-returning function is called by writing its name and argument list as part of an expression. A void function is called by writing its name and argument list as a complete C++ statement.

The C++ standard library is an integral part of every C++ system. The library contains many prewritten data types, functions, and other items that any programmer can use. These items are accessed by using #include directives to the C++ preprocessor, which inserts the appropriate header files into the program.

In output statements, the setw, showpoint, fixed, and setprecision manipulators control the appearance of values in the output. These manipulators do *not* affect the values actually stored in memory, only their appearance when displayed on the output device.

Not only should the output produced by a program be easy to read, but the format of the program itself should be clear and readable. C++ is a free-format language. A consistent style that uses indentation, blank lines, and spaces within lines helps you (and other programmers) understand and work with your programs.

Quick Check

1. Write a C++ constant declaration that gives the name PI to the value 3.14159. (pp. 105–106)
2. Declare an int variable named count and a float variable named sum. (pp. 106–107)

3. You want to divide 9 by 5.
    a. How do you write the expression if you want the result to be the floating-point value 1.8?
    b. How do you write it if you want only the integer quotient? (pp. 107–110)
4. What is the value of the following C++ expression?

    ```
    5 % 2
    ```

    (pp. 108–110)
5. What is the result of evaluating the expression

    ```
    (1 + 2 * 2) / 2 + 1
    ```

    (pp. 112–113)
6. How would you write the following formula as a C++ expression that produces a floating-point value as a result? (pp. 112–113)

$$\frac{9}{5}c + 32$$

7. Add type casts to the following statements to make the type conversions clear and explicit. Your answers should produce the same results as the original statements. (pp. 113–116)
    a. someFloat = 5 + someInt;
    b. someInt = 2.5 * someInt / someFloat;
8. You want to compute the square roots and absolute values of some floating-point numbers.
    a. Which C++ library functions would you use? (pp. 120–122)
    b. Which header file(s) must you #include in order to use these functions?
9. Which part of the following function call is its argument list? (p. 119)

    ```
    Square(someInt + 1)
    ```

10. In the statement

    ```
    alpha = 4 * Beta(gamma, delta) + 3;
    ```

    would you conclude that Beta is a value-returning function or a void function? (pp. 120–123)
11. In the statement

    ```
    Display(gamma, delta);
    ```

    would you conclude that Display is a value-returning function or a void function? (pp. 120–123)
12. Assume the float variable pay contains the value 327.66101. Using the fixed, setw, and setprecision manipulators, what output statement would you use to print pay in dollars and cents with three leading blanks? (pp. 124–128)
13. If the string variable str contains the string "Now is the time", what is output by the following statement? (pp. 131–136)

    ```
    cout << str.length() << ' ' << str.substr(1, 2) << endl;
    ```

14. Reformat the following program to make it clear and readable. (pp. 129–130)

```
//***********************************************************
              // SumProd program
   // This program computes the sum and product of two integers
//***********************************************************
#include <iostream>
using namespace std;
const int INT1=20;const int INT2=8;int main() { cout <<
"The sum of " << INT1 << " and "
<< INT2 << " is " << INT1+INT2 << endl;cout
<< "Their product is " << INT1*INT2 << endl;return 0; }
```

15. What should you do if a program fails to run correctly and the reason for the error is not immediately obvious? (p. 136)

Answers **1.** `const float PI = 3.14159;`
2. `int    count;`
   `float sum;`
3. a. `9.0 / 5.0` b. `9 / 5` **4.** The value is 1. **5.** The result is 3. **6.** `9.0 / 5.0 * c +`
`32.0` **7.** a. `someFloat = float(5 + someInt);` b. `someInt = int(2.5 *`
`float(someInt) / someFloat);` **8.** a. `sqrt` and `fabs` b. `math` **9.** `someInt + 1` **10.**
A value-returning function **11.** A void function **12.** `cout << fixed << setw(9) <<`
`setprecision(2) << pay;` **13.** 15 ow
14.
```
//***********************************************************
   // SumProd program
   // This program computes the sum and product of two integers
//***********************************************************
#include <iostream>

using namespace std;

const int INT1 = 20;
const int INT2 = 8;

int main()
{
    cout << "The sum of " << INT1 << " and " << INT2
         << " is " << INT1 + INT2 << endl;
    cout << "Their product is " << INT1 * INT2 << endl;
    return 0;
}
```

15. Get a fresh printout of the program, leave the computer, and study the program until you understand the cause of the problem. Then correct the algorithm and the program as necessary before you go back to the computer and make any changes in the program file.

Exam Preparation Exercises

1. Mark the following constructs either valid or invalid. Assume all variables are of type int.

	Valid	Invalid
a. x * y = c;	_____	_____
b. y = con;	_____	_____
c. const int x : 10;	_____	_____
d. int x;	_____	_____
e. a = b % c;	_____	_____

2. If alpha and beta are int variables with alpha containing 4 and beta containing 9, what value is stored into alpha in each of the following? Answer each part independently of the others.
   a. alpha = 3 * beta;
   b. alpha = alpha + beta;
   c. alpha++;
   d. alpha = alpha / beta;
   e. alpha--;
   f. alpha = alpha + alpha;
   g. alpha = beta % 6;

3. Compute the value of each legal expression. Indicate whether the value is an integer or a floating-point value. If the expression is not legal, explain why.

	Integer	Floating Point
a. 10.0 / 3.0 + 5 * 2	_____	_____
b. 10 % 3 + 5 % 2	_____	_____
c. 10 / 3 + 5 / 2	_____	_____
d. 12.5 + (2.5 / (6.2 / 3.1))	_____	_____
e. -4 * (-5 + 6)	_____	_____
f. 13 % 5 / 3	_____	_____
g. (10.0 / 3.0 % 2) / 3	_____	_____

4. What value is stored into the int variable result in each of the following?
   a. result = 15 % 4;
   b. result = 7 / 3 + 2;
   c. result = 2 + 7 * 5;
   d. result = 45 / 8 * 4 + 2;
   e. result = 17 + (21 % 6) * 2;
   f. result = int(4.5 + 2.6 * 0.5);

5. If a and b are int variables with a containing 5 and b containing 2, what output does each of the following statements produce?
   a. cout << "a = " << a << "b = " << b << endl;
   b. cout << "Sum:" << a + b << endl;
   c. cout << "Sum: " << a + b << endl;
   d. cout << a / b << " feet" << endl;

6. What does the following program print?

   ```
   #include <iostream>

   using namespace std;

   const int LBS = 10;
   ```

```
int main()
{
    int   price;
    int   cost;
    char ch;

    price = 30;
    cost = price * LBS;
    ch = 'A';
    cout << "Cost is " << endl;
    cout << cost << endl;
    cout << "Price is " << price << "Cost is " << cost << endl;
    cout << "Grade " << ch << " costs " << endl;
    cout << cost << endl;
    return 0;
}
```

7. Translate the following C++ code into algebraic notation. (All variables are `float` variables.)

```
y = -b + sqrt(b * b - 4.0 * a * c);
```

8. Given the following program fragment:

```
int    i;
int    j;
float z;


i = 4;
j = 17;
z = 2.6;
```

determine the value of each expression below. If the result is a floating-point value, include a decimal point in your answer.

```
a. i / float(j)
b. 1.0 / i + 2
c. z * j
d. i + j % i
e. (1 / 2) * i
f. 2 * i + j - i
g. j / 2
h. 2 * 3 - 1 % 3
i. i % j / i
j. int(z + 0.5)
```

9. To use each of the following statements, a C++ program must #include which header file(s)?

```
a. cout << x;
b. int1 = abs(int2);
c. y = sqrt(7.6 + x);
```

d. `cout << y << endl;`
e. `cout << setw(5) << someInt;`

10. Evaluate the following expressions. If the result is a floating-point number, include a decimal point in your answer.

    a. `fabs(-9.1)`
    b. `sqrt(49.0)`
    c. `3 * int(7.8) + 3`
    d. `pow(4.0, 2.0)`
    e. `sqrt(float(3 * 3 + 4 * 4))`
    f. `sqrt(fabs(-4.0) + sqrt(25.0))`

11. Show precisely the output of the following C++ program. Use a □ to indicate each blank.

    ```
    #include <iostream>
    #include <iomanip>     // For setw()

    using namespace std;

    int main()
    {
        char   ch;
        int    n;
        float  y;

        ch = 'A';
        cout << ch;
        ch = 'B';
        cout << ch << endl;
        n = 413;
        y = 21.8;
        cout << setw(5) << n << " is the value of n" << endl;
        cout << setw(7) << y << " is the value of y" << endl;
        return 0;
    }
    ```

12. Given that `x` is a `float` variable containing 14.3827, show the output of each statement below. Use a □ to indicate each blank. (Assume that `cout << fixed` has already executed.)

    a. `cout << "x is" << setw(5) << setprecision(2) << x;`
    b. `cout << "x is" << setw(8) << setprecision(2) << x;`
    c. `cout << "x is" << setw(0) << setprecision(2) << x;`
    d. `cout << "x is" << setw(7) << setprecision(3) << x;`

13. Given the statements

    ```
    string heading;
    string str;

    heading = "Exam Preparation Exercises";
    ```

what is the output of each code segment below?

```
a. cout << heading.length();
b. cout << heading.substr(6, 10);
c. cout << heading.find("Ex");
d. str = heading.substr(2, 24);
   cout << str.find("Ex");
e. str = heading.substr(heading.find("Ex") + 2, 24);
   cout << str.find("Ex");
f. str = heading.substr(heading.find("Ex") + 2,
                        heading.length() - heading.find("Ex") + 2);
   cout << str.find("Ex");
```

14. Formatting a program incorrectly causes an error. (True or False?)

Programming Warm-up Exercises

1. Change the program in Exam Preparation Exercise 6 so that it prints the cost for 15 pounds.
2. Write an assignment statement to calculate the sum of the numbers from 1 through *n* using Gauss's formula:

$$sum = \frac{n(n+1)}{2}$$

Store the result into the int variable sum.

3. Given the declarations

```
int   i;
int   j;
float x;
float y;
```

write a valid C++ expression for each of the following algebraic expressions.

a. $\dfrac{x}{y} - 3$ e. $\dfrac{i}{j}$ (the floating-point result)

b. $(x + y)(x - y)$ f. $\dfrac{i}{j}$ (the integer quotient)

c. $\dfrac{1}{x+y}$ g. $\dfrac{\dfrac{x+y}{3} - \dfrac{x-y}{3}}{4x}$

d. $\dfrac{1}{x} + y$

4. Given the declarations

```
int   i;
long  n;
float x;
float y;
```

write a valid C++ expression for each of the following algebraic expressions. Use calls to library functions wherever they are useful.

a. $|l|$ (absolute value)   e. $\dfrac{x^3}{y}$

b. $|n|$ f. $\sqrt{x^6 + y^5}$

c. $|x + y|$ g. $(x + \sqrt{y})^7$

d. $|x| + |y|$

5. Write expressions to compute both solutions for the quadratic formula. The formula is

$$\frac{-b \pm \sqrt{b^2 - 4ac}}{2a}$$

The ± means "plus or minus" and indicates that there are two solutions to the equation: one in which the result of the square root is added to $-b$ and one in which the result is subtracted from $-b$. Assume all variables are `float` variables.

6. Enter the following program into your computer and run it. In the initial comments, replace the items within parentheses with your own information. (Omit the parentheses.)

```
//**********************************
// Programming Assignment (assignment number)
// (your name)
// (date program was run)
// (description of the problem)
//**********************************
#include <iostream>

using namespace std;

const float DEBT = 300.0;       // Original value owed
const float PMT = 22.4;         // Payment
const float INT_RATE = 0.02;    // Interest rate

int main()
{
    float charge;       // Interest times debt
    float reduc;        // Amount debt is reduced
    float remaining;    // Remaining balance

    charge = INT_RATE * DEBT;
    reduc = PMT - charge;
    remaining = DEBT - reduc;
    cout << "Payment: " << PMT
         << " Charge: " << charge
         << " Balance owed: " << remaining << endl;
    return 0;
}
```

7. Enter the following program into your computer and run it. Add comments, using the pattern shown in Exercise 6 above. (Notice how hard it is to tell what the program does without the comments.)

    ```cpp
    #include <iostream>

    using namespace std;

    const int TOT_COST = 1376;
    const int POUNDS = 10;
    const int OUNCES = 12;

    int main()
    {
        int    totOz;
        float uCost;

        totOz = 16 * POUNDS;
        totOz = totOz + OUNCES;
        uCost = TOT_COST / totOz;
        cout << "Cost per unit: " << uCost << endl;
        return 0;
    }
    ```

8. Complete the following C++ program. The program should find and output the perimeter and area of a rectangle, given the length and the width. Be sure to label the output. And don't forget to use comments.

    ```cpp
    //************************************************
    // Rectangle program
    // This program finds the perimeter and the area
    // of a rectangle, given the length and width
    //************************************************
    #include <iostream>

    using namespace std;

    int main()
    {
        float length;       // Length of the rectangle
        float width;        // Width of the rectangle
        float perimeter;    // Perimeter of the rectangle
        float area;         // Area of the rectangle

        length = 10.7;
        width = 5.2;
    ```

9. Write an expression whose result is the position of the first occurrence of the characters "res" in a string variable named sentence. If the variable contains the first sentence of this question, then what is the result? (Look at the sentence carefully!)

10. Write a sequence of C++ statements to output the positions of the second and third occurrences of the characters "res" in the `string` variable named `sentence`. You may assume that there are always at least three occurrences in the variable. (*Hint:* Use the `substr` function to create a new string whose contents are the portion of `sentence` following an occurrence of "res".)

Programming Problems

1. C++ systems provide a header file `climits`, which contains declarations of constants related to the specific compiler and machine on which you are working. Two of these constants are `INT_MAX` and `INT_MIN`, the largest and smallest `int` values for your particular computer. Write a program to print out the values of `INT_MAX` and `INT_MIN`. The output should identify which value is `INT_MAX` and which value is `INT_MIN`. Be sure to include appropriate comments in your program, and use indentation as we do in the programs in this chapter.

2. Write a program that outputs three lines, labeled as follows:

   ```
   7 / 4 using integer division equals    <result>
   7 / 4 using floating-point division equals    <result>
   7 modulo 4 equals    <result>
   ```

   where <result> stands for the result computed by your program. Use named constants for 7 and 4 everywhere in your program (including the output statements) to make the program easy to modify. Be sure to include appropriate comments in your program, choose meaningful identifiers, and use indentation as we do in the programs in this chapter.

3. Write a C++ program that converts a Celsius temperature to its Fahrenheit equivalent. The formula is

$$Fahrenheit = \frac{9}{5}\ Celsius + 32$$

   Make the Celsius temperature a named constant so that its value can be changed easily. The program should print both the value of the Celsius temperature and its Fahrenheit equivalent, with appropriate identifying messages. Be sure to include appropriate comments in your program, choose meaningful identifiers, and use indentation as we do in the programs in this chapter.

4. Write a program to calculate the diameter, the circumference, and the area of a circle with a radius of 6.75. Assign the radius to a `float` variable, and then output the radius with an appropriate message. Declare a named constant `PI` with the value 3.14159. The program should output the diameter, the circumference, and the area, each on a separate line, with identifying labels. Print each value to five decimal places within a total fieldwidth of 10. Be sure to include appropriate comments in your program, choose meaningful identifiers, and use indentation as we do in the programs in this chapter.

5. You have bought a car, taking out a loan with an annual interest rate of 9%. You will make 36 monthly payments of $165.25 each. You want to keep track of the remaining balance you owe after each monthly payment. The formula for the remaining balance is

$$bal_k = pmt \left[\frac{1 - (1 + i)^{k - n}}{i} \right]$$

where

bal_k	=	balance remaining after the kth payment
k	=	payment number (1, 2, 3, ...)
pmt	=	amount of the monthly payment
i	=	interest rate per month (annual rate ÷ 12)
n	=	total number of payments to be made

Write a program to calculate and print the balance remaining after the first, second, and third monthly car payments. Before printing these three results, the program should output the values on which the calculations are based (monthly payment, interest rate, and total number of payments). Label all output with identifying messages, and print all money amounts to two decimal places. Be sure to include appropriate comments in your program, choose meaningful identifiers, and use indentation as we do in the programs in this chapter.

Case Study Follow-Up

1. What is the advantage of using named constants instead of literal constants in the Walk program?
2. Modify the Walk program to include a round-off factor so that the rounding of `miles` can be modified easily. Currently, the program uses a literal constant (10.0) in several places to round `miles` to the nearest tenth, requiring us to make multiple changes if we want a different round-off factor.
3. Should the round-off factor in Question 2 be a constant or a variable? Explain.
4. In the Walk program, a particular pattern of statements is repeated four times with small variations. Identify the repeating pattern. Next, circle those parts of the statements that vary with each repetition. Having done this, now modify the Walk program to work with a fifth distance measurement.

4

Program Input and the Software Design Process

GOALS

- To be able to construct input statements to read values into a program.
- To be able to determine the contents of variables assigned values by input statements.
- To be able to write appropriate prompting messages for interactive programs.
- To know when noninteractive input/output is appropriate and how it differs from interactive input/output.
- To be able to write programs that use data files for input and output.
- To understand the basic principles of object-oriented design.
- To be able to apply the functional decomposition methodology to solve a simple problem.
- To be able to take a functional decomposition and code it in C++, using self-documenting code.

A program needs data on which to operate. We have been writing all of the data values in the program itself, in literal and named constants. If this were the only way we could enter data, we would have to rewrite a program each time we wanted to apply it to a different set of values. In this chapter, we look at ways of entering data into a program while it is running.

Once we know how to input data, process the data, and output the results, we can begin to think about designing more complicated programs. We have talked about general problem-solving strategies and writing simple programs. For a simple problem, it's easy to choose a strategy, write the algorithm, and code the program. But as problems become more complex, we have to use a more organized approach. In the second part of this chapter, we look at two general methodologies for developing software: object-oriented design and functional decomposition.

Getting Data into Programs

One of the biggest advantages of computers is that a program can be used with many different sets of data. To do so, we must keep the data separate from the program until the program is executed. Then instructions in the program copy values from the data set into variables in the program. After storing these values into the variables, the program can perform calculations with them (see Figure 4-1).

FIGURE 4-1

Separating the Data from the Program

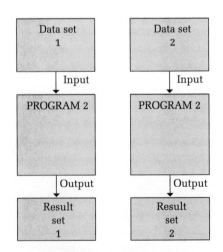

This program must be changed to work with different data values.

This program inputs its data from outside, so it can work with different data sets without being changed.

The process of placing values from an outside data set into variables in a program is called *input.* In widely used terminology, the computer is said to *read* outside data into the variables. The data for the program can come from an input device or from a file on an auxiliary storage device. We look at file input later in this chapter; here we consider the *standard input device,* the keyboard.

Input Streams and the Extraction Operator (>>)

The concept of a stream is fundamental to input and output in C++. As we stated in Chapter 3, you can think of an output stream as an endless sequence of characters going from your program to an output device. Likewise, think of an *input stream* as an endless sequence of characters coming into your program from an input device.

To use stream I/O, you must use the preprocessor directive

```
#include <iostream>
```

The header file iostream contains, among other things, the definitions of two data types: istream and ostream. These are data types representing input streams and output streams, respectively. The header file also contains declarations that look like this:

```
istream cin;
ostream cout;
```

The first declaration says that cin (pronounced "see-in") is a variable of type istream. The second says that cout (pronounced "see-out") is a variable of type ostream. Furthermore, cin is associated with the standard input device (the keyboard), and cout is associated with the standard output device (usually the display screen).

As you have already seen, you can output values to cout by using the insertion operator (<<), which is sometimes pronounced "put to":

```
cout << 3 * price;
```

In a similar fashion, you can input data from cin by using the *extraction operator* (>>), sometimes pronounced "get from":

```
cin >> cost;
```

When the computer executes this statement, it inputs the next number you type on the keyboard (425, for example) and stores it into the variable cost.

The extraction operator >> takes two operands. Its left-hand operand is a stream expression (in the simplest case, just the variable cin). Its right-hand operand is a variable into which we store the input data. For the time being, we assume the variable is of a simple type (`char`, `int`, `float`, and so forth). Later in the chapter we discuss the input of string data.

You can use the `>>` operator several times in a single input statement. Each occurrence extracts (inputs) the next data item from the input stream. For example, there is no difference between the statement

```
cin >> length >> width;
```

and the pair of statements

```
cin >> length;
cin >> width;
```

Using a sequence of extractions in one statement is a convenience for the programmer.

When you are new to C++, you may get the extraction operator (`>>`) and the insertion operator (`<<`) reversed. Here is an easy way to remember which one is which: Always begin the statement with either `cin` or `cout`, and use the operator that points in the direction in which the data is going. The statement

```
cout << someInt;
```

sends data from the variable `someInt` *to* the output stream. The statement

```
cin >> someInt;
```

sends data from the input stream *to* the variable `someInt`.

Here's the syntax template for an input statement:

InputStatement

cin >> Variable   **>>** Variable ... ;

Unlike the items specified in an output statement, which can be constants, variables, or complicated expressions, the items specified in an input statement can *only* be variable names. Why? Because an input statement indicates where input data values should be stored. Only variable names refer to memory locations where we can store values while a program is running.

When you enter input data at the keyboard, you must be sure that each data value is appropriate for the data type of the variable in the input statement.

Data Type of Variable in an >> Operation	Valid Input Data
char	A single printable character other than a blank
int	An int literal constant, optionally preceded by a sign
float	An int or float literal constant (possibly in scientific, E, notation), optionally preceded by a sign

Notice that when you input a number into a float variable, the input value doesn't have to have a decimal point. The integer value is automatically coerced to a float value. Any other mismatches, such as trying to input a float value into an int variable or a char value into a float variable, can lead to unexpected and sometimes serious results. Later in this chapter we discuss what might happen.

When looking for the next input value in the stream, the >> operator skips any leading *whitespace characters*. Whitespace characters are blanks and certain nonprintable characters such as the character that marks the end of a line. (We talk about this end-of-line character in the next section.) After skipping any whitespace characters, the >> operator proceeds to extract the desired data value from the input stream. If this data value is a char value, input stops as soon as a single character is input. If the data value is int or float, input of the number stops at the first character that is inappropriate for the data type, such as a whitespace character. Here are some examples, where i, j, and k are int variables, ch is a char variable, and x is a float variable:

Statement	Data	Contents After Input
1. cin >> i;	32	i = 32
2. cin >> i >> j;	4 60	i = 4, j = 60
3. cin >> i >> ch >> x;	25 A 16.9	i = 25, ch = 'A', x = 16.9
4. cin >> i >> ch >> x;	25	
	A	
	16.9	i = 25, ch = 'A', x = 16.9
5. cin >> i >> ch >> x;	25A16.9	i = 25, ch = 'A', x = 16.9
6. cin >> i >> j >> x;	12 8	i = 12, j = 8 (Computer waits for a third number)
7. cin >> i >> x;	46 32.4 15	i = 46, x = 32.4 (15 is held for later input)

Examples (1) and (2) are straightforward examples of integer input. Example (3) shows that you do not use quotes around character data values when they are input (quotes around character constants are needed in a program, though, to distinguish them from identifiers). Example (4) demonstrates how the process of skipping whitespace characters includes going on to the next line of input if necessary. Example (5) shows that the first character encountered that is inappropriate for a numeric data type ends the number. Input for the variable i stops at the input character A, after which the A is stored into ch, and then input for x stops at the end of the input line. Example (6) shows that if you are at the keyboard and haven't entered enough values to satisfy the input statement, the computer waits (and waits and waits. . .) for more data. Example (7) shows that if more values are entered than there are variables in the input statement, the extra values remain waiting in the input stream until they can be read by the next input statement. If there are extra values left when the program ends, the computer disregards them.

The Reading Marker and the Newline Character

To help explain stream input in more detail, we introduce the concept of the *reading marker*. The reading marker works like a bookmark, but instead of marking a place in a book, it keeps track of the point in the input stream where the computer should continue reading. The reading marker indicates the next character waiting to be read. The extraction operator >> leaves the reading marker on the character following the last piece of data that was input.

Each input line has an invisible end-of-line character (the *newline character*) that tells the computer where one line ends and the next begins. To find the next input value, the >> operator crosses line boundaries (newline characters) if it has to.

Where does the newline character come from? What is it? The answer to the first question is easy. When you are working at a keyboard, you generate a newline character yourself each time you hit the Return or Enter key. Your program also generates a newline character when it uses the endl manipulator in an output statement. The endl manipulator outputs a newline, telling the screen cursor to go to the next line. The answer to the second question varies from computer system to computer system. The newline character is a nonprintable control character that the system recognizes as meaning the end of a line, whether it's an input line or an output line.

In a C++ program, you can refer directly to the newline character by using the two symbols \n, a backslash and an n with no space between them. Although \n consists of two symbols, it refers to a single character—the newline character. Just as you can store the letter *A* into a char variable ch like this:

```
ch = 'A';
```

so you can store the newline character into a variable:

```
ch = '\n';
```

You also can put the newline character into a string, just as you can any printable character:

```
cout << "Hello\n";
```

This last statement has exactly the same effect as the statement

```
cout << "Hello" << endl;
```

But back to our discussion of input. Let's look at some examples using the reading marker and the newline character. In the following table, i is an int variable, ch is a char variable, and x is a float variable. The input statements produce the results shown. The part of the input stream printed in color is what has been extracted by input statements. The reading marker, denoted by the shaded block, indicates the next character waiting to be read. The \n denotes the newline character produced by striking the Return or Enter key.

Statements	Contents After Input	Marker Position in the Input Stream
1.		25 A 16.9\n
cin >> i;	i = 25	25 A 16.9\n
cin >> ch;	ch = 'A'	25 A 16.9\n
cin >> x;	x = 16.9	25 A 16.9 \n
2.		25\n
		A\n
		16.9\n
cin >> i;	i = 25	25 \n
		A\n
		16.9\n
cin >> ch;	ch = 'A'	25\n
		A \n
		16.9\n
cin >> x;	x = 16.9	25\n
		A\n
		16.9 \n

Statements	Contents After Input	Marker Position in the Input Stream
3.		25A16.9\n
cin >> i;	i = 25	25A16.9\n
cin >> ch;	ch = 'A'	25A16.9\n
cin >> x;	x = 16.9	25A16.9\n

Reading Character Data with the get Function

As we have discussed, the >> operator skips any leading whitespace characters (such as blanks and newline characters) while looking for the next data value in the input stream. Suppose that ch1 and ch2 are char variables and the program executes the statement

cin >> ch1 >> ch2;

If the input stream consists of

R 1

then the extraction operator stores 'R' into ch1, skips the blank, and stores '1' into ch2. (Note that the char value '1' is not the same as the int value 1. The two are stored completely differently in a computer's memory. The extraction operator interprets the same data in different ways, depending on the data type of the variable that's being filled.)

What if we had wanted to input *three* characters from the input line: the *R*, the blank, and the 1? With the extraction operator, it's not possible. Whitespace characters such as blanks are skipped over.

The istream data type provides a second way in which to read character data, in addition to the >> operator. You can use the get function, which inputs the very next character in the input stream without skipping any whitespace characters. A function call looks like this:

cin.get(someChar);

The get function is associated with the istream data type, and you must use dot notation to make a function call. (Recall that we used dot notation in Chapter 3 to invoke certain functions associated with the string type. Later in this chapter we explain the reason for dot notation.) To use the get function, you give the name of an istream variable (here, cin), then a dot (period), and then the function name and argument list. Notice that the call to get uses the syntax for calling a void function, not a value-returning function. The function call is a complete statement; it is not part of a larger expression.

The effect of the above function call is to input the next character waiting in the stream—even if it is a whitespace character like a blank—and store it into the variable `someChar`. The argument to the `get` function *must* be a variable, not a constant or arbitrary expression; we must tell the function where we want it to store the input character.

Using the `get` function, we now can input all three characters of the input line

```
R 1
```

We can use three consecutive calls to the `get` function:

```
cin.get(ch1);
cin.get(ch2);
cin.get(ch3);
```

or we can do it this way:

```
cin >> ch1;
cin.get(ch2);
cin >> ch3;
```

The first version is probably a bit clearer for someone to read and understand.

Here are some more examples of character input using both the `>>` operator and the `get` function. `ch1`, `ch2`, and `ch3` are all `char` variables. As before, \n denotes the newline character.

Statements	Contents After Input	Marker Position in the Input Stream
1.		A B\n
		CD\n
cin >> ch1;	ch1 = 'A'	A B\n
		CD\n
cin >> ch2;	ch2 = 'B'	A B\n
		CD\n
cin >> ch3;	ch3 = 'C'	A B\n
		CD\n
2.		A B\n
		CD\n
cin.get(ch1);	ch1 = 'A'	A B\n
		CD\n
cin.get(ch2);	ch2 = ' '	A B\n
		CD\n
cin.get(ch3);	ch3 = 'B'	A B\n
		CD\n

Statements	Contents After Input	Marker Position in the Input Stream
3.		A B\n CD\n
cin >> ch1;	ch1 = 'A'	A B\n CD\n
cin >> ch2;	ch2 = 'B'	A B\n CD\n
cin.get(ch3);	ch3 = '\n'	A B\n CD\n

*T*HEORETICAL FOUNDATIONS

More About Functions and Arguments

When your `main` function tells the computer to go off and follow the instructions in another function, `SomeFunc`, the `main` function is *calling* `SomeFunc`. In the call to `SomeFunc`, the arguments in the argument list are *passed* to the function. When `SomeFunc` finishes, the computer *returns* to the `main` function.

With some functions you have seen, like `sqrt` and `abs`, you can pass constants, variables, and arbitrary expressions to the function. The `get` function for reading character data, however, accepts only a variable as an argument. The `get` function stores a value into its argument when it returns, and only variables can have values stored into them while a program is running. Even though `get` is called as a void function—not a value-returning function—it *returns* or *passes back* a value through its argument list. The point to remember is that you can use arguments both to send data into a function and to get results back out.

Skipping Characters with the `ignore` Function

Most of us have a specialized tool lying in a kitchen drawer or in a toolbox. It gathers dust and cobwebs because we almost never use it. But when we suddenly need it, we're glad we have it. The `ignore` function associated with the `istream` type is like this specialized tool. You rarely have occasion to use `ignore`; but when you need it, you're glad it's available.

The `ignore` function is used to skip (read and discard) characters in the input stream. It is a function with two arguments, called like this:

```
cin.ignore(200, '\n');
```

The first argument is an `int` expression; the second, a `char` value. This particular function call tells the computer to skip the next 200 input characters *or* to skip characters until a newline character is read, whichever comes first.

Here are some examples that use a `char` variable `ch` and three `int` variables, `i`, `j`, and `k`:

Statements	Contents After Input	Marker Position in the Input Stream
1.		957 34 1235\n
		128 96\n
cin >> i >> j;	i = 957, j = 34	957 34█ 1235\n
		128 96\n
cin.ignore(100, '\n');		957 34 1235\n
		█128 96\n
cin >> k;	k = 128	957 34 1235\n
		128█96\n
2.		█A 22 B 16 C 19\n
cin >> ch;	ch = 'A'	A█22 B 16 C 19\n
cin.ignore(100, 'B');		A 22 B█16 C 19\n
cin >> i;	i = 16	A 22 B 16█C 19\n
3.		█ABCDEF\n
cin.ignore(2, '\n');		AB█CDEF\n
cin >> ch;	ch = 'C'	ABC█DEF\n

Example (1) shows the most common use of the `ignore` function, which is to skip the rest of the data on the current input line. Example (2) demonstrates the use of a character other than '\n' as the second argument. We skip over all input characters until a *B* has been found, then read the next input number into `i`. In both (1) and (2), we are focusing on the second argument to the `ignore` function, and we arbitrarily choose any large number, such as 100, for the first argument. In (3), we change our focus and concentrate on the first argument. Our intention is to skip the next two input characters on the current line.

Reading String Data

To input a character string into a `string` variable, we have two options. The first is to use the extraction operator (>>). When reading input characters into a `string` variable, the >> operator skips any leading whitespace characters such as blanks and newlines. It then reads successive characters into the variable, stopping at the first *trailing* whitespace character (which is not consumed, but remains as the first character waiting in the input stream). For example, assume we have the following code:

```
string firstName;
string lastName;

cin >> firstName >> lastName;
```

If the input stream initially looks like this (where □ denotes a blank):

□□Mary□Smith□□□18

then our input statement stores the four characters `Mary` into `firstName`, stores the five characters `Smith` into `lastName`, and leaves the input stream as

□□□18

Although the `>>` operator is widely used for string input, it has a potential drawback: it cannot be used to input a string that has blanks within it. (Remember that it stops reading as soon as it encounters a whitespace character.) This fact leads us to the second option for performing string input: the `getline` function. A call to this function looks like this:

```
getline(cin, myString);
```

The function call, which does not use dot notation, requires two arguments. The first is an input stream variable (here, `cin`) and the second is a `string` variable. The `getline` function does not skip leading whitespace characters and continues until it reaches the newline character '\n'. That is, `getline` reads and stores an entire input line, embedded blanks and all. Note that with `getline`, the newline character *is* consumed (but is not stored into the string variable). Given the code segment

```
string inputStr;
```

```
getline(cin, inputStr);
```

and the input line

□□Mary□Smith□□□18

the result of the call to `getline` is that all 17 characters on the input line (including blanks) are stored into `inputStr`, and the reading marker is positioned at the beginning of the next input line.

The following table summarizes the differences between the `>>` operator and the `getline` function when reading string data into `string` variables.

Statement	Skips Leading Whitespace?	Stops Reading When?
`cin >> inputStr;`	Yes	When a trailing whitespace character is encountered (which is *not* consumed)
`getline(cin, inputStr);`	No	When '\n' is encountered (which *is* consumed)

Interactive Input/Output

In Chapter 1, we defined an interactive program as one in which the user communicates directly with the computer. Many of the programs that we write are interactive. There is a certain "etiquette" involved in writing interactive programs that has to do with instructions for the user to follow.

To get data into an interactive program, we begin with *input prompts*, printed messages that explain what the user should enter. Without these messages, the user has no idea what data values to type. In many cases, a program also should print out all of the data values typed in so that the user can verify that they were entered correctly. Printing out the input values is called *echo printing*. Here's a program segment showing the proper use of prompts:

```
cout << "Enter the part number:" << endl;          // Prompt
cin >> partNumber;
cout << "Enter the quantity of this part ordered:"  // Prompt
    << endl;
cin >> quantity;
cout << "Enter the unit price for this part:"       // Prompt
    << endl;
cin >> unitPrice;
totalPrice = quantity * unitPrice;
cout << "Part " << partNumber                       // Echo print
    << ", quantity " << quantity
    << ", at $ " << setprecision(2) << unitPrice
    << " each" << endl;
cout << "totals $ " << totalPrice << endl;
```

And here's the output, with the user's input shown in color:

```
Enter the part number:
4671
Enter the quantity of this part ordered:
10
```

```
Enter the unit price for this part:
27.25
Part 4671, quantity 10, at $ 27.25 each
totals $ 272.50
```

The amount of information you should put into your prompts depends on who is going to be using a program. If you are writing a program for people who are not familiar with computers, your messages should be more detailed. For example, "Type a four-digit part number, then press the key marked Enter." If the program is going to be used frequently by the same people, you might shorten the prompts: "Enter PN" and "Enter Qty." If the program is for very experienced users, you can prompt for several values at once and have them type all of the values on one input line:

```
Enter PN, Qty, Unit Price:
4176 10 27.25
```

In programs that use large amounts of data, this method saves the user keystrokes and time. However, it also makes it easier for the user to enter values in the wrong order. In such situations, echo printing the data is especially important.

Whether a program should echo print its input or not also depends on how experienced the users are and on the task the program is to perform. If the users are experienced and the prompts are clear, as in the first example, then echo printing is probably not required. If the users are novices or multiple values can be input at once, echo printing should be used. If the program inputs a large quantity of data and the users are experienced, rather than echo print the data, it may be stored in a separate file that can be checked after all of the data is input. We discuss how to store data into a file later in this chapter.

Prompts are not the only way in which programs interact with users. It can be helpful to have a program print out some general instructions at the beginning ("Press Enter after typing each data value. Enter a negative number when done."). When data is not entered in the correct form, a message that indicates the problem should be printed. For users who haven't worked much with computers, it's important that these messages be informative and "friendly." The message

```
ILLEGAL DATA VALUES!!!!!!!
```

is likely to upset an inexperienced user. Moreover, it doesn't offer any constructive information. A much better message would be

```
That is not a valid part number.
Part numbers must be no more than four digits long.
Please reenter the number in its proper form:
```

In Chapter 5, we introduce the statements that allow us to test for erroneous data.

Noninteractive Input/Output

Although we tend to use examples of interactive I/O in this text, many programs are written using noninteractive I/O. A common example of noninteractive I/O on large computer systems is batch processing (see Chapter 1). Remember that in batch processing, the user and the computer do not interact while the program is running. This method is most effective when a program is going to input or output large amounts of data. An example of batch processing is a program that inputs a file containing semester grades for thousands of students and prints grade reports to be mailed out.

When a program must read in many data values, the usual practice is to prepare them ahead of time, storing them into a disk file. This allows the user to go back and make changes or corrections to the data as necessary before running the program. When a program is designed to print lots of data, the output can be sent directly to a high-speed printer or another disk file. After the program has been run, the user can examine the data at leisure. In the next section, we discuss input and output with disk files.

Programs designed for noninteractive I/O do not print prompting messages for input. It is a good idea, however, to echo print each data value that is read. Echo printing allows the person reading the output to verify that the input values were prepared correctly. Because noninteractive programs tend to print large amounts of data, their output often is in the form of a table—columns with descriptive headings.

Most C++ programs are written for interactive use. But the flexibility of the language allows you to write noninteractive programs as well. The biggest difference is in the input/output requirements. Noninteractive programs are generally more rigid about the organization and format of the input and output data.

File Input and Output

In everything we've done so far, we've assumed that the input to our programs comes from the keyboard and that the output from our programs goes to the screen. We look now at input/output to and from files.

Files

Earlier we defined a file as a named area in secondary storage that holds a collection of information (for example, the program code we have typed into the editor). The information in a file usually is stored on an auxiliary storage device, such as a disk. Our programs can read data from a file in the same way they read data from the keyboard, and they can write output to a disk file in the same way they write output to the screen.

Why would we want a program to read data from a file instead of the keyboard? If a program is going to read a large quantity of data, it is easier to enter the data into a file with an editor than to enter it while the program is running. With the editor, we can go back and correct mistakes. Also, we do not have to enter the data all at once; we can take a break and come back later. And if we want to rerun the program, having the data stored in a file allows us to do so without retyping the data.

Why would we want the output from a program to be written to a disk file? The contents of a file can be displayed on a screen or printed. This gives us the option of looking at the output over and over again without having to rerun the program. Also, the output stored in a file can be read into another program as input. For example, the Payroll program writes its output to a file named `payFile`. We can take `payFile` and read it into another program, perhaps one that prints out paychecks.

Using Files

If we want a program to use file I/O, we have to do four things:

1. Request the preprocessor to include the header file `fstream`.
2. Use declaration statements to declare the file streams we are going to use.
3. Prepare each file for reading or writing by using a function named `open`.
4. Specify the name of the file stream in each input or output statement.

Including the Header File `fstream`   Suppose we want the Walk program (p. 139) to read data from a file and to write its output to a file. The first thing we must do is use the preprocessor directive

```
#include <fstream>
```

Through the header file `fstream`, the C++ standard library defines two data types, `ifstream` and `ofstream` (standing for *input file stream* and *output file stream*). Consistent with the general idea of streams in C++, the `ifstream` data type represents a stream of characters coming from an input file, and `ofstream` represents a stream of characters going to an output file.

All of the `istream` operations you have learned about—the extraction operator (`>>`), the `get` function, and the `ignore` function—are also valid for the `ifstream` type. And all of the `ostream` operations, such as the insertion operator (`<<`) and the `endl`, `setw`, and `setprecision` manipulators, apply also to the `ofstream` type. To these basic operations, the `ifstream` and `ofstream` types add some more operations designed specifically for file I/O.

Declaring File Streams   In a program, you declare stream variables the same way that you declare any variable—you specify the data type and then the variable name:

```
int      someInt;
float    someFloat;
ifstream inFile;
ofstream outFile;
```

(You don't have to declare the stream variables `cin` and `cout`. The header file `iostream` already does this for you.)

For our Walk program, let's name the input and output file streams `inData` and `outData`. We declare them like this:

```
ifstream inData;      // Holds map distances in inches
ofstream outData;     // Holds walking distances in miles
```

Note that the `ifstream` type is for input files only, and the `ofstream` type is for output files only. With these data types, you cannot read from and write to the same file.

Opening Files   The third thing we have to do is prepare each file for reading or writing, an act called *opening a file*. Opening a file causes the computer's operating system to perform certain actions that allow us to proceed with file I/O.

In our example, we want to read from the file stream `inData` and write to the file stream `outData`. We open the relevant files by using these statements:

```
inData.open("walk.dat");
outData.open("results.dat");
```

Both of these statements are function calls (notice the telltale arguments—the mark of a function). In each function call, the argument is a literal string enclosed by quotes. The first statement is a call to a function named `open`, which is associated with the `ifstream` data type. The second is a call to another function (also named `open`) associated with the `ofstream` data type. As we have seen earlier, we use dot notation (as in inData.open) to call certain library functions that are tightly associated with data types.

Exactly what does an open function do? First, it associates a stream variable used in your program with a physical file on disk. Our first function call creates a connection between the stream variable inData and the actual disk file, named walk.dat. (Names of file streams must be identifiers; they are variables in your program. But some computer systems do not use this syntax for file names on disk. For example, many systems allow or even require a dot within a file name.) Similarly, the second function call associates the stream variable outData with the disk file results.dat. Associating a program's name for a file (outData) with the actual name for the file (results.dat) is much the same as associating a program's name for the standard output device (cout) with the actual device (the screen).

The next thing the open function does depends on whether the file is an input file or an output file. With an input file, the open function sets the file's reading marker to the first piece of data in the file. (Each input file has its own reading marker.)

With an output file, the open function checks to see whether the file already exists. If the file doesn't exist, open creates a new, empty file for you. If the file already exists, open erases the old contents of the file. Then the writing marker is set at the beginning of the empty file (see Figure 4-2). As output proceeds, each successive output operation advances the writing marker to add data to the end of the file.

FIGURE 4-2
The Effect of
Opening a File

FILE inData AFTER OPENING

FILE outData AFTER OPENING

inData

outData

Reading →
marker

Writing →
marker

Because the reason for opening files is to *prepare* the files for reading or writing, you must open the files before using any input or output statements that refer to the files. In a program, it's a good idea to open files right away to be sure that the files are prepared before the program attempts any file I/O.

⋮

```
int main()
{

    ⋮   } Declarations


    // Open the files

    inData.open("walk.dat");
    outData.open("results.dat");
      ⋮
}
```

Specifying File Streams in Input/Output Statements   There is just one more thing we have to do in order to use files. As we said earlier, all `istream` operations are also valid for the `ifstream` type, and all `ostream` operations are valid for the `ofstream` type. So, to read from or write to a file, all we need to do in our input and output statements is substitute the appropriate file stream variable for `cin` or `cout`. In our Walk program, we would use a statement like

```
inData >> distance1 >> distance2 >> distance3 >> distance4 >> scale;
```

to instruct the computer to read data from the file `inData` instead of from `cin`. Similarly, all of the output statements that write to the file `outData` would specify `outData`, not `cout`, as the destination:

```
outData << "Total mileage for the day is " << totMiles << " miles."
        << endl;
```

What is nice about C++ stream I/O is that we have a uniform syntax for performing I/O operations, regardless of whether we're working with the keyboard and screen, with files, or with other I/O devices.

An Example Program Using Files

The reworked Walk program is shown below. Now it reads its input from the file `inData` and writes its output to the file `outData`. Compare this program with the original version on page 139 and notice that the named constants have disappeared because the data is now input at execution time. Notice also that to set up the floating-point output format, the `fixed`, `showpoint`, and `setprecision` manipulators are applied to the `outData` stream variable, not to `cout`.

```cpp
//*******************************************************************
// Walk program
// This program computes the mileage (rounded to tenths of a mile)
// for each of four distances between points in a city, given
// the measurements on a map with a scale whose value is also
// input
//*******************************************************************
#include <iostream>
#include <iomanip>      // For setprecision()
#include <fstream>      // For file I/O

using namespace std;

int main()
{
    float     distance1;      // Measurement for first distance
    float     distance2;      // Measurement for second distance
    float     distance3;      // Measurement for third distance
    float     distance4;      // Measurement for fourth distance
    float     scale;          // Map scale (miles per inch)
    float     totMiles;       // Total of rounded mileages
    float     miles;          // An individual rounded mileage
    ifstream inData;          // Holds map distances in inches
    ofstream outData;         // Holds walking distances in miles

    outData << fixed << showpoint          // Set up floating-pt.
            << setprecision(1);            //    output format

    // Open the files

    inData.open("walk.dat");
    outData.open("results.dat");

    // Get data

    inData >> distance1 >> distance2 >> distance3 >> distance4
           >> scale;
```

```
// Initialize the total miles

totMiles = 0.0;

// Compute miles for each distance on the map

miles = float(int(distance1 * scale * 10.0 + 0.5)) / 10.0;
outData << "For a measurement of " << distance1
        << " the first distance is " << miles
        << " mile(s) long." << endl;
totMiles = totMiles + miles;

miles = float(int(distance2 * scale * 10.0 + 0.5)) / 10.0;
outData << "For a measurement of " << distance2
        << " the second distance is " << miles
        << " mile(s) long." << endl;
totMiles = totMiles + miles;

miles = float(int(distance3 * scale * 10.0 + 0.5)) / 10.0;
outData << "For a measurement of " << distance3
        << " the third distance is " << miles
        << " mile(s) long." << endl;
totMiles = totMiles + miles;

miles = float(int(distance4 * scale * 10.0 + 0.5)) / 10.0;
outData << "For a measurement of " << distance4
        << " the fourth distance is " << miles
        << " mile(s) long." << endl;
totMiles = totMiles + miles;

// Print the total miles

outData << endl;
outData << "Total mileage for the day is " << totMiles
        << " miles." << endl;
return 0;
}
```

Before running the program, you would use the editor to create and save a file walk.dat to serve as input. The contents of the file might look like this:

```
1.5 2.3 5.9 4.0 0.25
```

In writing the new Walk program, what happens if you mistakenly specify cout instead of outData in one of the output statements? Nothing disastrous; the output of that one statement merely goes to the screen instead of the output file. And what if, by mistake, you specify cin instead of inData in the input statement? The consequences are not as pleasant. When you run the program, the computer will appear to go dead (to *hang*). Here's the reason: Execution reaches the input statement and the computer waits for you to enter the data from the keyboard. But you don't know that the computer is waiting. There's no message on the screen prompting you for input, and you are assuming (wrongly) that the program is getting its input from a data file. So the computer waits, and you wait, and the computer waits, and you wait. Every programmer at one time or another has had the experience of thinking the computer has hung, when, in fact, it is working just fine, silently waiting for keyboard input.

Run-Time Input of File Names

Until now, our examples of opening a file for input have included code similar to the following:

```
ifstream inFile;

inFile.open("datafile.dat");
    ⋮
```

The open function associated with the ifstream data type requires an argument that specifies the name of the actual data file on disk. By using a literal string, as in the example above, the file name is fixed at compile time. Therefore, the program works only for this one particular disk file.

We often want to make a program more flexible by allowing the file name to be determined at *run time*. A common technique is to prompt the user for the name of the file, read the user's response into a variable, and pass the variable as an argument to the open function. In principle, the following code should accomplish what we want. Unfortunately, the compiler does not allow it.

```
ifstream inFile;
string    fileName;

cout << "Enter the input file name: ";
cin >> fileName;
inFile.open(fileName);              // Compile-time error
```

The problem is that the open function does not expect an argument of type string. Instead, it expects a *C string*. A C string (so named because it originated in the C language, the forerunner of C++) is a limited form of string whose properties we discuss much later in the book. A literal string, such as "datafile.dat", happens to be a C string and thus is acceptable as an argument to the open function.

To make the above code work correctly, we need to convert a `string` variable to a C string. The `string` data type provides a value-returning function named `c_str` that is applied to a `string` variable as follows:

```
fileName.c_str()
```

This function returns the C string that is equivalent to the one contained in the `fileName` variable. (The original string contained in `fileName` is not changed by the function call.) The primary purpose of the `c_str` function is to allow programmers to call library functions that expect C strings, not `string` strings, as arguments.

Using the `c_str` function, we can code the run-time input of a file name as follows:

```
ifstream inFile;
string    fileName;

cout << "Enter the input file name: ";
cin >> fileName;
inFile.open(fileName.c_str());
```

Input Failure

When a program inputs data from the keyboard or an input file, things can go wrong. Let's suppose that we're executing a program. It prompts us to enter an integer value, but we absentmindedly type some letters of the alphabet. The input operation fails because of the invalid data. In C++ terminology, the `cin` stream has entered the *fail state*. Once a stream has entered the fail state, any further I/O operations using that stream are considered to be null operations—that is, they have no effect at all. Unfortunately for us, *the computer does not halt the program or give any error message.* The computer just continues executing the program, silently ignoring each additional attempt to use that stream.

Invalid data is the most common reason for input failure. When your program inputs an `int` value, it is expecting to find only digits in the input stream, possibly preceded by a plus or minus sign. If there is a decimal point somewhere within the digits, does the input operation fail? Not necessarily; it depends on where the reading marker is. Let's look at an example.

Assume that a program has `int` variables `i`, `j`, and `k`, whose contents are currently 10, 20, and 30, respectively. The program now executes the following two statements:

```
cin >> i >> j >> k;
cout << "i: " << i << "  j: " << j << "  k: " << k;
```

If we type these characters for the input data:

```
1234.56 7 89
```

then the program produces this output:

```
i: 1234  j: 20  k: 30
```

Let's see why.

Remember that when reading int or float data, the extraction operator >> stops reading at the first character that is inappropriate for the data type (whitespace or otherwise). In our example, the input operation for i succeeds. The computer extracts the first four characters from the input stream and stores the integer value 1234 into i. The reading marker is now on the decimal point:

```
1234█56 7 89
```

The next input operation (for j) fails; an int value cannot begin with a decimal point. The cin stream is now in the fail state, and the current value of j (20) remains unchanged. The third input operation (for k) is ignored, as are all the rest of the statements in our program that read from cin.

Another way to make a stream enter the fail state is to try to open an input file that doesn't exist. Suppose that you have a data file on your disk named myfile.dat. In your program you have the following statements:

```
ifstream inFile;

inFile.open("myfil.dat");
inFile >> i >> j >> k;
```

In the call to the open function, you misspelled the name of your disk file. At run time, the attempt to open the file fails, so the stream inFile enters the fail state. The next three input operations (for i, j, and k) are null operations. Without issuing any error message, the program proceeds to use the (unknown) contents of i, j, and k in calculations. The results of these calculations are certain to be puzzling.

The point of this discussion is not to make you nervous about I/O but to make you aware. The Testing and Debugging section at the end of this chapter offers suggestions for avoiding input failure, and Chapters 5 and 6 introduce program statements that let you test the state of a stream.

Software Design Methodologies

Over the last two chapters and the first part of this one, we have introduced elements of the C++ language that let us input data, perform calculations, and output results. The programs we wrote were short and straightforward because the problems to be solved were simple. We are ready to write programs for more complicated problems, but first we need to step back and look at the overall process of programming.

As you learned in Chapter 1, the programming process consists of a problem-solving phase and an implementation phase. The problem-solving phase includes *analysis* (analyzing and understanding the problem to be solved) and *design* (designing a solution to the problem). Given a complex problem—one that results in a 10,000-line program, for example—it's simply not reasonable to skip the design process and go directly to writing C++ code. What we need is a systematic way of designing a solution to a problem, no matter how complicated the problem is.

In the remainder of this chapter, we describe two important methodologies for designing solutions to more complex problems: *functional decomposition* and *object-oriented design*. These methodologies help you create solutions that can be easily implemented as C++ programs. The resulting programs are readable, understandable, and easy to debug and modify.

One software design methodology that is in widespread use is known as **object-oriented design** (**OOD**). C++ evolved from the C language primarily to facilitate the use of the OOD methodology. In the next two sections, we present the essential concepts of OOD; we expand our treatment of the approach later in the book. OOD is often used in conjunction with the other methodology that we discuss in this chapter, **functional decomposition.**

Object-oriented design   A technique for developing software in which the solution is expressed in terms of objects—self-contained entities composed of data and operations on that data.

Functional decomposition   A technique for developing software in which the problem is divided into more easily handled subproblems, the solutions of which create a solution to the overall problem.

OOD focuses on entities (*objects*) consisting of data and operations on the data. In OOD, we solve a problem by identifying the components that make up a solution and identifying how those components interact with each other through operations on the data that they contain. The result is a design for a set of objects that can be assembled to form a solution to a problem. In contrast, functional decomposition views the solution to a problem as a task to be accomplished. It focuses on the sequence of operations that are required to complete the task. When the problem requires a sequence of steps that is long or complex, we divide it into subproblems that are easier to solve.

The choice of which methodology we use depends on the problem at hand. For example, a large problem might involve several sequential phases of processing, such as gathering data and verifying its correctness with noninteractive processing, analyzing the data interactively, and printing reports noninteractively at the conclusion of the analysis. This process has a natural functional decomposition. Each of the phases, however, may best be solved by a set of objects that represent the data and the operations that can be applied to it. Some of the individual operations may be sufficiently complex that they require further decomposition, either into a sequence of operations or into another set of objects.

If you look at a problem and see that it is natural to think about it in terms of a collection of component parts, then you should use OOD to solve it. For example, a banking problem may require a `checkingAccount` object with associated operations `OpenAccount`, `WriteCheck`, `MakeDeposit`, and `IsOverdrawn`. The `checkingAccount` object consists of not only data (the account number and current balance, for example) but also these operations, all bound together into one unit.

On the other hand, if you find that it is natural to think of the solution to the problem as a series of steps, then you should use functional decomposition. For example, when computing some statistical measures on a large set of real numbers, it is natural to decompose the problem into a sequence of steps that read a value, perform calculations, and then repeat the sequence. The C++ language and the standard library supply all of the operations that we need, and we simply write a sequence of those operations to solve the problem.

What Are Objects?

Let's take a closer look at what objects are and how they work before we examine OOD further. We said earlier that an object is a collection of data together with associated operations. Several programming languages, called *object-oriented programming languages,* have been created specifically to support OOD. Examples are C++, Java, Smalltalk, CLOS, Eiffel, and Object-Pascal. In these languages, a *class* is a programmer-defined data type from which objects are created. Although we did not say it at the time, we have been using classes and objects to perform input and output in C++. `cin` is an object of a data type (class) named `istream`, and `cout` is an object of a class `ostream`. As we explained earlier, the header file `iostream` defines the classes `istream` and `ostream` and also declares `cin` and `cout` to be objects of those classes:

```
istream cin;
ostream cout;
```

Similarly, the header file `fstream` defines classes `ifstream` and `ofstream`, from which you can declare your own input file stream and output file stream objects.

Another example you have seen already is `string`—a programmer-defined class from which you create objects by using declarations such as

```
string lastName;
```

In Figure 4-3, we picture the `cin` and `lastName` objects as entities that have a private part and a public part. The private part includes data and functions that the user cannot access and doesn't need to know about in order to use the object. The public part, shown as ovals in the side of the object, represents the object's *interface*. The interface consists of operations that are available to programmers wishing to use the object. In C++, public operations are written as functions and are known as *member functions*. Except for operations using symbols such as << and >>, a member function is invoked by giving the name of the class object, then a dot, and then the function name and argument list:

```
cin.ignore(100, '\n');
cin.get(someChar);
cin >> someInt;
len = lastName.length();
pos = lastName.find('A');
```

Object-Oriented Design

The first step in OOD is to identify the major objects in the problem, together with their associated operations. The final problem solution is ultimately expressed in terms of these objects and operations.

OOD leads to programs that are collections of objects. Each object is responsible for one part of the entire solution, and the objects communicate by accessing each other's member functions. There are many libraries of prewritten classes, including the C++ standard library, public libraries (called *freeware* or *shareware*), libraries that are sold commercially, and libraries that are developed by companies for their own use. In many cases, it is possible to browse through a library, choose classes you need for a problem, and assemble them to form a substantial portion of your program. Putting existing pieces together in this fashion is an excellent example of the building-block approach we discussed in Chapter 1.

FIGURE 4-3

Objects and Their
Operations

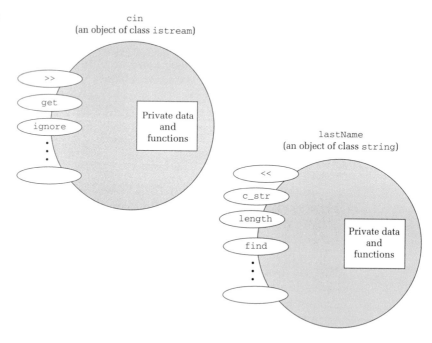

When there isn't a suitable class available in a library, it is necessary to define a new class. We see how this is done in Chapter 11. The design of a new class begins with the specification of its interface. We must decide what operations are needed on the outside of the class to make its objects useful. Once the interface is defined, we can design the implementation of the class, including all of its private members.

One of the goals in designing an interface is to make it flexible so the new class can be used in unforeseen circumstances. For example, we may provide a member function that converts the value of an object into a string, even though we don't need this capability in our program. When the time comes to debug the program, it may be very useful to display values of this type as strings.

Useful features are often absent from an interface, sometimes due to lack of foresight and sometimes for the purpose of simplifying the design. It is quite common to discover a class in a library that is almost right for your purpose but is missing some key feature. OOD addresses this situation with a concept called *inheritance,* which allows you to adapt an existing class to meet your particular needs. You can use inheritance to add features to a class (or restrict the use of existing features) without having to inspect and modify its source code. Inheritance is considered such an integral part of object-oriented programming that a separate term, *object-based programming,* is used to describe programming with objects but not inheritance.

In Chapter 14, we see how to define classes that inherit members from existing classes. Together, OOD, class libraries, and inheritance can dramatically reduce the time and effort required to design, implement, and maintain large software systems.

To summarize the OOD process: We identify the major components of a problem solution and how they interact. We then look in the available libraries for classes that correspond to the components. When we find a class that is almost right, we can use inheritance to adapt it. When we can't find a class that corresponds to a component, we must design a new class. Our design specifies the interface for the class, and we then implement the interface with public and private members as necessary. OOD isn't always used in isolation. Functional decomposition may be used in designing member functions within a class or in coordinating the interactions of objects.

In this section, we have presented only an introduction to OOD. A more complete discussion requires knowledge of topics that we explore in Chapters 5 through 10: flow of control, programmer-written functions, and more about data types. In Chapters 11 through 13, we learn how to write our own classes, and we return to OOD in Chapter 14. Until then, our programs are relatively small, so we use object-based programming and functional decomposition to arrive at our problem solutions.

Functional Decomposition

The second design technique we use is functional decomposition (it's also called *structured design*, *top-down design*, *stepwise refinement*, and *modular programming*). In functional decomposition, we work from the abstract (a list of the major steps in our solution) to the particular (algorithmic steps that can be translated directly into C++ code). You can also think of this as working from a high-level solution, leaving the details of implementation unspecified, down to a fully detailed solution.

The easiest way to solve a problem is to give it to someone else and say, "Solve this problem." This is the most abstract level of a problem solution: a single-statement solution that encompasses the entire problem without specifying any of the details of implementation. It's at this point that we programmers are called in. Our job is to turn the abstract solution into a concrete solution, a program.

If the solution clearly involves a series of major steps, we break it down (decompose it) into pieces. In the process, we move to a lower level of abstraction—that is, some of the implementation details (but not too many) are now specified. Each of the major steps becomes an independent subproblem that we can work on separately. In a very large project, one person (the *chief architect* or *team leader*) formulates the subproblems and then gives them to other members of the programming team, saying, "Solve this problem." In the case of a small project, we give the subproblems to ourselves. Then we choose one subproblem at a time to solve. We may break the chosen subproblem into another series of steps that, in turn, become smaller subproblems. Or we may identify components that are naturally represented as objects. The process continues until each subproblem cannot be divided further or has an obvious solution.

Why do we work this way? Why not simply write out all of the details? Because it is much easier to focus on one problem at a time. For example, suppose you are working on part of a program to output certain values and discover that you need a complex formula to calculate an appropriate fieldwidth for printing one of the values. Calculating fieldwidths is not the purpose of this part of the program. If you shift your focus to the calculation, you are likely to forget some detail of the overall output process. What you do is write down an abstract step—"Calculate the fieldwidth required"—and go on with the problem at hand. Once you've written the major steps, you can go back to solving the step that does the calculation.

By subdividing the problem, you create a hierarchical structure called a *tree structure*. Each level of the tree is a complete solution to the problem that is less abstract (more detailed) than the level above it. Figure 4-4 shows a generic solution tree for a problem. Steps that are shaded have enough implementation details to be translated directly into C++ statements. These are **concrete steps.** Those that are not shaded are **abstract steps;** they reappear as subproblems in the next level down. Each box in the figure represents a **module.** Modules are the basic building blocks in a functional decomposition. The diagram in Figure 4-4 is also called a *module structure chart.*

Concrete step   A step for which the implementation details are fully specified.

Abstract step   A step for which some implementation details remain unspecified.

Module   A self-contained collection of steps that solves a problem or subproblem; can contain both concrete and abstract steps.

Like OOD, functional decomposition uses the divide-and-conquer approach to problem solving. Both techniques break up large problems into smaller units that are easier to handle. The difference is that in OOD the units are objects, whereas the units in functional decomposition are modules representing algorithms.

Modules

A module begins life as an abstract step in the next-higher level of the solution tree. It is completed when it solves a given subproblem—that is, when

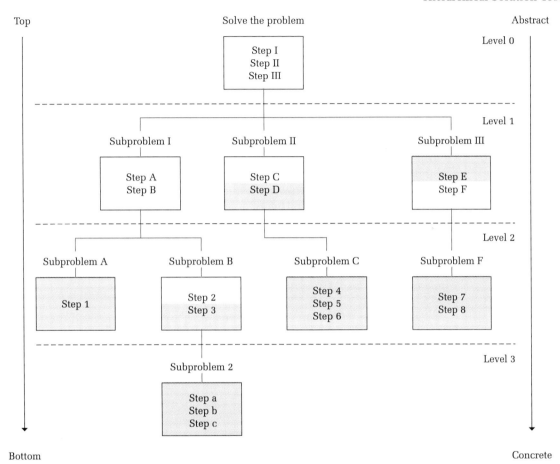

FIGURE 4-4
Hierarchical Solution Tree

it specifies a series of steps that does the same thing as the higher-level abstract step. At this stage, a module is **functionally equivalent** to the abstract step. (Don't confuse our use of *function* with C++ functions. Here we use the term to refer to the specific role that the module or step plays in an algorithmic solution.)

Functional equivalence A property of a module that performs exactly the same operation as the abstract step it defines. A pair of modules are also functionally equivalent to each other when they perform exactly the same operation.

In a properly written module, the only steps that directly address the given subproblem are concrete steps; abstract steps are used for significant new subproblems. This is called **functional cohesion.**

Functional cohesion   A property of a module in which all concrete steps are directed toward solving just one problem, and any significant subproblems are written as abstract steps.

The idea behind functional cohesion is that each module should do just one thing and do it well. Functional cohesion is not a well-defined property; there is no quantitative measure of cohesion. It is a product of the human need to organize things into neat chunks that are easy to understand and remember. Knowing which details to make concrete and which to leave abstract is a matter of experience, circumstance, and personal style. For example, you might decide to include a fieldwidth calculation in a printing module if there isn't so much detail in the rest of the module that it becomes confusing. On the other hand, if the calculation is performed several times, it makes sense to write it as a separate module and just refer to it each time you need it.

Writing Cohesive Modules   Here's one approach to writing modules that are cohesive:

1. Think about how you would solve the subproblem by hand.
2. Begin writing down the major steps.
3. If a step is simple enough that you can see how to implement it directly in C++, it is at the concrete level; it doesn't need any further refinement.
4. If you have to think about implementing a step as a series of smaller steps or as several C++ statements, it is still at an abstract level.
5. If you are trying to write a series of steps and start to feel overwhelmed by details, you probably are bypassing one or more levels of abstraction. Stand back and look for pieces that you can write as more abstract steps.

We could call this the "procrastinator's technique." If a step is cumbersome or difficult, put it off to a lower level; don't think about it today, think about it tomorrow. Of course, tomorrow does come, but the whole process can be applied again to the subproblem. A trouble spot often seems much simpler when you can focus on it. And eventually the whole problem is broken up into manageable units.

As you work your way down the solution tree, you make a series of design decisions. If a decision proves awkward or wrong (and many times it does!), you can backtrack (go back up the tree to a higher-level module) and try something else. You don't have to scrap your whole design—only the small part you are working on. There may be many intermediate steps and trial solutions before you reach a final design.

Pseudocode You'll find it easier to implement a design if you write the steps in pseudocode. *Pseudocode* is a mixture of English statements and C++-like control structures that can be translated easily into C++. (We've been using pseudocode in the algorithms in the Problem-Solving Case Studies.) When a concrete step is written in pseudocode, it should be possible to rewrite it directly as a C++ statement in a program.

Implementing the Design

The product of functional decomposition is a hierarchical solution to a problem with multiple levels of abstraction. Figure 4-5 shows a functional decomposition for the Walk program of Chapter 3. This kind of solution forms the basis for the implementation phase of programming.

How do we translate a functional decomposition into a C++ program? If you look closely at Figure 4-5, you can see that the concrete steps (those that are shaded) can be assembled into a complete algorithm for solving the problem. The order in which they are assembled is determined by their position in the tree. We start at the top of the tree, at level 0, with the first step, "Initialize the total miles." Because it is abstract, we must go to the next level, level 1. There we find a single concrete step that corresponds to this step; this step becomes the first part of our algorithm. Because the conversion process is now concrete, we can go back to level 0 and go on to the next step, computing the miles for each distance. We find that this step is abstract, but when we look at level 1, we see that it is broken into a series of abstract steps that are further expanded at level 2. Going through each of the abstract steps at level 1, we incorporate the corresponding concrete steps from level 2 into our algorithm. The last step at level 0 is abstract, so level 1 contains the corresponding concrete steps. Here's the resulting algorithm:

```
DISTANCE1 = 1.5
DISTANCE2 = 2.3
DISTANCE3 = 5.9
DISTANCE4 = 4.0
SCALE = 0.25
Set totMiles = 0.0
Set miles = float(int(DISTANCE1 * SCALE * 10.0 + 0.5)) / 10.0
Print DISTANCE1, miles
Add miles to totMiles
Set miles = float(int(DISTANCE2 * SCALE * 10.0 + 0.5)) / 10.0
Print DISTANCE2, miles
Add miles to totMiles
```

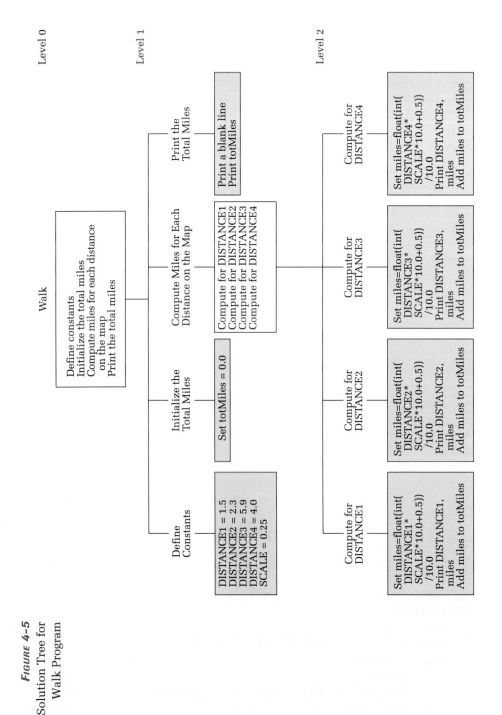

Figure 4-5
Solution Tree for Walk Program

Set miles = float(int(DISTANCE3 * SCALE * 10.0 + 0.5)) / 10.0
Print DISTANCE3, miles
Add miles to totMiles
Set miles = float(int(DISTANCE4 * SCALE * 10.0 + 0.5)) / 10.0
Print DISTANCE4, miles
Add miles to totMiles
Print a blank line
Print totMiles

From this algorithm we can construct a table of the constants and variables required, and then write the declarations and executable statements of the program.

In practice, you write your design not as a tree diagram but as a series of modules grouped by levels of abstraction, as we've done below.

Main Module   Level 0

```
Define constants
Initialize the total miles
Compute miles for each distance on the map
Print the total miles
```

Define Constants   Level 1

```
DISTANCE1 = 1.5
DISTANCE2 = 2.3
DISTANCE3 = 5.9
DISTANCE4 = 4.0
SCALE = 0.25
```

Initialize the Total Miles

```
Set totMiles = 0.0
```

Compute Miles for Each Distance on the Map

Compute for DISTANCE1
Compute for DISTANCE2
Compute for DISTANCE3
Compute for DISTANCE4

Print the Total Miles

Print a blank line
Print totMiles

Compute for DISTANCE1   Level 2

Set miles = float(int(DISTANCE1 * SCALE * 10.0 + 0.5)) / 10.0
Print DISTANCE1, miles
Add miles to totMiles

Compute for DISTANCE2

Set miles = float(int(DISTANCE2 * SCALE * 10.0 + 0.5)) / 10.0
Print DISTANCE2, miles
Add miles to totMiles

Compute for DISTANCE3

Set miles = float(int(DISTANCE3 * SCALE * 10.0 + 0.5)) / 10.0
Print DISTANCE3, miles
Add miles to totMiles

Compute for DISTANCE4

```
Set miles = float(int(DISTANCE4 * SCALE * 10.0 + 0.5)) / 10.0
Print DISTANCE4, miles
Add miles to totMiles
```

If you look at the C++ program for Walk, you can see that it closely resembles this solution. You can also see that the names of the modules have been paraphrased as comments in the code.

The type of implementation that we've introduced here is called *flat* or *inline implementation*. We are flattening the two-dimensional, hierarchical structure of the solution by writing all of the steps as one long sequence. This kind of implementation is adequate when a solution is short and has only a few levels of abstraction. The programs it produces are clear and easy to understand, assuming appropriate comments and good style.

Longer programs, with more levels of abstraction, are difficult to work with as flat implementations. In Chapter 7, you'll see that it is preferable to implement a hierarchical solution by using a *hierarchical implementation*. There we implement many of the modules by writing them as separate C++ functions, and the abstract steps in the design are replaced with calls to those functions.

One of the advantages of implementing modules as functions is that they can be called from different places in a program. For example, if a problem requires that the volume of a cylinder be computed in several places, we could write a single function to perform the calculation and simply call it in each place. This gives us a *semihierarchical implementation*. The implementation does not preserve a pure hierarchy because abstract steps at various levels of the solution tree share one implementation of a module (see Figure 4-6). A shared module actually falls outside the hierarchy because it doesn't really belong at any one level.

Another advantage of implementing modules as functions is that you can pick them up and use them in other programs. Over time, you will build a library of your own functions to complement those that are supplied by the C++ standard library.

We postpone a detailed discussion of hierarchical implementations until Chapter 7. For now, our programs remain short enough for flat implementations to suffice. Chapters 5 and 6 examine topics such as flow of control, preconditions and postconditions, interface design, side effects, and others you'll need in order to develop hierarchical implementations.

From now on, we use the following outline for the functional decompositions in our case studies, and we recommend that you adopt a similar outline in solving your own programming problems:

Problem statement
Input description
Output description
Discussion
Assumptions (if any)
Main module
Remaining modules by levels
Module structure chart

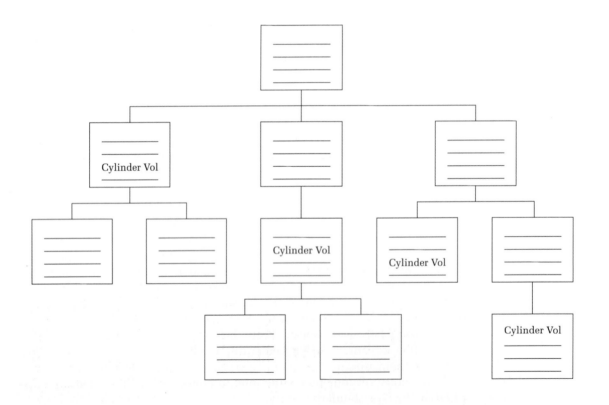

Cylinder Vol

Set volume = $\pi r^2 h$

FIGURE 4-6
A Semihierarchical Module Structure Chart with a Shared Module

In some of our case studies, the outline is reorganized, with the input and output descriptions following the discussion. In later chapters, we also expand the outline with additional sections. Don't think of this outline as a rigid prescription—it is more like a list of things to do. We want to be sure to do everything on the list, but the individual circumstances of each problem guide the order in which we do them.

A Perspective on Design

We have looked at two design methodologies, object-oriented design and functional decomposition. Until we learn about additional C++ language features that support OOD, we use functional decomposition (and object-based programming) in the next several chapters to come up with our problem solutions.

An important perspective to keep in mind is that functional decomposition and OOD are not separate, disjoint techniques. OOD decomposes a problem into objects. Objects not only contain data but also have associated operations. The operations on objects require algorithms. Sometimes the algorithms are complicated and must be decomposed into subalgorithms by using functional decomposition. Experienced programmers are familiar with both methodologies and know when to use one or the other, or a combination of the two.

Remember that the problem-solving phase of the programming process takes time. If you spend the bulk of your time analyzing and designing a solution, then coding and implementing the program take relatively little time.

SOFTWARE ENGINEERING TIP

Documentation

As you create your functional decomposition or object-oriented design, you are developing documentation for your program. *Documentation* includes the written problem specifications, design, development history, and actual code of a program.

Good documentation helps other programmers read and understand a program and is invaluable when software is being debugged and modified (maintained). If you haven't looked at your program for six months and need to change it, you'll be happy that you documented it well. Of course, if someone else has to use and modify your program, documentation is indispensable.

Documentation is both external and internal to the program. External documentation includes the specifications, the development history, and the design documents. Internal documentation includes the program format and **self-documenting code**—

meaningful identifiers and comments. You can use the pseudocode from the design process as comments in your programs.

This kind of documentation may be sufficient for someone reading or maintaining your programs. However, if a program is going to be used by people who are not programmers, you must provide a user's manual as well.

Be sure to keep documentation up-to-date. Indicate any changes you make in a program in all of the pertinent documentation. Use self-documenting code to make your programs more readable.

Self-documenting code   Program code containing meaningful identifiers as well as judiciously used clarifying comments.

Now let's look at a case study that demonstrates functional decomposition.

PROBLEM-SOLVING CASE STUDY

Stretching a Canvas

Problem: You are taking an art class in which you are learning to make your own painting canvas by stretching the cloth over a wooden frame and stapling it to the back of the frame. For a given size of painting, you must determine how much wood to buy for the frame, how large a piece of canvas to purchase, and the cost of the materials.

Input: Four floating-point numbers: the length and width of the painting, the cost per inch of the wood, and the cost per square foot of the canvas.

Output: Prompting messages, the input data (echo print), the length of wood to buy, the dimensions of the canvas, the cost of the wood, the cost of the canvas, and the total cost of the materials.

Discussion: The length of the wood is twice the sum of the length and width of the painting. The cost of the wood is simply its length times its cost per inch.

According to the art instructor, the dimensions of the canvas are the length and width of the painting, each with 5 inches added (for the part that wraps around to the back of the frame). The area of the canvas in square inches is its length times its width. However, we are given the cost for a square foot of the canvas. Thus, we must divide the area of the canvas by the number of square inches in a square foot (144) before multiplying by the cost.

Assumptions: The input values are positive (checking for erroneous data is not done).

Main Module   **Level 0**

Get length and width
Get wood cost
Get canvas cost
Compute dimensions and costs
Print dimensions and costs

Get Length and Width   **Level 1**

Print "Enter length and width of painting:"
Read length, width

Get Wood Cost

Print "Enter cost per inch of the framing wood in dollars:"
Read woodCost

Get Canvas Cost

Print "Enter cost per square foot of canvas in dollars:"
Read canvasCost

Compute Dimensions and Costs

Set lengthOfWood = (length + width) * 2
Set canvasWidth = width + 5
Set canvasLength = length + 5
Set canvasAreaInches = canvasWidth * canvasLength
Set canvasAreaFeet = canvasAreaInches / 144.0
Set totWoodCost = lengthOfWood * woodCost
Set totCanvasCost = canvasAreaFeet * canvasCost
Set totCost = totWoodCost + totCanvasCost

Print Dimensions and Costs

Print "For a painting", length, "in. long and", width, "in. wide,"
Print "you need to buy", lengthOfWood, "in. of wood, and"
Print "the canvas must be", canvasLength, "in. long and",
                    canvasWidth, "in. wide."

Print "Given a wood cost of $", woodCost, "per in."
Print "and a canvas cost of $", canvasCost, "per sq. ft.,"
Print "the wood will cost $", totWoodCost, ','
Print "the canvas will cost $", totCanvasCost, ','
Print "and the total cost of materials will be $", totCost, '.'

PROBLEM-SOLVING CASE STUDY cont'd.

Module Structure Chart:

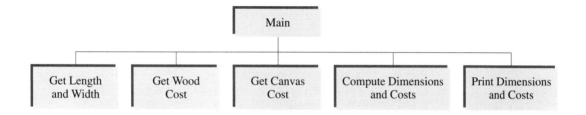

Variables

Name	Data Type	Description
length	float	Length of painting in inches
width	float	Width of painting in inches
woodCost	float	Cost of wood per inch in dollars
canvasCost	float	Cost of canvas per square foot
lengthOfWood	float	Amount of wood to buy
canvasWidth	float	Width of canvas to buy
canvasLength	float	Length of canvas to buy
canvasAreaInches	float	Area of canvas in square inches
canvasAreaFeet	float	Area of canvas in square feet
totCanvasCost	float	Total cost of canvas being bought
totWoodCost	float	Total cost of wood being bought
totCost	float	Total cost of materials

Constants

Name	Value	Description
SQ_IN_PER_SQ_FT	144.0	Number of square inches in one square foot

Here is the complete program. Notice how we've used the module names as comments to help distinguish the modules from one another in our flat implementation.

<u>*PROBLEM-SOLVING CASE STUDY cont'd.*</u>

(The following program is written in ISO/ANSI standard C++. If you are working with pre–standard C++, see the alternate version of the program in the PRE_STD directory of the program disk, available at the publisher's Web site, www.jbpub.com/disks.)

```cpp
//*****************************************************************
// Canvas program
// This program computes the dimensions and costs of materials
// to build a painting canvas of given dimensions. The user is
// asked to enter the length and width of the painting and the
// costs of the wood (per inch) and canvas (per square foot)
//*****************************************************************
#include <iostream>
#include <iomanip>     // For setprecision()

using namespace std;

const float SQ_IN_PER_SQ_FT = 144.0;     // Square inches per
                                         //    square foot
int main()
{
    float length;            // Length of painting in inches
    float width;             // Width of painting in inches
    float woodCost;          // Cost of wood per inch in dollars
    float canvasCost;        // Cost of canvas per square foot
    float lengthOfWood;      // Amount of wood to buy
    float canvasWidth;       // Width of canvas to buy
    float canvasLength;      // Length of canvas to buy
    float canvasAreaInches;  // Area of canvas in square inches
    float canvasAreaFeet;    // Area of canvas in square feet
    float totCanvasCost;     // Total cost of canvas being bought
    float totWoodCost;       // Total cost of wood being bought
    float totCost;           // Total cost of materials

    cout << fixed << showpoint;               // Set up floating-pt.
                                              //    output format

    // Get length and width

    cout << "Enter length and width of painting:" << endl;
    cin >> length >> width;

    // Get wood cost

    cout << "Enter cost per inch of the framing wood in dollars:"
         << endl;
    cin >> woodCost;
```

PROBLEM-SOLVING CASE STUDY cont'd.

```
// Get canvas cost

cout << "Enter cost per square foot of canvas in dollars:"
     << endl;
cin >> canvasCost;

// Compute dimensions and costs

lengthOfWood = (length + width) * 2;
canvasWidth = width + 5;
canvasLength = length + 5;
canvasAreaInches = canvasWidth * canvasLength;
canvasAreaFeet = canvasAreaInches / SQ_IN_PER_SQ_FT;
totWoodCost = lengthOfWood * woodCost;
totCanvasCost = canvasAreaFeet * canvasCost;
totCost = totWoodCost + totCanvasCost;

// Print dimensions and costs

cout << endl << setprecision(1);
cout << "For a painting " << length << " in. long and "
     << width << " in. wide," << endl;
cout << "you need to buy " << lengthOfWood << " in. of wood,"
     << " and" << endl;
cout << "the canvas must be " << canvasLength << " in. long"
     << " and " << canvasWidth << " in. wide." << endl;

cout << endl << setprecision(2);
cout << "Given a wood cost of $" << woodCost << " per in."
     << endl;
cout << "and a canvas cost of $" << canvasCost
     << " per sq. ft.," << endl;
cout << "the wood will cost $" << totWoodCost << ',' << endl;
cout << "the canvas will cost $" << totCanvasCost << ','
     << endl;
cout << "and the total cost of materials will be $" << totCost
     << '.' << endl;
return 0;
}
```

This is an interactive program. The data values are input while the program is executing. If the user enters this data:

```
24.0 36.0 0.08 2.80
```

then the dialogue with the user looks like this:

```
Enter length and width of painting:
24.0 36.0
Enter cost per inch of the framing wood in dollars:
0.08
Enter cost per square foot of canvas in dollars:
2.80

For a painting 24.0 in. long and 36.0 in. wide,
you need to buy 120.0 in. of wood, and
the canvas must be 29.0 in. long and 41.0 in. wide.

Given a wood cost of $0.08 per in.
and a canvas cost of $2.80 per sq. ft.,
the wood will cost $9.60,
the canvas will cost $23.12,
and the total cost of materials will be $32.72.
```

*B*ACKGROUND INFORMATION

Programming on Many Scales

To help you put the topics in this book into context, we describe in broad terms the way programming in its many forms is done in "the real world." Obviously, we can't cover every possibility, but we'll try to give you a flavor of the state of the art.

Programming projects range in size from the small scale, in which a student or computer hobbyist writes a short program to try out something new, to large-scale multicompany programming projects involving hundreds of people. Between these two extremes are efforts of many other sizes. There are people who use programming in their professions, even though it isn't their primary job. For example, a scientist might write a special-purpose program to analyze data from a particular experiment.

Even among professional programmers, there are many specialized programming areas. An individual might have a specialty in business data processing, in writing compilers or developing word processors (a specialty known as "tool making"), in research and development support, in graphical display development, in writing entertainment software, or in one of many other areas. However, one person can produce only fairly small programs (a few tens of thousands of lines of code at best). Work of this kind is called *programming in the small*.

A larger application, such as the development of a new operating system, might require hundreds of thousands or even millions of lines of code. Such large-scale projects require teams of programmers, many of them specialists, who must be organized in some manner or they waste valuable time just trying to communicate with one another.

Usually, a hierarchical organization is set up along the lines of the module structure chart. One person, the *chief architect* or *project director*, determines the basic structure of the program and then delegates the responsibility of implementing the major components. These components may be modules produced by a functional decomposition, or they might be classes and objects resulting from an object-oriented design. In smaller projects, the components may be delegated directly to programmers. In larger projects, the components may be given to team leaders, who divide them into subcomponents that are then delegated to individual programmers or groups of programmers. At each stage, the person in charge must have the knowledge and experience necessary to define the next-lower level of the hierarchy and to estimate the resources necessary to implement it. This sort of organization is called *programming in the large*.

Programming languages and software tools can help a great deal in supporting programming in the large. For example, if a programming language lets programmers develop, compile, and test parts of a program independently before they are put together, then it enables several people to work on the program simultaneously. Of course, it is hard to appreciate the complexity of programming in the large when you are writing a small program for a class assignment. However, the experience you gain in this course will be valuable as you begin to develop larger programs.

The following is a classic example of what happens when a large program is developed without careful organization and proper language support. In the 1960s, IBM developed a major new operating system called OS/360, which was one of the first true examples of programming in the large. After the operating system was written, more than 1000 significant errors were found. Despite years of trying to fix these errors, the programmers never did get the number of errors below 1000, and sometimes the "fixes" produced far more errors than they eliminated.

What led to this situation? Hindsight analysis showed that the code was badly organized and that different pieces were so interrelated that nobody could keep it all straight. A seemingly simple change in one part of the code caused several other parts of the system to fail. Eventually, at great expense, an entirely new system was created using better organization and tools.

In those early days of computing, everyone expected occasional errors to occur, and it was still possible to get useful work done with a faulty operating system. Today, however, computers are used more and more in critical applications such as medical equipment and aircraft control systems, where errors can prove fatal. Many of these applications depend on large-scale programming. If you were stepping onto a modern jetliner right now, you might well pause and wonder, "Just what sort of language and tools did they use when they wrote the programs for this thing?" Fortunately, most large software development efforts today use a combination of good methodology, appropriate language, and extensive organizational tools—an approach known as *software engineering*.

Testing and Debugging

An important part of implementing a program is testing it (checking the results). By now you should realize that there is nothing magical about the computer. It is infallible only if the person writing the instructions and entering the data is infallible. Don't trust it to give you the correct answers until you've verified enough of them by hand to convince yourself that the program is working.

From here on, these Testing and Debugging sections offer tips on how to test your programs and what to do if a program doesn't work the way you expect it to work. But don't wait until you've found a bug to read the Testing and Debugging sections. It's much easier to prevent bugs than to fix them.

When testing programs that input data values from a file, it's possible for input operations to fail. And when input fails in C++, the computer doesn't issue a warning message or terminate the program. The program simply continues executing, ignoring any further input operations on that file. The two most common reasons for input failure are invalid data and the *end-of-file error.*

An end-of-file error occurs when the program has read all of the input data available in the file and needs more data to fill the variables in its input statements. It might be that the data file simply was not prepared properly. Perhaps it contains fewer data items than the program requires. Or perhaps the format of the input data is wrong. Leaving out whitespace between numeric values is guaranteed to cause trouble. For example, we may want a data file to contain three integer values—25, 16, and 42. Look what happens with this data:

```
2516   42
```

and this code:

```
inFile >> i >> j >> k;
```

The first two input operations use up the data in the file, leaving the third with no data to read. The stream `inFile` enters the fail state, so `k` isn't assigned a new value and the computer quietly continues executing at the next statement in the program.

If the data file is prepared correctly and there is still an end-of-file error, the problem is in the program logic. For some reason, the program is attempting too many input operations. It could be a simple oversight such as specifying too many variables in a particular input statement. It could be a misuse of the `ignore` function, causing values to be skipped inadvertently. Or it could be a serious flaw in the algorithm. You should check all of these possibilities.

The other major source of input failure, invalid data, has several possi-ble causes. The most common is an error in the preparation or entry of the data. Numeric and character data mixed inappropriately in the input can cause the input stream to fail if it is supposed to read a numeric value but the reading marker is positioned at a character that isn't allowed in the number. Another cause is using the wrong variable name (which happens to be of the wrong data type) in an input statement. Declaring a variable to be of the wrong data type is a variation on the problem. Last, leaving out a variable (or including an extra one) in an input statement can cause the reading marker to end up positioned on the wrong type of data.

Another oversight, one that doesn't cause input failure but causes pro-grammer frustration, is to use `cin` or `cout` in an I/O statement when you meant to specify a file stream. If you mistakenly use `cin` instead of an input file stream, the program stops and waits for input from the keyboard. If you mistakenly use `cout` instead of an output file stream, you get unex-pected output on the screen.

By giving you a framework that can help you organize and keep track of the details involved in designing and implementing a program, func-tional decomposition (and, later, object-oriented design) should help you avoid many of these errors in the first place.

In later chapters, you'll see that you can test modules separately. If you make sure that each module works by itself, your program should work when you put all the modules together. Testing modules separately is less work than trying to test an entire program. In a smaller section of code, it's less likely that multiple errors will combine to produce behavior that is difficult to analyze.

Testing and Debugging Hints

1. Input and output statements always begin with the name of a stream object, and the >> and << operators point in the direction in which the data is going. The statement

    ```
    cout << n;
    ```

    sends data *to* the output stream `cout`, and the statement

    ```
    cin >> n;
    ```

    sends data *to* the variable n.

2. When a program inputs from or outputs to a file, be sure each I/O statement from or to the file uses the name of the file stream, not `cin` or `cout`.
3. The `open` function associated with an `ifstream` or `ofstream` object requires a C string as an argument. The argument cannot be a `string` object. At this point in the book, the argument can only be (a) a literal string or (b) the C string returned by the function call `myString.c_str()`, where `myString` is of type `string`.
4. When you open a data file for input, make sure that the argument to the `open` function supplies the correct name of the file as it exists on disk.
5. When reading a character string into a `string` object, the `>>` operator stops at, *but does not consume,* the first trailing whitespace character.
6. Be sure that each input statement specifies the correct number of variables and that each of those variables is of the correct data type.
7. If your input data is mixed (character and numeric values), be sure to deal with intervening blanks.
8. Echo print the input data to verify that each value is where it belongs and is in the proper format. (This is crucial, because an input failure in C++ doesn't produce an error message or terminate the program.)

Summary

Programs operate on data. If data and programs are kept separate, the data is available to use with other programs, and the same program can be run with different sets of input data.

The extraction operator (>>) inputs data from the keyboard or a file, storing the data into the variable specified as its right-hand operand. The extraction operator skips any leading whitespace characters to find the next data value in the input stream. The `get` function does not skip leading whitespace characters; it inputs the very next character and stores it into the `char` variable specified in its argument list. Both the `>>` operator and the `get` function leave the reading marker positioned at the next character to be read. The next input operation begins reading at the point indicated by the marker.

The newline character (denoted by \n in a C++ program) marks the end of a data line. You create a newline character each time you press the Return or Enter key. Your program generates a newline each time you use the `endl` manipulator or explicitly output the \n character. Newline is a control character; it does not print. It controls the movement of the screen cursor or the position of a line on a printer.

Interactive programs prompt the user for each data entry and directly inform the user of results and errors. Designing interactive dialogue is an exercise in the art of communication.

Noninteractive input/output allows data to be prepared before a program is run and allows the program to run again with the same data in the event that a problem crops up during processing.

Data files often are used for noninteractive processing and to permit the output from one program to be used as input to another program. To use these files, you must do four things: (1) include the header file `fstream`, (2) declare the file streams along with your other variable declarations, (3) prepare the files for reading or writing by calling the `open` function, and (4) specify the name of the file stream in each input or output statement that uses it.

Object-oriented design and functional decomposition are methodologies for tackling nontrivial programming problems. Object-oriented design produces a problem solution by focusing on objects and their associated operations. The first step is to identify the major objects in the problem and choose appropriate operations on those objects. An object is an instance of a data type called a class. During object-oriented design, classes can be designed from scratch, obtained from class libraries and used as is, or customized from existing classes by using the technique of inheritance. The result of the design process is a program consisting of self-contained objects that manage their own data and communicate by invoking each other's operations.

Functional decomposition begins with an abstract solution that then is divided into major steps. Each step becomes a subproblem that is analyzed and subdivided further. A concrete step is one that can be translated directly into C++; those steps that need more refining are abstract steps. A module is a collection of concrete and abstract steps that solves a subproblem. Programs can be built out of modules using a flat implementation, a hierarchical implementation, or a semihierarchical implementation.

Careful attention to program design, program formatting, and documentation produces highly structured and readable programs.

Quick Check

1. Write a C++ statement that inputs values from the standard input stream into two `float` variables, x and y. (pp. 155–158)
2. Your program is reading from the standard input stream. The next three characters waiting in the stream are a blank, a blank, and the letter *A*. Indicate what character is stored into the `char` variable ch by each of the following statements. (Assume the same initial stream contents for each.)

   a. `cin >> ch;`
   b. `cin.get(ch);`

   (pp. 158–162)
3. An input line contains a person's first, middle, and last names, separated by spaces. To read the entire name into a single `string` variable, which is appropriate: the `>>` operator or the `getline` function? (pp. 163–165)

4. Input prompts should acknowledge the user's experience.
    a. What sort of message would you have a program print to prompt a novice user to input a Social Security number?
    b. How would you change the wording of the prompting message for an experienced user? (pp. 165–166)
5. If a program is going to input 1000 numbers, is interactive input appropriate? (p. 167)
6. What four things must you remember to do in order to use data files in a C++ program? (pp. 168–171)
7. How many levels of abstraction are there in a functional decomposition before you reach the point at which you can begin coding a program? (pp. 181–191)
8. When is a flat implementation of a functional decomposition appropriate? (pp. 185–191)
9. Modules are the building blocks of functional decomposition. What are the building blocks of object-oriented design? (pp. 177–182)

Answers **1.** `cin >> x >> y;` **2.** a. 'A' b. ' ' (a blank) **3.** The `getline` function **4.** a. Please type a nine-digit Social Security number, then press the key marked Enter. b. Enter SSN. **5.** No. Batch input is more appropriate for programs that input large amounts of data. **6.** (1) Include the header file `fstream`. (2) Declare the file streams along with your other variable declarations. (3) Call the `open` function to prepare each file for reading or writing. (4) Specify the name of the file stream in each I/O statement that uses it. **7.** There is no fixed number of levels of abstraction. You keep refining the solution through as many levels as necessary until the steps are all concrete. **8.** A flat implementation is appropriate when a design is short and has just one or two levels of abstraction. **9.** The building blocks are objects, each of which has associated operations.

Exam Preparation Exercises

1. What is the main advantage of having a program input its data rather than writing all the data values as constants in the program?
2. Given these two lines of data:

    ```
    17 13
    7 3 24 6
    ```

    and this input statement:

    ```
    cin >> int1 >> int2 >> int3;
    ```

    a. What is the value of each variable after the statement is executed?
    b. What happens to any leftover data values in the input stream?
3. The newline character signals the end of a line.
    a. How do you generate a newline character when typing input data at the keyboard?
    b. How do you generate a newline character in a program's output?
4. When reading `char` data from an input stream, what is the difference between using the `>>` operator and using the `get` function?
5. Integer values can be read from the input data into `float` variables. (True or False?)

6. You may use either spaces or newlines to separate numeric data values being entered into a C++ program. (True or False?)

7. Consider this input data:

```
14 21 64
19 67 91
73 89 27
23 96 47
```

What are the values of the int variables a, b, c, and d after the following program segment is executed?

```
cin >> a;
cin.ignore(200, '\n');
cin >> b >> c;
cin.ignore(200, '\n');
cin >> d;
```

8. Given the input data

```
123W 56
```

what is printed by the output statement when the following code segment is executed?

```
int1 = 98;
int2 = 147;
cin >> int1 >> int2;
cout << int1 << ' ' << int2;
```

9. Given the input data

```
11 12.35 ABC
```

what is the value of each variable after the following statements are executed? Assume that i is of type int, x is of type float, and ch1 is of type char.
a. cin >> i >> x >> ch1 >> ch1;
b. cin >> ch1 >> i >> x;

10. Consider the input data

```
40 Tall Pine Drive
Sudbury, MA 01776
```

and the program code

```
string address;

cin >> address;
```

After the code is executed,
a. what string is contained in address?
b. where is the reading marker positioned?

11. Answer Exercise 10 again, replacing the input statement with

```
getline(cin, address);
```

12. Define the following terms as they apply to interactive input/output.
    a. Input prompt
    b. Echo printing
13. Correct the following program so that it reads a value from the file stream inData and writes it to the file stream outData.

```
#include <iostream>

using namespace std;

int main()
{
    int      n;
    ifstream inData;

    outData.open("results.dat");
    cin >> n;
    outData << n << endl;
    return 0;
}
```

14. Use your corrected version of the program in Exercise 13 to answer the following questions.
    a. If the file stream inData initially contains the value 144, what does it contain after the program is executed?
    b. If the file stream outData is initially empty, what are its contents after the program is executed?
15. List three characteristics of programs that are designed using a highly organized methodology such as functional decomposition or object-oriented design.
16. The get and ignore functions are member functions of the istream class. (True or False?)
17. The find and substr functions are member functions of the string class. (True or False?)
18. The getline function is a member function of the string class. (True or False?)

Programming Warm-up Exercises

1. Your program has three char variables: ch1, ch2, and ch3. Given the input data

   A B C\n

   write the input statement(s) required to store the A into ch1, the B into ch2, and the C into ch3. Note that each pair of input characters is separated by two blanks.
2. Change your answer to Exercise 1 so that the A is stored into ch1 and the next two blanks are stored into ch2 and ch3.

3. Write a single input statement that reads the input lines

   ```
   10.25    7.625\n
   8.5\n
   1.0\n
   ```

   and stores the four values into the float variables length1, height1, length2, and height2.
4. Write a series of statements that input the first letter of each of the following names into the char variables chr1, chr2, and chr3.

   ```
   Peter\n
   Kitty\n
   Kathy\n
   ```

5. Write a set of variable declarations and a series of input statements to read the following lines of data into variables of the appropriate type. You can make up the variable names. Notice that the values are separated from one another by a single blank and that there are no blanks to the left of the first character on each line.

   ```
   A 100 2.78 g 14\n
   207.98 w q 23.4 92\n
   R 42 L 27 R 63\n
   ```

6. Write a program segment that reads nine integer values from a file and writes them to the screen, three numbers per output line. The file is organized one value to a line.
7. Write a code segment for an interactive program to input values for a person's age, height, and weight and the initials of his or her first and last names. The numeric values are all integers. Assume that the person using the program is a novice user. How would you rewrite the code for an experienced user?
8. Fill in the blanks in the following program, which should read four values from the file stream dataIn and output them to the file stream resultsOut.

```
#include _____
#include _____
using _____
int main()
{
    int             val1;
    int             val2;
    int             val3;
    int             val4;
    _____      dataIn;
    ofstream        _____ ;
    _____ ("myinput.dat");
    _____ ("myoutput.dat");
    _____ >> val1 >> val2 >> val3 >> val4;
    _____ << val1 << val2 << val3 << val4 << endl;
    return 0;
}
```

9. Modify the program in Exercise 8 so that the name of the input file is prompted for and read in from the user at run time instead of being specified as a literal string.

10. Use functional decomposition to write an algorithm for starting the engine of an automobile with a manual transmission.

11. Use functional decomposition to write an algorithm for logging on to your computer system and entering and running a program. The algorithm should be simple enough for a novice user to follow.

12 The quadratic formula is

$$x = \frac{-b \pm \sqrt{b^2 - 4ac}}{2a}$$

Use functional decomposition to write an algorithm to read the three coefficients of a quadratic polynomial from a file (inQuad) and write the two floating-point solutions to another file (outQuad). Assume that the discriminant (the portion of the formula inside the square root) is nonnegative. You may use the standard library function sqrt. (Express your solution as pseudocode, not as a C++ program.)

Programming Problems

1. Write a functional decomposition and a C++ program to read an invoice number, quantity ordered, and unit price (all integers) and compute the total price. The program should write out the invoice number, quantity, unit price, and total price with identifying phrases. Format your program with consistent indentation, and use appropriate comments and meaningful identifiers. Write the program to be run interactively, with informative prompts for each data value.

2   How tall is a rainbow? Because of the way in which light is refracted by water droplets, the angle between the level of your eye and the top of a rainbow is always the same. If you know the distance to the rainbow, you can multiply it by the tangent of that angle to find the height of the rainbow. The magic angle is 42.3333333 degrees. The C++ standard library works in radians, however, so you have to convert the angle to radians with this formula:

$$radians = degrees \times \frac{\pi}{180}$$

where π equals 3.14159265.

Through the header file cmath, the C++ standard library provides a tangent function named tan. This is a value-returning function that takes a floating-point argument and returns a floating-point result:

```
x = tan(someAngle);
```

If you multiply the tangent by the distance to the rainbow, you get the height of the rainbow.

Write a functional decomposition and a C++ program to read a single floating-point value—the distance to the rainbow—and compute the height of the rainbow. The program should print the distance to the rainbow and its height, with phrases that identify which number is which. Display the floating-point values to four decimal places. Format your program with consistent indentation, and use appropriate comments and meaningful identifiers. Write the program so that it prompts the user for the input value.

3. Sometimes you can see a second, fainter rainbow outside a bright rainbow. This second rainbow has a magic angle of 52.25 degrees. Modify the program in Problem 2 so that it prints the height of the main rainbow, the height of the secondary rainbow, and the distance to the main rainbow, with a phrase identifying each of the numbers.

4. Write a program that reads a person's name in the format First Middle Last and then prints each of the names on a separate line. Following the last name, the program should print the initials for the name. For example, given the input James Tiberius Kirk, the program should output

```
James
Tiberius
Kirk
JTK
```

Assume that the first name begins in the first position on a line (there are no leading blanks) and that the names are separated from each other by a single blank.

Case Study Follow-Up

1. In the Canvas problem, look at the module structure chart and identify each level 1 module as an input module, a computational module, or an output module.

2. Redraw the module structure chart for the Canvas program so that level 1 contains modules named Get Data, Compute Values, and Print Results. Decide whether each of the level 1 modules in the original module structure chart corresponds directly to one of the three new modules or if it fits best as a level 2 module under one of the three. In the latter case, add the level 2 modules to the new module structure chart in the appropriate places.

3. Modify the Canvas program so that it reads the input data from a file rather than the keyboard. At run time, prompt the user for the name of the file containing the data.

5

Conditions, Logical Expressions, and Selection Control Structures

GOALS

- To be able to construct a simple logical (Boolean) expression to evaluate a given condition.
- To be able to construct a complex logical expression to evaluate a given condition.
- To be able to construct an If-Then-Else statement to perform a specific task.
- To be able to construct an If-Then statement to perform a specific task.
- To be able to construct a set of nested If statements to perform a specific task.
- To be able to determine the precondition and postcondition for a module and to use them to perform an algorithm walk-through.
- To be able to trace the execution of a C++ program.
- To be able to test and debug a C++ program.

So far, the statements in our programs have been executed in their physical order. The first statement is executed, then the second, and so on until all of the statements have been executed. But what if we want the computer to execute the statements in some other order? Suppose we want to check the validity of input data and then perform a calculation *or* print an error message, not both. To do so, we must be able to ask a question and then, based on the answer, choose one or another course of action.

The If statement allows us to execute statements in an order that is different from their physical order. We can ask a question with it and do one thing if the answer is yes (true) or another if the answer is no (false). In the first part of this chapter, we deal with asking questions; in the second part, we deal with the If statement itself.

Flow of Control

The order in which statements are executed in a program is called the **flow of control.** In a sense, the computer is under the control of one statement at a time. When a statement has been executed, control is turned over to the next statement (like a baton being passed in a relay race).

Flow of control   The order in which the computer executes statements in a program.

Flow of control is normally sequential (see Figure 5-1). That is, when one statement is finished executing, control passes to the next statement in the program. When we want the flow of control to be nonsequential, we

FIGURE 5-1
Sequential Control

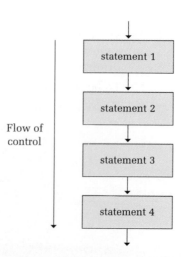

use **control structures,** special statements that transfer control to a statement other than the one that physically comes next. Control structures are so important that we focus on them in the remainder of this chapter and in the next four chapters.

Control structure   A statement used to alter the normally sequential flow of control.

Selection

We use a selection (or branching) control structure when we want the computer to choose between alternative actions. We make an assertion, a claim that is either true or false. If the assertion is true, the computer executes one statement. If it is false, it executes another (see Figure 5-2). The computer's ability to solve practical problems is a product of its ability to make decisions and execute different sequences of instructions.

The Payroll program in Chapter 1 shows the selection process at work. The computer must decide whether or not a worker has earned overtime pay. It does this by testing the assertion that the person has worked more

Figure 5-2
Selection
(Branching)
Control Structure

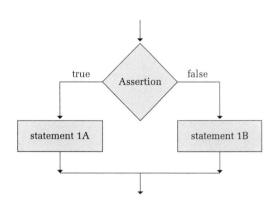

than 40 hours. If the assertion is true, the computer follows the instructions for computing overtime pay. If the assertion is false, the computer simply computes the regular pay. Before we examine selection control structures in C++, let's look closely at how we get the computer to make decisions.

Conditions and Logical Expressions

To ask a question in C++, we don't phrase it as a question; we state it as an assertion. If the assertion we make is true, the answer to the question is yes. If the statement is not true, the answer to the question is no. For example, if we want to ask, "Are we having spinach for dinner tonight?" we would say, "We are having spinach for dinner tonight." If the assertion is true, the answer to the question is yes. If not, the answer is no.

So, asking questions in C++ means making an assertion that is either true or false. The computer *evaluates* the assertion, checking it against some internal condition (the values stored in certain variables, for instance) to see whether it is true or false.

The `bool` Data Type

In C++, the `bool` data type is a built-in type consisting of just two values, the constants `true` and `false`. The reserved word `bool` is short for Boolean (pronounced 'BOOL-ē-un).* Boolean data is used for testing conditions in a program so that the computer can make decisions (with a selection control structure).

We declare variables of type `bool` the same way we declare variables of other types, that is, by writing the name of the data type and then an identifier:

```
bool dataOK;     // True if the input data is valid
bool done;       // True if the process is done
bool taxable;    // True if the item has sales tax
```

Each variable of type `bool` can contain one of two values: `true` or `false`. It's important to understand right from the beginning that `true` and `false` are not variable names and they are not strings. They are special constants in C++ and, in fact, are reserved words.

---

* The word *Boolean* is a tribute to George Boole, a nineteenth-century English mathematician who described a system of logic using variables with just two values, True and False. (See the May We Introduce box on page 224)

*B*ACKGROUND INFORMATION

Before the `bool` *Type*

The C language does not have a `bool` data type, and prior to the ISO/ANSI C++ language standard, neither did C++. In C and pre-standard C++, the value 0 represents *false*, and any nonzero value represents *true*. In these languages, it is customary to use the `int` type to represent Boolean data:

```
int dataOK;
   ⋮
dataOK = 1;    // Store "true" into dataOK
   ⋮
dataOK = 0;    // Store "false" into dataOK
```

To make the code more self-documenting, many C and pre-standard C++ programmers prefer to define their own Boolean data type by using a *Typedef statement*. This statement allows you to introduce a new name for an existing data type:

```
typedef int bool;
```

All this statement does is tell the compiler to substitute the word `int` for every occurrence of the word `bool` in the rest of the program. Thus, when the compiler encounters a statement such as

```
bool dataOK;
```

it translates the statement into

```
int dataOK;
```

With the Typedef statement and declarations of two named constants, `true` and `false`, the code at the beginning of this discussion becomes the following:

```
typedef int bool;
const int true = 1;
const int false = 0;
   ⋮
bool dataOK;
   ⋮
dataOK = true;
   ⋮
dataOK = false;
```

With standard C++, none of this is necessary because `bool` is a built-in type. If you are working with pre–standard C++, see Section D.4 of Appendix D for more information about defining your own `bool` type so that you can work with the programs in this book.

Logical Expressions

In programming languages, assertions take the form of *logical expressions* (also called *Boolean expressions*). Just as an arithmetic expression is made up of numeric values and operations, a logical expression is made up of logical values and operations. Every logical expression has one of two values: true or false.

Here are some examples of logical expressions:

- A Boolean variable or constant
- An expression followed by a relational operator followed by an expression
- A logical expression followed by a logical operator followed by a logical expression

Let's look at each of these in detail.

Boolean Variables and Constants   As we have seen, a Boolean variable is a variable declared to be of type `bool`, and it can contain either the value `true` or the value `false`. For example, if `dataOK` is a Boolean variable, then

```
dataOK = true;
```

is a valid assignment statement.

Relational Operators   Another way of assigning a value to a Boolean variable is to set it equal to the result of comparing two expressions with a *relational operator*. Relational operators test a relationship between two values.

Let's look at an example. In the following program fragment, `lessThan` is a Boolean variable and `i` and `j` are `int` variables:

```
cin >> i >> j;
lessThan = (i < j);   // Compare i and j with the "less than"
                      // relational operator, and assign the
                      // truth value to lessThan
```

By comparing two values, we assert that a relationship (like "less than") exists between them. If the relationship does exist, the assertion is true; if not, it is false. These are the relationships we can test for in C++:

Operator Relationship Tested

==	Equal to
!=	Not equal to
>	Greater than
<	Less than
>=	Greater than or equal to
<=	Less than or equal to

An expression followed by a relational operator followed by an expression is called a *relational expression*. The result of a relational expression is of type `bool`. For example, if x is 5 and y is 10, the following expressions all have the value `true`:

```
x != y
y > x
x < y
y >= x
x <= y
```

If x is the character 'M' and y is 'R', the values of the expressions are still `true` because the relational operator <, used with letters, means "comes before in the alphabet," or, more properly, "comes before in the collating sequence of the character set." For example, in the widely used ASCII character set, all of the uppercase letters are in alphabetical order, as are the lowercase letters, but all of the uppercase letters come before the lowercase letters. So

```
'M' < 'R'
```

and

```
'm' < 'r'
```

have the value `true`, but

```
'm' < 'R'
```

has the value `false`.

Of course, we have to be careful about the data types of things we compare. The safest approach is to always compare ints with ints, floats with `floats`, chars with chars, and so on. If you mix data types in a comparison, implicit type coercion takes place just as in arithmetic expressions. If an int value and a float value are compared, the computer temporarily coerces the int value to its `float` equivalent before making the comparison. As with arithmetic expressions, it's wise to use explicit type casting to make your intentions known:

```
someFloat >= float(someInt)
```

If you compare a `bool` value with a numeric value (probably by mistake), the value `false` is temporarily coerced to the number 0, and `true` is coerced to 1. Therefore, if `boolVar` is a `bool` variable, the expression

```
boolVar < 5
```

yields `true` because 0 and 1 both are less than 5.

Until you learn more about the char type in Chapter 10, be careful to compare char values only with other char values. For example, the comparisons

```
'0' < '9'
```

and

```
0 < 9
```

are appropriate, but

```
'0' < 9
```

generates an implicit type coercion and a result that probably isn't what you expect.

We can use relational operators not only to compare variables or constants, but also to compare the values of arithmetic expressions. In the following table, we compare the results of adding 3 to x and multiplying y by 10 for different values of x and y.

Value of x	Value of y	Expression	Result
12	2	x + 3 <= y * 10	true
20	2	x + 3 <= y * 10	false
7	1	x + 3 != y * 10	false
17	2	x + 3 == y * 10	true
100	5	x + 3 > y * 10	true

Caution: It's easy to confuse the assignment operator (=) and the == relational operator. These two operators have very different effects in a program. Some people pronounce the relational operator as "equals-equals" to remind themselves of the difference.

Comparing Strings Recall from Chapter 4 that string is a class—a programmer-defined type from which you declare variables that are more commonly called objects. Contained within each string object is a character string. The string class is designed such that you can compare these strings using the relational operators. Syntactically, the operands of a relational operator can either be two string objects, as in

```
myString < yourString
```

or a string object and a C string:

```
myString >= "Johnson"
```

However, the operands cannot both be C strings.

Comparison of strings follows the collating sequence of the machine's character set (ASCII, for instance). When the computer tests a relationship between two strings, it begins with the first character of each, compares them according to the collating sequence, and if they are the same repeats the comparison with the next character in each string. The character-by-character test proceeds until either a mismatch is found or the final characters have been compared and are equal. If all their characters are equal, then the two strings are equal. If a mismatch is found, then the string with the character that comes before the other is the "lesser" string.

For example, given the statements

```
string word1;
string word2;
```

```
word1 = "Tremendous";
word2 = "Small";
```

the relational expressions in the following table have the indicated values.

Expression	Value	Reason
word1 == word2	false	They are unequal in the first character.
word1 > word2	true	'T' comes after 'S' in the collating sequence.
word1 < "Tremble"	false	Fifth characters don't match, and 'b' comes before 'e'.
word2 == "Small"	true	They are equal.
"cat" < "dog"	Unpredictable	The operands cannot both be C strings.*

*The expression is syntactically legal in C++ but results in a *pointer* comparison, not a string comparison. Pointers are not discussed until Chapter 15.

In most cases, the ordering of strings corresponds to alphabetical ordering. But when strings have mixed-case letters, we can get nonalphabetical results. For example, in a phone book we expect to see Macauley before MacPherson, but the ASCII collating sequence places all uppercase letters before the lowercase letters, so the string "MacPherson" compares as less than "Macauley". To compare strings for strict alphabetical ordering, all the characters must be in the same case. In a later chapter we show an algorithm for changing the case of a string.

If two strings with different lengths are compared and the comparison is equal up to the end of the shorter string, then the shorter string compares as less than the longer string. For example, if word2 contains "Small", the expression

```
word2 < "Smaller"
```

yields true, because the strings are equal up to their fifth character position (the end of the string on the left), and the string on the right is longer.

Logical Operators   In mathematics, the *logical* (or *Boolean*) *operators* AND, OR, and NOT take logical expressions as operands. C++ uses special symbols for the logical operators: && (for AND), || (for OR), and ! (for NOT). By combining relational operators with logical operators, we can make more complex assertions. For example, suppose we want to determine whether a final score is greater than 90 *and* a midterm score is greater than 70. In C++, we would write the expression this way:

```
finalScore > 90 && midtermScore > 70
```

The AND operation (`&&`) requires both relationships to be true in order for the overall result to be true. If either or both of the relationships are false, the entire result is false.

The OR operation (`||`) takes two logical expressions and combines them. If *either* or *both* are true, the result is true. Both values must be false for the result to be false. Now we can determine whether the midterm grade is an A *or* the final grade is an A. If either the midterm grade or the final grade equals A, the assertion is true. In C++, we write the expression like this:

```
midtermGrade == 'A' || finalGrade == 'A'
```

The `&&` and `||` operators always appear between two expressions; they are binary (two-operand) operators. The NOT operator (`!`) is a unary (one-operand) operator. It precedes a single logical expression and gives its opposite as the result. If (`grade == 'A'`) is false, then `!(grade == 'A')` is true. NOT gives us a convenient way of reversing the meaning of an assertion. For example,

```
!(hours > 40)
```

is the equivalent of

```
hours <= 40
```

In some contexts, the first form is clearer; in others, the second makes more sense.

The following pairs of expressions are equivalent:

Expression	Equivalent Expression
`!(a == b)`	`a != b`
`!(a == b || a == c)`	`a != b && a != c`
`!(a == b && c > d)`	`a != b || c <= d`

Take a close look at these expressions to be sure you understand why they are equivalent. Try evaluating them with some values for a, b, c, and d. Notice the pattern: The expression on the left is just the one to its right with `!` added and the relational and logical operators reversed (for example, `==` instead of `!=` and `||` instead of `&&`). Remember this pattern. It allows you to rewrite expressions in the simplest form.*

---

* In Boolean algebra, the pattern is formalized by a theorem called *DeMorgan's law.*

Logical operators can be applied to the results of comparisons. They also can be applied directly to variables of type `bool`. For example, instead of writing

```
isElector = (age >= 18 && district == 23);
```

to assign a value to the Boolean variable `isElector`, we could use two intermediate Boolean variables, `isVoter` and `isConstituent`:

```
isVoter = (age >= 18);
isConstituent = (district == 23);
isElector = isVoter && isConstituent;
```

The two tables below summarize the results of applying `&&` and `||` to a pair of logical expressions (represented here by Boolean variables x and y).

Value of x	*Value of* y	*Value of* x `&&` y
true	true	true
true	false	false
false	true	false
false	false	false

Value of x	*Value of* y	*Value of* x `||` y
true	true	true
true	false	true
false	true	true
false	false	false

The following table summarizes the results of applying the `!` operator to a logical expression (represented by Boolean variable x).

Value of x	*Value of* !x
true	false
false	true

Technically, the C++ operators !, &&, and || are not required to have logical expressions as operands. Their operands can be of any simple data type, even floating-point types. If an operand is not of type bool, its value is temporarily coerced to type bool as follows: A 0 value is coerced to false, and any nonzero value is coerced to true. As an example, you sometimes encounter C++ code that looks like this:

```
float  height;
bool   badData;
  ⋮
cin >> height;
badData = !height;
```

The assignment statement says to set badData to true if the coerced value of height is false. That is, the statement really is saying, "Set badData to true if height equals 0.0." Although this assignment statement works correctly according to the C++ language, many programmers find the following statement to be more readable:

```
badData = (height == 0.0);
```

Throughout this text we apply the logical operators *only* to logical expressions, not to arithmetic expressions.

Caution: It's easy to confuse the logical operators && and || with two other C++ operators, & and |. We don't discuss the & and | operators here, but we'll tell you that they are used for manipulating individual bits within a memory cell—a role quite different from that of the logical operators. If you accidentally use & instead of &&, or | instead of ||, you won't get an error message from the compiler, but your program probably will compute wrong answers. Some programmers pronounce && as "and-and" and || as "or-or" to avoid making mistakes.

Short-Circuit Evaluation Consider the logical expression

```
i == 1 && j > 2
```

Some programming languages use *full evaluation* of logical expressions. With full evaluation, the computer first evaluates both subexpressions (both i == 1 and j > 2) before applying the && operator to produce the final result.

In contrast, C++ uses **short-circuit** (or **conditional**) **evaluation** of logical expressions. Evaluation proceeds from left to right, and the computer stops evaluating subexpressions as soon as possible—that is, as soon as it knows the truth value of the entire expression. How can the computer know if a lengthy logical expression yields true or false if it doesn't examine all the subexpressions? Let's look first at the AND operation.

An AND operation yields the value `true` only if both of its operands are `true`. In the expression above, suppose that the value of `i` happens to be 95. The first subexpression yields `false`, so it isn't necessary even to look at the second subexpression. The computer stops evaluation and produces the final result of `false`.

Short-circuit (conditional) evaluation   Evaluation of a logical expression in left-to-right order with evaluation stopping as soon as the final truth value can be determined.

With the OR operation, the left-to-right evaluation stops as soon as a subexpression yielding `true` is found. Remember that an OR produces a result of `true` if either one or both of its operands are `true`. Given this expression:

```
c <= d || e == f
```

if the first subexpression is `true`, evaluation stops and the entire result is `true`. The computer doesn't waste time with an unnecessary evaluation of the second subexpression.

MAY WE INTRODUCE

George Boole

Boolean algebra is named for its inventor, English mathematician George Boole, born in 1815. His father, a tradesman, began teaching him mathematics at an early age. But Boole initially was more interested in classical literature, languages, and religion—interests he maintained throughout his life. By the time he was 20, he had taught himself French, German, and Italian. He was well versed in the writings of Aristotle, Spinoza, Cicero, and Dante, and wrote several philosophical papers himself.

At 16, to help support his family, he took a position as a teaching assistant in a private school. His work there and a second teaching job left him little time to study. A few years later, he opened a school and began to learn higher mathematics on his own. In spite of his lack of formal training, his first scholarly paper was published in the *Cambridge Mathematical Journal* when he was just 24. Boole went on to publish over 50 papers and several major works before he died in 1864, at the peak of his career.

Boole's *The Mathematical Analysis of Logic* was published in 1847. It would eventually form the basis for the development of digital computers. In the book, Boole set forth the formal axioms of logic (much like the axioms of geometry) on which the field of symbolic logic is built.

Boole drew on the symbols and operations of algebra in creating his system of logic. He associated the value 1 with the universal set (the set representing everything in the universe) and the value 0 with the empty set, and restricted his system to these two quantities. He then defined operations that are analogous to subtraction, addition, and multiplication. Variables in the system have symbolic values. For example, if a Boolean variable *P* represents the set of all plants, then the expression 1 − *P* refers to the set of all things that are not plants. We can simplify the expression by using −*P* to mean "*not* plants." (0 − *P* is simply 0 because we can't remove elements from the empty set.) The subtraction operator in Boole's system corresponds to the ! (NOT) operator in C++. In a C++ program, we might set the value of the Boolean variable plant to true when the name of a plant is entered, whereas !plant is true when the name of anything else is input.

The expression 0 + *P* is the same as *P*. However, 0 + *P* + *F*, where *F* is the set of all foods, is the set of all things that are either plants or foods. So the addition operator in Boole's algebra is the same as the C++ || (OR) operator.

The analogy can be carried to multiplication: 0 × *P* is 0, and 1 × *P* is *P*. But what is *P* × *F*? It is the set of things that are both plants and foods. In Boole's system, the multiplication operator is the same as the && (AND) operator.

In 1854, Boole published *An Investigation of the Laws of Thought, on Which Are Founded the Mathematical Theories of Logic and Probabilities*. In the book, he described theorems built on his axioms of logic and extended the algebra to show how probabilities could be computed in a logical system. Five years later, Boole published *Treatise on Differential Equations*, then *Treatise on the Calculus of Finite Differences*. The latter is one of the cornerstones of numerical analysis, which deals with the accuracy of computations. (In Chapter 10, we examine the important role numerical analysis plays in computer programming.)

Boole received little recognition and few honors for his work. Given the importance of Boolean algebra in modern technology, it is hard to believe that his system of logic was not taken seriously until the early twentieth century. George Boole was truly one of the founders of computer science.

Precedence of Operators

In Chapter 3, we discussed the rules of precedence, the rules that govern the evaluation of complex arithmetic expressions. C++'s rules of precedence also govern relational and logical operators. Here's a list showing the order of precedence for the arithmetic, relational, and logical operators (with the assignment operator thrown in as well):

```
!    Unary +   Unary  -        Highest precedence
*      /     %
+      -
<      <=     >       >=
==     !=
&&
||
=                                Lowest precedence
```

Operators on the same line in the list have the same precedence. If an expression contains several operators with the same precedence, most of the operators group (or *associate*) from left to right. For example, the expression

```
a / b * c
```

means (a / b) * c, not a / (b * c). However, the unary operators (!, unary +, unary –) group from right to left. Although you'd never have occasion to use this expression:

```
!!badData
```

the meaning of it is `!(!badData)` rather than the meaningless `(!!)badData`. Appendix B, "Precedence of Operators," lists the order of precedence for all operators in C++. In skimming the appendix, you can see that a few of the operators associate from right to left (for the same reason we just described for the ! operator).

Parentheses are used to override the order of evaluation in an expression. If you're not sure whether parentheses are necessary, use them anyway. The compiler disregards unnecessary parentheses. So if they clarify an expression, use them. Some programmers like to include extra parentheses when assigning a relational expression to a Boolean variable:

```
dataInvalid = (inputVal == 0);
```

The parentheses are not needed; the assignment operator has the lowest precedence of all the operators we've just listed. So we could write the statement as

```
dataInvalid = inputVal == 0;
```

but some people find the parenthesized version more readable.

One final comment about parentheses: C++, like other programming languages, requires that parentheses always be used in pairs. Whenever you write a complicated expression, take a minute to go through and pair up all of the opening parentheses with their closing counterparts.

PEANUTS reprinted by permission of United Features Syndicate, Inc.

SOFTWARE ENGINEERING TIP

Changing English Statements into Logical Expressions

In most cases, you can write a logical expression directly from an English statement or mathematical term in an algorithm. But you have to watch out for some tricky situations. Remember our sample logical expression:

```
midtermGrade == 'A' || finalGrade == 'A'
```

In English, you would be tempted to write this expression: "Midterm grade or final grade equals A." In C++, you can't write the expression as you would in English. That is,

```
midtermGrade || finalGrade == 'A'
```

won't work because the `||` operator is connecting a `char` value (`midtermGrade`) and a logical expression (`finalGrade == 'A'`). The two operands of `||` should be logical expressions. (Note that this expression is wrong in terms of logic, but it isn't "wrong" to the C++ compiler. Recall that the `||` operator may legally connect two expressions of any data type, so this example won't generate a syntax error message. The program will run, but it won't work the way you intended.)

A variation of this mistake is to express the English assertion "*i* equals either 3 or 4" as

```
i == 3 || 4
```

Again, the syntax is correct but the semantics are not. This expression always evaluates to `true`. The first subexpression, `i == 3`, may be `true` or `false`. But the second subexpression, `4`, is nonzero and therefore is coerced to the value `true`. Thus, the `||` operation causes the entire expression to be `true`. We repeat: Use the `||` operator (and the `&&` operator) only to connect two logical expressions. Here's what we want:

```
i == 3 || i == 4
```

In math books, you might see a notation like this:

$$12 < y < 24$$

which means "*y* is between 12 and 24." This expression is legal in C++ but gives an unexpected result. First, the relation $12 < y$ is evaluated, giving the result `true` or `false`. The computer then coerces this result to 1 or 0 in order to compare it with the number 24. Because both 1 and 0 are less than 24, the result is always `true`. To write this expression correctly in C++, you must use the `&&` operator as follows:

```
12 < y && y < 24
```

Relational Operators with Floating-Point Types

So far, we've talked only about comparing `int`, `char`, and `string` values. Here we look at `float` values.

Do not compare floating-point numbers for equality. Because small errors in the rightmost decimal places are likely to arise when calculations are performed on floating-point numbers, two `float` values rarely are exactly equal. For example, consider the following code that uses two `float` variables named `oneThird` and `x`:

```
oneThird = 1.0 / 3.0;
x = oneThird + oneThird + oneThird;
```

We would expect `x` to contain the value 1.0, but it probably doesn't. The first assignment statement stores an *approximation* of 1/3 into `oneThird`, perhaps 0.333333. The second statement stores a value like 0.999999 into `x`. If we now ask the computer to compare `x` with 1.0, the comparison yields `false`.

Instead of testing floating-point numbers for equality, we test for *near* equality. To do so, we compute the difference between the two numbers and test to see if the result is less than some maximum allowable difference. For example, we often use comparisons like this:

```
fabs(r - s) < 0.00001
```

where `fabs` is the floating-point absolute value function from the C++ standard library. The expression `fabs(r - s)` computes the absolute value of the difference between two `float` variables `r` and `s`. If the difference is less than 0.00001, the two numbers are close enough to call them equal. We discuss this problem with floating-point accuracy in more detail in Chapter 10.

The If Statement

Now that we've seen how to write logical expressions, let's use them to alter the normal flow of control in a program. The *If statement* is the fundamental control structure that allows branches in the flow of control. With it, we can ask a question and choose a course of action: *If* a certain condition exists, *then* perform one action, *else* perform a different action.

At run time, the computer performs just one of the two actions, depending on the result of the condition being tested. Yet we must include the code for *both* actions in the program. Why? Because, depending on the circumstances, the computer can choose to execute *either* of them. The If statement gives us a way of including both actions in a program and gives the computer a way of deciding which action to take.

The If-Then-Else Form

In C++, the If statement comes in two forms: the *If-Then-Else* form and the *If-Then* form. Let's look first at the If-Then-Else. Here is its syntax template:

IfStatement (the If-Then-Else form)

```
if ( Expression )
    Statement1A
else
    Statement1B
```

The expression in parentheses can be of any simple data type. Almost without exception, this will be a logical (Boolean) expression; if not, its value is implicitly coerced to type `bool`. At run time, the computer evaluates the expression. If the value is `true`, the computer executes Statement1A. If the value of the expression is `false`, Statement1B is executed. Statement1A often is called the *then-clause*; Statement1B, the *else-clause*. Figure 5-3 illustrates the flow of control of the If-Then-Else. In the figure, Statement2 is the next statement in the program after the entire If statement.

FIGURE 5-3
If-Then-Else Flow
of Control

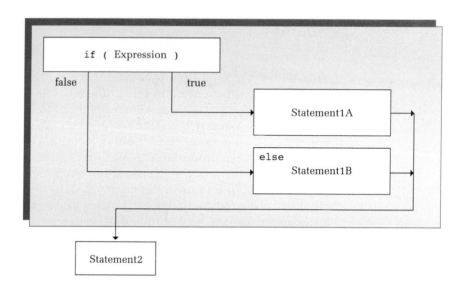

Notice that a C++ If statement uses the reserved words `if` and `else` but does not include the word *then*. Still, we use the term *If-Then-Else* because it corresponds to how we say things in English: "*If* something is true, *then* do this, *else* do that."

The code fragment below shows how to write an If statement in a program. Observe the indentation of the then-clause and the else-clause, which makes the statement easier to read. And notice the placement of the statement following the If statement.

```
if (hours <= 40.0)
    pay = rate * hours;
else
    pay = rate * (40.0 + (hours - 40.0) * 1.5);
cout << pay;
```

In terms of instructions to the computer, the above code fragment says, "If `hours` is less than or equal to 40.0, compute the regular pay and then go on to execute the output statement. But if `hours` is greater than 40, compute the regular pay and the overtime pay, and then go on to execute the output statement." Figure 5-4 shows the flow of control of this If statement.

If-Then-Else often is used to check the validity of input. For example, before we ask the computer to divide by a data value, we should be sure that the value is not zero. (Even computers can't divide something by zero. If you try, most computers halt the execution of your program.) If the divisor is zero, our program should print out an error message. Here's the code:

FIGURE 5-4

Flow of Control for
Calculating Pay

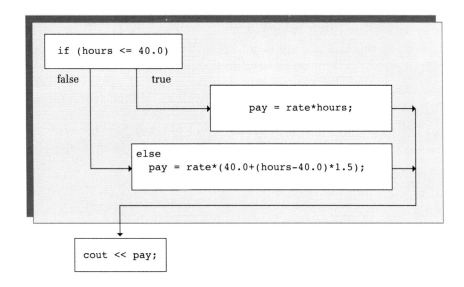

```
if (divisor != 0)
    result = dividend / divisor;
else
    cout << "Division by zero is not allowed." << endl;
```

As another example of an If-Then-Else, suppose we want to determine where in a string variable the first occurrence (if any) of the letter *A* is located. Recall from Chapter 3 that the string class has a member function named find, which returns the position where the item was found (or the named constant string::npos if the item wasn't found). The following code outputs the result of the search:

```
string myString;
string::size_type pos;
        ⋮
pos = myString.find('A');
if (pos == string::npos)
    cout << "No 'A' was found" << endl;
else
    cout << "An 'A' was found in position " << pos << endl;
```

Before we look any further at If statements, take another look at the syntax template for the If-Then-Else. According to the template, there is no semicolon at the end of an If statement. In all of the program fragments above—the worker's pay, division-by-zero, and string search examples—there seems to be a semicolon at the end of each If statement. However, the semicolons belong to the statements in the else-clauses in those examples; assignment statements end in semicolons, as do output statements. The If statement doesn't have its own semicolon at the end.

Blocks (Compound Statements)

In our division-by-zero example, suppose that when the divisor is equal to zero we want to do *two* things: print the error message *and* set the variable named `result` equal to a special value like 9999. We would need two statements in the same branch, but the syntax template seems to limit us to one.

What we really want to do is turn the else-clause into a *sequence* of statements. This is easy. Remember from Chapter 2 that the compiler treats the block (compound statement)

```
{
    ⋮
}
```

like a single statement. If you put a { } pair around the sequence of statements you want in a branch of the If statement, the sequence of statements becomes a single block. For example:

```
if (divisor != 0)
    result = dividend / divisor;
else
{
    cout << "Division by zero is not allowed." << endl;
    result = 9999;
}
```

If the value of `divisor` is 0, the computer both prints the error message and sets the value of `result` to 9999 before continuing with whatever statement follows the If statement.

Blocks can be used in both branches of an If-Then-Else. For example:

```
if (divisor != 0)
{
    result = dividend / divisor;
    cout << "Division performed." << endl;
}
else
{
    cout << "Division by zero is not allowed." << endl;
    result = 9999;
}
```

When you use blocks in an If statement, there's a rule of C++ syntax to remember: *Never use a semicolon after the right brace of a block.* Semicolons are used only to terminate simple statements such as assignment statements, input statements, and output statements. If you look at the examples above, you won't see a semicolon after the right brace that signals the end of each block.

MATTERS OF STYLE

Braces and Blocks

C++ programmers use different styles when it comes to locating the left brace of a block. The style we use puts the left and right braces directly below the words `if` and `else`, each brace on its own line:

```
if (n >= 2)
{
    alpha = 5;
    beta = 8;
}
else
{
    alpha = 23;
    beta = 12;
}
```

Another popular style is to place the left braces at the end of the `if` line and the `else` line; the right braces still line up directly below the words `if` and `else`. This way of formatting the If statement originated with programmers using the C language, the predecessor of C++.

```
if (n >= 2) {
    alpha = 5;
    beta = 8;
}
else {
    alpha = 23;
    beta = 12;
}
```

It makes no difference to the C++ compiler which style you use (and there are other styles as well). It's a matter of personal preference. Whichever style you use, though, you should always use the same style throughout a program. Inconsistency can confuse the person reading your program and give the impression of carelessness.

The If-Then Form

Sometimes you run into a situation where you want to say, "*If* a certain condition exists, *then* perform some action; otherwise, don't do anything." In other words, you want the computer to skip a sequence of instructions if a certain condition isn't met. You could do this by leaving the `else` branch empty, using only the null statement:

```
if (a <= b)
    c = 20;
else
    ;
```

Better yet, you can simply leave off the `else` part. The resulting statement is the If-Then form of the If statement. This is its syntax template:

IfStatement (the If-Then form)

```
if ( Expression )
    Statement
```

Here's an example of an If-Then. Notice the indentation and the placement of the statement that follows the If-Then.

```
if (age < 18)
    cout << "Not an eligible ";
cout << "voter." << endl;
```

This statement means that if `age` is less than 18, first print "Not an eligible " and then print "voter." If `age` is not less than 18, skip the first output statement and go directly to print "voter." Figure 5-5 shows the flow of control for an If-Then.

Like the two branches in an If-Then-Else, the one branch in an If-Then can be a block. For example, let's say you are writing a program to compute income taxes. One of the lines on the tax form reads "Subtract line 23 from line 17 and enter result on line 24; if result is less than zero, enter zero and check box 24A." You can use an If-Then to do this in C++:

```
result = line17 - line23;
if (result < 0.0)
{
    cout << "Check box 24A" << endl;
    result = 0.0;
}
line24 = result;
```

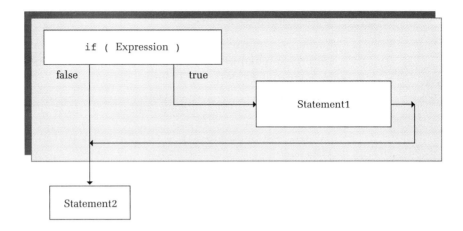

This code does exactly what the tax form says it should. It computes the result of subtracting line 23 from line 17. Then it looks to see if result is less than 0. If it is, the fragment prints a message telling the user to check box 24A and then sets result to 0. Finally, the calculated result (or 0, if the result is less than 0) is stored into a variable named line24.

What happens if we leave out the left and right braces in the code fragment above? Let's look at it:

```
result = line17 - line23;              // Incorrect version
if (result < 0.0)
    cout << "Check box 24A" << endl;
    result = 0.0;
line24 = result;
```

Despite the way we have indented the code, the compiler takes the then-clause to be a single statement—the output statement. If result is less than 0, the computer executes the output statement, then sets result to 0, and then stores result into line24. So far, so good. But if result is initially greater than or equal to 0, the computer skips the then-clause and proceeds to the statement following the If statement—the assignment statement that sets result to 0. The unhappy outcome is that result ends up as 0 no matter what its initial value was! The moral here is not to rely on indentation alone; you can't fool the compiler. If you want a compound statement for a then- or else-clause, you must include the left and right braces.

A Common Mistake

Earlier we warned against confusing the = operator and the == operator. Here is an example of a mistake that every C++ programmer is guaranteed to make at least once in his or her career:

```
cin >> n;
if (n = 3)                      // Wrong
    cout << "n equals 3";
else
    cout << "n doesn't equal 3";
```

This code segment *always* prints out

```
n equals 3
```

no matter what was input for n.

Here is the reason: We've used the wrong operator in the If test. The expression n = 3 is not a logical expression; it's called an *assignment expression*. (If an assignment is written as a separate statement ending with a semicolon, it's an assignment *statement*.) An assignment expression has a *value* (above, it's 3) and a *side effect* (storing 3 into n). In the If statement of our example, the computer finds the value of the tested expression to be 3. Because 3 is a nonzero value and thus is coerced to true, the then-clause is executed, no matter what the value of n is. Worse yet, the side effect of the assignment expression is to store 3 into n, destroying what was there.

Our intention is not to focus on assignment expressions; we discuss their use later in the book. What's important now is that you see the effect of using = when you meant to use ==. The program compiles correctly but runs incorrectly. When debugging a faulty program, always look at your If statements to see whether you've made this particular mistake.

Nested If Statements

There are no restrictions on what the statements in an If can be. Therefore, an If within an If is OK. In fact, an If within an If within an If is legal. The only limitation here is that people cannot follow a structure that is too involved, and readability is one of the marks of a good program.

When we place an If within an If, we are creating a *nested control structure*. Control structures nest much like mixing bowls do, with smaller ones tucked inside larger ones. Here's an example, written in pseudocode:

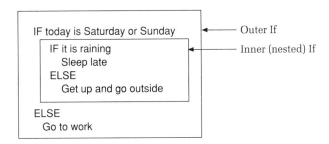

In general, any problem that involves a *multiway branch* (more than two alternative courses of action) can be coded using nested If statements. For example, to print out the name of a month given its number, we could use a sequence of If statements (unnested):

```
if (month == 1)
    cout << "January";
if (month == 2)
    cout << "February";
if (month == 3)
    cout << "March";
    ⋮
if (month == 12)
    cout << "December";
```

But the equivalent nested If structure,

```
if (month == 1)
    cout << "January";
else
    if (month == 2)              // Nested If
        cout << "February";
    else
        if (month == 3)          // Nested If
            cout << "March";
        else
            if (month == 4)              // Nested If
                ⋮
```

is more efficient because it makes fewer comparisons. The first version—
the sequence of independent If statements—always tests every condition
(all 12 of them), even if the first one is satisfied. In contrast, the nested If
solution skips all remaining comparisons after one alternative has been
selected. As fast as modern computers are, many applications require so
much computation that inefficient algorithms can waste hours of computer
time. Always be on the lookout for ways to make your programs more efficient, as long as doing so doesn't make them difficult for other programmers to understand. It's usually better to sacrifice a little efficiency for the
sake of readability.

In the last example, notice how the indentation of the then- and else-
clauses causes the statements to move continually the right. Instead, we
can use a special indentation style with deeply nested If-Then-Else statements to indicate that the complex structure is just choosing one of a set of
alternatives. This general multiway branch is known as an *If-Then-Else-If*
control structure:

```
if (month == 1)
    cout << "January";
else if (month == 2)            // Nested If
    cout << "February";
else if (month == 3)            // Nested If
    cout << "March";
else if (month == 4)            // Nested If
    ⋮
else
    cout << "December";
```

This style prevents the indentation from marching continuously to the
right. But, more important, it visually conveys the idea that we are using a
12-way branch based on the variable `month`.

It's important to note one difference between the sequence of If statements and the nested If: More than one alternative can be taken by the
sequence of Ifs, but the nested If can select only one. To see why this is
important, consider the analogy of filling out a questionnaire. Some questions are like a sequence of If statements, asking you to circle all the items
in a list that apply to you (such as all your hobbies). Other questions ask
you to circle only one item in a list (your age group, for example) and are
thus like a nested If structure. Both kinds of questions occur in programming problems. Being able to recognize which type of question is being
asked permits you to immediately select the appropriate control structure.

Another particularly helpful use of the nested If is when you want to
select from a series of consecutive ranges of values. For example, suppose
that we want to print out an appropriate activity for the outdoor temperature, given the following table.

Activity	Temperature
Swimming	Temperature > 85
Tennis	$70 < \text{temperature} \le 85$
Golf	$32 < \text{temperature} \le 70$
Skiing	$0 < \text{temperature} \le 32$
Dancing	Temperature ≤ 0

At first glance, you may be tempted to write a separate If statement for each range of temperatures. On closer examination, however, it is clear that these If conditions are interdependent. That is, if one of the statements is executed, none of the others should be executed. We really are selecting one alternative from a set of possibilities—just the sort of situation in which we can use a nested If structure as a multiway branch. The only difference between this problem and our earlier example of printing the month name from its number is that we must check ranges of numbers in the If expressions of the branches.

When the ranges are consecutive, we can take advantage of that fact to make our code more efficient. We arrange the branches in consecutive order by range. Then, if a particular branch has been reached, we know that the preceding ranges have been eliminated from consideration. Thus, the If expressions must compare the temperature to only the lowest value of each range.

```cpp
cout << "The recommended activity is ";
if (temperature > 85)
    cout << "swimming." << endl;
else if (temperature > 70)
    cout << "tennis." << endl;
else if (temperature > 32)
    cout << "golf." << endl;
else if (temperature > 0)
    cout << "skiing." << endl;
else
    cout << "dancing." << endl;
```

To see how this If-Then-Else-If structure works, consider the branch that tests for `temperature` greater than 70. If it has been reached, we know that `temperature` must be less than or equal to 85 because that condition causes this particular `else` branch to be taken. Thus, we only need to test whether `temperature` is above the bottom of this range (> 70). If that test fails, then we enter the next else-clause knowing that `temperature` must be less than or equal to 70. Each successive branch checks the bottom of its range until we reach the final `else`, which takes care of all the remaining possibilities.

Note that if the ranges aren't consecutive, then we must test the data value against both the highest and lowest value of each range. We still use an If-Then-Else-If because that is the best structure for selecting a single branch from multiple possibilities, and we may arrange the ranges in consecutive order to make them easier for a human reader to follow. But there is no way to reduce the number of comparisons when there are gaps between the ranges.

The Dangling `else`

When If statements are nested, you may find yourself confused about the `if`-`else` pairings. That is, to which `if` does an `else` belong? For example, suppose that if a student's average is below 60, we want to print "Failing"; if it is at least 60 but less than 70, we want to print "Passing but marginal"; and if it is 70 or greater, we don't want to print anything.

We code this information with an If-Then-Else nested within an If-Then:

```
if (average < 70.0)
    if (average < 60.0)
        cout << "Failing";
    else
        cout << "Passing but marginal";
```

How do we know to which `if` the `else` belongs? Here is the rule that the C++ compiler follows: In the absence of braces, an `else` is always paired with the closest preceding `if` that doesn't already have an `else` paired with it. We indented the code to reflect this pairing.

Suppose we write the fragment like this:

```
if (average >= 60.0)        // Incorrect version
    if (average < 70.0)
        cout << "Passing but marginal";
else
    cout << "Failing";
```

Here we want the `else` branch attached to the outer If statement, not the inner, so we indent the code as you see it. But indentation does not affect the execution of the code. Even though the `else` aligns with the first `if`, the compiler pairs it with the second `if`. An `else` that follows a nested If-Then is called a *dangling else*. It doesn't logically belong with the nested If but is attached to it by the compiler.

To attach the `else` to the first `if`, not the second, you can turn the outer then-clause into a block:

```
if (average >= 60.0)        // Correct version
{
    if (average < 70.0)
        cout << "Passing but marginal";
}
else
    cout << "Failing";
```

The { } pair indicates that the inner If statement is complete, so the else must belong to the outer if.

Testing the State of an I/O Stream

In Chapter 4, we talked about the concept of input and output streams in C++. We introduced the classes istream, ostream, ifstream, and ofstream. We said that any of the following can cause an input stream to enter the fail state:

- Invalid input data
- An attempt to read beyond the end of a file
- An attempt to open a nonexistent file for input

C++ provides a way to check whether a stream is in the fail state. In a logical expression, you simply use the name of the stream object (such as cin) as if it were a Boolean variable:

```
if (cin)
    ⋮


if ( !inFile )
    ⋮
```

When you do this, you are said to be **testing the state of the stream.** The result of the test is either true (meaning the last I/O operation on that stream succeeded) or false (meaning the last I/O operation failed).

Conceptually, you want to think of a stream object in a logical expression as being a Boolean variable with a value true (the stream state is OK) or false (the state isn't OK).

Notice in the second If statement above that we typed spaces around the expression !inFile. The spaces are not required by C++ but are there for readability. Without the spaces, it is harder to see the exclamation mark: if (!inFile).

Testing the state of a stream   The act of using a C++ stream object in a logical expression as if it were a Boolean variable; the result is `true` if the last I/O operation on that stream succeeded, and `false` otherwise.

In an If statement, the way you phrase the logical expression depends on what you want the then-clause to do. The statement

```
if (inFile)
    ⋮
```

executes the then-clause if the last I/O operation on `inFile` succeeded. The statement

```
if ( !inFile )
    ⋮
```

executes the then-clause if `inFile` is in the fail state. (And remember that once a stream is in the fail state, it remains so. Any further I/O operations on that stream are null operations.)

Here's an example that shows how to check whether an input file was opened successfully:

```cpp
#include <iostream>
#include <fstream>      // For file I/O

using namespace std;

int main()
{
    int       height;
    int       width;
    ifstream inFile;

    inFile.open("mydata.dat");          // Attempt to open input file
    if ( !inFile )                      // Was it opened?
    {
        cout << "Can't open the input file.";   // No--print message
        return 1;                                // Terminate program
    }
    inFile >> height >> width;
    ⋮
    return 0;
}
```

In this program, we begin by attempting to open the disk file `mydata.dat` for input. Immediately, we check to see whether the attempt succeeded. If it was successful, the value of the expression `!inFile` in the If statement is `false` and the then-clause is skipped. The program proceeds to read data from the file and then, presumably, to perform some computations. It concludes by executing the statement

```
return 0;
```

With this statement, the `main` function returns control to the computer's operating system. Recall that the function value returned by `main` is known as the exit status. The value 0 signifies normal completion of the program. Any other value (typically 1, 2, 3, …) means that something went wrong.

Let's trace through the program again, assuming we weren't able to open the input file. Upon return from the `open` function, the stream `inFile` is in the fail state. In the If statement, the value of the expression `!inFile` is `true`. Thus, the then-clause is executed. The program prints an error message to the user and then terminates, returning an exit status of 1 to inform the operating system of an abnormal termination of the program. (Our choice of the value 1 for the exit status is purely arbitrary. System programmers sometimes use several different values in a program to signal different reasons for program termination. But most people just use the value 1.)

Whenever you open a data file for input, be sure to test the stream state before proceeding. If you forget to, and the computer cannot open the file, your program quietly continues executing and ignores any input operations on the file.

P ROBLEM-SOLVING CASE STUDY

Warning Notices

Problem: Many universities send warning notices to freshmen who are in danger of failing a class. Your program should calculate the average of three test grades and print out a student's ID number, average, and whether or not the student is passing. Passing is a 60-point average or better. If the student is passing with less than a 70 average, the program should indicate that he or she is marginal.

Input: Student ID number (of type `long`) followed by three test grades (of type `int`). On some personal computers, the maximum `int` value is `32767`. The student ID number is of type `long` (meaning long integer) to accommodate larger values such as nine-digit Social Security numbers.

Output:

A prompt for input

The input values (echo print)

Student ID number, average grade, passing/failing message, marginal indication, and error message if any of the test scores are negative

Discussion: To calculate the average, we have to read in the three test scores, add them, and divide by 3.

To print the appropriate message, we have to determine whether or not the average is below 60. If it is at least 60, we have to determine if it is less than 70.

If you were doing this by hand, you probably would notice if a test grade was negative and question it. If the semantics of your data imply that the values should be nonnegative, then your program should test to be sure they are. We test to make sure each grade is nonnegative, using a Boolean variable to report the result of the test. Here is the main module for our algorithm.

Main Module   **Level 0**

```
Get data
Test data
IF data OK
        Calculate average
        Print message indicating status
ELSE
        Print "Invalid Data: Score(s) less than zero."
```

Which of these steps require(s) expansion? *Get data*, *Test data*, and *Print message indicating status* all require multiple statements in order to solve their particular subproblem. On the other hand, we can translate *Print "Invalid Data:..."* directly into a C++ output statement. What about the step *Calculate average*? We can write it as a single C++ statement, but there's another level of detail that we must fill in—the actual formula to be used. Because the formula is at a lower level of detail than the rest of the main module, we chose to expand *Calculate average* as a level 1 module.

Get Data   Level 1

```
Prompt for input
Read studentID, test1, test2, test3
Print studentID, test1, test2, test3
```

Test Data

```
IF test1 < 0 OR test2 < 0 OR test3 < 0
        Set dataOK = false
ELSE
        Set dataOK = true
```

Calculate Average

```
Set average = (test1 + test2 + test3) / 3.0
```

Print Message Indicating Status

```
Print average
IF average >= 60.0
        Print "Passing"
        IF average < 70.0
                Print " but marginal"
        Print '.'
ELSE
        Print "Failing."
```

<u>*PROBLEM-SOLVING CASE STUDY cont'd.*</u>

Module Structure Chart:

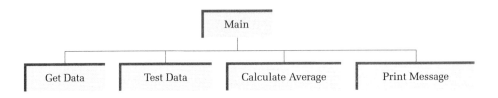

Variables

Name	Data Type	Description
average	float	Average of three test scores
studentID	long	Student's identification number
test1	int	Score for first test
test2	int	Score for second test
test3	int	Score for third test
dataOK	bool	True if data is correct

To save space, from here on we omit the list of constants and variables from the Problem-Solving Case Studies. But we recommend that you continue writing those lists as you design your own algorithms. The lists save you a lot of work when you are writing the declarations for your programs. Here is the program that implements our design.

(The following program is written in ISO/ANSI standard C++. If you are working with pre–standard C++, see the alternate version of the program in the PRE_STD directory of the program disk, available at the publisher's Web site, www.jbpub.com/disks.)

```
//**************************************************************
// Notices program
// This program determines (1) a student's average based on three
// test scores and (2) the student's passing/failing status
//**************************************************************
#include <iostream>
#include <iomanip>     // For setprecision()

using namespace std;
```

```
int main()
{
    float average;         // Average of three test scores
    long  studentID;       // Student's identification number
    int   test1;           // Score for first test
    int   test2;           // Score for second test
    int   test3;           // Score for third test
    bool  dataOK;          // True if data is correct

    cout << fixed << showpoint;           // Set up floating-pt.
                                          //   output format
    // Get data

    cout << "Enter a Student ID number and three test scores:"
         << endl;
    cin >> studentID >> test1 >> test2 >> test3;
    cout << "Student number: " << studentID << "  Test Scores: "
         << test1 << ", " << test2 << ", " << test3 << endl;

    // Test data

    if (test1 < 0 || test2 < 0 || test3 < 0)
        dataOK = false;
    else
        dataOK = true;

    if (dataOK)
    {
        // Calculate average

        average = float(test1 + test2 + test3) / 3.0;

        // Print message

        cout << "Average score is "
             << setprecision(2) << average << "--";
        if (average >= 60.0)
        {
            cout << "Passing";                    // Student is passing
            if (average < 70.0)
                cout << " but marginal";          // But marginal
            cout << '.' << endl;
        }
        else                                      // Student is failing
            cout << "Failing." << endl;
    }
```

```
        else                                  // Invalid data
            cout << "Invalid Data:  Score(s) less than zero." << endl;

        return 0;
    }
```

Here's a sample run of the program. Again, the input is in color.

```
Enter a Student ID number and three test scores:
9483681  73  62  68
Student Number: 9483681   Test Scores: 73, 62, 68
Average score is 67.67--Passing but marginal.
```

And here's a sample run with invalid data:

```
Enter a Student ID number and three test scores:
9483681  73  -10  62
Student Number: 9483681   Test Scores: 73, -10, 62
Invalid Data:  Score(s) less than zero.
```

In this program, we use a nested If structure that's easy to understand although somewhat inefficient. We assign a value to `dataOK` in one statement before testing it in the next. We could reduce the code by saying

```
dataOK = ! (test1 < 0 || test2 < 0 || test3 < 0);
```

Using DeMorgan's law, we also could write this statement as

```
dataOK = (test1 >= 0 && test2 >= 0 && test3 >= 0);
```

In fact, we could reduce the code even more by eliminating the variable `dataOK` and using

```
if (test1 >= 0 && test2 >= 0 && test3 >= 0)
    ⋮
```

in place of

```
if (dataOK)
    ⋮
```

To convince yourself that these three variations work, try them by hand with some test data.

If all of these statements do the same thing, how do you choose which one to use? If your goal is efficiency, the final variation—the compound condition in the main If statement—is best. If you are trying to express as clearly as possible what your code is doing, the longer form shown in the program may be best. The other variations lie somewhere in between. (However, some people would find the compound condition in the main If statement to be not only the most efficient but also the clearest to understand.) There are no absolute rules to follow here, but the general guideline is to strive for clarity, even if you must sacrifice a little efficiency.

Testing and Debugging

In Chapter 1, we discussed the problem-solving and implementation phases of computer programming. Testing is an integral part of both phases. Here we test both phases of the process used to develop the Notices program. Testing in the problem-solving phase is done after the solution is developed but before it is implemented. In the implementation phase, we test after the algorithm is translated into a program, and again after the program has compiled successfully. The compilation itself constitutes another stage of testing that is performed automatically.

Testing in the Problem-Solving Phase: The Algorithm Walk-Through

Determining Preconditions and Postconditions   To test during the problem-solving phase, we do a *walk-through* of the algorithm. For each module in the functional decomposition, we establish an assertion called a precondition and another called a postcondition. A **precondition** is an assertion that must be true before a module is executed in order for the module to execute correctly. A **postcondition** is an assertion that should be true after the module has executed, if it has done its job correctly. To test a module, we "walk through" the algorithmic steps to confirm that they produce the required postcondition, given the stated precondition.

Precondition   An assertion that must be true before a module begins executing.

Postcondition   An assertion that should be true after a module has executed.

Our algorithm has five modules: the main module, Get Data, Test Data, Calculate Average, and Print Message Indicating Status. Usually there is no precondition for a main module. Our main module's postcondition is that it outputs the correct results, given the correct input. More specifically, the postcondition for the main module is

- the computer has input four integer values into `studentID`, `test1`, `test2`, and `test3`.
- the input values have been echo printed.
- if the input is invalid, an error message has been printed; otherwise, the average of the last three input values has been printed, along with the message "Passing" if the average is greater than or equal to 70.0, "Passing but marginal." if the average is less than 70.0 and greater than or equal to 60.0, or "Failing." if the average is less than 60.0.

Because Get Data is the first module executed in the algorithm and because it does not assume anything about the contents of the variables it is about to manipulate, it has no precondition. Its postcondition is that it has input four integer values into `studentID`, `test1`, `test2`, and `test3`.

The precondition for module Test Data is that `test1`, `test2`, and `test3` have been assigned meaningful values. Its postcondition is that `dataOK` contains `true` if the values in `test1`, `test2`, and `test3` are non-negative; otherwise, `dataOK` contains `false`.

The precondition for module Calculate Average is that `test1`, `test2`, and `test3` contain meaningful values. Its postcondition is that the variable named `average` contains the mean (the average) of `test1`, `test2`, and `test3`.

The precondition for module Print Message Indicating Status is that `average` contains the mean of the values in `test1`, `test2`, and `test3`. Its postcondition is that the value in `average` has been printed, along with the message "Passing" if the average is greater than or equal to 70.0, "Passing but marginal." if the average is less than 70.0 and greater than or equal to 60.0, or "Failing." if the average is less than 60.0.

Below we summarize the module preconditions and postconditions in tabular form. In the table, we use *AND* with its usual meaning in an assertion—the logical AND operation. Also, a phrase like "someVariable is assigned" is an abbreviated way of asserting that `someVariable` has already been assigned a meaningful value.

Module	Precondition	Postcondition
Main	—	Four integer values have been input AND The input values have been echo printed AND If the input is invalid, an error message has been printed; otherwise, the average of the last three input values has been printed, along with a message indicating the student's status
Get Data	—	`studentID`, `test1`, `test2`, and `test3` have been input
Test Data	`test1`, `test2`, and `test3` are assigned	`dataOK` contains `true` if `test1`, `test2`, and `test3` are nonnegative; otherwise, `dataOK` contains `false`
Calculate Average	`test1`, `test2`, and `test3` are assigned	`average` contains the average of `test1`, `test2`, and `test3`
Print Message Indicating Status	`average` contains the average of `test1`, `test2`, and `test3`	The value of `average` has been printed, along with a message indicating the student's status

Performing the Algorithm Walk-Through Now that we've established the preconditions and postconditions, we walk through the main module. At this point, we are concerned only with the steps in the main module, so for now we assume that each lower-level module executes correctly. At each step, we must determine the current conditions. If the step is a reference to another module, we must verify that the precondition of that module is met by the current conditions.

By permission of Johnny Hart and Creators Syndicate, Inc.

We begin with the first statement in the main module. Get Data does not have a precondition, and we assume that Get Data satisfies its postcondition that it correctly inputs four integer values into `studentID`, `test1`, `test2`, and `test3`.

The precondition for module Test Data is that `test1`, `test2`, and `test3` are assigned values. This must be the case if Get Data's postcondition is true. Again, because we are concerned only with the step at level 0, we assume that Test Data satisfies its postcondition that `dataOK` contains `true` or `false`, depending on the input values.

Next, the If statement checks to see if `dataOK` is `true`. If it is, the algorithm performs the then-clause. Assuming that Calculate Average correctly calculates the mean of `test1`, `test2`, and `test3` and that Print Message Indicating Status prints the average and the appropriate message (remember, we're assuming that the lower-level modules are correct for now), then the If statement's then-clause is correct. If the value in `dataOK` is `false`, the algorithm performs the else-clause and prints an error message.

We now have verified that the main (level 0) module is correct, assuming the level 1 modules are correct. The next step is to examine each module at level 1 and answer this question: If the level 2 modules (if any) are assumed to be correct, does this level 1 module do what it is supposed to do? We simply repeat the walk-through process for each module, starting with its particular precondition. In this example, there are no level 2 modules, so the level 1 modules must be complete.

Get Data correctly reads in four values—`studentID`, `test1`, `test2`, and `test3`—thereby satisfying its postcondition. (The next refinement is to code this instruction in C++. Whether it is coded correctly or not is *not* an issue in this phase; we deal with the code when we perform testing in the implementation phase.)

Test Data checks to see if all three of the variables contain nonnegative scores. The If condition correctly uses OR operators to combine the relational expressions so that if any of them are `true`, the then-clause is executed. It thus assigns `false` to `dataOK` if any of the numbers are negative; otherwise, it assigns `true`. The module therefore satisfies its postcondition.

Calculate Average sums the three test scores, divides the sum by 3.0, and assigns the result to `average`. The required postcondition therefore is true.

Print Message Indicating Status outputs the value in `average`. It then tests whether `average` is greater than or equal to 60.0. If so, "Passing" is printed and it then tests whether `average` is less than 70.0. If so, the words "but marginal" are added after "Passing". On the other hand, if `average` is less than 60.0, the message "Failing." is printed. Thus the module satisfies its postcondition.

Once we've completed the algorithm walk-through, we have to correct any discrepancies and repeat the process. When we know that the modules do what they are supposed to do, we start translating the algorithm into our programming language.

A standard postcondition for any program is that the user has been notified of invalid data. You should *validate* every input value for which any restrictions apply. A data-validation If statement tests an input value and outputs an error message if the value is not acceptable. (We validated the data when we tested for negative scores in the Notices program.) The best place to validate data is immediately after it is input. To satisfy the data-validation postcondition, the Warning Notices algorithm also should test the input values to ensure that they aren't too large.

For example, if the maximum score on a test is 100, then module Test Data should check for values in `test1`, `test2`, and `test3` that are greater than 100. The printing of the error message also should be modified to indicate the particular error condition that occurred. It would be best if it also specified the score that is invalid. Such a change makes it clear that Test Data should be the module to print the error messages. If Test Data prints the error message, then the If-Then-Else in the main module can be rewritten as an If-Then.

Testing in the Implementation Phase

Now that we've talked about testing in the problem-solving phase, we turn to testing in the implementation phase. In this phase, you need to test at several points.

Code Walk-Through   After the code is written, you should go over it line by line to be sure that you've faithfully reproduced the algorithm—a process known as a *code walk-through*. In a team programming situation, you ask other team members to walk through the algorithm and code with you, to double-check the design and code.

Execution Trace   You also should take some actual values and hand-calculate what the output should be by doing an *execution trace* (or *hand trace*). When the program is executed, you can use these same values as input and check the results.

The computer is a very literal device—it does exactly what we tell it to do, which may or may not be what we want it to do. We try to make sure that a program does what we want by tracing the execution of the statements.

We use a nonsense program below to demonstrate the technique. We keep track of the values of the program variables on the right-hand side. Variables with undefined values are indicated with a dash. When a variable is assigned a value, that value is listed in the appropriate column.

	Value of		
Statement	*a*	*b*	*c*
`const int x = 5;`			
`int main()`			
`{`			
`    int a, b, c;`	—	—	—
`    b = 1;`	—	1	—
`    c = x + b;`	—	1	6
`    a = x + 4;`	9	1	6
`    a = c;`	6	1	6
`    b = c;`	6	6	6
`    a = a + b + c;`	18	6	6
`    c = c % x;`	18	6	1
`    c = c * a;`	18	6	18
`    a = a % b;`	0	6	18
`    cout << a << b`			
`        << c;`	0	6	18
`    return 0;`	0	6	18
`}`			

Now that you've seen how the technique works, let's apply it to the Notices program. We list only the executable statement portion here. The input values are 6483, 73, 62, and 60. (The table is on page 255.)

The then-clause of the first If statement is not executed for this input data, so we do not fill in any of the variable columns to its right. The same situation occurs with the else-clauses in the other If statements. The test data causes only the then-clauses to be executed. We always create columns for all of the variables, even if we know that some will stay empty. Why? Because it's possible that later we'll encounter an erroneous reference to an empty variable; having a column for the variable reminds us to check for just such an error.

	Value of					
Statement	*test 1*	*test 2*	*test 3*	*average*	*dataOK*	*student ID*
`cout << "Enter a Student ID number and three "`						
`    << "test scores:" << endl;`	—	—	—	—	—	—
`cin >> studentID >> test1 >> test2 >> test3;`	73	62	60	—	—	6483
`cout << "Student number: " << studentID`						
`    << "  Test Scores: " << test1 << ", "`						
`    << test2 << ", " << test3 << endl;`	73	62	60	—	—	6483
`if (test1 < 0 || test2 < 0 || test3 < 0)`	73	62	60	—	—	6483
`    dataOK = false;`						
`else`						
`    dataOK = true;`	73	62	60	—	true	6483
`if (dataOK)`	73	62	60	—	true	6483
`{`						
`    average = float(test1 + test2 + test3) /`						
`                3.0;`	73	62	60	67.67	true	6483
`    cout << "Average score is "`						
`        << setprecision(2) << average << "--";`	73	62	60	67.67	true	6483
`    if (average >= 60.0)`	73	62	60	67.67	true	6483
`    {`						
`        cout << "Passing";`	73	62	60	67.67	true	6483
`        if (average < 70.0)`	73	62	60	67.67	true	6483
`            cout << " but marginal";`	73	62	60	67.67	true	6483
`        cout << '.' << endl;`	73	62	60	67.67	true	6483
`    }`						
`    else`						
`        cout << "Failing." << endl;`						
`}`						
`else`						
`    cout << "Invalid Data:  Score(s) less "`						
`        << "than zero." << endl;`						
`return 0;`	73	62	60	67.67	true	6483

When a program contains branches, it's a good idea to retrace its execution with different input data so that each branch is traced at least once. In the next section, we describe how to develop data sets that test each of a program's branches.

Testing Selection Control Structures To test a program with branches, we need to execute each branch at least once and verify the results. For example, in the Notices program there are four If-Then-Else statements (see Figure 5-6). We need a series of data sets to test the different branches. For example, the following sets of input values for test1, test2, and test3 cause all of the branches to be executed:

	test1	test2	test3
Set 1	100	100	100
Set 2	60	60	63
Set 3	50	50	50
Set 4	−50	50	50

Figure 5-7 shows the flow of control through the branching structure of the Notices program for each of these data sets. Set 1 is valid and gives an average of 100, which is passing and not marginal. Set 2 is valid and gives an average of 61, which is passing but marginal. Set 3 is valid and gives an average of 50, which is failing. Set 4 has an invalid test grade, which generates an error message.

Every branch in the program is executed at least once through this series of test runs; eliminating any of the test data sets would leave at least one branch untested. This series of data sets provides what is called *minimum complete coverage* of the program's branching structure. Whenever you test a program with branches in it, you should design a series of tests that covers all of the branches. It may help to draw diagrams like those in Figure 5-7 so that you can see which branches are being executed.

FIGURE 5-6
Branching
Structure for
Notices Program

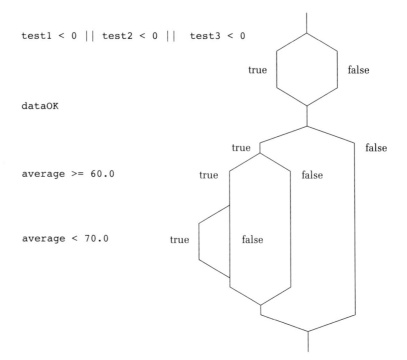

```
test1 < 0 || test2 < 0 ||  test3 < 0
```

```
dataOK
```

```
average >= 60.0
```

```
average < 70.0
```

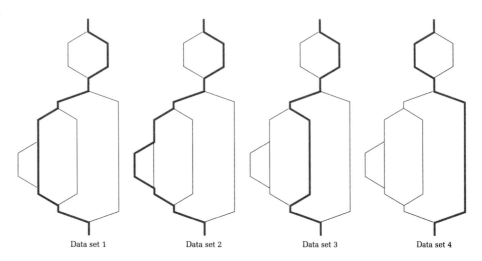

Data set 1   Data set 2   Data set 3   Data set 4

Because an action in one branch of a program often affects processing in a later branch, it is critical to test as many *combinations of branches*, or paths, through a program as possible. By doing so, we can be sure that there are no interdependencies that could cause problems. Of course, some combinations of branches may be impossible to follow. For example, if the else is taken in the first branch of the Notices program, the else in the second branch cannot be taken. Shouldn't we try all possible paths? Yes, in theory we should. However, the number of paths in even a small program can be very large.

The approach to testing that we've used here is called *code coverage* because the test data is designed by looking at the code of the program. Code coverage is also called *white box* (or *clear box*) *testing* because we are allowed to see the program code while designing the tests. Another approach to testing, *data coverage*, attempts to test as many allowable data values as possible without regard to the program code. Because we need not see the code in this form of testing, it is also called *black box testing*— we would design the same set of tests even if the code were hidden in a black box. Complete data coverage is as impractical as complete code coverage for many programs. For example, the Notices program reads four integer values and thus has approximately $(2 * \text{INT\_MAX})^4$ possible inputs. (INT_MAX and INT_MIN are constants declared in the header file climits. They represent the largest and smallest possible int values, respectively, on your particular computer and C++ compiler.)

Often, testing is a combination of these two strategies. Instead of trying every possible data value (data coverage), we examine the code (code coverage) and look for ranges of values for which processing is identical. Then we test the values at the boundaries and, sometimes, a value in the middle of each range. For example, a simple condition such as

```
alpha < 0
```

divides the integers into two ranges:

1. INT_MIN through −1
2. 0 through INT_MAX

Thus, we should test the four values INT_MIN, −1, 0, and INT_MAX. A compound condition such as

```
alpha >= 0 && alpha <= 100
```

divides the integers into three ranges:

1. `INT_MIN` through −1
2. 0 through 100
3. 101 through `INT_MAX`

Thus, we have six values to test. In addition, to verify that the relational operators are correct, we should test for values of 1 (> 0) and 99 (< 100).

Conditional branches are only one factor in developing a testing strategy. We consider more of these factors in later chapters.

The Test Plan

We've discussed strategies and techniques for testing programs, but how do you approach the testing of a specific program? You do it by designing and implementing a **test plan**—a document that specifies the test cases that should be tried, the reason for each test case, and the expected output. **Implementing a test plan** involves running the program using the data specified by the test cases in the plan and checking and recording the results.

Test plan A document that specifies how a program is to be tested.

Test plan implementation Using the test cases specified in a test plan to verify that a program outputs the predicted results.

The test plan should be developed together with the functional decomposition. As you create each module, write out its precondition and postcondition and note the test data required to verify them. Consider code coverage and data coverage to see if you've left out tests for any aspects of the program (if you've forgotten something, it probably also indicates that a precondition or postcondition is incomplete).

The following table shows a partial test plan for the Notices program. It has eight test cases. The first test case is just to check that the program echo prints its input properly. The next three cases test the different paths through the program for valid data. Three more test cases check that each of the scores is appropriately validated by separately entering an invalid score for each. The last test case checks the boundary where a score is considered valid—when it is 0. We could further expand this test plan to check the valid data boundary separately for each score by providing three test cases in which one score in each case is 0. We also could test the boundary conditions of the different paths for valid data. That is, we could check that averages of exactly 60 and 70, and slightly higher and slightly lower, produce the desired output. Case Study Follow-Up Exercise 1 asks you to complete this test plan and implement it.

Test Plan for Notices Program

Reason for Test Case	Input Values	Expected Output	Observed Output
Echo-print check	9999, 100, 100, 100	Student Number: 9999 Test Scores: 100, 100, 100	

Note to implementor: Once echo printing has been checked, it is omitted from the expected output column in subsequent test cases, but still appears in the program's output.

Passing scores	9999, 80, 70, 90	Average score is 80.00-- Passing.	
Passing but marginal scores	9999, 55, 65, 75	Average score is 65.00-- Passing but marginal.	
Failing scores	9999, 30, 40, 50	Average score is 40.00-- Failing.	
Invalid data, Test 1	9999, −1, 20, 30	Invalid Data: Score(s) less than zero.	
Invalid data, Test 2	9999, 10, −1, 30	Invalid Data: Score(s) less than zero.	
Invalid data, Test 3	9999, 10, 20, −1	Invalid Data: Score(s) less than zero.	
Boundary of valid data	9999, 0, 0, 0	Average score is 0.00-- Failing.	

Implementing a test plan does not guarantee that a program is completely correct. It means only that a careful, systematic test of the program has not demonstrated any bugs. The situation shown in Figure 5-8 is analogous to trying to test a program without a plan—depending only on luck, you may completely miss the fact that a program contains numerous errors. Developing and implementing a written test plan, on the other hand, casts a wide net that is much more likely to find errors.

Tests Performed Automatically During Compilation and Execution

Once a program is coded and test data has been prepared, it is ready for compiling. The compiler has two responsibilities: to report any errors and (if there are no errors) to translate the program into object code.

Errors can be syntactic or semantic. The compiler finds syntactic errors. For example, the compiler warns you when reserved words are misspelled, identifiers are undeclared, semicolons are missing, and operand types are mismatched. But it won't find all of your typing errors. If you type > instead of < , you won't get an error message; instead, you get erroneous results when you test the program. It's up to you to design a test plan and carefully check the code to detect errors of this type.

FIGURE 5-8

When You Test a Program Without a Plan, You Never Know What You Might Be Missing

Reprinted by permission of Jeff Griffin.

Semantic errors (also called *logic errors*) are mistakes that give you the wrong answer. They are more difficult to locate than syntactic errors and usually surface when a program is executing. C++ detects only the most obvious semantic errors—those that result in an invalid operation (dividing by zero, for example). Although semantic errors sometimes are caused by typing errors, they are more often a product of a faulty algorithm design. The lack of checking for test scores over 100 that we found in the algorithm walk-through for the Warning Notices problem is a typical semantic error.

By walking through the algorithm and the code, tracing the execution of the program, and developing a thorough test strategy, you should be able to avoid, or at least quickly locate, semantic errors in your programs.

Figure 5-9 illustrates the testing process we've been discussing. The figure shows where syntax and semantic errors occur and in which phase they can be corrected.

FIGURE 5-9

Testing Process

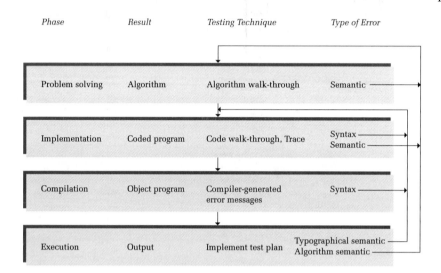

Testing and Debugging Hints

1. C++ has three pairs of operators that are similar in appearance but very different in effect: == and =, && and &, and | | and |. Double-check all of your logical expressions to be sure you're using the "equals-equals," "and-and," and "or-or" operators.

2. If you use extra parentheses for clarity, be sure that the opening and closing parentheses match up. To verify that parentheses are properly paired, start with the innermost pair and draw a line connecting them. Do the same for the others, working your way out to the outermost pair. For example,

Here is a quick way to tell whether you have an equal number of opening and closing parentheses. The scheme uses a single number (the "magic number"), whose value initially is 0. Scan the expression from left to right. At each opening parenthesis, add 1 to the magic number; at each closing parenthesis, subtract 1. At the final closing parenthesis, the magic number should be 0. For example,

```
if ((( total/scores) > 50) && ((total/(scores - 1)) < 100))
    0   123                2    1    23      4          32       10
```

3. Don't use =< to mean "less than or equal to"; only the symbol <= works. Likewise, => is invalid for "greater than or equal to"; you must use >= for this operation.

4. In an If statement, remember to use a { } pair if the then-clause or else-clause is a sequence of statements. And be sure not to put a semicolon after the right brace.

5. Echo print all input data. By doing so, you know that your input values are what they are supposed to be.

6. Test for bad data. If a data value must be positive, use an If statement to test the value. If the value is negative or 0, an error message should be printed; otherwise, processing should continue. For example, module Test Data in the Notices program could be rewritten to test for scores greater than 100 as follows (this change also requires that we remove the else branch in the main module):

```
dataOK = true;
if (test1 < 0 || test2 < 0 || test3 < 0)
{
    cout << "Invalid Data:  Score(s) less than zero." << endl;
    dataOK = false;
}
if (test1 > 100 || test2 > 100 || test3 > 100)
{
    cout << "Invalid Data:  Score(s) greater than 100." << endl;
    dataOK = false;
}
```

These If statements test the limits of reasonable scores, and the rest of the program continues only if the data values are reasonable.

7. Take some sample values and try them by hand as we did for the Notices program. (There's more on this method in Chapter 6.)

8. If your program reads data from an input file, it should verify that the file was opened successfully. Immediately after the call to the open function, an If statement should test the state of the file stream.

9. If your program produces an answer that does not agree with a value you've calculated by hand, try these suggestions:

   a. Redo your arithmetic.

   b. Recheck your input data.

   c. Carefully go over the section of code that does the calculation. If you're in doubt about the order in which the operations are performed, insert clarifying parentheses.

   d. Check for integer overflow. The value of an int variable may have exceeded INT_MAX in the middle of a calculation. Some systems give an error message when this happens, but most do not.

   e. Check the conditions in branching statements to be sure that the correct branch is taken under all circumstances.

Summary

Using logical expressions is a way of asking questions while a program is running. The program evaluates each logical expression, producing the value `true` if the expression is true or the value `false` if the expression is not true.

The If statement allows you to take different paths through a program based on the value of a logical expression. The If-Then-Else is used to choose between two courses of action; the If-Then is used to choose whether or not to take a particular course of action. The branches of an If-Then or If-Then-Else can be any statement, simple or compound. They can even be other If statements.

The algorithm walk-through requires us to define a precondition and a postcondition for each module in an algorithm. Then we need to verify that those assertions are true at the beginning and end of each module. By testing our design in the problem-solving phase, we can eliminate errors that can be more difficult to detect in the implementation phase.

An execution trace is a way of finding program errors once we've entered the implementation phase. It's a good idea to trace a program before you run it, so that you have some sample results against which to check the program's output. A written test plan is an essential part of any program development effort.

Quick Check

1. Write a C++ expression that compares the variable `letter` to the constant 'Z' and yields `true` if `letter` is less than 'Z'. (pp. 214–220)
2. Write a C++ expression that yields `true` if `letter` is between 'A' and 'Z' inclusive. (pp. 214–224)
3. What form of the If statement would you use to make a C++ program print out "Is an uppercase letter" if the value in `letter` is between 'A' and 'Z' inclusive, and print out "Is not an uppercase letter" if the value in `letter` is outside that range? (pp. 229–231)
4. What form of the If statement would you use to make a C++ program print out "Is a digit" only if the value in the variable `someChar` is between '0' and '9' inclusive? (pp. 234–236)
5. On a telephone, each of the digits 2 through 9 has a segment of the alphabet associated with it. What kind of control structure would you use to decide which segment a given letter falls into and to print out the corresponding digit? (pp. 236–240)
6. What is one postcondition that every program should have? (pp. 249–253)
7. In what phase of the program development process should you carry out an execution trace? (pp. 253–256)

8. You've written a program that prints out the corresponding digit on a phone, given a letter of the alphabet. Everything seems to work right except that you can't get the digit '5' to print out; you keep getting the digit '6'. What steps would you take to find and fix this bug? (pp. 256–259)

9. How do we satisfy the postcondition that the user has been notified of invalid data values? (pp. 249–253)

Answers **1.** letter < 'Z' **2.** letter >= 'A' && letter <= 'Z' **3.** The If-Then-Else form **4.** The If-Then form **5.** A nested If statement **6.** The user has been notified of invalid data values. **7.** The implementation phase **8.** Carefully review the section of code that should print out '5'. Check the branching condition and the output statement there. Try some sample values by hand. **9.** The program must validate every input for which any restrictions apply and print an error message if the data violates any of the restrictions.

Exam Preparation Exercises

1. Given these values for the Boolean variables x, y, and z:

   x = true, y = false, z = true

   evaluate the following logical expressions. In the blank next to each expression, write a T if the result is true or an F if the result is false.

   _____ a. x && y || x && z
   _____ b. (x || !y) && (!x || z)
   _____ c. x || y && z
   _____ d. !(x || y) && z

2. Given these values for variables i, j, p, and q:

   i = 10, j = 19, p = true, q = false

   add parentheses (if necessary) to the expressions below so that they evaluate to true.

   a. i == j || p
   b. i >= j || i <= j && p
   c. !p || p
   d. !q && q

3. Given these values for the int variables i, j, m, and n:

   i = 6, j = 7, m = 11, n = 11

   what is the output of the following code?

```
cout << "Madam";
if (i < j)
    if (m != n)
        cout << "How";
    else
        cout << "Now";
cout << "I'm";
if (i >= m)
    cout << "Cow";
else
    cout << "Adam";
```

4. Given the int variables x, y, and z, where x contains 3, y contains 7, and z contains 6, what is the output from each of the following code fragments?

    a. ```
    if (x <= 3)
          cout << x + y << endl;
       cout << x + y << endl;
    ```
    b. ```
    if (x != -1)
          cout << "The value of x is " << x << endl;
       else
          cout << "The value of y is " << y << endl;
    ```
    c. ```
    if (x != -1)
       {
          cout << x << endl;
          cout << y << endl;
          cout << z << endl;
       }
       else
          cout << "y" << endl;
          cout << "z" << endl;
    ```

5.  Given this code fragment:

    ```
    if (height >= minHeight)
        if (weight >= minWeight)
           cout << "Eligible to serve." << endl;
        else
           cout << "Too light to serve." << endl;
    else
        if (weight >= minWeight)
           cout << "Too short to serve." << endl;
        else
           cout << "Too short and too light to serve." << endl;
    ```

    a. What is the output when height exceeds minHeight and weight exceeds minWeight?
    b. What is the output when height is less than minHeight and weight is less than minWeight?

6. Match each logical expression in the left column with the logical expression in the right column that tests for the same condition.

_____ a. x < y && y < z	(1) !(x != y) && y == z
_____ b. x > y && y >= z	(2) !(x <= y || y < z)
_____ c. x != y || y == z	(3) (y < z || y == z) || x == y
_____ d. x == y || y <= z	(4) !(x >= y) && !(y >= z)
_____ e. x == y && y == z	(5) !(x == y && y != z)
    ```

7. The following expressions make sense but are invalid according to C++'s rules of syntax. Rewrite them so that they are valid logical expressions. (All the variables are of type int.)

    a. x < y <= z

    b. x, y, and z are greater than 0

    c. x is equal to neither y nor z

    d. x is equal to y and z

8. Given these values for the Boolean variables x, y, and z:

    x = true, y = true, z = false

    indicate whether each expression is true (T) or false (F).

    _____ a. !(y || z) || x

    _____ b. z && x && y

    _____ c. ! y || (z || !x)

    _____ d. z || (x && (y || z))

    _____ e. x || x && z

9. For each of the following problems, decide which is more appropriate, an If-Then-Else or an If-Then. Explain your answers.

    a. Students who are candidates for admission to a college submit their SAT scores. If a student's score is equal to or above a certain value, print a letter of acceptance for the student. Otherwise, print a rejection notice.

    b. For employees who work more than 40 hours a week, calculate overtime pay and add it to their regular pay.

    c. In solving a quadratic equation, whenever the value of the discriminant (the quantity under the square root sign) is negative, print out a message noting that the roots are complex (imaginary) numbers.

    d. In a computer-controlled sawmill, if a cross section of a log is greater than certain dimensions, adjust the saw to cut 4-inch by 8-inch beams; otherwise, adjust the saw to cut 2-inch by 4-inch studs.

10. What causes the error message "UNEXPECTED ELSE" when this code fragment is compiled?

```
if (mileage < 24.0)
{
    cout << "Gas ";
    cout << "guzzler.";
};
else
    cout << "Fuel efficient.";
```

11. The following code fragment is supposed to print "Type AB" when Boolean variables typeA and typeB are both true, and print "Type O" when both variables are false. Instead it prints "Type O" whenever just one of the variables is false. Insert a { } pair to make the code segment work the way it should.

```
if (typeA || typeB)
    if (typeA && typeB)
        cout << "Type AB";
else
    cout << "Type O";
```

12. The nested If structure below has five possible branches depending on the values read into char variables ch1, ch2, and ch3. To test the structure, you need five sets of data, each set using a different branch. Create the five test data sets.

```
cin >> ch1 >> ch2 >> ch3;
if (ch1 == ch2)
    if (ch2 == ch3)
        cout << "All initials are the same." << endl;
    else
        cout << "First two are the same." << endl;
else if (ch2 == ch3)
    cout << "Last two are the same." << endl;
else if (ch1 == ch3)
    cout << "First and last are the same." << endl;
else
    cout << "All initials are different." << endl;
```

   a. Test data set 1:   ch1 = _____   ch2 = _____   ch3 = _____
   b. Test data set 2:   ch1 = _____   ch2 = _____   ch3 = _____
   c. Test data set 3:   ch1 = _____   ch2 = _____   ch3 = _____
   d. Test data set 4:   ch1 = _____   ch2 = _____   ch3 = _____
   e. Test data set 5:   ch1 = _____   ch2 = _____   ch3 = _____

13. If x and y are Boolean variables, do the following two expressions test the same condition?

```
x != y
(x || y) && !(x && y)
```

14. The following If condition is made up of three relational expressions:

```
if (i >= 10 && i <= 20 && i != 16)
    j = 4;
```

If i contains the value 25 when this If statement is executed, which relational expression(s) does the computer evaluate? (Remember that C++ uses short-circuit evaluation.)

Programming Warm-up Exercises

1. Declare eligible to be a Boolean variable, and assign it the value true.
2. Write a statement that sets the Boolean variable available to true if numberOrdered is less than or equal to numberOnHand minus numberReserved.
3. Write a statement containing a logical expression that assigns true to the Boolean variable isCandidate if satScore is greater than or equal to 1100, gpa is not less than 2.5, and age is greater than 15. Otherwise, isCandidate should be false.
4. Given the declarations

```
bool leftPage;
int  pageNumber:
```

write a statement that sets leftPage to true if pageNumber is even. (*Hint:* Consider what the remainders are when you divide different integers by 2.)

5. Write an If statement (or a series of If statements) that assigns to the variable biggest the greatest value contained in variables i, j, and k. Assume the three values are distinct.

6. Rewrite the following sequence of If-Thens as a single If-Then-Else.

```
if (year % 4 == 0)
    cout << year << " is a leap year." << endl;
if (year % 4 != 0)
{
    year = year + 4 - year % 4;
    cout << year << " is the next leap year." << endl;
}
```

7. Simplify the following program segment, taking out unnecessary comparisons. Assume that age is an int variable.

```
if (age > 64)
    cout << "Senior voter";
if (age < 18)
    cout << "Under age";
if (age >= 18 && age < 65)
    cout << "Regular voter";
```

8. The following program fragment is supposed to print out the values 25, 60, and 8, in that order. Instead, it prints out 50, 60, and 4. Why?

```
length = 25;
width = 60;
if (length = 50)
    height = 4;
else
    height = 8;
cout << length << ' ' << width << ' ' << height << endl;
```

9. The following C++ program segment is almost unreadable because of the inconsistent indentation and the random placement of left and right braces. Fix the indentation and align the braces properly.

```
// This is a nonsense program
if (a > 0)
if (a < 20)
    {
    cout << "A is in range." << endl;
b = 5;
    }
        else
                {
cout << "A is too large." << endl;
    b = 3;
}
    else
cout << "A is too small." << endl;
        cout << "All done." << endl;
```

10. Given the `float` variables x1, x2, y1, y2, and m, write a program segment to find the slope of a line through the two points (x1, y1) and (x2, y2). Use the formula

$$m = \frac{y1 - y2}{x1 - x2}$$

to determine the slope of the line. If x1 equals x2, the line is vertical and the slope is undefined. The segment should write the slope with an appropriate label. If the slope is undefined, it should write the message "Slope undefined."

11. Given the `float` variables a, b, c, root1, root2, and discriminant, write a program segment to determine whether the roots of a quadratic polynomial are real or complex (imaginary). If the roots are real, find them and assign them to root1 and root2. If they are complex, write the message "No real roots."

    The formula for the solution to the quadratic equation is

$$\frac{-b \pm \sqrt{b^2 - 4ac}}{2a}$$

The ± means "plus or minus" and indicates that there are two solutions to the equation: one in which the result of the square root is added to −b and one in which the result is subtracted from −b. The roots are real if the discriminant (the quantity under the square root sign) is not negative.

12. The following program reads data from an input file without checking to see if the file was opened successfully. Insert statements that print an error message and terminate the program if the file cannot be opened.

```
#include <iostream>
#include <fstream>    // For file I/O

using namespace std;

int main()
{
    int      m;
    int      n;
    ifstream info;

    info.open("indata.dat");
    info >> m >> n;
    cout << "The sum of " << m << " and " << n
         << " is " << m + n << endl;
    return 0;
}
```

Programming Problems

1. Using functional decomposition, write a C++ program that inputs a single letter and prints out the corresponding digit on the telephone. The letters and digits on a telephone are grouped this way:

   2 = ABC   4 = GHI   6 = MNO   8 = TUV
   3 = DEF   5 = JKL   7 = PRS   9 = WXY

   No digit corresponds to either Q or Z. For these two letters, your program should print a message indicating that they are not used on a telephone.

   The program might operate like this:

   ```
   Enter a single letter, and I will tell you what the corresponding
   digit is on the telephone.
   R
   The digit 7 corresponds to the letter R on the telephone.
   ```

   Here's another example:

   ```
   Enter a single letter, and I will tell you what the corresponding
   digit is on the telephone.
   Q
   There is no digit on the telephone that corresponds to Q.
   ```

   Your program should print a message indicating that there is no matching digit for any nonalphabetic character the user enters. Also, the program should recognize only uppercase letters. Include the lowercase letters with the invalid characters.

   Prompt the user with an informative message for the input value, as shown above. The program should echo-print the input letter as part of the output.

   Use proper indentation, appropriate comments, and meaningful identifiers throughout the program.

2. People who deal with historical dates use a number called the *Julian day* to calculate the number of days between two events. The Julian day is the number of days that have elapsed since January 1, 4713 B.C. For example, the Julian day for October 16, 1956, is 2435763. There are formulas for computing the Julian day from a given date and vice versa.

   One very simple formula computes the day of the week from a given Julian day:

   $$day\ of\ the\ week = (Julian\ day + 1)\ \%\ 7$$

   where % is the C++ modulus operator. This formula gives a result of 0 for Sunday, 1 for Monday, and so on up to 6 for Saturday. For Julian day 2435763, the result is 2 (a Tuesday). Your job is to write a C++ program that inputs a Julian day, computes the day of the week using the formula, and then prints out the name of the day that corresponds to that number. If the maximum int value on your machine is small (32767, for instance), use the long data type instead of int. Be sure to echo-print the input data and to use proper indentation and comments.

Your output might look like this:

```
Enter a Julian day number:
2451545
Julian day number 2451545 is a Saturday.
```

3. You can compute the date for any Easter Sunday from 1982 to 2048 as follows (all variables are of type int):

```
a is year % 19
b is year % 4
c is year % 7
d is (19 * a + 24) % 30
e is (2 * b + 4 * c + 6 * d + 5) % 7
Easter Sunday is March (22 + d + e)*
```

Write a program that inputs the year and outputs the date (month and day) of Easter Sunday for that year. Echo-print the input as part of the output. For example:

```
Enter the year (for example, 1999):
1985
Easter is Sunday, April 7, in 1985.
```

4. The algorithm for computing the date of Easter can be extended easily to work with any year from 1900 to 2099. There are four years—1954, 1981, 2049, and 2076—for which the algorithm gives a date that is seven days later than it should be. Modify the program for Problem 3 to check for these years and subtract 7 from the day of the month. This correction does not cause the month to change. Be sure to change the documentation for the program to reflect its broadened capabilities.

5. Write a C++ program that calculates and prints the diameter, the circumference, or the area of a circle, given the radius. The program inputs two data items. The first is a character—'D' (for diameter), 'C' (for circumference), or 'A' (for area)—to indicate the calculation needed. The next data value is a floating-point number indicating the radius of the particular circle.

    The program should echo-print the input data. The output should be labeled appropriately and formatted to two decimal places. For example, if the input is

```
A 6.75
```

your program should print something like this:

```
The area of a circle with radius 6.75 is 143.14.
```

Here are the formulas you need:

Diameter = $2r$
Circumference = $2\pi r$
Area of a circle = πr^2

where r is the radius. Use 3.14159265 for π.

---

* Notice that this formula can give a date in April.

6. The factorial of a number n is $n * (n - 1) * (n - 2) * \ldots * 2 * 1$. Stirling's formula approximates the factorial for large values of n:

$$\frac{n^n\sqrt{2\pi n}}{e^n}$$

where $\pi = 3.14159265$ and $e = 2.718282$.

Write a C++ program that inputs an integer value (but stores it into a `float` variable n), calculates the factorial of n using Stirling's formula, assigns the (rounded) result to a `long` integer variable, and then prints the result appropriately labeled.

Depending on the value of n, you should obtain one of these results:

- A numerical result.
- If n equals 0, the factorial is defined to be 1.
- If n is less than 0, the factorial is undefined.
- If n is too large, the result exceeds LONG_MAX.

(LONG_MAX is a constant declared in the header file `climits`. It gives the maximum `long` value for your particular machine and C++ compiler.)

Because Stirling's formula is used to calculate the factorial of very large numbers, the factorial approaches LONG_MAX quickly. If the factorial exceeds LONG_MAX, it causes an arithmetic overflow in the computer, in which case the program either stops running or continues with a strange-looking integer result, perhaps negative. Before you write the program, then, you first must write a small program that lets you determine, by trial and error, the largest value of n for which your computer system can compute a factorial using Stirling's formula. After you've determined this value, you can write the program using nested Ifs that print different messages depending on the value of n. If n is within the acceptable range for your computer system, output the number and the result with an appropriate message. If n is 0, write the message, "The number is 0. The factorial is 1." If the number is less than 0, write "The number is less than 0. The factorial is undefined." If the number is greater than the largest value of n for which your computer system can compute a factorial, write "The number is too large."

Suggestion: Don't compute Stirling's formula directly. The values of n^n and e^n can be huge, even in floating-point form. Take the natural logarithm of the formula and manipulate it algebraically to work with more reasonable floating-point values. If r is the result of these intermediate calculations, the final result is e^r. Make use of the standard library functions `log` and `exp`, available through the header file `cmath`. These functions, described in Appendix C, compute the natural logarithm and natural exponentiation, respectively.

Case Study Follow-Up

1. a. Complete the test plan for the Notices program that was begun in the Testing and Debugging section on page 259. That section describes the remaining tests to be written.

    b. Implement the complete test plan and record the observed output.

2. Could the data validation test in the Notices program be changed to the following?

    ```
    dataOK = (test1 + test2 + test3) >= 0;
    ```

    Explain.

3. Modify the Notices program so that it prints "Passing with high marks." if the value in average is above 90.0.

4. If the Notices program is modified to input and average four scores, what changes (if any) to the control structures are required?

5. Change the Notices program so that it checks each of the test scores individually and prints error messages indicating which of the scores is invalid and why.

6. Rewrite the preconditions and postconditions for the modules in the Warning Notices algorithm to reflect the changes to the design of the Notices program requested in Case Study Follow-Up Exercise 4.

7. Write a test plan that achieves complete code coverage for the Notices program as modified in Case Study Follow-Up Exercise 4.

6

Looping

- To be able to construct syntactically correct While loops.
- To be able to construct count-controlled loops with a While statement.
- To be able to construct event-controlled loops with a While statement.
- To be able to use the end-of-file condition to control the input of data.
- To be able to use flags to control the execution of a While statement.
- To be able to construct counting loops with a While statement.
- To be able to construct summing loops with a While statement.
- To be able to choose the correct type of loop for a given problem.
- To be able to construct nested While loops.
- To be able to choose data sets that test a looping program comprehensively.

In Chapter 5, we said that the flow of control in a program can differ from the physical order of the statements. The *physical order* is the order in which the statements appear in a program; the order in which we want the statements to be executed is called the *logical order*.

The If statement is one way of making the logical order different from the physical order. Looping control structures are another. A **loop** executes the same statement (simple or compound) over and over, as long as a condition or set of conditions is satisfied.

Loop   A control structure that causes a statement or group of statements to be executed repeatedly.

In this chapter, we discuss different kinds of loops and how they are constructed using the While statement. We also discuss *nested loops* (loops that contain other loops) and introduce a notation for comparing the amount of work done by different algorithms.

The While Statement

The While statement, like the If statement, tests a condition. Here is the syntax template for the While statement:

WhileStatement

```
while ( Expression )
    Statement
```

and this is an example of one:

```
while (inputVal != 25)
    cin >> inputVal;
```

The While statement is a looping control structure. The statement to be executed each time through the loop is called the *body* of the loop. In the example above, the body of the loop is the input statement that reads in a value for `inputVal`. This While statement says to execute the body repeatedly as long as the input value does not equal 25. The While statement is completed (hence, the loop stops) when `inputVal` equals 25. The effect of this loop, then, is to consume and ignore all the values in the input stream until the number 25 is read.

Just like the condition in an If statement, the condition in a While statement can be an expression of any simple data type. Nearly always, it is a logical (Boolean) expression; if not, its value is implicitly coerced to type `bool` (recall that a zero value is coerced to `false`, and any nonzero value is coerced to `true`). The While statement says, "If the value of the expression is `true`, execute the body and then go back and test the expression again. If the expression's value is `false`, skip the body." The loop body is thus executed over and over as long as the expression is `true` when it is tested. When the expression is `false`, the program skips the body and execution continues at the statement immediately following the loop. Of course, if the expression is `false` to begin with, the body is not even executed. Figure 6-1 shows the flow of control of the While statement, where Statement1 is the body of the loop and Statement2 is the statement following the loop.

The body of a loop can be a compound statement (block), which allows us to execute any group of statements repeatedly. Most often we use While loops in the following form:

```
while (Expression)
{
   ⋮
}
```

In this structure, if the expression is `true`, the entire sequence of statements in the block is executed, and then the expression is checked again. If it is still `true`, the statements are executed again. The cycle continues until the expression becomes `false`.

Although in some ways the If and While statements are alike, there are fundamental differences between them (see Figure 6-2). In the If structure, Statement1 is either skipped or executed exactly once. In the While structure, Statement1 can be skipped, executed once, or executed over and over.

FIGURE 6-1

While Statement
Flow of Control

The If is used to *choose* a course of action; the While is used to *repeat* a course of action.

Phases of Loop Execution

The body of a loop is executed in several phases:

- The moment that the flow of control reaches the first statement inside the loop body is the **loop entry.**
- Each time the body of a loop is executed, a pass is made through the loop. This pass is called an **iteration.**
- Before each iteration, control is transferred to the **loop test** at the beginning of the loop.
- When the last iteration is complete and the flow of control has passed to the first statement following the loop, the program has **exited the loop.** The condition that causes a loop to be exited is the **termination condition.** In the case of a While loop, the termination condition is that the While expression becomes `false`.

FIGURE 6-2
A Comparison of If and While

IF-THEN STATEMENT

WHILE STATEMENT

Loop entry   The point at which the flow of control reaches the first statement inside a loop.

Iteration   An individual pass through, or repetition of, the body of a loop.

Loop test   The point at which the While expression is evaluated and the decision is made either to begin a new iteration or skip to the statement immediately following the loop.

Loop exit   The point at which the repetition of the loop body ends and control passes to the first statement following the loop.

Termination condition   The condition that causes a loop to be exited.

Notice that the loop exit occurs only at one point: when the loop test is performed. Even though the termination condition may become satisfied midway through the execution of the loop, the current iteration is completed before the computer checks the While expression again.

The concept of looping is fundamental to programming. In this chapter, we spend some time looking at typical kinds of loops and ways of implementing them with the While statement. These looping situations come up again and again when you are analyzing problems and designing algorithms.

Loops Using the While Statement

In solving problems, you will come across two major types of loops: **count-controlled loops,** which repeat a specified number of times, and **event-controlled loops,** which repeat until something happens within the loop.

Count-controlled loop   A loop that executes a specified number of times.

Event-controlled loop   A loop that terminates when something happens inside the loop body to signal that the loop should be exited.

If you are making an angel food cake and the recipe reads "Beat the mixture 300 strokes," you are executing a count-controlled loop. If you are making a pie crust and the recipe reads "Cut with a pastry blender until the mixture resembles coarse meal," you are executing an event-controlled loop; you don't know ahead of time the exact number of loop iterations.

Count-Controlled Loops

A count-controlled loop uses a variable we call the *loop control variable* in the loop test. Before we enter a count-controlled loop, we have to *initialize* (set the initial value of) the loop control variable and then test it. Then, as part of each iteration of the loop, we must *increment* (increase by 1) the loop control variable. Here's an example:

```
loopCount = 1;                         // Initialization
while (loopCount <= 10)                // Test
{
      .
      .                                // Repeated actions
      .
    loopCount = loopCount + 1;         // Incrementation
}
```

Here `loopCount` is the loop control variable. It is set to 1 before loop entry. The While statement tests the expression

```
loopCount <= 10
```

and executes the loop body as long as the expression is `true`. The dots inside the compound statement represent a sequence of statements to be repeated. The last statement in the loop body increments `loopCount` by adding 1 to it.

Look at the statement in which we increment the loop control variable. Notice its form:

```
variable = variable + 1;
```

This statement adds 1 to the current value of the variable, and the result replaces the old value. Variables that are used this way are called *counters*. In our example, `loopCount` is incremented with each iteration of the loop—we use it to count the iterations. The loop control variable of a count-controlled loop is always a counter.

We've encountered another way of incrementing a variable in C++. The incrementation operator (++) increments the variable that is its operand. The statement

```
loopCount++;
```

has precisely the same effect as the assignment statement

```
loopCount = loopCount + 1;
```

From here on, we typically use the ++ operator, as do most C++ programmers.

When designing loops, it is the programmer's responsibility to see that the condition to be tested is set correctly (initialized) before the While statement begins. The programmer also must make sure that the condition changes within the loop so that it eventually becomes `false`; otherwise, the loop is never exited.

```
loopCount = 1;                    ←Variable loopCount must be initialized
while (loopCount <= 10)
{
     ⋮
    loopCount++;                  ←loopCount must be incremented
}
```

A loop that never exits is called an *infinite loop* because, in theory, the loop executes forever. In the code above, omitting the incrementation of `loopCount` at the bottom of the loop leads to an infinite loop; the While expression is always `true` because the value of `loopCount` is forever 1. If your program goes on running for much longer than you expect it to, chances are that you've created an infinite loop. You may have to issue an operating system command to stop the program.

How many times does the loop in our example execute—9 or 10? To determine this, we have to look at the initial value of the loop control variable and then at the test to see what its final value is. Here we've initialized `loopCount` to 1, and the test indicates that the loop body is executed for each value of `loopCount` up through 10. If `loopCount` starts out at 1 and runs up to 10, the loop body is executed 10 times. If we want the loop to execute 11 times, we have to either initialize `loopCount` to 0 or change the test to

```
loopCount <= 11
```

Event-Controlled Loops

There are several kinds of event-controlled loops: sentinel-controlled, end-of-file-controlled, and flag-controlled. In all of these loops, the termination condition depends on some event occurring while the loop body is executing.

Sentinel-Controlled Loops   Loops often are used to read in and process long lists of data. Each time the loop body is executed, a new piece of data is read and processed. Often a special data value, called a *sentinel* or *trailer value*, is used to signal the program that there is no more data to be processed. Looping continues as long as the data value read is *not* the sentinel; the loop stops when the program recognizes the sentinel. In other words, reading the sentinel value is the event that controls the looping process.

A sentinel value must be something that never shows up in the normal input to a program. For example, if a program reads calendar dates, we could use February 31 as a sentinel value:

```
// This code is incorrect:

while ( !(month == 2 && day == 31) )
{
    cin >> month >> day;            // Get a date
        ⋮                          // Process it
}
```

There is a problem in the loop in the example above. The values of `month` and `day` are not defined before the first pass through the loop. Somehow we have to initialize these variables. We could assign them arbitrary values, but then we would run the risk that the first values input are the sentinel values, which would then be processed as data. Also, it's inefficient to initialize variables with values that are never used.

We can solve the problem by reading the first set of data values *before* entering the loop. This is called a *priming read*. (The idea is similar to priming a pump by pouring a bucket of water into the mechanism before starting it.) Let's add the priming read to the loop:

```
// This is still incorrect:

cin >> month >> day;                    // Get a date--priming read
while ( !(month == 2 && day == 31) )
{
    cin >> month >> day;                // Get a date
        ⋮                               // Process it
}
```

With the priming read, if the first values input are the sentinel values, then the loop correctly does not process them. We've solved one problem, but now there is a problem when the first values input are valid data. Notice that the first thing the program does inside the loop is to get a date, destroying the values obtained by the priming read. Thus, the first date in the data list is never processed. Given the priming read, the *first* thing that the loop body should do is process the data that's already been read. But then at what point do we read the next data set? We do this *last* in the loop. In this way, the While condition is applied to the next data set before it gets processed. Here's how it looks:

```
// This version is correct:

cin >> month >> day;                    // Get a date--priming read
while ( !(month == 2 && day == 31) )
{
        ⋮                               // Process it
    cin >> month >> day;                // Get the next date
}
```

This segment works fine. The first data set is read in; if it is not the sentinel, it gets processed. At the end of the loop, the next data set is read in, and we go back to the beginning of the loop. If the new data set is not the sentinel, it gets processed just like the first. When the sentinel value is read, the While expression becomes `false` and the loop exits (*without* processing the sentinel).

Many times the problem dictates the value of the sentinel. For example, if the problem does not allow data values of 0, then the sentinel value should be 0. Sometimes a combination of values is invalid. The combination of February and 31 as a date is such a case. Sometimes a range of values (negative numbers, for example) is the sentinel. And when you process `char` data one line of input at a time, the newline character (`'\n'`) often serves as the sentinel. Here's a code segment that reads and prints all of the characters on an input line (`inChar` is of type `char`):

```
cin.get(inChar);                         // Get first character
while (inChar != '\n')
{
    cout << inChar;                      // Echo it
    cin.get(inChar);                     // Get next character
}
```

(Notice that for this particular task we use the get function, not the >> operator, to input a character. Remember that the >> operator skips whitespace characters—including blanks and newlines—to find the next data value in the input stream. In this example, we want to input *every* character, even a blank and especially the newline character.)

When you are choosing a value to use as a sentinel, what happens if there aren't any invalid data values? Then you may have to input an extra value in each iteration, a value whose only purpose is to signal the end of the data. For example, look at this code segment:

```
cin >> dataValue >> sentinel;            // Get first data value
while (sentinel == 1)
{
       ⋮                                 // Process it
    cin >> dataValue >> sentinel;        // Get next data value
}
```

The second value on each line of the following data set is used to indicate whether or not there is more data. In this data set, when the sentinel value is 0, there is no more data; when it is 1, there is more data.

Data values	Sentinel values
↘	↓
10	1
0	1
−5	1
8	1
−1	1
47	0

What happens if you forget to enter the sentinel value? In an interactive program, the loop executes again, prompting for input. At that point, you can enter the sentinel value, but your program logic may be wrong if you already entered what you thought was the sentinel value. If the input to the program is from a file, once all the data has been read from the file, the loop body is executed again. However, there isn't any data left—because the computer has reached the end of the file—so the file stream enters the fail state. In the next section, we describe a way to use the end-of-file situation as an alternative to using a sentinel.

Before we go on, we mention an issue that is related not to the design of loops but to C++ language usage. In Chapter 5, we talked about the common mistake of using the assignment operator (=) instead of the relational operator (==) in an If condition. This same mistake can happen when you write While statements. See what happens when we use the wrong operator in the previous example:

```
cin >> dataValue >> sentinel;
while (sentinel = 1)                    // Whoops
{
    ⋮
    cin >> dataValue >> sentinel;
}
```

This mistake creates an infinite loop. The While expression is now an assignment expression, not a relational expression. The expression's value is 1 (interpreted in the loop test as `true` because it's nonzero), and its side effect is to store the value 1 into `sentinel`, replacing the value that was just input into the variable. Because the While expression is always `true`, the loop never stops.

End-of-File-Controlled Loops You already have learned that an input stream (such as `cin` or an input file stream) goes into the fail state (a) if it encounters unacceptable input data, (b) if the program tries to open a nonexistent input file, or (c) if the program tries to read past the end of an input file. Let's look at the third of these three possibilities.

After a program has read the last piece of data from an input file, the computer is at the end of the file (EOF, for short). At this moment, the stream state is all right. But if we try to input even one more data value, the stream goes into the fail state. We can use this fact to our advantage. To write a loop that inputs an unknown number of data items, we can use the failure of the input stream as a form of sentinel.

In Chapter 5, we described how to test the state of an I/O stream. In a logical expression, we use the name of the stream as though it were a Boolean variable:

```
if (inFile)
    ⋮
```

In a test like this, the result is `true` if the most recent I/O operation succeeded, or `false` if it failed. In a While statement, testing the state of a stream works the same way. Suppose we have a data file containing integer values. If `inData` is the name of the file stream in our program, here's a loop that reads and echoes all of the data values in the file:

```
inData >> intVal;                    // Get first value
while (inData)                        // While the input succeeded...
{
    cout << intVal << endl;          // Echo it
    inData >> intVal;                // Get next value
}
```

Let's trace this code, assuming there are three values in the file: 10, 20, and 30. The priming read inputs the value 10. The While condition is true because the input succeeded. Therefore, the computer executes the loop body. First the body prints out the value 10, and then it inputs the second data value, 20. Looping back to the loop test, the expression inData is true because the input succeeded. The body executes again, printing the value 20 and reading the value 30 from the file. Looping back to the test, the expression is true. Even though we are at the end of the file, the stream state is still OK—the previous input operation succeeded. The body executes a third time, printing the value 30 and executing the input statement. This time, the input statement fails; we're trying to read beyond the end of the file. The stream inData enters the fail state. Looping back to the loop test, the value of the expression is false and we exit the loop.

When we write EOF-controlled loops like the one above, we are expecting that the end of the file is the reason for stream failure. But keep in mind that *any* input error causes stream failure. The above loop terminates, for example, if input fails because of invalid characters in the input data. This fact emphasizes again the importance of echo printing. It helps us verify that all the data was read correctly before the EOF was encountered.

EOF-controlled loops are similar to sentinel-controlled loops in that the program doesn't know in advance how many data items are to be input. In the case of sentinel-controlled loops, the program reads until it encounters the sentinel value. With EOF-controlled loops, it reads until it reaches the end of the file.

Is it possible to use an EOF-controlled loop when we read from the standard input device (via the cin stream) instead of a data file? On many systems, yes. With the UNIX operating system, you can type Ctrl-D (that is, you hold down the Ctrl key and tap the D key) to signify end-of-file during interactive input. With the MS-DOS operating system, the end-of-file keystrokes are Ctrl-Z. Other systems use similar keystrokes. Here's a program segment that tests for EOF on the cin stream in UNIX:

```
cout << "Enter an integer (or Ctrl-D to quit): ";
cin >> someInt;
while (cin)
{
    cout << someInt << " doubled is " << 2 * someInt << endl;
    cout << "Next number (or Ctrl-D to quit): ";
    cin >> someInt;
}
```

Flag-Controlled Loops   A *flag* is a Boolean variable that is used to control
the logical flow of a program. We can set a Boolean variable to `true` before
a While loop; then, when we want to stop executing the loop, we reset it to
`false`. That is, we can use the Boolean variable to record whether or not
the event that controls the process has occurred. For example, the following code segment reads and sums values until the input value is negative.
(`nonNegative` is the Boolean flag; all of the other variables are of type
`int`.)

```
sum = 0;
nonNegative = true;                  // Initialize flag
while (nonNegative)
{
    cin >> number;
    if (number < 0)                  // Test input value
        nonNegative = false;         // Set flag if event occurred
    else
        sum = sum + number;
}
```

Notice that we can code sentinel-controlled loops with flags. In fact, this
code uses a negative value as a sentinel.

You do not have to initialize flags to `true`; you can initialize them to
`false`. If you do, you must use the NOT operator (`!`) in the While expression and reset the flag to `true` when the event occurs. Compare the code
segment above with the one below; both perform the same task. (Assume
that `negative` is a Boolean variable.)

```
sum = 0;
negative = false;                    // Initialize flag
while ( !negative )
{
    cin >> number;
    if (number < 0)                  // Test input value
        negative = true;             // Set flag if event occurred
    else
        sum = sum + number;
}
```

As one more example, look at the While statement in the Payroll program at the end of Chapter 1. This is a sentinel-controlled loop because an employee number (empNum) with a value of 0 is used to stop the loop. We could have used a flag instead, as follows. (moreData is a Boolean variable.)

```
cin >> empNum;
moreData = (empNum != 0);              // true if empNum != 0
while (moreData)
{
    ⋮
    cin >> empNum;                     // Get the next employee number
    moreData = (empNum != 0);          // Update the flag accordingly
}
```

Looping Subtasks

We have been looking at ways to use loops to affect the flow of control in programs. But looping by itself does nothing. The loop body must perform a task in order for the loop to accomplish something. In this section, we look at three tasks—counting, summing, and keeping track of a previous value—that often are used in loops.

Counting   A common task in a loop is to keep track of the number of times the loop has been executed. For example, the following program fragment reads and counts input characters until it comes to a period. (inChar is of type char; count is of type int.) The loop in this example has a counter variable, but the loop is not a count-controlled loop because the variable is not being used as a loop control variable.

```
count = 0;                        // Initialize counter
cin.get(inChar);                  // Read the first character
while (inChar != '.')
{
    count++;                      // Increment counter
    cin.get(inChar);              // Get the next character
}
```

The loop continues until a period is read. After the loop is finished, count contains one less than the number of characters read. That is, it counts the number of characters up to, but not including, the sentinel value (the period). Notice that if a period is the first character, the loop body is not entered and count contains a 0, as it should. We use a priming read here because the loop is sentinel-controlled.

The counter variable in this example is called an **iteration counter** because its value equals the number of iterations through the loop.

Iteration counter   A counter variable that is incremented with each iteration of a loop.

According to our definition, the loop control variable of a count-controlled loop is an iteration counter. However, as you've just seen, not all iteration counters are loop control variables.

Summing   Another common looping task is to sum a set of data values. Notice in the following example that the summing operation is written the same way, regardless of how the loop is controlled.

```
sum = 0;                              // Initialize the sum
count = 1;
while (count <= 10)
{
    cin >> number;                    // Input a value
    sum = sum + number;               // Add the value to sum
    count++;
}
```

We initialize sum to 0 before the loop starts so that the first time the loop body executes, the statement

```
sum = sum + number;
```

adds the current value of sum (0) to number to form the new value of sum. After the entire code fragment has executed, sum contains the total of the ten values read, count contains 11, and number contains the last value read.

Here count is being incremented in each iteration. For each new value of count, there is a new value for number. Does this mean we could decrement count by 1 and inspect the previous value of number? No. Once a new value has been read into number, the previous value is gone forever unless we've saved it in another variable. You'll see how to do that in the next section.

Let's look at another example. We want to count and sum the first ten odd numbers in a data set. We need to test each number to see if it is even or odd. (We can use the modulus operator to find out. If number % 2 equals 1, number is odd; otherwise, it's even.) If the input value is even, we do nothing. If it is odd, we increment the counter and add the value to our sum. We use a flag to control the loop because this is not a normal count-controlled loop. In the following code segment, all variables are of type int except the Boolean flag, lessThanTen.

```
count = 0;                              // Initialize event counter
sum = 0;                                // Initialize sum
lessThanTen = true;                     // Initialize loop control flag
while (lessThanTen)
{
    cin >> number;                      // Get the next value
    if (number % 2 == 1)                // Is the value odd?
    {
        count++;                        // Yes--Increment counter
        sum = sum + number;             // Add value to sum
        lessThanTen = (count < 10);     // Update loop control flag
    }
}
```

In this example, there is no relationship between the value of the counter variable and the number of times the loop is executed. We could have written the While expression this way:

```
while (count < 10)
```

but this might mislead a reader into thinking that the loop is count-controlled in the normal way. So, instead, we control the loop with the flag lessThanTen to emphasize that count is incremented only when an odd number is read. The counter in this example is an **event counter;** it is initialized to 0 and incremented only when a certain event occurs. The counter in the previous example was an *iteration counter;* it was initialized to 1 and incremented during each iteration of the loop.

Event counter   A variable that is incremented each time a particular event occurs.

Keeping Track of a Previous Value   Sometimes we want to remember the previous value of a variable. Suppose we want to write a program that counts the number of not-equal operators (!=) in a file that contains a C++ program. We can do so by simply counting the number of times an exclamation mark (!) followed by an equal sign (=) appears in the input. One way in which to do this is to read the input file one character at a time, keeping track of the two most recent characters, the current value and the previous value. In each iteration of the loop, a new current value is read and the old current value becomes the previous value. When EOF is reached, the loop is finished. Here's a program that counts not-equal operators in this way:

```cpp
//******************************************************************
// NotEqualCount program
// This program counts the occurrences of "!=" in a data file
//******************************************************************
#include <iostream>
#include <fstream>      // For file I/O

using namespace std;

int main()
{
    int     count;        // Number of != operators
    char    prevChar;     // Last character read
    char    currChar;     // Character read in this loop iteration
    ifstream inFile;      // Data file

    inFile.open("myfile.dat");          // Attempt to open input file
    if ( !inFile )                      // Was it opened?
    {
        cout << "** Can't open input file **"  // No--print message
            << endl;
        return 1;                               // Terminate program
    }
    count = 0;                  // Initialize counter
    inFile.get(prevChar);       // Initialize previous value
    inFile.get(currChar);       // Initialize current value
    while (inFile)              // While previous input succeeded...
    {
        if (currChar == '=' &&  // Test for event
            prevChar == '!')
            count++;            // Increment counter
        prevChar = currChar;    // Replace previous value
                                //    with current value
        inFile.get(currChar);   // Get next value
    }
    cout << count << " != operators were found." << endl;
    return 0;
}
```

Study this loop carefully. It's going to come in handy. There are many problems in which you must keep track of the last value read in addition to the current value.

How to Design Loops

It's one thing to understand how a loop works when you look at it and something else again to design a loop that solves a given problem. In this section, we look at how to design loops. We can divide the design process into two tasks: designing the control flow and designing the processing that takes place in the loop. We can in turn break each task into three phases: the task itself, initialization, and update. It's also important to specify the state of the program when it exits the loop, because a loop that leaves variables and files in a mess is not well designed.

There are seven different points to consider in designing a loop:

1. What is the condition that ends the loop?
2. How should the condition be initialized?
3. How should the condition be updated?
4. What is the process being repeated?
5. How should the process be initialized?
6. How should the process be updated?
7. What is the state of the program on exiting the loop?

We use these questions as a checklist. The first three help us design the parts of the loop that control its execution. The next three help us design the processing within the loop. The last question reminds us to make sure that the loop exits in an appropriate manner.

Designing the Flow of Control

The most important step in loop design is deciding what should make the loop stop. If the termination condition isn't well thought out, there's the potential for infinite loops and other mistakes. So here is our first question:

- What is the condition that ends the loop?

This question usually can be answered through a close examination of the problem statement. The following table lists some examples.

Key Phrase in Problem Statement	Termination Condition
"Sum 365 temperatures"	The loop ends when a counter reaches 365 (count-controlled loop).
"Process all the data in the file"	The loop ends when EOF occurs (EOF-controlled loop).
"Process until ten odd integers have been read"	The loop ends when ten odd numbers have been input (event counter).
"The end of the data is indicated by a negative test score"	The loop ends when a negative input value is encountered (sentinel-controlled loop).

Now we need statements that make sure the loop gets started correctly and statements that allow the loop to reach the termination condition. So we have to ask the next two questions:

- How should the condition be initialized?
- How should the condition be updated?

The answers to these questions depend on the type of termination condition.

Count-Controlled Loops   If the loop is count-controlled, we initialize the condition by giving the loop control variable an initial value. For count-controlled loops in which the loop control variable is also an iteration counter, the initial value is usually 1. If the process requires the counter to run through a specific range of values, the initial value should be the lowest value in that range.

The condition is updated by increasing the value of the counter by 1 for each iteration. (Occasionally, you may come across a problem that requires a counter to count from some value *down* to a lower value. In this case, the initial value is the greater value, and the counter is decremented by 1 for each iteration.) So, for count-controlled loops that use an iteration counter, these are the answers to the questions:

- Initialize the iteration counter to 1.
- Increment the iteration counter at the end of each iteration.

If the loop is controlled by a variable that is counting an event within the loop, the control variable usually is initialized to 0 and is incremented each time the event occurs. For count-controlled loops that use an event counter, these are the answers to the questions:

- Initialize the event counter to 0.
- Increment the event counter each time the event occurs.

Sentinel-Controlled Loops In sentinel-controlled loops, a priming read may be the only initialization necessary. If the source of input is a file rather than the keyboard, it also may be necessary to open the file in preparation for reading. To update the condition, a new value is read at the end of each iteration. So, for sentinel-controlled loops, we answer our questions this way:

- Open the file, if necessary, and input a value before entering the loop (priming read).
- Input a new value for processing at the end of each iteration.

EOF-Controlled Loops EOF-controlled loops require the same initialization as sentinel-controlled loops. You must open the file, if necessary, and perform a priming read. Updating the loop condition happens implicitly; the stream state is updated to reflect success or failure every time a value is input. However, if the loop doesn't read any data, it can never reach EOF, so updating the loop condition means the loop must keep reading data.

Flag-Controlled Loops In flag-controlled loops, the Boolean flag variable must be initialized to `true` or `false` and then updated when the condition changes.

- Initialize the flag variable to `true` or `false`, as appropriate.
- Update the flag variable as soon as the condition changes.

In a flag-controlled loop, the flag variable essentially remains unchanged until it is time for the loop to end. Then the code detects some condition within the process being repeated that changes the value of the flag (through an assignment statement). Because the update depends on what the process does, at times we have to design the process before we can decide how to update the condition.

Designing the Process Within the Loop

Once we've determined the looping structure itself, we can fill in the details of the process. In designing the process, we first must decide what we want a single iteration to do. Assume for a moment that the process is going to execute only once. What tasks must the process perform?

- What is the process being repeated?

To answer this question, we have to take another look at the problem statement. The definition of the problem may require the process to sum up data values or to keep a count of data values that satisfy some test. For example:

Count the number of integers in the file howMany.

This statement tells us that the process to be repeated is a counting operation.

Here's another example:

Read a stock price for each business day in a week and compute the average price.

In this case, part of the process involves reading a data value. We have to conclude from our knowledge of how an average is computed that the process also involves summing the data values.

In addition to counting and summing, another common loop process is reading data, performing a calculation, and writing out the result. Many other operations can appear in looping processes. We've mentioned only the simplest here; we look at some other processes later on.

After we've determined the operations to be performed if the process is executed only once, we design the parts of the process that are necessary for it to be repeated correctly. We often have to add some steps to take into account the fact that the loop executes more than once. This part of the design typically involves initializing certain variables before the loop and then reinitializing or updating them before each subsequent iteration.

- How should the process be initialized?
- How should the process be updated?

For example, if the process within a loop requires that several different counts and sums be performed, each must have its own statements to initialize variables, increment counting variables, or add values to sums. Just deal with each counting or summing operation by itself—that is, first write the initialization statement, and then write the incrementing or summing statement. After you've done this for one operation, you go on to the next.

The Loop Exit

When the termination condition occurs and the flow of control passes to the statement following the loop, the variables used in the loop still contain values. And if the cin stream has been used, the reading marker has been left at some position in the stream. Or maybe an output file has new contents. If these variables or files are used later in the program, the loop must leave them in an appropriate state. So, the final step in designing a loop is answering this question:

- What is the state of the program on exiting the loop?

Now we have to consider the consequences of our design and double-check its validity. For example, suppose we've used an event counter and that later processing depends on the number of events. It's important to be sure (with an algorithm walk-through) that the value left in the counter is the exact number of events—that it is not off by 1.

Look at this code segment:

```
commaCount = 1;                // This code is incorrect
cin.get(inChar);
while (inChar != '\n')
{
    if (inChar == ',')
        commaCount++;
    cin.get(inChar);
}
cout << commaCount << endl;
```

This loop reads characters from an input line and counts the number of commas on the line. However, when the loop terminates, commaCount equals the actual number of commas plus 1 because the loop initializes the event counter to 1 before any events take place. By determining the state of commaCount at loop exit, we've detected a flaw in the initialization. commaCount should be initialized to 0.

Designing correct loops depends as much on experience as it does on the application of design methodology. At this point, you may want to read through the Problem-Solving Case Study at the end of the chapter to see how the loop design process is applied to a real problem.

Nested Logic

In Chapter 5, we described nested If statements. It's also possible to nest While statements. Both While and If statements contain statements and are, themselves, statements. So the body of a While statement or the branch of an If statement can contain other While and If statements. By nesting, we can create complex control structures.

Suppose we want to extend our code for counting commas on one line, repeating it for all the lines in a file. We put an EOF-controlled loop around it:

```
cin.get(inChar);              // Initialize outer loop
while (cin)                   // Outer loop test
{
    commaCount = 0;           // Initialize inner loop
                              //    (Priming read is taken care of
                              //    by outer loop's priming read)
```

```
    while (inChar != '\n')      // Inner loop test
    {
        if (inChar == ',')
            commaCount++;
        cin.get(inChar);        // Update inner termination condition
    }
    cout << commaCount << endl;
    cin.get(inChar);            // Update outer termination condition
}
```

In this code, notice that we have omitted the priming read for the inner loop. The priming read for the outer loop has already "primed the pump." It would be a mistake to include another priming read just before the inner loop; the character read by the outer priming read would be destroyed before we could test it.

Let's examine the general pattern of a simple nested loop. The dots represent places where the processing and update may take place in the outer loop.

```
Initialize outer loop

while ( Outer loop condition )

{

        ⋮

   ┌──────────────────────────────────────────┐
   │ Initialize inner loop                      │
   │                                            │
   │ while ( Inner loop condition )             │
   │                                            │
   │ {                                          │
   │   Inner loop processing and update         │
   │ }                                          │
   └──────────────────────────────────────────┘


        ⋮

}
```

Notice that each loop has its own initialization, test, and update. It's possible for an outer loop to do no processing other than to execute the inner loop repeatedly. On the other hand, the inner loop might be just a small part of the processing done by the outer loop; there could be many statements preceding or following the inner loop.

Let's look at another example. For nested count-controlled loops, the pattern looks like this (where outCount is the counter for the outer loop, inCount is the counter for the inner loop, and limit1 and limit2 are the number of times each loop should be executed):

```
outCount = 1;                            // Initialize outer loop counter
while (outCount <= limit1)
{
    ⋮
    inCount = 1;                         // Initialize inner loop counter
    while (inCount <= limit2)
    {
        ⋮
        inCount++;                       // Increment inner loop counter
    }
    ⋮
    outCount++;                          // Increment outer loop counter
}
```

Here, both the inner and outer loops are count-controlled loops, but the pattern can be used with any combination of loops.

The following program fragment shows a count-controlled loop nested within an EOF-controlled loop. The outer loop inputs an integer value telling how many asterisks to print out across a row of the screen. (We use the numbers to the right of the code to trace the execution of the program.)

```
cin >> starCount;                             1
while (cin)                                    2
{
    loopCount = 1;                            3
    while (loopCount <= starCount)            4
    {
        cout << '*';                          5
        loopCount++;                          6
    }
    cout << endl;                             7
    cin >> starCount;                         8
}
cout << "Goodbye" << endl;                    9
```

To see how this code works, let's trace its execution with these data values (<EOF> denotes the end-of-file keystrokes pressed by the user):

```
3
1
<EOF>
```

We'll keep track of the variables `starCount` and `loopCount`, as well as the logical expressions. To do this, we've numbered each line (except those containing only a left or right brace). As we trace the program, we indicate the first execution of line 3 by 3.1, the second by 3.2, and so on.

Each loop iteration is enclosed by a large brace, and `true` and `false` are abbreviated as T and F (see Table 6-1).

Table 6-1   Code Trace

Statement	Variables		Logical Expressions		Output
	starCount	loopCount	cin	loopCount <= starCount	
1.1	3	—	—	—	—
2.1	3	—	T	—	—
3.1	3	1	—	—	—
4.1	3	1	—	T	—
5.1	3	1	—	—	★
6.1	3	2	—	—	—
4.2	3	2	—	T	—
5.2	3	2	—	—	★
6.2	3	3	—	—	—
4.3	3	3	—	T	—
5.3	3	3	—	—	★
6.3	3	4	—	—	—
4.4	3	4	—	F	—
7.1	3	4	—	—	\n (newline)
8.1	1	4	—	—	—
2.2	1	4	T	—	—
3.2	1	1	—	—	—
4.5	1	1	—	T	—
5.4	1	1	—	—	★
6.4	1	2	—	—	—
4.6	1	2	—	F	—
7.2	1	2	—	—	\n (newline)
8.2	1	2	—	—	—
	(null operation)				
2.3	1	2	F	—	—
9.1	1	2	—	—	Goodbye

Here's a sample run of the program. The user's input is in color. Again, the symbol <EOF> denotes the end-of-file keystrokes pressed by the user (the symbol would not appear on the screen).

```
3
***
1
*
<EOF>
Goodbye
```

Because `starCount` and `loopCount` are variables, their values remain the same until they are explicitly changed, as indicated by the repeating values in Table 6-1. The values of the logical expressions `cin` and `loopCount <= starCount` exist only when the test is made. We indicate this fact with dashes in those columns at all other times.

Designing Nested Loops

To design a nested loop, we begin with the outer loop. The process being repeated includes the nested loop as one of its steps. Because that step is more complex than a single statement, our functional decomposition methodology tells us to make it a separate module. We can come back to it later and design the nested loop just as we would any other loop.

For example, here's the design process for the preceding code segment:

1. *What is the condition that ends the loop?* EOF is reached in the input.
2. *How should the condition be initialized?* A priming read should be performed before the loop starts.
3. *How should the condition be updated?* An input statement should occur at the end of each iteration.
4. *What is the process being repeated?* Using the value of the current input integer, the code should print that many asterisks across one output line.
5. *How should the process be initialized?* No initialization is necessary.
6. *How should the process be updated?* A sequence of asterisks is output and then a newline character is output. There are no counter variables or sums to update.
7. *What is the state of the program on exiting the loop?* The `cin` stream is in the fail state (because the program tried to read past EOF), `starCount` contains the last integer read from the input stream, and the rows of asterisks have been printed along with a concluding message.

From the answers to these questions, we can write this much of the algorithm:

```
Read starCount
WHILE NOT EOF
      Print starCount asterisks
      Output newline
      Read starCount
Print "Goodbye"
```

After designing the outer loop, it's obvious that the process in its body (printing a sequence of asterisks) is a complex step that requires us to design an inner loop. So we repeat the methodology for the corresponding lower-level module:

1. *What is the condition that ends the loop?* An iteration counter exceeds the value of `starCount`.
2. *How should the condition be initialized?* The iteration counter should be initialized to 1.
3. *How should the condition be updated?* The iteration counter is incremented at the end of each iteration.
4. *What is the process being repeated?* The code should print a single asterisk on the standard output device.
5. *How should the process be initialized?* No initialization is needed.
6. *How should the process be updated?* No update is needed.
7. *What is the state of the program on exiting the loop?* A single row of asterisks has been printed, the writing marker is at the end of the current output line, and `loopCount` contains a value one greater than the current value of `starCount`.

Now we can write the algorithm:

```
Read starCount
WHILE NOT EOF
      Set loopCount = 1
      WHILE loopCount <= starCount
            Print ' * '
            Increment loopCount
      Output newline
      Read starCount
Print "Goodbye"
```

Of course, nested loops themselves can contain nested loops (called *doubly nested loops*), which can contain nested loops (*triply nested loops*), and so on. You can use this design process for any number of levels of nesting. The trick is to defer details by using the functional decomposition methodology—that is, focus on the outermost loop first and treat each new level of nested loop as a module within the loop that contains it.

It's also possible for the process within a loop to include more than one loop. For example, here's an algorithm that reads and prints people's names from a file, omitting the middle name in the output:

Read and print first name (ends with a comma)
WHILE NOT EOF
    Read and discard characters from middle name (ends with a comma)
    Read and print last name (ends at newline)
    Output newline
    Read and print first name (ends with a comma)

The steps for reading the first name, middle name, and last name require us to design three separate loops. All of these loops are sentinel-controlled.

This kind of complex control structure would be difficult to read if written out in full. There are simply too many variables, conditions, and steps to remember at one time. In the next two chapters, we examine the control structure that allows us to break programs down into more manageable chunks—the subprogram.

THEORETICAL FOUNDATIONS

Analysis of Algorithms

If you were given the choice of cleaning a room with a toothbrush or a broom, you probably would choose the broom. Using a broom sounds like less work than using a toothbrush. True, if the room were in a dollhouse, it might be easier to use the toothbrush, but in general a broom is the faster way to clean. If you were given the choice of adding numbers together with a pencil and paper or a calculator, you would probably choose the calculator because it is usually less work. If you were given the choice of walking or driving to a meeting, you would probably choose to drive; it sounds like less work.

What do these examples have in common? What do they have to do with computer science? In each of the situations mentioned, one of the choices seems to involve significantly less work. Precisely measuring the amount of work is difficult in each case because there are unknowns. How large is the room? How many numbers are there? How far away is the meeting? In each case, the unknown information is related to the size of the problem. If the problem is especially small (for example, adding 2 plus 2), our original estimate of which approach to take (using the calculator) might be wrong. However, our intuition is usually correct, because most problems are reasonably large.

In computer science, we need a way of measuring the amount of work done by an algorithm relative to the size of a problem, because there is usually more than one algorithm that solves any given problem. We often must choose the most efficient algorithm—the algorithm that does the least work for a problem of a given size.

The amount of work involved in executing an algorithm relative to the size of the problem is called the **complexity** of the algorithm. We would like to be able to look at an algorithm and determine its complexity. Then we could take two algorithms that perform the same task and determine which completes the task faster (requires less work).

Complexity A measure of the effort expended by the computer in performing a computation, relative to the size of the computation.

How do we measure the amount of work required to execute an algorithm? We use the total number of *steps* executed as a measure of work. One statement, such as an assignment, may require only one step; another, such as a loop, may require many steps. We define a step as any operation roughly equivalent in complexity to a comparison, an I/O operation, or an assignment.

Given an algorithm with just a sequence of simple statements (no branches or loops), the number of steps performed is directly related to the number of statements. When we introduce branches, however, we make it possible to skip some statements in the algorithm. Branches allow us to subtract steps without physically removing them from the algorithm because only one branch is executed at a time. But because we usually want to express work in terms of the worst-case scenario, we use the number of steps in the longest branch.

Now consider the effect of a loop. If a loop repeats a sequence of 15 simple statements 10 times, it performs 150 steps. Loops allow us to multiply the work done in an algorithm without physically adding statements.

Now that we have a measure for the work done in an algorithm, we can compare algorithms. For example, if algorithm A always executes 3124 steps and algorithm B always does the same task in 1321 steps, then we can say that algorithm B is more efficient—that is, it takes fewer steps to accomplish the same task.

If an algorithm, from run to run, always takes the same number of steps or fewer, we say that it executes in an amount of time bounded by a constant. Such algorithms are referred to as having *constant-time* complexity. Be careful: Constant time doesn't mean small; it means that the amount of work done does not exceed some amount from one run to another.

If a loop executes a fixed number of times, the work done is greater than the physical number of statements but still is constant. What happens if the number of loop iterations can change from one run to the next? Suppose a data file contains N data values to be processed in a loop. If the loop reads and processes one value during each iteration, then the loop executes N iterations. The amount of work done thus depends on a variable, the number of data values. The variable N determines the size of the problem in this example.

If we have a loop that executes N times, the number of steps to be executed is some factor times N. The factor is the number of steps performed within a single iteration of the loop. Specifically, the work done by an algorithm with a data-dependent loop is given by the expression

Steps performed
by the loop
$$\overbrace{S_1 \times N} + \underline{S_0}$$
Steps performed
outside the loop

where S_1 is the number of steps in the loop body (a constant for a given simple loop), N is the number of iterations (a variable representing the size of the problem), and S_0 is the number of steps outside the loop. Mathematicians call expressions of this form *linear;* hence, algorithms such as this are said to have *linear-time* complexity. Notice that if N grows very large, the term $S_1 \times N$ dominates the execution time. That is, S_0 becomes an insignificant part of the total execution time. For example, if S_0 and S_1 are each 20 steps, and N is 1,000,000, then the total number of steps is 20,000,020. The 20 steps contributed by S_0 are a tiny fraction of the total.

What about a data-dependent loop that contains a nested loop? The number of steps in the inner loop, S_2, and the number of iterations performed by the inner loop, L, must be multiplied by the number of iterations in the outer loop:

Steps performed   Steps performed   Steps performed outside
by the nested loop   by the outer loop   the outer loop

$$\overbrace{(S_2 \times L \times N)} \quad + \quad \overbrace{(S_1 \times N)} \quad + \quad \overbrace{S_0}$$

By itself, the inner loop performs $S_2 \times L$ steps, but because it is repeated N times by the outer loop, it accounts for a total of $S_2 \times L \times N$ steps. If L is a constant, then the algorithm still executes in linear time.

Now, suppose that for each of the N outer loop iterations, the inner loop performs N steps ($L = N$). Here the formula for the total steps is

$$(S_2 \times N \times N) + (S_1 \times N) + S_0$$

or

$$(S_2 \times N^2) + (S_1 \times N) + S_0$$

Because N^2 grows much faster than N (for large values of N), the inner loop term $(S_2 \times N^2)$ accounts for the majority of steps executed and of the work done. The corresponding execution time is thus essentially proportional to N^2. Mathematicians call this type of formula *quadratic.* If we have a doubly nested loop in which each loop depends on N, then the expression is

$$(S_3 \times N^3) + (S_2 \times N^2) + (S_1 \times N) + S_0$$

and the work and time are proportional to N^3 whenever N is reasonably large. Such a formula is called *cubic*.

The following table shows the number of steps required for each increase in the exponent of N, where N is a size factor for the problem, such as the number of input values.

N	N^0 *(Constant)*	N^1 *(Linear)*	N^2 *(Quadratic)*	N^3 *(Cubic)*
1	1	1	1	1
10	1	10	100	1,000
100	1	100	10,000	1,000,000
1,000	1	1,000	1,000,000	1,000,000,000
10,000	1	10,000	100,000,000	1,000,000,000,000

As you can see, each time the exponent increases by 1, the number of steps is multiplied by an additional order of magnitude (factor of 10). That is, if N is made 10 times greater, the work involved in an N^2 algorithm increases by a factor of 100, and the work involved in an N^3 algorithm increases by a factor of 1000. To put this in more concrete terms, an algorithm with a doubly nested loop in which each loop depends on the number of data values takes 1000 steps for 10 input values and 1 trillion steps for 10,000 values. On a computer that executes 10 million instructions per second, the latter case would take more than a day to run.

The table also shows that the steps outside of the innermost loop account for an insignificant portion of the total number of steps as N gets bigger. Because the innermost loop dominates the total time, we classify the complexity of an algorithm according to the highest order of N that appears in its complexity expression, called the *order of magnitude*, or simply the *order*, of that expression. So we talk about algorithms having "order N squared complexity" (or cubed or so on) or we describe them with what is called *Big-O notation*. We express the complexity by putting the highest-order term in parentheses with a capital O in front. For example, $O(1)$ is constant time, $O(N)$ is linear time, $O(N^2)$ is quadratic time, and $O(N^3)$ is cubic time.

Determining the complexities of different algorithms allows us to compare the work they require without having to program and execute them. For example, if you had an $O(N^2)$ algorithm and a linear algorithm that performed the same task, you probably would choose the linear algorithm. We say *probably* because an $O(N^2)$ algorithm actually may execute fewer steps than an $O(N)$ algorithm for small values of N. Remember that if the size factor N is small, the constants and lower-order terms in the complexity expression may be significant.

Let's look at an example. Suppose that algorithm A is $O(N^2)$ and that algorithm B is $O(N)$. For large values of N, we would normally choose algorithm B because it requires less work than A. But suppose that in algorithm B, $S_0 = 1000$ and $S_1 = 1000$. If $N = 1$, then algorithm B takes 2000 steps to execute. Now suppose that for algorithm A, $S_0 = 10$, $S_1 = 10$, and $S_2 = 10$. If $N = 1$, then algorithm A takes only 30 steps. Here is a table that compares the number of steps taken by these two algorithms for different values of N.

N	Algorithm A	Algorithm B
1	30	2000
2	70	3000
3	130	4000
10	1110	11,000
20	4210	21,000
30	9310	31,000
50	25,510	51,000
100	101,010	101,000
1,000	10,010,010	1,001,000
10,000	1,000,100,010	10,001,000

From this table we can see that the $O(N^2)$ algorithm A is actually faster than the $O(N)$ algorithm B, up to the point that N equals 100. Beyond that point, algorithm B becomes more efficient. Thus, if we know that N is always less than 100 in a particular problem, we would choose algorithm A. For example, if the size factor N is the number of test scores on an exam and the class size is limited to 30 students, algorithm A would be more efficient. On the other hand, if N is the number of scores at a university with 25,000 students, we would choose algorithm B.

Constant, linear, quadratic, and cubic expressions are all examples of *polynomial* expressions. Algorithms whose complexity is characterized by such expressions are therefore said to execute in *polynomial time* and form a broad class of algorithms that encompasses everything we've discussed so far.

In addition to polynomial-time algorithms, we encounter a logarithmic-time algorithm in Chapter 13. There are also factorial ($O(N!)$), exponential ($O(N^N)$), and hyperexponential ($O(N^{N^N})$) classes of algorithms, which can require vast amounts of time to execute and are beyond the scope of this book. For now, the important point to remember is that different algorithms that solve the same problem can vary significantly in the amount of work they do.

PROBLEM-SOLVING CASE STUDY

Average Income by Gender

Problem: You've been hired by a law firm that is working on a sex discrimination case. Your firm has obtained a file of incomes, `incFile`, that contains the salaries for every employee in the company being sued. Each salary amount is preceded by 'F' for female or 'M' for male. As a first pass in the analysis of this data, you've been asked to compute the average income for females and the average income for males.

Input: A file, `incFile`, of floating-point salary amounts, with one amount per line. Each amount is preceded by a character ('F' for female, 'M' for male). This code is the first character on each input line and is followed by a blank, which separates the code from the amount.

Output:

All the input data (echo print)
The number of females and their average income
The number of males and their average income

Discussion: The problem breaks down into three main steps. First, we have to process the data, counting and summing the salary amounts for each sex. Next, we compute the averages. Finally, we have to print the calculated results.

    The first step is the most difficult. It involves a loop with several subtasks. We use our checklist of questions to develop these subtasks in detail.

1. *What is the condition that ends the loop?* The termination condition is EOF on the file `incFile`. It leads to the following loop test (in pseudocode).

       WHILE NOT EOF on incFile

2. *How should the condition be initialized?* We must open the file for input, and a priming read must take place.
3. *How should the condition be updated?* We must input a new data line with a gender code and amount at the end of each iteration. Here's the resulting algorithm:

    Open incFile for input (and verify the attempt)
    Read sex and amount from incFile
    WHILE NOT EOF on incFile
      : (Process being repeated)
      Read sex and amount from incFile

4. *What is the process being repeated?* From our knowledge of how to compute an average, we know that we have to count the number of amounts and divide this number into the sum of the amounts. Because we have to do this separately for females and males, the process consists of four parts: counting the females and summing their incomes, and then counting the males and summing their incomes. We develop each of these in turn.

5. *How should the process be initialized?* `femaleCount` and `femaleSum` should be set to zero. `maleCount` and `maleSum` also should be set to zero.

6. *How should the process be updated?* When a female income is input, `femaleCount` is incremented and the income is added to `femaleSum`. Otherwise, an income is assumed to be for a male, so `maleCount` is incremented and the amount is added to `maleSum`.

7. *What is the state of the program on exiting the loop?* The file stream `incFile` is in the fail state, `femaleCount` contains the number of input values preceded by 'F', `femaleSum` contains the sum of the values preceded by 'F', `maleCount` contains the number of values not preceded by 'F', and `maleSum` holds the sum of those values.

From the description of how the process is updated, we can see that the loop must contain an If-Then-Else structure, with one branch for female incomes and the other for male incomes. Each branch must increment the correct event counter and add the income amount to the correct total. After the loop has exited, we have enough information to compute and print the averages, dividing each total by the corresponding count.

Assumptions: There is at least one male and one female among all the data sets. The only gender codes in the file are 'M' and 'F'—any other codes are counted as 'M'. (This last assumption invalidates the results if there are any illegal codes in the data. Case Study Follow-Up Exercise 1 asks you to change the program as necessary to address this problem.)

Now we're ready to write the complete algorithm:

Main Module   **Level 0**

Separately count females and males, and sum incomes
Compute average incomes
Output results

Separately Count Females and Males, and Sum Incomes   Level 1

```
Initialize ending condition
Initialize process
WHILE NOT EOF on incFile
        Update process
        Update ending condition
```

Compute Average Incomes

```
Set femaleAverage = femaleSum / femaleCount
Set maleAverage = maleSum / maleCount
```

Output Results

```
Print femaleCount and femaleAverage
Print maleCount and maleAverage
```

Initialize Ending Condition   Level 2

```
Open incFile for input (and verify the attempt)
Read sex and amount from incFile
```

Initialize Process

```
Set femaleCount = 0
Set femaleSum = 0.0
Set maleCount = 0
Set maleSum = 0.0
```

Update Process

Echo print sex and amount
IF sex is 'F'
       Increment femaleCount
       Add amount to femaleSum
ELSE
       Increment maleCount
       Add amount to maleSum

Update Ending Condition

Read sex and amount from incFile

Module Structure Chart:

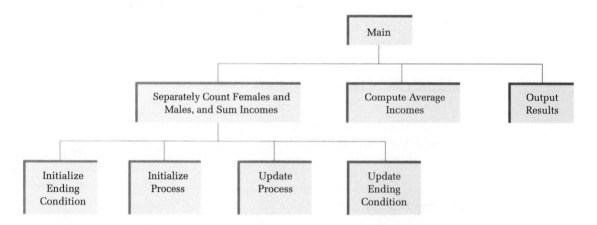

PROBLEM-SOLVING CASE STUDY cont'd.

(The following program is written in ISO/ANSI standard C++. If you are working with pre–standard C++, see the alternate version of the program in the PRE_STD directory of the program disk, available at the publisher's Web site, `www.jbpub.com/disks`.)

```
//****************************************************************
// Incomes program
// This program reads a file of income amounts classified by
// gender and computes the average income for each gender
//****************************************************************
#include <iostream>
#include <iomanip>      // For setprecision()
#include <fstream>      // For file I/O
#include <string>       // For string type

using namespace std;

int main()
{
    char     sex;             // Coded 'F' = female, 'M' = male
    int      femaleCount;     // Number of female income amounts
    int      maleCount;       // Number of male income amounts
    float    amount;          // Amount of income for a person
    float    femaleSum;       // Total of female income amounts
    float    maleSum;         // Total of male income amounts
    float    femaleAverage;   // Average female income
    float    maleAverage;     // Average male income
    ifstream incFile;         // File of income amounts
    string   fileName;        // External name of file

    cout << fixed << showpoint            // Set up floating-pt.
        << setprecision(2);               //    output format

    // Separately count females and males, and sum incomes

    // Initialize ending condition

    cout << "Name of the income data file: ";
    cin >> fileName;
    incFile.open(fileName.c_str());       // Open input file
    if ( !incFile )                       //    and verify attempt
    {
        cout << "** Can't open input file **" << endl;
        return 1;
    }
    incFile >> sex >> amount;             // Perform priming read
```

```
// Initialize process

femaleCount = 0;
femaleSum = 0.0;
maleCount = 0;
maleSum = 0.0;

while (incFile)
{
    // Update process

    cout << "Sex: " << sex << " Amount: " << amount << endl;
    if (sex == 'F')
    {
        femaleCount++;
        femaleSum = femaleSum + amount;
    }
    else
    {
        maleCount++;
        maleSum = maleSum + amount;
    }

    // Update ending condition

    incFile >> sex >> amount;
}

// Compute average incomes

femaleAverage = femaleSum / float(femaleCount);
maleAverage = maleSum / float(maleCount);

// Output results

cout << "For " << femaleCount << " females, the average "
     << "income is " << femaleAverage << endl;
cout << "For " << maleCount << " males, the average "
     << "income is " << maleAverage << endl;
return 0;
}
```

Testing: With an EOF-controlled loop, the obvious test cases are a file with data and an empty file. We should test input values of both 'F' and 'M' for the gender, and try some typical data (so we can compare the results with our hand-calculated values) and some atypical data (to see how the process behaves). An atypical data set for testing a counting operation is an empty file, which should result in a count of zero. Any other result for the count indicates an error. For a summing operation, atypical data might include negative or zero values.

The Incomes program is not designed to handle empty files or negative income values. An empty file causes both `femaleCount` and `maleCount` to equal zero at the end of the loop. Although this is correct, the statements that compute average income cause the program to crash because they divide by zero. A negative income would be treated like any other value, even though it is probably a mistake.

To correct these problems, we should insert If statements to test for the error conditions at the appropriate points in the program. When an error is detected, the program should print an error message instead of carrying out the usual computation. This prevents a crash and allows the program to keep running. We call a program that can recover from erroneous input and keep running a *robust program*.

Testing and Debugging

Loop-Testing Strategy

Even if a loop has been properly designed and verified, it is still important to test it rigorously because the chance of an error creeping in during the implementation phase is always present. Because loops allow us to input many data sets in one run, and because each iteration may be affected by preceding ones, the test data for a looping program is usually more extensive than for a program with just sequential or branching statements. To test a loop thoroughly, we must check for the proper execution of both a single iteration and multiple iterations.

Remember that a loop has seven parts (corresponding to the seven questions in our checklist). A test strategy must test each part. Although all seven parts aren't implemented separately in every loop, the checklist reminds us that some loop operations serve multiple purposes, each of which should be tested. For example, the incrementing statement in a count-controlled loop may be updating both the process and the ending condition, so it's important to verify that it performs both actions properly with respect to the rest of the loop.

To test a loop, we try to devise data sets that could cause the variables to go out of range or leave the files in improper states that violate either the loop postcondition (an assertion that must be true immediately after loop exit) or the postcondition of the module containing the loop.

It's also good practice to test a loop for four special cases: (1) when the loop is skipped entirely, (2) when the loop body is executed just once, (3) when the loop executes some normal number of times, and (4) when the loop fails to exit.

Statements following a loop often depend on its processing. If a loop can be skipped, those statements may not execute correctly. If it's possible to execute a single iteration of a loop, the results can show whether the body performs correctly in the absence of the effects of previous iterations, which can be very helpful when you're trying to isolate the source of an error. Obviously, it's important to test a loop under normal conditions, with a wide variety of inputs. If possible, you should test the loop with real data in addition to mock data sets. Count-controlled loops should be tested to be sure they execute exactly the right number of times. And finally, if there is any chance that a loop might never exit, your test data should try to make that happen.

Testing a program can be as challenging as writing it. To test a program, you need to step back, take a fresh look at what you've written, and then attack it in every way possible to make it fail. This isn't always easy to do, but it's necessary if your programs are going to be reliable. (A *reliable program* is one that works consistently and without errors regardless of whether the input data is valid or invalid.)

Test Plans Involving Loops

In Chapter 5, we introduced formal test plans and discussed the testing of branches. Those guidelines still apply to programs with loops, but here we provide some additional guidelines that are specific to loops.

Unfortunately, when a loop is embedded in a larger program, it sometimes is difficult to control and observe the conditions under which the loop executes using test data and output alone. In come cases we must use indirect tests. For example, if a loop reads floating-point values from a file and prints their average without echo printing them, you cannot tell directly that the loop processes all the data—if the data values in the file are all the same, then the average appears correct as long as even one of them is processed. You must construct the input file so that the average is a unique value that can be arrived at only by processing all the data.

To simplify our testing of such loops, we would like to observe the values of the variables associated with the loop at the start of each iteration. How can we observe the values of variables while a program is running? Two common techniques are the use of the system's *debugger* program and the use of extra output statements designed solely for debugging purposes. We discuss these techniques in the next section, Testing and Debugging Hints.

Now let's look at some test cases that are specific to the different types of loops that we've seen in this chapter.

Count-Controlled Loops   When a loop is count-controlled, you should include a test case that specifies the output for all the iterations. It may help to add an extra column to the test plan that lists the iteration number. If the loop reads data and outputs a result, then each input value should produce a different output to make it easier to spot errors. For example, in a loop that is supposed to read and print 100 data values, it is easier to tell that the loop executes the correct number of iterations when the values are 1, 2, 3, ..., 100 than if they are all the same.

If the program inputs the iteration count for the loop, you need to test the cases in which an invalid count, such as a negative number, is input (an error message should be output and the loop should be skipped), a count of 0 is input (the loop should be skipped), a count of 1 is input (the loop should execute once), and some typical number of iterations is input (the loop should execute the specified number of times).

Event-Controlled Loops   In an event-controlled loop, you should test the situation in which the event occurs before the loop, in the first iteration, and in a typical number of iterations. For example, if the event is that EOF occurs, then try an empty file, a file with one data set, and another with several data sets. If your testing involves reading from test files, you should attach printed copies of the files to the test plan and identify each in some way so that the plan can refer to them. It also helps to identify where each iteration begins in the Input and Expected Output columns of the test plan.

When the event is the input of a sentinel value, you need the following test cases: the sentinel is the only data set, the sentinel follows one data set, and the sentinel follows a typical number of data sets. Given that sentinel-controlled loops involve a priming read, it is especially important to verify that the first and last data sets are processed properly.

Testing and Debugging Hints

1. Plan your test data carefully to test all sections of a program.
2. Beware of infinite loops, in which the expression in the While statement never becomes `false`. The symptom: the program doesn't stop. If you are on a system that monitors the execution time of a program, you may see a message such as "TIME LIMIT EXCEEDED."

   If you have created an infinite loop, check your logic and the syntax of your loops. Be sure there's no semicolon immediately after the right parenthesis of the While condition:

   ```
   while (Expression);        // Wrong
      Statement
   ```

This semicolon causes an infinite loop in most cases; the compiler thinks the loop body is the null statement (the do-nothing statement composed only of a semicolon). In a count-controlled loop, make sure the loop control variable is incremented within the loop. In a flag-controlled loop, make sure the flag eventually changes.

And, as always, watch for the = versus == problem in While conditions as well as in If conditions. The line

```
while (someVar = 5)        // Wrong (should be ==)
```

produces an infinite loop. The value of the assignment (not relational) expression is always 5, which is interpreted as true.

3. Check the loop termination condition carefully and be sure that something in the loop causes it to be met. Watch closely for values that cause one iteration too many or too few (the "off-by-1" syndrome).

4. Remember to use the get function rather than the >> operator in loops that are controlled by detection of a newline character.

5. Perform an algorithm walk-through to verify that all of the appropriate preconditions and postconditions occur in the right places.

6. Trace the execution of the loop by hand with a code walk-through. Simulate the first few passes and the last few passes very carefully to see how the loop really behaves.

7. Use a *debugger* if your system provides one. A debugger is a program that runs your program in "slow motion," allowing you to execute one instruction at a time and to examine the contents of variables as they change. If you haven't already done so, check to see if a debugger is available on your system.

8. If all else fails, use *debug output statements*—output statements inserted into a program to help debug it. They output messages that indicate the flow of execution in the program or report the values of variables at certain points in the program.

    For example, if you want to know the value of variable beta at a certain point in a program, you could insert this statement:

```
cout << "beta = " << beta << endl;
```

If this output statement is in a loop, you will get as many values of beta output as there are iterations of the body of the loop.

After you have debugged your program, you can remove the debug output statements or just precede them with // so that they'll be treated as comments. (This practice is referred to as *commenting out* a piece of code.) You can remove the double slashes if you need to use the statements again.

9. An ounce of prevention is worth a pound of debugging. Use the checklist questions to design your loop correctly at the outset. It may seem like extra work, but it pays off in the long run.

Summary

The While statement is a looping construct that allows the program to repeat a statement as long as the value of an expression is true. When the value of the expression becomes false, the body of the loop is skipped and execution continues with the first statement following the loop.

With the While statement, you can construct several types of loops that you will use again and again. These types of loops fall into two categories: count-controlled loops and event-controlled loops.

In a count-controlled loop, the loop body is repeated a specified number of times. You initialize a counter variable right before the While statement. This variable is the loop control variable. The control variable is tested against the limit in the While expression. The last statement in the loop body increments the control variable.

Event-controlled loops continue executing until something inside the body signals that the looping process should stop. Event-controlled loops include those that test for a sentinel value in the data, for end-of-file, or for a change in a flag variable.

Sentinel-controlled loops are input loops that use a special data value as a signal to stop reading. EOF-controlled loops are loops that continue to input (and process) data values until there is no more data. To implement them with a While statement, you must test the state of the input stream by using the name of the stream object as if it were a Boolean variable. The test yields false when there are no more data values. A flag is a variable that is set in one part of the program and tested in another. In a flag-controlled loop, you must set the flag before the loop begins, test it in the While expression, and change it somewhere in the body of the loop.

Counting is a looping operation that keeps track of how many times a loop is repeated or how many times some event occurs. This count can be used in computations or to control the loop. A counter is a variable that is used for counting. It may be the loop control variable in a count-controlled loop, an iteration counter in a counting loop, or an event counter that counts the number of times a particular condition occurs in a loop.

Summing is a looping operation that keeps a running total of certain values. It is like counting in that the variable that holds the sum is initialized outside the loop. The summing operation, however, adds up unknown values; the counting operation adds a constant (1) to the counter each time.

When you design a loop, there are seven points to consider: how the termination condition is initialized, tested, and updated; how the process in the loop is initialized, performed, and updated; and the state of the program upon exiting the loop. By answering the checklist questions, you can bring each of these points into focus.

To design a nested loop structure, begin with the outermost loop. When you get to where the inner loop must appear, make it a separate module and come back to its design later.

The process of testing a loop is based on the answers to the checklist questions and the patterns the loop might encounter (for example, executing a single iteration, multiple iterations, an infinite number of iterations, or no iterations at all).

Quick Check

1. Write the first line of a While statement that loops until the value of the Boolean variable done becomes true. (pp. 276–279)
2. What are the four parts of a count-controlled loop? (pp. 280–282)
3. Should you use a priming read with an EOF-controlled loop? (pp. 285–287)
4. How is a flag variable used to control a loop? (pp. 287–288)
5. What is the difference between a counting operation in a loop and a summing operation in a loop? (pp. 288–291)
6. What is the difference between a loop control variable and an event counter? (pp. 288–291)
7. What kind of loop would you use in a program that reads the closing price of a stock for each day of the week? (pp. 292–296)
8. How would you extend the loop in Question 7 to make it read prices for 52 weeks? (pp. 296–302)
9. How would you test a program that is supposed to count the number of females and the number of males in a data set? (Assume that females are coded with 'F' in the data; males, with 'M'.) (pp. 313–315)

Answers **1.** while (!done) **2.** The process being repeated, plus initializing, testing, and incrementing the loop control variable **3.** Yes **4.** The flag is set outside the loop. The While expression checks the flag, and an If inside the loop resets the flag when the termination condition occurs. **5.** A counting operation increments by a fixed value with each iteration of the loop; a summing operation adds unknown values to the total. **6.** A loop control variable controls the loop; an event counter simply counts certain events during execution of the loop. **7.** Because there are five days in a business week, you would use a count-controlled loop that runs from 1 to 5. **8.** Nest the original loop inside a count-controlled loop that runs from 1 to 52. **9.** Run the program with data sets that have a different number of females and males, only females, only males, illegal values (other characters), and an empty input file.

Exam Preparation Exercises

1. In one or two sentences, explain the difference between loops and branches.
2. What does the following loop print out? (number is of type int.)

```
number = 1;
while (number < 11)
{
    number++;
    cout << number << endl;
}
```

3. By rearranging the order of the statements (don't change the way they are written), make the loop in Exercise 2 print the numbers from 1 through 10.
4. When the following code is executed, how many iterations of the loop are performed?

```
number = 2;
done = false;
while ( !done )
{
    number = number * 2;
    if (number > 64)
        done = true;
}
```

5. What is the output of this nested loop structure?

```
i = 4;
while (i >= 1)
{
    j = 2;
    while (j >= 1)
    {
        cout << j << ' ';
        j--;
    }
    cout << i << endl;
    i--;
}
```

6. The following code segment is supposed to write out the even numbers between 1 and 15. (n is an int variable.) It has two flaws in it.

```
n = 2;
while (n != 15)
{
    n = n + 2;
    cout << n << ' ';
}
```

   a. What is the output of the code as written?
   b. Correct the code so that it works as intended.

7. The following code segment is supposed to copy one line from the standard input device to the standard output device.

```
cin.get(inChar);
while (inChar != '\n')
{
    cin.get(inChar);
    cout << inChar;
}
```

   a. What is the output if the input line consists of the characters ABCDE?
   b. Rewrite the code so that it works properly.

8. Does the following program segment need any priming reads? If not, explain why. If so, add the input statement(s) in the proper place. (letter is of type char.)

```
while (cin)
{
    while (letter != '\n')
    {
        cout << letter;
        cin.get(letter);
    }
    cout << endl;
    cout << "Another line read..." << endl;
    cin.get(letter);
}
```

9. What sentinel value would you choose for a program that reads telephone numbers as integers?

10. Consider this program:

```
#include <iostream>

using namespace std;

const int LIMIT = 8;

int main()
{
    int   sum;
    int   i;
    int   number;
    bool  finished;

    sum = 0;
    i = 1;
    finished = false;
    while (i <= LIMIT && !finished)
    {
        cin >> number;
        if (number > 0)
            sum = sum + number;
        else if (number == 0)
            finished = true;
        i++;
    }
    cout << "End of test. " << sum << ' ' << number << endl;
    return 0;
}
```

and these data values:

```
5   6   -3   7   -4   0   5   8   9
```

a. What are the contents of sum and number after exit from the loop?

b. Do the data values fully test the program? Explain your answer.

11. Here is a simple count-controlled loop:

```
count = 1;
while (count < 20)
    count++;
```

a. List three ways of changing the loop so that it executes 20 times instead of 19.

b. Which of those changes makes the value of count range from 1 through 21?

12. What is the output of the following program segment? (All variables are of type int.)

```
i = 1;
while (i <= 5)
{
    sum = 0;
    j = 1;
    while (j <= i)
    {
        sum = sum + j;
        j++;
    }
    cout << sum << ' ';
    i++;
}
```

Programming Warm-up Exercises

1. Write a program segment that sets a Boolean variable dangerous to true and stops reading data if pressure (a float variable being read in) exceeds 510.0. Use dangerous as a flag to control the loop.

2. Write a program segment that counts the number of times the integer 28 occurs in a file of 100 integers.

3. Write a nested loop code segment that produces this output:

```
1
1 2
1 2 3
1 2 3 4
```

4. Write a program segment that reads a file of student scores for a class (any size) and finds the class average.

5. Write a program segment that reads in integers and then counts and prints out the number of positive integers and the number of negative integers. If a value is 0, it should not be counted. The process should continue until end-of-file occurs.

6. Write a program segment that adds up the even integers from 16 through 26, inclusive.

7. Write a program segment that prints out the sequence of all the hour and minute combinations in a day, starting with 1:00 A.M. and ending with 12:59 A.M.

8. Rewrite the code segment for Exercise 7 so that it prints the times in ten-minute intervals, arranged as a table with six columns and 24 rows.

9. Write a code segment that inputs one line of data containing an unknown number of character strings that are separated by spaces. The final value on the line is the sentinel string End. The segment should output the number of strings on the input line (excluding End), the number of strings that contained at least one letter *e*, and the percentage of strings that contained at least one *e*. (*Hint*: To determine if *e* occurs in a string, use the find function of the string class.)

10. Extend the code segment of Exercise 9 so that it processes all the lines in a data file inFile and prints the three pieces of information for each input line.

11. Modify the code segment of Exercise 10 so that it also keeps a count of the total number of strings in the file and the total number of strings containing at least one *e*. (Again, do not count the sentinel string on each line.) When EOF is reached, print the three pieces of information for the entire file.

Programming Problems

1. Write a functional decomposition and a C++ program that inputs an integer and a character. The output should be a diamond composed of the character and extending the width specified by the integer. For example, if the integer is 11 and the character is an asterisk (*), the diamond would look like this:

```
          *
         ***
        *****
       *******
      *********
     ***********
      *********
       *******
        *****
         ***
          *
```

If the input integer is an even number, it should be increased to the next odd number. Use meaningful variable names, proper indentation, appropriate comments, and good prompting messages.

2. Write a functional decomposition and a C++ program that inputs an integer larger than 1 and calculates the sum of the squares from 1 to that integer. For example, if the integer equals 4, the sum of the squares is 30 (1 + 4 + 9 + 16). The output should be the value of the integer and the sum, properly labeled. The program should repeat this process for several input values. A negative input value signals the end of the data.

3. You are putting together some music tapes for a party. You've arranged a list of songs in the order in which you want to play them. However, you would like to minimize the empty tape left at the end of each side of a cassette (the cassette plays for 45 minutes on a side). So you want to figure out the total time for a group of songs and see how well they fit. Write a functional decomposition and a C++ program to help you do this. The program should input a reference number and a time for each song until it encounters a reference number of

0. The times should each be entered as minutes and seconds (two integer values). For example, if song number 4 takes 7 minutes and 42 seconds to play, the data entered for that song would be

4   7   42

The program should echo print the data for each song and the current running time total. The last data entry (reference number 0) should not be added to the total time. After all the data has been read, the program should print a message indicating the time remaining on the tape.

If you are writing this program to read data from a file, the output should be in the form of a table with columns and headings. For example,

Song Number	Song Time Minutes	Seconds	Total Time Minutes	Seconds
------	-------	-------	-------	-------
1	5	10	5	10
2	7	42	12	52
5	4	19	17	11
3	4	33	21	44
4	10	27	32	11
6	8	55	41	6
0	0	1	41	6

There are 3 minutes and 54 seconds of tape left.

If you are using interactive input, your output should have prompting messages interspersed with the results. For example,

```
Enter the song number:
1
Enter the number of minutes:
5
Enter the number of seconds:
10
Song number 1, 5 minutes and 10 seconds
Total time is 5 minutes and 10 seconds.
For the next song,
Enter the song number:
  ⋮
```

Use meaningful variable names, proper indentation, and appropriate comments. If you're writing an interactive program, use good prompting messages. The program should discard any invalid data sets (negative numbers, for example) and print an error message indicating that the data set has been discarded and what was wrong with it.

4. Using functional decomposition, write a program that prints out the approximate number of words in a file of text. For our purposes, this is the same as the number of gaps following words. A *gap* is defined as one or more spaces in a row, so a sequence of spaces counts as just one gap. The newline character also counts as a gap. Anything other than a space or newline is considered to be part of a word. For example, there are 13 words in this sentence, according to our definition. The program should echo print the data.

Solve this problem with two different programs:

a. Use a `string` object into which you input each word as a string. This approach is quite straightforward.

b. Assume the `string` class does not exist, and input the data one character at a time. This approach is more complicated. (*Hint*: Only count a space as a gap if the previous character read is something other than a space.)

Use meaningful variable names, proper indentation, and appropriate comments. Thoroughly test the programs with your own data sets.

Case Study Follow-Up

1. Change the Incomes program so that it does the following:

   a. Prints an error message when a negative income value is input and then goes on processing any remaining data. The erroneous data should not be included in any of the calculations. Thoroughly test the modified program with your own data sets.

   b. Does not crash when there are no males in the input file or no females (or the file is empty). Instead, it should print an appropriate error message. Test the revised program with your own data sets.

   c. Rejects data sets that are coded with a letter other than 'F' or 'M' and prints an error message before continuing to process the remaining data. The program also should print a message indicating the number of erroneous data sets encountered in the file.

2. Develop a thorough set of test data for the Incomes program as modified in Exercise 1.

3. Modify the Incomes program so that it reports the highest and lowest incomes for each gender.

4. Develop a thorough set of test data for the Incomes program as modified in Exercise 3.

7

Functions

GOALS

- To be able to write a program that uses functions to reflect the structure of your functional decomposition.
- To be able to write a module of your own design as a void function.
- To be able to define a void function to do a specified task.
- To be able to distinguish between value and reference parameters.
- To be able to use arguments and parameters correctly.
- To be able to do the following tasks, given a functional decomposition of a problem:

    Determine what the parameter list should be for each module.

    Determine which parameters should be reference parameters and which should be value parameters.

    Code the program correctly.
- To be able to define and use local variables correctly.
- To be able to write a program that uses multiple calls to a single function.

You have been using C++ functions since we introduced standard library routines such as `sqrt` and `abs` in Chapter 3. By now, you should be quite comfortable with the idea of calling these subprograms to perform a task. So far, we have not considered how the programmer can create his or her own functions other than `main`. That is the topic of this chapter and the next.

You might wonder why we waited until now to look at user-defined subprograms. The reason, and the major purpose for using subprograms, is that we write our own value-returning functions and void functions to help organize and simplify larger programs. Until now, our programs have been relatively small and simple, so we didn't need to write subprograms. Now that we've covered the basic control structures, we are ready to introduce subprograms so that we can begin writing larger and more complex programs.

Functional Decomposition with Void Functions

As a brief refresher, let's review the two kinds of subprograms that the C++ language works with: value-returning functions and void functions. A value-returning function receives some data through its argument list, computes a single function value, and returns this function value to the calling code. The caller invokes (calls) a value-returning function by using its name and argument list in an expression:

```
y = 3.8 * sqrt(x);
```

In contrast, a void function (*procedure*, in some languages) does not return a function value. Nor is it called from within an expression. Instead, the function call appears as a complete, stand-alone statement. An example is the `get` function associated with the `istream` and `ifstream` classes:

```
cin.get(inputChar);
```

In this chapter, we concentrate exclusively on creating our own void functions. In Chapter 8, we examine how to write value-returning functions.

From the early chapters on, you have been designing your programs as collections of modules. Many of these modules are naturally implemented as *user-defined void functions*. We now look at how to turn the modules in your algorithms into user-defined void functions.

When to Use Functions

In general, you can code any module as a function, although some are so simple that this really is unnecessary. In designing a program, then, we frequently need to decide which modules should be implemented as functions. The decision should be based on whether the overall program is easier to understand as a result. Other factors can affect this decision, but for now this is the simplest heuristic (strategy) to use.

If a module is a single line only, it is usually best to write it directly in the program. Turning it into a function only complicates the overall program, which defeats the purpose of using subprograms. On the other hand, if a module is many lines long, it is easier to understand the program if the module is turned into a function.

Keep in mind that whether you choose to code a module as a function or not affects only the readability of the program and may make it more or less convenient to change the program later. Your choice does not affect the correct functioning of the program.

Writing Modules as Void Functions

It is quite simple to turn a module into a void function in C++. Basically, a void function looks like the `main` function except that the function heading uses `void` rather than `int` as the data type of the function. Additionally, the body of a void function does not contain a statement like

```
return 0;
```

as does `main`. A void function does not return a function value to its caller.

Let's look at a program using void functions. A friend of yours is returning from a long trip, and you want to write a program that prints the following message:

```
***************
***************
  Welcome Home!
***************
***************
***************
***************
```

Here is a design for the program.

Main   **Level 0**

Print two lines of asterisks
Print "Welcome Home!"
Print four lines of asterisks

Print 2 Lines   **Level 1**

Print 4 Lines

Print "**************"
Print "**************"
Print "**************"
Print "**************"

If we write the two first-level modules as void functions, the `main` function is simply

```
int main()
{
    Print2Lines();
    cout << "Welcome Home!" << endl;
    Print4Lines();
    return 0;
}
```

Notice how similar this code is to the main module of our functional decomposition. It contains two function calls—one to a function named `Print2Lines` and another to a function named `Print4Lines`. Both of these functions have empty argument lists.

The following code should look familiar to you, but look carefully at the function heading.

```
void Print2Lines()                              // Function heading
{
    cout << "***************" << endl;
    cout << "***************" << endl;
}
```

This segment is a *function definition*. A function definition is the code that extends from the function heading to the end of the block that is the body of the function. The function heading begins with the word `void`, signaling the compiler that this is not a value-returning function. The body of the function executes some ordinary statements and does *not* finish with a `return` statement to return a function value.

Now look again at the function heading. Just like any other identifier in C++, the name of a function cannot include blanks, even though our paper-and-pencil module names do. Following the function name is an empty argument list—that is, there is nothing between the parentheses. Later we see what goes inside the parentheses if a function uses arguments. Now let's put `main` and the other two functions together to form a complete program.

```
//****************************************************************
// Welcome program
// This program prints a "Welcome Home" message
//****************************************************************
#include <iostream>

using namespace std;

void Print2Lines();                             // Function prototypes
void Print4Lines();

int main()
{
    Print2Lines();                              // Function call
    cout << " Welcome Home!" << endl;
    Print4Lines();                              // Function call
    return 0;
}


//****************************************************************

void Print2Lines()                              // Function heading

// This function prints two lines of asterisks
```

```
{
    cout << "***************" << endl;
    cout << "***************" << endl;
}


//*****************************************************************

void Print4Lines()                          // Function heading

// This function prints four lines of asterisks

{
    cout << "***************" << endl;
    cout << "***************" << endl;
    cout << "***************" << endl;
    cout << "***************" << endl;
}
```

C++ function definitions can appear in any order. We could have chosen to place the main function last instead of first, but C++ programmers typically put main first and any supporting functions after it.

In the Welcome program, the two statements just before the main function are called *function prototypes*. These declarations are necessary because of the C++ rule requiring you to declare an identifier before you can use it. Our main function uses the identifiers Print2Lines and Print4Lines, but the definitions of those functions don't appear until later. We must supply the function prototypes to inform the compiler in advance that Print2Lines and Print4Lines are the names of functions, that they do not return function values, and that they have no arguments. We say more about function prototypes later in the chapter.

Because the Welcome program is so simple to begin with, it may seem more complicated with its modules written as functions. However, it is clear that it much more closely resembles our functional decomposition. This is especially true of the main function. If you handed this code to someone, the person could look at the main function (which, as we said, usually appears first) and tell you immediately what the program does—it prints two lines of something, prints "Welcome Home!", and prints four lines of something. If you asked the person to be more specific, he or she could then look up the details in the other function definitions. The person is able to begin with a top-level view of the program and then study the lower-level modules as necessary, without having to read the entire program or look at a module structure chart. As our programs grow to include many modules nested several levels deep, the ability to read a program in the same manner as a functional decomposition aids greatly in the development and debugging process.

MAY WE INTRODUCE

Charles Babbage

The British mathematician Charles Babbage (1791–1871) is generally credited with designing the world's first computer. Unlike today's electronic computers, however, Babbage's machine was mechanical. It was made of gears and levers, the predominant technology of the 1820s and 1830s.

Babbage actually designed two different machines. The first, called the Difference Engine, was to be used in computing mathematical tables. For example, the Difference Engine could produce a table of squares:

x	x^2
1	1
2	4
3	9
4	16
$\vdots$	$\vdots$

It was essentially a complex calculator that could not be programmed. Babbage's Difference Engine was designed to improve the accuracy of the computation of tables, not the speed. At that time, all tables were produced by hand, a tedious and error-prone job. Because much of science and engineering depended on accurate table information, an error could have serious consequences. Even though the Difference Engine could perform the calculations only a little faster than a human could, it did so without error. In fact, one of its most important features was that it would stamp its output directly onto copper plates, which could then be placed into a printing press, thereby avoiding even typographical errors.

By 1833, the project to build the Difference Engine had run into financial trouble. The engineer whom Babbage had hired to do the construction was dishonest and had drawn the project out as long as possible so as to extract more money from Babbage's sponsors in the British government. Eventually the sponsors became tired of waiting for the machine and withdrew their support. At about the same time, Babbage lost interest in the project because he had developed the idea for a much more powerful machine, which he called the Analytical Engine—a truly programmable computer.

The idea for the Analytical Engine came to Babbage as he toured Europe to survey the best technology of the time in preparation for constructing the Difference Engine. One of the technologies that he saw was the Jacquard automatic loom, in which a series of paper cards with punched holes was fed through the machine to produce a woven cloth pattern. The pattern of holes constituted a program for the loom and made it possible to weave patterns of arbitrary complexity automatically. In fact, its inventor even had a detailed portrait of himself woven by one of his machines.

Babbage realized that this sort of device could be used to control the operation of a computing machine. Instead of calculating just one type of formula, such a machine could be programmed to perform arbitrarily complex computations, including the manipulation of algebraic symbols. As his associate, Ada Lovelace (the world's first computer programmer), elegantly put it, "We may say most aptly that the Analytical Engine weaves algebraical patterns." It is clear that Babbage and Lovelace fully understood the power of a programmable computer and even contemplated the notion that someday such machines could achieve artificial thought.

Unfortunately, Babbage never completed construction of either of his machines. Some historians believe that he never finished them because the technology of the period could not support such complex machinery. But most feel that Babbage's failure was his own doing. He was both brilliant and somewhat eccentric (it is known that he was afraid of Italian organ grinders, for example). As a consequence, he had a tendency to abandon projects in midstream so that he could concentrate on newer and better ideas. He always believed that his new approaches would enable him to complete a machine in less time than his old ideas would.

When he died, Babbage had many pieces of computing machines and partial drawings of designs, but none of the plans were complete enough to produce a single working computer. After his death, his ideas were dismissed and his inventions ignored. Only after modern computers were developed did historians recognize the true importance of his contributions. Babbage recognized the potential of the computer an entire century before one was fully developed. Today, we can only imagine how different the world would be if he had succeeded in constructing his Analytical Engine.

An Overview of User-Defined Functions

Now that we've seen an example of how a program is written with functions, let's look briefly and informally at some of the more important points of function construction and use.

Flow of Control in Function Calls

We said that C++ function definitions can be arranged in any order, although main usually appears first. During compilation, the functions are translated in the order in which they physically appear. When the program is executed, however, control begins at the first statement in the main function, and the program proceeds in logical sequence. When a function call is encountered, logical control is passed to the first statement in that function's body. The statements in the function are executed in logical order. After the last one is executed, control returns to the point immediately following the function call. Because function calls alter the logical order of execution, functions are considered control structures. Figure 7-1 illustrates this physical versus logical ordering of functions. In the figure, functions A, B, and C are written in the physical order A, B, C but are executed in the order C, B, A.

In the Welcome program, execution begins with the first executable statement in the `main` function (the call to `Print2Lines`). When `Print2Lines` is called, control passes to its first statement and subsequent statements in its body. After the last statement in `Print2Lines` has executed, control returns to the `main` function at the point following the call (the output statement that prints "Welcome Home!").

Function Parameters

Looking at the Welcome program, you can see that `Print2Lines` and `Print4Lines` are very similar functions. They differ only in the number of lines that they print. Do we really need two different functions in this program? Maybe we should write only one function that prints *any* number of lines, where the "any number of lines" is passed as an argument by the caller (`main`). Here is a second version of the program, which uses only one function to do the printing. We call it NewWelcome.

FIGURE 7-1

Physical Versus
Logical Order of
Functions

Module Structure Chart

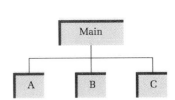

```
//*******************************************************************
// NewWelcome program
// This program prints a "Welcome Home" message
//*******************************************************************
#include <iostream>

using namespace std;

void PrintLines( int );                        // Function prototype

int main()
{
    PrintLines(2);
    cout << " Welcome Home!" << endl;
    PrintLines(4);
    return 0;
}


//*******************************************************************

void PrintLines( int numLines )

// This function prints lines of asterisks, where
// numLines specifies how many lines to print

{
    int count;       // Loop control variable

    count = 1;
    while (count <= numLines)
    {
        cout << "***************" << endl;
        count++;
    }
}
```

In the function heading of `PrintLines`, you see some code between
the parentheses that looks like a variable declaration. This is a *parameter
declaration*. As you learned in earlier chapters, arguments represent a way
for two functions to communicate with each other. Arguments enable the
calling function to input (pass) values to another function to use in its processing and—in some cases—to allow the called function to output (return)
results to the caller. The items listed in the call to a function are the **arguments.** The variables declared in the function heading are the **parameters.**
(Some programmers use the pair of terms *actual argument* and *formal
argument* instead of *argument* and *parameter*. Others use the term *actual
parameter* in place of *argument*, and *formal parameter* in place of *parame-*

ter.) Notice that the main function in the code above is a *parameterless* function.

Parameter   A variable declared in a function heading; also called *formal argument* or *formal parameter*.

Argument   A variable or expression listed in a call to a function; also called *actual argument* or *actual parameter*.

In the NewWelcome program, the arguments in the two function calls are the constants 2 and 4, and the parameter in the PrintLines function is named numLines. The main function first calls PrintLines with an argument of 2. When control is turned over to PrintLines, the parameter numLines is initialized to 2. Within PrintLines, the count-controlled loop executes twice and the function returns. The second time PrintLines is called, the parameter numLines is initialized to the value of the argument, 4. The loop executes four times, after which the function returns.

Although there is no benefit in doing so, we could write the main function this way:

```
int main()
{
    int lineCount;

    lineCount = 2;
    PrintLines(lineCount);
    cout << " Welcome Home!" << endl;
    lineCount = 4;
    PrintLines(lineCount);
    return 0;
}
```

In this version, the argument in each call to PrintLines is a variable rather than a constant. Each time main calls PrintLines, a copy of the argument's value is passed to the function to initialize the parameter numLines. This version shows that when you pass a variable as an argument, the argument and the parameter can have different names.

The NewWelcome program brings up a second major reason for using functions—namely, a function can be called from many places in the main function (or from other functions). Use of multiple calls can save a great deal of effort in coding many problem solutions. If a task must be done in more than one place in a program, we can avoid repetitive coding by writing it as a function and then calling it wherever we need it. Another example that illustrates this use of functions appears in the Problem-Solving Case Study at the end of this chapter.

If more than one argument is passed to a function, the arguments and parameters are matched by their relative positions in the two lists. For example, if you want `PrintLines` to print lines consisting of any selected character, not only asterisks, you might rewrite the function so that its heading is

```
void PrintLines( int  numLines,
             char whichChar )
```

and a call to the function might look like this:

```
PrintLines(3, '#');
```

The first argument, 3, is matched with `numLines` because `numLines` is the first parameter. Likewise, the second argument, '#', is matched with the second parameter, `whichChar`.

Syntax and Semantics of Void Functions

Function Call (Invocation)

To call (or invoke) a void function, we use its name as a statement, with the arguments in parentheses following the name. A **function call** in a program results in the execution of the body of the called function. This is the syntax template of a function call to a void function:

FunctionCall (to a void function)

FunctionName **(** ArgumentList **);**

Function call (to a void function)   A statement that transfers control to a void function. In C++, this statement is the name of the function, followed by a list of arguments.

According to the syntax template for a function call, the argument list is optional. A function is not required to have arguments. However, as the syntax template also shows, the parentheses are required even if the argument list is empty.

If there are two or more arguments in the argument list, you must separate them with commas. Here is the syntax template for ArgumentList:

ArgumentList

Expression **,** Expression . . .

When a function call is executed, the arguments are passed to the parameters according to their positions, left to right, and control is then transferred to the first executable statement in the function body. When the last statement in the function has executed, control returns to the point from which the function was called.

Function Declarations and Definitions

In C++, you must declare every identifier before it can be used. In the case of functions, a function's declaration must physically precede any function call.

A function declaration announces to the compiler the name of the function, the data type of the function's return value (either void or a data type like int or float), and the data types of the parameters it uses. The NewWelcome program shows a total of three function declarations. The first declaration (the statement labeled "Function prototype") does not include the body of the function. The remaining two declarations—for main and PrintLines—include bodies for the functions.

In C++ terminology, a function declaration that omits the body is called a **function prototype,** and a declaration that does include the body is a **function definition.** We can use a Venn diagram to picture the fact that all definitions are declarations, but not all declarations are definitions:

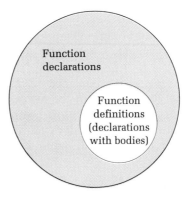

Function prototype   A function declaration without the body of the function.

Function definition   A function declaration that includes the body of the function.

Whether we are talking about functions or variables, the general idea in C++ is that a declaration becomes a definition if it also allocates memory space for the item. (There are exceptions to this rule of thumb, but we don't concern ourselves with them now.) For example, a function prototype is merely a declaration—that is, it specifies the properties of a function: its name, its data type, and the data types of its parameters. But a function definition does more; it causes the compiler to allocate memory for the instructions in the body of the function. (Technically, all of the variable declarations we've used so far have been variable *definitions* as well as declarations—they allocate memory for the variable. In Chapter 8, we see examples of variable declarations that aren't variable definitions.)

The rule throughout C++ is that you can declare an item as many times as you wish, but you can define it only once. In the NewWelcome program, we could include many function prototypes for `PrintLines` (though we'd have no reason to), but only one function definition is allowed.

Function Prototypes   We have said that the definition of the `main` function usually appears first in a program, followed by the definitions of all other functions. To satisfy the requirement that identifiers be declared before they are used, C++ programmers typically place all function prototypes near the top of the program, before the definition of `main`.

A function prototype (known as a *forward declaration* in some languages) specifies in advance the data type of the function value to be returned (or the word `void`) and the data types of the parameters. A prototype for a void function has the following form:

FunctionPrototype (for a void function)

```
void FunctionName ( ParameterList );
```

As you can see in the syntax template, no body is included for the function, and a semicolon terminates the declaration. The parameter list is optional, to allow for parameterless functions. If the parameter list is present, it has the following form:

ParameterList (in a function prototype)

DataType **&** VariableName **,** DataType **&** VariableName . . .

The ampersand (&) attached to the name of a data type is optional and has a special significance that we cover later in the chapter.

In a function prototype, the parameter list must specify the data types of the parameters, but their names are optional. You could write either

```
void DoSomething( int, float );
```

or

```
void DoSomething( int velocity, float angle );
```

Sometimes it's useful for documentation purposes to supply names for the parameters, but the compiler ignores them.

Function Definitions   You learned in Chapter 2 that a function definition consists of two parts: the function heading and the function body, which is syntactically a block (compound statement). Here's the syntax template for a function definition, specifically, for a void function:

FunctionDefinition (for a void function)

```
void FunctionName ( ParameterList )
{
      Statement
           ⋮
}
```

Notice that the function heading does *not* end in a semicolon the way a function prototype does. It is a common syntax error to put a semicolon at the end of the line.

The syntax of the parameter list differs slightly from that of a function prototype in that you *must* specify the names of all the parameters. Also, it's our style preference (but not a language requirement) to declare each parameter on a separate line:

ParameterList (in a function definition)

DataType **&** VariableName **,**
DataType **&** VariableName
⋮

Local Variables

Because a function body is a block, any function—not only the `main` function—can include variable declarations within its body. These variables are called **local variables** because they are accessible only within the block in which they are declared. As far as the calling code is concerned, they don't exist. If you tried to print the contents of a local variable from another function, a compile-time error such as "UNDECLARED IDENTIFIER" would occur. You saw an example of a local variable in the NewWelcome program—the `count` variable declared within the `PrintLines` function.

Local variable   A variable declared within a block and not accessible outside of that block.

In contrast to local variables, variables declared outside of all the functions in a program are called *global variables*. We return to the topic of global variables in Chapter 8.

Local variables occupy memory space only while the function is executing. At the moment the function is called, memory space is created for its local variables. When the function returns, its local variables are destroyed.* Therefore, every time the function is called, its local variables start out with their values undefined. Because every call to a function is independent of every other call to that same function, you must initialize the local variables within the function itself. And because local variables are destroyed when the function returns, you cannot use them to store values between calls to the function.

The following code segment illustrates each of the parts of the function declaration and calling mechanism that we have discussed.

```
#include <iostream>

using namespace std;

void TryThis( int, int, float );        // Function prototype
```

---

* We'll see an exception to this rule in the next chapter.

```
void TryThis( int, int, float );       // Function prototype

int main()                             // Function definition
{
    int    int1;                       // Variables local to main
    int    int2;
    float someFloat;
    ⋮
    TryThis(int1, int2, someFloat);    // Function call with three
                                       //   arguments
    ⋮
}

void TryThis( int    param1,           // Function definition with
              int    param2,           //   three parameters
              float param3 )
{
    int    i;                          // Variables local to TryThis
    float x;
    ⋮
}
```

The Return Statement

The `main` function uses the statement

```
return 0;
```

to return the value 0 (or 1 or some other value) to its caller, the operating system. Every value-returning function must return its function value this way.

A void function does not return a function value. Control returns from the function when it "falls off" the end of the body—that is, after the final statement has executed. As you saw in the NewWelcome program, the `PrintLines` function simply prints some lines of asterisks and then returns.

Alternatively, there is a second form of the Return statement. It looks like this:

```
return;
```

This statement is valid *only* for void functions. It can appear anywhere in the body of the function; it causes control to exit the function immediately and return to the caller. Here's an example:

```
void SomeFunc( int n )
{
    if (n > 50)
    {
        cout << "The value is out of range.";
        return;
    }
    n = 412 * n;
    cout << n;
}
```

In this (nonsense) example, there are two ways for control to exit the function. At function entry, the value of n is tested. If it is greater than 50, the function prints a message and returns immediately without executing any more statements. If n is less than or equal to 50, the If statement's then-clause is skipped and control proceeds to the assignment statement. After the last statement, control returns to the caller.

Another way of writing the above function is to use an If-Then-Else structure:

```
void SomeFunc( int n )
{
    if (n > 50)
        cout << "The value is out of range.";
    else
    {
        n = 412 * n;
        cout << n;
    }
}
```

If you asked different programmers about these two versions of the function, you would get differing opinions. Some prefer the first version, saying that it is most straightforward to use Return statements whenever it logically makes sense to do so. Others insist on the *single-entry, single-exit* approach in the second version. With this philosophy, control enters a function at one point only (the first executable statement) and exits at one point only (the end of the body). They argue that multiple exits from a function make the program logic hard to follow and difficult to debug. Other programmers take a position somewhere between these two philosophies, allowing occasional use of the Return statement when the logic is clear. Our advice is to use return sparingly; overuse can lead to confusing code.

MATTERS OF STYLE

Naming Void Functions

When you choose a name for a void function, keep in mind how calls to it will look. A call is written as a statement; therefore, it should sound like a command or an instruction to the computer. For this reason, it is a good idea to choose a name that is an imperative verb or has an imperative verb as part of it. (In English, an imperative verb is one representing a command: *Listen! Look! Do something!*) For example, the statement

```
Lines(3);
```

has no verb to suggest that it's a command. Adding the verb *Print* makes the name sound like an action:

```
PrintLines(3);
```

When you are picking a name for a void function, write down sample calls with different names until you come up with one that sounds like a command to the computer.

Header Files

From the very beginning, we have been using #include directives that request the C++ preprocessor to insert the contents of header files into our programs:

```
#include <iostream>
#include <cmath>       // For sqrt() and fabs()
#include <fstream>     // For file I/O
#include <climits>     // For INT_MAX and INT_MIN
```

Exactly what do these header files contain?

It turns out that there is nothing magical about header files. Their contents are nothing more than a series of C++ declarations. There are declarations of items such as named constants (INT_MAX, INT_MIN), classes (istream, ostream, string), and objects (cin, cout). But most of the items in a header file are function prototypes.

Suppose that your program needs to use the library function sqrt in a statement like this:

```
y = sqrt(x);
```

Every identifier must be declared before it can be used. If you forget to `#include` the header file `cmath`, the compiler gives you an "UNDE-CLARED IDENTIFIER" error message. The file `cmath` contains function prototypes for `sqrt` and other math-oriented library functions. With this header file included in your program, the compiler not only knows that the identifier `sqrt` is the name of a function but it also can verify that your function call is correct with respect to the number of arguments and their data types.

Header files save you the trouble of writing all of the library function prototypes yourself at the beginning of your program. With just one line—the `#include` directive—you cause the preprocessor to go out and find the header file and insert the prototypes into your program. In later chapters, we see how to create our own header files that contain declarations specific to our programs.

Parameters

When a function is executed, it uses the arguments given to it in the function call. How is this done? The answer to this question depends on the nature of the parameters. C++ supports two kinds of parameters: **value parameters** and **reference parameters.** With a value parameter, which is declared without an ampersand (&) at the end of the data type name, the function receives a copy of the argument's value. With a reference parameter, which is declared by adding an ampersand to the data type name, the function receives the location (memory address) of the caller's argument. Before we examine in detail the difference between these two kinds of parameters, let's look at an example of a function heading with a mixture of reference and value parameter declarations.

```
void Example( int&  param1,      // A reference parameter
              int   param2,      // A value parameter
              float param3 )     // Another value parameter
```

With simple data types—`int`, `char`, `float`, and so on—a value parameter is the default (assumed) kind of parameter. In other words, if you don't do anything special (add an ampersand), a parameter is assumed to be a value parameter. To specify a reference parameter, you have to go out of your way to do something extra (attach an ampersand).

Value parameter   A parameter that receives a copy of the value of the corresponding argument.

Reference parameter   A parameter that receives the location (memory address) of the caller's argument.

Let's look at both kinds of parameters, starting with value parameters.

Value Parameters

In the NewWelcome program, the `PrintLines` function heading is

```
void PrintLines( int numLines )
```

The parameter `numLines` is a value parameter because its data type name doesn't end in `&`. If the function is called using an argument `lineCount`,

```
PrintLines(lineCount);
```

then the parameter `numLines` receives a copy of the value of `lineCount`. At this moment, there are two copies of the data—one in the argument `lineCount` and one in the parameter `numLines`. If a statement inside the `PrintLines` function were to change the value of `numLines`, this change would not affect the argument `lineCount` (remember, there are two copies of the data). Using value parameters thus helps us avoid unintentional changes to arguments.

Because value parameters are passed copies of their arguments, anything that has a value may be passed to a value parameter. This includes constants, variables, and even arbitrarily complicated expressions. (The expression is simply evaluated and a copy of the result is sent to the corresponding value parameter.) For the `PrintLines` function, the following function calls are all valid:

```
PrintLines(3);
PrintLines(lineCount);
PrintLines(2 * abs(10 - someInt));
```

There must be the same number of arguments in a function call as there are parameters in the function heading.* Also, each argument should have the same data type as the parameter in the same position. Notice how each parameter in the following example is matched to the argument in the same position (the data type of each argument below is what you would assume from its name):

Function heading: `void ShowMatch(float num1, int num2, char letter)`

Function call: `ShowMatch(floatVariable, intVariable, charVariable);`

---

* This statement is not the whole truth. C++ has a special language feature—*default parameters*—that lets you call a function with fewer arguments than parameters. We do not cover default parameters in this book.

If the matched items are not of the same data type, implicit type coercion takes place. For example, if a parameter is of type int, an argument that is a float expression is coerced to an int value before it is passed to the function. As usual in C++, you can avoid unintended type coercion by using an explicit type cast or, better yet, by not mixing data types at all.

As we have stressed, a value parameter receives a copy of the argument, and therefore the caller's argument cannot be accessed directly or changed. When a function returns, the contents of its value parameters are destroyed, along with the contents of its local variables. The difference between value parameters and local variables is that the values of local variables are undefined when a function starts to execute, whereas value parameters are automatically initialized to the values of the corresponding arguments.

Because the contents of value parameters are destroyed when the function returns, they cannot be used to return information to the calling code. What if we *do* want to return information by modifying the caller's arguments? We must use the second kind of parameter available in C++: reference parameters. Let's look at these now.

Reference Parameters

A reference parameter is one that you declare by attaching an ampersand to the name of its data type. It is called a reference parameter because the called function can refer to the corresponding argument directly. Specifically, the function is allowed to inspect *and modify* the caller's argument.

When a function is invoked using a reference parameter, it is the *location* (memory address) of the argument, not its value, that is passed to the function. There is only one copy of the information, and it is used by both the caller and the called function. When a function is called, the argument and the parameter become synonyms for the same location in memory. Whatever value is left by the called function in this location is the value that the caller will find there. Therefore, you must be careful when using a reference parameter because any change made to it affects the argument in the calling code. Let's look at an example.

In Chapter 5, we wrote an If-Then-Else-If structure that prints an appropriate activity for a given outdoor temperature. Suppose we want a program that reads in a temperature from the user and prints the recommended activity. Here is its design.

Main   **Level 0**

```
Get temperature
Print activity
```

Get Temperature   **Level 1**

```
Prompt user for temperature
Read temperature
Echo print temperature
```

Print Activity

```
Print "The recommended activity is"
IF temperature > 85
        Print "swimming."
ELSE IF temperature > 70
        Print "tennis."
ELSE IF temperature > 32
        Print "golf."
ELSE IF temperature > 0
        Print "skiing."
ELSE
        Print "dancing."
```

Let's write the two level 1 modules as void functions, GetTemp and
PrintActivity, so that the main function looks like the main module of
our functional decomposition. Here is the resulting program.

```
//****************************************************************
// Activity program
// This program outputs an appropriate activity
// for a given temperature
//****************************************************************
#include <iostream>

using namespace std;

void GetTemp( int& );                          // Function prototypes
```

```
void PrintActivity( int );

int main()
{
    int temperature;     // The outside temperature

    GetTemp(temperature);                    // Function call
    PrintActivity(temperature);              // Function call
    return 0;
}

//*****************************************************************

void GetTemp( int& temp )                    // Reference parameter

// This function prompts for a temperature to be entered,
// reads the input value into temp, and echo prints it

{
    cout << "Enter the outside temperature:" << endl;
    cin >> temp;
    cout << "The current temperature is " << temp << endl;
}

//*****************************************************************

void PrintActivity( int temp )               // Value parameter

// Given the value of temp, this function prints a message
// indicating an appropriate activity

{
    cout << "The recommended activity is ";
    if (temp > 85)
        cout << "swimming." << endl;
    else if (temp > 70)
        cout << "tennis." << endl;
    else if (temp > 32)
        cout << "golf." << endl;
    else if (temp > 0)
        cout << "skiing." << endl;
    else
        cout << "dancing." << endl;
}
```

In the Activity program, the arguments in the two function calls are both named `temperature`. The parameter in `GetTemp` is a reference parameter named `temp`. The parameter in `PrintActivity` is a value parameter, also named `temp`.

The `main` function tells `GetTemp` where to leave the temperature by giving it the location of the variable `temperature` when it makes the function call. We *must* use a reference parameter here so that `GetTemp` knows where to deposit the result. In a sense, the parameter `temp` is just a convenient placeholder in the function definition. When `GetTemp` is called with `temperature` as its argument, all the references to `temp` inside the function actually are made to `temperature`. If the function were to be called again with a different variable as an argument, all the references to `temp` would actually refer to that other variable until the function returned control to `main`.

In contrast, `PrintActivity`'s parameter is a value parameter. When `PrintActivity` is called, `main` sends a copy of the value of `temperature` for the function to work with. It's appropriate to use a value parameter in this case because `PrintActivity` is not supposed to modify the argument `temperature`.

Because arguments and parameters can have different names, we can call a function at different times with different arguments. Suppose we wanted to change the Activity program to print an activity for both the indoor and outdoor temperatures. We could declare integer variables in the `main` function named `indoorTemp` and `outdoorTemp`, then write the body of `main` as follows:

```
GetTemp(indoorTemp);
PrintActivity(indoorTemp);
GetTemp(outdoorTemp);
PrintActivity(outdoorTemp)
return 0;
```

In `GetTemp` and `PrintActivity`, the parameters would receive values from, or pass values to, either `indoorTemp` or `outdoorTemp`.

The following table summarizes the usage of arguments and parameters.

Item	*Usage*
Argument	Appears in a function *call*. The corresponding parameter may be either a reference or a value parameter.
Value parameter	Appears in a function *heading*. Receives a *copy* of the value of the corresponding argument.
Reference parameter	Appears in a function *heading*. Receives the *address* of the corresponding argument.

An Analogy

Before we talk more about parameter passing, let's look at an analogy from daily life. You're at the local discount catalog showroom to buy a Father's Day present. To place your order, you fill out an order form. The form has places to write in the quantity of each item and its catalog number, and places where the order clerk will fill in the prices. You write down what you want and hand the form to the clerk. You wait for the clerk to check whether the items are available and calculate the cost. He returns the form, and you see that the items are in stock and the price is $48.50. You pay the clerk and go on about your business.

This illustrates how function calls work. The clerk is like a void function. You, acting as the `main` function, ask him to do some work for you. You give him some information: the item numbers and quantities. These are his input parameters. You wait until he returns some information to you: the availability of the items and their prices. These are the clerk's output parameters. The clerk does this task all day long with different input values. Each order activates the same process. The shopper waits until the clerk returns information based on the specific input.

The order form is analogous to the arguments of a function call. The spaces on the form represent variables in the `main` function. When you hand the form to the clerk, some of the places contain information and some are empty. The clerk holds the form while doing his job so he can write information in the blank spaces. These blank spaces correspond to reference parameters; you expect the clerk to return results to you in the spaces.

When the `main` function calls another function, reference parameters allow the called function to access and change the variables in the argument list. When the called function finishes, `main` continues, making use of whatever new information the called function left in the variables.

The parameter list is like the set of shorthand or slang terms the clerk uses to describe the spaces on the order form. For example, he may think in terms of "units," "codes," and "receipts." These are his terms (parameters) for what the order form calls "quantity," "catalog number," and "price" (the arguments). But he doesn't waste time reading the names on the form every time; he knows that the first item is the units (quantity), the second is the code (catalog number), and so on. In other words, he looks only at the position of each space on the form. This is how arguments are matched to parameters—by their relative positions in the two lists.

Matching Arguments with Parameters

Earlier we said that with reference parameters, the argument and the parameter become synonyms for the same memory location. When a function returns control to its caller, the link between the argument and the parameter is broken. They are synonymous only during a particular call to the function. The only evidence that a matchup between the two ever occurred is that the contents of the argument may have changed (see Figure 7-2).

Only a variable can be passed as an argument to a reference parameter because a function can assign a new value to the argument. (In contrast, remember that an arbitrarily complicated expression can be passed to a value parameter.) Suppose that we have a function with the following heading:

```
void DoThis( float val,      // Value parameter
             int&  count )   // Reference parameter
```

Then the following function calls are all valid.

```
DoThis(someFloat, someInt);
DoThis(9.83, intCounter);
DoThis(4.9 * sqrt(y), myInt);
```

When flow of control is in the `main` function,
`temperature` can be accessed as shown by the arrow.

When flow of control is in function `GetTemp`, every
reference to `temp` accesses the variable `temperature`.

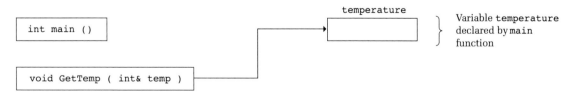

FIGURE 7-2

Using a Reference Parameter to Access an Argument

In the DoThis function, the first parameter is a value parameter, so any expression is allowed as the argument. The second parameter is a reference parameter, so the argument *must* be a variable name. The statement

```
DoThis(y, 3);
```

generates a compile-time error because the second argument isn't a variable name. Earlier we said the syntax template for an argument list is

ArgumentList

Expression **,** Expression . . .

But you must keep in mind that Expression is restricted to a variable name if the corresponding parameter is a reference parameter.

There is another important difference between value and reference parameters when it comes to matching arguments with parameters. With value parameters, we said that implicit type coercion occurs if the matched items have different data types (the value of the argument is coerced, if possible, to the data type of the parameter). In contrast, with reference parameters, the matched items *must* have exactly the same data type.

The following table summarizes the appropriate forms of arguments.

Parameter	*Argument*
Value parameter	A variable, constant, or arbitrary expression (type coercion may take place)
Reference parameter	A variable *only*, of exactly the same data type as the parameter

Finally, it is the programmer's responsibility to make sure that the argument list and parameter list match up semantically as well as syntactically. For example, suppose we had written the indoor/outdoor modification to the Activity program as follows.

```
int main()
{
    ⋮
    GetTemp(indoorTemp);
    PrintActivity(indoorTemp);
```

```
GetTemp(outdoorTemp);
PrintActivity(indoorTemp)     // Wrong argument
return 0;
}
```

The argument list in the last function call matches the corresponding parameter list in its number and type of arguments, so no syntax error would be signaled. However, the output would be erroneous because the argument is the wrong temperature value. Similarly, if a function has two parameters of the same data type, you must be careful that the arguments are in the right order. If they are in the wrong order, no syntax error will result, but the answers will be wrong.

THEORETICAL FOUNDATIONS

Argument-Passing Mechanisms

There are three major ways of passing arguments to and from subprograms. C++ supports only two of these mechanisms; however, it's useful to know about all three in case you have occasion to use them in another language.

C++ reference parameters employ a mechanism called a *pass by address* or *pass by location*. A memory address is passed to the function. Another name for this is a *pass by reference* because the function can refer directly to the caller's variable that is specified in the argument list.

C++ value parameters are an example of a *pass by value*. The function receives a copy of the value of the caller's argument. Passing by value can be less efficient than passing by address because the value of an argument may occupy many memory locations (as we see in Chapter 11), whereas an address usually occupies only a single location. For the simple data types int, char, bool, and float, the efficiency of either mechanism is about the same.

A third method of passing arguments is called a *pass by name*. The argument is passed to the function as a character string that must be interpreted by special run-time support software (called a *thunk*) supplied by the compiler. For example, if the name of a variable is passed to a function, the run-time interpreter looks up the name of the argument in a table of declarations to find the address of the variable. Passing by name can have unexpected results. If an argument has the same spelling as a local variable in the function, the function will refer to the local version of the variable instead of the variable in the calling code.

Some versions of the pass by name allow an expression or even a code segment to be passed to a function. Each time the function refers to the parameter, an interpreter performs the action specified by the parameter. An interpreter is similar to a compiler and nearly as complex. Thus, a pass by name is the least efficient of the three argument-passing mechanisms. Passing by name is supported by the ALGOL and LISP programming languages, but not by C++.

There are two different ways of matching arguments with parameters, although C++ supports only one of them. Most programming languages, C++ among them, match arguments and parameters by their relative positions in the argument and parameter lists. This is called *positional matching, relative matching*, or *implicit matching*. A few languages, such as Ada, also support *explicit* or *named matching*. In explicit matching, the argument list specifies the name of the parameter to be associated with each argument. Explicit matching allows arguments to be written in any order in the function call. The real advantage is that each call documents precisely which values are being passed to which parameters.

Designing Functions

We've looked at some examples of functions and defined the syntax of function prototypes and function definitions. But how do we design functions? First, we need to be more specific about what functions do. We've said that they allow us to organize our programs more like our functional decompositions, but what really is the advantage of doing that?

The body of a function is like any other segment of code, except that it is contained in a separate block within the program. Isolating a segment of code in a separate block means that its implementation details can be "hidden" from view. As long as you know how to call a function and what its purpose is, you can use it without looking at the code inside the function body. For example, you don't know how the code for a library function like sqrt is written (its implementation is hidden from view), yet you still can use it effectively.

The specification of what a function does and how it is invoked defines its **interface** (see Figure 7-3). By hiding a module implementation, or **encapsulating** the module, we can make changes to it without changing the main function, as long as the interface remains the same. For example, you might rewrite the body of a function using a more efficient algorithm.

Interface   A connecting link at a shared boundary that permits independent systems to meet and act on or communicate with each other. Also, the formal description of the purpose of a subprogram and the mechanism for communicating with it.

Encapsulation   Hiding a module implementation in a separate block with a formally specified interface.

FIGURE 7-3
Function Interface
(Visible) and
Implementation
(Hidden)

Heading: `void PrintActivity ( int temp )`
Precondition: `temp` is a temperature value in a valid range
Postcondition: A message has been printed indicating an
    appropriate activity given temperature `temp`

Implementation

Encapsulation is what we do in the functional decomposition process when we postpone the solution of a difficult subproblem. We write down its purpose, its precondition and postcondition, and what information it takes and returns, and then we write the rest of our design as if the subproblem had already been solved. We could hand this interface specification to someone else, and that person could develop a function for us that solves the subproblem. We needn't be concerned about how it works, as long as it conforms to the interface specification. Interfaces and encapsulation are the basis for *team programming,* in which a group of programmers work together to solve a large problem.

Thus, designing a function can (and should) be divided into two tasks: designing the interface and designing the implementation. We already know how to design an implementation—it is a segment of code that corresponds to an algorithm. To design the interface, we focus on the *what,* not the *how.* We must define the behavior of the function (what it does) and the mechanism for communicating with it.

You already know how to specify formally the behavior of a function. Because a function corresponds to a module, its behavior is defined by the precondition and postcondition of the module. All that remains is to define the mechanism for communicating with the function. To do so, make a list of the following items:

1. *Incoming values* that the function receives from the caller.
2. *Outgoing values* that the function produces and returns to the caller.
3. *Incoming/outgoing values*—values the caller has that the function changes (receives and returns).

Now decide which identifiers inside the module match the values in this list. These identifiers become the variables in the parameter list for the function. Then the parameters are declared in the function heading. All other variables that the function needs are local and must be declared within the body of the function. This process is repeated for all the modules at each level.

Let's look more closely at designing the interface. First we examine function preconditions and postconditions. After that, we consider in more detail the notion of incoming, outgoing, and incoming/outgoing parameters.

Writing Assertions as Program Comments

We have been writing module preconditions and postconditions as informal, English-language assertions. From now on, we include preconditions and postconditions as comments to document the interfaces of C++ functions. Here's an example:

```
void PrintAverage( float sum,
                   int   count )

// Precondition:
//      sum is assigned  &&  count > 0
// Postcondition:
//      The average sum/count has been output on one line

{
    cout << "Average is " << sum / float(count) << endl;
}
```

The precondition is an assertion describing everything that the function requires to be true at the moment the caller invokes the function. The postcondition describes the state of the program at the moment the function finishes executing.

You can think of the precondition and postcondition as a contract. The contract states that if the precondition is true at function entry, then the postcondition must be true at function exit. The *caller* is responsible for ensuring the precondition, and the *function code* must ensure the postcondition. If the caller fails to satisfy its part of the contract (the precondition), the contract is off; the function cannot guarantee that the postcondition will be true.

Above, the precondition warns the caller to make sure that sum has been assigned a meaningful value and to be sure that count is positive. If this precondition is true, the function guarantees it will satisfy the postcondition. If count isn't positive when PrintAverage is invoked, the effect of the function is undefined. (For example, if count equals 0, the postcondition surely isn't satisfied—the program crashes!)

Sometimes the caller doesn't need to satisfy any precondition before calling a function. In this case, the precondition can be written as the value `true` or simply omitted. In the following example, no precondition is necessary:

```
void Get2Ints( int& int1,
               int& int2 )

// Postcondition:
//     User has been prompted to enter two integers
//  && int1 == first input value
//  && int2 == second input value

{
    cout << "Please enter two integers: ";
    cin >> int1 >> int2;
}
```

In assertions written as C++ comments, we use either `&&` or AND to denote the logical AND operator, either `||` or OR to denote a logical OR, either `!` or NOT to denote a logical NOT, and `==` to denote "equals." (Notice that we do *not* use `=` to denote "equals." Even when we write program comments, we want to keep C++'s `==` operator distinct from the assignment operator.)

There is one final notation we use when we express assertions as program comments. Preconditions implicitly refer to values of variables at the moment the function is invoked. Postconditions implicitly refer to values at the moment the function returns. But sometimes you need to write a postcondition that refers to parameter values that existed at the moment the function was invoked. To signify "at the time of entry to the function," we attach the symbol `@entry` to the end of the variable name. Below is an example of the use of this notation. The `Swap` function exchanges, or swaps, the contents of its two parameters.

```
void Swap( int& firstInt,
           int& secondInt )

// Precondition:
//     firstInt and secondInt are assigned
// Postcondition:
//     firstInt == secondInt@entry
//  && secondInt == firstInt@entry

{
    int temporaryInt;
```

```
        temporaryInt = firstInt;
        firstInt = secondInt;
        secondInt = temporaryInt;
}
```

MATTERS OF STYLE

Function Preconditions and Postconditions

Preconditions and postconditions, when well written, are a concise but accurate description of the behavior of a function. A person reading your program should be able to see at a glance how to use the function by looking only at its interface (the function heading and the precondition and postcondition). The reader should never have to look into the code of the function body to understand the purpose of the function or how to use it.

A function interface describes *what* the function does, not the details of *how* it does it. For this reason, the postcondition should mention (by name) each outgoing parameter and its value but should not mention any local variables. Local variables are implementation details; they are irrelevant to the function's interface.

Documenting the Direction of Data Flow

Another helpful piece of documentation in a function interface is the direction of **data flow** for each parameter in the parameter list. Data flow is the flow of information between the function and its caller. We said earlier that each parameter can be classified as an *incoming* parameter, an *outgoing* parameter, or an *incoming/outgoing* parameter. (Some programmers refer to these as *input* parameters, *output* parameters, and *input/output* parameters.)

Data flow The flow of information from the calling code to a function and from the function back to the calling code.

For an incoming parameter, the direction of data flow is one-way—into the function. The function inspects and uses the current value of the parameter but does not modify it. In the function heading, we attach the comment

```
/* in */
```

to the declaration of the parameter. (Remember that C++ comments come in two forms. The first, which we use most often, starts with two slashes and extends to the end of the line. The second form encloses a comment between /* and */ and allows us to embed a comment within a line of code.) Here is the PrintAverage function with comments added to the parameter declarations:

```
void PrintAverage( /* in */ float sum,
                   /* in */ int   count )


// Precondition:
//     sum is assigned  &&  count > 0
// Postcondition:
//     The average sum/count has been output on one line


{
    cout << "Average is " << sum / float(count) << endl;
}
```

Passing by value is appropriate for each parameter that is incoming only. As you can see in the function body, PrintAverage does not modify the values of the parameters sum and count. It merely uses their current values. The direction of data flow is one-way—into the function.

The data flow for an outgoing parameter is one-way—out of the function. The function produces a new value for the parameter without using the old value in any way. The comment /* out */ identifies an outgoing parameter. Here we've added comments to the Get2Ints function heading:

```
void Get2Ints( /* out */ int& int1,
               /* out */ int& int2 )
```

Passing by reference must be used for an outgoing parameter. If you look back at the body of Get2Ints, you'll see that the function stores new values into the two variables (by means of the input statement), replacing whatever values they originally contained.

Finally, the data flow for an incoming/outgoing parameter is two-way—into and out of the function. The function uses the old value and also produces a new value for the parameter. We use /* inout */ to document this two-way direction of data flow. Here is an example of a function that uses two parameters, one of them incoming only and the other one incoming/outgoing:

```
void Calc( /* in */     int  alpha,
           /* inout */ int& beta  )

// Precondition:
//     alpha and beta are assigned
// Postcondition
//     beta == beta@entry * 7 - alpha

{
    beta = beta * 7 - alpha;
}
```

This function first inspects the incoming value of beta so that it can evaluate the expression to the right of the equal sign. Then it stores a new value into beta by using the assignment operation. The data flow for beta is therefore considered a two-way flow of information. A pass by value is appropriate for alpha (it's incoming only), but a pass by reference is required for beta (it's an incoming/outgoing parameter).

MATTERS OF STYLE

Formatting Function Headings

From here on, we follow a specific style when coding our function headings. Comments appear next to the parameters to explain how each parameter is used. Also, embedded comments indicate which of the three data flow categories each parameter belongs to (In, Out, or Inout).

```
void Print( /* in */     float val,     // Value to be printed
            /* inout */ int&  count )   // Number of lines printed
                                        //   so far
```

Notice that the first parameter above is a value parameter. The second is a reference parameter, presumably because the function changes the value of the counter.

We use comments in the form of rows of asterisks (or dashes or some other character) before and after a function to make the function stand out from the surrounding code. Each function also has its own block of introductory comments, just like those at the start of a program, as well as its precondition and postcondition.

It's important to put as much care into documenting each function as you would into the documentation at the beginning of a program.

The following table summarizes the correspondence between a parameter's data flow and the appropriate argument-passing mechanism.

Data Flow for a Parameter	Argument-Passing Mechanism
Incoming	Pass by value
Outgoing	Pass by reference
Incoming/outgoing	Pass by reference

There are exceptions to the guidelines in this table. C++ requires that I/O stream objects be passed by reference because of the way streams and files are implemented. We encounter another exception in Chapter 12.

SOFTWARE ENGINEERING TIP

Conceptual Versus Physical Hiding of a Function Implementation

In many programming languages, the encapsulation of an implementation is purely conceptual. If you want to know how a function is implemented, you simply look at the function body. C++, however, permits function implementations to be written and stored separately from the `main` function.

Larger C++ programs are usually split up and stored into separate files on a disk. One file might contain just the source code for the `main` function; another file, the source code for one or two functions invoked by `main`; and so on. This organization is called a *multifile program*. To translate the source code into object code, the compiler is invoked for each file independently of the others, possibly at different times. A program called the *linker* then collects all the resulting object code into a single executable program.

When you write a program that invokes a function located in another file, it isn't necessary for that function's source code to be available. All that's required is for you to include a function prototype so that the compiler can check the syntax of the call to the function. After the compiler is done, the linker finds the object code for that function and links it with your `main` function's object code. We do this kind of thing all the time when we invoke library functions. C++ systems supply only the object code, not the source code, for library functions like `sqrt`. The source code for their implementations are physically hidden from view.

One advantage of physical hiding is that it helps the programmer avoid the temptation to take advantage of any unusual features of a function's implementation. For example, suppose we want to change the Activity program to read temperatures and output activities repeatedly. Knowing that the `GetTemp` function doesn't perform range checking on the input value, we might be tempted to use –1000 as a sentinel for the loop:

```
int main()
{
    int temperature;

    GetTemp(temperature);
    while (temperature != -1000)
    {
        PrintActivity(temperature);
        GetTemp(temperature);
    }
    return 0;
}
```

This code works fine for now, but later another programmer decides to improve GetTemp so that it checks for a valid temperature range (as it should):

```
void GetTemp( /* out */ int& temp )

// This function prompts for a temperature to be entered, reads
// the input value, checks to be sure it is in a valid temperature
// range, and echo prints it

// Postcondition:
//      User has been prompted for a temperature value (temp)
//   && Error messages and additional prompts have been printed
//      in response to invalid data
//   && IF no valid data was encountered before EOF
//          Value of temp is undefined
//      ELSE
//          -50 <= temp <= 130  &&  temp has been printed

{
    cout << "Enter the outside temperature (-50 through 130): ";
    cin >> temp;
    while (cin &&                          // While not EOF and
           (temp < -50 || temp > 130))     //   temp is invalid...
    {
        cout << "Temperature must be"
             << " -50 through 130." << endl;
        cout << "Enter the outside temperature: ";
        cin >> temp;
    }
    if (cin)                               // If not EOF...
        cout << "The current temperature is "
             << temp << endl;
}
```

Unfortunately, this improvement causes the `main` function to be stuck in an infinite loop because `GetTemp` won't let us enter the sentinel value –1000. If the original implementation of `GetTemp` had been physically hidden, we would not have relied on the knowledge that it does not perform error checking. Instead, we would have written the `main` function in a way that is unaffected by the improvement to `GetTemp`:

```cpp
int main()
{
    int temperature;

    GetTemp(temperature);
    while (cin)                            // While not EOF...
    {
        PrintActivity(temperature);
        GetTemp(temperature);
    }
    return 0;
}
```

Later in the book, you learn how to write multifile programs and hide implementations physically. In the meantime, conscientiously avoid writing code that depends on the internal workings of a function.

PROBLEM-SOLVING CASE STUDY

Comparison of Furniture-Store Sales

Problem: A new regional sales manager for the Chippendale Furniture Stores has just come into town. She wants to see a monthly, department-by-department comparison, in the form of bar graphs, of the two Chippendale stores in town. The daily sales for each department are kept in each store's accounting files. Data on each store is stored in the following form:

Department ID number
Number of business days for the department
Daily sales for day 1
Daily sales for day 2
⋮
Daily sales for last day in period
Department ID number
Number of business days for the department
Daily sales for day 1
⋮

PROBLEM-SOLVING CASE STUDY *cont'd.*

The bar graph is to be printed in the following form:

```
Bar Graph Comparing Departments of Store #1 and Store #2

Store   Sales in 1,000s of dollars
   #    0          5         10        15        20        25
        |.........|.........|.........|.........|.........|

        Dept 1030
   1      ***********************
        Dept 1030
   2      ********************************************

        Dept 1210
   1      ****************************************************
        Dept 1210
   2      ********************************************

        Dept 2040
   1      **********************************************
        Dept 2040
   2      *****************************
```

As you can see from the bar graph, each star represents $500 in sales. No stars are printed if a department's sales are less than or equal to $250.

Input: Two data files (store1 and store2), each containing the following values for each department:

Department ID number (int)
Number of business days (int)
Daily sales (several float values)

Output: A bar graph showing total sales for each department.

Discussion: Reading the input data from both files is straightforward. To make the program flexible, we'll prompt the user for the names of the disk files, read the names as strings, and associate the strings with file stream objects (let's call them store1 and store2). We need to read a department ID number, the number of business days, and the daily sales for that department. After processing each department, we can read the data for the next department, continuing until we run out of departments (EOF is encountered). Because the reading process is the same for both store1 and store2, we can use one function for reading both files. All we have to do is pass the appropriate file stream as an argument to the function. We want total sales for each department, so this function has to sum the daily sales for a department as they are read. A function can be used to print the output heading. Another function can be used to print out each department's sales for the month in graphic form.

There are three loops in this program: one in the `main` function (to read and process the file data), one in the function that gets the data for one department (to read all the daily sales amounts), and one in the function that prints the bar graph (to print the stars in the graph). The loop for the `main` function tests for EOF on *both* `store1` and `store2`. One graph for each store must be printed for each iteration of this loop.

The loop for the `GetData` function requires an iteration counter that ranges from 1 through the number of days for the department. Also, a summing operation is needed to total the sales for the period.

At first glance, it might seem that the loop for the `PrintData` function is like any other counting loop, but let's look at how we would do this process by hand. Suppose we want to print a bar for the value 1850. We first make sure the number is greater than 250, then print a star and subtract 500 from the original value. We check again to see if the new value is greater than 250, then print a star and subtract 500. This process repeats until the resulting value is less than or equal to 250. Thus, the loop requires a counter that is decremented by 500 for each iteration, with a termination value of 250 or less. A star is printed for each iteration of the loop.

Function `PrintHeading` does not receive any values from `main`, nor does it return any. Thus, its parameter list is empty.

Function `GetData` receives the file stream object from `main` and returns it, modified, after having read some values. The function also returns to `main` the values of the department ID and its sales for the month. Thus, `GetData` has three parameters: the file stream object (with data flow Inout), department ID (data flow Out), and department sales (data flow Out).

Function `PrintData` must receive the department ID, store number, and department sales from the `main` function to print the bar graph for an input record. Therefore, the function has those three items as its parameters, all with data flow In.

We include one more function named `OpenForInput`. This function receives a file stream object, prompts the user for the name of the associated disk file, and attempts to open the file. The function returns the file stream object to its caller, either successfully opened or in the fail state (if the file could not be opened). The single parameter to this function—the file stream object—therefore has data flow Inout.

Assumptions: Each file is in order by department ID. Both stores have the same departments.

Main   **Level 0**

```
Open data files for input
IF either file could not be opened
        Terminate program
Print heading
Get data for a Store 1 department
Get data for a Store 2 department
WHILE NOT EOF on file store1 AND NOT EOF on file store2
        Print data for the Store 1 department
        Print data for the Store 2 department
        Get data for a Store 1 department
        Get data for a Store 2 department
```

Open for Input (Inout: someFile)   **Level 1**

```
Prompt user for name of disk file
Read fileName
Associate fileName with stream someFile,
        and try to open it
IF file could not be opened
        Print error message
```

Print Heading (No parameters)

```
Print chart title
Print heading
Print bar graph scale
```

Get Data (Inout: dataFile; Out: deptID, deptSales)

```
Read deptID from dataFile
IF EOF on dataFile
        Return
Read numDays from dataFile
Set deptSales = 0.0
Set day (loop control variable) = 1
WHILE day <= numDays
        Read sale from dataFile
        Add sale to deptSales
        Increment day
```

Print Data (In: deptID, storeNum, deptSales)

```
Print deptID
Print storeNum
WHILE deptSales > 250.0
        Print a '*'
        Subtract 500.0 from deptSales
Terminate current output line
```

To develop this functional decomposition, we had to make several passes through the design process, and several mistakes had to be fixed to arrive at the design you see here. Don't get discouraged if you don't have a perfect functional decomposition on the first try every time.

Module Structure Chart: Because we are expressing our modules as C++ functions, the module structure chart now includes the names of parameters and uses arrows to show the direction of data flow.

PROBLEM-SOLVING CASE STUDY cont'd.

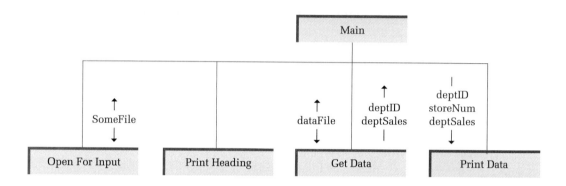

(The following program is written in ISO/ANSI standard C++. If you are working with pre–standard C++, see the alternate version of the program in the PRE_STD directory of the program disk, available at the publisher's Web site, www.jbpub.com/disks.)

```cpp
//*****************************************************************
// Graph program
// This program generates bar graphs of monthly sales
// by department for two Chippendale furniture stores, permitting
// department-by-department comparison of sales
//*****************************************************************
#include <iostream>
#include <iomanip>      // For setw()
#include <fstream>      // For file I/O
#include <string>       // For string type

using namespace std;

void GetData( ifstream&, int&, float& );
void OpenForInput( ifstream& );
void PrintData( int, int, float );
void PrintHeading();

int main()
{
    int     deptID1;        // Department ID number for Store 1
    int     deptID2;        // Department ID number for Store 2
    float   sales1;         // Department sales for Store 1
    float   sales2;         // Department sales for Store 2
```

```
ifstream store1;          // Accounting file for Store 1
ifstream store2;          // Accounting file for Store 2

cout << "For Store 1," << endl;
OpenForInput(store1);
cout << "For Store 2," << endl;
OpenForInput(store2);
if ( !store1 || !store2 )                 // Make sure files
    return 1;                             //    were opened

PrintHeading();

GetData(store1, deptID1, sales1);         // Priming reads
GetData(store2, deptID2, sales2);
while (store1 && store2)                   // While not EOF...
{
    cout << endl;
    PrintData(deptID1, 1, sales1);        // Process Store 1
    PrintData(deptID2, 2, sales2);        // Process Store 2
    GetData(store1, deptID1, sales1);
    GetData(store2, deptID2, sales2);
}
return 0;
}


//*****************************************************************

void OpenForInput( /* inout */ ifstream& someFile )    // File to be
                                                       // opened
// Prompts the user for the name of an input file
// and attempts to open the file

// Postcondition:
//     The user has been prompted for a file name
//  && IF the file could not be opened
//         An error message has been printed
// Note:
//     Upon return from this function, the caller must test
//     the stream state to see if the file was successfully opened

{
    string fileName;    // User-specified file name

    cout << "Input file name: ";
    cin >> fileName;
```

```
        someFile.open(fileName.c_str());
        if ( !someFile )
            cout << "** Can't open " << fileName << " **" << endl;
    }


//****************************************************************

void PrintHeading()

// Prints the title for the bar chart, a heading, and the numeric
// scale for the chart.  The scale uses one mark per $500

// Postcondition:
//      The heading for the bar chart has been printed

{
    cout
        << "Bar Graph Comparing Departments of Store #1 and Store #2"
        << endl << endl
        << "Store  Sales in 1,000s of dollars" << endl
        << " #    0         5        10        15        20        25"
        << endl
        << "      |.........|.........|.........|.........|.........|"
        << endl;
}


//****************************************************************

void GetData( /* inout */ ifstream& dataFile,    // Input file
              /* out */    int&      deptID,      // Department number
              /* out */    float&    deptSales )  // Department's
                                                  //   monthly sales

// Takes an input accounting file as a parameter, reads the
// department ID number and number of days of sales from that file,
// then reads one sales figure for each of those days, computing a
// total sales figure for the month.  This figure is returned in
// deptSales.  (If input of the department ID fails due to
// end-of-file, deptID and deptSales are undefined.)

// Precondition:
//     dataFile has been successfully opened
//  && For each department, the file contains a department ID,
//      number of days, and one sales figure for each day
// Postcondition:
//      IF input of deptID failed due to end-of-file
//         deptID and deptSales are undefined
```

PROBLEM-SOLVING CASE STUDY cont'd.

```
//     ELSE
//        The data file reading marker has advanced past one
//        department's data
//      && deptID == department ID number as read from the file
//      && deptSales == sum of the sales values for the department

{
    int   numDays;   // Number of business days in the month
    int   day;       // Loop control variable for reading daily sales
    float sale;      // One day's sales for the department

    dataFile >> deptID;
    if ( !dataFile )              // Check for EOF
        return;                   // If so, exit the function

    dataFile >> numDays;
    deptSales = 0.0;
    day = 1;                      // Initialize loop control variable
    while (day <= numDays)
    {
        dataFile >> sale;
        deptSales = deptSales + sale;
        day++;                    // Update loop control variable
    }
}

//*****************************************************************

void PrintData( /* in */ int   deptID,     // Department ID number
                /* in */ int   storeNum,   // Store number
                /* in */ float deptSales )  // Total sales for the
                                            //   department

// Prints the department ID number, the store number, and a
// bar graph of the sales for the department.  The bar graph
// is printed at a scale of one mark per $500

// Precondition:
//     deptID contains a valid department number
//   && storeNum contains a valid store number
//   && 0.0 <= deptSales <= 25000.0
// Postcondition:
//     A line of the bar chart has been printed with one * for
//     each $500 in sales, with remainders over $250 rounded up
//   && No stars have been printed for sales <= $250

{
```

```
cout << setw(12) << "Dept " << deptID << endl;
cout << setw(3) << storeNum << "        ";
while (deptSales > 250.0)
{
    cout << '*' ;                      // Print '*' for each $500
    deptSales = deptSales - 500.0;     // Update loop control
}                                      //    variable
cout << endl;
}
```

Testing: We should test this program with data files that contain the same number of data sets for both stores and with data files that contain different numbers of data sets for both stores. The case in which one or both of the files are empty also should be tested. The test data should include a set that generates a monthly sales figure of $0.00 and one that generates more than $25,000 in sales. We also should test the program to see what it does with negative days, negative sales, and mismatched department IDs. This series of tests would reveal that for this program to work correctly for the furniture-store employees who are to use it, we should add several checks for invalid data.

The main function of the Graph program not only reflects our functional decomposition but also contains multiple calls to OpenForInput, GetData, and PrintData. The resulting program is shorter and more readable than one in which the code for each function is physically duplicated.

Testing and Debugging

The parameters declared by a function and the arguments that are passed to the function by the caller must satisfy the interface to the function. Errors that occur with the use of functions often are due to an incorrect use of the interface between the calling code and the called function.

One source of errors is mismatched argument lists and parameter lists. The C++ compiler ensures that the lists have the same number of items and that they are compatible in type. It's the programmer's responsibility, however, to verify that each argument list contains the correct items. This is a matter of comparing the parameter declarations to the argument list in every call to the function. This job is much easier if the function heading gives each parameter a distinct name and describes its purpose in a comment. You can avoid mistakes in writing an argument list by using descriptive variable names in the calling code to suggest exactly what information is being passed to the function.

Another source of error is the failure to ensure that the precondition for a function is met before it is called. For example, if a function assumes that the input file is not at EOF when it is called, then the calling code must ensure that this is true before making the call to the function. If a function behaves incorrectly, review its precondition, then trace the program execution up to the point of the call to verify the precondition. You can waste a lot of time trying to locate an error in a correct function when the error is really in the part of the program prior to the call.

If the arguments match the parameters and the precondition is correctly established, then the source of the error is most likely in the function itself. Trace the function to verify that it transforms the precondition into the proper postcondition. Check that all local variables are initialized properly. Parameters that are supposed to return data to the caller must be declared as reference parameters (with an & symbol attached to the data type name).

An important technique for debugging a function is to use your system's debugger program, if one is available, to step through the execution of the function. If a debugger is not available, you can insert debug output statements to print the values of the arguments immediately before and after calls to the function. It also may help to print the values of all local variables at the end of the function. This information provides a snapshot of the function (a picture of its status at a particular moment in time) at its two most critical points, which is useful in verifying hand traces.

To test a function thoroughly, you must arrange the incoming values so that the precondition is pushed to its limits; then the postcondition must be verified. For example, if a function requires a parameter to be within a certain range, try calling the function with values in the middle of that range and at its extremes.

Testing a function also involves trying to arrange the data to *violate* its precondition. If the precondition can be violated, then errors may crop up that appear to be in the function being tested, when they are really in the main function or another function. For example, function PrintData in the Graph program assumes that a department's sales do not exceed $25,000. If a figure of $250,000 is entered by mistake, the main function does not check this number before the call, and the function tries to print a row of 500 stars. When this happens, you might assume that PrintData has gone haywire, but it's the main function's fault for not checking the validity of the data. (The program should perform this test in function GetData.) Thus, a side effect of one function can multiply and give the appearance of errors elsewhere in a program. We take a closer look at the concept of side effects in the next chapter.

The `assert` *Library Function*

We have discussed how function preconditions and postconditions are useful for debugging (by checking that the precondition of each function is true prior to a function call, and by verifying that each function correctly transforms the precondition into the postcondition) and for testing (by pushing the precondition to its limits and even violating it). To state the preconditions and postconditions for our functions, we've been writing the assertions as program comments:

```
// Precondition:
//      studentCount > 0
```

All comments, of course, are ignored by the compiler. They are not executable statements; they are for humans to examine.

On the other hand, the C++ standard library gives us a way in which to write *executable assertions*. Through the header file `cassert`, the library provides a void function named `assert`. This function takes a logical (Boolean) expression as an argument and halts the program if the expression is false. Here's an example:

```
#include <cassert>
    ⋮
assert(studentCount > 0);
average = sumOfScores / studentCount;
```

The argument to the `assert` function must be a valid C++ logical expression. If its value is `true`, nothing happens; execution continues on to the next statement. If its value is `false`, execution of the program terminates immediately with a message stating (a) the assertion as it appears in the argument list, (b) the name of the file containing the program source code, and (c) the line number in the program. In the example above, if the value of `studentCount` is less than or equal to 0, the program halts after printing a message like this:

```
Assertion failed: studentCount > 0, file myprog.cpp, line 48
```

(This message is potentially confusing. It doesn't mean that `studentCount` *is* greater than 0. In fact, it's just the opposite. The message tells you that the assertion `studentCount > 0` is *false*.)

Executable assertions have a profound advantage over assertions expressed as comments: the effect of a false assertion is highly visible (the program terminates with an error message). The `assert` function is therefore valuable in software testing. A program under development might be filled with calls to the `assert` function to help identify where errors are occurring. If an assertion is false, the error message gives the precise line number of the failed assertion.

Additionally, there is a way to "remove" the assertions without really removing them. If you use the preprocessor directive #define NDEBUG before including the header file cassert, like this:

```
#define NDEBUG
#include <cassert>
    ⋮
```

then all calls to the assert function are ignored when you run the program. (NDEBUG stands for "No debug," and a #define directive is a preprocessor feature that we don't discuss right now.) After program testing and debugging, programmers often like to "turn off" debugging statements yet leave them physically present in the source code in case they might need the statements later. Inserting the line #define NDEBUG turns off assertion checking without having to remove the assertions.

As useful as the assert function is, it has two limitations. First, the argument to the function must be expressed as a C++ logical expression. We can turn the comment

```
//   0.0 <= deptSales <= 25000.0
```

into an executable assertion with the statement

```
assert(0.0 <= deptSales && deptSales <= 25000.0);
```

But there is no easy way to turn the comment

```
//   For each department, the file contains a department ID,
//   number of days, and one sales figure for each day
```

into a C++ logical expression.

The second limitation is that the assert function is appropriate only for testing a program that is under development. A production program (one that has been completed and released to the public) must be robust and must furnish helpful error messages to the user of the program. You can imagine how baffled a user would be if the program suddenly quit and displayed an error message such as

```
Assertion failed: sysRes <= resCount, file newproj.cpp, line 298
```

Despite these limitations, you should consider using the assert function as a regular tool for testing and debugging your programs.

Testing and Debugging Hints

1. Follow documentation guidelines carefully when writing functions (see Appendix F). As your programs become more complex and therefore prone to errors, it becomes increasingly important to adhere to documentation and formatting standards. Even if the function name seems to reflect the process being done, describe that process in comments. Include comments stating the function precondition (if any) and postcondition to make the function interface complete. Use comments to explain the purposes of all parameters and local variables whose roles are not obvious.

2. Provide a function prototype near the top of your program for each function you've written. Make sure that the prototype and its corresponding function heading are an *exact* match (except for the absence of parameter names in the prototype).

3. Be sure to put a semicolon at the end of a function prototype. But do *not* put a semicolon at the end of the function heading in a function definition. Because function prototypes look so much like function headings, it's common to get one of them wrong.

4. Be sure the parameter list gives the data type of each parameter.

5. Use value parameters unless a result is to be returned through a parameter. Reference parameters can change the contents of the caller's argument; value parameters cannot.

6. In a parameter list, be sure the data type of each reference parameter ends with an ampersand (&). Without the ampersand, the parameter is a value parameter.

7. Make sure that the argument list of every function call matches the parameter list in number and order of items, and be very careful with their data types. The compiler will trap any mismatch in the number of arguments. But if there is a mismatch in data types, there may be no compile-time error. Specifically, with a pass by value, a type mismatch can lead to implicit type coercion rather than a compile-time error.

8. Remember that an argument matching a reference parameter *must* be a variable, whereas an argument matching a value parameter can be any expression that supplies a value of the same data type (except as noted in hint 7).

9. Become familiar with *all* the tools available to you when you're trying to locate the sources of errors—the algorithm walk-through, hand tracing, the system's debugger program, the `assert` function, and debug output statements.

Summary

C++ allows us to write programs in modules expressed as functions. The structure of a program, therefore, can parallel its functional decomposition even when the program is complicated. To make your main function look exactly like level 0 of your functional decomposition, simply write each lower-level module as a function. The `main` function then executes these other functions in logical sequence.

Functions communicate by means of two lists: the parameter list (which specifies the data type of each identifier) in the function heading, and the argument list in the calling code. The items in these lists must agree in number and position, and they should agree in data type.

Part of the functional decomposition process involves determining what data must be received by a lower-level module and what information must be returned from it. The names of these data items, together with the precondition and postcondition of a module, define its interface. The names of the data items become the parameter list, and the module name becomes the name of the function. With void functions, a call to the function is accomplished by writing the function's name as a statement, enclosing the appropriate arguments in parentheses.

C++ has two kinds of parameters: reference and value. Reference parameters have data types ending in & in the parameter list, whereas value parameters do not. Parameters that return values from a function must be reference parameters. All others should be value parameters. This minimizes the risk of errors, because only a copy of the value of an argument is passed to a value parameter, and thus the argument is protected from change.

In addition to the variables declared in its parameter list, a function may have local variables declared within it. These variables are accessible only within the block in which they are declared. Local variables must be initialized each time the function containing them is called because their values are destroyed when the function returns.

You may call functions from more than one place in a program. The positional matching mechanism allows the use of different variables as arguments to the same function. Multiple calls to a function, from different places and with different arguments, can simplify greatly the coding of many complex programs.

Quick Check

1. If a design has one level 0 module and three level 1 modules, how many C++ functions is the program likely to have? (pp. 326–330)
2. Does a C++ function have to be declared before it can be used in a function call? (p. 330)
3. What is the difference between a function declaration and a function definition in C++? (pp. 337–340)
4. Given the function heading

   ```
   void QuickCheck( int    size,
                    float& length,
                    char   initial )
   ```

   indicate which parameters are value parameters and which are reference parameters. (p. 344)

5. a. What would a call to the QuickCheck function look like if the arguments were the variables radius (a float), number (an int), and letter (a char)? (pp. 336–337)

    b. How is the matchup between these arguments and the parameters made? What information is actually passed from the calling code to the QuickCheck function, given these arguments? (pp. 344–353)

    c. Which of these arguments is (are) protected from being changed by the QuickCheck function? (pp. 344–353)

6. Where in a function are local variables declared, and what are their initial values equal to? (pp. 340–341)

7. You are designing a program and you need a void function that reads any number of floating-point values and returns their average. The number of values to be read is in an integer variable named dataPoints, declared in the calling code.

    a. How many parameters should there be in the parameter list, and what should their data type(s) be? (pp. 354–356)

    b. Which parameter(s) should be passed by reference and which should be passed by value? (pp. 354–361)

8. Describe one way in which you can use a function to simplify the coding of an algorithm. (pp. 335–336)

Answers   **1.** Four (including main)   **2.** Yes   **3.** A definition is a declaration that includes the function body.   **4.** length is a reference parameter; size and initial are value parameters.   **5.** a. QuickCheck(number, radius, letter); b. The matchup is done on the basis of the variables' positions in each list. Copies of the values of size and initial are passed to the function; the location (memory address) of length is passed to the function. c. size and initial are protected from change because only copies of their values are sent to the function.   **6.** In the block that forms the body of the function. Their initial values are undefined.   **7.** a. There should be two parameters: an int containing the number of values to be read and a float containing the computed average. b. The int should be a value parameter; the float should be a reference parameter.   **8.** The coding may be simplified if the function is called from more than one place in the program.

Exam Preparation Exercises

1. Define the following terms:

    function call   parameter
    argument list   argument
    parameterless function   local variable

2. Identify the following items in the program fragment shown below.

    function prototype   function definition
    function heading   parameters
    arguments   function call
    local variables   function body

```
void Test( int, int, int );

int main()
{
    int a;
    int b;
    int c;
    ⋮
    Test(a, c, b);
    Test(b, a, c);
    ⋮
}

void Test( int d,
           int e,
           int f )
{
    int g;
    int h;
    ⋮
}
```

3. For the program in Exercise 2, fill in the blanks below with variable names to show the matching that takes place between the arguments and parameters in each of the two calls to the Test function.

	First Call to Test			*Second Call to* Test	
	Parameter	*Argument*		*Parameter*	*Argument*
1.	_____	_____	1.	_____	_____
2.	_____	_____	2.	_____	_____
3.	_____	_____	3.	_____	_____

4. What is the output of the following program?

```
#include <iostream>

using namespace std;

void Print( int, int );

int main()
{
    int n;

    n = 3;
    Print(5, n);
    Print(n, n);
    Print(n * n, 12);
    return 0;
}
```

(continued on next page)

```
void Print( int a,
            int b )
{
    int c;

    c = 2 * a + b;
    cout << a << ' ' << b << ' ' << c << endl;
}
```

5. Using a reference parameter (passing by reference), the called function can obtain the initial value of an argument as well as change the value of the argument. (True or False?)

6. Using a value parameter, the value of a variable can be passed to a function and used for computation there without any modification of the caller's argument. (True or False?)

7. Given the declarations

```
const int ANGLE = 90;

char letter;
int  number;
```

indicate whether each of the following arguments would be valid using a pass by value, a pass by reference, or both.
a. `letter`
b. `ANGLE`
c. `number`
d. `number + 3`
e. `23`
f. `ANGLE * number`
g. `abs(number)`

8. A variable named `widgets` is stored in memory location 13571. When the statements

```
widgets = 23;
Drop(widgets);
```

are executed, what information is passed to the parameter in the `Drop` function? (Assume the parameter is a reference parameter.)

9. Assume that, in Exercise 8, the parameter within the `Drop` function is named `clunkers`. After the function body performs the assignment

```
clunkers = 77;
```

what is the value in `widgets`? in `clunkers`?

10. Using the data values

    3 2 4

    show what is printed by the following program.

    ```
    #include <iostream>

    using namespace std;

    void Test( int&, int&, int& );

    int main()
    {
        int a;
        int b;
        int c;

        Test(a, b, c);
        b = b + 10;
        cout << "The answers are " << b << ' ' << c << ' ' << a;
        return 0;
    }

    void Test( int& z,
               int& x,
               int& a )
    {
        cin >> z >> x >> a;
        a = z * x + a;
    }
    ```

11. The program below has a function named Change. Fill in the values of all variables before and after the function is called. Then fill in the values of all variables after the return to the main function. (If any value is undefined, write *U* instead of a number.)

    ```
    #include <iostream>

    using namespace std;

    void Change( int, int& );

    int main()
    {
        int a;
        int b;
    ```

```
        a = 10;
        b = 7;
        Change(a, b);
        cout << a << ' ' << b << endl;
        return 0;
    }

    void Change( int   x,
                      int& y )
    {
        int b;

        b = x;
        y = y + b;
        x = y;
    }
```

Variables in main just before Change is called:

a _____

b _____

Variables in Change at the moment control enters the function:

x _____

y _____

b _____

Variables in main after return from Change:

a _____

b _____

12. Show the output of the following program.

```
#include <iostream>

using namespace std;

void Test( int&, int );

int main()
{
    int d;
    int e;

    d = 12;
    e = 14;
    Test(d, e);
    cout << "In the main function after the first call, "
         << "the variables equal " << d << ' ' << e << endl;
    d = 15;
    e = 18;
    Test(e, d);
    cout << "In the main function after the second call, "
         << "the variables equal " << d << ' ' << e << endl;
    return 0;
}
```

```
void Test( int& s,
           int  t )
{
    s = 3;
    s = s + 2;
    t = 4 * s;
    cout << "In function Test, the variables equal "
         << s << ' ' << t << endl;
}
```

13. Number the marked statements in the following program to show the order in which they are executed (the logical order of execution).

```
#include <iostream>

using namespace std;

void DoThis( int&, int& );

int main()
{
    int number1;
    int number2;

____    cout << "Exercise ";
____    DoThis(number1, number2);
____    cout << number1 << ' ' << number2 << endl;
            return 0;
}

void DoThis( int& value1,
             int& value2 )
{
    int value3;

____    cin >> value3 >> value1;
____    value2 = value1 + 10;
}
```

14. If the program in Exercise 13 were run with the data values 10 and 15, what would be the values of the following variables just before execution of the Return statement in the main function?

number1 _____ number2 _____ value3 _____

Programming Warm-up Exercises

1. Write the function heading for a void function named PrintMax that accepts a pair of integers and prints out the greater of the two. Document the data flow of each parameter with /* in */, /* out */, or /* inout */.

2. Write the heading for a void function that corresponds to the following list.

   Rocket Simulation Module

Incoming	thrust (floating point)
Incoming/Outgoing	weight (floating point)
Incoming	timeStep (integer)
Incoming	totalTime (integer)
Outgoing	velocity (floating point)
Outgoing	outOfFuel (Boolean)

3. Write a void function that reads in a specified number of `float` values and returns their average. A call to this function might look like

   ```
   GetMeanOf(5, mean);
   ```

   where the first argument specifies the number of values to be read, and the second argument contains the result. Document the data flow of each parameter with `/* in */`, `/* out */`, or `/* inout */`.

4. Given the function heading

   ```
   void Halve( /* inout */ int& firstNumber,
               /* inout */ int& secondNumber )
   ```

   write the body of the function so that when it returns, the original values in firstNumber and secondNumber are halved.

5. Add comments to the preceding `Halve` function that state the function precondition and postcondition.

6. a. Write a single void function to replace the repeated pattern of statements you identified in Case Study Follow-Up Exercise 4 of Chapter 3. Document the data flow of the parameters with `/* in */`, `/* out */`, or `/* inout */`. Include comments giving the function precondition and postcondition.

   b. Show the function calls with arguments.

7. a. Write a void function that reads in data values of type `int` (heartRate) until a normal heart rate (from 60 through 80) is read or EOF occurs. The function has one parameter, named `normal`, that contains `true` if a normal heart rate was read or `false` if EOF occurred.

   b. Write a statement that invokes your function. You may use the same variable name for the argument and the parameter.

8. Consider the following function definition.

   ```
   void Rotate( /* inout */ int& firstValue,
                /* inout */ int& secondValue,
                /* inout */ int& thirdValue )
   {
       int temp;

       temp = firstValue;
       firstValue = secondValue;
       secondValue = thirdValue;
       thirdValue = temp;
   }
   ```

   a. Add comments to the function that tell a reader what the function does and what is the purpose of each parameter and local variable.

b. Write a program that reads three values into variables, echo prints them, calls the Rotate function with the three variables as arguments, and then prints the arguments after the function returns.

9. Modify the function in Exercise 8 to perform the same sort of operation on four values. Modify the program you wrote for part b of Exercise 8 to work with the new version of this function.

10. Write a void function named CountUpper that counts the number of uppercase letters on one line of input. The function should return this number to the calling code in a parameter named upCount.

11. Write a void function named AddTime that has three parameters: hours, minutes, and elapsedTime. elapsedTime is an integer number of minutes to be added to the starting time passed in through hours and minutes. The resulting new time is returned through hours and minutes. Here is an example, assuming that the arguments are also named hours, minutes, and elapsedTime:

Before Call to AddTime	After Call to AddTime
hours = 12	hours = 16
minutes = 44	minutes = 2
elapsedTime = 198	elapsedTime = 198

12. Write a void function named GetNonBlank that returns the first nonblank character it encounters in the standard input stream. In your function, use the cin.get function to read each character. (This GetNonBlank function is just for practice. It's unnecessary because you could use the >> operator, which skips leading blanks, to accomplish the same result.)

13. Write a void function named SkipToBlank that skips all characters in the standard input stream until a blank is encountered. In your function, use the cin.get function to read each character. (This function is just for practice. There's already a library function, cin.ignore, that allows you to do the same thing.)

14. Modify the function in Exercise 13 so that it returns a count of the number of characters that were skipped.

Programming Problems

1. Using functions, rewrite the program developed for Programming Problem 4 in Chapter 6. The program is to determine the number of words encountered in the input stream. For the sake of simplicity, we define a word to be any sequence of characters except whitespace characters (such as blanks and newlines). Words can be separated by any number of whitespace characters. A word can be any length, from a single character to an entire line of characters. If you are writing the program to read data from a file, then it should echo print the input. For an interactive implementation, you do not need to echo print for this program.

For example, for the following data, the program would indicate that 26 words were entered.

```
This isn't exactly an example of g00d english, but it
does demonstrate that a w0rd is just a se@uence of
characters              with0u+ any blank$.   #####   .......
```

As with Programming Problem 4 in Chapter 6, solve this problem with two different programs:

a. Use a string object into which you input each word as a string.

b. Assume the string class does not exist, and input the data one character at a time. (*Hint:* Consider turning the SkipToBlank function of Programming Warm-up Exercise 13 into a SkipToWhitespace function.)

Now that your programs are becoming more complex, it is even more important for you to use proper indentation and style, meaningful identifiers, and appropriate comments.

2. Write a C++ program that reads characters representing binary (base-2) numbers from a data file and translates them to decimal (base-10) numbers. The binary and decimal numbers should be output in two columns with appropriate headings. Here is a sample of the output:

```
Binary Number    Decimal Equivalent
     1                   1
    10                   2
    11                   3
 10000                  16
 10101                  21
```

There is only one binary number per input line, but an arbitrary number of blanks can precede the number. The program must read the binary numbers one character at a time. As each character is read, the program multiplies the total decimal value by 2 and adds either 1 or 0, depending on the input character. The program should check for bad data; if it encounters anything except a 0 or a 1, it should output the message "Bad digit on input."

As always, use appropriate comments, proper documentation and coding style, and meaningful identifiers throughout this program. You must decide which of your design modules should be coded as functions to make the program easier to understand.

3. Develop a functional decomposition and write a C++ program to print a calendar for one year, given the year and the day of the week that January 1 falls on. It may help to think of this task as printing 12 calendars, one for each month, given the day of the week on which a month starts and the number of days in the month. Each successive month starts on the day of the week that follows the last day of the preceding month. Days of the week should be numbered 0 through 6 for Sunday through Saturday. Years that are divisible by 4 are leap years. (Determining leap years actually is more complicated than this, but for this program it will suffice.) Here is a sample run for an interactive program:

```
What year do you want a calendar for?
2002
What day of the week does January 1 fall on?
(Enter 0 for Sunday, 1 for Monday, etc.)
2
```

```
        2002

        January
   S  M  T  W  T  F  S
   --------------------
         1  2  3  4  5
   6  7  8  9 10 11 12
  13 14 15 16 17 18 19
  20 21 22 23 24 25 26
  27 28 29 30 31

        February
   S  M  T  W  T  F  S
   --------------------
                  1  2
   3  4  5  6  7  8  9
  10 11 12 13 14 15 16
  17 18 19 20 21 22 23
  24 25 26 27 28

                 .
                 .
                 .

        December
   S  M  T  W  T  F  S
   --------------------
   1  2  3  4  5  6  7
   8  9 10 11 12 13 14
  15 16 17 18 19 20 21
  22 23 24 25 26 27 28
  29 30 31
```

When writing your program, be sure to use proper indentation and style, meaningful identifiers, and appropriate comments.

4. Write a functional decomposition and a C++ program with functions to help you balance your checking account. The program should let you enter the initial balance for the month, followed by a series of transactions. For each transaction entered, the program should echo print the transaction data, the current balance for the account, and the total service charges. Service charges are $0.10 for a deposit and $0.15 for a check. If the balance drops below $500.00 at any point during the month, a service charge of $5.00 is assessed for the month. If the balance drops below $50.00, the program should print a warning message. If the balance becomes negative, an additional service charge of $10.00 should be assessed for each check until the balance becomes positive again.

A transaction takes the form of a letter, followed by a blank and a float number. If the letter is a *C*, then the number is the amount of a check. If the letter is a *D*, then the number is the amount of a deposit. The last transaction consists of the letter *E*, with no number following it. A sample run might look like this:

```
Enter the beginning balance:
879.46
Enter a transaction:
C 400.00
Transaction: Check in amount of $400.00
Current balance: $479.46
Service charge: Check - $0.15
Service charge: Below $500 - $5.00
Total service charges: $5.15
Enter a transaction:
D 100.0
Transaction: Deposit in amount of $100.00
Current balance: $579.46
Service charge: Deposit - $0.10
Total service charges: $5.25
Enter a transaction:
E
Transaction: End
Current balance: $579.46
Total service charges: $5.25
Final balance: $574.21
```

As usual, your program should use proper style and indentation, meaningful identifiers, and appropriate comments. Also, be sure to check for data errors such as invalid transaction codes or negative amounts.

5. In this problem, you are to design and implement a Roman numeral calculator. The subtractive Roman numeral notation commonly in use today (such as IV, meaning 4) was used only rarely during the time of the Roman Republic and Empire. For ease of calculation, the Romans most frequently used a purely additive notation in which a number was simply the sum of its digits (4 equals IIII, in this notation). Each number starts with the digit of highest value and ends with the digit of smallest value. This is the notation we use in this problem.

Your program inputs two Roman numbers and an arithmetic operator and prints out the result of the operation, also as a Roman number. The values of the Roman digits are as follows:

I	1
V	5
X	10
L	50
C	100
D	500
M	1000

Thus, the number MDCCCCLXXXXVIIII represents 1999. The arithmetic operators that your program should recognize in the input are +, − , *, and /. These should perform the C++ operations of integer addition, subtraction, multiplication, and division.

One way of approaching this problem is to convert the Roman numbers into decimal integers, perform the required operation, and then convert the result back into a Roman number for printing. The following is a sample run of the program:

```
Enter the first number:
MCCXXVI
The first number is 1226
Enter the second number:
LXVIIII
The second number is 69
Enter the desired arithmetic operation:
+
The sum of MCCXXVI and LXVIIII is MCCLXXXXV (1295)
```

Your program should use proper style and indentation, appropriate comments, and meaningful identifiers. It also should check for errors in the input, such as illegal digits or arithmetic operators, and take appropriate actions when these are found. The program also might check to ensure that the numbers are in purely additive form—that is, digits are followed only by digits of the same or lower value.

6. Develop a functional decomposition and write a program to produce a bar chart of gourmet-popcorn production for a cooperative farm group on a farm-by-farm basis. The input to the program is a series of data sets, one per line, with each set representing the production for one farm. The output is a bar chart that identifies each farm and displays its production in pints of corn per acre.

   Each data set consists of the name of a farm, followed by a comma and one or more spaces, a `float` number representing acres planted, one or more spaces, and an `int` number representing pint jars of popcorn produced.

   The output is a single line for each farm, with the name of the farm starting in the first position on a line and the bar chart starting in position 30. Each mark in the bar chart represents 250 jars of popcorn per acre. The production goal for the year is 5000 jars per acre. A vertical bar should appear in the chart for farms with lower production, and a special mark is used for farms with production greater than or equal to 5000 jars per acre. For example, given the input file

```
Orville's Acres,   114.8  43801
Hoffman's Hills,    77.2  36229
Jiffy Quick Farm,   89.4  24812
Jolly Good Plantation,  183.2  104570
Organically Grown Inc.,  45.5  14683
```

the output would be

```
                        Pop CoOp
Farm Name                               Production in
                                        Thousands of
                                        Pint Jars per Acre
                                         1    2    3    4    5    6
                                        ---|---|---|---|---|---
Orville's Acres                         ***************      |
Hoffman's Hills                         ********************|
Jiffy Quick Farm                        ***********         |
Jolly Good Plantation                   *******************#***
Organically Grown Inc.                  *************        |
```

This problem should decompose neatly into several functions. You should write your program in proper programming style with appropriate comments. It should handle data errors (such as a farm name longer than 29 characters) without crashing.

Case Study Follow-Up

1. Write a separate function for the Graph program that creates a bar of asterisks in a string object, given a sales figure.
2. Rewrite the existing PrintData function so that it calls the function you wrote for Exercise 1.
3. Modify the Graph program to print an error message when a negative value is input for the number of days in a department's month.
4. Rewrite the Graph program to check for sales greater than $25,000. It should print a bar of asterisks out to the $25,000 mark and then print an exclamation point (!) at the end of the bar.
5. Write a program, to be run prior to the Graph program, that compares the two data files. The program should signal an error if it finds mismatched department ID numbers or if the files contain different numbers of departments.

Scope, Lifetime, and More on Functions

- To be able to do the following tasks, given a C++ program composed of several functions:

  Determine whether a variable is being referenced globally.

  Determine which variables are local variables.

  Determine which variables are accessible within a given block.

- To be able to determine the lifetime of each variable in a program.

- To understand and be able to avoid unwanted side effects.

- To know when to use a value-returning function.

- To be able to design and code a value-returning function for a specific task.

- To be able to invoke a value-returning function properly.

As programs get larger and more complicated, the number of identifiers in a program increases. We invent function names, variable names, constant identifiers, and so on. Some of these identifiers we declare inside blocks. Other identifiers—function names, for example—we declare outside of any block. This chapter examines the C++ rules by which a function may access identifiers that are declared outside its own block. Using these rules, we return to the discussion of interface design that we began in Chapter 7.

Finally, we look at the second kind of subprogram provided by C++: the *value-returning function*. Unlike void functions, which return results through the parameter list, a value-returning function returns a function value—to the expression from which it was how to write user-defined value-returning

cal variables are those declared inside a block, nction. Recall that local variables cannot be ck that contains them. The same access rule of named constants: Local constants may be in which they are declared.

Any block, not only a function body, can contain variable and constant declarations. For example, this If statement contains a block that declares a local variable n:

```
if (alpha > 3)
{
    int n;

    cin >> n;
    beta = beta + n;
}
```

As with any local variable, n cannot be accessed by any statement outside the block containing its declaration.

If we listed all the places from which an identifier could be accessed legally, we would describe that identifier's **scope of visibility** or **scope of access,** often just called its **scope.**

Scope   The region of program code where it is legal to reference (use) an identifier.

C++ defines several categories of scope for any identifier. We begin by describing three of these categories.

1. *Class scope.*   This term refers to the data type called a *class*, which we introduced briefly in Chapter 4. We postpone a detailed discussion of class scope until Chapter 11.
2. *Local scope.*   The scope of an identifier declared inside a block extends from the point of declaration to the end of that block. Also, the scope of a function parameter (formal parameter) extends from the point of declaration to the end of the block that is the body of the function.
3. *Global scope.*   The scope of an identifier declared outside all funtions and classes extends from the point of declaration to the en entire file containing the program code.

C++ function names have global scope. (There is an exce rule, which we discuss in Chapter 11 when we examine C++ a function name has been declared, the function can be other function in the rest of the program. In C++, there i local function—that is, you cannot nest a functi another function definition.

Global variables and constants are those decl In the following code fragment, gamma is a accessed directly by statements in main and

```
int gamma;     // Global variable

int main()
{
    gamma = 3;
       ⋮
}

void SomeFunc()
{
    gamma = 5;
       ⋮
}
```

When a function declares a local identifier with the same name as a global identifier, the local identifier takes precedence within the function. This principle is called **name precedence** or **name hiding.**

Name precedence   The precedence that a local identifier in a function has over a global identifier with the same name in any references that the function makes to that identifier; also called *name hiding.*

Here's an example that uses both local and global declarations:

```
#include <iostream>

using namespace std;
```

```
                 ...Func( float );
```

```
                                            l constant
                                            l variable
                                          r global variable
```

```
                                    // Assignment to global b
                                    // Assignment to global c
```

```
                                    // Prevents access to global c
```

```
                                    // Prevents access to global b
```

```
        b = 2.3;                     // Assignment to local b
        cout << "a = " << a;         // Output global a (17)
        cout << " b = " << b;        // Output local b (2.3)
        cout << " c = " << c;        // Output local c (42.8)
}
```

In this example, function SomeFunc accesses global constant a but declares its own local variable b and parameter c. Thus, the output would be

a = 17 b = 2.3 c = 42.8

Local variable b takes precedence over global variable b, effectively hiding global b from the statements in function SomeFunc. Parameter c also blocks access to global variable c from within the function. Function parameters act just like local variables in this respect; that is, parameters have local scope.

Scope Rules

When you write C++ programs, you rarely declare global variables. There are negative aspects to using global variables, which we discuss later. But when a situation crops up in which you have a compelling need for global variables, it pays to know how C++ handles these declarations. The rules for accessing identifiers that aren't declared locally are called **scope rules.**

Scope rules   The rules that determine where in the program an identifier may be accessed, given the point where that identifier is declared.

In addition to local and global access, the C++ scope rules define what happens when blocks are nested within other blocks. Anything declared in a block that contains a nested block is **nonlocal** to the inner block. (Global identifiers are nonlocal with respect to all blocks in the program.) If a block accesses any identifier declared outside its own block, it is a *nonlocal access.*

Nonlocal identifier   With respect to a given block, any identifier declared outside that block.

Here are the detailed scope rules, excluding class scope and certain language features we have not yet discussed:

1. A function name has global scope. Function definitions cannot be nested within function definitions.
2. The scope of a function parameter is identical to the scope of a local variable declared in the outermost block of the function body.
3. The scope of a global variable or constant extends from its declaration to the end of the file, except as noted in rule 5.
4. The scope of a local variable or constant extends from its declaration to the end of the block in which it is declared. This scope includes any nested blocks, except as noted in rule 5.
5. The scope of an identifier does not include any nested block that contains a locally declared identifier with the same name (local identifiers have name precedence).

Here is a sample program that demonstrates C++ scope rules. To simplify the example, only the declarations and headings are spelled out. Note how the While-loop body labeled Block3, located within function Block2, contains its own local variable declarations.

```cpp
// ScopeRules program

#include <iostream>

using namespace std;

void Block1( int, char& );
void Block2();

int  a1;        // One global variable
char a2;        // Another global variable

int main()
{
    ⋮
}

//*****************************************************************

void Block1( int    a1,        // Prevents access to global a1
             char&  b2 )       // Has same scope as c1 and d2
{
    int c1;         // A variable local to Block1
    int d2;         // Another variable local to Block1
    ⋮
}

//*****************************************************************
```

```
void Block2()
{
    int a1;         // Prevents access to global a1
    int b2;         // Local to Block2; no conflict with b2 in Block1

    while (...)
    {               // Block3
        int c1;     // Local to Block3; no conflict with c1 in Block1
        int b2;     // Prevents nonlocal access to b2 in Block2; no
                    //   conflict with b2 in Block1

        ⋮

    }
}
```

Let's look at the ScopeRules program in terms of the blocks it defines and see just what these rules mean. Figure 8-1 shows the headings and declarations in the ScopeRules program with the scopes of visibility indicated by boxes.

Anything inside a box can refer to anything in a larger surrounding box, but outside-in references aren't allowed. Thus, a statement in Block3 could access any identifier declared in Block2 or any global variable. A statement in Block3 could not access identifiers declared in Block1 because it would have to enter the Block1 box from outside.

Notice that the parameters for a function are inside the function's box, but the function name itself is outside. If the name of the function were inside the box, no function could call another function. This demonstrates merely that function names are globally accessible.

Imagine the boxes in Figure 8-1 as rooms with walls made of two-way mirrors, with the reflective side facing out and the see-through side facing in. If you stood in the room for Block3, you would be able to see out through all the surrounding rooms to the declarations of the global variables (and anything between). You would not be able to see into any other rooms (such as Block1), however, because their mirrored outer surfaces would block your view. Because of this analogy, the term *visible* is often used in describing a scope of access. For example, variable a2 is visible throughout the program, meaning that it can be accessed from anywhere in the program.

Figure 8-1 does not tell the whole story; it represents only scope rules 1 through 4. We also must keep rule 5 in mind. Variable a1 is declared in three different places in the ScopeRules program. Because of name precedence, Block2 and Block3 access the a1 declared in Block2 rather than the global a1. Similarly, the scope of the variable b2 declared in Block2 does *not* include the "hole" created by Block3, because Block3 declares its own variable b2.

FIGURE 8-1

Scope Diagram
for ScopeRules
Program

```
int  a1;
char a2;

int main()
{



}

void Block1(        int    a1,
                    char& b2 )

    {

        int c1;
        int d2;



}
void Block2()
{

        int a1;
        int b2;

        while (...)
        {              // Block3

            int c1;
            int b2;


        }

}
```

Name precedence is implemented by the compiler as follows. When an expression refers to an identifier, the compiler first checks the local declarations. If the identifier isn't local, the compiler works its way outward through each level of nesting until it finds an identifier with the same name. There it stops. If there is an identifier with the same name declared at a level even further out, it is never reached. If the compiler reaches the global declarations (including identifiers inserted by #include directives) and still can't find the identifier, an error message such as "UNDECLARED IDENTIFIER" is issued.

Such a message most likely indicates a misspelling or an incorrect capitalization, or it could mean that the identifier was not declared before the reference to it or was not declared at all. It may also indicate, however, that the blocks are nested so that the identifier's scope doesn't include the reference.

Variable Declarations and Definitions

In Chapter 7, you learned that C++ terminology distinguishes between a function declaration and a function definition. A function prototype is a declaration only—that is, it doesn't cause memory space to be reserved for the function. In contrast, a function declaration that includes the body is called a function definition. The compiler reserves memory for the instructions in the function body.

C++ applies the same terminology to variable declarations. A variable declaration becomes a variable definition if it also reserves memory for the variable. All of the variable declarations we have used from the beginning have been variable definitions. What would a variable declaration look like if it were *not* also a definition?

In the previous chapter, we talked about the concept of a multifile program, a program that physically occupies several files containing individual pieces of the program. C++ has a reserved word extern that lets you reference a global variable located in another file. A "normal" declaration such as

```
int someInt;
```

causes the compiler to reserve a memory location for someInt. On the other hand, the declaration

```
extern int someInt;
```

is known as an *external declaration*. It states that someInt is a global variable located in another file and that no storage should be reserved for it here. System header files such as iostream contain external declarations so that user programs can access important variables defined in system files. For example, iostream includes declarations like these:

```
extern istream cin;
extern ostream cout;
```

These declarations allow you to reference cin and cout as global variables in your program, but the variable definitions are located in another file supplied by the C++ system.

In C++ terminology, the statement

```
extern int someInt;
```

is a declaration but not a definition of someInt. It associates a variable name with a data type so that the compiler can perform type checking. But the statement

```
int someInt;
```

is both a declaration and a definition of someInt. It is a definition because it reserves memory for someInt. In C++, you can declare a variable or a function many times, but there can be only one definition.

Except in situations in which it's important to distinguish between declarations and definitions of variables, we'll continue to use the more general phrase *variable declaration* instead of the more specific *variable definition.*

Namespaces

For some time, we have been including the following using directive in our programs:

```
using namespace std;
```

What exactly is a namespace? As a general concept, *namespace* is another word for *scope*. However, as a specific C++ language feature, a namespace is a mechanism by which the programmer can create a named scope. For example, the standard header file cstdlib contains function prototypes for several library functions, one of which is the absolute value function, abs. The declarations are contained within a *namespace definition* as follows:

```
// In header file cstdlib:

namespace std
{
    ⋮
    int abs( int );
    ⋮
}
```

A namespace definition consists of the word namespace, then an identifier of the programmer's choice, and then the *namespace body* between braces. Identifiers declared within the namespace body are said to have *namespace scope.* Such identifiers cannot be accessed outside the body except by using one of three methods.

The first method, introduced in Chapter 2, is to use a qualified name: the name of the namespace, followed by the scope resolution operator (::), followed by the desired identifier. Here is an example:

```
#include <cstdlib>

int main()
{
    int alpha;
    int beta;
      ⋮
    alpha = std::abs(beta);      // A qualified name
      ⋮
}
```

The general idea is to inform the compiler that we are referring to the abs declared in the std namespace, not some other abs (such as a global function named abs that we might have written ourselves).

The second method is to use a statement called a *using declaration* as follows:

```
#include <cstdlib>

int main()
{
    int alpha;
    int beta;
    using std::abs;      // A using declaration
      ⋮
    alpha = abs(beta);
      ⋮
}
```

This using declaration allows the identifier abs to be used throughout the body of main as a synonym for the longer std::abs.

The third method—one with which we are familiar—is to use a using directive (not be confused with a using declaration).

```
#include <cstdlib>

int main()
{
    int alpha;
    int beta;
    using namespace std;      // A using directive
      ⋮
```

```
        alpha = abs(beta);
          ⋮
}
```

With a using directive, *all* identifiers from the specified namespace are accessible, but only in the scope in which the using directive appears. Above, the using directive is in local scope (it's within a block), so identifiers from the std namespace are accessible only within main. On the other hand, if we put the using directive outside all functions (as we have been doing), like this:

```
#include <cstdlib>

using namespace std;

int main()
{
    ⋮
}
```

then the using directive is in global scope; consequently, identifiers from the std namespace are accessible globally.

Placing a using directive in global scope can be a convenience. For example, all of the functions we write can refer to identifiers such as abs, cin, and cout without our having to insert a using directive locally in each function. However, global using directives are considered a bad idea when creating large, multifile programs. Programmers often make use of several libraries, not just the C++ standard library, when developing complex software. Two or more libraries may, just by coincidence, use the same identifier for completely different purposes. If global using directives are employed, *name clashes* (multiple definitions of the same identifier) can occur because all the identifiers have been brought into global scope. (C++ programmers refer to this as "polluting the global namespace.") Over the next several chapters, we continue to use global using directives for the std namespace because our programs are relatively small and therefore name clashes aren't likely.

Given the concept of namespace scope, we refine our description of C++ scope categories as follows.

1. *Class scope.* This term refers to the data type called a *class*. We postpone a detailed discussion of class scope until Chapter 11.
2. *Local scope.* The scope of an identifier declared inside a block extends from the point of declaration to the end of that block. Also, the scope of a function parameter (formal parameter) extends from the point of declaration to the end of the block that is the body of the function.

3. *Namespace scope.* The scope of an identifier declared in a namespace definition extends from the point of declaration to the end of the namespace body, *and* its scope includes the scope of a `using` directive specifying that namespace.

4. *Global* (or *global namespace*) *scope.* The scope of an identifier declared outside all namespaces, functions, and classes extends from the point of declaration to the end of the entire file containing the program code.

Note that these are general descriptions of scope categories and not scope rules. The descriptions do not account for name hiding (the redefinition of an identifier within a nested block).

Lifetime of a Variable

A concept related to but separate from the scope of a variable is its **lifetime**—the period of time during program execution when an identifier actually has memory allocated to it. We have said that storage for local variables is created (allocated) at the moment control enters a function. Then the variables are "alive" while the function is executing, and finally the storage is destroyed (deallocated) when the function exits. In contrast, the lifetime of a global variable is the same as the lifetime of the entire program. Memory is allocated only once, when the program begins executing, and is deallocated only when the entire program terminates. Observe that scope is a *compile-time* issue, but lifetime is a *run-time* issue.

Lifetime   The period of time during program execution when an identifier has memory allocated to it.

In C++, an **automatic variable** is one whose storage is allocated at block entry and deallocated at block exit. A **static variable** is one whose storage remains allocated for the duration of the entire program. All global variables are static variables. By default, variables declared within a block are automatic variables. However, you can use the reserved word `static` when you declare a local variable. If you do so, the variable is a static variable and its lifetime persists from function call to function call:

```
void SomeFunc()
{
    float  someFloat;       // Destroyed when function exits
    static int someInt;     // Retains its value from call to call
      ⋮
}
```

It is usually better to declare a local variable as static than to use a global variable. Like a global variable, its memory remains allocated throughout the lifetime of the entire program. But unlike a global variable, its local scope prevents other functions in the program from tinkering with it.

Automatic variable A variable for which memory is allocated and deallocated when control enters and exits the block in which it is declared.

Static variable A variable for which memory remains allocated throughout the execution of the entire program.

Initializations in Declarations

One of the most common things we do in programs is first declare a variable and then, in a separate statement, assign an initial value to the variable. Here's a typical example:

```
int sum;

sum = 0;
```

C++ allows you to combine these two statements into one. The result is known as an *initialization in a declaration*. Here we initialize sum in its declaration:

```
int sum = 0;
```

In a declaration, the expression that specifies the initial value is called an *initializer*. Above, the initializer is the constant 0. Implicit type coercion takes place if the data type of the initializer is different from the data type of the variable.

An automatic variable is initialized to the specified value each time control enters the block:

```
void SomeFunc( int someParam )
{
    int i = 0;                      // Initialized each time
    int n = 2 * someParam + 3;      // Initialized each time
      ⋮
}
```

In contrast, initialization of a static variable (either a global variable or a local variable explicitly declared static) occurs once only, the first time control reaches its declaration. Here's an example in which two local static variables are initialized only once (the first time the function is called):

```
void AnotherFunc( int param )
{
    static char ch = 'A';        // Initialized once only
    static int  m  = param + 1;  // Initialized once only
      ⋮
}
```

Although an initialization gives a variable an initial value, it is perfectly acceptable to reassign it another value during program execution.

There are differing opinions about initializing a variable in its declaration. Some programmers never do it, preferring to keep an initialization close to the executable statements that depend on that variable. For example,

```
int loopCount;
   ⋮
loopCount = 1;
while (loopCount <= 20)
{
   ⋮
}
```

Other programmers maintain that one of the most frequent causes of program errors is forgetting to initialize variables before using their contents; initializing each variable in its declaration eliminates these errors. As with any controversial topic, most programmers seem to take a position somewhere between these two extremes.

Interface Design

We return now to the issue of interface design, which we first discussed in Chapter 7. Recall that the data flow through a function interface can take three forms: incoming only, outgoing only, and incoming/outgoing. Any item that can be classified as purely incoming should be coded as a value parameter. Items in the remaining two categories (outgoing and incoming/outgoing) must be reference parameters; the only way the function can deposit results into the caller's arguments is to have the addresses of those arguments. For emphasis, we repeat the following table from Chapter 7.

Data Flow for a Parameter	Argument-Passing Mechanism
Incoming	Pass by value
Outgoing	Pass by reference
Incoming/outgoing	Pass by reference

As we said in the last chapter, there are exceptions to the guidelines in this table. C++ requires that I/O stream objects be passed by reference because of the way streams and files are implemented. We encounter another exception in Chapter 12.

Sometimes it is tempting to skip the interface design step when writing a function, letting it communicate with other functions by referencing global variables. Don't! Without the interface design step, you would actually be creating a poorly structured and undocumented interface. Except in well-justified circumstances, the use of global variables is a poor programming practice that can lead to program errors. These errors are extremely hard to locate and usually take the form of unwanted side effects.

Side Effects

Suppose you made a call to the `sqrt` library function in your program:

```
y = sqrt(x);
```

You expect the call to `sqrt` to do one thing only: compute the square root of the variable x. You'd be surprised if `sqrt` also changed the value of your variable x because `sqrt`, by definition, does not make such changes. This would be an example of an unexpected and unwanted **side effect.**

Side effect   Any effect of one function on another that is not a part of the explicitly defined interface between them.

Side effects are sometimes caused by a combination of reference parameters and careless coding in a function. Perhaps an assignment statement in the function stores a temporary result into one of the reference parameters, accidentally changing the value of an argument back in the calling code. As we mentioned before, using value parameters avoids this type of side effect by preventing the change from reaching the argument.

Side effects also can occur when a function accesses a global variable. An error in the function might cause the value of a global variable to be changed in an unexpected way, causing an error in other functions that access that variable.

The symptoms of a side-effect error are misleading because the trouble shows up in one part of the program when it really is caused by something in another part. To avoid such errors, the only external effect that a function should have is to transfer information through the well-structured interface of the parameter list (see Figure 8-2). If functions access nonlocal variables *only* through their parameter lists, and if all incoming-only parameters are value parameters, then each function is essentially isolated from other parts of the program and side effects cannot occur.

When a function is free of side effects, we can treat it as an independent module and reuse it in other programs. It is hazardous or impossible to reuse functions with side effects.

Here is a short example of a program that runs but produces incorrect results because of global variables and side effects.

```
//*******************************************************************
// Trouble program
// This is an example of poor program design, which
// causes an error when the program is executed
//*******************************************************************
#include <iostream>

using namespace std;

void CountChars();

int   count;            // Supposed to count input lines, but does it?
char ch;                // Holds one input character

int main()
{
    count = 0;
    cin.get(ch);
    while (cin)
    {
        count++;
        CountChars();
        cin.get(ch);
    }
    cout << count << " lines of input processed." << endl;
    return 0;
}


//*******************************************************************

void CountChars()

// Counts the number of characters on one input line
// and prints the count
// Note: main() has already read the first character on a line
```

```
{
    count = 0;                                      // Side effect
    while (ch != '\n')
    {
        count++;                                    // Side effect
        cin.get(ch);
    }
    cout << count << " characters on this line." << endl;
}
```

The Trouble program is supposed to count and print the number of characters on each line of input. After the last line has been processed, it should print the number of lines. Strangely enough, each time the program is run, it reports that the number of lines of input is the same as the number of characters in the last line of input. This is because the CountChars function accesses the global variable count and uses it to store the number of characters on each input line.

There is no reason for count to be a global variable. If a local variable count is declared in main and another local variable count is declared in CountChars, the program works correctly. There is no conflict between the two variables because each is visible only inside its own block.

The Trouble program also demonstrates one common exception to the rule of not accessing global variables. Technically, cin and cout are global objects declared in the header file iostream. The CountChars function reads and writes directly to these streams. To be absolutely correct, cin and cout should be passed as arguments to the function. However, cin

FIGURE 8-2
Side Effects

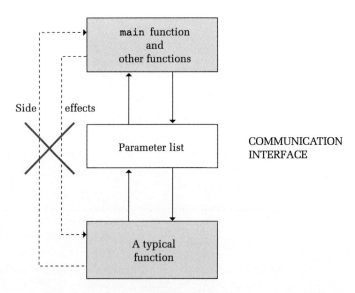

and cout are fundamental I/O facilities supplied by the standard library, and it is conventional for C++ functions to access them directly.

Global Constants

Contrary to what you might think, it is acceptable to reference named constants globally. Because the values of global constants cannot be changed while the program is running, no side effects can occur.

There are two advantages to referencing constants globally: ease of change, and consistency. If you need to change the value of a constant, it's easier to change only one global declaration than to change a local declaration in every function. By declaring a constant in only one place, we also ensure that all parts of the program use exactly the same value.

This is not to say that you should declare *all* constants globally. If a constant is needed in only one function, then it makes sense to declare it locally within that function.

At this point, you may want to turn to the first Problem-Solving Case Study at the end of this chapter. This case study further illustrates the interface design process and the use of value and reference parameters.

*M*AY WE INTRODUCE

Ada Lovelace

On December 10, 1815 (the same year in which George Boole was born), a daughter—Augusta Ada Byron—was born to Anna Isabella (Annabella) Byron and George Gordon, Lord Byron. In England at that time, Byron's fame derived not only from his poetry but also from his wild, scandalous behavior. The marriage was strained from the beginning, and Annabella left Byron shortly after Ada's birth. By April of 1816, the two had signed separation papers. Byron left England, never to return. Throughout the rest of his life, he regretted being unable to see his daughter. At one point, he wrote of her:

I see thee not. I hear thee not.
But none can be so wrapt in thee.

Before he died in Greece at age 36, he exclaimed,"Oh my poor dear child! My dear Ada! My God, could I but have seen her!"

Meanwhile, Annabella, who would eventually become a baroness in her own right, and who was educated as both a mathematician and a poet, carried on with Ada's upbringing and education. Annabella gave Ada her first instruction in mathematics, but it soon became clear that Ada was gifted in the subject and should receive more extensive tutoring. Ada received further training from Augustus DeMorgan, famous today for one of the basic theorems of Boolean algebra, the logical foundation for modern computers. By age 8, Ada had also demonstrated an interest in mechanical devices and was building detailed model boats.

When she was 18, Ada visited the Mechanics Institute to hear Dr. Dionysius Lardner's lectures on the Difference Engine, a mechanical calculating machine being built by Charles Babbage. She became so interested in the device that she arranged to be introduced to Babbage. It was said that, upon seeing Babbage's machine, Ada was the only person in the room to understand immediately how it worked and to recognize its significance. Ada and Charles Babbage became lifelong friends. She worked with him, helping to document his designs, translating writings about his work, and developing programs for his machines. In fact, today Ada is recognized as the first computer programmer in history, and the modern Ada programming language is named in her honor.

When Babbage designed his Analytical Engine, Ada foresaw that it could go beyond arithmetic computations and become a general manipulator of symbols, and that it would thus have far-reaching capabilities. She even suggested that such a device could eventually be programmed with rules of harmony and composition so that it could produce "scientific" music. In effect, Ada foresaw the field of artificial intelligence more than 150 years ago.

In 1842, Babbage gave a series of lectures in Turin, Italy, on his Analytical Engine. One of the attendees was Luigi Menabrea, who was so impressed that he wrote an account of Babbage's lectures. At age 27, Ada decided to translate the account into English with the intent of adding a few of her own notes about the machine. In the end, her notes were twice as long as the original material, and the document, "The Sketch of the Analytical Engine," became the definitive work on the subject.

It is obvious from Ada's letters that her "notes" were entirely her own and that Babbage was sometimes making unsolicited editorial changes. At one point, Ada wrote to him,

> I am much annoyed at your having altered my Note. You know I am always willing to make any required alterations myself, but that I cannot endure another person to meddle with my sentences.

Ada gained the title Countess of Lovelace when she married Lord William Lovelace. The couple had three children, whose upbringing was left to Ada's mother while Ada pursued her work in mathematics. Her husband was supportive of her work, but for a woman of that day, such behavior was considered almost as scandalous as some of her father's exploits.

Ada Lovelace died of cancer in 1852, just one year before a working Difference Engine was built in Sweden from one of Babbage's designs. Like her father, Ada lived only to age 36, and even though they led very different lives, she had undoubtedly admired him and taken inspiration from his unconventional, rebellious nature. In the end, Ada asked to be buried beside him at the family's estate.

Value-Returning Functions

In Chapter 7 and the first part of this chapter, we have been writing our own void functions. We now look at the second kind of subprogram in C++, the value-returning function. You already know several value-returning functions supplied by the C++ standard library: sqrt, abs, fabs, and others. From the caller's perspective, the main difference between void functions and value-returning functions is the way in which they are called. A call to a void function is a complete statement; a call to a value-returning function is part of an expression.

From a design perspective, value-returning functions are used when there is only one result returned by a function and that result is to be used directly in an expression. For example, suppose we are writing a program that calculates a prorated refund of tuition for students who withdraw in the middle of a semester. The amount to be refunded is the total tuition times the remaining fraction of the semester (the number of days remaining divided by the total number of days in the semester). The people who use the program want to be able to enter the dates on which the semester begins and ends and the date of withdrawal, and they want the program to calculate the fraction of the semester that remains.

Because each semester at this particular school begins and ends within one calendar year, we can calculate the number of days in a period by determining the day number of each date and subtracting the starting day number from the ending day number. The day number is the number associated with each day of the year if you count sequentially from January 1. December 31 has the day number 365, except in leap years, when it is 366. For example, if a semester begins on 1/3/01 and ends on 5/17/01, the calculation is as follows.

The day number of 1/3/01 is 3
The day number of 5/17/01 is 137
The length of the semester is 137 − 3 + 1 = 135

We add 1 to the difference of the days because we count the first day as part of the period.

The algorithm for calculating the day number for a date is complicated by leap years and by months of different lengths. We could code this algorithm as a void function named ComputeDay. The refund could then be computed by the following code segment.

```
ComputeDay(startMonth, startDay, startYear, start);
ComputeDay(lastMonth, lastDay, lastYear, last);
ComputeDay(withdrawMonth, withdrawDay, withdrawYear, withdraw);
fraction = float(last - withdraw + 1) / float(last - start + 1);
refund = tuition * fraction;
```

The first three arguments to ComputeDay are received by the function, and the last one is returned to the caller. Because ComputeDay returns only one value, we can write it as a value-returning function instead of a void function. Let's look at how the calling code would be written if we had a value-returning function named Day that returned the day number of a date in a given year.

```
start = Day(startMonth, startDay, startYear);
last = Day(lastMonth, lastDay, lastYear);
withdraw = Day(withdrawMonth, withdrawDay, withdrawYear);
fraction = float(last - withdraw + 1) / float(last - start + 1);
refund = tuition * fraction;
```

The second version of the code segment is much more intuitive. Because Day is a value-returning function, you know immediately that all its parameters receive values and that it returns just one value (the day number for a date).

Let's look at the function definition for Day. Don't worry about how Day works; for now, you should concentrate on its syntax and structure.

```
int Day( /* in */ int month,          // Month number, 1 - 12
         /* in */ int dayOfMonth,     // Day of month, 1 - 31
         /* in */ int year       )    // Year. For example, 2001

// This function computes the day number within a year, given
// the date. It accounts correctly for leap years. The
// calculation is based on the fact that months average 30 days
// in length. Thus, (month - 1) * 30 is roughly the number of
// days in the year at the start of any month. A correction
// factor is used to account for cases where the average is
// incorrect and for leap years. The day of the month is then
// added to produce the day number

// Precondition:
//     1 <= month <= 12
//  && dayOfMonth is in valid range for the month
//  && year is assigned
// Postcondition:
//     Function value == day number in the range 1 - 365
//                       (or 1 - 366 for a leap year)

{
    int correction = 0;   // Correction factor to account for leap
                          //   year and months of different lengths

    // Test for leap year
```

```
if (year % 4 == 0 && (year % 100 != 0 || year % 400 == 0))
    if (month >= 3)          // If date is after February 29
        correction = 1;      //   then add one for leap year

// Correct for different-length months

if (month == 3)
    correction = correction - 1;
else if (month == 2 || month == 6 || month == 7)
    correction = correction + 1;
else if (month == 8)
    correction = correction + 2;
else if (month == 9 || month == 10)
    correction = correction + 3;
else if (month == 11 || month == 12)
    correction = correction + 4;
return (month - 1) * 30 + correction + dayOfMonth;
}
```

The first thing to note is that the function definition looks like a void function, except for the fact that the heading begins with the data type `int` instead of the word `void`. The second thing to observe is the Return statement at the end, which includes an integer expression between the word `return` and the semicolon.

A value-returning function returns one value, not through a parameter but by means of a Return statement. The data type at the beginning of the heading declares the type of value that the function returns. This data type is called the *function type,* although a more precise term is **function value type** (or *function return type* or *function result type*).

Function value type   The data type of the result value returned by a function.

The last statement in the `Day` function evaluates the expression

```
(month - 1) * 30 + correction + dayOfMonth
```

and returns the result as the function value (see Figure 8-3).

You now have seen two forms of the Return statement. The form

```
return;
```

is valid *only* in void functions. It causes control to exit the function immediately and return to the caller. The second form is

```
return Expression;
```

FIGURE 8-3

Returning a
Function Value to
the Expression
That Called the
Function

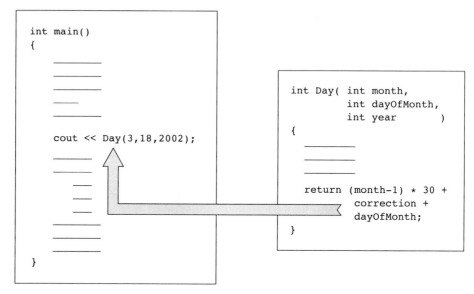

This form is valid *only* in a value-returning function. It returns control to the caller, sending back the value of Expression as the function value. (If the data type of Expression is different from the declared function type, its value is coerced to the correct type.)

In Chapter 7, we presented a syntax template for the function definition of a void function. We now update the syntax template to cover both void functions and value-returning functions:

FunctionDefinition

DataType FunctionName (ParameterList)
{
        Statement
        ⋮
}

If DataType is the word `void`, the function is a void function; otherwise, it is a value-returning function. Notice from the shading in the syntax template that DataType is optional. If you omit the data type of a function, `int` is assumed. We mention this point only because you sometimes encounter programs where DataType is missing from the function heading. Many programmers do not consider this practice to be good programming style.

The parameter list for a value-returning function has exactly the same form as for a void function: a list of parameter declarations, separated by commas. Also, a function prototype for a value-returning function looks just like the prototype for a void function except that it begins with a data type instead of `void`.

Let's look at two more examples of value-returning functions. The C++ standard library provides a power function, `pow`, that raises a floating-point number to a floating-point power. The library does not supply a power function for `int` values, so let's build one of our own. The function receives two integers, x and n (where $n \geq 0$), and computes x^n. We use a simple approach, multiplying repeatedly by x. Because the number of iterations is known in advance, a count-controlled loop is appropriate. The loop counts down to 0 from the initial value of n. For each iteration of the loop, x is multiplied by the previous product.

```
int Power( /* in */ int x,      // Base number
           /* in */ int n )     // Power to raise base to

// This function computes x to the n power

// Precondition:
//      x is assigned  &&  n >= 0  &&  (x to the n) <= INT_MAX
// Postcondition:
//      Function value == x to the n power

{
    int result;      // Holds intermediate powers of x

    result = 1;
    while (n > 0)
    {
        result = result * x;
        n--;
    }
    return result;
}
```

Notice the notation we use in the postcondition of a value-returning function. Because a value-returning function returns a single value, it is most concise if you simply state what that value equals. Except in complicated examples, the postcondition looks like this:

```
// Postcondition
//      Function value == ...
```

Another function that is used frequently in calculating probabilities is the factorial. For example, 5 factorial (written 5! in mathematical notation) is $5 \times 4 \times 3 \times 2 \times 1$. Zero factorial, by definition, equals 1. This function has one integer parameter. As with the `Power` function, we use repeated multiplication, but we decrement the multiplier on each iteration.

```
int Factorial( /* in */ int n )     // Number whose factorial is
                                    //   to be computed
// This function computes n!

// Precondition:
//      n >= 0  &&  n! <= INT_MAX
// Postcondition:
//      Function value == n!

{
    int result;      // Holds partial products

    result = 1;
    while (n > 0)
    {
        result = result * n;
        n--;
    }
    return result;
}
```

A call to the `Factorial` function might look like this:

```
combinations = Factorial(n) / (Factorial(m) * Factorial(n - m));
```

Boolean Functions

Value-returning functions are not restricted to returning numerical results. We can also use them, for example, to evaluate a condition and return a Boolean result. Boolean functions can be useful when a branch or loop depends on some complex condition. Rather than code the condition directly into the If or While statement, we can call a Boolean function to form the controlling expression.

Suppose we are writing a program that works with triangles. The program reads three angles as floating-point numbers. Before performing any calculations on those angles, however, we want to check that they really form a triangle by adding the angles to confirm that their sum equals 180 degrees. We can write a value-returning function that takes the three angles as parameters and returns a Boolean result. Such a function would look like this (recall from Chapter 5 that you should test floating-point numbers only for near equality):

```
#include <cmath>    // For fabs()
  ⋮
bool IsTriangle( /* in */ float angle1,    // First angle
                 /* in */ float angle2,    // Second angle
                 /* in */ float angle3 )   // Third angle

// This function checks to see if its three incoming values
// add up to 180 degrees, forming a valid triangle

// Precondition:
//     angle1, angle2, and angle3 are assigned
// Postcondition:
//    Function value == true, if (angle1 + angle2 + angle3) is
//                                within 0.00000001 of 180.0 degrees
//                   == false, otherwise

{
    return (fabs(angle1 + angle2 + angle3 - 180.0) < 0.00000001);
}
```

The following program fragment shows how the `IsTriangle` function might be called:

```
cin >> angleA >> angleB >> angleC;
if (IsTriangle(angleA, angleB, angleC))             // Function call
    cout << "The three angles form a valid triangle.";
else
    cout << "Those angles do not form a triangle.";
```

The If statement is much easier to understand with the function than it would be if the entire condition were coded directly. When a conditional test is at all complicated, a Boolean function is in order.

The C++ standard library provides a number of helpful functions that let you test the contents of char variables. To use them, you #include the header file cctype. Here are some of the available functions; Appendix C contains a more complete list.

Header File	Function	Function Type	Function Value
<cctype>	isalpha(ch)	int	Nonzero, if ch is a letter ('A'–'Z', 'a'–'z'); 0, otherwise
<cctype>	isalnum(ch)	int	Nonzero, if ch is a letter or a digit ('A'–'Z', 'a'–'z', '0'–'9'); 0, otherwise
<cctype>	isdigit(ch)	int	Nonzero, if ch is a digit ('0'–'9'); 0, otherwise
<cctype>	islower(ch)	int	Nonzero, if ch is a lowercase letter ('a'–'z'); 0, otherwise
<cctype>	isspace(ch)	int	Nonzero, if ch is a whitespace character (blank, newline, tab, carriage return, form feed); 0, otherwise
<cctype>	isupper(ch)	int	Nonzero, if ch is an uppercase letter ('A'–'Z'); 0, otherwise

Although they return int values, the "is..." functions behave like Boolean functions. They return an int value that is nonzero (coerced to true in an If or While condition) or 0 (coerced to false in an If or While condition). These functions are convenient to use and make programs more readable. For example, the test

```
if (isalnum(inputChar))
```

is easier to read and less prone to error than if you coded the test the long way:

```
if (inputChar >= 'A' && inputChar <= 'Z' ||
    inputChar >= 'a' && inputChar <= 'z' ||
    inputChar >= '0' && inputChar <= '9'    )
```

In fact, this complicated logical expression doesn't work correctly on some machines. We'll see why when we examine character data in Chapter 10.

MATTERS OF STYLE

Naming Value-Returning Functions

In Chapter 7, we said that it's good style to use imperative verbs when naming void functions. The reason is that a call to a void function is a complete statement and should look like a command to the computer:

```
PrintResults(a, b, c);
DoThis(x);
DoThat();
```

This naming scheme, however, doesn't work well with value-returning functions. A statement such as

```
z = 6.7 * ComputeMaximum(d, e, f);
```

sounds awkward when you read it aloud: "Set z equal to 6.7 times the *compute maximum* of d, e, and f."

With a value-returning function, the function call represents a value within an expression. Things that represent values, such as variables and value-returning functions, are best given names that are nouns or, occasionally, adjectives. See how much better this statement sounds when you pronounce it out loud:

```
z = 6.7 * Maximum(d, e, f);
```

You would read this as "Set z equal to 6.7 times the *maximum* of d, e, and f." Other names that suggest values rather than actions are SquareRoot, Cube, Factorial, StudentCount, SumOfSquares, and SocialSecurityNum. As you see, they are all nouns or noun phrases.

Boolean value-returning functions (and variables) are often named using adjectives or phrases beginning with *Is*. Here are a few examples:

```
while (Valid(m, n))
if (Odd(n))
if (IsTriangle(s1, s2, s3))
```

When you are choosing a name for a value-returning function, try to stick with nouns or adjectives so that the name suggests a value, not a command to the computer.

Interface Design and Side Effects

The interface to a value-returning function is designed in much the same way as the interface to a void function. We simply write down a list of what the function needs and what it must return. Because value-returning functions return only one value, there is only one item labeled "outgoing" in the list: the function return value. Everything else in the list is labeled "incoming," and there aren't any "incoming/outgoing" parameters.

Returning more than one value from a value-returning function (by modifying the caller's arguments) is a side effect and should be avoided. If your interface design calls for multiple values to be returned, then you should use a void function instead of a value-returning function.

A rule of thumb is never to use reference parameters in the parameter list of a value-returning function, but to use value parameters exclusively. Let's look at an example that demonstrates the importance of this rule. Suppose we define the following function:

```
int SideEffect( int& n )
{
    int result = n * n;

    n++;                    // Side effect
    return result;
}
```

This function returns the square of its incoming value, but it also increments the caller's argument before returning. Now suppose we call this function with the following statement:

```
y = x + SideEffect(x);
```

If x is originally 2, what value is stored into y? The answer depends on the order in which your compiler generates code to evaluate the expression. If the compiled code first calls the function, then the answer is 7. If it accesses x first in preparation for adding it to the function result, the answer is 6. This uncertainty is precisely why reference parameters shouldn't be used with value-returning functions. A function that causes an unpredictable result has no place in a well-written program.

An exception is the case in which an I/O stream object is passed to a value-returning function. Remember that C++ allows a stream object to be passed only to a reference parameter. Within a value-returning function, the only operation that should be performed is testing the state of the stream (for EOF or I/O errors). A value-returning function should not perform input or output operations. Such operations are considered to be side effects of the function. (We should point out that not everyone agrees with this point of view. Some programmers feel that performing I/O within a value-returning function is perfectly acceptable. You will find strong opinions on both sides of this issue.)

There is another advantage to using only value parameters in a value-returning function definition: You can use constants and expressions as arguments. For example, we can call the `IsTriangle` function using literals and other expressions:

```
if (IsTriangle(30.0, 60.0, 30.0 + 60.0))
    cout << "A 30-60-90 angle combination forms a triangle.";
else
    cout << "Something is wrong.";
```

When to Use Value-Returning Functions

There aren't any formal rules for determining when to use a void function and when to use a value-returning function, but here are some guidelines:

1. If the module must return more than one value or modify any of the caller's arguments, do not use a value-returning function.
2. If the module must perform I/O, do not use a value-returning function. (This guideline is not universally agreed upon.)
3. If there is only one value returned from the module and it is a Boolean value, a value-returning function is appropriate.
4. If there is only one value returned and that value is to be used immediately in an expression, a value-returning function is appropriate.
5. When in doubt, use a void function. You can recode any value-returning function as a void function by adding an extra outgoing parameter to carry back the computed result.
6. If both a void function and a value-returning function are acceptable, use the one you feel more comfortable implementing.

Value-returning functions were included in C++ to provide a way of simulating the mathematical concept of a function. The C++ standard library supplies a set of commonly used mathematical functions through the header file `cmath`. A list of these appears in Appendix C.

*B*ACKGROUND INFORMATION

Ignoring a Function Value

A peculiarity of the C++ language is that it lets you ignore the value returned by a value-returning function. For example, you could write the following statement in your program without any complaint from the compiler:

```
sqrt(x);
```

When this statement is executed, the value returned by `sqrt` is promptly discarded. This function call has absolutely no effect except to waste the computer's time by calculating a value that is never used.

Clearly, the above call to `sqrt` is a mistake. No programmer would write that statement intentionally. But C++ programmers occasionally write value-returning functions in a way that allows the caller to ignore the function value. Here is a specific example from the C++ standard library.

The library provides a function named `remove`, the purpose of which is to delete a disk file from the system. It takes a single argument—a C string specifying the name of the file—and it returns a function value. This function value is an integer notifying you of the status: 0 if the operation succeeded, and nonzero if it failed. Here is how you might call the `remove` function:

```
status = remove("junkfile.dat");
if (status != 0)
    PrintErrorMsg();
```

On the other hand, if you assume that the system always succeeds at deleting a file, you can ignore the returned status by calling `remove` as though it were a void function:

```
remove("junkfile.dat");
```

The `remove` function is sort of a hybrid between a void function and a value-returning function. Conceptually, it is a void function; its principal purpose is to delete a file, not to compute a value to be returned. Literally, however, it's a value-returning function. It does return a function value—the status of the operation (which you can choose to ignore).

In this book, we don't write hybrid functions. We prefer to keep the concept of a void function distinct from a value-returning function. But there are two reasons why every C++ programmer should know about the topic of ignoring a function value. First, if you accidentally call a value-returning function as if it were a void function, the compiler won't prevent you from making the mistake. Second, you sometimes encounter this style of coding in other people's programs and in the C++ standard library. Several of the library functions are technically value-returning functions, but the function value is used merely to return something of secondary importance such as a status value.

*P*ROBLEM-SOLVING CASE STUDY

Reformat Dates

Problem: You work for a company that publishes the schedules for international airlines. The firm must print three versions of the schedules because of the different formats for dates used around the world. Your job is to write a program that takes dates written in American format (mm/dd/yyyy) from file stream `dataIn` and converts them to British format (dd/mm/yyyy) and International Standards Organization (ISO) format (yyyy-mm-dd). The output should be a table written to file stream `dataOut` that contains the dates lined up in three columns as follows:

```
American Format      British Format        ISO Format

  mm/dd/yyyy            dd/mm/yyyy           yyyy-mm-dd
  mm/dd/yyyy            dd/mm/yyyy           yyyy-mm-dd
```

There is one small problem. Although the dates are in American format, one per line, embedded blanks can occur anywhere in the line. For example, the input file may look like this:

```
10/11/1935
1 1    / 2 3          / 1 9   2  6
               5/2/2004
05   /28                        /1965
7/   3/   19  56
```

Given this input, the output (written to file stream `dataOut`) would be

```
      American Format      British Format       ISO Format
         10/11/1935          11/10/1935        1935-10-11
         11/23/1926          23/11/1926        1926-11-23
         05/02/2004          02/05/2004        2004-05-02
         05/28/1965          28/05/1965        1965-05-28
         07/03/1956          03/07/1956        1956-07-03
```

Input: A data file (stream `dataIn`) containing dates, one per line, in American format, mm/dd/yyyy (may include embedded blanks).

The number of input lines is unknown. The program should continue to process input lines until EOF occurs.

Output: A file (stream `dataOut`) containing a table with each date in the following formats:

PROBLEM-SOLVING CASE STUDY cont'd.

mm/dd/yyyy   dd/mm/yyyy   yyyy–mm–dd

See the preceding sample output for the formatting of the table.

Discussion: It is easy for a human to scan the input line, skipping over the embedded blanks and the slash (/) to pick up each number. We also easily identify a one-character number. The key to this problem is making explicit what our eyes do implicitly.

First, we know that we cannot read values as int data because the digits may have blanks between them, and the terminating character may be a slash, a blank, or, in the case of the year, the newline character ('\n'). Therefore, we must read everything as char data.

We recognize the first character in the month because it is the first nonblank character on a line. If the next character is a digit, then we have the complete month, and we can skip over blanks and the slash. If the next character is not a digit, we must skip over blanks until we find a digit or a slash. If we find a slash, we know that the month is a one-digit month, and we must insert a leading zero. Once we have both characters of the month, we can store them into a string.

The same algorithm works for finding the day. The algorithm for finding the year is easier. Assuming that four digits are always present, we simply input four characters, skipping blanks along the way. Let's convert these observations into a functional decomposition.

Assumptions: Each line in dataIn contains a valid date in American format.

Main   **Level 0**

```
Open the input and output files
IF either file could not be opened
        Terminate program
Write headings
Get month
WHILE NOT EOF on dataIn
        Get day
        Get year
        Write date in American format
        Write date in British format
        Write date in ISO format
        Get month
```

Writing the headings can be done in a single C++ output statement, so we can code it directly in the `main` function instead of creating a separate module.

Open for Input (Inout: someFile)   **Level 1**

> We can reuse the Open for Input module from the Graph program in Chapter 7

Open for Output (Inout: someFile)

> We can modify the Open for Input module so that it opens an output file

Get Month (Inout: dataIn; Out: twoChars)

The parameter `twoChars` is a string variable that holds both digit characters of the month.

> Read firstChar from dataIn, skipping leading whitespace chars
> IF EOF on dataIn
>   Return
> Read secondChar from dataIn, skipping leading whitespace chars
> IF secondChar is '/'
>   Set secondChar = firstChar
>   Set firstChar = '0'
> ELSE
>   Read dummy from dataIn, skipping leading whitespace chars
> Set twoChars = firstChar
> Concatenate secondChar to twoChars

The else-clause uses a variable named dummy to move the reading marker past the slash if there is a two-digit month.

We must remember to test both one-digit and two-digit numbers, with the digits together and separated. We also must test digits at the beginning of the line and immediately before and after the slash.

Get Day (Inout: dataIn; Out: twoChars)

Because the reading marker is left pointing to the character immediately to the right of the slash, the Get Day module is identical to the Get Month module.

Get Year (Inout: dataIn; Out: year)

The outgoing parameter year is a string variable that holds the four digit characters of the month.

```
Set year = ""      (the null string)
Set loopCount = 1
WHILE loopCount ≤ 4
        Read digitChar from dataIn, skipping leading whitespace chars
        Concatenate digitChar to year
        Increment loopCount
```

The algorithm begins by storing the null string into year. Then, using a count-controlled loop, we input exactly four characters, concatenating each one to the end of year as we go.

Write Date in American Format (Inout: dataOut; In: month, day, year)

```
Write month, '/', day, '/', year to dataOut
```

PROBLEM-SOLVING CASE STUDY cont'd.

Write Date in British Format (Inout: dataOut; In: month, day, year)

> Write day, '/', month, '/', year to dataOut

Write Date in ISO Format (Inout: dataOut; In: month, day, year)

> Write year, '–', month, '–', day to dataOut

As we noted during the design phase, modules Get Month and Get Day are identical. We can replace them with a single module, Get Two Digits. We also can combine modules Write Date in American Format, Write Date in British Format, and Write Date in ISO Format into one module named Write. Here is the resulting module structure chart. The chart emphasizes the importance of interface design. The arrows indicate which identifiers are received or returned by each module.

Module Structure Chart:

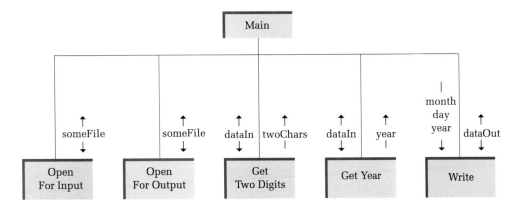

Here is the program that corresponds to our design. We have omitted the precondition and postcondition from the comments at the beginning of each function. Case Study Follow-Up Exercise 1 asks you to fill them in.

(The following program is written in ISO/ANSI standard C++. If you are working with pre–standard C++, see the alternate version of the program in the PRE_STD directory of the program disk, available at the publisher's Web site, www.jbpub.com/disks.)

```cpp
//*****************************************************************
// ConvertDates program
// This program reads dates in American form from an input file and
// writes them to an output file in American, British, and ISO form.
// No data validation is done on the input file
//*****************************************************************
#include <iostream>
#include <iomanip>    // For setw()
#include <fstream>    // For file I/O
#include <string>     // For string type

using namespace std;

void Get2Digits( ifstream&, string& );
void GetYear( ifstream&, string& );
void OpenForInput( ifstream& );
void OpenForOutput( ofstream& );
void Write( ofstream&, string, string, string );

int main()
{
    string    month;       // Both digits of month
    string    day;         // Both digits of day
    string    year;        // Four digits of year
    ifstream dataIn;       // Input file of dates
    ofstream dataOut;      // Output file of dates

    OpenForInput(dataIn);
    OpenForOutput(dataOut);
    if ( !dataIn || !dataOut )                  // Make sure files
        return 1;                               //    were opened

    dataOut << setw(20) << "American Format"    // Write headings
            << setw(20) << "British Format"
            << setw(20) << "ISO Format" << endl << endl;

    Get2Digits(dataIn, month);                  // Priming read
    while (dataIn)                              // While not EOF...
    {
```

```
            Get2Digits(dataIn, day);
            GetYear(dataIn, year);
            Write(dataOut, month, day, year);
            Get2Digits(dataIn, month);
        }
        return 0;
    }


//****************************************************************

void OpenForInput( /* inout */ ifstream& someFile )     // File to be
                                                        // opened
// Prompts the user for the name of an input file
// and attempts to open the file

// Postcondition: Exercise
//
// Note:
//      Upon return from this function, the caller must test
//      the stream state to see if the file was successfully opened

{
    string fileName;     // User-specified file name

    cout << "Input file name: ";
    cin >> fileName;

    someFile.open(fileName.c_str());
    if ( !someFile )
        cout << "** Can't open " << fileName << " **" << endl;
}

//****************************************************************

void OpenForOutput( /* inout */ ofstream& someFile )    // File to be
                                                        // opened
// Prompts the user for the name of an output file
// and attempts to open the file

// Postcondition: Exercise
//
// Note:
//      Upon return from this function, the caller must test
//      the stream state to see if the file was successfully opened

{
    string fileName;     // User-specified file name
```

```
        cout << "Output file name: ";
        cin >> fileName;

        someFile.open(fileName.c_str());
        if ( !someFile )
            cout << "** Can't open " << fileName << " **" << endl;
    }

//****************************************************************

void Get2Digits( /* inout */ ifstream& dataIn,      // Input file
                 /* out */    string&   twoChars )   // Two digits

// Reads characters up to a slash from dataIn and returns two
// digit characters in the string twoChars.  If only one digit
// is found before the slash, a leading '0' is inserted.
// (If input fails due to end-of-file, twoChars is undefined.)

// Precondition:  Exercise
// Postcondition: Exercise

{
    char firstChar;      // First character of a two-digit value
    char secondChar;     // Second character of value
    char dummy;          // To consume the slash, if necessary

    dataIn >> firstChar;
    if ( !dataIn )              // Check for EOF
        return;                 // If so, exit the function

    dataIn >> secondChar;
    if (secondChar == '/')
    {
        secondChar = firstChar;
        firstChar = '0';
    }
    else
        dataIn >> dummy;        // Consume the slash

    twoChars = firstChar;
    twoChars = twoChars + secondChar;
}

//****************************************************************

void GetYear( /* inout */ ifstream& dataIn,     // Input file
              /* out */    string&   year   )    // Four digits
                                                 //    of year
```

PROBLEM-SOLVING CASE STUDY cont'd.

```
// Reads characters from dataIn and returns four digit characters
// in the year string

// Precondition:  Exercise
// Postcondition: Exercise

{
    char digitChar;     // One digit of the year
    int  loopCount;     // Loop control variable

    year = "";
    loopCount = 1;
    while (loopCount <= 4)
    {
        dataIn >> digitChar;
        year = year + digitChar;
        loopCount++;
    }
}

//******************************************************************

void Write( /* inout */ ofstream& dataOut,     // Output file
            /* in */     string    month,      // Month string
            /* in */     string    day,        // Day string
            /* in */     string    year   )    // Year string

// Writes the date represented by month, day, and year to file
// dataOut in American, British, and ISO form

// Precondition:  Exercise
// Postcondition: Exercise

{
    dataOut << setw(9) << month << '/' << day << '/' << year;
    dataOut << setw(13) << day << '/' << month << '/' << year;
    dataOut << setw(16) << year << '-' << month
            << '-' << day << endl;
}
```

The `Write` function in this program contains only three statements in the body (and could have been written as a single, long output statement). We could just as easily have written these statements directly in the `main` function in place of the call to the function.

We don't mean to imply that you should never write a function with as few as one, two, or three statements. In some cases, decomposition of a problem makes a small function quite appropriate. When deciding whether to code a module directly in the next-higher level or as a function, ask yourself the following question: Which way will make the overall program easier to read, understand, and modify later? With experience, you will develop your own set of guidelines for making this decision. For example, if a two-line module is to be called from several places in the program, you should code it as a function. If it is called from only one place, it may be better to code it directly at the next-higher level, unless doing so would contribute to making the calling function too long.

Testing: The ConvertDates program allows a great deal of variation in the formatting of its input. Such flexibility makes it necessary to test the program with many combinations of input. The test data should include digits, slashes, and blanks in every valid arrangement and in some arrangements that are invalid.

Blanks can appear in a date in 11 places: between each pair of the 10 characters, before the first character, and after the last. At a minimum, we should test with a data set containing 11 dates in which a single blank appears in each of these positions. To be thorough, we should test all possible combinations of a blank or no blank in these positions. There are 2^{11} (or 2048) such combinations.

In theory, we also should test for combinations with single or multiple blanks in each position. If we check only for combinations of none, one, or two blanks in each position, then there are 3^{11} (or 177,147) such combinations. Creating such a comprehensive test data set by hand would be both difficult and time-consuming. However, we could write a program to generate it. Such programs, called *test generators,* often provide the simplest way of testing a program with a large test data set.

We actually can test the ConvertDates program with far fewer than 177,147 combinations of blanks, because we know that the >> operator is used to skip all blanks preceding a character. Thus, once we have verified that >> works correctly in one place in a date, it isn't necessary to test it for every combination of blanks in other places. In addition to testing for correctly skipping blanks, we must test that the program properly handles months and days with one or two digits. We should try a date in which the month and day are each a single digit, and another date in which they both have two digits.

Here is a sample test data file for the ConvertDates program:

10/23/1999
10/23/200 1

```
10/23/ 2002
10/23 /2003
10/2 3/2004
10/ 23/2005
10 /23/2006
1 0/23/2007
 10/23/2008
  1  0  /  2  3  /  2  0  0  9
1/2/1946
   1  /  2  /  1 946
```

For this data, here is the output from the program:

American Format	British Format	ISO Format
10/23/1999	23/10/1999	1999-10-23
10/23/2001	23/10/2001	2001-10-23
10/23/2002	23/10/2002	2002-10-23
10/23/2003	23/10/2003	2003-10-23
10/23/2004	23/10/2004	2004-10-23
10/23/2005	23/10/2005	2005-10-23
10/23/2006	23/10/2006	2006-10-23
10/23/2007	23/10/2007	2007-10-23
10/23/2008	23/10/2008	2008-10-23
10/23/2009	23/10/2009	2009-10-23
01/02/1946	02/01/1946	1946-01-02
01/02/1946	02/01/1946	1946-01-02

The ConvertDates program is actually too flexible in how it allows dates to be entered. For instance, a "digit" can be any nonblank character. Because slashes appear in the correct places, an input sequence such as

```
#$ / () / A@
```

is treated as a valid date. On the other hand, a seemingly valid date such as

```
12-27-65
```

is not recognized because dashes aren't valid separators. Furthermore, ConvertDates does not handle erroneous dates gracefully. If part of a date is missing, for example, the program may end up reading the remainder of the input file incorrectly. Case Study Follow-Up Exercise 2 asks you to add data validation to the ConvertDates program.

SOFTWARE ENGINEERING TIP

Control Abstraction, Functional Cohesion, and Communication Complexity

The ConvertDates program contains two different While loops. The control structure for this program has the potential to be fairly complex. Yet if you look at the individual modules, the most complicated control structure is a While loop without any If or While statements nested within it.

The complexity of a program is hidden by reducing each of the major control structures to an abstract action performed by a function call. In the ConvertDates program, for example, finding the year is an abstract action that appears as a call to GetYear. The logical properties of the action are separated from its implementation (a While loop). This aspect of a design is called **control abstraction**.

Control abstraction   The separation of the logical properties of an action from its implementation.

Control abstraction can serve as a guideline for deciding which modules to code as functions and which to code directly. If a module contains a control structure, it is a good candidate for being implemented as a function. On the other hand, the Write function lacks control abstraction. Its body is a sequence of three statements, which could just as well be located in the main function. But even if a module does not contain a control structure, you still want to consider other factors. Is it lengthy, or is it called from more than one place? If so, you should use a function.

Somewhat related to control abstraction is the concept of **functional cohesion,** which states that a module should perform exactly one abstract action.

Functional cohesion   The principle that a module should perform exactly one abstract action.

If you can state the action that a module performs in one sentence with no conjunctions (*and*s), then it is highly cohesive. A module that has more than one primary purpose lacks cohesion. Apart from main, all the functions in the ConvertDates program have good cohesion.

A module that only partially fulfills a purpose also lacks cohesion. Such a module should be combined with whatever other modules are directly related to it. For example, it would make no sense to have a separate function that prints the first digit of a date because printing a date is one abstract action.

A third and related aspect of a module's design is its **communication complexity**, the amount of data that passes through a module's interface—for example, the number of arguments. A module's communication complexity is often an indicator of its cohesiveness. Usually, if a module requires a large number of arguments, it either is trying to accomplish too much or is only partially fulfilling a purpose. You should step back and see if there is an alternative way of dividing up the problem so that a minimal amount of data is communicated between modules. The modules in ConvertDates have low communication complexity.

Communication complexity A measure of the quantity of data passing through a module's interface.

---

*P*ROBLEM-SOLVING CASE STUDY

Starship Weight and Balance

Problem: The company you work for has just upgraded its fleet of corporate aircraft by adding the Beechcraft Starship-1. As with any airplane, it is essential that the pilot know the total weight of the loaded plane at takeoff and its center of gravity. If the plane weighs too much, it won't be able to lift off. If its center of gravity is outside the limits established for the plane, it might be impossible to control. Either situation can lead to a crash. You have been asked to write a program that determines the weight and center of gravity of this new plane, based on the number of crew members and passengers as well as the weight of the baggage, closet contents, and fuel.

The Beechcraft Starship-1

Input: Number of crew members, number of passengers, weight of closet contents, baggage weight, fuel in gallons.

Output: Total weight, center of gravity.

Discussion: As with most real-world problems, the basic solution is simple but is complicated by special cases. We use value-returning functions to hide the complexity so that the `main` function remains simple.

The total weight is basically the sum of the empty weight of the airplane plus the weight of each of the following: crew members, passengers, baggage, contents of the storage closet, and fuel. We use the standard average weight of a person, 170 pounds, to compute the total weight of the people. The weight of the baggage and the contents of the closet are given. Fuel weighs 6.7 pounds per gallon. Thus, the total weight is

$$totalWeight = emptyWeight + (crew + passengers) \times 170 + baggage + closet + fuel \times 6.7$$

To compute the center of gravity, each weight is multiplied by its distance from the front of the airplane, and the products—called *moment arms* or simply *moments*—are then summed and divided by the total weight (see Figure 8-4). The formula is thus

$$centerOfGravity = (emptyMoment + crewMoment + passengerMoment + cargoMoment + fuelMoment) / totalWeight$$

The Starship-1 manual gives the distance from the front of the plane to the crew's seats, closet, baggage compartment, and fuel tanks. There are four rows of passenger seats, so this calculation depends on where the individual passengers sit. We have to make some assumptions about how passengers arrange themselves. Each row has two seats. The most popular seats are in row 2 because they are near the entrance and face forward. Once row 2 is filled, passengers usually take seats in row 1, facing their traveling companions. Row 3 is usually the next to fill up, even though it faces backward, because row 4 is a fold-down bench seat that is less comfortable than the armchairs in the forward rows. The following table gives the distance from the nose of the plane to each of the "loading stations."

PROBLEM-SOLVING CASE STUDY cont'd.

FIGURE 8-4
A Passenger
Moment Arm

Loading Station	Distance from Nose (inches)
Crew seats	143
Row 1 seats	219
Row 2 seats	265
Row 3 seats	295
Row 4 seats	341
Closet	182
Baggage	386

The distance for the fuel varies because there are several tanks, and the tanks are in different places. As fuel is added to the plane, it automatically flows into the different tanks so that the center of gravity changes as the tanks are filled. There are four formulas for computing the distance from the nose to the "center" of the fuel tanks, depending on how much fuel is being loaded into the plane. The following table lists these distance formulas.

Gallons of Fuel (G)	Distance (D) Formula
0–59	$D = 314.6 \times G$
60–360	$D = 305.8 + (-0.01233 \times (G - 60))$
361–520	$D = 303.0 + (0.12500 \times (G - 361))$
521–565	$D = 323.0 + (-0.04444 \times (G - 521))$

We define one value-returning function for each of the different moments, and we name these functions `CrewMoment`, `PassengerMoment`, `CargoMoment`, and `FuelMoment`. The center of gravity is then computed with the formula we gave earlier and the following arguments:

$$centerOfGravity = (CrewMoment(crew) + PassengerMoment(passengers) +$$
$$CargoMoment(closet, baggage) + FuelMoment(fuel) +$$
$$emptyMoment) / totalWeight$$

The empty weight of the Starship is 9887 pounds, and its empty center of gravity is 319 inches from the front of the airplane. Thus, the empty moment is 3,153,953 inch-pounds.

We now have enough information to write the algorithm to solve this problem. In addition to printing the results, we'll also print a warning message that states the assumptions of the program and tells the pilot to double-check the results by hand if the weight or center of gravity is near the allowable limits.

Main   **Level 0**

```
Get data
Set totalWt =
      EMPTY_WEIGHT + (passengers + crew) * 170 +
      baggage + closet + fuel * 6.7
Set centerOfGravity =
      (CrewMoment(crew) + PassengerMoment(passengers) +
      CargoMoment(closet, baggage) + FuelMoment(fuel) +
      EMPTY_MOMENT) / totalWt
Print totalWt, centerOfGravity
Print warning
```

Get Data (Out: crew, passengers, closet, baggage, fuel)   **Level 1**

```
Prompt for number of crew, number of passengers,
      weight in closet and baggage compartments,
      and gallons of fuel
Read crew, passengers, closet, baggage, fuel
Echo print the input
```

PROBLEM-SOLVING CASE STUDY cont'd.

Crew Moment (In: crew)

Out: Function value

```
Return crew * 170 * 143
```

Passenger Moment (In: passengers)

Out: Function value

```
Set moment = 0.0
IF passengers > 6
     Add (passengers – 6) * 170 * 341 to moment
     Set passengers = 6
IF passengers > 4
     Add (passengers – 4) * 170 * 295 to moment
     Set passengers = 4
IF passengers > 2
     Add (passengers – 2) * 170 * 219 to moment
     Set passengers = 2
IF passengers > 0
     Add passengers * 170 * 265 to moment
Return moment
```

Cargo Moment (In: closet, baggage)

Out: Function value

```
Return closet * 182 + baggage * 386
```

PROBLEM-SOLVING CASE STUDY cont'd.

Fuel Moment (In: fuel)

Out: Function value

```
Set fuelWt = fuel * 6.7
IF fuel < 60
        Set fuelDistance = fuel * 314.6
ELSE IF fuel < 361
        Set fuelDistance = 305.8 + (−0.01233 * (fuel − 60))
ELSE IF fuel < 521
        Set fuelDistance = 303.0 + ( 0.12500 * (fuel − 361))
ELSE
        Set fuelDistance = 323.0 + (−0.04444 * (fuel − 521))
Return fuelDistance * fuelWt
```

Print Warning (No parameters)

> Print a warning message about the assumptions of
> the program and when to double-check the results

Module Structure Chart: In the following chart, you'll see a new notation. The box corresponding to each value-returning function has an upward arrow originating at its right side. This arrow signifies the function value that is returned.

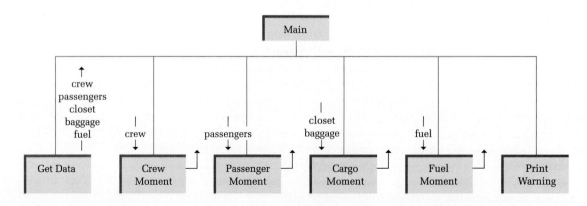

PROBLEM-SOLVING CASE STUDY cont'd.

(The following program is written in ISO/ANSI standard C++. If you are working with pre–standard C++, see the alternate version of the program in the PRE_STD directory of the program disk, available at the publisher's Web site, www.jbpub.com/disks.)

```cpp
//******************************************************************
// Starship program
// This program computes the total weight and center of gravity
// of a Beechcraft Starship-1, given the number of crew members
// and passengers, weight of closet and baggage compartment cargo,
// and gallons of fuel loaded.  It assumes that each person
// weighs 170 pounds, and that the fuel weighs 6.7 pounds per
// gallon.  Thus, the output is approximate and should be hand-
// checked if the Starship is loaded near its limits
//******************************************************************
#include <iostream>
#include <iomanip>      // For setw() and setprecision()

using namespace std;

const float PERSON_WT = 170.0;          // Average person weighs
                                        //    170 lbs.
const float LBS_PER_GAL = 6.7;          // Jet-A weighs 6.7 lbs.
                                        //    per gal.
const float EMPTY_WEIGHT = 9887.0;      // Standard empty weight
const float EMPTY_MOMENT = 3153953.0;   // Standard empty moment

float CargoMoment( int, int );
float CrewMoment( int );
float FuelMoment( int );
void GetData( int&, int&, int&, int&, int& );
float PassengerMoment( int );
void  PrintWarning();

int main()
{
    int   crew;             // Number of crew on board (1 or 2)
    int   passengers;       // Number of passengers (0 through 8)
    int   closet;           // Weight in closet (160 lbs. maximum)
    int   baggage;          // Weight of baggage (525 lbs. max.)
    int   fuel;             // Gallons of fuel (10 through 565 gals.)
    float totalWt;          // Total weight of the loaded Starship
    float centerOfGravity;  // Center of gravity of loaded Starship
```

```cpp
    cout << fixed << showpoint                   // Set up floating-pt.
         << setprecision(2);                     //    output format

    GetData(crew, passengers, closet, baggage, fuel);

    totalWt =
        EMPTY_WEIGHT + float(passengers + crew) * PERSON_WT +
        float(baggage + closet) + float(fuel) * LBS_PER_GAL;
    centerOfGravity =
        (CrewMoment(crew) + PassengerMoment(passengers) +
        CargoMoment(closet, baggage) + FuelMoment(fuel) +
        EMPTY_MOMENT) / totalWt;

    cout << "Total weight is " << totalWt << " pounds." << endl;
    cout << "Center of gravity is " << centerOfGravity
         << " inches from the front of the plane." << endl;
    PrintWarning();
    return 0;
}


//*****************************************************************

void GetData( /* out */ int& crew,           // Number of crew members
              /* out */ int& passengers,     // Number of passengers
              /* out */ int& closet,         // Weight of closet cargo
              /* out */ int& baggage,        // Weight of baggage
              /* out */ int& fuel         )  // Gallons of fuel

// Prompts for the input of crew, passengers, closet, baggage, and
// fuel values and returns the five values after echo printing them

// Postcondition:
//     All parameters (crew, passengers, closet, baggage, and fuel)
//     have been prompted for, input, and echo printed

{
    cout << "Enter the number of crew members." << endl;
    cin >> crew;
    cout << "Enter the number of passengers." << endl;
    cin >> passengers;
    cout << "Enter the weight, in pounds, of cargo in the" << endl
         << " closet, rounded up to the nearest whole number."
         << endl;
    cin >> closet;
    cout << "Enter the weight, in pounds, of cargo in the" << endl
         << " aft baggage compartment, rounded up to the" << endl
         << " nearest whole number." << endl;
```

```
        cin >> baggage;
        cout << "Enter the number of U.S. gallons of fuel" << endl
             << " loaded, rounded up to the nearest whole number."
             << endl;
        cin >> fuel;
        cout << endl;
        cout << "Starship loading data as entered:" << endl
             << "   Crew:            " << setw(6) << crew << endl
             << "   Passengers:      " << setw(6) << passengers << endl
             << "   Closet weight: " << setw(6) << closet << " pounds"
             << endl
             << "   Baggage weight:" << setw(6) << baggage << " pounds"
             << endl
             << "   Fuel:            " << setw(6) << fuel << " gallons"
             << endl << endl;
}


//****************************************************************

float CrewMoment( /* in */ int crew )    // Number of crew members

// Computes the crew moment arm in inch-pounds from the number of
// crew members.  Global constant PERSON_WT is used as the weight
// of each crew member

// Precondition:
//     crew == 1  OR  crew == 2
// Postcondition:
//     Function value == Crew moment arm, based on the crew parameter

{
    const float CREW_DISTANCE = 143.0;   // Distance to crew seats
                                         //    from front

    return float(crew) * PERSON_WT * CREW_DISTANCE;
}


//****************************************************************

float PassengerMoment( /* in */ int passengers )    // Number of
                                                    //    passengers

// Computes the passenger moment arm in inch-pounds from the number
// of passengers.  Global constant PERSON_WT is used as the weight
// of each passenger.  It is assumed that the first two passengers
// sit in row 2, the second two in row 1, the next two in row 3,
// and remaining passengers sit in row 4
```

```
// Precondition:
//     0 <= passengers <= 8
// Postcondition:
//     Function value == Passenger moment arm, based on the
//                       passengers parameter

{
    const float ROW1_DIST = 219.0;   // Distance to row 1 seats
                                     //    from front
    const float ROW2_DIST = 265.0;   // Distance to row 2 seats
    const float ROW3_DIST = 295.0;   // Distance to row 3 seats
    const float ROW4_DIST = 341.0;   // Distance to row 4 seats

    float moment = 0.0;               // Running total of moment as
                                     //    rows are added

    if (passengers > 6)                      // For passengers 7 and 8
    {
        moment = moment +
                float(passengers - 6) * PERSON_WT * ROW4_DIST;
        passengers = 6;                  // 6 remain
    }
    if (passengers > 4)                      // For passengers 5 and 6
    {
        moment = moment +
                float(passengers - 4) * PERSON_WT * ROW3_DIST;
        passengers = 4;                  // 4 remain
    }
    if (passengers > 2)                      // For passengers 3 and 4
    {
        moment = moment +
                float(passengers - 2) * PERSON_WT * ROW1_DIST;
        passengers = 2;                  // 2 remain
    }
    if (passengers > 0)                      // For passengers 1 and 2
        moment = moment +
                float(passengers) * PERSON_WT * ROW2_DIST;
    return moment;
}

//***************************************************************

float CargoMoment( /* in */ int closet,      // Weight in closet
                   /* in */ int baggage )    // Weight of baggage

// Computes the total moment arm for cargo loaded into the
// front closet and aft baggage compartment

// Precondition:
```

```
//       0 <= closet <= 160  &&   0 <= baggage <= 525
// Postcondition:
//       Function value == Cargo moment arm, based on the closet and
//                          baggage parameters

{
    const float CLOSET_DIST = 182.0;      // Distance from front
                                          //   to closet
    const float BAGGAGE_DIST = 386.0;     // Distance from front
                                          //   to bagg. comp.

    return float(closet) * CLOSET_DIST +
           float(baggage) * BAGGAGE_DIST;
}


//*****************************************************************

float FuelMoment( /* in */ int fuel )    // Fuel in gallons

// Computes the moment arm for fuel on board.  There are four
// different formulas for this calculation, depending on
// the amount of fuel, due to fuel tank layout.
// This function uses the global constant LBS_PER_GAL
// to compute the weight of the fuel

// Precondition:
//       10 <= fuel <= 565
// Postcondition:
//       Function value == Fuel moment arm, based on the
//                          fuel parameter

{
    float fuelWt;             // Weight of fuel in pounds
    float fuelDistance;       // Distance from front of plane

    fuelWt = float(fuel) * LBS_PER_GAL;
    if (fuel < 60)
        fuelDistance = float(fuel) * 314.6;
    else if (fuel < 361)
        fuelDistance = 305.8 + (-0.01233 * float(fuel - 60));
    else if (fuel < 521)
        fuelDistance = 303.0 + ( 0.12500 * float(fuel - 361));
    else
        fuelDistance = 323.0 + (-0.04444 * float(fuel - 521));
    return fuelDistance * fuelWt;
}


//*****************************************************************
```

```
void PrintWarning()

// Warns the user of assumptions made by the program
// and when to double-check the program's results

// Postcondition:
//      An informational warning message has been printed

{
    cout << endl
        << "Notice:  This program assumes that passengers" << endl
        << "  fill the seat rows in order 2, 1, 3, 4, and" << endl
        << "  that each passenger and crew member weighs " 
        << PERSON_WT << " pounds." << endl
        << "  It also assumes that Jet-A fuel weighs "
        << LBS_PER_GAL << " pounds" << endl
        << "  per U.S. gallon.  The center of gravity" << endl
        << "  calculations for fuel are approximate.  If" << endl
        << "  the aircraft is loaded near its limits, the" << endl
        << "  pilot's operating handbook should be used" << endl
        << "  to compute weight and center of gravity" << endl
        << "  with more accuracy." << endl;
}
```

Testing: Because someone could use the output of this program to make decisions that could result in property damage, injury, or death, it is essential to test the program thoroughly. In particular, it should be checked for maximum and minimum input values in different combinations. In addition, a wide range of test cases should be tried and verified against results calculated by hand. If possible, the program's output should be checked against sample calculations done by experienced pilots for actual flights.

Notice that the main function neglects to guarantee any of the function preconditions before calling the functions. If this program were actually to be used by pilots, it should have data validation checks added in the GetData function.

Testing and Debugging

One of the advantages of a modular design is that you can test it long before the code has been written for all of the modules. If we test each module individually, then we can assemble the modules into a complete program with much greater confidence that the program is correct. In this section, we introduce a technique for testing a module separately.

Stubs and Drivers

Suppose you were given the code for a module and your job was to test it. How would you test a single module by itself? First of all, it must be called by something (unless it is the `main` function). Second, it may have calls to other modules that aren't available to you. To test the module, you must fill in these missing links.

When a module contains calls to other modules, we can write dummy functions called **stubs** to satisfy those calls. A stub usually consists of an output statement that prints a message such as "Function such-and-such just got called." Even though the stub is a dummy, it allows us to determine whether the function is called at the right time by the `main` function or another function.

Stub A dummy function that assists in testing part of a program. A stub has the same name and interface as a function that actually would be called by the part of the program being tested, but it is usually much simpler.

A stub can also be used to print the set of values that are passed to it; this tells us whether or not the module being tested is supplying the correct information. Sometimes a stub assigns new values to its reference parameters to simulate data being read or results being computed in order to give the calling module something to keep working on. Because we can choose the values that are returned by the stub, we have better control over the conditions of the test run.

Here is a stub that simulates the `GetYear` function in the ConvertDates program by returning an arbitrarily chosen string.

```
void GetYear( /* inout */ ifstream& dataIn,       // Input file
              /* out */    string&    year )       // Four digits
                                                   //   of year

// Stub for GetYear function in the ConvertDates program

{
    cout << "GetYear was called here. Returning \"1948\"." << endl;
    year = "1948";
}
```

This stub is simpler than the function it simulates, which is typical because the object of using a stub is to provide a simple, predictable environment for testing a module.

In addition to supplying a stub for each call within the module, you must provide a dummy program—a **driver**—to call the module itself. A driver program contains the bare minimum of code required to call the module being tested.

Driver   A simple `main` function that is used to call a function being tested. The use of a driver permits direct control of the testing process.

By surrounding a module with a driver and stubs, you gain complete control of the conditions under which it executes. This allows you to test different situations and combinations that may reveal errors. For example, the following program is a driver for the `FuelMoment` function in the Starship program. Because `FuelMoment` doesn't call any other functions, no stubs are necessary.

```
//*****************************************************************
// FuelMomentDriver program
// This program provides an environment for testing the
// FuelMoment function in isolation from the Starship program
//*****************************************************************
#include <iostream>

using namespace std;

const float LBS_PER_GAL = 6.7;

float FuelMoment( int );

int main()
{
    int testVal;      // Test value for fuel in gallons

    cout << "Fuel moment for gallons from 10 through 565"
         << " in steps of 15:" << endl;
    testVal = 10;
    while (testVal <= 565)
    {
        cout << FuelMoment(testVal) << endl;
        testVal = testVal + 15;
    }
    return 0;
}

//*****************************************************************

float FuelMoment( /* in */ int Fuel )     // Fuel in gallons
```

```
{
    float fuelWt;            // Weight of fuel in pounds
    float fuelDistance;      // Distance from front of plane

    fuelWt = float(fuel) * LBS_PER_GAL;
    if (fuel < 60)
        fuelDistance = float(fuel) * 314.6;
    else if (fuel < 361)
        fuelDistance = 305.8 + (-0.01233 * float(fuel - 60));
    else if (fuel < 521)
        fuelDistance = 303.0 + ( 0.12500 * float(fuel - 361));
    else
        fuelDistance = 323.0 + (-0.04444 * float(fuel - 521));
    return fuelDistance * fuelWt;
}
```

Stubs and drivers are important tools in team programming. The programmers develop the overall design and the interfaces between the modules. Each programmer then designs and codes one or more of the modules and uses drivers and stubs to test the code. When all of the modules have been coded and tested, they are assembled into what should be a working program.

For team programming to succeed, it is essential that all of the module interfaces be defined explicitly and that the coded modules adhere strictly to the specifications for those interfaces. Obviously, global variable references must be carefully avoided in a team-programming situation because it is impossible for each person to know how the rest of the team is using every variable.

Testing and Debugging Hints

1. Make sure that variables used as arguments to a function are declared in the block where the function call is made.
2. Carefully define the precondition, postcondition, and parameter list to eliminate side effects. Variables used only in a function should be declared as local variables. *Do not* use global variables in your programs. (Exception: It is acceptable to reference `cin` and `cout` globally.)
3. If the compiler displays a message such as "UNDECLARED IDENTI-FIER," check that the identifier isn't misspelled (and that it is, in fact, declared), that the identifier is declared before it is referenced, and that the scope of the identifier includes the reference to it.
4. If you intend to use a local name that is the same as a nonlocal name, a misspelling in the local declaration will wreak havoc. The C++ compiler won't complain, but will cause every reference to the local name to go to the nonlocal name instead.

5. Remember that the same identifier cannot be used in both the parameter list and the outermost local declarations of a function.
6. With a value-returning function, be sure the function heading and prototype begin with the correct data type for the function return value.
7. With a value-returning function, don't forget to use a statement

   ```
   return Expression;
   ```

   to return the function value. Make sure the expression is of the correct type, or implicit type coercion will occur.
8. Remember that a call to a value-returning function is part of an expression, whereas a call to a void function is a separate statement. (C++ softens this distinction, however, by letting you call a value-returning function as if it were a void function, ignoring the return value. Be careful here.)
9. In general, don't use reference parameters in the parameter list of a value-returning function. A reference parameter must be used, however, when an I/O stream object is passed as a parameter.
10. If necessary, use your system's debugger (or use debug output statements) to indicate when a function is called and if it is executing correctly. The values of the arguments can be displayed immediately before the call to the function (to show the incoming values) and immediately after (to show the outgoing values). You also may want to display the values of local variables in the function itself to indicate what happens each time it is called.

Summary

The scope of an identifier refers to the parts of the program in which it is visible. C++ function names have global scope, as do the names of variables and constants that are declared outside all functions and namespaces. Variables and constants declared within a block have local scope; they are not visible outside the block. The parameters of a function have the same scope as local variables declared in the outermost block of the function.

With rare exceptions, it is not considered good practice to declare global variables and reference them directly from within a function. All communication between the modules of a program should be through the argument and parameter lists (and via the function value sent back by a value-returning function). The use of global constants, on the other hand, is considered to be an acceptable programming practice because it adds consistency and makes a program easier to change while avoiding the pitfalls of side effects. Well-designed and well-documented functions that are free of side effects can often be reused in other programs. Many programmers keep a library of functions that they use repeatedly.

The lifetime of a variable is the period of time during program execution when memory is allocated to it. Global variables have static lifetime (memory remains allocated for the duration of the program's execution). By default, local variables have automatic lifetime (memory is allocated and deallocated at block entry and block exit). A local variable may be given static lifetime by using the word `static` in its declaration. This variable has the lifetime of a global variable but the scope of a local variable.

C++ allows a variable to be initialized in its declaration. For a static variable, the initialization occurs once only—when control first reaches its declaration. An automatic variable is initialized each time control reaches the declaration.

C++ provides two kinds of subprograms, void functions and value-returning functions, for us to use. A value-returning function is called from within an expression and returns a single result that is used in the evaluation of the expression. For the function value to be returned, the last statement executed by the function must be a Return statement containing an expression of the appropriate data type.

All the scope rules, as well as the rules about reference and value parameters, apply to both void functions and value-returning functions. It is considered poor programming practice, however, to use reference parameters in a value-returning function definition. Doing so increases the potential for unintended side effects. (An exception is when I/O stream objects are passed as parameters. Other exceptions are noted in later chapters.)

We can use stubs and drivers to test functions in isolation from the rest of a program. They are particularly useful in the context of team-programming projects.

Quick Check

1. a. How can you tell if a variable that is referenced inside a function is local or global? (pp. 392–398)
   b. Where are local variables declared? (pp. 392–398)
   c. When does the scope of an identifier declared in block A exclude a block nested within block A? (pp. 392–398)
2. A program consists of two functions, `main` and `DoCalc`. A variable x is declared outside both functions. `DoCalc` declares two variables, a and b, within its body; b is declared as `static`. In what function(s) are each of a, b, and x visible, and what is the lifetime of each variable? (pp. 392–398, 403–404)
3. Why should you use value parameters whenever possible? Why should you avoid the use of global variables? (pp. 405–409, 420–421)
4. For each of the following, decide whether a value-returning function or a void function is the most appropriate implementation. (pp. 411–421)
   a. Selecting the larger of two values for further processing in an expression.
   b. Printing a paycheck.
   c. Computing the area of a hexagon.

    d. Testing whether an incoming value is valid and returning `true` if it is.

    e. Computing the two roots of a quadratic equation.

5.   What would the heading for a value-returning function named `Min` look like if it had two `float` parameters, `num1` and `num2`, and returned a `float` result? (pp. 411–421)

6.   What would a call to `Min` look like if the arguments were a variable named `deductions` and the literal `2000.0`? (pp. 411–421)

Answers   **1.** a. If the variable is not declared in either the body of the function or its parameter list, then the reference is global. b. Local variables are declared within a block (compound statement). c. When the nested block declares an identifier with the same name.   **2.** x is visible to both functions, but a and b are visible only within DoCalc. x and b are static variables; once memory is allocated to them, they are "alive" until the program terminates. a is an automatic variable; it is "alive" only while DoCalc is executing.   **3.** Both using value parameters and avoiding global variables will minimize side effects. Also, passing by value allows the arguments to be arbitrary expressions.   **4.** a. Value-returning function b. Void function c. Value-returning function d. Value-returning function e. Void function

5. `float Min( float num1,`
                 `float num2 )`

6. `smaller = Min(deductions, 2000.0);`

Exam Preparation Exercises

1.   If a function contains a locally declared variable with the same name as a global variable, no confusion results because references to variables in functions are first interpreted as references to local variables. (True or False?)

2.   Variables declared at the beginning of a block are accessible to all remaining statements in that block, including those in nested blocks (assuming the nested blocks don't declare local variables with the same names). (True or False?)

3.   Define the following terms.

    local variable   scope
    global variable side effects
    lifetime   name precedence (name hiding)

4.   What is the output of the following C++ program? (This program is an example of poor interface design practices.)

```
#include <iostream>

using namespace std;

void DoGlobal();
void DoLocal();
void DoReference( int& );
void DoValue( int );

int x;

int main()
{
    x = 15;
```

```
        DoReference(x);
        cout << "x = " << x << " after the call to DoReference."
            << endl;
        x = 16;
        DoValue(x);
        cout << "x = " << x << " after the call to DoValue."
            << endl;
        x = 17;
        DoLocal();
        cout << "x = " << x << " after the call to DoLocal."
            << endl;
        x = 18;
        DoGlobal();
        cout << "x = " << x << " after the call to DoGlobal."
            << endl;
        return 0;
}

void DoReference( int& a )
{
    a = 3;
}

void DoValue( int b )
{
    b = 4;
}

void DoLocal()
{
    int x;

    x = 5;
}

void DoGlobal()
{
    x = 7;
}
```

5. What is the output of the following program?

```
#include <iostream>

using namespace std;

void Test();

int main()
{
```

```
        Test ();
        Test ();
        Test ();
        return 0;
    }

void Test ()
{
    int i = 0;
    static int j = 0;

    i++;
    j++;
    cout << i << ' ' << j << endl;
}
```

6. The following function calculates the sum of the integers from 1 through n. However, it has an unintended side effect. What is it?

```
void SumInts ( int& n,
               int& sum )
{
    sum = 0;
    while (n >= 1)
    {
        sum = sum + n;
        n = n - 1;
    }
}
```

7. Given the function heading

```
bool HighTaxBracket ( int inc,
                      int ded )
```

is the following statement a legal call to the function if income and deductions are of type int?

```
if (HighTaxBracket (income, deductions))
    cout << "Upper Class";
```

8. The statement

```
Power (k, 1, m);
```

is a call to the void function whose definition follows. Rewrite the function as a value-returning function, then write a function call that assigns the function value to the variable m.

```
void Power ( float   base,
             int     exponent,
             float&  answer   )
{
    int i;
```

```
    answer = 1.0;
    i = 1;
    while (i <= exponent)
    {
        answer = answer * base;
        i++;
    }
}
```

9. You are given the following `Test` function and a C++ program in which the variables a, b, c, and `result` are declared to be of type `float`. In the calling code, a = −5.0, b = 0.1, and c = 16.2. What is the value of `result` when each of the following calls returns?

```
float Test( float x,
            float y,
            float z )
{
    if (x > y || y > z)
        return 0.5;
    else
        return -0.5;
}
```

   a. `result = Test(5.2, 5.3, 5.6);`
   b. `result = Test(fabs(a), b, c);`

10. What is wrong with each of the following C++ function definitions?
   a. `void Test1( int m,`
      `             int n )`

```
   {
       return 3 * m + n;
   }
```

   b. `float Test2( int   i,`
      `              float x )`

```
   {
       i = i + 7;
       x = 4.8 + float(i);
   }
```

11. Explain why it is risky to use a reference parameter as a parameter of a value-returning function.

Programming Warm-up Exercises

1. The following program is written with very poor style. For one thing, global variables are used in place of arguments. Rewrite it without global variables, using good programming style.

```
#include <iostream>
using namespace std;
void MashGlobals();
```

```
int a, b, c;
int main()
{
cin >> a >> b >> c;
MashGlobals();
cout << "a=" << a << ' ' << "b=" << b << ' '
<< "c=" << c << endl;
return 0;
}
void MashGlobals()
{
int temp;
temp = a + b;
a = b + c;
b = temp;
}
```

2. Write the heading for a value-returning function `Epsilon` that receives two `float` parameters named `high` and `low` and returns a `float` result.

3. Write the heading for a value-returning function named `NearlyEqual` that receives three `float` parameters—`num1`, `num2`, and `difference`—and returns a Boolean result.

4. Given the heading you wrote in Exercise 3, write the body of the function. The function returns `true` if the absolute value of the difference between `num1` and `num2` is less than the value in `difference` and returns `false` otherwise.

5. Write a value-returning function named `CompassHeading` that returns the sum of its four `float` parameters: `trueCourse`, `windCorrAngle`, `variance`, and `deviation`.

6. Write a value-returning function named `FracPart` that receives a floating-point number and returns the fractional part of that number. Use a single parameter named `x`. For example, if the incoming value of `x` is 16.753, the function return value is 0.753.

7. Write a value-returning function named `Circumf` that finds the circumference of a circle given the radius. The formula for calculating the circumference of a circle is π multiplied by twice the radius. Use 3.14159 for π.

8. Given the function heading

```
float Hypotenuse( float side1,
                  float side2 )
```

write the body of the function to return the length of the hypotenuse of a right triangle. The parameters represent the lengths of the other two sides. The formula for the hypotenuse is

$$\sqrt{side1^2 + side2^2}$$

9. Write a value-returning function named `FifthPow` that returns the fifth power of its `float` parameter.

10. Write a value-returning function named `Min` that returns the smallest of its three integer parameters.

11. The following If conditions work correctly on most, but not all, machines. Rewrite them using the "is..." functions from the C++ standard library (header file cctype).

    a. if (inChar >= '0' && inChar <= '9')
           DoSomething();
    b. if (inChar >= 'A' && inChar <= 'Z' ||
           inChar >= 'a' && inChar <= 'z'   )
           DoSomething();
    c. if (inChar >= 'A' && inChar <= 'Z' ||
           inChar >= '0' && inChar <= '9'   )
           DoSomething();
    d. if (inChar < 'a' || inChar > 'z')
           DoSomething();

12. Write a Boolean value-returning function IsPrime that receives an integer parameter n, tests it to see if it is a prime number, and returns true if it is. (A prime number is an integer greater than or equal to 2 whose only divisors are 1 and the number itself.) A call to this function might look like this:

    if (IsPrime(n))
        cout << n << " is a prime number.";

    (*Hint:* If n is not a prime number, it is exactly divisible by an integer in the range 2 through $\sqrt{n}$.)

13. Write a value-returning function named Postage that returns the cost of mailing a package, given the weight of the package in pounds and ounces and the cost per ounce.

Programming Problems

1. If a principal amount P, for which the interest is compounded Q times per year, is placed in a savings account, then the amount of money in the account (the balance) after N years is given by the following formula, where I is the annual interest rate as a floating-point number:

    $$balance = P \times \left(1 + \frac{I}{Q}\right)^{N \times Q}$$

    Write a C++ program that inputs the values for P, I, Q, and N and outputs the balance for each year up through year N. Use a value-returning function to compute the balance. Your program should prompt the user appropriately, label the output values, and have good style.

2. Euclid's algorithm is a method for finding the greatest common divisor (GCD) of two positive integers. It states that for any two positive integers M and N such that $M \le N$, the GCD is calculated as follows:

    a. Divide N by M.
    b. If the remainder $R = 0$, then the GCD = M.
    c. If $R > 0$, then M becomes N, and R becomes M, and repeat from step (a) until $R = 0$.

Write a program that uses a value-returning function to find the GCD of two numbers. The main function reads pairs of numbers from a file stream named dataFile. For each pair read in, the two numbers and the GCD should be labeled properly and written to a file stream named gcdList.

3. The distance to the landing point of a projectile, launched at an angle angle (in radians) with an initial velocity of velocity (in feet per second), ignoring air resistance, is given by the formula

$$distance = \frac{velocity^2 \times \sin{(2 \times angle)}}{32.2}$$

Write a C++ program that implements a game in which the user first enters the distance to a target. The user then enters the angle and velocity for launching a projectile. If the projectile comes within 0.1% of the distance to the target, the user wins the game. If the projectile doesn't come close enough, the user is told how far off the projectile is and is allowed to try again. If there isn't a winning input after five tries, then the user loses the game.

To simplify input for the user, your program should allow the angle to be input in degrees. The formula for converting degrees to radians is

$$radians = \frac{degrees \times 3.14159265}{180.0}$$

Each of the formulas in this problem should be implemented as a C++ value-returning function. Your program should prompt the user for input appropriately, label the output values, and have proper programming style.

4. Write a program that computes the number of days between two dates. One way of doing this is to have the program compute the Julian day number for each date and subtract one from the other. The Julian day number is the number of days that have elapsed since noon on January 1, 4713 B.C. The following algorithm can be used to calculate the Julian day number.

Given year (an integer, such as 2001), month (an integer from 1 through 12), and day (an integer from 1 through 31), if month is 1 or 2, then subtract 1 from year and add 12 to month.

If the date comes from the Gregorian calendar (later than October 15, 1582), then compute an intermediate result with the following formula (otherwise, let intRes1 equal 0):

$$intRes1 = 2 - year / 100 + year / 400 \quad \text{(integer division)}$$

Compute a second intermediate result with the formula

$$intRes2 = int(365.25 \times year)$$

Compute a third intermediate result with the formula

$$intRes3 = int(30.6001 \times (month + 1))$$

Finally, the Julian day number is computed with the formula

$$julianDay = intRes1 + intRes2 + intRes3 + day + 1720994.5$$

Your program should make appropriate use of value-returning functions in solving this problem. These formulas require nine significant digits; you may have to use the integer type long and the floating-point type double. Your program should prompt appropriately for input (the two dates) if it is to be run interactively. Use proper style with appropriate comments.

Case Study Follow-Up

1. Supply the missing precondition and postcondition in the comments at the beginning of each function in the ConvertDates program.
2. Add data validation to the ConvertDates program as follows.
    a. Have the program check the input characters and print an error message if any of the "digits" are not numeric characters ('0' through '9'). This validation test should be written as a separate function.
    b. Have the program check the date to be sure that it is valid. month should be in the range 01 through 12, and day should be in the appropriate range for the particular month. (For example, reject a date of 06/31/99 because June has only 30 days.) Remember that February can have either 28 or 29 days, depending on the year. This validation test should be written as a separate function.
3. Modify the ConvertDates program so that it can input the dates with digits separated by either slashes (/) or dashes (–).
4. In the Starship program, the main function neglects to guarantee any of the function preconditions before calling the functions. Modify the GetData function to validate the input data. When control returns from GetData, the main function should be able to assume that all the data values are within the proper ranges.

9

Additional Control Structures

GOALS

- To be able to write a Switch statement for a multiway branching problem.
- To be able to write a Do-While statement and contrast it with a While statement.
- To be able to write a For statement as an alternative to a While statement.
- To understand the purpose of the Break and Continue statements.
- To be able to choose the most appropriate looping statement for a given problem.

In the preceding chapters, we introduced C++ statements for sequence, selection, loop, and subprogram structures. In some cases, we introduced more than one way of implementing these structures. For example, selection may be implemented by an If-Then structure or an If-Then-Else structure. The If-Then is sufficient to implement any selection structure, but C++ provides the If-Then-Else for convenience because the two-way branch is frequently used in programming.

This chapter introduces five new statements that are also nonessential to, but nonetheless convenient for, programming. One, the Switch statement, makes it easier to write selection structures that have many branches. Two new looping statements, For and Do-While, make it easier to program certain types of loops. The other two statements, Break and Continue, are control statements that are used as part of larger looping and selection structures.

The Switch Statement

The Switch statement is a selection control structure that allows us to list any number of branches. In other words, it is a control structure for multi-way branches. A Switch is similar to nested If statements. The value of the **switch expression**—an expression whose value is matched with a label attached to a branch—determines which one of the branches is executed. For example, look at the following statement:

```
switch (letter)
{
    case 'X' : Statement1;
                 break;
    case 'L' :
    case 'M' : Statement2;
                 break;
    case 'S' : Statement3;
                 break;
    default  : Statement4;
}
Statement5;
```

In this example, `letter` is the switch expression. The statement means "If `letter` is 'X', execute Statement1 and break out of the Switch statement, continuing with Statement5. If `letter` is 'L' or 'M', execute Statement2 and continue with Statement5. If `letter` is 'S', execute Statement3 and continue with Statement5. If `letter` is none of the characters mentioned, execute Statement4 and continue with Statement5." The Break statement causes an immediate exit from the Switch statement. We'll see shortly what happens if we omit the Break statements.

Switch expression   The expression whose value determines which switch label is selected. It cannot be a floating-point or string expression.

The syntax template for the Switch statement is

SwitchStatement

```
switch ( IntegralOrEnumExpression )
{
        SwitchLabel ...   Statement
              ⋮
}
```

IntegralOrEnumExpression is an expression of integral type—char, short, int, long, bool—or of enum type (we discuss enum in the next chapter). The optional SwitchLabel in front of a statement is either a *case label* or a *default label:*

SwitchLabel

```
⎧  case ConstantExpression :
⎨
⎩  default :
```

In a case label, ConstantExpression is an integral or enum expression whose operands must be literal or named constants. The following are examples of constant integral expressions (where CLASS_SIZE is a named constant of type int):

```
3
CLASS_SIZE
'A'
2 * CLASS_SIZE + 1
```

The data type of ConstantExpression is coerced, if necessary, to match the type of the switch expression.

In our opening example that tests the value of `letter`, the following are the case labels:

```
case 'X' :
case 'L' :
case 'M' :
case 'S' :
```

As that example shows, a single statement may be preceded by more than one case label. Each case value may appear only once in a given Switch statement. If a value appears more than once, a syntax error results. Also, there can be only one default label in a Switch statement.

The flow of control through a Switch statement goes like this. First, the switch expression is evaluated. If this value matches one of the values in a case label, control branches to the statement following that case label. From there, control proceeds sequentially until either a Break statement or the end of the Switch statement is encountered. If the value of the switch expression doesn't match any case value, then one of two things happens. If there is a default label, control branches to the statement following that label. If there is no default label, all statements within the Switch are skipped and control simply proceeds to the statement following the entire Switch statement.

The following Switch statement prints an appropriate comment based on a student's grade (`grade` is of type `char`):

```
switch (grade)
{
    case 'A' :
    case 'B' : cout << "Good Work";
               break;
    case 'C' : cout << "Average Work";
               break;
    case 'D' :
    case 'F' : cout << "Poor Work";
               numberInTrouble++;
               break;                    // Unnecessary, but a good habit
}
```

Notice that the final Break statement is unnecessary. But programmers often include it anyway. One reason is that it's easier to insert another case label at the end if a Break statement is already present.

If `grade` does not contain one of the specified characters, none of the statements within the Switch is executed. Unless a precondition of the Switch statement is that `grade` is definitely one of 'A', 'B', 'C', 'D', or 'F', it would be wise to include a default label to account for an invalid grade:

```
switch (grade)
{
    case 'A' :
    case 'B' : cout << "Good Work";
               break;
    case 'C' : cout << "Average Work";
               break;
    case 'D' :
    case 'F' : cout << "Poor Work";
               numberInTrouble++;
               break;
    default  : cout << grade << " is not a valid letter grade.";
               break;
}
```

A Switch statement with a Break statement after each case alternative behaves exactly like an If-Then-Else-If control structure. For example, our Switch statement is equivalent to the following code:

```
if (grade == 'A' || grade == 'B')
    cout << "Good Work";
else if (grade == 'C')
    cout << "Average Work";
else if (grade == 'D' || grade == 'F')
{
    cout << "Poor Work";
    numberInTrouble++;
}
else
    cout << grade << " is not a valid letter grade.";
```

Is either of these two versions better than the other? There is no absolute answer to this question. For this particular example, our opinion is that the Switch statement is easier to understand because of its two-dimensional, table-like form. But some may find the If-Then-Else-If version easier to read. When implementing a multiway branching structure, our advice is to write down both a Switch and an If-Then-Else-If and then compare them for readability. Keep in mind that C++ provides the Switch statement as a matter of convenience. Don't feel obligated to use a Switch statement for every multiway branch.

Finally, we said we would look at what happens if you omit the Break statements inside a Switch statement. Let's rewrite our letter grade example without the Break statements:

```
switch (grade)      // Wrong version
{
    case 'A' :
    case 'B' : cout << "Good Work";
    case 'C' : cout << "Average Work";
    case 'D' :
    case 'F' : cout << "Poor Work";
                numberInTrouble++;
    default  : cout << grade << " is not a valid letter grade.";
}
```

If `grade` happens to be 'H', control branches to the statement at the default label and the output is

```
H is not a valid letter grade.
```

Unfortunately, this case alternative is the only one that works correctly. If `grade` is 'A', the resulting output is this:

```
Good WorkAverage WorkPoor WorkA is not a valid letter grade.
```

Remember that after a branch is taken to a specific case label, control proceeds sequentially until either a Break statement or the end of the Switch statement is encountered. Forgetting a Break statement in a case alternative is a very common source of errors in C++ programs.

MAY WE INTRODUCE

Admiral Grace Murray Hopper

From 1943 until her death on New Year's Day in 1992, Admiral Grace Murray Hopper was intimately involved with computing. In 1991, she was awarded the National Medal of Technology "for her pioneering accomplishments in the development of computer programming languages that simplified computer technology and opened the door to a significantly larger universe of users."

Admiral Hopper was born Grace Brewster Murray in New York City on December 9, 1906. She attended Vassar and received a Ph.D. in mathematics from Yale. For the next ten years, she taught mathematics at Vassar.

In 1943, Admiral Hopper joined the U.S. Navy and was assigned to the Bureau of Ordnance Computation Project at Harvard University as a programmer on the Mark I. After the war, she remained at Harvard as a faculty member and continued work on the Navy's Mark II and Mark III computers. In 1949, she joined Eckert-Mauchly Computer Corporation and worked on the UNIVAC I. It was there that she made a legendary contribution to computing: She discovered the first computer "bug"—a moth caught in the hardware.

Admiral Hopper had a working compiler in 1952, at a time when the conventional wisdom was that computers could do only arithmetic. Although not on the committee that designed the computer language COBOL, she was active in its design, implementation, and use. COBOL (which stands for Common Business-Oriented Language) was developed in the early 1960s and is still widely used in business data processing.

Admiral Hopper retired from the Navy in 1966, only to be recalled within a year to full-time active duty. Her mission was to oversee the Navy's efforts to maintain uniformity in programming languages. It has been said that just as Admiral Hyman Rickover was the father of the nuclear navy, Rear Admiral Hopper was the mother of computerized data automation in the Navy. She served with the Naval Data Automation Command until she retired again in 1986 with the rank of rear admiral. At the time of her death, she was a senior consultant at Digital Equipment Corporation.

During her lifetime, Admiral Hopper received honorary degrees from more than 40 colleges and universities. She was honored by her peers on several occasions, including the first Computer Sciences Man of the Year award given by the Data Processing Management Association, and the Contributions to Computer Science Education Award given by the Special Interest Group for Computer Science Education of the ACM (Association for Computing Machinery).

Admiral Hopper loved young people and enjoyed giving talks on college and university campuses. She often handed out colored wires, which she called nanoseconds because they were cut to a length of about one foot—the distance that light travels in a nanosecond (billionth of a second). Her advice to the young was, "You manage things, you lead people. We went overboard on management and forgot about leadership."

When asked which of her many accomplishments she was most proud of, she answered, "All the young people I have trained over the years."

The Do-While Statement

The Do-While statement is a looping control structure in which the loop condition is tested at the end (bottom) of the loop. This format guarantees that the loop body executes at least once. The syntax template for the Do-While is this:

DoWhileStatement

```
do
      Statement
while ( Expression ) ;
```

As usual in C++, Statement is either a single statement or a block. Also, note that the Do-While ends with a semicolon.

The Do-While statement

```
do
{
    Statement1;
    Statement2;
      ⋮
    StatementN;
} while (Expression);
```

means "Execute the statements between do and while as long as Expression still has the value true at the end of the loop."

Let's compare a While loop and a Do-While loop that do the same task: They find the first period in a file of data. Assume that there is at least one period in the file.

While Solution

```
dataFile >> inputChar;
while (inputChar != '.')
    dataFile >> inputChar;
```

Do-While Solution

```
do
    dataFile >> inputChar;
while (inputChar != '.');
```

The While solution requires a priming read so that `inputChar` has a value before the loop is entered. This isn't required for the Do-While solution because the input statement within the loop is executed before the loop condition is evaluated.

Let's look at another example. Suppose a program needs to read a person's age interactively. The program requires that the age be positive. The following loops ensure that the input value is positive before the program proceeds any further.

While Solution

```
cout << "Enter your age: ";
cin >> age;
while (age <= 0)
{
    cout << "Your age must be positive." << endl;
    cout << "Enter your age: ";
    cin >> age;
}
```

Do-While Solution

```
do
{
    cout << "Enter your age: ";
    cin >> age;
    if (age <= 0)
        cout << "Your age must be positive." << endl;
} while (age <= 0);
```

Notice that the Do-While solution does not require the prompt and input steps to appear twice—once before the loop and once within it—but it does test the input value twice.

We can also use the Do-While to implement a count-controlled loop *if* we know in advance that the loop body should always execute at least once. Below are two versions of a loop to sum the integers from 1 through n.

While Solution

```
sum = 0;
counter = 1;
while (counter <= n)
{
    sum = sum + counter;
    counter++;
}
```

Do-While Solution

```
sum = 0;
counter = 1;
do
{
    sum = sum + counter;
    counter++;
} while (counter <= n);
```

If n is a positive number, both of these versions are equivalent. But if n is 0 or negative, the two loops give different results. In the While version, the final value of sum is 0 because the loop body is never entered. In the Do-While version, the final value of sum is 1 because the body executes once and *then* the loop test is made.

Because the While statement tests the condition before executing the body of the loop, it is called a *pretest loop*. The Do-While statement does

FIGURE 9-1

Flow of Control: While and Do-While

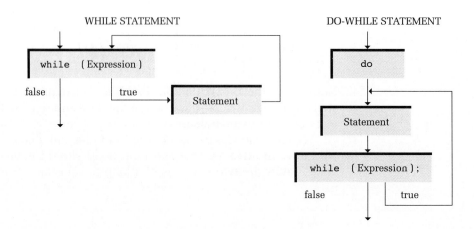

the opposite and thus is known as a *posttest loop.* Figure 9-1 compares the flow of control in the While and Do-While loops.

After we look at two other new looping constructs, we offer some guidelines for determining when to use each type of loop.

The For Statement

The For statement is designed to simplify the writing of count-controlled loops. The following statement prints out the integers from 1 through n:

```
for (count = 1; count <= n; count++)
    cout << count << endl;
```

This For statement means "Initialize the loop control variable count to 1. While count is less than or equal to n, execute the output statement and increment count by 1. Stop the loop after count has been incremented to n + 1."

In C++, a For statement is merely a compact notation for a While loop. In fact, the compiler essentially translates a For statement into an equivalent While loop as follows:

The syntax template for a For statement is

ForStatement

```
for ( InitStatement Expression1 ; Expression2 )
    Statement
```

Expression1 is the While condition. InitStatement can be one of the follow-ing: the null statement (just a semicolon), a declaration statement (which always ends in a semicolon), or an expression statement (an expression ending in a semicolon). Therefore, there is always a semicolon before Expression1. (This semicolon isn't shown in the syntax template because InitStatement always ends with its own semicolon.)

Most often, a For statement is written such that InitStatement initial-izes a loop control variable and Expression2 increments or decrements the loop control variable. Here are two loops that execute the same number of times (50):

```
for (loopCount = 1; loopCount <= 50; loopCount++)
    ⋮

for (loopCount = 50; loopCount >= 1; loopCount--)
    ⋮
```

Just like While loops, Do-While and For loops may be nested. For example, the nested For structure

```
for (lastNum = 1; lastNum <= 7; lastNum++)
{
    for (numToPrint = 1; numToPrint <= lastNum; numToPrint++)
        cout << numToPrint;
    cout << endl;
}
```

prints the following triangle of numbers.

```
1
12
123
1234
12345
123456
1234567
```

Although For statements are used primarily for count-controlled loops, C++ allows you to write *any* While loop by using a For statement. To use For loops intelligently, you should know the following facts.

1. In the syntax template, InitStatement can be the null statement, and Expression2 is optional. If Expression2 is omitted, there is no statement for the compiler to insert at the bottom of the loop. As a result, you could write the While loop

```
while (inputVal != 999)
    cin >> inputVal;
```

as the equivalent For loop

```
for ( ; inputVal != 999; )
    cin >> inputVal;
```

2. According to the syntax template, Expression1—the While condition—is optional. If you omit it, the expression `true` is assumed. The loop

```
for ( ; ; )
    cout "Hi" << endl;
```

is equivalent to the While loop

```
while (true)
    cout << "Hi" << endl;
```

Both of these are infinite loops that print "Hi" endlessly.

3. The initializing statement, InitStatement, can be a declaration with initialization:

```
for (int i = 1; i <= 20; i++)
    cout << "Hi" << endl;
```

Here, the variable i has local scope, even though there are no braces creating a block. The scope of i extends only to the end of the For statement. Like any local variable, i is inaccessible outside its scope (that is, outside the For statement). Because i is local to the For statement, it's possible to write code like this:

```
for (int i = 1; i <= 20; i++)
    cout << "Hi" << endl;
for (int i = 1; i <= 100; i++)
    cout << "Ed" << endl;
```

This code does *not* generate a compile-time error (such as "MULTIPLY DEFINED IDENTIFIER"). We have declared two distinct variables named i, each of which is local to its own For statement.*

As you have seen by now, the For statement in C++ is a very flexible structure. Its use can range from a simple count-controlled loop to a general-purpose, "anything goes" While loop. Some programmers squeeze a lot of work into the heading (the first line) of a For statement. For example, the program fragment

```
cin >> ch;
while (ch != '.')
    cin >> ch;
```

can be compressed into the following For loop:

```
for (cin >> ch; ch != '.'; cin >> ch)
    ;
```

Because all the work is done in the For heading, there is nothing for the loop body to do. The body is simply the null statement.

With For statements, our advice is to keep things simple. The trickier the code is, the harder it will be for another person (or you!) to understand your code and track down errors. In this book, we use For loops for count-controlled loops only.

The Break and Continue Statements

The Break statement, which we introduced with the Switch statement, is also used with loops. A Break statement causes an immediate exit from the innermost Switch, While, Do-While, or For statement in which it appears. Notice the word *innermost*. If break is in a loop that is nested inside another loop, control exits the inner loop but not the outer.

One of the more common ways of using break with loops is to set up an infinite loop and use If tests to exit the loop. Suppose we want to input ten pairs of integers, performing data validation and computing the square root of the sum of each pair. For data validation, assume that the first number of each pair must be less than 100 and the second must be greater than 50. Also, after each input, we want to test the state of the stream for EOF. Here's a loop using Break statements to accomplish the task:

---

* In versions of C++ prior to the ISO/ANSI language standard, i would not be local to the body of the loop. Its scope would extend to the end of the block surrounding the For statement. In other words, it would be as if i had been declared outside the loop. If you are using an older version of C++ and your compiler tells you something like "MULTIPLY DEFINED IDENTIFIER" in code similar to the pair of For statements above, simply choose a different variable name in the second For loop.

```
loopCount = 1;
while (true)
{
    cin >> num1;
    if ( !cin || num1 >= 100)
        break;
    cin >> num2;
    if ( !cin || num2 <= 50)
        break;
    cout << sqrt(float(num1 + num2)) << endl;
    loopCount++;
    if (loopCount > 10)
        break;
}
```

Note that we could have used a For loop to count from 1 to 10, breaking out of it as necessary. However, this loop is both count-controlled and event-controlled, so we prefer to use a While loop.

The above loop contains three distinct exit points. Some people vigorously oppose this style of programming, as it violates the single-entry, single-exit philosophy we discussed with multiple returns from a function. Is there any advantage to using an infinite loop in conjunction with break? To answer this question, let's rewrite the loop without using Break statements. The loop must terminate when num1 is invalid or num2 is invalid or loopCount exceeds 10. We'll use Boolean flags to signal invalid data in the While condition:

```
num1Valid = true;
num2Valid = true;
loopCount = 1;
while (num1Valid && num2Valid && loopCount <= 10)
{
    cin >> num1;
    if ( !cin || num1 >= 100)
        num1Valid = false;
    else
    {
        cin >> num2;
        if ( !cin || num2 <= 50)
            num2Valid = false;
        else
        {
            cout << sqrt(float(num1 + num2)) << endl;
            loopCount++;
        }
    }
}
```

One could argue that the first version is easier to follow and understand than this second version. The primary task of the loop body—computing the square root of the sum of the numbers—is more prominent in the first version. In the second version, the computation is obscured by being buried within nested Ifs. The second version also has a more complicated control flow.

The disadvantage of using `break` with loops is that it can become a crutch for those who are too impatient to think carefully about loop design. It's easy to overuse (and abuse) the technique. Here's an example, printing the integers 1 through 5:

```
i = 1;
while (true)
{
    cout << i;
    if (i == 5)
        break;
    i++;
}
```

There is no real justification for setting up the loop this way. Conceptually, it is a pure count-controlled loop, and a simple For loop does the job:

```
for (i = 1; i <= 5; i++)
    cout << i;
```

The For loop is easier to understand and is less prone to error.

A good rule of thumb is: Use `break` within loops only as a last resort. Specifically, use it only to avoid baffling combinations of multiple Boolean flags and nested Ifs.

Another statement that alters the flow of control in a C++ program is the Continue statement. This statement, valid only in loops, terminates the current loop iteration (but not the entire loop). It causes an immediate branch to the bottom of the loop—skipping the rest of the statements in the loop body—in preparation for the next iteration. Here is an example of a reading loop in which we want to process only the positive numbers in an input file:

```
for (dataCount = 1; dataCount <= 500; dataCount++)
{
    dataFile >> inputVal;
    if (inputVal <= 0)
        continue;
    cout << inputVal;
        ⋮
}
```

If `inputVal` is less than or equal to 0, control branches to the bottom of the loop. Then, as with any For loop, the computer increments `dataCount` and performs the loop test before going on to the next iteration.

The Continue statement is not used often, but we present it for completeness (and because you may run across it in other people's programs). Its primary purpose is to avoid obscuring the main process of the loop by indenting the process within an If statement. For example, the above code would be written without a Continue statement as follows:

```
for (dataCount = 1; dataCount <= 500; dataCount++)
{
    dataFile >> inputVal;
    if (inputVal > 0)
    {
        cout << inputVal;
        ⋮
    }
}
```

Be sure to note the difference between `continue` and `break`. The Continue statement means "Abandon the current iteration of the loop, and go on to the next iteration." The Break statement means "Exit the entire loop immediately."

Guidelines for Choosing a Looping Statement

Here are some guidelines to help you decide when to use each of the three looping statements (While, Do-While, and For).

1. If the loop is a simple count-controlled loop, the For statement is a natural. Concentrating the three loop control actions—initialize, test, and increment/decrement—into one location (the heading of the For statement) reduces the chances of forgetting to include one of them.
2. If the loop is an event-controlled loop whose body should execute at least once, a Do-While statement is appropriate.
3. If the loop is an event-controlled loop and nothing is known about the first execution, use a While (or perhaps a For) statement.
4. When in doubt, use a While statement.
5. An infinite loop with Break statements sometimes clarifies the code but more often reflects an undisciplined loop design. Use it only after careful consideration of While, Do-While, and For.

PROBLEM-SOLVING CASE STUDY

Monthly Rainfall Averages

Problem: Meteorologists have recorded monthly rainfall amounts at several sites throughout a region of the country. You have been asked to write an interactive program that lets the user enter one year's rainfall amounts at a particular site and prints out the average of the 12 values. After the data for a site is processed, the program asks whether the user would like to repeat the process for another recording site. A user response of 'y' means yes, and 'n' means no. The program must trap erroneous input data (negative values for rainfall amounts and invalid responses to the "Do you wish to continue?" prompt).

Input: For each recording site, 12 floating-point rainfall amounts. For each "Do you wish to continue?" prompt, either a 'y' or an 'n'.

Output: For each recording site, the floating-point average of the 12 rainfall amounts, displayed to two decimal places.

Discussion: A solution to this problem requires several looping structures. At the topmost level of the design, we need a loop to process the data from all the sites. Each iteration must process one site's data, then ask the user whether to continue with another recording site. The program does not know in advance how many recording sites there are, so the loop cannot be a count-controlled loop. Although we can make any of For, While, or Do-While work correctly, we'll use a Do-While under the assumption that the user definitely wants to process at least one site's data. Therefore, we can set up the loop so that it processes the data from a recording site and then, at the *bottom* of the loop, decides whether to iterate again.

Another loop is required to input 12 monthly rainfall amounts and form their sum. Using the summing technique we are familiar with by now, we initialize the sum to 0 before starting the loop, and each loop iteration reads another number and adds it to the accumulating sum. A For loop is appropriate for this task, because we know that exactly 12 iterations must occur.

We'll need two more loops to perform data validation—one loop to ensure that a rainfall amount is nonnegative and another to verify that the user types only 'y' or 'n' when prompted to continue. As we saw earlier in the chapter, Do-While loops are well suited to this kind of data validation. We want the loop body to execute at least once, reading an input value and testing for valid data. As long as the user keeps entering invalid data, the loop continues. Control exits the loop only when the user finally gets it right.

PROBLEM-SOLVING CASE STUDY _cont'd._

Assumptions: The user processes data for at least one site.

Main   **Level 0**

```
DO
      Get 12 rainfall amounts and sum them
      Print sum / 12
      Prompt user to continue
      Get yes or no response ('y' or 'n')
WHILE response is 'y'
```

Get 12 Amounts (Out: sum)   **Level 1**

```
Set sum = 0
FOR count going from 1 through 12
      Prompt user for a rainfall amount
      Get and verify one rainfall amount
      Add amount to sum
```

Get Yes or No (Out: response)

```
DO
      Read response
      IF response isn't 'y' or 'n'
              Print error message
WHILE response isn't 'y' or 'n'
```

Get One Amount (Out: amount)   **Level 2**

```
DO
        Read amount
        IF amount < 0.0
                Print error message
WHILE amount < 0.0
```

Module Structure Chart:

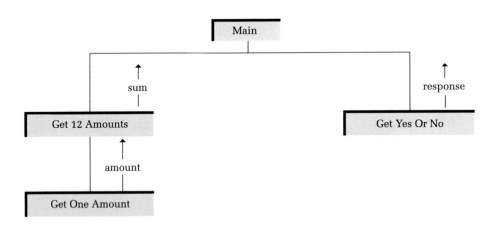

(The following program is written in ISO/ANSI standard C++. If you are working with pre–standard C++, see the alternate version of the program in the PRE_STD directory of the program disk, available at the publisher's Web site, www.jbpub.com/disks.)

PROBLEM-SOLVING CASE STUDY cont'd.

```cpp
//******************************************************************
// Rainfall program
// This program inputs 12 monthly rainfall amounts from a
// recording site and computes the average monthly rainfall.
// This process is repeated for as many recording sites as
// the user wishes.
//******************************************************************
#include <iostream>
#include <iomanip>      // For setprecision()

using namespace std;

void Get12Amounts( float& );
void GetOneAmount( float& );
void GetYesOrNo( char& );

int main()
{
    float sum;          // Sum of 12 rainfall amounts
    char  response;     // User response ('y' or 'n')

    cout << fixed << showpoint               // Set up floating-pt.
        << setprecision(2);                  //    output format

    do
    {
        Get12Amounts(sum);
        cout << endl << "Average rainfall is " << sum / 12.0
            << " inches" << endl << endl;
        cout << "Do you have another recording site? (y or n) ";
        GetYesOrNo(response);
    } while (response == 'y');
    return 0;
}

//******************************************************************

void Get12Amounts( /* out */ float& sum )   // Sum of 12 rainfall
                                            // amounts

// Inputs 12 monthly rainfall amounts, verifying that
// each is nonnegative, and returns their sum

// Postcondition:
//      12 rainfall amounts have been read and verified to be
//      nonnegative
//   && sum == sum of the 12 input values
```

PROBLEM-SOLVING CASE STUDY cont'd.

```cpp
{
    int   count;      // Loop control variable
    float amount;     // Rainfall amount for one month

    sum = 0;
    for (count = 1; count <= 12; count++)
    {
        cout << "Enter rainfall amount " << count << ": ";
        GetOneAmount(amount);
        sum = sum + amount;
    }
}

//****************************************************************

void GetYesOrNo( /* out */ char& response )    // User response char

// Inputs a character from the user and, if necessary,
// repeatedly prints an error message and inputs another
// character if the character isn't 'y' or 'n'

// Postcondition:
//      response has been input (repeatedly, if necessary, along
//      with output of an error message)
//   && response == 'y' or 'n'

{
    do
    {
        cin >> response;
        if (response != 'y' && response != 'n')
            cout << "Please type y or n: ";
    } while (response != 'y' && response != 'n');
}

//****************************************************************

void GetOneAmount( /* out */ float& amount )    // Rainfall amount
                                                // for one month

// Inputs one month's rainfall amount and, if necessary,
// repeatedly prints an error message and inputs another
// value if the value is negative
```

```
// Postcondition:
//     amount has been input (repeatedly, if necessary, along
//     with output of an error message)
//  && amount >= 0.0

{
    do
    {
        cin >> amount;
        if (amount < 0.0)
            cout << "Amount cannot be negative. Enter again: ";
    } while (amount < 0.0);
}
```

Testing: We should test two separate aspects of the Rainfall program. First, we should verify that the program works correctly given valid input data. Supplying arbitrary rainfall amounts of 0 or greater, we must confirm that the program correctly adds up the values and divides by 12 to produce the average. Also, we should make sure that the program behaves correctly whether we type 'y' or 'n' when prompted to continue.

The second aspect to test is the data validation code that we included in the program. When prompted for a rainfall amount, we should type negative numbers repeatedly to verify that an error message is printed and that we cannot escape the Do-While loop until we eventually type a nonnegative number. Similarly, when prompted to type 'y' or 'n' to process another recording site, we must press several incorrect keys to exercise the loop in the GetYesOrNo function. Here's a sample run showing the testing of the data validation code:

```
Enter rainfall amount 1: 0
Enter rainfall amount 2: 0
Enter rainfall amount 3: 0
Enter rainfall amount 4: 3.4
Enter rainfall amount 5: 9.6
Enter rainfall amount 6: 1.2
Enter rainfall amount 7: -3.4
Amount cannot be negative. Enter again: -9
Amount cannot be negative. Enter again: -4.2
Amount cannot be negative. Enter again: 1.3
Enter rainfall amount 8: 0
Enter rainfall amount 9: 0
Enter rainfall amount 10: 0
Enter rainfall amount 11: 0
Enter rainfall amount 12: 0
```

```
Average rainfall is 1.29 inches

Do you have another recording site? (y or n)  d
Please type y or n: q
Please type y or n: Y
Please type y or n: n
```

Testing and Debugging

The same testing techniques we used with While loops apply to Do-While and For loops. There are, however, a few additional considerations with these loops.

The body of a Do-While loop always executes at least once. Thus, you should try data sets that show the result of executing a Do-While loop the minimal number of times.

With a data-dependent For loop, it is important to test for proper results when the loop executes zero times. This occurs when the starting value is greater than the ending value (or less than the ending value if the loop control variable is being decremented).

When a program contains a Switch statement, you should test it with enough different data sets to ensure that each branch is selected and executed correctly. You should also test the program with a switch expression whose value is not in any of the case labels.

Testing and Debugging Hints

1. In a Switch statement, make sure there is a Break statement at the end of each case alternative. Otherwise, control "falls through" to the code in the next case alternative.
2. Case labels in a Switch statement are made up of values, not variables. They may, however, include named constants and expressions involving only constants.
3. A switch expression cannot be a floating-point or string expression, and case constants cannot be floating-point or string constants.
4. If there is a possibility that the value of the switch expression might not match one of the case constants, you should provide a `default` alternative.
5. Double-check long Switch statements to make sure that you haven't omitted any branches.
6. The Do-While loop is a posttest loop. If there is a possibility that the loop body should be skipped entirely, use a While statement or a For statement.

7. The For statement heading (the first line) always has three pieces within the parentheses. Most often, the first piece initializes a loop control variable, the second piece tests the variable, and the third piece increments or decrements the variable. The three pieces must be separated by semicolons. Any of the pieces can be omitted, but the semicolons still must be present.

8. With nested control structures, the Break statement can exit only one level of nesting—the innermost Switch or loop in which the `break` is located.

Summary

The Switch statement is a multiway selection statement. It allows the program to choose among a set of branches. A Switch containing Break statements can always be simulated by an If-Then-Else-If structure. If a Switch can be used, however, it often makes the code easier to read and understand. A Switch statement cannot be used with floating-point or string values in the case labels.

The Do-While is a general-purpose looping statement. It is like the While loop except that its test occurs at the end of the loop, guaranteeing at least one execution of the loop body. As with a While loop, a Do-While continues as long as the loop condition is `true`. A Do-While is convenient for loops that test input values and repeat if the input is not correct.

The For statement is also a general-purpose looping statement, but its most common use is to implement count-controlled loops. The initialization, testing, and incrementation (or decrementation) of the loop control variable are centralized in one location, the first line of the For statement.

The For, Do-While, and Switch statements are the ice cream and cake of C++. We can live without them if we absolutely must, but they are very nice to have.

Quick Check

1. Given a switch expression that is the `int` variable nameVal, write a Switch statement that prints your first name if nameVal = 1, your middle name if nameVal = 2, and your last name if nameVal = 3. (pp. 462–466])

2. How would you change the answer to Question 1 so that it prints an error message if the value is not 1, 2, or 3? (pp. 462–466)

3. What is the primary difference between a While loop and a Do-While loop? (pp. 468–471)

4. A certain problem requires a count-controlled loop that starts at 10 and counts down to 1. Write the heading (the first line) of a For statement that controls this loop. (pp. 471–474)

5. Within a loop, how does a Continue statement differ from a Break statement? (pp. 474–477)

6. What C++ looping statement would you choose for a loop that is both count-controlled and event-controlled and whose body might not execute even once? (p. 477)

Answers

1.
```
switch (nameVal)
{
    case 1 : cout << "Mary";
             break;
    case 2 : cout << "Lynn";
             break;
    case 3 : cout << "Smith";
             break;    // Not required
}
```

2.
```
switch (nameVal)
{
    case 1   : cout << "Mary";
               break;
    case 2   : cout << "Lynn";
               break;
    case 3   : cout << "Smith";
               break;
    default  : cout << "Invalid name value.";
               break;    // Not required
}
```

3. The body of a Do-While always executes at least once; the body of a While may not execute at all.   **4.** for (count = 10; count >= 1; count--)   **5.** A Continue statement terminates the current iteration and goes on to the next iteration (if possible). A Break statement causes an immediate loop exit.   **6.** A While (or perhaps a For) statement

Exam Preparation Exercises

1. Define the following terms:
   switch expression
   pretest loop
   posttest loop
2. A switch expression may be an expression that results in a value of type int, float, bool, or char. (True or False?)
3. The values in case labels may appear in any order, but duplicate case labels are not allowed within a given Switch statement. (True or False?)
4. All possible values for the switch expression must be included among the case labels for a given Switch statement. (True or False?)
5. Rewrite the following code fragment using a Switch statement.

```
if (n == 3)
    alpha++;
else if (n == 7)
    beta++;
else if (n == 10)
    gamma++;
```

6. What is printed by the following code fragment if n equals 3? (Be careful here.)

```
switch (n + 1)
{
    case 2  : cout << "Bill";
    case 4  : cout << "Mary";
    case 7  : cout << "Joe";
    case 9  : cout << "Anne";
    default : cout << "Whoops!";
}
```

7. If a While loop whose condition is `delta <= alpha` is converted into a Do-While loop, the loop condition of the Do-While loop is `delta > alpha`. (True or False?)

8. A Do-While statement always ends in a semicolon. (True or False?)

9. What is printed by the following program fragment, assuming the input value is 0? (All variables are of type int.)

```
cin >> n;
i = 1;
do
{
    cout << i;
    i++;
} while (i <= n);
```

10. What is printed by the following program fragment, assuming the input value is 0? (All variables are of type int.)

```
cin >> n;
for (i = 1; i <= n; i++)
    cout << i;
```

11. What is printed by the following program fragment? (All variables are of type int.)

```
for (i = 4; i >= 1; i--)
{
    for (j = i; j >= 1; j--)
        cout << j << ' ';
    cout << i << endl;
}
```

12. What is printed by the following program fragment? (All variables are of type int.)

```
for (row = 1; row <= 10; row++)
{
    for (col = 1; col <= 10 - row; col++)
        cout << '*';
    for (col = 1; col <= 2*row - 1; col++)
        cout << ' ';
    for (col = 1; col <= 10 - row; col++)
```

```
        cout << '*';
    cout << endl;
}
```

13. A Break statement located inside a Switch statement that is within a While loop causes control to exit the loop immediately. (True or False?)

Programming Warm-up Exercises

1. Write a Switch statement that does the following:
   If the value of grade is
   'A', add 4 to sum
   'B', add 3 to sum
   'C', add 2 to sum
   'D', add 1 to sum
   'F', print "Student is on probation"

2. Modify the code for Exercise 1 so that an error message is printed if grade does not equal one of the five possible grades.

3. Rewrite the Day function of Chapter 8 (pages 412–413), replacing the If-Then-Else-If structure with a Switch statement.

4. Write a program segment that reads and sums until it has summed ten data values or until a negative value is read, whichever comes first. Use a Do-While loop for your solution.

5. Rewrite the following code segment using a Do-While loop instead of a While loop.

```
cout << "Enter 1, 2, or 3: ";
cin >> response;
while (response < 1 || response > 3)
{
    cout << "Enter 1, 2, or 3: ";
    cin >> response;
}
```

6. Rewrite the following code segment using a While loop.

```
cin >> ch;
if (cin)
    do
    {
        cout << ch;
        cin >> ch;
    } while (cin);
```

7. Rewrite the following code segment using a For loop.

```
sum = 0;
count = 1;
while (count <= 1000)
{
    sum = sum + count;
    count++;
}
```

8. Rewrite the following For loop as a While loop.

```
for (m = 93; m >= 5; m--)
    cout << m << ' ' << m * m << endl;
```

9. Rewrite the following For loop using a Do-While loop.

```
for (k = 9; k <= 21; k++)
    cout << k << ' ' << 3 * k << endl;
```

10. Write a value-returning function that accepts two int parameters, base and exponent, and returns the value of base raised to the exponent power. Use a For loop in your solution.

11. Make the logic of the following loop easier to understand by using an infinite loop with Break statements.

```
sum = 0;
count = 1;
do
{
    cin >> int1;
    if ( !cin || int1 <= 0)
        cout << "Invalid first integer.";
    else
    {
        cin >> int2;
        if ( !cin || int2 > int1)
            cout << "Invalid second integer.";
        else
        {
            cin >> int3;
            if ( !cin || int3 == 0)
                cout << "Invalid third integer.";
            else
            {
                sum = sum + (int1 + int2) / int3;
                count++;
            }
        }
    }
} while (cin && int1 > 0 && int2 <= int1 && int3 != 0 &&
          count <= 100);
```

Programming Problems

1. Develop a functional decomposition and write a C++ program that inputs a two-letter abbreviation for one of the 50 states and prints out the full name of the state. If the abbreviation isn't valid, the program should print an error message and ask for an abbreviation again. The names of the 50 states and their abbreviations are given in the following table.

State	Abbreviation	State	Abbreviation
Alabama	AL	Montana	MT
Alaska	AK	Nebraska	NE
Arizona	AZ	Nevada	NV
Arkansas	AR	New Hampshire	NH
California	CA	New Jersey	NJ
Colorado	CO	New Mexico	NM
Connecticut	CT	New York	NY
Delaware	DE	North Carolina	NC
Florida	FL	North Dakota	ND
Georgia	GA	Ohio	OH
Hawaii	HI	Oklahoma	OK
Idaho	ID	Oregon	OR
Illinois	IL	Pennsylvania	PA
Indiana	IN	Rhode Island	RI
Iowa	IA	South Carolina	SC
Kansas	KS	South Dakota	SD
Kentucky	KY	Tennessee	TN
Louisiana	LA	Texas	TX
Maine	ME	Utah	UT
Maryland	MD	Vermont	VT
Massachusetts	MA	Virginia	VA
Michigan	MI	Washington	WA
Minnesota	MN	West Virginia	WV
Mississippi	MS	Wisconsin	WI
Missouri	MO	Wyoming	WY

(*Hint:* Use nested Switch statements, where the outer statement uses the first letter of the abbreviation as its switch expression.)

2. Write a functional decomposition and a C++ program that reads a date in numeric form and prints it in English. For example:

```
Enter a date in the form mm dd yyyy.
10  27  1942
October twenty-seventh, nineteen hundred forty-two.
```

Here is another example:

```
Enter a date in the form mm dd yyyy.
12  10  2010
December tenth, two thousand ten.
```

The program should print an error message for any invalid date, such as 2 29 1883 (1883 wasn't a leap year).

3. Write a C++ program that reads full names from an input file and writes the initials for the names to an output file stream named initials. For example, the input

```
John James Henry
```

should produce the output

```
JJH
```

The names are stored in the input file first name first, then middle name, then last name, separated by an arbitrary number of blanks. There is only one name per line. The first name or the middle name could be just an initial, or there may not be a middle name.

4. Write a functional decomposition and a C++ program that converts letters of the alphabet into their corresponding digits on the telephone. The program should let the user enter letters repeatedly until a 'Q' or a 'Z' is entered. (Q and Z are the two letters that are not on the telephone.) An error message should be printed for any nonalphabetic character that is entered.

The letters and digits on the telephone have the following correspondence.

ABC	=	2	DEF	=	3	GHI	= 4
JKL	=	5	MNO	=	6	PRS	= 7
TUV	=	8	WXY	=	9		

Here is an example:

```
Enter a letter: P
The letter P corresponds to 7 on the telephone.
Enter a letter: A
The letter A corresponds to 2 on the telephone.
Enter a letter: D
The letter D corresponds to 3 on the telephone.
Enter a letter: 2
Invalid letter. Enter Q or Z to quit.
Enter a letter: Z
Quit.
```

Case Study Follow-Up

1. Rewrite the GetYesOrNo and GetOneAmount functions in the Rainfall program, replacing the Do-While loops with While loops.
2. Rewrite the Get12Amounts function in the Rainfall program, replacing the For loop with a Do-While loop.
3. Rewrite the Get12Amounts function in the Rainfall program, replacing the For loop with a While loop.
4. In the GetYesOrNo function of the Rainfall program, is it possible to replace the If statement with a Switch statement? If so, is it advisable to do so?
5. In the GetOneAmount function of the Rainfall program, is it possible to replace the If statement with a Switch statement? If so, is it advisable to do so?

10

Simple Data Types: Built-In and User-Defined

GOALS

- To be able to identify all of the simple data types provided by the C++ language.
- To become familiar with specialized C++ operators and expressions.
- To be able to distinguish between external and internal representations of character data.
- To understand how floating-point numbers are represented in the computer.
- To understand how the limited numeric precision of the computer can affect calculations.
- To be able to select the most appropriate simple data type for a given variable.
- To be able to declare and use an enumeration type.
- To be able to use the For and Switch statements with user-defined enumeration types.
- To be able to distinguish a named user-defined type from an anonymous user-defined type.
- To be able to create a user-written header file.
- To understand the concepts of type promotion and type demotion.

This chapter represents a transition point in your study of computer science and C++ programming. So far, we have emphasized simple variables, control structures, and named processes (functions). After this chapter, the focus shifts to ways to structure (organize) data and to the algorithms necessary to process data in these structured forms. In order to make this transition, we must examine the concept of data type in greater detail.

Until now, we have worked primarily with the data types int, char, bool, and float. These four data types are adequate for solving a wide variety of problems. But certain programs need other kinds of data. In this chapter, we take a closer look at all of the simple data types that are part of the C++ language. As part of this look, we discuss the limitations of the computer in doing calculations. We examine how these limitations can cause numerical errors and how to avoid such errors.

There are times when even the built-in data types cannot adequately represent all the data in a program. C++ has several mechanisms for creating *user-defined* data types; that is, we can define new data types ourselves. This chapter introduces one of these mechanisms, the enumeration type. In subsequent chapters, we introduce additional user-defined data types.

Built-In Simple Types

In Chapter 2, we defined a data type as a specific set of data values (which we call the *domain*) along with a set of operations on those values. For the int type, the domain is the set of whole numbers from INT_MIN through INT_MAX, and the allowable operations we have seen so far are +, −, *, /, %, ++, --, and the relational and logical operations. The domain of the float type is the set of all real numbers that a particular computer is capable of representing, and the operations are the same as those for the int type except that modulus (%) is excluded. For the bool type, the domain is the set consisting of the two values true and false, and the allowable operations are the logical (!, &&, ||) and relational operations. The char type, though used primarily to manipulate character data, is classified as an integral type because it uses integers in memory to stand for characters. Later in the chapter we see how this works.

The int, char, bool, and float types have a property in common. The domain of each type is made up of indivisible, or atomic, data values. Data types with this property are called **simple** (or **atomic**) **data types.** When we say that a value is atomic, we mean that it has no component parts that can be accessed individually. For example, a single character of type char is atomic, but the string "Good Morning" is not (it is composed of 12 individual characters).

Simple (atomic) data type A data type in which each value is atomic (indivisible).

Another way of describing a simple type is to say that only one value can be associated with a variable of that type. In contrast, a *structured type* is one in which an entire collection of values is associated with a single variable of that type. For example, a string object represents a collection of characters that are given a single name. Beginning in Chapter 11, we look at structured types.

Figure 10-1 displays the simple types that are built into the C++ language. This figure is a portion of the complete diagram of C++ data types that you saw in Figure 3-1.

In this figure, one of the types—enum—is not actually a single data type in the sense that int and float are data types. Instead, it is a mechanism with which we can define our own simple data types. We look at enum later in the chapter.

The integral types char, short, int, and long represent nothing more than integers of different sizes. Similarly, the floating-point types float, double, and long double simply refer to floating-point numbers of different sizes. What do we mean by *sizes*?

In C++, sizes are measured in multiples of the size of a char. By definition, the size of a char is 1. On most—but not all—computers, the 1 means one byte. (Recall from Chapter 1 that a byte is a group of eight consecutive bits [1s or 0s].)

Let's use the notation *sizeof* (SomeType) to denote the size of a value of type SomeType. Then, by definition, *sizeof* (char) = 1. Other than char, the sizes of data objects in C++ are machine dependent. On one machine, it might be the case that

FIGURE 10-1
C++ Simple Types

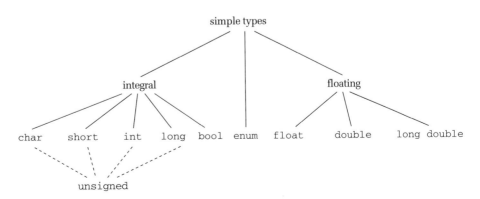

sizeof (char) = 1
sizeof (short) = 2
sizeof (int) = 4
sizeof (long) = 8

On another machine, the sizes might be as follows:

sizeof (char) = 1
sizeof (short) = 2
sizeof (int) = 2
sizeof (long) = 4

Despite these variations, the C++ language guarantees that the following statements are true:

- 1 = *sizeof* (char) ≤ *sizeof* (short) ≤ *sizeof* (int) ≤ *sizeof* (long).
- 1 ≤ *sizeof* (bool) ≤ *sizeof* (long).
- *sizeof* (float) ≤ *sizeof* (double) ≤ *sizeof* (long double).
- A char is at least 8 bits.
- A short is at least 16 bits.
- A long is at least 32 bits.

For numeric data, the size of a data object determines its **range of values.** Let's look in more detail at the sizes, ranges of values, and literal constants for each of the built-in types.

Range of values   The interval within which values of a numeric type must fall, specified in terms of the largest and smallest allowable values.

Integral Types

Before looking at how the sizes of integral types affect their possible values, we remind you that the reserved word unsigned may precede the name of certain integral types—unsigned char, unsigned short, unsigned int, unsigned long. Values of these types are nonnegative integers with values from 0 through some machine-dependent maximum value. Although we rarely use unsigned types in this book, we include them in this discussion for thoroughness.

Ranges of Values   The following table displays sample ranges of values for the char, short, int, and long data types and their unsigned variations.

Type	Size in Bytes*	Minimum Value*	Maximum Value*
char	1	−128	127
unsigned char	1	0	255
short	2	−32,768	32,767
unsigned short	2	0	65,535
int	2	−32,768	32,767
unsigned int	2	0	65,535
long	4	−2,147,483,648	2,147,483,647
unsigned long	4	0	4,294,967,295

* These values are for one particular machine. Your machine's values may be different.

C++ systems provide the header file `climits`, from which you can determine the maximum and minimum values for your machine. This header file defines the constants CHAR_MAX and CHAR_MIN, SHRT_MAX and SHRT_MIN, INT_MAX and INT_MIN, and LONG_MAX and LONG_MIN. The unsigned types have a minimum value of 0 and maximum values defined by UCHAR_MAX, USHRT_MAX, UINT_MAX, and ULONG_MAX. To find out the values specific to your computer, you could print them out like this:

```
#include <climits>
using namespace std;
    ⋮
cout << "Max. long = " << LONG_MAX << endl;
cout << "Min. long = " << LONG_MIN << endl;
    ⋮
```

Literal Constants In C++, the valid `bool` constants are `true` and `false`. Integer constants can be specified in three different number bases: decimal (base 10), octal (base 8), and hexadecimal (base 16). Just as the decimal number system has ten digits—0 through 9—the octal system has eight digits—0 through 7. The hexadecimal system has digits 0, 1, 2, 3, 4, 5, 6, 7, 8, 9, A, B, C, D, E, and F, which correspond to the decimal values 0 through 15. Octal and hexadecimal values are used in system software (compilers, linkers, and operating systems, for example) to refer directly to individual bits in a memory cell and to control hardware devices. These manipulations of low-level objects in a computer are the subject of more advanced study and are outside the scope of this book.

The following table shows examples of integer constants in C++. Notice that an `L` or a `U` (either uppercase or lowercase) can be added to the end of a constant to signify `long` or `unsigned`, respectively.

Constant	Type	Remarks
1658	int	Decimal (base-10) integer.
03172	int	Octal (base-8) integer. Begins with 0 (zero). Decimal equivalent is 1658.
0x67A	int	Hexadecimal (base-16) integer. Begins with 0 (zero), then either x or X. Decimal equivalent is 1658.
65535U	unsigned int	Unsigned constants end in U or u.
421L	long	Explicit long constant. Ends in L or l.
53100	long	Implicit long constant, assuming the machine's maximum int is, say, 32767.
389123487UL	unsigned long	Unsigned long constants end in UL or LU in any combination of uppercase and lowercase letters.

Notice that this table presents only numeric constants for the integral types. We discuss char constants later in a separate section.

Here is the syntax template for an integer constant:

IntegerConstant

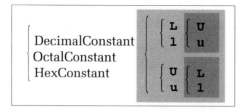

DecimalConstant is a nonzero digit followed, optionally, by a sequence of decimal digits:

DecimalConstant

NonzeroDigit DigitSeq

NonzeroDigit, DigitSeq, and Digit are defined as follows:

NonzeroDigit   **DigitSeq**   **Digit**

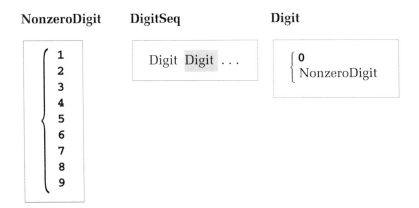

The second form of integer constant, OctalConstant, has the following syntax:

OctalConstant   **OctalDigit**

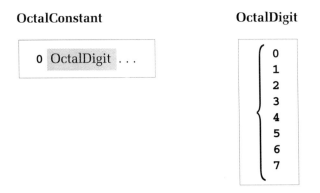

Finally, HexConstant is defined as

HexConstant   **HexDigit**

Floating-Point Types

Ranges of Values   Below is a table that gives sample ranges of values for the three floating-point types, `float`, `double`, and `long double`. In this table we show, for each type, the maximum positive value and the minimum positive value (a tiny fraction that is very close to 0). Negative numbers have the same range but the opposite sign. Ranges of values are expressed in exponential (scientific) notation, where 3.4E+38 means 3.4×10^{38}.

Type	Size in Bytes*	Minimum Positive Value*	Maximum Positive Value*
float	4	3.4E–38	3.4E+38
double	8	1.7E–308	1.7E+308
long double	10	3.4E–4932	1.1E+4932

*These values are for one particular machine. Your machine's values may be different.

The standard header file `cfloat` defines the constants `FLT_MAX` and `FLT_MIN`, `DBL_MAX` and `DBL_MIN`, and `LDBL_MAX` and `LDBL_MIN`. To determine the ranges of values for your machine, you could write a short program that prints out these constants.

Literal Constants When you use a floating-point constant such as 5.8 in a C++ program, its type is assumed to be `double` (double precision). If you store the value into a `float` variable, the computer coerces its type from `double` to `float` (single precision). If you insist on a constant being of type `float` rather than `double`, you can append an F or an f at the end of the constant. Similarly, a suffix of L or l signifies a `long double` constant. Here are some examples of floating-point constants in C++:

Constant	Type	Remarks
6.83	double	By default, floating-point constants are of type double.
6.83F	float	Explicit float constants end in F or f.
6.83L	long double	Explicit long double constants end in L or l.
4.35E-9	double	Exponential notation, meaning 4.35×10^{-9}.

Here's the syntax template for a floating-point constant in C++:

FloatingPtConstant

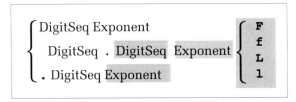

DigitSeq is the same as defined in the section on integer constants—a sequence of decimal (base-10) digits. The form of Exponent is the following:

Exponent

Additional C++ Operators

C++ has a rich, sometimes bewildering, variety of operators that allow you to manipulate values of the simple data types. Operators you have learned about so far include the assignment operator (=), the arithmetic operators (+, -, *, /, %), the increment and decrement operators (++, --), the relational operators (==, !=, <, <=, >, >=), and the logical operators (!, &&, ||). In certain cases, a pair of parentheses is also considered to be an operator—namely, the function call operator,

```
ComputeSum(x, y);
```

and the type cast operator,

```
y = float(someInt);
```

C++ also has many specialized operators that are seldom found in other programming languages. Here is a table of these additional operators. As you inspect the table, don't panic—a quick scan will do.

Operator	Remarks
Combined assignment operators	
+= Add and assign	
-= Subtract and assign	
*= Multiply and assign	
/= Divide and assign	
Increment and decrement operators	
++ Pre-increment	Example: ++someVar
++ Post-increment	Example: someVar++
-- Pre-decrement	Example: --someVar
-- Post-decrement	Example: --someVar

Operator	Remarks
Bitwise operators	Integer operands only
`<<` Left shift	
`>>` Right shift	
`&` Bitwise AND	
`|` Bitwise OR	
`^` Bitwise EXCLUSIVE OR	
`~` Complement (invert all bits)	
More combined assignment operators	Integer operands only
`%=` Modulus and assign	
`<<=` Shift left and assign	
`>>=` Shift right and assign	
`&=` Bitwise AND and assign	
`|=` Bitwise OR and assign	
`^=` Bitwise EXCLUSIVE OR and assign	
Other operators	
`()` Cast	
`sizeof` Size of operand in bytes	Form: `sizeof` Expr or `sizeof(`Type`)`
`?:` Conditional operator	Form: Expr1 `?` Expr2 `:` Expr3

The operators in this table, along with those you already know, comprise most—but not all—of the C++ operators. We introduce a few more operators in later chapters as the need arises.

Assignment Operators and Assignment Expressions

C++ has several assignment operators. The equal sign (=) is the basic assignment operator. When combined with its two operands, it forms an **assignment expression** (*not* an assignment statement). Every assignment expression has a *value* and a *side effect*, namely, that the value is stored into the object denoted by the left-hand side. For example, the expression

```
delta = 2 * 12
```

has the value 24 and the side effect of storing this value into `delta`.

In C++, any expression becomes an **expression statement** when it is terminated by a semicolon. All three of the following are valid C++ statements, although the first two have no effect whatsoever at run time:

```
23;
2 * (alpha + beta);
delta = 2 * 12;
```

The third expression statement *is* useful because of its side effect of storing 24 into `delta`.

Assignment expression   A C++ expression with (1) a value and (2) the side effect of storing the expression value into a memory location.

Expression statement   A statement formed by appending a semicolon to an expression.

Because an assignment is an expression, not a statement, you can use it anywhere an expression is allowed. Here is a statement that stores the value 20 into `firstInt`, the value 30 into `secondInt`, and the value 35 into `thirdInt`:

```
thirdInt = (secondInt = (firstInt = 20) + 10) + 5;
```

Some C++ programmers use this style of coding, but others find it hard to read and error-prone.

In Chapter 5, we cautioned against the mistake of using the = operator in place of the == operator:

```
if (alpha = 12)   // Wrong
   ⋮
else
   ⋮
```

The condition in the If statement is an assignment expression, not a relational expression. The value of the expression is 12 (interpreted in the If condition as `true`), so the else-clause is never executed. Worse yet, the side effect of the assignment expression is to store 12 into `alpha`, destroying its previous contents.

In addition to the = operator, C++ has several combined assignment operators (+=, *=, and the others listed in our table of operators). These operators have the following semantics:

Statement	*Equivalent Statement*
`i += 5;`	`i = i + 5;`
`pivotPoint *= n + 3;`	`pivotPoint = pivotPoint * (n + 3);`

The combined assignment operators are another example of "ice cream and cake." They are sometimes convenient for writing a line of code more compactly, but you can do just fine without them.

Increment and Decrement Operators

The increment and decrement operators (++ and --) operate only on variables, not on constants or arbitrary expressions. Suppose a variable someInt contains the value 3. The expression ++someInt denotes preincrementation. The side effect of incrementing someInt occurs first, so the resulting value of the expression is 4. In contrast, the expression someInt++ denotes post-incrementation. The value of the expression is 3, and *then* the side effect of incrementing someInt takes place. The following code illustrates the difference between pre- and post-incrementation:

```
int1 = 14;
int2 = ++int1;
// Assert: int1 == 15  &&  int2 == 15

int1 = 14;
int2 = int1++;
// Assert: int1 == 15  &&  int2 == 14
```

Using side effects in the middle of larger expressions is always a bit dangerous. It's easy to make semantic errors, and the code may be confusing to read. Look at this example:

```
a = (b = c++) * --d / (e += f++);
```

Some people make a game of seeing how much they can do in the fewest keystrokes possible. But they should remember that serious software development requires writing code that other programmers can read and understand. Overuse of side effects hinders this goal. By far the most common use of ++ and -- is to do the incrementation or decrementation as a separate expression statement:

```
count++;
```

Here, the value of the expression is unused, but we get the desired side effect of incrementing count. In this example, it doesn't matter whether you use pre-incrementation or post-incrementation. The choice is up to you.

Bitwise Operators

The bitwise operators listed in the operator table (<<, >>, &, |, and so forth) are used for manipulating individual bits within a memory cell. This book does not explore the use of these operators; the topic of bit-level operations is most often covered in a course on computer organization and assembly language programming. However, we point out two things about the bit-wise operators.

First, the built-in operators << and >> are the left shift and right shift operators, respectively. Their purpose is to take the bits within a memory cell and shift them to the left or right. Of course, we have been using these operators all along, but in an entirely different context—program input and output. The header file `iostream` uses an advanced C++ technique called *operator overloading* to give additional meanings to these two operators. An overloaded operator is one that has multiple meanings, depending on the data types of its operands. When looking at the << operator, the compiler determines by context whether a left shift operation or an output operation is desired. Specifically, if the first (left-hand) operand denotes an output stream, then it is an output operation. If the first operand is an integer variable, it is a left shift operation.

Second, we repeat our caution from Chapter 5: Do not confuse the && and || operators with the & and | operators. The statement

```
if (i == 3 & j == 4)    // Wrong
    k = 20;
```

is syntactically correct because & is a valid operator (the bitwise AND operator). The program containing this statement compiles correctly but executes incorrectly. Although we do not examine what the bitwise AND and OR operators do, just be careful to use the relational operators && and || in your logical expressions.

The Cast Operation

You have seen that C++ is very liberal about letting the programmer mix data types in expressions, in assignment operations, in argument passing, and in returning a function value. However, implicit type coercion takes place when values of different data types are mixed together. Instead of relying on implicit type coercion in a statement such as

```
intVar = floatVar;
```

we have recommended using an explicit type cast to show that the type conversion is intentional:

```
intVar = int(floatVar);
```

In C++, the cast operation comes in two forms:

```
intVar = int(floatVar);     // Functional notation
intVar = (int) floatVar;    // Prefix notation. Parentheses required
```

The first form is called functional notation because it looks like a function call. It isn't really a function call (there is no user-defined or predefined subprogram named int), but it has the syntax and visual appearance of a function call. The second form, prefix notation, doesn't look like any familiar language feature in C++. In this notation, the parentheses surround the name of the data type, not the expression being converted. Prefix notation is the only form available in the C language; C++ added the functional notation.

Although most C++ programmers use the functional notation for the cast operation, there is one restriction on its use. The data type name must be a single identifier. If the type name consists of more than one identifier, you *must* use prefix notation. For example,

```
myVar = unsigned int(someFloat);     // No
myVar = (unsigned int) someFloat;    // Yes
```

The sizeof Operator

The sizeof operator is a unary operator that yields the size, in bytes, of its operand. The operand can be a variable name, as in

```
sizeof someInt
```

or the operand can be the name of a data type, enclosed in parentheses:

```
sizeof(float)
```

You could find out the sizes of various data types on your machine by using code like this:

```
cout << "Size of a short is " << sizeof(short) << endl;
cout << "Size of an int is " << sizeof(int) << endl;
cout << "Size of a long is " << sizeof(long) << endl;
```

The ?: Operator

The last operator in our operator table is the ?: operator, sometimes called the conditional operator. It is a ternary (three-operand) operator with the following syntax:

ConditionalExpression

Expression1 **?** Expression2 **:** Expression3

Here's how it works. First, the computer evaluates Expression1. If the value is `true`, then the value of the entire expression is Expression2; otherwise, the value of the entire expression is Expression3. (Only one of Expression2 and Expression3 is evaluated.) A classic example of its use is to set a variable `max` equal to the larger of two variables `a` and `b`. Using an If statement, we would do it this way:

```
if (a > b)
    max = a;
else
    max = b;
```

With the `?:` operator, we can use the following assignment statement:

```
max = (a > b) ? a : b;
```

Here is another example. The absolute value of a number x is defined as

$$|x| = \begin{cases} x, & if\, x \geq 0 \\ -x, & if\, x < 0 \end{cases}$$

To compute the absolute value of a variable `x` and store it into `y`, you could use the `?:` operator as follows:

```
y = (x >= 0) ? x : -x;
```

In both the `max` and the absolute value examples, we used parentheses around the expression being tested. These parentheses are unnecessary because, as we'll see shortly, the conditional operator has very low precedence. But it is customary to include the parentheses for clarity.

Operator Precedence

Below is a summary of operator precedence for the C++ operators we have encountered so far, excluding the bitwise operators. (Appendix B contains the complete list.) In the table, the operators are grouped by precedence level, and a horizontal line separates each precedence level from the next-lower level.

Precedence (highest to lowest)

Operator	Associativity	Remarks
()	Left to right	Function call and function-style cast
++ --	Right to left	++ and -- as postfix operators
++ -- ! Unary + Unary -	Right to left	++ and -- as prefix operators
(cast) sizeof	Right to left	
* / %	Left to right	
+ -	Left to right	
< <= > >=	Left to right	
== !=	Left to right	
&&	Left to right	
||	Left to right	
?:	Right to left	
= += -= *= /=	Right to left	

The column labeled *Associativity* describes grouping order. Within a precedence level, most operators group from left to right. For example,

```
a - b + c
```

means

```
(a - b) + c
```

and not

```
a - (b + c)
```

Certain operators, though, group from right to left—specifically, the unary operators, the assignment operators, and the ?: operator. Look at the assignment operators, for example. The expression

```
sum = count = 0
```

means

```
sum = (count = 0)
```

This associativity makes sense because the assignment operation is naturally a right-to-left operation.

A word of caution: Although operator precedence and associativity dictate the *grouping* of operators with their operands, C++ does not define the *order* in which subexpressions are evaluated. Therefore, using side effects in expressions requires extra care. For example, if i currently contains 5, the statement

```
j = ++i + i;
```

stores either 11 or 12 into j, depending on the particular compiler being used. Let's see why. There are three operators in the expression statement above: =, ++, and +. The ++ operator has the highest precedence, so it operates just on i, not the expression i + i. The addition operator has higher precedence than the assignment operator, giving implicit parentheses as follows:

```
j = (++i + i);
```

So far, so good. But now we ask this question: In the addition operation, is the left operand or the right operand evaluated first? The C++ language doesn't dictate the order. If a compiler generates code to evaluate the left operand first, the result is 6 + 6, or 12. Another compiler might generate code to evaluate the right operand first, yielding 6 + 5, or 11. To be assured of left-to-right evaluation in this example, you should force the ordering with two separate statements:

```
++i;
j = i + i;
```

The moral here is that if you use multiple side effects in expressions, you increase the risk of unexpected or inconsistent results. For the newcomer to C++, it's better to avoid unnecessary side effects altogether.

Working with Character Data

We have been using `char` variables to store character data, such as the character 'A' or 'e' or '+':

```
char someChar;
    ⋮
someChar = 'A';
```

However, because `char` is defined to be an integral type and `sizeof(char)` equals 1, we also can use a `char` variable to store a small (usually one-byte) integer constant. For example,

```
char counter;
    ⋮
counter = 3;
```

On computers with a very limited amount of memory space, programmers sometimes use the `char` type to save memory when they are working with small integers.

A natural question to ask is, How does the computer know the difference between integer data and character data when the data is sitting in a memory cell? The answer is, The computer *can't* tell the difference! To explain this surprising fact, we must look more closely at how character data is stored in a computer.

Character Sets

Each computer uses a particular character set, the set of all possible characters with which it is capable of working. Two character sets widely in use today are the ASCII character set and the EBCDIC character set. ASCII is used by the vast majority of all computers, whereas EBCDIC is found primarily on IBM mainframe computers. ASCII consists of 128 different characters, and EBCDIC has 256 characters. Appendix E shows the characters that are available in these two character sets.

A more recently developed character set called *Unicode* allows many more distinct characters than either ASCII or EBCDIC. Unicode was invented primarily to accommodate the larger alphabets and symbols of various international human languages. In C++, the data type `wchar_t` rather than `char` is used for Unicode characters. In fact, `wchar_t` can be used for other, possibly infrequently used, "wide character" sets in addition to Unicode. In this book, we do not examine Unicode or the `wchar_t` type. We continue to focus our attention on the `char` type and the ASCII and EBCDIC character sets.

Whichever character set is being used, each character has an **external representation**—the way it looks on an I/O device like a printer—and an **internal representation**—the way it is stored inside the computer's memory unit. If you use the char constant 'A' in a C++ program, its external representation is the letter *A*. That is, if you print it out you see an *A*, as you would expect. Its internal representation, though, is an integer value. The 128 ASCII characters have internal representations 0 through 127; the EBCDIC characters, 0 through 255. For example, the ASCII table in Appendix E shows that the character 'A' has internal representation 65, and the character 'b' has internal representation 98.

External representation   The printable (character) form of a data value.

Internal representation   The form in which a data value is stored inside the memory unit.

Let's look again at the statement

```
someChar = 'A';
```

Assuming our machine uses the ASCII character set, the compiler translates the constant 'A' into the integer 65. We could also have written the statement as

```
someChar = 65;
```

Both statements have exactly the same effect—that of storing 65 into someChar. However, the second version is *not* recommended. It is not as understandable as the first version, and it is nonportable (the program won't work correctly on a machine that uses EBCDIC, which uses a different internal representation—193—for 'A').

Earlier we mentioned that the computer cannot tell the difference between character and integer data in memory. Both are stored internally as integers. However, when we perform I/O operations, the computer does the right thing—it uses the external representation that corresponds to the data type of the expression being printed. Look at this code segment, for example:

```
// This example assumes use of the ASCII character set
int   someInt = 97;
char someChar = 97;

cout << someInt << endl;
cout << someChar << endl;
```

When these statements are executed, the output is

```
97
a
```

When the << operator outputs someInt, it prints the sequence of characters 9 and 7. To output someChar, it prints the single character a. Even
though both variables contain the value 97 internally, the data type of each
variable determines how it is printed.

What do you think is output by the following sequence of statements?

```
char ch = 'D';

ch++;
cout << ch;
```

If you answered E, you are right. The first statement declares ch and initializes it to the integer value 68 (assuming ASCII). The next statement
increments ch to 69, and then its external representation (the letter *E*) is
printed. Extending this idea of incrementing a char variable, we could
print the letters *A* through *G* as follows:

```
char ch;

for (ch = 'A'; ch <= 'G'; ch++)
    cout << ch;
```

This code initializes ch to 'A' (65 in ASCII). Each time through the loop,
the external representation of ch is printed. On the final loop iteration, the
G is printed and ch is incremented to 'H' (72 in ASCII). The loop test is
then false, so the loop terminates.

C++ char Constants

In C++, char constants come in two different forms. The first form, which
we have been using regularly, is a single printable character enclosed by
apostrophes (single quotes):

```
'A'    '8'    ')'    '+'
```

Notice that we said *printable* character. Character sets include both printable characters and *control characters* (or *nonprintable characters*).
Control characters are not meant to be printed but are used to control the
screen, printer, and other hardware devices. If you look at the ASCII character table, you see that the printable characters are those with integer values 32–126. The remaining characters (with values 0–31 and 127) are
nonprintable control characters. In the EBCDIC character set, the control

characters are those with values 0–63 and 250–255 (and some that are intermingled with the printable characters). One control character you already know about is the newline character, which causes the screen cursor to advance to the next line.

To accommodate control characters, C++ provides a second form of `char` constant: the *escape sequence*. An escape sequence is one or more characters preceded by a backslash (\). You are familiar with the escape sequence \n, which represents the newline character. Here is the complete description of the two forms of `char` constant in C++:

1. A single printable character—except an apostrophe (') or backslash (\)—enclosed by apostrophes.
2. One of the following escape sequences, enclosed by apostrophes:

\n	Newline (Line feed in ASCII)
\t	Horizontal tab
\v	Vertical tab
\b	Backspace
\r	Carriage return
\f	Form feed
\a	Alert (a bell or beep)
\\	Backslash
\'	Single quote (apostrophe)
\"	Double quote (quotation mark)
\0	Null character (all 0 bits)
\ddd	Octal equivalent (one, two, or three octal digits specifying the integer value of the desired character)
\xddd	Hexadecimal equivalent (one or more hexadecimal digits specifying the integer value of the desired character)

Even though an escape sequence is written as two or more characters, each escape sequence represents a single character in the character set. The alert character (\a) is the same as what is called the BEL character in ASCII and EBCDIC. To ring the bell (well, these days, beep the beeper) on your computer, you can output the alert character like this:

```
cout << '\a';
```

In the list of escape sequences above, the entries labeled *Octal equivalent* and *Hexadecimal equivalent* let you refer to any character in your machine's character set by specifying its integer value in either octal or hexadecimal form.

Note that you can use an escape sequence within a string just as you can use any printable character within a string. The statement

```
cout << "\aWhoops!\n";
```

beeps the beeper, displays Whoops!, and terminates the output line. The statement

```
cout << "She said \"Hi\"";
```

outputs She said "Hi" and does not terminate the output line.

Programming Techniques

What kinds of things can we do with character data in a program? The possibilities are endless and depend, of course, on the particular problem we are solving. But several techniques are so widely used that it's worth taking a look at them.

Comparing Characters In previous chapters, you have seen examples of comparing characters for equality. We have used tests such as

```
if (ch == 'a')
```

and

```
while (inputChar != '\n')
```

Characters can also be compared by using <, <=, >, and >=. For example, if the variable firstLetter contains the first letter of a person's last name, we can test to see if the last name starts with *A* through *H* by using this test:

```
if (firstLetter >= 'A' && firstLetter <= 'H')
```

On one level of thought, a test like this is reasonable if you think of < as meaning "comes before" in the character set and > as meaning "comes after." On another level, the test makes even more sense when you consider that the underlying representation of a character is an integer number. The machine literally compares the two integer values using the mathematical meaning of less than or greater than.

When you write a logical expression to check whether a character lies within a certain range of values, you sometimes have to keep in mind the character set your machine uses. In Chapter 8, we hinted that a test like

```
if (ch >= 'a' && ch <= 'z')
```

works correctly on some machines but not on others. In ASCII, this If test behaves correctly because the lowercase letters occupy 26 consecutive positions in the character set. In EBCDIC, however, there is a gap between the lowercase letters *i* and *j* that includes nonprintable characters, and there is another gap between *r* and *s*. (There are similar gaps between the uppercase letters *I* and *J* and between *R* and *S*.) If your machine uses EBCDIC, you must rephrase the If test to be sure you include *only* the desired characters. A better approach, though, is to take advantage of the "is..." functions supplied by the standard library through the header file cctype. If you replace the above If test with this one:

```
if (islower(ch))
```

then your program is more portable; the test works correctly on any machine, regardless of its character set. It's a good idea to become well acquainted with these character-testing library functions (Appendix C). They can save you time and help you to write more portable programs.

Converting Digit Characters to Integers Suppose you want to convert a digit that is read in character form to its numeric equivalent. Because the digit characters '0' through '9' are consecutive in both the ASCII and EBCDIC character sets, subtracting '0' from any digit in character form gives the digit in numeric form:

```
'0' - '0' = 0
'1' - '0' = 1
'2' - '0' = 2
   ⋮
```

For example, in ASCII, '0' has internal representation 48 and '2' has internal representation 50. Therefore, the expression

```
'2' - '0'
```

equals $50 - 48$ and evaluates to 2.

Why would you want to do this? Recall that when the extraction operator (>>) reads data into an int variable, the input stream fails if an invalid character is encountered. (And once the stream has failed, no further input will succeed). Suppose you're writing a program that prompts an inexperienced user to enter a number from 1 through 5. If the input variable is of type int and the user accidentally types a letter of the alphabet, the program is in trouble. To defend against this possibility, you might read the user's response as a character and convert it to a number, performing error checking along the way. Here's a code segment that demonstrates the technique:

```
#include <cctype>    // For isdigit()
using namespace std;
   ⋮
void GetResponse( /* out */ int& response )
```

```
// Postcondition:
//      User has been prompted to enter a digit from 1
//      through 5 (repeatedly, and with error messages,
//      if data is invalid)
// && 1 <= response <= 5

{
    char inChar;
    bool badData = false;

    do
    {
        cout << "Enter a number from 1 through 5: ";
        cin >> inChar;
        if ( !isdigit(inChar) )
            badData = true;                     // It's not a digit
        else
        {
            response = int(inChar - '0');
            if (response < 1 || response > 5)
                badData = true;                 // It's a digit, but
        }                                       // it's out of range
        if (badData)
            cout << "Please try again." << endl;
    } while (badData);
}
```

Converting to Lowercase and Uppercase   When working with character data, you sometimes find that you need to convert a lowercase letter to uppercase, or vice versa. Fortunately, the programming technique required to do these conversions is easy—a simple call to a library function is all it takes. Through the header file cctype, the standard library provides not only the "is..." functions we have discussed, but also two value-returning functions named toupper and tolower. Here are their descriptions:

Header File	Function	Function Type	Function Value
<cctype>	toupper(ch)	char*	Uppercase equivalent of ch, if ch is a lowercase letter; ch, otherwise
<cctype>	tolower(ch)	char	Lowercase equivalent of ch, if ch is an uppercase letter; ch, otherwise

*Technically, both the argument and the return value are of type int. But conceptually, the functions operate on character data.

Notice that the value returned by each function is just the original character if the condition is not met. For example, tolower('M') returns the character 'm', whereas tolower('+') returns '+'.

A common use of these two functions is to let the user respond to certain input prompts by using either uppercase or lowercase letters. For example, if you want to allow either *Y* or *y* for a "Yes" response from the user, and either *N* or *n* for "No," you might do this:

```
#include <cctype>      // For toupper()
using namespace std;
      ⋮
cout << "Enter Y or N: ";
cin >> inputChar;
if (toupper(inputChar) == 'Y')
{
      ⋮
}
else if (toupper(inputChar) == 'N')
{
      ⋮
}
else
      PrintErrorMsg();
```

Below is a function named Lower, which is our implementation of the tolower function. (You wouldn't actually want to waste time by writing this function because tolower is already available to you.) This function returns the lowercase equivalent of an uppercase letter. In ASCII, each lowercase letter is exactly 32 positions beyond the corresponding uppercase letter. And in EBCDIC, the lowercase letters are 64 positions *before* their corresponding uppercase letters. To make our Lower function work on both ASCII-based and EBCDIC-based machines, we define a constant DISTANCE to have the value

```
'a' - 'A'
```

In ASCII, the value of this expression is 32. In EBCDIC, the value is –64.

```
#include <cctype>      // For isupper()
using namespace std;
      ⋮
char Lower( /* in */ char ch )

// Postcondition:
//      Function value == lowercase equivalent of ch, if ch is
//                        an uppercase letter
//                     == ch, otherwise

{
```

```
        const int DISTANCE = 'a' - 'A';   // Fixed distance between
                                          // uppercase and lowercase
                                          // letters
    if (isupper(ch))
        return ch + DISTANCE;
    else
        return ch;
}
```

Accessing Characters Within a String   In the last section, we gave the outline of a code segment that prompts the user for a "Yes" or "No" response. The code accepted a response of 'Y' or 'N' in uppercase or lowercase letters. If a problem requires the user to type the entire word *Yes* or *No* in any combination of uppercase and lowercase letters, the code becomes more complicated. Reading the user's response as a string into a `string` object named `inputStr`, we would need a lengthy If-Then-Else-If structure to compare `inputStr` to "yes", "Yes", "yEs", "yeS", and so on.

As an alternative, let's inspect only the first character of the input string, comparing it with 'Y', 'y', 'N', or 'n', and then ignore the rest of the string. The `string` class allows you to access an individual character in a string by giving its position number in square brackets:

StringObject [Position]

Within a string, the first character is at position 0, the second is at position 1, and so forth. Therefore, the value of Position must be greater than or equal to 0 and less than or equal to the string length minus 1. For example, if `inputStr` is a `string` object and `ch` is a `char` variable, the statement

```
ch = inputStr[2];
```

accesses the character at position 2 of the string (the third character) and copies it into `ch`.

Now we can sketch out the code for reading a "Yes" or "No" response, checking only the first letter of that response.

```
string inputStr;
    ⋮
cout << "Enter Yes or No: ";
cin >> inputStr;
if (toupper(inputStr[0]) == 'Y')
```

```
{
    ⋮
}
else if (toupper(inputStr[0]) == 'N')
{
    ⋮
}
else
    PrintErrorMsg();
```

More on Floating-Point Numbers

We have used floating-point numbers off and on since we introduced them in Chapter 2, but we have not examined them in depth. Floating-point numbers have special properties when used on the computer. Thus far, we've almost ignored these properties, but now it's time to consider them in detail.

Representation of Floating-Point Numbers

Let's assume we have a computer in which each memory location is the same size and is divided into a sign plus five decimal digits. When a variable or constant is defined, the location assigned to it consists of five digits and a sign. When an int variable or constant is defined, the interpretation of the number stored in that place is straightforward. When a float variable or constant is defined, the number stored there has both a whole number part and a fractional part, so it must be coded to represent both parts.

Let's see what such coded numbers might look like. The range of whole numbers we can represent with five digits is –99,999 through +99,999:

–99999 through +99999

| + | 9 | 9 | 9 | 9 | 9 | Largest positive number

| + | 0 | 0 | 0 | 0 | 0 | Zero

| – | 9 | 9 | 9 | 9 | 9 | Largest negative number

FIGURE 10-3 Coding Using Positive and Negative Exponents

Largest positive number: $+9999 \times 10^9$

Sign of number

Sign of exponent

Largest negative number: -9999×10^9

Smallest positive number: $+1 \times 10^{-9}$

Smallest negative number: -1×10^{-9}

sented exactly but −4,932,416 cannot, because our coding scheme limits us to four **significant digits.**

To extend our coding scheme to represent floating-point numbers, we must be able to represent negative exponents. Examples are

$$7394 \times 10^{-2} = 73.94$$

and

$$22 \times 10^{-4} = .0022$$

Because our scheme does not include a sign for the exponent, let's change it slightly. The existing sign becomes the sign of the exponent, and we add a sign to the far left to represent the sign of the number itself (see Figure 10-3).

All the numbers between -9999×10^9 and 9999×10^9 can now be represented accurately to four digits. Adding negative exponents to our scheme allows us to represent fractional numbers as small as 1×10^{-9}.

Figure 10-4 shows how we would encode some floating-point numbers. Note that our precision is still only four digits. The numbers 0.1032, −5.406, and 1,000,000 can be represented exactly. The number 476.0321, however, with seven significant digits, is represented as 476.0; the *321* cannot be represented. (We should point out that some computers perform *rounding* rather than simple truncation when discarding excess digits. Using our assumption of four significant digits, such a machine would store 476.0321 as 476.0 but would store 476.0823 as 476.1. We continue our discussion assuming simple truncation rather than rounding.)

FIGURE 10-4   Coding of Some Floating-Point Numbers

NUMBER	POWER OF TEN NOTATION	CODED REPRESENTATION							VALUE
		Sign		Exp					
0.1032	$+1032 \times 10^{-4}$	+	−	4	1	0	3	2	0.1032
−5.4060	-5406×10^{-3}	−	−	3	5	4	0	6	−5.406
−0.003	-3000×10^{-6}	−	−	6	3	0	0	0	−0.0030
476.0321	$+4760 \times 10^{-1}$	+	−	1	4	7	6	0	476.0
1,000,000	$+1000 \times 10^{3}$	+	+	3	1	0	0	0	1,000,000

Arithmetic with Floating-Point Numbers

When we use integer arithmetic, our results are exact. Floating-point arithmetic, however, is seldom exact. To understand why, let's add three floating-point numbers x, y, and z using our coding scheme.

First, we add x to y and then we add z to the result. Next, we perform the operations in a different order, adding y to z, and then adding x to that result. The associative law of arithmetic says that the two answers should be the same—but are they? Let's use the following values for x, y, and z:

$$x = -1324 \times 10^3 \qquad y = 1325 \times 10^3 \qquad z = 5424 \times 10^0$$

Here is the result of adding z to the sum of x and y:

$$
\begin{array}{lll}
(x) & -1324 \times 10^3 & \\
(y) & \underline{1325 \times 10^3} & \\
& 1 \times 10^3 & = 1000 \times 10^0 \\
\\
(x+y) & 1000 \times 10^0 & \\
(z) & \underline{5424 \times 10^0} & \\
& 6424 \times 10^0 & \leftarrow (x+y)+z
\end{array}
$$

Now here is the result of adding x to the sum of y and z:

$$
\begin{array}{llll}
(y) & 1325000 \times 10^0 & & \\
(z) & \underline{5424 \times 10^0} & & \\
& 1330424 \times 10^0 & = 1330 \times 10^3 & \text{(truncated to four digits)}
\end{array}
$$

$$
\begin{array}{lll}
(y + z) & 1330 \times 10^3 & \\
(x) & \underline{-1324 \times 10^3} & \\
& 6 \times 10^3 & = 6000 \times 10^0 \leftarrow x + (y + z)
\end{array}
$$

These two answers are the same in the thousands place but are different thereafter. The error behind this discrepancy is called **representational error.**

Because of representational errors, it is unwise to use a floating-point variable as a loop control variable. Because precision may be lost in calculations involving floating-point numbers, it is difficult to predict when (or even *if*) a loop control variable of type float (or double or long double) will equal the termination value. A count-controlled loop with a floating-point control variable can behave unpredictably.

Also because of representational errors, you should never compare floating-point numbers for exact equality. Rarely are two floating-point numbers exactly equal, and thus you should compare them only for near equality. If the difference between the two numbers is less than some acceptable small value, you can consider them equal for the purposes of the given problem.

Implementation of Floating-Point Numbers in the Computer

Let's formally define some of the terms we used informally in the previous sections.

Significant digits   Those digits from the first nonzero digit on the left to the last nonzero digit on the right (plus any 0 digits that are exact).

Precision   The maximum number of significant digits.

Representational error   Arithmetic error that occurs when the precision of the true result of an arithmetic operation is greater than the precision of the machine.

All computers limit the precision of floating-point numbers, although modern machines use binary rather than decimal arithmetic. In our representation, we used only 5 digits to simplify the examples, and some computers really are limited to only 4 or 5 digits of precision. A more typical system might provide 6 significant digits for float values, 15 digits for double values, and 19 for the long double type. We have shown only a single-digit exponent, but most systems allow 2 digits for the float type and up to 4-digit exponents for type long double.

When you declare a floating-point variable, part of the memory location is assumed to contain the exponent, and the number itself (called the *mantissa*) is assumed to be in the balance of the location. The system is called floating-point representation because the number of significant digits is fixed, and the decimal point conceptually is allowed to float (move to different positions as necessary). In our coding scheme, every number is stored as four digits, with the leftmost digit being nonzero and the exponent adjusted accordingly. Numbers in this form are said to be *normalized*. The number 1,000,000 is stored as

+	+	3	1	0	0	0

and 0.1032 is stored as

+	−	4	1	0	3	2

Normalization provides the maximum precision possible.

Model Numbers   Any real number that can be represented exactly as a floating-point number in the computer is called a *model number*. A real number whose value cannot be represented exactly is approximated by the model number closest to it. In our system with four digits of precision, 0.3021 is a model number. The values 0.3021409, 0.3021222, and 0.30209999999 are examples of real numbers that are represented in the computer by the same model number. The following table shows all of the model numbers for an even simpler floating-point system that has one digit in the mantissa and an exponent that can be −1, 0, or 1.

0.1×10^{-1}	0.1×10^{0}	$0.1 \times 10^{+1}$
0.2×10^{-1}	0.2×10^{0}	$0.2 \times 10^{+1}$
0.3×10^{-1}	0.3×10^{0}	$0.3 \times 10^{+1}$
0.4×10^{-1}	0.4×10^{0}	$0.4 \times 10^{+1}$
0.5×10^{-1}	0.5×10^{0}	$0.5 \times 10^{+1}$
0.6×10^{-1}	0.6×10^{0}	$0.6 \times 10^{+1}$
0.7×10^{-1}	0.7×10^{0}	$0.7 \times 10^{+1}$
0.8×10^{-1}	0.8×10^{0}	$0.8 \times 10^{+1}$
0.9×10^{-1}	0.9×10^{0}	$0.9 \times 10^{+1}$

The difference between a real number and the model number that represents it is a form of representational error called *rounding error.* We can measure rounding error in two ways. The *absolute error* is the difference between the real number and the model number. For example, the absolute error in representing 0.3021409 by the model number 0.3021 is 0.0000409. The *relative error* is the absolute error divided by the real number and sometimes is stated as a percentage. For example, 0.0000409 divided by 0.3021409 is 0.000135, or 0.0135%.

The maximum absolute error depends on the *model interval*—the difference between two adjacent model numbers. In our example, the interval between 0.3021 and 0.3022 is 0.0001. The maximum absolute error in this system, for this interval, is less than 0.0001. Adding digits of precision makes the model interval (and thus the maximum absolute error) smaller.

The model interval is not a fixed number; it varies with the exponent. To see why the interval varies, consider that the interval between 3021.0 and 3022.0 is 1.0, which is 10^4 times larger than the interval between 0.3021 and 0.3022. This makes sense, because 3021.0 is simply 0.3021 times 10^4. Thus, a change in the exponent of the model numbers adjacent to the interval has an equivalent effect on the size of the interval. In practical terms, this means that we give up significant digits in the fractional part in order to represent numbers with large integer parts. Figure 10-5 illustrates this by graphing all of the model numbers listed in the preceding table.

We also can use relative and absolute error to measure the rounding error resulting from calculations. For example, suppose we multiply 1.0005 by 1000. The correct result is 1000.5, but because of rounding error, our four-digit computer produces 1000.0 as its result. The absolute error of the computed result is 0.5, and the relative error is 0.05%. Now suppose we multiply 100,050.0 by 1000. The correct result is 100,050,000, but the computer produces 100,000,000 as its result. If we look at the relative error, it is still a modest 0.05%, but the absolute error has grown to 50,000. Notice that this example is another case of changing the size of the model interval.

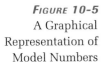

FIGURE 10-5
A Graphical
Representation of
Model Numbers

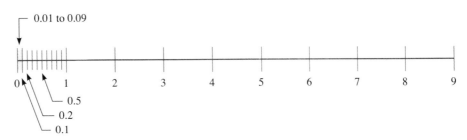

Whether it is more important to consider the absolute error or the relative error depends on the situation. It is unacceptable for an audit of a company to discover a $50,000 accounting error; the fact that the relative error is only 0.05% is not important. On the other hand, a 0.05% relative error is acceptable in representing prehistoric dates because the error in measurement techniques increases with age. That is, if we are talking about a date roughly 10,000 years ago, an absolute error of 5 years is acceptable; if the date is 100,000,000 years ago, then an absolute error of 50,000 years is equally acceptable.

Comparing Floating-Point Numbers We have cautioned against comparing floating-point numbers for exact equality. Our exploration of representational errors in this chapter reveals why calculations may not produce the expected results even though it appears that they should. In Chapter 5, we wrote an expression that compares two floating-point variables r and s for near equality using the floating-point absolute value function fabs:

```
fabs(r - s) < 0.00001
```

From our discussion of model numbers, you now can recognize that the constant 0.00001 in this expression represents a maximum absolute error. We can generalize this expression as

```
fabs(r - s) < ERROR_TERM
```

where ERROR_TERM is a value that must be determined for each programming problem.

What if we want to compare floating-point numbers with a relative error measure? We must multiply the error term by the value in the problem that the error is relative to. For example, if we want to test whether r and s are "equal" within 0.05% of s, we write the following expression:

```
fabs(r - s) < 0.0005 * s
```

Keep in mind that the choice of the acceptable error and whether it should be absolute or relative depends on the problem being solved. The error terms we have shown in our example expressions are completely arbitrary and may not be appropriate for most problems. In solving a problem that involves the comparison of floating-point numbers, you typically want an error term that is as small as possible. Sometimes the choice is specified in the problem description or is reasonably obvious. Some cases require careful analysis of both the mathematics of the problem and the representational limits of the particular computer. Such analyses are the domain of a branch of mathematics called *numerical analysis* and are beyond the scope of this text.

Underflow and Overflow   In addition to representational errors, there are two other problems to watch out for in floating-point arithmetic: *underflow* and *overflow*.

Underflow is the condition that arises when the value of a calculation is too small to be represented. Going back to our decimal representation, let's look at a calculation involving small numbers:

$$
\begin{array}{r}
4210 \times 10^{-8} \\
\times\, 2000 \times 10^{-8} \\
\hline
8420000 \times 10^{-16} \quad = 8420 \times 10^{-13}
\end{array}
$$

This value cannot be represented in our scheme because the exponent -13 is too small. Our minimum is -9. One way to resolve the problem is to set the result of the calculation to 0.0. Obviously, any answer depending on this calculation will not be exact.

Overflow is a more serious problem because there is no logical recourse when it occurs. For example, the result of the calculation

$$
\begin{array}{r}
9999 \times 10^{9} \\
\times\, 1000 \times 10^{9} \\
\hline
9999000 \times 10^{18} \quad = 9999 \times 10^{21}
\end{array}
$$

cannot be stored, so what should we do? To be consistent with our response to underflow, we could set the result to 9999×10^{9} (the maximum representable value in this case). Yet this seems intuitively wrong. The alternative is to stop with an error message.

C++ does not define what should happen in the case of overflow or underflow. Different implementations of C++ solve the problem in different ways. You might try to cause an overflow with your system and see what happens. Some systems may print a run-time error message such as

"FLOATING POINT OVERFLOW." On other systems, you may get the largest number that can be represented.

Although we are discussing problems with floating-point numbers, integer numbers also can overflow both negatively and positively. Most implementations of C++ ignore integer overflow. To see how your system handles the situation, you should try adding 1 to INT_MAX and −1 to INT_MIN. On most systems, adding 1 to INT_MAX sets the result to INT_MIN, a negative number.

Sometimes you can avoid overflow by arranging computations carefully. Suppose you want to know how many different five-card poker hands can be dealt from a deck of cards. What we are looking for is the number of *combinations* of 52 cards taken 5 at a time. The standard mathematical formula for the number of combinations of *n* things taken *r* at a time is

$$\frac{n!}{r!\,(n-r)!}$$

We could use the Factorial function we wrote in Chapter 8 and write this formula in an assignment statement:

```
hands = Factorial(52) / (Factorial(5) * Factorial(47));
```

The only problem is that 52! is a very large number (approximately 8.0658×10^{67}). And 47! is also large (approximately 2.5862×10^{59}). Both of these numbers are well beyond the capacity of most systems to represent exactly as integers (52! requires 68 digits of precision). Even though they can be represented on many machines as floating-point numbers, most of the precision is still lost. By rearranging the calculations, however, we can achieve an exact result on any system with 9 or more digits of precision. How? Consider that most of the multiplications in computing 52! are canceled when the product is divided by 47!

$$\frac{52!}{5! \times 47!} = \frac{52 \times 51 \times 50 \times 49 \times 48 \times 47 \times 46 \times 45 \times 44 \times \ldots}{(5 \times 4 \times 3 \times 2 \times 1) \times (47 \times 46 \times 45 \times 44 \times \ldots)}$$

So, we really only have to compute

```
hands = 52 * 51 * 50 * 49 * 48 / Factorial(5);
```

which means the numerator is 311,875,200 and the denominator is 120. On a system with 9 or more digits of precision, we get an exact answer: 2,598,960 poker hands.

Cancellation Error   Another type of error that can happen with floating-point numbers is called *cancellation error*, a form of representational error that occurs when numbers of widely differing magnitudes are added or subtracted. Let's look at an example:

$$(1 + 0.00001234 - 1) = 0.00001234$$

The laws of arithmetic say this equation should be true. But is it true if the computer does the arithmetic?

$$
\begin{array}{r}
100000000 \times 10^{-8} \\
+ \quad\quad 1234 \times 10^{-8} \\
\hline
100001234 \times 10^{-8}
\end{array}
$$

To four digits, the sum is 1000×10^{-3}. Now the computer subtracts 1:

$$
\begin{array}{r}
1000 \times 10^{-3} \\
-1000 \times 10^{-3} \\
\hline
0
\end{array}
$$

The result is 0, not .00001234.

Sometimes you can avoid adding two floating-point numbers that are drastically different in size by carefully arranging the calculations. Suppose a problem requires many small floating-point numbers to be added to a large floating-point number. The result is more accurate if the program first sums the smaller numbers to obtain a larger number and then adds the sum to the large number.

At this point, you may want to turn to the first Problem-Solving Case Study at the end of the chapter. This case study involves floating-point computations, and it addresses some of the issues you have learned about in this section.

*B*ACKGROUND INFORMATION

Practical Implications of Limited Precision

A discussion of representational, overflow, underflow, and cancellation errors may seem purely academic. In fact, these errors have serious practical implications in many problems. We close this section with three examples illustrating how limited precision can have costly or even disastrous effects.

During the Mercury space program, several of the spacecraft splashed down a considerable distance from their computed landing points. This delayed the recovery of the spacecraft and the astronaut, putting both in some danger. Eventually, the problem was traced to an imprecise representation of the Earth's rotation period in the program that calculated the landing point.

As part of the construction of a hydroelectric dam, a long set of high-tension cables had to be constructed to link the dam to the nearest power distribution point. The cables were to be several miles long, and each one was to be a continuous unit. (Because of the high power output from the dam, shorter cables couldn't be spliced together.) The cables were constructed at great expense and strung between the two points. It turned out that they were too short, however, so another set had to be manufactured. The problem was traced to errors of precision in calculating the length of the catenary curve (the curve that a cable forms when hanging between two points).

An audit of a bank turned up a mysterious account with a large amount of money in it. The account was traced to an unscrupulous programmer who had used limited precision to his advantage. The bank computed interest on its accounts to a precision of a tenth of a cent. The tenths of cents were not added to the customers' accounts, so the programmer had the extra tenths for all the accounts summed and deposited into an account in his name. Because the bank had thousands of accounts, these tiny amounts added up to a large amount of money. And because the rest of the bank's programs did not use as much precision in their calculations, the scheme went undetected for many months.

The moral of this discussion is twofold: (1) The results of floating-point calculations are often imprecise, and these errors can have serious consequences; and (2) if you are working with extremely large numbers or extremely small numbers, you need more information than this book provides and should consult a numerical analysis text.

SOFTWARE ENGINEERING TIP

Choosing a Numeric Data Type

A first encounter with all the numeric data types of C++ may leave you feeling overwhelmed. To help in choosing an alternative, you may even feel tempted to toss a coin. You should resist this temptation, because each data type exists for a reason. Here are some guidelines:

1. In general, `int` is preferable.

    As a rule, you should use floating-point types *only* when absolutely necessary—that is, when you definitely need fractional values. Not only is floating-point arithmetic subject to representational errors, it also is significantly slower than integer arithmetic on most computers.

    For ordinary integer data, use `int` instead of `char` or `short`. It's easy to make overflow errors with these smaller data types. (For character data, though, the `char` type is appropriate.)

2. Use `long` only if the range of `int` values on your machine is too restrictive.
   Compared to `int`, the `long` type requires more memory space and execution time.
3. Use `double` and `long double` only if you need enormously large or small numbers, or if your machine's `float` values do not carry enough digits of precision.
   The cost of using `double` and `long double` is increased memory space and execution time.
4. Avoid the `unsigned` forms of integral types.
   These types are primarily for manipulating bits within a memory cell, a topic this book does not cover. You might think that declaring a variable as `unsigned` prevents you from accidentally storing a negative number into the variable. However, the C++ compiler does *not* prevent you from doing so. Later in this chapter, we explain why.

By following these guidelines, you'll find that the simple types you use most often are `int` and `float`, along with `char` for character data and `bool` for Boolean data. Only rarely do you need the longer and shorter variations of these fundamental types.

User-Defined Simple Types

The concept of a data type is fundamental to all of the widely used programming languages. One of the strengths of the C++ language is that it allows programmers to create new data types, tailored to meet the needs of a particular program. Much of the remainder of this book is about user-defined data types. In this section, we examine how to create our own simple types.

The Typedef Statement

The *Typedef statement* allows you to introduce a new name for an existing type. Its syntax template is

TypedefStatement

> **typedef** ExistingTypeName NewTypeName ;

Before the `bool` data type was part of the C++ language, many programmers used code like the following to simulate a Boolean type:

```
typedef int Boolean;
const int TRUE = 1;
const int FALSE = 0;
  ⋮
Boolean dataOK;
  ⋮
dataOK = TRUE;
```

In this code, the Typedef statement causes the compiler to substitute the word `int` for every occurrence of the word `Boolean` in the rest of the program.

The Typedef statement provides a very limited way of defining our own data types. In fact, Typedef does not create a new data type at all: It merely creates an additional name for an existing data type. As far as the compiler is concerned, the domain and operations of the above `Boolean` type are identical to the domain and operations of the `int` type.

Despite the fact that Typedef cannot truly create a new data type, it is a valuable tool for writing self-documenting programs. Before `bool` was a built-in type, program code that used the identifiers `Boolean`, `TRUE`, and `FALSE` was more descriptive than code that used `int`, 1, and 0 for Boolean operations.

Names of user-defined types obey the same scope rules that apply to identifiers in general. Most types like `Boolean` above are defined globally, although it is reasonable to define a new type within a subprogram if that is the only place it is used. The guidelines that determine where a named constant should be defined apply also to data types.

Enumeration Types

C++ allows the user to define a new simple type by listing (enumerating) the literal values that make up the domain of the type. These literal values must be *identifiers*, not numbers. The identifiers are separated by commas, and the list is enclosed in braces. Data types defined in this way are called **enumeration types.** Here's an example:

```
enum Days {SUN, MON, TUE, WED, THU, FRI, SAT};
```

This declaration creates a new data type named `Days`. Whereas Typedef merely creates a synonym for an existing type, an enumeration type like `Days` is truly a new type and is distinct from any existing type.

The values in the Days type—SUN, MON, TUE, and so forth—are called **enumerators.** The enumerators are *ordered*, in the sense that SUN < MON < TUE ... < FRI < SAT. Applying relational operators to enumerators is like applying them to characters: The relation that is tested is whether an enumerator "comes before" or "comes after" in the ordering of the data type.

Enumeration type   A user-defined data type whose domain is an ordered set of literal values expressed as identifiers.

Enumerator   One of the values in the domain of an enumeration type.

Earlier we saw that the internal representation of a char constant is a nonnegative integer. The 128 ASCII characters are represented in memory as the integers 0 through 127. Values in an enumeration type are also represented internally as integers. By default, the first enumerator has the integer value 0, the second has the value 1, and so forth. Our declaration of the Days enumeration type is similar to the following set of declarations:

```
typedef int Days;
const int SUN = 0;
const int MON = 1;
const int TUE = 2;
   ⋮
const int SAT = 6;
```

If there is some reason that you want different internal representations for the enumerators, you can specify them explicitly like this:

```
enum Days {SUN = 4, MON = 18, TUE = 9, ... };
```

There is rarely any reason to assign specific values to enumerators. With the Days type, we are interested in the days of the week, not in the way the machine stores them internally. We do not discuss this feature any further, although you may occasionally see it in C++ programs.

Notice the style we use to capitalize enumerators. Because enumerators are, in essence, named constants, we capitalize the entire identifier. This is purely a style choice. Many C++ programmers use both uppercase and lowercase letters when they invent names for the enumerators.

Here is the syntax template for the declaration of an enumeration type. It is a simplified version; later in the chapter we expand it.

EnumDeclaration

enum Name **{** Enumerator **,** Enumerator ... **}** **;**

Each enumerator has the following form:

Enumerator

Identifier **=** ConstIntExpression

where the optional ConstIntExpression is an integer expression composed only of literal or named constants.

The identifiers used as enumerators must follow the rules for any C++ identifier. For example,

```
enum Vowel {'A', 'E', 'I', 'O', 'U'};     // Error
```

is not legal because the items are not identifiers. The declaration

```
enum Places {1st, 2nd, 3rd};     // Error
```

is not legal because identifiers cannot begin with digits. In the declarations

```
enum Starch {CORN, RICE, POTATO, BEAN};
enum Grain {WHEAT, CORN, RYE, BARLEY, SORGHUM};     // Error
```

type `Starch` and type `Grain` are legal individually, but together they are not. Identifiers in the same scope must be unique. `CORN` cannot be defined twice.

Suppose you are writing a program for a veterinary clinic. The program must keep track of different kinds of animals. The following enumeration type might be used for this purpose.

Type identifier   Literal values in the domain

enum Animals {RODENT, CAT, DOG, BIRD, REPTILE, HORSE, BOVINE, SHEEP};

Animals inPatient;
Animals outPatient;   Creation of two variables of type `Animals`

RODENT is a literal, one of the values in the data type Animals. Be sure you understand that RODENT is not a variable name. Instead, RODENT is one of the values that can be stored into the variables inPatient and outPatient. Let's look at the kinds of operations we might want to perform on variables of enumeration types.

Assignment   The assignment statement

inPatient = DOG;

does not assign to inPatient the character string "DOG", nor the contents of a variable named DOG. It assigns the *value* DOG, which is one of the values in the domain of the data type Animals.

Assignment is a valid operation, as long as the value being stored is of type Animals. Both of the statements

inPatient = DOG;
outPatient = inPatient;

are acceptable. Each expression on the right-hand side is of type Animals—DOG is a literal of type Animals, and inPatient is a variable of type Animals. Although we know that the underlying representation of DOG is the integer 2, the compiler prevents us from using this assignment:

inPatient = 2;   // Not allowed

Here is the precise rule:

Implicit type coercion is defined from an enumeration type to an integral type but not from an integral type to an enumeration type.

Applying this rule to the statements

someInt = DOG;   // Valid
inPatient = 2;   // Error

we see that the first statement stores 2 into someInt (because of implicit type coercion), but the second produces a compile-time error. The restriction against storing an integer value into a variable of type Animals is to keep you from accidentally storing an out-of-range value:

```
inPatient = 65;    // Error
```

Incrementation Suppose that you want to "increment" the value in inPatient so that it becomes the next value in the domain:

```
inPatient = inPatient + 1;    // Error
```

This statement is illegal for the following reason. The right-hand side is OK because implicit type coercion lets you add inPatient to 1; the result is an int value. But the assignment operation is not valid because you can't store an int value into inPatient. The statement

```
inPatient++;    // Error
```

is also invalid because the compiler considers it to have the same semantics as the assignment statement above. However, you can escape the type coercion rule by using an *explicit* type conversion—a type cast—as follows:

```
inPatient = Animals(inPatient + 1);    // Correct
```

When you use the type cast, the compiler assumes that you know what you are doing and allows it.

Incrementing a variable of enumeration type is very useful in loops. Sometimes we need a loop that processes all the values in the domain of the type. We might try the following For loop:

```
Animals patient;

for (patient=RODENT; patient <= SHEEP; patient++)   // Error
    ⋮
```

However, as we explained above, the compiler will complain about the expression patient++. To increment patient, we must use an assignment expression and a type cast:

```
for (patient=RODENT; patient <= SHEEP; patient=Animals(patient + 1))
    ⋮
```

The only caution here is that when control exits the loop, the value of `patient` is 1 *greater than* the largest value in the domain (`SHEEP`). If you want to use `patient` outside the loop, you must reassign it a value that is within the appropriate range for the `Animals` type.

Comparison   The most common operation performed on values of enumeration types is comparison. When you compare two values, their ordering is determined by the order in which you listed the enumerators in the type declaration. For instance, the expression

```
inPatient <= BIRD
```

has the value `true` if `inPatient` contains the value `RODENT`, `CAT`, `DOG`, or `BIRD`.

You can also use values of an enumeration type in a Switch statement. Because `RODENT`, `CAT`, and so on are literals, they can appear in case labels:

```
switch (inPatient)
{
    case RODENT   :
    case CAT      :
    case DOG      :
    case BIRD     : cout << "Cage ward";
                    break;
    case REPTILE  : cout << "Terrarium ward";
                    break;
    case HORSE    :
    case BOVINE   :
    case SHEEP    : cout << "Barn";
}
```

Input and Output   Stream I/O is defined only for the basic built-in types (`int`, `float`, and so on), not for user-defined enumeration types. Values of enumeration types must be input or output indirectly.

To input values, one strategy is to read a string that spells one of the constants in the enumeration type. The idea is to input the string and translate it to one of the literals in the enumeration type by looking only at as many letters as are necessary to determine what it is.

For example, the veterinary clinic program could read the kind of animal as a string, then assign one of the values of type `Animals` to that patient. *Cat, dog, horse,* and *sheep* can be determined by their first letter. *Bovine, bird, rodent,* and *reptile* cannot be determined until the second letter is examined. The following program fragment reads in a string representing an animal name and converts it to one of the values in type `Animals`.

```
#include <cctype>      // For toupper()
#include <string>      // For string type
    ⋮
string animalName;
    ⋮
cin >> animalName;
switch (toupper(animalName[0]))
{
    case 'R' : if (toupper(animalName[1]) == 'O')
                   inPatient = RODENT;
               else
                   inPatient = REPTILE;
               break;
    case 'C' : inPatient = CAT;
               break;
    case 'D' : inPatient = DOG;
               break;
    case 'B' : if (toupper(animalName[1]) == 'I')
                   inPatient = BIRD;
               else
                   inPatient = BOVINE;
               break;
    case 'H' : inPatient = HORSE;
               break;
    default  : inPatient = SHEEP;
}
```

Enumeration type values cannot be printed directly either. Printing is done by using a Switch statement that prints a character string corresponding to the value.

```
switch (inPatient)
{
    case RODENT  : cout << "Rodent";
                   break;
    case CAT     : cout << "Cat";
                   break;
    case DOG     : cout << "Dog";
                   break;
    case BIRD    : cout << "Bird";
                   break;
    case REPTILE : cout << "Reptile";
                   break;
    case HORSE   : cout << "Horse";
                   break;
    case BOVINE  : cout << "Bovine";
                   break;
    case SHEEP   : cout << "Sheep";
}
```

You might ask, Why not use just a pair of letters or an integer number as a code to represent each animal in a program? The answer is that we use enumeration types to make our programs more readable; they are another way to make the code more self-documenting.

Returning a Function Value   We have been using value-returning functions to compute and return values of built-in types such as `int`, `float`, and `char`:

```
int Factorial( int );
float CargoMoment( int );
```

C++ allows a function return value to be of *any* data type—built-in or user-defined—except an array (a data type we examine in later chapters).

In the last section, we wrote a Switch statement to convert an input string into a value of type `Animals`. Let's write a value-returning function that performs this task. Notice how the function heading declares the data type of the return value to be `Animals`.

```
Animals StrToAnimal( /* in */ string str )
{
    switch (toupper(str[0]))
    {
        case 'R' : if (toupper(str[1]) == 'O')
                       return RODENT;
                   else
                       return REPTILE;
        case 'C' : return CAT;
        case 'D' : return DOG;
        case 'B' : if (toupper(str[1]) == 'I')
                       return BIRD;
                   else
                       return BOVINE;
        case 'H' : return HORSE;
        default :  return SHEEP;
    }
}
```

In this function, why didn't we include a Break statement after each case alternative? Because when one of the alternatives executes a Return statement, control immediately exits the function. It's not possible for control to "fall through" to the next alternative.

Here is a sample of code that calls the `StrToAnimal` function:

```
enum Animals {RODENT, CAT, DOG, BIRD, REPTILE, HORSE, BOVINE, SHEEP};

Animals StrToAnimal( string );
  ⋮
int main()
{
    Animals inPatient;
    Animals outPatient;
    string  inputStr;
      ⋮
    cin >> inputStr;
    inPatient = StrToAnimal(inputStr);
      ⋮
    cin >> inputStr;
    outPatient = StrToAnimal(inputStr);
      ⋮
}
```

Named and Anonymous Data Types

The enumeration types we have looked at, `Animals` and `Days`, are called **named types** because their declarations included names for the types. Variables of these new data types are declared separately using the type identifiers `Animals` and `Days`.

Named type   A user-defined type whose declaration includes a type identifier that gives a name to the type.

C++ also lets us introduce a new type directly in a variable declaration. Instead of the declarations

```
enum CoinType {NICKEL, DIME, QUARTER, HALF_DOLLAR};
enum StatusType {OK, OUT_OF_STOCK, BACK_ORDERED};

CoinType   change;
StatusType status;
```

we could write

```
enum {NICKEL, DIME, QUARTER, HALF_DOLLAR} change;
enum {OK, OUT_OF_STOCK, BACK_ORDERED} status;
```

A new type declared in a variable declaration is called an **anonymous type** because it does not have a name—that is, it does not have a type identifier associated with it.

Anonymous type   A type that does not have an associated type identifier.

If we can create a data type in a variable declaration, why bother with a separate type declaration that creates a named type? Named types, like named constants, make a program more readable, more understandable, and easier to modify. Also, declaring a type and declaring a variable of that type are two distinct concepts; it is best to keep them separate.

We now give a more complete syntax template for an enumeration type declaration. This template shows that the type name is optional (yielding an anonymous type) and that a list of variables may optionally be included in the declaration.

EnumDeclaration

```
enum Name { Enumerator , Enumerator  ... } VariableName  ,  VariableName  ...  ;
```

User-Written Header Files

As you create your own user-defined data types, you often find that a data type can be useful in more than one program. For example, you may be working on several programs that need an enumeration type consisting of the names of the 12 months of the year. Instead of typing the statement

```
enum Months
{
    JANUARY, FEBRUARY, MARCH, APRIL, MAY, JUNE,
    JULY, AUGUST, SEPTEMBER, OCTOBER, NOVEMBER, DECEMBER
};
```

at the beginning of every program that uses the Months type, you can put this statement into a separate file named, say, months.h. Then you use months.h just as you use system-supplied header files such as iostream and cmath. By using an #include directive, you ask the C++ preprocessor to insert the contents of the file physically into your program. (Although many C++ systems use the filename extension .h [or no extension at all] to denote header files, other systems use extensions such as .hpp or .hxx.)

When you enclose the name of a header file in angle brackets, as in

```
#include <iostream>
```

the preprocessor looks for the file in the standard *include directory,* a directory that contains all the header files supplied by the C++ system. On the other hand, you can enclose the name of a header file in double quotes, like this:

```
#include "months.h"
```

In this case, the preprocessor looks for the file in the programmer's current directory. This mechanism allows us to write our own header files that contain type declarations and constant declarations. We can use a simple #include directive instead of retyping the declarations in every program that needs them (see Figure 10-6.)

More on Type Coercion

As you have learned over the course of several chapters, C++ performs implicit type coercion whenever values of different data types are used in the following:

1. Arithmetic and relational expressions
2. Assignment operations
3. Argument passing
4. Return of the function value from a value-returning function

For item 1—mixed type expressions—the C++ compiler follows one set of rules for type coercion. For items 2, 3, and 4, the compiler follows a second set of rules. Let's examine each of these two rules.

FIGURE 10-6
Including
Header Files

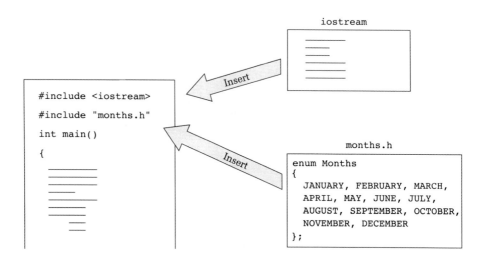

Type Coercion in Arithmetic and Relational Expressions

Suppose that an arithmetic expression consists of one operator and two operands—for example, `3.4*sum` or `var1/var2`. If the two operands are of different data types, then one of them is temporarily **promoted** (or **widened**) to match the data type of the other. To understand exactly what promotion means, let's look at the rule for type coercion in an arithmetic expression.*

Step 1:   Each `char`, `short`, `bool`, or enumeration value is promoted (widened) to `int`. If both operands are now `int`, the result is an `int` expression.

Step 2:   If step 1 still leaves a mixed type expression, the following precedence of types is used:

lowest $\longrightarrow$ highest

`int, unsigned int, long, unsigned long, float, double, long double`

The value of the operand of "lower" type is promoted to that of the "higher" type, and the result is an expression of that type.

A simple example is the expression `someFloat+2`. This expression has no `char`, `short`, `bool`, or enumeration values in it, so step 1 still leaves a mixed type expression. In step 2, `int` is a "lower" type than `float`, so the value 2 is coerced temporarily to the `float` value, say, 2.0. Then the addition takes place, and the type of the entire expression is `float`.

   This description of type coercion also holds for relational expressions such as

`someInt <= someFloat`

The value of `someInt` is temporarily coerced to floating-point representation before the comparison takes place. The only difference between arithmetic expressions and relational expressions is that the resulting type of a relational expression is always `bool`—the value `true` or `false`.

Promotion (widening)   The conversion of a value from a "lower" type to a "higher" type according to a programming language's precedence of data types.

---

* The rule we give for type coercion is a simplified version of the rule found in the C++ language definition. The complete rule has more to say about unsigned types, which we rarely use in this book.

Here is a table that describes the result of promoting a value from one simple type to another in C++:

From	To	Result of Promotion
double	long double	Same value, occupying more memory space
float	double	Same value, occupying more memory space
Integral type	Floating-point type	Floating-point equivalent of the integer value; fractional part is zero
Integral type	Its unsigned counterpart	Same value, if original number is nonnegative; a radically different positive number, if original number is negative
Signed integral type	Longer signed integral type	Same value, occupying more memory space
unsigned integral type	Longer integral type (either signed or unsigned)	Same nonnegative value, occupying more memory space

NOTE: The result of promoting a char to an int is compiler dependent. Some compilers treat char as unsigned char, so promotion always yields a nonnegative integer. With other compilers, char means signed char, so promotion of a negative value yields a negative integer.

The note at the bottom of the table suggests a potential problem if you are trying to write a portable C++ program. If you use the char type only to store character data, there is no problem. C++ guarantees that each character in a machine's character set (such as ASCII) is represented as a nonnegative value. Using character data, promotion from char to int gives the same result on any machine with any compiler.

But if you try to save memory by using the char type for manipulating small signed integers, then promotion of these values to the int type can produce different results on different machines! That is, one machine may promote negative char values to negative int values, whereas the same program on another machine might promote negative char values to *positive* int values. The moral is this: Unless you are squeezed to the limit for memory space, do not use char to manipulate small signed numbers. Use char only to store character data.

Type Coercion in Assignments, Argument Passing, and Return of a Function Value

In general, promotion of a value from one type to another does not cause loss of information. Think of promotion as moving your baseball cards from a small shoe box to a larger shoe box. All of the cards still fit into the new box and there is room to spare. On the other hand, **demotion** (or **narrowing**) of data values can potentially cause loss of information. Demotion is like moving a shoe box full of baseball cards into a smaller box—something has to be thrown out.

Demotion (narrowing)   The conversion of a value from a "higher" type to a "lower" type according to a programming language's precedence of data types. Demotion may cause loss of information.

Consider an assignment operation

$$v = e$$

where v is a variable and e is an expression. Regarding the data types of v and e, there are three possibilities:

1. If the types of v and e are the same, no type coercion is necessary.
2. If the type of v is "higher" than that of e (using the type precedence we explained with promotion), then the value of e is promoted to v's type before being stored into v.
3. If the type of v is "lower" than that of e, the value of e is demoted to v's type before being stored into v.

Demotion, which you can think of as shrinking a value, may cause loss of information:

- Demotion from a longer integral type to a shorter integral type (such as long to int) results in discarding the leftmost (most significant) bits in the binary number representation. The result may be a drastically different number.
- Demotion from a floating-point type to an integral type causes truncation of the fractional part (and an undefined result if the whole-number part will not fit into the destination variable). The result of truncating a negative number is machine dependent.
- Demotion from a longer floating-point type to a shorter floating-point type (such as double to float) may result in a loss of digits of precision.

Our description of type coercion in an assignment operation also holds for argument passing (the mapping of arguments onto parameters) and for returning a function value with a Return statement. For example, assume that INT_MAX on your machine is 32767 and that you have the following function:

```
void DoSomething( int n )
{
    ⋮
}
```

If the function is called with the statement

```
DoSomething(50000);
```

then the value 50000 (which is implicitly of type `long` because it is larger than `INT_MAX`) is demoted to a completely different, smaller value that fits into an `int` location. In a similar fashion, execution of the function

```
int SomeFunc( float x )
{
    ⋮
    return 70000;
}
```

causes demotion of the value 70000 to a smaller `int` value because `int` is the declared type of the function return value.

One interesting consequence of implicit type coercion is the futility of declaring a variable to be `unsigned`, hoping that the compiler will prevent you from making a mistake like this:

```
unsignedVar = -5;
```

The compiler does not complain at all. It generates code to coerce the `int` value to an `unsigned int` value. If you now print out the value of `unsignedVar`, you'll see a strange-looking positive integer. As we have pointed out before, `unsigned` types are most appropriate for advanced techniques that manipulate individual bits within memory cells. It's best to avoid using `unsigned` for ordinary numeric computations.

*P*ROBLEM-SOLVING CASE STUDY

Finding the Area Under a Curve

Problem: Find the area under the curve of the function X^3 over an interval specified by the user. In other words, given a pair of floating-point numbers, find the area under the graph of X^3 between those two numbers (see Figure 10-7).

Input: Two floating-point numbers specifying the interval over which to find the area, and an integer number of intervals to use in approximating the area.

PROBLEM-SOLVING CASE STUDY cont'd.

FIGURE 10-7

Area Under Graph
of X^3 Between 0
and 3

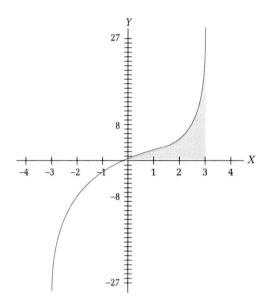

Output: The input data (echo print) and the value calculated for the area over the given interval.

Discussion: Our approach is to compute an approximation to this area. If the area under the curve is divided into equal, narrow, rectangular strips, the sum of the areas of these rectangles is close to the actual area under the curve (see Figure 10-8). The narrower the rectangles, the more accurate the approximation should be.

We can use a value-returning function to compute the area of each rectangle. The user enters the low and high values for X, as well as the number of rectangles into which the area should be subdivided (divisions). The width of a rectangle is then

```
(high - low) / divisions
```

The height of a rectangle equals the value of X^3 when X is at the horizontal midpoint of the rectangle. The area of a rectangle equals its height times its width. Because the leftmost rectangle has its midpoint at

```
(low + width/2.0)
```

its area equals the following (see Figure 10-9):

PROBLEM-SOLVING CASE STUDY cont'd.

FIGURE 10-8
Approximation
of Area Under a
Curve

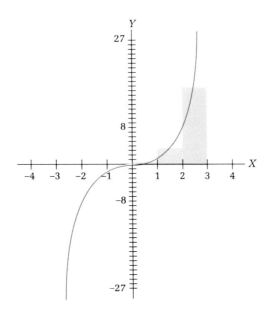

FIGURE 10-9
Area of the Left-
most Rectangle

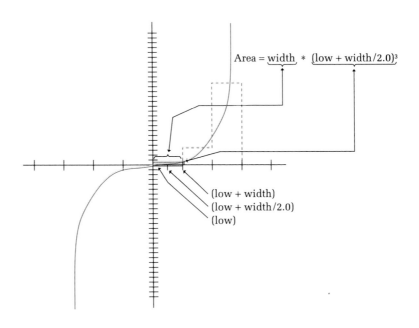

`(low + width/2.0)`^{3} `* width`

The second rectangle has its left edge at the point where *X* equals

`low + width`

and its area equals the following (see Figure 10-10):

`(low + width + width/2.0)`^{3} `* width`

The left edge of each rectangle is at a point that is `width` greater than the left edge of the rectangle to its left. Thus, we can step through the rectangles by using a count-controlled loop with the number of iterations equal to the value of `divisions`. This loop contains a second counter (not the loop control variable) starting at `low` and counting by steps of `width` up to (`high − width`). Two counters are necessary because the second counter must be of type `float`, and it is poor programming technique to have a loop control variable be a `float` variable. For each iteration of this loop, we compute the area of the corresponding rectangle and add this value to the total area under the curve.

We want a value-returning function to compute the area of a rectangle, given the position of its left edge and its width. Let's also make X^3 a separate function named `Funct`, so we can substitute other mathematical func-

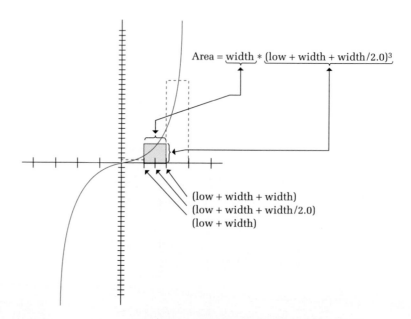

FIGURE 10-10
Area of the
Second
Rectangle

tions in its place without changing the rest of the design. Our program can then be converted quickly to find the area under the curve of any single-variable function.

Here is our design:

Main   **Level 0**

> Get data
> Set width = (high – low) / divisions
> Set area = 0.0
> Set leftEdge = low
> FOR count going from 1 through divisions
>   Set area = area + RectArea(leftEdge, width)
>   Set leftEdge = leftEdge + width
> Print area

RectArea (In: leftEdge, width)   **Level 1**

  Out: Function value

> Return Funct(leftEdge + width/2.0) * width

Get Data (Out: low, high, divisions)

> Prompt for low and high
> Read low, high
> Prompt for divisions
> Read divisions
> Echo print input data

Funct (In: x)   **Level 2**

  Out: Function value

> Return x * x * x

Module Structure Chart:

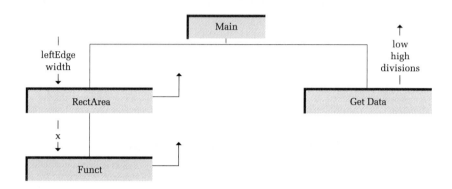

(The following program is written in ISO/ANSI standard C++. If you are working with pre–standard C++, see the alternate version of the program in the PRE_STD directory of the program disk, available at the publisher's Web site, www.jbpub.com/disks.)

```
//*****************************************************************
// Area program
// This program finds the area under the curve of a mathematical
// function in a specified interval.  Input consists of two float
// values and one int.  The first two are the low, high values for
// the interval.  The third is the number of slices to be used in
// approximating the area.  As written, this program finds the
// area under the curve of the function x cubed; however, any
// single-variable function may be substituted for the function
// named Funct
//*****************************************************************
#include <iostream>
#include <iomanip>      // For setprecision()

using namespace std;

float Funct( float );
void  GetData( float&, float&, int& );
float RectArea( float, float );

int main()
{
    float low;          // Lowest value in the desired interval
    float high;         // Highest value in the desired interval
    float width;        // Computed width of a rectangular slice
    float leftEdge;     // Left edge point in a rectangular slice
    float area;         // Total area under the curve
```

PROBLEM-SOLVING CASE STUDY cont'd.

```
int    divisions;   // Number of slices to divide the interval by
int    count;       // Loop control variable

cout << fixed << showpoint;              // Set up floating-pt.
                                         //    output format
GetData(low, high, divisions);
width = (high - low) / float(divisions);
area = 0.0;
leftEdge = low;

// Calculate and sum areas of slices

for (count = 1; count <= divisions; count++)
{
    area = area + RectArea(leftEdge, width);
    leftEdge = leftEdge + width;
}

// Print result

cout << "The result is equal to "
     << setprecision(7) << area << endl;
return 0;
}

//**************************************************************

void GetData( /* out */ float& low,          // Bottom of interval
              /* out */ float& high,         // Top of interval
              /* out */ int&   divisions )   // Division factor

// Prompts for the input of low, high, and divisions values
// and returns the three values after echo printing them

// Postcondition:
//     All parameters (low, high, and divisions)
//     have been prompted for, input, and echo printed
{

    cout << "Enter low and high values of desired interval"
         << " (floating point)." << endl;
    cin >> low >> high;
    cout << "Enter the number of divisions to be used (integer)."
         << endl;
    cin >> divisions;
    cout << "The area is computed over the interval "
         << setprecision(7) << low << endl
         << "to " << high << " with " << divisions
         << " subdivisions of the interval." << endl;
}
```

PROBLEM-SOLVING CASE STUDY cont'd.

```
//*****************************************************************

float RectArea( /* in */ float leftEdge,     // Left edge point of
                                             //    rectangle
               /* in */ float width   )      // Width of rectangle

// Computes the area of a rectangle that starts at leftEdge and is
// "width" units wide.  The rectangle's height is given by the value
// computed by Funct at the horizontal midpoint of the rectangle

// Precondition:
//      leftEdge and width are assigned
// Postcondition:
//      Function value == area of specified rectangle

{
    return Funct(leftEdge + width / 2.0) * width;
}


//*****************************************************************

float Funct( /* in */ float x )     // Value to be cubed

// Computes x cubed.  You may replace this function with any
// single-variable function

// Precondition:
//      The absolute value of x cubed does not exceed the
//      machine's maximum float value
// Postcondition:
//      Function value == x cubed

{
    return x * x * x;
}
```

Testing: We should test this program with sets of data that include positive, negative, and zero values. It is especially important to try to input values of 0 and 1 for the number of divisions. The results from the program should be compared against values calculated by hand using the same algorithm and against the true value of the area under the curve of X^3, which is given by the formula

$$\frac{1}{4} \times (high^4 - low^4)$$

PROBLEM-SOLVING CASE STUDY cont'd.

(This formula comes from the mathematical topic of calculus. What we have been referring to as the area under the curve in the interval a to b is called the *integral* of the function from a to b.)

Let's consider for a moment the effects of representational error on this program. The user specifies the low and high values of the interval, as well as the number of subdivisions to be used in computing the result. The more subdivisions used, the more accurate the result should be because the rectangles are narrower and thus approximate more closely the shape of the area under the curve. It seems that we can obtain precise results by using a large number of subdivisions. In fact, however, there is a point beyond which an increase in the number of subdivisions *decreases* the precision of the results. If we specify too many subdivisions, the area of an individual rectangle becomes so small that the computer can no longer represent its value accurately. Adding all those inaccurate values produces a total area that has an even greater error.

*P*ROBLEM-SOLVING CASE STUDY

Rock, Paper, Scissors

Problem: Play the children's game Rock, Paper, Scissors. In this game, two people simultaneously choose one of the following: rock, paper, or scissors. Whether a player wins or loses depends not only on that player's choice but also on the opponent's choice. The rules are as follows:

Rock breaks scissors; rock wins.
Paper covers rock; paper wins.
Scissors cut paper; scissors win.
All matching combinations are ties.
The overall winner is the player who wins the most individual games.

Input: A series of letters representing player A's plays (`fileA`, one letter per line) and a series of letters representing player B's plays (`fileB`, one letter per line), with each play indicated by 'R' (for Rock), 'P' (for Paper), or 'S' (for Scissors).

Output: For each game, the game number and the player who won that game; at the end, the total number of games won by each player, and the overall winner.

Discussion: We assume that everyone has played this game and understands it. Therefore, our discussion centers on how to simulate the game in a program.

THE FAR SIDE   By GARY LARSON

Before paper and fire

In the algorithm we developed to read in animal names, we used as input a string containing the entire animal name and translated the string into a corresponding literal in an enumeration type. Here, we show an alternative approach. For input, we use a single character to stand for rock, paper, or scissors. We input 'R', 'P', or 'S' and convert the letter to a value of an enumeration type made up of the literals ROCK, PAPER, and SCISSORS.

Each player creates a file composed of a series of the letters 'R', 'P', and 'S', representing a series of individual games. A pair of letters is read, one from each file, and converted into the appropriate enumeration type literals. Let's call each literal a play. The plays are compared, and a winner is determined. The number of games won is incremented for the winning player each time. The game is over when there are no more plays (the files are empty).

Assumptions: The game is over when one of the files runs out of plays.

Main   **Level 0**

```
Open data files (and verify success)
Get plays
WHILE NOT EOF on fileA AND NOT EOF on fileB
        IF plays are legal
                    Process plays
        ELSE
                    Print an error message
        Get plays
Print big winner
```

Get Plays (Out: playForA, playForB, legal)   **Level 1**

```
Read charForA (player A's play) from fileA
Read charForB (player B's play) from fileB
IF EOF on fileA OR EOF on fileB
        Return
Set legal =  (charForA is 'R', 'P', or 'S') AND
                    (charForB is 'R', 'P', or 'S')
IF legal
        Set playForA = ConversionValue(charForA)
        Set playForB = ConversionValue(charForB)
```

Process Plays (In: gameNumber, playForA, playForB; Inout: winsForA, winsForB)

```
IF playForA = = playForB
        Print gameNumber, " is a tie"
ELSE IF    playForA = = PAPER AND playForB = = ROCK OR
           playForA = = SCISSORS AND playForB = = PAPER OR
           playForA = = ROCK AND playForB = = SCISSORS
        Record a win for Player A, incrementing winsForA (the number
            of games won by Player A)
ELSE
        Record a win for Player B, incrementing winsForB
```

PROBLEM-SOLVING CASE STUDY cont'd.

Print Big Winner (In: winsForA, winsForB)

```
Print winsForA
Print winsForB
IF winsForA > winsForB
      Print "Player A has won the most games."
ELSE IF winsForB > winsForA
      Print "Player B has won the most games."
ELSE
      Print "Players A and B have tied."
```

ConversionValue (In: someChar)
Out: Function value

Level 2

```
SWITCH someChar
      'R': Return ROCK
      'P': Return PAPER
      'S': Return SCISSORS
```

Record a Win (In: player, gameNumber; Inout: numOfWins)

```
Print message saying which player has won game number gameNumber
Increment numOfWins by 1
```

Now we are ready to code the simulation of the game. We must remember to initialize our counters. We assumed that we knew the game number for each game, yet nowhere have we kept track of the game number. We need to add a counter to our loop in the main module. Here's the revised main module:

PROBLEM-SOLVING CASE STUDY cont'd.

Main

```
Open data files (and verify success)
Set winsForA and winsForB = 0
Set gameNumber = 0
Get plays
WHILE NOT EOF on fileA AND NOT EOF on fileB
        Increment gameNumber by 1
        IF plays are legal
                Process plays
        ELSE
                Print an error message
        Get plays
Print big winner
```

Module Structure Chart:

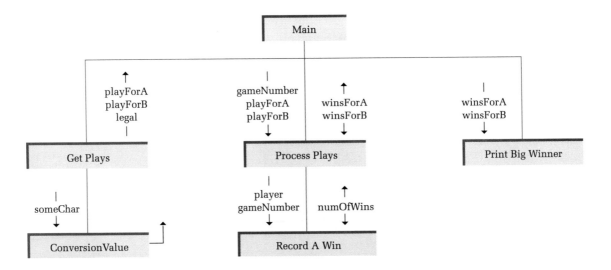

(The following program is written in ISO/ANSI standard C++. If you are working with pre–standard C++, see the alternate version of the program in the PRE_STD directory of the program disk, available at the publisher's Web site, www.jbpub.com/disks.)

```cpp
//*******************************************************************
// Game program
// This program simulates the children's game Rock, Paper, and
// Scissors.  Each game consists of inputs from two players,
// coming from fileA and fileB.  A winner is determined for each
// individual game and for the games overall
//*******************************************************************
#include <iostream>
#include <fstream>     // For file I/O

using namespace std;

enum PlayType {ROCK, PAPER, SCISSORS};

PlayType ConversionVal( char );
void GetPlays( ifstream&, ifstream&, PlayType&, PlayType&, bool& );
void PrintBigWinner( int, int );
void ProcessPlays( int, PlayType, PlayType, int&, int& );
void RecordAWin( char, int, int& );

int main()
{
    PlayType playForA;              // Player A's play
    PlayType playForB;              // Player B's play
    int      winsForA = 0;          // Number of games A wins
    int      winsForB = 0;          // Number of games B wins
    int      gameNumber = 0;        // Number of games played
    bool     legal;                 // True if play is legal
    ifstream fileA;                 // Player A's plays
    ifstream fileB;                 // Player B's plays

    // Open the input files

    fileA.open("filea.dat");
    fileB.open("fileb.dat");
    if ( !fileA || !fileB )
    {
        cout << "** Can't open input file(s) **" << endl;
        return 1;
    }

    // Play a series of games and keep track of who wins

    GetPlays(fileA, fileB, playForA, playForB, legal);
    while (fileA && fileB)
    {
        gameNumber++;
```

PROBLEM-SOLVING CASE STUDY cont'd.

```
              if (legal)
                  ProcessPlays(gameNumber, playForA, playForB, winsForA,
                                 winsForB);
              else
                  cout << "Game number " << gameNumber
                          << " contained an illegal play." << endl;
              GetPlays(fileA, fileB, playForA, playForB, legal);
          }

          // Print overall winner

          PrintBigWinner(winsForA, winsForB);

          return 0;
      }

      //****************************************************************

      void GetPlays( /* inout */ ifstream& fileA,        // Plays for A
                     /* inout */ ifstream& fileB,        // Plays for B
                     /* out */   PlayType& playForA,     // A's play
                     /* out */   PlayType& playForB,     // B's play
                     /* out */   bool&     legal     )   // True if plays
                                                          //   are legal

      // Reads the players' plays from the data files, converts the plays
      // from char form to PlayType form, and reports whether the plays
      // are legal.  If end-of-file is encountered on either file, the
      // outgoing parameters are undefined.

      // Precondition:
      //     fileA and fileB have been successfully opened
      // Postcondition:
      //     IF input from either file failed due to end-of-file
      //         playForA, playForB, and legal are undefined
      //     ELSE
      //         Player A's play has been read from fileA and Player B's
      //         play has been read from fileB
      //       && IF both plays are legal
      //            legal == TRUE
      //          && playForA == PlayType equivalent of Player A's play
      //                         char
      //          && playForB == PlayType equivalent of Player B's play
      //                         char
      //        ELSE
      //            legal == FALSE
      //          && playForA and playForB are undefined
```

PROBLEM-SOLVING CASE STUDY cont'd.

```
{
    char charForA;        // Player A's input
    char charForB;        // Player B's input

    fileA >> charForA;              // Skip whitespace, including newline
    fileB >> charForB;
    if ( !fileA || !fileB )
        return;

    legal = (charForA=='R' || charForA=='P' || charForA=='S') &&
            (charForB=='R' || charForB=='P' || charForB=='S');
    if (legal)
    {
        playForA = ConversionVal(charForA);
        playForB = ConversionVal(charForB);
    }
}


//******************************************************************

PlayType ConversionVal( /* in */ char someChar )    // Play character

// Converts a character into an associated PlayType value

// Precondition:
//      someChar == 'R' or 'P' or 'S'
// Postcondition:
//      Function value == ROCK, if someChar == 'R'
//                     == PAPER, if someChar == 'P'
//                     == SCISSORS, if someChar == 'S'

{
    switch (someChar)
    {
        case 'R': return ROCK;       // No break needed after
        case 'P': return PAPER;      //   return statement
        case 'S': return SCISSORS;
    }
}


//******************************************************************

void ProcessPlays( /* in */     int      gameNumber,   // Game number
                   /* in */     PlayType playForA,      // A's play
                   /* in */     PlayType playForB,      // B's play
                   /* inout */ int&      winsForA,      // A's wins
                   /* inout */ int&      winsForB  )    // B's wins
```

<u>*PROBLEM-SOLVING CASE STUDY cont'd.*</u>

```
// Determines whether there is a winning play or a tie.  If there
// is a winner, the number of wins of the winning player is
// incremented.  In all cases, a message is written

// Precondition:
//     All arguments are assigned
// Postcondition:
//     IF Player A won
//         winsForA == winsForA@entry + 1
//     ELSE IF Player B won
//         winsForB == winsForB@entry + 1
//  && A message, including gameNumber, has been written specifying
//     either a tie or a winner

{
    if (playForA == playForB)
        cout << "Game number " << gameNumber << " is a tie."
             << endl;
    else if (playForA == PAPER && playForB == ROCK ||
            playForA == SCISSORS && playForB == PAPER ||
            playForA == ROCK && playForB == SCISSORS)
        RecordAWin('A', gameNumber, winsForA);       // Player A wins
    else
        RecordAWin('B', gameNumber, winsForB);       // Player B wins
}


//*************************************************************

void RecordAWin( /* in */    char player,        // Winning player
                 /* in */    int  gameNumber,    // Game number
                 /* inout */ int& numOfWins  )   // Win count

// Outputs a message telling which player has won the current game
// and updates that player's total

// Precondition:
//     player == 'A' or 'B'
//  && gameNumber and numOfWins are assigned
// Postcondition:
//     A winning message, including player and gameNumber, has
//     been written
//  && numOfWins == numOfWins@entry + 1

{
    cout << "Player " << player << " has won game number "
         << gameNumber << '.' << endl;
    numOfWins++;
}
```

```
//*******************************************************************
void PrintBigWinner( /* in */ int winsForA,      // A's win count
                     /* in */ int winsForB )     // B's win count

// Prints number of wins for each player and the
// overall winner (or tie)

// Precondition:
//     winsForA and winsForB are assigned
// Postcondition:
//     The values of winsForA and winsForB have been output
//  && A message indicating the overall winner (or a tie) has been
//     output

{
    cout << endl;
    cout << "Player A has won " << winsForA << " games." << endl;
    cout << "Player B has won " << winsForB << " games." << endl;
    if (winsForA > winsForB)
        cout << "Player A has won the most games." << endl;
    else if (winsForB > winsForA)
        cout << "Player B has won the most games." << endl;
    else
        cout << "Players A and B have tied." << endl;
}
```

Testing: We tested the Game program with the following files. They are listed side by side so that you can see the pairs that made up each game. Note that each combination of 'R', 'P', and 'S' is used at least once. In addition, there is an erroneous play character in each file.

fileA	fileB
R	R
S	S
S	S
R	S
R	P
P	P
P	P
R	S
S	T
A	P
P	S
P	R
S	P
R	S

```
R               S
P               P
S               R
```

Given the data in these files, the program produced the following output.

```
Game number 1 is a tie.
Game number 2 is a tie.
Game number 3 is a tie.
Player A has won game number 4.
Player B has won game number 5.
Game number 6 is a tie.
Game number 7 is a tie.
Player A has won game number 8.
Game number 9 contained an illegal play.
Game number 10 contained an illegal play.
Player B has won game number 11.
Player A has won game number 12.
Player A has won game number 13.
Player A has won game number 14.
Player A has won game number 15.
Game number 16 is a tie.
Player B has won game number 17.


Player A has won 6 games.
Player B has won 3 games.
Player A has won the most games.
```

An examination of the output shows it to be correct: Player A did win six games, player B did win three games, and player A won the most games. This one set of test data is not enough to test the program completely, though. It should be run with test data in which player B wins, player A and player B tie, `fileA` is longer than `fileB`, and `fileB` is longer than `fileA`.

Testing and Debugging

Floating-Point Data

When a problem requires the use of floating-point numbers that are extremely large, small, or precise, it is important to keep in mind the limitations of the particular system you are using. When testing a program that performs floating-point calculations, determine the acceptable margin of error beforehand, and then design your test data to try to push the program beyond those limits. Carefully check the accuracy of the computed results.

(Remember that when you hand-calculate the correct results, a pocket cal-culator may have *less* precision than your computer system.) If the pro-gram produces acceptable results when given worst-case data, it probably performs correctly on typical data.

Coping with Input Errors

Several times in this book, we've had our programs test for invalid data and write an error message. Writing an error message is certainly neces-sary, but it is only the first step. We must also decide what the program should do next. The problem itself and the severity of the error should determine what action is taken in any error condition. The approach taken also depends on whether or not the program is being run interactively.

In a program that reads its data only from an input file, there is no interaction with the person who entered the data. The program, therefore, should try to adjust for the bad data items, if at all possible.

If the invalid data item is not essential, the program can skip it and continue; for example, if a program averaging test grades encounters a neg-ative test score, it could simply skip the negative score. If an educated guess can be made about the probable value of the bad data, it can be set to that value before being processed. In either event, a message should be written stating that an invalid data item was encountered and outlining the steps that were taken. Such messages form an *exception report*.

If the data item is essential and no guess is possible, processing should be terminated. A message should be written to the user with as much infor-mation as possible about the invalid data item.

In an interactive environment, the program can prompt the user to sup-ply another value. The program should indicate to the user what is wrong with the original data. Another possibility is to write out a list of actions and ask the user to choose among them.

These suggestions on how to handle bad data assume that the program recognizes bad data values. There are two approaches to error detection: passive and active. Passive error detection leaves it to the system to detect errors. This may seem easier, but the programmer relinquishes control of processing when an error occurs. An example of passive error detection is the system's division-by-zero error.

Active error detection means having the program check for possible errors and determine an appropriate action if an error occurs. An example of active error detection would be to read a value and use an If statement to see if the value is 0 before dividing it into another number.

The Area program in the first Problem-Solving Case Study uses *no* error detection. If the input is typed incorrectly, the program either crashes (if `divisions` is 0) or produces erroneous output (if `high` < `low`). Case Study Follow-Up Exercise 2 asks you to supply active error detection for these situations.

Testing and Debugging Hints

1. Avoid using unnecessary side effects in expressions. The test

   ```
   if ((x = y) < z)
      ⋮
   ```

   is less clear and more prone to error than the equivalent sequence of statements

   ```
   x = y;
   if (y < z)
      ⋮
   ```

   Also, if you accidentally omit the parentheses around the assignment operation, like this:

   ```
   if (x = y < z)
   ```

   then, according to C++ operator precedence, x is *not* assigned the value of y. It is assigned the value 1 or 0 (the coerced value of the Boolean result of the relational expression y < z).

2. Programs that rely on a particular machine's character set may not run correctly on another machine. Check to see what character-handling functions are supplied by the standard library. Functions such as `tolower`, `toupper`, `isalpha`, and `iscntrl` automatically account for the character set being used.

3. Don't directly compare floating-point values for equality. Instead, check them for near equality. The tolerance for near equality depends on the particular problem you are solving.

4. Use integers if you are dealing with whole numbers only. Any integer can be represented exactly by the computer, as long as it is within the machine's allowable range of values. Also, integer arithmetic is faster than floating-point arithmetic on most machines.

5. Be aware of representational, cancellation, overflow, and underflow errors. If possible, try to arrange calculations in your program to keep floating-point numbers from becoming too large or too small.

6. If your program increases the value of a positive integer and the result suddenly becomes a negative number, you should suspect integer overflow. On most computers, adding 1 to `INT_MAX` yields `INT_MIN`, a negative number.

7. Except when you really need to, avoid mixing data types in expressions, assignment operations, argument passing, and the return of a function value. If you must mix types, explicit type casts can prevent unwelcome surprises caused by implicit type coercion.

8. Consider using enumeration types to make your programs more readable, understandable, and modifiable.

9. Avoid anonymous data typing. Give each user-defined type a name.

10. Enumeration type values cannot be input or output directly.

11. Type demotion can lead to decreased precision or corruption of data.

Summary

A data type is a set of values (the domain) along with the operations that can be applied to those values. Simple data types are data types whose values are atomic (indivisible).

The integral types in C++ are `char`, `short`, `int`, `long`, and `bool`. The most commonly used integral types are `int` and `char`. The `char` type can be used for storing small (usually one-byte) numeric integers or, more often, for storing character data. Character data includes both printable and nonprintable characters. Nonprintable characters—those that control the behavior of hardware devices—are expressed in C++ as escape sequences such as `\n`. Each character is represented internally as a nonnegative integer according to the particular character set (such as ASCII or EBCDIC) that a computer uses.

The floating-point types built into the C++ language are `float`, `double`, and `long double`. Floating-point numbers are represented in the computer with a mantissa and an exponent. This representation permits numbers that are much larger or much smaller than those that can be represented with the integral types. Floating-point representation also allows us to perform calculations on numbers with fractional parts.

However, there are drawbacks to using floating-point numbers in arithmetic calculations. Representational errors, for example, can affect the accuracy of a program's computations. When using floating-point numbers, keep in mind that if two numbers are vastly different from each other in size, adding or subtracting them can produce the wrong answer. Remember, also, that the computer has a limited range of numbers that it can represent. If a program tries to compute a value that is too large or too small, an error message may result when the program executes.

C++ allows the programmer to define additional data types. The Typedef statement is a simple mechanism for renaming an existing type, although the result is not truly a new data type. An enumeration type, created by listing the identifiers that make up the domain, is a new data type that is distinct from any existing type. Values of an enumeration type may be assigned, compared in relational expressions, used as case labels in a Switch statement, passed as arguments, and returned as function values. Enumeration types are extremely useful in the writing of clear, self-documenting programs. In succeeding chapters, we look at language features that let us create even more powerful user-defined types.

Quick Check

1. The C++ simple types are divided into integral types, floating-point types, and enum types. What are the five integral types (ignoring the unsigned variations) and the three floating-point types? (pp. 494–496)
2. What is the difference between an expression and an expression statement in C++? (pp. 503–505)
3. Assume that the following code segment is executed on a machine that uses the ASCII character set. What is the final value of the char variable someChar? Give both its external and internal representations. (pp. 511–513)

```
someChar = 'T';
someChar = someChar + 4;
```

4. Why is it inappropriate to use a variable of a floating-point type as a loop control variable? (pp. 520–531)
5. If a computer has four digits of precision, what would be the result of the following addition operation? (pp. 520–531)

$$400400.000 + 199.9$$

6. When choosing a data type for a variable that stores whole numbers only, why should int be your first choice? (pp. 531–532)
7. Declare an enumeration type named AutoMakes, consisting of the names of five of your favorite car manufacturers. (pp. 533–541)
8. Given the type declaration

```
enum VisibleColors
{
    RED, ORANGE, YELLOW, GREEN, BLUE, INDIGO, VIOLET
};
```

write the first line of a For statement that "counts" from RED through VIOLET. Use a loop control variable named rainbow that is of type VisibleColors. (pp. 533–541)
9. Why is it better to use a named type than an anonymous type? (pp. 541–542)
10. Suppose that many of your programs need an enumeration type named Days and another named Months. If you place the type declarations into a file named calendar.h, what would an #include directive look like that inserts these declarations into a program? (pp. 542–543)
11. In arithmetic and relational expressions, which of the following could occur: type promotion, type demotion, or both? (pp. 543–547)

Answers **1.** The integral types are char, short, int, long, and bool. The floating-point types are float, double, and long double. **2.** An expression becomes an expression statement when it is terminated by a semicolon. **3.** The external representation is the letter *X*; the internal representation is the integer 88. **4.** Because representational errors can cause the loop termination condition to be evaluated with unpredictable results. **5.** 400500.000 (Actually, 4.005E+5) **6.** Floating-point arithmetic is subject to numerical inaccuracies and is slower than integer arithmetic on most machines. Use of the smaller integral types, char and short, can more easily lead to overflow errors. The long type usually requires more memory than int, and the arithmetic is usually slower. **7.** enum AutoMakes {SAAB, JAGUAR,

CITROEN, CHEVROLET, FORD}; **8.** for (rainbow = RED; rainbow <= VIOLET; rainbow = VisibleColors(rainbow + 1)) **9.** Named types make a program more readable, more understandable, and easier to modify. **10.** #include "calendar.h" **11.** Type promotion

Exam Preparation Exercises

1. Every C++ compiler guarantees that sizeof(int) < sizeof(long). (True or False?)
2. Classify each of the following as either an expression or an expression statement.
   a. sum = 0
   b. sqrt(x)
   c. y = 17;
   d. count++
3. Rewrite each statement as described.
   a. Using the += operator, rewrite the statement

   sumOfSquares = sumOfSquares + x * x;

   b. Using the decrement operator, rewrite the statement

   count = count - 1;

   c. Using a single assignment statement that uses the ?: operator, rewrite the statement

   if (n > 8)
       k = 32;
   else
       k = 15 * n;

4. What is printed by each of the following program fragments? (In both cases, ch is of type char.)
   a. for (ch = 'd'; ch <= 'g'; ch++)
       cout << ch;
   b. ch = 'F';
       cout << ch << ' ' << int(ch);   // Assume ASCII
5. What is printed by the following output statement?

   cout << "Notice that\nthe character \\ is a backslash.\n";

6. If a system supports ten digits of precision for floating-point numbers, what are the results of the following computations?
   a. 1.4E+12 + 100.0
   b. 4.2E-8 + 100.0
   c. 3.2E-5 + 3.2E+5
7. Define the following terms:

   mantissa   significant digits
   exponent   overflow
   representational error

8. Given the type declaration

   ```
   enum Agents {SMITH, JONES, GRANT, WHITE};
   ```

   does the expression `JONES > GRANT` have the value `true` or `false`?
9. Given the following declarations,

   ```
   enum Perfumes {POISON, DIOR_ESSENCE, CHANEL_NO_5, COTY};
   Perfumes sample;
   ```

   indicate whether each statement below is valid or invalid.
   a. `sample = POISON;`
   b. `sample = 3;`
   c. `sample++;`
   d. `sample = Perfumes(sample + 1);`
10. Using the declarations

    ```
    enum SeasonType {WINTER, SPRING, SUMMER, FALL};
    SeasonType season;
    ```

    indicate whether each statement below is valid or invalid.
    a. `cin >> season;`
    b. `if (season >= SPRING)`
       ⋮
    c. `for (season = WINTER; season <= SUMMER; season =`
                                     `SeasonType(season + 1))`

       ⋮
11. Given the following program fragment,

    ```
    enum Colors {RED, GREEN, BLUE};
    ```

    ```
    Colors myColor;
    enum {RED, GREEN, BLUE} yourColor;
    ```

    the data type of `myColor` is a named type, and the data type of `yourColor` is an anonymous type. (True or False?)
12. If you have written your own header file named `mytypes.h`, then the preprocessor directive

    ```
    #include <mytypes.h>
    ```

    is the correct way to insert the contents of the header file into a program. (True or False?)
13. In each of the following situations, indicate whether promotion or demotion occurs. (The names of the variables are meant to suggest their data types.)
    a. Execution of the assignment operation `someInt = someFloat`
    b. Evaluation of the expression `someFloat + someLong`
    c. Passing the argument `someDouble` to the parameter `someFloat`
    d. Execution of the following statement within an `int` function:

       ```
       return someShort;
       ```

14. Active error detection leaves error hunting to C++ and the operating system, whereas passive error detection requires the programmer to do the error hunting. (True or False?)

Programming Warm-up Exercises

1. Find out the maximum and minimum values for each of the C++ integral and floating-point types on your machine. These values are declared as named constants in the files `climits` and `cfloat` in the standard include directory.

2. Using a combination of printable characters and escape sequences within *one* literal string, write a single output statement that does the following in the order shown:
   - Prints `Hello`
   - Prints a (horizontal) tab character
   - Prints `There`
   - Prints two blank lines
   - Prints `"Ace"` (including the double quotes)

3. Write a While loop that copies all the characters (including whitespace characters) from an input file stream `inFile` to an output file stream `outFile`, except that every lowercase letter is converted to uppercase. Assume that both files have been opened successfully before the loop begins. The loop should terminate when end-of-file is detected.

4. Given the following declarations

   ```
   int   n;
   char ch1;
   char ch2;
   ```

   and given that n contains a two-digit number, translate n into two single characters such that `ch1` holds the higher-order digit, and `ch2` holds the lower-order digit. For example, if n = 59, `ch1` would equal '5', and `ch2` would equal '9'. Then output the two digits as characters in the same order as the original numbers. (*Hint:* Consider how you might use the / and % operators in your solution.)

5. In a program you are writing, a `float` variable `beta` potentially contains a very large number. Before multiplying `beta` by 100.0, you want the program to test whether it is safe to do so. Write an If statement that tests for a possible overflow *before* multiplying by 100.0. Specifically, if the multiplication would lead to overflow, print a message and don't perform the multiplication; otherwise, go ahead with the multiplication.

6. Declare an enumeration type for the course numbers of computer courses at your school.

7. Declare an enumeration type for the South American countries.

8. Declare an enumeration type for the work days of the week (Monday through Friday).

9. Write a value-returning function that converts the first two letters of a work day into the type declared in Exercise 8.

10. Write a void function that prints a value of the type declared in Exercise 8.

11. Using a loop control variable `today` of the type declared in Exercise 8, write a For loop that prints out all five values in the domain of the type. To print each value, invoke the function of Exercise 10.

12. Below is a function that is supposed to return the ratio of two integers, rounded up or down to the nearest integer.

```
int Ratio( /* in */ int int1,
           /* in */ int int2 )
{
    return float(int1) / float(int2);
}
```

Sometimes this function returns an incorrect result. Describe what the problem is in terms of type promotion or demotion and fix the problem.

Programming Problems

1. Read in the lengths of the sides of a triangle and determine whether the triangle is isosceles (two sides are equal), equilateral (three sides are equal), or scalene (no sides are equal). Use an enumeration type whose enumerators are ISOSCELES, EQUILATERAL, and SCALENE.

    The lengths of the sides of the triangle are to be entered as integer values. For each set of sides, print out the kind of triangle or an error message saying that the three sides do not make a triangle. (For a triangle to exist, any two sides together must be longer than the remaining side.) Continue analyzing triangles until end-of-file occurs.

2. Write a C++ program that reads a single character from 'A' through 'Z' and produces output in the shape of a pyramid composed of the letters up to and including the letter that is input. The top letter in the pyramid should be 'A', and on each level, the next letter in the alphabet should fall between two copies of the letter that was introduced in the level above it. For example, if the input is 'E', the output looks like the following:

```
    A
   ABA
  ABCBA
 ABCDCBA
ABCDEDCBA
```

3. Read in a floating-point number character by character, ignoring any characters other than digits and a decimal point. Convert the valid characters into a single floating-point number and print the result. Your algorithm should convert the whole number part to an integer and the fractional part to an integer and combine the two integers as follows:

$$\text{Set result} = \text{wholePart} + \text{fractionalPart} / (10^{\text{number of digits in fraction}})$$

For example, 3A4.21P6 would be converted into 34 and 216, and the result would be the value of the sum

$$34 + \frac{216}{1000}$$

You may assume that the number has at least one digit on either side of the decimal point.

4. The program that plays Rock, Paper, and Scissors takes its input from two files. Rewrite the program so that it uses interactive input from two players. The main module should be as follows:

```
DO
    Get command
    IF command is CONTINUE
        Play game
    ELSE IF command is PRINT_STATS
        Print statistics
WHILE command isn't STOP
```

command should be a variable of an enumeration type whose enumerators are CONTINUE, PRINT_STATS, and STOP. The statistics to be printed are the current game number, the current number of wins for the first player, and the current number of wins for the second player. The Get Command module should begin by asking if the players want to see the current statistics. If they do not, the first player should be prompted to enter a 'C' to continue or an 'S' to stop. If the first player wishes to continue, ask the second player; command should be CONTINUE if both players enter a 'C', and STOP otherwise. If both players wish to continue, the first player and then the second player should be prompted to enter a play.

Case Study Follow-Up

1. In the Area program, it would be more efficient to go directly from midpoint to midpoint and not use the left edge of a rectangle at all. How would you change the program to use this approach?
2. The following exercises pertain to the Area program.
    a. Why does the program crash if the user enters 0 for divisions?
    b. Add active error detection to the GetData function so that, upon return from the function, it is guaranteed that divisions > 0 and high ≥ low.
3. Enter and repeatedly run the Area program to observe the effect of increasing the number of divisions. On each run, enter 0 for low and 2 for high. Start with one division, then use 10, 100, 1000, 10,000, 100,000, and 1,000,000 divisions on successive runs.
    a. What is the result from each run?
    b. Does the result ever equal the exact answer, 4.0? If so, which run gives the correct answer? If not, which run comes closest? Does it help to use even more divisions?
    c. Approximately how long does the computer take to execute each of the runs? From these times, estimate how long it would take to execute with 100,000,000 divisions.
4. Repeat Exercise 3, using 0 for low and 1000 for high.

5. What is the advantage of converting 'R', 'P', and 'S' into values of an enumeration type in the Rock, Paper, Scissors case study?
6. Modify the Game program so that it prompts the user for the names of the two external files before opening them.
7. Write a comprehensive test plan for the Game program.
8. Implement your test plan for the Game program.

11

Structured Types, Data Abstraction, and Classes

G O A L S

- To be able to declare a record (struct) data type, a data structure whose components may be heterogeneous.
- To be able to access a member of a record variable.
- To be able to define a hierarchical record structure.
- To be able to access values stored in a hierarchical record variable.
- To understand the general concept of a C++ union type.
- To understand the difference between specification and implementation of an abstract data type.
- To be able to declare a C++ class type.
- To be able to declare class objects, given the declaration of a class type.
- To be able to write client code that invokes class member functions.
- To be able to implement class member functions.
- To understand how encapsulation and information hiding are enforced by the C++ compiler.
- To be able to organize the code for a C++ class into two files: the specification (.h) file and the implementation file.
- To be able to write a C++ class constructor.

In the last chapter, we examined the concept of a data type and looked at how to define simple data types. In this chapter, we expand the definition of a data type to include structured types, which represent collections of components that are referred to by a single name. We begin with a discussion of structured types in general and then examine two structured types provided by the C++ language: the struct and the union.

Next, we introduce the concept of *data abstraction,* the separation of a data type's logical properties from its implementation. Data abstraction is important because it allows us to create data types not otherwise available in a programming language. Another benefit of data abstraction is the ability to produce *off-the-shelf software*—pieces of software that can be used over and over again in different programs either by the creator of the software or by any programmer wishing to use them.

The primary concept for practicing data abstraction is the *abstract data type.* In this chapter, we examine abstract data types in depth and introduce the C++ language feature designed expressly for creating abstract data types: the *class.* We conclude with two case studies that demonstrate data abstraction, abstract data types, and C++ classes.

Simple Versus Structured Data Types

In Chapter 10, we examined simple, or atomic, data types. A value in a simple type is a single data item; it cannot be broken down into component parts. For example, each int value is a single integer number and cannot be further decomposed. In contrast, a **structured data type** is one in which each value is a *collection* of component items. The entire collection is given a single name, yet each component can still be accessed individually. An example of a structured data type in C++ is the string class, used for creating and manipulating strings. When you declare a variable myString to be of type string, myString does not represent just one atomic data value; it represents an entire collection of characters. But each of the components in the string can be accessed individually (by using an expression such as myString[3], which accesses the char value at position 3).

Structured data type   A data type in which each value is a collection of components and whose organization is characterized by the method used to access individual components. The allowable operations on a structured data type include the storage and retrieval of individual components.

Simple data types, both built-in and user-defined, are the building blocks for structured types. A structured type gathers together a set of com-

FIGURE 11-1
Atomic (Simple)
and Structured
Data Types

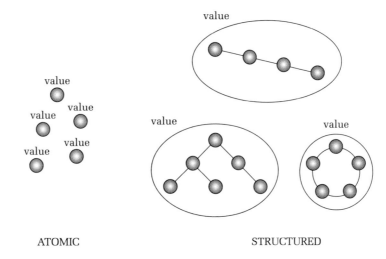

FIGURE 11-2
C++ Structured
Types

ponent values and usually imposes a specific arrangement on them (see Figure 11-1). The method used to access the individual components of a structured type depends on how the components are arranged. As we discuss various ways of structuring data, we look at the corresponding access mechanisms.

Figure 11-2 shows the structured types available in C++. This figure is a portion of the complete diagram presented in Figure 3-1.

In this chapter, we examine the struct, union, and class types. Array data types are the topic of Chapter 12.

Records (C++ Structs)

In computer science, a **record** is a heterogeneous structured data type. By *heterogeneous*, we mean that the individual components of a record can be of different data types. Each component of a record is called a **field** of the

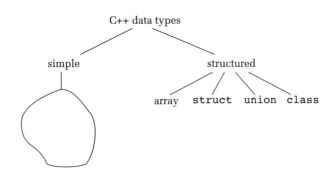

record, and each field is given a name called the *field name*. C++ uses its own terminology with records. A record is called a **structure**, the fields of a record are called **members** of the structure, and each member has a *member name*.

Record (structure, in C++)   A structured data type with a fixed number of components that are accessed by name. The components may be heterogeneous (of different types).

Field (member, in C++)   A component of a record.

In C++, record data types are most commonly declared according to the following syntax:

StructDeclaration

```
struct TypeName
{
      MemberList
};
```

where TypeName is an identifier giving a name to the data type, and MemberList is defined as

MemberList

```
DataType MemberName ;
DataType MemberName ;
      ⋮
```

The reserved word `struct` is an abbreviation for *structure*, the C++ term for a record. Because the word *structure* has many other meanings in computer science, we'll use *struct* or *record* to avoid any possible confusion about what we are referring to.

You probably recognize the syntax of a member list as being nearly identical to a series of variable declarations. Be careful: A `struct` declaration is a type declaration, and we still must declare variables of this type for any memory locations to be associated with the member names. As an example, let's use a struct to describe a student in a class. We want to store the first and last names, the overall grade point average prior to this class, the grade on programming assignments, the grade on quizzes, the final exam grade, and the final course grade.

```
// Type declarations

enum GradeType {A, B, C, D, F};

struct StudentRec
{
    string     firstName;
    string     lastName;
    float      gpa;             // Grade point average
    int        programGrade;    // Assume 0..400
    int        quizGrade;       // Assume 0..300
    int        finalExam;       // Assume 0..300
    GradeType courseGrade;
};

// Variable declarations

StudentRec firstStudent;
StudentRec student;
int        grade;
```

Notice, both in this example and in the syntax template, that a `struct` declaration ends with a semicolon. By now, you have learned not to put a semicolon after the right brace of a compound statement (block). However, the member list in a `struct` declaration is not considered to be a compound statement; the braces are simply required syntax in the declaration. A `struct` declaration, like all C++ declaration statements, must end with a semicolon.

`firstName`, `lastName`, `gpa`, `programGrade`, `quizGrade`, `finalExam`, and `courseGrade` are member names within the `struct` type `StudentRec`. These member names make up the member list. Note that each member name is given a type. Also, member names must be unique within a `struct` type, just as variable names must be unique within a block.

`firstName` and `lastName` are of type `string`. `gpa` is a `float` member. `programGrade`, `quizGrade`, and `finalExam` are `int` members. `courseGrade` is of an enumeration data type made up of the grades A through D and F.

None of these struct members are associated with memory locations until we declare a variable of the `StudentRec` type. `StudentRec` is merely a pattern for a struct (see Figure 11-3). The variables `firstStudent` and `student` are variables of type `StudentRec`.

FIGURE 11-3

Pattern for a Struct

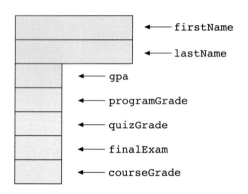

Accessing Individual Components

To access an individual member of a struct variable, you give the name of the variable, followed by a dot (period), and then the member name. This expression is called a **member selector**. The syntax template is

MemberSelector

StructVariable . MemberName

This syntax for selecting individual components of a struct is often called *dot notation*. To access the grade point average of `firstStudent`, we would write

`firstStudent.gpa`

To access the final exam score of `student`, we would write

`student.finalExam`

Member selector   The expression used to access components of a struct variable. It is formed by using the struct variable name and the member name, separated by a dot (period).

The component of a struct accessed by the member selector is treated just like any other variable of the same type. It may be used in an assignment statement, passed as an argument, and so on. Figure 11-4 shows the struct variable `student` with the member selector for each member. In this example, we assume that some processing has already taken place, so values are stored in some of the components.

Let's demonstrate the use of these member selectors. Using our `student` variable, the following code segment reads in a final exam grade; adds up the program grade, the quiz grade, and the final exam grade; and then assigns a letter grade to the result.

```
cin >> student.finalExam;
grade = student.finalExam + student.programGrade +
        student.quizGrade;
if (grade >= 900)
    student.courseGrade = A;
else if (grade >= 800)
    student.courseGrade = B;
else  .
        .
        .
```

Aggregate Operations on Structs

In addition to accessing individual components of a struct variable, we can in some cases use **aggregate operations**. An aggregate operation is one that manipulates the struct as an entire unit.

Aggregate operation   An operation on a data structure as a whole, as opposed to an operation on an individual component of the data structure.

The following table summarizes the aggregate operations that are allowed on struct variables.

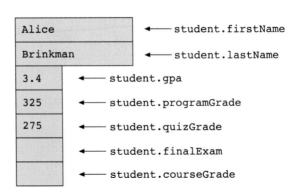

Figure 11-4
Struct Variable
`student` with
Member Selectors

Aggregate Operation	Allowed on Structs?
I/O	No
Assignment	Yes
Arithmetic	No
Comparison	No
Argument passage	Yes, by value or by reference
Return as a function's return value	Yes

According to the table, one struct variable can be assigned to another. However, both variables must be declared to be of the same type. For example, given the declarations

```
StudentRec student;
StudentRec anotherStudent;
```

the statement

```
anotherStudent = student;
```

copies the entire contents of the struct variable `student` to the variable `anotherStudent`, member by member.

On the other hand, aggregate arithmetic operations and comparisons are not allowed (primarily because they wouldn't make sense):

```
student = student * anotherStudent;    // Not allowed
if (student < anotherStudent)          // Not allowed
```

Furthermore, aggregate I/O is not permitted:

```
cin >> student;                        // Not allowed
```

We must input or output a struct variable one member at a time:

```
cin >> student.firstName;
cin >> student.lastName;
⋮
```

According to the table, an entire struct can be passed as an argument, either by value or by reference, and a struct can be returned as the value of a value-returning function. Let's define a function that takes a `StudentRec` variable as a parameter.

The task of this function is to determine if a student's grade in a course is consistent with his or her overall grade point average (GPA). We define *consistent* to mean that the course grade corresponds correctly to the rounded GPA. The GPA is calculated on a four-point scale, where A is 4, B is 3, C is 2, D is 1, and F is 0. If the rounded GPA is 4 and the course grade is A, then the function returns `true`. If the rounded GPA is 4 and the course grade is not A, then the function returns `false`. Each of the other grades is tested in the same way.

The `Consistent` function is coded below. The parameter `aStudent`, a struct variable of type `StudentRec`, is passed by value.

```
bool Consistent( /* in */ StudentRec aStudent )

// Precondition:
//      0.0 <= aStudent.gpa <= 4.0
// Postcondition:
//      Function value == true, if the course grade is consistent
//                                   with the overall GPA
//                       == false, otherwise

{
    int roundedGPA = int(aStudent.gpa + 0.5);

    switch (roundedGPA)
    {
        case 0: return (aStudent.courseGrade == F);
        case 1: return (aStudent.courseGrade == D);
        case 2: return (aStudent.courseGrade == C);
        case 3: return (aStudent.courseGrade == B);
        case 4: return (aStudent.courseGrade == A);
    }
}
```

More About Struct Declarations

To complete our initial look at C++ structs, we give a more complete syntax template for a `struct` type declaration:

StructDeclaration

```
struct TypeName
{
        MemberList
} VariableList ;
```

As you can see in the syntax template, two items are optional: TypeName (the name of the `struct` type being declared), and VariableList (a list of variable names between the right brace and the semicolon). Our examples thus far have declared a type name but have not included a variable list. The variable list allows you not only to declare a `struct` type but also to declare variables of that type, all in one statement. For example, you could write the declarations

```
struct StudentRec
{
    string firstName;
    string lastName;
        ⋮
};

StudentRec firstStudent;
StudentRec student;
```

more compactly in the form

```
struct StudentRec
{
    string firstName;
    string lastName;
        ⋮
} firstStudent, student;
```

In this book, we avoid combining variable declarations with type declarations, preferring to keep the two notions separate.

If you omit the type name but include the variable list, you create an anonymous type:

```
struct
{
    int    firstMember;
    float secondMember;
} someVar;
```

Here, `someVar` is a variable of an anonymous type. No other variables of that type can be declared because the type has no name. Therefore, `someVar` cannot participate in aggregate operations such as assignment or argument passage. The cautions given in Chapter 10 against anonymous typing of enumeration types apply to `struct` types as well.

Hierarchical Records

We have seen examples in which the components of a record are simple variables and strings. A component of a record can also be another record. Records whose components are themselves records are called **hierarchical records.**

Hierarchical record   A record in which at least one of the components is itself a record.

Let's look at an example in which a hierarchical structure is appropriate. A small machine shop keeps information about each of its machines. There is descriptive information, such as the identification number, a description of the machine, the purchase date, and the cost. Statistical information is also kept, such as the number of down days, the failure rate, and the date of last service. What is a reasonable way of representing all this information? First, let's look at a flat (nonhierarchical) record structure that holds this information.

```
struct MachineRec
{
    int     idNumber;
    string  description;
    float   failRate;
    int     lastServicedMonth;   // Assume 1..12
    int     lastServicedDay;     // Assume 1..31
    int     lastServicedYear;    // Assume 1900..2050
    int     downDays;
    int     purchaseDateMonth;   // Assume 1..12
    int     purchaseDateDay;     // Assume 1..31
    int     purchaseDateYear;    // Assume 1900..2050
    float   cost;
};
```

The MachineRec type has 11 members. There is so much detailed information here that it is difficult to quickly get a feeling for what the record represents. Let's see if we can reorganize it into a hierarchical structure that makes more sense. We can divide the information into two groups: information that changes and information that does not. There are also two dates to be kept: date of purchase and date of last service. These observations suggest use of a record describing a date, a record describing the statistical data, and an overall record containing the other two as components. The following type declarations reflect this structure.

```
struct DateType
{
    int month;    // Assume 1..12
    int day;      // Assume 1..31
    int year;     // Assume 1900..2050
};
struct StatisticsType
{
    float     failRate;
    DateType lastServiced;
    int       downDays;
};
struct MachineRec
{
    int           idNumber;
    string        description;
    StatisticsType history;
    DateType      purchaseDate;
    float         cost;
};
```

```
MachineRec machine;
```

The contents of a machine record are now much more obvious. Two of the components of the `struct` type `MachineRec` are themselves structs: `purchaseDate` is of `struct` type `DateType`, and `history` is of `struct` type `StatisticsType`. One of the components of `struct` type `StatisticsType` is a struct of type `DateType`.

How do we access the components of a hierarchical structure such as this one? We build the accessing expressions (member selectors) for the members of the embedded structs from left to right, beginning with the struct variable name. Here are some expressions and the components they access:

Expression	*Component Accessed*
`machine.purchaseDate`	`DateType` struct variable
`machine.purchaseDate.month`	`month` member of a `DateType` struct variable
`machine.purchaseDate.year`	`year` member of a `DateType` struct variable
`machine.history.lastServiced.year`	`year` member of a `DateType` struct variable contained in a struct of type `StatisticsType`

Figure 11-5 is a pictorial representation of machine with values. Look carefully at how each component is accessed.

Unions

In Figure 11-2, we presented a diagram showing the four structured types available in C++. We have discussed struct types and now look briefly at *union* types.

In C++, a union is defined to be a struct that holds only one of its members at a time during program execution. Here is a declaration of a union type and a union variable:

```
union WeightType
{
    long   wtInOunces;
    int    wtInPounds;
    float  wtInTons;
};

WeightType weight;
```

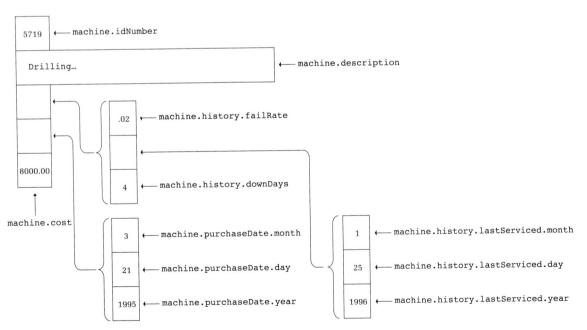

FIGURE 11-5

Hierarchical Records in machine Variable

The syntax for declaring a `union` type is identical to that of a `struct` type, except that the word `union` is substituted for `struct`.

At run time, the memory space allocated to the variable `weight` does *not* include room for three distinct components. Instead, `weight` can contain only one of the following: *either* a `long` value *or* an `int` value *or* a `float` value. The assumption is that the program will never need a weight in ounces, a weight in pounds, and a weight in tons simultaneously while executing. The purpose of a union is to conserve memory by forcing several values to use the same memory space, one at a time. The following code shows how the `weight` variable might be used.

```
weight.wtInTons = 4.83;
  ⋮
// Weight in tons is no longer needed. Reuse the memory space.

weight.wtInPounds = 35;
  ⋮
```

After the last assignment statement, the previous `float` value 4.83 is gone, replaced by the `int` value 35.

It's quite reasonable to argue that a union is not a data structure at all. It does not represent a collection of values; it represents only a single value from among several *potential* values. On the other hand, unions are grouped together with the structured types because of their similarity to structs.

There is much more to be said about unions, including subtle issues related to their declaration and usage. However, these issues are more appropriate in an advanced study of data structures and system programming. We have introduced unions only to present a complete picture of the structured types provided by C++ and to acquaint you with the general idea in case you encounter unions in other C++ programs.

Data Abstraction

As the software we develop becomes more complex, we design algorithms and data structures in parallel. We progress from the logical or abstract data structure envisioned at the top level through the refinement process until we reach the concrete coding in C++. We have illustrated two ways of representing the logical structure of a machine record in a shop inventory. The first used a record in which all the components were defined (made concrete) at the same time. The second used a hierarchical record in which the dates and statistics describing a machine's history were defined in lower-level records.

Let's look again at the two different ways in which we represented our logical data structure.

```
// **************** Version 1 ****************

struct MachineRec
{
    int     idNumber;
    string description;
    float   failRate;
    int     lastServicedMonth;  // Assume 1..12
    int     lastServicedDay;    // Assume 1..31
    int     lastServicedYear;   // Assume 1900..2050
    int     downDays;
    int     purchaseDateMonth;  // Assume 1..12
    int     purchaseDateDay;    // Assume 1..31
    int     purchaseDateYear;   // Assume 1900..2050
    float   cost;
};


// **************** Version 2 ****************

struct DateType
{
    int month;   // Assume 1..12
    int day;     // Assume 1..31
    int year;    // Assume 1900..2050
};
struct StatisticsType
{
    float    failRate;
    DateType lastServiced;
    int      downDays;
};
struct MachineRec
{
    int           idNumber;
    string        description;
    StatisticsType history;
    DateType      purchaseDate;
    float         cost;
};
```

Which of these two representations is better? The second one is better for two reasons.

First, it groups elements together logically. The statistics and the dates are entities within themselves. We may want a date or a machine history in another record structure. If we define the dates and statistics only within

`MachineRec` (as in the first structure), we would have to define them again for every other data structure that needs them, giving us multiple definitions of the same logical entity.

Second, the details of the entities (statistics and dates) are pushed down to a lower level in the second structure. The principle of deferring details to as low a level as possible should be applied to designing data structures as well as to designing algorithms. How a machine history or a date is represented is not relevant to our concept of a machine record, so the details need not be specified until it is time to write the algorithms to manipulate those members.

Pushing the implementation details of a data type to a lower level separates the logical description from the implementation. This concept is analogous to control abstraction, which we discussed in Chapter 8. The separation of the logical properties of a data type from its implementation details is called **data abstraction,** which is a goal of effective programming and the foundation upon which abstract data types are built. (We explore the concept of abstract data types in the next section.)

Data abstraction   The separation of a data type's logical properties from its implementation.

Eventually, all the logical properties must be defined in terms of concrete data types and routines written to manipulate them. If the implementation is properly designed, we can use the same routines to manipulate the structure in a wide variety of applications. For example, if we have a routine to compare dates, we can use that routine to compare dates representing days on which equipment was bought or maintained, or dates representing people's birthdays. The concept of designing a low-level structure and writing routines to manipulate it is the basis for C++ `class` types, which we examine later in the chapter.

Abstract Data Types

We live in a complex world. Throughout the course of each day, we are constantly bombarded with information, facts, and details. To cope with complexity, the human mind engages in *abstraction*—the act of separating the essential qualities of an idea or object from the details of how it works or is composed.

With abstraction, we focus on the *what*, not the *how*. For example, our understanding of automobiles is largely based on abstraction. Most of us know *what* the engine does (it propels the car), but fewer of us know—or want to know—precisely *how* the engine works internally. Abstraction allows us to discuss, think about, and use automobiles without having to know everything about how they work.

In the world of software design, it is now recognized that abstraction is an absolute necessity for managing immense, complex software projects. In introductory computer science courses, programs are usually small (perhaps 50 to 200 lines of code) and understandable in their entirety by one person. However, large commercial software products composed of hundreds of thousands—even millions—of lines of code cannot be designed, understood, or tested thoroughly without using abstraction in various forms. To manage complexity, software developers regularly use two important abstraction techniques: control abstraction and data abstraction.

In Chapter 8, we defined control abstraction as the separation of the logical properties of an action from its implementation. We engage in control abstraction whenever we write a function that reduces a complicated algorithm to an abstract action performed by a function call. By invoking a library function, as in the expression

```
4.6 + sqrt(x)
```

we depend only on the function's *specification,* a written description of what it does. We can use the function without having to know its *implementation* (the algorithms that accomplish the result). By invoking the sqrt function, our program is less complex because all the details involved in computing square roots are absent.

Abstraction techniques also apply to data. Every data type consists of a set of values (the domain) along with a collection of allowable operations on those values. In the preceding section, we described data abstraction as the separation of a data type's logical properties from its implementation details. Data abstraction comes into play when we need a data type that is not built into the programming language. We can define the new data type as an **abstract data type (ADT)**, concentrating only on its logical properties and deferring the details of its implementation.

Abstract data type A data type whose properties (domain and operations) are specified independently of any particular implementation.

As with control abstraction, an abstract data type has both a specification (the *what*) and an implementation (the *how*). The specification of an ADT describes the characteristics of the data values as well as the behavior of each of the operations on those values. The user of the ADT needs to understand only the specification, not the implementation, in order to use it. Here's a very informal specification of a list ADT:

TYPE
  IntList
DOMAIN
  Each IntList value is a collection of up to 100 separate integer numbers.
OPERATIONS
  Insert an item into the list.
  Delete an item from the list.
  Search the list for an item.
  Return the current length of the list.
  Sort the list into ascending order.
  Print the list.

Notice the complete absence of implementation details. We have not mentioned how the data might actually be stored in a program or how the operations might be implemented. Concealing the implementation details reduces complexity for the user and also shields the user from changes in the implementation.

Below is the specification of another ADT, one that might be useful for representing time in a program.

TYPE
  TimeType
DOMAIN
  Each TimeType value is a time of day in the form of hours, minutes, and
  seconds.
OPERATIONS
  Set the time.
  Print the time.
  Increment the time by one second.
  Compare two times for equality.
  Determine if one time is "less than" (comes before) another.

The specification of an ADT defines abstract data values and abstract operations for the user. Ultimately, of course, the ADT must be implemented in program code. To implement an ADT, the programmer must do two things:

1. Choose a concrete **data representation** of the abstract data, using data types that already exist.
2. Implement each of the allowable operations in terms of program instructions.

Data representation   The concrete form of data used to represent the abstract values of an abstract data type.

To implement the IntList ADT, we could choose a concrete data representation consisting of two items: a 100-element data structure (such as an *array*, the topic of the next chapter) and an `int` variable that keeps track of the current length of the list. To implement the IntList operations, we must create algorithms based on the chosen data representation. In the next two chapters, we discuss in detail the array data structure and its use in implementing list ADTs.

To implement the TimeType ADT, we might use three `int` variables for the data representation—one for the hours, one for the minutes, and one for the seconds. Or we might use three strings as the data representation. The specification of the ADT does not confine us to any particular data representation. As long as we satisfy the specification, we are free to choose among alternative data representations and their associated algorithms. Our choice may be based on time efficiency (the speed at which the algorithms execute), space efficiency (the economical use of memory space), or simplicity and readability of the algorithms. Over time, you will acquire knowledge and experience that help you decide which implementation is best for a particular context.

*T*HEORETICAL FOUNDATIONS

Categories of Abstract Data Type Operations

In general, the basic operations associated with an abstract data type fall into three categories: **constructors, transformers,** and **observers.**

Constructor   An operation that creates a new instance (variable) of an ADT.

Transformer   An operation that builds a new value of the ADT, given one or more previous values of the type.

An operation that creates a new instance of an ADT (such as a list) is a constructor. Operations that insert an item into a list and delete an item from a list are transformers. An operation that takes one list and appends it to the end of a second list is also a transformer.

Observer   An operation that allows us to observe the state of an instance of an ADT without changing it.

A Boolean function that returns `true` if a list is empty and `false` if it contains any components is an example of an observer. A Boolean function that tests to see if a certain value is in the list is another observer.

Some operations are combinations of observers and constructors. An operation that takes two lists and merges them into a (new) third list is both an observer (of the two existing lists) and a constructor (of the third list).

In addition to the three basic categories of ADT operations, a fourth category is sometimes defined: **iterators.**

Iterator   An operation that allows us to process—one at a time—all the components in an instance of an ADT.

An example of an iterator is an operation that returns the first item in a list when it is called initially and returns the next one with each successive call.

C++ Classes

In previous chapters, we have treated data values as passive quantities to be acted upon by functions. In Chapter 10, we viewed Rock, Paper, Scissors game plays as passive data, and we implemented operations as

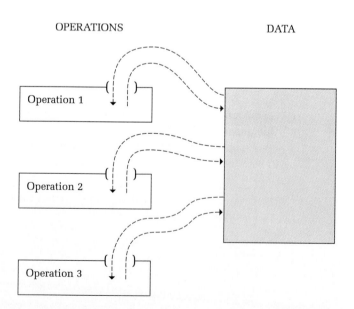

FIGURE 11-6
Data and
Operations as
Separate Entities

OPERATIONS   DATA

Operation 1

Operation 2

Operation 3

functions that took `PlayType` values as parameters. Similarly, earlier in this chapter we treated a student record as a passive quantity, using a struct as the data representation and implementing the operation `Consistent` as a function receiving a struct as a parameter (see Figure 11-6).

This separation of operations and data does not correspond very well with the notion of an abstract data type. After all, an ADT consists of *both* data values and operations on those values. It is preferable to view an ADT as defining an *active* data structure—one that combines both data and operations into a single, cohesive unit (see Figure 11-7). C++ supports this view by providing a built-in structured type known as a **class.**

In Figure 11-2, we listed the four structured types available in the C++ language: the array, the struct, the union, and the class. A class is a structured type provided specifically for representing abstract data types. A class is similar to a struct but is nearly always designed so that its components (**class members**) include not only data but also functions that manipulate that data. Here is a C++ class declaration corresponding to the TimeType ADT that we defined in the previous section:

```cpp
class TimeType
{
public:
    void Set( int, int, int );
    void Increment();
    void Write() const;
    bool Equal( TimeType ) const;
    bool LessThan( TimeType ) const;
private:
    int hrs;
    int mins;
    int secs;
};
```

(For now, you should ignore the word `const` appearing in some of the function prototypes. We explain this use of `const` later in the chapter.)

FIGURE 11-7

Data and Operations Bound into a Single Unit

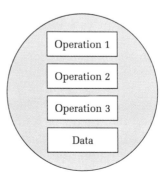

The TimeType class has eight members—five member functions (Set, Increment, Write, Equal, LessThan) and three member variables (hrs, mins, secs). As you might guess, the three member variables form the concrete data representation for the TimeType ADT. The five member functions correspond to the operations we listed for the TimeType ADT: set the time (to the hours, minutes, and seconds passed as arguments to the Set function), increment the time by one second, print the time, compare two times for equality, and determine if one time is less than another. Although the Equal function compares two TimeType variables for equality, its parameter list has only one parameter—a TimeType variable. Similarly, the LessThan function has only one parameter, even though it compares two times. We'll see the reason later.

Like a struct declaration, the declaration of TimeType defines a data type but does not create variables of the type. Class variables (more often referred to as **class objects** or **class instances**) are created by using ordinary variable declarations:

```
TimeType startTime;
TimeType endTime;
```

Any software that declares and manipulates TimeType objects is called a **client** of the class.

Class   A structured type in a programming language that is used to represent an abstract data type.

Class member   A component of a class. Class members may be either data or functions.

Class object (class instance)   A variable of a class type.

Client   Software that declares and manipulates objects of a particular class.

As you look at the preceding declaration of the TimeType class, you can see the reserved words public and private, each followed by a colon. Data and/or functions declared between the words public and private constitute the public interface; clients can access these class members directly. Class members declared after the word private are considered private information and are inaccessible to clients. If client code attempts to access a private item, the compiler signals an error.

Private class members can be accessed only by the class's member functions. In the TimeType class, the private variables hrs, mins, and secs can be accessed only by the member functions Set, Increment, Write, Equal, and LessThan, not by client code. This separation of class members into private and public parts is a hallmark of ADT design. To preserve the properties of an ADT correctly, an instance of the ADT should be manipulated *only* through the operations that form the public interface. We have more to say about this issue later in the chapter.

MATTERS OF STYLE

Declaring Public and Private Class Members

C++ does not require you to declare public and private class members in a fixed order. Several variations are possible.

By default, class members are private; the word `public` must be used to "open up" any members for public access. Therefore, we could write the `TimeType` class declaration as follows:

```
class TimeType
{
    int hrs;
    int mins;
    int secs;
public:
    void Set( int, int, int );
    void Increment();
    void Write() const;
    bool Equal( TimeType ) const;
    bool LessThan( TimeType ) const;
};
```

By default, the variables `hrs`, `mins`, and `secs` are private. The public part extends from the word `public` to the end of the class declaration.

Even with the private part located first, some programmers use the reserved word `private` to be as explicit as possible:

```
class TimeType
{
private:
    int hrs;
    int mins;
    int secs;
public:
    void Set( int, int, int );
    void Increment();
    void Write() const;
    bool Equal( TimeType ) const;
    bool LessThan( TimeType ) const;
};
```

Our preference is to locate the public part first so as to focus attention on the public interface and deemphasize the private data representation:

```
class TimeType
{
public:
    void Set( int, int, int );
    void Increment();
    void Write() const;
    bool Equal( TimeType ) const;
    bool LessThan( TimeType ) const;
private:
    int hrs;
    int mins;
    int secs;
};
```

We use this style throughout the remainder of the book.

Regarding public versus private accessibility, we can now describe more fully the difference between C++ structs and classes. C++ defines a struct to be a class whose members are all, by default, public. In contrast, members of a class are, by default, private. Furthermore, it is most common to use only data, not functions, as members of a struct. Note that you *can* declare struct members to be private and you *can* include member functions in a struct, but then you might as well use a class!

Classes, Class Objects, and Class Members

It is important to restate that a class is a type, not a data object. Like any type, a class is a pattern from which you create (or *instantiate*) many objects of that type. Think of a type as a cookie cutter and objects of that type as the cookies.

The declarations

```
TimeType time1;
TimeType time2;
```

create two objects of the TimeType class: time1 and time2. Each object has its own copies of hrs, mins, and secs, the private data members of the class. At a given moment during program execution, time1's copies of hrs, mins, and secs might contain the values 5, 30, and 10; and time2's copies might contain the values 17, 58, and 2. Figure 11-8 is a visual image of the class objects time1 and time2.

(In truth, the C++ compiler does not waste memory by placing duplicate copies of a member function—say, Increment—into both time1 and time2. The compiler generates just one physical copy of Increment, and any class object executes this one copy of the function. Nevertheless, the diagram in Figure 11-8 is a good mental picture of two different class objects.)

FIGURE 11-8
Conceptual View of Two Class Objects

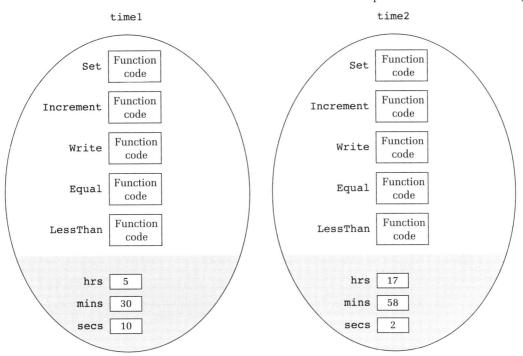

Be sure you are clear about the difference between the terms *class object* and *class member*. Figure 11-8 depicts two objects of the TimeType class, and each object has eight members.

Built-in Operations on Class Objects

In many ways, programmer-defined classes are like built-in types. You can declare as many objects of a class as you like. You can pass class objects as arguments to functions and return them as function values. Like any variable, a class object can be automatic (created each time control reaches its declaration and destroyed when control exits its surrounding block) or static (created once when control reaches its declaration and destroyed when the program terminates).

In other ways, C++ treats structs and classes differently from built-in types. Most of the built-in operations do not apply to structs or classes. You cannot use the + operator to add two TimeType objects, nor can you use the == operator to compare two TimeType objects for equality.

Two built-in operations that are valid for struct and class objects are member selection (.) and assignment (=). As with structs, you select an individual member of a class by using dot notation. That is, you write the name of the class object, then a dot, then the member name. The statement

```
time1.Increment();
```

invokes the `Increment` function for the `time1` object, presumably to add one second to the time stored in `time1`. The other built-in operation, assignment, performs aggregate assignment of one class object to another with the following semantics: If x and y are objects of the same class, then the assignment x = y copies the data members of y into x. Below is a fragment of client code that demonstrates member selection and assignment.

```
TimeType time1;
TimeType time2;
int      inputHrs;
int      inputMins;
int      inputSecs;

time1.Set(5, 20, 0);
// Assert: time1 corresponds to 5:20:0

cout << "Enter hours, minutes, seconds: ";
cin >> inputHrs >> inputMins >> inputSecs;
time2.Set(inputHrs, inputMins, inputSecs);

if (time1.LessThan(time2))
    DoSomething();

time2 = time1;                        // Member-by-member assignment
time2.Write();
// Assert: 5:20:0 has been output
```

Earlier we remarked that the `Equal` and `LessThan` functions have only one parameter each, even though they are comparing two `TimeType` objects. In the If statement of the code segment above, we are comparing `time1` and `time2`. Because `LessThan` is a class member function, we invoke it by giving the name of a class object (`time1`), then a dot, then the function name (`LessThan`). Only one item remains unspecified: the class object with which `time1` should be compared (`time2`). Therefore, the `LessThan` function requires only one parameter, not two. Here is another way of explaining it: If a class member function represents a binary (two-operand) operation, the first operand appears to the left of the dot operator, and the second operand is in the parameter list. (To generalize, an *n*-ary operation has *n* − 1 operands in the parameter list. Thus, a unary operation—such as `Write` or `Increment` in the `TimeType` class—has an empty parameter list.)

In addition to member selection and assignment, a few other built-in operators are valid for class objects and structs. These operators are used for manipulating memory addresses, and we defer discussing them until later in the book. For now, think of . and = as the only valid built-in operators.

From the very beginning, you have been working with C++ classes in a particular context: input and output. The standard header file `iostream` contains the declarations of two classes—`istream` and `ostream`—that manage a program's I/O. The C++ standard library declares `cin` and `cout` to be objects of these classes:

```
istream cin;
ostream cout;
```

The `istream` class has many member functions, two of which—the `get` function and the `ignore` function—you have already seen in statements like these:

```
cin.get(someChar);
cin.ignore(200, '\n');
```

As with any C++ class object, we use dot notation to select a particular member function to invoke.

You also have used C++ classes when performing file I/O. The header file `fstream` contains declarations for the `ifstream` and `ofstream` classes. The client code

```
ifstream dataFile;

dataFile.open("input.dat");
```

declares an `ifstream` class object named `dataFile`, then invokes the class member function `open` to try to open a file `input.dat` for input.

We do not examine in detail the `istream`, `ostream`, `ifstream`, and `ofstream` classes and all of their member functions. To study these would be beyond the goals of this book. What is important to recognize is that classes and objects are fundamental to all I/O activity in a C++ program.

Class Scope

We said earlier that member names must be unique within a struct. Additionally, in Chapter 8 we mentioned four kinds of scope in C++: local scope, global scope, namespace scope, and *class scope*. Class scope applies to the member names within structs, unions, and classes. To say that a member name has class scope means that the name is bound to that class (or struct or union). If the same identifier happens to be declared outside the class, the two identifiers are unrelated. Let's look at an example.

The `TimeType` class has a member function named `Write`. In the same program, another class (say, `SomeClass`) could also have a member function named `Write`. Furthermore, the program might have a global `Write` function that is completely unrelated to any classes. If the program has statements like

```
TimeType   checkInTime;
SomeClass someObject;
int        n;
  ⋮
checkInTime.Write();
someObject.Write();
Write(n);
```

then the C++ compiler has no trouble distinguishing among the three `Write` functions. In the first two function calls, the dot notation denotes class member selection. The first statement invokes the `Write` function of the `TimeType` class, and the second statement invokes the `Write` function of the `SomeClass` class. The final statement does not use dot notation, so the compiler knows that the function being called is the global `Write` function.

Information Hiding

Conceptually, a class object has an invisible wall around it. This wall, called the **abstraction barrier,** protects private data and functions from being accessed by client code. The barrier also prohibits the class object from directly accessing data and functions outside the object. This barrier is a critical characteristic of classes and abstract data types.

For a class object to share information with the outside world (that is, with clients), there must be a gap in the abstraction barrier. This gap is the public interface—the class members declared to be `public`. The only way that a client can manipulate the internals of the class object is indirectly—through the operations in the public interface. Engineers have a similar concept called a **black box.** A black box is a module or device whose inner workings are hidden from view. The user of the black box depends only on the written specification of *what* it does, not on *how* it does it. The user connects wires to the interface and assumes that the module works correctly by satisfying the specification (see Figure 11-9).

In software design, the black box concept is referred to as **information hiding.** Information hiding protects the user of a class from having to know all the details of its implementation. Information hiding also assures the

FIGURE 11-9
A Black Box

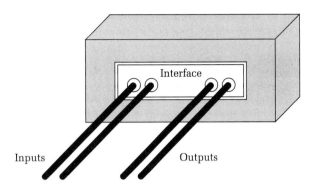

class's implementor that the user cannot directly access any private code or data and compromise the correctness of the implementation.

You have been introduced to encapsulation and information hiding before. In Chapter 7, we discussed the possibility of hiding a function's implementation in a separate file. In this chapter, you'll see how to hide the implementations of class member functions by placing them in files that are separate from the client code.

Abstraction barrier   The invisible wall around a class object that encapsulates implementation details. The wall can be breached only through the public interface.

Black box   An electrical or mechanical device whose inner workings are hidden from view.

Information hiding   The encapsulation and hiding of implementation details to keep the user of an abstraction from depending on or incorrectly manipulating these details.

The creator of a C++ class is free to choose which members are private and which are public. However, making data members public (as in a struct) allows the client to inspect and modify the data directly. Because information hiding is so fundamental to data abstraction, most classes exhibit a typical pattern: The private part contains data, and the public part contains the functions that manipulate the data.

The `TimeType` class exemplifies this organization. The data members `hrs`, `mins`, and `secs` are private, so the compiler prohibits a client from accessing these members directly. The following client statement therefore results in a compile-time error:

```
TimeType checkInTime;

checkInTime.hrs = 9;    // Prohibited in client code
```

Because only the class's member functions can access the private data, the creator of the class can offer a reliable product, knowing that external access to the private data is impossible. If it is acceptable to let the client *inspect* (but not modify) private data members, a class might provide observer functions. The TimeType class has three such functions: Write, Equal, and LessThan. Because these observer functions are not intended to modify the private data, they are declared with the word const following the parameter list:

```
void Write() const;
bool Equal( TimeType ) const;
bool LessThan( TimeType ) const;
```

C++ refers to these functions as *const member functions*. Within the body of a const member function, a compile-time error occurs if any statement tries to modify a private data member. Although not required by the language, it is good practice to declare as const those member functions that do not modify private data.

Specification and Implementation Files

An abstract data type consists of two parts: a specification and an implementation. The specification describes the behavior of the data type without reference to its implementation. The implementation creates an abstraction barrier by hiding the concrete data representation as well as the code for the operations.

The TimeType class declaration serves as the specification of TimeType. This declaration presents the public interface to the user in the form of function prototypes. To implement the TimeType class, we must provide function definitions (declarations with bodies) for all the member functions.

In C++, it is customary (though not required) to package the class declaration and the class implementation into separate files. One file—the *specification file*—is a header (.h) file containing only the class declaration. The second file—the *implementation file*—contains the function definitions for the class member functions. Let's look first at the specification file.

The Specification File

Below is the specification file for the TimeType class. On our computer system, we have named the file timetype.h. The class declaration is the same as we presented earlier, with one important exception: We include function preconditions and postconditions to specify the semantics of the member functions as unambiguously as possible for the user of the class.

```
//****************************************************************
// SPECIFICATION FILE (timetype.h)
// This file gives the specification
// of a TimeType abstract data type
//****************************************************************

class TimeType
{
public:
    void Set( /* in */ int hours,
              /* in */ int minutes,
              /* in */ int seconds );
        // Precondition:
        //      0 <= hours <= 23  &&  0 <= minutes <= 59
        //   && 0 <= seconds <= 59
        // Postcondition:
        //      Time is set according to the incoming parameters
        // NOTE:
        //      This function MUST be called prior to
        //      any of the other member functions

    void Increment();
        // Precondition:
        //      The Set function has been invoked at least once
        // Postcondition:
        //      Time has been advanced by one second, with
        //      23:59:59 wrapping around to 0:0:0

    void Write() const;
        // Precondition:
        //      The Set function has been invoked at least once
        // Postcondition:
        //      Time has been output in the form HH:MM:SS

    bool Equal( /* in */ TimeType otherTime ) const;
        // Precondition:
        //      The Set function has been invoked at least once
        //      for both this time and otherTime
        // Postcondition:
        //      Function value == true, if this time equals otherTime
        //                     == false, otherwise

    bool LessThan( /* in */ TimeType otherTime ) const;
        // Precondition:
        //      The Set function has been invoked at least once
        //      for both this time and otherTime
```

```
             //  && This time and otherTime represent times in the
             //      same day
             // Postcondition:
             //      Function value == true, if this time is earlier
             //                               in the day than otherTime
             //                          == false, otherwise
      private:
         int hrs;
         int mins;
         int secs;
   };
```

Notice the preconditions for the `Increment`, `Write`, `Equal`, and `LessThan` functions. It is the responsibility of the client to set the time before incrementing, printing, or testing it. If the client fails to set the time, the effect of each of these functions is undefined.

In principle, a specification file should not reveal any implementation details to the user of the class. The file should specify *what* each member function does without disclosing how it does it. However, as you can see in the class declaration, there is one implementation detail that is visible to the user: the concrete data representation of our ADT that is listed in the private part. However, the data representation is still considered hidden information in the sense that the compiler prohibits client code from accessing the data directly.

The Implementation File

The specification (`.h`) file for the `TimeType` class contains only the class declaration. The implementation file must provide the function definitions for all the class member functions. In the opening comments of the implementation file below, we document the file name as `timetype.cpp`. Your system may use a different file name suffix for source code files, perhaps `.c`, `.C`, or `.cxx`.

We recommend that you first skim the C++ code below, not being too concerned about the new language features such as prefixing the name of each function with the symbols

```
TimeType::
```

Immediately following the program code, we explain the new features.

```
//**********************************************************************
// IMPLEMENTATION FILE (timetype.cpp)
// This file implements the TimeType member functions
//**********************************************************************
```

```
#include "timetype.h"
#include <iostream>

using namespace std;

// Private members of class:
//      int hrs;
//      int mins;
//      int secs;

//****************************************************************

void TimeType::Set( /* in */ int hours,
                    /* in */ int minutes,
                    /* in */ int seconds )

// Precondition:
//      0 <= hours <= 23  &&  0 <= minutes <= 59
//      && 0 <= seconds <= 59
// Postcondition:
//      hrs == hours  &&  mins == minutes  &&  secs == seconds
// NOTE:
//      This function MUST be called prior to
//      any of the other member functions

{
    hrs = hours;
    mins = minutes;
    secs = seconds;
}

//****************************************************************

void TimeType::Increment()

// Precondition:
//      The Set function has been invoked at least once
// Postcondition:
//      Time has been advanced by one second, with
//      23:59:59 wrapping around to 0:0:0

{
    secs++;
    if (secs > 59)
    {
        secs = 0;
        mins++;
        if (mins > 59)
        {
```

```
            mins = 0;
            hrs++;
            if (hrs > 23)
                hrs = 0;
        }
    }
}

//******************************************************************

void TimeType::Write() const

// Precondition:
//      The Set function has been invoked at least once
// Postcondition:
//      Time has been output in the form HH:MM:SS

{
    if (hrs < 10)
        cout << '0';
    cout << hrs << ':';
    if (mins < 10)
        cout << '0';
    cout << mins << ':';
    if (secs < 10)
        cout << '0';
    cout << secs;
}

//******************************************************************

bool TimeType::Equal( /* in */ TimeType otherTime ) const

// Precondition:
//      The Set function has been invoked at least once
//      for both this time and otherTime
// Postcondition:
//      Function value == true, if this time equals otherTime
//                     == false, otherwise

{
    return (hrs == otherTime.hrs && mins == otherTime.mins &&
            secs == otherTime.secs);
}

//******************************************************************
```

```
bool TimeType::LessThan( /* in */ TimeType otherTime ) const

// Precondition:
//      The Set function has been invoked at least once
//      for both this time and otherTime
//   && This time and otherTime represent times in the
//      same day
// Postcondition:
//      Function value == true,  if this time is earlier
//                               in the day than otherTime
//                    == false,  otherwise

{
    return (hrs < otherTime.hrs ||
           hrs == otherTime.hrs && mins < otherTime.mins ||
           hrs == otherTime.hrs && mins == otherTime.mins
                               && secs < otherTime.secs);
}
```

This implementation file demonstrates several important points.

1. The file begins with the preprocessor directive

   ```
   #include "timetype.h"
   ```

   Both the implementation file and the client code must #include the specification file. Figure 11-10 pictures this shared access to the specification file. This sharing guarantees that all declarations related to an abstraction are consistent. That is, both client.cpp and timetype.cpp must reference the same declaration of the TimeType class located in timetype.h.

2. Near the top of the implementation file we have included a comment that restates the private members of the TimeType class.

   ```
   // Private members of class:
   //      int hrs;
   //      int mins;
   //      int secs;
   ```

   This comment reminds the reader that any references to these identifiers are references to the private class members.

3. In the heading of each function definition, the name of the member function is prefixed by the class name (TimeType) and the C++ scope resolution operator (::). As we discussed earlier, it is possible for several different classes to have member functions with the same name, say, Write. In addition, there may be a global Write function that is not a member of any class. The scope resolution operator eliminates any uncertainty about which particular function is being defined.

FIGURE 11-10
Shared Access to a
Specification File

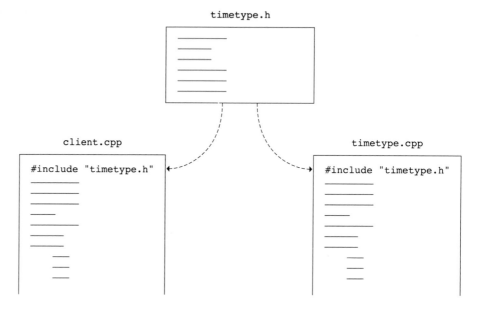

4. Although clients of a class must use the dot operator to refer to class members (for example, startTime.Write()), members of a class refer to each other directly without using dot notation. Looking at the bodies of the Set and Increment functions, you can see that the statements refer directly to the member variables hrs, mins, and secs without using the dot operator.

An exception to this rule occurs when a member function manipulates two or more class objects. Consider the Equal function. Suppose that the client code has two class objects, startTime and endTime, and uses the statement

```
if (startTime.Equal(endTime))
    ⋮
```

At execution time, the startTime object is the object for which the Equal function is invoked. In the body of the Equal function, the relational expression

```
hrs == otherTime.hrs
```

refers to class members of two different class objects. The unadorned identifier hrs refers to the hrs member of the class object for which the function is invoked (that is, startTime). The expression otherTime.hrs refers to the hrs member of the class object that is passed as a function argument: endTime.

5. Write, Equal, and LessThan are observer functions; they do not modify the private data of the class. Because we have declared these to be const member functions, the compiler prevents them from assigning new values to the private data. The use of const is both an aid to the user of the class (as a visual signal that this function does not modify any private data) and an aid to the class implementor (as a way of preventing accidental modification of the data). Note that the word const must appear in both the function prototype (in the class declaration) and the heading of the function definition.

Compiling and Linking a Multifile Program

Now that we have created a specification file and an implementation file for our TimeType class, how do we (or any other programmer) make use of these files in our programs? Let's begin by looking at the notion of *separate compilation* of source code files.

In earlier chapters, we have referred to the concept of a multifile program—a program divided up into several files containing source code. In C++, it is possible to compile each of these files separately and at different times. The compiler translates each source code file into an object code file. Figure 11-11 shows a multifile program consisting of the source code files myprog.cpp, file2.cpp, and file3.cpp. We can compile each of these files independently, yielding object code files myprog.obj, file2.obj, and file3.obj. Although each .obj file contains machine language code, it is not yet in executable form. The system's linker program brings the object code together to form an executable program file. (In Figure 11-11, we use the file name suffixes .cpp, .obj, and .exe. Your C++ system may use different file name conventions.)

Files such as file2.cpp and file3.cpp typically contain function definitions for functions that are called by the code in myprog.cpp. An important benefit of separate compilation is that modifying the code in just one file requires recompiling only that file. The new .obj file is then relinked with the other existing .obj files. Of course, if a modification to one file affects the code in another file—for example, changing a function's interface by altering the number or data types of the function parameters— then the affected files also need to be modified and recompiled.

Returning to our TimeType class, let's assume we have used the system's editor to create the timetype.h and timetype.cpp files. Now we can compile timetype.cpp into object code. If we are working at the operating system's command line, we use a command similar to the following:

```
cc -c timetype.cpp
```

FIGURE 11-11

Separate
Compilation and
Linking

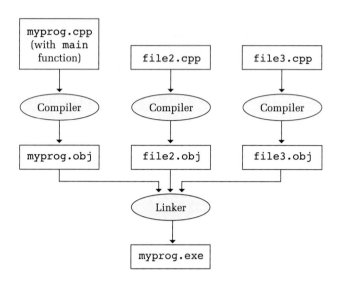

In this example, we assume that cc is the name of a command that invokes either the C++ compiler or the linker or both, depending on various options given on the command line. The command-line option -c means, on many systems, "compile but do not link." In other words, this command produces an object code file, say, timetype.obj, but does not attempt to link this file with any other file.

A programmer wishing to use the TimeType class will write code that #includes the file timetype.h, then declares and uses TimeType objects:

```
#include "timetype.h"
    ⋮
TimeType appointment;

appointment.Set(15, 30, 0);
appointment.Write();
    ⋮
```

If this client code is in a file named diary.cpp, an operating system command like

```
cc diary.cpp timetype.obj
```

compiles the client program into object code, links this object code with timetype.obj, and produces an executable program (see Figure 11-12). The mechanics of compiling, linking, and executing vary from one computer system to another. Our examples using the cc command assume you are working at the operating system's command line. Many C++ sys-

FIGURE 11-12

Linking with the
TimeType
Implementation
File

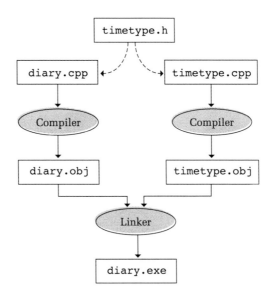

tems provide an *integrated environment*—a program that bundles the editor, the compiler, and the linker into one package. Integrated environments put you back into the editor when a compile-time or link-time error occurs, pinpointing the location of the error. Some integrated environments also manage *project files*. Project files contain information about all the constituent files of a multifile program. With project files, the system automatically recompiles or relinks any files that have become out-of-date because of changes to other files of the program.

Whichever environment you use—the command-line environment or an integrated environment—the overall process is the same: You compile the individual source code files into object code, link the object files into an executable program, then execute the program.

Before leaving the topic of multifile programs, we stress an important point. Referring to Figure 11-12, the files timetype.h and timetype.obj must be available to users of the TimeType class. The user needs to examine timetype.h to see what TimeType objects do and how to use them. The user must also be able to link his or her program with timetype.obj to produce an executable program. But the user does *not* need to see timetype.cpp. The implementation of TimeType should be treated as a black box. The main purpose of abstraction is to simplify the programmer's job by reducing complexity. Users of an abstraction should not have to look at its implementation to learn how to use it, nor should they write programs that depend on implementation details. In the latter case, any changes in the implementation could "break" the user's programs. In Chapter 7, the Software Engineering Tip box entitled "Conceptual Versus Physical Hiding of a Function Implementation" discussed the hazards of writing code that relies on implementation details.

Guaranteed Initialization with Class Constructors

The `TimeType` class we have been discussing has a weakness. It depends on the client to invoke the `Set` function before calling any other member function. For example, the `Increment` function's precondition is

```
// Precondition:
//      The Set function has been invoked at least once
```

If the client fails to invoke the `Set` function first, this precondition is false and the contract between the client and the function implementation is broken. Because classes nearly always encapsulate data, the creator of a class should not rely on the user to initialize the data. If the user forgets to do so, unpleasant results may occur.

C++ provides a mechanism, called a *class constructor,* to guarantee the initialization of a class object. A constructor is a member function that is implicitly invoked whenever a class object is created.

A constructor function has an unusual name: the name of the class itself. Let's change the `TimeType` class by adding two class constructors:

```
class TimeType
{
public:
    void Set( int, int, int );
    void Increment();
    void Write() const;
    bool Equal( TimeType ) const;
    bool LessThan( TimeType ) const;
    TimeType( int, int, int );          // Constructor
    TimeType();                         // Constructor
private:
    int hrs;
    int mins;
    int secs;
};
```

This class declaration includes two constructors, differentiated by their parameter lists. The first has three `int` parameters, which, as we will see, are used to initialize the private data when a class object is created. The second constructor is parameterless and initializes the time to some default value, such as 0:0:0. A parameterless constructor is known in C++ as a *default constructor.*

Constructor declarations are unique in two ways. First, as we have mentioned, the name of the function is the same as the name of the class. Second, the data type of the function is omitted. The reason is that a constructor cannot return a function value. Its purpose is only to initialize a class object's private data.

In the implementation file, the function definitions for the two `TimeType` constructors might look like the following:

```
//***************************************************************

TimeType::TimeType( /* in */ int initHrs,
                    /* in */ int initMins,
                    /* in */ int initSecs )
// Constructor

// Precondition:
//     0 <= initHrs <= 23  &&  0 <= initMins <= 59
//  && 0 <= initSecs <= 59
// Postcondition:
//     hrs == initHrs  &&  mins == initMins  &&  secs == initSecs

{
    hrs = initHrs;
    mins = initMins;
    secs = initSecs;
}


//***************************************************************

TimeType::TimeType()

// Default constructor

// Postcondition:
//     hrs == 0  &&  mins == 0  &&  secs == 0

{
    hrs = 0;
    mins = 0;
    secs = 0;
}
```

Invoking a Constructor

Although a constructor is a member of a class, it is never invoked using dot notation. A constructor is automatically invoked whenever a class object is created. The client declaration

```
TimeType lectureTime(10, 30, 0);
```

includes an argument list to the right of the name of the class object being declared. When this declaration is encountered at execution time, the first (parameterized) constructor is automatically invoked, initializing the private data of `lectureTime` to the time 10:30:0. The client declaration

```
TimeType startTime;
```

has no argument list after the identifier `startTime`. The default (parameterless) constructor is implicitly invoked, initializing `startTime`'s private data to the time 0:0:0.

Remember that a declaration in C++ is a genuine statement and can appear anywhere among executable statements. Placing declarations among executable statements is extremely useful when creating class objects whose initial values are not known until execution time. Here's an example:

```
cout << "Enter appointment time in hours, minutes, and seconds: ";
cin >> hours >> minutes >> seconds;

TimeType appointmentTime(hours, minutes, seconds);

cout << "The appointment time is ";
appointmentTime.Write();
  ⋮
```

Revised Specification and Implementation Files for `TimeType`

By including constructors for the `TimeType` class, we are sure that each class object is initialized before any subsequent calls to the class member functions. One of the constructors allows the client code to specify an initial time; the other creates an initial time of 0:0:0 if the client does not specify a time. Because of these constructors, it is *impossible* for a `TimeType` object to be in an uninitialized state after it is created. As a result, we can delete from the `TimeType` specification file the warning to call `Set` before calling any other member functions. Also, we can remove all of the function preconditions that require `Set` to be called previously. Here is the revised `TimeType` specification file:

```
//************************************************************************
// SPECIFICATION FILE (timetype.h)
// This file gives the specification
// of a TimeType abstract data type
//************************************************************************
```

```
class TimeType
{
public:
    void Set( /* in */ int hours,
              /* in */ int minutes,
              /* in */ int seconds );
        // Precondition:
        //     0 <= hours <= 23  &&  0 <= minutes <= 59
        //  && 0 <= seconds <= 59
        // Postcondition:
        //     Time is set according to the incoming parameters

    void Increment();
        // Postcondition:
        //     Time has been advanced by one second, with
        //     23:59:59 wrapping around to 0:0:0

    void Write() const;
        // Postcondition:
        //     Time has been output in the form HH:MM:SS

    bool Equal( /* in */ TimeType otherTime ) const;
        // Postcondition:
        //     Function value == true, if this time equals otherTime
        //                    == false, otherwise

    bool LessThan( /* in */ TimeType otherTime ) const;
        // Precondition:
        //     This time and otherTime represent times in the
        //     same day
        // Postcondition:
        //     Function value == true, if this time is earlier
        //                             in the day than otherTime
        //                    == false, otherwise

    TimeType( /* in */ int initHrs,
              /* in */ int initMins,
              /* in */ int initSecs );
        // Precondition:
        //     0 <= initHrs <= 23  &&  0 <= initMins <= 59
        //  && 0 <= initSecs <= 59
        // Postcondition:
        //     Class object is constructed
        //  && Time is set according to the incoming parameters

    TimeType();
        // Postcondition:
        //     Class object is constructed  &&  Time is 0:0:0
```

```
private:
    int hrs;
    int mins;
    int secs;
};
```

To save space, we do not include the revised implementation file here. The only changes are as follows:

1. The inclusion of the function definitions for the two class constructors, which we presented earlier.
2. The deletion of all function preconditions stating that the Set function must be invoked previously.

At this point, you may wonder whether we need the Set function at all. After all, both the Set function and the parameterized constructor seem to do the same thing—set the time according to values passed as arguments—and the implementations of the two functions are essentially identical. The difference is that Set can be invoked for an existing class object whenever and as often as we wish, whereas the parameterized constructor is invoked once only—at the moment a class object is created. Therefore, we retain the Set function to provide maximum flexibility to clients of the class.

Guidelines for Using Class Constructors

The class is an essential language feature for creating abstract data types in C++. The class mechanism is a powerful design tool, but along with this power come rules for using classes correctly.

C++ has some very intricate rules about using constructors, many of which relate to language features we have not yet discussed. Below are some guidelines that are pertinent at this point.

1. A constructor cannot return a function value, so the function is declared without a return value type.
2. A class may provide several constructors. When a class object is declared, the compiler chooses the appropriate constructor according to the number and data types of the arguments to the constructor.
3. Arguments to a constructor are passed by placing the argument list immediately after the name of the class object being declared:

   ```
   SomeClass anObject(arg1, arg2);
   ```

4. If a class object is declared without an argument list, as in the statement

   ```
   SomeClass anObject;
   ```

then the effect depends upon what constructors (if any) the class provides.

If the class has no constructors at all, memory is allocated for anObject but its private data members are in an uninitialized state.

If the class does have constructors, then the default (parameterless) constructor is invoked if there is one. If the class has constructors but no default constructor, a syntax error occurs.

Before leaving the topic of constructors, we give you a brief preview of another special member function supported by C++: the *class destructor.* Just as a constructor is implicitly invoked when a class object is created, a destructor is implicitly invoked when a class object is destroyed—for example, when control leaves the block in which a local object is declared. A class destructor is named the same as a constructor except that the first character is a tilde (~):

```
class SomeClass
{
public:
    ⋮
    SomeClass();      // Constructor
    ~SomeClass();     // Destructor
private:
    ⋮
};
```

In the next few chapters, we won't be using destructors; the kinds of classes we'll be writing have no need to perform special actions at the moment a class object is destroyed. In Chapter 15, we explore destructors in detail and describe the situations in which you need to use them.

PROBLEM-SOLVING CASE STUDY

Manipulating Dates

Dates are often necessary pieces of information. In programs, our processing of dates may call for us to compare two dates, print a date, or determine the date a certain number of days in the future. The machine shop example had a date as part of the data. In fact, the machine shop example had two dates: the date of purchase and the date of last service. Each time we needed a date, we defined it again.

Let's stop this duplication of effort and do the job once and for all—let's write the code to support a date as an abstract data type.

The format for this case study needs to be a little different. Because we are developing only one software component—an ADT—and not a complete program, we omit the Input and Output sections. Instead, we include two sections entitled Specification of the ADT and Implementation of the ADT.

Problem: Design and implement an ADT to represent a date. Make the domain and operations general enough to be used in any program that needs to perform these operations on dates. The informal specification of the ADT is given below.

TYPE
　　DateType
DOMAIN
　　Each DateType value is a single date after the year 1582 A.D. in the form of month, day, and year.
OPERATIONS
　　Construct a new DateType instance.
　　Set the date.
　　Inspect the date's month.
　　Inspect the date's day.
　　Inspect the date's year.
　　Print the date.
　　Compare two dates for "before," "equal," or "after."
　　Increment the date by one day.

Discussion: We create the DateType ADT in two stages: specification, followed by implementation. The result of the first stage is a C++ specification (.h) file containing the declaration of a DateType class. This file must describe for the user the precise semantics of each ADT operation. The informal specification given above would be unacceptable to the user of the ADT. The descriptions of the operations are too imprecise and ambiguous to be helpful to the user.

The second stage—implementation—requires us to (a) choose a concrete data representation for a date, and (b) implement each of the operations as a C++ function definition. The result is a C++ implementation file containing these function definitions.

Specification of the ADT: The domain of our ADT is the set of all dates after the year 1582 A.D. in the form of a month, a day, and a year. We restrict the year to be after 1582 A.D. in order to simplify the ADT operations (ten days were skipped in 1582 in switching from the Julian to the Gregorian calendar).

To represent the DateType ADT as program code, we use a C++ class named `DateType`. The ADT operations become public member functions of the class. Let's now specify the operations more carefully.

Construct a new DateType instance: For this operation, we use a C++ default constructor that initializes the date to January 1 of the year 1583. The client code can reset the date at any time using the "Set the date" operation.

Set the date: The client must supply three arguments for this operation: month, day, and year. Although we haven't yet determined a concrete data representation for a date, we must decide what data types the client should use for these arguments. We choose integers, where the month must be in the range 1 through 12, the day must be in the range 1 through the maximum number of days in the month, and the year must be greater than 1582. Notice that these range restrictions will become the precondition for invoking this operation.

Inspect the date's month, inspect the date's day, and inspect the date's year: All three of these operations are observer operations. They give the client access, indirectly, to the private data. In the `DateType` class, we represent these operations as value-returning member functions with the following prototypes:

```
int Month();
int Day();
int Year();
```

Why do we need these observer operations? Why not simply let the data representation of the month, day, and year be public instead of private so that the client can access the values directly? The answer is that the client should be allowed to inspect *but not modify* these values. If the data were public, a client could manipulate the data incorrectly (such as incrementing January 31 to January 32), thereby compromising the correct behavior of the ADT.

Print the date: This operation prints the date on the standard output device in the following form:

```
January 12, 2001
```

Compare two dates: This operation compares two dates and determines whether the first one comes before the second one, they are the same, or the first one comes after the second one. To indicate the result of the comparison, we define an enumeration type with three values:

```
enum RelationType {BEFORE, SAME, AFTER};
```

Then we can code the comparison operation as a class member function that returns a value of type `RelationType`. Here is the function prototype:

```
RelationType ComparedTo( /* in */ DateType otherDate ) const;
```

Because this is a class member function, the date being compared to `otherDate` is the class object for which the member function is invoked. For example, the following client code tests to see whether `date1` comes before `date2`.

```
DateType date1;
DateType date2;
   ⋮
if (date1.ComparedTo(date2) == BEFORE)
    DoSomething();
```

Increment the date by one day: This operation advances the date to the next day. For example, given the date March 31, 2000, this operation changes the date to April 1, 2000.

We are now almost ready to write the C++ specification file for our `DateType` class. However, the class declaration requires us to include the private part—the private variables that are the concrete data representation of the ADT. Choosing a concrete data representation properly belongs in the ADT implementation phase, not the specification phase. But to satisfy the C++ class declaration requirement, we now choose a data representation. The simplest representation for a date is three `int` values—one each for the month, day, and year. Here, then, is the specification file containing the `DateType` class declaration (along with the declaration of the `RelationType` enumeration type).

```
//*****************************************************************
// SPECIFICATION FILE (datetype.h)
// This file gives the specification of a DateType abstract data
// type and provides an enumeration type for comparing dates
//*****************************************************************
```

```
enum RelationType {BEFORE, SAME, AFTER};

class DateType
{
public:
    void Set( /* in */ int newMonth,
              /* in */ int newDay,
              /* in */ int newYear  );
        // Precondition:
        //     1 <= newMonth <= 12
        //  && 1 <= newDay <= maximum no. of days in month newMonth
        //  && newYear > 1582
        // Postcondition:
        //     Date is set according to the incoming parameters

    int Month() const;
        // Postcondition:
        //     Function value == this date's month

    int Day() const;
        // Postcondition:
        //     Function value == this date's day

    int Year() const;
        // Postcondition:
        //     Function value == this date's year

    void Print() const;
        // Postcondition:
        //     Date has been output in the form
        //         month day, year
        //     where the name of the month is printed as a string

    RelationType ComparedTo( /* in */ DateType otherDate ) const;
        // Postcondition:
        //     Function value == BEFORE, if this date is
        //                                 before otherDate
        //                    == SAME, if this date equals otherDate
        //                    == AFTER, if this date is
        //                                 after otherDate

    void Increment();
        // Postcondition:
        //     Date has been advanced by one day

    DateType();
        // Postcondition:
```

PROBLEM-SOLVING CASE STUDY cont'd.

```
        //      New DateType object is constructed with a
        //      month, day, and year of 1, 1, and 1583
private:
    int mo;
    int day;
    int yr;
};
```

Implementation of the ADT: We have already chosen a concrete data representation for a date, shown in the specification file as the int variables mo, day, and yr. Now we must implement each class member function, placing the function definitions into a C++ implementation file named, say, datetype.cpp. As we implement the member functions, we also discuss testing strategies that can help to convince us that the implementations are correct.

The class constructor, Set, Month, Day, and Year functions: The implementations of these functions are so straightforward that no discussion is needed.

The class constructor DateType ( )

```
Set mo = 1
Set day = 1
Set yr = 1583
```

Set (In: newMonth, newDay, newYear)

```
Set mo = newMonth
Set day = newDay
Set yr = newYear
```

Month ( )

Out: Function value

```
Return mo
```

Day ( )

    Out: Function value

```
Return day
```

Year ( )

    Out: Function value

```
Return yr
```

Testing: The `Month`, `Day`, and `Year` observer functions can be used to verify that the class constructor and `Set` functions work correctly. The code

```
DateType someDate;

cout << someDate.Month() << ' ' << someDate.Day() << ' '
     << someDate.Year() << endl;
```

should print out `1 1 1583`. To test the `Set` function, it is sufficient to set a `DateType` object to a few different values (obeying the precondition for the `Set` function), then print out the month, day, and year as above.

The `Print` function   The date is to be printed in the form month, day, comma, and year. We need a blank to separate the month and the day, and a comma followed by a blank to separate the day and the year. Because the month is represented as an integer in the range 1 through 12, we can use a Switch statement to print out the month in word form.

Print ( )

```
SWITCH mo
      1:  Print "January"
      2:  Print "February"
          ⋮
     12:  Print "December"
Print ' ', day, ", ", yr
```

Testing: In testing the `Print` function, we should print each month at least once. Both the year and the day should be tested at their end points and at several points between.

The `ComparedTo` *function:* If we were to compare two dates in our heads, we would look first at the years. If the years were different, we would immediately know which date came first. If the years were the same, we would look at the months. If the months were the same, we would have to look at the days. As so often happens, we can use this algorithm directly in our function.

ComparedTo (In: otherDate)

Out: Function value

```
IF yr < otherDate.yr
        Return BEFORE
IF yr > otherDate.yr
        Return AFTER

// Years are equal.  Compare months
IF mo < otherDate.mo
        Return BEFORE
IF mo > otherDate.mo
        Return AFTER

// Years and months are equal.  Compare days
IF day < otherDate.day
        Return BEFORE
IF day > otherDate.day
        Return AFTER

// Years, months, and days are equal
Return SAME
```

Testing: In testing this function, we should ensure that each path is taken at least once. Case Study Follow-Up Exercises 2 and 3 ask you to design test data for this function and to write a driver that does the testing.

The `Increment` *function:* The algorithm to increment the date is similar to our earlier algorithm for incrementing a `TimeType` value by one second. If the current date plus 1 is still within the same month, we are done. If the current date plus 1 is within the next month, then we must increment the month and reset the day to 1. Finally, we must not forget to increment the year when the month changes from December to January.

To determine whether the current date plus 1 is within the current month, we add 1 to the current day and compare this value with the maximum number of days in the current month. In this comparison, we must remember to check for leap year if the month is February.

Increment ( )

```
Increment day by 1
IF day > number of days in month "mo"
      Set day = 1
      Increment mo by 1
      IF mo > 12
            Set mo = 1
            Increment yr by 1
```

We can code the algorithm for finding the number of days in a month as a separate function—an auxiliary ("helper") function that is not a member of the `DateType` class. The number of days in February might need to be adjusted for leap year, so this function must receive as parameters both a month and a year.

DaysInMonth (In: month, year)

   Out: Function value

```
SWITCH month
      1, 3, 5, 7, 8, 10, 12 : Return 31
      4, 6, 9, 11 : Return 30
      2 :   // It's February.  Check for leap year
            IF (year MOD 4 is 0 AND year MOD 100 isn't 0)
            OR year MOD 400 is 0
                  Return 29
      ELSE
            Return 28
```

Testing: To test the `Increment` function, we need to create a driver that calls the function with different values for the date. Values that cause the month to change must be tested, as well as values that cause the year to change. Leap year must be tested, including years with the last two digits 00. Case Study Follow-Up Exercises 4 and 5 ask you to carry out this testing.

Here is the implementation file that contains function definitions for all of the ADT operations:

```cpp
//*****************************************************************
// IMPLEMENTATION FILE (datetype.cpp)
// This file implements the DateType member functions
//*****************************************************************
#include "datetype.h"
#include <iostream>

using namespace std;

// Private members of class:
//      int mo;
//      int day;
//      int yr;

int DaysInMonth( int, int );   // Prototype for auxiliary function

//*****************************************************************

DateType::DateType()

// Constructor

// Postcondition:
//      mo == 1  &&  day == 1  &&  yr == 1583

{
    mo = 1;
    day = 1;
    yr = 1583;
}

//*****************************************************************

void DateType::Set( /* in */ int newMonth,
                    /* in */ int newDay,
                    /* in */ int newYear  )

// Precondition:
//      1 <= newMonth <= 12
```

PROBLEM-SOLVING CASE STUDY *cont'd.*

```cpp
//    && 1 <= newDay <= maximum no. of days in month newMonth
//    && newYear > 1582
// Postcondition:
//      mo == newMonth  &&  day == newDay  &&  yr == newYear

{
    mo = newMonth;
    day = newDay;
    yr = newYear;
}

//****************************************************************

int DateType::Month() const

// Postcondition:
//      Function value == mo

{
    return mo;
}

//****************************************************************

int DateType::Day() const

// Postcondition:
//      Function value == day

{
    return day;
}

//****************************************************************

int DateType::Year() const

// Postcondition:
//      Function value == yr

{
    return yr;
}

//****************************************************************
```

PROBLEM-SOLVING CASE STUDY *cont'd.*

```cpp
void DateType::Print() const

// Postcondition:
//      Date has been output in the form
//          month day, year
//      where the name of the month is printed as a string

{
    switch (mo)
    {
        case 1 : cout << "January";
                break;
        case 2 : cout << "February";
                break;
        case 3 : cout << "March";
                break;
        case 4 : cout << "April";
                break;
        case 5 : cout << "May";
                break;
        case 6 : cout << "June";
                break;
        case 7 : cout << "July";
                break;
        case 8 : cout << "August";
                break;
        case 9 : cout << "September";
                break;
        case 10 : cout << "October";
                 break;
        case 11 : cout << "November";
                 break;
        case 12 : cout << "December";
    }
    cout << ' ' << day << ", " << yr;
}

//******************************************************************

RelationType DateType::ComparedTo(
                        /* in */ DateType otherDate ) const

// Postcondition:
//      Function value == BEFORE, if this date is
//                                   before otherDate
//                     == SAME, if this date equals otherDate
//                     == AFTER, if this date is
//                                   after otherDate
//
```

PROBLEM-SOLVING CASE STUDY cont'd.

```
{
    if (yr < otherDate.yr)             // Compare years
        return BEFORE;
    if (yr > otherDate.yr)
        return AFTER;

    if (mo < otherDate.mo)             // Years are equal. Compare
        return BEFORE;                 //    months
    if (mo > otherDate.mo)
        return AFTER;

    if (day < otherDate.day)           // Years and months are equal.
        return BEFORE;                 //    Compare days
    if (day > otherDate.day)
        return AFTER;

    return SAME;                       // Years, months, and days
}                                      //    are equal

//******************************************************************

void DateType::Increment()

// Postcondition:
//     Date has been advanced by one day

{
    day++;
    if (day > DaysInMonth(mo, yr))
    {
        day = 1;
        mo++;
        if (mo > 12)
        {
            mo = 1;
            yr++;
        }
    }
}

//******************************************************************

int DaysInMonth( /* in */ int month,
                 /* in */ int year  )

// Returns the number of days in month "month", taking
// leap year into account
```

PROBLEM-SOLVING CASE STUDY cont'd.

```
// Precondition:
//     1 <= month <= 12  &&  year > 1582
// Postcondition:
//     Function value == number of days in month "month "

{
    switch (month)
    {
        case 1: case 3: case 5: case 7: case 8: case 10: case 12:
            return 31;
        case 4: case 6: case 9: case 11:
            return 30;
        case 2:    // It's February.  Check for leap year
            if ((year % 4 == 0 && year % 100 != 0) ||
                 year % 400 == 0)
                return 29;
            else
                return 28;
    }
}
```

A date is a logical entity for which we now have developed an implementation. We have designed, implemented, and tested a date ADT that we (or any programmer) can use whenever we have a date as part of our program data. If we discover in the future that additional operations on a date would be useful, we can implement, test, and add them to our set of date operations.

We have said that data abstraction is an important principle of software design. What we have done here is an example of data abstraction. From now on, when a problem needs a date, we can stop our decomposition at the logical level. We do not need to worry about implementing a date each time.

PROBLEM-SOLVING CASE STUDY

Birthday Calls

Problem: Everyone has at least one friend who always remembers everyone's birthday. Each year when we receive greetings on our birthday from this friend, we promise to do better about remembering others' birthdays. Let's write a program to go through your address book and print the names and phone numbers of all the people who have birthdays within the next two weeks, so you can give them a call. Here, the "address book" is a data file containing information about your friends.

Input: Today's date (from the keyboard); and a list of names, phone numbers, and birth dates (from file `friendFile`). Entries in this file are in the form

```
John Arbuthnot
(493) 384-2938
 1/12/1970

Mary Smith
(123) 123-4567
10/12/1960
```

Output: The names, phone numbers, and birthdays of any friends whose birthdays are within the next two weeks. A sample of the output is

```
John Arbuthnot
(493) 384-2938
January 12, 2001
```

Note that the date printed is the friend's next birthday, not the friend's birth date.

Discussion: As we start our design phase for this problem, we call all the information about one person an *entry*. An entry consists of the following items: first name, last name, phone number, and birth date. To go any further, we must decide how we will represent these items as a C++ data structure. And we must design specific algorithms associated with our data structure.

Two of the items are names—that is, sequences of alphabetic characters. We can represent them as strings. The area code and local phone number could both be integer numbers, but we would like to store the hyphen that is between the third and fourth digits of the local number, because this is how phone numbers are usually printed. Therefore, we make the area code an integer, but we make the local phone number a string. (We assume that an area code is 100 or greater so that we don't have to worry about how to print leading zeros in area codes such as 052. A Case Study Follow-Up exercise asks you to rethink this assumption.) Because a phone number has two components—an area code and a local number—it makes sense to represent it as a struct:

```
struct PhoneType
{
    int      areaCode;
    string number;
};
```

Finally, we represent a birth date as a `DateType` object, where `DateType` is the class we developed in the preceding case study.

Putting this all together, we define the following `struct` type to represent an entry for one person.

```
struct EntryType
{
    string     firstName;
    string     lastName;
    PhoneType phone;
    DateType   birthDate;
};
```

`firstName`, `lastName`, `phone`, and `birthDate` are member names within the `struct` type `EntryType`. The members `firstName` and `lastName` are strings of type `string`, phone is a struct of type

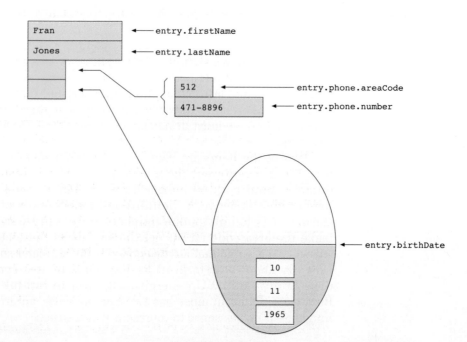

FIGURE 11-13
Struct Variable
entry, of type
EntryType

PhoneType, and birthDate is a class object of type DateType. Notice that EntryType is a hierarchical record type, because the phone member is also a record. A complete entry with values stored in a struct variable named entry is shown in Figure 11-13.

When looking for birthdays, we are interested in month and day only—the year is not important. If we were going through a conventional address book checking for birthdays by hand, we would write down the month and day of the date two weeks away and compare it to the month and day of each friend's birth date.

We can use the same algorithm in our program. Using the DateType class that we developed, the member function Increment can be used to calculate the date two weeks (14 days) from the current date. We can use the class member function ComparedTo to determine whether a friend's birthday lies between the current date and the date two weeks away, inclusive. How do we ignore the year? We set the year of each friend's birth date to the current year for the comparison. However, if the current date plus 14 days is in the next year, and the friend's birthday is in January, then we must set the year to the current year plus 1 for the comparison to work correctly.

Data Structures:

The DateType class, for manipulating dates.

A struct type PhoneType that stores an area code (integer) and a local phone number (string).

A struct type EntryType that stores a first name (string), a last name (string), a telephone number of type PhoneType, and a birth date of type DateType.

Main   **Level 0**

```
Open friendFile for input (and verify success)
Get current date into class object currentDate
Set targetDate = currentDate
FOR count going from 1 through 14
      targetDate.Increment()

Get entry
WHILE NOT EOF on friendFile
      IF targetDate.Year() isn't currentDate.Year() AND
                      entry.birthDate.Month() is 1
            Set birthdayYear = targetDate.Year()
      ELSE
            Set birthdayYear = currentDate.Year()
      birthday.Set(entry.birthDate.Month(), entry.birthDate.Day(), birthdayYear)
      IF birthday.ComparedTo(currentDate) ≥ SAME AND
                      birthday.ComparedTo(targetDate) ≤ SAME
            Print entry
      Get entry
```

Get Current Date (Out: currentDate)   **Level 1**

```
Prompt user for current date
Read month, day, year
currentDate.Set(month, day, year)
```

PROBLEM-SOLVING CASE STUDY cont'd.

Get Entry (Inout: friendFile; Out: entry)

> Read entry.firstName from friendFile
> IF EOF on friendFile
>   Return
> Read entry.lastName from friendFile
>
> // Below, dummy is a char variable to consume the '(' and ')'
> Read dummy, entry.phone.areaCode,
>   dummy, entry.phone.number from friendFile
>
> // Below, dummy consumes the '/' and '/'
> Read month, dummy, day, dummy, year from friendFile
>
> entry.birthDate.Set(month, day, year)

Print Entry (In: entry, birthday)

> Print entry.firstName, ' ', entry.lastName
> Print '(', entry.phone.areaCode, ')', entry.phone.number
> birthday.Print()

Because the `DateType` member functions (`Increment`, `ComparedTo`, and so on) already exist, no more decomposition is necessary.

Module Structure Chart:

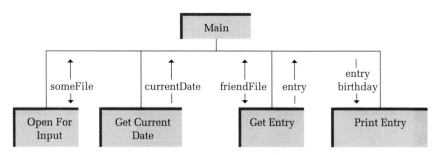

Below is the BirthdayCalls program that implements our design. By using the preexisting `DateType` class, the program is significantly shorter and easier to understand than if it included all the code to manipulate dates. All we have to do is `#include` the header file `datetype.h` to make use of `DateType` class objects. To run the program, we link its object code file with the `DateType` object code file, the place where all the `DateType` implementation details are hidden.

(The following program is written in ISO/ANSI standard C++. If you are working with pre–standard C++, see the alternate version of the program in the PRE_STD directory of the program disk, available at the publisher's Web site, `www.jbpub.com/disks`.)

```cpp
//******************************************************************
// BirthdayCalls program
// A data file contains people's names, phone numbers, and birth
// dates.  This program reads a date from standard input, calculates
// a date two weeks away, and prints the names, phone numbers, and
// birthdays of all those in the file whose birthdays come on or
// before the date two weeks away
//******************************************************************
#include "datetype.h"
#include <iostream>
#include <fstream>     // For file I/O
#include <string>      // For string type

using namespace std;

struct PhoneType
{
    int     areaCode;
    string number;
};
struct EntryType
{
    string     firstName;
    string     lastName;
    PhoneType phone;
    DateType  birthDate;
};

void GetCurrentDate( DateType& );
void GetEntry( ifstream&, EntryType& );
void OpenForInput( ifstream& );
void PrintEntry( EntryType, DateType );
```

PROBLEM-SOLVING CASE STUDY cont'd.

```cpp
int main()
{
    ifstream  friendFile;     // Input file of friends' records
    EntryType entry;          // Current record from friendFile
                              //   being checked
    DateType  currentDate;    // Month, day, and year of current day
    DateType  birthday;       // Date of next birthday
    DateType  targetDate;     // Two weeks from current date
    int       birthdayYear;   // Year of next birthday
    int       count;          // Loop counter

    OpenForInput(friendFile);
    if ( !friendFile )
        return 1;

    GetCurrentDate(currentDate);
    targetDate = currentDate;
    for (count = 1; count <= 14; count++)
        targetDate.Increment();

    GetEntry(friendFile, entry);
    while (friendFile)
    {
        if (targetDate.Year() != currentDate.Year() &&
                entry.birthDate.Month() == 1)
            birthdayYear = targetDate.Year();
        else
            birthdayYear = currentDate.Year();
        birthday.Set(entry.birthDate.Month(), entry.birthDate.Day(),
                    birthdayYear);
        if (birthday.ComparedTo(currentDate) >= SAME &&
                birthday.ComparedTo(targetDate) <= SAME)
            PrintEntry(entry, birthday);
        GetEntry(friendFile, entry);
    }
    return 0;
}

//****************************************************************

void OpenForInput( /* inout */ ifstream& someFile )    // File to be
                                                       // opened
// Prompts the user for the name of an input file
// and attempts to open the file
```

PROBLEM-SOLVING CASE STUDY cont'd.

```
// Postcondition:
//      The user has been prompted for a file name
//   && IF the file could not be opened
//          An error message has been printed
// Note:
//      Upon return from this function, the caller must test
//      the stream state to see if the file was successfully opened

{
        .
        .           (Same as in ConvertDates program of Chapter 8)
        .
}


//*****************************************************************

void GetCurrentDate( /* out */ DateType& currentDate )    // Today's
                                                          //    date
// Reads the current date from standard input

// Postcondition:
//      User has been prompted for the current month, day, and year
//   && currentDate is set according to the input values

{
    int month;
    int day;
    int year;

    cout << "Enter current date as three integers, separated by"
         << " spaces: MM DD YYYY" << endl;
    cin >> month >> day >> year;
    currentDate.Set(month, day, year);
}


//*****************************************************************

void GetEntry(
      /* inout */ ifstream&  friendFile,    // Input file of records
      /* out */    EntryType& entry       )    // Next record from file

// Reads an entry from file friendFile

// Precondition:
//      friendFile is open for input
// Postcondition:
```

```
//      IF input of the firstName member failed due to end-of-file
//          entry is undefined
//      ELSE
//          All members of entry are filled with the values
//          for one person read from friendFile

{
    char dummy;    // Used to input and ignore certain characters
    int  month;
    int  day;
    int  year;

    friendFile >> entry.firstName;
    if ( !friendFile )
        return;
    friendFile >> entry.lastName;

    friendFile >> dummy                    // Consume '('
               >> entry.phone.areaCode
               >> dummy                    // Consume ')'
               >> entry.phone.number;

    friendFile >> month
               >> dummy                    // Consume '/'
               >> day
               >> dummy                    // Consume '/'
               >> year;
    entry.birthDate.Set(month, day, year);
}


//****************************************************************

void PrintEntry( /* in */ EntryType entry,     // Friend's record
                 /* in */ DateType  birthday ) // Friend's birthday
                                               //   this year
// Prints the name, phone number, and birthday

// Precondition:
//     entry is assigned
// Postcondition:
//     entry.firstName, entry.lastName, entry.phone, and birthday
//     have been printed

{
    cout << entry.firstName << ' ' << entry.lastName << endl;
    cout << '(' << entry.phone.areaCode << ") "
```

```
                << entry.phone.number << endl;
        birthday.Print();
        cout << endl << endl;
    }
```

Testing: The only portions of this program that need to be checked are the `main` function and the input and output routines. The operations on dates have already been tested thoroughly.

The logic in the `main` function is straightforward. The test data should include birthdays less than two weeks away, exactly two weeks away, and more than two weeks away. The current date should include the cases in which two weeks away is within the same month, within the next month, and within the next year.

Testing and Debugging

Testing and debugging a C++ class amounts to testing and debugging each member function of the class. All of the techniques you have learned about—algorithm walk-throughs, code walk-throughs, hand traces, test drivers, verification of preconditions and postconditions, the system debugger, the `assert` function, and debug outputs—may be brought into play.

Consider how we might test this chapter's `TimeType` class. Here is the class declaration, abbreviated by leaving out the function preconditions and postconditions:

```
class TimeType
{
public:
    void Set( /* in */ int hours,
              /* in */ int minutes,
              /* in */ int seconds );
        // Precondition: ...
        // Postcondition: ...

    void Increment();
        // Postcondition: ...

    void Write() const;
        // Postcondition: ...

    bool Equal( /* in */ TimeType otherTime ) const;
        // Postcondition: ...

    bool LessThan( /* in */ TimeType otherTime ) const;
```

```
        // Precondition: ...
        // Postcondition: ...

    TimeType( /* in */ int initHrs,
              /* in */ int initMins,
              /* in */ int initSecs );
        // Precondition: ...
        // Postcondition: ...

    TimeType();
        // Postcondition: ...
private:
    int hrs;
    int mins;
    int secs;
};
```

To test this class fully, we must test each of the member functions. Let's step through the process of testing just one of them: the `Increment` function.

When we implemented the `Increment` function, we presumably started with a pseudocode algorithm, performed an algorithm walk-through, and translated the pseudocode into the following C++ function:

```
void TimeType::Increment()

// Postcondition:
//      Time has been advanced by one second, with
//      23:59:59 wrapping around to 0:0:0

{
    secs++;
    if (secs > 59)
    {
        secs = 0;
        mins++;
        if (mins > 59)
        {
            mins = 0;
            hrs++;
            if (hrs > 23)
                hrs = 0;
        }
    }
}
```

Now we perform a code walk-through, verifying that the C++ code faithfully matches the pseudocode algorithm. At this point (or earlier, during the algorithm walk-through), we do a hand trace to confirm that the logic is correct.

For the hand trace we should pick values of hrs, mins, and secs that ensure code coverage. To execute every path though the control flow, we need cases in which the following conditions occur:

1. The first If condition is false.
2. The first If condition is true and the second is false.
3. The first If condition is true, the second is true, and the third is false.
4. The first If condition is true, the second is true, and the third is true.

Below is a table displaying values of hrs, mins, and secs that correspond to these four cases. For each case we also write down what we hope will be the values of the variables after executing the algorithm.

	Initial Values				Expected Results		
Case	hrs	mins	secs		hrs	mins	secs
1	10	5	30		10	5	31
2	4	6	59		4	7	0
3	13	59	59		14	0	0
4	23	59	59		0	0	0

Using the initial values for each case, a hand trace of the code confirms that the algorithm produces the desired results.

Finally, we write a test driver for the Increment function, just to be sure that our understanding of the algorithm logic is the same as the computer's! Here is a possible test driver:

```cpp
#include <iostream>
#include "timetype.h"

using namespace std;

int main()
{
    TimeType time;
    int     hours;
    int     minutes;
    int     seconds;

    cout << "Enter a time (use hours < 0 to quit): ";
    cin >> hours >> minutes >> seconds;
    while (hours >= 0)
```

```
    {
        time.Set(hours, minutes, seconds);
        time.Increment();
        cout << "Incremented time is ";
        time.Write();
        cout << endl;
        cout << "Enter a time (use hours < 0 to quit): ";
        cin >> hours >> minutes >> seconds;
    }
    return 0;
}
```

The `timetype.cpp` implementation file only needs to contain function definitions for the following member functions: `Set`, `Increment`, `Write`, and the default constructor. The other member functions do not need to be implemented yet. Now we compile the test driver and `timetype.cpp`, link the two object files, and execute the program. For input data, we supply at least the four test cases discussed earlier. The program's output should match the desired results.

Now that we have tested the `Increment` function, we can apply the same steps to the remaining class member functions. We can create a separate test driver for each function, or we can write just one driver that tests all of the functions. The disadvantage of writing just one driver is that devising different combinations of input values to test several functions at once can quickly become complicated.

Before leaving the topic of testing a class, we must emphasize an important point. Even though a class has been tested thoroughly, it is still possible for errors to arise. Let's look at two examples using the `TimeType` class. The first example is the client statement

```
time.Set(24, 0, 0);
```

The second example is the comparison

```
if (time1.LessThan(time2))
    ⋮
```

where the programmer intends `time1` to be 11:00:00 on a Wednesday and `time2` to be 1:20:00 on a Thursday. (The result of the test is `false`, not `true` as the programmer expects.) Do you see the problem? In each example, the client has violated the function precondition. The precondition of `Set` requires the first argument to have a value from 0 through 23. The precondition of `LessThan` requires the two times to be on the same day, not on two different days.

If a class has been well tested and there are errors when client code uses the class, always check the member function preconditions. You can waste many hours trying to debug a class member function when, in fact, the function is correct. The error may lie in the client code.

Testing and Debugging Hints

1. The declarations of `struct` and `class` types must end with semi-colons.
2. Be sure to specify the full member selector when referencing a component of a struct variable or class object.
3. Avoid using anonymous `struct` types.
4. Regarding semicolons, the declarations and definitions of class member functions are treated the same as any C++ function. The member function prototype, located in the class declaration, ends with a semi-colon. The function heading—the part of the function definition preceding the body—does not end with a semicolon.
5. When implementing a class member function, don't forget to prefix the function name with the name of the class and the scope resolution operator (`::`).

```
void TimeType::Increment()
{
    ⋮
}
```

6. For now, the only built-in operations that apply to struct variables and class objects are member selection (`.`) and assignment (`=`). To perform other operations, such as comparing two struct variables or class objects, you must access the components individually (in the case of struct variables) or write class member functions (in the case of class objects).
7. If a class member function inspects but does not modify the private data, it is a good idea to make it a `const` member function.
8. A class member function does not use dot notation to access private members of the class object for which the function is invoked. In contrast, a member function *must* use dot notation to access the private members of a class object that is passed to it as an argument.
9. To avoid errors caused by uninitialized data, it is good practice to always include a class constructor when designing a class.
10. A class constructor is declared without a return value type and cannot return a function value.
11. If a client of a class has errors that seem to be related to the class, start by checking the preconditions of the class member functions. The errors may be in the client, not the class.

Summary

In addition to being able to create user-defined atomic data types, we can create structured data types. In a structured data type, a name is given to an entire group of components. With many structured types, the group can be accessed as a whole, or each individual component can be accessed separately.

The record is a data structure for grouping together heterogeneous data—data items that are of different types. Individual components of a record are accessed by name. In C++, records are referred to as *structures* or as structs. We can use a struct variable to refer to the struct as a whole, or we can use a member selector to access any individual member (component) of the struct. Entire structs of the same type may be assigned directly to each other, passed as arguments, or returned as function return values. Comparison of structs, however, must be done member by member. Reading and writing of structs must also be done member by member.

Data abstraction is a powerful technique for reducing the complexity and increasing the reliability of programs. Separating the properties of a data type from the details of its implementation frees the user of the type from having to write code that depends on a particular implementation of the type. This separation also assures the implementor of the type that client code cannot accidentally compromise a correct implementation.

An abstract data type (ADT) is a type whose specification is separate from its implementation. The specification announces the abstract properties of the type. The implementation consists of (a) a concrete data representation and (b) the implementations of the ADT operations. In C++, an ADT can be realized by using the class mechanism. A class is similar to a struct, but the members of a class are not only data but also functions. Class members can be designated as public or private. Most commonly, the private members are the concrete data representation of the ADT, and the public members are the functions corresponding to the ADT operations.

Among the public member functions of a class, the programmer often includes one or more class constructors—functions that are invoked automatically whenever a class object is created.

Separate compilation of program units is central to the separation of specification from implementation. The declaration of a C++ class is typically placed in a specification (.h) file, and the implementations of the class member functions reside in another file: the implementation file. The client code is compiled separately from the class implementation file, and the two resulting object code files are linked together to form an executable file. Through separate compilation, the user of an ADT can treat the ADT as an off-the-shelf component without ever seeing how it is implemented.

Quick Check

1. Write the type declaration for a `struct` data type named `PersonRec` with three members: `age`, `height`, and `weight`. All three members are intended to store integer values, with `height` and `weight` representing height in inches and weight in pounds, respectively. (pp. 579–586)
2. Assume a variable named `now`, of type `PersonRec`, has been declared. Write assignment statements to store into `now` the data for a 28-year old person measuring 5'6" and weighing 140 pounds. (pp. 579–586)
3. Declare a hierarchical record type named `HistoryRec` that consists of two members of type `PersonRec`. The members are named `past` and `present`. (pp. 587–589)
4. Assume a variable named `history`, of type `HistoryRec`, has been declared. Write assignment statements to store into the `past` member of `history` the data for a 15-year-old person measuring 5'0" and weighing 96 pounds. Write the assignment statement that copies the contents of variable `now` into the `present` member of `history`. (pp. 587–589)
5. What is the primary purpose of C++ `union` types? (pp. 589–590)
6. The specification of an ADT describes only its properties (the domain and allowable operations). To implement the ADT, what two things must a programmer do? (pp. 592–595)
7. Write a C++ class declaration for the following Checkbook ADT. Do not implement the ADT other than to include in the private part a concrete data representation for the current balance. All monetary amounts are to be represented as floating-point numbers.

   TYPE
       Checkbook
   DOMAIN
       Each instance of the Checkbook type is a value representing one customer's current checking account balance.
   OPERATIONS
       Open the checking account, specifying an initial balance.
       Write a check for a specified amount.
       Deposit a specified amount into the checking account.
       Return the current balance.

   (pp. 596–600)
8. Write a segment of client code that declares two `Checkbook` objects, one for a personal checkbook and one for a business account. (pp. 596–600)
9. For the personal checkbook in Question 8, write a segment of client code that opens the account with an initial balance of $300.00, writes two checks for $50.25 and $150.00, deposits $87.34 into the account, and prints out the resulting balance. (pp. 600–603)
10. Implement the following `Checkbook` member functions. (pp. 608–613)
    a. `Open`
    b. `WriteCheck`
    c. `CurrentBalance`

11. A compile-time error occurs if a client of Checkbook tries to access the private class members directly. Give an example of such a client statement. (pp. 604–605)

12. In which file—the specification file or the implementation file—would the solution to Question 7 be located? In which file would the solution to Question 10 be located? (pp. 606–613)

13. For the Checkbook class, replace the Open function with two C++ class constructors. One (the default constructor) initializes the account balance to zero. The other initializes the balance to an amount passed as an argument. (pp. 616–621)

    a. Revise the class declaration.

    b. Implement the two class constructors.

Answers

1.  ```
    struct PersonRec
    {
        int age;
        int height;
        int weight;
    };
    ```

2.  ```
    now.age = 28;
    now.height = 66;
    now.weight = 140;
    ```

3.  ```
    struct HistoryRec
    {
        PersonRec past;
        PersonRec present;
    };
    ```

4.  ```
    history.past.age = 15;
    history.past.height = 60;
    history.past.weight = 96;
    history.present = now;
    ```

5. The primary purpose is to save memory by forcing different values to share the same memory space, one at a time.   **6.** a. Choose a concrete data representation of the abstract data, using data types that already exist. b. Implement each of the allowable operations in terms of program instructions.

7.  ```
    class Checkbook
    {
    public:
        void Open( /* in */ float initBalance );
        void WriteCheck( /* in */ float amount );
        void Deposit( /* in */ float amount );
        float CurrentBalance() const;
    private:
        float balance;
    };
    ```

8.  ```
    Checkbook personalAcct;
    Checkbook businessAcct;
    ```

9.  ```
    personalAcct.Open(300.0);
    personalAcct.WriteCheck(50.25);
    personalAcct.WriteCheck(150.0);
    personalAcct.Deposit(87.34);
    cout << '$' << personalAcct.CurrentBalance() << endl;
    ```
    ```

10. a.
```
void Checkbook::Open( /* in */ float initBalance )
{
    balance = initBalance;
}
```
b.
```
void Checkbook::WriteCheck( /* in */ float amount )
{
    balance = balance - amount;
}
```
c.
```
float Checkbook::CurrentBalance() const
{
    return balance;
}
```

11. `personalAcct.balance = 10000.0;`

12. The C++ class declaration of Question 7 would be located in the specification file. The C++ function definitions of Question 10 would be located in the implementation file.

13. a.
```
class Checkbook
{
public:
    void WriteCheck( /* in */ float amount );
    void Deposit( /* in */ float amount );
    float CurrentBalance() const;
    Checkbook();
    Checkbook( /* in */ float initBalance );
private:
    float balance;
};
```
b.
```
Checkbook::Checkbook()
{
    balance = 0.0;
}
Checkbook::Checkbook( /* in */ float initBalance )
{
    balance = initBalance;
}
```

Exam Preparation Exercises

1. Define the following terms that relate to records (structs in C++):
   record
   member
   member selector
   hierarchical record

2. Declare a `struct` type named `RecType` to contain an integer variable representing a person's number of dependents, a floating-point variable representing the person's salary, and a Boolean variable indicating whether the person has major medical insurance coverage (`true`) or basic company coverage only (`false`).

3. Using the second version of the `MachineRec` type in this chapter (p. 588), the code below is supposed to print a message if a machine has not been serviced within the current year. The code has an error. Correct the error by using a proper member selector in the If statement.

```
DateType    currentDate;
MachineRec machine;
   ⋮
if (machine.lastServiced.year != currentDate.year)
      PrintMsg();
```

4. Given the declarations

```
struct NameType
{
     string first;
     string last;
};
struct AddrType
{
     string city;
     string state;
     long    zipCode;
};
struct PersonType
{
     NameType name;
     AddrType address;
};


PersonType person;
```

   write C++ code that stores the following information into person:
   Beverly Johnson
   2638 Oak Dr.
   La Crosse, WI 54601

5. The specification of an abstract data type (ADT) should not mention implementation details. (True or False?)

6. Below are some real-world objects you might want to represent in a program as ADTs. For each, give some abstract operations that might be appropriate. (Ignore the concrete data representation for each object.)
   a. A thesaurus
   b. An automatic dishwasher
   c. A radio-controlled model airplane

7. Consider the following C++ class declaration and client code:

Class Declaration	*Client Code*

```
class SomeClass                  SomeClass object1;
{                                SomeClass object2;
public:                          int       m;
     void Func1( int n );
     int  Func2( int n ) const;  object1.Func1(3);
     void Func3();               m = object2.Func2(5);
private:
     int someInt;
};
```

a. List all the identifiers that refer to data types (both built-in and programmer-defined).

b. List all the identifiers that are names of class members.

c. List all the identifiers that are names of class objects.

d. List the names of all member functions that are allowed to inspect the private data.

e. List the names of all member functions that are allowed to modify the private data.

f. In the implementation of SomeClass, which one of the following would be the correct function definition for Func3?

```
i.   void Func3()
     {
           ⋮
     }
ii.  void SomeClass::Func3()
     {
           ⋮
     }
iii. SomeClass::void Func3()
     {
           ⋮
     }
```

8. If you do not use the reserved words public and private, all members of a C++ class are private and all members of a struct are public. (True or False?)

9. Define the following terms:

instantiate

const member function

specification file

implementation file

10. To the TimeType class we wish to add three observer operations: CurrentHrs, CurrentMins, and CurrentSecs. These operations simply return the current values of the private data to the client. We can amend the class declaration by inserting the following function prototypes into the public part:

```
int CurrentHrs() const;
     // Postcondition:
     //      Function value == hours part of the time of day

int CurrentMins() const;
     // Postcondition:
     //      Function value == minutes part of the time of day

int CurrentSecs() const;
     // Postcondition:
     //      Function value == seconds part of the time of day
```

Write the function definitions for these three functions as they would appear in the implementation file.

11. Answer the following questions about Figure 11-11, which illustrates the process of compiling and linking a multifile program.
    a. If only the file `myprog.cpp` is modified, which files must be recompiled?
    b. If only the file `myprog.cpp` is modified, which files must be relinked?
    c. If only the files `file2.cpp` and `file3.cpp` are modified, which files must be recompiled? (Assume that the modifications do not affect existing code in `myprog.cpp`.)
    d. If only the files `file2.cpp` and `file3.cpp` are modified, which files must be relinked? (Assume that the modifications do not affect existing code in `myprog.cpp`.)

12. Define the following terms:
    separate compilation
    C++ class constructor
    default constructor

13. The following class has two constructors among its public member functions:

```
class SomeClass
{
public:
    float Func1() const;
      ⋮
    SomeClass( /* in */ float f );
        // Precondition:
        //      f is assigned
        // Postcondition:
        //      Private data is initialized to f
    SomeClass();
        // Postcondition:
        //      Private data is initialized to 8.6
private:
    float someFloat;
};
```

Write declarations for the following class objects.
    a. An object `obj1`, initialized to 0.0.
    b. An object `obj2`, initialized to 8.6.

14. The C++ compiler will signal a syntax error in the following class declaration. What is the error?

```
class SomeClass
{
public:
    void Func1( int n );
    int  Func2();
    int  SomeClass();
private:
    int privateInt;
};
```

Programming Warm-up Exercises

1. a. Write a `struct` declaration to contain the following information about a
       student:
       Name (string of characters)
       Social Security number (string of characters)
       Year (freshman, sophomore, junior, senior)
       Grade point average (floating-point number)
       Sex (M, F)
    b. Declare a struct variable of the type in part (a), and write a program segment
       that prints the information in each member of the variable.

2. a. Declare a `struct` type named `AptType` for an apartment locator service. The
       following information should be included:
       Landlord (string of characters)
       Address (string of characters)
       Bedrooms (integer)
       Price (floating-point number)
    b. Declare `anApt` to be a variable of type `AptType`.
    c. Write a function to read values into the members of a variable of type
       `AptType`. (The struct variable should be passed as an argument.) The order
       in which the data is read is the same as that of the items in the struct.

3. Write a hierarchical C++ `struct` declaration to contain the following informa-
    tion about a student:
    Name (string of characters)
    Student ID number
    Credit hours to date
    Number of courses taken
    Date first enrolled (month and year)
    Year (freshman, sophomore, junior, senior)
    Grade point average
    Each `struct` and enumeration type should have a separate type declaration.

4. You are writing the subscription renewal system for a magazine. For each sub-
    scriber, the system is to keep the following information:
    Name (first, last)
    Address (street, city, state, zip code)
    Expiration date (month, year)
    Date renewal notice was sent (month, day, year)
    Number of renewal notices sent so far
    Number of years for which subscription is being renewed (0 for renewal not yet
    received; otherwise, 1, 2, or 3 years)
    Whether or not the subscriber's name may be included in a mailing list for sale
    to other companies
    Write a hierarchical record type declaration to represent this information. Each
    subrecord should be declared separately as a named data type.

5. The `TimeType` class supplies two member functions, `Equal` and `LessThan`, that
    correspond to the relational operators `==` and `<` Show how *client code* can sim-
    ulate the other four relational operators (`!=`, `<=`, `>`, and `>=`) using only the `Equal`
    and `LessThan` functions. Specifically, express each of the following
    pseudocode statements in C++, where `time1` and `time2` are objects of type
    `TimeType`.

    a. IF time1 ≠ time2

      Set n = 1

    b. IF time1 ≤ time2

      Set n = 5

    c. IF time1 > time2

      Set n = 8

    d. IF time1 ≥ time2

      Set n = 5

6. In reference to Programming Warm-up Exercise 5, make life easier for the user of the `TimeType` class by adding new member functions `NotEqual`, `LessOrEqual`, `GreaterThan`, and `GreaterOrEqual` to the class.

    a. Show the function specifications (prototypes and preconditions and post-conditions) as they would appear in the new class declaration.

    b. Write the function definitions as they would appear in the implementation file. (*Hint:* Instead of writing the algorithms from scratch, simply have the function bodies invoke the existing functions `Equal` and `LessThan`. And remember: Class members can refer to each other directly without using dot notation.)

7. Enhance the `TimeType` class by adding a new member function `WriteAmPm`. This function prints the time in 12-hour rather than 24-hour form, adding *AM* or *PM* at the end. Show the function specification (prototype and precondition and postcondition) as it would appear in the new class declaration. Then write the function definition as it would appear in the implementation file.

8. Add a member function named `Minus` to the `TimeType` class. This value-returning function yields the difference in seconds between the times represented by two class objects. Show the function specification (prototype and precondition and postcondition) as it would appear in the new class declaration. Then write the function definition as it would appear in the implementation file.

9. a. Design the data sets necessary to thoroughly test the `LessThan` function of the `TimeType` class.

    b. Write a driver and test the `LessThan` function using your test data.

10. a. Design the data sets necessary to thoroughly test the `Write` function of the `TimeType` class.

    b. Write a driver and test the `Write` function using your test data.

11. a. Design the data sets necessary to thoroughly test the `WriteAmPm` function of Programming Warm-Up Exercise 7.

    b. Write a driver and test the `WriteAmPm` function using your test data.

12. Reimplement the `TimeType` class so that the private data representation is a single variable:

```
long secs;
```

This variable represents time as the number of seconds since midnight. *Do not change the public interface in any way.* The user's view is still hours, minutes, and seconds, but the class's view is seconds since midnight.

    Notice how this data representation simplifies the `Equal` and `LessThan` functions but makes the other operations more complicated by converting seconds back and forth to hours, minutes, and seconds. Use auxiliary functions, hidden inside the implementation file, to perform these conversions instead of duplicating the algorithms in several places.

Programming Problems

1. The Emerging Manufacturing Company has just installed its first computer and hired you as a junior programmer. Your first program is to read employee pay data and produce two reports: (1) an error and control report, and (2) a report on pay amounts. The second report must contain a line for each employee and a line of totals at the end of the report.

   Input:
   Transaction File
   Set of three job site number/name pairs
   One line for each employee containing ID number, job site number, and number of hours worked

   These data items have been presorted by ID number.

   Master File
   ID number
   Name
   Pay rate per hour
   Number of dependents
   Type of employee (1 is management, 0 is union)
   Job site
   Sex (M, F)

   This file is ordered by ID number.
   NOTE: (1) Union members, unlike management, get time and a half for hours over 40. (2) The tax formula for tax computation is as follows: If number of dependents is 1, tax rate is 15%. Otherwise, the tax rate is the greater of 2.5% and

   $$\left[1 - \left(\frac{No.\ of\ dep.}{No.\ of\ dep.\ +\ 6} \right) \right] \times 15\%$$

   Output:
   Error and Control Report
   Lists the input lines for which there is no corresponding master record, or where the employees' job site numbers do not agree with those in the master file. Continues processing with the next line of data.
   Gives the total number of employee records that were processed correctly during the run.

   Payroll Report (Labeled for Management)
   Contains a line for each employee showing the name, ID number, job site name, gross pay, and net pay.
   Contains a total line showing the total amount of gross pay and total amount of net pay.

2. You have taken a job with the IRS because you want to learn how to save on your income tax. They want you to write a toy tax computing program so that they can get an idea of your programming abilities. The program reads in the names of the members of families and each person's income, and computes the tax that the family owes. You may assume that people with the same last name who appear consecutively in the input are in the same family. The number of deductions that a family can count is equal to the number of people listed in

that family in the input data. Tax is computed as follows:

adjusted income $=$ income $-$ (5000 $\times$ number of deductions)

$$\text{tax rate} = \begin{cases} \text{adjusted income}/100{,}000 \text{ if income} < 60{,}000 \\ 50\%, \text{ otherwise} \end{cases}$$

tax $=$ tax rate $\times$ adjusted income

There will be no refunds, so you must check for people whose tax would be negative and set it to zero.

Input entries are in the following form:

Last name First name Total income

Sample Data:
```
Jones Ralph 19765.43
Jones Mary 8532.00
Jones Francis 0
Atwell Humphrey 5678.12
Murphy Robert 13432.20
Murphy Ellen 0
Murphy Paddy 0
Murphy Eileen 0
Murphy Conan 0
Murphy Nora 0
```

Input:
The data as described above, with end-of-file indicating the end of the input data.

Output:
A table containing all the families, one family per line, with each line containing the last name of the family, their total income, and their computed tax.

3. A rational number is a number that can be expressed as a fraction whose numerator and denominator are integers. Examples of rational numbers are 0.75 (which is 3/4) and 1.125 (which is 9/8). The value π is not a rational number; it cannot be expressed as the ratio of two integers.

Working with rational numbers on a computer is often a problem. Inaccuracies in floating-point representation can yield imprecise results. For example, the result of the C++ expression

```
1.0 / 3.0 * 3.0
```

is likely to be a value like 0.999999 rather than 1.0.

Design, implement, and test a Rational class that represents a rational number as a pair of integers instead of a single floating-point number. The Rational class should have two class constructors. The first one lets the client specify an initial numerator and denominator. The other—the default constructor—creates the rational number 0, represented as a numerator of 0 and a denominator of 1. The segment of client code

```
Rational num1(1, 3);
Rational num2(3, 1);
Rational result;

cout << "The product of ";
```

```
num1.Write();
cout << " and ";
num2.Write();
cout << " is ";
result = num1.MultipliedBy(num2);
result.Write();
```

would produce the output

```
The product of 1/3 and 3/1 is 1/1
```

At the very least, you should provide the following operations:
- Constructors for explicit as well as default initialization of Rational objects.
- Arithmetic operations that add, subtract, multiply, and divide two Rational objects. These should be implemented as value-returning functions, each returning a Rational object.
- A Boolean operation that compares two Rational objects for equality.
- An output operation that displays the value of a Rational object in the form numerator/denominator.

Include any additional operations that you think would be useful for a rational number class.

4. A complex ("imaginary") number has the form $a + bi$, where i is the square root of -1. Here, a is called the real part and b is called the imaginary part. Alternatively, $a + bi$ can be expressed as the ordered pair of real numbers (a, b).

   Arithmetic operations on two complex numbers (a, b) and (c, d) are as follows:

$$(a,b) + (c,d) = (a + c, b + d)$$
$$(a,b) - (c,d) = (a - c, b - d)$$
$$(a,b) \times (c,d) = (a \times c - b \times d, a \times d + b \times c)$$
$$(a,b) \div (c,d) = \left(\frac{a \times c + b \times d}{c^2 + d^2}, \frac{b \times c + a \times d}{c^2 + d^2} \right)$$

Also, the absolute value (or magnitude) of a complex number is defined as

$$|(a,b)| = \sqrt{a^2 + b^2}$$

Design, implement, and test a complex number class that represents the real and imaginary parts as double-precision values (data type double) and provides at least the following operations:
- Constructors for explicit as well as default initialization. The default initial value should be (0.0, 0.0).
- Arithmetic operations that add, subtract, multiply, and divide two complex numbers. These should be implemented as value-returning functions, each returning a class object.
- A complex absolute value operation.
- Two observer operations, RealPart and ImagPart, that return the real and imaginary parts of a complex number.

5. Design, implement, and test a countdown timer class named `Timer`. This class mimics a real-world timer by counting off seconds, starting from an initial value. When the timer reaches zero, it beeps (by sending the alert character, '\a', to the standard output device). Some appropriate operations might be the following:
   - Create a timer, initializing it to a specified number of seconds.
   - Start the timer.
   - Reset the timer to some value.

   When the `Start` operation is invoked, it should repeatedly decrement and output the current value of the timer approximately every second. To delay the program for one second, use a For loop whose body does absolutely nothing; that is, its body is the null statement. Experiment with the number of loop iterations to achieve as close to a one-second delay as you can.

   If your C++ system provides functions to clear the screen and to position the cursor anywhere on the screen, you might want to do the following. Begin by clearing the screen. Then, always display the timer value at the same position in the center of the screen. Each output should overwrite the previous value displayed, just like a real-world timer.

Case Study Follow-Up

1. Classify each of the eight member functions of the `DateType` class as a constructor, a transformer, or an observer operation.
2. Write a test plan for testing the `ComparedTo` function of the `DateType` class.
3. Write a driver to implement your test plan for the `ComparedTo` function.
4. Write a test plan for testing the `Increment` function of the `DateType` class.
5. Write a driver to implement your test plan for the `Increment` function.
6. In the BirthdayCalls program, we represented a person's area code as an `int` value. Printing an `int` area code works fine for North American phone numbers, where area codes are greater than 200. But international area codes may start with a zero. Our program would print an area code of 052 as 52. Suggest two ways of accommodating international area codes so that leading zeros are printed.
7. Write a test plan for the BirthdayCalls program.
8. Implement your test plan for the BirthdayCalls program.
9. Modify the BirthdayCalls program as follows. Add an additional date called `babyBoomerDate`. As the first action in the program, read a value for `babyBoomerDate`. Keep track of how many friends were born before `babyBoomerDate` and how many were born on or after that date. Print these two counts at the end of the program.

12

Arrays

G O A L S

- To be able to declare a one-dimensional array.
- To be able to perform fundamental operations on a one-dimensional array:

    Assign a value to an array component.

    Access a value stored in an array component.

    Fill an array with data, and process the data in the array.

- To be able to initialize a one-dimensional array in its declaration.
- To be able to pass one-dimensional arrays as arguments to functions.
- To be able to use arrays of records and class objects.
- To be able to apply subarray processing to a given one-dimensional array.
- To be able to declare and use a one-dimensional array with index values that have semantic content.
- To be able to declare a two-dimensional array.
- To be able to perform fundamental operations on a two-dimensional array:

    Access a component of the array.

    Initialize the array.

    Print the values in the array.

    Process the array by rows.

    Process the array by columns.

- To be able to declare a two-dimensional array as a parameter.
- To be able to view a two-dimensional array as an array of arrays.
- To be able to declare and process a multidimensional array.

Data structures play an important role in the design process. The choice of data structure directly affects the design because it determines the algorithms used to process the data. In Chapter 11, we saw how the record (struct) and the class give us the ability to refer to an entire group of components by one name. This simplifies the design of many programs.

In many problems, however, a data structure has so many components that it is difficult to process them if each one must have a unique member name. For example, the IntList abstract data type (ADT) we proposed briefly in Chapter 11 represents a collection of up to 100 integer values. If we used a struct or a class to hold these values, we would need to invent 100 different member names, write 100 different input statements to read values into the members, and write 100 different output statements to display the values—an incredibly tedious task! An *array*—the fourth of the structured data types supported by C++—is a data type that allows us to program operations of this kind with ease.

In this chapter, we examine array data types as provided by the C++ language; in Chapter 13, we show how to combine classes and arrays to implement an ADT such as IntList.

One-Dimensional Arrays

If we wanted to input 1000 integer values and print them in reverse order, we could write a program of this form:

```
//***************************
// ReverseNumbers program
//***************************
#include <iostream>

using namespace std;

int main()
{
    int value0;
    int value1;
    int value2;
        ⋮
    int value999;

    cin >> value0;
    cin >> value1;
    cin >> value2;
        ⋮
    cin >> value999;
```

```
    cout << value999 << endl;
    cout << value998 << endl;
    cout << value997 << endl;
       ⋮
    cout << value0 << endl;
    return 0;
}
```

This program is over 3000 lines long, and we have to use 1000 separate variables. Note that all the variables have the same name except for an appended number that distinguishes them. Wouldn't it be convenient if we could put the number into a counter variable and use For loops to go from 0 through 999, and then from 999 back down to 0? For example, if the counter variable were `number`, we could replace the 2000 original input/output statements with the following four lines of code (we enclose `number` in brackets to set it apart from `value`):

```
for (number = 0; number < 1000; number++)
    cin >> value[number];
for (number = 999; number >= 0; number--)
    cout << value[number] << endl;
```

This code fragment is correct in C++ *if* we declare `value` to be a *one-dimensional array,* which is a collection of variables—all of the same type—in which the first part of each variable name is the same, and the last part is an *index value* enclosed in square brackets. In our example, the value stored in `number` is called the *index*.

The declaration of a one-dimensional array is similar to the declaration of a simple variable (a variable of a simple data type), with one exception: You must also declare the size of the array. To do so, you indicate within brackets the number of components in the array:

```
int value[1000];
```

This declaration creates an array with 1000 components, all of type `int`. The first component has index value 0, the second component has index value 1, and the last component has index value 999.

Here is the complete ReverseNumbers program, using array notation. This is certainly much shorter than our first version of the program.

```
//****************************
// ReverseNumbers program
//****************************
#include <iostream>

using namespace std;
```

```
int main()
{
    int value[1000];
    int number;

    for (number = 0; number < 1000; number++)
        cin >> value[number];
    for (number = 999; number >= 0; number--)
        cout << value[number] << endl;
    return 0;
}
```

As a data structure, an array differs from a struct or class in two fundamental ways:

1. An array is a *homogeneous* data structure (all components are of the same data type), whereas structs and classes are heterogeneous types (their components may be of different types).
2. A component of an array is accessed by its *position* in the structure, whereas a component of a struct or class is accessed by an identifier (the member name).

Let's now define arrays formally and look at the rules for accessing individual components.

Declaring Arrays

A **one-dimensional array** is a structured collection of components (often called *array elements*) that can be accessed individually by specifying the position of a component with a single index value. (Later in the chapter, we introduce multidimensional arrays, which are arrays that have more than one index value.)

One-dimensional array A structured collection of components, all of the same type, that is given a single name. Each component (array element) is accessed by an index that indicates the component's position within the collection.

Here is a syntax template describing the simplest form of a one-dimensional array declaration:

ArrayDeclaration

DataType ArrayName **[** ConstIntExpression **]** **;**

In the syntax template, DataType describes what is stored in each component of the array. Array components may be of almost any type, but for now we limit our discussion to atomic components. ConstIntExpression is an integer expression composed only of literal or named constants. This expression, which specifies the number of components in the array, must have a value greater than 0. If the value is *n*, the range of index values is 0 through *n* − 1, not 1 through *n*. For example, the declarations

```
float angle[4];
int   testScore[10];
```

create the arrays shown in Figure 12-1. The `angle` array has four components, each capable of holding one `float` value. The `testScore` array has a total of ten components, all of type `int`.

Accessing Individual Components

Recall that to access an individual component of a struct or class, we use dot notation—the name of the struct variable or class object, followed by a period, followed by the member name. In contrast, to access an individual array component, we write the array name, followed by an expression enclosed in square brackets. The expression specifies which component to access. The syntax template for accessing an array component is

FIGURE 12-1

`angle` and
`testScore` Arrays

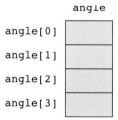

ArrayComponentAccess

ArrayName [IndexExpression]

The index expression may be as simple as a constant or a variable name or as complex as a combination of variables, operators, and function calls. Whatever the form of the expression, it must result in an integer value. Index expressions can be of type `char`, `short`, `int`, `long`, or `bool` because these are all integral types. Additionally, values of enumeration types can be used as index expressions, with an enumeration value implicitly coerced to an integer.

The simplest form of index expression is a constant. Using our `angle` array, the sequence of assignment statements

```
angle[0] = 4.93;
angle[1] = -15.2;
angle[2] = 0.5;
angle[3] = 1.67;
```

fills the array components one at a time (see Figure 12-2).

Each array component—`angle[2]`, for instance—can be treated exactly the same as any simple variable of type `float`. For example, we can do the following to the individual component `angle[2]`:

`angle[2] = 9.6;`	Assign it a value.
`cin >> angle[2];`	Read a value into it.
`cout << angle[2];`	Write its contents.
`y = sqrt(angle[2]);`	Pass it as an argument.
`x = 6.8 * angle[2] + 7.5;`	Use it in an arithmetic expression.

Let's look at index expressions that are more complicated than constants. Suppose we declare a 1000-element array of `int` values with the statement

```
int value[1000];
```

FIGURE 12-2

angle Array with Values

and execute the following two statements.

```
value[counter] = 5;
if (value[number+1] % 10 != 0)
    ⋮
```

In the first statement, 5 is stored into an array component. If `counter` is 0, 5 is stored into the first component of the array. If `counter` is 1, 5 is stored into the second place in the array, and so forth.

In the second statement, the expression `number+1` selects an array component. The specific array component accessed is divided by 10 and checked to see if the remainder is nonzero. If `number+1` is 0, we are testing the value in the first component; if `number+1` is 1, we are testing the second place; and so on. Figure 12-3 shows the index expression as a constant, a variable, and a more complex expression.

Note that we have seen the use of square brackets before. In earlier chapters, we said that the `string` class allows you to access an individual character within a string:

```
string aString;

aString = "Hello";
cout << aString[1];     // Prints 'e'
```

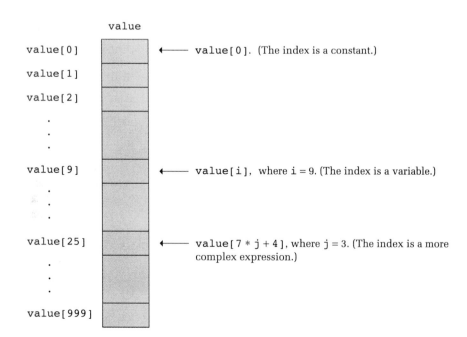

FIGURE 12-3

An Index as a Constant, a Variable, and an Arbitrary Expression

`value`

`value[0]` ←—— `value[0]`. (The index is a constant.)

`value[1]`

`value[2]`

`value[9]` ←—— `value[i]`, where i = 9. (The index is a variable.)

`value[25]` ←—— `value[7 * j + 4]`, where j = 3. (The index is a more complex expression.)

`value[999]`

Although string is a class, not an array, the string class was written using the advanced C++ technique of *operator overloading* to give the [] operator another meaning (string component selection) in addition to its standard meaning (array element selection). The result is that a string object is similar to an array of characters but has special properties.

Out-of-Bounds Array Indexes

Given the declaration

```
float alpha[100];
```

the valid range of index values is 0 through 99. What happens if we execute the statement

```
alpha[i] = 62.4;
```

when i is less than 0 or when i is greater than 99? The result is that a memory location outside the array is accessed. C++ does not check for invalid (*out-of-bounds*) array indexes either at compile time or at run time. If i happens to be 100 in the statement above, the computer stores 62.4 into the next memory location past the end of the array, destroying whatever value was contained there. It is entirely the programmer's responsibility to make sure that an array index does not step off either end of the array.

Out-of-bounds array index An index value that, in C++, is either less than 0 or greater than the array size minus 1.

Array-processing algorithms often use For loops to step through the array elements one at a time. Here is a loop to zero out our 100-element alpha array (i is an int variable):

```
for (i = 0; i < 100; i++)
    alpha[i] = 0.0;
```

We could also write the first line as

```
for (i = 0; i <= 99; i++)
```

However, C++ programmers commonly use the first version so that the number in the loop test (100) is the same as the array size. With this pattern, it is important to remember to test for *less-than*, not less-than-or-equal.

Initializing Arrays in Declarations

You learned in Chapter 8 that C++ allows you to initialize a variable in its declaration:

```
int delta = 25;
```

The value 25 is called an initializer. You also can initialize an array in its declaration, using a special syntax for the initializer. You specify a list of initial values for the array elements, separate them with commas, and enclose the list within braces:

```
int age[5] = {23, 10, 16, 37, 12};
```

In this declaration, `age[0]` is initialized to 23, `age[1]` is initialized to 10, and so on. There must be at least one initial value between the braces. If you specify too many initial values, you get a syntax error message. If you specify too few, the remaining array elements are initialized to zero.

Arrays follow the same rule as simple variables about the time(s) at which initialization occurs. A static array (one that is either global or declared as `static` within a block) is initialized once only, when control reaches its declaration. An automatic array (one that is local and not declared as `static`) is reinitialized each time control reaches its declaration.

An interesting feature of C++ is that you are allowed to omit the size of an array when you initialize it in a declaration:

```
float temperature[] = {0.0, 112.37, 98.6};
```

The compiler figures out the size of the array (here, 3) according to how many initial values are listed. In general, this feature is not particularly useful. In Chapter 13, though, we'll see that it can be convenient for initializing certain kinds of `char` arrays called C strings.

(Lack of) Aggregate Array Operations

In Chapter 11, we defined an aggregate operation as an operation on a data structure as a whole. Some programming languages allow aggregate operations on arrays, but C++ does not. If x and y are declared as

```
int x[50];
int y[50];
```

there is no aggregate assignment of y to x:

```
x = y;    // Not valid
```

To copy array y into array x, you must do it yourself, element by element:

```
for (index = 0; index < 50; index++)
    x[index] = y[index];
```

Similarly, there is no aggregate comparison of arrays:

```
if (x == y)    // Not valid
```

nor can you perform aggregate I/O of arrays:

```
cout << x;    // Not valid
```

or aggregate arithmetic on arrays:

```
x = x + y;    // Not valid
```

(C++ allows one exception for I/O, which we discuss in Chapter 13. Aggregate I/O is permitted for C strings, which are special kinds of char arrays.) Finally, it's not possible to return an entire array as the value of a value-returning function:

```
return x;    // Not valid
```

The only thing you can do to an array as a whole is to pass it as an argument to a function:

```
DoSomething(x);
```

Passing an array as an argument gives the function access to the entire array. The following table compares arrays, structs, and classes with respect to aggregate operations.

Aggregate Operation	Arrays	Structs and Classes
I/O	No (except C strings)	No
Assignment	No	Yes
Arithmetic	No	No
Comparison	No	No
Argument passage	By reference only	By value or by reference
Return as a function's return value	No	Yes

Later in the chapter, we look in detail at passing arrays as arguments.

Examples of Declaring and Accessing Arrays

We now look in detail at some specific examples of declaring and accessing arrays. Here are some declarations that a program might use to analyze occupancy rates in an apartment building:

```
const int BUILDING_SIZE = 350;   // Number of apartments

int occupants[BUILDING_SIZE];    // occupants[i] is the number of
                                 //    occupants in apartment i
int totalOccupants;              // Total number of occupants
int counter;                     // Loop control and index variable
```

occupants is a 350-element array of integers (see Figure 12-4). occupants[0] = 3 if the first apartment has three occupants; occupants[1] = 5 if the second apartment has five occupants; and so on. If values have been stored into the array, then the following code totals the number of occupants in the building.

```
totalOccupants = 0;
for (counter = 0; counter < BUILDING_SIZE; counter++)
    totalOccupants = totalOccupants + occupants[counter];
```

The first time through the loop, counter is 0. We add the contents of totalOccupants (that is, 0) to the contents of occupants[0], storing the result into totalOccupants. Next, counter becomes 1 and the loop test occurs. The second loop iteration adds the contents of totalOccupants to the contents of occupants[1], storing the result into totalOccupants. Now counter becomes 2 and the loop test is made. Eventually, the loop adds the contents of occupants[349] to the sum and increments counter to 350. At this point, the loop condition is false, and control exits the loop.

Note how we used the named constant BUILDING_SIZE in both the array declaration and the For loop. When constants are used in this manner, changes are easy to make. If the number of apartments changes from 350 to 400, we need to change only one line: the const declaration of BUILDING_SIZE. If we had used the literal value 350 in place of BUILD-ING_SIZE, we would need to update several of the statements in the code above, and probably many more throughout the rest of the program.

FIGURE 12-4

occupants Array

occupants

occupants[0]

occupants[1]

occupants[2]

.
.
.

occupants[349]

Because an array index is an integer value, we access the components by their position in the array—that is, the first, the second, the third, and so on. Using an int index is the most common way of thinking about an array. C++, however, provides more flexibility by allowing an index to be of any integral type or enumeration type. (The index expression still must evaluate to an integer in the range from 0 through one less than the array size.) The next example shows an array in which the indexes are values of an enumeration type.

```
enum Drink {ORANGE, COLA, ROOT_BEER, GINGER_ALE, CHERRY, LEMON};

float salesAmt[6];  // Array of 6 floats, to be indexed by Drink type
Drink flavor;       // Variable of the index type
```

Drink is an enumeration type in which the enumerators ORANGE, COLA, ..., LEMON have internal representations 0 through 5, respectively. salesAmt is a group of six float components representing dollar sales figures for each kind of drink (see Figure 12-5). The following code prints the values in the array (see Chapter 10 to review how to increment values of enumeration types in For loops).

FIGURE 12-5

salesAmt Array

salesAmt

salesAmt[ORANGE] (i.e., salesAmt[0])

salesAmt[COLA] (i.e., salesAmt[1])

salesAmt[ROOT_BEER] (i.e., salesAmt[2])

salesAmt[GINGER_ALE] (i.e., salesAmt[3])

salesAmt[CHERRY] (i.e., salesAmt[4])

salesAmt[LEMON] (i.e., salesAmt[5])

FIGURE 12-6

grade Array with Values

```
for (flavor = ORANGE; flavor <= LEMON; flavor = Drink(flavor + 1))
    cout << salesAmt[flavor] << endl;
```

Here is one last example.

```
const int NUM_STUDENTS = 10;

char grade[NUM_STUDENTS];    // Array of 10 student letter grades
int  idNumber;               // Student ID number (0 through 9)
```

The grade array is pictured in Figure 12-6. Values are shown in the components, which implies that some processing of the array has already occurred. Following are some simple examples showing how the array might be used.

`cin >> grade[2];`	Reads the next nonwhitespace character from the input stream and stores it into the component in grade indexed by 2.
`grade[3] = 'A';`	Assigns the character 'A' to the component in grade indexed by 3.
`idNumber = 5;`	Assigns 5 to the index variable idNumber.

```grade[idNumber] = 'C';```	Assigns the character 'C' to the component of grade indexed by idNumber (that is, by 5).
```for (idNumber = 0; idNumber < NUM_STUDENTS;``` `idNumber++)` `cout << grade[idNumber];`	Loops through the grade array, printing each component. For this loop, the output would be FBCAFCAACB.
```for (idNumber = 0; idNumber < NUM_STUDENTS;``` `idNumber++)` `cout << "Student " << idNumber` `<< " Grade " << grade[idNumber]` `<< endl;`	Loops through grade, printing each component in a more readable form.

In the last example, idNumber is used as the index, but it also has semantic content—it is the student's identification number. The output would be

```
Student 0 Grade F
Student 1 Grade B
   ⋮
Student 9 Grade B
```

Passing Arrays as Arguments

In Chapter 8, we said that if a variable is passed to a function and it is not to be changed by the function, then the variable should be passed by value instead of by reference. We specifically excluded stream variables (such as those representing data files) from this rule and said that there would be one more exception. Arrays are this exception.

By default, C++ simple variables are always passed by value. To pass a simple variable by reference, you must append an ampersand (&) to the data type name in the function's parameter list:

```
int SomeFunc( float param1,    // Pass-by-value
               char& param2 )   // Pass-by-reference
{
     ⋮
}
```

It is impossible to pass a C++ array by value; arrays are *always* passed by reference. Therefore, you never use & when declaring an array as a parameter. When an array is passed as an argument, its **base address**—the memory address of the first element of the array—is sent to the function. The function then knows where the caller's actual array is located and can access any element of the array.

Base address   The memory address of the first element of an array.

Here is a C++ function that will zero out a one-dimensional float array of any size:

```
void ZeroOut( /* out */ float arr[],
              /* in */   int   numElements )
{
    int i;

    for (i = 0; i < numElements; i++)
        arr[i] = 0.0;
}
```

In the parameter list, the declaration of arr does not include a size within the brackets. If you include a size, the compiler ignores it. The compiler only wants to know that it is a float array, not a float array of any particular size. Therefore, in the ZeroOut function you must include a second parameter—the number of array elements—in order for the For loop to work correctly.

The calling code can invoke the ZeroOut function for a float array of any size. The following code fragment makes function calls to zero out two arrays of different sizes. Notice how an array parameter is declared in a function prototype.

```
void ZeroOut( float[], int );    // Function prototype
  ⋮
int main()
{
    float velocity[30];
    float refractionAngle[9000];
      ⋮
    ZeroOut(velocity, 30);
    ZeroOut(refractionAngle, 9000);
      ⋮
}
```

With simple variables, passing by value prevents a function from modifying the caller's argument. Although you cannot pass arrays by value in C++, you can still prevent the function from modifying the caller's array.

To do so, you use the reserved word const in the declaration of the parameter. Below is a function that copies one int array into another. The first parameter—the destination array—is expected to be modified, but the second array is not.

```
void Copy( /* out */      int destination[],
           /* in */  const int source[],
           /* in */        int size          )
{
    int i;

    for (i = 0; i < size; i++)
        destination[i] = source[i];

}
```

The word const guarantees that any attempt to modify the source array within the Copy function results in a compile-time error.

Here's a table that summarizes argument passage for simple variables and one-dimensional arrays:

Argument	Parameter Declaration for a Pass by Value	Parameter Declaration for a Pass by Reference
Simple variable	int cost	int& price
Array	Impossible*	int arr[]

*However, prefixing the array declaration with the word const prevents the function from modifying the parameter.

One final remark about argument passage: It is a common mistake to pass an array *element* to a function when passing the entire array was intended. For example, our ZeroOut function expects the base address of a float array to be sent as the first argument. In the following code fragment, the function call is an error.

```
float velocity[30];
   ⋮
ZeroOut(velocity[30], 30);    // Error
```

First of all, velocity[30] denotes a single array element—one floating-point number—and not an entire array. Furthermore, there is no array element with an index of 30. The indexes for the velocity array run from 0 through 29.

*B*ACKGROUND INFORMATION

C, C++, and Arrays as Arguments

Some programming languages allow arrays to be passed either by value or by reference. Remember that with passing by value, a copy of the argument is sent to the function. When an array is passed by value, the entire array is copied. Not only is extra space required in the function to hold the copy, but the copying itself takes time. Passing by reference requires only that the address of the argument be passed to the function, so when an array is passed by reference, just the address of the first array component is passed. Thus, passing large arrays by reference saves both memory and time.

The C programming language—the direct predecessor of C++—was designed to be a system programming language. System programs, such as compilers, assemblers, linkers, and operating systems, must be both fast and economical with memory space. In the design of the C language, passing arrays by value was judged to be an unnecessary language feature. Serious system programmers never used a pass by value when working with arrays. Therefore, both C and C++ pass arrays only by reference.

Of course, using a reference parameter can lead to inadvertent errors if the values are changed within the function. In early versions of the C language, there was no way to protect the caller's array from being modified by the function.

C++ (and recent versions of C) added the ability to declare an array parameter as const. By declaring the array as const, a compile-time error occurs if the function attempts to modify the array. As a result, C++ supports the efficiency of passing arrays by reference yet also provides the protection (through const) of passing by value.

Whenever your design of a function's interface identifies an array parameter as incoming-only (to be inspected but not modified by the function), declare the array as const to obtain the same protection as passing by value.

Assertions About Arrays

In assertions written as comments, we often need to refer to a range of array elements:

```
// Assert: alpha[i] through alpha[j] have been printed
```

To specify such ranges, it is more convenient to use an abbreviated notation consisting of two dots:

```
// Assert: alpha[i]..alpha[j] have been printed
```

or, more briefly:

```
// Assert: alpha[i..j] have been printed
```

Note that this dot-dot notation is not valid syntax in C++ language statements. We are talking only about comments in a program.

As an example of the use of this notation, here is how we would write the precondition and postcondition for our ZeroOut function:

```
void ZeroOut( /* out */ float arr[],
              /* in */  int   numElements )

// Precondition:
//     numElements is assigned
// Postcondition:
//     arr[0..numElements-1] == 0.0

{
    int i;

    for (i = 0; i < numElements; i++)
        arr[i] = 0.0;
}
```

Using Typedef with Arrays

In Chapter 10, we discussed the Typedef statement as a way of giving an additional name to an existing data type. We said that before bool became a built-in type in C++, programmers often used a Typedef statement such as the following:

```
typedef int Boolean;
```

We can also use Typedef to give a name to an array type. Here's an example:

```
typedef float FloatArr[100];
```

This statement says that the type FloatArr is the same as the type "100-element array of float." (Notice that the array size in brackets comes at the very end of the statement.) We can now declare variables to be of type FloatArr:

```
FloatArr angle;
FloatArr velocity;
```

The compiler essentially translates these declarations into

```
float angle[100];
float velocity[100];
```

In this book, we don't often use Typedefs to give names to one-dimensional array types. However, when we discuss multidimensional arrays later in the chapter, we'll see that the technique can come in handy.

Arrays of Records and Class Objects

Although arrays with atomic components are very common, many applications require a collection of records or class objects. For example, a business needs a list of parts records, and a teacher needs a list of students in a class. Arrays are ideal for these applications. We simply define an array whose components are records or class objects.

Arrays of Records

Let's define a grade book to be a collection of student records as follows:

```
const int MAX_STUDENTS = 150;

enum GradeType {A, B, C, D, F};

struct StudentRec
{
    string    stuName;
    float     gpa;
    int       examScore[4];
    GradeType courseGrade;
};

StudentRec gradeBook[MAX_STUDENTS];
int        count;
```

This data structure can be visualized as shown in Figure 12-7.

An element of gradeBook is selected by an index. For example, gradeBook[2] is the third component in the array gradeBook. Each component of gradeBook is a record of type StudentRec. To access the course grade of the third student, we use the following expression:

FIGURE 12-7
gradeBook Array
with Records as
Elements

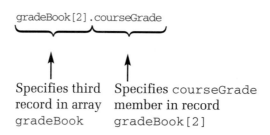

The record component `gradeBook[2].examScore` is an array. We can access the individual elements in this component just as we would access the elements of any other array: We give the name of the array followed by the index, which is enclosed in brackets.

The following code fragment prints the name of each student in the class:

```
for (count = 0; count < MAX_STUDENTS; count++)
    cout << gradeBook[count].stuName << endl;
```

Arrays of Class Objects

The syntax for declaring and using arrays of class objects is the same as for arrays of structs. Given the `TimeType` class of Chapter 11, we can maintain a collection of ten appointment times by starting with the declaration

```
TimeType appointment[10];
```

This statement creates a ten-element array named `appointment`, in which each element is a `TimeType` object. The following statements set the first two appointment times to 8:45:00 and 10:00:00.

```
appointment[0].Set(8, 45, 0);
appointment[1].Set(10, 0, 0);
```

To output all ten appointment times, we would write

```
for (index = 0; index < 10; index++)
{
    appointment[index].Write();
    cout << endl;
}
```

Recall that the `TimeType` class has two constructors defined for it. One is the default (parameterless) constructor, which sets the time for a newly created object to 00:00:00. The other is a parameterized constructor with which the client code can specify an initial time when the class object is created. How are constructors handled when you declare an array of class objects? Here is the rule in C++:

If a class has at least one constructor, and an array of class objects is declared:

```
SomeClass arr[50];
```

then one of the constructors *must* be the default (parameterless) constructor. This constructor is invoked for each element of the array.

Therefore, with our declaration of the `appointment` array

```
TimeType appointment[10];
```

the default constructor is called for all ten array elements, setting each time to an initial value of 00:00:00.

▆ *Special Kinds of Array Processing*

Two types of array processing occur especially often: using only part of the declared array (a subarray) and using index values that have specific meaning within the problem (indexes with semantic content). We describe both of these methods briefly here and give further examples in the remainder of the chapter.

Subarray Processing

The *size* of an array—the declared number of array components—is established at compile time. We have to declare it to be as big as it would ever need to be. Because the exact number of values to be put into the array often depends on the data itself, however, we may not fill all of the array components with values. The problem is that to avoid processing empty ones, we must keep track of how many components are actually filled.

As values are put into the array, we keep a count of how many components are filled. We then use this count to process only components that have values stored in them. Any remaining places are not processed. For example, if there are 250 students in a class, a program to analyze test grades would set aside 250 locations for the grades. However, some students may be absent on the day of the test. So the number of test grades must be counted, and that number, rather than 250, is used to control the processing of the array.

If the number of data items actually stored in an array is less than its declared size, functions that receive array parameters must also receive the number of data items as a parameter. For example,

```
void Print( /* in */ const char grade[],      // Array for up to
                                              //    250 students
               /* in */       int  numGrades )  // Number of grades
                                              //    actually in array
```

The first case study at the end of this chapter demonstrates the technique of subarray processing.

Indexes with Semantic Content

In some problems, an array index has meaning beyond simple position; that is, the index has *semantic content*. An example is the salesAmt array we showed earlier. This array is indexed by a value of enumeration type Drink. The index of a specific sales amount is the kind of soft drink sold; for example, salesAmt[ROOT_BEER] is the dollar sales figure for root beer.

The next section gives additional examples of indexes with semantic content.

Two-Dimensional Arrays

A one-dimensional array is used to represent items in a list or sequence of values. In many problems, however, the relationships between data items are more complex than a simple list. A **two-dimensional array** is used to represent items in a table with rows and columns, provided each item in the table is of the same data type. Two-dimensional arrays are useful for representing board games, such as chess, tic-tac-toe, or Scrabble, and in computer graphics, where the screen is thought of as a two-dimensional array. A component in a two-dimensional array is accessed by specifying the row and column indexes of the item in the array. This is a familiar task. For example, if you want to find a street on a map, you look up the street name on the back of the map to find the coordinates of the street, usually a letter and a number. The letter specifies a column to look on, and the number specifies a row. You find the street where the row and column meet.

Two-dimensional array   A collection of components, all of the same type, structured in two dimensions. Each component is accessed by a pair of indexes that represent the component's position in each dimension.

Figure 12-8 shows a two-dimensional array with 100 rows and 9 columns. The rows are accessed by an integer ranging from 0 through 99; the columns are accessed by an integer ranging from 0 through 8. Each component is accessed by a row-column pair—for example, 0, 5.

A two-dimensional array is declared in exactly the same way as a one-dimensional array, except that sizes must be specified for two dimensions. Below is the syntax template for declaring an array with more than one dimension, along with an example.

ArrayDeclaration

DataType ArrayName **[** ConstIntExpression **]**   **[** ConstIntExpression **]** . . . **;**

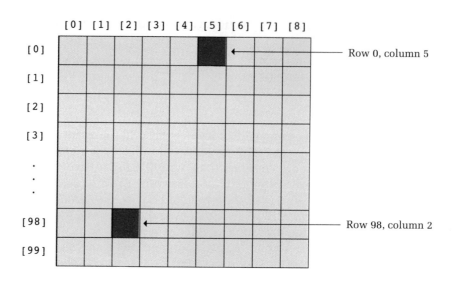

FIGURE 12-8

A Two-Dimensional Array

Row 0, column 5

Row 98, column 2

```
const int NUM_ROWS = 100;
const int NUM_COLS = 9;
   ⋮
float alpha[NUM_ROWS][NUM_COLS];
```

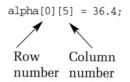

First   Second
dimension dimension

This example declares alpha to be a two-dimensional array, all of whose components are float values. The declaration creates the array that is pictured in Figure 12-8.

To access an individual component of the alpha array, two expressions (one for each dimension) are used to specify its position. Each expression is in its own pair of brackets next to the name of the array:

alpha[0][5] = 36.4;

Row   Column
number number

The syntax template for accessing an array component is

ArrayComponentAccess

ArrayName **[** IndexExpression **]**   **[** IndexExpression **]** . . .

As with one-dimensional arrays, each index expression must result in an integer value.

Let's look now at some examples. Here is the declaration of a two-dimensional array with 364 integer components ($52 \times 7 = 364$):

```
int hiTemp[52][7];
```

hiTemp is an array with 52 rows and 7 columns. Each place in the array (each component) can contain any int value. Our intention is that the array contains high temperatures for each day in a year. Each row represents one of the 52 weeks in a year, and each column represents one of the 7 days in a week. (To keep the example simple, we ignore the fact that there are 365—and sometimes 366—days in a year.) The expression hiTemp[2][6] refers to the int value in the third row (row 2) and the seventh column (column 6). Semantically, hiTemp[2][6] is the temperature for the seventh day of the third week. The code fragment shown in Figure 12-9 would print the temperature values for the third week.

Another representation of the same data might be as follows:

FIGURE 12-9
hiTemp Array

```
// Print temperature values
//    for 3rd week (row 2)

for (day = 0; day < 7; day++)
    cout << ' ' << hiTemp[2][day];
```

```
enum DayType
{
     MONDAY, TUESDAY, WEDNESDAY, THURSDAY, FRIDAY, SATURDAY, SUNDAY
};

int hiTemp[52][7];
```

Here, `hiTemp` is declared the same as before, but we can use an expression of type `DayType` for the column index. `hiTemp[2][SUNDAY]` corresponds to the same component as `hiTemp[2][6]` in the first example. (Recall that enumerators such as MONDAY, TUESDAY, ... are represented internally as the integers 0, 1, 2, ...) If `day` is of type `DayType` and `week` is of type `int`, the code fragment shown in Figure 12-10 sets the entire array to 0. (Notice that by using `DayType`, the temperature values in the array begin with the first Monday of the year, not necessarily with January 1.)

Another way of looking at a two-dimensional array is to see it as a structure in which each component has two features. For example, in the following code,

```
enum Colors {RED, ORANGE, YELLOW, GREEN, BLUE, INDIGO, VIOLET};
enum Makes
{
     FORD, TOYOTA, HYUNDAI, JAGUAR, CITROEN, BMW, FIAT, SAAB
};
const int NUM_COLORS = 7;
const int NUM_MAKES = 8;
```

FIGURE 12-10
hiTemp Array
(Alternate Form)

```
// Initialize entire array to zero

for (week = 0; week < 52; week++)
    for (day = MONDAY; day <= SUNDAY;
                       day = DayType(day + 1))
        hiTemp[week][day] = 0;
```

```
float crashRating[NUM_COLORS][NUM_MAKES];    // Array of crash
                                             // likelihoods by color
                                             // and make
  ⋮
crashRating[BLUE][JAGUAR] = 0.83;            // Blue Jaguars have a crash
                                             //   likelihood of 0.83
crashRating[RED][FORD] = 0.19;               // Red Fords have a crash
                                             //   likelihood of 0.19
```

the data structure uses one dimension to represent the color and the other to represent the make of automobile. In other words, both indexes have semantic content—a concept we discussed in the previous section.

Processing Two-Dimensional Arrays

Processing data in a two-dimensional array generally means accessing the array in one of four patterns: randomly, along rows, along columns, or throughout the entire array. Each of these may also involve subarray processing.

The simplest way to access a component is to look directly in a given location. For example, a user enters map coordinates that we use as indexes into an array of street names to access the desired name at those coordinates. This process is referred to as *random access* because the user may enter any set of coordinates at random.

There are many cases in which we might wish to perform an operation on all the elements of a particular row or column in an array. Consider the hiTemp array defined previously, in which the rows represent weeks of the year and the columns represent days of the week. If we wanted the average high temperature for a given week, we would sum the values in that row and divide by 7. If we wanted the average for a given day of the week, we would sum the values in that column and divide by 52. The former case is access by row; the latter case is access by column.

Now suppose that we wish to determine the average for the year. We must access every element in the array, sum them, and divide by 364. In this case, the order of access—by row or by column—is not important. (The same is true when we initialize every element of an array to zero.) This is access throughout the array.

There are times when we must access every array element in a particular order, either by rows or by columns. For example, if we wanted the average for every week, we would run through the entire array, taking each row in turn. However, if we wanted the average for each day of the week, we would run through the array a column at a time.

Let's take a closer look at these patterns of access by considering four common examples of array processing.

1. Sum the rows.
2. Sum the columns.
3. Initialize the array to all zeros (or some special value).
4. Print the array.

First, let's define some constants and variables using general identifiers, such as `row` and `col`, rather than problem-dependent identifiers. Then let's look at each algorithm in terms of generalized two-dimensional array processing.

```
const int NUM_ROWS = 50;
const int NUM_COLS = 50;

int arr[NUM_ROWS][NUM_COLS];     // A two-dimensional array
int row;                         // A row index
int col;                         // A column index
int total;                       // A variable for summing
```

Sum the Rows

Suppose we want to sum row number 3 (the fourth row) in the array and print the result. We can do this easily with a For loop:

```
total = 0;
for (col = 0; col < NUM_COLS; col++)
    total = total + arr[3][col];
cout << "Row sum: " << total << endl;
```

This For loop runs through each column of `arr`, while keeping the row index fixed at 3. Every value in row 3 is added to `total`.

Now suppose we want to sum and print two rows—row 2 and row 3. We can use a nested loop and make the row index a variable:

```
for (row = 2; row < 4; row++)
{
    total = 0;
    for (col = 0; col < NUM_COLS; col++)
        total = total + arr[row][col];
    cout << "Row sum: " << total << endl;
}
```

The outer loop controls the rows, and the inner loop controls the columns. For each value of row, every column is processed; then the outer loop moves to the next row. In the first iteration of the outer loop, row is held at 2 and col goes from 0 through NUM_COLS−1. Therefore, the array is accessed in the following order:

```
arr[2][0]   [2][1]   [2][2]   [2][3] ... [2][NUM_COLS-1]
```

In the second iteration of the outer loop, row is incremented to 3, and the array is accessed as follows:

```
arr[3][0]   [3][1]   [3][2]   [3][3] ... [3][NUM_COLS-1]
```

We can generalize this row processing to run through every row of the array by having the outer loop run from 0 through NUM_ROWS−1. However, if we want to access only part of the array (subarray processing), given variables declared as

```
int rowsFilled;    // Data is in 0..rowsFilled-1
int colsFilled;    // Data is in 0..colsFilled-1
```

then we write the code fragment as follows:

```
for (row = 0; row < rowsFilled; row++)
{
    total = 0;
    for (col = 0; col < colsFilled; col++)
        total = total + arr[row][col];
    cout << "Row sum: " << total << endl;
}
```

Figure 12-11 illustrates subarray processing by row.

Sum the Columns

Suppose we want to sum and print each column. The code to perform this task follows. Again, we have generalized the code to sum only the portion of the array that contains valid data.

```
for (col = 0; col < colsFilled; col++)
{
    total = 0;
    for (row = 0; row < rowsFilled; row++)
        total = total + arr[row][col];
    cout << "Column sum: " << total << endl;
}
```

In this case, the outer loop controls the column, and the inner loop controls the row. All the components in the first column are accessed and summed before the outer loop index changes and the components in the second column are accessed. Figure 12-12 illustrates subarray processing by column.

Initialize the Array

As with one-dimensional arrays, we can initialize a two-dimensional array either by initializing it in its declaration or by using assignment statements. If the array is small, it is simplest to initialize it in its declaration. To initialize a two-row by three-column array to look like this:

```
14   3  −5
 0  46   7
```

Figure 12-11
Partial Array
Processing by Row

we can use the following declaration.

```
int arr[2][3] =
{
    {14, 3, -5},
    {0, 46, 7}
};
```

In this declaration, the initializer list consists of two items, each of which is itself an initializer list. The first inner initializer list stores 14, 3, and −5 into row 0 of the array; the second stores 0, 46, and 7 into row 1. The use of two initializer lists makes sense if you think of each row of the two-dimensional array as a one-dimensional array of three ints. The first initializer list initializes the first array (the first row), and the second list initializes the second array (the second row). Later in the chapter, we revisit this notion of viewing a two-dimensional array as an array of arrays.

Initializing an array in its declaration is impractical if the array is large. For a 100-row by 100-column array, you don't want to list 10,000 values. If the values are all different, you should store them into a file and input them into the array at run time. If the values are all the same, the usual approach is to use nested For loops and an assignment statement. Here is a general-purpose code segment that zeros out an array with NUM_ROWS rows and NUM_COLS columns:

FIGURE 12-12

Partial Array
Processing by
Column

```
for (row = 0; row < NUM_ROWS; row++)
    for (col = 0; col < NUM_COLS; col++)
        arr[row][col] = 0;
```

In this case, we initialized the array a row at a time, but we could just as easily have run through each column instead. The order doesn't matter as long as we access every element.

Print the Array

If we wish to print out an array with one row per line, then we have another case of row processing:

```
#include <iomanip>    // For setw()
    ⋮
for (row = 0; row < NUM_ROWS; row++)
{
    for (col = 0; col < NUM_COLS; col++)
        cout << setw(15) << arr[row][col];
    cout << endl;
}
```

This code fragment prints the values of the array in columns that are 15 characters wide. As a matter of proper style, this fragment should be preceded by code that prints headings over the columns to identify their contents.

There's no rule that we have to print each row on a line. We could turn the array sideways and print each column on one line simply by exchanging the two For loops. When you are printing a two-dimensional array, you must consider which order of presentation makes the most sense and how the array fits on the page. For example, an array with 6 columns and 100 rows would be best printed as 6 columns, 100 lines long.

Almost all processing of data stored in a two-dimensional array involves either processing by row or processing by column. In most of our examples the index type has been int, but the pattern of operation of the loops is the same no matter what types the indexes are.

The looping patterns for row processing and column processing are so useful that we summarize them below. To make them more general, we use minRow for the first row number and minCol for the first column number. Remember that row processing has the row index in the outer loop, and column processing has the column index in the outer loop.

Row Processing

```
for (row = minRow; row < rowsFilled; row++)
    for (col = minCol; col < colsFilled; col++)
        ⋮               // Whatever processing is required
```

Column Processing

```
for (col = minCol; col < colsFilled; col++)
    for (row = minRow; row < rowsFilled; row++)
        ⋮               // Whatever processing is required
```

Passing Two-Dimensional Arrays as Arguments

Earlier in the chapter, we said that when one-dimensional arrays are declared as parameters in a function, the size of the array usually is omitted from the square brackets:

```
void SomeFunc( /* inout */ float alpha[],
               /* in */    int   size   )
{
    ⋮
}
```

If you include a size in the brackets, the compiler ignores it. As you learned, the base address of the caller's argument (the memory address of the first array element) is passed to the function. The function works for an argument of any size. Because the function cannot know the size of the caller's array, we either pass the size as an argument—as in SomeFunc above—or use a named constant if the function always operates on an array of a certain size.

When a two-dimensional array is passed as an argument, again the base address of the caller's array is sent to the function. But you cannot leave off the sizes of both of the array dimensions. You can omit the size of the first dimension (the number of rows) but not the second (the number of columns). Here is the reason.

In the computer's memory, C++ stores two-dimensional arrays in row order. Thinking of memory as one long line of memory cells, the first row of the array is followed by the second row, which is followed by the third, and so on (see Figure 12-13). To locate beta[1][0] in this figure, a function that receives beta's base address must be able to know that there are four elements in each row—that is, that the array consists of four columns. Therefore, the declaration of a parameter must always state the number of columns:

```
void AnotherFunc( /* inout */ int beta[][4] )
{
    ⋮
}
```

Furthermore, the number of columns declared for the parameter must be *exactly* the same as the number of columns in the caller's array. As you can tell from Figure 12-13, if there is any discrepancy in the number of columns, the function will access the wrong array element in memory.

Our AnotherFunc function works for a two-dimensional array of any number of rows, as long as it has exactly four columns. In practice, we seldom write programs that use arrays with a varying number of rows but the same number of columns. To avoid problems with mismatches in argument and parameter sizes, it's practical to use a Typedef statement to define a two-dimensional array type and then declare both the argument and the parameter to be of that type. For example, we might make the declarations

```
const int NUM_ROWS = 10;
const int NUM_COLS = 20;
typedef int ArrayType[NUM_ROWS][NUM_COLS];
```

and then write the following general-purpose function that initializes all elements of an array to a specified value:

```
void Initialize( /* out */ ArrayType arr,      // Array to initialize
                 /* in */   int       initVal) // Initial value

// Initializes each element of arr to initVal

// Precondition:
//      initVal is assigned
// Postcondition:
//      arr[0..NUM_ROWS-1][0..NUM_COLS-1] == initVal
```

FIGURE 12-13
Memory Layout for
a Two-Row by
Four-Column
Array

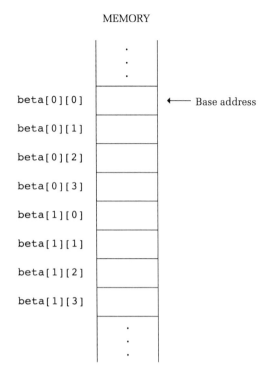

```
{
    int row;
    int col;

    for (row = 0; row < NUM_ROWS; row++)
        for (col = 0; col < NUM_COLS; col++)
            arr[row][col] = initVal;
}
```

The calling code could then declare and initialize one or more arrays of type `ArrayType` by making calls to the `Initialize` function. For example,

```
ArrayType delta;
ArrayType gamma;

Initialize(delta, 0);
Initialize(gamma, -1);
    ⋮
```

Another Way of Defining Two-Dimensional Arrays

We hinted earlier that a two-dimensional array can be viewed as an array of arrays. This view is supported by C++ in the sense that the components of a one-dimensional array do not have to be atomic. The components can themselves be structured—structs, class objects, even arrays. For example, our hiTemp array could be declared as follows.

```
typedef int WeekType[7];    // Array type for 7 temperature readings

WeekType hiTemp[52];        // Array of 52 WeekType arrays
```

With this declaration, the 52 components of the hiTemp array are one-dimensional arrays of type WeekType. In other words, hiTemp has two dimensions. We can refer to each row as an entity: hiTemp[2] refers to the array of temperatures for week 2. We can also access each individual component of hiTemp by specifying both indexes: hiTemp[2][0] accesses the temperature on the first day of week 2.

Does it matter which way we declare a two-dimensional array? Not to C++. The choice should be based on readability and understandability. Sometimes the features of the data are shown more clearly if both indexes are specified in a single declaration. At other times, the code is clearer if one dimension is defined first as a one-dimensional array type.

Here is an example of when it is advantageous to define a two-dimensional array as an array of arrays. If the rows have been defined first as a one-dimensional array type, each row can be passed to a function whose parameter is a one-dimensional array of the same type. For example, the following function calculates and returns the maximum value in an array of type WeekType.

```
int Maximum( /* in */ const WeekType data )   // Array to be examined

// Precondition:
//      data[0..6] are assigned
// Postcondition:
//      Function value == maximum value in data[0..6]

{
    int max;       // Temporary max. value
    int index;     // Loop control and index variable
```

```
    max = data[0];
    for (index = 1; index < 7; index++)
        if (data[index] > max)
            max = data[index];
    return max;
}
```

Our two-part declaration of hiTemp permits us to call Maximum using a component of hiTemp as follows.

```
highest = Maximum(hiTemp[20]);
```

Row 20 of hiTemp is passed to Maximum, which treats it like any other one-dimensional array of type WeekType (see Figure 12-14). It makes sense to pass the row as an argument because both it and the function parameter are of the same named type, WeekType.

With hiTemp declared as an array of arrays, we can output the maximum temperature of each week of the year with the following code:

```
cout << " Week  Maximum" << endl
     << "Number Temperature" << endl;
for (week = 0; week < 52; week++)
    cout << setw(6) << week
         << setw(9) << Maximum(hiTemp[week]) << endl;
```

FIGURE 12-14
A One-Dimensional Array of One-Dimensional Arrays

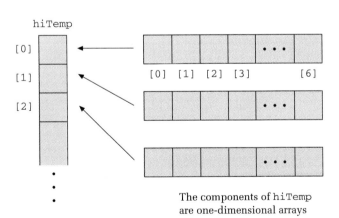

The components of hiTemp are one-dimensional arrays of type WeekType.

Multidimensional Arrays

C++ does not place a limit on the number of dimensions that an array can have. We can generalize our definition of an array to cover all cases.

Array   A collection of components, all of the same type, ordered on N dimensions ($N \geq 1$). Each component is accessed by N indexes, each of which represents the component's position within that dimension.

You might have guessed from the syntax templates that you can have as many dimensions as you want. How many should you have in a particular case? Use as many as there are features that describe the components in the array.

Take, for example, a chain of department stores. Monthly sales figures must be kept for each item by store. There are three important pieces of information about each item: the month in which it was sold, the store from which it was purchased, and the item number. We can define an array type to summarize this data as follows:

```
const int NUM_ITEMS = 100;
const int NUM_STORES = 10;

typedef int SalesType[NUM_STORES][12][NUM_ITEMS];

SalesType sales;    // Array of sales figures
int       item;
int       store;
int       month;
int       numberSold;
int       currentMonth;
```

A graphic representation of the `sales` array is shown in Figure 12-15.

The number of components in `sales` is 12,000 (10 × 12 × 100). If sales figures are available only for January through June, then half the array is empty. If we want to process the data in the array, we must use subarray processing. The following program fragment sums and prints the total number of each item sold this year to date by all stores.

FIGURE 12-15
Graphical
Representation of
sales Array

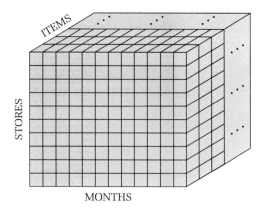

```
for (item = 0; item < NUM_ITEMS; item++)
{
    numberSold = 0;
    for (store = 0; store < NUM_STORES; store++)
        for (month = 0; month <= currentMonth; month++)
            numberSold = numberSold + sales[store][month][item];
    cout << "Item #" << item << " Sales to date = " << numberSold
        << endl;
}
```

Because item controls the outer For loop, we are summing each item's sales by month and store. If we want to find the total sales for each store, we use store to control the outer For loop, summing its sales by month and item with the inner loops.

```
for (store = 0; store < NUM_STORES; store++)
{
    numberSold = 0;
    for (item = 0; item < NUM_ITEMS; item++)
        for (month = 0; month <= currentMonth; month++)
            numberSold = numberSold + sales[store][month][item];
    cout << "Store #" << store << " Sales to date = " << numberSold
        << endl;
}
```

It takes two loops to access each component in a two-dimensional array; it takes three loops to access each component in a three-dimensional array. The task to be accomplished determines which index controls the outer loop, the middle loop, and the inner loop. If we want to calculate monthly sales by store, `month` controls the outer loop and `store` controls the middle loop. If we want to calculate monthly sales by item, `month` controls the outer loop and `item` controls the middle loop.

If we want to keep track of the departments that sell each item, we can add a fourth dimension.

```
enum Departments {A, B, C, D, E, F, G};
const int NUM_DEPTS = 7;
typedef int SalesType[NUM_STORES][12][NUM_ITEMS][NUM_DEPTS];
```

How would we visualize this new structure? Not very easily! Fortunately, we do not have to visualize a structure in order to use it. If we want the number of sales in store 1 during June for item number 4 in department C, we simply access the array element

```
sales[1][5][4][C]
```

When a multidimensional array is declared as a parameter in a function, C++ requires you to state the sizes of all dimensions except the first. For our four-dimensional version of `SalesType`, a function heading would look either like this:

```
void DoSomething( /* inout */ int arr[][12][NUM_ITEMS][NUM_DEPTS] )
```

or, better yet, like this:

```
void DoSomething( /* inout */ SalesType arr )
```

The second version is the safest (and the most uncluttered to look at). It ensures that the sizes of all dimensions of the parameter match those of the argument exactly. With the first version, the reason that you must declare the sizes of all but the first dimension is the same as we discussed earlier for two-dimensional arrays. Because arrays are stored linearly in memory (one array element after another), the compiler must use this size information to locate correctly an element that lies within the array.

Problem-Solving Case Study

Comparison of Two Lists

Problem: You are writing a program for an application that does not tolerate erroneous input data. Therefore, the data values are prepared by entering them twice into one file. The file contains two lists of positive integer numbers, separated by a negative number. These two lists of numbers should be identical; if they are not, then a data entry error has occurred. For example, if the input file contains the sequence of numbers 17, 14, 8, −5, 17, 14, 8, then the two lists of three numbers are identical. However, the sequence 17, 14, 8, −5, 17, 12, 8 shows a data entry error.

You decide to write a separate program to compare the lists and print out any pairs of numbers that are not the same. The exact number of integers in each list is unknown, but each list has no more than 500.

Input: A file (`dataFile`) containing two lists of positive integers. The lists are separated by a negative integer, and both lists have the same number of integers.

Output: A statement that the lists are identical, or a list of the pairs of values that do not match.

Discussion: Because the lists are in the same file, the first list has to be read and stored until the negative number is read. Then the second list can be read and compared with the first list.

If we were checking the lists by hand, we would write the numbers from the first list on a pad of paper, one per line. The line number would correspond to the number's position in the list; that is, the first number would be on the first line, the second number on the second line, and so on. The first number in the second list would then be compared to the number on the first line, the second number to the number on the second line, and so forth.

We use an array named `firstList` to represent the pad of paper. Its declaration looks like this:

```
const int MAX_NUMBER = 500;    // Maximum in each list

int firstList[MAX_NUMBER];     // Holds first list
```

Because the first array component has index 0, we must think of our pad of paper as having its lines numbered from 0, not 1.

Now we can complete the design and program for our problem.

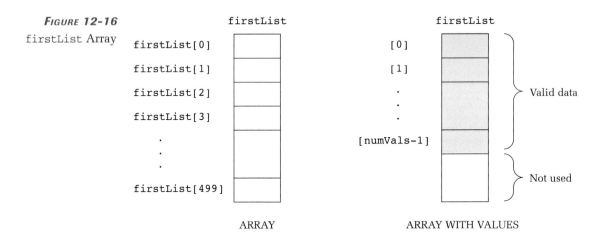

FIGURE 12-16

firstList Array

ARRAY

ARRAY WITH VALUES

Assumption: The two lists to be compared have the same number of integers.

Data Structures: A one-dimensional int array (firstList) to hold the first list of numbers. If numVals is the actual number of values in each list, only positions 0 through numVals − 1 of the array will be filled (see Figure 12-16).

Main   **Level 0**

```
Open dataFile (and verify success)
Read first list
Set allOK = true
Compare lists, changing allOK if necessary
IF allOK
    Print "The two lists are identical"
```

In the module Read First List, the first input value is stored into firstList[0], the second into firstList[1], the third into firstList[2]. This implies that we need a counter to keep track of which number is being read. When the negative number is encountered, the counter tells us how many of the 500 places set aside were actually needed. We can use this value (call it numVals) to control the reading and comparing loop in the Compare Lists module. This is an example of subarray processing.

Read First List (Inout: dataFile; Out: numVals, firstList)   Level 1

```
Set counter = 0
Read number from dataFile
WHILE number >= 0
        Set firstList[counter] = number
        Increment counter
        Read number from dataFile
Set numVals= counter
```

Compare Lists (In: firstList, numVals; Inout: dataFile, allOK)

```
FOR counter going from 0 through numVals–1
        Read number from second list
        IF numbers not the same
                Set allOK = false
                Print both numbers
```

Numbers Not the Same   Level 2

```
number != firstList[counter]
```

Print Both Numbers

```
Print firstList[counter], number
```

PROBLEM-SOLVING CASE STUDY cont'd.

Because the last two modules are only one line each, we can code them directly in the Compare Lists module.

Module Structure Chart:

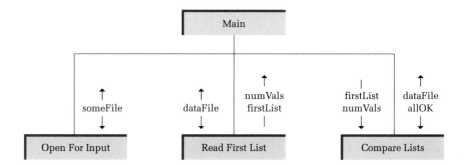

(The following program is written in ISO/ANSI standard C++. If you are working with pre–standard C++, see the alternate version of the program in the PRE_STD directory of the program disk, available at the publisher's Web site, www.jbpub.com/disks.)

```
//******************************************************************
// CheckLists program
// There are two lists of positive integers in a data file,
// separated by a negative integer.  This program compares the two
// lists.  If they are identical, a message is printed.  If not,
// nonmatching pairs are printed.  Assumption: The number of values
// in both lists is the same and is <= 500
//******************************************************************
#include <iostream>
#include <iomanip>     // For setw()
#include <fstream>     // For file I/O
#include <string>      // For string class

using namespace std;

const int MAX_NUMBER = 500;     // Maximum in each list

void CompareLists( const int[], int, ifstream&, bool& );
void OpenForInput( ifstream& );
```

PROBLEM-SOLVING CASE STUDY cont'd.

```
void ReadFirstList( int[], int&, ifstream& );

int main()
{
    int      firstList[MAX_NUMBER];    // Holds first list
    bool     allOK;                    // True if lists are identical
    int      numVals;                  // No. of values in first list
    ifstream dataFile;                 // Input file

    OpenForInput(dataFile);
    if ( !dataFile )
        return 1;

    ReadFirstList(firstList, numVals, dataFile);
    allOK = true;
    CompareLists(firstList, numVals, dataFile, allOK);
    if (allOK)
        cout << "The two lists are identical" << endl;
    return 0;
}

//******************************************************************

void OpenForInput( /* inout */ ifstream& someFile )    // File to be
                                                       // opened
// Prompts the user for the name of an input file
// and attempts to open the file

{
    .
    .        (Same as in ConvertDates program of Chapter 8)
    .
}

//******************************************************************

void ReadFirstList(
            /* out */    int      firstList[],    // Filled first list
            /* out */    int&     numVals,        // Number of values
            /* inout */ ifstream& dataFile    )   // Input file

// Reads the first list from the data file
// and counts the number of values in the list

// Precondition:
//     dataFile has been successfully opened for input
//  && The no. of input values in the first list <= MAX_NUMBER
```

```
// Postcondition:
//     numVals == number of input values in the first list
//     && firstList[0..numVals-1] contain the input values

{
    int counter;      // Index variable
    int number;       // An input value

    counter = 0;
    dataFile >> number;
    while (number >= 0)
    {
        firstList[counter] = number;
        counter++;
        dataFile >> number;
    }
    numVals = counter;
}


//*****************************************************************

void CompareLists(
    /* in */      const int        firstList[],    // 1st list of numbers
    /* in */                int       numVals,      // Number in 1st list
    /* inout */            ifstream& dataFile,      // Input file
    /* inout */            bool&     allOK      )   // True if lists match

// Reads the second list of numbers
// and compares it to the first list

// Precondition:
//     allOK is assigned
//     && numVals <= MAX_NUMBER
//     && firstList[0..numVals-1] are assigned
//     && The two lists have the same number of values
// Postcondition:
//     Values from the second list have been read from the
//         input file
//     && IF all values in the two lists match
//             allOK == allOK@entry
//         ELSE
//             allOK == false
//           && The positions and contents of mismatches have been
//               printed
```

```
{
    int counter;      // Loop control and index variable
    int number;       // An input value

    for (counter = 0; counter < numVals; counter++)
    {
        dataFile >> number;
        if (number != firstList[counter])
        {
            allOK = false;
            cout << "Position " << counter << ": "
                 << setw(4) << firstList[counter] << " != "
                 << setw(4) << number << endl;
        }
    }
}
```

Testing: The program is run with two sets of data, one in which the two lists are identical and one in which there are errors. The data and the results from each are shown below.

Data Set 1	*Data Set 2*
21	21
32	32
76	76
22	22
21	21
-4	-4
21	21
32	32
76	176
22	12
21	21

Output	*Output*
The two lists are identical.	Position 2: 76 != 176
	Position 3: 22 != 12

PROBLEM-SOLVING CASE STUDY

City Council Election

Problem: There has just been a hotly contested city council election. In four voting precincts, citizens have cast their ballots for four candidates. Let's do an analysis of the votes for the four candidates by precinct. We want to know how many votes each candidate received in each precinct, how many total votes each candidate received, and how many total votes were cast in each precinct.

Input: An arbitrary number of votes in a file `voteFile`, with each vote represented as a pair of numbers: a precinct number (1 through 4) and a candidate number (1 through 4); and candidate names, entered from the keyboard (to be used for printing the output).

Output: The following three items, written to a file `reportFile`: a tabular report showing how many votes each candidate received in each precinct, the total number of votes for each candidate, and the total number of votes in each precinct.

Discussion: The data consists of a pair of numbers for each vote. The first number is the precinct number; the second number is the candidate number.

If we were doing the analysis by hand, our first task would be to go through the data, counting how many people in each precinct voted for each candidate. We would probably create a table with precincts down the side and candidates across the top. Each vote would be recorded as a hash mark in the appropriate row and column (see Figure 12-17).

When all of the votes had been recorded, a sum of each column would tell us how many votes each candidate had received. A sum of each row would tell us how many people had voted in each precinct.

As is so often the case, we can use this by-hand algorithm directly in our program. We can create a two-dimensional array in which each component is a counter for the number of votes for a particular candidate in each

FIGURE 12-17
Vote-Counting
Table

Precinct	Smith	Jones	Adams	Smiley
1	ꟷꟷꟷ ꟷꟷ	ꟷꟷ	ꟷꟷꟷ ꟷꟷꟷ ꟷꟷ	ꟷꟷꟷ
2	ꟷꟷꟷ ꟷꟷꟷ	ꟷꟷ	ꟷꟷꟷ	ꟷꟷꟷ
3	ꟷꟷ	ꟷꟷꟷ ꟷꟷꟷ	ꟷꟷꟷ ꟷꟷꟷ ꟷꟷꟷ	ꟷꟷꟷ
4	ꟷꟷꟷ	ꟷꟷꟷ ꟷꟷꟷ	ꟷꟷꟷ ꟷꟷꟷ	ꟷꟷ

FIGURE 12-18
Data Structures for
Election Program

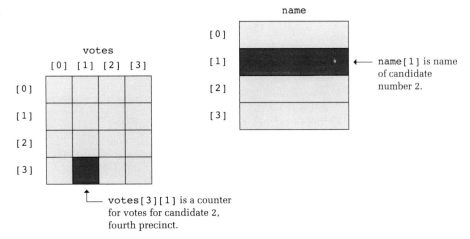

votes

votes[3][1] is a counter
for votes for candidate 2,
fourth precinct.

name

name[1] is name
of candidate
number 2.

precinct; for example, the value indexed by [2][1] would be the counter for the votes in precinct 2 for candidate 1. Well, not quite. C++ arrays are indexed beginning at 0, so the correct array component would be indexed by [1][0]. When we input a precinct number and candidate number, we must remember to subtract 1 from each before indexing into the array. Likewise, we must add 1 to an array index that represents a precinct number or candidate number before printing it out.

Data Structures:

A two-dimensional array named votes, where the rows represent precincts and the columns represent candidates
A one-dimensional array of strings containing the names of the candidates, to be used for printing (see Figure 12-18).

In the design that follows, we use the named constants NUM_PRECINCTS and NUM_CANDIDATES in place of the literal constants 4 and 4.

Main   Level 0

Open voteFile for input (and verify success)
Open reportFile for output (and verify success)
Get candidate names
Set votes array to 0
Read precinct, candidate from voteFile
WHILE NOT EOF on voteFile
     Increment votes[precinct–1][candidate–1] by 1
     Read precinct, candidate from voteFile
Write report to reportFile
Write totals per candidate to reportFile
Write totals per precinct to reportFile

Get Candidate Names (Out: name)   Level 1

Print "Enter the names of the candidates, one per line,
              in the order they appear on the ballot."
FOR candidate going from 0 through NUM_CANDIDATES – 1
     Read name[candidate]

Note that each candidate's name is stored in the slot in the name array corresponding to his or her candidate number (minus 1). These names are useful when the totals are printed.

Set Votes to Zero (Out: votes)

FOR each precinct
     FOR each candidate
          Set votes[precinct][candidate] = 0

Write Report (In: votes, name; Inout: reportFile)

```
// Set up headings
FOR each candidate
        Write name[candidate] to reportFile
Write newline to reportFile
// Print array by row
FOR each precinct
        FOR each candidate
                Write votes[precinct][candidate] to reportFile
        Write newline to reportFile
```

Write Totals per Candidate (In: votes, name; Inout: reportFile)

```
FOR each candidate
        Set total = 0
        // Compute column sum
        FOR each precinct
                Add votes[precinct][candidate] to total
Write "Total votes for", name[candidate], total to reportFile
```

Write Totals per Precinct (In: votes; Inout: reportFile)

```
FOR each precinct
        Set total = 0
        // Compute row sum
        FOR each candidate
                Add votes[precinct][candidate] to total
Write "Total votes for precinct", precinct, ':', total to reportFile
```

Module Structure Chart:

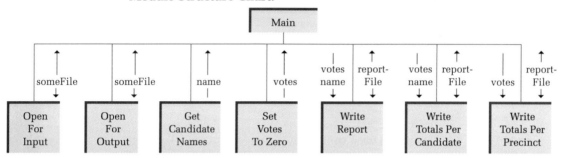

(The following program is written in ISO/ANSI standard C++. If you are working with pre–standard C++, see the alternate version of the program in the PRE_STD directory of the program disk, available at the publisher's Web site, www.jbpub.com/disks.)

```
//******************************************************************
// Election program
// This program reads votes represented by precinct number and
// ballot position from a data file, calculates the sums per
// precinct and per candidate, and writes all totals to an
// output file
//******************************************************************
#include <iostream>
#include <iomanip>      // For setw()
#include <fstream>      // For file I/O
#include <string>       // For string class

using namespace std;

const int NUM_PRECINCTS = 4;
const int NUM_CANDIDATES = 4;

typedef int VoteArray[NUM_PRECINCTS][NUM_CANDIDATES];
                               // 2-dimensional array type
                        //    for votes
```

```
void GetNames( string[] );
void OpenForInput( ifstream& );
void OpenForOutput( ofstream& );
void WritePerCandidate( const VoteArray, const string[],
                         ofstream& );
void WritePerPrecinct( const VoteArray, ofstream& );
void WriteReport( const VoteArray, const string[], ofstream& );
void ZeroVotes( VoteArray );

int main()
{
    string     name[NUM_CANDIDATES];  // Array of candidate names
    VoteArray votes;              // Totals for precincts vs. candidates
    int        candidate;         // Candidate number input from voteFile
    int        precinct;          // Precinct number input from voteFile
    ifstream   voteFile;          // Input file of precincts, candidates
    ofstream   reportFile;        // Output file receiving summaries

    OpenForInput(voteFile);
    if ( !voteFile )
        return 1;
    OpenForOutput(reportFile);
    if ( !reportFile )
        return 1;

    GetNames(name);
    ZeroVotes(votes);

    // Read and tally votes

    voteFile >> precinct >> candidate;
    while (voteFile)
    {
        votes[precinct-1][candidate-1]++;
        voteFile >> precinct >> candidate;
    }

    // Write results to report file

    WriteReport(votes, name, reportFile);
    WritePerCandidate(votes, name, reportFile);
    WritePerPrecinct(votes, reportFile);
```

```
        return 0;
}

//*****************************************************************

void OpenForInput( /* inout */ ifstream& someFile )    // File to be
                                                        // opened
// Prompts the user for the name of an input file
// and attempts to open the file

{
      .
      .          (Same as in ConvertDates program of Chapter 8)
      .
}

//*****************************************************************

void OpenForOutput( /* inout */ ofstream& someFile )   // File to be
                                                        // opened
// Prompts the user for the name of an output file
// and attempts to open the file

{
      .
      .          (Same as in ConvertDates program of Chapter 8)
      .
}

//*****************************************************************

void GetNames( /* out */ string name[] )    // Array of candidate
                                             //    names
// Reads the candidate names from standard input

// Postcondition:
//      The user has been prompted to enter the candidate names
//   && name[0..NUM_CANDIDATES-1] contain the input names,
//      truncated to 10 characters each

{
    string inputStr;      // An input string
    int    candidate;     // Loop counter
```

PROBLEM-SOLVING CASE STUDY cont'd.

```cpp
        cout << "Enter the names of the candidates, one per line,"
             << endl << "in the order they appear on the ballot."
             << endl;

        for (candidate = 0; candidate < NUM_CANDIDATES; candidate++)
        {
            cin >> inputStr;
            name[candidate] = inputStr.substr(0, 10);
        }
}

//******************************************************************

void ZeroVotes( /* out */ VoteArray votes )  // Array of vote totals

// Zeros out the votes array

// Postcondition:
//     All votes[0..NUM_PRECINCTS-1][0..NUM_CANDIDATES-1] == 0

{
    int precinct;        // Loop counter
    int candidate;       // Loop counter

    for (precinct = 0; precinct < NUM_PRECINCTS; precinct++)
        for (candidate = 0; candidate < NUM_CANDIDATES; candidate++)
            votes[precinct][candidate] = 0;
}

//******************************************************************

void WriteReport(
        /* in */     const VoteArray votes,       // Total votes
        /* in */     const string    name[],      // Candidate names
        /* inout */          ofstream& reportFile )  // Output file

// Writes the vote totals in tabular form to the report file

// Precondition:
//     votes[0..NUM_PRECINCTS-1][0..NUM_CANDIDATES] are assigned
//   && name[0..NUM_CANDIDATES-1] are assigned
// Postcondition:
//     The name array has been output across one line, followed by
//     the votes array, one row per line
```

```
{
    int precinct;        // Loop counter
    int candidate;       // Loop counter

    // Set up headings

    reportFile << "              ";
    for (candidate = 0; candidate < NUM_CANDIDATES; candidate++)
        reportFile << setw(12) << name[candidate];
    reportFile << endl;

    // Print array by row

    for (precinct = 0; precinct < NUM_PRECINCTS; precinct++)
    {
        reportFile << "Precinct" << setw(4) << precinct + 1;
        for (candidate = 0; candidate < NUM_CANDIDATES; candidate++)
            reportFile << setw(12) << votes[precinct][candidate];
        reportFile << endl;
    }
    reportFile << endl;
}

//*****************************************************************

void WritePerCandidate(
        /* in */     const VoteArray votes,       // Total votes
        /* in */     const string    name[],      // Candidate names
        /* inout */       ofstream& reportFile )   // Output file

// Sums the votes per person and writes the totals to the
// report file

// Precondition:
//     votes[0..NUM_PRECINCTS-1][0..NUM_CANDIDATES] are assigned
//  && name[0..NUM_CANDIDATES-1] are assigned
// Postcondition:
//     For each person i, name[i] has been output,
//     followed by the sum
//     votes[0][i] + votes[1][i] + ... + votes[NUM_PRECINCTS-1][i]
```

PROBLEM-SOLVING CASE STUDY cont'd.

```cpp
{
    int precinct;        // Loop counter
    int candidate;       // Loop counter
    int total;           // Total votes for a candidate

    for (candidate = 0; candidate < NUM_CANDIDATES; candidate++)
    {
        total = 0;

        // Compute column sum

        for (precinct = 0; precinct < NUM_PRECINCTS; precinct++)
            total = total + votes[precinct][candidate];

        reportFile << "Total votes for"
                   << setw(10) << name[candidate] << ":"
                   << setw(3) << total << endl;
    }
    reportFile << endl;
}

//******************************************************************

void WritePerPrecinct(
        /* in */      const VoteArray votes,        // Total votes
        /* inout */        ofstream& reportFile )    // Output file

// Sums the votes per precinct and writes the totals to the
// report file

// Precondition:
//     votes[0..NUM_PRECINCTS-1][0..NUM_CANDIDATES] are assigned
// Postcondition:
//     For each precinct i, the value i+1 has been output,
//     followed by the sum
//     votes[i][0] + votes[i][1] + ... + votes[i][NUM_CANDIDATES-1]

{
    int precinct;        // Loop counter
    int candidate;       // Loop counter
    int total;           // Total votes for a precinct
```

```
for (precinct = 0; precinct < NUM_PRECINCTS; precinct++)
{
    total = 0;

    // Compute row sum

    for (candidate = 0; candidate < NUM_CANDIDATES; candidate++)
        total = total + votes[precinct][candidate];

    reportFile << "Total votes for precinct"
               << setw(3) << precinct + 1 << ':'
               << setw(3) << total << endl;
}
}
```

Testing: This program was executed with the data listed below. (We list the data in three columns to save space.) The names of the candidates entered from the keyboard were Smith, Jones, Adams, and Smiley. In this data set, there is at least one vote for each candidate in each precinct. Case Study Follow-Up Exercise 4 asks you to outline a complete testing strategy for this program.

Input Data

1 1	3 1	3 3
1 1	4 3	4 4
1 2	3 4	4 4
1 2	3 2	4 3
1 3	3 3	4 4
1 4	2 1	4 4
2 2	2 3	4 1
2 2	4 3	4 2
2 3	4 4	2 4
2 1	3 2	4 4

The output, which was written to file `reportFile`, is shown below.

		Jones	Smith	Adams	Smiley
Precinct	1	2	2	1	1
Precinct	2	2	2	2	1
Precinct	3	1	2	2	1
Precinct	4	1	1	3	6

```
Total votes for      Jones:  6
Total votes for      Smith:  7
Total votes for      Adams:  8
Total votes for     Smiley:  9

Total votes for precinct  1:  6
Total votes for precinct  2:  7
Total votes for precinct  3:  6
Total votes for precinct  4: 11
```

Testing and Debugging

One-Dimensional Arrays

The most common error in processing arrays is an out-of-bounds array index. That is, the program attempts to access a component using an index that is either less than 0 or greater than the array size minus 1. For example, given the declarations

```
char line[100];
int  counter;
```

the following For statement would print the 100 elements of the `line` array and then print a 101st value—the value that resides in memory immediately beyond the end of the array.

```
for (counter = 0; counter <= 100; counter++)
    cout << line[counter];
```

This error is easy to detect, because 101 characters get printed instead of 100. The loop test should be `counter < 100`. But you won't always use a simple For statement when accessing arrays. Suppose we read data into the `line` array in another part of the program. Let's use a While statement that reads to the newline character:

```
counter = 0;
cin.get(ch);
while (ch != '\n')
{
    line[counter] = ch;
    counter++;
    cin.get(ch);
}
```

This code seems reasonable enough, but what if the input line has more than 100 characters? After the hundredth character is read and stored into the array, the loop continues to execute with the array index out of bounds. Characters are stored into memory locations past the end of the array, wiping out other data values (or even machine language instructions in the program!).

The moral is: When processing arrays, give special attention to the design of loop termination conditions. Always ask yourself if the loop could possibly keep running after the last array component has been processed.

Whenever an array index goes out of bounds, the first suspicion should be a loop that fails to terminate properly. The second thing to check is any array access involving an index that is based on input data or a calculation. When an array index is input as data, a data validation check is an absolute necessity.

Complex Structures

As we have demonstrated in many examples in this chapter and the last, it is possible to combine data structures in various ways: structs whose components are structs, structs whose components are arrays, arrays whose components are structs or class objects, arrays whose components are arrays (multidimensional arrays), and so forth. When arrays, structs, and class objects are combined, there can be confusion about precisely where to place the operators for array element selection ([]) and struct or class member selection (.).

To summarize the correct placement of these operators, let's use the StudentRec type we introduced in this chapter:

```
struct StudentRec
{
    string     stuName;
    float      gpa;
    int        examScore[4];
    GradeType  courseGrade;
};
```

If we declare a variable of type StudentRec,

```
StudentRec student;
```

then what is the syntax for selecting the first exam score of the student (that is, for selecting element 0 of the examScore member of student)? The dot operator is a binary (two-operand) operator; its left operand denotes a struct variable, and its right operand is a member name:

StructVariable.MemberName

The `[]` operator is a unary (one-operand) operator; it comes immediately after an expression denoting an array:

Array [IndexExpression]

Therefore, the expression

```
student
```

denotes a struct variable, the expression

```
student.examScore
```

denotes an array, and the expression

```
student.examScore[0]
```

denotes an integer—the integer located in element 0 of the `student.examScore` array.

With arrays of structs or class objects, again you have to be sure that the `[]` and `.` operators are in the proper positions. Given the declaration

```
StudentRec gradeBook[150];
```

we can access the `gpa` member of the first element of the `gradeBook` array with the expression

```
gradeBook[0].gpa
```

The index `[0]` is correctly attached to the identifier `gradeBook` because `gradeBook` is the name of an array. Furthermore, the expression

```
gradeBook[0]
```

denotes a struct, so the dot operator selects the `gpa` member of this struct.

Multidimensional Arrays

Errors with multidimensional arrays usually fall into two major categories: index expressions that are out of order and index range errors.

Suppose we were to expand the Election program to accommodate ten candidates and four precincts. Let's declare the `votes` array as

```
int votes[4][10];
```

The first dimension represents the precincts, and the second represents the candidates. An example of the first kind of error—incorrect order of the index expressions—would be to print out the `votes` array as follows.

```
for (precinct = 0; precinct < 4; precinct++)
{
    for (candidate = 0; candidate < 10; candidate++)
        cout << setw(4) << votes[candidate][precinct];
    cout << endl;
}
```

The output statement specifies the array indexes in the wrong order. The loops march through the array with the first index ranging from 0 through 9 (instead of 0 through 3) and the second index ranging from 0 through 3 (instead of 0 through 9). The effect of executing this code may vary from system to system. The program may output the wrong array components and continue executing, or the program may crash with a memory access error.

An example of the second kind of error—an incorrect index range in an otherwise correct loop—can be seen in this code:

```
for (precinct = 0; precinct < 10; precinct++)
{
    for (candidate = 0; candidate < 4; candidate++)
        cout << setw(4) << votes[precinct][candidate];
    cout << endl;
}
```

Here, the output statement correctly uses `precinct` for the first index and `candidate` for the second. However, the For statements use incorrect upper limits for the index variables. As with the preceding example, the effect of executing this code is undefined but is certainly wrong. A valuable way to prevent this kind of error is to use named constants instead of the literals 10 and 4. In the case study, we used NUM_PRECINCTS and NUM_CANDIDATES. You are much more likely to spot an error (or to avoid making an error in the first place) if you write something like this:

```
for (precinct = 0; precinct < NUM_PRECINCTS; precinct++)
```

than if you use a literal constant as the upper limit for the index variable.

Testing and Debugging Hints

1. When an individual component of a one-dimensional array is accessed, the index must be within the range 0 through the array size minus 1. Attempting to use an index value outside this range causes your program to access memory locations outside the array.

2. The individual components of an array are themselves variables of the component type. When values are stored into an array, they should either be of the component type or be explicitly converted to the component type; otherwise, implicit type coercion occurs.

3. C++ does not allow aggregate operations on arrays. There is no aggregate assignment, aggregate comparison, aggregate I/O, or aggregate arithmetic. You must write code to do all of these operations, one array element at a time.

4. Omitting the size of a one-dimensional array in its declaration is permitted only in two cases: (1) when an array is declared as a parameter in a function heading and (2) when an array is initialized in its declaration. In all other declarations, you *must* specify the size of the array with a constant integer expression.

5. If an array parameter is incoming-only, declare the parameter as `const` to prevent the function from modifying the caller's argument accidentally.

6. Don't pass an individual array component as an argument when the function expects to receive the base address of an entire array.

7. The size of an array is fixed at compile time, but the number of values actually stored there is determined at run time. Therefore, an array must be declared to be as large as it could ever be for the particular problem. Subarray processing is used to process only the components that have data in them.

8. When functions perform subarray processing on a one-dimensional array, pass both the array name and the number of data items actually stored in the array.

9. With multidimensional arrays, use the proper number of indexes when referencing an array component, and make sure the indexes are in the correct order.

10. In loops that process multidimensional arrays, double-check the upper and lower bounds on each index variable to be sure they are correct for that dimension of the array.

11. When declaring a multidimensional array as a parameter, you must state the sizes of all but the first dimension. Also, these sizes must agree exactly with the sizes of the caller's argument.

12. To eliminate the chances of the size mismatches referred to in item 11, use a Typedef statement to define a multidimensional array type. Declare both the argument and the parameter to be of this type.

Summary

The one-dimensional array is a homogeneous data structure that gives a name to a sequential group of like components. Each component is accessed by its relative position within the group (rather than by name, as in a struct or class), and each component is a variable of the component type. To access a particular component, we give the name of the array and an index that specifies which component of the group we want. The index can be an expression of any integral type, as long as it evaluates to an integer from 0 through the array size minus 1. Array components can be accessed in random order directly, or they can be accessed sequentially by stepping through the index values one at a time.

Two-dimensional arrays are useful for processing information that is represented naturally in tabular form. Processing data in two-dimensional arrays usually takes one of two forms: processing by row or processing by column. An array of arrays, which is useful if rows of the array must be passed as arguments, is an alternative way of defining a two-dimensional array.

A multidimensional array is a collection of like components that are ordered on more than one dimension. Each component is accessed by a set of indexes, one for each dimension, that represents the component's position on the various dimensions. Each index may be thought of as describing a feature of a given array component.

Quick Check

1. Declare a one-dimensional array named `quizAnswer` that contains 12 components indexed by the integers 0 through 11. The component type is `bool`. (pp. 664–667)
2. Given the declarations

   ```
   const int SIZE = 30;

   char firstName[SIZE];
   ```

   a. Write an assignment statement that stores 'A' into the first component of array `firstName`. (pp. 667–669)
   b. Write an output statement that prints the value of the fourteenth component of array `firstName`. (pp. 667–669)
   c. Write a For statement that fills array `firstName` with blanks. (p. 670)
3. Declare a five-element one-dimensional `int` array named `oddNums`, and initialize it (in its declaration) to contain the first five odd integers, starting with 1. (p. 671)

4. Give the function heading for a void function named `SomeFunc`, where
   a. `SomeFunc` has a single parameter: a one-dimensional `float` array x that is an Inout parameter.
   b. `SomeFunc` has a single parameter: a one-dimensional `float` array x that is an In parameter.
   (pp. 676–678)

5. Given the declaration

   ```
   StudentRec gradeBook[150];
   ```

   where `StudentRec` is the `struct` type defined in this chapter, do the following.
   a. Write an assignment statement that records the fact that the tenth student has a grade point average of 3.25.
   b. Write an assignment statement that records the fact that the fourth student scored 78 on the third exam. (pp. 681–683)

6. Given the declarations in Question 2 and the following program fragment, which reads characters into array `firstName` until a blank is encountered, write a For statement that prints out the portion of the array that is filled with input data. (p. 684)

   ```
   n = 0;
   cin.get(letter);
   while (letter != ' ')
   {
       firstName[n] = letter;
       n++;
       cin.get(letter);
   }
   ```

7. Define an enumeration type for the musical notes A through G (excluding sharps and flats). Then declare a one-dimensional array in which the index values represent musical notes, and the component type is `float`. Finally, show an example of a For loop that prints out the contents of the array. (p. 684)

8. Declare a two-dimensional array, named `plan`, with 30 rows and 10 columns. The component type of the array is `float`. (p. 685–689)

9. a. Assign the value 27.3 to the component in row 13, column 7 of the array `plan` from Question 8. (pp. 685–689)
   b. Nested For loops can be used to sum the values in each row of array `plan`. What range of values would the outer For loop count through to do this? (pp. 690–691)
   c. Nested For loops can be used to sum the values in each column of array `plan`. What range of values would the outer For loop count through to do this? (pp. 691–692)
   d. Write a program fragment that initializes array `plan` to all zeros. (pp. 692–694)

e. Write a program fragment that prints the contents of array plan, one row per line of output. (pp. 694–695)

10. Suppose array plan is passed as an argument to a function in which the corresponding parameter is named someArray. What would the declaration of someArray look like in the parameter list? (pp. 695–697)

11. Given the declarations

```
typedef int OneDimType[100];


OneDimType twoDim[40];
```

rewrite the declaration of twoDim without referring to type OneDimType. (pp. 698–699)

12. Given the declarations

```
const int SIZE = 10;
typedef char FourDim[SIZE][SIZE][SIZE][SIZE-1];


FourDim quick;
```

a. How many components does array quick contain? (pp. 700–702)
b. Write a program fragment that fills array quick with blanks. (pp. 700–702)

Answers

1. `bool quizAnswer[12];`
2. a. `firstName[0] = 'A';`
   b. `cout << firstName[13];`
   c. `for (index = 0; index < SIZE; index++)`
      `    firstName[index] = ' ';`
3. `int oddNums[5] = {1, 3, 5, 7, 9};`
4. a. `void SomeFunc( float x[] )`
   b. `void SomeFunc( const float x[] )`
5. a. `gradeBook[9].gpa = 3.25;`
   b. `gradeBook[3].examScore[2] = 78;`
6. `for (index = 0; index < n; index++)`
   `    cout << firstName[index];`
7. `enum NoteType {A, B, C, D, E, F, G};`
   `float noteVal[7];`
   `NoteType index;`
   `for (index = A; index <= G; index = NoteType(index + 1))`
   `    cout << noteVal[index] << endl;`
8. `float plan[30][10];`
9. a. `plan[13][7] = 27.3;`
   b. `for (row = 0; row < 30; row++)`
   c. `for (col = 0; col < 10; col++)`
   d. `for (row = 0; row < 30; row++)`
      `    for (col = 0; col < 10; col++)`
      `        plan[row][col] = 0.0;`

e. for (row = 0; row < 30; row++)
    {
        for (col = 0; col < 10; col++)
            cout << setw(8) << plan[row][col];
        cout << endl;
    }

10. Either
        float someArray[30][10]
    or
        float someArray[][10]

11. int twoDim[40][100];

12. a. Nine thousand ($10 \times 10 \times 10 \times 9$)
    b. for (dim1 = 0; dim1 < SIZE; dim1++)
            for (dim2 = 0; dim2 < SIZE; dim2++)
                for (dim3 = 0; dim3 < SIZE; dim3++)
                    for (dim4 = 0; dim4 < SIZE - 1; dim4++)
                        quick[dim1][dim2][dim3][dim4] = ' ';

Exam Preparation Exercises

1. Every component in an array must have the same type, and the number of components is fixed at compile time. (True or False?)
2. The components of an array must be of an integral or enumeration type. (True or False?)
3. Declare one-dimensional arrays according to the following descriptions.
    a. A 24-element float array
    b. A 500-element int array
    c. A 50-element double-precision floating-point array
    d. A 10-element char array
4. Write a code fragment to do the following tasks:
    a. Declare a constant named CLASS_SIZE representing the number of students in a class.
    b. Declare a one-dimensional array quizAvg of size CLASS_SIZE whose components will contain floating-point quiz score averages.
5. Write a code fragment to do the following tasks:
    a. Declare an enumeration type BirdType made up of bird names.
    b. Declare a one-dimensional int array sightings that is to be indexed by BirdType.
6. Given the declarations

    const int SIZE = 100;

    enum Colors
    {
        BLUE, GREEN, GOLD, ORANGE, PURPLE, RED, WHITE, BLACK
    };

```
int     count[8];
Colors cIndex;                    // Index for count array
Colors rainbow[SIZE];
int     rIndex;                   // Index for rainbow array
```

write code fragments to do the following tasks:

a. Set count to all zeros.

b. Set rainbow to all WHITE.

c. Count the number of times GREEN appears in rainbow.

d. Print the value in count indexed by BLUE.

e. Total the values in count.

7. What is the output of the following program? The data for the program is given below it.

```cpp
#include <iostream>

using namespace std;

int main()
{
    int a[100];
    int b[100];
    int j;
    int m;
    int sumA = 0;
    int sumB = 0;
    int sumDiff = 0;

    cin >> m;
    for (j = 0; j < m; j++)
    {
        cin >> a[j] >> b[j];
        sumA = sumA + a[j];
        sumB = sumB + b[j];
        sumDiff = sumDiff + (a[j] - b[j]);
    }
    for (j = m - 1; j >= 0; j--)
        cout << a[j] << ' ' << b[j] << ' '
             << a[j] - b[j] << endl;
    cout << endl;
    cout << sumA << ' ' << sumB << ' ' << sumDiff << endl;
    return 0;
}
```

Data

```
    5
11  15
19  14
 4   2
17   6
 1   3
```

8. A person wrote the following code fragment, intending to print 10 20 30 40.

```
int arr[4] = {10, 20, 30, 40};
int index;

for (index = 1; index <= 4; index++)
    cout << ' ' << arr[index];
```

Instead, the code printed 20 30 40 24835. Explain the reason for this output.

9. Given the declarations

```
int sample[8];
int i;
int k;
```

show the contents of the array sample after the following code segment is executed. Use a question mark to indicate any undefined values in the array.

```
for (k = 0; k < 8; k++)
    sample[k] = 10 - k;
```

10. Using the same declarations given for Exercise 9, show the contents of the array sample after the following code segment is executed.

```
for (i = 0; i < 8; i++)
    if (i <= 3)
        sample[i] = 1;
    else
        sample[i] = -1;
```

11. Using the same declarations given for Exercise 9, show the contents of the array sample after the following code segment is executed.

```
for (k = 0; k < 8; k++)
    if (k % 2 == 0)
        sample[k] = k;
    else
        sample[k] = k + 100;
```

12. What are the two basic differences between a record and an array?

13. If the members of a record are all the same data type, an array data structure could be used instead. (True or False?)

14. For each of the following descriptions of data, determine which general type of data structure (array, record, array of records, or hierarchical record) is appropriate.
    a. A payroll entry with a name, address, and pay rate.
    b. A person's address.
    c. An inventory entry for a part.
    d. A list of addresses.
    e. A list of hourly temperatures.
    f. A list of passengers on an airliner, including names, addresses, fare class, and seat assignment.
    g. A departmental telephone directory with last name and extension number.

15. Given the declarations

```
const int NUM_SCHOOLS = 10;
const int NUM_SPORTS = 3;
enum SportType {FOOTBALL, BASKETBALL, VOLLEYBALL};

int   kidsInSports[NUM_SCHOOLS][NUM_SPORTS];
float costOfSports[NUM_SPORTS][NUM_SCHOOLS];
```

answer the following questions:
a. What is the number of rows in `kidsInSports`?
b. What is the number of columns in `kidsInSports`?
c. What is the number of rows in `costOfSports`?
d. What is the number of columns in `costOfSports`?
e. How many components does `kidsInSports` have?
f. How many components does `costOfSports` have?
g. What kind of processing (row or column) would be needed to total the amount of money spent on each sport?
h. What kind of processing (row or column) would be needed to total the number of children participating in sports at a particular school?

16. Given the following code segments, draw the arrays and their contents after the code is executed. Indicate any undefined values with the letter *U.*
a. `int exampleA[4][3];`
```
      int i, j;

      for (i = 0; i < 4; i++)
          for (j = 0; j < 3; j++)
              exampleA[i][j] = i * j;
```
b. `int exampleB[4][3];`
```
      int i, j;

      for (i = 0; i < 3; i++)
          for (j = 0; j < 3; j++)
              exampleB[i][j] = (i + j) % 3;
```
c. `int exampleC[8][2];`
```
      int i, j;

      exampleC[7][0] = 4;
      exampleC[7][1] = 5;
      for (i = 0; i < 7; i++)
      {
          exampleC[i][0] = 2;
          exampleC[i][1] = 3;
      }
```

17. a. Define enumeration types for the following:
   `TeamType` made up of classes (freshman, sophomore, etc.) on your campus
   `ResultType` made up of game results (won, lost, or tied)

b. Using Typedef, declare a two-dimensional integer array type named Outcome, intended to be indexed by TeamType and ResultType.

c. Declare an array variable standings to be of type Outcome.

d. Give a C++ statement that increases the number of freshman wins by 1.

18. The following code fragment includes a call to a function named DoSomething.

```
typedef float ArrType[100][20];

ArrType x;
    ⋮
DoSomething(x);
```

Indicate whether each of the following would be valid or invalid as the function heading for DoSomething.

a. `void DoSomething( /* inout */ ArrType arr )`

b. `void DoSomething( /* inout */ float arr[100][20] )`

c. `void DoSomething( /* inout */ float arr[100][] )`

d. `void DoSomething( /* inout */ float arr[][20] )`

e. `void DoSomething( /* inout */ float arr[][] )`

f. `void DoSomething( /* inout */ float arr[][10] )`

19. Declare the two-dimensional array variables described below. Use proper style.

a. An array with five rows and six columns that contains Boolean values.

b. An array, indexed from 0 through 39 and 0 through 199, that contains float values.

c. A char array with rows indexed by a type

```
enum FruitType {LEMON, PEAR, APPLE, ORANGE};
```

and columns indexed by the integers 0 through 15.

20. A logging operation keeps records of 37 loggers' monthly production for purposes of analysis, using the following array structure:

```
const int NUM_LOGGERS = 37;

int logsCut[NUM_LOGGERS][12];   // Logs cut per logger per month
int monthlyHigh;
int monthlyTotal;
int yearlyTotal;
int high;
int month;
int bestMonth;
int logger;
int bestLogger;
```

a. The following statement assigns the January log total for logger number 7 to monthlyTotal. (True or False?)

```
monthlyTotal = logsCut[7][0];
```

b. The following statements compute the yearly total for logger number 11. (True or False?)

```
    yearlyTotal = 0;
    for (month = 0; month < NUM_LOGGERS; month++)
        yearlyTotal = yearlyTotal + logsCut[month][10];
```

c. The following statements find the best logger (most logs cut) in March. (True or False?)

```
    monthlyHigh = 0;
    for (logger = 0; logger < NUM_LOGGERS; logger++)
        if (logsCut[logger][2] > monthlyHigh)
        {
            bestLogger = logger;
            monthlyHigh = logsCut[logger][2];
        }
```

d. The following statements find the logger with the highest monthly production and the logger's best month. (True or False?)

```
    high = -1;
    for (month = 0; month < 12; month++)
        for (logger = 0; logger < NUM_LOGGERS; logger++)
            if (logsCut[logger][month] > high)
            {
                high = logsCut[logger][month];
                bestLogger = logger;
                bestMonth = month;
            }
```

21. Declare the `float` array variables described below. Use proper style.
   a. A three-dimensional array in which the first dimension is indexed from 0 through 9, the second dimension is indexed by an enumeration type representing the days of the week, and the third dimension is indexed from 0 through 20.
   b. A four-dimensional array in which the first two dimensions are indexed from 0 through 49, and the third and fourth are indexed by any valid ASCII character.

Programming Warm-up Exercises

Use the following declarations in Exercises 1–7. You may declare any other variables that you need.

```
    const int NUM_STUDS = 100;   // Number of students

    bool failing[NUM_STUDS];
    bool passing[NUM_STUDS];
    int  grade;
    int  score[NUM_STUDS];
```

1. Write a C++ function that initializes all components of `failing` to `false`. The `failing` array is a parameter.

2. Write a C++ function that has `failing` and `score` as parameters. Set the components of `failing` to `true` wherever the corresponding value in `score` is less than 60.

3. Write a C++ function that has `passing` and `score` as parameters. Set the components of `passing` to `true` wherever the corresponding value in `score` is greater than or equal to 60.

4. Write a C++ value-returning function `PassTally` that takes `passing` as a parameter and reports how many components in `passing` are `true`.

5. Write a C++ value-returning function `Error` that takes `passing` and `failing` as parameters. `Error` returns `true` if any corresponding components in `passing` and `failing` are the same.

6. Write a C++ value-returning function that takes `grade` and `score` as parameters. The function reports how many values in `score` are greater than or equal to `grade`.

7. Write a C++ function that takes `score` as a parameter and reverses the order of the components in `score`; that is, `score[0]` goes into `score[NUM_STUDS-1]`, `score[1]` goes into `score[NUM_STUDS-2]`, and so on.

8. Write a program segment to read in a set of part numbers and associated unit costs. Use an array of structs with two members, `number` and `cost`, to represent each pair of input values. Assume the end-of-file condition terminates the input.

9. Below is the specification of a "safe array" class, which halts the program if an array index goes out of bounds. (Recall that C++ does not check for out-of-bounds indexes when you use built-in arrays.)

```
const int MAX_SIZE = 200;

class IntArray
{
public:
    int ValueAt( /* in */ int i ) const;
        // Precondition:
        //      i is assigned
        // Postcondition:
        //      IF i >= 0  &&  i < declared size of array
        //          Function value == value of array element
        //                              at index i
        //      ELSE
        //          Program has halted with error message

    void Store( /* in */ int val,
                /* in */ int i   );
        // Precondition:
        //      val and i are assigned
        // Postcondition:
        //      IF i >= 0  &&  i < declared size of array
        //          val is stored in array element i
        //      ELSE
        //          Program has halted with error message
```

```
        IntArray( /* in */ int arrSize );
            // Precondition:
            //      arrSize is assigned
            // Postcondition:
            //      IF arrSize >= 1  &&  arrSize <= MAX_SIZE
            //          Array created with all array elements == 0
            //      ELSE
            //          Program has halted with error message
    private:
        int arr[MAX_SIZE];
        int size;
    };
```

Implement each member function as it would appear in the implementation file. To halt the program, use the `exit` function supplied by the C++ standard library through the header file `cstdlib` (see Appendix C).

10. Write a C++ value-returning function that returns `true` if all the values in a certain subarray of a two-dimensional array are positive, and returns `false` otherwise. The array (of type `ArrayType`), the number of columns in the subarray, and the number of rows in the subarray should be passed as arguments.

11. Write a C++ function `Copy` that takes a two-dimensional `int` array `data`, defined to be NUM_ROWS by NUM_COLS, and copies the values into a second array `data2`, defined the same way. `data` and `data2` are of type `TwoDimType`. The constants NUM_ROWS and NUM_COLS may be accessed globally.

12. Write a C++ function that finds the largest value in a two-dimensional `float` array of 50 rows and 50 columns.

13. Using the declarations in Exam Preparation Exercise 15, write functions, in proper style, to do the following tasks. Only constants may be accessed globally.

    a. Determine which school spent the most money on football.

    b. Determine which sport the last school spent the most money on.

    c. Determine which school had the most students playing basketball.

    d. Determine in which sport the third school had the most students participating.

    e. Determine the total amount spent by all the schools on volleyball.

    f. Determine the total number of students who played any sport. (Assume that each student played only one sport.)

    g. Determine which school had the most students participating in sports.

    h. Determine which was the most popular sport in terms of money spent.

    i. Determine which was the most popular sport in terms of student participation.

14. Given the following declarations

```
const int NUM_DEPTS = 100;
const int NUM_STORES = 10;
const int NUM_MONTHS = 12;

typedef int SalesType[NUM_STORES][NUM_MONTHS][NUM_DEPTS];
```

write a C++ function to initialize an array of type SalesType to 0. The constants NUM_STORES, NUM_MONTHS, and NUM_DEPTS may be accessed globally. The array should be a parameter.

15. Sales figures are kept on items sold by store, by department, and by month. Write a C++ function to calculate and print the total number of items sold during the year by each department in each store. The data is stored in an array of type SalesType as defined in Programming Warm-up Exercise 14. The array containing the data should be a parameter. The constants NUM_STORES, NUM_MONTHS, and NUM_DEPTS may be accessed globally.

16. Write a C++ value-returning function that returns the sum of the elements in a specified row of a two-dimensional array. The array, the number of filled-in columns, and which row is to be totaled should be parameters.

Programming Problems

1. The local baseball team is computerizing its records. You are to write a program that computes batting averages. There are 20 players on the team, identified by the numbers 1 through 20. Their batting records are coded in a file as follows. Each line contains four numbers: the player's identification number and the number of hits, walks, and outs he or she made in a particular game. Here is a sample:

```
3   2   1   1
```

The example above indicates that during a game, player number 3 was at bat four times and made 2 hits, 1 walk, and 1 out. For each player there are several lines in the file. Each player's batting average is computed by adding the player's total number of hits and dividing by the total number of times at bat. A walk does not count as either a hit or a time at bat when the batting average is being calculated. Your program prints a table showing each player's identification number, batting average, and number of walks. (Be careful: The players' identification numbers are 1 through 20, but C++ array indexes start at 0.)

2   Write a program that calculates the mean and standard deviation of integers stored in a file. The output should be of type float and should be properly labeled and formatted to two decimal places. The formula for calculating the mean of a series of integers is to add all the numbers, then divide by the number of integers. Expressed in mathematical terms, the mean $\overline{X}$ of N numbers X_1, X_2, ... X_N is

$$\overline{X} = \frac{\sum\limits_{i=1}^{N} X_i}{N}$$

To calculate the standard deviation of a series of integers, subtract the mean from each integer (you may get a negative number) and square the result, add all these squared differences, divide by the number of integers minus 1, then take the square root of the result. Expressed in mathematical terms, the standard deviation S is

$$S = \sqrt{\frac{\sum\limits_{i=1}^{N} (X_i - \overline{X})^2}{N-1}}$$

3. One of the local banks is gearing up for a big advertising campaign and would like to see how long its customers are waiting for service at drive-up windows. Several employees have been asked to keep accurate records for the 24-hour drive-up service. The collected information, which is read from a file, consists of the time the customer arrived in hours, minutes, and seconds; the time the customer actually was served; and the ID number of the teller. Write a program that does the following:

   a. Reads in the wait data.

   b. Computes the wait time in seconds.

   c. Calculates the mean, standard deviation (defined in Programming Problem 2), and range.

   d. Prints a single-page summary showing the values calculated in part c.

   Input

   The first data line contains a title.

   The remaining lines each contain a teller ID, an arrival time, and a service time. The times are broken up into integer hours, minutes, and seconds according to a 24-hour clock.

   Processing

   Calculate the mean and the standard deviation.

   Locate the shortest wait time and the longest wait time for any number of records up to 100.

   Output

   The input data (echo print).

   The title.

   The following values, all properly labeled: number of records, mean, standard deviation, and range (minimum and maximum).

4. Your history professor has so many students in her class that she has trouble determining how well the class does on exams. She has discovered that you are a computer whiz and has asked you to write a program to perform some simple statistical analyses on exam scores. Your program must work for any class size up to 100. Write and test a computer program that does the following:

   a. Reads the test grades from file inData.

   b. Calculates the class mean, standard deviation (defined in Programming Problem 2), and percentage of the test scores falling in the ranges <10, 10–19, 20–29, 30–39, ... , 80–89, and ≥90.

   c. Prints a summary showing the mean and the standard deviation, as well as a histogram showing the percentage distribution of test scores.

   Input

   The first data line contains the number of exams to be analyzed and a title for the report.

   The remaining lines have ten test scores on each line until the last line, and one to ten scores on the last. The scores are all integers.

   Output

   The input data as they are read.

   A report consisting of the title that was read from the data, the number of scores, the mean, the standard deviation (all clearly labeled), and the histogram.

5. The final exam in your psychology class consists of 30 multiple-choice questions. Your instructor says that if you write the program to grade the finals, you won't have to take the exam.

   Input

   The first data line contains the key to the exam. The correct answers are the first 30 characters; they are followed by an integer number that says how many students took the exam (call it *n*).

   The next *n* lines contain student answers in the first 30 character positions, followed by the student's name in the next 10 character positions.

   Output

   For each student—the student's name; followed by the number of correct answers; followed by *PASS* if the number correct is 60 percent or better, or *FAIL* otherwise.

6. Write an interactive program that plays tic-tac-toe. Represent the board as a 3 × 3 character array. Initialize the array to blanks and ask each player in turn to input a position. The first player's position is marked on the board with an *O*, and the second player's position is marked with an *X*. Continue the process until a player wins or the game is a draw. To win, a player must have three marks in a row, in a column, or on a diagonal. A draw occurs when the board is full and no one has won.

   Each player's position should be input as indexes into the tic-tac-toe board— that is, a row number, a space, and a column number. Make the program user-friendly.

   After each game, print out a diagram of the board showing the ending positions. Keep a count of the number of games each player has won and the number of draws. Before the beginning of each game, ask each player if he or she wishes to continue. If either player wishes to quit, print out the statistics and stop.

7. Photos taken in space by the Galileo spacecraft are sent back to earth as a stream of numbers. Each number represents a level of brightness. A large number represents a high brightness level, and a small number represents a low level. Your job is to take a matrix (a two-dimensional array) of the numbers and print it as a picture.

   One approach to generating a picture is to print a dark character (such as a $) when the brightness level is low, and to print a light character (such as a blank or a period) when the level is high. Unfortunately, errors in transmission sometimes occur. Thus, your program should first attempt to find and correct these errors. Assume a value is in error if it differs by more than 1 from each of its four neighboring values. Correct the erroneous value by giving it the average of its neighboring values, rounded to the nearest integer.

   Example:

	5	
4	2	5
	5	

   The 2 would be regarded as an error and would be given a corrected value of 5.

   Note that values on the corners or boundaries of the matrix have to be processed differently than the values on the interior. Your program should print an image of the uncorrected picture and then an image of the corrected picture.

8. The following diagram represents an island surrounded by water (shaded area).

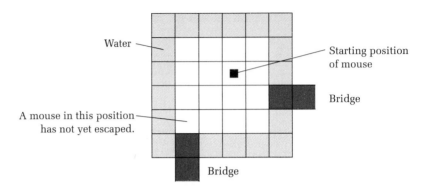

Two bridges lead out of the island. A mouse is placed on the black square. Write a program to make the mouse take a walk across the island. The mouse is allowed to travel one square at a time, either horizontally or vertically. A random number from 1 through 4 should be used to decide which direction the mouse is to take.* The mouse drowns when he hits the water; he escapes when he enters a bridge. You may generate a random number up to 100 times. If the mouse does not find his way by the hundredth try, he will die of starvation. Restart the mouse in a reinitialized array and go back and repeat the whole process. Count the number of times he escapes, drowns, and starves.

Input

First input line—the size of the array, including border of water and bridges (not larger than 20 × 20)

Next *N* input lines—the rows of the two-dimensional array, where the positions containing negative numbers represent the water, the positions in the edge containing a 0 represent the bridges, the position containing a 1 represents the starting position of the mouse, and all other positions contain 0s

Output

A line stating whether the mouse escaped, drowned, or starved

A line showing the mouse's starting position and the position of the two bridges

A map showing the frequency of the mouse's visits to each position

You should print the items above (double spaced between trips) for each trip by the mouse.

---

* Through the header file cstdlib, the C++ standard library supplies a value-returning, parameterless function named rand. Each time it is called, rand returns a random int in the range 0 through RAND_MAX, a constant defined in cstdlib (usually the same as INT_MAX). The following statement assigns to randNum a random integer in the range 1 through 4:

randNum = rand() % 4 + 1;

See Appendix C for further details.

9. In competitive diving, each diver makes three dives of varying degrees of difficulty. Nine judges score each dive from 0 through 10 in steps of 0.5. The total score is obtained by discarding the lowest and highest of the judges' scores, adding the remaining scores, and then multiplying the scores by the degree of difficulty. The divers take turns, and when the competition is finished, they are ranked according to score. Write a program to calculate the outcome of a competition, using the following input and output specifications.

   Input

   Number of divers

   Diver's name (ten characters), difficulty (`float`), and judges' ratings (nine `floats`)

   There is a line of data for each diver for each dive. All the data for Dive 1 are grouped together, then all for Dive 2, then all for Dive 3.

   Output

   The input data, echo printed in tabular form with appropriate headings—for example, Name, Difficulty, judge's number (1–9)

   A table that contains the following information:

   > Name   Dive 1   Dive 2   Dive 3   Total

   where Name is the diver's name; Dive 1, Dive 2, and Dive 3 are the total points received for a single dive, as described above; and Total is the overall total

Case Study Follow-Up

1. In the CheckLists program, the `ReadFirstList` function declares a parameter `firstList`. Would it be all right to prefix the declaration of `firstList` with the word `const`? Explain.
2. The CheckLists program compares two lists of integers. Exactly what changes would be necessary for the program to compare two lists of `float` values?
3. Modify the CheckLists program so that it works even if the lists are not the same length or they contain more than 500 values. Print appropriate error messages and stop the comparison.
4. Outline a testing strategy that fully tests the Election program.
5. The Election program is designed for 4 precincts and 4 candidates. Modify the program so that it works for 12 precincts and 3 candidates.

13

Array-Based Lists

G O A L S

- To be able to insert a value into a list.
- To be able to delete a specific value from a list.
- To be able to search for a specific value in a list.
- To be able to sort the components of a list into ascending or descending order.
- To be able to insert a value into a sorted list.
- To be able to delete a specific value from a sorted list.
- To be able to search for a specific value in a sorted list using a linear search.
- To be able to search for a specific value using a binary search.
- To be able to declare and use C strings.

Chapter 12 introduced the array, a data structure that is a collection of components of the same type given a single name. In general, a one-dimensional array is a structure used to hold a list of items. In this chapter, we examine algorithms that build and manipulate data stored as a list in a one-dimensional array. These algorithms are implemented as general-purpose functions that can be modified easily to work with many kinds of lists.

We also consider the *C string*, a special kind of built-in one-dimensional array that is used for storing character strings. We conclude with a case study that uses list algorithms developed in this chapter.

The List as an Abstract Data Type

As defined in Chapter 12, a one-dimensional array is a built-in data structure that consists of a fixed number of homogeneous components. One use for an array is to store a list of values. A list may contain fewer values than the number of places reserved in the array. In Chapter 12's Comparison of Two Lists case study, we used a variable numVals to keep track of the number of values currently stored in the array, and we employed subarray processing to prevent processing array components that were not part of the list of values. In Figure 12-16, you can see that the *array* goes from firstList[0] through firstList[499], but the *list* stored in the array goes from firstList[0] through firstList[numVals-1]. The number of places in the array is fixed, but the number of values in the list stored there may vary.

For a moment, let's think of the concept of a list not in terms of arrays but as a separate data type. We can define a **list** as a varying-length, linear collection of homogeneous components. That's quite a mouthful. By *linear* we mean that each component (except the first) has a unique component that comes before it and each component (except the last) has a unique component that comes after it. The **length** of a list—the number of values currently stored in the list—can vary during the execution of the program.

List   A variable-length, linear collection of homogeneous components.

Length   The number of values currently stored in a list.

Like any data type, a list must have associated with it a set of allowable operations. What kinds of operations would we want to define for a list? Here are some possibilities: create a list, add an item to a list, delete an item from a list, print a list, search a list for a particular value, sort a list into alphabetical or numerical order, and so on. When we define a data

type formally—by specifying its properties and the operations that preserve those properties—we are creating an abstract data type (ADT). In fact,
in Chapter 11 we proposed an ADT named IntList, a data type for a list of
up to 100 integer values. At the time, we did not implement this ADT
because we did not have at our disposal a suitable concrete data representation. Now that we are familiar with the idea of using a one-dimensional
array to represent a list, we can combine C++ classes and arrays to implement list ADTs.

Let's generalize the IntList ADT by (a) allowing the components to be
of *any* simple type or of type `string`, (b) replacing the maximum length of
100 with a maximum of `MAX_LENGTH`, a defined constant, and (c) including a wider variety of allowable operations. Here is the specification of the
more general ADT:

TYPE
  List
DOMAIN
  Each instance of type List is a collection of up to MAX_LENGTH compo-
  nents, each of type ItemType.
OPERATIONS
  Create an initially empty list.
  Report whether the list is empty (`true` or `false`).
  Report whether the list is full (`true` or `false`).
  Return the current length of the list.
  Insert an item into the list.
  Delete an item from the list.
  Search for a specified item, returning `true` or `false` according to
    whether the item is present in the list.
  Sort the list into ascending order.
  Print the list.

We can use a C++ class named `List` to represent the List ADT in our
programs. For the concrete data representation, we use two items: a one-
dimensional array to hold the list items, and an `int` variable that stores the
current length of the list. When we compile the `List` class, we need to
supply definitions for `MAX_LENGTH` and `ItemType`:

```
const int MAX_LENGTH = [_____] ;     // Maximum possible number of
                                       //    components needed
typedef [_____] ItemType;            // Type of each component
                                       //    (a simple type or the
                                       //     string class)
```

Here is the specification file for our List ADT. Notice that we use 50 for
`MAX_LENGTH` and `int` for `ItemType`. Notice also that the abstract operation

Create an initially empty list is implemented as the class constructor
List().

```
//*****************************************************************
// SPECIFICATION FILE (list.h)
// This file gives the specification of a list abstract data type.
// The list components are not assumed to be in order by value
//*****************************************************************

const int MAX_LENGTH = 50;       // Maximum possible number of
                                 //   components needed
typedef int ItemType;            // Type of each component
                                 //   (a simple type or string class)

class List
{
public:
    bool IsEmpty() const;
        // Postcondition:
        //     Function value == true, if list is empty
        //                    == false, otherwise

    bool IsFull() const;
        // Postcondition:
        //     Function value == true, if list is full
        //                    == false, otherwise

    int Length() const;
        // Postcondition:
        //     Function value == length of list

    void Insert( /* in */ ItemType item );
        // Precondition:
        //     NOT IsFull()
        //  && item is assigned
        // Postcondition:
        //     item is in list
        //  && Length() == Length()@entry + 1

    void Delete( /* in */ ItemType item );
        // Precondition:
        //     NOT IsEmpty()
        //  && item is assigned
        // Postcondition:
        //     IF item is in list at entry
        //           First occurrence of item is no longer in list
        //        && Length() == Length()@entry - 1
        //     ELSE
        //           List is unchanged
```

```
    bool IsPresent( /* in */ ItemType item ) const;
        // Precondition:
        //     item is assigned
        // Postcondition:
        //     Function value == true, if item is in list
        //                    == false, otherwise

    void SelSort();
        // Postcondition:
        //     List components are in ascending order of value

    void Print() const;
        // Postcondition:
        //     All components (if any) in list have been output

    List();
        // Constructor
        // Postcondition:
        //     Empty list is created
private:
    int     length;
    ItemType data[MAX_LENGTH];
};
```

In Chapter 11, we classified ADT operations as constructors, transformers, observers, and iterators. IsEmpty, IsFull, Length, IsPresent, and Print are observers. Insert, Delete, and SelSort are transformers. The class constructor is an ADT constructor operation.

The private part of the class declaration shows our data representation of a list: an int variable and an array (see Figure 13-1). However, notice that the preconditions and postconditions of the member functions mention nothing about an array. The abstraction is a list, not an array. The user of the class is interested only in manipulating lists of items and does not care how we implement a list. If we change to a different data representation (as we do in Chapter 15), neither the public interface nor the client code needs to be changed.

We now consider how to implement each of the ADT operations, given that the list items are stored in an array. Before we do so, however, we must distinguish between lists whose components must always be kept in alphabetical or numerical order (*sorted lists*) and lists in which the components are not arranged in any particular order (*unsorted lists*). We begin with unsorted lists.

FIGURE 13-1

myList, a Class
Object of
Type List

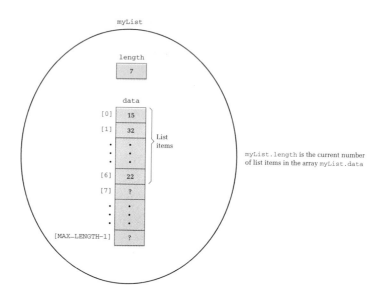

myList.length is the current number
of list items in the array myList.data

Unsorted Lists

Basic Operations

As we discussed in Chapter 11, an ADT is typically implemented in C++ by using a pair of files: the specification file (such as the preceding list.h file) and the implementation file, which contains the implementations of the class member functions. Here is how the implementation file list.cpp starts out:

```
//***********************************************************************
// IMPLEMENTATION FILE (list.cpp)
// This file implements the List class member functions
// List representation: a one-dimensional array and a length
//                      variable
//***********************************************************************
#include "list.h"
#include <iostream>

using namespace std;

// Private members of class:
//     int       length;              Length of the list
//     ItemType  data[MAX_LENGTH];    Array holding the list
```

Let's look now at the implementations of the basic list operations.

Creating an Empty List As Figure 13-1 shows, the list exists in the array elements data[0] through data[length-1]. To create an empty list, it is sufficient to set the length member to 0. We do not need to store any special values into the `data` array to make the list empty, because only those values in `data[0]` through `data[length-1]` are processed by the list algorithms.

In the `List` class, the appropriate place to initialize the list to be empty is the class constructor:

```
List::List()

// Constructor

// Postcondition:
//      length == 0

{
    length = 0;
}
```

One thing you will notice as we go through the `List` member functions is that the *implementation assertions* (the preconditions and postconditions appearing in the implementation file) are often stated differently from the *abstract assertions* (those located in the specification file). Abstract assertions are written in terms that are meaningful to the user of the ADT; implementation details should not be mentioned. In contrast, implementation assertions can be made more precise by referring directly to variables and algorithms in the implementation code. In the case of the `List` class constructor, the abstract postcondition is simply that an empty list has been created. On the other hand, the implementation postcondition

```
// Postcondition:
//      length == 0
```

is phrased in terms of our private data representation.

The IsEmpty Operation   This operation returns `true` if the list is empty and `false` if the list is not empty. Using our convention that `length` equals 0 if the list is empty, the implementation of this operation is straightforward.

```
bool List::IsEmpty() const

// Reports whether list is empty

// Postcondition:
//      Function value == true, if length == 0
//                     == false, otherwise

{
    return (length == 0);
}
```

The IsFull Operation   The list is full if there is no more room in the array holding the list items—that is, if the list length equals MAX_LENGTH.

```
bool List::IsFull() const

// Reports whether list is full

// Postcondition:
//     Function value == true, if length == MAX_LENGTH
//                    == false, otherwise

{
    return (length == MAX_LENGTH);
}
```

The Length Operation   This operation simply returns to the client the current length of the list.

```
int List::Length() const

// Returns current length of list

// Postcondition:
//     Function value == length

{
    return length;
}
```

The Print Operation   To output the components of the list, we can simply use a For loop that steps through the data array, printing each array element in sequence.

```
void List::Print() const

// Prints the list

// Postcondition:
//     Contents of data[0..length-1] have been output

{
    int index;     // Loop control and index variable

    for (index = 0; index < length; index++)
        cout << data[index] << endl;
}
```

Insertion and Deletion

To devise an algorithm for inserting a new item into the list, we first observe that we are working with an unsorted list and that the values do not have to be maintained in any particular order. Therefore, we can store a new value into the next available position in the array—data[length]—and then increment length. This algorithm brings up a question: Do we need to check that there is room in the list for the new item? We have two choices. The Insert function can test length against MAX_LENGTH and return an error flag if there isn't any room, or we can let the client code make the test before calling Insert (that is, make it a precondition that the list is not full). If you look back at the List class declaration in list.h, you can see that we have chosen the second approach. The client can use the IsFull operation to make sure the precondition is true. If the client fails to satisfy the precondition, the contract between client and function is broken, and the function is not required to satisfy the postcondition.

```
void List::Insert( /* in */ ItemType item )

// Inserts item into the list

// Precondition:
//      length < MAX_LENGTH
//   && item is assigned
// Postcondition:
//      data[length@entry] == item
//   && length == length@entry + 1

{
    data[length] = item;
    length++;
}
```

Deleting a component from a list consists of two parts: finding the component and removing it from the list. Before we can write the algorithm, we must know what to do if the component is not there. *Delete* can mean "Delete, if it's there" or "Delete, it *is* there." According to the List class declaration in list.h, we assume the first meaning; the code for the first definition works for the second as well but is not as efficient. We must start at the beginning of the list and search for the value to be deleted. If we find it, how do we remove it? We take the last value in the list (the one stored in data[length-1]), put it where the item to be deleted is located, and then decrement length. Moving the last item from its original position is appropriate only for an unsorted list because we don't need to preserve the order of the items in the list.

The definition "Delete, if it's there" requires a searching loop with a compound condition. We examine each component in turn and stop looking when we find the item to be deleted or when we have looked at all the items and know that it is not there.

```
void List::Delete( /* in */ ItemType item )

// Deletes item from the list, if it is there

// Precondition:
//      length > 0
//   && item is assigned
// Postcondition:
//      IF item is in data array at entry
//          First occurrence of item is no longer in array
//        && length == length@entry - 1
//      ELSE
//          length and data array are unchanged

{
    int index = 0;      // Index variable

    while (index < length && item != data[index])
        index++;

    if (index < length)
    {                                        // Remove item
        data[index] = data[length-1];
        length--;
    }
}
```

To see how the While loop and the subsequent If statement work, let's look at the two possibilities: Either item is in the list or it is not. If item is in the list, the loop terminates when the expression index < length is true and the expression item != data[index] is false. After the loop exit, the If statement finds the expression index < length to be true and removes the item. On the other hand, if item is not in the list, the loop terminates when the expression index < length is false—that is, when index becomes equal to length. Subsequently, the If condition is false, and the function returns without changing anything.

Sequential Search

In the Delete function, the algorithm we used to search for the item to be deleted is known as a *sequential* or *linear search* in an unsorted list. We use the same algorithm to implement the `IsPresent` function of the `List` class.

```
bool List::IsPresent( /* in */ ItemType item ) const

// Searches the list for item, reporting whether it was found

// Precondition:
//      item is assigned
// Postcondition:
//      Function value == true, if item is in data[0..length-1]
//                     == false, otherwise

{
    int index = 0;      // Index variable

    while (index < length && item != data[index])
        index++;

    return (index < length);
}
```

This algorithm is called a sequential search because we start at the beginning of the list and look at each item in sequence. We stop the search as soon as we find the item we are looking for (or when we reach the end of the list, concluding that the desired item is not present in the list).

We can use this algorithm in any program requiring a list search. In the form shown, it searches a list of `ItemType` components, provided that `ItemType` is an integral type or the `string` class. To use the function with a list of floating-point values, we must modify it so that the While statement tests for near equality rather than exact equality (for the reasons discussed in Chapter 10). In the following statement, we assume that `EPSILON` is defined as a global constant.

```
while (index < length && fabs(item - data[index]) >= EPSILON)
    index++;
```

The sequential search algorithm finds the first occurrence of the searched-for item. How would we modify it to find the last occurrence? We would initialize `index` to `length`–1 and decrement `index` each time through the loop, stopping when we found the item we wanted or when `index` became –1.

Before we leave this search algorithm, let's introduce a variation that makes the program more efficient, although a little more complex. The While loop contains a compound condition: It stops when it either finds `item` or reaches the end of the list. We can insert a copy of `item` into `data[length]`—that is, into the array component beyond the end of the list—as a sentinel. By doing so, we are guaranteed to find `item` in the list.

FIGURE 13-2
Sequential Search
with Copy of item
in data[length]

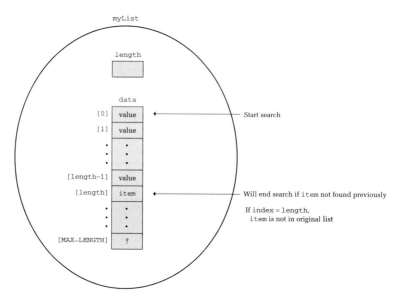

Then we can eliminate the condition that checks for the end of the list (index < length) (see Figure 13-2). Eliminating a condition saves the computer the time that would be required to test it. In this case, we save time during every iteration of the loop, so the savings add up quickly. Note, however, that we are gaining efficiency at the expense of space. We must declare the array size to be 1 larger than MAX_LENGTH to hold the sentinel value if the list becomes full. That is, we must change the private part of the class declaration as follows:

```
class List
{
    ⋮
private:
    int      length;
    ItemType data[MAX_LENGTH+1];
};
```

Figure 13-2 reflects this change. The last array element shows an index of MAX_LENGTH rather than MAX_LENGTH-1, as in Figure 13-1.

The following function, IsPresent2, implements this new algorithm. After the search loop terminates, the function returns true if index is less than length; otherwise, it returns false.

```
bool List::IsPresent2( /* in */ ItemType item ) const

// Searches the list for item, reporting whether it was found

// Precondition:
//      item is assigned
```

```
// Postcondition:
//     data[0..length-1] are the same as at entry
//  && data[length] is overwritten to aid in the search
//  && Function value == true, if item is in data[0..length-1]
//                    == false, otherwise

{
    int index = 0;      // Index variable

    data[length] = item;            // Store item at position beyond
                                    //   end of list
    while (item != data[index])
        index++;

    return (index < length);
}
```

Note that the declaration of our `List` class in the file `list.h` includes the member function `IsPresent` but not `IsPresent2`. We have presented `IsPresent2` only to show you an alternative approach to implementing the search operation.

Sorting

Although we are implementing an unsorted list ADT, there are times when the user of the `List` class may want to rearrange the list components into a certain order just before calling the `Print` function. For example, the user might want to put a list of stock numbers into either ascending or descending order, or the user might want to put a list of words into alphabetical order. In software development, arranging list items into order is a very common operation and is known as **sorting.**

Sorting   Arranging the components of a list into order (for instance, words into alphabetical order or numbers into ascending or descending order).

If you were given a sheet of paper with a column of 20 numbers on it and were asked to write the numbers in ascending order, you would probably do the following:

1. Make a pass through the list, looking for the smallest number.
2. Write it on the paper in a second column.
3. Cross the number off the original list.
4. Repeat the process, always looking for the smallest number remaining in the original list.
5. Stop when all the numbers have been crossed off.

We can implement this algorithm directly in C++, but we need two arrays—one for the original list and a second for the sorted list. If the list is large, we might not have enough memory for two copies of it. Also, how do we "cross off" an array component? We could simulate crossing off a value by replacing it with some dummy value like INT_MAX. That is, we would set the value of the crossed-off variable to something that would not interfere with the processing of the rest of the components. However, a slight variation of our hand-done algorithm allows us to sort the components *in place*. We do not have to use a second array; we can put a value into its proper place in the list by having it swap places with the component currently in that position.

We can state the algorithm as follows. We search for the smallest value in the list and exchange it with the component in the first position in the list. We search for the next-smallest value in the list and exchange it with the component in the second position in the list. This process continues until all the components are in their proper places.

FOR count going from 0 through length–2
    Find minimum value in data[count .. length–1]
    Swap minimum value with data[count]

Figure 13-3 illustrates how this algorithm works.

Observe that we perform length–1 passes through the list because count runs from 0 through length–2. The loop does not need to be executed when count equals length–1 because the last value, data[length–1], is in its proper place after the preceding components have been sorted.

This sort, known as the *straight selection sort,* belongs to a class of sorts called selection sorts. There are many types of sorting algorithms. Selection sorts are characterized by finding the smallest (or largest) value left in the unsorted portion at each iteration and swapping it with the value indexed by the iteration counter. Swapping the contents of two variables requires a temporary variable so that no values are lost (see Figure 13-4).

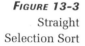

FIGURE 13-3

Straight
Selection Sort

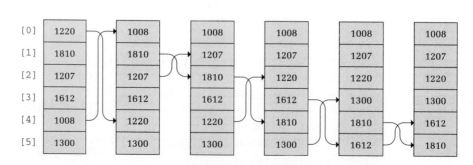

FIGURE 13-4
Swapping the
Contents of Two
Variables, x and y

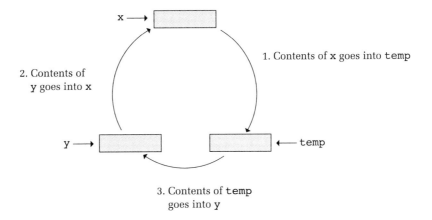

Here is the code for the sorting operation of the List class:

```
void List::SelSort()

// Sorts list into ascending order

// Postcondition:
//     data array contains the same values as data@entry, rearranged
//     into ascending order

{
    ItemType temp;              // Temporary variable
    int     passCount;          // Loop control variable
    int     searchIndx;         // Loop control variable
    int     minIndx;            // Index of minimum so far

    for (passCount = 0; passCount < length - 1; passCount++)
    {
        minIndx = passCount;

        // Find the index of the smallest component
        // in data[passCount..length-1]

        for (searchIndx = passCount + 1; searchIndx < length;
                                            searchIndx++)
            if (data[searchIndx] < data[minIndx])
                minIndx = searchIndx;

        // Swap data[minIndx] and data[passCount]

        temp = data[minIndx];
        data[minIndx] = data[passCount];
        data[passCount] = temp;
    }
}
```

Note that with each pass through the outer loop, we are looking for the minimum value in the rest of the list (data[passCount] through data[length-1]). Therefore, minIndx is initialized to passCount and the inner loop runs from searchIndx equal to passCount+1 through length-1. Upon exit from the inner loop, minIndx contains the position of the smallest value. (Note that the If statement is the only statement in the loop.)

Note also that we may swap a component with itself, which occurs if no value in the remaining list is smaller than data[passCount]. We could avoid this unnecessary swap by checking to see if minIndx is equal to passCount. Because this comparison would be made during each iteration of the outer loop, it is more efficient not to check for this possibility and just to swap something with itself occasionally. If the components we are sorting are much more complex than simple numbers, we might reconsider this decision.

This algorithm sorts the components into ascending order. To sort them into descending order, we would scan for the maximum value instead of the minimum value. To do so, we would simply change the relational operator in the inner loop from < to >. Of course, minIndx would no longer be an appropriate identifier and should be changed to maxIndx.

By providing the user of the List class with a sorting operation, we have not turned our unsorted list ADT into a sorted list ADT. The Insert and Delete algorithms we wrote do not preserve ordering by value. Insert places a new item at the end of the list, regardless of its value, and Delete moves the last item to a different position in the list. After SelSort has executed, the list items remain in sorted order only until the next insertion or deletion takes place. We now look at a sorted list ADT in which all the list operations cooperate to preserve the sorted order of the list components.

Sorted Lists

In the List class, the IsPresent and IsPresent2 algorithms both assume that the list to be searched is unsorted. A drawback to searching an unsorted list is that we must scan the entire list to discover that the search item is not there. Think what it would be like if your city telephone book contained people's names in random rather than alphabetical order. To look up Mary Anthony's phone number, you would have to start with the first name in the phone book and scan sequentially, page after page, until you found it. In the worst case, you might have to examine tens of thousands of names only to find out that Mary's name is not in the book.

Of course, telephone books *are* alphabetized, and the alphabetical ordering makes searching easier. If Mary Anthony's name is not in the book, you discover this fact quickly by starting with the A's and stopping the search as soon as you have passed the place where her name should be.

Let's define a sorted list ADT in which the components always remain in order by value, no matter what operations are applied. Below is the slist.h file that contains the declaration of a SortedList class.

```
//******************************************************************
// SPECIFICATION FILE (slist.h)
// This file gives the specification of a sorted list abstract data
// type.  The list components are maintained in ascending order
// of value
//******************************************************************

const int MAX_LENGTH = 50;        // Maximum possible number of
                                  //   components needed
                                  // Requirement:
                                  //   MAX_LENGTH <= INT_MAX/2
typedef int ItemType;             // Type of each component
                                  //   (a simple type or string class)

class SortedList
{
public:
    bool IsEmpty() const;
        // Postcondition:
        //      Function value == true, if list is empty
        //                     == false, otherwise

    bool IsFull() const;
        // Postcondition:
        //      Function value == true, if list is full
        //                     == false, otherwise

    int Length() const;
        // Postcondition:
        //      Function value == length of list

    void Insert( /* in */ ItemType item );
        // Precondition:
        //      NOT IsFull()
        //   && item is assigned
        // Postcondition:
        //      item is in list
        //   && Length() == Length()@entry + 1
        //   && List components are in ascending order of value

    void Delete( /* in */ ItemType item );
        // Precondition:
        //      NOT IsEmpty()
```

```
        //    && item is assigned
        // Postcondition:
        //       IF item is in list at entry
        //            First occurrence of item is no longer in list
        //            && Length() == Length()@entry - 1
        //            && List components are in ascending order of value
        //       ELSE
        //            List is unchanged

    bool IsPresent( /* in */ ItemType item ) const;
        // Precondition:
        //       item is assigned
        // Postcondition:
        //       Function value == true, if item is in list
        //                      == false, otherwise

    void Print() const;
        // Postcondition:
        //       All components (if any) in list have been output

    SortedList();
        // Constructor
        // Postcondition:
        //       Empty list is created
private:
    int       length;
    ItemType data[MAX_LENGTH];
    void      BinSearch( ItemType, bool&, int& ) const;
};
```

How does the declaration of `SortedList` differ from the declaration of our original `List` class? Apart from a few changes in the documentation comments, there are only two differences:

1. The `SortedList` class does not supply a sorting operation to the client. Such an operation is needless, because the list components are assumed to be kept in sorted order at all times.

2. The `SortedList` class has an additional class member in the private part: a `BinSearch` function. This function is an auxiliary ("helper") function that is used only by other class member functions and is inaccessible to clients. We discuss its purpose when we examine the class implementation.

Let's look at what changes, if any, are required in the algorithms for the ADT operations, given that we are now working with a sorted list instead of an unsorted list.

Basic Operations

The algorithms for the class constructor, IsEmpty, IsFull, Length, and Print are identical to those in the List class. The constructor sets the private data member length to 0, IsEmpty reports whether length equals 0, IsFull reports whether length equals MAX_LENGTH, Length returns the value of length, and Print outputs the list items from first to last.

Insertion

To add a new value to an already sorted list, we could store the new value at data[length], increment length, and sort the array again. However, such a solution is *not* an efficient way of solving the problem. Inserting five new items results in five separate sorting operations.

   If we were to insert a value by hand into a sorted list, we would write the new value out to the side and draw a line showing where it belongs. To find this position, we start at the top and scan the list until we find a value greater than the one we are inserting. The new value goes in the list just before that point.

   We can use a similar process in our Insert function. We find the proper place in the list using the by-hand algorithm. Instead of writing the value to the side, we shift all the values larger than the new one down one place to make room for it. The main algorithm is expressed as follows, where item is the value being inserted.

```
WHILE place not found AND more places to look
   IF item > current component in list
            Increment current position
   ELSE
            Place found
Shift remainder of list down
Insert item
Increment length
```

Assuming that index is the place where item is to be inserted, the algorithm for Shift List Down is

```
Set data[length]     =     data[length–1]
Set data[length–1]   =     data[length–2]
   ⋮                          ⋮
Set data[index+1]    =     data[index]
```

This algorithm is illustrated in Figure 13-5.

FIGURE 13-5
Inserting into a
Sorted List

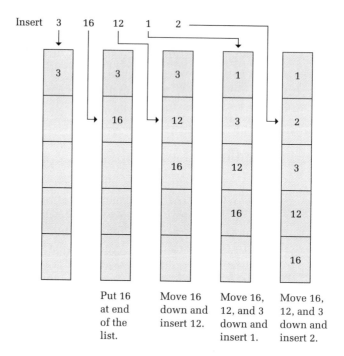

This algorithm is based on how we would accomplish the task by hand. Often, such an adaptation is the best way to solve a problem. However, in this case, further thought reveals a slightly better way. Notice that we search from the front of the list (people always do), and we shift down from the end of the list upward. We can combine the searching and shifting by beginning at the *end* of the list.

If item is the new item to be inserted, compare item to the value in data[length-1]. If item is *less*, put data[length-1] into data[length] and compare item to the value in data[length-2]. This process continues until you find the place where item is greater than or equal to the item in the list. Store item directly below it. Here is the algorithm:

```
Set index = length – 1
WHILE index ≥ 0 AND item < data[index]
    Set data[index + 1] = data[index]
    Decrement index
Set data[index + 1] = item
Increment length
```

What about duplicates? The algorithm continues until an item is found that is less than the one we are inserting. Therefore, the new item is inserted below a duplicate value (if one is there). Here is the code:

```
void SortedList::Insert( /* in */ ItemType item )

// Inserts item into the list

// Precondition:
//      length < MAX_LENGTH
//   && data[0..length-1] are in ascending order
//   && item is assigned
// Postcondition:
//      item is in the list
//   && length == length@entry + 1
//   && data[0..length-1] are in ascending order

{
    int index;      // Index and loop control variable

    index = length - 1;
    while (index >= 0 && item < data[index])
    {
        data[index+1] = data[index];
        index--;
    }
    data[index+1] = item;           // Insert item
    length++;
}
```

Notice that this algorithm works even if the list is empty. When the list is empty, `length` is 0 and the body of the While loop is not entered. So `item` is stored into `data[0]`, and `length` is incremented to 1. Does the algorithm work if `item` is the smallest? The largest? Let's see. If `item` is the smallest, the loop body is executed `length` times, and `index` is −1. Thus, `item` is stored into position 0, where it belongs. If `item` is the largest, the loop body is not entered. The value of `index` is still `length − 1`, so `item` is stored into `data[length]`, where it belongs.

Are you surprised that the general case also takes care of the special cases? This situation does not happen all the time, but it occurs often enough that it is good programming practice to start with the general case. If we begin with the special cases, we usually generate a correct solution, but we may not realize that we don't need to handle the special cases separately. So begin with the general case, then treat as special cases only those situations that the general case does not handle correctly.

This algorithm is the basis for another general-purpose sorting algorithm—an *insertion sort*. In an insertion sort, values are inserted one at a time into a list that was originally empty. An insertion sort is often used when input data must be sorted; each value is put into its proper place as it is read. We use this technique in the Problem-Solving Case Study at the end of this chapter.

Sequential Search

When we search for an item in an unsorted list, we won't discover that the item is missing until we reach the end of the list. If the list is already sorted, we know that an item is missing when we pass the place where it should be in the list. For example, if a list contains the values

```
 7
11
13
76
98
102
```

and we are looking for 12, we need only compare 12 with 7, 11, and 13 to know that 12 is not in the list.

If the search item is greater than the current list component, we move on to the next component. If the item is equal to the current component, we have found what we are looking for. If the item is less than the current component, then we know that it is not in the list. In either of the last two cases, we stop looking. We can restate this algorithmically with the following code, in which found is set to true if the search item was found.

```
// Sequential search in a sorted list

index = 0;
while (index < length && item > data[index])
    index++;

found = (index < length && item == data[index]);
```

On average, searching a sorted list in this way takes the same number of iterations to find an item as searching an unsorted list. The advantage of this new algorithm is that we find out sooner if an item is missing. Thus, it is slightly more efficient; however, it works only on a sorted list.

We do not use this algorithm to implement the SortedList::
IsPresent function. There is a better algorithm, which we look at next.

Binary Search

There is a second search algorithm on a sorted list that is considerably faster both for finding an item and for discovering that an item is missing. This algorithm is called a *binary search*. A binary search is based on the principle of successive approximation. The algorithm divides the list in half (divides by 2—that's why it's called *binary* search) and decides which half to look in next. Division of the selected portion of the list is repeated until the item is found or it is determined that the item is not in the list.

This method is analogous to the way in which we look up a word in a dictionary. We open the dictionary in the middle and compare the word with one on the page that we turned to. If the word we're looking for comes before this word, we continue our search in the left-hand section of the dictionary. Otherwise, we continue in the right-hand section of the dictionary. We repeat this process until we find the word. If it is not there, we realize that either we have misspelled the word or our dictionary isn't complete.

The algorithm for a binary search is given below. The list of values is in the array data, and the value being looked for is item (see Figure 13-6).

1. Compare item to data[middle]. If item = data[middle], then we have found it. If item < data[middle], then look in the first half of data. If item > data[middle], then look in the second half of data.
2. Redefine data to be the half of data that we search next, and repeat step 1.
3. Stop when we have found item or know it is missing. We know it's missing when there is nowhere else to look and we still have not found it.

This algorithm should make sense. With each comparison, at best, we find the item for which we are searching; at worst, we eliminate half of the remaining list from consideration.

We need to keep track of the first possible place to look (first) and the last possible place to look (last). At any one time, we are looking only

FIGURE 13-6
Binary Search

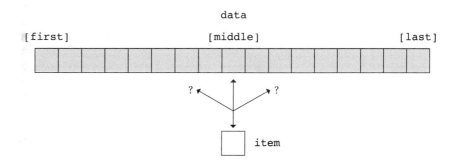

in data[first] through data[last]. When the function begins, first is set to 0 and last is set to length−1 to encompass the entire list.

Our three previous search algorithms have been Boolean observer operations. They just answer the question, Is this item in the list? Let's code the binary search as a void function that not only asks if the item is in the list but also asks which one it is (if it's there). To do so, we need to add two parameters to the parameter list: a Boolean flag found (to tell us whether the item is in the list) and an integer variable position (to tell us which item it is). If found is false, position is undefined.

```
void SortedList::BinSearch(
       /* in */  ItemType item,         // Item to be found
       /* out */ bool&    found,         // True if item is found
       /* out */ int&     position ) const // Location if found

// Searches list for item, returning the index
// of item if item was found.

// Precondition:
//     length <= INT_MAX / 2
//   && data[0..length-1] are in ascending order
//   && item is assigned
// Postcondition:
//     IF item is in the list
//         found == true  &&  data[position] contains item
//     ELSE
//         found == false  &&  position is undefined

{
    int first = 0;           // Lower bound on list
    int last = length - 1;   // Upper bound on list
    int middle;              // Middle index

    found = false;
    while (last >= first && !found)
    {
        middle = (first + last) / 2;
        if (item < data[middle])
            // Assert: item is not in data[middle..last]
            last = middle - 1;
        else if (item > data[middle])
            // Assert: item is not in data[first..middle]
            first = middle + 1;
        else
            // Assert: item == data[middle]
            found = true;
    }
    if (found)
        position = middle;
}
```

Should BinSearch be a public member of the SortedList class? No. The function returns the index of the array element where the item was found. An array index is useless to a client of SortedList. The array containing the list items is encapsulated within the private part of the class and is inaccessible to clients. If you review the SortedList class declaration, you'll see that BinSearch is a *private*, not public, class member. We intend to use it as a helper function when we implement the public operations IsPresent and Delete.

Let's do a code walk-through of the binary search algorithm. The value being searched for is 24. Figure 13-7a shows the values of first, last, and middle during the first iteration. In this iteration, 24 is compared with 103, the value in data[middle]. Because 24 is less than 103, last becomes middle-1 and first stays the same. Figure 13-7b shows the situation during the second iteration. This time, 24 is compared with 72, the value in data[middle]. Because 24 is less than 72, last becomes middle-1 and first again stays the same.

In the third iteration (Figure 13-7c), middle and first are both 0. The value 24 is compared with 12, the value in data[middle]. Because 24 is greater than 12, first becomes middle+1. In the fourth iteration (Figure 13-7d), first, last, and middle are all the same. Again, 24 is compared with the value in data[middle]. Because 24 is less than 64, last becomes middle-1. Now that last is less than first, the process stops; found is false.

The binary search is the most complex algorithm that we have examined so far. The following table shows first, last, middle, and data[middle] for searches of the values 106, 400, and 406, using the same data as in the previous example. Examine the results in this table carefully.

item	first	last	middle	data[middle]	*Termination of Loop*
106	0	10	5	103	
	6	10	8	200	
	6	7	6	106	found = true
400	0	10	5	103	
	6	10	8	200	
	9	10	9	300	
	10	10	10	400	found = true
406	0	10	5	103	
	6	10	8	200	
	9	10	9	300	
	10	10	10	400	
	11	10			last < first
					found = false

FIGURE 13-7
Code Walk-
Through of
BinSearch
Function (Search
Item Is 24)

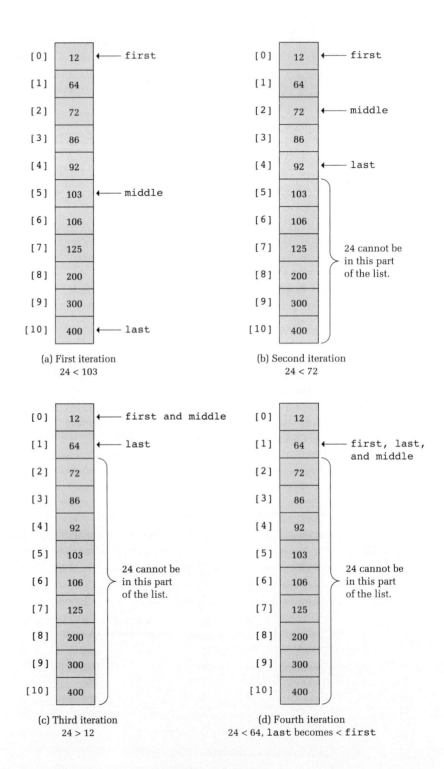

(a) First iteration
24 < 103

(b) Second iteration
24 < 72

(c) Third iteration
24 > 12

(d) Fourth iteration
24 < 64, last becomes < first

The calculation

```
middle = (first + last) / 2;
```

explains why the function precondition restricts the value of `length` to `INT_MAX/2`. If the item being searched for happens to reside in the last position of the list (for example, when `item` equals 400 in our sample list), then `first + last` equals `length + length`. If `length` is greater than `INT_MAX/2`, the sum `length + length` would produce an integer overflow.

Notice in the table that whether we searched for 106, 400, or 406, the loop never executed more than four times. It never executes more than four times in a list of 11 components because the list is being cut in half each time through the loop. The table below compares a sequential search and a binary search in terms of the average number of iterations needed to find an item.

	Average Number of Iterations	
Length of List	Sequential Search	Binary Search
10	5.5	2.9
100	50.5	5.8
1000	500.5	9.0
10,000	5000.5	12.4

If the binary search is so much faster, why not use it all the time? It certainly is faster in terms of the number of times through the loop, but more computations are performed within the binary search loop than in the other search algorithms. So if the number of components in the list is small (say, less than 20), the sequential search algorithms are faster because they perform less work at each iteration. As the number of components in the list increases, the binary search algorithm becomes relatively more efficient. Remember, however, that the binary search requires the list to be sorted, and sorting takes time. Keep three factors in mind when you are deciding which search algorithm to use:

1. The length of the list to be searched
2. Whether or not the list is already sorted
3. The number of times the list is to be searched

Given the `BinSearch` function (a private member of the `SortedList` class), it's easy to implement the `IsPresent` function (a public member of the class).

```
bool SortedList::IsPresent( /* in */ ItemType item ) const

// Searches the list for item, reporting whether it was found

// Precondition:
//     length <= INT_MAX / 2
//  && data[0..length-1] are in ascending order
//  && item is assigned
// Postcondition:
//     Function value == true, if item is in data[0..length-1]
//                    == false, otherwise

{
    bool found;       // True if item is found
    int position;     // Required (but unused) argument for
                      //    the call to BinSearch

    BinSearch(item, found, position);
    return found;
}
```

The body of `IsPresent` calls `BinSearch`, obtaining the result of the search in the variables `found` and `position`. Like the children's game of Pass It On, `IsPresent` receives the value of `found` from `BinSearch` and simply passes it on to the client (via the `return` statement). The body of `IsPresent` is not interested in where the item was found, so it ignores the value returned in the `position` argument. Why did we include this third argument when we designed `BinSearch`? The answer is that the `Delete` operation, which we look at next, calls `BinSearch` and *does* use the `position` argument.

Deletion

In the `List::Delete` function, we deleted an item by moving up the last component in the list to fill the deleted item's position. Although this algorithm is fine for unsorted lists, it won't work for sorted lists. Moving the last component to an arbitrary position in the list is almost certain to disturb the sorted order of the components. We need a new algorithm for sorted lists.

Let's call `BinSearch` to tell us the position of the item to be deleted. Then we can "squeeze out" the deleted item by shifting up all the remaining array elements by one position:

BinSearch(item, found, position)
IF found
   Shift remainder of list up
   Decrement length

The algorithm for Shift List Up is

Set data[position]   =   data[position+1]
Set data[position+1] =   data[position+2]
       ⋮   ⋮
Set data[length-2]   =   data[length-1]

Here is the coded version of this algorithm:

```
void SortedList::Delete( /* in */ ItemType item )

// Deletes item from the list, if it is there

// Precondition:
//     0 < length <= INT_MAX/2
//     && data[0..length-1] are in ascending order
//     && item is assigned
// Postcondition:
//     IF item is in data array at entry
//           First occurrence of item is no longer in array
//         && length == length@entry - 1
//         && data[0..length-1] are in ascending order
//     ELSE
//         length and data array are unchanged

{
    bool found;        // True if item is found
    int position;      // Position of item, if found
    int index;         // Index and loop control variable

    BinSearch(item, found, position);
    if (found)
    {
        // Shift data[position..length-1] up one position

        for (index = position; index < length - 1; index++)
            data[index] = data[index+1];
        length--;
    }
}
```

THEORETICAL FOUNDATIONS

Complexity of Searching and Sorting

We introduced Big-*O* notation in Chapter 6 as a way of comparing the work done by different algorithms. Let's apply it to the algorithms that we've developed in this chapter and see how they compare with each other. In each algorithm, we start with a list containing some number of values, *N*.

In the worst case, our `List::IsPresent` function scans all *N* values to locate an item. Thus, it requires *N* steps to execute. On average, `List::IsPresent` takes roughly *N*/2 steps to find an item; however, recall that in Big-*O* notation, we ignore constant factors (as well as lower-order terms). Thus, function `List::IsPresent` is an order *N*–that is, an *O(N)*–algorithm.

`List::IsPresent2` is also an *O(N)* algorithm because even though we saved a comparison on each loop iteration, the same number of iterations are performed. However, making the loop more efficient without changing the number of iterations decreases the constant (the number of steps) that *N* is multiplied by in the algorithm's work formula. Thus, function `List::IsPresent2` is said to be a constant factor faster than `List::IsPresent`.

What about the algorithm we presented for a sequential search in a sorted list? The number of iterations is decreased for the case in which the item is missing from the list. However, all we have done is take a case that would require *N* steps and reduce its time, on average, to *N*/2 steps. Therefore, this algorithm is also *O(N)*.

Now consider `BinSearch`. In the worst case, it eliminates half of the remaining list components on each iteration. Thus, the worst-case number of iterations is equal to the number of times *N* must be divided by 2 to eliminate all but one value. This number is computed by taking the logarithm, base 2, of *N* (written $\log_2 N$). Here are some examples of $\log_2 N$ for different values of *N*:

N	$Log_2 N$
2	1
4	2
8	3
16	4
32	5
1024	10
32,768	15
1,048,576	20
33,554,432	25
1,073,741,824	30

As you can see, for a list of over 1 billion values, `BinSearch` takes only 30 iterations. It is definitely the best choice for searching large lists. Algorithms such as `BinSearch` are said to be of *logarithmic order.*

Now let's turn to sorting. Function `SelSort` contains nested For loops. The total number of iterations is the product of the iterations performed by the two loops. The outer loop executes *N* – 1 times. The inner loop also starts out executing *N* – 1 times, but steadily decreases until it performs just one iteration: The inner loop executes *N*/2 iterations. The total number of iterations is thus

$$\frac{(N-1) \times N}{2}$$

Ignoring the constant factor and lower-order term, this is N^2 iterations, and `SelSort` is an $O(N^2)$ algorithm. Whereas `BinSearch` takes only 30 iterations to search a sorted array of 1 billion values, putting the array into order takes `SelSort` approximately 1 billion times 1 billion iterations!

We mentioned that the `SortedList::Insert` algorithm forms the basis for an insertion sort, in which values are inserted into a sorted list as they are input. On average, `SortedList::Insert` must shift down half of the values (*N*/2) in the list; thus, it is an $O(N)$ algorithm. If `SortedList::Insert` is called for each input value, we are executing an $O(N)$ algorithm *N* times; therefore, an insertion sort is an $O(N^2)$ algorithm.

Is every sorting algorithm $O(N^2)$? Most of the simpler ones are, but $O(N \times \log_2 N)$ sorting algorithms exist. Algorithms that are $O(N \times \log_2 N)$ are much closer in performance to $O(N)$ algorithms than are $O(N^2)$ algorithms. For example, if *N* is 1 million, then an $O(N^2)$ algorithm takes a million times a million (1 trillion) iterations, but an $O(N \times \log_2 N)$ algorithm takes only 20 million iterations—that is, it is 20 times slower than the $O(N)$ algorithm but 50,000 times faster than the $O(N^2)$ algorithm.

Now let's turn our attention to another example of array-based lists—a special kind of array that is useful when working with alphanumeric character data.

Understanding Character Strings

Ever since Chapter 2, we have been using the `string` class to store and manipulate character strings.

```
string name;

name = "James Smith";
len = name.length();
    ⋮
```

In some contexts, we think of a string as a single unit of data. In other contexts, we treat it as a group of individually accessible characters. In particular, we think of a string as a variable-length, linear collection of homogeneous components (of type char). Does this sound familiar? It should. As an abstraction, a string is a list of characters that, at any moment in time, has a length associated with it.

Thinking of a string as an ADT, how would we implement the ADT? There are many ways to implement strings. Programmers have specified and implemented their own string classes—the string class from the standard library, for instance. And the C++ language has its own built-in notion of a string: the **C string.** In C++, a string constant (or string literal, or literal string) is a sequence of characters enclosed by double quotes:

```
"Hi"
```

A string constant is stored as a char array with enough components to hold each specified character plus one more—the *null character.* The null character, which is the first character in both the ASCII and EBCDIC character sets, has internal representation 0. In C++, the escape sequence \0 stands for the null character. When the compiler encounters the string "Hi" in a program, it stores the three characters 'H', 'i', and '\0' into a three-element, anonymous (unnamed) char array as follows:

Unnamed array

[0]	'H'
[1]	'i'
[2]	'\0'

The C string is the only kind of C++ array for which there exists an aggregate constant—the string constant. Notice that in a C++ program, the symbols 'A' denote a single character, whereas the symbols "A" denote two: the character 'A' and the null character.*

In addition to C string constants, we can create C string *variables.* To do so, we explicitly declare a char array and store into it whatever characters we want to, finishing with the null character. Here's an example:

---

* *C string* is not an official term used in C++ language manuals. Such manuals typically use the term *string.* However, we use *C string* to distinguish between the general concept of a string and the built-in array representation defined by the C and C++ languages.

```
char myStr[8];    // Room for 7 significant characters plus '\0'

myStr[0] = 'H';
myStr[1] = 'i';
myStr[2] = '\0';
```

C string   In C and C++, a null-terminated sequence of characters stored in a `char` array.

In C++, all C strings (constants or variables) are assumed to be null-terminated. This convention is agreed upon by all C++ programmers and standard library functions. The null character serves as a sentinel value; it allows algorithms to locate the end of the string. For example, here is a function that determines the length of any C string, not counting the terminating null character:

```
int StrLength( /* in */ const char str[] )

// Precondition:
//      str holds a null-terminated string
// Postcondition:
//      Function value == number of characters in str (excluding '\0')

{
    int i = 0;    // Index variable

    while (str[i] != '\0')
        i++;
    return i;
}
```

The value of `i` is the correct value for this function to return. If the array being examined is

[0]	'B'
[1]	'y'
[2]	'\0'
[3]	
	. . .

then i equals 2 at loop exit. The string length is therefore 2.

     The argument to the StrLength function can be a C string variable, as in the function call

```
cout << StrLength(myStr);
```

or it can be a string constant:

```
cout << StrLength("Hello");
```

In the first case, the base address of the myStr array is sent to the function, as we discussed in Chapter 12. In the second case, a base address is also sent to the function—the base address of the unnamed array that the compiler has set aside for the string constant.

     There is one more thing we should say about our StrLength function. A C++ programmer would not actually write this function. The standard library supplies several string-processing functions, one of which is named strlen and does exactly what our StrLength function does. Later in the chapter, we look at strlen and other library functions.

Initializing C Strings

In Chapter 12, we showed how to initialize an array in its declaration by specifying a list of initial values within braces, like this:

```
int delta[5] = {25, -3, 7, 13, 4};
```

To initialize a C string variable in its declaration, you could use the same technique:

```
char message[8] = {'W', 'h', 'o', 'o', 'p', 's', '!', '\0'};
```

However, C++ allows a more convenient way to initialize a C string. You can simply initialize the array by using a string constant:

```
char message[8] = "Whoops!";
```

This shorthand notation is unique to C strings because there is no other kind of array for which there are aggregate constants.

We said in Chapter 12 that you can omit the size of an array when you initialize it in its declaration (in which case, the compiler determines its size). This feature is often used with C strings because it keeps you from having to count the number of characters. For example,

```
char promptMsg[] = "Enter a positive number:";   // Size is 25
char errMsg[] = "Value must be positive.";       // Size is 24
```

Be very careful about one thing: C++ treats initialization (in a declaration) and assignment (in an assignment statement) as two distinct operations. Different rules apply. Remember that array initialization is legal, but aggregate array assignment is not.

```
char myStr[20] = "Hello";    // OK
   ⋮
myStr = "Howdy";             // Not allowed
```

C String Input and Output

In Chapter 12, we emphasized that C++ does not provide aggregate operations on arrays. There is no aggregate assignment, aggregate comparison, or aggregate arithmetic on arrays. We also said that aggregate input/output of arrays is not possible, with one exception. C strings are that exception. Let's look first at output.

To output the contents of an array that is *not* a C string, you aren't allowed to do this:

```
int alpha[100];
   ⋮
cout << alpha;    // Not allowed
```

Instead, you must write a loop and print the array elements one at a time. However, aggregate output of a null-terminated `char` array (that is, a C string) is valid. The C string can be a constant (as we've been doing since Chapter 2):

```
cout << "Results are:";
```

or it can be a variable:

```
char msg[8] = "Welcome";
    ⋮
cout << msg;
```

In both cases, the insertion operator (<<) outputs each character in the array until the null character is found. It is up to you to double-check that the terminating null character is present in the array. If not, the << operator will march through the array and into the rest of memory, printing out bytes until—just by chance—it encounters a byte whose integer value is 0.

To input C strings, we have several options. The first is to use the extraction operator (>>), which behaves exactly the same as with `string` class objects. When reading input characters into a C string variable, the >> operator skips leading whitespace characters and then reads successive characters into the array, stopping at the first trailing whitespace character (which is not consumed, but remains as the first character waiting in the input stream). The >> operator also takes care of adding the null character to the end of the string. For example, assume we have the following code:

```
char firstName[31];    // Room for 30 characters plus '\0'
char lastName[31];

cin >> firstName >> lastName;
```

If the input stream initially looks like this (where ❏ denotes a blank):

❏❏John❏Smith❏❏❏25

then our input statement stores 'J', 'o', 'h', 'n', and '\0' into `firstName[0]` through `firstName[4]`; stores 'S', 'm', 'i', 't', 'h', and '\0' into `lastName[0]` through `lastName[5]`; and leaves the input stream as

❏❏❏25

The >> operator, however, has two potential drawbacks.

1. If the array isn't large enough to hold the sequence of input characters (and the '\0'), the >> operator will continue to store characters into memory past the end of the array.
2. The >> operator cannot be used to input a string that has blanks within it. (It stops reading as soon as it encounters the first whitespace character.)

To cope with these limitations, we can use a variation of the get function, a member of the istream class. We have used the get function to input a single character, even if it is a whitespace character:

```
cin.get(inputChar);
```

The get function also can be used to input C strings, in which case the function call requires two arguments. The first is the array name and the second is an int expression.

```
cin.get(myStr, charCount + 1);
```

The get function does not skip leading whitespace characters and continues until it either has read charCount characters or it reaches the newline character '\n', whichever comes first. It then appends the null character to the end of the string. With the statements

```
char oneLine[81];    // Room for 80 characters plus '\0'
  ⋮
cin.get(oneLine, 81);
```

the get function reads and stores an entire input line (to a maximum of 80 characters), embedded blanks and all. If the line has fewer than 80 characters, reading stops at '\n' but does not consume it. The newline character is now the first one waiting in the input stream. To read two consecutive lines worth of strings, it is necessary to consume the newline character:

```
char dummy;
  ⋮
cin.get(string1, 81);
cin.get(dummy);          // Eat newline before next "get"
cin.get(string2, 81);
```

The first function call reads characters up to, but not including, the '\n'. If the input of dummy were omitted, then the input of string2 would read *no* characters because '\n' would immediately be the first character waiting in the stream.

Finally, the ignore function—introduced in Chapter 4—can be useful in conjunction with the get function. Recall that the statement

```
cin.ignore(200, '\n');
```

says to skip at most 200 input characters but stop if a newline was read. (The newline character *is* consumed by this function.) If a program inputs a long string from the user but only wants to retain the first four characters of the response, here is a way to do it:

```
char response[5];        // Room for 4 characters plus '\0'

cin.get(response, 5);    // Input at most 4 characters
cin.ignore(100, '\n');   // Skip remaining chars up to and
                         //   including '\n'
```

The value 100 in the last statement is arbitrary. Any "large enough" number will do.

Here is a table that summarizes the differences between the >> operator and the `get` function when reading C strings:

Statement	Skips Leading Whitespace?	Stops Reading When?
`cin >> inputStr;`	Yes	At the first trailing whitespace character (which is *not* consumed)
`cin.get(inputStr, 21);`	No	When either 20 characters are read or '\n' is encountered (which is *not* consumed)

Finally, we revisit a topic that came up in Chapter 4. Certain library functions and member functions of system-supplied classes require C strings as arguments. An example is the `ifstream` class member function named `open`. To open a file, we pass the name of the file as a C string, either a constant or a variable:

```
ifstream file1;
ifstream file2;
char     fileName[51];   // Max. 50 characters plus '\0'

file1.open("students.dat");
cin.get(fileName, 51);            // Read at most 50 characters
cin.ignore(100, '\n');            // Skip rest of input line
file2.open(fileName);
```

As discussed in Chapter 4, if our file name is contained in a `string` class object, we still can use the `open` function, *provided* we use the `string` class member function named `c_str` to convert the string to a C string:

```
ifstream inFile;
string    fileName;

cin >> fileName;
inFile.open(fileName.c_str());
```

Comparing these two code segments, you can observe a major advantage of the `string` class over C strings: A string in a `string` class object has unbounded length, whereas the length of a C string is bounded by the array size, which is fixed at compile time.

C String Library Routines

Through the header file `cstring`, the C++ standard library provides a large assortment of C string operations. In this section, we discuss three of these library functions: `strlen`, which returns the length of a string; `strcmp`, which compares two strings using the relations less-than, equal, and greater-than; and `strcpy`, which copies one string to another. Here is a summary of `strlen`, `strcmp`, and `strcpy`:

Header File	Function	Function Value	Effect
`<cstring>`	`strlen(str)`	Integer length of `str` (excluding '\0')	Computes length of `str`
`<cstring>`	`strcmp(str1, str2)`	An integer < 0, if `str1` < `str2` The integer 0, if `str1` = `str2` An integer > 0, if `str1` > `str2`	Compares `str1` and `str2`
`<cstring>`	`strcpy(toStr, fromStr)`	Base address of `toStr` (usually ignored)	Copies `fromStr` (including '\0') to `toStr`, overwriting what was there; `toStr` must be large enough to hold the result

The `strlen` function is similar to the `StrLength` function we wrote earlier. It returns the number of characters in a C string prior to the terminating '\0'. Here's an example of a call to the function:

```
#include <cstring>
    ⋮
char subject[] = "Computer Science";

cout << strlen(subject);    // Prints 16
```

The `strcpy` routine is important because aggregate assignment with the = operator is not allowed on C strings. In the following code fragment, we show the wrong way and the right way to perform a string copy.

```
#include <cstring>
    ⋮
char myStr[100];
    ⋮
myStr = "Abracadabra";            // No
strcpy(myStr, "Abracadabra");     // Yes
```

In `strcpy`'s argument list, the destination string is the one on the left, just as an assignment operation transfers data from right to left. It is the caller's responsibility to make sure that the destination array is large enough to hold the result.

The `strcpy` function is technically a value-returning function; it not only copies one C string to another, but also returns as a function value the base address of the destination array. The reason why the caller would want to use this function value is not at all obvious, and we don't discuss it here. Programmers nearly always ignore the function value and simply invoke `strcpy` as if it were a void function (as we did above). You may wish to review the Background Information box in Chapter 8 entitled "Ignoring a Function Value."

The `strcmp` function is used for comparing two strings. The function receives two C strings as parameters and compares them in *lexicographic* order (the order in which they would appear in a dictionary)—the same ordering used in comparing `string` class objects. Given the function call `strcmp(str1, str2)`, the function returns one of the following int values: a negative integer, if `str1` < `str2` lexicographically; the value 0, if `str1` = `str2`; or a positive integer, if `str1` > `str2`. The precise values of the negative integer and the positive integer are unspecified. You simply test to see if the result is less than 0, 0, or greater than 0. Here is an example:

```
if (strcmp(str1, str2) < 0)   // If str1 is less than str2 ...
   ⋮
```

We have described only three of the string-handling routines provided by the standard library. These three are the most commonly needed, but there are many more. If you are designing or maintaining programs that use C strings extensively, you should read the documentation on strings for your C++ system.

String Class or C Strings?

When working with string data, should you use a class like `string`, or should you use C strings? From the standpoints of clarity, versatility, and ease of use, there is no contest. Use a string class. The standard library `string` class provides strings of unbounded length, aggregate assignment, aggregate comparison, concatenation with the + operator, and so forth.

However, it is still useful to be familiar with C strings. Among the thousands of software products currently in use that are written in C and C++, most (but a declining percentage) use C strings to represent string data. In your next place of employment, if you are asked to modify or upgrade such software, understanding C strings is essential. Additionally, *using* a string class is one thing; *implementing* it is another. Someone must implement the class using a concrete data representation. In your employment, that someone might be you, and the underlying data representation might very well be a C string!

*P*ROBLEM-SOLVING CASE STUDY

Exam Attendance

Problem: You are the grader for a U.S. government class of 200 students.The instructor has asked you to prepare two lists: students taking an exam and students who have missed it. The catch is that he wants the lists before the exam is over. You decide to write a program for your notebook computer that takes each student's name as the student enters the exam room and prints the lists of absentees and attendees for your instructor.

Input:
A list of last names of the students in the class (file `roster`), which was obtained from a master list in order of Social Security number
Each student's last name as he or she enters the room (standard input device)
(In this class, there are no duplicate last names.)

Output:
A list of those students taking the exam
A list of those students who are absent

Discussion: How would you take attendance by hand? You would stand at the door with a class roster. As each student came in, you would check off his or her name. When all the students had entered, you would go through the roster, making a list of those present. Then you would do the same for those who were absent.

This by-hand algorithm can serve as a model for your program. As each student enters the room, you enter his or her name at the keyboard. Your program scans the list of students for that name and marks that the student is present. When the last student has entered, you can enter a special sentinel name, perhaps "EndData," to signal the program to print the lists.

You can simulate "Mark that the student is present" by maintaining two lists: notCheckedIn, which initially contains all the student names, and thosePresent, which is initially empty. To mark a student present, delete his or her name from the notCheckedIn list and insert it into the thosePresent list. After all students have entered the exam room, the two lists contain the names of those absent and those present.

Your program must prepare the initial list of students in notCheckedIn from the class roster file, which is ordered by Social Security number. If you enter the names directly from the roster, they will not be in alphabetical order. Does that matter? Yes, in this case it does matter. The size of the class is 200, and the students need to enter the exam room with minimum delay (because most arrive just before the exam starts).

The length of the list and the speed required suggest that a binary search is appropriate. A binary search requires that the list be in sorted order. The names in the input file are not in alphabetical order, so your program must sort them. You can input all the names at once and then sort them using a function like SelSort, or you can use an insertion sort, inserting each name into its proper place as it is read. You decide to take the second approach because you can use the SortedList class of this chapter directly. This class provides such an Insert operation as well as a BinSearch operation.

Data Structures and Objects:
A SortedList object containing names of students not yet checked in
    (notCheckedIn)
A SortedList object containing names of students who have checked in
    (thosePresent)

Main   **Level 0**

> Open roster file for input (and verify success)
> Get class roster
> Check in students
> Print lists

Get Class Roster (Inout: notCheckedIn, roster)   **Level 1**

> Read stuName from roster file
> WHILE NOT EOF on roster
>   notCheckedIn.Insert(stuName)
>   Read stuName from roster file

Check in Students (Inout: notCheckedIn, thosePresent)

> Print "Enter last name"
> Read stuName
> WHILE stuName isn't "EndData"
>   Process stuName
>   Print "Enter last name"
>   Read stuName

Process Name (In: stuName; Inout: notCheckedIn, thosePresent) Level 2

> IF notCheckedIn.IsPresent(stuName)
>   thosepresent.Insert(stuName)
>   notCheckedIn.Delete(stuName)
> ELSE
>   Print "Name not on roster."

PROBLEM-SOLVING CASE STUDY *cont'd.*

Print (In: notCheckedIn, thosePresent)   **Level 1**

> Print "The following students are taking the exam."
> thosePresent.Print()
> Print "The following students have missed the exam."
> notCheckedIn.Print()

The design is now ready to be coded.

Because our program uses the `SortedList` class, we need

```
#include "slist.h"
```

to insert the appropriate declarations into the program. But we must make sure that `MAX_LENGTH` and `ItemType` in the file `slist.h` are correct for our problem. Our lists should hold up to 200 student names, and the type of each list component is `string`. Thus, we edit `slist.h` as follows:

```
const int MAX_LENGTH = 200;
typedef string ItemType;
```

Then we recompile `slist.cpp` into `slist.obj`. To run our Exam program, we link its object code file with the object code file `slist.obj`.

Module Structure Chart:

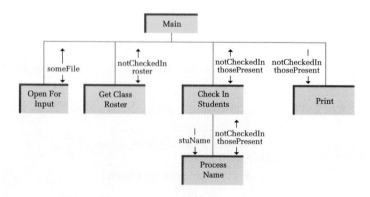

PROBLEM-SOLVING CASE STUDY cont'd.

(The following program is written in ISO/ANSI standard C++. If you are working with pre–standard C++, see the alternate version of the program in the PRE_STD directory of the program disk, available at the publisher's Web site, www.jbpub.com/disks.)

```cpp
//*****************************************************************
// Exam program
// This program compares students who come to take an exam against
// a class roster.  A list of students who took the exam and a list
// of students who missed the exam are printed.
// Assumption: Max. number of student names in roster file is
// MAX_LENGTH, which is defined in slist.h
//*****************************************************************
#include <iostream>
#include <fstream>       // For file I/O
#include <string>        // For string class
#include "slist.h"       // For SortedList class

const string END_DATA = "EndData";     // Sentinel value for
                                       //    student name

void CheckInStudents( SortedList&, SortedList& );
void GetClassRoster( SortedList&, ifstream& );
void OpenForInput( ifstream& );
void Print( SortedList, SortedList );
void ProcessName( string, SortedList&, SortedList& );

int main()
{
    SortedList notCheckedIn;   // List of students not yet checked in
    SortedList thosePresent;   // List of students present at exam
    ifstream roster;           // Input file to be analyzed

    OpenForInput(roster);
    if ( !roster )
        return 1;

    GetClassRoster(notCheckedIn, roster);
    CheckInStudents(notCheckedIn, thosePresent);
    Print(notCheckedIn, thosePresent);
    return 0;
}


//*****************************************************************
```

PROBLEM-SOLVING CASE STUDY cont'd.

```cpp
void OpenForInput( /* inout */ ifstream& someFile )     // File to be
                                                        // opened
// Prompts the user for the name of an input file
// and attempts to open the file

{
    .
    .          (Same as in previous case studies)
    .
}


//******************************************************************

void GetClassRoster(
        /* inout */ SortedList& notCheckedIn,     // List of students
        /* inout */ ifstream&   roster       )   // Roster data file

// Reads the class roster from the data file

// Precondition:
//     notCheckedIn is the empty list
// Precondition:
//     The roster file has been successfully opened for input
//  && The no. of student names in the file <= MAX_LENGTH (defined
//        in slist.h)
// Postcondition:
//     notCheckedIn contains the student names read from the file

{
    string stuName;        // An input student name

    roster >> stuName;
    while (roster)
    {
        notCheckedIn.Insert(stuName);
        roster >> stuName;
    }
}


//******************************************************************

void CheckInStudents(
        /* inout */ SortedList& notCheckedIn,     // List of students
        /* inout */ SortedList& thosePresent )    // List of students

// Inputs student names from standard input,
// marking students present
```

PROBLEM-SOLVING CASE STUDY cont'd.

```
// Precondition:
//     notCheckedIn contains names of all students in class
//   && thosePresent is empty
// Postcondition:
//     The user has been repeatedly prompted to enter student names
//   && thosePresent contains all the valid input names
//   && notCheckedIn contains all student names except the valid
//         input names
//   && For all input names not found in the notCheckedIn list,
//         an error message has been printed

{
    string stuName;      // Name of student who is checking in

    cout << "Enter last name: ";
    cin >> stuName;
    while (stuName != END_DATA)
    {
        ProcessName(stuName, notCheckedIn, thosePresent);
        cout << "Enter last name: ";
        cin >> stuName;
    }
}


//*****************************************************************

void ProcessName(
        /* in */    string        stuName,        // Input student name
        /* inout */ SortedList& notCheckedIn,    // List of students
        /* inout */ SortedList& thosePresent )   // List of students

// Searches for stuName in the notCheckedIn list.  If stuName
// is found, it is inserted into thosePresent and deleted from
// notCheckedIn.  Otherwise, an error message is printed.

// Precondition:
//     stuName is assigned
// Postcondition:
//     IF stuName is in notCheckedIn@entry
//         stuName is in thosePresent
//      && stuName is not in notCheckedIn
//     ELSE
//         An error message has been printed

{
    if (notCheckedIn.IsPresent(stuName))
    {
```

```
                    thosePresent.Insert(stuName);
                    notCheckedIn.Delete(stuName);
            }
        else
            cout << "Name not on roster." << endl;
    }


//**************************************************************

void Print( /* in */ SortedList notCheckedIn,    // List of students
            /* in */ SortedList thosePresent )   // List of students

// Prints the names of those taking the exam, then the names
// of those who are absent

// Postcondition:
//      Contents of thosePresent and notCheckedIn have been printed

{
    cout << endl << "The following students are taking the exam."
        << endl;
    thosePresent.Print();

    cout << endl << "The following students have missed the exam."
        << endl;
    notCheckedIn.Print();
}
```

Testing: The list manipulation operations `Insert`, `Delete`, `BinSearch`, and `Print` must be tested with different sized lists: an empty list, a one-item list, a list of maximum length, and several sizes in between. The `BinSearch` routine must be tested by searching for items that are in the list, items that are not in the list, at least one item that compares less than the first item in the list, at least one item that compares greater than the last item in the list, the last item, and the first item.

In testing the overall logic of the program, names read from the keyboard must be spelled incorrectly as well as correctly. The following data represents a sample data set.

Roster File

```
Dale
MacDonald
Weems
Vitek
Westby
Smith
```

```
Jamison
Jones
Kirshen
Gleason
Thompson
Ripley
Lilly
Headington
```

Copy of the Screen During the Run

```
Input file name: roster.dat
Enter last name: Weems
Enter last name: Dale
Enter last name: McDonald
Name not on roster.
Enter last name: MacDonald
Enter last name: Vitek
Enter last name: Westby
Enter last name: Gleason
Enter last name: EndData

The following students are taking the exam.
Dale
Gleason
MacDonald
Vitek
Weems
Westby

The following students have missed the exam.
Headington
Jamison
Jones
Kirshen
Lilly
Ripley
Smith
Thompson
```

By assuming that all students have unique last names, we have simplified the problem somewhat. Case Study Follow-Up Exercise 1 asks you to expand the program to account for duplicate last names.

Testing and Debugging

In this chapter, we have discussed, designed, and coded algorithms to construct and manipulate items in a list. In addition to the basic list operations `IsFull`, `IsEmpty`, `Length`, and `Print`, the algorithms included three sequential searches, a binary search, insertion into sorted and unsorted lists, deletion from sorted and unsorted lists, and a selection sort. We have already tested `SortedList::Insert`, `SortedList::Delete`, and `SortedList::BinSearch` in conjunction with the case study. Now we need to test the other searching algorithms and the functions `List::Insert`, `List::Delete`, and `List::SelSort`. We can use the same scheme that we used to test `BinSearch` to test the other search algorithms. We should test `List::Insert`, `List::Delete`, and `List::SelSort` with lists containing no components, one component, two components, MAX_LENGTH − 1 components, and MAX_LENGTH components.

When we wrote the precondition that the list was not full for operation `List::Insert`, we indicated that we could handle the problem another way—we could include an error flag in the function's parameter list. The function would call `IsFull` and set the error flag. The insertion would not take place if the error flag were set to `true`. Both options are acceptable ways of handling the problem. The important point is that we clearly state whether the calling code or the called function is to check for the error condition. However, it is the calling code that must decide what to do when an error condition occurs. In other words, if errors are handled by means of preconditions, then the user must write the code to guarantee the preconditions. If errors are handled by flags, then the user must write the code to monitor the error flags.

Testing and Debugging Hints

1. Review the Testing and Debugging Hints for Chapter 12. They apply to all one-dimensional arrays, including C strings.
2. Make sure that every C string is terminated with the null character. String constants are automatically null-terminated by the compiler. On input, the >> operator and the `get` function automatically add the null character. If you store characters into a C string individually or manipulate the array in any way, be sure to account for the null character.
3. Remember that C++ treats C string initialization (in a declaration) as different from C string assignment. Initialization is allowed, but assignment is not.
4. Aggregate input/output is allowed for C strings but not for other array types.

5. If you use the >> operator to input into a C string variable, be sure the array is large enough to hold the null character plus the longest sequence of (nonwhitespace) characters in the input stream.

6. With C string input, the >> operator stops at, *but does not consume,* the first trailing whitespace character. Likewise, if the get function stops reading early because it encounters a newline character, the newline character is not consumed.

7. When you use the strcpy library function, ensure that the destination array is at least as large as the array from which you are copying.

8. General-purpose functions (such as ADT operations) should be tested outside the context of a particular program, using a test driver.

9. Choose test data carefully so that you test all end conditions and some in the middle. End conditions are those that reach the limits of the structure used to store them. For example, in a list, there should be test data in which the number of components is 0, 1, and MAX_LENGTH, as well as between 1 and MAX_LENGTH.

Summary

This chapter has provided practice in working with lists stored in one-dimensional arrays. We have examined algorithms that insert, delete, search, and sort data stored in a list, and we have written functions to implement these algorithms. We can use these functions again and again in different contexts because they are members of general-purpose C++ classes (List and SortedList) that represent list ADTs.

C strings are a special case of char arrays in C++. The last significant character must be followed by a null character to mark the end of the string. C strings are less versatile than a string class. However, it pays to understand how they work because many existing programs in C and C++ use them, and string classes often use C strings as the underlying data representation.

Quick Check

1. The following code fragment implements the "Delete, if it's there" meaning for the Delete operation in an unsorted list. Change it so that the other meaning is implemented; that is, there is a precondition that the item *is* in the list. (pp. 751–752)

```
index = 0;
while (index < length && item != data[index])
    index++;
if (index < length)
{                                        // Remove item
    data[index] = data[length-1];
    length--;
}
```

2. In a sequential search of an unsorted array of 1000 values, what is the average number of loop iterations required to find a value? What is the maximum number of iterations? (pp. 772–773)

3. The following program fragment sorts list items into ascending order. Change it to sort into descending order. (pp. 755–758)

```
for (passCount = 0; passCount < length - 1; passCount++)
{
    minIndx = passCount;
    for (searchIndx = passCount + 1; searchIndx < length;
                                            searchIndx++)
        if (data[searchIndx] < data[minIndx])
            minIndx = searchIndx;
    temp = data[minIndx];                   // Swap
    data[minIndx] = data[passCount];
    data[passCount] = temp;
}
```

4. Describe how the `SortedList::Insert` operation can be used to build a sorted list from unsorted input data. (pp. 761–764)

5. Describe the basic principle behind the binary search algorithm. (pp. 765–769)

6. Using Typedef, define an array data type for a C string of up to 15 characters plus the null character. Declare an array variable of this type, initializing it to your first name. Then use a library function to replace the contents of the variable with your last name (up to 15 characters). (pp. 773–783)

Answers

1.
```
index = 0;
while (item != data[index])
    index++;
data[index] = data[length-1];
length--;
```

2. The average number is 500 iterations. The maximum is 1000 iterations.   **3.** The only required change is to replace the < symbol in the inner loop with a >. As a matter of style, the name `minIndx` should be changed to `maxIndx`.   **4.** The list initially has a length of 0. Each time a data value is read, insertion adds the value to the list in its correct position. When all the data values have been read, they are in the array in sorted order.   **5.** The binary search takes advantage of sorted list values, looking at a component in the middle of the list and deciding whether the search value precedes or follows the midpoint. The search is then repeated on the appropriate half, quarter, eighth, and so on, of the list until the value is located.

6.
```
typedef char String15[16];

String15 name = "Anna";

strcpy(name, "Rodriguez");
```

Exam Preparation Exercises

1. What three factors should you consider when you are deciding which search algorithm to use on a list?
2. The following values are stored in an array in ascending order.

   28 45 97 103 107 162 196 202 257

   Applying function `List::Search2` to this array, search for the following values and indicate how many comparisons are required to either find the number or find that it is not in the list.
   a. 28
   b. 32
   c. 196
   d. 194
3. Repeat Exercise 2, applying the algorithm for a sequential search in a sorted list (page 764).
4. The following values are stored in an array in ascending order.

   29 57 63 72 79 83 96 104 114 136

   Apply function `SortedList::BinSearch` with `item = 114` to this list, and trace the values of `first`, `last`, and `middle`. Indicate any undefined values with a *U*.
5. A binary search is always better to use than a sequential search. (True or False?)
6. a. Using Typedef, define a data type `NameType` for a C string of at most 40 characters plus the null character.
   b. Declare a variable `oneName` to be of type `NameType`.
   c. Declare `employeeName` to be a 100-element array whose elements are C strings of type `NameType`.
7. Given the declarations

   ```
   typedef char NameString[21];
   typedef char WordString[11];

   NameString firstName;
   NameString lastName;
   WordString word;
   ```

   mark the following statements valid or invalid. (Assume the header file cstring has been included.)
   a. ```
      i = 0;
      while (firstName[i] != '\0')
      {
          cout << firstName[i];
          i++;
      }
      ```
   b. `cout << lastName;`
   c. ```
      if (firstName == lastName)
          n = 1;
      ```
   d. ```
      if (strcmp(firstName, lastName) == 0)
          m = 8;
      ```
   e. `cin >> word;`
      ```

    f. `lastName = word;`

    g. `if (strcmp(NameString, "Hi") < 0)`
           `n = 3;`

    h. `if (firstName[2] == word[5])`
           `m = 4;`

8. Given the declarations

```
typedef char String20[21];
typedef char String30[31];

String20 rodent;
String30 mammal;
```

write code fragments for the following tasks. (If the task is not possible, say so.)

  a. Store the string "Moose" into `mammal`.

  b. Copy whatever string is in `rodent` into `mammal`.

  c. If the string in `mammal` is greater than "Opossum" lexicographically, increment a variable `count`.

  d. If the string in `mammal` is less than or equal to "Jackal", decrement a variable `count`.

  e. Store the string "Grey-tipped field shrew" into `rodent`.

  f. Print the length of the string in `rodent`.

9. Given the declarations

```
const int NUMBER_OF_BOOKS = 200;

typedef char BookName[31];
typedef char PersonName[21];

BookName    bookOut[NUMBER_OF_BOOKS];
PersonName  borrower[NUMBER_OF_BOOKS];
BookName    bookIn;
PersonName  name;
```

mark the following statements valid or invalid. (Assume the header file `cstring` has been included.)

  a. `cout << bookIn;`

  b. `cout << bookOut;`

  c. `for (i = 0; i < NUMBER_OF_BOOKS; i++)`
       `cout << bookOut[i] << endl;`

  d. `if (bookOut[3] > bookIn)`
       `cout << bookIn;`

  e. `for (i = 0; i < NUMBER_OF_BOOKS; i++)`
       `if (strcmp(bookIn, bookOut[i]) == 0)`
          `cout << bookIn << ' ' << borrower[i] << endl;`

  f. `bookIn = "Don Quixote";`

  g. `cout << name[2];`

10. Write code fragments to perform the following tasks, using the declarations given in Exercise 9. Assume that the books listed in `bookOut` have been borrowed by the person listed in the corresponding position of `borrower`.

a. Write a code fragment to print each book borrowed by name.
b. Write a code fragment to count the number of books borrowed by name.
c. Write a code fragment to count the number of copies of bookIn that have been borrowed.
d. Write a code fragment to count the number of copies of bookIn that have been borrowed by name.

Programming Warm-up Exercises

1. Write a C++ Boolean function named Exclusive that has three parameters: item (of type ItemType), list1, and list2 (both of type List as defined in this chapter). The function returns true if item is present in either list1 or list2 but not both.

2. To this chapter's List class, we wish to add a value-returning member function named Occurrences that receives a single parameter, item, and returns the number of times item occurs in the list. Write the function definition as it would appear in the implementation file.

3. Repeat Exercise 2 for the SortedList class.

4. To this chapter's List class, we wish to add a Boolean member function named GreaterFound that receives a single parameter, item, and searches the list for a value greater than item. If such a value is found, the function returns true; otherwise, it returns false. Write the function definition as it would appear in the implementation file.

5. Repeat Exercise 4 for the SortedList class.

6. The SortedList::Insert function inserts items into the list in ascending order. Rewrite it so that it inserts items in descending order.

7. Rewrite the SortedList::Delete function so that it removes all occurrences of item from the list.

8. Modify function SortedList::BinSearch so that position is where item should be inserted when found is false.

9. Rewrite function SortedList::Insert so that it implements the first insertion algorithm discussed for sorted lists. That is, the place where the item should be inserted is found by searching from the beginning of the list. When the place is found, all the items from the insertion point to the end of the list are shifted down one position. (Assume that BinSearch has been modified as in Exercise 8.) Write the function definition as it would appear in the implementation file.

10. To the SortedList class, we wish to add a member function named Component that returns a component of the list if a given position number (pos) is in the range 0 through length − 1. The function should also return a Boolean flag named valid that is false if pos is outside this range. Write the function definition as it would appear in the implementation file.

11. To the SortedList class, we wish to add a Boolean member function named Equal that has a single parameter named otherList, which is an object of type SortedList. This function compares two lists for equality: the one represented by otherList and the one represented by the class object for which the function is called. The function returns true if the two lists are of the same length and each element in one list equals the corresponding element in the other list. Here is an example of a call to the Equal function:

```
if (myList.Equal(yourList))
    ⋮
```

Assume the `Component` function of Exercise 10 has been added as a member of the `SortedList` class. Write the function definition as it would appear in the implementation file.

Programming Problems

1. A company wants to know the percentages of total sales and total expenses attributable to each salesperson. Each person has a pair of data lines. The first line contains his or her name, last name first. The second line contains his or her sales (`int`) and expenses (`float`). Write a program that produces a report with a header line containing the total sales and total expenses. Following this header should be a table with each salesperson's name, percentage of total sales, and percentage of total expenses, sorted by salesperson's name.

    Use one of the list classes developed in this chapter, modifying it as follows. `ItemType` should be a `struct` type that holds one salesperson's information. Therefore, the list is a list of structs. Some member functions of the list class must be modified to accommodate this `ItemType`. For example, comparisons involving list components must be changed to comparisons involving *members* of list components (which are structs). Also, include a `Component` member function in your list class (see Programming Warm-up Exercise 10) to allow the client code to access components of the list.

2. Only authorized shareholders are allowed to attend a stockholders' meeting. Write a program to read a person's name from the keyboard, check it against a list of shareholders, and print a message saying whether or not the person may attend the meeting. The list of shareholders is in a file `inFile` in the following format: first name, blank, last name. Use the end-of-file condition to stop reading the file. The maximum number of shareholders is 1000.

    The user should be prompted to enter his or her name in the same format as is used for the data in the file. If the name does not appear on the list, the program should repeat the instructions on how to enter the name and then tell the user to try again. A message saying that the person may not enter should be printed only after he or she has been given a second chance to enter the name. The prompt to the user should include the message that a *Q* should be entered to end the program.

3. Enhance the program in Problem 2 as follows:
    a. Print a report showing the number of stockholders at the time of the meeting, how many were present at the meeting, and how many people who tried to enter were denied permission to attend.
    b. Follow this summary report with a list of the names of the stockholders, with either *Present* or *Absent* after each name.

4. An advertising company wants to send a letter to all its clients announcing a new fee schedule. The clients' names are on several different lists in the company. The various lists are merged to form one file, `clientNames`, but obviously, the company does not want to send a letter twice to anyone.

Write a program that removes any names appearing on the list more than once. On each line of data, there is a four-digit code number, followed by a blank and then the client's name. For example, Amalgamated Steel is listed as

```
0231 Amalgamated Steel
```

Your program is to output each client's code and name, but no duplicates should be printed.

Use one of the list classes developed in this chapter, modifying it as follows. ItemType should be a `struct` type that holds one company's information. Therefore, the list is a list of structs. Some member functions of the list class must be modified to accommodate this ItemType. For example, comparisons involving list components must be changed to comparisons involving *members* of list components (which are structs).

Case Study Follow-Up

1. The Exam program assumes that the students have unique last names. Rewrite the program so that it accommodates duplicate last names. Assume now that each line in the `roster` file contains a student's first and last names, with last name first.

2. The Exam program uses an insertion sort, placing each student's name into its proper place in the list as it is input. How would you rewrite the program to input all the names at once and then sort them using SelSort?

3. The Exam program uses a binary search to search the student list. Assuming a list of 200 students, how many loop iterations are required to determine that a student is absent? How many iterations would be required if we had used the algorithm for a sequential search of a sorted list instead of BinSearch?

4. Write a test plan for the functions SortedList::Insert and SortedList:: BinSearch, assuming ItemType is int.

5. Write a test driver to implement your test plan.

14

Object-Oriented Software Development

GOALS

- To be able to distinguish between structured (procedural) programming and object-oriented programming.
- To be able to define the characteristics of an object-oriented programming language.
- To be able to create a new C++ class from an existing class by using inheritance.
- To be able to create a new C++ class from an existing class by using composition.
- To be able to distinguish between static and dynamic binding of operations to objects.
- To be able to apply the object-oriented design methodology to solve a problem.
- To be able to take an object-oriented design and code it in C++.

In Chapter 11, we introduced the concept of data abstraction—the separation of the logical properties of a data type from the details of how it is implemented. We expanded on this concept by defining the notion of an abstract data type (ADT) and by using the C++ class mechanism to incorporate both data and operations into a single data type. In that chapter and Chapter 13, we saw how an object of a given class maintains its own private data and is manipulated by calling its public member functions.

In this chapter, we examine how classes and objects can be used to guide the entire software development process. Although the design phase precedes the implementation phase in the development of software, we reverse the order of presentation in this chapter. We begin with *object-oriented programming,* a topic that includes design but is more about implementation issues. We describe the basic principles, terminology, and programming language features associated with the object-oriented approach. After presenting these fundamental concepts, we look more closely at the design phase—*object-oriented design.*

Object-Oriented Programming

Until now, we have used functional decomposition (also called *structured design*), in which we decompose a problem into modules, where each module is a self-contained collection of steps that solves one part of the overall problem. The process of implementing a functional decomposition is often called **structured** (or **procedural**) **programming.** Some modules are translated directly into a few programming language instructions, whereas others are coded as functions with or without arguments. The end result is a program that is a collection of interacting functions (see Figure 14-1). Throughout structured design and structured programming, data is considered a passive quantity to be acted upon by control structures and functions.

Structured design is satisfactory for programming in the small (a concept we discussed in Chapter 4) but often does not "scale up" well for programming in the large. In building large software systems, structured design has two important limitations. First, the technique yields an inflexible structure. If the top-level algorithm requires modification, the changes may force many lower-level algorithms to be modified as well. Second, the technique does not lend itself easily to code reuse. By *code reuse* we mean the ability to use pieces of code—either as they are or adapted slightly—in other sections of the program or in other programs. It is rare to be able to take a complicated C++ function and reuse it easily in a different context.

A methodology that often works better for creating large software systems is object-oriented design (OOD), which we introduced briefly in Chapter 4. OOD decomposes a problem into objects—self-contained entities composed of data and operations on the data. The process of imple-

FIGURE 14-1

Program Resulting
from Structured
(Procedural)
Programming

PROGRAM

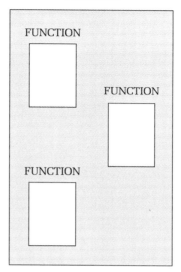

menting an object-oriented design is called **object-oriented programming (OOP).** The end result is a program that is a collection of interacting objects (see Figure 14-2). In OOD and OOP, data plays a leading role; the primary contribution of algorithms is to implement the operations on objects. In this chapter, we'll see why OOD tends to result in programs that are more flexible and conducive to code reuse than programs produced by structured design.

Several programming languages have been created specifically to support OOD and OOP: C++, Java, Smalltalk, Simula, CLOS, Objective-C, Eiffel, Actor, Object-Pascal, recent versions of Turbo Pascal, and others. These languages, called *object-oriented programming languages*, have facilities for

1. Data abstraction
2. Inheritance
3. Dynamic binding

You have already seen that C++ supports data abstraction through the class mechanism. Some non-OOP languages also have facilities for data abstraction. But only OOP languages support the other two concepts—*inheritance* and *dynamic binding*. Before we define these two concepts, we discuss some of the fundamental ideas and terminology of object-oriented programming.

FIGURE 14-2
Program Resulting
from Object-
Oriented
Programming

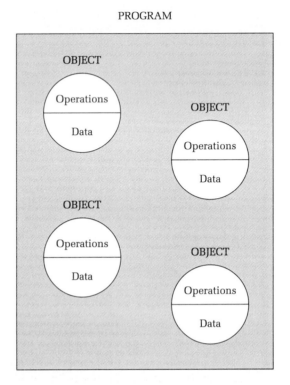

PROGRAM

Structured (procedural) programming   The construction of programs that are collections of interacting functions or procedures.

Object-oriented programming (OOP)   The use of data abstraction, inheritance, and dynamic binding to construct programs that are collections of interacting objects.

Objects

The major principles of OOP originated as far back as the mid-1960s with a language called Simula. However, much of the current terminology of OOP is due to Smalltalk, a language developed in the late 1970s at Xerox's Palo Alto Research Center. In OOP, the term *object* has a very specific meaning: It is a self-contained entity encapsulating data and operations on the data. In other words, an object represents an instance of an ADT. More specifically, an object has an internal *state* (the current values of its private data, called *instance variables*), and it has a set of *methods* (public operations). Methods are the only means by which an object's state can be inspected or modified by another object. An object-oriented program consists of a collection of objects, communicating with one another by *message passing*. If object A wants object B to perform some task, object A sends a message containing the name of the object (B, in this case) and the name of the particular method to execute. Object B responds by executing this method in its own way, possibly changing its state and sending messages to other objects as well.

As you can tell, an object is quite different from a traditional data structure. A C++ struct is a passive data structure that contains only data and is acted upon by a program. In contrast, an object is an active data structure; the data and the code that manipulates the data are bound together within the object. In OOP jargon, an object knows how to manipulate itself.

The vocabulary of Smalltalk has influenced the vocabulary of OOP. The literature of OOP is full of phrases such as "methods," "instance variables," and "sending a message to." Here are some OOP terms and their C++ equivalents:

OOP	C++
Object	Class object or class instance
Instance variable	Private data member
Method	Public member function
Message passing	Function call (to a public member function)

In C++, we define the properties and behavior of objects by using the class mechanism. Within a program, classes can be related to each other in various ways. The three most common relationships are as follows:

1. Two classes are independent of each other and have nothing in common.
2. Two classes are related by *inheritance*.
3. Two classes are related by *composition*.

The first relationship—none—is not very interesting. Let's look at the other two—inheritance and composition.

Inheritance

In the world at large, it is often possible to arrange concepts into an *inheritance hierarchy*—a hierarchy in which each concept inherits the properties of the concept immediately above it in the hierarchy. For example, we might classify different kinds of vehicles according to the inheritance hierarchy in Figure 14-3. Moving down the hierarchy, each kind of vehicle is more specialized than its *parent* (and all of its *ancestors*) and is more general than its *child* (and all of its *descendants*). A wheeled vehicle inherits properties common to all vehicles (it holds one or more people and carries them from place to place) but has an additional property that makes it more specialized (it has wheels). A car inherits properties common to all wheeled vehicles but also has additional, more specialized properties (four wheels, an engine, a body, and so forth).

The inheritance relationship can be viewed as an *is-a relationship*. Every two-door car is a car, every car is a wheeled vehicle, and every wheeled vehicle is a vehicle.

OOP languages provide a way of creating inheritance relationships among classes. In these languages, **inheritance** is the mechanism by which one class acquires the properties of another class. You can take an existing class A (called the **base class** or **superclass**) and create from it a new class B (called the **derived class** or **subclass**). The derived class B inherits all the properties of its base class A. In particular, the data and operations defined for A are now also defined for B. (Notice the is-a relationship—every B is also an A.) The idea, next, is to specialize class B, usually by adding specific properties to those already inherited from A. Let's look at an example in C++.

Inheritance   A mechanism by which one class acquires the properties—the data and operations—of another class.

Base class (superclass)   The class being inherited from.

Derived class (subclass)   The class that inherits.

FIGURE 14-3
Inheritance
Hierarchy

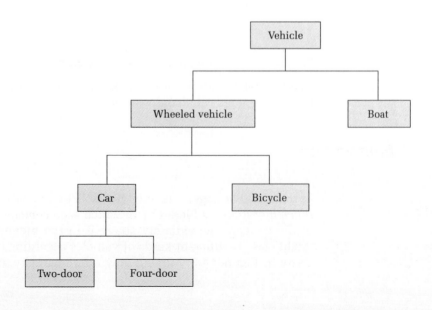

Deriving One Class from Another

Suppose that someone has already written a `Time` class with the following specification, abbreviated by omitting the preconditions and postconditions:

```
class Time
{
public:
    void Set( /* in */ int hours,
              /* in */ int minutes,
              /* in */ int seconds );
    void Increment();
    void Write() const;
    Time( /* in */ int initHrs,       // Constructor
          /* in */ int initMins,
          /* in */ int initSecs );
    Time();                           // Default constructor,
private:                              //    setting time to 0:0:0
    int hrs;
    int mins;
    int secs;
};
```

This class is the same as our `TimeType` class of Chapter 11, simplified by omitting the `Equal` and `LessThan` member functions. Figure 14-4 displays a *class interface diagram* for the `Time` class. The public interface, shown as ovals in the side of the large circle, consists of the operations available to

FIGURE 14-4
Class Interface
Diagram for `Time`
Class

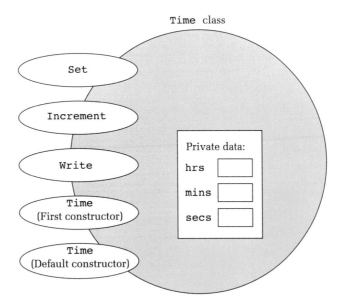

client code. The private data items shown in the interior are inaccessible to clients.

Suppose that we want to modify the Time class by adding, as private data, a variable of an enumeration type indicating the (American) time zone—EST for Eastern Standard Time, CST for Central Standard Time, MST for Mountain Standard Time, PST for Pacific Standard Time, EDT for Eastern Daylight Time, CDT for Central Daylight Time, MDT for Mountain Daylight Time, or PDT for Pacific Daylight Time. We'll need to modify the Set function and the class constructors to accommodate a time zone value. And the Write function should print the time in the form

```
12:34:10 CST
```

The Increment function, which advances the time by one second, does not need to be changed.

To add these time zone features to the Time class, the conventional approach would be to obtain the source code found in the time.cpp implementation file, analyze in detail how the class is implemented, then modify and recompile the source code. This process has several draw-backs. If Time is an off-the-shelf class on a system, the source code for the implementation is probably unavailable. Even if it is available, modifying it may introduce bugs into a previously debugged solution. Access to the source code also violates a principal benefit of abstraction: Users of an abstraction should not need to know how it is implemented.

In C++, as in other OOP languages, there is a far quicker and safer way in which to add time zone features: Use inheritance. Let's derive a new class from the Time class and then specialize it. This new, extended time class—call it ExtTime—inherits the members of its base class, Time. Here is the declaration of ExtTime:

```
enum ZoneType {EST, CST, MST, PST, EDT, CDT, MDT, PDT};

class ExtTime : public Time
{
public:
    void Set( /* in */ int      hours,
              /* in */ int      minutes,
              /* in */ int      seconds,
              /* in */ ZoneType timeZone );
    void Write() const;
    ExtTime( /* in */ int      initHrs,        // Constructor
             /* in */ int      initMins,
             /* in */ int      initSecs,
             /* in */ ZoneType initZone );
```

```
        ExtTime();                          // Default constructor,
                                            //    setting time to
private:                                    //    0:0:0 EST
    ZoneType zone;
};
```

The opening line

```
class ExtTime : public Time
```

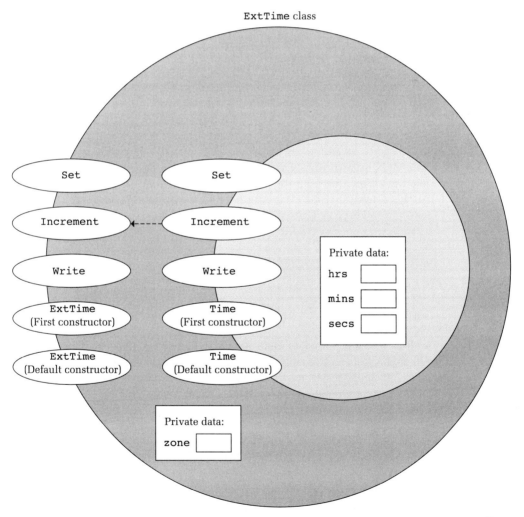

ExtTime class

FIGURE 14-5
Class Interface Diagram for ExtTime Class

states that `ExtTime` is derived from `Time`. The reserved word `public` declares `Time` to be a *public base class* of `ExtTime`. This means that all public members of `Time` (except constructors) are also public members of `ExtTime`. In other words, `Time`'s member functions `Set`, `Increment`, and `Write` can also be invoked for `ExtTime` objects.* However, the public part of `ExtTime` specializes the base class by reimplementing (redefining) the inherited functions `Set` and `Write` and by providing its own constructors.

The private part of `ExtTime` declares that a new private member is added: `zone`. The private members of `ExtTime` are therefore `hrs`, `mins`, `secs` (all inherited from `Time`), and `zone`. Figure 14-5 pictures the relationship between the `ExtTime` and `Time` classes.

This diagram shows that each `ExtTime` object has a `Time` object as a *subobject*. Every `ExtTime` is a `Time`, and more. C++ uses the terms *base class* and *derived class* instead of *superclass* and *subclass*. The terms *superclass* and *subclass* can be confusing because the prefix *sub-* usually implies something smaller than the original (for example, a subset of a mathematical set). In contrast, a subclass is often "bigger" than its superclass—that is, it has more data and/or functions.

In Figure 14-5, you see an arrow between the two ovals labeled `Increment`. Because `Time` is a public base class of `ExtTime`, and because `Increment` is not redefined by `ExtTime`, the `Increment` function available to clients of `ExtTime` is the same as the one inherited from `Time`. We use the arrow between the corresponding ovals to indicate this fact. (Notice in the diagram that `Time`'s constructors are operations on `Time`, not on `ExtTime`. The `ExtTime` class must have its own constructors.)

SOFTWARE ENGINEERING TIP

Inheritance and Accessibility

With C++, it is important to understand that inheritance does not imply accessibility. Although a derived class inherits the members of its base class, both private and public, it cannot access the private members of the base class. Figure 14-5 shows the variables `hrs`, `mins`, and `secs` to be encapsulated within the `Time` class. Neither external client code nor `ExtTime` member functions can refer to these three vari-

---

* If a class declaration omits the word `public` and begins as

`class DerivedClass : BaseClass`

or if it explicitly uses the word `private`,

`class DerivedClass : private BaseClass`

then `BaseClass` is called a *private base class* of `DerivedClass`. Public members of `BaseClass` are *not* public members of `DerivedClass`. That is, clients of `DerivedClass` cannot invoke `BaseClass` operations on `DerivedClass` objects. We do not work with private base classes in this book.

ables directly. If a derived class were able to access the private members of its base class, any programmer could derive a class from another and then write code to directly inspect or modify the private data, defeating the benefits of encapsulation and information hiding.

Specification of the `ExtTime` Class

Below is the fully documented specification of the `ExtTime` class. Notice that the preprocessor directive

```
#include "time.h"
```

is necessary for the compiler to verify the consistency of the derived class with its base class.

```
//*****************************************************************
// SPECIFICATION FILE (exttime.h)
// This file gives the specification of an ExtTime abstract data
// type.  The Time class is a public base class of ExtTime, so
// public operations of Time are also public operations of ExtTime.
//*****************************************************************
#include "time.h"

enum ZoneType {EST, CST, MST, PST, EDT, CDT, MDT, PDT};

class ExtTime : public Time
{
public:
    void Set( /* in */ int       hours,
              /* in */ int       minutes,
              /* in */ int       seconds,
              /* in */ ZoneType timeZone );
        // Precondition:
        //     0 <= hours <= 23  &&  0 <= minutes <= 59
        //  && 0 <= seconds <= 59  &&  timeZone is assigned
        // Postcondition:
        //     Time is set according to the incoming parameters

    void Write() const;
        // Postcondition:
        //     Time has been output in the form HH:MM:SS ZZZ
        //     where ZZZ is the time zone

    ExtTime( /* in */ int       initHrs,
             /* in */ int       initMins,
             /* in */ int       initSecs,
             /* in */ ZoneType initZone );
```

```
            // Precondition:
            //     0 <= initHrs <= 23  &&  0 <= initMins <= 59
            //  && 0 <= initSecs <= 59  &&  initZone is assigned
            // Postcondition:
            //     Class object is constructed
            //  && Time is set according to the incoming parameters

        ExtTime();
            // Postcondition:
            //     Class object is constructed
            //  && Time is 0:0:0 Eastern Standard Time
    private:
        ZoneType zone;
    };
```

With this new class, the programmer can set the time with a time zone (via a class constructor or the redefined Set function), output the time with its time zone (via the redefined Write function), and increment the time by one second (via the inherited Increment function):

```
// Client code:

#include "exttime.h"
   ⋮
ExtTime time1(8, 35, 0, PST);
ExtTime time2;                      // Default constructor called

time2.Write();                      // Outputs 0:0:0 EST
cout << endl;

time2.Set(16, 49, 23, CDT);
time2.Write();                      // Outputs 16:49:23 CDT
cout << endl;

time1.Increment();
time1.Increment();
time1.Write();                      // Outputs 08:35:02 PST
cout << endl;
   ⋮
```

Implementation of the ExtTime Class

The implementation of the ExtTime class needs to deal only with the new features that are different from Time. Specifically, we must write code to redefine the Set and Write functions and we must write the two constructors.

With derived classes, constructors are subject to special rules. At run time, the base class constructor is implicitly called first, before the body of the derived class's constructor executes. Additionally, if the base class constructor requires arguments, these arguments must be passed by the derived class's constructor. To see how these rules pertain, let's examine the implementation file exttime.cpp (see Figure 14-6).

Figure 14-6
ExtTime
Implementation
File

```
//******************************************************************
// IMPLEMENTATION FILE (exttime.cpp)
// This file implements the ExtTime member functions.
// The Time class is a public base class of ExtTime
//******************************************************************
#include "exttime.h"
#include <iostream>
#include <string>

using namespace std;

// Additional private members of class:
//      ZoneType zone;


//******************************************************************

ExtTime::ExtTime( /* in */ int      initHrs,
                  /* in */ int      initMins,
                  /* in */ int      initSecs,
                  /* in */ ZoneType initZone )


    : Time(initHrs, initMins, initSecs)


// Constructor

// Precondition:
//      0 <= initHrs <= 23   &&   0 <= initMins <= 59
//   && 0 <= initSecs <= 59  &&  initZone is assigned
// Postcondition:
//      Time is set according to initHrs, initMins, and initSecs
//       (via call to base class constructor)
//   && zone == initZone

{
    zone = initZone;
}


//******************************************************************

ExtTime::ExtTime()
```

FIGURE 14-6
ExtTime
Implementation
File
(continued)

```
// Default constructor

// Postcondition:
//      Time is 0:0:0 (via implicit call to base class's
//      default constructor)
//   && zone == EST

{
    zone = EST;
}


//*******************************************************************

void ExtTime::Set( /* in */ int       hours,
                   /* in */ int       minutes,
                   /* in */ int       seconds,
                   /* in */ ZoneType timeZone )

// Precondition:
//     0 <= hours <= 23  &&  0 <= minutes <= 59
//   && 0 <= seconds <= 59  &&  timeZone is assigned
// Postcondition:
//     Time is set according to hours, minutes, and seconds
//   && zone == timeZone

{
    Time::Set(hours, minutes, seconds);
    zone = timeZone;
}


//*******************************************************************

void ExtTime::Write() const

// Postcondition:
//     Time has been output in the form HH:MM:SS ZZZ
//     where ZZZ is the time zone

{
    static string zoneString[8] =
    {
        "EST", "CST", "MST", "PST", "EDT", "CDT", "MDT", "PDT"
    };

    Time::Write();
    cout << ' ' << zoneString[zone];
}
```

In the first constructor in Figure 14-6, notice the syntax by which a constructor passes arguments to its base class constructor:

```
ExtTime::ExtTime( /* in */ int      initHrs,
                  /* in */ int      initMins,
                  /* in */ int      initSecs,
                  /* in */ ZoneType initZone )

    : Time(initHrs, initMins, initSecs)      ←    Constructor initializer

{
    zone = initZone;
}
```

After the parameter list to the `ExtTime` constructor (but before its body), you insert what is called a *constructor initializer*—a colon and then the name of the base class along with the arguments to *its* constructor. When an `ExtTime` object is created with a declaration such as

```
ExtTime time1(8, 35, 0, PST);
```

the `ExtTime` constructor receives four arguments. The first three are simply passed along to the `Time` class constructor by means of the constructor initializer. After the `Time` class constructor has executed (creating the base class subobject as shown in Figure 14-5), the body of the `ExtTime` constructor executes, setting `zone` equal to the fourth argument.

The second constructor in Figure 14-6 (the default constructor) does not need a constructor initializer; there are no arguments to pass to the base class's default constructor. When an `ExtTime` object is created with the declaration

```
ExtTime time2;
```

the `ExtTime` class's default constructor first implicitly calls `Time`'s default constructor, after which its body executes, setting `zone` to EST.

Next, look at the `Set` function in Figure 14-6. This function reimplements the `Set` function inherited from the base class. Consequently, there are two distinct `Set` functions, one a public member of the `Time` class, the other a public member of the `ExtTime` class. Their full names are `Time::Set` and `ExtTime::Set`. In Figure 14-6, the `ExtTime::Set` function begins by "reaching up" into its base class and calling `Time::Set` to set the hours, minutes, and seconds. (Remember that a class derived from `Time` cannot access the private data `hrs`, `mins`, and `secs` directly; these variables are private to the `Time` class.) The function then finishes by assigning a value to `ExtTime`'s private data, the `zone` variable.

The Write function in Figure 14-6 uses a similar strategy. It reaches up into its base class and invokes `Time::Write` to output the hours, minutes, and seconds. Then it outputs a string corresponding to the time zone. (Recall that a value of enumeration type cannot be output directly in C++. If we were to print the value of `zone` directly, the output would be an integer from 0 through 7—the internal representations of the `ZoneType` values.) The Write function establishes an array of eight strings and selects the correct string by using `zone` to index into the array. Why is `zoneString` declared to be `static`? Remember that by default, local variables in C++ are automatic variables—that is, memory is allocated for them when the function begins execution and is deallocated when the function returns. With `zoneString` declared as `static`, the array is allocated once only, when the program begins execution, and remains allocated until the program terminates. From function call to function call, the computer does not waste time creating and destroying the array.

Now we can compile the file `exttime.cpp` into an object code file, say, `exttime.obj`. After writing a test driver and compiling it into `test.obj`, we obtain an executable file by linking three object files:

1. `test.obj`
2. `exttime.obj`
3. `time.obj`

We can then test the resulting program.

The remarkable thing about derived classes and inheritance is that modification of the base class is unnecessary. The source code for the implementation of the `Time` class may be unavailable. Yet variations of this ADT can continue to be created without that source code, in ways the creator never even considered. Through classes and inheritance, OOP languages facilitate code reuse. A class such as `Time` can be used as-is in many different contexts, or it can be adapted to a particular context by using inheritance. Inheritance allows us to create *extensible* data abstractions—a derived class typically extends the base class by including additional private data or public operations or both.

Avoiding Multiple Inclusion of Header Files

We saw that the specification file `exttime.h` begins with an `#include` directive to insert the file `time.h`:

```
#include "time.h"

enum ZoneType {EST, CST, MST, PST, EDT, CDT, MDT, PDT};

class ExtTime : public Time
{
    ⋮
};
```

Now think about what happens if a programmer using the ExtTime class already has included time.h for other purposes, overlooking the fact that exttime.h also includes it:

```
#include "time.h"
#include "exttime.h"
```

The preprocessor inserts the file time.h, then exttime.h, and then time.h a second time (because exttime.h also includes time.h). The result is a compile-time error, because the Time class is defined twice.

The widely used solution to this problem is to write time.h this way:

```
#ifndef TIME_H
#define TIME_H
class Time
{
    ⋮
};
#endif
```

The lines beginning with "#" are directives to the preprocessor. TIME_H (or any identifier you wish to use) is a preprocessor identifier, not a C++ program identifier. In effect, these directives say:

If the preprocessor identifier TIME_H is not already defined, then

1. define TIME_H as an identifier known to the preprocessor,

and

2. let the declaration of the Time class pass through to the compiler.

If a subsequent #include "time.h" is encountered, the test #ifndef TIME_H will fail. The Time class declaration will not pass through to the compiler a second time.

Composition

Earlier we said that two classes typically exhibit one of the following relationships: They are independent of each other, they are related by inheritance, or they are related by **composition.** Composition (or **containment**) is the relationship in which the internal data of one class A includes an object of another class B. Stated another way, a B object is contained within an A object.

Composition (containment) A mechanism by which the internal data (the state) of one class includes an object of another class.

C++ does not have (or need) any special language notation for composition. You simply declare an object of one class to be one of the data members of another class. Let's look at an example.

Design of a `TimeCard` Class

You are developing a program to manage a factory's payroll. Employees are issued time cards containing their ID numbers. When reporting for work, an employee "punches in" by inserting the card into a clock, which punches the current time onto the card. When leaving work, the employee takes a new card and "punches out" to record the departure time. For your program, you decide that you need a `TimeCard` ADT to represent an employee's time card. The abstract data consists of an ID number and a time. The abstract operations include Punch the Time, Print the Time Card Data, constructor operations, and others. To implement the ADT, you must choose a concrete data representation for the abstract data and you must implement the operations. Assuming an employee ID number is a large integer value, you choose the `long` data type to represent the ID number. To represent time, you remember that one of your friends has already written and debugged a `Time` class (we'll use the one from earlier in this chapter). At this point, you create a `TimeCard` class declaration as follows:

```
#include "time.h"
   ⋮
class TimeCard
{
public:
    void Punch( /* in */ int hours,
                /* in */ int minutes,
                /* in */ int seconds );
    void Print() const;
      ⋮
    TimeCard( /* in */ long idNum,
              /* in */ int  initHrs,
              /* in */ int  initMins,
              /* in */ int  initSecs );
    TimeCard();
private:
    long id;
    Time timeStamp;
};
```

FIGURE 14-7
Class Interface Diagram for TimeCard Class

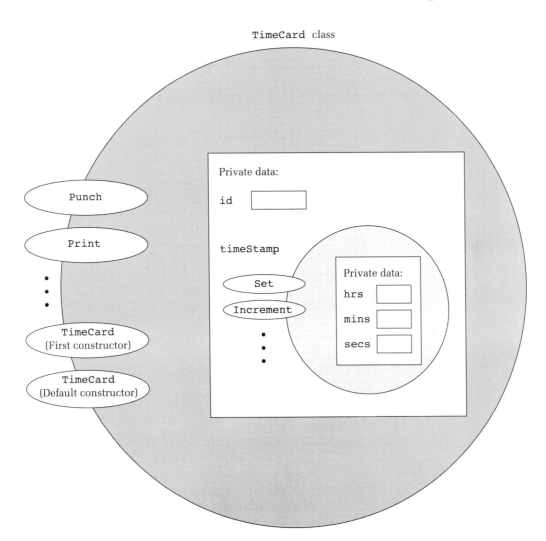

In designing the TimeCard class, you have used composition; a TimeCard object is composed of a Time object (and a long variable). Composition creates a *has-a relationship*—a TimeCard object *has a* Time object as a subobject (see Figure 14-7).

Implementation of the `TimeCard` Class

The private data of `TimeCard` consists of a `long` variable named `id` and a `Time` object named `timeStamp`. The `TimeCard` member functions can manipulate `id` by using ordinary built-in operations, but they must manipulate `timeStamp` through the member functions defined for the `Time` class. For example, you could implement the `Print` and `Punch` functions as follows:

```
void TimeCard::Print() const
{
    cout << "ID: "  << id << " Time: " ;
    timeStamp.Write();
}


void TimeCard::Punch( /* in */ int hours,
                      /* in */ int minutes,
                      /* in */ int seconds )
{
    timeStamp.Set(hours, minutes, seconds);
}
```

Implementing the class constructors is a bit more complicated to describe. Let's start with an implementation of the first constructor shown in the `TimeCard` class declaration:

```
TimeCard::TimeCard( /* in */ long idNum,
                    /* in */ int  initHrs,
                    /* in */ int  initMins,
                    /* in */ int  initSecs )

    : timeStamp(initHrs, initMins, initSecs)     ← Constructor initializer

{
    id = idNum;
}
```

This is the second time we've seen the unusual notation—the constructor initializer—inserted between the parameter list and the body of a constructor. The first time was when we implemented the parameterized `ExtTime` class constructor (Figure 14-6). There, we used the constructor initializer to pass some of the incoming arguments to the base class constructor. Here, we use a constructor initializer to pass some of the arguments to a member object's (`timeStamp`'s) constructor. Whether you are using inheritance or composition, the purpose of a constructor initializer is the same: to pass arguments to another constructor. The only difference is the following: With inheritance, you specify the name of the *base class* prior to the argument list, as follows.

```
ExtTime::ExtTime( /* in */ int       initHrs,
                  /* in */ int       initMins,
                  /* in */ int       initSecs,
                  /* in */ ZoneType initZone )

    : Time(initHrs, initMins, initSecs)
```

With composition, you specify the name of the *member object* prior to the argument list:

```
TimeCard::TimeCard( /* in */ long idNum,
                    /* in */ int  initHrs,
                    /* in */ int  initMins,
                    /* in */ int  initSecs )

   : timeStamp(initHrs, initMins, initSecs)
```

Furthermore, if a class has several members that are objects of classes with parameterized constructors, you form a list of constructor initializers separated by commas:

```
SomeClass::SomeClass( ... )

    : memberObject1(arg1, arg2), memberObject2(arg3)
```

Having discussed both inheritance and composition, we can give a complete description of the order in which constructors are executed:

> *Given a class X, if X is a derived class, its base class constructor is executed first. Next, constructors for member objects (if any) are executed. Finally, the body of X's constructor is executed.*

When a TimeCard object is created, the constructor for its timeStamp member is first invoked. After the timeStamp object is constructed, the body of TimeCard's constructor is executed, setting the id member equal to idNum.

The second constructor shown in the TimeCard class declaration—the default constructor—has no parameters and could be implemented as follows:

```
TimeCard::TimeCard()
{
    id = 0;
}
```

In this case, what happened to construction of the timeStamp member object? We didn't include a constructor initializer, so the timeStamp object is first constructed using the *default* constructor of the Time class, after which the body of the TimeCard constructor is executed. The result is a time card having a time stamp of 0:0:0 and an ID number of 0.

Dynamic Binding and Virtual Functions

Early in the chapter, we said that object-oriented programming languages provide language features that support three concepts: data abstraction, inheritance, and dynamic binding. The phrase *dynamic binding* means, more specifically, *dynamic binding of an operation to an object*. To explain this concept, let's begin with an example.

Given the Time and ExtTime classes of this chapter, the following code creates two class objects and outputs the time represented by each.

```
Time    startTime(8, 30, 0);
ExtTime endTime(10, 45, 0, CST);

startTime.Write();
cout << endl;
endTime.Write();
cout << endl;
```

This code fragment invokes two different Write functions, even though the functions appear to have the same name. The first function call invokes the Write function of the Time class, printing out three values: hours, minutes, and seconds. The second call invokes the Write function of the ExtTime class, printing out four values: hours, minutes, seconds, and time zone. In this code fragment, the compiler uses **static** (compile-time) **binding** of the operation (Write) to the appropriate object. The compiler can easily determine which Write function to call by checking the data type of the associated object.

Static binding   The compile-time determination of which function to call for a particular object.

In some situations, the compiler cannot determine the type of an object, and the binding of an operation to an object must occur at run time. One situation, which we look at now, involves passing class objects as arguments.

The basic C++ rule for passing class objects as arguments is that the argument and its corresponding parameter must be of identical type. With inheritance, though, C++ relaxes the rule. You may pass an object of a child class *C* to an object of its parent class *P*, but not the other way around—that is, you cannot pass an object of type *P* to an object of type *C*. More generally, you can pass an object of a descendant class to an object of any of its ancestor classes. This rule has a tremendous benefit—it allows us to write a single function that applies to any descendant class instead of writing a different function for each. For example, we could write a fancy Print function that takes as an argument an object of type Time or any class descended from Time:

```
void Print( /* in */ Time someTime )
{
    cout << "*************************" << endl;
    cout << "** The time is ";
    someTime.Write();
    cout << endl;
    cout << "*************************" << endl;
}
```

Given the code fragment

```
Time     startTime(8, 30, 0);
ExtTime endTime(10, 45, 0, CST);

Print(startTime);
Print(endTime);
```

the compiler lets us pass either a Time object or an ExtTime object to the Print function. Unfortunately, the output is not what we would like. When endTime is printed, the time zone CST is missing from the output. Let's see why.

The Slicing Problem

Our Print function uses passing by value for the parameter someTime. Passing by value sends a copy of the argument to the parameter. Whenever you pass an object of a child class to an object of its parent class using a pass by value, only the data members they have in common are copied. Remember that a child class is often "larger" than its parent—that is, it contains additional data members. For example, a Time object has three data members (hrs, mins, and secs), but an ExtTime object has four data members (hrs, mins, secs, and zone). When the larger class object is copied to the smaller parameter using a pass by value, the extra data members are discarded or "sliced off." This situation is called the *slicing problem* (see Figure 14-8).

Figure 14-8
The Slicing Problem Resulting from Passing by Value

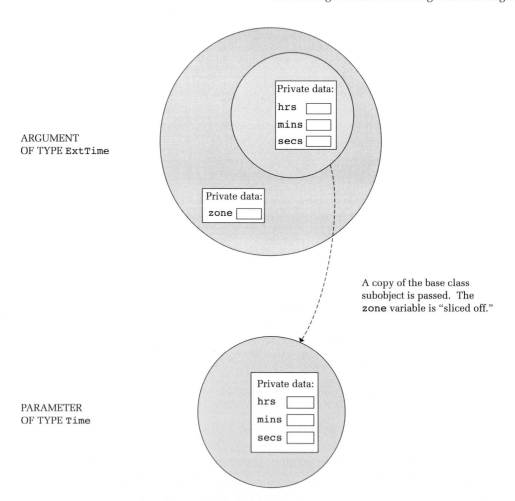

(The slicing problem also occurs with assignment operations. In the statement

```
parentClassObject = childClassObject;
```

only the data members that the two objects have in common are copied. Additional data members contained in `childClassObject` are not copied.)

With passing by reference, the slicing problem does not occur because the *address* of the caller's argument is sent to the function. Let's change the heading of our `Print` function so that `someTime` is a reference parameter:

```
void Print( /* in */ Time& someTime )
```

Now when we pass endTime as the argument, its address is sent to the function. Its time zone member is not sliced off because no copying takes place. But to our dismay, the Print function *still* prints only three of endTime's data members—hours, minutes, and seconds.

Within the Print function, the difficulty is that static binding is used in the statement

```
someTime.Write();
```

The compiler must generate machine language code for the Print function at compile time, but the type of the actual argument (Time or ExtTime) isn't known until run time. How can the compiler know which Write function to use—Time::Write or ExtTime::Write? The compiler cannot know, so it uses Time::Write because the parameter someTime is of type Time. Therefore, the Print function always prints just three values—hours, minutes, and seconds—regardless of the type of the argument. Fortunately, C++ provides a very simple solution to our problem: *virtual functions*.

Virtual Functions

Suppose we make one small change to our Time class declaration: We begin the declaration of the Write function with the reserved word virtual.

```
class Time
{
public:
    ⋮
    virtual void Write() const;
    ⋮
private:
    ⋮
};
```

Declaring a member function to be virtual instructs the compiler to generate code that guarantees **dynamic** (run-time) **binding** of a function to an object. That is, the determination of which function to call is postponed until run time. (Note that to make Write a virtual function, the word virtual appears in one place only—the Time class declaration. It does not appear in the Write function definition that is located in the time.cpp file, nor does it appear in any descendant class—such as ExtTime—that redefines the Write function.)

Dynamic binding   The run-time determination of which function to call for a particular object.

Virtual functions work in the following way. If a class object is passed *by reference* to some function, and if the body of that function contains a statement

```
param.MemberFunc( ... );
```

then

1. If `MemberFunc` is not a virtual function, the type of the *parameter* determines which function to call. (Static binding is used.)
2. If `MemberFunc` is a virtual function, the type of the *argument* determines which function to call. (Dynamic binding is used.)

With just one word—`virtual`—the difficulties we encountered with our `Print` function disappear entirely. If we declare `Write` to be a virtual function in the `Time` class, the function

```
void Print( /* in */ Time& someTime )
{
    ⋮
    someTime.Write();
    ⋮
}
```

works correctly for arguments either of type `Time` or of type `ExtTime`. The correct `Write` function (`Time::Write` or `ExtTime::Write`) is invoked because the argument carries the information necessary at run time to choose the appropriate function. Deriving a new and unanticipated class from `Time` presents no complications. If this new class redefines the `Write` function, then our `Print` function still works correctly. Dynamic binding ensures that each object knows how to print itself, and the appropriate version will be invoked. In OOP terminology, `Write` is a **polymorphic operation**—an operation that has multiple meanings depending on the type of the object that responds to it at run time.

Polymorphic operation   An operation that has multiple meanings depending on the type of the object to which it is bound at run time.

Here are some things to know about using virtual functions in C++:

1. To obtain dynamic binding, you must use passing by reference when passing a class object to a function. If you use passing by value, the compiler does not use the `virtual` mechanism; instead, member slicing and static binding occur.
2. In the declaration of a virtual function, the word `virtual` appears only in the base class, not in any derived class.
3. If a base class declares a virtual function, it *must* implement that function, even if the body is empty.
4. A derived class is not required to provide its own reimplementation of a virtual function. In this case, the base class's version is used by default.
5. A derived class cannot redefine the function return type of a virtual function.

Object-Oriented Design

We have looked at language features that let us implement an object-oriented design. Now let's turn to the phase that precedes implementation—OOD itself.

A computer program usually models some real-life activity or concept. A banking program models the real-life activities associated with a bank. A spreadsheet program models a real spreadsheet, a large paper form used by accountants and financial planners. A robotics program models human perception and human motion.

Nearly always, the aspect of the world that we are modeling (the *application domain* or *problem domain*) consists of objects—checking accounts, bank tellers, spreadsheet rows, spreadsheet columns, robot arms, robot legs. The computer program that solves the real-life problem also includes objects (the *solution domain*)—counters, lists, menus, windows, and so forth. OOD is based on the philosophy that programs are easier to write and understand if the major objects in a program correspond closely to the objects in the problem domain.

There are many ways in which to perform object-oriented design. Different authors advocate different techniques. Our purpose is not to choose one particular technique or to present a summary of all the techniques. Rather, our purpose is to describe a three-step process that captures the essence of OOD:

1. Identify the objects and operations.
2. Determine the relationships among objects.
3. Design the driver.

In this section, we do not show a complete example of an object-oriented design of a problem solution—we save that for the Problem-Solving Case Study at the end of the chapter. Instead, we describe the important issues involved in each of the three steps.

Step 1: Identify the Objects and Operations

Recall that structured design (functional decomposition) begins with identification of the major actions the program is to perform. In contrast, OOD begins by identifying the major objects and the associated operations on those objects. In both design methods, it is often difficult to see where to start.

To identify solution-domain objects, a good way to start is to look at the problem domain. More specifically, go to the problem definition and look for important nouns and verbs. The nouns (and noun phrases) may suggest objects; the verbs (and verb phrases) may suggest operations. For example, the problem definition for a banking program might include the following sentences:

... The program must handle a customer's savings account. The customer is allowed to deposit funds into the account and withdraw funds from the account, and the bank must pay interest on a quarterly basis. ...

In these sentences, the key nouns are

Savings account
Customer

and the key verb phrases are

Deposit funds
Withdraw funds
Pay interest

Although we are working with a very small portion of the entire problem definition, the list of nouns suggests two potential objects: `savingsAccount` and `customer`. The operations on a `savingsAccount` object are suggested by the list of verb phrases—namely, `Deposit`, `Withdraw`, and `PayInterest`. What are the operations on a `customer` object? We would need more information from the rest of the problem definition in order to answer this question. In fact, `customer` may not turn out to be a useful object at all. The nouns-and-verbs technique is only a starting point—it points us to *potential* objects and operations.

Determining which nouns and verbs are significant is one of the most difficult aspects of OOD. There are no cookbook formulas for doing so, and there probably never will be. Not all nouns become objects, and not all verbs become operations. The nouns-and-verbs technique is imperfect, but it does give us a first approximation to a solution.

The solution domain includes not only objects drawn from the problem domain but also *implementation-level* objects. These are objects that do not model the problem domain but are used in building the program itself. In systems with graphical user interfaces—Microsoft Windows or the Macintosh operating system, for example—a program may need several kinds of implementation-level objects: window objects, menu objects, objects that respond to mouse clicks, and so on. Objects such as these are often available in class libraries so that we don't need to design and implement them from scratch each time we need them in different programs.

Step 2: Determine the Relationships Among Objects

After selecting potential objects and operations, the next step is to examine the relationships among the objects. In particular, we want to see whether certain objects might be related either by inheritance or by composition. Inheritance and composition relationships not only pave the way for code reuse—as we emphasized in our discussion of OOP—but also simplify the design and allow us to model the problem domain more accurately. For example, the banking problem may require several kinds of savings accounts—one for general customers, another for preferred customers, and another for children under the age of 12. If these are all variations on a basic savings account, the is-a relationship (and, therefore, inheritance) is probably appropriate. Starting with a SavingsAccount class that provides operations common to any savings account, we could design each of the other accounts as a child class of SavingsAccount, concentrating our efforts only on the properties that make each one different from the parent class.

Sometimes the choice between inheritance and composition is not immediately clear. Earlier we wrote a TimeCard class to represent an employee's time card. Given an existing Time class, we used composition to relate TimeCard and Time—the private part of the TimeCard class was composed of a Time object (and an ID number). We could also have used inheritance. We could have derived class TimeCard from Time (inheriting the hours, minutes, and seconds members) and then specialized it by adding an extra data member (the ID number) and the extra operations of Punch, Print, and so forth. Both inheritance and composition give us four private data members: hours, minutes, seconds, and ID number. However, the use of inheritance means that all of the Time operations are also valid for TimeCard objects. A user of the TimeCard class could—either intentionally or accidentally—invoke operations such as Set and Increment, which are not appropriate operations on a time card. Furthermore, inheritance leads to a confused design in this example. It is not true that a TimeCard *is a* Time; rather, a TimeCard *has a* Time (and an ID number). In general, the best design strategy is to use inheritance for is-a relationships and composition for has-a relationships.

Step 3: Design the Driver

The final step is to design the driver—the top-level algorithm. In OOD, the driver is the glue that puts the objects (along with their operations) together. When implementing the design in C++, the driver becomes the `main` function.

Notice that structured design *begins* with the design of the top-level algorithm, whereas OOD *ends* with the top-level algorithm. In OOD, most of the control flow has already been designed in steps 1 and 2; the algorithms are located within the operations on objects. As a result, the driver often has very little to do but process user commands or input some data and then delegate tasks to various objects.

SOFTWARE ENGINEERING TIP

The Iterative Nature of Object-Oriented Design

Software developers, researchers, and authors have proposed many different strategies for performing OOD. Common to nearly all of these strategies are three fundamental steps:

1. Identify the objects and operations.
2. Determine the relationships among objects.
3. Design the driver.

Experience with large software projects has shown that these three steps are not necessarily sequential—step 1, step 2, step 3, then we are done. In practice, step 1 occurs first, but only as a first approximation. During steps 2 and 3, new objects or operations may be discovered, leading us back to step 1 again. It is realistic to think of steps 1 through 3 not as a sequence but as a loop.

Furthermore, each step is an iterative process within itself. Step 1 may entail working and reworking our view of the objects and operations. Similarly, steps 2 and 3 often involve experimentation and revision. In any step, we may conclude that a potential object is not useful after all. Or we might decide to add or eliminate operations on a particular object.

There is always more than one way to solve a problem. Iterating and reiterating through the design phase leads to insights that produce a better solution.

Implementing the Design

In OOD, when we first identify an object, it is an *abstract object.* We do not immediately choose an exact data representation for that object. Similarly, the operations on objects begin as *abstract operations,* because there is no initial attempt to provide algorithms for these operations.

Eventually, we have to implement the objects and operations. For each abstract object, we must

- Choose a suitable data representation.
- Create algorithms for the abstract operations.

To select a data representation for an object, the C++ programmer has three options:

1. Use a built-in data type.
2. Use an existing ADT.
3. Create a new ADT.

For a given object, a good rule of thumb is to consider these three options in the order listed. A built-in type is the most straightforward to use and understand, and operations on these types are already defined by the language. If a built-in type is not adequate to represent an object, you should survey available ADTs in a class library (either the system's or your own) to see if any are a good match for the abstract object. If no suitable ADT exists, you must design and implement a new ADT to represent the object.

Fortunately, even if you must resort to option 3, the mechanisms of inheritance and composition allow you to combine options 2 and 3. When we needed an `ExtTime` class earlier in the chapter, we used inheritance to build on an existing `Time` class. And when we created a `TimeCard` class, we used composition to include a `Time` object in the private data.

In addition to choosing a data representation for the abstract object, we must implement the abstract operations. With OOD, the algorithms that implement the abstract operations are often short and straightforward. We have seen numerous examples in this chapter and in Chapters 11 and 13 in which the code for ADT operations is only a few lines long. But this is not always the case. If an operation is extremely complex, it may be best to treat the operation as a new problem and use functional decomposition on the control flow. In this situation, it is appropriate to apply both functional decomposition and object-oriented methodologies together. Experienced programmers are familiar with both methodologies and use them either independently or in combination with each other. However, the software development community is becoming increasingly convinced that although functional decomposition is important for designing low-level algorithms and operations on ADTs, the future in developing huge software systems lies in OOD and OOP.

PROBLEM-SOLVING CASE STUDY

Time Card Lookup

Problem: In this chapter, we talked about a factory that is computerizing its employee time card information. Work on the software has already begun, and you have been hired to join the effort. Each morning after the employees have punched in, the time card data (ID number and time stamp) for all employees is written to a file named `punchInFile`. Your task is to write a program that inputs the data from this file and allows the user to look up the time stamp (punch-in time) for any employee. The program should prompt the user for an ID number, look up that employee's time card information, and print it out. This interactive lookup process is repeated until the user types a negative number for the employee ID. The factory has, at most, 500 employees. If `punchInFile` contains more than 500 time cards, the excess time cards should be ignored and a warning message printed.

Input: Employee time card information (file stream `punchInFile`) and a sequence of employee ID numbers to be looked up (standard input device).

Each line in `punchInFile` contains an employee's ID number (`long` integer) and the time he or she punched in (three integers—hours, minutes, and seconds):

```
246308 7 45 50
129336 8 15 29
```

The end-of-file condition signals the end of the input data.

Interactive input from the user consists of employee ID numbers, entered one at a time in response to a prompt. A negative ID number signals the end of the interactive input.

PROBLEM-SOLVING CASE STUDY *cont'd.*

Output: For each employee ID that is input from the user, the corresponding time at which the employee punched in (or a message if the program cannot find a time card for the employee).

Below is a sample of the run-time dialogue. The user's input is highlighted.

```
Enter an employee ID (negative to quit): 129336
ID: 129336 Time: 08:15:29

Enter an employee ID (negative to quit): 222000
222000 has not punched in yet.

Enter an employee ID (negative to quit): -3
```

Discussion: Using structured design (functional decomposition), we would begin by thinking about the overall flow of control and the major actions to be performed. With object-oriented design, we consider the overall flow of control *last*.

We begin our design by identifying objects and their associated operations. The best place to start is by examining the problem domain. In object-oriented fashion, we search for important nouns and noun phrases in the problem definition. Here is a list of candidate objects (potential objects):

Factory
Employee
File punchInFile
ID number
Time card
Time stamp (punch-in time)
User

Reviewing this list, we conclude that the first two candidates—factory and employee—are probably not objects in the solution domain. In the problem we are to solve, a factory and an employee have no useful properties or interesting operations. Also, we can eliminate the last candidate listed—a user. *User* is merely a noun appearing in the problem definition; it has nothing to do with the problem domain. At this point, we can pare down our list of potential objects to the following:

File punchInFile
ID number
Time card
Time stamp

To determine operations on these objects, we look for significant verb phrases in the problem definition. Here are some possibilities:

Punch a time card
Input data from the file
Look up time card information
Print out time card information
Input an employee ID

To associate these operations with the appropriate objects, let's make an *object table* as follows:

Object	Operation
File `punchInFile`	Input data from the file
ID number	Input an employee ID
Time card	Punch a time card
	Look up time card information
	Print out time card information
Time stamp	—

Analyzing the object table, we see that something is not quite right. For one thing, "Look up time card information" is not an operation on a single time card—it's more properly an operation that applies to a *collection* of time cards. What we're missing is an object that represents a list of time cards. That is, the program should read all the time cards from the data file and store them into a list. From this list, our program can look up the time card that matches a particular employee ID. Notice that this new object—the time card list—is an implementation-level object rather than a problem-domain object. This object is not readily apparent in the problem domain, yet we need it in order to design and implement the program.

Another thing we notice in the object table is the absence of any operations on the time stamp object. A little thought should convince us that this object simply represents the time of day. As with the `Time` class we discussed in this chapter, suitable operations might be to set the time and to print the time.

Here is a revised object table that includes the time card list object and refines the operations that might be suitable for each object:

Object	Operation
File `punchInFile`	Open the file
	Input data from the file
ID number	Input an employee ID
	Print an employee ID
Time card	Set the ID number on a time card
	Inspect the ID number on a time card
	Punch the time stamp on a time card
	Inspect the time stamp on a time card
	Print the time card information
Time card list	Read all time cards into the list
	Look up time card information
Time stamp	Set the time of day
	Print the time

The second major step in OOD is to determine the relationships among the objects. Specifically, we're looking for inheritance and composition relationships. Our object table does not reveal any inheritance relationships. Using *is-a* as a guide, we cannot say that a time card is a kind of time stamp or vice versa, that a time card list is a kind of time card or vice versa, and so on. However, we find several composition relationships. Using *has-a* as a guide, we see that a time card has a time stamp as part of its state, a time card has an ID number as part of its state, and a time card list has several time cards as part of its state (see Figure 14-9). Discovery of these relationships helps us to further refine the design (and implementation) of the objects.

Now that we have determined a reasonable set of objects and operations, let's look at each object in detail. Keep in mind that the decisions we have made are not necessarily final. We may change our minds as we proceed, perhaps adding and deleting objects and operations as we focus in on a solution. Remember that OOD is an iterative process, characterized by experimentation and revision.

The `punchInFile` Object: This object represents an ordinary kind of input file with the ordinary operations of opening the file and reading from the file. No further design of this object is necessary. To implement the object, the obvious choice for a data representation is the `ifstream` class supplied by the C++ standard library. The `ifstream` class provides operations for opening and reading from a file, so we don't need to implement these operations ourselves.

The ID Number Object: This object merely represents an integer number (possibly large), and the only abstract operations we have identified are input and output. Therefore, the built-in `long` type is the most straightforward data representation. To implement the abstract operations of input and output we can simply use the << and >> operators.

The Time Stamp Object: The time stamp object represents a time of day. There is no built-in type we can use as a data representation, but we can use an existing class—the `Time` class we worked with earlier in the chapter. The complete specification of the `Time` class appears below.

```
//*****************************************************************
// SPECIFICATION FILE (time.h)
// This file gives the specification of a Time abstract data type
//*****************************************************************
#ifndef TIME_H
#define TIME_H

class Time
{
public:
    void Set( /* in */ int hours,
              /* in */ int minutes,
              /* in */ int seconds );
        // Precondition:
        //     0 <= hours <= 23  &&  0 <= minutes <= 59
```

FIGURE 14-9

Composition Relationships Among Objects

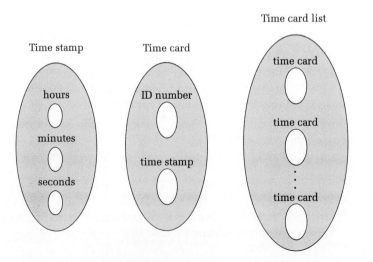

```
                    //   && 0 <= seconds <= 59
                    // Postcondition:
                    //     Time is set according to the incoming parameters

            void Increment();
                    // Postcondition:
                    //     Time has been advanced by one second, with
                    //     23:59:59 wrapping around to 0:0:0

            void Write() const;
                    // Postcondition:
                    //     Time has been output in the form HH:MM:SS

            Time( /* in */ int initHrs,
                  /* in */ int initMins,
                  /* in */ int initSecs );
                    // Precondition:
                    //     0 <= initHrs <= 23  &&  0 <= initMins <= 59
                    //  && 0 <= initSecs <= 59
                    // Postcondition:
                    //     Class object is constructed
                    //  && Time is set according to the incoming parameters

            Time();
                    // Postcondition:
                    //     Class object is constructed  &&  Time is 0:0:0
        private:
            int hrs;
            int mins;
            int secs;
        };
        #endif
```

(We surround the code with the preprocessor directives

```
#ifndef TIME_H
#define TIME_H
  ⋮
#endif
```

to prevent multiple inclusion of the Time class declaration in cases where a new class is created from Time by inheritance or composition. You may wish to review the section "Avoiding Multiple Inclusion of Header Files" in this chapter.)

You have already seen the implementations of the Time class member functions. They are the same as in the TimeType class of Chapter 11.

By declaring a time stamp object to be of type `Time`, we can simply implement our time stamp operations as calls to the `Time` class member functions:

```
Time timeStamp;

timeStamp.Set(hours, minutes, seconds);
timeStamp.Write();
```

Notice that the abstract operations we listed for a time stamp do not include an increment operation. Should we rewrite the `Time` class to eliminate the `Increment` function? No. Wherever possible, we want to reuse existing code. Let's use the `Time` class as it exists. The presence of the `Increment` function does no harm. We simply have no need to invoke it on behalf of a time stamp object.

Testing: Testing the `Time` class amounts to testing each of its member functions. In the Testing and Debugging section of Chapter 11, we described at length how to test a similar class, `TimeType`. `Time` is identical to `TimeType` except for the absence of two member functions, `Equal` and `LessThan`.

The Time Card Object: A time card object represents a pair of values: an employee ID number and a time stamp. The abstract operations are those we listed in our object table. There is no built-in type or existing C++ class that we can use directly to represent a time card, so we'll design a new class. (We sketched a `TimeCard` class earlier in the chapter, but it was not complete.)

Here is a possible specification of the class. Notice that we have added a new operation that did not appear in our object table: a class constructor.

```
//******************************************************************
// SPECIFICATION FILE (timecard.h)
// This file gives the specification of a TimeCard ADT
//******************************************************************
#ifndef TIMECARD_H
#define TIMECARD_H

#include "time.h"

class TimeCard
{
public:
    void Punch( /* in */ int hours,
```

```
                        /* in */ int minutes,
                        /* in */ int seconds );
        // Precondition:
        //      0 <= hours <= 23   &&  0 <= minutes <= 59
        //   && 0 <= seconds <= 59
        // Postcondition:
        //      Time is punched according to the incoming parameters

    void SetID( /* in */ long idNum );
        // Precondition:
        //      idNum is assigned
        // Postcondition:
        //      ID number on the time card is idNum

    long IDPart() const;
        // Postcondition:
        //      Function value == ID number on the time card

    Time TimePart() const;
        // Postcondition:
        //      Function value == time stamp on the time card

    void Print() const;
        // Postcondition:
        //      Time card has been output in the form
        //          ID: 235658 Time: 08:14:25

    TimeCard();
        // Postcondition:
        //      Class object is constructed with an ID number of 0
        //      and a time of 0:0:0
private:
    long id;
    Time timeStamp;
};
#endif
```

The private part of this class declaration shows very clearly the composition relationship we proposed earlier—namely, that a time card object is composed of an ID number object and a time stamp object.

To implement the abstract operations on a time stamp, we must implement the `TimeCard` class member functions. Earlier in the chapter, we showed how to implement the constructor, `Punch`, and `Print` functions, so we do not repeat the discussion here. Now we must implement `SetID`, `IDPart`, and `TimePart`. These are easy. The body of `SetID` merely sets the private variable `id` equal to the incoming parameter, `idNum`:

```
id = idNum;
```

The body of `IDPart` needs only to return the current value of `id`, and the body of `TimePart` simply returns the current value of the private object `timeStamp`. Here is the implementation file containing the definitions of all the `TimeCard` member functions:

```cpp
//*******************************************************************
// IMPLEMENTATION FILE (timecard.cpp)
// This file implements the TimeCard class member functions
//*******************************************************************
#include "timecard.h"
#include <iostream>

using namespace std;

// Private members of class:
//      long id;
//      Time timeStamp;


//*******************************************************************

TimeCard::TimeCard()

// Default constructor

// Postcondition:
//      Time is 0:0:0 (via implicit call to timeStamp object's
//      default constructor)
//   && id == 0

{
    id = 0;
}


//*******************************************************************

void TimeCard::Punch( /* in */ int hours,
                      /* in */ int minutes,
                      /* in */ int seconds )
```

PROBLEM-SOLVING CASE STUDY cont'd.

```
// Precondition:
//     0 <= hours <= 23  &&  0 <= minutes <= 59
//  && 0 <= seconds <= 59
// Postcondition:
//     Time is punched according to hours, minutes, and seconds

{
    timeStamp.Set(hours, minutes, seconds);
}

//****************************************************************

void TimeCard::SetID( /* in */ long idNum )

// Precondition:
//     idNum is assigned
// Postcondition:
//     id == idNum

{
    id = idNum;
}

//****************************************************************

long TimeCard::IDPart() const

// Postcondition:
//     Function value == id

{
    return id;
}

//****************************************************************

Time TimeCard::TimePart() const

// Postcondition:
//     Function value == timeStamp

{
    return timeStamp;
}

//****************************************************************
```

```
void TimeCard::Print() const

// Postcondition:
//     Time card has been output in the form
//        ID: 235658 Time: 08:14:25

{
    cout << "ID: " << id << " Time: ";
    timeStamp.Write();
}
```

Testing: These functions are all very easy to test. Because the `Time` class has already been tested and debugged, the `Punch` function (which calls `Time::Set`) and the `Print` function (which calls `Time::Write`) should work correctly. Also, none of the `TimeCard` member functions use loops or branching, so it is sufficient to write a single test driver that calls each of the member functions, supplying argument values that satisfy the preconditions.

The Time Card List Object: This object represents a list of time cards. Once again, we'll write a new C++ class for this list because no built-in type or existing class will do.

In Chapter 13, we introduced the list as an ADT and examined typical list operations: insert an item into the list, delete an item, report whether the list is full, report whether the list is empty, search for a particular item, sort the list items into order, print the entire list, and so forth. Should we include all these operations when designing our list of time cards? Probably not. It's unlikely that a list of time cards would be considered general-purpose enough to warrant the effort. Let's stick to the operations we listed in the object table:

Read all time cards into the list
Look up time card information

To choose a data representation for the list, let's review the relationships among the objects in our program. We said that the time card list object is composed of time card objects. Therefore, we can use a 500-element array of `TimeCard` class objects to represent the list, along with an integer variable indicating the length of the list (the number of array elements that are actually in use).

Before we write the specification of the `TimeCardList` class, let's review the operations once more. The lookup operation must search the array for a particular time card. Because the array is potentially very large (500 elements), a binary search is better than a sequential search. However, a binary search requires the array elements to be in sorted order. We must either insert each time card into its proper place as it is read from the data file or sort the time cards after they have been read. Chapter 13's Exam Attendance case study used the former approach. For variety, let's take the latter approach and add another operation—a sorting operation. (We'll use the selection sort we developed in Chapter 13.) Finally, we need one more operation to initialize the private data: a class constructor. Here is the resulting class specification:

```cpp
//*********************************************************************
// SPECIFICATION FILE (tclist.h)
// This file gives the specification of TimeCardList, an ADT for a
// list of TimeCard objects.
//*********************************************************************
#ifndef TCLIST_H
#define TCLIST_H

#include "timecard.h"
#include <fstream>

using namespace std;

const int MAX_LENGTH = 500;    // Maximum number of time cards

class TimeCardList
{
public:
    void ReadAll( /* inout */ ifstream& inFile );
        // Precondition:
        //     inFile has been opened for input
        // Postcondition:
        //     List contains at most MAX_LENGTH employee time cards
        //     as read from inFile. (Excess time cards are ignored
        //     and a warning message is printed)

    void SelSort();
        // Postcondition:
        //     List components are in ascending order of employee ID

    void BinSearch( /* in */  long      idNum,
                    /* out */ bool&     found,
                    /* out */ TimeCard& card  ) const;
        // Precondition:
        //     List components are in ascending order of employee ID
        //  && idNum is assigned
        // Postcondition:
        //     IF time card for employee idNum is in list
```

```
        //              found == true  &&  card == time card for idNum
        //      ELSE
        //              found == false  &&  value of card is undefined

    TimeCardList();
        // Postcondition:
        //      Empty list created
private:
    int     length;
    TimeCard data[MAX_LENGTH];
};
#endif
```

The `BinSearch` function is a little different from the one we presented in Chapter 13. There, it was a private member function that returned the index of the array element where the item was found. Here, `BinSearch` is a public member function that returns the entire time card to the client.

Now we must implement the `TimeCardList` member functions. Let's begin with the class constructor. Remember that when a class X is composed of objects of other classes, the constructors for those objects are executed before the body of X's constructor is executed. When the `TimeCardList` constructor is called, all 500 `TimeCard` objects in the private `data` array are first constructed. These objects are constructed via implicit calls to the `TimeCard` class's default constructor. (Recall from Chapter 12 that an array of class objects is constructed using the class's default constructor, not a parameterized constructor.) After the `data` array elements are constructed, there is nothing left to do but to set the private variable `length` equal to 0:

```
TimeCardList::TimeCardList()

// Postcondition:
//      Each element of data array has an ID number of 0
//      and a time of 0:0:0 (via implicit call to each array
//      element's default constructor)
//  && length == 0

{
    length = 0;
}
```

To implement the `ReadAll` member function, we use a loop that reads each employee's data (ID number and hours, minutes, and seconds of the punch-in time) and stores the data into the next unused element of the data array. The loop terminates either when end-of-file occurs or when the length of the array reaches MAX_LENGTH. After exiting the loop, we are to print a warning message if more data exists in the file (that is, if end-of-file has not occurred).

ReadAll (Inout: inFile)

```
Read idNum, hours, minutes, seconds from inFile
WHILE NOT EOF on inFile AND length < MAX_LENGTH
        data[length].SetID(idNum)
        data[length].Punch(hours, minutes, seconds)
        Increment length by 1
        Read idNum, hours, minutes, seconds from inFile
IF NOT EOF on inFile
        Print warning that remaining time cards will be ignored
```

The implementation of the SelSort member function has to be slightly different from the one we developed in Chapter 13. Remember that SelSort finds the minimum value in the list and swaps it with the value in the first place in the list. Then the next-smallest value in the list is swapped with the value in the second place. This process continues until all the values are in order. The location in this algorithm that we must change is where the minimum value is determined. Instead of comparing two time cards in the list (which doesn't make any sense), we compare the *ID numbers* on the time cards. To inspect the ID number on a time card, we use the observer function IDPart provided by the TimeCard class. The statement that did the comparison in the original SelSort function must be changed from

```
if (data[searchIndx] < data[minIndx])
```

to

```
if (data[searchIndx].IDPart() < data[minIndx].IDPart())
```

We must make a similar change in the BinSearch function. The original version in Chapter 13 compared the search item with list components directly. Here, we cannot compare the search item (an ID number of type long) with a list component (an object of type TimeCard). Again, we must use the IDPart observer function to inspect the ID number on a time card.

Below is the implementation file for the `TimeCardList` class.

```
//*****************************************************************
// IMPLEMENTATION FILE (tclist.cpp)
// This file implements the TimeCardList class member functions.
// List representation: an array of TimeCard objects and an
// integer variable giving the current length of the list
//*****************************************************************
#include "tclist.h"
#include <iostream>

using namespace std;

// Private members of class:
//     int       length;               Current length of list
//     TimeCard data[MAX_LENGTH];      Array of TimeCard objects


//*****************************************************************

TimeCardList::TimeCardList()

// Default constructor

// Postcondition:
//     Each element of data array has an ID number of 0
//     and a time of 0:0:0 (via implicit call to each array
//     element's default constructor)
//  && length == 0

{
    length = 0;
}


//*****************************************************************

void TimeCardList::ReadAll( /* inout */ ifstream& inFile )

// Precondition:
//     inFile has been opened for input
// Postcondition:
//     data[0..length-1] contain employee time cards as read
//     from inFile
//  && 0 <= length <= MAX_LENGTH
//  && IF inFile contains more than MAX_LENGTH time cards
//         Warning message has been printed and excess time cards
//         are ignored
```

```
{
    long idNum;        // Employee ID number
    int  hours;        // Employee punch-in time
    int  minutes;
    int  seconds;

    inFile >> idNum >> hours >> minutes >> seconds;
    while (inFile && length < MAX_LENGTH)
    {
        data[length].SetID(idNum);
        data[length].Punch(hours, minutes, seconds);
        length++;
        inFile >> idNum >> hours >> minutes >> seconds;
    }
    if (inFile)
        // Assert: inFile is not at end-of-file
        cout << "More than " << MAX_LENGTH << " time cards "
             << "in input file.  Remainder are ignored." << endl;
}

//***************************************************************

void TimeCardList::SelSort()

// Postcondition:
//     data array contains the same values as data@entry, rearranged
//     into ascending order of employee ID

{
    TimeCard temp;         // Used for swapping
    int      passCount;    // Loop control variable
    int      searchIndx;   // Loop control variable
    int      minIndx;      // Index of minimum so far

    for (passCount = 0; passCount < length - 1; passCount++)
    {
        minIndx = passCount;

        // Find the index of the smallest component
        // in data[passCount..length-1]

        for (searchIndx = passCount + 1; searchIndx < length;
                                          searchIndx++)
            if (data[searchIndx].IDPart() < data[minIndx].IDPart())
                minIndx = searchIndx;
```

```
                    // Swap data[minIndx] and data[passCount]

                    temp = data[minIndx];
                    data[minIndx] = data[passCount];
                    data[passCount] = temp;
                }
            }


    //****************************************************************

    void TimeCardList::BinSearch( /* in */   long       idNum,
                                  /* out */ bool&      found,
                                  /* out */ TimeCard& card  ) const

    // Precondition:
    //     data[0..length-1] are in ascending order of employee ID
    //  && idNum is assigned
    // Postcondition:
    //     IF time card for employee idNum is in list at position i
    //         found == true  &&  card == data[i]
    //     ELSE
    //         found == false  &&  value of card is undefined

    {
        int first = 0;          // Lower bound on list
        int last = length - 1;  // Upper bound on list
        int middle;             // Middle index

        found = false;
        while (last >= first && !found)
        {
            middle = (first + last) / 2;
            if (idNum < data[middle].IDPart())
                // Assert: idNum is not in data[middle..last]
                last = middle - 1;
            else if (idNum > data[middle].IDPart())
                // Assert: idNum is not in data[first..middle]
                first = middle + 1;
            else
                // Assert: idNum is in data[middle]
                found = true;
        }
        if (found)
            card = data[middle];
    }
```

Testing: If we step back and think about it, we realize that if we write a test driver for the `TimeCardList` class, we will have written the main driver for the entire program! The big picture is that our program is to read in all the file data (function `ReadAll`), sort the time cards into order (function `SelSort`), and look up the time card information for various employees (function `BinSearch`). Therefore, we defer a discussion of testing until we have looked at the main driver.

The Driver: The final step in OOD is to design the driver—the top-level algorithm. As is usually the case in OOD, the driver has very little to do but coordinate the objects that have already been designed.

Main   **Level 0**

```
Create empty list of time cards named punchInList
Open punchInFile for input and verify success
punchInList.ReadAll(punchInFile)
punchInList.SelSort()

Get idNum from user
WHILE idNum ≥ 0
       punchInList.BinSearch(idNum, found, punchInCard)
       IF found
               punchInCard.Print()
       ELSE
               Print idNum, " has not punched in yet."
       Get idNum from user
```

Get ID (Out: idNum)   **Level 1**

```
Print blank line
Prompt user for an ID number
Read idNum
```

Module Structure Chart:

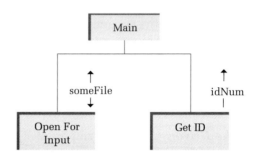

The PunchIn program showing the implementation of the driver follows. We use

```
#include "timecard.h"
```

to insert the TimeCard class declaration into the program, and we use

```
#include "tclist.h"
```

to insert the TimeCardList class declaration. (Recall that tclist.h also happens to #include the header file timecard.h. Thus, timecard.h gets inserted into our program twice. If we had not used the #ifndef directive at the beginning of timecard.h, we would now get a compile-time error for declaring the TimeCard class twice.)

To run the program, we link its object code file with the object code files tclist.obj, timecard.obj, and time.obj.

(The following program is written in ISO/ANSI standard C++. If you are working with pre–standard C++, see the alternate version of the program in the PRE_STD directory of the program disk, available at the publisher's Web site, www.jbpub.com/disks.)

```
//*****************************************************************
// PunchIn program
// A data file contains time cards for employees who have punched
// in for work.  This program reads in the time cards from the
// input file, then reads employee ID numbers from the standard
// input.  For each ID number, the program looks up the employee's
// punch-in time and displays it to the user
//*****************************************************************
#include <iostream>
#include <fstream>       // For file I/O
#include <string>        // For string class
```

PROBLEM-SOLVING CASE STUDY cont'd.

```cpp
#include "timecard.h"    // For TimeCard class
#include "tclist.h"      // For TimeCardList class

void GetID( long& );
void OpenForInput( ifstream& );

int main()
{
    ifstream     punchInFile;     // Input file of time cards
    TimeCardList punchInList;     // List of time cards
    TimeCard     punchInCard;     // A single time card
    long         idNum;           // Employee ID number
    bool         found;           // True if idNum found in list

    OpenForInput(punchInFile);
    if ( !punchInFile )
        return 1;

    punchInList.ReadAll(punchInFile);
    punchInList.SelSort();

    GetID(idNum);
    while (idNum >= 0)
    {
        punchInList.BinSearch(idNum, found, punchInCard);
        if (found)
        {
            punchInCard.Print();
            cout << endl;
        }
        else
            cout << idNum << " has not punched in yet." << endl;
        GetID(idNum);
    }
    return 0;
}

//****************************************************************

void OpenForInput( /* inout */ ifstream& someFile )    // File to be
                                                       // opened

// Prompts the user for the name of an input file
// and attempts to open the file

// Postcondition:
//     The user has been prompted for a file name
//  && IF the file could not be opened
```

PROBLEM-SOLVING CASE STUDY cont'd.

```
//              An error message has been printed
// Note:
//      Upon return from this function, the caller must test
//      the stream state to see if the file was successfully opened

{
        •
    •   (Same as in previous case studies)
        •
}

//****************************************************************

void GetID( /* out */ long& idNum )     // Employee ID number

// Prompts for and reads an employee ID number

// Postcondition:
//      idNum == value read from standard input

{
    cout << endl;
    cout << "Enter an employee ID (negative to quit): ";
    cin >> idNum;
}
```

Testing: To test this program, we begin by preparing an input file that contains time card information for, say, five employees. The data should be in random order of employee ID to verify that the sorting routine works properly. Using this input file, we run the program and supply the following interactive input: the ID numbers of all five employees in the data file (the program should print their punch-in times), a few ID numbers that are not in the data file (the program should print the message that these employees have not checked in yet), and a negative ID number (the program should quit). If the program tells us that one of the five employees in the data file has not checked in yet or prints a punch-in time for one of the employees not in the data file, the fault clearly lies with the punchInList object—the object responsible for reading the file, sorting, and searching. Using a hand trace, the system debugger, or debug output statements, we should check the TimeCardList member functions in the following order: ReadAll (to verify that the file data was read into the list correctly), SelSort (to confirm that the time card information ends up in ascending order of ID number), then BinSearch (to ensure that items in the list are indeed found and that items not in the list are reported as not there).

One more thing needs to be tested. If the data file contains more than MAX_LENGTH time cards, the ReadAll function should print a warning message and ignore the excess time cards. To test this feature, we obviously don't want to create an input file with over 500 time cards. Instead, we go into tclist.h and change the const definition of MAX_LENGTH from 500 to a more manageable value—3, for example. We then recompile only tclist.cpp and relink all four object code files. When we run the program, it should read only the first three time cards from the file, print a warning message, and work with a list of only three time cards. Here is a sample run of the program using 3 as the value of MAX_LENGTH:

Input File

```
398405 7 45 04
290387 7 48 10
193847 7 53 20
938473 7 55 14
837485 8 00 00
385473 8 05 45
573920 8 12 13
483948 8 14 45
```

Copy of the Screen During the Run

```
Input file name: punchin.dat
More than 3 time cards in input file.  Remainder are ignored.

Enter an employee ID (negative to quit): 398405
ID: 398405 Time: 07:45:04

Enter an employee ID (negative to quit): 193847
ID: 193847 Time: 07:53:20

Enter an employee ID (negative to quit): 290387
ID: 290387 Time: 07:48:10

Enter an employee ID (negative to quit): 938473
938473 has not punched in yet.

Enter an employee ID (negative to quit): 111111
111111 has not punched in yet.

Enter an employee ID (negative to quit): -5
```

After testing this aspect of the program, we must not forget to change the value of MAX_LENGTH back to 500, recompile tclist.cpp, and relink the object code files.

Testing and Debugging

Testing and debugging an object-oriented program is largely a process of testing and debugging the C++ classes on which the program is built. The top-level driver also needs testing, but this testing is usually uncomplicated—OOD tends to result in a simple driver.

To review how to test a C++ class, you should refer back to the Testing and Debugging section of Chapter 11. There we walked through the process of testing each member function of a class. We made the observation that you could write a separate test driver for each member function or you could write just one test driver that tests all of the member functions. The latter approach is recommended only for classes that have a few simple member functions.

When an object-oriented program uses inheritance and composition, the order in which you test the classes is, in a sense, predetermined. If class X is derived from class Y or contains an object of class Y, you cannot test X until you have designed and implemented Y. Thus, it makes sense to test and debug the lower-level class (class Y) before testing class X. This chapter's Problem-Solving Case Study demonstrated this sequence of testing. We tested the lowest level class—the Time class—first. Next, we tested the TimeCard class, which contains a Time object. Finally, we tested the TimeCardList class, which contains an array of TimeCard objects. The general principle is that if class X is built on class Y (through inheritance or composition), the testing of X is simplified if Y is already tested and is known to behave correctly.

Testing and Debugging Hints

1. Review the Testing and Debugging Hints for Chapter 11. They apply to the design and testing of C++ classes, which are at the heart of OOP.
2. When using inheritance, don't forget to include the word public when declaring the derived class:

```
class DerivedClass : public BaseClass
{
    ⋮
};
```

The word public makes BaseClass a public base class of DerivedClass. That is, clients of DerivedClass can apply any public BaseClass operation (except constructors) to a DerivedClass object.

3. The header file containing the declaration of a derived class must #include the header file containing the declaration of the base class.
4. Although a derived class inherits the private and public members of its base class, it cannot directly access the inherited private members.
5. If a base class has a constructor, it is invoked before the body of the derived class's constructor is executed. If the base class constructor requires arguments, you must pass these arguments using a constructor initializer:

```
DerivedClass::DerivedClass( ... )
    : BaseClass(arg1, arg2)
{
    ⋮
}
```

If you do not include a constructor initializer, the base class's default constructor is invoked.

6. If a class has a member that is an object of another class and this member object's constructor requires arguments, you must pass these arguments using a constructor initializer:

```
SomeClass::SomeClass( ... )
    : memberObject(arg1, arg2)
{
    ⋮
}
```

If there is no constructor initializer, the member object's default constructor is invoked.

7. To obtain dynamic binding of an operation to an object when passing class objects as arguments, you must
   - Pass the object using passing by reference.
   - Declare the operation to be virtual in the class declaration.
8. If a base class declares a virtual function, it *must* implement that function even if the body is empty.
9. A derived class cannot redefine the function return type of a virtual function.

Summary

Object-oriented design (OOD) decomposes a problem into objects—self-contained entities in which data and operations are bound together. In OOD, data is treated as an active, rather than passive, quantity. Each object is responsible for one part of the solution, and the objects communicate by invoking each other's operations.

OOD begins by identifying potential objects and their operations. Examining objects in the problem domain is a good way to begin the process. The next step is to determine the relationships among the objects using inheritance (to express is-a relationships) and composition (to express has-a relationships). Finally, a driver algorithm is designed to coordinate the overall flow of control.

Object-oriented programming (OOP) is the process of implementing an object-oriented design by using language mechanisms for data abstraction, inheritance, and dynamic binding. Inheritance allows any programmer to take an existing class (the base class) and create a new class (the derived class) that inherits the data and operations of the base class. The derived class then specializes the base class by adding new private data, adding new operations, or reimplementing inherited operations—all without analyzing and modifying the implementation of the base class in any way. Dynamic binding of operations to objects allows objects of many different derived types to respond to a single function name, each in its own way. Together, inheritance and dynamic binding have been shown to reduce dramatically the time and effort required to customize existing ADTs. The result is truly reusable software components whose applications and lifetimes extend beyond those conceived of by the original creator.

Quick Check

1. Fill in the blanks: Structured (procedural) programming results in a program that is a collection of interacting _____, whereas OOP results in a program that is a collection of interacting _____. (pp. 802–805)
2. Name the three language features that characterize object-oriented programming languages. (pp. 802–805)
3. Given the class declaration

```
class Point
{
public:
    int X_Coord() const;       // Return the x-coordinate
    int Y_Coord() const;       // Return the y-coordinate
    Point( /* in */ int initX,  // Constructor
           /* in */ int initY );
private:
    int x;
    int y;
};
```

and the type declaration

```
enum StatusType {ON, OFF};
```

declare a class `Pixel` that inherits from class `Point`. Class `Pixel` has an additional data member of type `StatusType` named `status`; it has an additional member function `CurrentStatus` that returns the value of `status`; and it supplies its own constructor that receives three parameters. (pp. 805–812)

4. Write a client statement that creates a `Pixel` object named `onePixel` with an initial (*x*, *y*) position of (3, 8) and a status of `OFF`. (pp. 805–812)

5. Assuming `somePixel` is an object of type `Pixel`, write client code that prints out the current *x*- and *y*-coordinates and status of `somePixel`. (pp. 805–812)

6. Write the function definitions for the `Pixel` class constructor and the `CurrentStatus` function. (pp. 812–817)

7. Fill in the private part of the following class declaration, which uses composition to define a `Line` object in terms of two `Point` objects. (pp. 817–819)

```
class Line
{
public:
    Point StartingPoint() const;    // Return line's starting point
    Point EndingPoint() const;      // Return line's ending point
    float Length() const;           // Return length of the line
    Line( /* in */ int startX,      // Constructor
          /* in */ int startY,
          /* in */ int endX,
          /* in */ int endY    );
private:


};
```

8. Write the function definition for the `Line` class constructor. (pp. 820–822)

9. What is the difference between static and dynamic binding of an operation to an object? (pp. 822–827)

10. Although there are many specific techniques for performing OOD, this chapter uses a three-step process. What are these three steps? (pp. 827–830)

11. When selecting a data representation for an abstract object, what three choices does the C++ programmer have? (pp. 831–832)

Answers **1.** functions, objects **2** Data abstraction, inheritance, dynamic binding
3.
```
class Pixel : public Point
{
public:
    StatusType CurrentStatus() const;
    Pixel( /* in */ int        initX,
           /* in */ int        initY,
```

```
                  /* in */ StatusType initStatus );
      private:
          StatusType status;
      };
```
4. `Pixel onePixel(3, 8, OFF);`
5.
```
   cout << "x-coordinate: " << somePixel.X_Coord() << endl;
   cout << "y-coordinate: " << somePixel.Y_Coord() << endl;
   if (somePixel.CurrentStatus() == ON)
       cout << "Status: on" << endl;
   else
       cout << "Status: off" << endl;
```
6.
```
   Pixel::Pixel( /* in */ int          initX,
                 /* in */ int          initY,
                 /* in */ StatusType initStatus )

       : Point(initX, initY)               // Constructor initializer
   {
       status = initStatus;
   }
```
7.
```
   Point startPt;
   Point endPt;
```
8.
```
   Line::Line( /* in */ int startX,
               /* in */ int startY,
               /* in */ int endX,
               /* in */ int endY    )

       : startPt(startX, startY), endPt(endX, endY)
   {
       // Empty body--nothing more to do
   }
```
9. With static binding, the determination of which function to call for an object occurs at compile time. With dynamic binding, the determination of which function to call for an object occurs at run time. **10.** Identify the objects and operations, determine the relationships among the objects, and design the driver. **11.** Use a built-in data type, use an existing ADT, or create a new ADT.

Exam Preparation Exercises

1. Define the following terms:

structured design	method (of an object)
code reuse	is-a relationship
state (of an object)	has-a relationship
instance variable (of an object)	

2. In C++, inheritance allows a derived class to access directly all of the functions and data of its base class. (True or False?)

3. Given an existing class declaration

```
class Sigma
{
public:
    void Write() const;
        :
private:
    int n;
};
```

a programmer derives a new class `Epsilon` as follows:

```
class Epsilon : Sigma
{
public:
    void Twist();
    Epsilon( /* in */ float initVal );
private:
    float x;
};
```

Then the following client code results in a compile-time error:

```
Epsilon someObject(4.8);

someObject.Write();    // Error
```

a. Why is the call to the `Write` function erroneous?
b. How would you fix the problem?

4. Consider the following two class declarations:

```
class Abc
{
public:
    void DoThis();
private:
    void DoThat();
    int   alpha;
    int   beta;
};
```

```
class Xyz : public Abc
{
public:
    void TryIt();
private:
    int gamma;
};
```

For *each* class, do the following:

a. List all private data members.

b. List all private data members that the class's member functions can reference directly.

c. List all functions that the class's member functions can invoke.

d. List all member functions that a client of the class may legally invoke.

5. A class X uses both inheritance and composition as follows. X is derived from class Y and has a member that is an object of class Z. When an object of class X is created, in what order are the constructors for classes X, Y, and Z executed?

6. With argument passing in C++, you can pass an object of an ancestor class to a parameter that is an object of a descendant class. (True or False?)

7. Consider the following two class declarations:

```
class A
{
public:
    virtual void Write() const;
    A( /* in */ char ch );
private:
    char c;
};
```

```
class B : public A
{
public:
    void Write() const;
    B( /* in */ char ch1,
       /* in */ char ch2 );
private:
    char d;
};
```

Let the implementations of the constructors and Write functions be as follows:

```
A::A( /* in */ char ch )
{
    c = ch;
}
```

```
void A::Write() const
{
    cout << c;
}
```

```
B::B( /* in */ char ch1,
      /* in */ char ch2 )

    : A(ch1)
{
    d = ch2;
}

void B::Write() const
{
    A::Write();
    cout << d;
}
```

Suppose that we declare two class objects, `objectA` and `objectB`:

```
A objectA('x');
B objectB('y', 'z');
```

a. If we write a global function `PrintIt`, defined as

```
void PrintIt( /* in */ A someObject )
{
    someObject.Write();
}
```

then what is printed by the following code segment?

```
PrintIt(objectA);
cout << endl;
PrintIt(objectB);
```

b. Repeat part (a), assuming that `PrintIt` uses passing by reference instead of passing by value:

```
void PrintIt( /* in */ A& someObject )
{
    someObject.Write();
}
```

c. Repeat part (b), assuming that `Write` is *not* a virtual function.

8. Define the following terms associated with object-oriented design:
   problem domain
   solution domain
   implementation-level object

9. Mark each of the following statements as True or False.
   a. Every noun and noun phrase in a problem definition becomes an object in the solution domain.
   b. For a given problem, there are usually more objects in the solution domain than in the problem domain.
   c. In the three-step process for performing object-oriented design, all decisions made during each step are final.
10. For each of the following design methodologies, at what general time (beginning, middle, end) is the driver—the top-level algorithm—designed?
    a. Object-oriented design
    b. Structured design
11. Fill in each blank below with either *is-a* or *has-a*.
    In general, the best strategy in object-oriented design is to use inheritance for _____ relationships and composition for _____ relationships.

Programming Warm-up Exercises

1. For the Line class of Quick Check Question 7, implement the StartingPoint and EndingPoint member functions.
2. For the Line class of Quick Check Question 7, implement the Length member function. *Hint:* The distance between two points (x_1, y_1) and (x_2, y_2) is

$$\sqrt{(x_1 - x_2)^2 + (y_1 - y_2)^2}$$

3. The following class represents a person's mailing address in the United States.

```
class Address
{
public:
    void Write() const;
    Address( /* in */ string newStreet,
             /* in */ string newCity,
             /* in */ string newState,
             /* in */ string newZip    );
private:
    string street;
    string city;
    string state;
    string zipCode;
};
```

Using inheritance, we want to derive an international address class, InterAddress, from the Address class. For this exercise, an international address has all the attributes of a U.S. address plus a country code (a string indicating the name of the country). The public operations of InterAddress are Write (which reimplements the Write function inherited from Address) and a class constructor that receives five parameters (street, city, state, zip code, and country code). Write a class declaration for the InterAddress class.

4. Implement the InterAddress class constructor.
5. Implement the Write function of the InterAddress class.
6. Write a global function PrintAddress that takes a single parameter and uses dynamic binding to print either a U.S. address or an international address. Make the necessary change(s) in the declaration of the Address class so that PrintAddress executes correctly.
7. In Chapter 11, we developed a TimeType class (page 619) and a DateType class (page 625). Using composition, we want to create a TimeAndDay class that contains both a TimeType object and a DateType object. The public operations of the TimeAndDay class should be Set (with six parameters to set the time and day), Increment, Write, and a default constructor. Write a class declaration for the TimeAndDay class.
8. Implement the TimeAndDay default constructor.
9. Implement the Set function of the TimeAndDay class.
10. Implement the Increment function of the TimeAndDay class. (*Hint:* If the time part is incremented to midnight, increment the date part.)
11. Implement the Write function of the TimeAndDay class.

Programming Problems

1. Your parents are thinking of opening a video rental store. Because they are helping with your tuition, they ask you to write a program to handle their inventory.

   What are the major objects in a rental store? They are the items to be rented and the people who rent them. You begin with the abstraction of the items to be rented—video tapes. To determine the characteristics of a video object, you jot down a list of questions.

   - Should the object be one physical video tape, or should it be a title (to allow for multiple copies of a video)?
   - What information about each title should be kept?
   - Should the object contain a place for the card number of the person who has it rented?
   - If there are multiple copies, is it important to keep track of specific copies?
   - What operations should a video object be able to execute?

You decide that the basic object is the title, not an individual tape. The number of copies owned can be a data member of the object. Other data members should include the title, the movie stars, the producer, the director, and the production company. The system eventually must be able to track who has rented which videos, but this is not a property of the video object itself. You'll worry about how to represent the "has rented" object later. For now, who has which specific copy is not important.

The video object must have operations to initialize it and access the various data members. In addition, the object should adjust the number of copies (up or down), determine if a copy is available, check in a copy, and check out a copy. Because you will need to create a list of videos later, you decide to include operations that compare titles and print titles.

You decide to stop at this point, implement the video object, and test it before going on to the rest of the design.

2. Having completed the design and testing of the video object in Programming Problem 1, you are ready to continue with the original problem. Write a program to do the following tasks.

   a. Create a list of video objects.
   b. Search the list for a particular title.
   c. Determine if there are any copies of a particular video currently in the store.
   d. Print the list of video titles.

3. Now that the video inventory is under control, determine the characteristics of the customer and define a customer object. Write the operations and test them. Using this representation of a customer, write a program to do the following tasks.

   a. Create a list of customers.
   b. Search the list by customer name.
   c. Search the list by customer identification number.
   d. Print the list of customer names.

4. Combine the list of video objects and the list of customer objects into a program with the following capabilities.

   a. Check out a video.
   b. Check in a video.
   c. Determine how many videos a customer has (by customer identification number).
   d. Determine which customers have a certain video checked out (by title). (*Hint:* Create a hasVideo object that has a video title and a customer number.)

Case Study Follow-Up

1. Write a test plan for testing the TimeCard class.
2. Write a test driver to implement your test plan for the TimeCard class.

3. Object-oriented design makes code reuse easier and leads to flexible programs. See how easy it is to modify the case study's main driver so that it inputs *two* files (punchInFile and punchOutFile) and outputs not only the punch-in time but also the punch-out time for each employee whose ID is entered by the user. Make these modifications.

4. Revise the TimeCardList class by removing the SelSort function and modifying ReadAll so that it inserts each time card into its proper place in the list as it is read from the input file. Give both the specification and the implementation of the revised class.

15

Pointers, Dynamic Data, and Reference Types

G O A L S

- To be able to declare variables of pointer types.
- To be able to take the addresses of variables and to access the variables through pointers.
- To be able to write an expression that selects a member of a class, struct, or union that is pointed to by a pointer.
- To be able to create and access dynamic data.
- To be able to destroy dynamic data.
- To be able to declare and initialize variables of reference types.
- To be able to access variables that are referenced by reference variables.
- To understand the difference between deep and shallow copy operations.
- To understand how C++ defines the term *initialization*.
- To be able to identify the four member functions needed by a C++ class that manipulates dynamic data.
- To be able to use pointers to improve program efficiency.

In the preceding chapters, we have looked at the simple types and structured types available in C++. There are only two built-in data types left to cover: **pointer** types and **reference** types (see Figure 15-1). These types are simple data types, yet in Figure 15-1 we list them separately from the other simple types because their purpose is so special. We refer to pointer types and reference types as *address types*. A variable of one of these types does not contain a data value; it contains the *memory address* of another variable or structure. Address types have two main purposes: They can make a program more efficient—either in terms of speed or in terms of memory usage—and they can be used to build complex data structures. In this chapter, we demonstrate how they make a program more efficient. Chapter 16 explains how to build complex structures using address types.

Pointers

In many ways, we've saved the best till last. Pointer types are the most interesting data types of all. Pointers are what their name implies: variables that tell where to find something else; that is, pointers contain the addresses or locations of other variables.

Pointer type   A simple data type consisting of an unbounded set of values, each of which addresses or otherwise indicates the location of a variable of a given type. Among the operations defined on pointer variables are assignment and testing for equality.

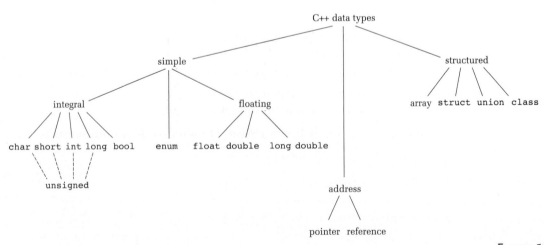

FIGURE 15-1
C++ Data Types

Let's begin this discussion by looking at how pointer variables are declared in C++.

Pointer Variables

Surprisingly, the word *pointer* isn't used in declaring pointer variables; the symbol * is used instead. The declaration

```
int* intPtr;
```

states that `intPtr` is a variable that can point to (that is, contain the address of) an `int` variable. Here is the syntax template for declaring pointer variables:

PointerVariableDeclaration

$$\left\{\begin{array}{l} \text{DataType* Variable ;} \\ \text{DataType *Variable , *Variable \dots ;} \end{array}\right.$$

The syntax template shows two forms, one for declaring a single variable and the other for declaring several variables. In the first form, the compiler does not care where the asterisk is placed. Both of the following declarations are equivalent:

```
int* intPtr;
int *intPtr;
```

Although C++ programmers use both styles, we prefer the first. Attaching the asterisk to the data type name instead of the variable name readily suggests that `intPtr` is of type "pointer to `int`."

According to the syntax template, if you declare several variables in one statement you must precede each variable name with an asterisk. Otherwise, only the first variable is taken to be a pointer variable. The compiler interprets the statement

```
int* p, q;
```

as if it were written

```
int* p;
int  q;
```

To avoid unintended errors when declaring pointer variables, it is safest to declare each variable in a separate statement.

Given the declarations

```
int   beta;
int*  intPtr;
```

we can make `intPtr` point to `beta` by using the unary `&` operator, which is called the *address-of* operator. At run time, the assignment statement

```
intPtr = &beta;
```

takes the memory address of `beta` and stores it into `intPtr`. Alternatively, we could initialize `intPtr` in its declaration as follows:

```
int   beta;
int*  intPtr = &beta;
```

Suppose that `intPtr` and `beta` happen to be located at memory addresses 5000 and 5008, respectively. Then storing the address of `beta` into `intPtr` results in the relationship pictured in Figure 15-2.

Because actual numeric addresses are generally unknown to the C++ programmer, it is more common to display the relationship between a pointer and a pointed-to variable by using rectangles and arrows as in Figure 15-3.

To access a variable that a pointer points to, we use the unary `*` operator—the *dereference* or *indirection* operator. The expression

```
*intPtr
```

FIGURE 15-2
Machine-Level
View of a Pointer
Variable

FIGURE 15-3
Abstract Diagram
of a Pointer
Variable

denotes the variable pointed to by `intPtr`. In our example, `intPtr` currently points to `beta`, so the statement

```
*intPtr = 28;
```

dereferences `intPtr` and stores the value 28 into `beta`. This statement represents **indirect addressing** of `beta`; the machine first accesses `intPtr`, then uses its contents to locate `beta`. In contrast, the statement

```
beta = 28;
```

represents **direct addressing** of `beta`. Direct addressing is like opening a post office box (P.O. Box 15, for instance) and finding a package, whereas indirect addressing is like opening P.O. Box 15 and finding a note that says your package is sitting in P.O. Box 23.

Direct addressing   Accessing a variable in one step by using the variable name.

Indirect addressing   Accessing a variable in two steps by first using a pointer that gives the location of the variable.

Continuing with our example, if we execute the statements

```
*intPtr = 28;
cout << intPtr << endl;
cout << *intPtr << endl;
```

then the output is

```
5008
28
```

The first output statement prints the contents of `intPtr` (5008); the second prints the contents of the variable pointed to by `intPtr` (28).

Let's look at a more involved example of declaring pointers, taking addresses, and dereferencing pointers. The following program fragment declares several types and variables. In this code, the `TimeType` class is the C++ class we developed in Chapter 11, with member functions `Set`, `Increment`, `Write`, `Equal`, and `LessThan`.

```
#include "timetype.h"    // For TimeType class
    ⋮
enum ColorType {RED, GREEN, BLUE};
struct PatientRec
{
    int idNum;
    int height;
    int weight;
};

int        alpha;
ColorType  color;
PatientRec patient;
TimeType   startTime(8, 30, 0);

int*        intPtr = &alpha;
ColorType*  colorPtr = &color;
PatientRec* patientPtr = &patient;
TimeType*   timePtr = &startTime;
```

The variables `intPtr`, `colorPtr`, `patientPtr`, and `timePtr` are all pointer variables. `intPtr` points to (contains the address of) a variable of type `int`, `colorPtr` points to a variable of type `Color`, `patientPtr` points to a struct variable of type `PatientRec`, and `timePtr` points to a class object of type `TimeType`.

The expression `*intPtr` denotes the variable pointed to by `intPtr`. The pointed-to variable can contain any `int` value. The expression `*colorPtr` denotes a variable of type `ColorType`. It can contain RED, GREEN, or BLUE. The expression `*patientPtr` denotes a struct variable of type `PatientRec`. Furthermore, the expressions `(*patientPtr).idNum`, `(*patientPtr).height`, and `(*patientPtr).weight` denote the idNum, height, and weight members of `*patientPtr`. Notice how the accessing expression is built.

`patientPtr`	A pointer variable of type "pointer to `PatientRec`."
`*patientPtr`	A struct variable of type `PatientRec`.
`(*patientPtr).weight`	The weight member of a struct variable of type `PatientRec`.

The expression `(*patientPtr).weight` is a mixture of pointer dereferencing and struct member selection. The parentheses are necessary because the dot operator has higher precedence than the dereference operator (see Appendix B for C++ operator precedence). Without the parentheses, the expression `*patientPtr.weight` would be interpreted wrongly as `*(patientPtr.weight)`.

When a pointer points to a struct (or a class or a union) variable, enclosing the pointer dereference within parentheses can become tedious.

In addition to the dot operator, C++ provides another member selection operator: ->. This *arrow operator* consists of two consecutive symbols: a hyphen and a greater-than symbol. By definition,

PointerExpression **->** MemberName

is equivalent to

(*PointerExpression).MemberName

Therefore, we can write (*patientPtr).weight as patientPtr->weight.

The general guideline for choosing between the two member selection operators (dot and arrow) is the following:

Use the dot operator if the first operand denotes a struct, class, or union variable; use the arrow operator if the first operand denotes a *pointer* to a struct, class, or union variable.

If we want to increment and print the TimeType class object pointed to by timePtr, we could use either the statements

```
(*timePtr).Increment();
(*timePtr).Write();
```

or the statements

```
timePtr->Increment();
timePtr->Write();
```

And if we had declared an array of pointers

```
PatientRec* patPtrArray[20];
```

and initialized the array elements, then we could access the idNum member of the fourth patient as follows:

```
patPtrArray[3]->idNum
```

Pointed-to variables can be used in the same way as any other variable. The following statements are all valid:

```
*intPtr = 250;
*colorPtr = RED;
patientPtr->idNum = 3245;
patientPtr->height = 64;
patientPtr->weight = 114;
patPtrArray[3]->idNum = 6356;
patPtrArray[3]->height = 73;
patPtrArray[3]->weight = 185;
```

Figure 15-4 shows the results of these assignments.

FIGURE 15-4
Results of
Assignment
Statements

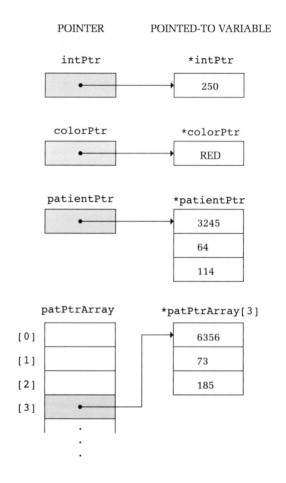

At this point, you may be wondering why we should use pointers at all. Instead of making `intPtr` point to `alpha` and storing 250 into `*intPtr`, why not just store 250 directly into `alpha`? The truth is that there is no good reason to program this way; on the contrary, the examples we have shown would make a program more roundabout and confusing. The major use of pointers in C++ is to manipulate *dynamic variables*— variables that come into existence at execution time only as they are needed. Later in the chapter, we show how to use pointers to create dynamic variables. In the meantime, let's continue with some of the basic aspects of pointers themselves.

Pointer Expressions

You learned in the early chapters that an arithmetic expression is made up of variables, constants, operator symbols, and parentheses. Similarly, pointer expressions are composed of pointer variables, pointer constants, certain allowable operators, and parentheses. We have already discussed pointer variables—variables that hold addresses of other variables. Let's look now at pointer constants.

In C++, there is only one literal pointer constant: the value 0. The pointer constant 0, called the *null pointer,* points to absolutely nothing. The statement

```
intPtr = 0;
```

stores the null pointer into `intPtr`. This statement does *not* cause `intPtr` to point to memory location zero; the null pointer is guaranteed to be distinct from any actual memory address. Because the null pointer does not point to anything, we diagram the null pointer as follows, instead of using an arrow to point somewhere:

intPtr

Instead of using the constant 0, many programmers prefer to use the named constant NULL that is supplied by the standard header file `cstddef`:

```
#include <cstddef>
   ⋮
intPtr = NULL;
```

As with any named constant, the identifier NULL makes a program more self-documenting. Its use also reduces the chance of confusing the null pointer with the integer constant 0.

It is an error to dereference the null pointer, as it does not point to anything. The null pointer is used only as a special value that a program can test for:

```
if (intPtr == NULL)
    DoSomething();
```

We'll see examples of using the null pointer later in this chapter and in Chapter 16.

Although 0 is the only literal constant of pointer type, there is another pointer expression that is considered to be a constant pointer expression: an array name without any index brackets. The value of this expression is the base address (the address of the first element) of the array. Given the declarations

```
int  arr[100];
int* ptr;
```

the assignment statement

```
ptr = arr;
```

has exactly the same effect as

```
ptr = &arr[0];
```

Both of these statements store the base address of arr into ptr.

Although we did not explain it at the time, you have already used the fact that an array name without brackets is a pointer expression. Consider the following code, which calls a ZeroOut function to zero out an array whose size is given as the second argument:

```
int main()
{
    float velocity[30];
        ⋮
    ZeroOut(velocity, 30);
        ⋮
}
```

In the function call, the first argument—an array name without index brackets—is a pointer expression. The value of this expression is the base address of the velocity array. This base address is passed to the function. We can write the ZeroOut function in one of two ways. The first approach—one that you have seen many times—declares the first parameter to be an array of unspecified size.

```
void ZeroOut ( /* out */ float arr[],
               /* in */  int   size  )
{
    int i;

    for (i = 0; i < size; i++)
        arr[i] = 0.0;
}
```

Alternatively, we can declare the parameter to be of type float*, because the parameter simply holds the address of a float variable (the address of the first array element).

```
void ZeroOut( /* out */ float* arr,
              /* in */   int    size )
{
     ⋮   // Function body is unchanged
}
```

Whether we declare the parameter as float arr[] or as float* arr, the result is exactly the same to the C++ compiler: Within the ZeroOut function, arr is a simple variable that points to the beginning of the caller's actual array (see Figure 15-5).

Even though arr is a pointer variable within the ZeroOut function, we are still allowed to attach an index expression to the name arr:

```
arr[i] = 0.0;
```

Indexing a pointer variable is made possible by the following rule in C++:

Indexing is valid for *any* pointer expression, not only an array name. (However, indexing a pointer makes sense only if the pointer points to an array.)

We have now seen four C++ operators that are valid for pointers: =, *, ->, and []. The following table lists the most common operations that may be applied to pointers.

FIGURE 15-5
A Parameter
Pointing to the
Caller's Argument

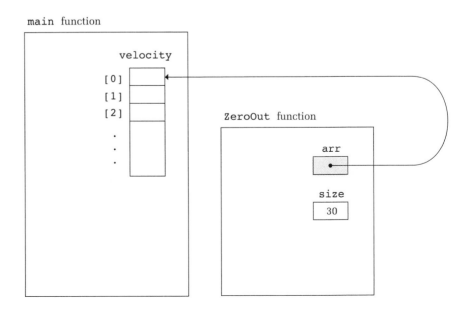

Operator	Meaning	Example	Remarks

=	Assignment	`ptr = &someVar;`
		`ptr1 = ptr2;`
		`ptr = 0;`
			Except for the null pointer, both operands must be of the same data type.

*	Dereference	`*ptr`	
==, !=, <, <=, >, and >=	Relational operators	`ptr1 == ptr2`	The two operands must be of the same data type.
!	Logical NOT	`!ptr`	The result is `true` if the operand is 0 (the null pointer), else the result is `false`.
[]	Index (or subscript)	`ptr[4]`	The indexed pointer should point to an array.
->	Member selection	`ptr->height`	Selects a member of the class, struct, or union variable that is pointed to.

Notice that the logical NOT operator can be used to test for the null pointer:

```
if ( !ptr )
    DoSomething();
```

Some people find this notation confusing because `ptr` is a pointer expression, not a Boolean expression. We prefer to phrase the test this way for clarity:

```
if (ptr == NULL)
    DoSomething();
```

When looking at the table, it is important to keep in mind that the operations listed are operations on pointers, *not* on the pointed-to variables. For example, if `intPtr1` and `intPtr2` are variables of type `int*`, the test

```
if (intPtr1 == intPtr2)
```

compares the pointers, not what they point to. In other words, we are comparing memory addresses, not `int`s. To compare the integers that `intPtr1` and `intPtr2` point to, we would need to write

```
if (*intPtr1 == *intPtr2)
```

In addition to the operators we have listed in the table, the following C++ operators may be applied to pointers: ++, --, +, -, +=, and -=. These operators perform arithmetic on pointers that point to arrays. For example, the expression ptr++ causes ptr to point to the next element of the array, regardless of the size in bytes of each array element. And the expression ptr + 5 accesses the array element that is five elements beyond the one currently pointed to by ptr. We'll say no more about these operators or about pointer arithmetic; the topic of pointer arithmetic is off the main track of what we want to emphasize in this chapter. Instead, we proceed now to explore one of the most important uses of pointers: the creation of dynamic data.

Dynamic Data

In Chapter 8, we described two categories of program data in C++: static data and automatic data. Any global variable is static, as is any local variable explicitly declared as static. The lifetime of a static variable is the lifetime of the entire program. In contrast, an automatic variable—a local variable not declared as static—is allocated (created) when control reaches its declaration and deallocated (destroyed) when control exits the block in which the variable is declared.

With the aid of pointers, C++ provides a third category of program data: **dynamic data.** Dynamic variables are not declared with ordinary variable declarations; they are explicitly allocated and deallocated at execution time by means of two special operators, new and delete. When a program requires an additional variable, it uses new to allocate the variable. When the program no longer needs the variable, it uses delete to deallocate it. The lifetime of a dynamic variable is therefore the time between the execution of new and the execution of delete. The advantage of being able to create new variables at execution time is that we don't have to create any more of them than we need.

Dynamic data   Variables created during execution of a program by means of special operations. In C++, these operations are new and delete.

The new operation has two forms, one for allocating a single variable and one for allocating an array. Here is the syntax template:

AllocationExpression

$$\left\{ \begin{array}{l} \textbf{new } \text{DataType} \\[1em] \textbf{new } \text{DataType } [\text{ IntExpression }] \end{array} \right.$$

The first form is used for creating a single variable of type DataType. The second form creates an array whose elements are of type DataType; the desired number of array elements is given by IntExpression. Here is an example that demonstrates both forms of the new operation:

```
int*  intPtr;
char* nameStr;
```

`intPtr = new int;`	Creates a variable of type `int` and stores its address into `intPtr`.
`nameStr = new char[6];`	Creates a six-element `char` array and stores the base address of the array into `nameStr`.

Normally, the new operator does two things: It creates an uninitialized variable (or an array) of the designated type, and it returns a pointer to this variable (or the base address of an array). However, if the computer system has run out of space available for dynamic data, the program terminates with an error message.*

Variables created by new are said to be on the **free store** (or **heap**), a region of memory set aside for dynamic variables. The new operator obtains a chunk of memory from the free store, and, as we will see, the delete operator returns it to the free store.

Free store (heap)   A pool of memory locations reserved for allocation and deallocation of dynamic data.

A dynamic variable is unnamed and cannot be directly addressed. It must be indirectly addressed through the pointer returned by the new operator. Below is an example of creating dynamic data and then accessing the

---

* Technically, if the new operator finds that no more memory is available, it generates what is called a bad_alloc exception—a topic we do not discuss further. Unless we write additional program code to deal explicitly with this bad_alloc exception, the program simply terminates with a message such as "ABNORMAL PROGRAM TERMINATION."

In pre–standard C++, an entirely different approach was used. If new found no more memory available, it returned the null pointer rather than a pointer to a newly allocated object. The code invoking new could then test the returned pointer to see whether the allocation succeeded.

data through pointers. The code begins by initializing the pointer variables in their declarations.

```
#include <cstring>    // For strcpy()
   ⋮
int*  intPtr = new int;
char* nameStr = new char[6];

*intPtr = 357;
strcpy(nameStr, "Ben");
```

Recall from Chapter 13 that the `strcpy` library function requires two arguments, each being the base address of a `char` array. For the first argument, we are passing the base address of the dynamic array on the free store. For the second argument, the compiler passes the base address of the anonymous array where the C string "Ben" (including the terminating null character) is located. Figures 15-6a and 15-6b picture the effect of executing this code segment.

a. `int*  intPtr = new int;`
   `char* nameStr = new char[6];`

b. `*intPtr = 357;`
   `strcpy(nameStr, "Ben");`

FIGURE 15-6

Allocating Dynamic Data on the Free Store

Dynamic data can be destroyed at any time during the execution of a program when it is no longer needed. The built-in operator `delete` is used to destroy a dynamic variable. The `delete` operation has two forms, one for deleting a single variable, the other for deleting an array:

DeallocationExpression

> **delete** Pointer
>
> **delete []** Pointer

Using the previous example, we can deallocate the dynamic data pointed to by `intPtr` and `nameStr` with the following statements.

`delete intPtr;`	Returns the variable pointed to by `intPtr` to the free store to be used again. The value of `intPtr` is then undefined.
`delete [] nameStr;`	Returns the array pointed to by `nameStr` to the free store to be used again. The value of `nameStr` is then undefined.*

After execution of these statements, the values of `intPtr` and `nameStr` are undefined; they may or may not still point to the deallocated data. Before using these pointers again, you must assign new values to them (that is, store new memory addresses into them).

Until you gain experience with the `new` and `delete` operators, it is important to pronounce the statement

```
delete intPtr;
```

accurately. Instead of saying "Delete `intPtr`," it is better to say "Delete the variable *pointed to* by `intPtr`." The `delete` operation does not delete the pointer; it deletes the pointed-to variable.

When using the `delete` operator, you should keep two rules in mind.

1. Applying `delete` to the null pointer does no harm; the operation simply has no effect.

---

* The syntax for deallocating an array, `delete [] nameStr`, may not be accepted by some prestandard compilers. Early versions of the C++ language required the array size to be included within the brackets: `delete [6] nameStr`. If your compiler complains about the empty brackets, include the array size.

2. Excepting rule 1, the `delete` operator must only be applied to a pointer value that was obtained previously from the `new` operator.

The second rule is important to remember. If you apply `delete` to an arbitrary memory address that is not in the free store, the result is undefined and could prove to be very unpleasant.

Finally, remember that a major reason for using dynamic data is to economize on memory space. The `new` operator lets you create variables only as they are needed. When you are finished using a dynamic variable, you should `delete` it. It is counterproductive to keep dynamic variables when they are no longer needed—a situation known as a **memory leak.** If this is done too often, you may run out of memory.

Memory leak The loss of available memory space that occurs when dynamic data is allocated but never deallocated.

Let's look at another example of using dynamic data.

```
int* ptr1 = new int;     // Create a dynamic variable
int* ptr2 = new int;     // Create a dynamic variable

*ptr2 = 44;              // Assign a value to a dynamic variable
*ptr1 = *ptr2;           // Copy one dynamic variable to another
ptr1 = ptr2;             // Copy one pointer to another
delete ptr2;             // Destroy a dynamic variable
```

Here is a more detailed description of the effect of each statement:

`int* ptr1 = new int;`	Creates a pair of dynamic variables of type `int` and stores their locations into `ptr1` and `ptr2`.
`int* ptr2 = new int;`	The values of the dynamic variables are undefined even though the pointer variables now have values (see Figure 15-7a).
`*ptr2 = 44;`	Stores the value 44 into the dynamic variable pointed to by `ptr2` (see Figure 15-7b).
`*ptr1 = *ptr2;`	Copies the contents of the dynamic variable `*ptr2` to the dynamic variable `*ptr1` (see Figure 15-7c).
`ptr1 = ptr2;`	Copies the contents of the pointer variable `ptr2` to the pointer variable `ptr1` (see Figure 15-7d).

```
delete ptr2;
```
Returns the dynamic variable *ptr2 back to the free store to be used again. The value of ptr2 is undefined (see Figure 15-7e).

In Figure 15-7d, notice that the variable pointed to by ptr1 before the assignment statement is still there. It cannot be accessed, however, because no pointer is pointing to it. This isolated variable is called an **inaccessible object.** Leaving inaccessible objects on the free store should be considered a logic error and is a cause of memory leaks.

Notice also that in Figure 15-7e ptr1 is now pointing to a variable that, in principle, no longer exists. We call ptr1 a **dangling pointer.** If the program later dereferences ptr1, the result is unpredictable. The pointed-to value might still be the original one (44), or it might be a different value stored there as a result of reusing that space on the free store.

Inaccessible object   A dynamic variable on the free store without any pointer pointing to it.

Dangling pointer   A pointer that points to a variable that has been deallocated.

Both situations shown in Figure 15-7e—an inaccessible object and a dangling pointer—can be avoided by deallocating *ptr1 before assigning ptr2 to ptr1, and by setting ptr1 to NULL after deallocating *ptr2.

```
#include <cstddef>    // For NULL
   ⋮
int* ptr1 = new int;
int* ptr2 = new int;

*ptr2 = 44;
*ptr1 = *ptr2;
delete ptr1;          // Avoid an inaccessible object
ptr1 = ptr2;
delete ptr2;
ptr1 = NULL;          // Avoid a dangling pointer
```

Figure 15-8 shows the results of executing this revised code segment.

Reference Types

According to Figure 15-1, there is only one built-in type remaining: the **reference type.** Like pointer variables, reference variables contain the addresses of other variables. The statement

INITIAL CONDITIONS

a. `int* ptr1 = new int;`
   `int* ptr2 = new int;`

b. `*ptr2 = 44;`

c. `*ptr1 = *ptr2;`

d. `ptr1 = ptr2;`

e. `delete ptr2;`

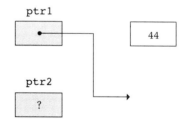

FIGURE 15-7
Results from Sample Code Segment

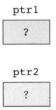

ptr1

ptr2

INITIAL CONDITIONS

a. `int* ptr1 = new int;`
   `int* ptr2 = new int;`

b. `*ptr2 = 44;`

c. `*ptr1 = *ptr2;`

d. `delete ptr1;`

e. `ptr1 = ptr2;`

f. `delete ptr2;`

g. `ptr1 = NULL;`

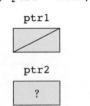

FIGURE 15-8
Results from Sample Code Segment After It Was Modified

```
int& intRef;
```

declares that `intRef` is a variable that can contain the address of an `int` variable. Here is the syntax template for declaring reference variables:

ReferenceVariableDeclaration

$$\begin{cases} \text{DataType}\textbf{\&} \;\; \text{Variable} \; \textbf{;} \\[2ex] \text{DataType} \;\; \textbf{\&}\text{Variable} \; \textbf{,} \; \textbf{\&}\text{Variable} \; \dots \textbf{;} \end{cases}$$

Although reference variables and pointer variables both contain addresses of data objects, there are two fundamental differences. First, the dereferencing and address-of operators (`*` and `&`) are not used with reference variables. After a reference variable has been declared, the compiler *invisibly* dereferences every single appearance of that reference variable. This difference is illustrated below:

Using a Reference Variable	**Using a Pointer Variable**

```int gamma = 26;```
```int& intRef = gamma;```
```// Assert: intRef points```
```//   to gamma```
	```int gamma = 26;```
	```int* intPtr = γ```
	```// Assert: intPtr points```
	```// to gamma```

```intRef = 35;``` ```// Assert: gamma == 35```	```*intPtr = 35;``` ```// Assert: gamma == 35```
```intRef = intRef + 3;``` ```// Assert: gamma == 38```	```*intPtr = *intPtr + 3;``` ```// Assert: gamma == 38```

Some programmers like to think of a reference variable as an *alias* for another variable. In the preceding code, we can think of `intRef` as an alias for `gamma`. After `intRef` is initialized in its declaration, everything we do to `intRef` is actually happening to `gamma`.

The second difference between reference and pointer variables is that the compiler treats a reference variable as if it were a *constant* pointer. It cannot be reassigned after being initialized. In fact, absolutely no operations apply directly to a reference variable except initialization. (In this context, C++ defines initialization to mean (a) explicit initialization in a declaration, (b) implicit initialization by passing an argument to a parameter, or (c) implicit initialization by returning a function value.) For example, the statement

```
intRef++;
```

does not increment `intRef`; it increments the variable to which `intRef` points. Why? Because the compiler implicitly dereferences each appearance of the name `intRef`.

The principal advantage of reference variables, then, is notational convenience. Unlike pointer variables, reference variables do not require the programmer to continually prefix the variable with an asterisk in order to access the pointed-to variable.

Reference type   A simple data type consisting of an unbounded set of values, each of which is the address of a variable of a given type. The only operation defined on a reference variable is initialization, after which every appearance of the variable is implicitly dereferenced.

A common use of reference variables is to pass nonarray arguments by reference instead of by value (as we have been doing ever since Chapter 7). Suppose the programmer wants to exchange the contents of two `float` variables with the function call

```
Swap(alpha, beta);
```

Because C++ normally passes simple variables by value, the following code fails:

```
void Swap( float x, float y )
// Caution: This routine does not work
{
    float temp = x;

    x = y;
    y = temp;
}
```

By default, C++ passes the two arguments by value. That is, *copies* of `alpha`'s and `beta`'s values are sent to the function. The local contents of `x` and `y` are exchanged within the function, but the caller's arguments `alpha` and `beta` remain unchanged. To correct this situation, we have two options. The first is to send the addresses of `alpha` and `beta` explicitly by using the address-of operator (`&`):

```
Swap(&alpha, &beta);
```

The function must then declare the parameters to be pointer variables:

```
void Swap( float* px, float* py )
{
    float temp = *px;

    *px = *py;
    *py = temp;
}
```

This approach is necessary in the C language, which has pointer variables but not reference variables.

The other option is to use reference variables to eliminate the need for explicit dereferencing:

```
void Swap( float& x, float& y )
{
    float temp = x;

    x = y;
    y = temp;
}
```

In this case, the function call does not require the address-of operator (&) for the arguments:

```
Swap(alpha, beta);
```

The compiler implicitly generates code to pass the addresses, not the contents, of `alpha` and `beta`. This method of passing nonarray arguments by reference is the one that we have been using all along and continue to use throughout the book.

By now, you have probably noticed that the ampersand (&) has several meanings in the C++ language. To avoid errors, it pays to keep these meanings distinct from each other. Below is a table that summarizes the different uses of the ampersand. Note that a *prefix* operator is one that precedes its operand(s), an *infix* operator lies between its operands, and a *postfix* operator comes after its operand(s).

Position	Usage	Meaning
Prefix	&Variable	Address-of operation
Infix	Expression & Expression	Bitwise AND operation (mentioned, but not explored, in Chapter 10)
Infix	Expression && Expression	Logical AND operation
Postfix	DataType&	Data type (specifically, a reference type) *Exception*: To declare two variables of reference type, the & must be attached to each variable name: `int &var1, &var2;`

Classes and Dynamic Data

When programmers use C++ classes, it is often useful for class objects to create dynamic data on the free store. Let's consider writing a variation of the `DateType` class of Chapter 11. In addition to a month, day, and year, we want each class object to store a message string such as "My birthday" or "Meet Al." When a client program prints a date, this message string will be printed next to the date. The obvious thing to do is to use an object of class `string` to hold the message string. However, to demonstrate allocation and deallocation of dynamic data, let's use a C string to hold the message.

To keep the example simple, we supply only a bare minimum of public member functions. We begin with the class declaration for a `Date` class, abbreviated by leaving out the function preconditions and postconditions.

```
class Date
{
public:
    void Print() const;                        // Output operation
    Date( /* in */ int       initMo,           // Constructor
          /* in */ int       initDay,
          /* in */ int       initYr,
          /* in */ const char* msgStr );
private:
    int    mo;
    int    day;
    int    yr;
    char*  msg;
};
```

In the class constructor's parameter list, we could just as well have declared `msgStr` as

```
const char[] msgStr
```

instead of

```
const char* msgStr
```

Remember that both of these declarations are equivalent as far as the C++ compiler is concerned. They both mean that the parameter being received is the base address of a C string.

As you can see in the private part of the class declaration, the private variable `msg` is a pointer, not a `char` array. If we declared `msg` to be an array of fixed size, say, 30, the array might be either too large or too small to hold the `msgStr` string that the client passes through the constructor's argument list. Instead, the class constructor will dynamically allocate a `char` array of just the right size on the free store and make `msg` point to this array. Here is the implementation of the class constructor as it would appear in the implementation file:

```
#include <cstring>    // For strcpy() and strlen()
    ⋮
Date::Date( /* in */ int          initMo,
            /* in */ int          initDay,
            /* in */ int          initYr,
            /* in */ const char* msgStr  )
{
    mo = initMo;
    day = initDay;
    yr = initYr;
    msg = new char[strlen(msgStr) + 1];
    // Assert:
    //      Storage for dynamic C string is now on free store
    //      and its base address is in msg
    strcpy(msg, msgStr);
    // Assert:
    //      Incoming string has been copied to free store
}
```

The constructor begins by copying the first three incoming parameters into the appropriate private variables. Next, we use the `new` operator to allocate a `char` array on the free store. (We add 1 to the length of the incoming string to leave room for the terminating `'\0'` character.) Finally, we use `strcpy` to copy all the characters from the `msgStr` array to the new dynamic array. If the client code declares two class objects with the statements

```
Date date1(4, 15, 2001, "My birthday");
Date date2(5, 12, 2001, "Meet Al");
    ⋮
```

then the two class objects point to dynamic `char` arrays as shown in Figure 15-9.

Figure 15-9 illustrates an important concept: a `Date` class object does not encapsulate an array—it only encapsulates *access* to the array. The array itself is located externally (on the free store), not within the protective abstraction barrier of the class object. This arrangement does not violate the principle of information hiding, however. The only access to the array is through the pointer variable `msg`, which is a private class member and is therefore inaccessible to clients.

Notice that the `Date` class allocates dynamic data, but we have made no provision for deallocating the dynamic data. To deal adequately with class objects that point to dynamic data, we need more than just a class constructor. We need an entire group of class member functions: a class constructor, a *class destructor*, a *deep copy operation*, and a *class copy-constructor*. One by one, we will explain each of these new functions. But first, here is the overall picture of what our new class declaration looks like:

```
class Date
{
public:
    void Print() const;                        // Output operation
    void CopyFrom( /* in */ Date otherDate );  // Deep copy operation
    Date( /* in */ int        initMo,          // Constructor
          /* in */ int        initDay,
          /* in */ int        initYr,
          /* in */ const char* msgStr );
```

FIGURE 15-9

Class Objects Pointing to Dynamically Allocated C Strings

```
        Date( const Date& otherDate );          // Copy-constructor
        ~Date();                                 // Destructor
    private:
        int     mo;
        int     day;
        int     yr;
        char*   msg;
    };
```

This class declaration includes function prototypes for all four of the member functions we said we are going to need: constructor, destructor, deep copy operation, and copy-constructor. Before proceeding, let's define more precisely the semantics of each member function by furnishing the function preconditions and postconditions. We have placed the complete specification of the Date class in its own figure—Figure 15-10—so that we can refer to it later.

FIGURE 15-10
Specification of
the Date Class

```
//*****************************************************************
// SPECIFICATION FILE (date.h)
// This file gives the specification of a Date abstract data
// type representing a date and an associated message
//*****************************************************************

class Date
{
public:
    void Print() const;
        // Postcondition:
        //      Date and message have been output in the form
        //          month day, year     message
        //      where the name of the month is printed as a string

    void CopyFrom( /* in */ Date otherDate );
        // Postcondition:
        //      This date is a copy of otherDate, including
        //      the message string

    Date( /* in */ int            initMo,
          /* in */ int            initDay,
          /* in */ int            initYr,
          /* in */ const char* msgStr  );
        // Constructor
        // Precondition:
        //      1 <= initMo <= 12
        //   && 1 <= initDay <= maximum number of days in initMo
        //   && 1582 < initYr
        //   && msgStr is assigned
        // Postcondition:
```

FIGURE 15-10

Specification of
the Date Class

(continued)

```
            //     New class object is constructed with a date of
            //        initMo, initDay, initYr and a message string msgStr

        Date( const Date& otherDate );
            // Copy-constructor
            // Postcondition:
            //     New class object is constructed with date and
            //        message string the same as otherDate's
            // Note:
            //     This constructor is implicitly invoked whenever a
            //     Date object is passed by value, is returned as a
            //     function value, or is initialized by another
            //     Date object in a declaration

        ~Date();
            // Destructor
            // Postcondition:
            //     Message string is destroyed
    private:
        int   mo;
        int   day;
        int   yr;
        char* msg;
};
```

Class Destructors

The Date class of Figure 15-10 provides a destructor function named
~Date. A class destructor, identified by a tilde (~) preceding the name of
the class, can be thought of as the opposite of a constructor. Just as a constructor is implicitly invoked when control reaches the declaration of a
class object, a destructor is implicitly invoked when the class object is
destroyed. A class object is destroyed when it "goes out of scope." (An
automatic object goes out of scope when control leaves the block in which
it is declared. A static object goes out of scope when program execution
terminates.) The following block—which might be a function body, for
example—includes remarks at the locations where the constructor and
destructor are invoked:

```
{
    Date conf(1, 30, 2002, "Conference");        ← Constructor is invoked
                                                    here
        ⋮
}               ← Destructor is invoked here because conf goes out of scope
```

In the implementation file `date.cpp`, the implementation of the class destructor is very simple:

```
Date::~Date()

// Destructor

// Postcondition:
//      Array pointed to by msg is no longer on the free store
{
    delete [] msg;
}
```

You cannot pass arguments to a destructor and, as with a class constructor, you must not declare the data type of the function.

Until now, we have not needed class destructors. In all previous examples of classes, the private data has been enclosed entirely within the abstraction barrier of the class. For example, in Chapter 11, a `TimeType` class object encapsulates all of its data:

startTime

hrs	8
mins	30
secs	20

When `startTime` goes out of scope, destruction of `startTime` implies destruction of all of its component data.

With the `Date` class, four data items are enclosed within the abstraction barrier, but the array is not (see Figure 15-9). Without the destructor function `~Date`, destruction of a class object would deallocate the *pointer* to the dynamic array, but would not deallocate the array itself. The result would be a memory leak; the dynamic array would remain allocated but no longer accessible.

Shallow Versus Deep Copying

Next, let's look at the `CopyFrom` function of the `Date` class (see Figure 15-10). This function is designed to copy one class object to another, *including the dynamic message array*. With the built-in assignment operator (=), assignment of one class object to another copies only the class members; it does *not* copy any data pointed to by the class members. For example, given the `date1` and `date2` objects of Figure 15-9, the effect of the assignment statement

```
date1 = date2;
```

is shown in Figure 15-11. The result is called a **shallow copy** operation. The pointer is copied, but the pointed-to data is not.

Shallow copying is perfectly fine if none of the class members are pointers. But if one or more members are pointers, then shallow copying may be erroneous. In Figure 15-11, the dynamic array originally pointed to by the date1 object has been left inaccessible.

What we want is a **deep copy** operation—one that duplicates not only the class members but also the pointed-to data. The CopyFrom function of the Date class performs a deep copy. Here is the function implementation:

```
void Date::CopyFrom( /* in */ Date otherDate )

// Postcondition:
//      mo == otherDate.mo
//   && day == otherDate.day
//   && yr == otherDate.yr
//   && msg points to a duplicate of otherDate's message string
//      on the free store

{
    mo = otherDate.mo;
    day = otherDate.day;
    yr = otherDate.yr;
    delete [] msg;                              // Deallocate the
                                                //   original array

    msg = new char[strlen(otherDate.msg) + 1]; // Allocate a new
                                                //   array

    strcpy(msg, otherDate.msg);                 // Copy the chars

}
```

FIGURE 15-11

A Shallow Copy
Caused by the
Assignment
date1 = date2

First, the function copies the month, day, and year from the `otherDate` object into the current object. Next, the function deallocates the current object's dynamic array from the free store, allocates a new dynamic array, and copies all elements of `otherDate`'s array into the new array. The result is therefore a deep copy—two identical class objects pointing to two identical (but *separate*) dynamic arrays. Given our `date1` and `date2` objects of Figure 15-9, the statement

```
date1.CopyFrom(date2);
```

yields the result shown in Figure 15-12. Compare this figure with the shallow copy pictured in Figure 15-11.

Shallow copy   An operation that copies one class object to another without copying any pointed-to data.

Deep copy   An operation that not only copies one class object to another but also makes copies of any pointed-to data.

Class Copy-Constructors

As we have just discussed, the built-in assignment operator (=) leads to a shallow copy when class objects point to dynamic data. The issue of deep versus shallow copying can also appear in another context: initialization of one class object by another. C++ defines initialization to mean the following:

1. Initialization in a variable declaration

    ```
    Date date1 = date2;
    ```

2. Passing a copy of an argument to a parameter (that is, passing by value)

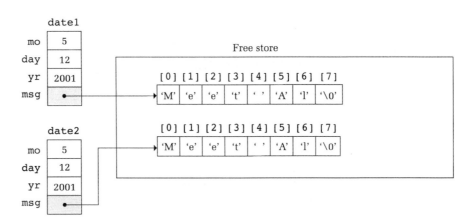

FIGURE 15-12

A Deep Copy

3. Returning an object as the value of a function

```
return someObject;
```

By default, C++ performs such initializations using shallow copy semantics. In other words, the newly created class object is initialized via a member-by-member copy of the old object without regard for any data to which the class members may point. For our Date class, the result would again be two class objects pointing to the same dynamic data.

To handle this situation, C++ has a special kind of constructor known as a *copy-constructor*. In a class declaration, its prototype has the following form:

```
class SomeClass
{
public:
     ⋮
    SomeClass( const SomeClass& someObject );    // Copy-constructor
     ⋮
};
```

Notice that the function prototype does not use any special words to suggest that this is a copy-constructor. You simply have to recognize the pattern of symbols: the class name followed by a parameter list, which contains a single parameter of type

```
const SomeClass&
```

For example, our Date class declaration in Figure 15-10 shows the prototype of the copy-constructor to be

```
Date( const Date& otherDate );
```

If a copy-constructor is present, the default method of initialization (member-by-member copying) is inhibited. Instead, the copy-constructor is implicitly invoked whenever one class object is initialized by another. The following implementation of the copy-constructor for the Date class shows the steps that are involved:

```
Date::Date( const Date& otherDate )

// Copy-constructor

// Postcondition:
//      mo == otherDate.mo
//   && day == otherDate.day
//   && yr == otherDate.yr
```

```
//   && msg points to a duplicate of otherDate's message string
//      on the free store

{
    mo = otherDate.mo;
    day = otherDate.day;
    yr = otherDate.yr;
    msg = new char[strlen(otherDate.msg) + 1];
    strcpy(msg, otherDate.msg);
}
```

The body of the copy-constructor function differs from the body of the `CopyFrom` function in only one line of code: The `CopyFrom` function executes

```
delete [] msg;
```

before allocating a new array. The difference between these two functions is that `CopyFrom` is copying to an *existing* class object (which is already pointing to a dynamic array that must be deallocated), whereas the copy-constructor is creating a new class object that doesn't already exist.

Notice the use of the reserved word `const` in the parameter list of the copy-constructor. The word `const` ensures that the function cannot alter `otherDate`, even though `otherDate` is passed by reference.

As with any nonarray variable in C++, a class object can be passed to a function either by value or by reference. Because C++ defines initialization to include passing by value, copy-constructors are vitally important when class objects point to dynamic data. Assume that we did not include a copy-constructor for the `Date` class, and assume that the following call to the `DoSomething` function uses a pass by value:

```
int main()
{
    Date quizDate(2, 18, 2002, "Geography quiz");
      ⋮
    DoSomething(quizDate);
      ⋮
```

Without a copy-constructor, `quizDate` would be copied to the `DoSomething` function's parameter using a shallow copy. A copy of `quizDate`'s dynamic array would *not* be created for use within `DoSomething`. Both `quizDate` and the parameter within `DoSomething` would point to the same dynamic array (see Figure 15-13). If the `DoSomething` function were to modify the dynamic array (thinking it is working on a *copy* of the original), then after the function returns, `quizDate` would point to a corrupted dynamic array.

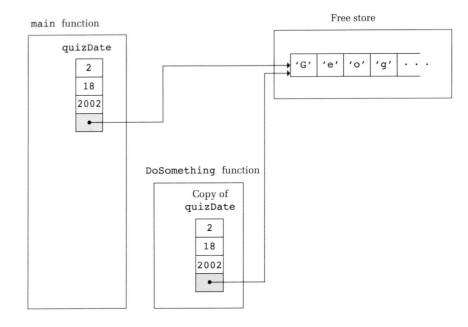

FIGURE 15-13
Shallow Copy
Caused by a Pass
by Value without a
Copy-Constructor

In summary, the default operations of assignment and initialization may be dangerous when class objects point to dynamic data on the free store. Member-by-member assignment and initialization cause only pointers to be copied, not the pointed-to data. If a class allocates and deallocates data on the free store, it almost certainly needs the following suite of member functions to ensure deep copying of dynamic data:

```
class SomeClass
{
public:
    ⋮
    void CopyFrom( SomeClass anotherObject );
        // A deep copy operation

    SomeClass( ... );
        // Constructor, to create data on the free store

    SomeClass( const SomeClass& anotherObject );
        // Copy-constructor, for deep copying in initializations

    ~SomeClass();
        // Destructor, to clean up the free store
```

```
private:
    ⋮
};
```

At the beginning of this chapter, we said that pointers are used for two reasons: to make a program more efficient—either in speed or in memory usage—and to create complex data structures (called *linked structures*). We give examples of the use of pointers to make a program more efficient in the case studies in this chapter. Linked structures are covered in Chapter 16.

PROBLEM-SOLVING CASE STUDY

Personnel Records

Problem: We have a file of personnel records, and there is a great deal of data associated with each person. The task is to read in these records, sort them alphabetically by last name, and print out the sorted records.

Input: A file of personnel records (masterFile), in which each record corresponds to the data type PersonnelData in the declarations below.

```
struct AddressType
{
    string street;
    string city;
    string state;
};
struct PersonnelData
{
    string      lastName;
    string      firstName;
    AddressType address;
    string      workHistory;
    string      education;
    string      payrollData;
};
```

Each of the eight character strings (last name, first name, street address, city, state, work history, education, and payroll data) is on a separate line in masterFile, and each string may contain embedded blanks.

The number of records in the file is unknown. The maximum number of employees that the company has ever had is 1000.

Output: The contents of `masterFile` with the records in alphabetical order by last name.

Discussion: Using object-oriented design (OOD) to solve this problem, we begin by identifying potential objects and their operations. Recall that a good way to start is to examine the problem definition, looking for important nouns and noun phrases (to find objects) and important verbs and verb phrases (to find operations). Additionally, implementation-level objects usually are necessary in the solution. Here is an object table for this problem:

Object	Operation
File `masterFile`	Open the file
	Input data from the file
Personnel record	Read a record
	Print a record
Record list	Read all personnel records into the list
	Sort
	Print all records in the list

Notice that the record list object is an implementation-level object. This object is not readily apparent in the problem domain, yet we need it in order for the operation of sorting to make any sense. ("Sort" is not an operation on an individual personnel record; it is an operation on a *list* of records.)

The second major step in OOD is to determine if there are any inheritance or composition relationships among the objects. Using *is-a* as a guide, we do not find any inheritance relationships. However, the record list object and the personnel record object clearly are related by composition. That is, a record list *has a* personnel record within it (in fact, it probably contains many personnel records). Discovery of this relationship helps us as we proceed to design and implement each object.

The `masterFile` *Object:*   For the concrete representation of this object, we can use the `ifstream` class supplied by the standard library. Then the abstract operations of opening a file and reading data are naturally implemented by using the operations already provided by the `ifstream` class.

The Personnel Record Object: We could implement this object by using a C++ class, hiding the data members as private data and supplying public operations for reading and writing the members. (Also, we might need to provide observer and transformer operations that retrieve and store the values of individual members.) Instead, let's treat this particular object as passive data (in the form of a struct with all members public) rather than as an active object with associated operations. We'll use the struct declarations shown earlier (`AddressType` and `PersonnelData`), and we can implement the reading and writing operations by using the >> and << operators to input and output individual members of the struct.

The Record List Object: This object represents a list of personnel records. Thinking of a list as an ADT, we can use a C++ class to conceal the private data representation and provide public operations to read records into the list, sort the list, and print the list.

To choose a concrete data representation for the list, we remember the composition relationship we proposed—namely, that a record list is composed of one or more personnel record objects. Therefore, we could use a 1000-element array of `PersonnelData` structs, along with an integer variable to keep track of the length of the list. But there are two disadvantages to using an array of structs in this particular problem.

First, the `PersonnelData` structs are quite large (let's say 1000 bytes each). If we declare a 1000-element array of these structs, the compiler reserves 1,000,000 bytes of memory even though the input file may contain only a few records!

Second, the act of sorting an array of structs can take a lot of time. Consider the selection sort we introduced in Chapter 13. In the `SelSort` function, the contents of two variables are swapped during each iteration. Swapping two simple variables is a fast operation. If large structs are being sorted, however, swapping two of them can be time-consuming. The C++ code to swap two structs is the same, regardless of the size of the structs— ordinary assignment statements will do. But the length of time to make the swap varies greatly depending on the size of the structs. For example, it may take ten times as long to swap structs with 20 members as it does to swap structs with 2 members.

If we are dealing with large structs, we can make the sorting operation more efficient and save memory by making the structs dynamic variables and by sorting pointers to the structs rather than sorting the structs themselves. This way, only simple pointer variables are swapped on each iteration, rather than whole structs.

The `SelSort` function has to be modified somewhat to sort large structs rather than simple variables. The structs themselves are dynami-

cally allocated, and a pointer to each is stored in an array. It is these pointers that are swapped when the algorithm calls for exchanging two values.

We have to declare an array ptrList, which holds pointers to the personnel records, to be the maximum size we might need. However, we create each PersonnelData variable only when we need it. Therefore, room
for 1000 pointers is set aside in memory for the ptrList array, but at run
time there are only as many PersonnelData variables in memory as there
are records in the file (see Figure 15-14).

The ptrList array before and after sorting is shown in Figure 15-15.
Note that when the algorithm wants to swap the contents of two structs, we
swap the pointers instead.

Now that we have chosen a concrete data representation for the personnel record list, we should review the ADT operations once more. We
identified three operations: read all the records into the list, sort the list,
and print all the records in the list. Because our data representation uses
dynamically allocated data, we must consider supplying additional operations: a class constructor, a class destructor, a class copy-constructor, and a
deep copy operation. At a minimum, we need a constructor to initialize
the private data and a destructor to deallocate all the PersonnelData
variables from the free store. (Case Study Follow-Up Exercise 3 asks you to
write the copy-constructor and deep copy operations.)

Below is the specification of the RecordList class. Notice that we use
a Typedef statement to define the identifier PersonPtr as a synonym for
the type PersonnelData*. Thereafter, we can declare the ptrList array
as

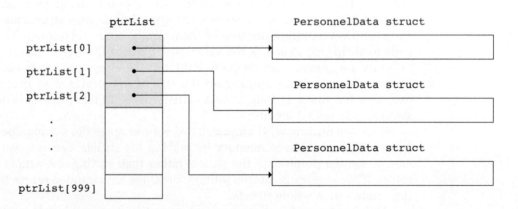

Figure 15-14
Array of Pointers to PersonnelData Structs

```
PersonPtr ptrList[MAX_EMPL];
```

instead of

```
PersonnelData* ptrList[MAX_EMPL];
```

```
//****************************************************************
// SPECIFICATION FILE (reclist.h)
// This file gives the specification of RecordList, an ADT for a
// list of personnel records.
//****************************************************************
#ifndef RECLIST_H
#define RECLIST_H

#include <fstream>    // For file I/O
#include <string>     // For string class

using namespace std;

const int MAX_EMPL = 1000;      // Maximum number of employees

struct AddressType
{
    string street;
    string city;
    string state;
};
struct PersonnelData
```

BEFORE SORTING   AFTER SORTING

Figure 15-15
ptrList Array Before and After Sorting

PROBLEM-SOLVING CASE STUDY cont'd.

```
{
    string      lastName;
    string      firstName;
    AddressType address;
    string      workHistory;
    string      education;
    string      payrollData;
};

typedef PersonnelData* PersonPtr;

class RecordList
{
public:
    void ReadAll( /* inout */ ifstream& inFile );
        // Precondition:
        //     inFile has been opened for input
        //  && inFile contains at most MAX_EMPL records
        // Postcondition:
        //     List contains employee records as read from inFile

    void SelSort();
        // Postcondition:
        //     List is in ascending order of employee last name

    void PrintAll();
        // Postcondition:
        //     All employee records have been written to
        //     standard output

    RecordList();
        // Postcondition:
        //     Empty list created

    ~RecordList();
        // Postcondition:
        //     List destroyed
private:
    PersonPtr ptrList[MAX_EMPL];
    int       length;
};
#endif
```

Now we are ready to implement the `RecordList` member functions. We begin with the class constructor, whose sole task is to initialize the private variable `length` to 0.

The class constructor RecordList ( )

```
Set length = 0
```

To implement the `ReadAll` member function, we use a loop that repeatedly does the following: allocates a dynamic `PersonnelData` struct, reads an employee record into that struct, and stores the pointer to that struct into the next unused element of the `ptrList` array.

ReadAll (Inout: inFile)

```
Set aPerson = new PersonnelData              // Allocate a dynamic struct
Get a record from inFile into
        the struct pointed to by aPerson
WHILE NOT EOF on inFile
        Set ptrList[length] = aPerson        // Store pointer into array
        Increment length
        Set aPerson = new PersonnelData      // Allocate a dynamic struct
        Get a record from inFile into
                the struct pointed to by aPerson
```

The pseudocode step "Get a record from inFile ... " appears twice in `ReadAll`. This step breaks down into several substeps: read the last name, check for end-of-file, read the first name, and so on. To avoid physically writing down the substeps twice, let's write a separate "helper" function named `GetRecord`. In `GetRecord`'s parameter list, `aPerson` is a pointer to a `PersonnelData` struct.

GetRecord (Inout: inFile; In: aPerson)

Read aPerson->lastName from inFile
IF EOF on inFile
     Return
Read aPerson->firstName from inFile
Read aPerson->address.street from inFile
Read aPerson->address.city from inFile
Read aPerson->address.state from inFile
Read aPerson->workHistory from inFile
Read aPerson->education from inFile
Read aPerson->payrollData from inFile

The `SelSort` function is nearly the same as in Chapter 13. The original `SelSort` finds the minimum value in the list and swaps it with the value in the first place in the list. Then the next-smallest value in the list is swapped with the value in the second place. This process continues until all the values are in order. The location in this algorithm that we must change is where the minimum value is determined. Instead of comparing two components in the list, we compare the last-name members in the structs to which these components point. The statement that did the comparison in the original `SelSort` function must be changed from

```
if (data[searchIndx] < data[minIndx])
```

to

```
if (ptrList[searchIndx]->lastName
       < ptrList[minIndx]->lastName)
```

The remaining member functions—`PrintAll` and the class destructor—are straightforward to implement.

PrintAll ( )

```
FOR index going from 0 through length – 1
     Print ptrList[index]->lastName, ", ", ptrList[index]->firstName
     Print ptrList[index]->address.street
     Print ptrList[index]->address.city, ", ", ptrList[index]->address.state
     Print ptrList[index]->workHistory
     Print ptrList[index]->education
     Print ptrList[index]->payrollData
```

The class destructor ~RecordList ( )

```
FOR index going from 0 through length – 1
     Deallocate the struct pointed to by ptrList[index]
```

Below is the implementation file for the `RecordList` class.

```cpp
//***************************************************************
// IMPLEMENTATION FILE (reclist.cpp)
// This file implements the RecordList class member functions.
// List representation: an array of pointers to PersonnelData
// structs and an integer variable giving the current length
// of the list
//***************************************************************
#include "reclist.h"
#include <iostream>
#include <cstddef>        // For NULL

using namespace std;

// Private members of class:
//     PersonPtr ptrList[MAX_EMPL];   Array of pointers
//     int       length;             Number of valid pointers
//                                       in ptrList

void GetRecord( ifstream&, PersonPtr );   // Prototype for "helper"
                                          //    function
```

PROBLEM-SOLVING CASE STUDY *cont'd.*

```cpp
//*****************************************************************

RecordList::RecordList()

// Default constructor

// Postcondition:
//     length == 0

{
    length = 0;
}

//*****************************************************************

RecordList::~RecordList()

// Destructor

// Postcondition:
//     Structs pointed to by ptrList[0..length-1]
//     are no longer on the free store

{
    int index;    // Loop control variable

    for (index = 0; index < length; index++)
        delete ptrList[index];
}

//*****************************************************************

void GetRecord( /* inout */ ifstream& inFile,
                /* in */     PersonPtr aPerson )

// Reads one record from file inFile

// Precondition:
//     inFile is open for input
//  && aPerson points to a valid PersonnelData struct
// Postcondition:
//     IF input of the lastName member failed due to end-of-file
//         The contents of *aPerson are undefined
//     ELSE
//         All members of *aPerson are filled with the values
//         for one person read from inFile
```

```
{
    getline(inFile, aPerson->lastName);
    if ( !inFile )
        return;
    getline(inFile, aPerson->firstName);
    getline(inFile, aPerson->address.street);
    getline(inFile, aPerson->address.city);
    getline(inFile, aPerson->address.state);
    getline(inFile, aPerson->workHistory);
    getline(inFile, aPerson->education);
    getline(inFile, aPerson->payrollData);
}

//****************************************************************

void RecordList::ReadAll( /* inout */ ifstream& inFile )

// Precondition:
//     inFile has been opened for input
//  && inFile contains at most MAX_EMPL records
// Postcondition:
//     ptrList[0..length-1] point to dynamic structs
//     containing values read from inFile

{

    PersonPtr aPerson;    // Pointer to newly input record

    aPerson = new PersonnelData;
    GetRecord(inFile, aPerson);
    while (inFile)
    {
        ptrList[length] = aPerson;        // Store pointer into array
        length++;
        aPerson = new PersonnelData;
        GetRecord(inFile, aPerson);
    }
}

//****************************************************************

void RecordList::SelSort()

// Sorts ptrList so that the pointed-to structs are in
// ascending order of last name

// Precondition:
//     ptrList[0..length-1] point to valid PersonnelData structs
```

PROBLEM-SOLVING CASE STUDY cont'd.

```
// Postcondition:
//     ptrList contains the same values as ptrList@entry, rearranged
//     so that consecutive elements of ptrList point to structs in
//     ascending order of last name

{
    PersonPtr tempPtr;       // Used for swapping
    int       passCount;     // Loop control variable
    int       searchIndx;    // Loop control variable
    int       minIndx;       // Index of minimum so far

    for (passCount = 0; passCount < length - 1; passCount++)
    {
        minIndx = passCount;

        // Find the index of the pointer to the alphabetically first
        // last name remaining in ptrList[passCount..length-1]

        for (searchIndx = passCount + 1; searchIndx < length;
                                                   searchIndx++)
            if (ptrList[searchIndx]->lastName
                 < ptrList[minIndx]->lastName)
                minIndx = searchIndx;

        // Swap ptrList[minIndx] and ptrList[passCount]

        tempPtr = ptrList[minIndx];
        ptrList[minIndx] = ptrList[passCount];
        ptrList[passCount] = tempPtr;
    }
}

//*****************************************************************

void RecordList::PrintAll()

// Precondition:
//     ptrList[0..length-1] point to valid PersonnelData structs
// Postcondition:
//     Contents of the structs pointed to by ptrList[0..length-1]
//     have been written to standard output

{
    int index;    // Loop control variable

    for (index = 0; index < length; index++)
    {
```

```
        cout << ptrList[index]->lastName << ", "
            << ptrList[index]->firstName << endl;
        cout << ptrList[index]->address.street << endl;
        cout << ptrList[index]->address.city << ", "
            << ptrList[index]->address.state << endl;
        cout << ptrList[index]->workHistory << endl;
        cout << ptrList[index]->education << endl;
        cout << ptrList[index]->payrollData << endl << endl;
    }
}
```

Testing: As with any C++ class, testing RecordList amounts to testing
each of its member functions. To test the ReadAll function, a test driver
that invokes only ReadAll would not be useful; we would also need to
invoke PrintAll to check the results. Likewise, a test driver cannot
invoke only PrintAll without first putting something into the list (by
invoking ReadAll). Thus, a minimal test driver must open a data file, call
ReadAll, then call PrintAll. But now the test driver is almost identical
to the main driver for the entire program, the only difference being that the
main driver calls SelSort after calling ReadAll. Therefore, we postpone
a detailed discussion of testing until we have written the main driver.

The Driver: The third step in OOD is to design the driver—the top-level
algorithm. In this program, all the driver has to do is invoke the operations
of the masterFile object and the record list object.

Main   **Level 0**

> Create empty list of personnel records named list
> Open masterFile for input and verify success
> list.ReadAll(masterFile)
> list.SelSort()
> list.PrintAll()

Assumption: File masterFile contains no more than 1000 personnel
records.

Module Structure Chart:

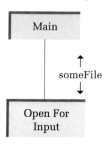

Below is the SortWithPointers program that implements our design. To run the program, we compile the source code files `reclist.cpp` and `sortwithpointers.cpp` into object code files `reclist.obj` and `sortwithpointers.obj`, then link the object code files to produce an executable file.

(The following program is written in ISO/ANSI standard C++. If you are working with pre–standard C++, see the alternate version of the program in the PRE_STD directory of the program disk, available at the publisher's Web site, `www.jbpub.com/disks`.)

```cpp
//*****************************************************************
// SortWithPointers program
// This program reads personnel records from a data file,
// sorts the records alphabetically by last name,
// and writes them to the standard output device.
// Assumption: The input file contains at most 1000 records
//*****************************************************************
#include <iostream>
#include <fstream>      // For file I/O
#include <string>       // For string class (for OpenForInput function)
#include "reclist.h" // For RecordList class

using namespace std;

void OpenForInput( ifstream& );

int main()
{
    RecordList list;               // List of personnel records
    ifstream    masterFile;        // Input file of personnel records
```

```
        OpenForInput(masterFile);
        if ( !masterFile )
            return 1;

        list.ReadAll(masterFile);
        list.SelSort();
        list.PrintAll();
        return 0;
}


//******************************************************************


void OpenForInput( /* inout */ ifstream& someFile )    // File to be
                                                       // opened
// Prompts the user for the name of an input file
// and attempts to open the file

{
        .
        .    (Same as in previous case studies)
        .
}
```

Testing: To test this program, we begin by preparing an input file that contains personnel information for, say, ten employees. The data should be in random order by employee last name to make sure that the sorting routine works properly. Given this input data, we expect the program to output the personnel records in ascending order of last name.

File Data	**Expected Output**
Adams	Adams
: } Remainder of Adams's data	: } Remainder of Adams's data
Gordon	Cava
: } Remainder of Gordon's data	: } Remainder of Cava's data
Cava	Gleason
⋮	⋮
Sheehan	Gordon
⋮	⋮
McCorkle	Kirshen
⋮	⋮
Pinard	McCorkle
⋮	⋮
Ripley	Pinard
⋮	⋮

Kirshen	Ripley
⋮	⋮
Gleason	Sheehan
⋮	⋮
Thompson	Thompson

If we run the program and find too many or too few employee records printed out, or if the records are not in alphabetical order, the problem lies in the record list object—the object responsible for reading the file, sorting, and printing. Using a hand trace, the system debugger, or debug output statements, we should check the RecordList member functions in the following order: ReadAll (to verify that the file data was read into the list correctly), SelSort (to confirm that the records are ordered by employee last name), then PrintAll (to ensure that all records are output properly).

After the program works correctly for the file of test data, we should also run the program against the following files: a nonexistent file and an empty file. With a nonexistent file, the program should halt after the OpenForInput function prints its error message. With an empty file, the program should terminate successfully but produce no output at all. (Look at the loops in the ReadAll, SelSort, and PrintAll functions to see why.)

Are we required to test the program with a file of more than 1000 employee records? No. Clearly, the program would misbehave if the index into the ptrList array exceeded 999. However, our program correctly satisfies the problem definition, which states a precondition for the entire program—namely, that the input file contains at most 1000 records. The user of the program must be informed of this precondition and is expected to comply. If the problem definition were changed to eliminate this precondition, then, of course, we would have to modify the program to deal with an input file that is too long.

One final remark: For the SelSort function, what we have tested is that the program correctly sorts the data using pointers to dynamic variables of type PersonnelData. But the output may still be slightly wrong. Because SelSort compares the strings that make up the last names, it orders the names according to the machine's particular character set. As we mentioned earlier in the book, such comparisons can lead to problems when uppercase and lowercase characters are mixed. For example, in the ASCII set, Macartney would come *after* MacDonald. Case Study Follow-Up Exercise 1 asks you to modify SelSort so that it orders names regardless of the case of the individual characters.

PROBLEM-SOLVING CASE STUDY

Dynamic Arrays

Problem: In Chapter 12, Programming Warm-up Exercise 9 described a "safe array" class (IntArray) that prevents array indexes from going out of bounds. The public member functions were as follows: a class constructor, to create an array of up to MAX_SIZE elements and initialize all elements to 0; a Store function, to store a value into a particular array element; and a ValueAt function, to retrieve the value of an array element. We want to enhance the IntArray class so that a client of the class can create an array of *any* size—a size that is not bounded by a constant MAX_SIZE. Furthermore, the client should be able to specify the array size at execution time rather than at compile time.

In this case study, we omit the Input and Output sections because we are developing only a C++ class, not a complete program. Instead, we include two sections entitled Specification of the Class and Implementation of the Class.

Discussion: In Chapter 12's IntArray class, the private part includes a fixed-size array of MAX_SIZE (which is 200) elements:

```
class IntArray
{
    ⋮
private:
    int arr[MAX_SIZE];
    int size;
};
```

Each class object contains an array of exactly 200 elements, whether the client needs that many or not. If the client requires fewer than 200 elements, then memory is wasted. If more than 200 elements are needed, the class cannot be used.

The disadvantage of any built-in array, such as arr in the IntArray class, is that its size must be known *statically* (at compile time). In this case study, we want to be able to specify the array size *dynamically* (at execution time). Therefore, we must design and implement a class (call it DynArray) that allocates dynamic data on the free store—specifically, an integer array of any size specified by the client code. The private part of our class will no longer include an entire array; rather, it will include a pointer to a dynamically allocated array:

```
class DynArray
{
```

```
    ⋮
private:
    int* arr;
    int  size;
};
```

Figure 15-9 depicted exactly the same strategy of keeping a pointer within a class object and letting it point to a dynamic array on the free store.

Specification of the Class: In choosing public operations for the DynArray class, we will retain the three operations from the IntArray class: ValueAt, Store, and a class constructor. The job of the constructor, when it receives a parameter arrSize, will be to allocate a dynamic array of exactly arrSize elements—no more and no less. Because DynArray class objects point to dynamic data on the free store, we also need a deep copy operation, a class copy-constructor, and a class destructor. Here is the specification of DynArray, complete with preconditions and postconditions for the member functions.

```
//******************************************************************
// SPECIFICATION FILE (dynarray.h)
// This file gives the specification of an integer array class
// that allows
//     1. Run-time specification of array size
//     2. Trapping of invalid array indexes
//     3. Aggregate copying of one array to another
//     4. Aggregate array initialization (for parameter passing by
//        value, function value return, and initialization in a
//        declaration)
//******************************************************************

class DynArray
{
public:
    int ValueAt( /* in */ int i ) const;
        // Precondition:
        //      i is assigned
        // Postcondition:
        //      IF i >= 0  &&  i < declared size of array
        //          Function value == value of array element
        //                                  at index i
        //      ELSE
        //          Program has halted with error message
```

```
void Store( /* in */ int val,
            /* in */ int i   );
    // Precondition:
    //     val and i are assigned
    // Postcondition:
    //     IF i >= 0  &&  i < declared size of array
    //         val is stored in array element i
    //     ELSE
    //         Program has halted with error message

void CopyFrom( /* in */ DynArray array2 );
    // Postcondition:
    //     IF there is enough memory for a deep copy of array2
    //         This object is a copy of array2 (deep copy)
    //     ELSE
    //         Program has halted with error message

DynArray( /* in */ int arrSize );
    // Constructor
    // Precondition:
    //     arrSize is assigned
    // Postcondition:
    //     IF arrSize >= 1  &&  There is enough memory
    //         Array of size arrSize is created with all
    //         array elements == 0
    //     ELSE
    //         Program has halted with error message

DynArray( const DynArray& array2 );
    // Copy-constructor
    // Postcondition:
    //     IF there is enough memory
    //         New array is created with size and contents
    //         the same as array2 (deep copy)
    //     ELSE
    //         Program has halted with error message
    // Note:
    //     This constructor is implicitly invoked whenever a
    //     DynArray object is passed by value, is returned as
    //     a function value, or is initialized by another
    //     DynArray object in a declaration

~DynArray();
    // Destructor
    // Postcondition:
    //     Array is destroyed
```

```
private:
    int* arr;
    int  size;
};
```

Below is a simple client program that creates two class objects, x and y, stores the values 100, 101, 102, ... into x, copies object x to object y, and prints out the contents of y.

```
#include "dynarray.h"
#include <iostream>

using namespace std;

int main()
{
    int numElements;    // Array size
    int index;          // Array index

    cout << "Enter the array size: ";
    cin >> numElements;

    Dynarray x(numElements);
    Dynarray y(numElements);

    for (index = 0; index < numElements; index++)
        x.Store(index + 100, index);
    y.CopyFrom(x);
    for (index = 0; index < numElements; index++)
        cout << y.ValueAt(index);
    return 0;
}
```

If the input value for numElements is 20, the class constructor creates a 20-element array for x and initializes all elements to 0. Similarly, y is created with all 20 elements initialized to 0. After using the Store function to store 20 new values into x, the program does an aggregate copy of x to y using the CopyFrom operation. Then the program outputs the 20 elements of y, which should be the same as the values contained in x. Finally, both class objects go out of scope (because control exits the block in which they are declared), causing the class destructor to be executed for each object. Each call to the destructor deallocates a dynamic array from the free store, as we'll see when we look at the implementations of the class member functions.

Implementation of the Class: Next, we implement each class member function, placing the function definitions into a C++ implementation file dynarray.cpp. As we implement the member functions, we also discuss appropriate testing strategies.

The class constructor and destructor: According to the specification file, the class constructor should allocate an array of size arrSize, and the destructor should deallocate the array. The constructor must also verify that arrSize is at least 1. If this condition is met and allocation of the dynamic data succeeded, the constructor sets each array element to 0. (If the new operator fails to allocate the dynamic array, the program automatically terminates with an error message, thereby satisfying the stated postcondition.)

The class constructor DynArray (In: arrSize)

```
IF arrSize < 1
      Print error message
      Halt the program
Set size = arrSize
Set arr = new int[size]           // Allocate a dynamic array
FOR i going from 0 through size – 1
      Set arr[i] = 0
```

The class destructor ~DynArray ( )

```
Deallocate the array pointed to by arr
```

In the constructor, we allocate an integer array of arrSize elements and store its base address into the pointer variable arr. Remember that in C++ any pointer can be indexed by attaching an index expression in brackets. Therefore, the assignment statement

```
arr[i] = 0;
```

does exactly what we want it to do: it stores 0 into element i of the array pointed to by arr.

Testing: Two things should be tested in the constructor: the If statement and the initialization loop. To test the If statement, we should try different values of the parameter `arrSize`: negative, 0, and positive. Negative and 0 values should cause the program to halt. To test the initialization loop, we can create a class object, use the `ValueAt` function to output the array elements, and verify that the elements are all 0:

```
DynArray testArr(50);

for (index = 0; index < 50; index++)
    cout << testArr.ValueAt(index) << endl;
```

Regarding the class destructor, there is nothing to test. The function simply deallocates the dynamic array from the free store.

The `ValueAt` and `Store` functions: The essence of each of these functions is simple: The `Store` function stores a value into the array, and `ValueAt` retrieves a value. Additionally, the function postconditions require each function to halt the program if the index is out of bounds.

ValueAt (In: i)

   Out: Function value

```
IF i < 0 OR i ≥ size
        Print error message
        Halt the program
Return arr[i]
```

Store (In: val, i)

```
IF i < 0 OR i ≥ size
        Print error message
        Halt the program
Set arr[i] = val
```

Testing: To test these functions, valid indexes (0 through `size`–1) as well as invalid indexes should be passed as arguments. Case Study Follow-Up Exercises 5 and 6 ask you to design test data for these finctions and to write drivers that do the testing.

The class copy-constructor: This function is called whenever a new class object is created *and* initialized to be a copy of an existing class object.

The class copy-constructor DynArray (In: array2)

```
Set size = array2.size
Set arr = new int[size]          // Allocate a dynamic array
FOR i going from 0 through size – 1
        Set arr[i] = array2.arr[i]
```

Testing: A copy-constructor is implicitly invoked whenever a class object is passed by value as an argument, is returned as a function value, or is initialized by another class object in a declaration. To test the copy-constructor, you could write a function that receives a DynArray object by value, outputs the contents (to confirm that the values of the array elements are the same as in the caller's argument), and modifies some of the array elements. On return from the function, the calling code should print out the contents of the original array, which should be unchanged from the time before the function call. In other words, you want to verify that when the function modified some array elements, it was working on a *copy* of the argument, not on the argument itself.

The CopyFrom function: This function is nearly the same as the copy-constructor; it performs a deep copy of one class object to another. The important difference is that whereas the copy-constructor creates a *new* class object to copy to, the CopyFrom function is applied to an *existing* class object. The only difference in the two algorithms, then, is that CopyFrom must begin by deallocating the dynamic array that is currently being pointed to.

CopyFrom (In: array2)

> Deallocate the dynamic array pointed to by arr
> Set size = array2.size
> Set arr = new int[size]   // Allocate a new dynamic array
> FOR i going from 0 through size – 1
>   Set arr[i] = array2.arr[i]

Testing: To test the `CopyFrom` function, we can use the client code we presented earlier:

```
for (index = 0; index < numElements; index++)
    x.Store(index + 100, index);
y.CopyFrom(x);
for (index = 0; index < numElements; index++)
    cout << y.ValueAt(index);
```

If the value of `numElements` is 20, the output should be the values 100 through 119, demonstrating that `y` is a copy of `x`.

Translating all of these pseudocode algorithms into C++, we obtain the following implementation file for the `DynArray` class.

```
//****************************************************************
// IMPLEMENTATION FILE (dynarray.cpp)
// This file implements the DynArray class member functions
//****************************************************************
#include "dynarray.h"
#include <iostream>
#include <cstddef>      // For NULL
#include <cstdlib>      // For exit()

using namespace std;

// Private members of class:
//     int* arr;              Pointer to array on free store
//     int  size;             Size of array


//****************************************************************

DynArray::DynArray( /* in */ int arrSize )

// Constructor
```

```
// Precondition:
//      arrSize is assigned
// Postcondition:
//      IF arrSize >= 1  &&  There is room on free store
//           New array of size arrSize is created on free store
//         && arr == base address of new array
//         && size == arrSize
//         && arr[0..size-1] == 0
//      ELSE
//           Program has halted with error message

{
    int i;    // Array index

    if (arrSize < 1)
    {
        cout << "** In DynArray constructor, invalid size: "
            << arrSize << " **" << endl;
        exit(1);
    }
    size = arrSize;
    arr = new int[size];
    for (i = 0; i < size; i++)
        arr[i] = 0;
}


//******************************************************************

DynArray::DynArray( const DynArray& array2 )

// Copy-constructor

// Postcondition:
//      IF there is room on free store
//           New array of size array2.size is created on free store
//         && arr == base address of new array
//         && size == array2.size
//         && arr[0..size-1] == array2.arr[0..size-1]
//      ELSE
//           Program has halted with error message

{
    int i;    // Array index
```

```
            size = array2.size;
            arr = new int[size];
            for (i = 0; i < size; i++)
                arr[i] = array2.arr[i];
    }


    //*****************************************************************


    DynArray::~DynArray()

    // Destructor

    // Postcondition:
    //      Array pointed to by arr is no longer on the free store

    {
        delete [] arr;
    }


    //*****************************************************************


    int DynArray::ValueAt( /* in */ int i ) const

    // Precondition:
    //      i is assigned
    // Postcondition:
    //      IF i >= 0  &&  i < size
    //          Function value == arr[i]
    //      ELSE
    //          Program has halted with error message

    {
        if (i < 0 || i >= size)
        {
            cout << "** In ValueAt function, invalid index: "
                << i << " **" << endl;
            exit(1);
        }
        return arr[i];
    }


    //*****************************************************************


    void DynArray::Store( /* in */ int val,
                          /* in */ int i   )
```

```
// Precondition:
//     val and i are assigned
// Postcondition:
//     IF i >= 0  &&  i < size
//        arr[i] == val
//     ELSE
//        Program has halted with error message

{
    if (i < 0 || i >= size)
    {
        cout << "** In Store function, invalid index: "
            << i << " **" << endl;
        exit(1);
    }
    arr[i] = val;
}


//******************************************************************

void DynArray::CopyFrom( /* in */ DynArray array2 )

// Postcondition:
//     Array pointed to by arr@entry is no longer on free store
//  && IF free store has room for an array of size array2.size
//        New array of size array2.size is created on free store
//        && arr == base address of new array
//        && size == array2.size
//        && arr[0..size-1] == array2.arr[0..size-1]
//     ELSE
//        Program has halted with error message

{
    int i;     // Array index

    delete [] arr;
    size = array2.size;
    arr = new int[size];
    for (i = 0; i < size; i++)
        arr[i] = array2.arr[i];
}
```

Testing and Debugging

Programs that use pointers are more difficult to write and debug than programs without pointers. Indirect addressing never seems quite as "normal" as direct addressing when you want to get at the contents of a variable.

The most common errors associated with the use of pointer variables are as follows:

1. Confusing the pointer variable with the variable it points to
2. Trying to dereference the null pointer or an uninitialized pointer
3. Inaccessible objects
4. Dangling pointers

Let's look at each of these in turn.

If `ptr` is a pointer variable, care must be taken not to confuse the expressions `ptr` and `*ptr`. The expression

```
ptr
```

accesses the variable `ptr` (which contains a memory address). The expression

```
*ptr
```

accesses the variable that `ptr` points to.

`ptr1 = ptr2`	Copies the contents of `ptr2` into `ptr1`.
`*ptr1 = *ptr2`	Copies the contents of the variable pointed to by `ptr2` into the variable pointed to by `ptr1`.
`*ptr1 = ptr2`	Illegal—one is a pointer and one is a variable being pointed to.
`ptr1 = *ptr2`	Illegal—one is a pointer and one is a variable being pointed to.

The second common error is to dereference the null pointer or an uninitialized pointer. On some systems, an attempt to dereference the null pointer produces a run-time error message such as "NULL POINTER DEREFERENCE," followed immediately by termination of the program. When this event occurs, you have at least some notion of what went wrong with the program. The situation is worse, though, if your program dereferences an uninitialized pointer. In the code fragment

```
int   num;
int*  intPtr;

num = *intPtr;
```

the variable `intPtr` has not been assigned any value before we dereference it. Initially, it contains some meaningless value such as 315988, but the computer does not know that it is meaningless. The machine simply accesses memory location 315988 and copies whatever it finds there into num. There is no way to test whether a pointer variable contains an undefined value. The only advice we can give is to check the code carefully to make sure that every pointer variable is assigned a value before being dereferenced.

The third error—leaving inaccessible objects on the free store—usually results from either a shallow copy operation or incorrect use of the new operator. In Figure 15-11, we showed how the built-in assignment operator causes a shallow copy; the dynamic data object originally pointed to by one pointer variable remains allocated but inaccessible. Misuse of the new operator also can leave dynamic data inaccessible. Execution of the code fragment

```
float* floatPtr;

floatPtr = new float;
*floatPtr = 38.5;
floatPtr = new float;
```

creates an inaccessible object: the dynamic variable containing 38.5. The problem is that we assigned a new value to `floatPtr` in the last statement without first deallocating the variable it pointed to. To guard against this kind of error, examine every use of the new operator in your code. If the associated variable currently points to data, delete the pointed-to data before executing the new operation.

Finally, dangling pointers are a source of errors and can be difficult to detect. One cause of dangling pointers is deallocating a dynamic data object that is pointed to by more than one pointer. Figures 15-7d and 15-7e pictured this situation. A second cause of dangling pointers is returning a pointer to an automatic variable from a function. The following function, which returns a function value of type `int*`, is erroneous.

```
int* Func()
{
    int n;
      ⋮
    return &n;
}
```

Remember that automatic variables are implicitly created at block entry and implicitly destroyed at block exit. The above function returns a pointer to the local variable n, but n disappears as soon as control exits the function. The caller of the function therefore receives a dangling pointer. Dangling pointers are hazardous for the same reason that uninitialized pointers are hazardous: When your program dereferences incorrect pointer values, it will access memory locations whose contents are unknown.

Testing and Debugging Hints

1. To declare two pointer variables in the same statement, you must use

   ```
   int *p, *q;
   ```

   You cannot use

   ```
   int* p, q;
   ```

   Similarly, you must use

   ```
   int &m, &n;
   ```

   to declare two reference variables in the same statement.
2. Do not confuse a pointer with the variable it points to.
3. Before dereferencing a pointer variable, be sure it has been assigned a meaningful value other than NULL.
4. Pointer variables must be of the same data type to be compared or assigned to one another.
5. In an expression, an array name without any index brackets is a pointer expression; its value is the base address of the array. The array name is considered a *constant* expression, so it cannot be assigned to. The following code shows correct and incorrect assignments.

   ```
   int  arrA[5] = {10, 20, 30, 40, 50};
   int  arrB[5] = {60, 70, 80, 90, 100};
   int* ptr;

   ptr = arrB;      // OK--you can assign to a variable
   arrA = arrB;     // Wrong--you cannot assign to a constant
   ```
6. If ptr points to a struct, union, or class variable that has an int member named age, the expression

   ```
   *ptr.age
   ```

is incorrect. You must either enclose the dereference operation in parentheses:

```
(*ptr).age
```

or use the arrow operator:

```
ptr->age
```

7. The `delete` operator must be applied to a pointer whose value was previously returned by new. Also, the `delete` operation leaves the value of the pointer variable undefined; do not use the variable again until you have assigned it a new value.

8. A function must not return a pointer to automatic local data, or else a dangling pointer will result.

9. If `ptrA` and `ptrB` point to the same dynamic data object, the statement

```
delete ptrA;
```

makes `ptrB` a dangling pointer. You should now assign `ptrB` the value NULL rather than leave it dangling.

10. Deallocate dynamic data when it is no longer needed. Memory leaks can cause you to run out of memory space.

11. Inaccessible objects—another cause of memory leaks—are caused by

    a. shallow copying of pointers that point to dynamic data. When designing C++ classes whose objects point to dynamic data, be sure to provide a deep copy operation and a copy-constructor.

    b. using the new operation when the associated variable already points to dynamic data. Before executing new, use `delete` to deallocate the data that is currently pointed to.

Summary

Pointer types and reference types are simple data types for storing memory addresses. Variables of these types do not contain data; rather, they contain the addresses of other variables or data structures. Pointer variables require explicit dereferencing using the * operator. Reference variables are dereferenced implicitly and are commonly used to pass nonarray arguments by reference.

A powerful use of pointers is to create dynamic variables. The pointer is created at compile time, but the data to which the pointer points is created at run time. The built-in operator new creates a variable on the free store (heap) and returns a pointer to that variable. A dynamic variable is not given a name, but rather is accessed through a pointer variable.

The use of dynamic data saves memory space because a variable is created only when it is needed at run time. When a dynamic variable is no longer needed, it can be deallocated (using `delete`) and the memory space can be used again. The use of dynamic data can also save machine time when large structures are being sorted. The pointers to the large structures, rather than the large structures themselves, can be rearranged.

When C++ class objects point to data on the free store, it is important to distinguish between shallow and deep copy operations. A shallow copy of one class object to another copies only the pointers and results in two class objects pointing to the same dynamic variable. A deep copy results in two distinct copies of the pointed-to data. Therefore, classes that manipulate dynamic data usually require a complete collection of support routines: one or more constructors, a destructor (for cleaning up the free store), a deep copy operation, and a copy-constructor (for deep copying during initialization of one class object by another).

Quick Check

1. How would you declare each of the following pointer variables? (868–879)
   a. A variable `intPtr` that can point to a single `int` variable.
   b. A variable `arrPtr` that can point to a `float` array.
   c. A variable `recPtr` that can point to a structure of the following type.

   ```
   struct RecType
   {
       int    age;
       float height;
       float weight;
   };
   ```

2. Given the declarations

   ```
   int    someVal;
   float velocity[10];
   ```

   and the declarations in Question 1, answer the following.
   a. How would you make `intPtr` point to `someVal` and then use `intPtr` to store 25 into `someVal`?
   b. How would you make `arrPtr` point to `velocity` and then use `arrPtr` to store 6.43 into the third element of `velocity`? (pp. 868–879)

3. Given the declaration

   ```
   RecType oneRec;
   ```

   and the declarations in Question 1, answer the following.
   a. How would you make `recPtr` point to `oneRec`?
   b. What are two different expressions using `recPtr` that will store 120.5 into the `weight` member of `oneRec`? (pp. 868–879)

4. a. In a single statement, declare a pointer variable named dblPtr and initialize it to the address of a newly created dynamic variable of type double. Then, in a second statement, store 98.32586728 into the dynamic variable.

    b. In a single statement, declare a pointer variable named list and initialize it to the base address of a newly created dynamic array of 50 int elements. Then give a section of code that will zero out the array. (pp. 879–884)

5. Given the variables dblPtr and list of Question 4, show how to deallocate the dynamic data pointed to by dblPtr and list. (pp. 879–884)

6. Given the declaration and initialization

    ```
    float delta = -42.7;
    ```

    how would you declare a variable gamma to be of type "reference to float" and initialize it to contain the memory address of delta? (pp. 884–889)

7. Using the variable gamma of Question 6, how would you store the value 12.9 into delta? (pp. 884–889)

8. Which kind of copy operation—deep or shallow—copies one pointer to another without copying any pointed-to data? (pp. 890–897)

9. As defined by C++, assignment (using an assignment expression) and initialization are two different things. What are the three ways in which one C++ class object is initialized by another? (pp. 897–898)

10. In designing a C++ class whose class objects point to dynamic data, what are the four member functions you should provide? (pp. 900–901)

11. What are two ways in which pointers may be used to improve program efficiency? (p. 932)

Answers

1.  ```
    int*       intPtr;
    float*     arrPtr;
    RecType* recPtr;
    ```
2. a. ```
        intPtr = &someVal;
        *intPtr = 25;
        ```
    b.  ```
        arrPtr = velocity; (or arrPtr = &velocity[0];)
        arrPtr[2] = 6.43;
        ```
3. a. ```
        recPtr = &oneRec;
        ```
    b.  ```
        (*recPtr).weight = 120.5;
        recPtr->weight = 120.5;
        ```
4. a. ```
        double* dblPtr = new double;
        *dblPtr = 98.32586728;
        ```
    b.  ```
        int* list = new int[50];
            for (i = 0; i < 50; i++)
                list[i] = 0;
        ```
5.  ```
    delete dblPtr;
    delete [] list;
    ```
6. float& gamma = delta;   7. gamma = 12.9; (Remember that once a reference variable is initialized, each appearance of the variable is *implicitly* dereferenced.)   **8.** Shallow copying copies one pointer to another without copying any pointed-to data.   **9.** a. Passing a class object as an argument using a pass by value. b. Initializing a class object in its declaration. c. Returning a class object as a function value.   **10.** The class needs one or more constructors (to create the dynamic data), a destructor (to clean up the free store), a deep copy operation, and a copy-constructor (for deep copying during initializations).   **11.** Pointers, when used with dynamic data, improve memory efficiency because we create only as many dynamic variables as are needed. With respect to time

efficiency, it is faster to move pointers than to move large data structures, as in the case of sorting large structs.

Exam Preparation Exercises

1. How does a variable of type `float*` differ from a variable of type `float`?
2. Show what is output by the following C++ code. If an unknown value gets printed, write a *U*.

```cpp
int main()
{
    int   m;
    int   n;
    int*  p = &m;
    int*  q;

    *p = 27;
    cout << *p << ' ' << *q << endl;
    q = &n;
    n = 54;
    cout << *p << ' ' << *q << endl;
    p = &n;
    *p = 6;
    cout << *p << ' ' << n << endl;
    return 0;
}
```

3. Given the declarations

```cpp
struct PersonType
{
    string lastName;
    char   firstInitial;
};
typedef PersonType* PtrType;

PersonType onePerson;
PtrType    ptr = &onePerson;
```

tell whether each statement below is valid or invalid.

```
a. ptr.lastName = "Alvarez";
b. (*ptr).lastName = "Alvarez";
c. *ptr.lastName = "Alvarez";
d. ptr->lastName = "Alvarez";
e. *ptr->lastName = "Alvarez";
```

4. What C++ built-in operation releases the space reserved for a dynamic variable back to the system?

5. Given the declarations

```
int* ptrA;
int* ptrB;
```

tell whether each code segment below results in an inaccessible object, a dangling pointer, or neither.

a.
```
ptrA = new int;
ptrB = new int;
*ptrA = 345;
ptrB = ptrA;
```

d.
```
ptrA = new int;
ptrB = new int;
*ptrA = 345;
*ptrB = *ptrA;
```

b.
```
ptrA = new int;
*ptrA = 345;
ptrB = ptrA;
delete ptrA;
```

e.
```
ptrA = new int;
ptrB = new int;
*ptrA = 345;
ptrB = new int;
*ptrB = *ptrA;
```

c.
```
ptrA = LocationOfAge();
```

where function `LocationOfAge` is defined as

```
int* LocationOfAge()
{
    int age;

    cout << "Enter your age: ";
    cin >> age;
    return &age;
}
```

6. The only operation that affects the contents of a reference variable is initialization. (True or False?)

7. Given the declarations

```
int  n;
int& r = n;
```

what does the following statement do?

```
r = 2 * r;
```

a. It doubles the contents of n.
b. It doubles the contents of r.
c. It doubles the contents of the variable that n points to.
d. It doubles the contents of both r and n.
e. Nothing—it results in a compile-time error.

8. Define the following terms:
   deep copy
   shallow copy
   class destructor
   class copy-constructor

9. By default, C++ performs both assignment and initialization of class objects using shallow copying. (True or False?)

10. Given the class declaration

```
class TestClass
{
public:
    void Write();
    TestClass( /* in */ int initValue );
    ~TestClass();
private:
    int privateData;
};
```

suppose that the member functions are implemented as follows:

```
void TestClass::Write()
{
    cout << "Private data is " << privateData << endl;
}


TestClass::TestClass( /* in */ int initValue )
{
    privateData = initValue;
    cout << "Constructor executing" << endl;
}


TestClass::~TestClass()
{
    cout << "Destructor executing" << endl;
}
```

What is the output of the following program?

```
#include "testclass.h"
#include <iostream>

using namespace std;

int main()
{
    int       count;
    TestClass anObject(5);

    for (count = 1; count <= 3; count++)
        anObject.Write();
    return 0;
}
```

11. Given the TestClass class of Exercise 10, what is the output of the following program?

```
#include "testclass.h"
#include <iostream>
```

```
using namespace std;

int main()
{
    int count;

    for (count = 1; count <= 3; count++)
    {
        TestClass anObject(count);
        anObject.Write();
    }
    return 0;
}
```

12. Let x and y be class objects of the DynArray class developed in this chapter.

```
DynArray x(100);
DynArray y(100);
```

What is the output of each of the following code segments?

a. ```
x.Store(425, 10);
y.CopyFrom(x);
x.Store(250, 10);
cout << x.ValueAt(10) << endl;
cout << y.ValueAt(10) << endl;
```

b. ```
x.Store(425, 10);
y = x;
x.Store(250, 10);
cout << x.ValueAt(10) << endl;
cout << y.ValueAt(10) << endl;
```

13. Given a class named IntList, which of the following is the correct function prototype for the class copy-constructor?

a. `void IntList( IntList otherList );`
b. `IntList( IntList& otherList );`
c. `IntList( const IntList otherList );`
d. `void IntList( const IntList& otherList );`
e. `IntList( const IntList& otherList );`

14. How can the use of pointers make a program run faster?

Programming Warm-up Exercises

1. a. Declare a pointer variable p and initialize it to point to a char variable named ch.
   b. Declare a pointer variable q and initialize it to point to the first element of a long array named arr.
   c. Declare a pointer variable r and initialize it to point to a variable named box of type

```
struct BoxType
{
    int length;
    int width;
    int height;
};
```

2. Using the variables p, q, and r of Exercise 1, write code to do the following:
   a. Store '@' into the variable pointed to by p.
   b. Store 959263 into the first element of the array pointed to by q.
   c. Store a length, width, and height of 12, 14, and 5 into the variable pointed to by r.

3. Write a Boolean value-returning function that takes two pointer variables—ptr1 and ptr2—as parameters. Both variables point to float data. The function should return true if the two pointers point to the same variable, and false otherwise.

4. Write a Boolean value-returning function that takes two pointer variables—ptr1 and ptr2—as parameters. Both variables point to float data. The function should return true if the values in the pointed-to variables are identical, and false otherwise.

5. Given the code segment

```
struct GradeType
{
    int  score;
    char grade;
};
typedef GradeType* PtrType;

PtrType p1;
PtrType p2;
PtrType p3;
PtrType p4;
    ⋮
p4 = PtrToMax(p1, p2, p3);
```

the PtrToMax function returns a pointer: the value of p1, p2, or p3, whichever points to the struct with the highest value of score. Implement the PtrToMax function.

6. Write an If statement that compares the two dynamic int variables pointed to by variables p and q, puts the smaller into an int variable named smaller, and destroys the original two dynamic variables.

7. Declare all variables used in Exercise 6.

8. Given the declarations

```
int    numLetters;   // No. of letters in user's last name
int    i;            // Index variable
char* list;          // Pointer to array of letters in
                     //    user's last name
```

write a section of code that prompts the user for the number of letters in his or her last name, dynamically creates a `char` array of exactly the right size to hold the letters, inputs the letters, prints out the letters in reverse order (last through first), and deallocates the array.

9. Pretend that C++ provides pointer types but not reference types. Rewrite the following function using pointer variables instead of reference variables.

```
void AddAndIncr( /* in */     int  int1,
                 /* inout */ int& int2,
                 /* out */    int& sum  )
{
    sum = int1 + int2;
    int2++;
}
```

10. For the function of Exercise 9, change the function call

```
AddAndIncr(m, n, theirSum);
```

so that it corresponds to the new version of the function.

Programming Problems

1. Given two arrays a and b, we can define the relation a < b to mean a[0] < b[0] *and* a[1] < b[1] *and* a[2] < b[2], and so forth. (If the two arrays are of different sizes, the relation is defined only through the size of the smaller array.) We can define the other relational operators likewise. Enhance this chapter's DynArray class by adding two Boolean member functions, LessThan and Equal.

   These functions can be thought of as *deep comparison* operations because the dynamic arrays on the free store are to be compared element by element. In other words, the function call

   ```
   arr1.LessThan(arr2)
   ```

   returns true if arr1's array elements are pairwise less than arr2's elements.

   Test your two new functions with suitable test drivers and comprehensive sets of test data.

2. Referring to Programming Problem 1, the client code can simulate the other four relational operators (!=, <=, >, and >=) using only the Equal and LessThan functions. However, you could make the class easier to use by supplying additional member functions NotEqual, LessOrEqual, GreaterThan, and GreaterOrEqual. Add these functions to the DynArray class in addition to Equal and LessThan. (*Hint:* Instead of writing each of the algorithms from scratch, simply have the function bodies invoke the existing functions Equal and LessThan. And remember: Class members can refer to each other directly without using dot notation.)

   Test your new functions with suitable test drivers and comprehensive sets of test data.

3. The size of a built-in array is fixed statically (at compile time). The size of a dynamic array can be specified dynamically (at run time). In both cases, however, once memory has been allocated for the array, the array size cannot change while the program is executing. In this problem, you are to design and test a C++ class that represents an *expandable array*—one that can grow in size at run time.

   Using this chapter's `DynArray` class as a starting point, create a class named `ExpArray`. This class has all of `DynArray`'s member functions plus one more:

```
void ExpandBy( /* in */ int n );
    // Precondition:
    //     n > 0
    // Postcondition:
    //     Size of array has increased by n elements
    //   && All of the additional n elements equal zero
```

   Here is an example of client code:

```
ExpArray myArray(100);
// Assert: Class object created with array size 100
   ⋮
myArray.ExpandBy(50);
// Assert: Array size is now 150
```

   (*Hint:* To expand the array, you should allocate a new, larger dynamic array on the free store, copy the values from the old dynamic array to the new, and deallocate the old array.)

   Test your class with a suitable test driver and a comprehensive set of test data. Note that your test driver should exercise the other class member functions to be sure they still work correctly.

Case Study Follow-Up

1. Rewrite the `RecordList::SelSort` function from the SortWithPointers program so that it correctly orders the structs regardless of whether characters in the last names are uppercase or lowercase. (*Hint:* Temporarily convert all the characters in both strings to uppercase before making the comparison.)
2. Rewrite the `RecordList::SelSort` function from the SortWithPointers program so that it orders the structs by last name, then first name (in case two or more people have the same last name).
3. We want to add two member functions to the `RecordList` class of the SortWithPointers program: a copy-constructor and a deep copy operation.
   a. Give the specification of the copy-constructor (as it would appear in the class declaration), then give the implementation of the function.
   b. Give the specification of a `CopyFrom` function (as it would appear in the class declaration), then give the implementation of the function.
4. In the Dynamic Arrays case study, suppose that the `DynArray` class had been written to store `float` rather than `int` values:

```
class DynArray
{
```

```
public:
    float ValueAt( /* in */ int i ) const;
    void Store( /* in */ float val,
                /* in */ int   i  );
    void CopyFrom( /* in */ DynArray array2 );
    DynArray( /* in */ int arrSize );
    DynArray( const DynArray& array2 );
    ~DynArray();
private:
    float* arr;
    int    size;
};
```

Indicate precisely how the implementation of each of the six member functions would differ from the code presented in the case study.

5. a. Design the data sets necessary to thoroughly test the ValueAt function of the DynArray class (pages 918–927).
    b. Write a driver and test the ValueAt function using your test data.
6. a. Design the data sets necessary to thoroughly test the Store function of the DynArray class (pages 918–927).
    b. Write a driver and test the Store function using your test data.

16

Linked Structures

- To understand the concept of a linked data structure.
- To be able to declare the data types and variables needed for a dynamic linked list.
- To be able to print the contents of a linked list.
- To be able to insert new items into a linked list.
- To be able to delete items from a linked list.

In the last chapter, we saw that C++ has a mechanism for creating dynamic variables. These dynamic variables, which can be of any simple or structured type, can be created or destroyed at any time during execution of the program using the operators new and delete. A dynamic variable is referenced not by a name but through a pointer that contains its location (address). Every dynamic variable has an associated pointer by which it can be accessed. We used dynamic variables to save space and machine time. In this chapter, we see how to use them to build data structures that can grow and shrink as the program executes.

Sequential Versus Linked Structures

As we have pointed out in previous chapters, many problems in computing involve lists of items. A list is an abstract data type (ADT) with certain allowable operations: searching the list, sorting it, printing it, and so forth. The structure we have used as the concrete data representation of a list is the array, a sequential structure. By *sequential structure* we mean that successive components of the array are located next to each other in memory.

If the list we are implementing is a sorted list—one whose components must be kept in ascending or descending order—certain operations are efficiently carried out using an array representation. For example, searching a sorted list for a particular value is done quickly by using a binary search. However, inserting and deleting items from a sorted list are inefficient with an array representation. To insert a new item into its proper place in the list, we must shift array elements down to make room for the new item (see Figure 16-1). Similarly, deleting an item from the list requires that we shift up all the array elements following the one to be deleted.

FIGURE 16-1
Inserting into a
Sequential
Representation of a
Sorted List

a. Array before inserting the value 25

data[0]	4
data[1]	16
data[2]	39
data[3]	46
data[4]	58

b. Array after inserting the value 25

data[0]	4
data[1]	16
data[2]	25
data[3]	39
data[4]	46
data[5]	58

When insertions and deletions are frequent, there is a better data representation for a list: the **linked list.** A linked list is a collection of items, called *nodes*, that can be scattered about in memory, not necessarily in consecutive memory locations. Each node, typically represented as a struct, consists of two members:

1. A component member, which contains one of the data values in the list
2. A link member, which gives the location of the next node in the list

Component	Link
(Data)	(Location of next node)

Figure 16-2 shows an abstract diagram of a linked list. An arrow is used in the link member of each node to indicate the location of the next node. The slash (/) in the link member of the last node signifies the end of the list. The separate variable head is not a node in the linked list; its purpose is to give the location of the first node.

Accessing the items in a linked list is a little like playing the children's game of treasure hunt—each child is given a clue to the hiding place of the next clue, and the chain of clues eventually leads to the treasure.

As you look at Figure 16-2, you should observe two things. First, we have deliberately arranged the nodes in random positions. We have done this to emphasize the fact that the items in a linked list are not necessarily in adjacent memory locations (as they are in the array representation of Figure 16-1). Second, you may already be thinking of pointers when you see the arrows in the figure because we drew pointer variables this way in Chapter 15. But so far, we have carefully avoided using the word *pointer;* we said only that the link member of a node gives the location of the next node. As we will see, there are two ways in which to implement a linked list. One way is to store it in an array of structs, a technique that does not use pointers at all. The second way is to use dynamic data and pointers. Let's begin with the first of these two techniques.

FIGURE 16-2
A Linked List

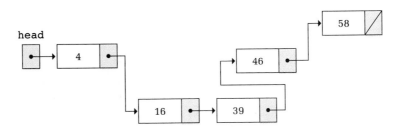

Linked list   A list in which the order of the components is determined by an explicit link member in each node, rather than by the sequential order of the components in memory.

Array Representation of a Linked List

A linked list can be represented as an array of structs. For a linked list of int components, we use the following declarations:

```
struct NodeType
{
    int component;
    int link;
};

NodeType node[1000];    // Max. 1000 nodes
int      head;
```

The nodes all reside in an array named node. Each node has two members: component (in this example, an int data value) and link, which contains the *array index* of the next node in the list. The last node in the list will have a link member of –1. Because –1 is not a valid array index in C++, it is suitable as a special "end-of-list" value. The variable head contains the

FIGURE 16-3

Array Representation of a Linked List

head		component	link
2	node[0]	58	–1
	node[1]		
	node[2]	4	5
	node[3]		
	node[4]	46	0
	node[5]	16	7
	node[6]		
	node[7]	39	4
	.		
	.		
	.		

array index of the first node in the list. Figure 16-3 illustrates an array representation of the linked list of Figure 16-2.

Compare Figures 16-1 and 16-3. Figure 16-1 shows a list represented directly as an array. Figure 16-3 shows a list represented as a linked list, which, in turn, is represented as an array (of structs). We said that when insertions and deletions occur frequently, it is better to use a linked list to represent a list than it is to use an array directly. Let's see why.

Figure 16-1 showed the effect of inserting 25 into the list; we had to shift array elements 2, 3, 4, ... down to insert the value 25 into element 2. If the list is long, we might have to move hundreds or thousands of numbers. In contrast, inserting the value 25 into the linked list of Figure 16-3 requires *no* movement of existing data. We simply find an unused slot in the array, store 25 into the `component` member, and adjust the `link` member of the node containing 16 (see Figure 16-4).

Before we introduce the second technique for implementing a linked list—the use of dynamic data and pointers—let's step back and look at the big picture. We are interested in the list as an ADT. Because it is an ADT, we must implement it using some existing data representation. One data representation is the built-in array, a sequential structure. Another data representation is the linked list, a linked structure. But a linked list is, itself, an ADT and requires a concrete data representation—an array of structs, for example. To help visualize all these relationships, we use an *implementation hierarchy diagram*, such as the one shown in Figure 16-5. In this diagram, each data type is implemented by using the data type(s) directly below it in the hierarchy.

FIGURE 16-4

Array Representation of Linked List After 25 Was Inserted

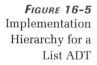

FIGURE 16-5
Implementation
Hierarchy for a
List ADT

Dynamic Data Representation of a Linked List

Representing a list either as an array or as a linked list stored in an array of structs has a disadvantage: The size of the array is fixed and cannot change while the program is executing. Yet when we are working with lists, we often have no idea how many components we will have. The usual approach in this situation is to declare an array large enough to hold the maximum amount of data we can logically expect. Because we usually have less data than the maximum, memory space is wasted on the unused array elements.

There is an alternative technique in which the list components are dynamic variables that are created only as they are needed. We represent the list as a linked list whose nodes are dynamically allocated on the free store, and the link member of each node contains the memory address of the next dynamic node. In this data representation, called a **dynamic linked list,** the arrows in the diagram of Figure 16-2 really do represent pointers (and the slash in the last node is the null pointer). We access the list with a pointer variable that holds the address of the first node in the list. This pointer variable, named head in Figure 16-2, is called the **external pointer** or **head pointer.** Every node after the first node is accessed by using the link member in the node before it.

Such a list can expand or contract as the program executes. To insert a new item into the list, we allocate more space on the free store. To delete an item, we deallocate the memory assigned to it. We don't have to know in advance how long the list will be. The only limitation is the amount of available memory space. Data structures built using this technique are called **dynamic data structures.**

Dynamic data structure A data structure that can expand and contract during execution.

Dynamic linked list A linked list composed of dynamically allocated nodes that are linked together by pointers.

External (head) pointer A pointer variable that points to the first node in a dynamic linked list.

To create a dynamic linked list, we begin by allocating the first node and saving the pointer to it in the external pointer. We then allocate a second node and store the pointer to it into the link member of the first node. We continue this process—allocating a new node and storing the pointer to it into the link member of the previous node—until we have finished adding nodes to the list.

Let's look at how we can use C++ pointer variables to create a dynamic linked list of `float` values. We begin with the declarations

```
typedef float ComponentType;

struct NodeType
{
    ComponentType component;
    NodeType*      link;
};
typedef NodeType* NodePtr;

NodePtr head;                // External pointer to list
NodePtr currPtr;             // Pointer to current node
NodePtr newNodePtr;          // Pointer to newest node
```

The order of these declarations is important. The Typedef for `NodePtr` refers to the identifier `NodeType`, so the declaration of `NodeType` must come first. (Remember that C++ requires every identifier to be declared before it is used.) Within the declaration of `NodeType`, we would like to declare `link` to be of type `NodePtr`, but we can't because the identifier `NodePtr` hasn't been declared yet. However, C++ allows *forward* (or *incomplete*) *declarations* of structs, classes, and unions:

```
typedef float ComponentType;

struct  NodeType;            // Forward (incomplete) declaration
typedef NodeType* NodePtr;

struct NodeType              // Complete declaration
{
    ComponentType component;
```

```
    NodePtr        link;
};
```

The advantage of using a forward declaration is that we can declare the type of `link` to be `NodePtr` just as we declare `head`, `currPtr`, and `newNodePtr` to be of type `NodePtr`.

Given the declarations above, the following code fragment creates a dynamic linked list with the values 12.8, 45.2, and 70.1 as the components in the list.

```
#include <cstddef>    // For NULL
   ⋮
head = new NodeType;
head->component = 12.8;
newNodePtr = new NodeType;
newNodePtr->component = 45.2;
head->link = newNodePtr;
currPtr = newNodePtr;
newNodePtr = new NodeType;
newNodePtr->component = 70.1;
currPtr->link = newNodePtr;
newNodePtr->link = NULL;
currPtr = newNodePtr;
```

Let's go through each of these statements, describing in words what is happening and showing the linked list as it appears after the execution of the statement.

`head = new NodeType;`   A dynamic variable of type `NodeType` is created. The pointer to this new node is stored into `head`. Variable `head` is the external pointer to the list we are building.

`head->component = 12.8;`   The value 12.8 is stored into the component member of the first node.

(see diagram next page)

```
newNodePtr = new NodeType;
```

A dynamic variable of type NodeType is created. The pointer to this new node is stored into newNodePtr.

```
newNodePtr->component = 45.2;
```

The value 45.2 is stored into the component member of the new node.

```
head->link = newNodePtr;
```

The pointer to the new node containing 45.2 in its component member is copied into the link member of *head. Variable newNodePtr still points to this new node. The node can be accessed either as *newNodePtr or as *(head->link).

```
currPtr = newNodePtr;
```

The pointer to the new node is copied into `currPtr`. Now `currPtr`, `newNodePtr`, and `head->link` all point to the node containing 45.2 as its component.

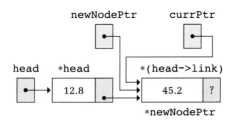

```
newNodePtr = new NodeType;
```

A dynamic variable of type `NodeType` is created. The pointer to this new node is stored into `newNodePtr`.

```
newNodePtr->component = 70.1;
```

The value 70.1 is stored into the `component` member of the new node.

`currPtr->link = newNodePtr;`

The pointer to the new node containing 70.1 in the `component` member is copied into the `link` member of the node that contains 45.2.

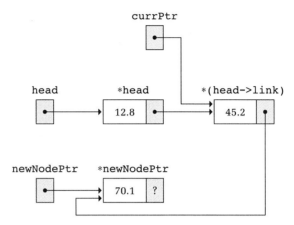

`newNodePtr->link = NULL;`

The special pointer constant `NULL` is stored into the `link` member of the last node in the list. When used in the `link` member of a node, `NULL` means the end of the list. `NULL` is shown in the diagram as a / in the `link` member.

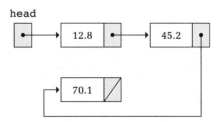

`currPtr = newNodePtr;`

`currPtr` is updated.

We would like to generalize this algorithm so that we can use a loop to create a dynamic linked list of any length. In the algorithm, we used three pointers:

1. head, which was used in creating the first node in the list and became the external pointer to the list.
2. newNodePtr, which was used in creating a new node when it was needed.
3. currPtr, which was updated to always point to the last node in the linked list.

When building any dynamic linked list by adding each new node to the end of the list, we always need three pointers to perform these functions. The algorithm that we used is generalized below to build a linked list of int numbers read from the standard input device. It is assumed that the user types in at least one number.

```
Set head = new NodeType
Read head->component
Set currPtr = head

Read inputVal
WHILE NOT EOF
        Set newNodePtr = new NodeType
        Set newNodePtr->component = inputVal
        Set currPtr->link = newNodePtr
        Set currPtr = newNodePtr
        Read inputVal
Set currPtr->link = NULL
```

The following code segment implements this algorithm. For variety, we define the component type to be int rather than float.

```
typedef int ComponentType;

struct   NodeType;                    // Forward declaration
typedef NodeType* NodePtr;

struct NodeType
{
    ComponentType component;
    NodePtr        link;
};
```

```
NodePtr       head;              // External pointer to list
NodePtr       newNodePtr;        // Pointer to newest node
NodePtr       currPtr;           // Pointer to last node
ComponentType inputVal;

head = new NodeType;
cin >> head->component;
currPtr = head;

cin >> inputVal;
while (cin)
{
    newNodePtr = new NodeType;          // Create new node
    newNodePtr->component = inputVal;   // Set its component value
    currPtr->link = newNodePtr;         // Link node into list
    currPtr = newNodePtr;               // Set currPtr to last node
    cin >> inputVal;
}
currPtr->link = NULL;                    // Mark end of list
```

Let's do a code walk-through and see just how this algorithm works.

`head = new NodeType;`	A variable of type `NodeType` is created. The pointer is stored into `head`. Variable `head` will remain unchanged as the pointer to the first node (that is, `head` is the external pointer to the list).
`cin >> head->component;`	The first number is read into the `component` member of the first node in the list.
`currPtr = head;`	`currPtr` now points to the last node (the only node) in the list.
`cin >> inputVal;`	The next number (if there is one) is read into variable `inputVal`.
`while (cin)` `{`	An event-controlled loop is used to read input values until end-of-file occurs.
`newNodePtr = new NodeType;`	Another variable of type `NodeType` is created, with `newNodePtr` pointing to it.
`newNodePtr->component = inputVal;`	The current input value is stored into the `component` member of the newly created node.
`currPtr->link = newNodePtr;`	The pointer to the new node is stored into the `link` member of the last node in the list.

`currPtr = newNodePtr;`	`currPtr` is again pointing to the last node in the list.
`cin >> inputVal;`	The next input value (if there is one) is read in.
`}`	The loop body repeats again.
`currPtr->link = NULL;`	The `link` member of the last node is assigned the special end-of-list value `NULL`.

Following is the linked list that results when the program is run with the numbers 32, 78, 99, and 21 as data. The final values are shown for the auxiliary variables.

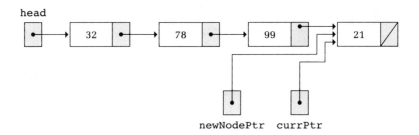

Algorithms on Dynamic Linked Lists

Now that we have looked at two examples of creating a dynamic linked list, let's look at algorithms that process nodes in a linked list. We need to be able to insert a node into a list, delete a node from a list, print the data values in a list, and so forth. For each of these operations, we make use of the fact that NULL is in the link member of the last node. NULL can be assigned to any pointer variable. It means that the pointer points to nothing. Its importance lies in the fact that we can compare the link member of each node to NULL to see when we have reached the end of the list.

As we develop these algorithms, we do so in the following context. We want to write a C++ class for a list (not linked list) ADT. As emphasized in Figure 16-5, a list ADT can be implemented in several ways. We choose a dynamic linked list as the data representation for a list, and we create the SortedList2 class whose specification is shown in Figure 16-6. (We use the name SortedList2 to distinguish this class from the SortedList class of Chapter 13.)

FIGURE 16-6

Specification of
the SortedList2
Class

```
//*********************************************************************
// SPECIFICATION FILE (slist2.h)
// This file gives the specification of a sorted list abstract data
// type. The list components are maintained in ascending order of
// value
//*********************************************************************

typedef int ComponentType;     // Type of each component
                               //    (a simple type or the string type)

struct NodeType;               // Forward declaration
                               //    (Complete declaration is
                               //    hidden in implementation file)
class SortedList2
{
public:
    bool IsEmpty() const;
        // Postcondition:
        //      Function value == true, if list is empty
        //                     == false, otherwise

    void Print() const;
        // Postcondition:
        //      All components (if any) in list have been output

    void InsertTop( /* in */ ComponentType item );
        // Precondition:
        //      item < first component in list
        // Postcondition:
        //      item is first component in list
        //   && List components are in ascending order

    void Insert( /* in */ ComponentType item );
        // Precondition:
        //      item is assigned
        // Postcondition:
        //      item is in list
        //   && List components are in ascending order

    void DeleteTop( /* out */ ComponentType& item );
        // Precondition:
        //      NOT IsEmpty()
        // Postcondition:
        //      item == first component in list at entry
        //   && item is no longer in list
        //   && List components are in ascending order

    void Delete( /* in */ ComponentType item );
        // Precondition:
```

FIGURE 16-6

Specification of
the SortedList2
Class

(continued)

```
//      item is somewhere in list
// Postcondition:
//      First occurrence of item is no longer in list
//   && List components are in ascending order

SortedList2();
    // Constructor
    // Postcondition:
    //      Empty list is created

SortedList2( const SortedList2& otherList );
    // Copy-constructor
    // Postcondition:
    //      List is created as a duplicate of otherList

~SortedList2();
    // Destructor
    // Postcondition:
    //      List is destroyed
private:
    NodeType* head;
};
```

In the class declaration, notice that the preconditions and postconditions of the member functions mention nothing about linked lists. The abstraction is a list, not a linked list. The user of the class is interested only in manipulating lists of items and does not care how we implement a list. If we change to a different implementation—an array, for example—the public interface remains valid.

The private data of the SortedList2 class consists of a single item: a pointer variable head. This variable is the external pointer to a dynamic linked list. As with any C++ class, different class objects have their own copies of the private data. For example, if the client code declares and manipulates two class objects like this:

```
SortedList2 list1;
SortedList2 list2;

list1.Insert(352);
list1.Insert(48);
list2.Insert(12);
    ⋮
if ( !list2.IsEmpty() )
    list2.DeleteTop(item);
```

then each of the two objects list1 and list2 has its own private head variable and maintains its own dynamic linked list on the free store.

In Figure 16-6, the specification file `slist2.h` declares a type `NodeType`, but only as a forward declaration. The only reason we need to declare the identifier `NodeType` in the specification file is so that the data type of the private variable `head` can be specified. In the spirit of information hiding, we place the complete declaration of `NodeType` into the implementation file `slist2.cpp`. The complete declaration is an implementation detail that the user does not need to know about. Here's how `slist2.cpp` starts out:

```
//*****************************************************************
// IMPLEMENTATION FILE (slist2.cpp)
// This file implements the SortedList2 class member functions
// List representation: a linked list of dynamic nodes
//*****************************************************************
#include "slist2.h"
#include <iostream>
#include <cstddef>      // For NULL

using namespace std;

typedef NodeType* NodePtr;
struct NodeType
{
    ComponentType  component;
    NodePtr        link;
};

// Private members of class:
//      NodePtr head;               External pointer to linked list
  ⋮
```

To illustrate some commonly used algorithms on dynamic linked lists, let's look at the implementations of the `SortedList2` member functions. Creating an empty linked list is the easiest of the algorithms, so we begin there.

Creating an Empty Linked List   To create a linked list with no nodes, all that is necessary is to assign the external pointer the value NULL. For the `SortedList2` class, the appropriate place to do this is in the class constructor:

```
SortedList2::SortedList2()

// Constructor

// Postcondition:
//      head == NULL
```

```
{
    head = NULL;
}
```

As we discussed in Chapter 13, the implementation assertions (the preconditions and postconditions appearing in the implementation file) are often stated differently from the abstract assertions (those located in the specification file). Abstract assertions are written in terms that are meaningful to the user of the ADT; implementation details should not be mentioned. In contrast, implementation assertions can be made more precise by referring directly to variables and algorithms in the implementation code. In the case of the SortedList2 class constructor, the abstract postcondition is simply that an empty list (not a linked list) has been created. On the other hand, the implementation postcondition

```
// Postcondition:
//      head == NULL
```

is phrased in terms of our private data (head) and our particular list implementation (a dynamic linked list).

Testing for an Empty Linked List   The SortedList2 member function IsEmpty returns true if the list is empty and false if the list is not empty. Using a dynamic linked list representation, we return true if head contains the value NULL, and false otherwise:

```
bool SortedList2::IsEmpty() const

// Postcondition:
//      Function value == true, if head == NULL
//                     == false, otherwise

{
    return (head == NULL);
}
```

Printing a Linked List   To print the components of a linked list, we need to access the nodes one at a time. This requirement implies an event-controlled loop, where the event that stops the loop is reaching the end of the list. The loop control variable is a pointer that is initialized to the external pointer and is advanced from node to node by setting it equal to the link member of the current node. When the loop control pointer equals NULL, the last node has been accessed.

Print ( )

> Set currPtr = head
> WHILE currPtr doesn't equal NULL
>   Print component member of *currPtr
>   Set currPtr = link member of *currPtr

Note that this algorithm works correctly even if the list is empty (head equals NULL).

```
void SortedList2::Print() const

// Postcondition:
//      component members of all nodes (if any) in linked list
//      have been output

{
    NodePtr currPtr = head;     // Loop control pointer

    while (currPtr != NULL)
    {
        cout << currPtr->component << endl;
        currPtr = currPtr->link;
    }
}
```

Let's do a code walk-through using the following list.

currPtr = head;   currPtr and head both point to
                                              the first node in the list.

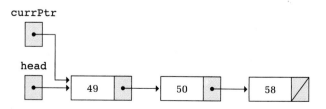

`while (currPtr != NULL)`	The loop body is entered because `currPtr` is not NULL.
`cout << currPtr->component << endl;` `currPtr = currPtr->link;`	The number 49 is printed. `currPtr` now points to the second node in the list.

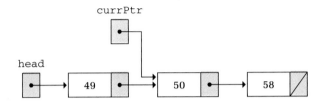

`while (currPtr != NULL)`	The loop body repeats because `currPtr` is not NULL.
`cout << currPtr->component << endl;` `currPtr = currPtr->link;`	The number 50 is printed. `currPtr` now points to the third node in the list.

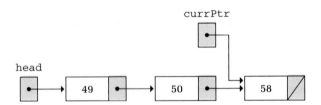

`while (currPtr != NULL)`	The loop body repeats because `currPtr` is not NULL.
`cout << currPtr->component << endl;` `currPtr = currPtr->link;`	The number 58 is printed. `currPtr` is now NULL.

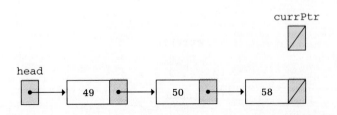

```
while (currPtr != NULL)                    The loop body is not
                                            repeated because currPtr
                                            is NULL.
```

Inserting into a Linked List A function for inserting a component into a linked list must have an argument: the item to be inserted. The phrase *inserting into a linked list* could mean either inserting the component at the top of the list (as the first node) or inserting the component into its proper place according to some ordering (alphabetic or numeric). Let's examine these two situations separately.

Inserting a component at the top of a list is easy because we don't have to search the list to find where the item belongs.

InsertTop (In: item)

```
Set newNodePtr = new NodeType
Set component member of *newNodePtr = item
Set link member of *newNodePtr = head
Set head = newNodePtr
```

This algorithm is coded in the following function.

```
void SortedList2::InsertTop( /* in */ ComponentType item )

// Precondition:
//      component members of list nodes are in ascending order
//   && item < component member of first list node
// Postcondition:
//      New node containing item is at top of linked list
//   && component members of list nodes are in ascending order

{
    NodePtr newNodePtr = new NodeType;      // Temporary pointer

    newNodePtr->component = item;
    newNodePtr->link = head;
    head = newNodePtr;
}
```

The function precondition states that `item` must be smaller than the value in the first node. This precondition is not a requirement of linked lists in general. However, the `SortedList2` abstraction we are implementing is a sorted list. The precondition/postcondition contract states that *if* the client sends a value smaller than the first one in the list, then the function guarantees to preserve the ascending order. If the client violates the precondition, the contract is broken.

The following code walk-through shows the steps in inserting a component with the value 20 as the first node in the linked list that was printed in the last section.

`newNodePtr = new NodeType;`   A new node is created.
`newNodePtr->component = item;`   The number 20 is stored into the
                                                              `component` member of the new
                                                              node.

`newNodePtr->link = head;`   The `link` member of `*newNodePtr`
                                                    now points to the first node in the
                                                    list.

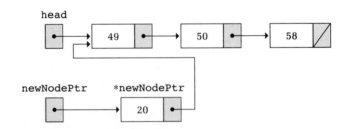

`head = newNodePtr;`   The external pointer to the list now
                                          points to the node containing the
                                          new component.

To insert a component into its proper place in a sorted list, we have to loop through the nodes until we find where the component belongs. Because the SortedList2 class keeps components in ascending order, we can recognize where a component belongs by finding the node that contains a value greater than the one being inserted. Our new node should be inserted directly before the node with that value; therefore, we must keep track of the node before the current one in order to insert our new node. We use a pointer prevPtr to point to this previous node. This method leads to the following algorithm:

Insert (In: item)

```
Set newNodePtr = new NodeType
Set component member of *newNodePtr = item
Set prevPtr = NULL
Set currPtr = head
WHILE item > component member of *currPtr
        Set prevPtr = currPtr
        Set currPtr = link member of *currPtr
Insert *newNodePtr between *prevPtr and *currPtr
```

This algorithm is basically sound, but there are problems with it in special cases. If the new component is larger than all other components in the list, the event that stops the loop (finding a node whose component is larger than the one being inserted) does not occur. When the end of the list is reached, the While condition tries to dereference currPtr, which now contains NULL. On some systems, the program will crash. We can take care of this case by using the following expression to control the While loop:

currPtr isn't NULL AND item > component member of *currPtr

This expression keeps us from dereferencing the null pointer because C++ uses short-circuit evaluation of logical expressions. If the first part evaluates to false—that is, if currPtr equals NULL—the second part of the expression, which dereferences currPtr, is not evaluated.

There is one more point to consider in our algorithm: the special case in which the list is empty or the new value is less than the first component in the list. The variable prevPtr remains NULL in this case, and *newNodePtr must be inserted at the top instead of between *prevPtr and *currPtr.

The following function implements our algorithm with these changes incorporated.

```
void SortedList2::Insert( /* in */ ComponentType item )

// Precondition:
//      component members of list nodes are in ascending order
//   && item is assigned
// Postcondition:
//      New node containing item is in its proper place
//         in linked list
//   && component members of list nodes are in ascending order

{
    NodePtr currPtr;       // Moving pointer
    NodePtr prevPtr;       // Pointer to node before *currPtr
    NodePtr newNodePtr;    // Pointer to new node

    // Set up node to be inserted

    newNodePtr = new NodeType;
    newNodePtr->component = item;

    // Find previous insertion point

    prevPtr = NULL;
    currPtr = head;
    while (currPtr != NULL && item > currPtr->component)
    {
        prevPtr = currPtr;
        currPtr = currPtr->link;
    }

    // Insert new node

    newNodePtr->link = currPtr;
    if (prevPtr == NULL)
        head = newNodePtr;
    else
        prevPtr->link = newNodePtr;
}
```

Let's go through this code for each of the three cases: inserting at the top (`item` is 20), inserting in the middle (`item` is 60), and inserting at the end (`item` is 100). Each insertion begins with the list below.

Insert(20)

```
newNodePtr = new NodeType;
newNodePtr->component = item;
prevPtr = NULL;
currPtr = head;
```

These four statements initialize the variables used in the searching process. The variables their contents are shown below.

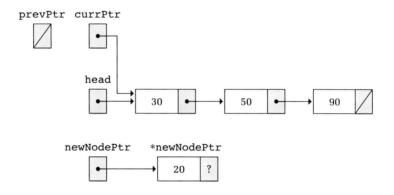

```
while (currPtr != NULL &&
    item > currPtr->component)


newNodePtr->link = currPtr;


if (prevPtr == NULL)
head = newNodePtr;
```

Because 20 is less than 30, the expression is `false` and the loop body is not entered.

`link` member of `*newNodePtr` now points to `*currPtr`.

Because `prevPtr` is NULL, the then-clause is executed and 20 is inserted at the top of the list.

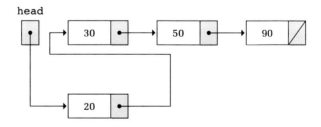

Insert(60)

```
newNodePtr = new NodeType;
newNodePtr->component = item;
prevPtr = NULL;
currPtr = head;
```

These four statements initialize the variables used in the searching process. The variables and their contents are shown below.

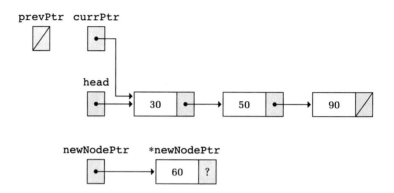

```
while (currPtr != NULL &&
    item > currPtr->component)

prevPtr = currPtr;
currPtr = currPtr->link;
```

Because 60 is greater than 30, this expression is true and the loop body is entered.
Pointer variables are advanced.

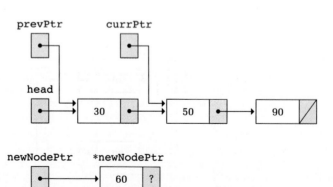

```
while (currPtr != NULL &&
    item > currPtr->component)

prevPtr = currPtr;
currPtr = currPtr->link;
```

Because 60 is greater than 50,
this expression is true and the
loop body is repeated.
Pointer variables are advanced.

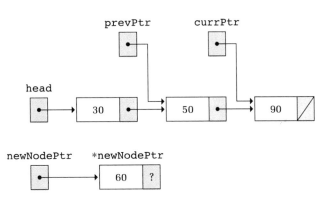

```
while (currPtr != NULL &&
    item > currPtr->component)

newNodePtr->link = currPtr;
```

Because 60 is not greater than 90,
the expression is false and
the loop body is not repeated.
link member of *newNodePtr
now points to *currPtr.

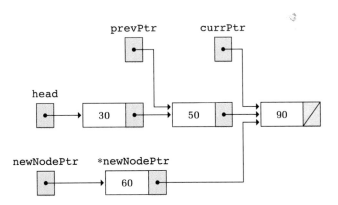

```
if (prevPtr == NULL)
prevPtr->link = newNodePtr;
```

Because `prevPtr` does not equal `NULL`, the else-clause is executed. The completed list is shown with the auxiliary variables removed.

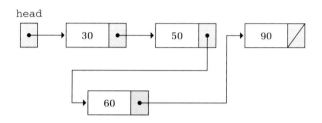

Insert(100)

We do not repeat the first part of the search, but pick up the walk-through where `prevPtr` is pointing to the node whose component is 50, and `currPtr` is pointing to the node whose component is 90.

```
while (currPtr != NULL &&
    item > currPtr->component)

prevPtr = currPtr;
currPtr = currPtr->link;
```

Because 100 is greater than 90, this expression is `true` and the loop body is repeated. The pointer variables are advanced.

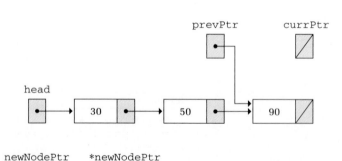

```
while (currPtr != NULL &&
    item > currPtr->component)

newNodePtr->link = currPtr;
```

Because `currPtr` equals `NULL`, the expression is `false` and the loop body is not repeated. `NULL` is copied into `link` member of `*newNodePtr`.

```
if (prevPtr == NULL)
    prevPtr->link = newNodePtr;
```

Because `prevPtr` does not equal `NULL`, the else-clause is executed. Node `*newNodePtr` is inserted after `*prevPtr`. The list is shown with auxiliary variables removed.

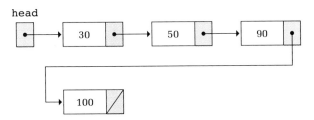

Deleting from a Linked List   To delete an existing node from a linked list, we have to loop through the nodes until we find the node we want to delete. We look at the mirror image of our insertions: deleting the top node and deleting a node whose component is equal to an incoming parameter.

To delete the first node, we just change the external pointer to point to the second node (or to contain NULL if we are deleting the only node in a one-node list). The value in the node being deleted can be returned as an outgoing parameter. Notice the precondition for the following function: The client must not call the function if the list is empty.

```
void SortedList2::DeleteTop( /* out */ ComponentType& item )

// Precondition:
//     Linked list is not empty (head != NULL)
//   && component members of list nodes are in ascending order
// Postcondition:
//     item == component member of first list node at entry
//   && Node containing item is no longer in linked list
//   && component members of list nodes are in ascending order

{
    NodePtr tempPtr = head;     // Temporary pointer

    item = head->component;
    head = head->link;
    delete tempPtr;
}
```

We don't show a complete code walk-through because the code is so straightforward. Instead, we show the state of the data structure in two stages: after the first two statements and at the end. We use one of our previous lists. Following is the data structure after the execution of the first two statements in the function.

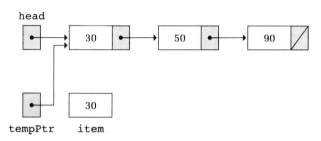

After the execution of the function, the structure is as follows:

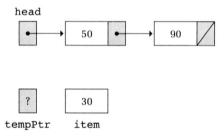

The function for deleting a node whose component contains a certain value is similar to the Insert function. The difference is that we are looking for a match, not a component member greater than our item. Because the function precondition states that the component we are looking for is definitely in the list, our loop control is simple. We don't have to worry about dereferencing the null pointer.

As in the Insert function, we need the node before the one that is to be deleted so we can change its link member. In the following function, we demonstrate another technique for keeping track of the previous node. Instead of comparing item with the component member of *currPtr, we compare it with the component member of the node pointed to by currPtr->link; that is, we compare item with currPtr->link->component. When currPtr->link->component is equal to item, *currPtr is the previous node.

```
void SortedList2::Delete( /* in */ ComponentType item )

// Precondition:
//     item == component member of some list node
//   && component members of list nodes are in ascending order
// Postcondition:
//     Node containing first occurrence of item is no longer in
//        linked list
//   && component members of list nodes are in ascending order

{
    NodePtr delPtr;      // Pointer to node to be deleted
    NodePtr currPtr;     // Loop control pointer

    // Check if item is in first node

    if (item == head->component)
    {
        // Delete first node

        delPtr = head;
        head = head->link;
    }
    else
    {
        // Search for node in rest of list

        currPtr = head;
        while (currPtr->link->component != item)
            currPtr = currPtr->link;

        // Delete *(currPtr->link)

        delPtr = currPtr->link;
        currPtr->link = currPtr->link->link;
    }
    delete delPtr;
}
```

Let's delete the node whose component is 90. The structure is shown below, with the nodes labeled as they are when the While statement is reached.

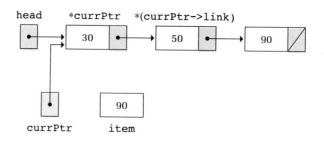

`while (currPtr->link->component != item)` Because 50 is not equal to 90, the loop body is entered.

`currPtr = currPtr->link;`   Pointer is advanced.

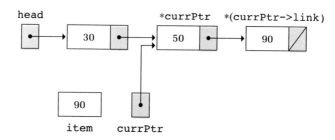

`while (currPtr->link->component != item)` Because 90 is equal to 90, the loop is exited.

`delPtr = currPtr->link;`
`currPtr->link = currPtr->link->link;`   The `link` member of the node whose component is 90 is copied into the `link` member of the node whose component is 50. The `link` member equals NULL in this case.

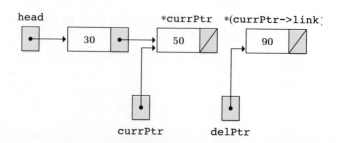

```
delete delPtr;
```

Memory allocated to `*delPtr` (the node that was deleted) is returned to the free store. The value of `delPtr` is undefined.

Note that NULL was stored into `currPtr->link` only because the node whose component is 90 was the last one in the list. If there had been more nodes beyond this one, a pointer to the next node would have been stored into `currPtr->link`.

Pointer Expressions

As you can see from the `SortedList2::Delete` function, pointer expressions can be quite complex. Let's look at some examples.

`p`, `q`, and `r` point to nodes in a dynamic linked list. The nodes themselves are `*p`, `*q`, and `*r`. Use the preceding diagram to convince yourself that the following are true.

```
p->link == q
*(p->link) is the same node as *q
p->link->link == r
*(p->link->link) is the same node as *r
q->link == r
*(q->link) is the same node as *r
```

And remember the semantics of assignment statements for pointers.

`p = q;`   Assigns the contents of pointer `q` to pointer `p`.

`*p = *q;`   Assigns the contents of the variable pointed to by `q` to the variable pointed to by `p`.

Classes and Dynamic Linked Lists

In Chapter 15, we said that classes whose objects manipulate dynamic data on the free store should provide not only a class constructor but also a destructor, a deep copy operation, and a copy-constructor. The SortedList2 class includes all of these except (to keep the example simpler) a deep copy operation. Let's look at the class destructor.

The purpose of the destructor is to deallocate the dynamic linked list when a SortedList2 class object is destroyed. Without a destructor, the linked list would be left behind on the free store, still allocated but inaccessible. The code for the destructor is easy to write. Using the existing member functions IsEmpty and DeleteTop, we simply march through the list and delete each node:

```
SortedList2::~SortedList2()

// Destructor

// Postcondition:
//      All linked list nodes have been deallocated from free store

{
    ComponentType temp;     // Temporary variable

    while ( !IsEmpty() )
        DeleteTop(temp);
}
```

The copy-constructor is harder to write. Before we look at it, we must stress the importance of providing a copy-constructor whenever we also provide a destructor. Pretend that SortedList2 doesn't have a copy-constructor, and suppose that a client passes a class object to a function using a pass by value. (Remember that passing an argument by value sends a *copy* of the value of the argument to the function.) Within the function, the parameter is initialized to be a copy of the caller's class object, including the caller's value of the private variable head. At this point, both the argument and the parameter are pointing to the same dynamic linked list. When the client function returns, the class destructor is invoked for the parameter, destroying the only copy of the linked list. Upon return from the function, the caller's linked list has disappeared!

By providing a copy-constructor, we ensure deep copying of an argument to a parameter whenever a pass by value occurs. The implementation of the copy-constructor, shown below, employs a commonly used algorithm for creating a new linked list as a copy of another.

```
SortedList2::SortedList2( const SortedList2& otherList )

// Copy-constructor

// Postcondition:
//     IF otherList.head == NULL   (i.e., the other list is empty)
//         head == NULL
//     ELSE
//         head points to a new linked list that is a copy of
//         the linked list pointed to by otherList.head

{
    NodePtr fromPtr;      // Pointer into list being copied from
    NodePtr toPtr;        // Pointer into new list being built

    if (otherList.head == NULL)
    {
        head = NULL;
        return;
    }

    // Copy first node

    fromPtr = otherList.head;
    head = new NodeType;
    head->component = fromPtr->component;

    // Copy remaining nodes

    toPtr = head;
    fromPtr = fromPtr->link;
    while (fromPtr != NULL)
    {
        toPtr->link = new NodeType;
        toPtr = toPtr->link;
        toPtr->component = fromPtr->component;
        fromPtr = fromPtr->link;
    }
    toPtr->link = NULL;
}
```

Choice of Data Representation

We have looked in detail at two ways of representing lists of components:
one in which the components are physically next to each other (a direct
array representation, as in Figure 16-1), and one in which the components

are only logically next to each other (a linked list). Furthermore, a linked list is an abstraction that can be implemented either by using an array of structs or by using dynamically allocated structs and pointers (a dynamic linked list).

Let's compare the array representation with the dynamic linked list representation. (Throughout this discussion, we use *array* to mean a direct array representation, not an array of structs forming a linked list.) We look at common operations on lists and examine the advantages and disadvantages of each representation for each operation.

Common Operations

1. Read the components into an initially empty list.
2. Access all the components in the list in sequence.
3. Insert or delete the first component in a list.
4. Insert or delete the last component in a list.
5. Insert or delete the nth component in a list.
6. Access the nth component in a list.
7. Sort the components in a list.
8. Search the list for a specific component.

Reading components into a list is faster with an array representation than with a dynamic linked list because the new operation doesn't have to be executed for each component. Accessing the components in sequence takes approximately the same time with both structures.

Inserting or deleting the first component is much faster using a linked representation. Remember that with an array, all the other list items have to be shifted down (for an insertion) or up (for a deletion). Conversely, inserting or deleting the last component is much more efficient with an array; there is direct access to the last component, and no shifting is required. In a linked representation, the entire list must be searched to find the last component.

On average, the time spent inserting or deleting the nth component is about equal for the two types of lists. A linked representation would be better for small values of n, and an array representation would be better for values of n near the end of the list.

Accessing the nth element is *much* faster in an array representation. We can access it directly by using $n - 1$ as the index into the array. In a linked representation, we have to access the first $n - 1$ components sequentially to reach the nth one.

For many sorting algorithms, including the selection sort, the two representations are approximately equal in efficiency. However, there are some sophisticated, very fast sorting algorithms that rely on direct access to array elements by using array indexes. These algorithms are not suitable for a linked representation, which requires sequential access to the components.

In general, searching a sorted list for a specific component is much faster in an array representation because a binary search can be used. When the components in the list to be searched are not in sorted order, the two representations are about the same.

When you are trying to decide whether to use an array representation or a linked representation, determine which of these common operations are likely to be applied most frequently. Use your analysis to determine which structure would be better in the context of your particular problem.

There is one additional point to consider when deciding whether to use an array or a dynamic linked list. How accurately can you predict the maximum number of components in the list? Does the number of components in the list fluctuate widely? If you know the maximum and it remains fairly constant, an array representation is fine in terms of memory usage. Otherwise, it is better to choose a dynamic linked representation in order to use memory more efficiently.

*P*ROBLEM-SOLVING CASE STUDY

Simulated Playing Cards

Problem: As an avid card player, you plan to write a program to play solitaire once you have become thoroughly comfortable with dynamic data structures. As a prelude to that program, you decide to design a C++ class that models a pile of playing cards. The pile could be a discard pile, a pile of cards face up on the table, or even a full deck of unshuffled cards. The card pile will be structured as a dynamic linked list.

In this case study, we omit the Input and Output sections because we are developing only a C++ class, not a complete program. Instead, we include two sections entitled Specification of the Class and Implementation of the Class.

Discussion: Thinking of a card pile as an ADT, what kinds of operations would we like to perform on this ADT? You might come up with a different list, but here are some operations we have chosen:

Create an empty pile
Put a new card onto the pile
Take a card from the pile
Determine the current length of the pile
Inspect the *n*th card in the pile

We can base our design roughly on the `SortedList2` class of this chapter, but there are some differences. First, we should consider a card pile to be an unsorted list, not a sorted list, because the cards can be in random order in the pile. Second, the last two operations listed above were not present in SortedList2. These operations allow more flexibility in asking questions about the list. If we use a private variable to keep track of the current length of the list, we can ask at any time how many cards are in a pile. We also can simulate looking at a face-up pile of cards by using the last operation to inspect any card in the pile without removing it.

Before we write the class specification, we must decide how to represent an individual playing card. The suit of a card can be represented using an enumeration type. Rank can be represented using the numbers 1 through 13, with the ace as a 1 and the king as a 13. Each card is then represented as a struct with two members, suit and rank:

```
enum Suits {CLUB, DIAMOND, HEART, SPADE};

struct CardType
{
    Suits suit;
    int   rank;      // Range 1 (ace) through 13 (king)
};
```

Below is the specification file cardpile.h, which provides the client with declarations for the CardType type and the CardPile class.

```
//*******************************************************************
// SPECIFICATION FILE (cardpile.h)
// This file gives the specifications of
//    1. CardType--a data type representing an ordinary playing card
//    2. CardPile--an unsorted list ADT representing a pile
//        of playing cards
//*******************************************************************
#ifndef CARDPILE_H
#define CARDPILE_H

enum Suits {CLUB, DIAMOND, HEART, SPADE};

struct CardType
{
    Suits suit;
    int   rank;      // Range 1 (ace) through 13 (king)
};

struct NodeType;          // Forward declaration (Complete declaration
                          // is hidden in implementation file)
```

PROBLEM-SOLVING CASE STUDY cont'd.

```
class CardPile
{
public:
    int Length() const;
        // Postcondition:
        //      Function value == number of cards in pile

    CardType CardAt( /* in */ int n ) const;
        // Precondition:
        //      n >= 1  &&  n <= Length()
        // Postcondition:
        //      Function value == card at position n in pile

    void InsertTop( /* in */ CardType newCard );
        // Precondition:
        //      newCard is assigned
        // Postcondition:
        //      newCard is at top of pile

    void RemoveTop( /* out */ CardType& topCard );
        // Precondition:
        //      Length() > 0
        // Postcondition:
        //      topCard == value of first component in pile at entry
        //   && topCard is no longer in pile

    CardPile();
        // Postcondition:
        //      Empty pile is created

    CardPile( const CardPile& otherPile );
        // Postcondition:
        //      Pile is created as a duplicate of otherPile

    ~CardPile();
        // Postcondition:
        //      Pile is destroyed
private:
    NodeType* head;
    int       listLength;
};

#endif
```

Implementation of the Class: For the data representation of a card pile, we use a linked list. Furthermore, we implement the linked list using dynamic data and pointers. Each node is of type NodeType, whose complete declaration (hidden in the implementation file) is as follows:

```
typedef NodeType* NodePtr;
struct NodeType
{
    CardType card;
    NodePtr  link;
};
```

The private variable head is the external pointer to the linked list, and the private variable listLength keeps track of the current length of the list.

The class constructor, copy-constructor, and destructor: These functions are essentially identical to those in the SortedList2 class. The only significant difference is in the constructor. In addition to setting head to NULL, the constructor must set listLength to 0.

The InsertTop and RemoveTop functions: These functions are the same as InsertTop and DeleteTop in the SortedList2 class, with the following differences. After inserting a new node, InsertTop must increment listLength; after deleting a node, RemoveTop must decrement listLength.

The Length function: Because the private variable listLength always indicates the current length of the list, no looping and counting are required. The function body is a single statement:

```
return listLength;
```

The CardAt function: To access the card at position n in the pile, we must start at the front of the list and sequence our way through the first $n - 1$ nodes. When we get to the desired node, we return the card member of the node as the function return value.

CardAt (In: n)

```
Set currPtr = head
FOR count going from 1 through n – 1
        Set currPtr = link member of *currPtr
Return card member of *currPtr
```

Here is the implementation file containing the definitions of the `CardPile` member functions:

```cpp
//******************************************************************
// IMPLEMENTATION FILE (cardpile.cpp)
// This file implements the CardPile class member functions
// List representation: a linked list of dynamic nodes
//******************************************************************
#include "cardpile.h"
#include <cstddef>      // For NULL

using namespace std;

typedef NodeType* NodePtr;
struct NodeType
{
    CardType card;
    NodePtr  link;
};

// Private members of class:
//      NodePtr head;           External pointer to linked list
//      int     listLength;     Current length of list


//******************************************************************

CardPile::CardPile()

// Constructor

// Postcondition:
//      head == NULL  &&  listLength == 0

{
    head = NULL;
    listLength = 0;
}
```

```
//******************************************************************

CardPile::CardPile( const CardPile& otherPile )

// Copy-constructor

// Postcondition:
//      listLength == otherPile.listLength
//   && IF otherPile.head == NULL
//          head == NULL
//      ELSE
//          head points to a new linked list that is a copy of
//          the linked list pointed to by otherPile.head

{
    NodePtr toPtr;        // Pointer into new list being built
    NodePtr fromPtr;      // Pointer into list being copied from

    listLength = otherPile.listLength;
    if (otherPile.head == NULL)
    {
        head = NULL;
        return;
    }

    // Copy first node

    fromPtr = otherPile.head;
    head = new NodeType;
    head->card = fromPtr->card;

    // Copy remaining nodes

    toPtr = head;
    fromPtr = fromPtr->link;
    while (fromPtr != NULL)
    {
        toPtr->link = new NodeType;
        toPtr = toPtr->link;
        toPtr->card = fromPtr->card;
        fromPtr = fromPtr->link;
    }
    toPtr->link = NULL;
}

//******************************************************************
```

```
CardPile::~CardPile()

// Destructor

// Postcondition:
//     All linked list nodes have been deallocated from free store

{
    CardType temp;     // Temporary variable

    while (listLength > 0)
        RemoveTop(temp);
}

//****************************************************************

int CardPile::Length() const

// Postcondition:
//     Function value == listLength

{
    return listLength;
}

//****************************************************************

CardType CardPile::CardAt( /* in */ int n ) const

// Precondition:
//     1 <= n <= listLength
// Postcondition:
//     Function value == card member of list node at position n

{
    int     count;          // Loop control variable
    NodePtr currPtr = head;    // Moving pointer variable

    for (count = 1; count < n; count++)
        currPtr = currPtr->link;
    return currPtr->card;
}

//****************************************************************

void CardPile::InsertTop( /* in */ CardType newCard )
```

PROBLEM-SOLVING CASE STUDY cont'd.

```
// Precondition:
//     newCard is assigned
// Postcondition:
//     New node containing newCard is at top of linked list
//  && listLength == listLength@entry + 1

{
    NodePtr newNodePtr = new NodeType;     // Temporary pointer

    newNodePtr->card = newCard;
    newNodePtr->link = head;
    head = newNodePtr;
    listLength++;
}


//****************************************************************

void CardPile::RemoveTop( /* out */ CardType& topCard )

// Precondition:
//     listLength > 0
// Postcondition:
//     topCard == card member of first list node at entry
//  && Node containing topCard is no longer in linked list
//  && listLength == listLength@entry - 1

{
    NodePtr tempPtr = head;     // Temporary pointer

    topCard = head->card;
    head = head->link;
    delete tempPtr;
    listLength--;
}
```

PROBLEM-SOLVING CASE STUDY

Solitaire Simulation

Problem: There is a solitaire game that is quite simple but seems difficult to win. Let's write a program to play the game, then run it a number of times to see if it really is that difficult to win or if we have just been unlucky.

Although this card game is played with a regular poker or bridge deck, the rules deal with suits only; the face values (ranks) are ignored. The rules are listed below. Rules 1 and 2 are initialization.

1. Take a deck of playing cards and shuffle it.
2. Place four cards side by side, left to right, face up on the table.
3. If the four cards (or the rightmost four if there are more than four on the table) are of the same suit, move them to a discard pile. Otherwise, if the first one and the fourth one (of the rightmost four cards) are of the same suit, move the other two cards (second and third) to a discard pile. Repeat until no cards can be removed.
4. Take the next card from the shuffled deck and place it face up to the right of those already there. Repeat this step if there are fewer than four cards face up (assuming there are more cards in the deck).
5. Repeat steps 3 and 4 until there are no more cards in the deck. You win if all the cards are on the discard pile.

Figure 16-7 walks us through the beginning of a typical game to demonstrate how the rules operate. Remember that the game deals with suits only. There must be at least four cards face up on the table before the rules can be applied.

Input: The number of times the simulation is to be run (`numberOf-Games`), the number of times the deck is to be shuffled between games (`numberOfShuffles`), and an initial seed value for a random number generator (`seed`). We discuss the `seed` variable later.

Output: The number of games played and the number of games won.

Discussion: A program that plays a game is an example of a *simulation program*. The program simulates what a human does when playing the game. Programs that simulate games or real-world processes are very common in computing.

In developing a simulation, object-oriented design helps us decide how to represent the physical items being simulated. In a card game, the basic item is, of course, a card. A deck of cards becomes a list of 52 cards in the program. We can use a variation of the `CardPile` class developed in the previous case study to represent the deck.

Cards face up on the table and in the discard pile must also be simulated in this program. Putting a card face up on the table means that a card is being taken from the deck and put onto the table where the player can see it. The cards on the table can be represented by a `CardPile` class object. The rules that determine whether or not cards can be moved to the

PROBLEM-SOLVING CASE STUDY cont'd.

FIGURE 16-7

Solitaire Game

Initialize with the first 4 cards.

Remove the 2 inner cards.
Add 2 cards (need at least 4 cards to play).

Remove all 4 cards.
Add 4 more cards.

Remove the 2 inner cards.
Add 2 cards until another match.

Remove the 2 inner cards from group of last 4.

Remove the last 4 cards.
Add cards until another match.

Remove the 2 inner cards from group of last 4.
Add cards until another match.

Remove all 4 cards.

.
.
.

discard pile are applied to the top four cards in this list—that is, the last four cards put into the list.

The discard pile is also a list of cards and can be represented as a CardPile class object. If no cards remain on the table (they are all on the discard pile) at the end of the game, then the player has won. If any cards remain on the table face up, the player has lost.

A linked list is a good choice for representing these three lists (the deck, the cards face up on the table, and the discard pile). The simulation requires a lot of deleting from one list and inserting into another list, and these operations are quite efficient with a linked list.

Using dynamic variables to represent our lists instead of a direct array representation saves memory space. If an array representation were used, three arrays of 52 components each would have to be created. In a dynamic linked representation, we use only 52 components in all, because a card can be in only one list at a time.

In our object-oriented design, we have now identified three objects: a card deck, an on-table pile, and a discard pile. A fourth object we'll use is a player object. This object can be thought of as a manager—it is responsible for coordinating the three card pile objects and playing the game according to the rules.

To determine the relationships among these four objects, we observe that the three card pile objects are independent of each other and are not related by inheritance or composition. However, the player object is composed of the other three objects—it *has a* deck, an on-table pile, and a discard pile as part or all of its internal data. This relationship is seen more clearly when we design and implement the player object.

The On-Table Pile and Discard Pile Objects: We can represent these objects directly using the CardPile class from the previous case study.

The Card Deck Object: We could represent this object using the CardPile class, but a full deck of cards is more specialized than an ordinary card pile. For example, the CardPile class constructor creates an empty pile, whereas we would like a new card deck to be created as a list of all 52 cards, arranged in order by suit and rank. Also, we would like to include two more operations that are appropriate for a card deck—one to shuffle the deck, the other to recreate the deck at the end of each game by gathering together all 52 cards from the on-table pile and the discard pile.

The easiest way to add these new operations to the CardPile class is to use inheritance. From the CardPile class we can derive a new CardDeck class that inherits the CardPile class members and adds the new functions. Inheritance is appropriate here because a card deck *is a* card pile (and more). Here is the class specification:

```
//********************************************************************
// SPECIFICATION FILE (carddeck.h)
// This file gives the specification of a CardDeck class, derived
// from the CardPile class using inheritance
//********************************************************************
#ifndef CARDDECK_H
#define CARDDECK_H

#include "cardpile.h"

const int DECK_SIZE = 52;

class CardDeck : public CardPile
{
public:
    void Shuffle( /* in */ int numberOfShuffles);
        // Precondition:
        //      Length of deck == DECK_SIZE
        //   && numberOfShuffles is assigned
        // Postcondition:
        //      The order of components in the deck has been
        //      rearranged numberOfShuffles times, randomly

    void Recreate( /* inout */ CardPile& pile1,
                   /* inout */ CardPile& pile2 );
        // Gathers cards from two piles and puts them back into deck
        // Precondition:
        //      Length of deck == 0
        //   && (Length of pile1 + length of pile2) == DECK_SIZE
        // Postcondition:
        //      Deck is the list consisting of all cards from
        //      pile1@entry followed by all cards from pile2@entry
        //   && Length of deck == DECK_SIZE
        //   && Length of pile1 == 0  &&  Length of pile2 == 0

    CardDeck();
        // Postcondition:
        //      List of DECK_SIZE components is created
        //      representing a standard deck of playing cards
        //   && Cards are in order by suit and by rank
private:
    void Merge( CardPile&, CardPile& );
};

#endif
```

Notice in the CardDeck class declaration that the private part does not include any additional data members. The only private data is the data inherited from the CardPile class. However, the private part declares a member function named Merge. This function is not accessible to clients of CardDeck. As we see shortly, the Merge function is a "helper" function that is used by the Shuffle member function.

Now we implement the CardDeck member functions. We begin with the class constructor.

The class constructor CardDeck ( )

When a CardDeck class object is created, the constructor for its base class (CardPile) is implicitly executed first, creating an empty list. Starting with the empty list, we can generate the first card—the ace of clubs—and insert it into the list. The balance of the 52 cards can be generated in a loop. After every 13th card, we increment the suit and reset the rank to 1.

```
Set tempCard.suit = CLUB
Set tempCard.rank = 1
InsertTop(tempCard)                          // Insert into deck
FOR count going from 2 through 52
      Increment tempCard.rank
      IF tempCard.rank > 13
            Increment tempCard.suit
            Set tempCard.rank = 1
      InsertTop(tempCard)                     // Insert into deck
```

Although we don't use the rank of a card, we leave it there because we may want to print out the contents of the list during debugging. Also, the CardDeck class may be used in other simulations. The class should be tested with a complete representation of a deck of cards

Shuffle (In: numberOfShuffles)

When a human shuffles a deck of cards, he or she divides the deck into two nearly equal parts and then merges the two parts again. This process can be simulated directly (a simulation within a simulation). The list representing the deck can be divided into two lists, `halfA` and `halfB`. Then these two lists can be merged again. We use a random number generator to determine how many cards go into `halfA`. The rest go into `halfB`.

Through the header file `cstdlib`, the C++ standard library provides two functions for producing random numbers. The first, named `rand`, has the following prototype:

```
int rand();
```

Each time this function is called, it returns a random integer in the range 0 through RAND_MAX, a constant defined in `cstdlib`. (RAND_MAX is typically the same as INT_MAX.) Because we want our random number to be in the range 1 through 52, we use the conversion formula

Set sizeOfCut = rand( ) MOD 52 + 1

or, in C++,

```
sizeOfCut = rand() % 52 + 1;
```

Random number generators use an initial *seed* value from which to start the sequence of random numbers. The C++ library function `srand` lets you specify an initial seed before calling `rand`. The prototype for `srand` is

```
void srand( unsigned int );
```

If you do not call `srand` before the first call to `rand`, an initial seed of 1 is assumed. As you'll see in the initialization portion of our `main` function, we input an initial seed value from the user and pass it as an argument to `srand`.

```
FOR count1 going from 1 through numberOfShuffles
        Create empty list halfA
        Create empty list halfB
        Set sizeOfCut = rand( ) MOD 52 + 1
        Move sizeOfCut cards from deck to halfA
        Move remaining 52–sizeOfCut cards from deck to halfB
        IF sizeOfCut <= 26
                Merge(halfA, halfB)
        ELSE
                Merge(halfB, halfA)
```

Merge (Inout: shorterList, longerList)

The merge algorithm takes a component alternately from each list without regard to the contents of the component. We call the `Merge` function with two arguments: the shorter list and the longer list.

```
WHILE more cards in shorterList
        shorterList.RemoveTop(tempCard)
        InsertTop(tempCard)                        // Insert into deck
        longerList.RemoveTop(tempCard)
        InsertTop(tempCard)
WHILE more cards in longerList
        longerList.RemoveTop(tempCard)
        InsertTop(tempCard)
```

Recreate (Inout: pile1, pile2)

The `Recreate` function takes an empty deck (an empty list) and gathers cards from two piles, putting them back into the deck.

PROBLEM-SOLVING CASE STUDY cont'd.

```
WHILE more cards in pile1
      pile1.RemoveTop(tempCard)
      InsertTop(tempCard)                        // Insert into deck
WHILE more cards in pile2
      pile2.RemoveTop(tempCard)
      InsertTop(tempCard)
```

Below is the implementation file for the `CardDeck` member functions.

```cpp
//*****************************************************************
// IMPLEMENTATION FILE (carddeck.cpp)
// This file implements the CardDeck class member functions.
// The CardPile class is a public base class of CardDeck
//*****************************************************************
#include "carddeck.h"
#include <cstdlib>      // For rand()

using namespace std;

const int HALF_DECK = 26;

// Additional private members of class (beyond those
// inherited from CardPile):
//      void Merge( CardPile&, CardPile& );      Used by the Shuffle
//                                               function


//*****************************************************************

CardDeck::CardDeck()

// Constructor--creates a list of DECK_SIZE components representing
// a standard deck of playing cards

// Postcondition:
//      After empty linked list created (via implicit call to base
//      class constructor), all DECK_SIZE playing cards have been
//      inserted into deck in order by suit and by rank

{
    int      count;      // Loop counter
    CardType tempCard;   // Temporary card
```

```
        tempCard.suit = CLUB;
        tempCard.rank = 1;
        InsertTop(tempCard);

        // Loop to create balance of deck

        for (count = 2; count <= DECK_SIZE; count++)
        {
            // Increment rank

            tempCard.rank++;

            // Test for change of suit

            if (tempCard.rank > 13)
            {
                tempCard.suit = Suits(tempCard.suit + 1);
                tempCard.rank = 1;
            }
            InsertTop(tempCard);
        }
}

//******************************************************************

void CardDeck::Shuffle( /* in */ int numberOfShuffles)

// Rearranges the deck (the list of DECK_SIZE components) into a
// different order.  The list is divided into two parts, which are
// then merged.  The process is repeated numberOfShuffles times

// Precondition:
//     Length of deck == DECK_SIZE
//   && numberOfShuffles is assigned
// Postcondition:
//     The order of components in the deck has been rearranged
//     numberOfShuffles times, randomly

{
    CardType tempCard;     // Temporary card
    int      count1;       // Loop counter
    int      count2;       // Loop counter
    int      sizeOfCut;    // Size of simulated cut
```

```
            for (count1 = 1; count1 <= numberOfShuffles; count1++)
            {
                CardPile halfA;     // Half of the list, initially empty
                CardPile halfB;     // Half of the list, initially empty

                sizeOfCut = rand() % DECK_SIZE + 1;

                // Divide deck into two parts

                for (count2 = 1; count2 <= sizeOfCut; count2++)
                {
                    RemoveTop(tempCard);
                    halfA.InsertTop(tempCard);
                }
                for (count2 = sizeOfCut+1; count2 <= DECK_SIZE; count2++)
                {
                    RemoveTop(tempCard);
                    halfB.InsertTop(tempCard);
                }
                if (sizeOfCut <= HALF_DECK)
                    Merge(halfA, halfB);
                else
                    Merge(halfB, halfA);
            }
        }


//******************************************************************

void CardDeck::Merge( /* inout */ CardPile& shorterList,
                      /* inout */ CardPile& longerList  )

// Merges shorterList and longerList into deck

// Precondition:
//     Length of shorterList > 0  &&  Length of longerList > 0
//   && Length of deck == 0
// Postcondition:
//     Deck is the list of cards obtained by merging
//     shorterList@entry and longerList@entry into one list
//   && Length of shorterList == 0
//   && Length of longerList == 0

{
    CardType tempCard;    // Temporary card

    // Take one card from each list alternately
```

```
        while (shorterList.Length() > 0)
        {
            shorterList.RemoveTop(tempCard);
            InsertTop(tempCard);
            longerList.RemoveTop(tempCard);
            InsertTop(tempCard);
        }

        // Copy remainder of longer list to deck

        while (longerList.Length() > 0)
        {
            longerList.RemoveTop(tempCard);
            InsertTop(tempCard);
        }
    }

//*****************************************************************

void CardDeck::Recreate( /* inout */ CardPile& pile1,
                         /* inout */ CardPile& pile2 )

// Gathers cards from two piles and puts them back into deck

// Precondition:
//     Length of deck == 0
//  && (Length of pile1 + length of pile2) == DECK_SIZE
// Postcondition:
//     Deck is the list consisting of all cards from pile1@entry
//     followed by all cards from pile2@entry
//  && Length of deck == DECK_SIZE
//  && Length of pile1 == 0  &&  Length of pile2 == 0

{
    CardType tempCard;     // Temporary card

    while (pile1.Length() > 0)
    {
        pile1.RemoveTop(tempCard);
        InsertTop(tempCard);
    }
    while (pile2.Length() > 0)
    {
        pile2.RemoveTop(tempCard);
        InsertTop(tempCard);
    }
}
```

The Player Object: This object manages the playing of the solitaire game. It encapsulates the card deck, on-table pile, and discard pile objects and is responsible for moving cards from one pile to another according to the rules of the game.

To represent the player object, we design a `Player` class with the following specification:

```cpp
//***********************************************************************
// SPECIFICATION FILE (player.h)
// This file gives the specification of a Player class that manages
// the playing of a solitaire game
//***********************************************************************
#ifndef PLAYER_H
#define PLAYER_H

#include "cardpile.h"
#include "carddeck.h"

class Player
{
public:
    void PlayGame( /* in */  int    numberOfShuffles,
                   /* out */ bool& won                 );
        // Precondition:
        //     numberOfShuffles is assigned
        // Postcondition:
        //     After deck has been shuffled numberOfShuffles times,
        //     one game of solitaire has been played
        //  && won == true, if the game was won
        //          == false, otherwise
private:
    CardDeck deck;
    CardPile onTable;
    CardPile discardPile;

    void TryRemove();
    void MoveFour();
    void MoveTwo();
};

#endif
```

The `Player` class has one public operation, `PlayGame`, that plays one game of solitaire and reports whether the game was won or lost. The private part of the class consists of three class objects—deck, `onTable`, and `discardPile`—and three private member functions. These "helper" functions are used in the playing of the game and are not accessible to clients of the class.

PlayGame (In: numberOfShuffles; Out: won)

```
deck.Shuffle(numberOfShuffles)
WHILE more cards in deck
        // Turn up a card
        deck.RemoveTop(tempCard)
        onTable.InsertTop(tempCard)
        // Try to remove it
        TryRemove( )
Set won = (onTable.Length( ) equals 0)
deck.Recreate(onTable, discardPile)
```

TryRemove ( )

To remove cards, we first need to check the first and fourth cards. If these do not match, we can't move any cards. If they do match, we check to see how many can be moved. This process continues until there are fewer than four cards face up on the table or until no move can be made.

```
Set moveMade = true
WHILE onTable.Length( ) >= 4 AND moveMade
      IF suit of onTable.CardAt(1) matches suit of onTable.CardAt(4)
              IF suit of onTable.CardAt(1) matches suit of onTable.CardAt(2) AND
                          suit of onTable.CardAt(1) matches suit of onTable.CardAt(3)
              Move four cards from onTable to discardPile
          ELSE
                  Move two cards—the second and third—from onTable to discardPile
      ELSE
              Set moveMade = false
```

<u>*PROBLEM-SOLVING CASE STUDY cont'd.*</u>

MoveFour ( )

```
FOR count going from 1 through 4
    onTable.RemoveTop(tempCard)
    discardPile.InsertTop(tempCard)
```

MoveTwo ( )

```
Save top card from onTable
Move top card from onTable to discardPile
Move top card from onTable to discardPile
Restore original top card to onTable
```

The implementations of the `Player` class member functions are shown in the `player.cpp` file below.

```cpp
//***********************************************************
// IMPLEMENTATION FILE (player.cpp)
// This file implements the Player class member functions
//***********************************************************
#include "player.h"

// Private members of class
//     CardDeck deck;              Deck of cards
//     CardPile onTable;           Cards face up on the table
//     CardPile discardPile;       Cards on discard pile
//
//     void TryRemove( CardPile&, CardPile& );
//     void MoveFour( CardPile&, CardPile& );
//     void MoveTwo( CardPile&, CardPile& );

//***********************************************************

void Player::PlayGame( /* in */  int    numberOfShuffles,
                       /* out */ bool& won                )

// Places each card in the deck face up on the table
// and applies rules for moving
```

PROBLEM-SOLVING CASE STUDY cont'd.

```
// Precondition:
//      numberOfShuffles is assigned
// Postcondition:
//      After deck has been shuffled numberOfShuffles times,
//      all cards have been moved one at a time from deck to onTable
//  && Cards have (possibly) been moved from onTable to discardPile
//      according to the rules of the game
//  && won == true, if the game was won
//          == false, otherwise

{
    CardType tempCard;     // Temporary card

    deck.Shuffle(numberOfShuffles);
    while (deck.Length() > 0)
    {
        deck.RemoveTop(tempCard);
        onTable.InsertTop(tempCard);
        TryRemove();
    }
    won = (onTable.Length() == 0);
    deck.Recreate(onTable, discardPile);
}


//******************************************************************


void Player::TryRemove()

// If the first (top) four cards in onTable are the same suit,
// they are moved to discardPile.  If the first card and the fourth
// card are the same suit, the second and third card are moved from
// onTable to discardPile.  This process continues until no further
// moves can be made

// Precondition:
//      Length of onTable > 0
// Postcondition:
//      Cards have (possibly) been moved from onTable to discardPile
//      according to the above rules

{
    bool moveMade = true;     // True if a move has been made

    while (onTable.Length() >= 4 && moveMade)
        if (onTable.CardAt(1).suit == onTable.CardAt(4).suit)
```

PROBLEM-SOLVING CASE STUDY cont'd.

```
                    // A move will be made

                    if (onTable.CardAt(1).suit == onTable.CardAt(2).suit &&
                        onTable.CardAt(1).suit == onTable.CardAt(3).suit)
                        MoveFour();   // Four alike
                    else
                        MoveTwo();    // 1st and 4th alike
                else
                    moveMade = false;
    }


//****************************************************************

void Player::MoveFour()

// Moves the first four cards from onTable to discardPile

// Precondition:
//      Length of onTable >= 4
// Postcondition:
//      The first four cards have been removed from onTable and
//      placed at the front of discardPile

{
    CardType tempCard;    // Temporary card
    int      count;       // Loop counter

    for (count = 1; count <= 4; count++)
    {
        onTable.RemoveTop(tempCard);
        discardPile.InsertTop(tempCard);
    }
}


//****************************************************************

void Player::MoveTwo()

// Moves the second and third cards from onTable to discardPile

// Precondition:
//      Length of onTable >= 4
// Postcondition:
//      The second and third cards have been removed from onTable and
//      placed at the front of discardPile
//   && The first card in onTable at entry is still the first card
//      in onTable
```

```
{
    CardType tempCard;      // Temporary card
    CardType firstCard;     // First card in onTable

    // Remove and save first card

    onTable.RemoveTop(firstCard);

    // Move second card

    onTable.RemoveTop(tempCard);
    discardPile.InsertTop(tempCard);

    // Move third card

    onTable.RemoveTop(tempCard);
    discardPile.InsertTop(tempCard);

    // Restore first card

    onTable.InsertTop(firstCard);
}
```

The Driver: We have now designed and implemented all the objects responsible for playing the solitaire game. All that remains is to write the top-level algorithm (the driver).

Main   **Level 0**

Create player—an object of type Player
Set gamesWon = 0
Prompt for and input numberOfGames
Prompt for and input numberOfShuffles
Prompt for and input seed
Use seed to initialize the random number generator

FOR gamesPlayed going from 1 through numberOfGames
    player.PlayGame(numberOfShuffles, won)
    IF won
        Increment gamesWon
Print numberOfGames
Print gamesWon

PROBLEM-SOLVING CASE STUDY cont'd.

Module Structure Chart:

```
┌──────────┐
│   Main   │
└──────────┘
```

(The following program is written in ISO/ANSI standard C++. If you are working with pre–standard C++, see the alternate version of the program in the PRE_STD directory of the program disk, available at the publisher's Web site, www.jbpub.com/disks.)

```cpp
//*******************************************************************
// Solitaire program
// This program is a simulation of a card game.
// See text for rules of the game
//*******************************************************************
#include "player.h"      // For Player class
#include <iostream>
#include <cstdlib>       // For srand()

using namespace std;

int main()
{
    Player player;              // Card-playing manager
    int    numberOfShuffles;    // Number of shuffles per game
    int    numberOfGames;       // Number of games to play
    int    gamesPlayed;         // Number of games played
    int    gamesWon;            // Number of games won
    int    seed;                // Used with random no. generator
    bool   won;                 // True if a game has been won

    gamesWon = 0;
    cout << "Enter number of games to play: ";
    cin >> numberOfGames;
    cout << "Enter number of shuffles per game: ";
    cin >> numberOfShuffles;
    cout << "Enter integer seed for random no. generator: ";
    cin >> seed;
    srand(seed);                        // Seed the random no. generator

    for (gamesPlayed=1; gamesPlayed <= numberOfGames; gamesPlayed++)
    {
        player.PlayGame(numberOfShuffles, won);
        if (won)
            gamesWon++;
```

```
    }
    cout << endl;
    cout << "Number of games played: " << numberOfGames << endl;
    cout << "Number of games won: " << gamesWon << endl;
    return 0;
}
```

Testing: To test this program exhaustively, all possible configurations of a deck of 52 cards have to be generated. Although this is theoretically possible, it is not realistic. There are 52! (52 factorial) possible arrangements of a deck of cards, and 52! equals

$$52 \times 51 \times 50 \times \ldots 2 \times 1$$

This is a large number. Try multiplying it out.

Therefore, another method of testing is required. At a minimum, the questions to be examined are the following:

1. Does the program recognize a winning hand?
2. Does the program recognize a losing hand?

To answer these questions, we must examine at least one hand declared to be a winner and several hands declared to be losers. Specifying 20 as the number of games to play, we ran the program to see if there were any winning hands. There were none.

From past experience, we know this solitaire game is difficult. We let the simulation run, specifying 100 games and an initial seed of 3. There were two winning hands. Intermediate output statements were put in to examine the winning hands. They were correct. Several losing hands were also printed; they were indeed losing hands. Satisfied that the program was working correctly, we set up runs that varied in length, number of shuffles, and seed for the random number generator. The results are listed below. There is no strategy behind the particular choices of inputs; they are random.

Number of Games	Number of Shuffles	Seed	Games Won
100	1	3	2
100	2	4	0
500	3	4	3
1000	6	3	6
5000	10	327	11
10,000	4	4	40
10,000	4	3	45
10,000	4	120	44

Testing and Debugging

Testing and debugging a linked structure is complicated by the fact that each item in the structure contains not only a data portion but also a link to the next item. Algorithms must correctly account for both the data and the link.

When linked lists are implemented with dynamic data and pointers, the errors discussed in Chapter 15 can crop up: memory leaks, dangling pointers, and attempts to dereference a null pointer or an uninitialized pointer. Below are suggestions to help you locate such errors or avoid them in the first place.

Testing and Debugging Hints

1. Review the Testing and Debugging Hints for Chapter 15. They apply to the pointers and dynamic data that are used in dynamic linked lists.
2. Be sure that the link member in the last node of a dynamic linked list has been set to NULL.
3. When visiting the components in a dynamic linked list, be sure that you test for the end of the list in such a way that you don't try to dereference the null pointer. On many systems, dereferencing the null pointer causes a run-time error.
4. Be sure to initialize the external pointer to each dynamic data structure.
5. Do not use

    ```
    currPtr++;
    ```

    to make currPtr point to the next node in a dynamic linked list. The list nodes are not necessarily in consecutive memory locations on the free store.
6. Keep close track of pointers. Changing pointer values prematurely may cause problems when you try to get back to the pointed-to variable.
7. If a C++ class that points to dynamic data has a class destructor but not a copy-constructor, do not pass a class object to a function using a pass by value. A shallow copy occurs, and both the parameter and the argument point to the same dynamic data. When the function returns, the parameter's destructor is executed, destroying the argument's dynamic data.

Summary

Dynamic data structures grow and contract during run time. They are made up of nodes that contain two kinds of members: the component, and one or more pointers to nodes of the same type. The pointer to the first node is saved in a variable called the external pointer to the structure.

A linked list is a data structure in which the components are logically next to each other rather than physically next to each other as they are in an array. A linked list can be represented either as an array of structs or as a collection of dynamic nodes, linked together by pointers. The end of a dynamic linked list is indicated by the special pointer constant NULL. Common operations on linked lists include inserting a node, deleting a node, and traversing the list (visiting each node from first to last).

In this chapter, we used linked lists to implement lists. But linked lists are also used to implement many data structures other than lists. The study of data structures forms a major topic in computer science. Entire books and courses are developed to cover the subject. A solid understanding of the fundamentals of linked lists is a prerequisite to creating more complex structures.

Quick Check

1. What distinguishes a linked list from an array? (pp. 944–946)
2. Nodes in a linked list structure must contain a link member. (True or False?) (pp. 944–950)
3. The number of elements in a dynamic data structure must be determined before the program is compiled. (True or False?) (pp. 948–949)
4. When printing the contents of a dynamically allocated linked list, what operation advances the current node pointer to the next node? (pp. 960–963)
5. What is the difference between the operations of inserting a new item at the top of a linked list and inserting the new item into its proper position in a sorted list? (pp. 963–971)
6. In deleting an item from a linked list, why do we need to keep track of the previous node (the node before the one to be deleted)? (pp. 971–975)

Answers **1.** Arrays are data structures whose components are located next to each other in memory. Linked lists are data structures in which the locations of the components are defined by an explicit link member in each node. **2.** True; every node (except the first) is accessed by using the link member in the node before it. **3.** False; we do not have to know in advance how large it has to be. (In fact, we rarely know.) The only limitation is the amount of memory space available on the free store. **4.** The current node pointer is set equal to the link member of the current node. **5.** When inserting an item into position, the list must first be searched to find the proper place. We don't have to search the list when inserting at the top. **6.** Because we must set the link member of the previous node equal to the link member of the current node as part of the deletion operation.

Exam Preparation Exercises

1. Given the `SortedList2` class of this chapter and a client's declaration

   ```
   SortedList2 myList;
   ```

   what is the output of each of the following code segments?

   a. `myList.InsertTop(30);`
      `myList.InsertTop(20);`
      `myList.InsertTop(10);`
      `myList.Print();`

   b. `myList.Insert(10);`
      `myList.Insert(20);`
      `myList.Insert(30);`
      `myList.Print();`

2. In a linked list, components are only logically next to each other, whereas in an array they are also physically next to each other. (True or False?)

3. Which of the following can be used to implement a list ADT?
   a. An array of the component type
   b. A linked list implemented using an array of structs
   c. A linked list implemented using dynamic structs and pointers

4. The following declarations for a node of a linked list are not acceptable to the C++ compiler:

   ```
   typedef T* P;
   struct T
   {
       float x;
       P      link;
   };
   ```

   Correct the problem by inserting another declaration before the Typedef statement.

5. What is the primary benefit of dynamic data structures?

6. This chapter's `SortedList2` class represents a sorted list ADT. To make an *unsorted* list ADT, which of the following member functions could be removed: `IsEmpty`, `Print`, `InsertTop`, `Insert`, `DeleteTop`, and `Delete`?

7. Use the C++ code below to identify the values of the variables and Boolean comparisons that follow. The value may be undefined, or the expression may be invalid.

   ```
   struct NodeType;
   typedef NodeType* NodePtr;

   struct NodeType
   {
       int      number;
       char     character;
       NodePtr link;
   };

   NodePtr currPtr = NULL;
   NodePtr firstPtr = NULL;
   NodePtr lastPtr = NULL;

   currPtr = new NodeType;
   currPtr->number = 13;
   ```

```
currPtr->character = 'z';
currPtr->link = new NodeType;
lastPtr = currPtr->link;
lastPtr->number = 9;
firstPtr = new NodeType;
lastPtr->link = firstPtr;
firstPtr->number = 9;
firstPtr->character = 'h';
firstPtr->link = currPtr;
        ⋮
```

Expression	*Value*
a. `firstPtr->link->number`	_____
b. `firstPtr->link->link->character`	_____
c. `firstPtr->link == lastPtr`	_____
d. `currPtr->link->number`	_____
e. `currPtr->link == *lastPtr`	_____
f. `firstPtr == lastPtr->link`	_____
g. `firstPtr->number < firstPtr->link->number`	_____

8. Choose the best data structure (array or dynamic linked list) for each of the following situations. Assume unlimited memory but limited time.
   a. A list of the abbreviations for the 50 states
   b. A fixed list of 1000 to 4000 (usually 1500) elements that has elements printed according to position requests that are input to the program
   c. A list of an unknown number of elements that is read, then printed in reverse order

9. Choose the best data structure (array or dynamic linked list) for each of the following situations. Assume limited memory but unlimited time.
   a. A list of the abbreviations for the 50 states
   b. A fixed list of 1000 to 4000 (usually 1500) elements that has elements printed according to position requests that are input to the program
   c. A list of an unknown number of elements that is read, then printed in reverse order

10. What is the output of the following C++ code, given the input data 5, 6, 3, and 1?

```
struct PersonNode;
typedef PersonNode* PtrType;

struct PersonNode
{
    int      ssNum;
    PtrType next;
};

int      ssNumber;
PtrType ptr;
PtrType head = NULL;
```

```
cin >> ssNumber;
while (cin)
{
    ptr = new PersonNode;
    ptr->ssNum = ssNumber;
    ptr->next = head;
    head = ptr;
    cin >> ssNumber;
}
ptr = head;
while (ptr != NULL)
{
    cout << ptr->ssNum;
    ptr = ptr->next;
}
```

Programming Warm-up Exercises

1. To the SortedList2 class of this chapter, add a value-returning member function named Length that counts and returns the number of nodes in a list.

2. To the SortedList2 class, add a value-returning member function named Sum that returns the sum of all the data values in a list.

3. To the SortedList2 class, add a Boolean member function named IsPresent that searches a list for a particular value (passed as an argument) and returns true if the value is found.

4. To the SortedList2 class, add a Boolean member function named Equal that compares two class objects and returns true if the two lists they represent are identical.

5. The SortedList2 class provides a copy-constructor but not a deep copy operation. Add a CopyFrom function to the SortedList2 class that performs a deep copy of one class object to another.

6. To avoid special handling of empty linked lists for insertion and deletion routines, some programmers prefer to keep a dummy node permanently in the list. (The list is considered empty if it contains only the dummy node.) Rewrite the SortedList2 class to use a dummy node whose component value is equal to a constant named DUMMY. Do not keep any unnecessary code. (*Hint:* The first element of the list follows the dummy node.)

7. Given the declarations

```
struct NodeType;
typedef NodeType* NodePtr;

struct NodeType
{
    int     number;
    NodePtr link;
};
```

and the function prototype

```
void Exchange( /* in */ NodePtr head,
               /* in */ int     key );
```

implement the Exchange function. The function searches a linked list for the value given by key and exchanges it with the number preceding it in the list. If key is the first value in the list or if key is not found, then no exchange occurs.

8. Using the type declarations given in Exercise 7, write a function that reorganizes the items in a linked list so that the last item is first, the second to last is second, and so forth. (*Hint:* Use a temporary list.)

Programming Problems

1. In the Solitaire program in this chapter, all insertions into a linked list are made using the function InsertTop, and all the deletions are made using RemoveTop. In some cases, this is inefficient. For example, function CardDeck::Recreate takes the cards from onTable and moves them one by one to the deck. Then the cards on discardPile are moved one by one to the deck. It would be more efficient simply to concatenate (join) the deck list and the onTable list, then concatenate the resulting list and the discardPile list.

   To the CardPile class, add a member function whose specification is the following:

```
void Concat( /* inout */ CardPile& otherList );
    // Postcondition:
    //     This list and otherList are concatenated (the front
    //     of otherList@entry is joined to the rear of this list)
    // && otherList is empty
```

   Implement and test the Concat member function. Use it in the CardDeck::Recreate function of the Solitaire program to make the program more efficient.

2. In Chapter 11, the BirthdayCalls program uses a DateType class to process address book information found in a file friendFile. Entries in friendFile are in the form

```
John Arbuthnot
(493) 384-2938
1/12/1970

Mary Smith
(123) 123-4567
10/12/1960
```

   Write a program to read in the entries from friendFile and store them into a dynamic linked list ordered by birth date. The output should consist of a listing by month of the names and telephone numbers of the people who have birthdays each month.

3. In Chapter 15, the Personnel Records case study reads a file of personnel records, sorts the records alphabetically, and prints out the sorted records. Rewrite the program so that it reads each record and stores it into its proper position in a sorted list. Implement the list as a dynamic linked list using this chapter's SortedList2 class as a model. Note that the limit of 1000 employee records is no longer relevant because you are using a dynamic data structure.

4. This chapter's SortedList2 class implements a sorted list ADT by using a linked list. In turn, the linked list is implemented by using dynamic data and pointers. Reimplement the linked list using an array of structs. You will have to manage a "free store" within the array—the collection of currently unused array elements. To mimic the new and delete operations, your implementation will need two auxiliary functions that obtain and release space on the "free store."

Case Study Follow-Up

1. The CardDeck class is derived from the CardPile class using inheritance.
   a. List the names of all the public members of the CardDeck class.
   b. List the names of all the private members of the CardDeck class.
2. In the Shuffle function of the CardDeck class, why are the declarations of halfA and halfB located inside the body of the For loop? What would happen if the declarations were placed outside the loop at the top of the function?
3. Give the Player class more responsibility by making it prompt for and input the number of shuffles and the random number seed. Encapsulate the numberOfShuffles and seed variables within the Player class, and add two member functions named GetNumShuffles and GetSeed. Show the new class declaration and the implementations of the two new functions. Also, rewrite the main function, given these changes.

17

Recursion

G O A L S

- To be able to identify the base case(s) and the general case in a recursive definition.
- To be able to write a recursive algorithm for a problem involving only simple variables.
- To be able to write a recursive algorithm for a problem involving structured variables.
- To be able to write a recursive algorithm for a problem involving linked lists.

In C++, any function can call another function. A function can even call itself! When a function calls itself, it is making a **recursive call.** The word *recursive* means "having the characteristic of coming up again, or repeating." In this case, a function call is being repeated by the function itself. Recursion is a powerful technique that can be used in place of iteration (looping).

Recursive solutions are generally less efficient than iterative solutions to the same problem. However, some problems lend themselves to simple, elegant, recursive solutions and are exceedingly cumbersome to solve iteratively. Some programming languages, such as early versions of FORTRAN, BASIC, and COBOL, do not allow recursion. Other languages are especially oriented to recursive algorithms—LISP is one of these. C++ lets us take our choice: We can implement both iterative and recursive algorithms.

Our examples are broken into two groups: problems that use only simple variables and problems that use structured variables. If you are studying recursion before reading Chapter 11 on structured data types, then cover only the first set of examples and leave the rest until you have completed the chapters on structured data types.

What Is Recursion?

You may have seen a set of gaily painted Russian dolls that fit inside one another. Inside the first doll is a smaller doll, inside of which is an even smaller doll, inside of which is yet a smaller doll, and so on. A recursive algorithm is like such a set of Russian dolls. It reproduces itself with smaller and smaller examples of itself until a solution is found—that is, until there are no more dolls.The recursive algorithm is implemented by using a function that makes recursive calls to itself.

Recursive call   A function call in which the function being called is the same as the one making the call.

In Chapter 8, we wrote a function named `Power` that calculates the result of raising an integer to a positive power. If X is an integer and N is a positive integer, the formula for X^N is

$$X^N = \underbrace{X \times X \times X \times X \times X \times \ldots \times X}_{N \text{ times}}$$

We could also write this formula as

$$X^N = X \times \underbrace{(X \times X \times \ldots \times X)}_{(N-1) \text{ times}}$$

or even as

$$X^N = X \times X \times \underbrace{(X \times X \times \ldots \times X)}_{(N-2) \text{ times}}$$

In fact, we can write the formula most concisely as

$$X^N = X \times X^{N-1}$$

This definition of X^N is a classic **recursive definition**—that is, a definition given in terms of a smaller version of itself.

Recursive definition   A definition in which something is defined in terms of smaller versions of itself.

X^N is defined in terms of multiplying X times X^{N-1}. How is X^{N-1} defined? Why, as $X \times X^{N-2}$, of course! And X^{N-2} is $X \times X^{N-3}$; X^{N-3} is $X \times X^{N-4}$; and so on. In this example, "in terms of smaller versions of itself" means that the exponent is decremented each time.

When does the process stop? When we have reached a case for which we know the answer without resorting to a recursive definition. In this example, it is the case where N equals 1: X^1 is X. The case (or cases) for which an answer is explicitly known is called the **base case.** The case for which the solution is expressed in terms of a smaller version of itself is called the **recursive** or **general case.** A **recursive algorithm** is an algorithm that expresses the solution in terms of a call to itself, a recursive call. A recursive algorithm must terminate; that is, it must have a base case.

Base case   The case for which the solution can be stated nonrecursively.

General case   The case for which the solution is expressed in terms of a smaller version of itself; also known as *recursive case*.

Recursive algorithm   A solution that is expressed in terms of (a) smaller instances of itself and (b) a base case.

Figure 17-1 shows a recursive version of the Power function with the base case and the recursive call marked. The function is embedded in a program that reads in a number and an exponent and prints the result.

FIGURE 17-1

Power Function

```
//**********************************************************************
// Exponentiation program
//**********************************************************************
#include <iostream>

using namespace std;

int Power( int, int );

int main()
{
    int number;             // Number that is being raised to power
    int exponent;           // Power the number is being raised to

    cin >> number >> exponent;
    cout << Power(number, exponent);  <——————— // Nonrecursive call
    return 0;
}


//**********************************************************************

int Power( /* in */ int x,    // Number that is being raised to power
           /* in */ int n )   // Power the number is being raised to

// Computes x to the n power by multiplying x times the result of
// computing x to the n - 1 power.

// Precondition:
//      x is assigned  &&  n > 0
// Postcondition:
//      Function value == x raised to the power n
// Note:
//      Large exponents may result in integer overflow

{
    if (n == 1)
        return x;  <———————————————————————— // Base case
    else
        return x * Power(x, n - 1);  <——————— // Recursive call
}
```

Each recursive call to Power can be thought of as creating a completely new copy of the function, each with its own copies of the parameters x and n. The value of x remains the same for each version of Power, but the value of n decreases by 1 for each call until it becomes 1.

Let's trace the execution of this recursive function, with number equal to 2 and exponent equal to 3. We use a new format to trace recursive routines: We number the calls and then discuss what is happening in paragraph form.

Call 1: Power is called by main, with number equal to 2 and expo-nent equal to 3. Within Power, the parameters x and n are initialized to 2 and 3, respectively. Because n is not equal to 1, Power is called recursively with x and n − 1 as arguments. Execution of Call 1 pauses until an answer is sent back from this recursive call.

Call 2: x is equal to 2 and n is equal to 2. Because n is not equal to 1, the function Power is called again, this time with x and n − 1 as argu-ments. Execution of Call 2 pauses until an answer is sent back from this recursive call.

Call 3: x is equal to 2 and n is equal to 1. Because n equals 1, the value of x is to be returned. This call to the function has finished executing, and the function return value (which is 2) is passed back to the place in the statement from which the call was made.

Call 2: This call to the function can now complete the statement that contained the recursive call because the recursive call has returned. Call 3's return value (which is 2) is multiplied by x. This call to the function has finished executing, and the function return value (which is 4) is passed back to the place in the statement from which the call was made.

Call 1: This call to the function can now complete the statement that contained the recursive call because the recursive call has returned. Call 2's return value (which is 4) is multiplied by x. This call to the function has finished executing, and the function return value (which is 8) is passed back to the place in the statement from which the call was made. Because the first call (the nonrecursive call in main) has now completed, this is the final value of the function Power.

This trace is summarized in Figure 17-2. Each box represents a call to the Power function. The values for the parameters for that call are shown in each box.

What happens if there is no base case? We have **infinite recursion,** the recursive equivalent of an infinite loop. For example, if the condition

```
if (n == 1)
```

were omitted, Power would be called over and over again. Infinite recur-sion also occurs if Power is called with n less than or equal to 0.

Infinite recursion   The situation in which a function calls itself over and over end-lessly.

In actuality, recursive calls can't go on forever. Here's the reason. When a function is called, either recursively or nonrecursively, the com-puter system creates temporary storage for the parameters and the func-tion's (automatic) local variables. This temporary storage is a region of memory called the *run-time stack*. When the function returns, its parame-

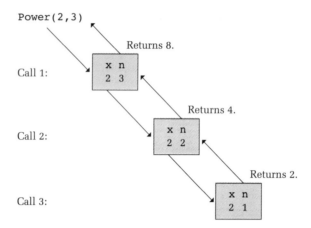

FIGURE 17-2
Execution of
Power(2, 3)

ters and local variables are released from the run-time stack. With infinite recursion, the recursive function calls never return. Each time the function calls itself, a little more of the run-time stack is used to store the new copies of the variables. Eventually, all the memory space on the stack is used. At that point, the program crashes with an error message such as "RUN-TIME STACK OVERFLOW" (or the computer may simply hang).

Recursive Algorithms with Simple Variables

Let's look at another example: calculating a factorial. The factorial of a number N (written $N!$) is N multiplied by $N - 1$, $N - 2$, $N - 3$, and so on. Another way of expressing factorial is

$$N! = N \times (N - 1)!$$

This expression looks like a recursive definition. $(N - 1)!$ is a smaller instance of $N!$—that is, it takes one less multiplication to calculate $(N - 1)!$ than it does to calculate $N!$ If we can find a base case, we can write a recursive algorithm. Fortunately, we don't have to look too far: $0!$ is defined in mathematics to be 1.

Factorial (In: n)

```
IF n is 0
        Return 1
ELSE
        Return n * Factorial(n – 1)
```

This algorithm can be coded directly as follows.

```
int Factorial ( /* in */ int n )

// Precondition:
//     n >= 0
// Postcondition:
//     Function value == n!
// Note:
//     Large values of n may cause integer overflow

{
    if (n == 0)
        return 1;                       // Base case
    else
        return n * Factorial(n - 1);    // General case
}
```

Let's trace this function with an original n of 4.

Call 1: n is 4. Because n is not 0, the `else` branch is taken. The Return statement cannot be completed until the recursive call to `Factorial` with n − 1 as the argument has been completed.

Call 2: n is 3. Because n is not 0, the `else` branch is taken. The Return statement cannot be completed until the recursive call to `Factorial` with n − 1 as the argument has been completed.

Call 3: n is 2. Because n is not 0, the `else` branch is taken. The Return statement cannot be completed until the recursive call to `Factorial` with n − 1 as the argument has been completed.

Call 4: n is 1. Because n is not 0, the `else` branch is taken. The Return statement cannot be completed until the recursive call to `Factorial` with n − 1 as the argument has been completed.

Call 5: n is 0. Because n equals 0, this call to the function returns, sending back 1 as the result.

Call 4: The Return statement in this copy can now be completed. The value to be returned is n (which is 1) times 1. This call to the function returns, sending back 1 as the result.

Call 3: The Return statement in this copy can now be completed. The value to be returned is n (which is 2) times 1. This call to the function returns, sending back 2 as the result.

Call 2: The Return statement in this copy can now be completed. The value to be returned is n (which is 3) times 2. This call to the function returns, sending back 6 as the result.

Call 1: The Return statement in this copy can now be completed. The value to be returned is n (which is 4) times 6. This call to the function returns, sending back 24 as the result. Because this is the last of the calls to `Factorial`, the recursive process is over. The value 24 is returned as the

FIGURE 17-3

Execution of
Factorial(4)

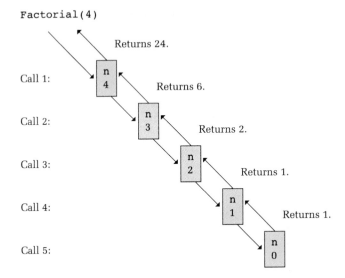

final value of the call to Factorial with an argument of 4. Figure 17-3 summarizes the execution of the Factorial function with an argument of 4.

Let's organize what we have done in these two solutions into an outline for writing recursive algorithms.

1. Understand the problem. (We threw this in for good measure; it is always the first step.)
2. Determine the base case(s).
3. Determine the recursive case(s).

We have used the factorial and the power algorithms to demonstrate recursion because they are easy to visualize. In practice, one would never want to calculate either of these functions using the recursive solution. In both cases, the iterative solutions are simpler and much more efficient because starting a new iteration of a loop is a faster operation than calling a function. Let's compare the code for the iterative and recursive versions of the factorial problem.

Iterative Solution

```
int Factorial ( /* in */ int n )
{
    int factor;
    int count;

    factor = 1;
    for (count = 2; count <= n; count++)
        factor = factor * count;
    return factor;
}
```

Recursive Solution

```
int Factorial ( /* in */ int n )
{
    if (n == 0)
        return 1;
    else
        return n * Factorial(n - 1);
}
```

The iterative version has two local variables, whereas the recursive version has none. There are usually fewer local variables in a recursive routine than in an iterative routine. Also, the iterative version always has a loop, whereas the recursive version always has a selection statement—either an If or a Switch. A branching structure is the main control structure in a recursive routine. A looping structure is the main control structure in an iterative routine.

In the next section, we examine a more complicated problem—one in which the recursive solution is not immediately apparent.

Towers of Hanoi

One of your first toys may have been three pegs with colored circles of different diameters. If so, you probably spent countless hours moving the circles from one peg to another. If we put some constraints on how the circles or discs can be moved, we have an adult game called the Towers of Hanoi. When the game begins, all the circles are on the first peg in order by size, with the smallest on the top. The object of the game is to move the circles, one at a time, to the third peg. The catch is that a circle cannot be placed on top of one that is smaller in diameter. The middle peg can be used as an auxiliary peg, but it must be empty at the beginning and at the end of the game.

To get a feel for how this might be done, let's look at some sketches of what the configuration must be at certain points if a solution is possible. We use four circles or discs. The beginning configuration is:

To move the largest circle (circle 4) to peg 3, we must move the three smaller circles to peg 2. Then circle 4 can be moved into its final place:

Let's assume we can do this. Now, to move the next largest circle (circle 3) into place, we must move the two circles on top of it onto an auxiliary peg (peg 1 in this case):

To get circle 2 into place, we must move circle 1 to another peg, freeing circle 2 to be moved to its place on peg 3:

The last circle (circle 1) can now be moved into its final place, and we are finished:

Notice that to free circle 4, we had to move three circles to another peg. To free circle 3, we had to move two circles to another peg. To free circle 2, we had to move one circle to another peg. This sounds like a recursive algorithm: To free the nth circle, we have to move $n - 1$ circles. Each stage can be thought of as beginning again with three pegs, but with one less circle each time. Let's see if we can summarize this process, using n instead of an actual number.

Get N Circles Moved from Peg 1 to Peg 3

Get n – 1 circles moved from peg 1 to peg 2
Move nth circle from peg 1 to peg 3
Get n – 1 circles moved from peg 2 to peg 3

This algorithm certainly sounds simple; surely there must be more. But this really is all there is to it.

Let's write a recursive function that implements this algorithm. We can't actually move discs, of course, but we can print out a message to do so. Notice that the beginning peg, the ending peg, and the auxiliary peg keep changing during the algorithm. To make the algorithm easier to follow, we call the pegs `beginPeg`, `endPeg`, and `auxPeg`. These three pegs, along with the number of circles on the beginning peg, are the parameters of the function.

We have the recursive or general case, but what about a base case? How do we know when to stop the recursive process? The clue is in the expression "Get *n* circles moved." If we don't have any circles to move, we don't have anything to do. We are finished with that stage. Therefore, when the number of circles equals 0, we do nothing (that is, we simply return).

```
void DoTowers(
    /* in */ int circleCount,     // Number of circles to move
    /* in */ int beginPeg,        // Peg containing circles to move
    /* in */ int auxPeg,          // Peg holding circles temporarily
    /* in */ int endPeg        )  // Peg receiving circles being moved
{
    if (circleCount > 0)
    {
        // Move n - 1 circles from beginning peg to auxiliary peg

        DoTowers(circleCount - 1, beginPeg, endPeg, auxPeg);
        cout << "Move circle from peg " << beginPeg
             << " to peg " << endPeg << endl;

        // Move n - 1 circles from auxiliary peg to ending peg

        DoTowers(circleCount - 1, auxPeg, beginPeg, endPeg);
    }
}
```

It's hard to believe that such a simple algorithm actually works, but we'll prove it to you. Following is a driver program that calls the `DoTowers` function. Output statements have been added so you can see the values of the arguments with each recursive call. Because there are two recursive calls within the function, we have indicated which recursive statement issued the call.

```cpp
//*****************************************************************
// TestTowers program
// This program, a test driver for the DoTowers function, reads in
// a value from standard input and passes this value to DoTowers
//*****************************************************************
#include <iostream>
#include <iomanip>     // For setw()

using namespace std;

void DoTowers( int, int, int, int );

int main()
{
    int circleCount;     // Number of circles on starting peg

    cout << "Input number of circles: ";
    cin >> circleCount;
    cout << "OUTPUT WITH " << circleCount << " CIRCLES" << endl
         << endl;
    cout << "CALLED FROM  #CIRCLES" << setw(8) << "BEGIN"
         << setw(8) << "AUXIL." << setw(5) << "END"
         << "      INSTRUCTIONS" << endl
         << endl;
    cout << "Original    :";
    DoTowers(circleCount, 1, 2, 3);
    return 0;
}


//*****************************************************************

void DoTowers(
    /* in */ int circleCount,    // Number of circles to move
    /* in */ int beginPeg,       // Peg containing circles to move
    /* in */ int auxPeg,         // Peg holding circles temporarily
    /* in */ int endPeg     )    // Peg receiving circles being moved

// This recursive function moves circleCount circles from beginPeg
// to endPeg.  All but one of the circles are moved from beginPeg
// to auxPeg, then the last circle is moved from beginPeg to endPeg,
// and then the circles are moved from auxPeg to endPeg.
// The subgoals of moving circles to and from auxPeg are what
// involve recursion
```

```
// Precondition:
//     All parameters are assigned  &&  circleCount >= 0
// Postcondition:
//     The values of all parameters have been printed
//  && IF circleCount > 0
//        circleCount circles have been moved from beginPeg to
//        endPeg in the manner detailed above
//     ELSE
//        No further actions have taken place

{
    cout << setw(6) << circleCount << setw(9) << beginPeg
        << setw(7) << auxPeg << setw(7) << endPeg << endl;
    if (circleCount > 0)
    {
        cout << "From  first:";
        DoTowers(circleCount - 1, beginPeg, endPeg, auxPeg);
        cout << setw(58) << "Move circle " << circleCount
            << " from " << beginPeg << " to " << endPeg << endl;
        cout << "From second:";
        DoTowers(circleCount - 1, auxPeg, beginPeg, endPeg);
    }
}
```

The output from a run with three circles follows. "Original" means that the parameters listed beside it are from the nonrecursive call, which is the first call to `DoTowers`. "From first" means that the parameters listed are for a call issued from the first recursive statement. "From second" means that the parameters listed are for a call issued from the second recursive statement. Notice that a call cannot be issued from the second recursive statement until the preceding call from the first recursive statement has completed execution.

```
OUTPUT WITH 3 CIRCLES

CALLED FROM   #CIRCLES   BEGIN   AUXIL.   END   INSTRUCTIONS

Original   :      3        1       2       3
From  first:      2        1       3       2
From  first:      1        1       2       3
From  first:      0        1       3       2
                                                Move circle 1 from 1 to 3
From second:      0        2       1       3
                                                Move circle 2 from 1 to 2
From second:      1        3       1       2
From  first:      0        3       2       1
                                                Move circle 1 from 3 to 2
```

From second:	0	1	3	2

Move circle 3 from 1 to 3

From second:	2	2	1	3
From first:	1	2	3	1
From first:	0	2	1	3

Move circle 1 from 2 to 1

Move circle 2 from 2 to 3

From second:	0	3	2	1

From second:	1	1	2	3
From first:	0	1	3	2

Move circle 1 from 1 to 3

From second:	0	2	1	3

Recursive Algorithms with Structured Variables

In our definition of a recursive algorithm, we said there were two cases: the recursive or general case, and the base case for which an answer can be expressed nonrecursively. In the general case for all our algorithms so far, an argument was expressed in terms of a smaller value each time. When structured variables are used, the recursive case is often in terms of a smaller structure rather than a smaller value; the base case occurs when there are no values left to process in the structure.

We examine a recursive algorithm for printing the contents of a one-dimensional array of *n* elements to show what we mean.

Print Array

IF more elements
       Print the value of the first element
       Print array of n − 1 elements

The recursive case is to print the values in an array that is one element "smaller"; that is, the size of the array decreases by 1 with each recursive call. The base case is when the size of the array becomes 0—that is, when there are no more elements to print.

Our arguments must include the index of the first element (the one to be printed). How do we know when there are no more elements to print (that is, when the size of the array to be printed is 0)? We know we have printed the last element in the array when the index of the next element to be printed is beyond the index of the last element in the array. Therefore, the index of the last array element must be passed as an argument. We call the indexes `first` and `last`. When `first` is greater than `last`, we are finished. The name of the array is `data`.

```
void Print( /* in */ const int data[],    // Array to be printed
             /* in */           int first,  // Index of first element
             /* in */           int last )  // Index of last element
{
    if (first <= last)
    {                                              // Recursive case
        cout << data[first] << endl;
        Print(data, first + 1, last);
    }
    // Empty else-clause is the base case
}
```

Here is a code walk-through of the function call

```
Print(data, 0, 4);
```

using the pictured array.

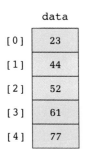

Call 1: `first` is 0 and `last` is 4. Because `first` is less than `last`, the value in `data[first]` (which is 23) is printed. Execution of this call pauses while the array from `first + 1` through `last` is printed.

Call 2: `first` is 1 and `last` is 4. Because `first` is less than `last`, the value in `data[first]` (which is 44) is printed. Execution of this call pauses while the array from `first + 1` through `last` is printed.

Call 3: `first` is 2 and `last` is 4. Because `first` is less than `last`, the value in `data[first]` (which is 52) is printed. Execution of this call pauses while the array from `first + 1` through `last` is printed.

Call 4: `first` is 3 and `last` is 4. Because `first` is less than `last`, the value in `data[first]` (which is 61) is printed. Execution of this call pauses while the array from `first + 1` through `last` is printed.

Call 5: `first` is 4 and `last` is 4. Because `first` is equal to `last`, the value in `data[first]` (which is 77) is printed. Execution of this call pauses while the array from `first + 1` through `last` is printed.

Call 6: `first` is 5 and `last` is 4. Because `first` is greater than `last`, the execution of this call is complete. Control returns to the preceding call.

Call 5: Execution of this call is complete. Control returns to the preceding call.

Calls 4, 3, 2, and 1: Each execution is completed in turn, and control returns to the preceding call.

Notice that once the deepest call (the call with the highest number) was reached, each of the calls before it returned without doing anything. When no statements are executed after the return from the recursive call to the function, the recursion is known as **tail recursion.** Tail recursion often indicates that the problem could be solved more easily using iteration. We used the array example because it made the recursive process easy to visualize; in practice, an array should be printed iteratively.

Tail recursion A recursive algorithm in which no statements are executed after the return from the recursive call.

Figure 17-4 shows the execution of the Print function with the values of the parameters for each call. Notice that the array gets smaller with each recursive call (data[first] through data[last]). If we want to print

Print(data, 0, 4)

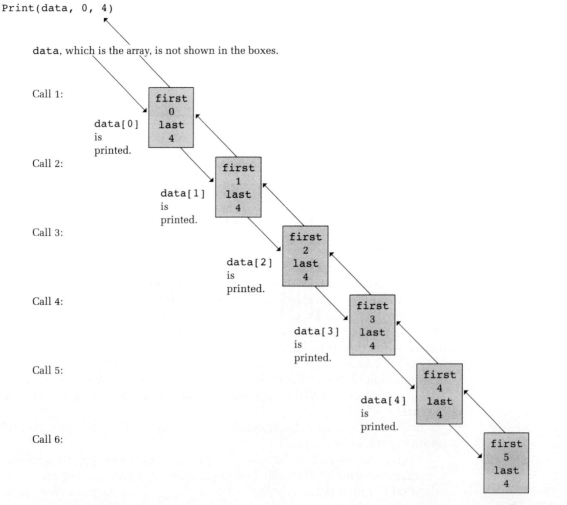

FIGURE 17-4

Execution of Print(data, 0, 4)

the array elements in reverse order recursively, all we have to do is inter-change the two statements within the If statement.

Recursion Using Pointer Variables

The previous recursive algorithm using a one-dimensional array could have been done much more easily using iteration. Now we look at two algorithms that cannot be done more easily with iteration: printing a linked list in reverse order and creating a duplicate copy of a linked list.

Printing a Dynamic Linked List in Reverse Order

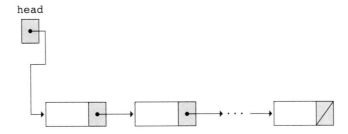

Printing a list in order from first to last is easy. We set a running pointer (ptr) equal to head and cycle through the list until ptr becomes NULL.

Print List (In: head)

```
Set ptr = head
WHILE ptr is not NULL
        Print ptr->component
        Set ptr = ptr->link
```

To print the list in reverse order, we must print the value in the last node first, then the value in the next-to-last node, and so on. Another way of expressing this is to say that we do not print a value until the values in all the nodes following it have been printed. We might visualize the process as the first node's turning to its neighbor and saying, "Tell me when you have printed your value. Then I'll print my value." The second node says to its neighbor, "Tell me when you have printed your value. Then I'll print mine." That node, in turn, says the same to its neighbor, and this continues until there is nothing to print.

Because the number of neighbors gets smaller and smaller, we seem to have the makings of a recursive solution. The end of the list is reached when the running pointer is NULL. When that happens, the last node can print its value and send the message back to the one before it. That node can then print its value and send the message back to the one before it, and so on.

RevPrint (In: head)

> IF head is not NULL
> > RevPrint rest of nodes in list
> > Print current node in list

This algorithm can be coded directly as the following function:

```
void RevPrint ( /* in */ NodePtr head )

// Precondition:
//      head points to a list node (or == NULL)
// Postcondition:
//      IF head != NULL
//          All nodes following *head have been output,
//          then *head has been output
//      ELSE
//          No action has taken place

{
    if (head != NULL)
    {
        RevPrint(head->link);                       // Recursive call
        cout << head->component << endl;
    }
    // Empty else-clause is the base case
}
```

This algorithm seems complex enough to warrant a code walk-through. We use the following list:

Call 1: head points to the node containing 45 and is not NULL. Execution of this call pauses until the recursive call with the argument head->link has been completed.

Call 2: head points to the node containing 78 and is not NULL. Execution of this call pauses until the recursive call with the argument head->link has been completed.

Call 3: head points to the node containing 1066 and is not NULL. Execution of this call pauses until the recursive call with the argument head->link has been completed.

Call 4: head points to the node containing 1492 and is not NULL. Execution of this call pauses until the recursive call with the argument head->link has been completed.

Call 5: head is NULL. Execution of this call is complete. Control returns to the preceding call.

Call 4: head->component (which is 1492) is printed. Execution of this call is complete. Control returns to the preceding call.

Call 3: head->component (which is 1066) is printed. Execution of this call is complete. Control returns to the preceding call.

Call 2: head->component (which is 78) is printed. Execution of this call is complete. Control returns to the preceding call.

Call 1: head->component (which is 45) is printed. Execution of this call is complete. Because this is the nonrecursive call, execution continues with the statement immediately following RevPrint(head).

Figure 17-5 shows the execution of the RevPrint function. The parameters are pointers (memory addresses), so we use → 45 to mean the pointer to the node whose component is 45.

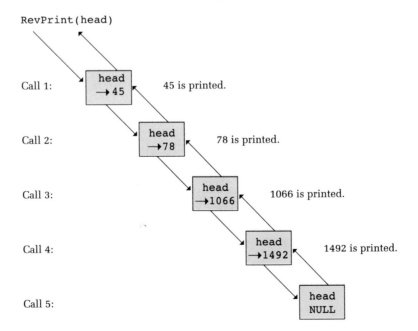

FIGURE 17-5

Execution of RevPrint(head)

Copying a Dynamic Linked List

When working with linked lists, we sometimes need to create a duplicate copy (a *clone*) of a linked list. For example, in Chapter 16, we wrote a copy-constructor for the SortedList2 class. This copy-constructor creates a new class object to be a clone of another class object, including its dynamic linked list.

Suppose that we want to write a value-returning function that receives the external pointer to a linked list (head), makes a clone of the linked list, and returns the external pointer to the new list as the function value. A typical call to the function would be the following:

```
NodePtr head;
NodePtr newListHead;
   ⋮
newListHead = PtrToClone(head);
```

Using iteration to copy a linked list is rather complicated. The following algorithm is essentially the same as the one used in the SortedList2 copy-constructor.

PtrToClone (In: head)   **// Iterative algorithm**

  Out: Function value

IF head is NULL
        Return NULL

// Copy first node
Set fromPtr = head
Set cloneHead = new NodeType
Set cloneHead–>component = fromPtr–>component

// Copy remaining nodes
Set toPtr = cloneHead
Set fromPtr = fromPtr–>link
WHILE fromPtr is not NULL
        Set toPtr–>link = new NodeType
        Set toPtr = toPtr–>link
        Set toPtr–>component = fromPtr–>component
        Set fromPtr = fromPtr–>link
Set toPtr–>link = NULL
Return cloneHead

A recursive solution to this problem is far simpler, but it requires us to think recursively. To clone the first node of the original list, we can allocate a new dynamic node and copy the component value from the original node into the new node. However, we cannot yet fill in the link member of the new node. We must wait until we have cloned the second node so that we can store its address into the link member of the first node. Likewise, the cloning of the second node cannot complete until we have finished cloning the third node. Eventually, we clone the last node of the original list and set the link member of the cloned node to NULL. At this point, the last node returns its own address to the next-to-last node, which stores the address into its link member. The next-to-last node returns its own address to the node before it, and so forth. The process completes when the first node returns its address to the first (nonrecursive) call, yielding an external pointer to the new linked list.

PtrToClone (In: fromPtr)   **// Recursive algorithm**

  Out: Function value

```
IF fromPtr is NULL
        Return NULL
ELSE
        Set toPtr = new NodeType
        Set toPtr->component = fromPtr->component
        Set toPtr->link = PtrToClone(fromPtr->link)
        Return toPtr
```

Like the solution to the Towers of Hanoi problem, this looks too simple; yet, it is the algorithm. Because the argument that is passed to each recursive call is fromPtr->link, the number of nodes left in the original list gets smaller with each call. The base case occurs when the pointer into the original list becomes NULL. Below is the C++ function that implements the algorithm.

```
NodePtr PtrToClone( /* in */ NodePtr fromPtr )

// Precondition:
//      fromPtr points to a list node (or == NULL)
// Postcondition:
//      IF fromPtr != NULL
//              A clone of the entire sublist starting with *fromPtr
//              is on the free store
//          && Function value == pointer to front of this sublist
//      ELSE
//              Function value == NULL
```

```
{
    NodePtr toPtr;          // Pointer to newly created node

    if (fromPtr == NULL)
        return NULL;                        // Base case
    else
    {                                       // Recursive case
        toPtr = new NodeType;
        toPtr->component = fromPtr->component;
        toPtr->link = PtrToClone(fromPtr->link);
        return toPtr;
    }
}
```

Let's perform a code walk-through of the function call

```
newListHead = PtrToClone(head);
```

using the following list:

Call 1: fromPtr points to the node containing 49 and is not NULL. A new node is allocated and its component value is set to 49.

Execution of this call pauses until the recursive call with argument fromPtr->link has been completed.

Call 2: fromPtr points to the node containing 50 and is not NULL. A new node is allocated and its component value is set to 50.

Execution of this call pauses until the recursive call with argument `fromPtr->link` has been completed.

Call 3: `fromPtr` points to the node containing 58 and is not NULL. A new node is allocated and its component value is set to 58.

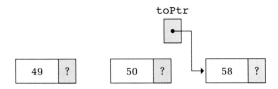

Execution of this call pauses until the recursive call with argument `fromPtr->link` has been completed.

Call 4: `fromPtr` is NULL. The list is unchanged.

Execution of this call is complete. NULL is returned as the function value to the preceding call.

Call 3: Execution of this call resumes by assigning the returned function value (NULL) to `toPtr->link`.

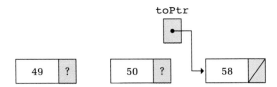

Execution of this call is complete. The value of `toPtr` is returned to the preceding call.

Call 2: Execution of this call resumes by assigning the returned function value (the address of the third node) to `toPtr->link`.

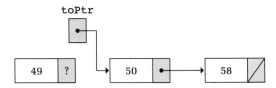

Execution of this call is complete. The value of `toPtr` is returned to the preceding call.

Call 1: Execution of this call resumes by assigning the returned function value (the address of the second node) to `toPtr->link`.

toPtr

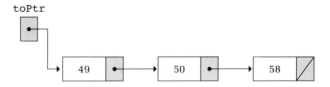

Execution of this call is complete. Because this is the nonrecursive call, the value of `toPtr` is returned to the assignment statement containing the original call. The variable `newListHead` now points to a clone of the original list.

newListHead

Recursion or Iteration?

Recursion and iteration are alternative ways of expressing repetition in a program. When iterative control structures are used, processes are made to repeat by embedding code in a looping structure such as a While, For, or Do-While. In recursion, a process is made to repeat by having a function call itself. A selection statement is used to control the repeated calls.

Which is better to use—recursion or iteration? There is no simple answer to this question. The choice usually depends on two issues: efficiency and the nature of the problem being solved.

Historically, the quest for efficiency, in terms of both execution speed and memory usage, has favored iteration over recursion. Each time a recursive call is made, the system must allocate stack space for all parameters and (automatic) local variables. The overhead involved in any function call is time-consuming. On early, slow computers with limited memory capacity, recursive algorithms were visibly—sometimes painfully—slower than the iterative versions. However, studies have shown that on modern, fast computers, the overhead of recursion is often so small that the increase in computation time is almost unnoticeable to the user. Except in cases where efficiency is absolutely critical, then, the choice between recursion and iteration more often depends on the second issue—the nature of the problem being solved.

Consider the factorial and power algorithms we discussed earlier in the chapter. In both cases, iterative solutions were obvious and easy to devise. We imposed recursive solutions on these problems only to demonstrate how recursion works. As a rule of thumb, if an iterative solution is more obvious or easier to understand, use it; it will be more efficient. However, there are problems for which the recursive solution is more obvious or easier to devise, such as the Towers of Hanoi problem. (It turns out that the Towers of Hanoi problem is surprisingly difficult to solve using iteration.) Computer science students should be aware of the power of recursion. If the definition of a problem is inherently recursive, then a recursive solution should certainly be considered.

PROBLEM-SOLVING CASE STUDY

Converting Decimal Integers to Binary Integers

Problem: Convert a decimal (base-10) integer to a binary (base-2) integer.

Discussion: The algorithm for this conversion is as follows:

1. Take the decimal number and divide it by 2.
2. Make the remainder the rightmost digit in the answer.
3. Replace the original dividend with the quotient.
4. Repeat, placing each new remainder to the left of the previous one.
5. Stop when the quotient is 0.

This is clearly an algorithm for a calculator and paper and pencil. Expressions such as "to the left of" certainly cannot be implemented in C++ as yet. Let's do an example—convert 42 from base 10 to base 2—to get a feel for the algorithm before we try to write a computer solution. Remember, the quotient in one step becomes the dividend in the next.

Step 1
$$21 \leftarrow \text{Quotient}$$
$$2\,\overline{)42}$$
$$\underline{4}$$
$$2$$
$$\underline{2}$$
$$0 \leftarrow \text{Remainder}$$

Step 2
$$10 \leftarrow \text{Quotient}$$
$$2\,\overline{)21}$$
$$\underline{2}$$
$$1$$
$$\underline{0}$$
$$1 \leftarrow \text{Remainder}$$

Step 3
$$5 \leftarrow \text{Quotient}$$
$$2\,\overline{)10}$$
$$\underline{10}$$
$$0 \leftarrow \text{Remainder}$$

Step 4
$$2 \leftarrow \text{Quotient}$$
$$2\,\overline{)5}$$
$$\underline{4}$$
$$1 \leftarrow \text{Remainder}$$

Step 5
$$1 \leftarrow \text{Quotient}$$
$$2\overline{)2}$$
$$\underline{2}$$
$$0 \leftarrow \text{Remainder}$$

Step 6
$$0 \leftarrow \text{Quotient}$$
$$2\overline{)1}$$
$$\underline{0}$$
$$1 \leftarrow \text{Remainder}$$

The answer is the sequence of remainders from last to first. Therefore, the decimal number 42 is 101010 in binary.

It looks as though the problem can be implemented with a straightforward iterative algorithm. Each remainder is obtained from the MOD operation (% in C++), and each quotient is the result of the / operation.

```
WHILE number > 0
    Set remainder = number MOD 2
    Print remainder
    Set number = number / 2
```

Let's do a walk-through to test this algorithm.

Number	Remainder
42	0
21	1
10	0
5	1
2	0
1	1

Answer:	0	1	0	1	0	1
(remainder from step	1	2	3	4	5	6)

The answer is backwards! An iterative solution (using only simple variables) doesn't work. We need to print the last remainder first. The first remainder should be printed only after the rest of the remainders have been calculated and printed.

In our example, we should print 42 MOD 2 after (42 / 2) MOD 2 has been printed. But this, in turn, means that we should print (42 / 2) MOD 2 after ((42 / 2) / 2) MOD 2 has been printed. Now this begins to look like a recursive definition. We can summarize by saying that, for any given number, we should print number MOD 2 after (number / 2) MOD 2 has been printed. This becomes the following algorithm:

Convert (In: number)

```
IF number > 0
    Convert(number / 2)
    Print number MOD 2
```

If number is 0, we have called `Convert` as many times as we need to and can begin printing the answer. The base case is simply when we stop making recursive calls. The recursive solution to this problem is encoded in the `Convert` function.

```
void Convert( /* in */ int number )     // Number being converted
                                        //    to binary
// Precondition:
//      number >= 0
// Postcondition:
//      IF number > 0
//          number has been printed in binary (base 2) form
//      ELSE
//          No action has taken place

{
    if (number > 0)
    {
        Convert(number / 2);                    // Recursive call
        cout << number % 2;
    }
    // Empty else-clause is the base case
}
```

Let's do a code walk-through of `Convert(10)`. We pick up our original example at step 3, where the dividend is 10.

Call 1: `Convert` is called with an argument of 10. Because number is not equal to 0, the then-clause is executed. Execution pauses until the recursive call to `Convert` with an argument of (number / 2) has completed.

Call 2: number is 5. Because number is not equal to 0, execution of this call pauses until the recursive call with an argument of (number / 2) has completed.

Call 3: number is 2. Because number is not equal to 0, execution of this call pauses until the recursive call with an argument of (number / 2) has completed.

Call 4: number is 1. Because number is not equal to 0, execution of this call pauses until the recursive call with an argument of (number / 2) has completed.

Call 5: number is 0. Execution of this call to `Convert` is complete. Control returns to the preceding call.

Call 4: Execution of this call resumes with the statement following the recursive call to `Convert`. The value of number % 2 (which is 1) is printed. Execution of this call is complete.

Call 3: Execution of this call resumes with the statement following the recursive call to Convert. The value of number % 2 (which is 0) is printed. Execution of this call is complete.

Call 2: Execution of this call resumes with the statement following the recursive call to Convert. The value of number % 2 (which is 1) is printed. Execution of this call is complete.

Call 1: Execution of this call resumes with the statement following the recursive call to Convert. The value of number % 2 (which is 0) is printed. Execution of this call is complete. Because this is the nonrecursive call, execution resumes with the statement immediately following the original call.

Figure 17-6 shows the execution of the Convert function with the values of the parameters.

*P*ROBLEM-SOLVING CASE STUDY

Minimum Value in an Integer Array

Problem: Find the minimum value in an integer array indexed from 0 through size − 1.

Discussion: This problem is easy to solve iteratively, but the objective here is to think recursively. The problem has to be stated in terms of a smaller case of itself. Because this is a problem using an array, a smaller case involves a smaller array. The minimum value in an array of size size is the smaller of data[size−1] and the smallest value in the array from data[0]...data[size−2].

Minimum (In: data, size)

```
Set minSoFar = Minimum(data, size − 1)
IF data[size−1] < minSoFar
      Return data[size−1]
ELSE
      Return minSoFar
```

PROBLEM-SOLVING CASE STUDY cont'd.

FIGURE 17-6

Execution of
Convert(10)

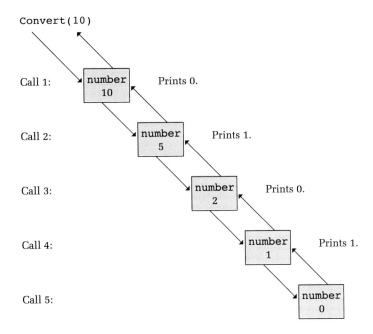

This algorithm looks reasonable. All we need is a base case. Because each recursive call reduces the size of the array by 1, our base case occurs when size is 1. We know the minimum value for this call: It is the only value in the array.

```
int Minimum(
        /* in */ const int data[],    // Array of integers to examine
        /* in */       int size   )   // One greater than index of
                                      //   last number in array
// Precondition:
//     data[0..size-1] are assigned
//   && size >= 1
// Postcondition:
//     Function value == smallest number in data[0..size-1]

{
    int minSoFar;        // Minimum returned from recursive call
```

FIGURE 17-7
Execution of
Minimum(data,5)

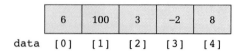

data   [0]   [1]   [2]   [3]   [4]

Minimum(data,5)

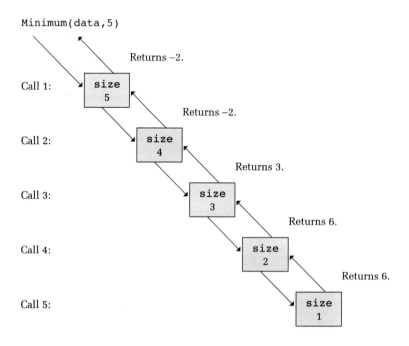

```
if (size == 1)
    return data[0];                           // Base case
else                                          // Recursive case
{
    minSoFar = Minimum(data, size-1);
    if (data[size-1] < minSoFar)
        return data[size-1];
    else
        return minSoFar;
}
}
```

We do not provide a code walk-through for this function. A diagram showing the parameters for each call appears in Figure 17-7.

Testing: To test this function, we need a driver program that reads values into an array, calls the function, and prints the result. The cases to be tested are the end cases (the minimum value is the first in the array, and the minimum value is the last in the array) and several cases between.

Testing and Debugging

Recursion is a powerful technique when used correctly. Improperly used, recursion can cause errors that are difficult to diagnose. The best way to debug a recursive algorithm is to construct it correctly in the first place. To be realistic, however, we give a few hints about where to look if an error occurs.

Testing and Debugging Hints

1. Be sure there is a base case. If there is no base case, the algorithm continues to issue recursive calls until all memory has been used. Each time the function is called, either recursively or nonrecursively, stack space is allocated for the parameters and automatic local variables. If there is no base case to end the recursive calls, the run-time stack eventually overflows. An error message such as "STACK OVERFLOW" indicates that the base case is missing.
2. Be sure you have not used a While structure. The basic structure in a recursive algorithm is the If statement. There must be at least two cases: the recursive case and the base case. If the base case does nothing, the else-clause is omitted. The selection structure, however, must be there. If a While statement is used in a recursive algorithm, the While statement usually should not contain a recursive call.
3. As with nonrecursive functions, do not reference global variables directly within a recursive function unless you have justification for doing so.
4. Parameters that relate to the size of the problem must be value parameters, not reference parameters. The arguments that relate to the size of the problem are usually expressions. Arbitrary expressions can be passed only to value parameters.
5. Use your system's debugger program (or use debug output statements) to trace a series of recursive calls. Inspecting the values of parameters and local variables often helps to locate errors in a recursive algorithm.

Summary

A recursive algorithm is expressed in terms of a smaller instance of itself. It must include a recursive case, for which the algorithm is expressed in terms of itself, and a base case, for which the algorithm is expressed in nonrecursive terms.

In many recursive problems, the smaller instance refers to a numeric argument that is being reduced with each call. In other problems, the smaller instance refers to the size of the data structure being manipulated.

The base case is the one in which the size of the problem (value or structure) reaches a point for which an explicit answer is known.

In the example for finding the minimum using recursion, the size of the problem was the size of the array being searched. When the array size became 1, the solution was known. If there is only one array element, it is clearly the minimum (as well as the maximum).

In the Towers of Hanoi game, the size of the problem was the number of discs to be moved. When there was only one left on the beginning peg, it could be moved to its final destination.

Quick Check

1. What distinguishes the base case from the recursive case in a recursive algorithm? (pp. 1014–1015)
2. What is the base case in the Towers of Hanoi algorithm? (pp. 1021–1025)
3. In working with simple variables, the recursive case is often stated in terms of a smaller value. What is typical of the recursive case in working with structured variables? (pp. 1026–1036)
4. In printing a linked list in reverse order recursively, what is the base case? (pp. 1029–1031)

Answers **1.** The base case is the simplest case, the case for which the solution can be stated nonrecursively.   **2.** When there are no more circles left to move.   **3.** It is often stated in terms of a smaller structure.   **4.** When the value of the current node pointer is NULL.

Exam Preparation Exercises

1. Recursion is an example of
    a. selection
    b. a data structure
    c. repetition
    d. data-flow programming
2. A void function can be recursive, but a value-returning function cannot. (True or False?)
3. When a function is called recursively, the arguments and automatic local variables of the calling version are saved until its execution is resumed. (True or False?)
4. Given the recursive formula $F(N) = -F(N-2)$, with base case $F(0) = 1$, what are the values of $F(4)$, $F(6)$, and $F(5)$? (If any of the values are undefined, say so.)
5. What algorithm error(s) leads to infinite recursion?
6. What control structure appears most commonly in a recursive function?
7. If you develop a recursive algorithm that employs tail recursion, what should you consider?
8. A recursive algorithm depends on making something smaller. When the algorithm works on a data structure, what may become smaller?
    a. Distance from a position in the structure.
    b. The data structure.
    c. The number of variables in the recursive function.

9. What is the name of the memory area used by the computer system to store a function's parameters and automatic local variables?

10. Given the following input data (where \n denotes the newline character):

    ABCDE\n

    what is the output of the following program?

```
#include <iostream>

using namespace std;

void Rev();

int main()
{
    Rev();
    cout << endl;
    return 0;
}

//************************************

void Rev()
{
    char ch;

    cin.get(ch);
    if (ch != '\n')
    {
        Rev();
        cout << ch;
    }
}
```

11. Repeat Exercise 10, replacing the Rev function with the following version:

```
void Rev()
{
    char ch;

    cin.get(ch);
    if (ch != '\n')
    {
        cout << ch;
        Rev();
    }
}
```

12. Given the following input:

    15
    23

21
19

what is the output of the following program?

```cpp
#include <iostream>

using namespace std;

void PrintNums();

int main()
{
    PrintNums();
    cout << endl;
    return 0;
}

//****************************************

void PrintNums()
{
    int n;

    cin >> n;
    if (cin)                    // If not EOF...
    {
        cout << n << ' ';
        PrintNums();
        cout << n << ' ';
    }
}
```

Programming Warm-up Exercises

1. Write a C++ value-returning function that implements the recursive formula $F(N) = F(N-1) + F(N-2)$ with base cases $F(0) = 1$ and $F(1) = 1$.

2. Add whatever is necessary to fix the following function so that Func(3) equals 10.

```cpp
int Func( /* in */ int n )
{
    return Func(n - 1) + 3;
}
```

3. Rewrite the following DoubleSpace function without using recursion.

```cpp
void DoubleSpace( /* inout */ ifstream& inFile )
{
    char ch;
```

```
        inFile.get(ch);
        if (inFile)              // If not EOF...
        {
            cout << ch;
            if (ch == '\n')
                cout << endl;
            DoubleSpace();
        }
    }
```

4. Rewrite the following `PrintSquares` function using recursion.

```
void PrintSquares()
{
    int count;

    for (count = 1; count <= 10; count++)
        cout << count << ' ' << count * count;
}
```

5. Modify the `Factorial` function of this chapter to print its parameter and returned value indented two spaces for each level of call to the function. The call `Factorial(3)` should produce the following output:

```
3
  2
    1
      0
      1
    1
  2
6
```

6. Write a recursive value-returning function that sums the integers from 1 through *N*.

7. Rewrite the following function so that it is recursive.

```
void PrintSqRoots( /* in */ int n )
{
    int i;

    for (i = n; i > 0; i--)
        cout << i << ' ' << sqrt(double(i)) << endl;
}
```

8. The `RevPrint` function of this chapter prints the contents of a dynamic linked list in reverse order. Write a recursive function that prints the contents in forward order.

9. The `Print` function of this chapter prints the contents of an array from first element to last. Write a recursive function that prints from last element to first.

10. Given the following declarations:

```
struct NodeType;
typedef NodeType* PtrType;

struct NodeType
{
    int     info;
    PtrType link;
};

PtrType head;
int     key;
```

write a recursive value-returning function that searches a dynamic linked list for the integer value key. If the value is in the list, the function should return a pointer to the node where it was found. If the value is not in the list, the function should return NULL.

Programming Problems

1. Use recursion to solve the following problem.

A *palindrome* is a string of characters that reads the same forward and backward. Write a program that reads in strings of characters and determines if each string is a palindrome. Each string is on a separate input line. Echo print each string, followed by "Is a palindrome" if the string is a palindrome or "Is not a palindrome" if the string is not a palindrome. For example, given the input string

```
Able was I, ere I saw Elba.
```

the program would print "Is a palindrome." In determining whether a string is a palindrome, consider uppercase and lowercase letters to be the same and ignore punctuation characters.

2. Write a program to place eight queens on a chessboard in such a way that no queen is attacking any other queen. This is a classic problem that lends itself to a recursive solution. The chessboard should be represented as an 8 × 8 Boolean array. If a square is occupied by a queen, the value is true; otherwise, the value is false. The status of the chessboard when all eight queens have been placed is the solution.

3. A maze is to be represented by a 10 × 10 array of an enumeration type composed of three values: PATH, HEDGE, and EXIT. There is one exit from the maze. Write a program to determine if it is possible to exit the maze from a given starting point. You may move vertically or horizontally in any direction that contains PATH; you may not move to a square that contains HEDGE. If you move into a square that contains EXIT, you have exited.

The input data consists of two parts: the maze and a series of starting points. The maze is entered as ten lines of ten characters (P, H, and E). Each succeeding line contains a pair of integers that represents a starting point (that is, row and column numbers). Continue processing entry points until end-of-file occurs.

4. A group of soldiers is overwhelmed by an enemy force. Only one person can go for help because they have only one horse. To decide which soldier should go for help, they put their names in a helmet and put one slip of paper for each soldier with a number on it in another helmet. For example, if there are five soldiers, then the second helmet contains five pieces of paper with the numbers 1 through 5 each written on a separate slip.

    The soldiers arrange themselves in a circle and pull a name and a number from the helmets. Starting with the person whose name was pulled, they count off in a clockwise direction until they reach the number that was pulled. When the count stops, that soldier is eliminated from the circle. This continues until there is one soldier left, and that soldier rides for help.

    Implement this process in C++. The names are stored in a file, and the last name in the file is followed by the word STOP. Use a circular linked list to represent the soldiers (a circular linked list is one in which the link member of the last node points back to the first node instead of containing NULL). Use recursive functions to count around the circle and eliminate the soldiers. Output the total number of soldiers in the group, the names of the soldiers who were eliminated, and the name of the soldier who will go for help.

Case Study Follow-Up

1. What is the base case in the recursive Convert function?
2. In the recursive Minimum function, what is the first array index to be evaluated? Explain.
3. Rewrite the Minimum function, assuming the data structure is a dynamic linked list of integers instead of an array.

Appendix A   Reserved Words

The following identifiers are *reserved words*—identifiers with predefined meanings in the C++ language. The programmer cannot declare them for other uses (for example, variable names) in a C++ program.

and	double	not	this
and_eq	dynamic_cast	not_eq	throw
asm	else	operator	true
auto	enum	or	try
bitand	explicit	or_eq	typedef
bitor	export	private	typeid
bool	extern	protected	typename
break	false	public	union
case	float	register	unsigned
catch	for	reinterpret_cast	using
char	friend	return	virtual
class	goto	short	void
compl	if	signed	volatile
const	inline	sizeof	wchar_t
const_cast	int	static	while
continue	long	static_cast	xor
default	mutable	struct	xor_eq
delete	namespace	switch	
do	new	template	

Appendix B   Operator Precedence

The following table summarizes C++ operator precedence. Several operators are not discussed in this book (typeid, the comma operator, ->*, and .*, for instance). For information on these operators, see Stroustrup's *The C++ Programming Language,* Third Edition (Addison-Wesley, 1997).

In the table, the operators are grouped by precedence level (highest to lowest), and a horizontal line separates each precedence level from the next-lower level.

In general, the binary operators group from left to right; the unary operators, from right to left; and the ?: operator, from right to left. Exception: The assignment operators group from right to left.

Precedence (highest to lowest)

Operator	Associativity	Remarks
`::`	Left to right	Scope resolution (binary)
`::`	Right to left	Global access (unary)
`()`	Left to right	Function call and function-style cast
`[]  ->  .`	Left to right	
`++  --`	Right to left	++ and -- as postfix operators
`typeid  dynamic_cast`	Right to left	
`static_cast  const_cast`	Right to left	
`reinterpret_cast`	Right to left	
`++  --  !  Unary +  Unary -`	Right to left	++ and -- as prefix operators
`~  Unary *  Unary &`	Right to left	
`(cast)  sizeof  new  delete`	Right to left	
`->*  .*`	Left to right	
`*  /  %`	Left to right	
`+  -`	Left to right	
`<<  >>`	Left to right	
`<  <=  >  >=`	Left to right	
`==  !=`	Left to right	
`&`	Left to right	
`^`	Left to right	
`|`	Left to right	
`&&`	Left to right	
`||`	Left to right	
`?:`	Right to left	
`=  +=  -=  *=  /=  %=`	Right to left	
`<<=  >>=  &=  |=  ^=`	Right to left	
`throw`	Right to left	
`,`	Left to right	The sequencing operator, not the separator

Appendix C   A Selection of Standard Library Routines

The C++ standard library provides a wealth of data types, functions, and named constants. This appendix details only some of the more widely used library facilities. It is a good idea to consult the manual for your particular system to see what other types, functions, and constants the standard library provides.

This appendix is organized alphabetically according to the header file your program must #include before accessing the listed items. For example, to use a mathematics routine such as sqrt, you would #include the header file cmath as follows:

```
#include <cmath>
using namespace std;
  ⋮
y = sqrt(x);
```

Note that every identifier in the standard library is defined to be in the namespace std. Without the using directive above, you would write

```
y = std::sqrt(x);
```

C.1   The Header File cassert

assert(booleanExpr)
  Argument: A logical (Boolean) expression
  Effect: If the value of booleanExpr is true, execution of the program simply continues. If the value of booleanExpr is false, execution terminates immediately with a message stating the Boolean expression, the name of the file containing the source code, and the line number in the source code.
  Function return value: None (a void function)
  Note: If the preprocessor directive #define NDEBUG is placed before the directive #include <cassert>, all assert statements are ignored.

C.2   The Header File cctype

isalnum(ch)
  Argument: A char value ch
  Function return value: An int value that is
  - nonzero (true), if ch is a letter or a digit character ('A'–'Z', 'a'–'z', '0'–'9')
  - 0 (false), otherwise

`isalpha(ch)`
> *Argument:* A `char` value `ch`
> *Function return value:* An `int` value that is
> - nonzero (`true`), if `ch` is a letter ('A'–'Z', 'a'–'z')
> - 0 (`false`), otherwise

`iscntrl(ch)`
> *Argument:* A `char` value `ch`
> *Function return value:* An `int` value that is
> - nonzero (`true`), if `ch` is a control character (in ASCII, a character with the value 0–31 or 127)
> - 0 (`false`), otherwise

`isdigit(ch)`
> *Argument:* A `char` value `ch`
> *Function return value:* An `int` value that is
> - nonzero (`true`), if `ch` is a digit character ('0'–'9')
> - 0 (`false`), otherwise

`isgraph(ch)`
> *Argument:* A `char` value `ch`
> *Function return value:* An `int` value that is
> - nonzero (`true`), if `ch` is a nonblank printable character (in ASCII, '!' through '~')
> - 0 (`false`), otherwise

`islower(ch)`
> *Argument:* A `char` value `ch`
> *Function return value:* An `int` value that is
> - nonzero (`true`), if `ch` is a lowercase letter ('a'–'z')
> - 0 (`false`), otherwise

`isprint(ch)`
> *Argument:* A `char` value `ch`
> *Function return value:* An `int` value that is
> - nonzero (`true`), if `ch` is a printable character, including the blank (in ASCII, ' ' through '~')
> - 0 (`false`), otherwise

`ispunct(ch)`
> *Argument:* A `char` value `ch`
> *Function return value:* An `int` value that is
> - nonzero (`true`), if `ch` is a punctuation character (equivalent to `isgraph(ch) && !isalnum(ch)`)
> - 0 (`false`), otherwise

`isspace(ch)`

   Argument: A `char` value `ch`
   Function return value: An `int` value that is
   - nonzero (`true`), if `ch` is a whitespace character (blank, newline, tab, carriage return, form feed)
   - 0 (`false`), otherwise

`isupper(ch)`

   Argument: A `char` value `ch`
   Function return value: An `int` value that is
   - nonzero (`true`), if `ch` is an uppercase letter ('A'–'Z')
   - 0 (`false`), otherwise

`isxdigit(ch)`

   Argument: A `char` value `ch`
   Function return value: An `int` value that is
   - nonzero (`true`), if `ch` is a hexadecimal digit ('0'–'9', 'A'–'F', 'a'–'f')
   - 0 (`false`), otherwise

`tolower(ch)`

   Argument: A `char` value `ch`
   Function return value: A character that is
   - the lowercase equivalent of `ch`, if `ch` is an uppercase letter
   - `ch`, otherwise

`toupper(ch)`

   Argument: A `char` value `ch`
   Function return value: A character that is
   - the uppercase equivalent of `ch`, if `ch` is a lowercase letter
   - `ch`, otherwise

C.3 The Header File `cfloat`

This header file supplies named constants that define the characteristics of floating-point numbers on your particular machine. Among these constants are the following:

`FLT_DIG`   Approximate number of significant digits in a `float` value on your machine
`FLT_MAX`   Maximum positive `float` value on your machine
`FLT_MIN`   Minimum positive `float` value on your machine
`DBL_DIG`   Approximate number of significant digits in a `double` value on your machine
`DBL_MAX`   Maximum positive `double` value on your machine
`DBL_MIN`   Minimum positive `double` value on your machine
`LDBL_DIG`   Approximate number of significant digits in a `long double` value on your machine

LDBL_MAX   Maximum positive long double value on your machine
LDBL_MIN   Minimum positive long double value on your machine

C.4   The Header File climits

This header file supplies named constants that define the limits of integer values on your particular machine. Among these constants are the following:

CHAR_BITS   Number of bits in a byte on your machine (8, for example)
CHAR_MAX   Maximum char value on your machine
CHAR_MIN   Minimum char value on your machine
SHRT_MAX   Maximum short value on your machine
SHRT_MIN   Minimum short value on your machine
INT_MAX   Maximum int value on your machine
INT_MIN   Minimum int value on your machine
LONG_MAX   Maximum long value on your machine
LONG_MIN   Minimum long value on your machine
UCHAR_MAX   Maximum unsigned char value on your machine
USHRT_MAX   Maximum unsigned short value on your machine
UINT_MAX   Maximum unsigned int value on your machine
ULONG_MAX   Maximum unsigned long value on your machine

C.5   The Header File cmath

In the math routines listed below, the following notes apply.

1. Error handling for incalculable or out-of-range results is system dependent.
2. All arguments and function return values are technically of type double (double-precision floating-point). However, single-precision (float) values may be passed to the functions.

acos(x)
   Argument: A floating-point expression x, where $-1.0 \le x \le 1.0$
   Function return value: Arc cosine of x, in the range 0.0 through π

asin(x)
   Argument: A floating-point expression x, where $-1.0 \le x \le 1.0$
   Function return value: Arc sine of x, in the range $-\pi/2$ through $\pi/2$

atan(x)
   Argument: A floating-point expression x
   Function return value: Arc tangent of x, in the range $-\pi/2$ through $\pi/2$

ceil(x)
   Argument: A floating-point expression x
   Function return value: "Ceiling" of x (the smallest whole number $\ge x$)

cos(angle)
   Argument: A floating-point expression angle, measured in radians
   Function return value: Trigonometric cosine of angle

cosh(x)
   Argument: A floating-point expression x
   Function return value: Hyperbolic cosine of x

exp(x)
   Argument: A floating-point expression x
   Function return value: The value e(2.718...) raised to the power x

fabs(x)
   Argument: A floating-point expression x
   Function return value: Absolute value of x

floor(x)
   Argument: A floating-point expression x
   Function return value: "Floor" of x (the largest whole number $\leq$ x)

log(x)
   Argument: A floating-point expression x, where x > 0.0
   Function return value: Natural logarithm (base e) of x

log10(x)
   Argument: A floating-point expression x, where x > 0.0
   Function return value: Common logarithm (base 10) of x

pow(x, y)
   Arguments: Floating-point expressions x and y. If x = 0.0, y must be positive; if x $\leq$ 0.0, y must be a whole number
   Function return value: x raised to the power y

sin(angle)
   Argument: A floating-point expression angle, measured in radians
   Function return value: Trigonometric sine of angle

sinh(x)
   Argument: A floating-point expression x
   Function return value: Hyperbolic sine of x

sqrt(x)
   Argument: A floating-point expression x, where x $\geq$ 0.0
   Function return value: Square root of x

tan(angle)
  Argument: A floating-point expression `angle`, measured in radians
  Function return value: Trigonometric tangent of `angle`

tanh(x)
  Argument: A floating-point expression `x`
  Function return value: Hyperbolic tangent of `x`

C.6   The Header File `cstddef`

This header file defines a few system-dependent constants and data types. From this header file, the only item we use in this book is the following symbolic constant:

NULL   The null pointer constant 0

C.7   The Header File `cstdlib`

abs(i)
  Argument: An `int` expression `i`
  Function return value: An `int` value that is the absolute value of `i`

atof(str)
  Argument: A C string (null-terminated `char` array) `str` representing a floating point number, possibly preceded by whitespace characters and a '+' or '−'
  Function return value: A `double` value that is the floating-point equivalent of the characters in `str`
  Note: Conversion stops at the first character in `str` that is inappropriate for a floating-point number. If no appropriate characters were found, the return value is system dependent.

atoi(str)
  Argument: A C string (null-terminated `char` array) `str` representing an integer number, possibly preceded by whitespace characters and a '+' or '−'
  Function return value: An `int` value that is the integer equivalent of the characters in `str`
  Note: Conversion stops at the first character in `str` that is inappropriate for an integer number. If no appropriate characters were found, the return value is system dependent.

atol(str)
  Argument: A C string (null-terminated `char` array) `str` representing a long integer, possibly preceded by whitespace characters and a '+' or '−'

Function return value:	A `long` value that is the long integer equivalent of the characters in `str`
Note:	Conversion stops at the first character in `str` that is inappropriate for a `long` integer number. If no appropriate characters were found, the return value is system dependent.

`exit(exitStatus)`

Argument:	An `int` expression `exitStatus`
Effect:	Program execution terminates immediately with all files properly closed
Function return value:	None (a void function)
Note:	By convention, `exitStatus` is 0 to indicate normal program completion and is nonzero to indicate an abnormal termination.

`labs(i)`

Argument:	A `long` expression `i`
Function return value:	A `long` value that is the absolute value of `i`

`rand()`

Argument:	None
Function return value:	A random `int` value in the range 0 through `RAND_MAX`, a constant defined in `cstdlib` (`RAND_MAX` is usually the same as `INT_MAX`)
Note:	See `srand` below.

`srand(seed)`

Argument:	An `int` expression `seed`, where $seed \geq 0$
Effect:	Using `seed`, the random number generator is initialized in preparation for subsequent calls to the `rand` function.
Function return value:	None (a void function)
Note:	If `srand` is not called before the first call to `rand`, a `seed` value of 1 is assumed.

`system(str)`

Argument:	A C string (null-terminated `char` array) `str` representing an operating system command, exactly as it would be typed by a user on the operating system command line
Effect:	The operating system command represented by `str` is executed.
Function return value:	An `int` value that is system dependent
Note:	Programmers often ignore the function return value, using the syntax of a void function call rather than a value-returning function call.

C.8 The Header File `cstring`

The header file `cstring` (not to be confused with the header file named `string`) supports manipulation of C strings (null-terminated `char` arrays).

`strcat(toStr, fromStr)`

Arguments:	C strings (null-terminated `char` arrays) `toStr` and `fromStr`, where `toStr` must be large enough to hold the result
Effect:	`fromStr`, including the null character '\0', is concatenated (joined) to the end of `toStr`.
Function return value:	The base address of `toStr`
Note:	Programmers usually ignore the function return value, using the syntax of a void function call rather than a value-returning function call.

`strcmp(str1, str2)`

Arguments:	C strings (null-terminated `char` arrays) `str1` and `str2`
Function return value:	An `int` value < 0, if `str1` < `str2` lexicographically
	The `int` value 0, if `str1` = `str2` lexicographically
	An `int` value > 0, if `str1` > `str2` lexicographically

`strcpy(toStr, fromStr)`

Arguments:	`toStr` is a `char` array and `fromStr` is a C string (null-terminated `char` array), and `toStr` must be large enough to hold the result
Effect:	`fromStr`, including the null character '\0', is copied to `toStr`, overwriting what was there.
Function return value:	The base address of `toStr`
Note:	Programmers usually ignore the function return value, using the syntax of a void function call rather than a value-returning function call.

`strlen(str)`

Argument:	A C string (null-terminated `char` array) `str`
Function return value:	An `int` value ≥ 0 that is the length of `str` (excluding the '\0')

C.9 The Header File `string`

This header file supplies a programmer-defined data type (specifically, a *class*) named `string`. Associated with the `string` type are a data type `string::size_type` and a named constant `string::npos`, defined as follows:

`string::size_type`	An unsigned integer type related to the number of characters in a string
`string::npos`	The maximum value of type `string::size_type`

There are dozens of functions associated with the `string` type. Below are several of the most important ones. In the descriptions, s is assumed to be a variable (an *object*) of type `string`.

`s.c_str()`
Arguments:	None
Function return value:	The base address of a C string (null-terminated `char` array) corresponding to the characters stored in s

`s.find(arg)`
Argument:	An expression of type `string` or `char`, or a C string (such as a literal string)
Function return value:	A value of type `string::size_type` that gives the starting position in s where `arg` was found. If `arg` was not found, the return value is `string::npos`.
Note:	Positions of characters within a string are numbered starting at 0.

`getline(inStream, s)`
Arguments:	An input stream `inStream` (of type `istream` or `ifstream`) and a `string` object s
Effect:	Characters are input from `inStream` and stored into s until the newline character is encountered. (The newline character is consumed but not stored into s.)
Function return value:	Although the function technically returns a value (which we do not discuss here), programmers usually invoke the function as though it were a void function.

`s.length()`
Arguments:	None
Function return value:	A value of type `string::size_type` that gives the number of characters in the string

`s.size()`
Arguments:	None
Function return value:	The same as `s.length()`

`s.substr(pos, len)`
Arguments:	Two unsigned integers, `pos` and `len`, representing a position and a length. The value of `pos` must be less than `s.length()`.
Function return value:	A temporary `string` object that holds a substring of at most `len` characters, starting at position `pos` of s. If `len` is too large, it means "to the end" of the string in s.
Note:	Positions of characters within a string are numbered starting at 0.

Appendix D   Using This Book with a Prestandard Version of C++

D.1   The `string` Type

Prior to the ISO/ANSI C++ language standard, the standard library did not provide a `string` data type. Compiler vendors often supplied their own programmer-defined types with names like `String`, `StringType`, and so on. The syntax and semantics of string operations often varied from vendor to vendor.

For readers with prestandard compilers, the authors of this book have created a data type named `StrType` that mimics a subset of the standard `string` type. The subset is sufficient to match the string operations displayed throughout this book.

The files related to `StrType` are available for download from the publisher's Web site (www.jbpub.com). Among the files is one called `README.TXT`, which explains how to compile the source code and link it with the programs you write. Another file is the header file `strtype.h`, which contains important declarations that define the `StrType` type. Programs that use `StrType` must `#include` this header file:

```
#include "strtype.h"
```

In the `#include` directive, you cannot place the file name in angle brackets (< >), which tell the preprocessor to look for the file in the standard include directory. Instead, you enclose the file name in double quotes (" "). The double quotes tell the preprocessor to look for the file in the programmer's current directory. Therefore, to use `StrType` in your program, you must (a) verify that the file `strtype.h` is in the directory in which you are currently working on your program, and (b) make sure your program uses the directive

```
#include "strtype.h"
```

Additional directions are given in `README.TXT`.

Throughout this book you can use `StrType` instead of the `string` data type as follows. First, in your variable declarations, substitute the word `StrType` for `string` as the name of the data type. Second, change the directive `#include <string>` to `#include "strtype.h"`. For example, instead of

```
#include <string>
   ⋮
string lastName;
```

you would write

```
#include "strtype.h"
   ⋮
StrType lastName;
```

Finally, there is a restriction on performing input into `StrType` variables. Chapter 4 discusses the use of the `>>` operator and the `getline` function to input characters into a string variable. Using >> with StrType variables, at most 1023 characters can be read and stored into one variable. In practice, however, this isn't much of a restriction. It would be extremely rare for an input string to consist of that many characters. Input using getline is also restricted to 1023 characters. In the function call

```
getline(cin, myString);
```

in which myString is a StrType variable, the getline function does not skip leading white-space characters and continues until it either has read 1023 characters or it reaches the newline character '\n', whichever comes first. That is, getline reads and stores an entire input line (to a maximum of 1023 characters), embedded blanks and all. Note that for an input line of 1023 characters or less, the newline character *is* consumed (but is not stored into myString).

D.2   Standard Header Files and Namespaces

Historically, the standard header files in both C and C++ had file names ending in .h (meaning "header file"). Certain header files—for example, iostream.h, iomanip.h, and fstream.h—related specifically to C++. Others, such as math.h, stddef.h, stdlib.h, and string.h, were carried over from the C standard library and were available to both C and C++ programs. When you used an #include directive such as

```
#include <math.h>
```

near the beginning of your program, all identifiers declared in math.h were introduced into your program in global scope (as discussed in Chapter 8). With the advent of the *namespace* mechanism in ISO/ANSI standard C++ (see Chapter 2 and, in more detail, Chapter 8), all of the standard header files were modified so that identifiers are declared within a namespace called std. In standard C++, when you #include a standard header file, the identifiers therein are not automatically placed into global scope.

To preserve compatibility with older versions of C++ that still need the original files iostream.h, math.h, and so forth, the new standard header files are renamed as follows: The C++-related header files have the .h removed, and the header files from the C library have the .h removed *and* the letter *c* inserted at the beginning. Here is a list of the old and new names for some of the most commonly used header files.

Old Name	New Name
iostream.h	iostream
iomanip.h	iomanip
fstream.h	fstream
assert.h	cassert
ctype.h	cctype
float.h	cfloat
limits.h	climits
math.h	cmath
stddef.h	cstddef

```
stdlib.h        cstdlib
string.h        cstring
```

Be careful: The last entry in the list above refers to the C language concept of a string and is unrelated to the `string` type defined in the C++ standard library.

If you are working with a prestandard compiler that does not recognize the new header file names or namespaces, simply substitute the old header file names for the new ones as you encounter them in the book. For example, where we have written

```
#include <iostream>
using namespace std;
```

you would write

```
#include <iostream.h>
```

For compatibility, C++ systems are likely to retain both versions of the header files for some time to come.

D.3   The `fixed` and `showpoint` Manipulators

Chapter 3 introduces five manipulators for formatting the output: `endl`, `setw`, `fixed`, `showpoint`, and `setprecision`. If you are using a prestandard compiler with the header file `iostream.h`, the `fixed` and `showpoint` manipulators may not be available.

In place of the following code shown in Chapter 3,

```
#include <iostream>
using namespace std;
  ⋮
cout << fixed << showpoint;           // Set up floating-pt.
                                      //   output format
```

you can substitute the following code:

```
#include <iostream.h>
  ⋮
cout.setf(ios::fixed, ios::floatfield);
cout.setf(ios::showpoint);
```

These two statements employ some advanced C++ notation. Our advice is simply to use the statements just as you see them and not worry about the details. Here's the general idea. `setf` is a void function associated with the `cout` stream. (Note that the dot, or period, between `cout` and `setf` is required.) The first function call ensures that floating-point numbers are always printed in decimal form rather than scientific notation. The second function call specifies that the decimal point should always be printed, even for whole numbers. In other words, these two function calls accomplish the same effect as the `fixed` and `showpoint` manipulators.

Note: If your compiler complains about the syntax `ios::fixed`, `ios::floatfield`, or `ios::showpoint`, you may have to replace `ios` with `ios_base` as follows:

```
cout.setf(ios_base::fixed, ios_base::floatfield);
cout.setf(ios_base::showpoint);
```

D.4   The `bool` Type

Before the ISO/ANSI C++ language standard, C++ did not have a `bool` data type. Some pre-standard compilers implemented the `bool` type before the standard was approved, but others did not. If your compiler does not recognize the `bool` type, the following discussion will assist you in writing programs that are compatible with those in this book.

In versions of C++ without the `bool` type, the value 0 represents *false*, and any nonzero value represents *true*. It is customary in pre–standard C++ to use the `int` type to represent Boolean data:

```
int dataOK;
  ⋮
dataOK = 1;    // Store "true" into dataOK
  ⋮
dataOK = 0;    // Store "false" into dataOK
```

To make the code more self-documenting, many pre–standard C++ programmers define their own Boolean data type by using a *Typedef statement*. This statement allows you to introduce a new name for an existing data type:

```
typedef int bool;
```

All this statement does is tell the compiler to substitute the word `int` for every occurrence of the word `bool` in the rest of the program. Thus, when the compiler encounters a statement such as

```
bool dataOK;
```

it translates the statement into

```
int dataOK;
```

With the Typedef statement and declarations of two named constants, `true` and `false`, the code at the beginning of this discussion becomes the following:

```
typedef int bool;
const int true = 1;
const int false = 0;
  ⋮
```

```
bool dataOK;
  ⋮
dataOK = true;
  ⋮
dataOK = false;
```

Throughout the book, our programs use the words `bool`, `true`, and `false` when manipulating Boolean data. If your compiler recognizes `bool` as a built-in type, there is nothing you need to do. Otherwise, here are three steps you can take.

1. Use your system's editor to create a file containing the following lines:

```
#ifndef BOOL_H
#define BOOL_H
typedef int bool;
const int true = 1;
const int false = 0;
#endif
```

   Don't worry about the meaning of the first, second, and last lines. They are explained in Chapter 14. Simply type the lines as you see them above.

2. Save the file you created in step 1, giving it the name `bool.h`. Save this file into the same directory in which you work on your C++ programs.

3. Near the top of every program in which you need `bool` variables, type the line

```
#include "bool.h"
```

   Be sure to surround the file name with double quotes, not angle brackets (< >). The quotes tell the preprocessor to look for `bool.h` in your current directory rather than the C++ system directory.

With `bool`, `true`, and `false` defined in this fashion, the programs in this book run correctly, and you can use `bool` in your own programs, even if it is not a built-in type.

Appendix E   Character Sets

The following charts show the ordering of characters in two widely used character sets: ASCII (American Standard Code for Information Interchange) and EBCDIC (Extended Binary Coded Decimal Interchange Code). The internal representation for each character is shown in decimal. For example, the letter *A* is represented internally as the integer 65 in ASCII and as 193 in EBCDIC. The space (blank) character is denoted by a "☐".

Left Digit(s)	Right Digit				ASCII					
	0	*1*	*2*	*3*	*4*	*5*	*6*	*7*	*8*	*9*
0	NUL	SOH	STX	ETX	EOT	ENQ	ACK	BEL	BS	HT
1	LF	VT	FF	CR	SO	SI	DLE	DC1	DC2	DC3
2	DC4	NAK	SYN	ETB	CAN	EM	SUB	ESC	FS	GS
3	RS	US	□	!	"	#	$	%	&	´
4	(	)	*	+	,	–	.	/	0	1
5	2	3	4	5	6	7	8	9	:	;
6	<	=	>	?	@	A	B	C	D	E
7	F	G	H	I	J	K	L	M	N	O
8	P	Q	R	S	T	U	V	W	X	Y
9	Z	[	\	]	^	_	`		a	b	c
10	d	e	f	g	h	i	j	k	l	m
11	n	o	p	q	r	s	t	u	v	w
12	x	y	z	{	|	}	~	DEL		

Codes 00–31 and 127 are the following nonprintable control characters:

NUL	Null character	VT	Vertical tab	SYN	Synchronous idle
SOH	Start of header	FF	Form feed	ETB	End of transmitted block
STX	Start of text	CR	Carriage return	CAN	Cancel
ETX	End of text	SO	Shift out	EM	End of medium
EOT	End of transmission	SI	Shift in	SUB	Substitute
ENQ	Enquiry	DLE	Data link escape	ESC	Escape
ACK	Acknowledge	DC1	Device control one	FS	File separator
BEL	Bell character (beep)	DC2	Device control two	GS	Group separator
BS	Back space	DC3	Device control three	RS	Record separator
HT	Horizontal tab	DC4	Device control four	US	Unit separator
LF	Line feed	NAK	Negative acknowledge	DEL	Delete

Left Digit(s)	Right Digit	EBCDIC									
		0	1	2	3	4	5	6	7	8	9
6						□					
7						¢	.	<	(	+	|
8		&									
9		!	$	*	)	;	¬	−	/		
10								^	,	%	_
11		>	?								
12			`	:	#	@	´	=	"		a
13		b	c	d	e	f	g	h	i		
14							j	k	l	m	n
15		o	p	q	r						
16			~	s	t	u	v	w	x	y	z
17									\	{	}
18		[	]								
19				A	B	C	D	E	F	G	
20		H	I								J
21		K	L	M	N	O	P	Q	R		
22								S	T	U	V
23		W	X	Y	Z						
24		0	1	2	3	4	5	6	7	8	9

In the EBCDIC table, nonprintable control characters—codes 00–63, 250–255, and those for which empty spaces appear in the chart—are not shown.

Appendix F   Program Style, Formatting, and Documentation

Throughout this text, we encourage the use of good programming style and documentation. Although the programs you write for class assignments may not be looked at by anyone except the person grading your work, outside of class you will write programs that will be used by others.

Useful programs have very long lifetimes, during which they must be modified and updated. When maintenance work must be done, either you or another programmer will have to do it. Good style and documentation are essential if another programmer is to understand and work with your program. You will also discover that after not working with your own program for a few months, you'll be amazed at how many of the details you've forgotten.

F.1 General Guidelines

The style used in the programs and fragments throughout this text provides a good starting point for developing your own style. Our goals in creating this style were to make it simple, consistent, and easy to read.

Style is of benefit only for a human reader of your program—differences in style make no difference to the computer. Good style includes the use of meaningful variable names, comments, and indentation of control structures, all of which help others to understand and work with your program. Perhaps the most important aspect of program style is consistency. If the style within a program is not consistent, then it becomes misleading and confusing.

Sometimes, a particular style is specified for you by your instructor or by the company you work for. When you are modifying someone else's code, you should use his or her style in order to maintain consistency within the program. However, you will also develop your own, personal programming style based on what you've been taught, your own experience, and your personal taste.

F.2 Comments

Comments are extra information included to make a program easier to understand. You should include a comment anywhere the code is difficult to understand. However, don't overcomment. Too many comments in a program can obscure the code and be a source of distraction.

In our style, there are four basic types of comments: headers, declarations, in-line, and sidebar.

Header comments appear at the top of the program and should include your name, the date that the program was written, and its purpose. It is also useful to include sections describing input, output, and assumptions. Think of the header comments as the reader's introduction to your program. Here is an example:

```
// This program computes the sidereal time for a given date and
// solar time.
//
// Written By: Your Name
//
// Date Completed: 4/8/02
//
// Input: A date and time in the form MM DD YYYY HH MM SS
//
// Output: Sidereal time in the form HH MM SS
//
// Assumptions: Solar time is specified for a longitude of 0
//       degrees (GMT, UT, or Z time zone)
```

Header comments should also be included for all user-defined functions (see Chapters 7 and 8).

Declaration comments accompany the constant and variable declarations in the program. Anywhere that an identifier is declared, it is helpful to include a comment that explains its purpose. In programs in the text, declaration comments appear to the right of the identifier being declared. For example:

```
const float E = 2.71828;      // The base of the natural logarithms

float deltaX;                 // The difference in the x direction
float deltaY;                 // The difference in the y direction
```

Notice that aligning the comments gives the code a neater appearance and is less distracting.

In-line comments are used to break long sections of code into shorter, more comprehensible fragments. These are often the names of modules in your algorithm design, although you may occasionally choose to include other information. It is generally a good idea to surround in-line comments with blank lines to make them stand out. For example:

```
// Prepare file for reading

scoreFile.open("scores.dat");

// Get data

scoreFile >> test1 >> weight1;
scoreFile >> test2 >> weight2;
scoreFile >> test3 >> weight3;

// Print heading

cout << "Test Score   Weight" << endl;
```

Even if comments are not used, blank lines can be inserted wherever there is a logical break in the code that you would like to emphasize.

Sidebar comments appear to the right of executable statements and are used to shed light on the purpose of the statement. Sidebar comments are often just pseudocode statements from the lowest levels of your design. If a complicated C++ statement requires some explanation, the pseudocode statement should be written to the right of the C++ statement. For example:

```
while (file1 && file2)    // While neither file is empty...
{
    ⋮
```

In addition to the four main types of comments that we have discussed, there are some miscellaneous comments that we should mention. After the `main` function, we recommend using a row of asterisks (or dashes or equal signs or ...) in a comment before and after each function to help it to stand out. For example:

```
//******************************************************************

void PrintSecondHeading()
{
    ⋮
```

```
}

//*************************************************************
```

In this text, we use C++'s alternative comment form

```
/* Some comment */
```

to document the flow of information for each parameter of a function:

```
void GetData( /* out */ int age,          // Patient's age
              /* out */ int weight )      // Patient's weight
{
    ⋮
}

void Print( /* in */      float val,      // Value to be printed
            /* inout */ int&  count )     // Number of lines printed
                                          //   so far
{
    ⋮
}
```

(Chapter 7 describes the purpose of labeling each parameter as `/* in */`, `/* out */`, or `/* inout */`.)

Programmers sometimes place a comment after the right brace of a block (compound statement) to indicate which control structure the block belongs to:

```
while (num >= 0)
{
    ⋮

    if (num == 25)
    {
        ⋮
    } // if
} // while
```

Attaching comments in this fashion can help to clarify the code and aid in debugging mismatched braces.

F.3   Identifiers

The most important consideration in choosing a name for a data item or function in a program is that the name convey as much information as possible about what the data item is or what the function does. The name should also be readable in the context in which it is used. For example, the following names convey the same information but one is more readable than the other:

```
datOfInvc        invoiceDate
```

Identifiers for types, constants, and variables should be nouns, whereas names of void functions (non-value-returning functions) should be imperative verbs or phrases containing imperative verbs. Because of the way that value-returning functions are invoked, their names should be nouns or occasionally adjectives. Here are some examples:

Variables	`address, price, radius, monthNumber`
Constants	`PI, TAX_RATE, STRING_LENGTH, ARRAY_SIZE`
Data types	`NameType, CarMakes, RoomLists, Hours`
Void functions	`GetData, ClearTable, PrintBarChart`
Value-returning functions	`CubeRoot, Greatest, Color, AreaOf, IsEmpty`

Although an identifier may be a series of words, very long identifiers can become quite tedious and can make the program difficult to read.

The best approach to designing an identifier is to try writing out different names until you reach an acceptable compromise—and then write an especially informative declaration comment next to the declaration.

Capitalization is another consideration when choosing an identifier. C++ is a case-sensitive language; that is, uppercase and lowercase letters are distinct. Different programmers use different conventions for capitalizing identifiers. In this text, we begin each variable name with a lowercase letter and capitalize the beginning of each successive English word. We begin each function name and data type name with a capital letter and, again, capitalize the beginning of each successive English word. For named constants, we capitalize the entire identifier, separating successive English words with underscore (_) characters. Keep in mind, however, that C++ reserved words such as `main`, `if`, and `while` are always lowercase letters, and the compiler will not recognize them if you capitalize them differently.

F.4   Formatting Lines and Expressions

C++ allows you to break a long statement in the middle and continue onto the next line. (However, you cannot split a line in the middle of an identifier, a literal constant, or a string.) When you must split a line, it's important to choose a breaking point that is logical and readable. Compare the readability of the following code fragments.

```
cout << "For a radius of " << radius << " the diameter of the cir"
    << "cle is " << diameter << endl;
```

```
cout << "For a radius of " << radius
     << " the diameter of the circle is " << diameter << endl;
```

When you must split an expression across multiple lines, try to end each line with an operator. Also, try to take advantage of any repeating patterns in the expression. For example,

```
meanOfMaxima = (Maximum(set1Value1, set1Value2, set1Value3) +
                Maximum(set2Value1, set2Value2, set2Value3) +
                Maximum(set3Value1, set3Value2, set3Value3)) / 3.0;
```

When writing expressions, also keep in mind that spaces improve readability. Usually you should include one space on either side of the = operator and most other operators. Occasionally, spaces are left out to emphasize the order in which operations are performed. Here are some examples:

```
if (x+y > y+z)
    maximum = x + y;
else
    maximum = y + z;
hypotenuse = sqrt(a*a + b*b);
```

F.5 Indentation

The purpose of indenting statements in a program is to provide visual cues to the reader and to make the program easier to debug. When a program is properly indented, the way the statements are grouped is immediately obvious. Compare the following two program fragments:

```
while (count <= 10)                 while (count <= 10)
{                                   {
cin >> num;                             cin >> num;
if (num == 0)                           if (num == 0)
{                                       {
count++;                                    count++;
num = 1;                                    num = 1;
}                                       }
cout << num << endl;                    cout << num << endl;
cout << count << endl;                  cout << count << endl;
}                                   }
```

As a basic rule in this text, each nested or lower-level item is indented by four spaces. Exceptions to this rule are parameter declarations and statements that are split across two or more lines. Indenting by four spaces is a matter of personal preference. Some people prefer to indent by three, five, or even more than five spaces.

In this book, we indent the entire body of a function. Also, in general, any statement that is part of another statement is indented. For example, the If-Then-Else contains two parts, the then-clause and the else-clause. The statements within both clauses are indented four spaces beyond the beginning of the If-Then-Else statement. The If-Then statement is indented like the

If-Then-Else, except that there is no else-clause. Here are examples of the If-Then-Else and the If-Then:

```
if (sex == MALE)
{
    maleSalary = maleSalary + salary;
    maleCount++;
}
else
    femaleSalary = femaleSalary + salary;

if (count > 0)
    average = total / count;
```

For nested If-Then-Else statements that form a generalized multiway branch (the If-Then-Else-If, described in Chapter 5), a special style of indentation is used in the text. Here is an example:

```
if (month == JANUARY)
    monthNumber = 1;
else if (month == FEBRUARY)
    monthNumber = 2;
else if (month == MARCH)
    monthNumber = 3;
else if (month == APRIL)
    ⋮
else
    monthNumber = 12;
```

The remaining C++ statements all follow the basic indentation guideline mentioned previously. For reference purposes, here are examples of each.

```
while (count <= 10)
{
    cin >> value;
    sum = sum + value;
    count++;
}

do
{
    GetAnswer(letter);
    PutAnswer(letter);
} while (letter != 'N');

for (count = 1; count <= numSales; count++)
    cout << '*';
```

```
for (count = 10; count >= 1; count--)
{
    inFile >> dataItem;
    outFile << dataItem << ' ' << count << endl;
}

switch (color)
{
    RED     : cout << "Red";
              break;
    ORANGE  : cout << "Orange";
              break;
    YELLOW  : cout << "Yellow";
              break;
    GREEN   :
    BLUE    :
    INDIGO  :
    VIOLET  : cout << "Short visible wavelengths";
              break;
    WHITE   :
    BLACK   : cout << "Not valid colors";
              color = NONE;
}
```

Glossary

Abstract data type A data type whose properties (domain and operations) are specified independently of any particular implementation.

Abstract step A step for which some implementation details remain unspecified.

Abstraction barrier The invisible wall around a class object that encapsulates implementation details. The wall can be breached only through the public interface.

Aggregate operation An operation on a data structure as a whole, as opposed to an operation on an individual component of the data structure.

Algorithm A step-by-step procedure for solving a problem in a finite amount of time.

Anonymous type A type that does not have an associated type identifier.

Argument A variable or expression listed in a call to a function; also called *actual argument* or *actual parameter*.

Argument list A mechanism by which functions communicate with each other.

Arithmetic/logic unit (ALU) The component of the central processing unit that performs arithmetic and logical operations.

Array A collection of components, all of the same type, ordered on N dimensions ($N \geq 1$). Each component is accessed by N indexes, each of which represents the component's position within that dimension.

Assembler A program that translates an assembly language program into machine code.

Assembly language A low-level programming language in which a mnemonic is used to represent each of the machine language instructions for a particular computer.

Assignment expression A C++ expression with (1) a value and (2) the side effect of storing the expression value into a memory location.

Assignment statement A statement that stores the value of an expression into a variable.

Automatic variable A variable for which memory is allocated and deallocated when control enters and exits the block in which it is declared.

Auxiliary storage device A device that stores data in encoded form outside the computer's main memory.

Base address The memory address of the first element of an array.

Base case The case for which the solution can be stated nonrecursively.

Base class (superclass) The class being inherited from.

Binary operator An operator that has two operands.

Black box An electrical or mechanical device whose inner workings are hidden from view.

C string In C and C++, a null-terminated sequence of characters stored in a `char` array.

Central processing unit (CPU) The part of the computer that executes the instructions (program) stored in memory; made up of the arithmetic/logic unit and the control unit.

Class A structured type in a programming language that is used to represent an abstract data type.

Class member A component of a class. Class members may be either data or functions.

Class object (class instance) A variable of a class type.

Client Software that declares and manipulates objects of a particular class.

Communication complexity A measure of the quantity of data passing through a module's interface.

Compiler A program that translates a high-level language into machine code.

Complexity A measure of the effort expended by the computer in performing a computation, relative to the size of the computation.

Composition (containment) A mechanism by which the internal data (the state) of one class includes an object of another class.

Computer A programmable device that can store, retrieve, and process data.

Computer program A sequence of instructions to be performed by a computer.

Computer programming The process of planning a sequence of steps for a computer to follow.

Concrete step A step for which the implementation details are fully specified.

Constructor An operation that creates a new instance (variable) of an ADT.

Control abstraction The separation of the logical properties of an action from its implementation.

Control structure A statement used to alter the normally sequential flow of control.

Control unit The component of the central processing unit that controls the actions of the other components so that instructions (the program) are executed in the correct sequence.

Count-controlled loop A loop that executes a specified number of times.

Dangling pointer A pointer that points to a variable that has been deallocated.

Data Information in a form a computer can use.

Data abstraction The separation of a data type's logical properties from its implementation.

Data flow The flow of information from the calling code to a function and from the function back to the calling code.

Data representation The concrete form of data used to represent the abstract values of an abstract data type.

Data type A specific set of data values, along with a set of operations on those values.

Declaration A statement that associates an identifier with a data object, a function, or a data type so that the programmer can refer to that item by name.

Deep copy An operation that not only copies one class object to another but also makes copies of any pointed-to data.

Demotion (narrowing) The conversion of a value from a "higher" type to a "lower" type according to a programming language's precedence of data types. Demotion may cause loss of information.

Derived class (subclass) The class that inherits.

Direct addressing Accessing a variable in one step by using the variable name.

Documentation The written text and comments that make a program easier for others to understand, use, and modify.

Driver A simple `main` function that is used to call a function being tested. The use of a driver permits direct control of the testing process.

Dynamic binding The run-time determination of which function to call for a particular object.

Dynamic data Variables created during execution of a program by means of special operations. In C++, these operations are `new` and `delete`.

Dynamic data structure A data structure that can expand and contract during execution.

Dynamic linked list A linked list composed of dynamically allocated nodes that are linked together by pointers.

Editor An interactive program used to create and modify source programs or data.

Encapsulation Hiding a module implementation in a separate block with a formally specified interface.

Enumeration type A user-defined data type whose domain is an ordered set of literal values expressed as identifiers.

Enumerator One of the values in the domain of an enumeration type.

Evaluate To compute a new value by performing a specified set of operations on given values.

Event counter A variable that is incremented each time a particular event occurs.

Event-controlled loop A loop that terminates when something happens inside the loop body to signal that the loop should be exited.

Expression An arrangement of identifiers, literals, and operators that can be evaluated to compute a value of a given type.

Expression statement A statement formed by appending a semicolon to an expression.

External (head) pointer A pointer variable that points to the first node in a dynamic linked list.

External representation The printable (character) form of a data value.

Field (member, in C++) A component of a record.

File A named area in secondary storage that is used to hold a collection of data; the collection of data itself.

Flow of control The order in which the computer executes statements in a program.

Free store (heap) A pool of memory locations reserved for allocation and deallocation of dynamic data.

Function A subprogram in C++.

Function call (function invocation) The mechanism that transfers control to a function.

Function call (to a void function) A statement that transfers control to a void function. In C++, this statement is the name of the function, followed by a list of arguments.

Function definition A function declaration that includes the body of the function.

Function prototype A function declaration without the body of the function.

Function value type The data type of the result value returned by a function.

Functional cohesion A property of a module in which all concrete steps are directed toward solving just one problem, and any significant subproblems are written as abstract steps. Also, the principle that a module should perform exactly one abstract action.

Functional decomposition A technique for developing software in which the problem is divided into more easily handled subproblems, the solutions of which create a solution to the overall problem.

Functional equivalence A property of a module that performs exactly the same operation as the abstract step it defines. A pair of modules are also functionally equivalent to each other when they perform exactly the same operation.

General case The case for which the solution is expressed in terms of a smaller version of itself; also known as *recursive case.*

Hardware The physical components of a computer.

Hierarchical record A record in which at least one of the components is itself a record.

Identifier A name associated with a function or data object and used to refer to that function or data object.

Inaccessible object A dynamic variable on the free store without any pointer pointing to it.

Indirect addressing Accessing a variable in two steps by first using a pointer that gives the location of the variable.

Infinite recursion The situation in which a function calls itself over and over endlessly.

Information Any knowledge that can be communicated.

Information hiding The encapsulation and hiding of implementation details to keep the user of an abstraction from depending on or incorrectly manipulating these details.

Inheritance A mechanism by which one class acquires the properties—the data and operations—of another class.

Input/output (I/O) devices The parts of the computer that accept data to be processed (input) and present the results of that processing (output).

Interactive system   A system that allows direct communication between user and computer.

Interface   A connecting link at a shared boundary that permits independent systems to meet and act on or communicate with each other. Also, the formal description of the purpose of a subprogram and the mechanism for communicating with it.

Internal representation   The form in which a data value is stored inside the memory unit.

Iteration   An individual pass through, or repetition of, the body of a loop.

Iteration counter   A counter variable that is incremented with each iteration of a loop.

Iterator   An operation that allows us to process—one at a time—all the components in an instance of an ADT.

Length   The number of values currently stored in a list.

Lifetime   The period of time during program execution when an identifier has memory allocated to it.

Linked list   A list in which the order of the components is determined by an explicit link member in each node, rather than by the sequential order of the components in memory.

List   A variable-length, linear collection of homogeneous components.

Literal value   Any constant value written in a program.

Local variable   A variable declared within a block and not accessible outside of that block.

Loop   A control structure that causes a statement or group of statements to be executed repeatedly.

Loop entry   The point at which the flow of control reaches the first statement inside a loop.

Loop exit   The point at which the repetition of the loop body ends and control passes to the first statement following the loop.

Loop test   The point at which the While expression is evaluated and the decision is made either to begin a new iteration or skip to the statement immediately following the loop.

Machine language   The language, made up of binary-coded instructions, that is used directly by the computer.

Member selector   The expression used to access components of a struct or class variable. It is formed by using the struct or class variable name and the member name, separated by a dot (period).

Memory leak   The loss of available memory space that occurs when dynamic data is allocated but never deallocated.

Memory unit   Internal data storage in a computer.

Metalanguage   A language that is used to write the syntax rules for another language.

Mixed type expression   An expression that contains operands of different data types; also called *mixed mode expression.*

Module A self-contained collection of steps that solves a problem or subproblem; can contain both concrete and abstract steps.

Name precedence The precedence that a local identifier in a function has over a global identifier with the same name in any references that the function makes to that identifier; also called *name hiding.*

Named constant (symbolic constant) A location in memory, referenced by an identifier, that contains a data value that cannot be changed.

Named type A user-defined type whose declaration includes a type identifier that gives a name to the type.

Nonlocal identifier With respect to a given block, any identifier declared outside that block.

Object-oriented design (OOD) A technique for developing software in which the solution is expressed in terms of objects—self-contained entities composed of data and operations on that data.

Object-oriented programming (OOP) The use of data abstraction, inheritance, and dynamic binding to construct programs that are collections of interacting objects.

Object program The machine language version of a source program.

Observer An operation that allows us to observe the state of an instance of an ADT without changing it.

One-dimensional array A structured collection of components, all of the same type, that is given a single name. Each component (array element) is accessed by an index that indicates the component's position within the collection.

Operating system A set of programs that manages all of the computer's resources.

Out-of-bounds array index An index value that, in C++, is either less than 0 or greater than the array size minus 1.

Parameter A variable declared in a function heading; also called *formal argument* or *formal parameter.*

Peripheral device An input, output, or auxiliary storage device attached to a computer.

Pointer type A simple data type consisting of an unbounded set of values, each of which addresses or otherwise indicates the location of a variable of a given type. Among the operations defined on pointer variables are assignment and testing for equality.

Polymorphic operation An operation that has multiple meanings depending on the type of the object to which it is bound at run time.

Postcondition An assertion that should be true after a module has executed.

Precision The maximum number of significant digits.

Precondition An assertion that must be true before a module begins executing.

Programming Planning or scheduling the performance of a task or an event.

Programming language A set of rules, symbols, and special words used to construct a computer program.

Promotion (widening) The conversion of a value from a "lower" type to a "higher" type according to a programming language's precedence of data types.

Range of values The interval within which values of a numeric type must fall, specified in terms of the largest and smallest allowable values.

Record (structure, in C++) A structured data type with a fixed number of components that are accessed by name. The components may be heterogeneous (of different types).

Recursive algorithm A solution that is expressed in terms of (a) smaller instances of itself and (b) a base case.

Recursive call A function call in which the function being called is the same as the one making the call.

Recursive definition A definition in which something is defined in terms of smaller versions of itself.

Reference parameter A parameter that receives the location (memory address) of the caller's argument.

Reference type A simple data type consisting of an unbounded set of values, each of which is the address of a variable of a given type. The only operation defined on a reference variable is initialization, after which every appearance of the variable is implicitly dereferenced.

Representational error Arithmetic error that occurs when the precision of the true result of an arithmetic operation is greater than the precision of the machine.

Reserved word A word that has special meaning in C++; it cannot be used as a programmer-defined identifier.

Scope The region of program code where it is legal to reference (use) an identifier.

Scope rules The rules that determine where in the program an identifier may be accessed, given the point where that identifier is declared.

Self-documenting code Program code containing meaningful identifiers as well as judiciously used clarifying comments.

Semantics The set of rules that determines the meaning of instructions written in a programming language.

Shallow copy An operation that copies one class object to another without copying any pointed-to data.

Short-circuit (conditional) evaluation Evaluation of a logical expression in left-to-right order with evaluation stopping as soon as the final truth value can be determined.

Side effect Any effect of one function on another that is not a part of the explicitly defined interface between them.

Significant digits Those digits from the first nonzero digit on the left to the last nonzero digit on the right (plus any 0 digits that are exact).

Simple (atomic) data type A data type in which each value is atomic (indivisible).

Software Computer programs; the set of all programs available on a computer.

Software engineering The application of traditional engineering methodologies and techniques to the development of software.

Software piracy The unauthorized copying of software for either personal use or use by others.

Sorting Arranging the components of a list into order (for instance, words into alphabetical order or numbers into ascending or descending order).

Source program A program written in a high-level programming language.

Static binding The compile-time determination of which function to call for a particular object.

Static variable A variable for which memory remains allocated throughout the execution of the entire program.

Structured data type A data type in which each value is a collection of components and whose organization is characterized by the method used to access individual components. The allowable operations on a structured data type include the storage and retrieval of individual components.

Structured (procedural) programming The construction of programs that are collections of interacting functions or procedures.

Stub A dummy function that assists in testing part of a program. A stub has the same name and interface as a function that actually would be called by the part of the program being tested, but it is usually much simpler.

Switch expression The expression whose value determines which switch label is selected. It cannot be a floating-point or string expression.

Syntax The formal rules governing how valid instructions are written in a programming language.

Tail recursion A recursive algorithm in which no statements are executed after the return from the recursive call.

Termination condition The condition that causes a loop to be exited.

Test plan A document that specifies how a program is to be tested.

Test plan implementation Using the test cases specified in a test plan to verify that a program outputs the predicted results.

Testing the state of a stream The act of using a C++ stream object in a logical expression as if it were a Boolean variable; the result is `true` if the last I/O operation on that stream succeeded, and `false` otherwise.

Transformer An operation that builds a new value of the ADT, given one or more previous values of the type.

Two-dimensional array A collection of components, all of the same type, structured in two dimensions. Each component is accessed by a pair of indexes that represent the component's position in each dimension.

Type casting The explicit conversion of a value from one data type to another; also called type conversion.

Type coercion The implicit (automatic) conversion of a value from one data type to another.

Unary operator An operator that has just one operand.

Value parameter A parameter that receives a copy of the value of the corresponding argument.

Value-returning function A function that returns a single value to its caller and is invoked from within an expression.

Variable A location in memory, referenced by an identifier, that contains a data value that can be changed.

Virus A computer program that replicates itself, often with the goal of spreading to other computers without authorization, and possibly with the intent of doing harm.

Void function (procedure) A function that does not return a function value to its caller and is invoked as a separate statement.

Answers to Selected Exercises

Chapter 1 Exam Preparation Exercises

2. Input: Source code file (program in a high-level language such as C++)
   Output: Object code file (machine language program). Some compilers also output a listing (a copy of the program with error messages and other information inserted).

4. The following are peripheral devices: disk drive, magnetic tape drive, printer, CD-ROM drive, auxiliary storage, LCD screen, and mouse. The arithmetic/logic unit, the memory, and the control unit are not peripherals.

Chapter 1 Case Study Follow-Up

1. There are many valid solutions to this question. Here is one way of dividing the problem:

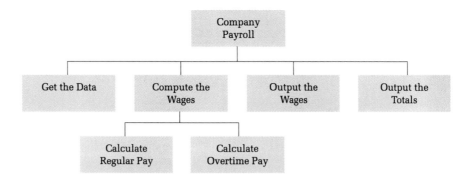

4. The remarks preceded by // are comments. The compiler ignores comments. They are included to help people (including the programmer) understand the program.

Chapter 2 Exam Preparation Exercises

1. a. invalid   b. valid   c. valid   d. invalid   e. valid   f. invalid   g. valid
   h. invalid

3. program—15; algorithm—14; compiler—3; identifier—1; compilation phase—12; execution phase—10; variable—11; constant—2; memory—13; syntax—6; semantics—8; block—7

4. a. reserved   b. programmer-defined   c. programmer-defined   d. reserved
   e. programmer-defined

7. a. s1 = blues2 = bird
   b. Result:bluebird
   c. Result: bluebird
   d. Result: blue bird

8. A rolling
   stone   ← One blank line

   gathers

                            ← Three blank lines

   nomoss
11. False
14. 1425B Elm St.
    Amaryllis, Iowa

Chapter 2   Programming Warm-up Exercises

2.
```
cout << "The moon" << endl;
cout << "is" << endl;
cout << "blue." << endl;
```
3.
```
string make;
string model;
string color;
string plateType;
char   classification;
```

Chapter 2   Case Study Follow-Up

1. In the line

   ```
   cout << "beautiful Panhard, Texas! Now " << first << "I realize"
   ```

   replace `Panhard, Texas` with `Wormwood, Massachusetts`.
3. To insert blank lines in the form letter, you would use additional `endl` manipulators
   after the line

   ```
   cout << "Argyle M. Sneeze" << endl << endl << endl << endl;
   ```

   For example, to add two more blank lines, the code would be

   ```
   cout << "Argyle M. Sneeze" << endl << endl << endl << endl;
   cout << endl << endl;
   cout << "* Measured around the circumference of the packing"
   ```

Chapter 3   Exam Preparation Exercises

3. a. Floating point: 13.3333 b. Integer: 2 c. Integer: 5 d. Floating point: 13.75
   e. Integer: −4 f. Integer: 1 g. Illegal: 10.0 / 3.0 is a floating-point expression, but the %
   operator requires integer operands.
6.
```
Cost is
300
Price is 30Cost is 300
Grade A costs
300
```
9. a. `iostream` b. `cstdlib` c. `cmath` d. `iostream` e. `iostream` and `iomanip`
14. False

Chapter 3   Programming Warm-up Exercises

1. Only one line needs to be changed. In the following declaration, change 10 to 15:

   ```
   const int LBS = 10;
   ```

2. `sum = n * (n + 1) / 2;`
5. `discriminant = sqrt(b * b - 4.0 * a * c);`
   `denominator = 2.0 * a;`
   `solution1 = (-b + discriminant) / denominator;`
   `solution2 = (-b - discriminant) / denominator;`
9. The expression is `sentence.find("res")`. The first occurrence of the string "res" occurs at position 12.

Chapter 3   Case Study Follow-Up

1. The named constants make the program easier to read and understand. Also, to change one of the constants, you only need to change one line (the constant declaration) instead of changing every occurrence of the literal constant throughout the program.
2. Declare a constant `ROUND_FACTOR` (defined to be equal to the desired rounding factor, such as 100.0 for hundredths) and replace every occurrence of 10.0 with `ROUND_FACTOR`.

Chapter 4   Exam Preparation Exercises

2. a. `int1` contains 17, `int2` contains 13, and `int3` contains 7.
   b. The leftover values remain waiting in the input stream. These values will be read by subsequent input statements (or they will be ignored if no more input statements are executed).
6. True
8. `123 147`
13. Errors in the program are as follows:
    - The declaration of `outData` is missing:

      ```
      ofstream outData;
      ```

    - The opening of the input file is missing:

      ```
      inData.open("myfile.dat");
      ```

    - The statement

      ```
      cin >> n;
      ```

      does not read from the input file. Change `cin` to `inData`.
14. With the corrected version of the program in Exercise 13, file stream `inData` will still contain the value 144 after the program is executed. File stream `outData` will contain 144, followed by a newline character.
18. False. Class member functions are invoked by using dot notation.

Chapter 4   Programming Warm-up Exercises

1. `cin >> ch1 >> ch2 >> ch3;`
3. `cin >> length1 >> height1 >> length2 >> height2;`
4. In the following, the value 100 is arbitrary. Any value greater than 4 will work.

```
cin.get(chr1);
cin.ignore(100, '\n');
cin.get(chr2);
cin.ignore(100, '\n');
cin.get(chr3);
cin.ignore(100, '\n');
```

8.
```
#include <iostream>
#include <fstream>

using namespace std;

int main()
{
    int     val1;
    int     val2;
    int     val3;
    int     val4;
    ifstream dataIn;
    ofstream resultsOut;

    dataIn.open("myinput.dat");
    resultsOut.open("myoutput.dat");
    dataIn >> val1 >> val2 >> val3 >> val4;
    resultsOut << val1 << val2 << val3 << val4 << endl;
    return 0;
}
```

10. Note that the problem statement said nothing about getting into the car, adjusting seatbelts, checking the mirror, or driving away. Presumably those tasks, along with starting the car, are subtasks of a larger design such as "Go to the store." Here we are concerned only with starting the car itself.

Main Module

> Ensure car won't roll.
> Disengage gears.
> Attempt ignition.

Ensure Car Won't Roll

> Engage parking brake.
> Turn wheels into curb.

Disengage Gears

> Push in clutch with left foot.
> Move gearshift to neutral.
> Release clutch.

Attempt Ignition
>Insert key into ignition slot.
>Turn key to ON position.
>Pump accelerator once.
>Turn key to START position.
>Release after engine catches or 5 seconds, whichever comes first.

Chapter 4 Case Study Follow-Up

1. Get Length and Width, Get Wood Cost, and Get Canvas Cost are input modules. Compute Dimensions and Costs is a computational module. Print Dimensions and Costs is an output module.

Chapter 5 Exam Preparation Exercises

2. a. No parentheses are needed. b. No parentheses are needed. c. No parentheses are needed. d. `!(q && q)`
6. a. 4 b. 2 c. 5 d. 3 e. 1
9. a. If-Then-Else b. If-Then c. If-Then d. If-Then-Else
10. The error message is printed because there is a semicolon after the right brace of a block (compound statement).
13. Yes

Chapter 5 Programming Warm-up Exercises

2. In the following statement, the outer parentheses are not required but are included for readability.

```
available = (numberOrdered <= (numberOnHand - numberReserved));
```

4. In the following statement, the outer parentheses are not required but are included for readability.

```
leftPage = (pageNumber % 2 == 0);
```

6.
```
if (year % 4 == 0)
    cout << year << " is a leap year." << endl;
else
{
    year = year + 4 - year % 4;
    cout << year << " is the next leap year." << endl;
}
```

7.
```
if (age > 64)
    cout << "Senior voter";
else if (age < 18)
    cout << "Under age";
else
    cout << "Regular voter";
```

9.
```
// This is a nonsense program
if (a > 0)
    if (a < 20)
    {
        cout << "A is in range." << endl;
        b = 5;
    }
    else
    {
        cout << "A is too large." << endl;
        b = 3;
    }
else
    cout << "A is too small." << endl;
cout << "All done." << endl;
```

Chapter 5   Case Study Follow-Up

2. No. The data is only valid if each test score is nonnegative. Modifying the code to test whether the sum of the test scores is nonnegative will not catch the following invalid case: test1 = 100, test2 = 80, test3 = −20.

4. To input and compute the average of four scores, one control structure would need to be changed. The statement

```
if (test1 < 0 || test2 < 0 || test3 < 0)
    dataOK = false;
else
    dataOK = true;
```

would need to be replaced with

```
if (test1 < 0 || test2 < 0 || test3 < 0 || test4 < 0)
    dataOK = false;
else
    dataOK = true;
```

Note that the program would require other changes, but this is the only control structure that would need to be changed.

Chapter 6   Exam Preparation Exercises

3.
```
number = 1;
while (number < 11)
{
    cout << number << endl;
    number++;
}
```

4. Six iterations are performed.

9. Telephone numbers read in as integers have many different values that could be used as sentinels. In the United States, a standard telephone number is a positive seven-digit integer (ignoring area codes) and cannot start with 0, 1, 411, or 911. Therefore, a reasonable sentinel may be negative, greater than 9999999, or less than 2000000.

11. a. (1) Change < to <=. (2) Change 1 to 0. (3) Change 20 to 21.
    b. Changes (1) and (3) make count range from 1 through 21. Change (2) makes count range from 0 through 20.

Chapter 6   Programming Warm-up Exercises

1.
```
dangerous = false;
while ( !dangerous )
{
    cin >> pressure;
    if (pressure > 510.0)
        dangerous = true;
}
```

or

```
dangerous = false;
while ( !dangerous )
{
    cin >> pressure;
    dangerous = (pressure > 510.0);
}
```

2.
```
count28 = 0;
loopCount = 1;
while (loopCount <= 100)
{
    inputFile >> number;
    if (number == 28)
        count28++;
    loopCount++;
}
```

5.
```
positives = 0;
negatives = 0;
cin >> number;
while (cin)          // While NOT EOF...
{
    if (number > 0)
        positives++;
    else if (number < 0)
        negatives++;
    cin >> number;
}
cout << "Number of positive numbers: " << positives << endl;
cout << "Number of negative numbers: " << negatives << endl;
```

6.  ```
    sum = 0;
    evenInt = 16;
    while (evenInt <= 26)
    {
        sum = sum + evenInt;
        evenInt = evenInt + 2;
    }
    ```

7.  ```
    hour = 1;
    minute = 0;
    am = true;
    done = false;
    while ( !done )
    {
        cout << hour << ':';
        if (minute < 10)
            cout << '0';
        cout << minute;
        if (am)
            cout << " A.M." << endl;
        else
            cout << " P.M." << endl;

        minute++;
        if (minute > 59)
        {
            minute = 0;
            hour++;
            if (hour == 13)
                hour = 1;
            else if (hour == 12)
                am = !am;
        }
        if (hour == 1 && minute == 0 && am)
            done = true;
    }
    ```

Chapter 6   Case Study Follow-Up

1. a. In the While loop, check for a negative income amount before processing it:

    ```
    incFile >> sex >> amount;
    femaleCount = 0;
    femaleSum = 0.0;
    maleCount = 0;
    maleSum = 0.0;

    while (incFile)
    {
        cout << "Sex: " << sex << " Amount: " << amount << endl;
    ```

```
        if (amount < 0.0)                    // Check for invalid salary
            cout << "** Bad data--negative salary **" << endl;
        else
            if (sex == 'F')
            {
                femaleCount++;
                femaleSum = femaleSum + amount;
            }
            else
            {
                maleCount++;
                maleSum = maleSum + amount;
            }
        incFile >> sex >> amount;
    }
```

2. Set 1:

   Empty file

   Set 2 (no males) :

   F 30000

   Set 3 (no females):

   M 30000

   Set 4 (invalid sex codes and income values):

   F 64000

   R 20000

   M 40000

   F −15000

   M 50000

   G 30000

   M −30000

   F 20000

Chapter 7   Exam Preparation Exercises

4. 5 3 13
   3 3 9
   9 12 30
7. For passing by value, parts (a) through (g) are all valid. For passing by reference, only parts (a) and (c) are valid.
8. 13571 (the memory address of the variable widgets).
10. The answers are 12 10 3
11. Variables in main just before Change is called: a = 10 and b = 7. Variables in Change at the moment control enters the function (before any statements are executed): x = 10, y = 7, and the value of b is undefined. Variables in main after return from Change: a = 10 (x in Change is a value parameter, so the argument a is not modified) and b = 17.

Chapter 7 Programming Warm-up Exercises

2.  ```
    void RocketSimulation( /* in */      float   thrust,
                           /* inout */ float&  weight,
                           /* in */      int     timeStep,
                           /* in */      int     totalTime,
                           /* out */     float&  velocity,
                           /* out */     bool&   outOfFuel )
    ```

5.  ```
    void Halve( /* inout */ int& firstNumber,
                /* inout */ int& secondNumber )

    // Precondition:
    //      firstNumber and secondNumber are assigned
    // Postcondition:
    //      firstNumber == firstNumber@entry / 2
    //   && secondNumber == secondNumber@entry / 2

    {
        ⋮
    }
    ```

7. a. Function definition:

    ```
    void ScanHeart( /* out */ bool& normal )

    // Postcondition:
    //      normal == true, if a normal heart rate (60-80) was input
    //                      before EOF occurred
    //             == false, otherwise
    {
        int heartRate;

        cin >> heartRate;
        while ((heartRate < 60 || heartRate > 80) && cin)
            cin >> heartRate;

        // At loop exit, either (heartRate >= 60 && heartRate <= 80)
        // or EOF occurred

        normal = (heartRate >= 60 && heartRate <= 80);
    }
    ```

    b. Function invocation:

    ```
    ScanHeart(normal);
    ```

8. a. Function definition:

    ```
    void Rotate( /* inout */ int& firstValue,
                 /* inout */ int& secondValue,
                 /* inout */ int& thirdValue  )
    ```

```
// This function takes three parameters and returns their values
// in a shifted order

// Precondition:
//      firstValue, secondValue, and thirdValue are assigned
// Postcondition:
//      firstValue == secondValue@entry
//   && secondValue == thirdValue@entry
//   && thirdValue == firstValue@entry

{
    int temp;      // Temporary holding variable

    // Save value of first parameter

    temp = firstValue;

    // Shift values of next two parameters

    firstValue = secondValue;
    secondValue = thirdValue;

    // Replace value of final parameter with saved value

    thirdValue = temp;
}
```

b. Test program:

```
#include <iostream>

using namespace std;

void Rotate( int&, int&, int& );

int main()
{
    int int1;      // First input value
    int int2;      // Second input value
    int int3;      // Third input value

    cout << "Enter three values: ";
    cin >> int1 >> int2 >> int3;

    cout << "Before: " << int1 << ' ' << int2 << ' '
        << int3 << endl;
    Rotate(int1, int2, int3);
    cout << "After: " << int1 << ' ' << int2 << ' '
        << int3 << endl;
    return 0;
}
// The Rotate function, as above, goes here
```

Chapter 7 Case Study Follow-Up

2.  ```
    void PrintData( /* in */ int    deptID,
                    /* in */ int    storeNum,
                    /* in */ float  deptSales )
    {
        string bar;     // Bar of asterisks

        cout << setw(12) << "Dept " << deptID << endl;
        cout << setw(3) << storeNum << "      ";
        bar = BarOfAsterisks(deptSales);
        cout << bar << endl;

    }
    ```

3. The GetData function would have the following statement added after the input statement that reads in numDays:

    ```
    if (numDays < 0)
        cout << "** Data error--number of days for dept. " << deptId
             << " is negative **" << endl;
    ```

Chapter 8 Exam Preparation Exercises

1. True
5. 1 1
    1 2
    1 3
7. Yes
11. It is risky to use a reference parameter as a parameter of a value-returning function because it provides a mechanism for side effects to escape from the function. A value-returning function usually is designed to return a single result (the function value), which is then used in the expression that called the function. If a value-returning function declares a reference parameter and modifies the parameter (hence, the caller's argument), that function is returning more than one result, which is not obvious from the way the function is invoked. (However, an I/O stream variable *must* be declared as a reference parameter, even in a value-returning function.)

Chapter 8 Programming Warm-up Exercises

3.  ```
    bool NearlyEqual( /* in */ float num1,
                      /* in */ float num2,
                      /* in */ float difference )
    ```
5.  ```
    float CompassHeading( /* in */ float trueCourse,
                          /* in */ float windCorrAngle,
                          /* in */ float variance,
                          /* in */ float deviation    )


    // Precondition:
    //      All parameters are assigned
    // Postcondition:
    //      Function value == trueCourse + windCorrAngle +
    //                        variance + deviation
    ```
    ```

```
{
    return trueCourse + windCorrAngle + variance + deviation;
}
```

8. Function body for Hypotenuse function (assuming the header file cmath has been included in order to access the sqrt function):

```
{
    return sqrt(side1*side1 + side2*side2);
}
```

13. Below, the type of costPerOunce and the function return type are float so that the cost can be expressed in terms of dollars and cents (e.g., 1.23 means $1.23). These types could be int if the cost were expressed in terms of cents only (e.g., 123 means $1.23).

```
float Postage( /* in */ int    pounds,
               /* in */ int    ounces,
               /* in */ float costPerOunce )

// Precondition:
//    pounds >= 0  &&  ounces >= 0  &&  costPerOunce >= 0.0
// Postcondition:
//    Function value == (pounds * 16 + ounces) * costPerOunce

{
    return (pounds * 16 + ounces) * costPerOunce;
}
```

Chapter 8   Case Study Follow-Up

3. Only the Get2Digits function needs to be modified. The test for whether the second character is a slash needs to be changed from

```
if (secondChar == '/')
```

to

```
if (secondChar == '/' || secondChar == '-')
```

4. Change the body of GetData so that it begins as follows:

```
{
    bool badData;   // True if an input value is invalid

    badData = true;
    while (badData)
    {
        cout << "Enter the number of crew (1 or 2)." << endl;
        cin >> crew;
        badData = (crew < 1 || crew > 2);
        if (badData)
            cout << "Invalid number of crew members." << endl;
    }
```

```
            badData = true;
            while (badData)
            {
                cout << "Enter the number of passengers (0 through 8)."
                    << endl;
                cin >> passengers;
                badData = (passengers < 0 || passengers > 8);
                if (badData)
                    cout << "Invalid number of passengers." << endl;
            }
```

Continue in this manner to validate the closet weight (0–160 pounds), baggage weight (0–525 pounds), and amount of fuel loaded (10–565 gallons).

Chapter 9   Exam Preparation Exercises

2. False
4. False
6. MaryJoeAnneWhoops!
9. 1
13. False

Chapter 9   Programming Warm-up Exercises

```
1.  switch (grade)
    {
        case 'A' : sum = sum + 4;
                   break;
        case 'B' : sum = sum + 3;
                   break;
        case 'C' : sum = sum + 2;
                   break;
        case 'D' : sum++;
                   break;
        case 'F' : cout << "Student is on probation" << endl;
                   break;     // Not required
    }
2.  switch (grade)
    {
        case 'A' : sum = sum + 4;
                   break;
        case 'B' : sum = sum + 3;
                   break;
        case 'C' : sum = sum + 2;
                   break;
        case 'D' : sum++;
                   break;
        case 'F' : cout << "Student is on probation" << endl;
                   break;
```

```
                    break;     // Not required
    }
```

5.
```
   do
   {
       cout << "Enter 1, 2, or 3: ";
       cin >> response;
   } while (response < 1 || response > 3);
```

6.
```
   cin >> ch;
   while (cin)
   {
       cout << ch;
       cin >> ch;
   }
```

10. This solution returns proper results only if the precondition shown in the comments is true. Note that it returns the correct result for $base^0$, which is 1.

```
int Power( /* in */ int base,
           /* in */ int exponent )


// Precondition:
//      base is assigned  &&  exponent >= 0
//   && (base to the exponent power) <= INT_MAX
// Postcondition:
//      Function value == base to the exponent power


{
    int result = 1;      // Holds intermediate powers of base
    int count;           // Loop control variable

    for (count = 1; count <= exponent; count++)
        result = result * base;
    return result;
}
```

Chapter 9   Case Study Follow-Up

1.
```
void GetYesOrNo( /* out */ char& response )    // User response char
{
    cin >> response;
    while (response != 'y' && response != 'n')
    {
        cout << "Please type y or n: ";
        cin >> response;
    }
}
```

```
void GetOneAmount( /* out */ float& amount )    // Rainfall amount
                                                // for one month
{
    cin >> amount;
    while (amount < 0.0)
    {
        cout << "Amount cannot be negative. Enter again: ";
        cin >> amount;
    }
}
```

Chapter 10   Exam Preparation Exercises

3. a. `sumOfSquares += x * x;`
   b. `count--;`
      or
      `--count;`
   c. `k = (n > 8) ? 32 : 15 * n;`
5. Notice that
   the character \ is a backslash.
6. a. 1.4E+12 (to 10 digits)   b. 100.0 (to 10 digits)   c. 3.2E+5 (to 10 digits)
9. a. valid   b. invalid   c. invalid   d. valid
12. False. The angle brackets (< >) should be quotation marks.

Chapter 10   Programming Warm-up Exercises

2. `cout << "Hello\tThere\n\n\n\"Ace\"";`
6. `enum CourseType {CS101, CS200, CS210, CS350, CS375, CS441};`
8. `enum DayType {MONDAY, TUESDAY, WEDNESDAY, THURSDAY, FRIDAY};`
9.

```
DayType CharToDay( /* in */ char ch1,
                   /* in */ char ch2 )

// Precondition:
//      ch1=='M' OR ch1=='W' OR ch1=='F' OR
//      (ch1=='T' && ch2=='U') OR (ch1=='T' && ch2=='H')
// Postcondition:
//      Function value == MONDAY, if ch1=='M'
//                     == TUESDAY, if (ch1=='T' && ch2=='U')
//                     == WEDNESDAY, if ch1=='W'
//                     == THURSDAY, if (ch1=='T' && ch2=='H')
//                     == FRIDAY, if ch1=='F'

{
    switch (ch1)
    {
        case 'M' : return MONDAY;
        case 'T' : if (ch2 == 'U')
                        return TUESDAY;
                   else
                        return THURSDAY;
```

```
                    case 'W' : return WEDNESDAY;
                    case 'F' : return FRIDAY;
                }
        }
```

Chapter 10   Case Study Follow-Up

5. The readability of the program is enhanced because we are using the actual values rather than char codes for the plays.

7. The data used in the book is a good data set. It tests each combination of 'R', 'P', and 'S' at least once and has an error in each data file. However, a comprehensive test plan must include data sets to test the following situations:

   - Player A wins.
   - Player B wins.
   - The game is a tie.
   - There is an error in both files at the same position.
   - fileA does not have enough plays.
   - fileB does not have enough plays.
   - Neither file has enough plays.

   Your test plan should include the data used for each case and the expected results.

Chapter 11   Exam Preparation Exercises

2.
```
struct RecType
{
    int    numDependents;
    float  salary;
    bool   hasMajorMed;
};
```

7. a. SomeClass and int b. Func1, Func2, Func3, and someInt c. object1 and object2 d. Func1, Func2, and Func3 e. Func1 and Func3 f. part (ii)

8. True

11. a. Only myprog.cpp must be recompiled. b. All of the object (.obj) files must be relinked. c. Only file2.cpp and file3.cpp must be recompiled. d. All of the object (.obj) files must be relinked.

Chapter 11   Programming Warm-up Exercises

1. a.
```
enum YearType {FRESHMAN, SOPHOMORE, JUNIOR, SENIOR};
enum SexType {M, F};

struct PersonType
{
    string    name;
    string    ssNumber;
    YearType  year;
    float     gpa;
    SexType   sex;
};
```

b.

```
PersonType person;
    ⋮
cout << person.name << endl;
cout << person.ssNumber << endl;
switch (person.year)
{
    FRESHMAN   : cout << "Freshman" << endl;
                 break;
    SOPHOMORE : cout << "Sophomore" << endl;
                 break;
    JUNIOR     : cout << "Junior" << endl;
                 break;
    SENIOR     : cout << "Senior" << endl;
}
cout << person.gpa << endl;
if (person.sex == M)
    cout << "Male" << endl;
else
    cout << "Female" << endl;
```

3.
```
enum YearType {FRESHMAN, SOPHOMORE, JUNIOR, SENIOR};
struct DateType
{
    int month;
    int year;
};

struct StudentType
{
    string    name;
    long      studentID;
    int       hoursToDate;
    int       coursesToDate;
    DateType  firstEnrolled;
    YearType  year;
    float     gpa;
};
```

5. a. `if ( !time1.Equal(time2) )`
      `n = 1;`
   b. `if (time1.LessThan(time2) || time1.Equal(time2))`
      `n = 5;`
   c. `if (time2.LessThan(time1))`
      `n = 8;`
   d. `if ( !time1.LessThan(time2) )`
      `n = 5;`
      or
      `if (time2.LessThan(time1) || time2.Equal(time1))`
      `n = 5;`

7. Function specification (within the `TimeType` class declaration):

```
void WriteAmPm() const;
    // Postcondition:
    //      Time has been output in 12-hour form
    //           HH:MM:SS AM   or   HH:MM:SS PM
```

Function definition (omitting the postcondition to save space):

```
void TimeType::WriteAmPm() const
{
    bool am;        // True if AM should be printed
    int  tempHrs;   // Value of hours to be printed

    am = (hrs <= 11);
    if (hrs == 0)
        tempHrs = 12;
    else if (hrs >= 13)
        tempHrs = hrs - 12;
    else
        tempHrs = hrs;

    if (tempHrs < 10)
        cout << '0';
    cout << tempHrs << ':';
    if (mins < 10)
        cout << '0';
    cout << mins << ':';
    if (secs < 10)
        cout << '0';
    cout << secs;
    if (am)
        cout << " AM";
    else
        cout << " PM";
}
```

8. Function specification (within the `TimeType` class declaration):

```
long Minus( /* in */ TimeType time2 ) const;
    // Precondition:
    //      This time and time2 represent times in the same day
    // Postcondition:
    //      Function value == (this time) - time2, in seconds
```

Function definition (omitting the precondition and postcondition to save space):

```
long TimeType::Minus( /* in */ TimeType time2 ) const
{
    long thisTimeInSecs;   // This time in seconds since midnight
    long time2InSecs;      // time2 in seconds since midnight
```

```
                    // Using 3600 seconds per hour and 60 seconds per minute...

                    thisTimeInSecs = long(hrs)*3600 + long(mins)*60 + long(secs);
                    time2InSecs = long(time2.hrs)*3600 + long(time2.mins)*60 +
                                  long(time2.secs);
                    return thisTimeInSecs - time2InSecs;
                }
```

Chapter 11 Case Study Follow-Up

1. The class constructor DateType() is a constructor operation. Set and Increment are transformers. Month, Day, Year, Print, and ComparedTo are observers.

6. Assuming a variable areaCode is of type int, one solution is to print a leading zero if the area code is less than 100:

```
if (areaCode < 100)
    cout << '0';
cout << areaCode;
```

Another solution is to declare an area code to be a string rather than an int, thereby reading or printing exactly three characters each time I/O takes place.

Chapter 12 Exam Preparation Exercises

1. True
5. a. enum BirdType {CARDINAL, BLUEJAY, HUMMINGBIRD, ROBIN};
   b. int sightings[4];
7. 1 3 -2
   17 6 11
   4 2 2
   19 14 5
   11 15 -4

   52 40 12

9. sample [0] [1] [2] [3] [4] [5] [6] [7]

10	9	8	7	6	5	4	3

14. a. hierarchical record   b. record   c. record   d. array of records   e. array   f. array of hierarchical records   g. array of records
18. a. valid   b. valid   c. invalid   d. valid   e. invalid   f. invalid
20. a. True   b. False   c. True   d. True

Chapter 12 Programming Warm-up Exercises

1.
```
void Initialize( /* out */ bool failing[] )

// Postcondition:
//     failing[0..NUM_STUDS-1] == false

{
```

```
          int index;    // Loop control and index variable

          for (index = 0; index < NUM_STUDS; index++)
              failing[index] = false;
      }
```

3.  ```
    void SetPassing( /* inout */      bool passing[],
                     /* in */    const int  score[]   )
    ```

    ```
    // Precondition:
    //     score[0..NUM_STUDS-1] are assigned
    // Postcondition:
    //     For all i, where 0 <= i <= NUM_STUDS-1,
    //         IF score[i] >= 60, THEN passing[i] == true

    {
        int index;    // Loop control and index variable

        for (index = 0; index < NUM_STUDS; index++)
            if (score[index] >= 60)
                passing[index] = true;
    }
    ```

8. Below, assume the input will never exceed 500 parts.

    ```
    const int MAX_PARTS = 500;

    struct PartType
    {
        int    number;
        float cost;
    };

    PartType part[MAX_PARTS];
    int      count = 0;

    cin >> part[count].number >> part[count].cost;
    while (cin)
    {
        count++;
        cin >> part[count].number >> part[count].cost;
    }
    ```

11. ```
    void Copy( /* in */  const TwoDimType data,
               /* out */       TwoDimType data2 )
    ```

    ```
    // Precondition:
    //     data[0..NUM_ROWS-1][0..NUM_COLS-1] are assigned
    // Postcondition:
    //     data2[0..NUM_ROWS-1][0..NUM_COLS-1] ==
    //         corresponding elements of array "data"
    ```

```
        {
            int row;        // Loop control and index variable
            int col;        // Loop control and index variable

            for (row = 0; row < NUM_ROWS; row++)
                for (col = 0; col < NUM_COLS; col++)
                    data2[row][col] = data[row][col];
        }
```

16. Below, assume ArrayType is a two-dimensional integer array type with NUM_ROWS rows and NUM_COLS columns.

```
int RowSum( /* in */ const ArrayType arr,
            /* in */       int         whichRow,
            /* in */       int         colsFilled )

// Precondition:
//     colsFilled <= NUM_COLS  &&  whichRow < NUM_ROWS
//  && arr[whichRow][0..colsFilled-1] are assigned
// Postcondition:
//     Function value == arr[whichRow][0] + ...
//                              + arr[whichRow][colsFilled-1]

{
    int col;        // Loop control and index variable
    int sum = 0;    // Accumulating sum

    for (col = 0; col < colsFilled; col++)
        sum = sum + arr[whichRow][col];
    return sum;
}
```

Chapter 12 Case Study Follow-Up

1. No. If firstList were declared to be a const parameter, the compiler would not allow the function body to modify the array. Specifically, the statement

```
firstList[counter] = number;
```

would generate a compile-time error.

5. Only two lines in the program need to be changed—the constant declarations for NUM_PRECINCTS and NUM_CANDIDATES:

```
const int NUM_PRECINCTS = 12;
const int NUM_CANDIDATES = 3;
```

Chapter 13 Exam Preparation Exercises

6. a typedef char NameType[41];
   b. NameType oneName;
   c. NameType employeeName[100];

7.   a. valid b. valid c. invalid d. valid e. valid f. invalid g. invalid h. valid
9.   a. valid b. invalid c. valid d. invalid e. valid f. invalid g. valid

Chapter 13   Programming Warm-up Exercises

2.
```
int List::Occurrences( /* in */ ItemType item )

// Precondition:
//      item is assigned
// Postcondition:
//      Function value == number of occurrences of value "item"
//                        in data[0..length-1]

{
    int index;         // Loop control and index variable
    int counter = 0;   // Number of occurrences of item

    for (index = 0; index < length; index++)
        if (data[index] == item)
            counter++;
    return counter;
}
```

8. The `SortedList::BinSearch` function remains the same until the last If statement. This statement should be replaced with the following:

```
if (found)
    position = middle;
else
    position = first;
```

Also, the function postcondition should read as follows:

```
//      IF item is in list
//          found == true  &&  data[position] contains item
//      ELSE
//          found == false  &&  position is where item belongs
```

10.
```
void SortedList::Component(
        /* in */   int       pos,      // Desired position
        /* out */  ItemType& item,     // Item retrieved
        /* out */  bool&     valid )   // True if pos is valid

// Precondition:
//      pos is assigned
// Postcondition:
//      IF 0 <= pos < length
//          valid == true
//        && item == data[pos]
//      ELSE
//          valid == false
```

```
        {
            valid = (pos >= 0 && pos < length);
            if (valid)
                item = data[pos];
        }
```

Chapter 13   Case Study Follow-Up

3. Using a binary search, the number of loop iterations for an unsuccessful search of 200 items is 8 (because $\log_2 128 = 7$ and $\log_2 256 = 8$). Using a sequential search of a sorted list, the worst-case number of loop iterations is 200, the best case is 1 iteration, and the average is 100.

Chapter 14   Exam Preparation Exercises

2. False
4. *Class Abc:*
   a. The private data members are `alpha` and `beta`.
   b. Functions `DoThis` and `DoThat` can reference `alpha` and `beta` directly.
   c. Functions `DoThis` and `DoThat` can invoke each other directly.
   d. Clients can invoke `DoThis`.
   Class Xyz:
   a. The private data members are `alpha`, `beta`, and `gamma`.
   b. Function `TryIt` can reference only `gamma` directly.
   c. Function `TryIt` can invoke the parent class's `DoThis` function directly. The syntax for the function call is `Abc::DoThis()`.
   d. Clients can invoke `DoThis` and `TryIt`.
7. a. Member slicing occurs, and static binding is used. The output is

      x

      y

   b. Member slicing does not occur, and dynamic binding is used. The output is

      x

      yz

   c. Member slicing does not occur, but static binding is used. The output is

      x

      y

9. a. False   b. True   c. False

Chapter 14   Programming Warm-up Exercises

2.
```
   #include <cmath>    // For sqrt()
     ⋮
   float Line::Length() const

   // Postcondition:
   //     Function value == length of this line
```

```
    {
        float diffX;    // Difference in x coordinates
        float diffY;    // Difference in y coordinates

        diffX = startPt.X_Coord() - endPt.X_Coord();
        diffY = startPt.Y_Coord() - endPt.Y_Coord();
        return sqrt(diffX*diffX + diffY*diffY);
    }
```

3.
```
    class InterAddress : public Address
    {
    public:
        void Write() const;
            // Postcondition:
            //      Address has been output

        InterAddress( /* in */ string newStreet,
                      /* in */ string newCity,
                      /* in */ string newState,
                      /* in */ string newZip,
                      /* in */ string newCountry );
            // Precondition:
            //      All parameters are assigned
            // Postcondition:
            //      Class object is constructed with private data
            //      initialized by the incoming parameters
    private:
        string country;
    };
```

7.
```
    class TimeAndDay
    {
    public:
        void Set( /* in */ int hours,
                  /* in */ int minutes,
                  /* in */ int seconds,
                  /* in */ int month,
                  /* in */ int day,
                  /* in */ int year    );
            // Precondition:
            //      0 <= hours <= 23  &&   0 <= minutes <= 59
            //   && 0 <= seconds <= 59  &&  1 <= month <= 12
            //   && 1 <= day <= maximum no. of days in month
            //   && year > 1582
            // Postcondition:
            //      Time and date are set according to the
            //      incoming parameters

        void Increment();
            // Postcondition:
```

```
        //        Time has been advanced by one second, with
        //        23:59:59 wrapping around to 0:0:0
        //     && IF new time is 0:0:0
        //              Date has been advanced to the next day

     void Write() const;
        // Postcondition:
        //        Time and date have been output in the form
        //           HH:MM:SS   month day, year

     TimeAndDay();
        // Postcondition:
        //        Class object is constructed with a time of 0:0:0
        //        and a date of January 1, 1583
  private:
     TimeType time;
     DateType date;
  };
```

Chapter 15   Exam Preparation Exercises

4. The `delete` operation releases the space reserved for a dynamic variable back to the system.
5. a. inaccessible object   b. dangling pointer   c. dangling pointer   d. neither   e. inaccessible object
7. The correct answer is (a).
11.
```
Constructor executing
Private data is 1
Destructor executing
Constructor executing
Private data is 2
Destructor executing
Constructor executing
Private data is 3
Destructor executing
```
13. The correct answer is (e).

Chapter 15   Programming Warm-up Exercises

1.   a. `char* p = &ch;`
     b. `long* q = arr;`
        or
        `long* q = &arr[0];`
     c. `BoxType* r = &box;`

2.   a. `*p = '@';`
     b. `*q = 959263;`
     c. `r->length = 12;`   `(*r).length = 12;`
        `r->width = 14;`   *or*   `(*r).width = 14;`
        `r->height = 5;`   `(*r).height = 5;`

6.  ```
    if (*p < *q)
        smaller = *p;
    else
        smaller = *q;
    delete p;
    delete q;
    ```

10. `AddAndIncr(m, &n, &theirSum);`

Chapter 15   Case Study Follow-Up

4. Change the function headings for `ValueAt` and `Store` so that the data types match those in the function prototypes. The bodies of `ValueAt`, `Store`, and the destructor do not need to be changed. Change the bodies of the constructor, copy-constructor, and `CopyFrom` functions by replacing

    ```
    arr = new int[size];
    ```

    with

    ```
    arr = new float[size];
    ```

Chapter 16   Exam Preparation Exercises

2. True
5. Dynamic data structures can expand and contract during program execution.
8. a. array   b. array   c. dynamic linked list

Chapter 16   Programming Warm-up Exercises

1. Function specification (within the `SortedList2` class declaration):

    ```
    int Length() const;
        // Postcondition:
        //      Function value == number of components in list
    ```

    Function definition:

    ```
    int SortedList2::Length() const
    {
        NodePtr currPtr = head;     // Loop control pointer
        int     count = 0;          // Number of nodes in list

        while (currPtr != NULL)
        {
            count++;
            currPtr = currPtr->link;
        }
        return count;
    }
    ```
    ```

5. The function heading is

```
void SortedList2::CopyFrom( /* in */ SortedList2 otherList )
```

(with a corresponding function prototype in the class declaration). The function body begins by deallocating the linked list pointed to by the current class object:

```
ComponentType temp;    // Temporary variable

while ( !IsEmpty() )
    DeleteTop(temp);
```

After this deallocation, the rest of the body is identical to the body of the copy-constructor.

Chapter 16   Case Study Follow-Up

1. a. The functions `Length`, `CardAt`, `InsertTop`, `RemoveTop`, `Shuffle`, `Recreate`, and the class constructor are public members of the `CardDeck` class.
    b. The variables `head` and `listLength` and the function `Merge` are private members of the `CardDeck` class.

Chapter 17   Exam Preparation Exercises

2. False. Both void functions and value-returning functions can be recursive.
4. $F(4) = 1$, $F(6) = -1$, and $F(5)$ is undefined.
6. A selection control structure—either an If or a Switch statement
9. The run-time stack

Chapter 17   Programming Warm-up Exercises

1.
```
int F( /* in */ int n )
{
    if (n == 0 || n == 1)
        return 1;
    else
        return F(n - 1) + F(n - 2);
}
```

3.
```
void DoubleSpace( /* inout */ ifstream& inFile )
{
    char ch;

    inFile.get(ch);
    while (inFile)               // While not EOF...
    {
        cout << ch;
        if (ch == '\n')
            cout << endl;
        inFile.get(ch);
    }
}
```

8. In the If statement of the RevPrint function, change the sequence

```
RevPrint(head->link);                          // Recursive call
cout << head->component << endl;
```

to

```
cout << head->component << endl;
RevPrint(head->link);                          // Recursive call
```

and reword the function postcondition accordingly.

Chapter 17 Case Study Follow-Up

2. 0, the index of the first array element. The recursive algorithm starts at the fifth element but recursively calls itself until it reaches the first element, which is stored into minSoFar; then it compares minSoFar to the second element, and so on.

< > (angle brackets), 79, 542
{ } (braces). *See* Braces ({ })
: (colon). *See* Colon (:)
, (comma). *See* Comma (,)
- (minus sign). *See* Minus sign (-)
. (period). *See* Period (.)
:: (scope resolution operator), 79, 611
; (semicolon). *See* Semicolon (;)
/ (slash). *See* Slash (/)
& (ampersand). *See* Ampersand (&)
' (apostrophe). *See* Apostrophe (')
* (asterisk). *See* Asterisk (*)
\ (backslash)
    for escape sequences, 514
    in output statements, 71
[ ] (brackets), 665, 667, 686, 877–878
^ (caret), 503
" (double quotation mark). *See* Double quotation mark (")
= (equal sign). *See* Equal sign (=)
! (exclamation point). *See* Exclamation point (!)
> (greater-than symbol). *See* Greater-than symbol (>)
< (less-than symbol). *See* Less-than symbol (<)
( ) (parentheses). *See* Parentheses ( )
% (percent sign). *See* Percent sign (%)
+ (plus sign). *See* Plus sign (+)
# (pound sign), 78, 817
? (question mark), 507–508
~ (tilde)
    for bitwise operations, 503
    for destructors, 621, 894
_ (underscore), 52, 56, 65
| (vertical bar). *See* Vertical bar (|)

\a escape sequence, 514
abs function, 121
Absolute error, 526
Absolute values
    conditional statements for, 508
    for floating-point number comparisons, 228
Abstract assertions, 749, 960
Abstract data types (ADTs), 592–606. *See also* Classes
    lists as, 744–748, 947
    operations for, 595–596
Abstract object, 831
Abstract steps, 182
Abstraction
    control, 434
    data, 590–592
    in software design, 592
Abstraction barriers, 604–606
Access
    to array components, 667–670, 673–676, 686–687, 689
    to class members, 598–600, 604–606, 810–811

    to identifiers. *See* Scope
    with inheritance, 810–811
    to standard library functions, 409
    to structure members, 582–583, 588
Active data structures, 597–598
Active error detection, 566
Activity program, 347–348, 362–363
Actor language, 803
Actual parameters, 119, 334
Addition, 108
    in assignment operators, 502
    precedence of, 112
Address, parameter passing by, 353
Address-of operator (&), 870, 887, 889–890
Addresses, 58, 868
    as argument, 676–678, 695
    data types for, 868
    as parameters, 344, 346
    pointer types. *See* Pointers
    reference type for, 887
Aggregate operations, 671–673
Airplane weight and balance case study, 435–447
Alert, escape sequence for, 514
ALGOL language, 354
Algorithms, 4–6. *See also* Problem-solving techniques
    for company payroll, 36–40
    efficiency of, 302–306
    implementing, 7
    recursive. *See* Recursion
    walk-through, 6, 249–253
Allocating
    dynamic data, 879–882
    memory for variables, 338, 399
    nodes, 948–956
Alphabetizing. *See* Sorting
ALU (arithmetic/logic unit), 16, 17
Ampersand (&)
    as address-of operator, 870, 887, 889–890
    in assertion comments, 357
    for bit manipulation, 223, 503, 505, 506
    in AND operator (&&), 220–223, 226, 227, 357, 506, 509
    precedence of, 226, 509
    for reference parameters, 344, 346
Analogies for problem-solving, 31–32
Analysis and specification problem-solving phase, 177
Analytical Engine, 331–332, 410
Ancestors of classes, 806
AND operator (&&), 506
    in assertion comments, 357
    in logical expressions, 220–223, 227
    precedence of, 226, 509
Angle brackets (< >), 79, 542
Anonymous data types, 541–542, 586

Apostrophe (')
    for char constants, 59, 63, 513–514
    escape sequence for, 514
Application domain in object-oriented design, 827
Area program, 552–554
Area under curves case study, 547–555
Argument list, 119, 352, 618, 620
Arguments, 334–335. *See also* Parameters
    arrays as, 672–673, 676–678, 695–699
    in constructors, 618, 620
    objects as, 823
    passing, 162, 353–354, 546
    reference variables as, 888–889
Arithmetic
    expressions, 112–116, 544–545
    floating-point numbers and, 523–524
    mixing data types in, 113–116
    operators for, 107–110
    with pointers, 879
    precedence rules in, 112–113
    type coercion in, 113–116, 544–545
Arithmetic/logic unit (ALU), 16, 17
Arranging. *See* Sorting
Array index, 946
Arrays, 664. *See also* One-dimensional arrays; Two-
    dimensional arrays
    accessing components in, 667–670, 673–676,
        686–687, 689
    of arrays, 698
    copying, 678
    declaring, 665–667, 671, 673–676, 687, 697
    dynamic, case study, 917–927
    dynamic data in, 879–884
    initializing, 671, 693–694, 697
    for linked lists, 946–948, 977–979
    minimum value in, 1040–1042
    multidimensional, 700–702, 723–724
    names of, 876
    of objects, 683
    passing, 672–673, 676–678, 695–699
    of pointers, 873
    printing, 694–695, 1026–1029
    of records, 681–683
    strings as, 774–776
    subarrays, 684
    testing and debugging, 721–725
    type definitions with, 680–681
Arrow operator (->), 873, 877–878
Arrows, BNF, 52
Arrows in linked lists, 945
Ascending sorts, 758
ASCII character set, 59n
    character representations in, 511–513
    letters in, 515

Asking questions in problem-solving, 30–31
Assemblers, 11
Assembly language, 10, 24
assert function, 374–375
Assertions
    for arrays, 679–680
    as comments, 356–358
    and control structures, 213–214
    executable, 374
    implementation and abstract, 749, 960
Assignment operator (=), 67, 219, 236, 502–504
    for pointers, 877–878, 895
    precedence of, 226, 509
    for struct and class objects, 584, 601
    for type coercion, 546
Assignments, 66–70
    of class members, 601–602
    of enumeration types, 536–537
    expressions, side effects from, 236, 503–504
    mixing data types in, 113–115
    of pointers, 878
    of records (structs), 584
    slicing problem with, 823–825
    of strings, 777
    type coercion in, 113–115, 546
Associativity of operators, 112–113, 509–510
Asterisk (*)
    in combined assignment operators, 502, 504
    in comments, 39, 72
    for multiplication, 108, 502, 509
    with pointers, 869, 872, 877–878
    precedence of, 112, 226, 509
Atomic data types, 494–495
Attendance case study, 783–791
Automatic arrays, 671
Automatic variables, 403–404
Auxiliary storage devices, 16, 18
Average income by gender case study, 307–313
Average rainfall case study, 478–484

\b escape sequence, 514
B language, 25
Babbage, Charles, 331–332, 410
Back ups, 18
Backslash (\)
    for escape sequences, 514
    in output statements, 71
Backspace, escape sequence for, 514
Backups, 86
Backus, John, 52
Backus-Naur Form (BNF), 52
Bar (|). *See* Vertical bar (|)
Bar charts in sales case study, 363–364
Base addresses of arrays, 677, 695, 876

Base case in recursion, 1015
Base classes, 806
Basic Combined Programming Language (BCPL), 24–25
BASIC language, 13, 1014
Batch processing, 23, 167
BCPL (Basic Combined Programming Language), 24–25
Beechcraft Starship-1 weight and balance case study, 435–447
Beep, escape sequence for, 514
Bell, escape sequence for, 514
Big-*O* notation, 305, 772
Binary numbers, 59
    codes for, 8–9
    converting decimal numbers to, 1037–1040
Binary operators, 108
Binary search, 765–770
Binding of operations to objects, 822–827
BinSearch function
    efficiency of, 769, 772–773
    in SortedList class, 766–767
    in TimeCardList class, 843–844, 848
    walk-through of, 767–769
Birthday calls case study, 634–644
BirthdayCalls program, 640–644
Bits, 9
Bitwise operators, 223, 503, 505–506
Black box, 604–605
Black box testing, 258
Blank characters
    in input data, 157, 160
    in lines, 82–83
    in strings, 123–126, 164, 778, 779
Blank lines
    in output, 81–82
    in programs, 75
Blocks, 75–77
    braces for, 76, 232–233
    for functions, 354
    with if statements, 232–233, 240–241
    nested, 395–398
    with while statements, 277
BNF (Backus-Naur Form), 52
Body
    of functions, 49, 55, 73, 354
    of loops, 277
    of namespace, 400
Boldface text in syntax diagrams, 53
bool data type, 214
    as atomic data type, 494
    constants, 497
Boole, George, 214n, 224–225
Boolean constants, 216
Boolean expressions. *See* Logical expressions
Boolean functions, 419

Boolean operators. *See* Logical operators
Boolean variables, 216
Braces ({ })
    in array initializations, 671, 776–777
    for blocks, 76, 232–233
    for enumeration types, 533
    in functions, 49, 73
    with if statements, 232–233, 235, 240, 241
    positioning, 233
    in syntax templates, 53, 55
Brackets
    for array index values ([ ]), 665, 667, 686, 877–878
    for preprocessor directives (< >), 79, 542–543
Branching, 14. *See also* Control structures
    with do-while, 468–471
    with if. *See* if statements
    with switch, 462–466
break statements
    with loops, 474–476
    with switch statements, 462–466
Bugs. *See* Errors; Side effects
Building-block problem-solving approach, 34, 38
Byron, Anna Isabella, 409
Byron, Lord, 409
Bytes, 9, 495

C strings. *See* Strings
CalcPay function (Payroll), 39–40
Calculations. *See also* Expressions
Calculators
    Difference Engine, 331, 410
    mechanical, 117
Calculus, 117
Calling functions, 49–50, 119–120, 160–161, 162, 335, 336–337
Calls, recursive, 1014
Cancellation error, 530
Candidate votes case study, 710–721
Canvas case study, 192–198
Canvas program, 196–197
Capitalization. *See also* Uppercase letters
    of constant identifiers, 65–66, 132
    of enumerators, 534
Card game simulation, 986–1005
CardAt function (CardPile class), 981, 982, 985
CardDeck class
    constructors for, 991, 994–995
    implementation file for, 994–997
    specification file for, 990–991
carddeck.cpp file, 994–997
carddeck.h file, 990–991
CardPile class
    constructors for, 982, 983

destructor for, 982, 985
    implementation file for, 983–986
    specification file for, 980–981
cardpile.cpp file, 983–986
cardpile file, 980–981
Caret (^), 503
CargoMoment function (Starship), 444–445
Carriage return, escape sequence for, 514
Case labels for switch statements, 463–464
Case of characters. *See also* Letters
    converting, 517–519
    with identifiers, 57, 65–66
Cast operations. *See* Type casting
cctype file, 417–418, 517
CD-ROM drives, 18
Center of gravity case study, 435–447
Central processing unit (CPU), 16, 17
char data type, 58, 59–60, 511
    as atomic data type, 494
    collating sequences for, 60, 217
    comparing, 60, 515–516
    constants, 63–64, 513–515
    converting case of, 517–519
    converting to integers, 516–517
    with input statements, 157, 158–161
    range of values for, 496–497
    representation of, 103, 104, 511–513
    using, 532
Character sets, 59–60, 511–513
Characters. *See also* char data type
    accessing within string, 519–520
    bytes for, 9
    case of, 57, 517–519
    nonprintable, 158, 513
    null, 774–775
CHAR_MAX constant, 497
CHAR_MIN constant, 497
Charts in sales case study, 363–364
CheckInStudents function (Exam), 788–789
CheckLists program, 706–709
Chief architects, 181, 199
Children of classes, 806
Chips, 19
cin stream
    accessing, 408
    using, 155–158
cin.get function, 160–162, 779–780
cin.ignore function, 162–163, 780
City council election case study, 710–721
Class interface diagrams, 807–808
Classes, 596–598
    composition in, 817–822
    constructors for. *See* Constructors
    copy-constructors for, 897–901

copying in, 895–897
    for dates, 890–893
    declaring, 598–600
    deriving, 807–810
    destructors for, 621, 894–895
    dynamic binding in, 822–827
    dynamic data with, 890–901
    implementation files for, 608–613
    inheritance in, 180, 805–817
    for input and output, 603
    for linked lists, 976–977
    members of, 179, 598–601, 604–606, 810–811
    objects of. *See* Objects
    scope in, 393, 402, 603–604
    specification files for, 606–608
    testing and debugging, 644–648
Clear box testing, 258
Clients of classes, 598
climits file, 497
CLOS language, 178, 803
cmath file, 121, 344
COBOL language, 467, 1014
Code, 8–9. *See also* Programming
    for algorithms, 7
    coverage, 258
    reusing, 802, 816
    self-documenting, 191–192
    walk-throughs, 253
Cohesion, functional, 184–185, 434
Cohesive modules, 184–185
Collating sequences, 60, 217–218
Collections
    linear, 774
    lists, 834
    in structured data types, 578
Colon (:)
    in BNF, 52
    in conditional operator (?:), 507–508
    in constructor initializers, 815
    in scope resolution operators, 79, 611
Columns in two-dimensional arrays, 685
    looping for, 695
    summing, 691–692
Combined assignment operators, 502–503
    and pointers, 879
    precedence of, 226, 509
    semantics for, 504
Comma (,)
    in array initializations, 671
    in constructor initializers, 821
    in enumeration types, 533
    in numbers, 103
    in parameter lists, 119, 337, 415
Command line, compiling from, 614

Comments, 39, 72–73
    assertions as, 356–358
    for data flow, 358–359
    for declarations, 63, 65
    embedded, 359
    in function headings, 360
    notation for, 680
Communication complexity, 434–435
Company payroll case study, 36–40
CompareTo function (DateType class), 625, 628, 632–633
CompareLists function (CheckLists), 708–709
Comparing
    characters, 60, 515–516
    dates, 624, 628
    with enumeration types, 538
    floating point numbers, 228, 524, 527–528
    relational operators for, 216–219
    strings, 781, 782–783
Comparison case study, 703–709
Compilers and compilation, 12, 13–14, 84–85
    for multifile programs, 361, 613–616
    tests performed during, 260–261
Compile-time, 403
Complex structures, testing, 722–723
Complexity
    of algorithms, 302–306
    communication, 434–435
    in searches, 772–773
Component members in linked lists, 945, 946
Composition
    in classes, 817–822
    in object-oriented design, 829
Compound statements. *See* Blocks
ComputeDay program, 412–413
Computer programming. *See* Programming
Computer programs. *See* Programs
Computer resources, use of, 28–29
Computers, 2, 3, 16–25
Concatenation operator (+), 68–69, 135
Concrete steps, 182
Conditional evaluation of logical expressions, 223–224
Conditional operator (?:), 503, 507–508
Conditions
    for flow of control. *See* Control structures
    and logical expressions, 214–224
    relational operators for, 216–219
Consistent function, 585
const reserved word
    for arrays, 678
    for constant declarations, 64–65
    in copy-constructors, 899
Constant time execution, 303

Constants
    in array indexes, 668–669
    char, 513–515
    comments for, 73
    declaring, 63–64
    floating-point, 501–502
    global, 409
    integer, 497–500
    for literals, 106
    as parameters, 120, 162, 335, 345
    pointer, 875
    scope of, 392–393
    string, 774–775, 777
Constructor initializers, 815, 820–821
Constructors, 595
    for CardDeck class, 991, 994–995
    for CardPile class, 982, 983
    for Date class, 890–891, 898
    for DateType class, 626, 630
    for derived classes, 812
    for DynArray class, 919, 921–922, 924–925
    execution order of, 821
    for ExtTime class, 813–814
    guidelines for, 620–621
    initializing, 616–621
    invoking, 617–618
    for List class, 749
    for RecordList class, 907, 910
    for SortedList2 class, 958
    for Time class, 837
    for TimeCard class, 820–822, 839
    for TimeCardList class, 844
    for TimeType class, 616–617
Constructs, 51
Containment, 817–822
Contest letter case study, 86–91
continue statements, 476–477
Control abstraction, 434
Control characters, 513
Control structures, 14, 212–214
    break statements, 462–466, 474–476
    continue statements, 476–477
    do-while loops, 468–471
    efficiency in, 302–306
    for loops, 471–474, 670, 690–691, 701–702
    functions as, 332–333
    if statements. *See* if statements
    nested, 236–241
    switch statements, 462–466
    testing, 241–243, 256–259
    while loops, 276–278, 296–302, 468–471
Control unit, 16, 17
ConversionVal function (Game), 562
Convert function, 1039–1040

`ConvertDates` program, 428–431, 447
Converting
    case of characters, 517–519
    decimal numbers to binary, 1037–1040
Converting dates case study, 423–433
Copy-constructors, 897–901
    for `CardPile` class, 982, 984
    for `DynArray` class, 919, 923, 925–926
    for `SortedList2` class, 976–977
`Copy` function, 678
`CopyFrom` function
    in `Date` class, 893, 895–897
    in `DynArray` class, 919, 924, 927
Copying
    arrays, 672, 678
    in classes, 895–897
    linked lists, 1032–1036
    strings, 781, 782
`cos` function, 121
Count-controlled loops
    with `do-while` statements, 469–470
    in flow design, 293
    with `for` statements, 471–474
    in nested loops, 297–298
    testing, 315
    with `while` statements, 280–282
Counter variables, 281, 288–289
Counting in loops, 288–289, 290–292
Counting votes case study, 710–721
`cout` stream, 155
    accessing, 408
    using, 49, 70–72
`.cpp` files
    for class implementations, 608
    linking, 613
CPU (central processing unit), 16, 17
Crashes from infinite recursion, 1018
`CrewMoment` function (`Starship`), 443
`cstdlib` file, 121, 400, 992
`c_str` function, 175, 781
`cstring` file, 781
Ctrl-D keys, 286
Ctrl-Z keys, 286
Cubic time execution, 305
Curly braces ({ }). *See* Braces ({ })
Curves, area under, 547–555

Dangling `else` problem, 240–241
Dangling pointers, 884, 929
Data, 8
    coverage, 258
    inputting, 154–165
    privacy of, 27
    representation of. *See* Representation

    storing, 58–59
    validation of, 253
Data abstraction, 578, 590–592
Data-dependent loops, 304
Data flow, documenting, 358–360
Data objects, 61
Data types, 58–61
    abstract. *See* Abstract data types (ADTs); Classes
    anonymous, 541–542, 586
    for array indexes, 674
    `bool`, 214, 494, 497
    built-in, 494–502
    choosing, 531–532
    in comparisons, 218
    constants, 497–500, 501–502
    in declarations, 62
    defining, 215–216, 532–533
    demoting, 545–547
    floating-point. *See* Floating-point data types
    with input statements, 157
    integral. *See* Integral data types
    named, 541–542
    for parameters, 337, 346
    pointers. *See* Pointers
    promoting, 544–545
    range of values for, 496–497, 500–501
    simple, 494–502
    structured. *See* Arrays; Records; Classes
    testing and debugging, 565–567
    type coercion and type casting with, 113–116, 346, 502–503, 506–507
    user-defined, 532–543
    using, 531–532
`Date` class
    constructors for, 890–891, 898
    declaring, 890–893
    destructor for, 894–895
    specification file for, 893–894
Date manipulation case study, 621–634
`date.h` file, 893–894
Dates
    in Birthday calls case study, 634–644
    classes for, 890–893
    comparing, 624, 628
    incrementing, 624, 629–630
    printing, 623, 627–628
    reformatting, program for, 423–433
`DateType` class
    constructor for, 626, 630
    implementation file for, 630–634
    specification file for, 624–626
    testing, 627, 630
`datetype.cpp` file, 630–634
`datetype.h` file, 624–626

Day function (DateType class), 625, 631
DaysInMonth function (DateType class), 633–634
DBL_MAX constant, 501
DBL_MIN constant, 501
de Fermat, Pierre, 117
Deallocating memory, 880, 882–883
Debugger programs, 314
Debugging, 85, 91–92
    algorithm walk-through in, 251–253
    array-based lists, 792–793
    classes, 644–648
    complex structures, 722–723
    conditional expressions, 262–263
    data types, 565–567
    expressions and function calls, 141
    functions, 372–373, 376
    input, 566
    linked lists, 1006
    loops, 313–316, 484–485
    modular design in, 446–450
    multidimensional arrays, 723–724
    object-oriented programming, 854–855
    one-dimensional arrays, 721–722
    pointers, 928–931
    preconditions and postconditions in, 249–251
    programs, 7, 136, 200–202
    recursion, 1043
    searches, 792–793
Decimal numbers
    constants, 498–499
    converting to binary, 1037–1040
    representing, 9
Decimal places in output statements, 127
Decimal point
    in floating-point numbers, 104
    in input data, 157
    in output formatting, 127
Decisions in programming. *See* Control structures
Declarations, 61–66
    in blocks, 77
    of classes, 598–600
    of constants, 63–64, 105–106
    file stream, 169
    in for statements, 472
    forward, 338, 949
    of functions, 330, 337–340
    initializations in, 404–405
    of objects, 600
    of one-dimensional arrays, 665–667, 671, 673–676
    of parameters, 334
    of pointers, 869–871, 871
    of records (structs), 580–581
    of two-dimensional arrays, 687, 697
    of unions, 589–590
    of variables, 62–63, 106–107, 399–400

Decrement operator, 110–111, 502
    with pointers, 879
    side effects from, 505
Deep copying in class, 896
Default constructors, 616, 821
Default parameters, 345n
Default switch statement labels, 463, 465
#define directive, 375, 817
Definitions
    for data types, 215–216, 532–533
    for functions, 73–74, 76, 329, 337–340
    recursive, 1015
    for variables, 399–400
Delete functions
    for List class, 746, 752
    for SortedList class, 759–760, 770–771
    for SortedList2 class, 957–958
delete operator, 879, 882–883
DeleteTop function (SortedList2 class), 957, 971–972
Deleting
    files, 422
    linked list items, 971–975
    sorted list items, 770–771
    unsorted list items, 751–752
DeMorgan, Augustus, 409
DeMorgan's Law, 221n, 248
Demotion of data types, 545–547
Dereference operator, 870–871, 872
Dereferencing
    pointers, 870–871, 878
    reference variables, 887
Derived classes, 806
    constructors for, 812
    deriving, 807–810
Descendants of classes, 806
Descending sorts, 758
Designs
    of functions, 354–356
    implementing, 185–191
    of interfaces, 405–409, 420–421
    of loops, 292–296, 300–302
    object-oriented. *See* Object-oriented design (OOD)
    functional decomposition, 181–191
Destructors, 621
    for CardPile class, 982, 985
    for Date class, 894–895
    for DynArray class, 919, 921, 926
    purpose of, 894–895
    for RecordList class, 909, 910
    for SortedList2 class, 958, 976
Diagrams, syntax, 52–53
Difference Engine, 331, 410
Differential calculus, 117
Digits
    in BNF, 52

significant, 522, 524
syntax templates for, 54, 499
Direct addressing, 871
Directives, preprocessor, 78, 542–543, 817
Disk drives, 18
Disk files. *See* Files
Divide and conquer techniques, 33–34, 37
Division, 108
    in assignment operators, 502
    with mixed data types, 116
    precedence of, 112
    by zero, 109
do-while statements, 468–471
Documentation, 8
    data flow, 358–360
    in function headings, 358–359
    interfaces as, 358
    self-documenting code, 191–192
Domains
    of data types, 494
    in object-oriented design, 827
Dot (.). *See* Period (.)
Dot-dot notation, 679–680
Dot notation, 131, 582, 601–602, 604, 873
DoTowers function (TestTowers), 1023, 1024–1025
double data type, 121
    constants, 501
    demoting, 546
    promoting, 545
    ranges of, 500
    using, 532
Double quotation mark (")
    for blanks, 83
    escape sequence for, 514
    for header files, 543
    for string constants, 60, 63, 71, 774
Doubly nested loops, 301
Drivers, 447–449
    in object-oriented design, 830
    for PunchIn, 849–852
    for RecordList class, 913
Dynamic arrays case study, 917–927
Dynamic binding, 803, 822–827
Dynamic data, 879–884, 890–901
Dynamic data structures, 948–949
Dynamic linked lists, 948–949
    algorithms for, 956–975
    classes and, 976–977
    copying, 1032–1036
    creating, 948–953
    pointer expressions for, 975
    printing, 1028–1031
DynArray class, 918
    constructor for, 919, 921–922, 924–925
    destructor for, 919, 921, 926

implementation file for, 924–927
specification file for, 918–920
dynarray.cpp file, 924–927
dynarray.h file, 918–920

EBCDIC character set
    character representations in, 511
    control characters in, 513
    letters in, 515–516
Echo printing, 165–167
Editors, 23, 84
Efficiency
    of algorithms, 302–306
    of loops, 302–306
    readability compared, 238
    of searches, 769
Eiffel language, 178, 803
Election case study, 710–721
Election program, 714–721
Elements in one-dimensional arrays, 666
else-clause. *See* if statements
Embedded comments, 359, 360
Employee time card lookup case study, 832–854
Empty lists, 748–749, 959–960
Empty sets, 225
Empty strings, 60
Encapsulation of functions, 354–355
Encryption, 27
End-of-file-controlled loops, 285–287, 294, 298–299
endl manipulator, 72, 81, 82, 124, 128
Enter key, newline characters from, 158
Entering programs, 83–84
Entry conditions in assertion comments, 356
Enumeration types, 533–541
    for array indexes, 674
    assignment with, 536–537
    as atomic data type, 495
    comparisons with, 538
    function values returned with, 540–541
    incrementation with, 537–538
    input and output with, 538–540
    named and anonymous, 541–542
Enumerators, 534–535
EOF-controlled loops, 285–287, 294, 298–299
Equal function (TimeType class), 602, 606, 607, 610, 619
Equal sign (=). *See also* Assignment operator (=)
    in combined assignment operators, 226, 502, 503,
        504, 509, 879
    in constant declarations, 65
    in equals operator (==), 219, 226, 236, 357, 509, 878
    precedence of, 226, 509
    in relational operators, 226, 509, 515, 878
Equals relational operator (==), 217, 219, 236, 357
    for pointers, 878
    precedence of, 226, 509

Errors. *See also* Side effects
  cancellation, 530
  input, 566
  logic (semantic), 85, 261
  representational, 524
  syntax, 51, 85, 260
Escape sequences, 158–159, 514–515
Ethics, 25–30
Etiquette in interactive input, 165
Evaluating expressions, 67–68, 223–224
Event-controlled loops, 280
  end-of-file-controlled, 285–287, 294, 298–299
  flag-controlled, 287–288, 294
  sentinel-controlled, 282–285, 294
  testing, 315
Event counters in loops, 290
Exactness of floating-point numbers, 105, 524
Exam attendance case study, 783–791
Exam program, 787–790
Exception reports, 566
Exclamation point (!). *See also* NOT operator (!)
  in assertion comments, 357
  in not equal to (!=) operator, 217, 509, 878
  precedence of, 226, 509
.exe files, 613
Executable assertions, 374
Executable statements, 66–72
Execution, program, 7, 13, 84–85
  tests performed during, 260–261
  tracing, 253–256
Exit status, 75, 243
Exiting
  functions, 341–342
  loops, 278–279, 292–293, 295–296, 474–477
Explicit parameter matching, 354
Exponential class algorithms, 306
Exponentiation program, 1016
Exponents
  in floating-point numbers, 105, 521–522
  syntax templates for, 502
Expression statements, 503–504
Expressions, 411
  arithmetic, 112–116, 544–545
  for array indexes, 667–669
  in assignments, 67, 503–504
  in comparisons, 218–219
  evaluating, 67–68, 223–224
  with increment and decrement operators, 505
  logical, 216–224
  as parameters, 162, 345
  for pointers, 874–879, 975
  relational, 217, 544–545
  switch, 462–463
  type coercion in, 544–545

Extensible data abstractions, 816
extern reserved word, 399
External declarations, 399
External pointers for linked lists, 948–949
External representation of characters, 512
External variables, 399–400
Extraction operator (>>), 778–780
  inputting with, 155–158
  for strings, 163–164
ExtTime class
  constructors for, 813–814
  implementation file for, 813–814
  specification file for, 811–812
exttime.cpp file, 813–814
exttime.h file, 811–812

\f escape sequence, 514
F with constants, 501
fabs function, 121, 228
Factorial class algorithms, 306
Factorial function
  using iteration, 415–416
  using recursion, 1018–1021
Fail state, 175
  in EOF-controlled loops, 286
  in sentinel-controlled loops, 285
  testing for, 241–243
Failing notices case study, 243–249
False values, 214
Fear of starting, 35
Fetch-execute cycle, 18
Fields
  output, 125
  record. *See* Members of structures
Fieldwidth specifications, 125
Files, 83, 168
  deleting, 422
  header. *See* Header files
  input from, 167–175
  in input/output statements, 171
  opening, 169–171, 242–243
  project, 615
  run-time input of names for, 174–175
  sample program using, 172–174
  streams for, 168–169
find function, 132–134, 136
fixed manipulator, 124, 128
Flag-controlled loops, 287–288, 294
Flat implementation, 189
float data type, 58
  as atomic data type, 494
  constants, 501
  with input statements, 157

promoting, 545
ranges of, 500–501
Floating-point data types, 104–105
    arithmetic with, 523–524
    cancellation errors in, 530
    comparing, 228, 524, 527–528
    constants, 501–502
    demoting, 546
    division with, 108–109
    implementation of, 524–530
    with input statements, 157
    mixing with integers, 113–116, 544
    overflow of, 528–529
    precision of, 105, 521–523, 524, 530–531
    promoting, 544–545
    ranges of, 500–501
    representation of, 520–523
    testing and debugging, 565–566
    underflow of, 528
Flow of control. *See* Control structures
FLT_MAX constant, 501
FLT_MIN constant, 501
for loops
    for arrays, 670, 690–691, 701–702
    for count-controlled loops, 471–474
Form feed, escape sequence for, 514
Form letter case study, 86–91
Formal parameters, 334
Formatting
    function headings, 360–361
    output, 123–128
    programs, 129–130
FormLetter program, 88–90
FORTRAN language, 1014
Forward declarations, 338, 949
Free format, 129
Free store, 880
Freeware, 179
fstream file, 168–169, 603
FuelMoment function (Starship), 445, 448–449
Full logical expression evaluation, 223
Funct function (Area), 554
Function return values
    data types for, 413
    with enumeration types, 540–541
    ignoring, 421–422
    from main, 50, 75, 243
    records (structs) as, 584
    type coercion in, 545–547
Function value type, 413
Functional cohesion, 184–185, 434
Functional decomposition, 181–191
Functional equivalence, 183
Functional notation for type casting, 507

Functions, 48–49
    abstraction with, 434
    Boolean, 416–418
    calling, 49–50, 119–120, 160–161, 162, 335, 336–337
    declaring, 330, 337–340
    definitions for, 73–74, 76, 329, 337–340
    designing, 354–356
    and flow of control, 332–333
    header files for, 343–344
    headings for, 55, 73, 329, 360–361
    integrating, 547–555
    library. *See* Library functions
    local variables in, 340–341
    modules as, 327–330
    names for, 330, 343, 393, 419
    observer, 595
    parameters for. *See* Parameters
    prototypes for, 330, 337, 338
    recursive. *See* Recursion
    return statement in, 55, 341–342, 413
    return values from. *See* Function return values
    testing and debugging, 372–373, 376
    value-returning, 50, 118–120, 411–422
    virtual, 825–827
    void, 122–123
Furniture store sales case study, 363–372

Game program, 560–564
Games
    rock, paper, scissors, 555–565
    solitaire simulation, 986–1005
    Towers of Hanoi, 1021–1026
Gender and income case study, 307–313
General case in recursion, 1015
get function, 160–162, 779–780
Get12Amounts function (Rainfall), 481–482
GetClassRoster function (Exam), 788
GetCurrentDate function (BirthdayCalls), 642
GetData functions
    in Area, 553–554
    in Graph, 370–371
    in Starship, 442–443
Get2Digits function (ConvertDates), 430
GetEntry function (BirthdayCalls), 642–643
GetID function (PunchIn), 852
getline function, 164–165
GetNames function (Election), 716–717
GetOneAmount function (Rainfall), 482–483
GetPlays function (Game), 561–562
GetRecord function (RecordList class), 908, 910–911
GetTemp function (Activity), 347, 348, 362–363
GetYear function (ConvertDates), 430–431, 447
GetYesOrNo function (Rainfall), 482

Global constants, 409
Global scope, 393, 403
Global variables
    in functions, 340
    lifetime of, 403
    side effects with, 406–409
`Graph` program, 368–372
Greater-than symbol (>)
    as angle brackets, 79, 542–543
    in arrow operator (->), 873, 877–878
    in BNF, 52
    in character comparisons, 515
    in extraction operator (>>), 155–156, 163–164,
        778–780
    precedence of, 226, 509
    in relational operators, 217, 226, 509
    in right shift operator (>>), 503, 505, 506
Grouping order of operators, 112–113, 509–510

`.h` files. *See* Header files
Hand tracing program execution, 253–256
Hardware, 17–19
Has-a relationships, 819
Head pointers for linked lists, 947, 948
Header files
    for class specifications, 606
    contents of, 78–79
    including, 121, 168–169, 343–344
    multiple inclusion of, 816–817
    user-written, 542–543
Headings for function, 55, 73, 329, 360–361
Heap, 880
Heterogeneous data types, 579
Heuristics, 327
Hexadecimal numbers
    escape sequence with, 514
    representation of integers, 497–500
Hexagrammum mysticum, 117
Hiding
    in classes, 604–606
    function implementation, 354, 361–363
    variable names, 394–395
Hierarchical records, 587–589
Hierarchies
    in implementation, 189
    inheritance. *See* Inheritance
High-level programming languages, 12–13
Homogeneous data structures, 666
Hopper, Grace Murray, 466–467
Horizontal spacing in output, 124–125
Horizontal tab, escape sequence for, 514
`.hpp` files, 542
`.hxx` files, 542
Hybrid functions, 422

Hyperexponential class algorithms, 306
Hyphen (-). *See* Minus sign (-)

I/O. *See* Input; Output
Identification stage in object-oriented design, 828–829
Identifiers, 52, 53–54, 56–57
    capitalization of, 65–66, 132
    declaring, 61–66
    for enumeration types, 533–535
    for file streams, 169
    meaningful, 57–58
    scope of, 392–403
`IDPart` function (`TimeCard` class), 839, 841
`if` statements, 229–236
    blocks with, 232–233, 240–241
    dangling `else` with, 240–241
    equal signs in, 236
    If-Then-Else form, 229–231
    If-Then-Else-If form, 238–240
    If-Then form, 234–235
    nested, 236–241
    `switch` statements compared,
        465–466
    testing, 241–243, 256–259
    `while` statements compared, 277
`#ifndef` directive, 817
`ifstream` class, 168–169, 603
`ignore` function, 162–163, 779–780
Implementation
    of algorithms, 7
    of designs, 185–191
    of floating-point numbers, 524–530
    of functions, hiding, 354, 361–363
    of object-oriented design, 831–832
    of programs, 3–4, 253–259
    specification compared, 593
Implementation assertions, 749, 960
Implementation files, 608–613
    for `CardDeck` class, 994–997
    for `CardPile` class, 983–986
    for `DateType` class, 630–634
    for `DynArray` class, 924–927
    for `ExtTime` class, 813–814
    for `List` class, 748
    for `Player` class, 1000–1003
    for `RecordList` class, 909–913
    for `SortedList2` class, 959
    for `TimeCard` class, 820–822, 840–842
    for `TimeCardList` class, 846–848
    for `TimeType` class, 608–611
Implementation hierarchy diagrams, 947
Implementation-level objects, 829
Implicit parameter matching, 354
In-place sorting, 756

Inaccessible objects, 884
#include directives, 817
    in implementation files, 611
    for library files, 79, 121, 343–344
    for user-written header files, 543
Include directory, 79, 543
Income by gender case study, 307–313
Incomes program, 311–312
Incoming/outgoing parameters, 358, 359
Incoming/outgoing values in interfaces, 355
Incoming parameters, 358, 359
Incoming values in interfaces, 355
Incomplete declarations, 949
Increment functions
    in DateType class, 625, 629–630, 633
    in Time class, 837
    in TimeType class, 607, 609–610, 619, 645
Increment operator (++), 110–111, 502
    with pointers, 879
    precedence of, 509
    side effects from, 505
Incrementing
    dates, 624, 629–630
    with enumeration types, 537–538
    loop control variables, 280–282, 293
Indentation
    of blocks, 77
    of if statements, 230
    for readability, 129
Indexes in arrays, 665
    data types for, 674
    expressions for, 667–669
    out-of-bounds, 670
    with pointers, 877–878
    semantic content in, 684–685
Indirect addressing, 871
Indirection operator, 870–871, 872
Infinite loops, 5, 281
    from assignment expressions, 285
    exiting, 474–477
Infinite recursion, 1017–1018
Infix operators, 889
Information, 8
Information hiding, 604–606
Inheritance, 803, 805–817
    accessibility with, 810–811
    in deriving classes, 807–810
    in object-oriented design, 180, 829
Inheritance hierarchy, 805
Initialization
    of constructors, 616–621
    in declarations, 404–405
    in for statements, 472
    of loop control variables, 280–282, 293

    of objects, 897–901
    of one-dimensional arrays, 671
    of strings, 776–777
    of two-dimensional arrays, 693–694, 697
Initialize function, 697
Initializers, 404
Inline implementation, 189
Input, 154–165
    in batch processing, 167
    of characters, 160–162
    classes for, 603
    devices for, 16, 17
    with enumeration types, 538–540
    errors in, 566
    extraction operator for, 155–158
    failures in, 175–176
    from files, 167–175
    files for. See Files
    with get, 160–162
    if statements for, 230–231
    interactive, 165–167
    prompts for, 37, 165–167
    reading marker and newline character in, 158–160
    skipping characters in, 162–163, 779–780
    of strings, 777–781
    of structure (struct) members, 584
    testing and debugging, 566
    validating, 253
Input files, opening, 170
Insert functions
    in List class, 746, 751
    in SortedList class, 759, 763, 773
    in SortedList2 class, 957, 965–971
Inserting items
    into linked lists, 963–971
    into sorted lists, 761–764
    into unsorted lists, 751
Insertion operator (<<), 70–72, 778
Insertion sort, 764
InsertTop functions
    in CardPile class, 981, 982, 985–986
    in SortedList2 class, 957, 963–965
Instance variables, 804–805
Instances of classes, 598
Instantiating objects, 600
int data type, 50, 58, 103
    for array indexes, 674, 687
    as atomic data type, 494
    for Boolean data, 215
    with input statements, 157
    promoting, 545
    range of values for, 496–497
    using, 531–532

Integral data types
> constants, 497–500
> converting characters to, 516–517
> demoting, 546
> division with, 108–109
> functions returning, 50
> with input statements, 157
> mixing with floating-point numbers, 113–116
> overflow of, 529
> promoting, 545
> range of values for, 496–497
> representation of, 103, 104

Integrated circuits, 19

Integrated environments, compiling and linking from, 615

Integrating function, 547–555

Interactive input, 165–167

Interactive systems, 23

Interfaces, 22–23
> designing, 405–409, 420–421
> documentation in, 358
> for functions, 354–356
> in team programming, 355

Internal representation of characters, 512

Internet, 23

Interpreters, 13–14, 353

INT_MAX constant, 494, 497

INT_MIN constant, 494, 497

Invalid data
> input failures from, 175–176
> testing for, 566

Investigation of the Laws of Thought, An (Boole), 225

Invoking
> constructors, 617–618
> functions, 49–50, 119–120, 160–161, 162, 335, 336–337

iomanip file, 124

iostream file
> contents of, 155, 603
> external variables in, 399
> including, 74, 78

Is-a relationships, 806

isalnum function, 418

isalpha function, 418

isdigit function, 418

IsEmpty function
> for List class, 746, 749
> for SortedList class, 759
> for SortedList2 class, 957

IsFull function
> for List class, 746, 750
> for SortedList class, 759

islower function, 418

IsPresent2 function (List class), 754–755, 772

IsPresent functions
> for List class, 747, 772
> for SortedList class, 753, 760, 770

isspace function, 418

istream class, 155, 160, 162, 603

IsTriangle function, 417–418

isupper function, 418

Iteration counters, 289

Iterations
> in loops, 278–279, 288–289
> in object-oriented design, 830
> recursion compared, 1036–1037

Iterators, 596

Jacquard automatic loom, 331

Java language, 14, 178, 803

Java Virtual Machine (JVM), 14

Keyboards, 17, 155. *See also* Input

L with constants, 497, 501

Labels for switch statements, 463–464

labs function, 121

Languages
> object-oriented, 803
> programming, 6, 10–16

Laptop computers, 19

Lardner, Dionysius, 410

LCD (liquid crystal display) screens, 17

LDBL_MAX constant, 501

LDBL_MIN constant, 501

Leading zeros in numbers, 104

Leaks, memory, 883, 895

Left shift operator (<<), 503, 505, 506

Length function, 131–132, 136
> for CardPile class, 981, 982, 985
> for List class, 746, 750
> for SortedList class, 759

Length of strings, 774–776, 781–782

Less-than symbol (<)
> in angle brackets, 79, 542–543
> in BNF, 52
> with character comparisons, 515
> in insertion operator (<<), 70, 778
> in left-shift operator (<<), 503, 505, 506
> precedence of, 226, 509
> in relational operators, 217

LessThan function (TimeType class), 602, 606, 607, 611, 619

Letters
> converting case of, 517–519
> in EBCDIC character set, 515
> in identifiers, 56, 57, 65–66
> syntax template for, 54

Lexicographic order, 782
Library functions, 179
    including, 102, 120–122
    prototypes for, 344
Life cycles in programming, 8
Lifetime of variables, 403–405, 879
Line feed, escape sequence for, 514
Linear collections, 774
Linear searches, 752–755
Linear time execution, 304
Link members in linked lists, 945, 946
Linked lists, 944–946
    array representation of, 946–948
    copying, 1032–1036
    data representation choices for, 977–979
    deleting items from, 971–975
    dynamic. *See* Dynamic linked lists
    inserting items into, 963–971
    pointer expressions for, 975
    printing, 960–963, 1029–1031
    recursion with, 1029–1036
    sorting, 978
    testing and debugging, 960, 1006
Linkers, 361
Linking programs, 85, 361, 613–616
Liquid crystal display (LCD) screens, 17
LISP language
    interpreters in, 13
    parameter passing in, 354
    recursion in, 1014
List class, 745, 748
List comparison case study, 703–709
list.cpp file, 748
list.h file, 746–747, 751
Lists
    as abstract data type, 744–748, 947
    empty, 748–749, 959–960
    linked. *See* Dynamic linked lists; Linked lists
    searching in, 752–755, 764–770, 772–773
    sorted, 758–771
    sorting, 755–758, 772–773, 978
    unsorted, 748–758
Literal strings, 174
Literal values
    for constants, 64, 106
    in enumeration types, 533
Local area networks (LANs), 23
Local scope, 393, 402
Local variables
    in functions, 340–341
    lifetime of, 403
    scope of, 392
Location, parameter passing by, 353
Logarithmic order, 773

Logarithmic time, 306
Logging off from workstations, 86
Logging on to workstations, 83
Logic
    errors in, 85, 261
    symbolic, 224–225
Logical execution order, 276
Logical expressions, 216–224
    logical operators in, 220–223
    relational operators for, 216–219
Logical operators
    in assertion comments, 357
    in logical expressions, 220–223
    with pointers, 878–879
long data type, 121
    range of values for, 496–497
    representation of, 103, 104, 105
    using, 532
Long-haul networks, 23
Long words, 9
LONG_MAX constant, 497
LONG_MIN constant, 497
Loop control variables, 281, 293
Loop entry, 278–279
Loop test, 278–279
Loops, 14
    for arrays, 690–691, 701–702
    choosing, 477
    count-controlled, 280–282, 293, 297–298, 469–474
    counting in, 288–289, 290–292
    designing, 292–296, 300–302
    do-while, 468–471
    efficiency in, 302–306
    event-controlled, 280, 282–288, 294, 315
    exiting, 278–279, 292–293, 295–296, 474–477
    flow of control in, 292–294
    for, 471–474
    infinite. *See* Infinite loops
    nested, 276, 296–302
    phases in, 278–279
    process within, 294–295
    and recursion. *See* Recursion
    subtasks in, 288–292
    summing in, 289–290
    testing and debugging, 313–316, 484–485
    variable tracking in, 290–292
    while, 276–278
Lovelace, Ada, 332, 409–410
Lower function, 518–519
Lowercase letters
    converting characters to, 517–519
    in identifiers, 57, 65–66

Machine-independent code, 12
Machine language, 10, 613
`MachineRec` program, 591
Magnetic tape drives, 18
`main` function, 49–50
 exit status of, 50, 75, 243
 flow of control from, 332
 position of, 330
 syntax template for, 55
Mainframes, 19
Maintenance programming phase, 4, 8
Manipulating date case study, 621–634
Manipulators, 72, 124–126
Mantissa, 525
Map measurement case study, 137–141
Matching parameters, 350–353, 696
Mathematical Analysis of Logic, The (Boole), 224
Maximum values
 conditional statements for, 508
 for floating-point numbers, 500–501
 for integers, 497
Means-ends analysis, 32–33, 37
Measurement case study, 137–141
Mechanical calculators, 117
Member selectors, 582–583
Members of classes
 accessing, 598–600, 604–606, 810–811
 functions for, 179
 objects compared, 601
 public and private, 179, 604
 scope of, 603–604
Members of structures (`structs`), 580
 accessing, 582–583, 588
 data types for, 584
 input for, 584
 names of, 580
Memory, 58
 allocating, 338, 399
 corrupted by out-of-bounds array indexes, 670
 dynamic data in, 879–884
 lifetime of variables in, 403
 for linked lists, 948
 for local variables, 340
 pointers to. *See* Pointers
Memory cells, 16
Memory leaks, 883, 895
Memory locations, 16
Memory units, 16
Menabrea, Luigi, 410
Mental blocks, 35
`Merge` function (`CardDeck` class), 991, 993, 996–997
Merging solutions in problem-solving, 34
Messages
 for objects, 804
 prompting, 37, 166

Metalanguages, 51, 52–53
Methods in objects, 804–805
Minimum complete coverage of branches, 256
`Minimum` function, 1041–1042
Minimum values
 in arrays, 1040–1042
 for floating-point numbers, 500–501
 for integers, 497
Minus sign (-)
 in arrow operator (->), 873, 877–878
 in decrement operator (--), 111, 502, 505, 879
 for negation, 103, 108
 precedence of, 112, 226
 for subtraction, 108
Mixed data types
 in comparisons, 218
 in expressions, 113–116
 in parameters, 346
Mixed type expressions, 115
Mnemonics, 10
Model interval, 526
Model numbers, 525–527
Modeling in object-oriented design, 827
Modular programming
 testing and debugging, 446–450
 in functional decomposition, 181–191
Module structure charts, 182
 for `Area` program, 552
 for `BirthdayCalls` program, 639
 for `Canvas` program, 195
 for `CheckLists` program, 706
 for `ConvertDates` program, 427
 for `Election` program, 714
 for `Exam` program, 786
 for `Game` program, 560
 for `Graph` program, 367–368
 for `Incomes` program, 310
 for `Notices` program, 246
 for `PunchIn` program, 850
 for `Rainfall` program, 480
 for `RecordList` class, 914
 for `Solitaire` program, 1004
 for `Starship` program, 440
Modules, 182–185, 327–330
Modulus operator (%), 108–109, 289
 for number conversion, 1038
 precedence of, 112
Moment arms, 436
Monitors, 17
`Month` function (`DateType` class), 625, 631
Monthly rainfall case study, 478–484
Mouse, 17
`MoveFour` function (`Player` class), 1000, 1002
`MoveTwo` function (`Player` class), 1000, 1002–1003
MS-DOS operating system, 286

Multiway branches, 237
Multidimensional arrays, 700–702, 723–724
Multifile programs, 361
    compiling and linking, 613–616
    external variables in, 399–400
Multiple exits in functions, 342
Multiple inclusion of header files, 816–817
Multiplication, 108
    in assignment operators, 502
    precedence of, 112

\n escape sequence, 158–159, 514
Name, parameter passing by, 353–354
Name precedence, 394–395, 398
Named constants, 64, 105–106
Named data types, 541–542
Named parameter passing, 354
Names
    of arrays, 876
    clashes of, 402
    of enumeration types, 541–542
    of files, run-time input of, 174–175
    of functions, 330, 343, 393, 419
    for workstation logons, 83
    of parameters, 339, 349
    of structure (struct) members, 580
    of user-defined types, 532
    of variables. *See* Identifiers
Namespace scope, 400, 403
Namespaces, 79–80, 400–403
Narrowing of data types, 545–547
Naur, Peter, 52
NDEBUG, 375
Negative exponents, 522
Negative numbers, 103
Nesting
    blocks, 395–398
    if statements, 236–241
    for statements, 472
    while statements, 296–302
Networks, 23
new operator, 879–880
Newline characters, 158–160
    escape sequence for, 514
    with string input, 779–780
NewWelcome program, 333–334
Nibbles, 9
Nodes
    allocating, 948–956
    in linked lists, 945
Nonlocal access, 395
Nonprintable characters, 158, 513
Nonterminal symbols, 52
Nonzero digits, syntax templates for, 499

Normalization, 525
Not equal to operator (!=), 217, 509, 878
NOT operator (!)
    in assertion comments, 357
    in logical expressions, 220–223
    with pointers, 878
    precedence of, 226, 509
Notebook computers, 19
NotEqualCount program, 291
Notices program, 246–248
Null characters
    escape sequence for, 514
    in strings, 774–775
NULL constant
    for linked lists, 948, 956
    for pointers, 875
Null pointers, 875, 928
Null statement, 76
    with if statements, 234
    with for statements, 472, 473
Null strings, 60
Number bases, 497–500
Number sign (#), 78, 817
Number systems, 8–9
Numbers. *See also* Floating-point data types; Integral data
    types
    converting, 1037–1040
    declarations for, 105–107
    operators for, 107–110
Numerical analysis, 528
Nybbles, 9

Object code (.obj) files, 613
Object-oriented design (OOD), 177–178, 179–181, 802, 827–830
    driver design in, 830
    identification stage in, 828–829
    implementing, 831–832
    iterative nature of, 830
    relationships in, 829, 835
    in time card lookup case study, 832–854
Object-oriented programming languages, 803
Object-oriented programming (OOP), 802–804
    composition in, 817–822
    dynamic binding in, 822–827
    inheritance in, 805–817
    objects in, 804–805
    testing and debugging, 854–855
Object-Pascal language, 178, 803
Object programs, 12
Object tables, 834
Objective C language, 803
Objects, class, 598
    as arguments, 823

arrays of, 683
declaring, 600
dynamic binding of operations to, 822–827
and dynamic data, 890–901
initializing, 897–901
in object-oriented design, 177, 828–829
in object-oriented programming, 804–805
operations on, 601–603
Observer functions, 595
Octal numbers
escape sequence with, 514
representation of integers, 497–500
zeros for, 104
Off-the-shelf software, 578
ofstream class, 168–169, 603
One-dimensional arrays, 664–681. *See also* Lists
accessing components in, 667–670, 673–676
aggregate operations on, 671–673
as arguments, 678–679
assertions for, 679–680
copying, 672, 678
declaring, 665–667, 671, 673–676
initializing, 671
naming, 680–681
out-of-bounds array indexes with, 670
passing, 672–673, 676–678
printing, 1026–1029
subarray processing, 684
testing and debugging, 721–725
open function, 169–171, 780
OpenForInput functions
in BirthdayCalls, 641–642
in CheckLists, 707
in ConvertDates, 429
in Election, 716
in Exam, 788
in PunchIn, 851–852
in SortWithPointers, 915
OpenForOutput functions
in ConvertDates, 429–430
in Election, 716
Opening files, 169–171, 242–243
Operating systems, 23
design problems in, 199
main called by, 50
UNIX, 24
Operations
for abstract data types, 595–596
on classes, 601–603
in object-oriented design, 828–829
with pointers, 878–879
with reference types, 887
on structures (structs), 583–585
Operator overloading, 506, 670

Operators. *See also* Assignment operator (=)
address-of (&), 870, 887, 889–890
arithmetic, 107–110
arrow (->), 873, 877–878
associativity of, 112–113, 509–510
bitwise, 223, 503, 505–506
cast ( ), 114, 503, 507
combined assignment, 226, 502–503, 504, 509, 879
concatenation (+), 68–69, 135
conditional (?:), 503, 507–508
decrement (--), 110–111, 502, 505, 879
in expressions, 68, 221
extraction (>>), 155–158, 163–164, 778–780, 780
increment (++), 110–111, 502, 505, 509, 879
insertion (<<), 70–72, 778
left shift (<<), 503, 505, 506
logical, 220–223, 357, 878–879
modulus (%), 108–109, 112, 289, 1038
NOT (!), 220–223, 226, 357, 509, 878
OR (| |), 220–223, 227, 357, 506
precedence of, 112, 225–228, 508–510
relational, 216–219, 228, 878
remainder (%), 108, 112, 1038
right shift (>>), 503, 506
scope resolution (::), 79, 611
sizeof, 503, 507
OR operator (| |), 506
in assertion comments, 357
in logical expressions, 220–223, 227
Order of instructions. *See* Control structures
Ordering. *See* Sorting
Orders of magnitude, 305
OS/360 operating system, 199
ostream class, 155, 603
Out-of-bounds array indexes, 670
Outgoing parameters, 358, 359
Outgoing values in interfaces, 355
Output, 49, 70–72
classes for, 603
devices for, 16, 17, 70
with enumeration types, 538–540
files for. *See* Files
formatting, 81–83
manipulators for, 124–126
spacing in, 123–126
of strings, 777–781
Output files, opening, 170
Output streams. *See* Streams
Overflow
floating-point, 528–529
integer, 104, 529

Parameterless functions, 335
Parameters, 119, 333–336. *See also* Arguments

analogy demonstrating, 350
data flow documentation for, 358–360
declaring, 334
matching, 336, 350–353, 696
names for, 339, 349
records as, 584
reference, 344, 346–349, 405–406, 420–421, 824–825
scope of, 395
side effects from, 406–409, 420–421
syntax templates for, 339
type coercion in, 346, 352
value, 344, 345–346, 349
Parentheses ( )
    for cast operations, 114, 503, 507
    for functions, 55, 75, 336, 502
    for `if` statements, 229
    for pointer dereferencing, 872
    for precedence, 112, 226, 509
    for `sizeof` operator, 507
Parents of classes, 806
Pascal, Blaise, 117–118
Pascal, Etienne, 117
Pascal's law, 118
Pascal's theorem, 117
Pascal's triangle, 117
`PassengerMoment` function (`Starship`), 443–444
Passing
    arrays, 672–673, 676–678, 695–699
    messages, 804–805
    parameters, 162, 353–354, 546
Passive error detection, 566
Passwords, 83
Payroll case study, 36–40
`Payroll` program, 39–40
PCs (personal computers), 19
Percent sign (%)
    as modulus operator, 108–109, 112, 289, 1038
    precedence of, 112, 226, 509
    as remainder operator, 108, 112, 1038
Period (.). *See also* Decimal point
    as dot operator, 582, 601–602, 872, 873
    precedence of, 872
    in syntax templates (...), 54, 55
Peripheral devices, 19
Personal computers (PCs), 19
Personnel records case study, 901–916
Phases
    in loops, 278–279
    in programming, 3–8, 177
Physical execution order, 276
`Player` class
    implementation file for, 1000–1003
    specification file for, 998

`player.cpp` file, 1000–1003
`player.h` file, 998
`PlayGame` function (`Player` class), 998–999, 1000–1001
Playing cards, simulated, 979–986
Plus sign (+)
    for addition, 108
    in combined assignment operator (+=), 502, 504, 879
    for concatenation, 68, 135
    in increment operator (++), 110–111, 502, 509, 879
    precedence of, 112, 226, 509
Pointers, 868–879
    arithmetic with, 879
    array names as, 876
    arrays of, 873
    constants, 875
    dangling, 884, 929
    declaring, 869–871, 871
    for dynamic data, 879–884
    expressions for, 874–879, 975
    for linked lists. *See* Dynamic linked lists
    null, 875, 928
    operations with, 878–879
    recursion with, 1029–1036
    sorting with, 903–904, 916
    testing and debugging, 928–931
    variables for, 869–874
Poker hands, number of, 529
Polymorphic operations, 826
Polynomial expressions, 306
Polynomial time, 306
Portable code, 12
Positional parameter matching, 336, 350–353, 696
Post-incrementation, 505
Postconditions
    assertions for, 356
    function, 358
    in problem-solving, 249–251
Postfix operators, 111, 889
Posttest loops, 471
Pound sign (#), 78, 817
`pow` function, 121, 415
Power, turning off, 86
`Power` function
    using iteration, 415–416
    using recursion, 1014–1018
Pre-incrementation, 505
Precedence
    name, 394–395, 398
    of operators, 112, 225–228, 508–510
Precision of floating-point numbers, 105, 521–523, 524, 530–531

Preconditions
  assertions for, 356
  function, 358
  in problem-solving, 249–251
  in specification files, 608
Prefix notation for type casting, 507
Prefix operators, 111, 889
Preprocessor, 78–79, 542–543, 817
Pretest loops, 471
Priming reads
  with `do-while` statements, 469
  in event-controlled loops, 282
`Print` functions
  for arrays, 1027–1028
  in `Date` class, 893
  in `DateType` class, 625, 627–628, 632
  dynamic binding with, 823
  in `Exam`, 790
  in `List` class, 747, 750
  in `SortedList` class, 760
  in `SortedList2` class, 957, 960–963
  in `TimeCard` class, 820, 839, 842
Printable characters, 513
`PrintActivity` function (`Activity`), 347, 348
`PrintAll` function (`RecordList` class), 906, 909, 912–913
`PrintBigWinner` function (`Game`), 564
`PrintData` function (`Graph`), 371–372
`PrintEntry` function (`BirthdayCalls`), 643–644
Printers, 17
`PrintHeading` function (`Graph`), 369, 370
Printing
  arrays recursively, 1026–1029
  dates, 623, 627–628
  echo, 165–167
  with enumeration types, 539
  linked lists, 960–963, 1029–1031
  two-dimensional arrays, 694–695
  using recursion, 1026–1029
`PrintLines` function (`NewWelcome`), 334
`Print2Lines` function (`Welcome`), 328
`Print4Lines` function (`Welcome`), 328
`PrintName` program, 74–75
`PrintWarning` function (`Starship`), 446
Privacy of data, 27
Private base classes, 810n
Private class members
  as abstraction barrier, 604–606
  accessing, 598, 599–600, 810–811
  in implementation files, 611
  for objects, 179
`private` reserved word, 598
Problem domain in object-oriented design, 827
Problem-solving programming phase, 3–4, 177

Problem-solving techniques, 30–36
  algorithm walk-through in, 249–253
  algorithmic, 36
  analogies for, 31–32
  asking questions, 30–31
  building-block approach, 34, 38
  divide and conquer, 33–34, 37
  looking for familiar, 31
  means-ends analysis, 32–33, 37
  for mental blocks, 35
  merging solutions, 34
  preconditions and postconditions in, 249–251
Procedural programming, 802–804
Procedures, 122–123. *See also* Functions
`ProcessName` function (`Exam`), 789–790
`ProcessPlays` function (`Game`), 563
Procrastinator's technique, 184
Professional ethics/responsibilities, 25–30
Programmers, 3
Programming, 2–3
  design implementation in, 185–191
  languages for, 6, 10–16
  modules in, 182–185
  object-oriented. *See* Object-oriented programming (OOP)
  object-oriented design for, 177–178, 179–181
  phases in, 3–8, 177
  scales in, 198–199, 802
  style in. *See* Style in programming
  functional decomposition for, 181–191
Programming in the large, 199
Programming in the small, 198
Programs, 3
  blocks in, 75–77
  compiling and running, 84–85, 613–616
  constructing, 73–80
  data types in, 58–61
  debugging, 85. *See* also Debugging
  entering, 83–84
  executing, 7, 13
  formatting, 129–130
  identifiers in, 56–57
  implementation of, 253–259
  input/output for. *See* Input; Output
  multifile, 361, 399–400, 613–616
  structure of, 48–51
  syntax and semantics in, 51
  syntax template for, 73
  testing, 7, 200–202
  tracing execution of, 253–256
Project directors, 199
Project files, 615
Prolog language, 13
Promotion of data types, 544–545

Prompting messages, 37, 166
Properties, inheriting. *See* Inheritance
Prototypes
  function, 330, 337, 338
  header files for, 344
Provincial Letters (Pascal), 118
Pseudocode, 185
PtrToClone function, 1032–1036
Public base classes, 810
Public class interface, 598, 599–600
  for information sharing, 604–606
  for objects, 179
  for Time class, 807–808
public reserved word, 598
Punch function (TimeCard class), 820, 838–839, 840–841
PunchIn program, 850–852

Quadratic time execution, 304
Qualified names, 79
Question mark (?), 507–508
Questions, asking, 30–31
Quotation marks (' "). *See* Apostrophe ('); Double
  quotation mark (")

\r escape sequence, 514
Rainfall averages case study, 478–484
Rainfall program, 481–483
Raising integers to power function
  using iteration, 415–416
  using recursion, 1014–1018
RAM (random access memory), 16n. *See also* Memory
rand function, 992
RAND_MAX constant, 992
Random access methods, 689
Random numbers, 992
Range of values
  for array indexes, 667
  for floating-point numbers, 500–501
  for integers, 496–497
Readability. *See also* Style in programming
  blank lines for, 75
  efficiency compared, 238
  enumeration types for, 540
  fieldwidth specifications for, 126
  functions for, 327
  with if statements, 230
  meaningful identifiers for, 57–58
  program formatting for, 129–130
  of two-dimensional array declarations, 698
ReadAll functions
  in RecordList class, 906, 907, 911
  in TimeCardList class, 843, 846–847
ReadFirstList function (CheckLists), 707–708
Reading data, 155, 160–162

Reading marker
  in opening files, 170
  operations of, 158–160
Reads, priming, 282, 469
Real numbers. *See* Floating-point data types
reclist.cpp file, 909–913
reclist.h file, 905–906
reclist.obj file, 914
RecordAWin function (Game), 563
RecordList class, 904–905
  constructor for, 907, 910
  destructor for, 909, 910
  implementation file for, 909–913
  specification file for, 905–906
Records (structs), 579–582
  accessing members of, 582–583, 588
  arrays of, 681–683
  assignment of, 584
  classes compared, 600
  declaring, 580–581
  as function return values, 584
  hierarchical, 587–589
  operations on, 583–585
  as parameters, 584
  pointers for, 873
  syntax templates for, 580, 585
  variables for, 581, 586
Recreate function (CardDeck class), 990, 993–994, 997
RectArea function (Area), 554
Recursion, 1014
  factorial function, 1018–1021
  infinite, 1017–1018
  iteration compared, 1036–1037
  with linked lists, 1029–1036
  for minimum array value, 1040–1042
  for number conversion, 1037–1040
  with pointer variables, 1029–1036
  power function using, 1014–1018
  for printing arrays, 1026–1029
  testing and debugging, 1043
  Towers of Hanoi game, 1021–1026
Recursive algorithm, 1015
Recursive calls, 1014
Recursive definition, 1015
Reference
  array passing by, 676–678,
    695–699
  parameter passing by, 353, 359
Reference parameters, 344, 346–349
  for dynamic binding, 824–825
  side effects from, 406, 420–421
Reference types, 884–890
Reformatting dates case study, 423–433
Relational expressions, 217, 544–545

Relational operators
    with floating-point numbers, 228
    with logical expressions, 216–219
    with pointers, 878
Relationships in object-oriented design, 829, 835
Relative error, 526
Relative parameter matching, 354
Reliable programs, 314
Remainder operator (%), 108
    for number conversion, 1038
    precedence of, 112
remove function, 422
RemoveTop function (CardPile class), 981, 982, 986
Repeating actions, 14. *See also* Loops
Representation
    of abstract data, 594
    of characters, 511–513
    of enumeration types, 533–541
    of floating-point numbers, 520–523
Representational error, 524
Reserved words, 56–57, 66
Return key, newline characters from, 158
return statement, 55, 341–342, 413
Return values. *See* Function return values
Returning from functions, 55, 162, 341–342, 413
Reusing code, 802, 816
ReverseNumbers program, 664–666
RevPrint function, 1030–1031
Right-justified fields, 125
Right shift operator (>>), 503, 506
Ritchie, Dennis, 24–25
Robust programs, 313
Rock, paper, scissors case study, 555–565
Rounding
    floating-point numbers, 115, 522
    with type casting, 115
Rounding error, 526
Rows in two-dimensional arrays, 685
    looping for, 695
    summing, 690–691
Running programs, 84–85
Run-time, 403
    input of file names, 174–175
    stack, 1017–1018

Safe array class, 917
Sales case study, 363–372
Scales in programming, 198–199, 802
Scientific notation, 105, 126
Scope, 392–403
    categories of, 393, 402–403
    in classes, 393, 402, 603–604

namespace as, 400
    rules, 395–398
    of user-defined types, 533
Scope resolution operator (::), 79, 611
ScopeRules program, 396–397
Searches
    complexity in, 772–773
    in sorted lists, 764–770
    testing and debugging, 792–793
    in unsorted lists, 752–755
Secondary storage devices, 16, 18
Seed value for random numbers, 992
Selection control structures, 14, 213–214
Selection sorts, 756
Self-documenting code, 191–192
SelSort function
    complexity in, 773
    in List class, 747, 757
    in RecordList class, 906, 911–912
    in TimeCardList class, 843, 847–848
Semantic content in array indexes, 684–685
Semantics
    errors in, 85, 261
    and syntax, 51
Semicolon (;)
    for assignment statements, 77, 231
    in declarations, 62, 77, 581
    for do-while statements, 468
    for expression statements, 503
    in for statements, 472
    and function definitions, 339
    and if statements, 231, 232
    for input statements, 232
    as null statement, 76
    for output statements, 77, 231
Semihierarchical implementation, 189
Sentinel-controlled loops, 282–285, 294
Sentinel values, 753
Separate compilation of source code files, 613
Sequences, 14
Sequential flow of control, 212–213
Sequential searches
    efficiency of, 769
    in sorted lists, 764
    testing and debugging, 792–793
    in unsorted lists, 752–755
Sequential structures, 14, 944–946
Servers, 22
Set functions
    in DateType class, 625, 630–631
    in ExtTime class, 811, 814, 815
    in Time class, 836–837
    in TimeType class, 607, 609, 619, 620
SetID function (TimeCard class), 839, 841

setprecision manipulator, 124, 127–128
Sets, 225
setw manipulator, 124, 125–126, 128
Sex discrimination case study, 307–313
Shallow copying in classes, 896–897
Shareware, 179
Shickard, Wilhelm, 117
Shift operators, 503, 505, 506
Short-circuit evaluation, 223–224
short data type
    range of values for, 496–497
    representation of, 103
    size of, 495
Short words, 9
showpoint manipulator, 124, 127, 128
SHRT_MAX constant, 497
SHRT_MIN constant, 497
Shuffle function (CardDeck class), 990, 992, 995–996
Side effects
    from assignment expressions, 236, 503–504
    from global variables, 406–409
    with increment and decrement operators, 505
    and interface design, 420–421
    from operator associativity, 510
    from parameters, 406, 420–421
Significant digits, 522, 524
Signs
    for exponents, 522
    for floating-point numbers, 520–523
Simple data types, 494–502
    structured compared, 578–589
    user-defined, 532–543
Simula language, 803, 804
Simulations
    playing cards, 979–986
    rock, paper, scissors game, 555–565
    solitaire game, 986–1005
sin function, 121
Single-entry/single-exit approach to functions, 342
Single quotation mark ('). *See* Apostrophe (')
Size
    of arrays, 665, 671, 677, 917
    of data types, 495–496
size function, 132, 136
sizeof operator, 503, 507
Sketch of the Analytical Engine, The (Lovelace), 410
Skipping input characters, 162–163, 779–780
Slash (/)
    in assignment operators, 502
    in comments, 39, 72
    for division, 108
    as null pointer, 945
    precedence of, 112, 226, 509
Slicing problem, 823–825

slist2.cpp file, 959
slist.h file, 759–760
slist2.h file, 957–958
Smalltalk language, 178, 803, 804, 805
Software, 19, 23
Software engineering, 29–30
Software piracy, 26–27
Solitaire program, 1004–1005
Solitaire simulation, 986–1005
Solution domain in object-oriented design, 827
Sorted lists, 758–771
    inserting into, 761–764
    searching in, 764–770
SortedList2 class, 957–958, 959
Sorting
    complexity in, 772–773
    linked lists, 978
    with pointers, 903–904, 916
    unsorted lists, 755–758
SortWithPointers program, 914–915
sortwithpointers.cpp file, 914
sortwithpointers.obj file, 914
Source code files
    hiding, 361–363
    separate compilation of, 613
Source programs, 12
Spaces
    in input data, 157, 160
    in strings, 123–126, 778, 779
Spacing in output, 123–126
Specification files, 606–608
    for CardDeck class, 990–991
    for CardPile class, 980–981
    for Date class, 893–894
    for DateType class, 624–626
    for DynArray class, 918–920
    for ExtTime class, 811–812
    for List class, 746–747
    for Player class, 998
    for RecordList class, 905–906
    for SortedList class, 759–760
    for SortedList2 class, 957–958
    for Time class, 836–837
    for TimeCard class, 838–839
    for TimeCardList class, 843–844
    for TimeType class, 607–608
sqrt function, 121, 344
Square brackets ([ ]), 665, 667, 686, 877–878
srand function, 992
Standard data types. *See* Data types
Standard input device, 155
Standard library, 60. *See also* Library functions
Standard output device, 70
Standards for programming languages, 12

`Starship` program, 441–446, 448–449
Starship weight and balance case study, 435–447
Statements. *See also* Assignments; Control structures
    compound. *See* Blocks
    expression, 503–504
    null, 76, 234, 472, 473
    syntax template for, 76
States of objects, 804
Static arrays, 671
Static binding, 822
`static` reserved word, 403
Static variables, 403–404
`std`, 79–80
Stepwise refinement in program design, 181–191
Storage, 16, 18, 58–59
Storage class, 403
`Store` function (`DynArray` class), 919, 926–927
Store sales case study, 363–372
Straight selection sort, 756
`strcmp` function, 781, 782–783
`strcpy` function, 781, 782, 881
Streams, 70, 155
    for files, 168–169
    testing state of, 241–243
`string` class, 578
`string` data type, 60–61, 578
String expressions, 68–70
Strings
    as abstract data types, 774
    as arrays of characters, 774–776
    blanks in, 123–126, 164, 778, 779
    comparing, 219–220, 781, 782–783
    constants, 774–775, 777
    copying, 781, 782
    empty, 60
    initializing, 776–777
    input of, 777–781
    length of, 775–776, 781–782
    literal, 174
    newline characters in, 159
    null, 60
    operations for, 131–135
    output of, 71, 777–781
    as parameters, 353
    testing and debugging, 792–793
    variables, 131–135, 774–775
`strlen` function, 776, 781–782
`StrLength` function, 775
Stroustrup, Bjarne, 25
`StrToAnimal` function, 540–541
`struct` reserved word, 580. *See also* Records
Structure of programs, 48–51
Structured data types, 578
Structured design, 181–191

Structured programming, 802–804
Structures, 580. *See also* Records
    classes compared, 600
    control. *See* Control structures
    simple data types compared, 495, 578–589
Stubs, 447
Style in programming, 7
    brace positioning, 233
    capitalization. *See* Capitalization
    class member declarations, 599–600
    comments, 72–73
    data flow documentation, 358–360
    data structure considerations, 590–592
    function headings, 360–361
    function interfaces, 358
    function names, 419
    meaningful identifiers, 57–58
    program formatting, 129–130
    void function names, 343
Subarray processing, 684
Subclass, 806
Subobject, 810
Subprograms, 14–16. *See also* Functions
`substr` function, 134–136, 136
Subtraction, 108
    in assignment operators, 502
    precedence of, 112
Summing
    columns in two-dimensional arrays, 691–692
    loops for, 289–290
    rows in two-dimensional arrays, 690–691
Superclass, 806
Supercomputers, 22
`Swap` function, 357–358, 888–889
Swapping sorts, 756
`switch` statement, 462–466
Symbolic constants, 64
Symbolic logic, 224–225
Syntax, 51
Syntax diagrams, 52–53
Syntax errors, 51, 85, 260
Syntax templates, 53–55
    for argument list, 337, 352
    for arrays, 666, 667
    for assignment statements, 67
    for blocks, 75
    for conditional expressions, 508
    for constant declarations, 64
    for constants, 498–500
    for digits, 54, 499
    for `do-while` statements, 468
    for dynamic allocation, 880
    for enumeration types, 535, 542
    for exponents, 502

for floating-point constant, 501
for `for` statements, 472
for function calls, 119, 336
for function definitions, 74, 76, 339, 414
for function prototypes, 338
for identifiers, 56
for If-Then-Else statements, 229
for If-Then statements, 234
for input statements, 156
for letters, 54
for `main` function, 55
for member list, 580
for member selectors, 582
for nonzero digits, 499
for output statements, 71, 124
for parameters, 339
for pointer variable declarations, 869
for programs, 73
for records (struct), 580, 585
for reference variable, 887
for statements, 76
for switch labels, 463
for `switch` statements, 463
for two-dimensional arrays, 685, 687
for `typedef` statements, 532
for variable declarations, 62
for `while` statements, 276
System programs, 679
System software, 23, 497

\t escape sequence, 514
Tab, escape sequence for, 514
Tail recursion, 1027–1028
Tape drives, 19
`tclist.cpp` file, 846–848
`tclist.h` file, 843–844
Team leaders, 181
Team programming, 199, 355
Templates, syntax. *See* Syntax templates
Temporary variables in exchange sorts, 756
Terminal symbols, 52
Termination conditions for loops, 278–279
Ternary operators, 507
Test generators, 432
Test plan, 259–260, 314–315
Testing, 91–92
    algorithm walk-through in, 251–253
    `Area` program, 554–555
    array-based lists, 792–793
    assertions in control structures, 213–214
    automatic, 260–261
    `BirthdayCalls` program, 644
    `CheckLists` program, 709
    classes, 644–648

complex structures, 722–723
conditional expressions, 262–263
control structures, 256–259
`ConvertDates` program, 432–433
data types, 565–567
`DateType` class, 627, 628, 630
`DynArray` class, 923, 924
`Election` program, 720–721
expressions and function calls, 141
functions, 372–373, 376
`Game` program, 564–565
`Graph` program, 372
in implementation programming phase, 253–259
input, 566
linked lists, 960, 1006
loops, 313–316, 484–485
`Minimum` function, 1042
modular design, 446–450
multidimensional arrays, 723–724
object-oriented programming, 854–855
one-dimensional arrays, 721–722
pointers, 928–931
preconditions and postconditions in, 249–251
programs, 7, 200–202
`PunchIn` program, 852–854
`Rainfall` program, 483–484
`RecordList` class, 913
recursion, 1043
searches, 792–793
`Solitaire` program, 1005
`SortWithPointers` program, 915–916
`Starship` program, 446
stream states, 241–243
`Time` class, 838
`TimeCard` class, 842
`TimeCardList` class, 849
`TimeType` class, 644–648
`TestTowers` program, 1024–1025
then-clause. *See* `if` statements
Thunks, 353
Tilde (~)
    for bitwise operations, 503
    for destructors, 621, 894
Time card lookup case study, 832–854
Time class, 808–810
`Time` class, 808
    constructors for, 837
    specification file for, 836–837
Time zones for `Time` class, 808–810
`TimeCard` class
    constructors for, 820–822, 839
    declaring, 818–819
    implementation file for, 820–822, 840–842
    specification file for, 838–839
`timecard.cpp` file, 840–842

`timecard.h` file, 838–839
`TimeCardList` class
    constructor for, 844
    implementation file for, 846–848
    specification file for, 843–844
`time.h` file, 836–837
`TimePart` function (`TimeCard` class), 839, 841
`TimeType` class
    compiling and linking, 613–615
    constructors for, 616–617
    declaring, 599–600
    implementation file for, 608–611, 618–620
    members of, 597
    specification file for, 607–608, 618–620
    testing and debugging, 644–648
`timetype.cpp` file, 608–611
`timetype.h` file, 606, 607–608
`tolower` function, 517–518
Tool making, 198
Top-down program design. *See* Functional decomposition
`toupper` function, 517–518
Towers of Hanoi game, 1021–1026
Tracing program execution, 253–256
Trailer values, 282
Transformers, 595
Treatise on Differential Equations (Boole), 225
Treatise on the Calculus of Finite Differences (Boole), 225
Tree structures in program design, 182
Triply nested loops, 301
`Trouble` program, 407–408
True values, 214
Truncation
    of floating-point numbers, 522
    with type coercion, 114
`TryRemove` function (`Player` class), 999, 1001–1002
Turbo Pascal language, 803
Two-dimensional arrays, 685–689
    accessing components in, 686–687, 689
    as arguments, 695–699
    as arrays of arrays, 698
    declaring, 687, 697
    initializing, 693–694, 697
    printing, 694–695
    processing, 689–695
    summing columns in, 691–692
    summing rows in, 690–691
Type casting, 113–116, 506–507
    in arithmetic expressions, 116
    in assignments, 114–115
    with enumeration types, 537
    operator for, 502
Type coercion, 113–116
    in arithmetic expressions, 115, 544–545
    in assignments, 113–115, 545–547

    with enumeration types, 537
    in expressions, 543–547
    with parameters, 346, 352, 545–547
`typedef` statements, 215
    with arrays, 680–681
    limitations of, 532–533
Types. *See* Data types

`U` with constants, 497
`UCHAR_MAX` constant, 497
`UINT_MAX` constant, 497
`ULONG_MAX` constant, 497
Unary operators, 108, 111, 226
`UNDECLARED IDENTIFIER` message, 71, 340, 398
Undefined pointers, 880
Underflow of floating-point numbers, 528
Underscore (_), 52, 56, 65
Unicode, 59n, 511
Unions, 589–590
Universal sets, 225
UNIX operating system, 24, 286
`unsigned` reserved word, 103, 496–497, 532, 545
Unsorted lists, 748–758
    deleting in, 751–752
    inserting in, 751
    searching in, 752–755
    sorting, 755–758
Uppercase letters
    converting characters to, 517–518
    for enumerators, 534
    in identifiers, 57, 65–66
User-defined data types, 58
    anonymous, 541–542, 586
    enumeration, 533–541
    header files, 542–543
    `typedef` for, 532–533
User names, 83
User-written header files, 542–543
User-defined void functions, 327
`USHRT_MAX` constant, 497
`using` declaration, 401
`using` directive, 80, 400, 401–402

`\v` escape sequence, 514
Validation, data, 253
Value, parameter passing by, 353, 359
Value parameters, 344, 345–346, 349
Value-returning functions, 50, 118–120, 123, 411–422. *See also* Functions
`ValueAt` function (`DynArray` class), 918, 926
Values
    in assignment expressions, 503
    literal, 64, 106, 533

parameter passing by, 345, 349
range of, 496–497, 500–501
return. *See* Function return values
true and false, 214
variable, 62
Variable identifier, 62
Variable name, 62
Variables
    in array indexes, 668
    Boolean, 216
    class, 598
    comments for, 73
    counter, 281, 288–289
    declaring, 62–63, 106–107, 399–400
    defining, 399–400
    dynamic, 879–884
    in expressions, 67
    external, 399–400
    in for statements, 472
    in functions, 340–341
    hiding, 394–395
    inaccessible, 884
    initializing, 404–405
    in input statements, 156–157
    lifetime of, 403–405
    in loops, 281, 290–292, 293
    as members of objects, 598
    memory for, 338, 340, 399
    names of. *See* Identifiers
    as parameters, 162, 334, 335, 345
    for pointers, 869–874
    pointers to. *See* Pointers
    for records (structs), 581, 586
    for recursion, 1021
    reference, 884–890
    scope of, 392
    side effects with, 406–409
    string, 131–135, 774–775
    swapping values of, 756
    union, 589
Vertical bar (|)
    for bit manipulation, 223, 503, 505
    in BNF, 52
    in OR operator (| |), 220–223, 227, 357, 506
    precedence of, 226, 509
Vertical tab, escape sequence for, 514
Video displays, 17, 70
Virtual functions, 825–827
virtual reserved word, 825
Virus, 28–29
Visibility, 397. *See* Scope
Void functions, 122–123. *See also* Functions
    calling, 335, 336–337
    defining and declaring, 337–340

    modules as, 327–330
    names for, 343
    prototypes for, 338–339
void reserved word, 327
Vote counting case study, 710–721

Walk program, 139–141, 172–173
Walk-throughs, 249–253
Warning notices case study, 243–249
Weight and balance of airplane case study, 435–447
Welcome program, 329–330, 333
while statements, 276–278. *See also* Loops
    do-while statements compared, 468–471
    nested, 296–302
White box testing, 258
Whitespace characters
    with input, 157, 160
    with strings, 778, 779
    trailing, 163
Wide area networks (WANs), 23
Widening of data types, 544–545
Width of output fields, 125–126
Words, 9
Workstations, 22, 83, 86
World Wide Web, 23
Write functions
    in ConvertDates program, 431
    in ExtTime class, 811, 814, 816
    in Time class, 837
    in TimeType class, 604, 606, 607, 610, 619
WritePerCandidate function (Election), 718–719
WritePerPrecinct function (Election), 719–720
WriteReport function (Election), 717–718

X for hexadecimal numbers, 500, 514

Year function (DateType class), 625, 631

\0 sequence, 514
ZeroOut function, 677
Zeros
    for array index values, 667
    division by, 109
    for false values, 215
    for octal numbers, 104
ZeroVotes function (Election), 717